THE SCOUTING REPORT: 1987

THE SCOUTING REPORT: 1987

An in-depth analysis of the strengths
and weaknesses of every
active major league baseball player

by
Larry Dierker
Jim Kaat
Harmon Killebrew
Jim Rooker

Edited by
Marybeth Sullivan

PERENNIAL LIBRARY

HARPER & ROW, PUBLISHERS, New York
Cambridge, Philadelphia, San Francisco, Washington
London, Mexico City, São Paulo, Singapore, Sydney

The player photographs which appear in THE SCOUTING REPORT were furnished individually by the 26 teams that comprise Major League Baseball. Their cooperation is gratefully acknowledged: Baltimore Orioles, Boston Red Sox, California Angels, Chicago White Sox, Cleveland Indians, Detroit Tigers, Kansas City Royals, Milwaukee Brewers, Minnesota Twins, New York Yankees, Oakland A's, Seattle Mariners, Texas Rangers, Toronto Blue Jays, Atlanta Braves, Chicago Cubs, Cincinnati Reds, Houston Astros, Los Angeles Dodgers, Montreal Expos, New York Mets, Philadelphia Phillies, Pittsburgh Pirates, St. Louis Cardinals, San Diego Padres and San Francisco Giants.

THE SCOUTING REPORT: 1987

Designer: Marybeth Sullivan

ISSN: 0743-1309
ISBN: 0-06-096136-8

CONTENTS

Who's Off Base Here?

I suppose it's not unusual to be conned.

When President Reagan stood before the American people last November and denied that the government's deal to send military arms to Iran was related to the release of three American hostages, well, I thought I had heard it all before. Over the past two months, we had been treated like jackasses by institutions we had come to trust. In September, the CBS television network had the audacity to tell its loyal "Dallas" viewers that the program's 1985 season "was all a dream," ABC's "Dynasty" fans were to believe that daughter Amanda had lost her British accent and changed her face over the summer and *then* President Reagan insisted that the freedom of Soviet-captured American journalist Richard Daniloff was not in exchange for an accused Soviet spy being held by the United States.

It all made me roar when, in the midst of the Iran arms controversy, when accusations and denials were rampant, Jack Morris began his trek across the country to try to exercise his rights as a free agent and to find a new team. Up until then, I admit, I believed that there was a chance that all 26 major league owners were acting independently to trim their payroll and might not be in collusion. But *come on! Yankee owner George Steinbrenner says he can't afford the winningest righthanded starting pitcher in this decade?*

How seriously are we supposed to take this stuff?

Does Mike Scott scuff the ball or are the Mets crybabies? Did Lenny Dykstra cork his bat to help push his three post-season home runs over the fence last year? Are there no more drugs in baseball? Maybe the National Hockey League really can't control its violence. Or instant replays will make football a better game. Or that Sugar Ray Leonard didn't want the Hagler fight just for the money. Or, for that matter, the addition of the designated hitter is bad.

But we turn to baseball to avoid heady politicism, don't we? And we should. I do. I don't want to bring comparisons of matters of global thermonuclear warfare to stadiums and arenas, but the sports pages just look different now. I'm less inclined to believe the sincerity of statements made that don't make sense.

Maybe I just woke up. But maybe I'm not the only one.

I can't make President Reagan come clean. I can't make the major league owners admit that they're playing games they shouldn't be playing. And I can't stop athletes from making all those silly statements about drive and the desire for excellence during contract years. But I can make sure that this is an honest book. It's such a small thing in the scope of the world, but it matters to me.

So . . . read, relax, enjoy the season. The sun is shining, the kids are here, the veterans are here. Heck, they've even brought bats and balls!

Mary Beth Sullivan

Managing Editor

The Format:

THE SCOUTING REPORT: 1987 is divided into two sections: first, the 14 teams of the American League, followed by the 12 teams of the National League. Player reports are located alphabetically with their team, with the exception of some players who are used on a limited basis; these players appear at the end of their team's section.

Free agency and trades make it impossible to keep up with all of the players' movements--use the index located on page 647 to locate players who have been traded to or signed by other teams since this book went to press.

One of the most popular features of THE SCOUTING REPORT is the batter's chart; reviewing the diagrams before each game could help you follow a pitcher's strategy to a particular batter and pick up the subtleties of defensive alignments:

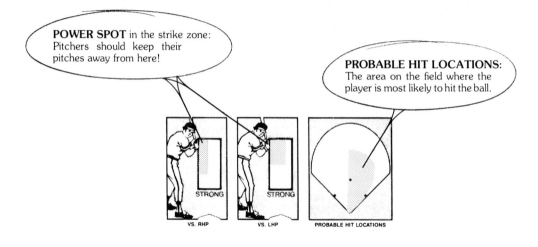

POWER SPOT in the strike zone: Pitchers should keep their pitches away from here!

PROBABLE HIT LOCATIONS: The area on the field where the player is most likely to hit the ball.

STRONG   STRONG

VS. RHP   VS. LHP   PROBABLE HIT LOCATIONS

EDITORIAL STAFF

The following are the unsung heroes of major league baseball, the beat writers. These professionals work under deadline all season long, travel across the country week after week and are still at the ballpark writing their game stories or features hours after the last fan has left the stadium. They work hard to bring the game to you and they all turned in stellar performances for THE SCOUTING REPORT: 1987.

Jim Corbett, Westchester-Rockland Newspapers
Tom Flaherty, Milwaukee Journal
Bud Geracie, San Jose Mercury News
Joe Giuliotti, Boston Herald
Scott Gregor, Arlington Heights Daily Herald
Paul Hagan, Philadelphia Daily News
Bob Hertzel, Pittsburgh Press
Greg Hoard, Cincinnati Enquirer
Paul Hoynes, Cleveland Plain Dealer
Rick Hummell, St. Louis Post-Dispatch
Mark Kriedler, San Diego Union
Tim Kurkjian, Baltimore Morning Sun
Neil MacCarl, Toronto Star
Ivy McLemore, Houston Post

Fred Mitchell, Chicago Tribune
Kevin Modesti, Los Angeles Daily News
Bob Nightengale, Kansas City Times
Tom Pedulla, Westchester-Rockland Newspapers
Nick Peters, Oakland Tribune
Vern Plagenhoef, Booth Group
Rusty Pray, Camden Courier Post
Charlie Scoggins, Lowell Sun
Terry Scott, TSI Communications
Tom Singer, Los Angeles Herald-Examiner
Howard Sinker, Minneapolis Star and Tribune
Bill Stetka, Towson Times
Jim Street, Seattle Post-Intelligencer
Tim Tucker, Atlanta Journal

Acknowledgments

Congratulations are in order for ace copyeditor Jim Armstrong of Harper & Row Publishers who has worked expertly on all five editions of this book. Gratitude is due to Dan Bial, a supportive, understanding editor who shows more patience and grace in a day than many people exhibit in a lifetime. I also extend my best wishes to Rick Rennert, a fastidious editor who is generous with kind words.

It has been my good fortune to work with the authors of this edition, Larry Dierker, Jim Kaat, Jim Rooker and Harmon Killebrew, four gentlemen who have trusted me to bring their evaluations of major league ballplayers to you, the fans. I am happy to have had that opportunity.

There is an Australian lass, Georgia Miller, who cheerily accepted the challenge of cutting and pasting a large portion of this project and a slightly off-center artist named Rose Petersons who contributed tremendously in bringing THE SCOUTING REPORT: 1987 to life. Tucked away in a tiny village just north of Manhattan is an erudite newspaper publisher named Richard Abel who gave me the kind of attentive service customers can only dream about. And everyone should have a friend like Sue Schwer, you know, the type who says, "Oh no, no way," but then does it anyway. Then there is my younger sister, Eileen, who continues to let me think I'm teaching her the ways of the world--when all along, it's me who's learning.

My mother, father, brothers and friends all help, too. They leave me alone when I'm working. There's a lot to be said for that--I'm not sure what it is, but thanks anyway.

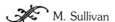 M. Sullivan

THE AUTHORS

Larry Dierker

Larry Dierker burst upon the major league scene almost directly out of high school, pitching just part of one season in the minor leagues before coming to the big show at the age of 18.

A member of a pitching staff that became one of the most dominating in baseball, with fastballers like Don Wilson, Ken Forsch, Tom Griffin, Jim Ray and J.R. Richard, Dierker pitched for 14 major league seasons, the first 13 of which were with the Houston Astros.

Dierker was one of the first 20-game winners in Astros' history when he put together a 20-13 season with a 2.33 ERA in 1969. From 1969 until 1972, he was one of the league's best pitchers, compiling 63 victories against just 39 losses.

Dierker capped his career on July 9, 1976, when he pitched a no-hitter against the Montreal Expos.

Larry's playing career came to an end in 1977. Two years later he joined the Astros' broadcast team. He has provided the reports on the players of the National League West for THE SCOUTING REPORT: 1987.

Jim Kaat

Jim Kaat pitched in four decades, lasting 25 years in the major leagues after his 1959 debut with the Washington Senators. Kaat's 898 games pitched are fifth on the all-time list.

THE AUTHORS

(Jim Kaat cont'd)

But Kaat was more than durable through a career that saw him pitch with Washington, Minnesota, the White Sox, Phillies, Yankees and St. Louis Cardinals. He was also good. He won 283 games and lost 237, with a career ERA of 3.43. Kaat's best season was 1966, when he was 25-13. He won 20 on two other occasions, going 21-13 in 1974 and 20-14 in 1975.

An all-around athlete, Kaat won the Gold Glove for pitchers for an incredible 16 consecutive seasons.

Last season Kaat was a broadcaster for New York Yankees' telecasts. Jim has evaluated the players of the American League East for THE SCOUTING REPORT: 1987.

Harmon Killebrew

Harmon Killebrew was one of the greatest home run hitters in baseball history and was elected to the Hall of Fame in Cooperstown in 1984.

A muscular, stout man, Killebrew hit 573 home runs during his career, the game's fifth highest total. Only two players hit home runs at a more frequent pace.

Killebrew, who broke into the major leagues in 1954 with the Washington Senators and spent most of his career with Minnesota, won the American League home run title six times and the RBI crown on three occasions.

(Harmon Killebrew cont'd)

Splitting his time mostly between first and third base, Killebrew hit 40 or more homers in eight different seasons, including his best year--1969--when he hit .276 with 49 home runs despite a league-leading 145 walks.

Killebrew serves as a color commentator on Twins' games today. He has offered his opinions on the strengths and weaknesses of the players of the American League West for THE SCOUTING REPORT: 1987.

Jim Rooker

The Detroit Tigers signed Jim Rooker as an outfielder, but he made his way to the major leagues as a lefthanded pitcher, debuting with the Tigers in 1968.

Traded to Kansas City in 1969, Rooker struggled with the American League through the 1972 season, after which he was dealt to the Pittsburgh Pirates for his best seasons.

Although Rooker was 103-109 for his career, as a Pirate he was 82-65. Rooker's best seasons came in 1976 when he was 15-8 with a 3.35 ERA and 1974 when he was 15-11 with a 2.77 ERA.

If there was one memorable game in Rooker's career, it came in Game 5 of the 1979 World Series. Called upon to start against Baltimore with the Pirates trailing three games to one, Rooker pitched five innings allowing only one run. The Pirates went on to win the game and the World Series.

THE AUTHORS

(Jim Rooker cont'd)

Known as a good-hitting pitcher, Rooker completed his career with a .201 lifetime batting average and seven homers--two of them coming in one game with Kansas City off, ironically, his co-author, Jim Kaat.

Rooker begins his seventh season as a broadcaster of Pirates' games. Jim has provided THE SCOUTING REPORT: 1987 with his judgments on the players of the National League East.

Marybeth Sullivan

Marybeth Sullivan has been the Managing Editor of THE SCOUTING REPORT since it was first published in 1983. She holds a degree in Recreation Education from the State University of New York College at Cortland. Marybeth served as Recreation Supervisor for a community in Westchester County, New York, for three years before turning her attentions to major league baseball. Credited with uncovering the secrets of scouting reports for sports fans, she is also an accomplished stoneware potter and has sold her work throughout New York State.

As a catcher for her summer softball team, Marybeth has infuriated her pitching staff by calling for split-finger fastballs.

THE MANAGERS

MANAGERS - AMERICAN LEAGUE

CAL RIPKEN, Sr.
BALTIMORE ORIOLES

Born: 12-17-35 in Aberdeen, MD
Major League Playing Experience:
   none
Major League Coaching Experience:
   1976-86: bullpen coach and
   third base coach, Baltimore Orioles
Major League Managing Experience:
   none

IN THE CLUBHOUSE:

Cal Ripken, Sr. faces a rare situation in the Orioles' clubhouse this season. In addition to taking the helm for the first time in his major league career, he will also have one and possibly two sons on his team. Cal, Jr. is, of course, Baltimore's stalwart shortstop, but younger brother Billy has been rated as a fine prospect with a shot at the second base job this year.

The Ripkens represent only the third father/son, manager/player relationship in major league history (Yogi and Dale Berra, NY Yankees, 1985, and Connie and Earle Mack, Philadelphia Athletics, 1910-11, 1914, the others).

The Ripkens face a potentially awkward situation in their new roles as Sr. as manager and Jr. as player. Differences of opinion between the manager and the team are a matter of course in this business and one or the other might find himself caught in the middle somewhere along the line. Both are highly respected throughout baseball, however, and are likely to handle whatever situation comes their way.

As the new manager of the Baltimore Orioles, Ripken asks that his players come to the park promptly and ready to work. He knows all of them well from his service as third-base coach, a position he had held since 1977. Nonetheless, he enters into a new, more distant relationship with the players. That is likely to require an adjustment by both parties.

IN THE DUGOUT:

In describing his own managerial philosophy, longtime Baltimore manager Earl Weaver said, "The key to winning baseball games is pitching, fundamentals and three-run homers."

For years, that formula worked well for this club. But the O's didn't hit many three-run homers in 1986 and Ripken will be forced to roll the dice more often in an attempt to reverse the club's fortunes.

The Orioles are in a state of transition; and while they know where they've been, they are not quite sure where

(Cal Ripken, Sr. - continued)

they're going. Ripken will have to adapt to the skills of his given personnel. Thirteen infielders were scheduled to report to the club's Miami complex this spring in hopes of filling the team's gaping holes both at second and third base. At one time, precise execution of fundamentals was the Orioles' style. That is no longer the case. But Ripken was there when the club excelled at all of the little things and remembers their importance as a precursor to winning. He is expected to stress the basics.

THE PITCHING STAFF:

Baltimore's pitching staff was always able to save the game. But over the past few years, the staff has grown weak. This is an area of great concern to Ripken. The Orioles ranked 10th among the 14 clubs in the American League with an uncharacteristic 4.30 ERA last season.

Ripken must work to restore the confidence of Mike Boddicker, who has slumped badly in the second half of the season in each of the last two years.

Mike Flanagan, Scott McGregor and Ken Dixon all must be watched closely. Flanagan, at 7-11, comes off his only losing record over a full major league season. In 1986, McGregor and Dixon were rocked for 35 and 33 home runs, respectively.

Ripken must pick his spots for bullpen ace Don Aase, who will have to be used extensively but carefully. A good supporting cast is lacking. Ripken will put leads in Aase's hands and leave them there. Aase is not about to be lifted because a pinch-hitter comes up. "I don't care if the guy stands on the middle of home plate," Ripken has said.

OVERALL:

Ripken gets his shot at the top spot this season after having served 30 years in the Orioles organization. When he was a non-playing minor league skipper, he endured only one losing season. Ripken is a born and raised Oriole, a fine and dedicated baseball man who has earned this opportunity.

Unfortunately for Ripken, he enters at one of the most difficult times in the franchise's history. He inherits a club that finished last for the only time in its history and endured its first losing season since 1967.

The Orioles are not ready to win. No matter what Ripken does, he doesn't appear to have the horses to win the race this season. It would be unfortunate for him if the front office uses him as a scapegoat in the uncertain times ahead.

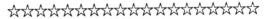

MANAGERS - AMERICAN LEAGUE

JOHN McNAMARA
BOSTON RED SOX

Born: *6-4-32 in Sacramento, CA*
Major League Playing Experience:
   none
Minor League Managing Experience:
   1959-68: Kansas City A's system
Major League Coaching Experience:
   1971-73: San Francisco Giants
   1978: California Angels
Major League Managing Experience:
   1969-70, 1974-77, 1979-84:
   Oakland A's, San Diego Padres,
   Cincinnati Reds, California Angels
   1985 to present: Boston Red Sox

IN THE CLUBHOUSE:

John McNamara is as steady as they come, which is one reason he was named American League Manager of the Year last year as he guided Boston to its first division title since 1975.

McNamara doesn't rattle and his players have become a stronger team because of it. McNamara lives the cliche about taking one game at a time, and never gets too high or too low. While skeptics waited for the Red Sox to tumble from the AL East lead last season and reporters reminded the manager and his players of past collapses, McNamara tersely replied that this was a different manager, a different team and a different year.

McNamara's players know he will --literally--fight for them. When a fan at Yankee Stadium made off with outfielder Jim Rice's cap last season, Rice leaped into the stands in pursuit, closely followed by his teammates. They were followed by their 54-year-old manager. "I won't have my players going over the railing without me," McNamara explained later, although he also acknowledged, "I'm too old to be doing that stuff."

IN THE DUGOUT:

McNamara makes the best of what he has, which means he must operate rather conservatively. The Red Sox have little speed and finished last in the AL with 41 stolen bases, 23 fewer than next-to-last Baltimore. McNamara can't sit back and wait for the home run, either, because the Red Sox mustered only 144 of those in 1986. Only three teams had less power than the BoSox last year.

What McNamara does have is a one-base-at-a-time attack led by some outstanding veteran hitters. They are willing to give themselves up, hit behind baserunners to move men over. McNamara further capitalizes on their skills with the timely hit-and-run.

(John McNamara - continued)

McNamara's lineups and changes are predictable, which provides further stability for his players. He will not back down from difficult decisions. In the World Series last year, for instance, he consistently used rookie Mike Greenwell in place of veteran designated hitter Don Baylor as a pinch-hitter. Although Greenwell was 0-for-3 with two strikeouts in the Series, McNamara kept faith in Greenwell.

THE PITCHING STAFF:

McNamara describes himself as being pitching-oriented. His effectiveness at handling his pitching staff is his greatest strength as a manager.

Roger Clemens and Bruce Hurst have both realized their potential under McNamara. He also coaxed 16 victories out of combustible Dennis "Oil Can" Boyd.

McNamara recognized the abilities of reliever Calvin Schiraldi and didn't hesitate to install him as the stopper in August upon his promotion from Triple-A. Schiraldi responded with nine saves during the pennant drive.

McNamara faces two confidence-building projects on his 1987 pitching staff: Oil Can Boyd and Calvin Schiraldi. Boyd needs coddling and patience and Schiraldi needs reassurance following his shaky post-season performance last year. On both counts, McNamara has his hands full.

OVERALL:

McNamara endured a brutal winter of second-guessing after the New York Mets rallied from deficits of 2-0 and 3-2 to take the World Series in seven games. McNamara's worst moment came in the 10th inning of Game 6 as the Mets staved off elimination with an improbable three-run rally. The game was won when Mookie Wilson's routine grounder slipped through the legs of Bill Buckner at first base. Why, McNamara's critics cried, was the gimpy-legged Buckner still in the game when Dave Stapleton finished seven post-season games at first?

The ghosts of losses past notwithstanding, McNamara is a fine manager who has produced division titles in both leagues.

With the exception of catcher Rich Gedman, the Boston club remains essentially the very same club this season as the one that took the World Series to seven games last October. There remain many observers who feel that Boston won the AL East last year only because the rest of the division simply fell apart. Whatever the case, McNamara's Band faces a tough battle this season.

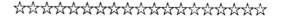

GENE MAUCH
CALIFORNIA ANGELS

Born: *11-18-25 in Salinas, KS*

Major League Playing Experience:

1944-57: shortstop, Brooklyn Dodgers, Los Angeles Dodgers, Pittsburgh Pirates, Chicago Cubs, Boston Braves, Milwaukee Braves, Boston Red Sox, Minnesota Twins, St. Louis Cardinals

Minor League Managing Experience:

1953, 1958-59: Milwaukee Braves' system

Major League Managing Experience:

1960-81: Philadelphia Phillies, Montreal Expos, Minnesota Twins, California Angels (and Director of Player Development, 1981)
1985 to present: California Angels

IN THE CLUBHOUSE:

Gene Mauch, known as the "Little General," isn't necessarily liked, but he *is* respected. "He's a stoic SOB, but he's no robot," Reggie Jackson once said of Mauch. "He's shown me compassion."

Players may not always agree with the moves Mauch makes, but they know and appreciate that the manager has given each matter careful consideration. Mauch is a serious man who lives and breathes baseball. He expects his players to behave and perform like major leaguers. It's when they fail to do that that the trouble starts.

Mauch is tagged as the greatest manager never to win a world championship. That label has been invoked with increasingly regularity as Mauch's 25-year string of futility increases and he is unable to shake the ghosts of past seasons that haunt him. Mauch's 1964 Philadelphia Phillies were guilty of one of baseball's all-time great collapses. They blew a 6½-game lead with 12 to play as Mauch went with a two-man rotation of Jim Bunning and Chris Short in the last two weeks. His 1982 California Angels squandered a 2-0 lead in their best-of-five American League Championship Series against Milwaukee. In 1986, California came within one strike of clinching its first AL pennant in Game 5 of its ALCS against Boston, only to fall in seven games.

Given that history, Mauch may have reached the point where he no longer has his players' trust at crucial times.

IN THE DUGOUT:

A game against the New York Yankees during the stretch run in September 1986 illustrates well Mauch's determination to follow previous patterns no matter what the current circumstances. Lefthanded hitting Reggie Jackson, a typically streaky slugger, had gone 2-for-3 with two home runs against Doug Drabek, a rookie righthander. With nasty lefthander Dave Righetti pitching, Mauch didn't let Jackson hit again. Jackson had had one hit and nine strikeouts in 18 previous at-bats

(Gene Mauch - continued)

against Righetti. With a large crowd screaming "Reg-gie! Reg-gie!," righthanded pinch-hitter Rick Burleson struck out.

Mauch's teams excel in the basics. California ranked second in the AL in 1986 in fielding. Mauch makes extensive use of the bunt, and his players are accomplished at using this weapon, which is too often spurned by modern-day players.

Mauch's lineups are completely unpredictable. He often does not decide them until shortly before game time, but they are the product of much deliberation.

THE PITCHING STAFF:

Mauch generally goes by the book, and this may have cost him and the Angels the 1986 ALCS. Righthander Mike Witt was clinging to a 5-4 lead, having surrendered a two-run ninth-inning homer to Don Baylor, and was within an out of clinching the pennant. Mauch pulled his ace, who had recorded 18 victories in the regular season, in favor of lefthander Gary Lucas to face lefthanded hitting Rich Gedman. The catcher had gone 3-for-3 with a homer against Witt. Lucas had fanned Gedman the night before and another time in a key spot during the regular season.

Lucas' first and only pitch struck Gedman. Mauch then switched to his righthanded--ailing--relief ace, Donnie Moore, who also ultimately failed him. Mauch was severely second-guessed for not sticking with Witt.

Mauch clearly defines roles for his pitchers and rarely deviates. He has done well overall in developing the confidence of Witt and Kirk McCaskill. Mauch may have to make more pitching moves than usual this season if Moore is not fully recovered from shoulder problems.

OVERALL:

There is no question Mauch is a good manager. His teams are efficient and steady during the regular season and he has given the Angels two division winners in the last five years. But his horrible post-season history is a stigma he seems incapable of shaking, and it overshadows any other good he does.

☆☆☆☆☆☆☆☆☆☆☆☆☆☆☆☆☆☆☆☆

JIM FREGOSI
CHICAGO WHITE SOX

Born: *4-4-42 in San Francisco, CA*

Major League Playing Experience:

1962-78: shortstop, Los Angeles Dodgers, California Angels, New York Mets, Texas Rangers, Pittsburgh Pirates

Major League Managing Experience:

1979-81: California Angels
1986 to present: Chicago White Sox

(Jim Fregosi - continued)
IN THE CLUBHOUSE:

Jim Fregosi was intent on establishing a respectful distance after replacing popular Tony LaRussa during last season. He wanted it clear who was boss and went about creating a businesslike atmosphere.

Soon after he took the job, Fregosi made the clubhouse off-limits to the players' children. The move wasn't applauded, but Fregosi made his point.

In September, when the White Sox were playing with the hopelessness of a team long left behind by the pennant race, which they were, Fregosi criticized his players to the press, questioning their desire and work ethic and emphasizing that the games were meaningful toward establishing the proper attitude for 1987. He was right, of course, but a less forceful manager wouldn't have spoken his mind.

Fregosi is equally forceful in letting players know his door is open. He talked, for instance, with disgruntled veteran Carlton Fisk, who was concerned about his role. No role ever was defined for Fisk, but at least he did not become openly disruptive.

IN THE DUGOUT:

Fregosi insists his players master the basics and is disappointed in this regard in the young players rising through the White Sox system. The manager demands that the plays that *have* to be made *are* made.

Young center fielder John Cangelosi found himself on the bench after he allowed Bob Boone, California's aged catcher, to score from second base on a deep fly ball. Fregosi felt Cangelosi's momentum should not have delayed his throw as long as it did.

Fregosi will have to be a magician offensively because his attack has countless deficiencies entering the 1987 season. The White Sox were last in the American League in average (.247), runs scored (644) and home runs (121) last year. Fregosi will be hard pressed to improve the Sox offense unless Greg Walker is fully recovered from a broken right wrist last season and Fisk has one more big year left in him.

THE PITCHING STAFF:

Fregosi's goal when he became manager was to get the White Sox' team ERA below 4.00. He achieved that at 3.93. Fregosi and pitching coach Dick Bosman worked extensively with enigmatic righthander Jose DeLeon between starts, with Bosman catching and Fregosi observing from behind the mound. There was dramatic improvement. Veteran lefthander Floyd Bannister improved after Fregosi convinced him to junk a big curve and throw his change-up and slider more.

Fregosi constantly stresses mechanics. Young righthander Joel Davis was returned to the minors last season partly because Fregosi thought that his delivery was poor and that he was risking serious injury if he continued to throw with bad mechanics.

(Jim Fregosi - continued)

Fregosi trusts his instinct in deciding whether to change pitchers. If he doesn't like what he sees, the sign goes to the bullpen regardless of what is said in the meeting on the mound.

Joe Cowley was nearly lifted from the no-hitter he hurled against California last September. Although Cowley allowed nothing resembling a hit, he bunched three of his seven walks in the sixth inning, then fell behind Reggie Jackson 3-1. Jackson lofted a sacrifice fly for the Angels' only run in the 7-1 no-hitter. Had Jackson walked, Fregosi later said, Cowley would have been history instead of making a little bit of it.

OVERALL:

Fregosi did about as well as could be expected in 1986 after entering an extremely difficult situation. He replaced a very popular manager in Tony LaRussa and the 1986 front office, led by the colorful but unsuccessful Ken "Hawk" Harrelson, was in chaos. Fregosi's goal entering his first full season must be to get the White Sox thinking positively again. That would at least be a start.

☆☆☆☆☆☆☆☆☆☆☆☆☆☆☆☆☆☆

PAT CORRALES
CLEVELAND INDIANS
Born: 3-20-41 in Los Angeles, CA
Major League Playing Experience:
    1964-73: catcher, Philadelphia Phillies,
    St. Louis Cardinals, Cincinnati Reds,
    San Diego Padres
Minor League Managing Experience:
    1975: San Diego Padres' system
Major League Managing Experience:
    1978-80: Texas Rangers
    1982-83: Philadelphia Phillies
    1983 to present: Cleveland Indians

IN THE CLUBHOUSE:

Pat Corrales won't win any popularity contests. He cares only about his team's performance and in that regard seems to get the most out of his players.

Corrales does not communicate a great deal in the clubhouse, which is unsettling to some team members, particularly those who are not regulars. His bench players often feel as though they are kept in the dark.

Corrales commands respect, but his respectful distance may be a bit too far. He is not easy to get to know and like.

IN THE DUGOUT:

Corrales is very aggressive and the Indians reflect this. The Indians paced the American League last year with

MANAGERS - AMERICAN LEAGUE

(Pat Corrales - continued)

141 stolen bases and had six players in double figures in that category. Corrales is a manager who makes things happen offensively.

Corrales also is not afraid to shuffle the deck if the club is struggling. His move of switch-hitter Tony Bernazard to the leadoff spot not only roused Bernazard but enlivened the entire Indians attack.

Last season, Cleveland went on to lead the league in average (.284) and in runs scored (831). And that was without a full year's worth of production from rookie star Cory Snyder, who was not promoted to the Indians until June 12.

With the firepower at Corrales' disposal, scoring runs is definitely not a problem.

Defensively, a project for Corrales has been shortstop Julio Franco, a gifted, if erratic, athlete. There are signs Corrales' teachings are getting through to Franco. Although Franco committed 19 errors last year, that represented a reduction of 17 from 1985.

THE PITCHING STAFF:

Corrales makes logical moves only to see them fail because of his staff's shortcomings. There have been countless times when Corrales brings in a righthander to face a righthanded hitter, or a southpaw for a lefty, and the results are negative.

In these instances, Corrales might be the target of criticism, but he has done his best to put his club in a position to win. He simply does not have enough good arms.

Some of the burden of a poor bullpen is eased by the presence of developing knuckleballer Tom Candiotti, who tossed a league-leading 17 complete games last year. Because of that, Candiotti will receive considerations for longer stints that other starters might not get.

Corrales faces a decision on Scott Bailes, a talented lefthander he helped develop as a rookie by consistently using him in tight spots, even if he had fared poorly in his previous outing. Bailes was moved into the rotation later in the season and wound up with 10 victories and seven saves. Corrales must decide where Bailes will be most valuable.

Corrales uses hard-throwing Ernie Camacho as the Indians' bullpen stopper. Camacho isn't always right on, and on days when he isn't right, Corrales might well march to the mound and raise hell with his bullpen ace. On days when Camacho doesn't respond, Corrales will pull him before he has a chance to do further damage.

OVERALL:

The Indians' front office has patiently stayed with Corrales. It has been a decision which is paying dividends. Corrales, though he downplays his club's chances, has the Indians in position to contend, if not in 1987 then surely in '88. The Indians improved to 84-78 in

(Pat Corrales - continued)

1986 after a 60-102 disaster the year before. As a resounding vote of confidence, the Indians awarded Corrales a perpetual contract after the 102-loss campaign in 1985.

Until the Indians' fifth-place finish in 1986, they had placed last or next-to-last in the American League East every year since 1977. When the Indians finally win their first pennant since 1954, the crusty Corrales deserves to be in the dugout.

☆☆☆☆☆☆☆☆☆☆☆☆☆☆☆☆☆☆☆

SPARKY ANDERSON
DETROIT TIGERS

Born: 2-22-34 in Bridgewater, SD
Major League Playing Experience:
  1959: infielder, Philadelphia Phillies
Minor League Managing Experience:
  1964: Washington Senators/
  Milwaukee Braves' system
  1965-67: St. Louis' system
  1968: Cincinnati Reds' system
Major League Managing Experience:
  1970-78: Cincinnati Reds
  1979 to present: Detroit Tigers

IN THE CLUBHOUSE:

However George "Sparky" Anderson's plan is outlined, it is a good one. He is the first manager to win more than 100 games in a season and a World Series in each league.

Sparky guided Detroit to a world championship in 1984. He motored Cincinnati's Big Red Machine to two World Series victories, four pennants and five National League West titles from 1970-78.

Sparky is best known for his outrageous statements, usually verbal pats on the backs for his players that are too grand for even them to believe.

He once mentioned Mickey Mahler, a journeyman pitcher, in the same breath as Dwight Gooden. Another time he said Howard Johnson had a "mortal lock" on third base. Johnson was traded soon afterward. A long at-bat by Dave Bergman against Toronto in May 1984 was "the greatest at-bat in the history of baseball." And so on. And on, sometimes.

Sparky will get tough when necessary. When Kirk Gibson was a young, developing outfielder, Anderson once yanked him in the middle of an inning to prove his point. Gibson met with Sparky before the next game and the problem was behind them.

The manager insists his players wear jackets and ties on the road and firmly believes good appearance and discipline are related to performance.

(Sparky Anderson - continued)
IN THE DUGOUT:

Sparky adjusts well to the talent he has. He has used the stolen base more in the last couple of years in an attempt to enliven the Tigers' attack.

He doesn't run his club too often, however, because he doesn't have to. Tiger Stadium helped Detroit lead the American League last year with 198 home runs. Each member of the infield belted at least 20 homers and Gibson is a well-established slugger in the outfield.

Defensively, the Tigers returned in 1986 to their usual fine form under Anderson. They ranked third in the league in fielding percentage last year after an error-filled 1985 season. Sparky had been unable to motivate the club, and perhaps even himself, after the Tigers' dominant '84 campaign.

THE PITCHING STAFF:

Sparky owns a well-earned reputation as "Captain Hook." The one starter who receives special consideration, of course, is ace Jack Morris, the winningest pitcher in the majors in the 1980s. Morris registered 15 complete games in 1986, Sparky notwithstanding.

Morris, once compared by the manager to "a high-strung racehorse," may be more difficult to handle than usual after a bitter experience as an unwanted free agent forced him to submit to arbitration with Detroit.

Another delicate situation will be the handling of screwballer Willie Hernandez, who has been the bullpen ace for this club over the last couple of years. Sparky is grooming hard-throwing youngster Eric King for that role. He will need to nurture King and give him work and still protect the ego of the veteran Hernandez.

Anderson is not overly swayed by statistics and past performance. He perhaps best espoused his philosophy last season. After Frank Tanana defeated Kansas City for his seventh victory in 27 decisions against the Royals, Anderson was asked if he was surprised. "What was was. What is is," he answered enigmatically.

OVERALL:

There is some discontent with Anderson in the Motor City now after two straight also-ran showings since the Tigers' world championship year of 1984. The spark has sometimes been missing, leading the manager himself to wonder aloud about his own motivation. The situation bears watching, although it is impossible to picture Sparky out of baseball or out of a Tigers uniform.

BILLY GARDNER
KANSAS CITY ROYALS
Born: 7-19-27 in New London, CT
Major League Playing Experience:
  1954-64: New York Giants, Baltimore Orioles, Washington Senators, Minnesota Twins, New York Yankees, Boston Red Sox
Minor League Managing Experience:
  1967-71: Red Sox system
  1972-76: Royals system
  1979-80: Expos system
Major League Coaching Experience:
  1965-66: Boston Red Sox
  1977-78: Montreal Expos
  early 1981: Minnesota Twins
Major League Managing Experience:
  1981-85: Minnesota Twins

IN THE CLUBHOUSE:

Billy Gardner could not have begun his job as manager of the Royals under more difficult circumstances. He was hired to manage the Kansas City club on February 23rd this year, when Dick Howser realized--on the third day of spring training workouts--that his battle with brain cancer left him too weak to steer a big league ballclub.

The Royals hired Gardner as third base coach last winter. He had an inkling he might manage the Royals some time in the future. But he was misty-eyed as he repeatedly told reporters on the day of Howser's resignation: "I just didn't think it'd happen this quick."

The change in managers was regrettable and painful, but it will benefit the club in the short term. Tension had filled the clubhouse since last July, when Howser's grave illness was initially discovered. Concern over Howser's condition made it diffcult for the members of the organization to go about everyday business, and the Royals failed to make their customary second-half run last season.

Gardner is regarded as a fairly relaxed manager, easy to work for as long as players perform. He is very visible in the clubhouse and will stop to joke or just chat with the ballplayers. The club will be paying close attention to Howser's condition throughout the season, but Gardner's presence as manager should make it easier for the ballplayers to persevere on the field.

IN THE DUGOUT:

Gardner is well suited to the challenge facing him. He is familiar with the organization, having managed in the Royals' minor league system from 1972 to 1976. He guided the Royals' Double-A affiliate at Jacksonville, Fla., to consecutive Southern League division titles in

1973 and '74. In 1976, he took Triple-A Omaha to the American Association crown. Current second baseman Frank White was among the players under Gardner's leadership in the minors. Gardner should have no trouble gaining the confidence of his new team.

A USA TODAY players' poll in 1984 ranked Gardner as AL Manager of the Year after he guided the Minnesota Twins to second place in the West behind Kansas City.

Most significantly, Gardner has better offensive talent to work with this season than his predecessors did. Howser and interim manager Mike Ferraro watched helplessly last year as the opposition consistently pitched around the dangerous George Brett, ultimately issuing him 80 walks. There simply was no one to protect Brett in the lineup. As a result, the Royals scored the second fewest runs (654) in the league and ranked 12th with 137 home runs.

That will change with the offseason addition of Danny Tartabull, who collected 25 homers and 96 RBIs as a rookie with Seattle. His acquisition ended a two-year search for a power-hitting outfielder and will make life more pleasant not only for Brett but for Gardner as well.

THE PITCHING STAFF:

The pitching staff figures to be the area of greatest concern for Gardner in that he will need time to learn the staff and develop a feel for it.

Gardner will probably pay closest attention to starter Bret Saberhagen and short reliever Dan Quisenberry. The young Saberhagen went from a 20-6 Cy Young, World Series MVP year in 1985 to 7-12 in 1986. Quisenberry, a veteran of seven major league seasons, plunged from a league-leading 37 saves in the Royals' world championship season to 12 last year and lost his stature as bullpen ace. Quisenberry is eager to regain his stopper status if Gardner will let him.

The Royals' youth-oriented staff led the American League with a 3.82 ERA last year, giving Gardner plenty of pitching material to work with.

OVERALL:

Howser piloted the Royals to three division championships in the five full seasons he managed them. The club always responded to his patient, confident handling. It remains to be seen how the shaken Royals will adjust to Gardner.

☆☆☆☆☆☆☆☆☆☆☆☆☆☆☆☆☆☆☆

TOM TREBELHORN
MILWAUKEE BREWERS
Born: *1-27-48 in Portland, OR*
Major League Playing Experience:
  none
Minor League Coaching Experience:
  1978-81: Pittsburgh Pirates' system
Minor League Managerial Experience:
  1975-77: Oakland A's system
  1979: Cleveland Indians' system
  1982-83: Pittsburgh Pirates' system
  1985: Milwaukee Brewers' system
Major League Coaching Experience:
  1984-85: third base coach,
  Milwaukee Brewers
Major League Managerial Experience:
  1986: less than one month

IN THE CLUBHOUSE:

Tom Trebelhorn describes himself as "confrontive." The term, as the Brewers' new manager uses it, does not refer to one who constantly seeks confrontations, but to one who tackles matters head on.

If Trebelhorn likes what he sees, he'll let the player know it right away. If there is a problem, Trebelhorn will take steps to correct it at the first appropriate moment. Players will know where Trebelhorn stands.

Trebelhorn is a great believer in team meetings. He estimates there might be as many as five get-tough sessions and 125 quick get-togethers this year over the course of the 162-game season.

Trebelhorn wants his players to know everything he knows about an opponent. He doesn't want Milwaukee to lose because a detail was overlooked.

It is not surprising Trebelhorn puts such emphasis on instructing. He is a certified teacher with a degree from Portland State University in social science and math. He continued his offseason employment as a substitute teacher in the Portland area even after being named Brewers manager.

IN THE DUGOUT:

George Bamberger, Trebelhorn's predecessor, was known as a sit-back-and-wait manager. Trebelhorn represents a dramatic shift in style for a club that ranked 12th among 14 AL teams with 667 runs scored.

He will use the hit-and-run much more extensively and regards at least five Brewers players as having the potential to steal 20 bases or more. Look for Milwaukee runners to be consistently moving on 2-2 and 3-2 counts.

When Trebelhorn first managed in the minor leagues, he became well known for a freewheeling style that put his clubs at the top of the circuit in stolen bases. But stolen bases alone were not winning ballgames for his

MANAGERS - AMERICAN LEAGUE

(Tom Trebelhorn - continued)

clubs; as a result, Trebelhorn has come to a more conservative view on the value of the stolen base, saying he no longer regards it as a terrific weapon but merely as a good one.

Trebelhorn will make full use of his bench. He believes someone good enough to be in the majors is good enough to play.

Trebelhorn is confident the Brewers can significantly improve defensively this year--but that will be a chore. Milwaukee ranked 12th in the league last year in defense and made 40 errors in their last 34 games. The new manager feels that more concentration on defensive fundamentals is the cure.

THE PITCHING STAFF:

Trebelhorn places great faith in his bullpen and won't hesitate to yank a starter when trouble is brewing. He expects to have three or four relievers on his 1987 staff notch 45-55 appearances each.

Trebelhorn is determined to avoid a situation in which the pitcher warming in the bullpen has better stuff than the one still in the game. Even workhorse Teddy Higuera, the staff ace and one of the league's premier pitchers, may find himself with fewer complete games.

Trebelhorn has great faith in the one-two punch of righthander Mark Clear and lefthander Dan Plesac in the pen. As long as either is effective, Trebelhorn will be inclined not to make a change because of a pinch-hitter. Although the highly regarded Plesac is seen as having potential as a starter, Trebelhorn is committed to him in relief.

OVERALL:

Trebelhorn was a surprise choice to those outside the Milwaukee organization after Bamberger resigned. The club's choice appears to be a good one because the Brewers are depending on the development of young players. A manager with the patience of a teacher is required, and Trebelhorn, by vocation, is exactly that. He realizes the Brewers are rebuilding and can bear the growing pains as long as development continues.

☆☆☆☆☆☆☆☆☆☆☆☆☆☆☆☆☆

TOM KELLY
MINNESOTA TWINS

Born: 8-15-50 in Graceville, MN
Major League Playing Experience:
   1975: third baseman, Minnesota Twins
Minor League Managing Experience:
   1977-82: Minnesota Twins' system
Major League Coaching Experience:
   1983-86: third base coach,
   Minnesota Twins
Major League Managing Experience:
   1986 to present: Minnesota Twins

(Tom Kelly - continued)

IN THE CLUBHOUSE:

Tom Kelly enters his first full season with a great advantage: his players really wanted him to get the job. Kelly replaced former manager Ray Miller in September last season and was well liked.

Most of the Twins know Kelly from the minor leagues. He has their respect and confidence. He will not need the time a new manager typically requires to learn what makes each player tick. Judging by the Twins' response, Kelly has the right touch.

Kelly is aware of the importance of the proper clubhouse attitude and firmly believes that a positive attitude is directly related to a winning performance.

IN THE DUGOUT:

Kelly manages by instinct. He is aware of the statistics available on matchups, but believes they are often misleading. If Kelly's heart tells him something the numbers don't, the heart wins every time.

The Twins are known for their reliance on home runs, especially in the Metrodome, better known as the Homerdome.

The Twins do pack power. They ranked second in the American League with 196 homers and feature such sluggers as Kirby Puckett (31 homers in '86), Gary Gaetti (34) and Kent Hrbek (29).

Kelly believes, however, that the launching pad effect of the Metrodome is exaggerated. He vows not sit back and wait for the three-run home run, reasoning, "Why wait for something that might never happen?" To force action, he will move runners with the hit-and-run and bunt more often than his predecessors and generally try to instill a more aggressive approach.

THE PITCHING STAFF:

To develop this club's pitching staff into an effective bunch represents Kelly's stiffest challenge this season. In 1986, the Twins ranked last in the American League with a 4.77 ERA. Their bullpen ranked next-to-last in the majors with 24 saves.

Kelly will put all of his effort into fashioning a bullpen, which could be the key to improving his heavily worked, inconsistent starters.

Kelly is working to build the confidence of converted starter Mark Portugal, a righthander being counted on to develop into the bullpen stopper this year.

He also is banking on George Frazier, another righthander, to complement Portugal. Neither has demonstrated the ability to do what Kelly will be asking, but Kelly has no other choice than to hope for the best. He is not willing to simply look on while his starters fail.

OVERALL:

As this season begins, Kelly will be on his honeymoon,

MANAGERS - AMERICAN LEAGUE

(Tom Kelly - continued)

the length of which will be determined by the team's success. He is a popular figure who will please Twins fans simply by improving on last year's 71-91, sixth-place finish in the AL West.

LOU PINIELLA
NEW YORK YANKEES

Born: 8-28-43 in Tampa, FL
Major League Playing Experience:
  1964: Baltimore Orioles
  1968-84: outfielder, Cleveland Indians
  Kansas City Royals, New York Yankees
Major League Coaching Experience:
  1984-85: hitting instructor,
  New York Yankees
Major League Managing Experience:
  1986 to present: New York Yankees

IN THE CLUBHOUSE:

Members of the New York Yankees rejoiced at the hiring of Lou Piniella before the 1986 season for a number of reasons.

First, they liked his personality and style when he played for the Yankees and valued him when he was their batting instructor. Secondly, he was not Billy Martin, the disliked manager he replaced.

After one full season, Piniella still has the players' favor. But he still has to prove to them that *he* is in charge of the lineup, not meddling owner George Steinbrenner. Last season, for instance, when Dave Winfield was briefly platooned in right field, the 10-time All-Star suggested the move was Steinbrenner's. Piniella did not deny the charge.

Throughout his career as a player, Piniella was notorious for his hot temper. During a batting slump, say, no watercooler was safe from his wrath. But with only a few exceptions during his first year as manager last season, Piniella did a good job at controlling his emotions during and after games. Yankee players almost welcomed his rare temper tantrums, feeling they were good for both him and them as a time-tested means of blowing off steam.

IN THE DUGOUT:

Piniella was not decisive enough in his handling of players as a rookie manager. He would make plans for individual players, but then abruptly abandoned the blueprint.

When young slugger Dan Pasqua was called up from the minors in May, for instance, Piniella first promised that Pasqua would play. Pasqua was used irregularly until Piniella finally decided to go with a set linep late in

(Lou Piniella - continued)

the season. The manager later admitted that he should have stuck with a set lineup sooner.

Piniella is not afraid of unorthodox moves. In an emergency last season, Piniella used Don Mattingly, a Gold Glove first baseman who is lefthanded, at third base. Mattingly sparkled in the hot corner and Piniella beamed. In another experiment, Piniella took Rickey Henderson, one of the greatest leadoff hitters in baseball history, and moved him lower in the order. The idea was dropped after one game, but at least Piniella was willing to attempt something radically different while the club was slumping.

Piniella urges the Yankees to play aggressively, and they do. He vowed to stress baserunning and the ability to move runners as he prepared for spring training this year.

THE PITCHING STAFF:

Piniella showed his inexperience in handling the pitching staff. Early last season, he had little feel for the proper moment to remove his starting pitchers. At times, the sign to the bullpen seemed premature. On other occasions, it appeared he allowed starters to talk him into leaving them in, with poor results.

Piniella is blessed with the ability to analyze the strengths and weaknesses of opposing pitchers as well as his own staff. As his initial managerial campaign wore on, he learned to trust his instinct more rather than what pitchers, catchers and even coaches were telling him.

Piniella never faltered in his commitment to Dave Righetti, even as the bullpen ace slumped early in the 1986 season. Righetti justified that faith by achieving a major league record of 46 saves.

OVERALL:

Piniella has perhaps the most difficult managerial job in all of baseball. He is faced with the impatient Steinbrenner, a massive press corps, and a team of high-salaried stars often upset with the quirks of an unpredictable ownership. Despite the shortcomings that might be expected of a rookie manager in Piniella's precarious position, particularly one with no minor league managerial experience, he did well. More is expected the second time around.

MANAGERS - AMERICAN LEAGUE

TONY LaRUSSA
OAKLAND A's

Born: 10-4-44 in Tampa, FL
Major League Playing Experience:
  1963-73: Kansas City/Oakland A's,
  Atlanta Braves, Chicago Cubs
Minor League Managing Experience:
  1978: Chicago White Sox's system
Major League Coaching Experience:
  1978: Chicago White Sox
Major League Managing Experience:
  1979-86: Chicago White Sox
  1986 to present: Oakland A's

IN THE CLUBHOUSE:

Oakland hired Tony LaRussa soon after firing easygoing Jackie Moore. The A's brought in LaRussa to be a "presence," according to Sandy Alderson, vice president of baseball operations.

Among other things, LaRussa is most certainly a "presence." What else would you expect from a 1978 graduate of Florida State University's Law School who generally spends his offseason working for a Sarasota, Florida law firm.

LaRussa's aura is achieved through respect and friendship. LaRussa reaches out to his players and most respond with fierce loyalty. When LaRussa was on the verge of being fired as Chicago White Sox manager after six full seasons in that position, players rallied behind their leader. T-shirts reading "Save the Skipper" appeared throughout the clubhouse. LaRussa has won over the A's in the same way.

IN THE DUGOUT:

LaRussa is very active. He is quick to shuffle his lineup if he doesn't like what he's been seeing and he uses his bench extensively, which contributes to team morale. He is skillful at finding the proper role for a player and at recognizing when those particular talents are needed.

LaRussa is a very positive person in the dugout. He is confident in his abilities, having guided an unspectacular Chicago White Sox club to a 99-63 record in 1983 and the American League West title. He inspires confidence. He will not let his team give up on a game.

LaRussa virtually always goes with the percentages, a trait sometimes used as a knock against him. He studies computer information to determine trends and will count on history repeating itself.

LaRussa's teams are fundamentally sound. Offensively, he will adjust to his players' abilities. He is limited in Oakland because his most dangerous hitter, *Rookie of the Year* Jose Canseco, is as noted for his many strikeouts as for his mammoth home runs.

(Tony LaRussa - continued)

Canseco fanned 175 times to go with 33 home runs and 117 RBIs last year.

Still, the A's have fine speed overall and tied for second in the league with 139 stolen bases in 1986. LaRussa will have them among the leaders in that category again.

THE PITCHING STAFF:

LaRussa trusts his pitchers more than many managers. When he goes to the mound, it is usually with an open mind. Not surprisingly, established starters get the benefit of the doubt.

Once LaRussa goes to his bullpen, it usually means a series of changes because of his unswerving faith in the percentages.

Changes may be more frequent than usual because Oakland's middle relinspis sorely lacking. LaRussa always shows great faith in his bullpen stoppers and Jay Howell will be no exception. A problem will occur if Howell breaks down physically, which the hard-thrower often does.

LaRussa's greatest challenge in his handling of an injury-plagued, problem-filled staff is his treatment of two temperamental but very talented pitchers from the Dominican Republic, Joaquin Andujar and Jose Rijo.

LaRussa is trying to coax Andujar into ending his feuds with umpires (Joaquin, you will remember, was dragged from the diamond after being ejected in the seventh game of the 1985 World Series). Rijo is overpowering--when he has his control.

OVERALL:

LaRussa worked wonders with the A's after taking over on July 7. He inherited a 32-52 last-place wreck. More than anything, he transformed the attitudes of the players. He suddenly had them thinking like winners and they started winning, finishing 76-86, tied for Kansas City for third in the AL West. That represented a significant turnaround for a franchise that had not placed higher than fourth since winning the division under Billy Martin in the strike-interrupted 1981 season.

LaRussa will be aided in his first full season by the momentum generated late last summer. He has the full confidence of front office officials who were sold on LaRussa even before they interviewed him. They are more convinced than ever that they made the perfect choice. They also understand that LaRussa has an improving club--made at least more appealing by the addition of Mr. October, Reggie Jackson--but understand the club has too many deficiences for Jackson to be an October hero one more time.

☆☆☆☆☆☆☆☆☆☆☆☆☆☆☆☆☆☆☆☆☆☆

MANAGERS - AMERICAN LEAGUE

DICK WILLIAMS
SEATTLE MARINERS

Born: 5-7-28 in St. Louis, MO
Major League Playing Experience:
1951-64: infielder/outfielder,
Brooklyn Dodgers, Baltimore Orioles,
Cleveland Indians, Kansas City A's,
Boston Red Sox
Minor League Managing Experience:
1965-66: Boston Red Sox's system
Major League Managing Experience:
1967-69, 1971-85: Boston Red Sox,
Oakland A's, California Angels,
Montreal Expos, San Diego Padres
1986 to present: Seattle Mariners

IN THE CLUBHOUSE:

"It's possible I may be overdemanding for some players. But I'm not hired to be a nice guy. I'm hired to win baseball games."

Dick Williams, the demanding man behind that quote, wins. He's made four trips to the World Series with three different teams over the course of his major league managerial career. If not for the success of his teams, he would have been out of baseball long ago.

Williams' reputation as a rebuilder is well established. The Mariners, who have never had a winning season, are in desperate need of that kind of help.

When he was hired last May, Williams said that the first step he would take with this club was to develop a positive attitude. Much of his energy will be devoted to that this season. Williams' history is to rouse poor clubs to great heights. But that is in the short term; his pattern for the long term is abrasive. As Williams' tenure increases with a particular club, his players' tolerance for his tough-guy approach dwindles. By the end, he is disliked by most everyone in the clubhouse and front office and is even despised by a few.

Needless to say, Williams demands hard work and competence. He will not make excuses for his players. Danny Tartabull was traded despite 25 home runs and 96 RBIs as a rookie. The official reason for the trade given by the Mariners is that the club (most likely Williams) did not like Tartabull's work habits.

IN THE DUGOUT:

Williams experimented with his personnel upon replacing the fired Chuck Cottier last season and found much of the material to his disliking. Williams never found a suitable leadoff hitter, which is essential to the aggressive style he wants to implement.

Williams is further hindered by what seems to be the

(Dick Williams - continued)

Mariners' penchant for striking out (it was against this club that Roger Clemens set a major league strikeout record last year for a nine-inning game by fanning 20 batters).

Jim Presley, one of Williams' big guns with 27 homers and 107 RBIs, fanned 172 times in 1986. Phil Bradley, despite a .310 average, went down on strikes 134 times. Williams thus must think twice before flashing the steal and hit-and-run signs he favors.

Williams is not afraid to make major adjustments and his experiments are often brilliant strokes. Tartabull's bat, for instance, woke up after Williams switched him from second base to the outfield last season.

Williams will continue to juggle his lineup. The Mariners were active at the winter meetings and a drastic overhaul is anticipated until the new manager feels comfortable with the personnel. Williams will insist on it.

THE PITCHING STAFF:

It will be interesting to see how Williams handles the Mariners' young, erratic, still-promising pitchers.

The Mariners are loaded with good arms who were high draft choices. Former first-round picks Mike Moore, Billy Swift and Mike Morgan have all been major disappointments to date.

Mark Langston, a third-round pick, has been a highly erratic pitcher, being either overpowering or way wild. Williams will also have two more youngsters to handle this year, Scott Bankhead from Kansas City and Dennis Powell from Los Angeles. The lot of them should keep Williams busy.

In the club's haste to improve, Seattle is thought to have rushed and mishandled most of their pitchers. That notwithstanding, Williams must make relatively quick judgments on all of them. It's a case of do the job or else.

Williams may have to stick with his starters longer than he wants to because the bullpen is a potential disaster. Lefthander Matt Young, a converted starter who emerged as the club leader with 13 saves, was dealt to the Dodgers over the winter.

OVERALL:

Williams and the Mariners may regret their marriage. The organization has been accused of paying more attention to the payroll than to the won-lost column. Williams starts his first full season with a plethora of problems. He is capable, however, of taking a club with little material and transforming it into a contender.

Williams at least started in the right frame of mind. "I'm going to try to be nicer here," he said upon taking the job. "My wife says, 'Be nice, be nice.' "

MANAGERS - AMERICAN LEAGUE

BOBBY VALENTINE
TEXAS RANGERS

Born: 5-13-50 in Stamford, CT
Major League Playing Experience:
1969-79: infielder/outfielder,
Los Angeles Dodgers, California Angels,
San Diego Padres, New York Mets,
Seattle Mariners
Major League Coaching Experience:
1983-85: third base coach,
New York Mets
Major League Managing Experience:
1985 to present: Texas Rangers

IN THE CLUBHOUSE:

"I find out where they come from and meet them halfway. It's easier to find the key to open that door if in fact you know the neighborhood a guy's living in."

That Bobby Valentine statement best summarizes what this manager is about. He not only knows the neighborhoods his players live in, but he could probably tell you about their wives, children and pets, too. Valentine cares about his players. In fact, he regards "empathy"as his greatest asset.

Valentine is in many ways a clone of Los Angeles Dodgers manager Tommy Lasorda, whom he played for and remains close to. Valentine has some Hollywood in him, with the ability to entertain reporters and audiences everywhere. He is forever bubbly, an attitude reflected in slogans hanging in the Rangers' clubhouse. "Winning is an attitude," reads one. "You can if you believe you can," booms another. One would think major leaguers are too sophisticated for such basic motivation. But given the attitudinal turnaround of the Rangers under this enthusiastic manager, apparently not.

IN THE DUGOUT:

Valentine is extremely aggressive, a quality that helped shorten his promising playing career as a No. 1 draft choice. On May 17, 1973, as a left fielder for the California Angels, he raced to the wall in pursuit of a fly ball off the bat of Oakland's Dick Green. The ball cleared the wall and Valentine broke his right leg in two places in a collision with the fence. He was never the same player after that.

Still, Valentine has never wavered in his belief that the game must be played with abandon. His aggressiveness, however, will sometimes run the Rangers out of innings: Texas had the most runners caught stealing of any American League club (86).

More significantly, though, the Rangers set a club record with 771 runs in 1986, Valentine's first full season, and were shut out only four times, matching the world champion New York Mets for the lowest total in the majors.

(Bobby Valentine - continued)
THE PITCHING STAFF:

Valentine's pitchers are routinely observed throwing balls as part of their pre-game preparation--footballs, that is.

Valentine and pitching coach Tom House, who at last check was writing his doctoral dissertation on terminal adolescence in professional sports, believe throwing the pigskin in tight spirals helps discipline pitchers' mechanics on the mound.

Valentine reversed the Rangers' fortunes by risking everything on young, unproven pitchers with an abundance of raw talent. He rolled the dice, for instance, with righthander Bobby Witt, an extremely hard thrower who had never won a professional game before last season. Witt wound up breaking an American League record with 22 wild pitches--*but*, thanks to Valentine's patience and careful handling, Witt won his last seven decisions.

Valentine also groomed Mitch Williams, an unbridled lefthander who walked 117 batters in 99 innings with Class A Salem in 1985. Williams led the majors in '86 with 80 appearances and is on the verge of becoming a premier bullpen stopper.

OVERALL:

Many believe the Baseball Writers' Association of America should have named Valentine the American League Manager of the Year instead of Boston's John McNamara. The upstart Rangers gained 25 additional wins, the greatest improvement of any major league team and the fifth greatest one-year improvement since divisional play began in 1969. He gave young players an opportunity to make the difference for this club and they did. He allowed Pete Incaviglia to make the leap from college ball to the majors and stuck with Incaviglia even after the slugger produced just six hits in his first 50 at-bats. Valentine's faith, as usual, was rewarded. Incaviglia tied a club record by clouting 30 home runs, only the 16th player in major league history to hit that many in his first season.

MANAGERS - AMERICAN LEAGUE

JIMY WILLIAMS
TORONTO BLUE JAYS

Born: 10-4-43 in Arroyo Grande,CA
Major League Playing Experience:
1966-67: shortstop,
St. Louis Cardinals
Minor League Managing Experience:
1974-79: California Angels' and
St. Louis Cardinals' systems
Major League Coaching Experience:
1980-85: third base coach,
Toronto Blue Jays
Major League Managing Experience:
1986 to present: Toronto Blue Jays

IN THE CLUBHOUSE:

Jimy Williams, who was promoted from third base coach to manager after the 1985 season when Bobby Cox left to become Atlanta's general manager, proved his managerial mettle early.

The Jays, riding high after their first division title, stumbled badly at the start of Williams' tenure and dropped 18 of their first 30 games. Another manager might have responded with a series of desperate moves. Not Williams. He kept his poise and the Blue Jays kept their poise, regrouping to climb back into the AL East race. The Jays were not eliminated until they lost to the eventual division winners, the Boston Red Sox, in late September. The comeback is quite a credit to the Jays and their manager.

Williams is a quiet sort who fits in well with the Toronto ballclub. He has continued one of his chores as a coach, which is to pitch batting practice. He blends in easily before games and players can feel he is one with them.

IN THE DUGOUT:

Williams was wise in choosing to follow Cox's lead in the handling of personnel. It was, after all, a proven formula.

Cox used many lefty/righty switches, the most successful being the strict platoon of Garth Iorg and Rance Mulliniks at third base. Williams stayed with that pattern.

Williams also approached the club with an open mind. Breaking-ball specialist Mark Eichhorn attended spring training in 1986 as a non-roster player. He finished the season with 14 victories and 10 saves and was a perfect complement to fireballing Tom Henke. Williams began 1986 with Tony Fernandez batting second. He was soon moved up to leadoff and responded with 213 hits, which was the most in major league history by a shortstop.

Williams deserves credit as well for the Jays' excellent play in the field. They led the American League with a .984 fielding percentage last season.

(Jimy Williams - continued)
THE PITCHING STAFF:

Williams' biggest problem on the Blue Jay pitching staff this season is Dave Stieb. The performance of the author of the autobiography "Tomorrow I'll Be Perfect" hasn't been close to that.

Stieb is the key to the staff and Williams has had many difficult moments on the mound with the temperamental righthander.

Williams spent a lot of time at the mound overall as the Jays recorded just 16 complete games (only the Texas Rangers and New York Yankees had fewer).

Williams has an outstanding one-two punch in the bullpen in Henke and Eichhorn and he goes with it often. Williams got himself in trouble when he lifted starters in favor of other relievers, however. It is up to the Jays' starters to develop more consistency this year.

Williams likes to play the lefty/righty percentages although, as would be expected, Henke is given every opportunity to close out a game.

OVERALL:

Williams did well as a rookie manager, particularly considering that he replaced a popular predecessor. Williams has the transition from coach to manager behind him. As a further advantage, he has the momentum of a strong finish in 1986. Beyond that, the club already has shown itself capable of winning the division.

With that comes the pressure of getting it done. A middle-of-the-pack showing in a difficult division could doom Williams.

CHUCK TANNER
ATLANTA BRAVES

Born: *7-4-29 in New Castle, PA*
Major League Playing Experience:
   1955-62: outfielder,
   Milwaukee Braves, Chicago Cubs, Cleveland Indians, Los Angeles Angels
Minor League Managing Experience:
   1963-70: Los Angeles Angels' system
Major League Managing Experience:
   1970-1985: Chicago White Sox, Oakland A's, Pittsburgh Pirates
   1986 to present: Atlanta Braves

IN THE CLUBHOUSE:

Until the last couple of years, the one trait of teams managed by Chuck Tanner has been that they were loose and ready to play when it came time for the game.

Tanner is a master of clubhouse psychology. He has taken the likes of Richie Allen and turned him into an MVP. He put together a clubhouse full of mavericks back in the '70s to make a world championship team in Pittsburgh.

Over the past few seasons, however, the Tanner magic has been lost. Whether or not it is because baseball players are a different breed now or because Tanner has become more withdrawn from his players, there can be no doubt that Tanner failed to convince the likes of George Hendrick, Bill Madlock and John Candelaria to produce up to their capabilities when he managed them in Pittsburgh.

At Atlanta, Tanner inherited a team that seemed to need his touch, yet no one individual player's production increased significantly last year. In fact, the contributions of several key Braves players declined.

IN THE DUGOUT:

The one thing certain about the way Chuck Tanner manages a game is that nothing is certain. Tanner plays hunches and loves the trick play.

One of his greatest moments as a manager came in Pittsburgh in 1979 when he sent lefthanded John Milner up to pinch-hit against lefthander Tug McGraw in a crucial game. Milner hit a grand slam home run.

Tanner has been known to play a seven-man infield, to use a pet trick bunt play with runners at first and third and to use a pitcher in the outfield so that he can return him to the mound later in the game.

Although he tries all these trick plays, Tanner would rather see Dale Murphy or Willie Stargell hitting a home run. He would prefer to pepper his lineup with power hitters.

Tanner managed the Oakland A's when that team broke the major league record for stolen bases (in 1976), yet he has placed much less emphasis on the stolen base

(Chuck Tanner - continued)

in recent years. His penchant for power is understandable as Tanner now manages a club whose home park, Atlanta-Fulton County Stadium, is known as "The Launching Pad."

Tanner likes veteran ballplayers. And he has had quite a few of them in Atlanta. He also likes to list his lineup in ink every day and would prefer not to platoon his position players. Still, Tanner makes good use of his entire roster and last season, blessed with a veteran bench, used the likes of Chris Chambliss and Ted Simmons at every opportunity.

THE PITCHING STAFF:

Tanner likes a five-man starting rotation but does not feel as though each pitcher must complete what he starts. If he gets seven innings from a starter, Tanner is happy. Traditionally, Tanner has been known as being one who goes quickly to his bullpen and brags that he converted Goose Gossage and Terry Forster into relievers when both were still young starting pitchers.

He has relied on the likes of Gossage and Kent Tekulve to save games for him and last year made great use of rookie lefthander Paul Assenmacher and veteran Gene Garber in the absence of the injured Bruce Sutter.

OVERALL:

Tanner's reputation has been tarnished the past three seasons with last-place finishes, but he steadfastly maintains that his style is the right one. Tanner's greatest skills are his ability to adapt his game to the type of team he has and his ability to sell his players on the virtues of what he is doing. Once he gets his team to believe in him, he can win.

☆☆☆☆☆☆☆☆☆☆☆☆☆☆☆☆☆

GENE MICHAEL
CHICAGO CUBS

Born: *6-2-38 in Kent, OH*
Major League Playing Experience:
   1966-75: shortstop,
   Pittsburgh Pirates, Los Angeles Dodgers, New York Yankees, Detroit Tigers
Minor League Managing Experience:
   1979: New York Yankees' system
Major League Coaching Experience:
   1978-86: first and third base coach, New York Yankees
Major League Managing Experience:
   1980-82: New York Yankees
   1986 to present: Chicago Cubs

(Gene Michael - continued)

IN THE CLUBHOUSE:

At first glance, one might think that Gene Michael's occupation is that of a social studies teacher in high school. He's Mr. Nice Guy, Mr. Average, a soft-spoken sort who does not come on strong.

In fact, Michael's meetings with the Cubs over the final weeks of last season were more like teaching sessions than a forum in which he listed his concerns: there was little yelling and screaming.

Michael did not have much time to prove himself during his stay with the Cubs last season following the firing of Jim Frey in June. Early on, Michael turned the handling of the game over to coach John Vukovich while he learned the league.

IN THE DUGOUT:

It seems as though Michael is going to attempt to bring something to the Cubs that they have not had much of in the past: a running game.

Playing in the friendly confines of Wrigley Field, the Cubs have traditionally been built around power, with plodders holding down most of the key spots. Michael, however, likes to run and will do his best to turn loose the players at his disposal who can motor.

Ryne Sandberg and Bob Dernier were the only two running threats last year but young Chico Walker was given freedom to run under Michael in September. Michaels' green light allowed Walker to tie the team record with 15 stolen bases in the month.

Michael is not the type of manager who platoons and will go with the set lineup that has become a Chicago tradition. What he is going to try to do is blend some youth together with the veterans. In 1987, Michael is likely to give rookie outfielder Rafael Palmeiro a shot at winning the left-field job while at the same time trying to figure out who will play at third base.

THE PITCHING STAFF:

The biggest change Michael will affect on the pitching staff is his insistence that they not be psyched out by Wrigley Field. In the past, Cubs pitchers avoided the inside corner of the plate in fear of seeing baseballs fly into the bleachers.

Michael insists his pitchers use the entire plate and pitch inside. He brought in pitching coach Herm Starrette to establish that philosophy.

Last September Michael looked at his younger starting pitchers like Jamie Moyer, Drew Hill and Greg Maddux, liked what he saw and is expected to work them into his staff. This is not to say that he will abandon veteran starters such as Rick Sutcliffe, Dennis Eckersley and Scott Sanderson. Michael is going to need every ounce of strength the starters have because he does not have a deep bullpen. Lee Smith is his only dependable shortman and he needs to enter a game very late to work his magic.

OVERALL:

Michael is used to difficult situations, having managed the New York Yankees for George Steinbrenner. Michael's experience in the hot seat will come in handy in Chicago because that's pretty much where he finds himself now. He is managing a team that has decayed with age and that finished in fifth-place last season. What's more, the Cubs have been grooming coach John Vukovich to manage eventually and he will be looking over Michael's shoulder should he fail to produce a miracle with the Cubs.

☆☆☆☆☆☆☆☆☆☆☆☆☆☆☆☆☆☆☆☆

PETE ROSE
CINCINNATI REDS
Born: *4-14-41 in Cincinnati, OH*
Major League Playing Experience:
*1963 to present: outfielder,
first baseman, Cincinnati Reds,
Philadelphia Phillies, Montreal Expos*
Major League Managing Experience:
1984 to present: Cincinnati Reds

IN THE CLUBHOUSE:

If Pete Rose has an effect on a team, it is more in the clubhouse than on the field. This effect will be doubled when he finally accepts the fact that his playing days are over and that from here on in, it's Pete Rose, Manager.

Rose's enthusiasm for the game and his will to win are contagious. When the Cincnnati Reds were the dominant team in the 1970s, it was as much because of Rose's determination as it was anything else. It is significant to understand how difficult it is to repeat as world champions; in the 1970s there were three repeat winners: Oakland, Cincinnati and the Yankees. Each team was driven by the personality of a Reggie Jackson, Billy Martin or Pete Rose.

Rose has managed to accept the need for younger players while making the difficult decision to ease out his friends and long-time teammates, the likes of shortstop Dave Concepcion and Tony Perez.

As would be expected, Rose leans on his veteran players. The acquisition of Buddy Bell and the latitude given Bell through some lean times indicate Rose's respect for time-tested, gritty ballplayers.

Rose has been accused of having difficulty accepting young players who do not display his same unquenchable thirst for the game. This was evidenced last season when Kal Daniels found it difficult to win a starting postion.

IN THE DUGOUT:

Rose gets his real test this season as a manager now

(Pete Rose - continued)

that George Scherger, upon whom Rose leaned for advice while he was a player-manager, has retired.

Rose likes to manage an aggressive type of game and will allow those runners who can do it to run on their own.

His strategy is mostly old school. A switch-hitter himself, Rose likes to platoon and set up lefty vs. righty situations, particularly with his younger players.

He will play for the big inning, centered around the power potential of Eric Davis and Dave Parker.

THE PITCHING STAFF:

Rose has not been able to get maximum performances out of his starting pitchers and, in the final analysis, that has killed the Reds.

With one of the best bullpens in the National League in Ron Robinson from the right side and John Franco from the left, Rose should be quicker with the hook than he has been to date. Last season, Rose discovered the awesome potential of rookie shortman lefthander Rob Murphy, who went 6-0 with an incredible 0.72 ERA. If these three relievers aren't a deep bullpen, what's the point of having them?

In the two years Rose has managed the Reds, starter Mario Soto has not pitched well. Soto underwent arm surgery last year and his recovery and his willingness to perform at the top of his game for Rose is one of the key items for the Reds in 1987.

On the positive side, Rose made a good move last year by converting Ted Power from relief into the starting rotation.

OVERALL:

This is a crucial year for Pete Rose as a manager. A year ago there were those who thought his club was talented enough to win the West. But the Reds got off to a horrendous start and could not recover. This year, however, there are many organizations who are drooling over the young talent the Reds have gathered. It is up to Rose to mold that raw talent into a team and get 162 games' worth of production out of it.

HAL LANIER
HOUSTON ASTROS
Born: 7-4-42 in Denton, NC
Major League Playing Experience:
   1964-73: second baseman/shortstop,
   San Francisco, New York Yankees
Minor League Managing Experience:
   1976-1980: St. Louis Cardinals' system
Major League Coaching Experience:
   1981-85: first and third base coach,
   St. Louis Cardinals
Major League Managing Experience:
   1986 to present: Houston Astros

IN THE CLUBHOUSE:

Although the generation gap between Hal Lanier and his players is relatively small, he keeps his distance from his players. Last season, he used coach Gene Tenace, who is himself not far removed from his days as a major leaguer, as a liason to hear the players' complaints.

If Lanier had a problem with an individual player, he called a player in for a one-on-one session. These discussions were private and their content was kept from the media as much as possible.

Lanier likes a team which is fundamentally sound and does not make mistakes on the field. As a result, he prefers veteran players. More than anything else, gaffes in the field set Lanier afire.

IN THE DUGOUT:

Seldom does a manager in his first season win the kind of universal respect that Hal Lanier received after winning the National League Western Division title last year. Normally, a winning rookie manager is looked upon as a man who inherited a talented team, but this is not the attitude toward Lanier throughout the league. Indeed, Lanier had to call upon all the skills he learned at the knee of Whitey Herzog in St. Louis to pull it off and in so doing quickly established his style as a manager.

Lanier is a gambling manager, one who will steal a base and demand the bases be run aggressively. He'll make use of the squeeze play and the hit-and-run.

Lanier uses his entire roster well, platooning where necessary, such as the way he platooned veterans Phil Garner and Denny Walling at third base and Dickie Thon and Craig Reynolds at shortstop in 1986.

THE PITCHING STAFF:

If Lanier inherited any great talent on the Astros' 1986 team, it was in his pitching staff. He was smart enough to give Mike Scott the ball every fifth day and that resulted

(Hal Lanier - continued)

in the Cy Young Award for the split-finger ace.

However, Lanier had to do a lot of scrambling with his pitchers during the season and proved himself capable. When Nolan Ryan was injured, Lanier did not allow the Astro staff to crumble. He nursed a brilliant season out of rookie Jim Deshaies and allowed Charlie Kerfeld to be his outrageous self while filling the setup role to perfection.

Lanier is one of the modern-day managers who relies heavily on the bullpen but found himself without a talented lefthander upon whom he could rely. Because of this, he had to pick his spots carefully for his ace, Dave Smith, and did so with such expertise that Smith finished with 33 saves in 54 appearances.

OVERALL:

A managerial star was born last season in Hal Lanier, who skillfully handled a Houston team that was in need of guidance to the divisional title. Lanier, while far more low-key than his mentor in St. Louis, has adopted a number of Whitey Herzog's best points and blended it with his own background to create a unique style that is capable of drawing the most out of a team.

☆☆☆☆☆☆☆☆☆☆☆☆☆☆☆☆☆☆☆

TOMMY LASORDA
LOS ANGELES DODGERS

Born: 9-22-27 in Norristown, PA
Major League Playing Experience:
    1954-56: pitcher,
    Brooklyn Dodgers, Kansas City Athletics
Minor League Managing Experience:
    1965-72: Los Angeles Dodgers' system
Major League Managing Experience:
    1977 to present: Los Angeles Dodgers

IN THE CLUBHOUSE:

The walls of Tommy Lasorda's Dodger Stadium office tell a story. There are pictures of Lasorda with everyone from Ted Williams to Ronald Reagan. There is a full wall devoted to his friend Frank Sinatra.

But there is more. There is a picture of Lasorda in a whirlpool with his pitcher Jerry Reuss. In many ways, that one picture exposes the essence of Tommy Lasorda. He is the LA manager, and often comes on as all glitz and show biz but the man can handle his players. From a flake like Jay Johnstone or a character like Reuss to Steve Garvey and his three-piece-suit image, Lasorda has always found a way to blend the individuals into a team of baseball players. He will joke with some, push others. His ultimate yardstick has been each

(Tommy Lasorda - continued)

player's accomplishments on the field.

Lasorda has a great knack of keeping his team loose, whether it be by kidding with them, offering them a taste of the never-ending stream of food that passes through his office or by introducing them to the dozens of celebrities who pass through his office.

IN THE DUGOUT:

Lasorda would prefer to be the big inning manager he was when he could turn to Ron Cey, Steve Garvey or Dusty Baker to slash him a home run. He still looks for power in the likes of Mike Marshall, Pedro Guerrero and Franklin Stubbs.

But Lasorda is more of a chameleon as a manager. If a stolen base or a hit-and-run is called for, he'll use it. Davey Lopes never complained about being held back as a basestealer under Lasorda and Mariano Duncan won't either.

Lasorda would like to have a set lineup and go with it 150 games a year, but an assortment of injuries to key players has made that impossible in the recent past.

THE PITCHING STAFF:

Lasorda has always been blessed with superior starting pitching, a Dodger trademark since the Brooklyn days. What's more, behind that he has always had a dependable bullpen upon which he could rely.

Lasorda does not have a set manner of handling pitchers. With Fernando Valenzuela, who can finish what he starts, he has infinite patience. However, he is not as calm when watching a young pitcher try to work his way out of a jam and will be quicker with the hook with an unproven challenger.

OVERALL:

Tommy Lasorda does not get credit for being as successful a manager as he is. His team is always relaxed and ready to play. His bluster and his name-dropping detracts from the fact that he is both a psychologist and a man capable of handling his pitching staff.

☆☆☆☆☆☆☆☆☆☆☆☆☆☆☆☆☆☆

BUCK RODGERS
MONTREAL EXPOS

Born: 8-16-38 in Delaware, OH
Major League Playing Experience:
  1961-69: catcher,
  Los Angeles Angels, California Angels
Minor League Managing Experience:
  1975, 1977: San Francisco Giants' system
Major League Coaching Experience:
  1970-74: pitching coach,
  Minnesota Twins
  1976: coach, San Francisco Giants
  1978-80: third base coach,
  Milwaukee Brewers
Major League Managing Experience:
  1980-82: Milwaukee Brewers
  1985 to present: Montreal Expos

IN THE CLUBHOUSE:

When Buck Rodgers was hired by the Expos in 1984, Montreal management's idea was to replace the ultra-intense Bill Virdon with a more easy-going, new generation manager. Rodgers has filled that role.

Seldom shaken, Rodgers has suffered through a couple of injury-filled seasons without blowing his cool in the clubhouse. He handles his players with a soft touch.

If Rodgers has any great attribute, it's his patience. When he decides he is going to give a player a chance to prove himself, he goes all the way with that player. Two years ago he did so with Herm Winningham, only to have Winningham eventually fail to make it.

This past season, Rodgers' patience was seen in centerfielder Mitch Webster who, after some rough times, panned out and gave the Expos a big lift in center field.

IN THE DUGOUT:

Bob Rodgers is the type of manager who plays for the big inning, even though injuries to key players last year cost him a power-oriented team. Neither Hubie Brooks nor Andres Galarraga, who were initially counted on for power, batted 400 times. Despite the fact that the Expos were leading the majors in home runs for the first month and a half of the season, Montreal hit fewer home runs than every team in the National League except the anemic 1986 St. Louis Cardinals.

Rodgers did not quit looking for the big inning,

(Buck Rodgers - continued)

however. No team used the sacrifice bunt less often than did his Expos: Rodgers called for the sac bunt once every three games.

Rather than bunt, he prefers the stolen base and the hit-and-run. But last season, Rodgers found himself with no one available to execute either maneuver, and he had to scramble for production. This meant taking Tim Raines, who is one of the game's top two leadoff hitters (Rickey Henderson is the other), and dropping him into the No. 3 spot in the order.

For the most part, Rodgers likes to use veteran players over young ballplayers and prefers to use a set lineup and avoid platooning.

THE PITCHING STAFF:

Because his club was short on starting pitching in 1986, Rodgers managed his games with the intent of going to his bullpen (if he had a lead) by the sixth or seventh inning. For two straight years, he has used the bullpen duet of Tim Burke followed by Jeff Reardon with great success.

Burke is the setup man and he has pitched 146 times with a 18-11 record over the past two seasons, leaving the final inning or so for Reardon, who has saved 41 and 35 games in each of the last two seasons.

Rodgers made good use of his only real lefthanded reliever, Bob McClure, but was handicapped because McClure had no help from the left side.

This quick hook has not sat well with his starting pitchers, who have been vocal in their opposition to coming out of games so quickly.

Rodgers likes a five-man rotation but last year had trouble keeping five starters healthy. He did discover a star in Floyd Youmans, who at 22 years old struck out 202 batters in 219 innings. Youmans is now the man around whom Rodgers' rotation will be built.

OVERALL:

Rodgers walked into a deteriorating situation in Montreal and has survived despite many setbacks. In the face of injuries, declining attendance and a history of an underachieving club, Rodgers has been unflappable.

To this point, he has given Montreal exactly what they wanted. Now, however, the job gets tougher; Expos' management wants a pennant.

DAVEY JOHNSON
NEW YORK METS

Born: 1-30-43 in Orlando, FL

Major League Playing Experience:

    1965-1978: second baseman,
    Baltimore Orioles, Atlanta Braves, Philadelphia
    Phillies, Chicago Cubs
    1975-76: Yomiuri Giants, Japan

Minor League Managing Experience:

    1979-1983: Mets' system

Major League Managing Experience:

    1984 to present: New York Mets

IN THE CLUBHOUSE:

Davey Johnson spends a lot of pre-game time out of his office and in the clubhouse with his players. He is not, however, above lowering the boom, as he has done on talented outfielder Darryl Strawberry on a couple of occasions. Johnson deals individually with his players, often wandering around the clubhouse after a game with a beer in his hand, as if to show the players that he once roamed the clubhouses, too.

IN THE DUGOUT:

Davey Johnson is one of the new breed of computerized managers. He makes good use of statistics indicating who hits lefthanders and who hits righthanders. He is not, however, a slave to a digital printout, though some have given him an underserved bad rap for his computer affinity. Johnson often manages by the seat of his pants and sticks to some old-fashioned intuitions.

He platooned Wally Backman, a switch-hitter, at second base with Tim Teufel last season because Backman does not hit well as a righthanded batter. When Darryl Strawberry had trouble hitting lefthanders, he sat him right down.

Yet Johnson etches nothing in stone. He opened the year platooning Ray Knight with Howard Johnson at third base, but when Knight got hot he allowed him to win the job.

With Keith Hernandez, Gary Carter and Strawberry in the heart of his lineup, Johnson naturally plays for the big inning, though he is not afraid to run with Lenny Dykstra or Backman.

He believes in his veterans but trusts his feelings about younger players as well. He stuck with Wally Backman several seasons ago through thick and thin and last year gave rookie Kevin Mitchell a chance when George Foster went sour. Johnson also likes to make use of veterans off his bench, men like Lee Mazzilli or Danny Heep.

Johnson learned the intricacies of involving the entire roster to weave a successful season under the tutelage of

(Davey Johnson - continued)

Earl Weaver when Johnson was a player for him in Baltimore.

THE PITCHING STAFF:

As a manager, Johnson is smart enough to write the name Gooden as his starter on Monday, Ojeda on Tuesday, Darling on Wednesday, Fernandez on Thursday, Aguilera on Friday and back to Gooden again on Saturday. That's really handling pitchers.

In reality, Johnson has been masterful in handling this talented staff. He seldom pushes Gooden, for example, and won't risk the young golden-armed pitcher's future to win just one game.

Johnson has also built one of baseball's best bullpens with Jesse Orosco coming from the left side and Roger McDowell from the right. When the game is on the line, these are the two men who will be there.

Often Johnson will match a relief pitcher to a starter. For example, he'll follow Fernandez, who has a rising fastball, with McDowell, who gives a completely different look as a sinkerball pitcher.

He is confident in the ability of his pitching staff and issued the fewest intentional walks in baseball last year.

OVERALL:

Many people think of Johnson as being arrogant, but when you win 108 games, it is hard not to be. Johnson is more involved in the game than might be immediately apparent. Although he may be chattering away with his staff or the players in the dugout, his mind is always on the top step.

☆☆☆☆☆☆☆☆☆☆☆☆☆☆☆☆☆☆

JOHN FELSKE
PHILADELPHIA PHILLIES

Born: 5-30-42 in Chicago, IL

Major League Playing Experience:

    1968: Chicago Cubs
    1972-73: Milwaukee Brewers

Minor League Managing Experience:

    1974-79: Milwaukee Brewers' system,
    1982-83: Philadelphia Phillies' system

Major League Coaching Experience:

    1980-81: bullpen coach,
    Toronto Blue Jays
    1984: bench coach,
    Philadelphia Phillies

Major League Managing Experience:

    1985 to present: Philadelphia Phillies

(John Felske - continued)

IN THE CLUBHOUSE:

John Felske is a low-key sort of guy who tries to stay out of the limelight. Unlike a manager like Tommy Lasorda or Sparky Anderson, he is not a high-profile media personality.

However, Felske seems to be liked by his players. He doesn't rip them in print and is patient with them.

Felske will kid with his players around the batting cage but doesn't spend a lot of time kidding with them in the locker room.

IN THE DUGOUT:

Last year the Phillies gathered a house full of speed in Juan Samuel, Jeff Stone, Gary Redus and Von Hayes and many expected them to steal 250 or more bases.

It didn't happen, however, and it was due largely to Felske's reluctance to use the running game to his advantage. He is not an adventurer or a gambler.

He seems to be wary of the second guess and, because of it, he gets second guessed for a lack of aggressiveness in the Phillies' game.

Felske's greatest strength is his patience. He is willing to stick with a player, as he did this past season with outfielder Glenn Wilson, who got off to a miserable start only to come on late in the year and finish among the RBI leaders.

Felske goes mostly with a set lineup that includes Mike Schmidt, Wilson and Von Hayes. That accounts for why he plays for the big inning rather than uses the bunt.

THE PITCHING STAFF:

Felske defined the roles of his pitching staff well last year and let them go about doing their job.

Early in the season, he made Tom Hume and Kent Tekulve, two veteran relievers who had once been cast in the role of stopper, into middle relievers. He convinced each man that this was the right spot for him and got exceptional years out of both, using them to set up his short man, Steve Bedrosian.

Until Steve Carlton was released, Felske had the one-time ace lefthander on his staff and, along with the rest of the Phillies organization, could only hope that Carlton still had some pitches left in him. Felske opened the year giving Carlton free rein and leaving him in far too long. When that didn't work, he went to a quick hook, yanking Carlton at the first sign of trouble. Felske also made an interesting move when he took Don Carman, who was having trouble in the bullpen, and converted him into a starting pitcher.

OVERALL:

John Felske doesn't appear to be the type of manager who will manage his way toward victories or away from losses. He will ride with the flow of the game and let the players' chart their own course. He seems to be more reflective as to what is going on around him than he is able to dictate results. Because he is so low key, he probably doesn't get whatever credit is coming his way.

JIM LEYLAND
PITTSBURGH PIRATES
Born: 12-15-44 in Toledo, Ohio
Major League Playing Experience:
 none
Minor League Coaching Experience:
 1970: Detroit Tigers' system
Minor League Managing Experience:
 1971-1981: Detroit Tigers' system
Major League Coaching Experience:
 1982-1985: third base coach and outfield instructor Chicago White Sox
Major League Managing Experience:
 1985: one-day replacement for suspended Chicago White Sox manager Tony LaRussa
 1986 to present: Pittsburgh Pirates

IN THE CLUBHOUSE:

Jim Leyland is a player's manager. Having spent 18 years bouncing around the minor leagues as a catcher without much talent, he became a major league manager-for-a-day for the Chicago White Sox in 1985 when he was an interim replacement for Tony LaRussa. He became the full-time skipper of the Pirates for the 1986 season.

As a result of his minor league toils, Leyland has developed an appreciation for the skills required for big league success.

Leyland is the type who will pat a player on the back when it's necessary to lift or reward a player for a job well done. His attention to the player's plight has earned him a great deal of loyalty and respect among his players after just one season as their manager.

Leyland is not all Mr. Nice Guy, however. He does have a fiery personality and sometimes it is accompanied by a short fuse. He made headlines on numerous occasions last season after a couple of violent clubhouse

(Jim Leyland - continued)
meetings--in some instances flipping a food table and filling the room with obscenities.

IN THE DUGOUT:

Because the 1986 Pirates were lacking in so many areas, Leyland had to platoon a lot and go with young players. Over the course of last year, he used 98 *different lineups.*

However, once Barry Bonds arrived from the minors, Leyland was able to settle down his team somewhat. He stuck with Bonds every day in center field, with Johnny Ray at second base, Jim Morrison at third base and Tony Pena catching. If given his druthers, Leyland would prefer not to be a master juggler of big leaguers, but to have a set lineup.

Leyland does like to play a gambling game, often encouraging the stolen base and employing the hit-and-run. Last season, he trailed Dwight Gooden and the Mets, 5-0, in one game when he turned his baserunners loose and almost stole a victory from the World Champions before losing, 7-5.

The speedy style paid off as the Pirates, despite lacking real power, were in the middle of the league in runs scored.

THE PITCHING STAFF:

Leyland judges each pitcher and each game on its own merits. He will allow a veteran such as Rick Reuschel to stick in there a lot longer than a young, inexperienced pitcher such as Bob Kipper.

The Pirates were pitching-thin last season and, because of the lack of good arms, Leyland had to do a lot of experimenting. He believes in having a "stopper" out of the bullpen and spent part of the season giving Jim Winn, Cecilio Guante, Barry Jones and Don Robinson chances to win that spot.

Leyland uses all of his pitchers, and last year, he experimented with his rotation almost to some excess: 12 different pitchers started games for the Pirates in 1986. He does not play hunches when it comes to pitching, using a lefthander to get out lefthanded hitters and switching to a righthander when a pinch-hitter is sent up.

OVERALL:

Somehow, Jim Leyland managed to make a success out of a first season that saw him lose 98 games. He spent considerable energies trying to instill an overall aggressive attitude among the team's individuals. He is popular with the fans and his players and is the kind of man who will grow in the job if given long enough in a very difficult situation.

WHITEY HERZOG
ST. LOUIS CARDINALS

Born: *11-9-31 in New Athens, IL*
Major League Playing Experience:
1956-1963: outfielder/first baseman, Washington Senators, Kansas City Athletics, Baltimore Orioles, Detroit Tigers
Director of Player Development:
1967-72: New York Mets
Major League Coaching Experience:
1965-66: Kansas City A's, New York Mets
1974-75: California Angels
Major League Managing Experience:
1973-79: Texas Rangers, California Angels Kansas City Royals
1980 to present: St. Louis Cardinals

IN THE CLUBHOUSE:

Perhaps nothing says more about Whitey Herzog's ability to get the most out of his players than the fact that the temperamental pitcher Joaquin Andujar not only won 20 or more games for him in two consecutive years, but actually said that he wanted to play for no other manager than Whitey for the next 100 years.

Herzog has only two rules: be on time and play hard. His players appreciate his straightforward, no-nonsense approach.

A one-time utility player, Herzog has a knack of keeping his utilitymen happy.

IN THE DUGOUT:

Whitey Herzog likes a team with speed and is willing to employ it to its fullest. He has a loud voice in player procurement and has built a team of rabbits. He is not afraid to turn them loose, no matter what the score.

With Vince Coleman, Willie McGee and Ozzie Smith, he uses the stolen base as some teams use the home run. It is an intimidating threat that some have criticized him for using even when the game is seemingly won for his club; yet, while teams do not stop trying to hit home runs when leading 8-0, Herzog will not stop running with the score 8-0.

Not surprisingly, Herzog uses the squeeze play more than any other manager.

He believes in defense as well as speed and when he won the pennant two years ago, he did so on the strength of those two items. However, last season he could not make up for a team batting average of .236, which was 14 points lower than any other team in the National League, nor could he make up for a lack of power as his team hit only 58 home runs.

He doesn't mix up his lineup too often and prefers to

MANAGERS - NATIONAL LEAGUE

(Whitey Herzog - continued)
grind it out with his starting players if possible, allowing second baseman Tommy Herr, Ozzie Smith, McGee and Coleman to play as much as they want.

THE PITCHING STAFF:

Herzog may be the most astute man in the business when it comes to squeezing the most out of a pitching staff. He is a master of the bullpen, and won a pennant in 1982 with Bruce Sutter as his bullpen star by using him in every key situation. Then, when Sutter was gone, Herzog went to a "bullpen by committee" in 1985, and got as much production out of a group that included no one single star.

Last year he brought along rookie Todd Worrell to the point that he broke the rookie save record by 12 saves. Worrell now gives Herzog the stopper to go to that Sutter once was.

Herzog is firm with his pitching decisions. He expects his starters to give him seven good innings and then he marches to the mound to call for the door-slammer. Once he goes to the mound, there is no talking him out out of removing a pitcher.

OVERALL:

Whitey Herzog is considered to be among the game's two or three best managers. He has won five division titles in 11 seasons as a manager. If a poll was taken among the players, it would probably show that most of them would want to play at least one year for Herzog before they were through.

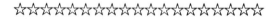

LARRY BOWA
SAN DIEGO PADRES
Born: 12-6-45 in Sacramento, CA
Major League Playing Experience:
  1970-83: shortstop,
  Philadelphia Phillies, Chicago Cubs, NY Mets
Minor League Managing Experience:
  1986: San Diego Padres' system
Major League Managing Experience:
  none

IN THE CLUBHOUSE:

Larry Bowa says he was hired by the Padres to be a cross between Dick Williams, who was too cantankerous to get along with his players, and Steve Boros, who was too laid back to motivate them.

Bowa is less than two years removed from playing in the major leagues and is younger than some of today's

(Larry Bowa - continued)
active players. Because of this he has to work hard to avoid being "one of the boys."

Bowa managed one season in the minor leagues, winning the Pacific Coast League pennant at Hawaii last year and he had difficulties handling his players early in the season. He could not differentiate between those who needed a pat on the back and those who needed to be disciplined.

He said this aspect of the game, learning to give individual treatment to players who needed it, was more difficult than handling the pitching staff.

He was extremely rough at first and was upset by the work habits of his players. He often would hold morning workouts on the day of games. While he says he will not be that extreme in the major leagues, he will be pushing for players to spend extra time working on areas where they are weak.

Bowa also plans on being a disciplinarian and will not hesitate to use fines or bench players as his tools of order.

IN THE DUGOUT:

Bowa's managerial style has been predetermined by the Padres' recent moves toward more speed and youth. He will run with this club and plans to play an aggressive offensive game built around the hitting of Tony Gwynn. Bowa also hopes to make more use of shortstop Gary Templeton's talents by hitting him higher in the order than the No. 8 spot.

Bowa, a slap hitter who used his speed to his advantage when he was a player, will hit-and-run, bunt and steal with the likes of newcomer Stanley Jefferson and Gwynn.

Always a fiery character as a player, Bowa promises to speak his piece when he disagrees with an umpire.

THE PITCHING STAFF:

Bowa inherits a veteran pitching staff with a deep bullpen and he plans to make good use of that bullpen. Few rookie managers have a Goose Gossage to save games for them, to say nothing of Lance McCullers and lefthander Craig Lefferts.

Bowa will have to experiment early in the season before he develops a personality as to how long he will go with his pitchers. He does plan to use a five-man starting rotation

OVERALL:

It is easy to see a lot of Billy Martin in Larry Bowa as he takes his first managerial job in the majors. Like Martin, Bowa is a player who made more of his talent because of an insatiable desire to succeed and is a man who has had

(Larry Bowa - continued)

(Roger Craig - continued)

his share of battles with umpires and reporters. Bowa, however, seems more capable of handling the people around him so that he can hold onto a job.

ROGER CRAIG
SAN FRANCISCO GIANTS

Born: 2-17-30 in Durham, NC

Major League Playing Experience:
1955-66: pitcher,
Brooklyn Dodgers, Los Angeles Dodgers, New York Mets, St. Louis Cardinals, Cincinnati Reds, Philadelphia Phillies

Major League Coaching Experience:
1974-75: pitching coach,
Houston Astros
1976-77: San Diego Padres
1980-84: Detroit Tigers

Minor League Coaching Experience:
1973: Los Angeles Dodgers' system

Minor League Managing Experience:
1968: Los Angeles Dodgers' system

Major League Managing Experience:
1986 to present: San Francisco Giants

IN THE CLUBHOUSE:

The thing Roger Craig does best with a team is pump it full of positive thoughts. He is a master at keeping players from getting down on themselves and in drawing out the best they have to offer.

There were numerous examples of this last season. Rookie pitcher Kelly Downs came up from the minors and lost four games in a row. Craig, however, kept encouraging him and Downs responded by winning his final four decisions with a 1.81 ERA over his last eight starts.

Another example is what Craig did with veteran Juan Berenguer. The righthander was considered washed up with Detroit but Craig took a chance on him. Berenguer was a winning pitcher at Detroit while Craig was the Tigers' pitching coach, but fell apart when Craig left. Reuinted with Craig in San Francisco, Berenguer again became productive.

Craig does not look at whether a player is young or a veteran, but watches for results. He gave rookie Will Clark the first-base job to open the season and reconstructed the career of veteran pitcher Mike LaCoss, benefiting as LaCoss was 9-3 at the All-Star break.

IN THE DUGOUT:

The evidence of good managing comes in winning games you shouldn't. The Giants, a team that lost 100 games in 1985, came from behind more often than any other National League team to win games last season, doing it 40 times under Craig, 24 of those 40 victories coming after the sixth inning. Craig was able to accomplish this because he was seldom outmanaged. Craig used his bench to perfection, leading the majors in pinch-hit production, led by Candy Maldonado and Harry Spilman.

Craig likes to play an aggressive game offensively with an emphasis on the hit-and-run and the stolen base. He is not a slave to the mythical "book," sometimes going against the lefty/righty routine.

Craig pays great attention to statistics, much as does the Mets' Davey Johnson and as did Earl Weaver. If a platoon situation is called for, he uses it, but he doesn't look to platoon players.

THE PITCHING STAFF:

Craig is, of course, the guru of the split-finger fastball and as such has taught the pitch to many of his pitchers. Beyond that, however, he has instilled a "can-do" attitude in each of his players.

Craig took Mike Krukow, a career .500 pitcher, and made a 20-game winner out of him and had a similar effect on the entire staff.

Even though the starting rotation was often in a shambles due to injury, the Giants finished with a 3.33 ERA, third in league behind New York and Houston, the division winners.

Craig knows the fine points of pitching so well that he seldom allows a starter to go one batter too far and, even though his bullpen was one of the club's weaker points, he was able to make good use of it.

OVERALL:

Roger Craig proved last season that he is more than just a man capable of handling pitchers as he took the Giants, a team that had lost 100 games in 1985, and through shrewd managing and positive psychology had them in first place in the West for 47 days during the 1986 season.

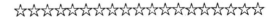

1986 AMERICAN LEAGUE LEADERS

BATTING AVERAGE:
Wade Boggs, Boston, .357
Don Mattingly, New York, .352

HOME RUNS:
Jesse Barfield, Toronto, 40
Dave Kingman, Oakland, 35

HITS:
Don Mattingly, New York, 238
Kirby Puckett, Seattle, 223

DOUBLES:
Don Mattingly, New York, 53
Wade Boggs, Boston, 47

TRIPLES:
Brett Butler, Cleveland, 14
Ruben Sierra, Texas, 10

RUNS:
Rickey Henderson, New York, 130
Kirby Puckett, Seattle, 119

RUNS BATTED IN:
Joe Carter, Cleveland, 121
Jose Canseco, Oakland, 117

GAME-WINNING RBI:
George Bell, Toronto, 15
Cal Ripken, Baltimore, 15
Don Mattingly, New York, 15

WALKS:
Wade Boggs, Boston, 105
Dwight Evans, Boston, 97

STOLEN BASES:
Rickey Henderson, New York, 87
Gary Pettis, California, 50
John Cangelosi, Chicago, 50

WON-LOST:
Roger Clemens, Boston, 24-4
Teddy Higuera, Milwaukee, 20-11

ERA:
Roger Clemens, Boston, 2.48
Teddy Higuera, Milwaukee, 2.79

GAMES:
Mitch Williams, Texas, 80
Dave Righetti, New York, 74

COMPLETE GAMES:
Tom Candiotti, Cleveland, 17
Bert Blyleven, Minnesota, 16

INNINGS PITCHED:
Bert Blyleven, Minnesota, 271.2
Roger Clemens, Boston, 254.1

STRIKEOUTS:
Mark Langston, Seattle, 245
Roger Clemens, Boston, 238

SHUTOUTS:
Jack Morris, Detroit, 6
Bruce Hurst, Boston, 4

SAVES:
Dave Righetti, New York, 46
Don Aase,.Baltimore, 34

1986 NATIONAL LEAGUE LEADERS

BATTING AVERAGE:
Tim Raines, Montreal, .334
Steve Sax, Los Angeles, .332

HOME RUNS:
Mike Schmidt, Philadelphia, 37
Glenn Davis, Houston, 31

HITS:
Tony Gwynn, San Diego, 211
Steve Sax, Los Angeles, 210

DOUBLES:
Von Hayes, Philadelphia, 48
Steve Sax, Los Angeles, 43

TRIPLES:
Mitch Webster, Montreal, 13
Juan Samuel, Philadelphia, 12

RUNS:
Tony Gwynn, San Diego, 107
Von Hayes, Philadelphia, 107

RUNS BATTED IN:
Mike Schmidt, Philadelphia, 119
Dave Parker, Cincinnati, 116

GAME-WINNING RBI:
Gary Carter, New York, 16
Glenn Davis, Houston, 16

WALKS:
Keith Hernandez, New York, 94
Mike Schmidt, Philadelphia, 89

STOLEN BASES:
Vince Coleman, St. Louis, 107
Eric Davis, Cincinnati, 80

WON-LOST:
Fernando Valenzuela, Los Angeles, 21-11
Mike Krukow, San Francisco, 20-9

ERA:
Mike Scott, Houston, 2.22
Bob Ojeda, New York, 2.57

GAMES:
Craig Lefferts, San Diego, 83
Roger McDowell, New York, 75

COMPLETE GAMES:
Fernando Valenzuela, Los Angeles, 20
Dwight Gooden, New York, 12

INNINGS PITCHED:
Mike Scott, Houston, 275.1
Fernando Valenzuela, Los Angeles, 269.1

STRIKEOUTS:
Mike Scott, Houston, 306
Fernando Valenzuela, Los Angeles, 242

SHUTOUTS:
Bob Knepper, Houston, 5
Mike Scott, Houston, 5

SAVES:
Todd Worrell, St. Louis, 36
Jeff Reardon, Montreal, 35

THE PLAYERS

BALTIMORE ORIOLES

PITCHING:

Many pitchers have come back from severe arm injuries, but few have ever come back to throw as hard as Don Aase. His career was virtually over after an injury to his right elbow in 1982. But in 1986, he was the best reliever in the league for four months.

He finished with 34 saves, the most in club history and most ever for a pitcher on a last place team. In one season, he came within seven saves of matching his career total in 168 relief appearances.

Aase throws hard. Then, he throws harder. Then harder. In the end, he's throwing 94 MPH straight over the top. He can rocket his heater at the same velocity (some say more) than before the operation.

Aase works fast. He challenges every hitter. He fears no one. He enjoys the it's-him-or-me confrontation against the great hitters in the league. He doesn't need to pitch inside or even keep the ball down, he is *that* overpowering. His control has always been somewhat erratic, but when he was throwing close to 95 MPH, it doesn't matter much.

At the height of his success last season, Aase would blow hitters away with his fastball, but every so often toss in a little slider. He also showed a new slow curveball that, though seldom used, was devastating next to the fastball. When he had all three pitches working right, he was close to unhittable.

The key to 1986 for Aase--at least for the first four months--was his resiliency. After pitching three straight days only once in 1985 and not always bouncing back well on one day's rest, Aase was there when needed almost every time in 1986. Eventually, however, the overwork tired him out. After the beginning of August, his ERA was 5.32, and he got only six saves.

Though he was never disabled last year, Aase's right elbow needed to be rested more than once for a week each time; he lost some of his velocity. The pitches he was getting up were being hit hard after August. He didn't throw his slider or slow curveball for strikes, so opposing hitters waited for his fastball. He needed a rest towards the end of the season,

DON AASE
RHP, No. 41
RR, 6'3", 222 lbs.
ML Svc: 9 years
Born: 9-8-54 in
Orange, CA

1986 STATISTICS

W	L	ERA	G	GS	CG	SV	IP	H	R	ER	BB	SO
6	7	2.98	66	0	0	34	81.2	71	29	27	28	67

CAREER STATISTICS

W	L	ERA	G	GS	CG	SV	IP	H	R	ER	BB	SO
61	54	3.74	325	91	22	75	956.2	948	428	398	371	552

but the Orioles had no one to take his place. The team struggled.

Last year was Aase's first full season as a stopper. The 1987 season should be interesting to see how his arm bounces back. It is rare that a power pitcher--especially a reliever--can have two dominating seasons back-to-back. That's why it's important for him to continue to improve his breaking ball and give the hitters something else to ponder.

FIELDING:

Aase is a big man: 6'3", 215 pounds. He is not a quick man, either, and therefore is, at best, an average fielder. Still, few people bunted on him last season.

His move to first is nothing special. He is a fast worker, however, and often throws to first to keep runners honest.

OVERALL:

Aase was the Orioles' MVP last year. If they are to contend in the American League East this year, he will need to have an equally good year--maybe better.

Kaat: "Confidence-wise, Don has finally hit the level that many people in baseball have been expecting for some time. For this season, all he needs is a one or two good set-up men to take the burden off him. And he's *got* to use the breaking ball."

BALTIMORE ORIOLES

PITCHING:

On June 20th last year, Mike Boddicker was 10-1 with a 3.48 ERA and had allowed 77 hits (eight homers) in 93 innings. After that, however, he fell off the ladder: he went 4-11 with a 5.60 ERA, allowing 137 hits (18 homers) in 125 1/3 innings. He finished 14-12 with a 4.70 ERA. He has lost 29 games over the last two years.

In 1986, Boddicker's problem was not that he was tipping off his change-up, as he did when he slumped at the end of 1985. Rather, a strained tendon suffered in his right middle finger in the middle of April affected him the rest of the year. The ache made it hard for him to throw his famous foshball correctly (the fosh is part forkball, part screwball, part everything) and Boddicker even struggled with his change-up, which is a key pitch for him.

The slow stuff is Boddicker's strength. His wide-breaking curveball is one of the best in baseball. He often jokes about the lack of velocity on his fastball, but it's a little quicker than many batters think--like 86 MPH. But his key is control, out-thinking the hitter and fooling him with a variety of curveballs and change-ups. He can change speeds on all his pitches. Boddicker comes at the hitter from many angles, even dropping down from the side.

And, he's a battler. Boddicker is one of the most competitive pitchers in the American League. He hates to miss a start, he hates to lose, he hates getting hit. He never complains about injuries. He is fearless. He would challenge Babe Ruth. But he's not a strikeout pitcher, so he depends a great deal on his defense, which wasn't very good last year.

Last year, the home run ball hurt Boddicker badly after never hurting him before. Because he isn't overpowering, if he misses by a couple inches, he can be in trouble. He didn't win after August 4th last year mainly because he'd make one bad pitch that would cost him the victory. The injured finger didn't help in that respect, but he said it had almost healed over the off-season.

MIKE BODDICKER
RHP, No. 52
RR, 5'11", 182 lbs.
ML Svc: 4 years
Born: 8-23-57 in
 Cedar Rapids, IA

1986 STATISTICS

W	L	ERA	G	GS	CG	SV	IP	H	R	ER	BB	SO
14	12	4.70	33	33	7	0	218.1	214	125	114	74	175

CAREER STATISTICS

W	L	ERA	G	GS	CG	SV	IP	H	R	ER	BB	SO
63	49	3.60	136	126	42	0	900.2	837	409	360	315	584

FIELDING:

A great third baseman in college, Boddicker can be considered one of the game's best athletes. Therefore, he is one of the game's best fielding pitchers. There is no sense bunting on him. He has not made a fielding error in his big league career.

His errors come from throwing to first too often to keep runners close. The reason he has to do that is because he is easy to run on. It's not that his delivery is particularly slow, but as a breaking ball pitcher, many of his pitches are. Therefore, every year the number of runners who steal successfully on him is astounding. He improved it somewhat last year, but not enough.

OVERALL:

He is the ace of the staff, the stopper, the guy the club looks to in times of need. He is one of the league's top pitchers.

Kaat: "Mike is a steady guy with a very good curveball. And he can adjust in the middle of a game to go with what's working for him. I'm optimistic that with the everyday lineup they have, he will be do better as the team does."

BALTIMORE ORIOLES

HITTING:

After sitting out a year and then spending most of the 1985 season in the minor leagues, Juan Bonilla got a new lease on life last year with the Orioles. He was impressive in the field and at the plate, made the team as a utility infielder in spring training and saw action in 102 games. He hit over .300 for two months before finishing the season at .243.

Last year, compared to his years with San Diego, Bonilla was more patient at the plate. In the National League, if a pitcher gambled on the first pitch and got a strike to get ahead on the count, Bonilla would chase anything. Last year, he was a little more disciplined: he walked 25 times. You can't categorize him as a high- or low-ball hitter, but one can say that he is a wild swinger. He can be made to look bad on outside pitches, but he has the ability to go with the pitch and take it to right field. Like a lot of free swingers, he has great trouble with breaking balls in the dirt.

Bonilla is in a Catch-22 situation. His strength should be as a No. 2 hitter, because of his ability to go away with the pitch. But because he swings and misses so many pitches, managers are reluctant to hit him in that spot. The Orioles even used him often to lead off, something he'd never done before last year.

BASERUNNING:

He has some speed, but Bonilla is not called on to steal. He is a capable bunter, able to go for the base hit and move the runners up with a sacrifice when needed.

FIELDING:

Bonilla has some flair with the glove. In the National League, he really put on a show. He

JUAN BONILLA
INF, No. 3
RR, 5'9", 170 lbs.
ML Svc: 4 years
Born: 2-12-56 in
Santurce, PR

1986 STATISTICS

AVG	G	AB	R	H	2B	3B	HR	RBI	BB	SO	SB
.243	102	284	33	69	10	1	1	18	25	21	0

CAREER STATISTICS

AVG	G	AB	R	H	2B	3B	HR	RBI	BB	SO	SB
.257	406	1407	139	361	47	9	6	98	111	102	7

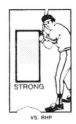  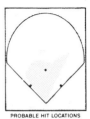

STRONG VS. RHP   STRONG VS. LHP   PROBABLE HIT LOCATIONS

has a little of the hot dog in him and had the reputation of looking as though he was careless at times. But after getting a second chance with the Orioles last year, he wiped a lot of the mustard off. He played mostly at third base, but is very adept at turning the double play as a second baseman. He has a quick release.

OVERALL:

Bonilla has the quickness to play third base and the range to play second base. And he seems to have put a bad situation in San Diego behind him.

Kaat: "His value is that he can play a couple positions, plus he's not timid off the bench in a pinch-hitting role because he's an aggressive hitter."

BALTIMORE ORIOLES

PITCHING:

Like Don Aase, Rich Bordi ran out of steam the final two months of the 1986 season. By the first week of August last year, Bordi had a 3.09 ERA. After that, however, he went 2-3 with a 7.91 ERA. He finished with a 4.46 ERA and 14 homers allowed in 107 innings.

For the first four months of the year, Bordi was Aase's set-up man. He worked mainly in middle relief, protected a lead and handed it over to Aase. He had no problem pitching two straight days, he had no problem pitching six innings at a time and he even started one game in July. If Aase needed a day off in short relief, Bordi got that call, too. He had three saves.

Bordi has a better-than-average fastball which he throws mainly three-quarters. Because of his long, rangy build, he can be a mass of arms and legs to a hitter.

He has always had good control. His curveball is above-average. He is developing a forkball or split-finger fastball as an extra pitch. His pitch selection can be shaky sometimes. For instance, he can blow away a hitter with fastballs, then go to a breaking ball, and get hurt badly by it.

Although he was a workhorse for four months, there's always concern about his back. It stiffens up regularly, and at times he has to inform the manager that he can't pitch that night. Simple running bothers his back enough that he gets his work done on an exercise bike.

FIELDING:

Because of his size and lankiness, he's not a

RICH BORDI
RHP, No. 42
RR, 6'7", 220 lbs.
ML Svc: 4 years
Born: 4-18-59 in
*   San Francisco, CA*

1986 STATISTICS

W	L	ERA	G	GS	CG	SV	IP	H	R	ER	BB	SO
6	4	4.46	52	1	0	3	107	105	56	53	41	83

CAREER STATISTICS

W	L	ERA	G	GS	CG	SV	IP	H	R	ER	BB	SO
17	18	4.00	155	14	3	10	330.2	335	162	147	104	218

particularly adept fielder. He is not quick or agile. His pickoff move is nothing special, either, but it's a little better than some righthanders on the staff. He is careful to keep runners close.

OVERALL:

Bordi is a very valuable man for Aase. With the addition of Dave Schmidt and Mark Williamson, his role hasn't changed, but it's obvious he'll have more help. This will be the first time in a while that he will be with the same team for two straight years. That will help, too.

Kaat: "Last year, I didn't think they defined a role enough for him. He can be very versatile. He can be like Bob Shirley is for the Yankees or Steve Crawford for the Red Sox. If they find a specific role, he can be a big help."

BALTIMORE ORIOLES

HITTING:

For four years, Rick Burleson was virtually wiped off the baseball map. But the same attitude which earned him a reputation as a hard-nosed player goaded him into an overall successful comeback from a series of shoulder injuries.

He has lost none of his baseball instincts. If anything, the long layoff brought him back with a rookie's spirit. Burleson spent much of his inactive years in weight rooms, rebuilding his torn shoulder muscles. As a result, he bulked up quite a bit.

Remembered as a line drive contact hitter, he was stronger, with greater power (25% of his hits in 1986 went for extra bases), without any loss of feel for the strike zone.

In trying to make the most of limited playing time last year, he often became too aggressive at the plate and developed the habit of chasing high fastballs. Since he was used as a DH, he felt pressured to bat out of character. Rick is still more valuable in the lineup as a table-setter who relies on his ability to make contact and guide the ball.

BASERUNNING:

The inactivity was most telling in Burleson's legs. He is two steps slower down the line than when he last played regularly (1982). He may not have the speed to steal the extra base but he is alert enough to take it if the defense gives it to him.

FIELDING:

Burleson probably ranked as the AL's top shortstop at the time of his injury. His calling card was a shotgun arm, which has lost a few calibres. To reduce wear on the shoulder, Rick now throws mostly sidearm, sometimes even lower, and relies on a quick release.

Both his reduced range and arm strength now make him better suited to play second base (where Baltimore plans to start him).

RICK BURLESON
2B/DH, No. 7
RR, 5'10", 160 lbs.
ML Svc: 13 years
Born: 4-29-51 in
Lynwood, CA

1986 STATISTICS											
AVG	G	AB	R	H	2B	3B	HR	RBI	BB	SO	SB
.284	93	271	35	77	14	0	5	29	33	32	1

CAREER STATISTICS											
AVG	G	AB	R	H	2B	3B	HR	RBI	BB	SO	SB
.275	1284	4933	630	1358	242	22	48	435	403	447	72

  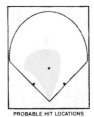

VS. RHP   VS. LHP   PROBABLE HIT LOCATIONS

He'll need help in positioning until he learns to play the hitters, and he still has to prove he can turn the pivot from that side. He'll have problems making the jerky throw from the middle and on slow-hit balls.

OVERALL:

Burleson spent last year grumbling about not getting the chance to prove he can play second base regularly. A new team now gives him that chance. As unlikely as it sounds, he is a better hitter than when last seen. If he's made to feel like a valuable cog, no one does more for a team's chemistry than Rooster.

Killebrew: "Rick again demonstrated his fierce competitiveness by making an improbable comeback. He's a valuable addition to the Orioles because he can help that club in a lot of ways."

BALTIMORE ORIOLES

PITCHING:

He is strong as a bull, can throw 140 pitches per game, can throw over 90 MPH and is a battler. Yet last year, Ken Dixon gave up some of the longest home runs in history. He gave up home runs to such power immortals as John Moses, Jim Sundberg and Cecil Fielder. During one stretch, he gave up 19 homers in 47 innings.

Dixon finished with an 11-13 record a 4.58 ERA and did not win from the first day of August to the middle of September. He threw 33 home run pitches in 203 innings. No one knows why. All agree that shouldn't happen.

He throws hard enough to be overpowering and strike people out: he can throw in the low 90s. His curveball is very effective, also. He entered 1986 needing another pitch, so he developed a change-up which was somewhat effective early, but not later. It still needs work. He is not afraid to throw inside. He's not afraid to challenge hitters. He's not afraid of using any pitch. Perhaps a little forethought borne of fear might help Dixon.

He is a uniquely confident guy. Every time he would give up a homer, he would later say that he didn't know how the hitter hit the pitch that far. He may be a little too cocky for his own good, but last year may have humbled him slightly. But he's got good enough stuff to be cocky.

His problems are the routine types of mistakes made by a young pitcher. The deeper in the count he gets, the better pitches he has to make. And he wasn't always able to do that, which led to the many, damaging home runs. With more experience, there's no reason why he can't develop into a solid big league winner.

Dixon, remember, has only pitched one full year in a big league starting rotation. He is 26 years old, but really doesn't have the

KEN DIXON
RHP, No. 39
SR, 5'11", 192 lbs.
ML Svc: 2 years
Born: 10-17-60 in Monroe, VA

1986 STATISTICS

W	L	ERA	G	GS	CG	SV	IP	H	R	ER	BB	SO
11	13	4.58	35	33	2	0	202.1	194	111	103	83	170

CAREER STATISTICS

W	L	ERA	G	GS	CG	SV	IP	H	R	ER	BB	SO
19	18	4.17	71	53	5	1	377.1	352	185	175	151	286

experience of a 26-year-old. If he can continue to develop the change-up, he could be very tough.

FIELDING:

A terrific football running back in high school, he is an outstanding athlete. With teammate Mike Boddicker, the Orioles have two of the best-fielding pitchers in baseball. He is quick, agile and strong.

But like most of the other righthanders on this staff, he has trouble holding runners on. Runners who can get a good jump distract him. It's something that he continues to work on vigorously.

OVERALL:

Kaat: "He lost sight of how to get hitters out. His problem was not using a quality pitch at a time when he needed to polish off a hitter. He needs to learn to change speeds more often. But he has a good fastball and good stuff. I look for him--with added experience-- to do well."

BALTIMORE ORIOLES

BIG, BREAKING CURVEBALL

PITCHING:

Mike Flanagan's final record for 1986 was 7-11, his ERA was 4.24 and he had two complete games. He won his third start of the season, but didn't win again until July 1st. But that doesn't tell what type of season he had. He was much better than that.

For the first thing, the Baltimore defense was his worst enemy. It seems as if every time he pitched, the defense would self-destruct. There would be times when he walked off the mound, and you couldn't believe that he had given up 5 or 7 runs.

Last August 23rd, at age 34, Flanagan was clocked at 90 MPH on the radar gun for what he says is the first time in his career. He can still bore the fastball in on all hitters, meaning he still likes to pitch inside. He throws what many people call a "heavy ball." He throws mostly three-quarters, but drops down sidearm against some lefthanded hitters. Sometimes he turns over his fastball, making it somewhat like a sinker.

His curveball--a big breaking one--isn't as good as it was during his Cy Young season in 1979, but it's still one of the better ones in the league. His change-up is thrown mainly to righthanded hitters, but can be used against anyone.

The problem last year was that Flanagan got too caught up in throwing the curveball and the change-up, meantime forgetting about the fastball. He later admitted it was a major mistake. He came up as a power pitcher, but because of a variety of injuries, he had to become more of a finesse pitcher. But after June last year, he returned to his powerful style, began challenging more hitters, and was successful.

He is basically a ground-ball pitcher and the Orioles' defensive problems at third base hurt him worse than anyone else on the pitching staff. When a sure double play ball somehow wound up in left field as a single, it flustered Flanagan. New manager Cal Ripken, Sr. said Flanagan changed his pitching style because of it. But he knows what style he wants this year. Now if he gets some luck . . .

MIKE FLANAGAN
LHP, No. 46
LL, 6'0", 194 lbs.
ML Svc: 11 years
Born: 12-16-51 in Manchester, NH

1986 STATISTICS

W	L	ERA	G	GS	CG	SV	IP	H	R	ER	BB	SO
7	11	4.24	29	28	2	0	172	179	95	81	66	96

CAREER STATISTICS

W	L	ERA	G	GS	CG	SV	IP	H	R	ER	BB	SO
136	103	3.84	328	311	94	1	2090	2090	9.66	892	656	1175

FIELDING:

In January 1985, Flanagan tore his Achilles tendon. In 1983, he tore ligaments in his left knee. Each has taken away from his quickness and agility. He is now just an average fielding pitcher.

But he makes up for it with his pickoff move, which is one of the best in baseball. He is very clever with it, too, not showing his best move until he believes he's got the runner leaning. Baserunners have never been able to distract him.

OVERALL:

Over the last two months last year, Flanagan felt that he threw the ball as well as he's thrown it in years. The Orioles may need him to do that all season this year.

Kaat: "Boddicker, Dixon and Flanagan all feed off one another. If one goes out and give seven good innings, it makes them all better. Flanagan is one of those guys who really knows how to pitch. If something isn't working a particular night, he can make an adjustment.

"He is so good at changing speeds. He should be at a time when he's ready to have one of his better years. He's very capable of coming up with a big year."

BALTIMORE ORIOLES

PITCHING:

In case you forgot, Brad Havens was involved in the trade which sent Rod Carew from Minnesota to California in 1979. He made his big league debut in 1981, was in the Twins starting rotation for all of 1982 (going 10-14), started 1983 with the Twins, but was back in the minor leagues by the middle of that season.

He has been around even though he's only 27 years old. The Orioles made him a relief pitcher in 1985, and he's still adjusting to the role. He's also still adjusting to his new pitching style.

Havens used to have a big, full windup. He used to try to throw every pitch through the wall. Now, he's cut his windup in half, doesn't grunt and looks to throw more strikes. He hasn't mastered it, but if hard work counts for anything, this guy would get an A for effort.

Havens showed flashes of brilliance last year. He throws around 90 MPH and has an above-average curveball. All are thrown from three-quarters. He is not afraid to go after hitters or pitch inside, although he still isn't sure where all his pitches are going. His lack of location is what generally causes his problems. He wild-pitched home two runs last year.

His strength is his resiliency and his desire. He wants the ball whenever possible, be it short, middle or long relief. He once pitched 6 1/3 standout innings last year, took one day off, then pitched the next.

But it took its toll. He had to sit out the final two weeks when his left shoulder went what he called "dead." He worked with weights six days a week, 75 minutes a day from October to January to strengthen it. From January 1st through spring training, he did the same routine for 50 minutes a day. The life has now returned to his arm, but the Orioles are

BRAD HAVENS
LHP, No. 47
LL, 6'1", 196 lbs.
ML Svc: 3 years
Born: 11-17-59 in
Highland Park, MI

1986 STATISTICS

W	L	ERA	G	GS	CG	SV	IP	H	R	ER	BB	SO
3	3	4.56	46	0	0	1	71	64	37	36	29	57

CAREER STATISTICS

W	L	ERA	G	GS	CG	SV	IP	H	R	ER	BB	SO
21	32	5.05	117	59	6	1	452.1	471	271	254	181	288

hoping he can control that life this year.

FIELDING:

Not good, not bad. He's a good enough athlete that he shouldn't struggle, but he tends to rush himself sometimes. His pickoff move is very ordinary for a lefthander. Actually, it would be very ordinary for a righthander, too.

OVERALL:

He's bidding for the lefthanded reliever spot that new manager Cal Ripken, Sr. so badly wants to fill. The job is Havens' if he can throw more strikes. He's the type of guy you don't give up on because of his physical attributes.

Kaat: "He's better as a starting pitcher. I don't think he has the mental makeup to be a reliever. He lacks that aggressiveness in the late innings. But they need a lefthander to go against a lefthander in middle relief. Still, I think he's a starting pitcher."

BALTIMORE ORIOLES

HITTING:

Terry Kennedy underwent a strange transformation during his six years with the San Diego Padres. Once a power monger who drove in 195 runs in two seasons, he had become almost exclusively a slap hitter by the end of the 1986 campaign, punching the ball to the opposite field.

That would be fine, except that given Kennedy's large frame it seems reasonable to expect him to hit for more power. Kennedy says that he never was a power hitter but simply enjoyed good power numbers as a natural result of hitting the ball well (which he admits he hasn't done for the past three seasons).

Kennedy is notoriously mechanical and cerebral when it comes to his offense and is prone to overthinking. He is at his best when he resists the temptation to guess at pitches and situations and simply swings away.

When he does make solid contact, it's usually on a low fastball. Kennedy still has plenty of muscle to get the ball out of the park and he won 10 games with hits in 1986.

BASERUNNING:

A rigorous diet brought Kennedy to spring training camp in 1986 about 15 pounds lighter than the year before and it showed in his movement around the bases. Kennedy is still a liability on the paths, but less so than he once was.

FIELDING:

Though he's been criticzed for his slow footwork, average arm and reluctance to block home plate on close plays, Kennedy has developed into one of the game's best signal-callers. This skill, one of the most difficult to gauge, became apparent during the Padres' championship season in 1984 and he's constantly improved since then.

TERRY KENNEDY
C, No. 16
LR, 6'4", 224 lbs.
ML Svc: 8 years
Born: 6-4-56 in
Euclid, OH

1986 STATISTICS

AVG	G	AB	R	H	2B	3B	HR	RBI	BB	SO	SB
.264	141	432	46	114	22	1	12	57	37	74	0

CAREER STATISTICS

AVG	G	AB	R	H	2B	3B	HR	RBI	BB	SO	SB
.272	962	3373	347	916	177	10	82	477	238	565	3

  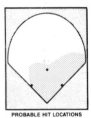

VS. RHP VS. LHP PROBABLE HIT LOCATIONS

Kennedy has an encyclopaedic knowledge of opposing batters and can get his pitchers to throw what he wants. His throwing arm is better than it was and the loss of weight enabled Kennedy to get up more quickly for the throw to second.

OVERALL:

His off-season trade to Baltimore may be just what Kennedy needed. He expressed the opinion during the 1986 season that perhaps it was time for a change of scenery. It's likely, of course, that he'll see fewer fastballs in the American League but the feeling of starting over may compensate for that.

Kennedy's field performance often is tied to his state of mind. The trade may be the event that revives his stagnant career.

BALTIMORE ORIOLES

HITTING:

Lee Lacy is an ideal No. 2 hitter. He knows the game well and has the ability to go to right field, which is one of the things you look for in that position. He likes to swing the bat, too, and he strikes out a bit more than expected from a contact hitter.

But Lacy can hit in several spots. He is a fastball hitter with some power to all parts of the field. He can surprise the opposition from time to time, as he did last year when he hit three home runs in a game at Yankee Stadium. He likes to take a rip at the first fastball he sees over the plate.

Once a pitcher gets ahead of him, Lacy is not a patient hitter. He doesn't want to walk: he wants to hit. He has a big swing and pitchers try to keep the fastball in on him. Righthanders often get Lacy fishing by throwing him breaking balls outside, but if Ripken and Murray are producing, Lacy sees more fastballs.

LEE LACY
RF, No. 27
RR, 6'1", 195 lbs.
ML Svc: 14 years
Born: 4-10-49 in
Longview, TX

1986 STATISTICS

AVG	G	AB	R	H	2B	3B	HR	RBI	BB	SO	SB
.287	130	491	77	141	18	0	11	47	37	71	4

CAREER STATISTICS

AVG	G	AB	R	H	2B	3B	HR	RBI	BB	SO	SB
.289	1436	4291	615	1240	194	39	84	430	340	608	182

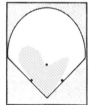

VS. RHP   VS. LHP   PROBABLE HIT LOCATIONS

BASERUNNING:

Lacy has excellent speed and gets out of the batter's box quickly. He and Alan Wiggins could steal a lot if they were allowed to go, but with Cal Ripken and Eddie Murray behind them, that probably won't happen.

Lacy is an aggressive baserunner and a hard slider. Sometimes, he is too aggressive, but his speed usually overcomes that.

FIELDING:

For years, Lacy was platooned and didn't play every day. Infrequent appearances in the field affects a player's judgment, concentration and reaction. Playing every day, Lacy has shown himself to be an average outfielder; he can go for the ball in any direction and has a

decent arm, but his throws are sometimes erratic.

OVERALL:

Age should not be a factor with Lacy, who has only been a regular for three years. He looks to be in good shape. He may serve as DH this year to improve the Orioles' outfield defense, and probably would be agreeable to that role under the new manager.

Kaat: "The better year Alan Wiggins has, the better year Lacy will have. With nobody on base, he becomes a big swinger. Lacy has to imagine someone's always on base and just make contact. He'll still hit a few homers that way."

BALTIMORE ORIOLES

HITTING:

Smooth-swinging Fred Lynn has always been a pleasure to watch. He is a good fastball hitter with power from right field to left-center field. He is a quality hitter that a pitcher can't pitch any one way to get out consistently.

His swing is such that he hasn't had to alter his style, whether he was breaking in with the Red Sox in Fenway Park, playing with the Angels in Anaheim Stadium, or now with the Orioles in Memorial Stadium. He uses the whole field, which is to his advantage with his ability.

Lefthanders try to pitch him up and in. Righthanders throw the fastball away and mix it up with breaking balls. You don't see him get caught out in front too much, except by certain lefthanders. But in general, Lynn hits lefthanders quite well because he stays in against them.

BASERUNNING:

Lynn may steal a half-dozen bases a year. He steals when it's least expected, and often goes when the pitcher ignores him as a runner. He has better-than-average speed on a non-stealing team and is an excellent baserunner.

FIELDING:

His smoothness extends to his style in the field. He glides to balls and looks nonchalant, but Lynn is an aggressive center fielder. His arm is not quite as strong as it once was, but his great instincts and excellent range he makes up for anything he has lost.

He is not afraid to crash into walls and fences to make catches, despite the risk of injury.

FRED LYNN
CF, No. 19
LL, 6'1", 185 lbs.
ML Svc: 13 years
Born: 2-3-52 in
Chicago, IL

1986 STATISTICS

AVG	G	AB	R	H	2B	3B	HR	RBI	BB	SO	SB
.287	112	397	67	114	13	1	23	67	53	59	2

CAREER STATISTICS

AVG	G	AB	R	H	2B	3B	HR	RBI	BB	SO	SB
.292	1537	5589	906	1632	336	40	241	926	716	847	64

  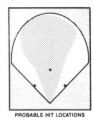

VS. RHP   VS. LHP   PROBABLE HIT LOCATIONS

OVERALL:

If he played 162 games a year, Lynn might surpass teammates Eddie Murray or Cal Ripken with his output. But that's been the criticism of him: his durability. Lynn has been an All-Star when he's been in there, but only once in the last seven years has he missed fewer than 20 games.

Kaat: "He has to prove to the baseball world that he's truly a 'gamer.' He brings it on himself when he doesn't play against a Ron Guidry, a Jimmy Key or other such tough lefthanders. He's too good a player, too good an athlete, to miss so many games. You have to wonder why he misses so many opportunities against lefties."

PITCHING:

How many active lefthanded relievers have done more than this guy? Not many. In his prime, he was a sneaky-fast pitcher with a great, great curveball that gave lefthander hitters boatloads of trouble.

Well, he's 36 years old now and past his prime. Last season, he pitched only 16 innings before being placed on the disabled list for the third (and last) time the day before the All-Star break. His left shoulder was in intense pain again.

It was diagnosed as a "worn out" rotator cuff, a nasty phrase for a pitcher. He had it operated on last fall, and spent the whole winter rehabilitating it. Whether he can come back remains to be seen, but he vows to pitch again sometime this season. But that seems doubtful due to the severity of the injury.

If he can pitch effectively again, it would be a major plus for the Orioles, who need a solid lefthander in the bullpen. When he's right, Martinez sets a hitter up and gets him out with the curveball. He makes batters chase it down and out of the strike zone. But he has not had the great curveball since 1983.

He cannot succeed without it because though his fastball was underrated at its peak, it still wasn't enough to get out the top righthanded hitters. He totaled only four saves in 70 innings in 1985. Last year was a waste.

FIELDING:

Martinez may look lean, but he is

TIPPY MARTINEZ
LHP, No. 23
LL, 5'10", 179 lbs.
ML Svc: 12 years
Born: 5-31-50 in
LaJunta, CO

1986 STATISTICS

W	L	ERA	G	GS	CG	SV	IP	H	R	ER	BB	SO
0	2	5.63	14	0	0	1	16	18	10	10	12	11

CAREER STATISTICS

W	L	ERA	G	GS	CG	SV	IP	H	R	ER	BB	SO
55	42	3.38	543	2	0	115	831	724	348	312	421	628

sometimes slow covering first base. He is, at best, an average fielder. He once picked off three men in one inning against the Blue Jays in 1983, and has kept on doing a good job holding runners on since.

OVERALL:

It will be a minor miracle if he is able to bounce back from the his serious injury problems in 1986. He is paid through 1987, and said he wants to earn that money. He is not pushing his recovery, but badly wants to pitch again.

Kaat: "If he stays healthy, he could be one of the two set-up men the Orioles are looking for. With that curveball, he could be especially effective against lefthanders. He's not a real blower, but he has a good fastball."

BALTIMORE ORIOLES

PITCHING:

The Orioles had two complete-game shutouts last season. Both came in September, both were thrown by Scott McGregor, who finally reminded people of his old self. You remember McGregor: he's the guy who has the second most victories (105) in this decade behind Jack Morris (123).

McGregor's season looked dismal; he finished with an 11-15 record (the most losses in the AL East) and a 4.52 ERA. The home run ball hurt him again: in 203 innings, he threw 35 homers. He gave up 27 first-inning runs, and lasted less than five innings 10 times.

His early problems were simple: he was afraid to throw strikes, and he was afraid to throw his fastball, which travels (at best) 83 MPH. This affected his control--he threw five wild pitches last year, which is two more than he had thrown in his previous 705 innings. The fear of throwing strikes made him pitch scared and ineffectively.

It also took away from his curveball, which is still one of the better ones in the league. It took away from his change-up, which is still one of the better ones in the league. At times, McGregor said he felt like he had never pitched before. He nibbled too much, tried to be too fine. And when he missed in the strike zone, the result was usually a monstrous home run. He must have his good control if he is to win games.

But September saved McGregor's season. In the final two months of the 1986 season, he adopted an aggressive attitude and began throwing his fastball again--as he had done during his glory years. He began throwing more strikes, gained confidence and was using 100 pitches for an entire game instead of 120 in six innings.

McGregor's herky-jerky motion can be a detriment because it messes with his mechanics, but it also throws off hitters because he make the ball hard to pick up. That deception plus his unusual gift for changing speeds on every pitch makes him quite tough to hit. He often checks the difference in MPH between his fastball and change-up. He wants to make certain that his change-up is coming in at the batter at considerably less velocity than his fastball--or

SCOTT McGREGOR
LHP, No. 16
SL, 6'1", 192 lbs.
ML Svc: 10 years
Born: 1-18-54 in
Inglewood, CA

1986 STATISTICS

W	L	ERA	G	GS	CG	SV	IP	H	R	ER	BB	SO
11	15	4.52	34	33	4	0	203	216	110	102	57	95

CAREER STATISTICS

W	L	ERA	G	GS	CG	SV	IP	H	R	ER	BB	SO
136	98	3.84	326	290	82	5	2038.2	2106	944	869	476	855

he won't be effective.

When the fastball wasn't working last season, McGregor began tinkering with a slider, but it's doubtful it could be useful because he doesn't throw hard enough. But as he has proved for 10 years--including last September--it doesn't matter how hard you throw, but *where* you throw it.

FIELDING:

A good athlete who outhit George Brett in high school, McGregor has good hands and is surprisingly quick. He is smart, too: he'll never throw to the wrong base.

His pickoff move is not as good as Mike Flanagan's, but it's good enough. But if a runner gets a good jump, he will probably steal successfully because of McGregor's deliberate motion and his propensity to use slow stuff.

OVERALL:

McGregor is 33 years old, and though some believe he's well past his prime, others think he has a lot of good pitching left in him. This year is very important for him.

Kaat: "Scott has struggled in the last two years. But if he can get his aggressiveness back, he can be successful. Because he's a finesse pitcher, he has to get ahead in the count more often. But overall, I look for him to bounce back in 1987."

BALTIMORE ORIOLES

HITTING:

Despite the fact that Eddie Murray had career-lows in seven offensive categories (including 17 homers, 84 RBIs and only four game-winning RBIs) last year, he still led the Orioles in RBIs and batting average (.305). He was slowed by a spring training ankle injury and went on to miss 25 games, the most in his 10-year career.

Still, it was an excellent year by almost anyone's standards. Murray is a switch-hitter who is equally good from either side of the plate. And he has made himself a better hitter through the years by developing the ability to wait and hit the off-speed pitch while remaining quick enough to get around on a fastball.

He has power to all fields from both sides of the plate and there's little difference in his average and home run ratio from either side. He stays in on the pitch more from the right side, which is his natural side, and tends to pull away from a pitch from the left side to move toward first base, which is a natural tendency by a lefthander. His stance from both sides is a slightly open crouch.

Like many switch-hitters, Murray is a better low-ball hitter lefthanded and a high-ball hitter righthanded. But there is no one way to attack him. Pitchers have to mix up their pattern, not only from game to game, but from at-bat to at-bat, to have any chance at success.

BASERUNNING:

If Murray was called on to steal, he could. He is not a gambler on the bases. He does not slide well and is more of a station-to-station runner.

FIELDING:

Murray can be outstanding in the field (he's a former Gold Glover), but he has slipped a little defensively over the last couple of years. He has a good arm, especially in making the

EDDIE MURRAY
1B, No. 33
SR, 6'2", 215 lbs.
ML Svc: 10 years
Born: 2-24-56 in
Los Angeles, CA

1986 STATISTICS

AVG	G	AB	R	H	2B	3B	HR	RBI	BB	SO	SB
.305	137	495	61	151	25	1	17	84	78	49	3

CAREER STATISTICS

AVG	G	AB	R	H	2B	3B	HR	RBI	BB	SO	SB
.299	1499	5624	884	1679	296	20	275	1015	708	768	55

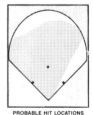

force-out at second base, but has had trouble with pickoff throws to second in the last few seasons. He covers the bunt as well as any first baseman in the American League.

OVERALL:

Murray went through a tough season mentally as well as physically last year. For the first time, the people in Baltimore seemed to see an attitude flaw in Murray. That'll be the key to his season this year: whether or not he returns to favor as a favorite son.

Kaat: "The change of managers to Cal Ripken should have a positive effect on Eddie. Murray is the kind of player who needs to play on a good or excellent club so he can rise above that level. He has had several MVP years, but someone else always seemed to have a slightly better year. It wouldn't be surprising to see him bounce back from last season and have an MVP-type year again this season."

BALTIMORE ORIOLES

HITTING:

For the fourth consecutive year, Cal Ripken led American League shortstops in home runs (18) and RBIs (81) last year. He led the Orioles in seven offensive categories. And yet, these numbers were low for Ripken.

Like Eddie Murray, Ripken covers the whole strike zone very well. He prefers his pitches inside and is a better low-ball hitter and he doesn't go to the opposite field as much as he did when he first came up. But the more experience he's gotten, the more he has come to know the pitchers, the better he has become at getting his pitch.

If the Oriole lineup stays intact, with Alan Wiggins and Lee Lacy getting on in front of him and Eddie Murray and Fred Lynn healthy behind him, Ripken should hit well. If the batters ahead of him are getting on base, he will adjust. If the others aren't producing, Ripken has to take on more responsibility.

BASERUNNING:

Ripken has average speed but great instincts on the bases. He gets a keen knowledge of the game from his father, Cal, Sr., the Orioles' new manager. Ripken is into the game and aware of how to run the bases and knows when to take the extra base.

FIELDING:

Ripken made only 13 errors last season and led American League shortstops in assists. He is right up there with the best of them, but he doesn't get as much credit because of his size. He looks like a lumbering athlete, but he has big steps to get to balls, an excellent sense and knowledge of where to play hitters, and a strong arm.

There has been talk of moving him to third base, but it won't happen soon. he has played 765 straight games, the 10th longest streak in history, and hasn't missed an inning since 1982.

CAL RIPKEN
SS, No. 8
RR, 6'4", 218 lbs.
ML Svc: 5 years
Born: 8-24-60 in
 Havre de Grace, MD

1986 STATISTICS

AVG	G	AB	R	H	2B	3B	HR	RBI	BB	SO	SB
.282	162	627	98	177	35	1	25	81	70	60	4

CAREER STATISTICS

AVG	G	AB	R	H	2B	3B	HR	RBI	BB	SO	SB
.289	830	3210	529	927	183	20	133	472	313	417	11

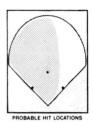

VS. RHP   VS. LHP   PROBABLE HIT LOCATIONS

OVERALL:

Ripken and Murray need to complement each other. The better year one has, the better year the other has. If one's not doing well, the other isn't going to get the pitches to hit.

Kaat: "I don't expect that Cal will have any trouble adjusting to his father as the manager of the club. He is such a level-headed guy, and they've both been in the Oriole organization a long time, that I'm sure they will both ease quickly in this relationship. If his father had come from another organization to take the Oriole job, there might be some pressure. But they're used to being with each other by now.

"Cal is one of the best all-around players in the league. He can't carry the entire club, however, and will need the entire Oriole machine to function well around him if he is to be as effective as he can."

PITCHING:

After a rather lengthy stay with the Texas Rangers, Dave Schmidt has suddenly become a man on the move. That doesn't necessarily mean his value has dropped, it just *may* be increasing.

Schmidt doesn't get a whole lot of attention, but he has effectively gone about his job throughout his career. He is best known for throwing a wicked slider, but he also throws a good change-up and sinker. His fastball is a bit lacking, but he can throw it in the mid-80s.

Schmidt has become a good middle relief man for several reasons. The biggest plus is his effectiveness against both right- and lefthanders. Last year, both sides hit him at an identical .264 clip. His control is very good with the exception of a wild pitch here and there and he is skilled at keeping the ball down. He runs into long ball trouble when his fastball takes off on him.

Schmidt has the perfect demeanor for relief pitching. Few things bother him on the mound and he thrives on pressure. He's not afraid to back batters off the plate.

FIELDING:

Schmidt's pickoff move to first base slipped a bit last season, when baserunners had a high stolen base percentage against him. He also slacked off as a fielder, but has been

DAVE SCHMIDT
RHP, No. 24
RR, 6'1", 185 lbs.
ML Svc: 5 years
Born: 4-22-57 in
Niles, MI

1986 STATISTICS

W	L	ERA	G	GS	CG	SV	IP	H	R	ER	BB	SO
3	6	3.31	49	1	0	8	92.1	94	37	34	27	67

CAREER STATISTICS

W	L	ERA	G	GS	CG	SV	IP	H	R	ER	BB	SO
23	28	3.18	221	14	1	34	436.1	435	179	154	119	270

steady over the course of his career. He gets over to first base quickly.

OVERALL:

Schmidt is a quality competitor and should turn out to be a solid acquisition for the White Sox. He has pitched short relief before and could fill that role, but he's much better working longer shifts.

Killebrew: "Schmidt is a perfect example of what a middle reliever should be like. He's tough out there and really challenges the hitters."

BALTIMORE ORIOLES

HITTING:

Powerfully built lefthanded-hitting Larry Sheets built solidly upon his 1985 rookie season last year, hitting one more home run (18) while raising his average 10 points (.272) and his RBIs by 10 (to 60). He has improved, and has the work ethics to continue to improve. He is probably the prototypic designated hitter.

Sheets is mostly a pull hitter, but he can and will go the other way when fooled. He likes the low fastball. There is one area where he must improve to play regularly, and that is hitting against lefthanded pitchers. Partly because they give him trouble with the breaking ball, but partly because he has been protected from facing lefthanders, he rarely gets to bat against them.

Sheets is a bit too impatient when he gets behind in the count and when men are on base, but he showed improvement last year and should continue in that regard. He has a bright future at the plate.

BASERUNNING:

Sheets is no threat on the bases. He is fundamentally sound and has good instincts, but he simply has no speed. He doesn't get a good jump out of the box or off the bases.

FIELDING:

Sheets will not find himself playing in the field very often. He is not a good defensive player, but his categorization stops just short of "butcher." He'll catch what he gets to and has an average arm. It's just that his speed--or lack of it--restricts his defensive ability. He is fundamentally sound, just slow.

He has worked at catching in recent years, but at this stage is only an emergency fill-in.

LARRY SHEETS
DH/OF, No. 18
LR, 6'3", 225 lbs.
ML Svc: 2 years
Born: 12-6-59 in
Staunton, VA

1986 STATISTICS

AVG	G	AB	R	H	2B	3B	HR	RBI	BB	SO	SB
.272	112	338	42	92	17	1	18	60	21	56	2

CAREER STATISTICS

AVG	G	AB	R	H	2B	3B	HR	RBI	BB	SO	SB
.271	233	682	88	185	26	1	36	112	50	111	2

  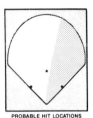

VS. RHP   VS. LHP   PROBABLE HIT LOCATIONS

He still is learning the fundamentals of the trade and has to think too much about what he is doing to be thrust into a pressure situation behind the plate.

OVERALL:

With another year's worth of experience, Sheets should be an even better hitter. He learns quickly and has taken instruction well from Oriole coaches Frank Robinson and Cal Ripken, Sr., who now is his manager.

Kaat: "His role depends on how they maneuver the other hitters from the outfield, Lacy, Shelby and Young. Sheets probably will end up as the lefthanded DH again, but will benefit from playing against lefthanded pitchers."

BALTIMORE ORIOLES

HITTING:

Once deemed the center fielder of the future by the Orioles, John Shelby has struggled to regain the form that had him inked in as Al Bumbry's replacement several seasons ago. He saw a lot of playing time in all three outfield spots last year, but still batted only .228 and drew only 18 walks.

Shelby is a switch-hitter who likes the high strike from both sides of the plate. He has a tendency to chase bad pitches, both high and away, and he's not good on the breaking ball. But much of his problem is a product of not being an everyday player.

His home run production is not up there, but he'll pop your eyes open on occasion. He had a career-high 11 home runs last year.

With his speed, Shelby would be an ideal leadoff or No. 2 hitter. But he doesn't walk and is not a particularly good bunter, and he hasn't hit consistently to get on base in those roles.

BASERUNNING:

Shelby has excellent speed and stole 18 bases last year, but he is not a particularly great baserunner. He simply doesn't have the instincts. That is where he could use some help; perhaps if the Orioles brought in a Lou Brock or Maury Wills, as other teams have done in past years, to work with Shelby, it could help him become a better runner. It could salvage a position for him.

FIELDING:

Shelby's defensive ability brought him to the majors. He has good range and gets a good jump on the ball and has a strong arm. He has some trouble hitting the cutoff man, but as with his hitting, much of his defensive play probably would improve if he were to

JOHN SHELBY
OF, No. 37
SR, 6'1", 178 lbs.
ML Svc: 4 years
Born: 2-23-58 in Lexington, KY

1986 STATISTICS
AVG	G	AB	R	H	2B	3B	HR	RBI	BB	SO	SB
.228	135	404	54	92	14	4	11	49	18	75	18

CAREER STATISTICS
AVG	G	AB	R	H	2B	3B	HR	RBI	BB	SO	SB
.240	491	1354	188	325	50	13	30	135	63	260	52

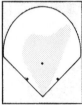

VS. RHP   VS. LHP   PROBABLE HIT LOCATIONS

play every day.

Shelby will get a shot to win one of the flank positions in the Oriole outfield this year. Fred Lynn still is the center fielder, and no one is going to beat him out.

OVERALL:

Shelby's value is that he's a switch-hitter, he has speed and is a good defensive player to use for the late innings.

Kaat: "Unfortunately for him, Shelby's future with the Orioles depends on how the other guys perform, how healthy they are. When Lynn and Lacy are healthy, he'll get less playing time. And if they need somebody with some pop in his bat, there are other players the Orioles will turn to before Shelby."

BALTIMORE ORIOLES

HITTING:

Alan Wiggins got into manager Earl Weaver's doghouse last year and never got out, and it affected every aspect of his game. If he is right, he could be one of the better leadoff hitters in the game. He has speed, draws walks and can get base hits.

Wiggins is a switch-hitter with no power from either side of the plate. Lefthanded pitchers have been able to knock the bat out of his hands. As a lefthanded batter, he has a little quicker stroke. He has a little slap stroke from both sides of the plate. If he played on AstroTurf, Wiggins would be the ideal leadoff man and his average would improve automatically by 30 points.

He likes the pitch out over the plate and pitchers try to overpower him with fastballs.

Wiggins will attempt to bunt to get on base-- and infielders know it. It puts more pressure on them, but he didn't show the punch needed last year to drive a ball past the corners to make infielders back off.

BASERUNNING:

The ability is there. Wiggins is very fast and could steal 75 bases if turned loose. That wasn't Earl Weaver's style, so it will depend on new manager Cal Ripken, Sr. as to how much Wiggins is allowed to run.

Wiggins has had a tendency to fall asleep on the bases, however. He gets picked off too often, something that Ripken will try to work on just as Weaver did.

FIELDING:

Wiggins was an outfielder and doesn't have the ideally fluid moves of a second baseman. But he can get the job done when he concentrates. Too often, his nonchalant

ALAN WIGGINS
2B, No. 2
SR, 6'2", 164 lbs.
ML Svc: 5 years
Born: 2-17-58 in
Los Angeles, CA

1986 STATISTICS

AVG	G	AB	R	H	2B	3B	HR	RBI	BB	SO	SB
.251	71	239	30	60	3	1	0	11	22	20	21

CAREER STATISTICS

AVG	G	AB	R	H	2B	3B	HR	RBI	BB	SO	SB
.263	546	1941	309	510	57	17	4	103	207	159	222

VS. RHP — STRONG VS. LHP — STRONG PROBABLE HIT LOCATIONS

attitude led to errors on routine plays.

He has very good range, although he has had trouble going back on balls hit into shallow right and center field. He retreats like an outfielder and pop flies give him trouble.

OVERALL:

From a manager's standpoint, the challenge is in keeping Wiggins mentally sharp throughout the whole season. He can go into a closet for a while. If he gets his mind together, he could give the Orioles an excellent leadoff man.

Kaat: "Wiggins should be a much better player than his stats show. He should be a .290-.300 hitter, which isn't many more hits, especially for someone with his bunting ability and speed."

BALTIMORE ORIOLES

HITTING:

In the second half of 1985, Mike Young looked like the second coming of Eddie Murray. He hit 20 home runs and had 50 RBIs in a 51-game span from midseason to September. Young's hitting was phenomenal back then. But just as dramatically, his lack of contact last season was phenomenal, too. In 1986, he went 103 at-bats without a home run and finished with only nine. He drove in only 42 runs and struck out 90 times. Young was a major disappointment last year.

This switch-hitting outfielder has a big swing from a crouch. His stance is much like Murray's, and he has power to all fields. From the right side, he likes pitches up in the strike zone. From the left side, he likes the low ball. He is weaker from the right side.

Young chases breaking balls and did not make enough contact last year from either side of the plate. As a lefthanded hitter, righthanded pitchers threw him up-and-in, jamming him with strikes or getting him to swing at pitches off the inside part of the plate. He must adjust by laying off that pitch or by backing off the plate to be able to get the bat out in front.

Young must learn to make contact again to change the way pitchers' approach his at-bat.

BASERUNNING:

Young has good speed, but he's not a good baserunner. His lack of baserunning skills probably goes back to the Oriole philosophy, which has been an emphasis on power rather than hit-and-run and stealing bases.

If the O's didn't have Murray and Cal Ripken, the club would have a lot of players with decent basestealing ability who they could utilize to play a different style offense. Young is one of those speedy types.

FIELDING:

When it comes to defense, Young falls into

MIKE YOUNG
LF, No. 43
SR, 6'2", 198 lbs.
ML Svc: 3 years
Born: 3-20-60 in Oakland, CA

1986 STATISTICS

AVG	G	AB	R	H	2B	3B	HR	RBI	BB	SO	SB
.252	117	369	43	93	15	1	9	42	49	90	3

CAREER STATISTICS

AVG	G	AB	R	H	2B	3B	HR	RBI	BB	SO	SB
.257	409	1258	181	323	56	5	54	177	157	313	11

VS. RHP   VS. LHP   PROBABLE HIT LOCATIONS

the same category as Lee Lacy. Because he hasn't played regularly in one spot, his judgment, concentration and reactions are not what they should be.

Young is simply an average outfielder. His speed helps him to overcome errors in judgment at times, and he makes accurate--if not overpowering--throws. He has been used in both right and left field, and the latter appears to be the more suitable spot for him.

OVERALL:

Young is caught in a quandary. He needs to make better contact with the pitch, but the best way for him to do that is to cut down on his swing. He may sacrifice power if he does that, however.

Kaat: "As a player, you don't like to win this award, but Young is the kind of guy who could win Comeback Player of the Year if he returns to his 1985 form. He has tremendous ability."

BALTIMORE ORIOLES

JIM DWYER
OF, No. 9
LL, 5'10", 182 lbs.
ML Svc: 12 years
Born: 1-3-50 in
Evergreen Park, IL

HITTING, BASERUNNING, FIELDING:

Jim Dwyer is the ideal lefthanded pinch-hitter. He has the experience to handle that role and is a good situation hitter. He can make contact--and with power. He is an outstanding clutch hitter.

Dwyer is a decent player in all phases of the game, but his past performance makes him an excellent man to have on the bench and available late in the game. He is a low fastball hitter who primarily pulls the ball.

He is a pretty good bunter, and is not afraid to use that tool when the situation arises.

Dwyer is an average runner who uses his experience as much as his speed on the bases. He can steal an occasional base and is an aggressive slider when it comes to breaking up the double play. He gets out of the batter's box quickly.

It's not that he *can't* play in the field, it's just that he hasn't had the opportunity. Dwyer can be used at all three outfield positions and first base. Left and right field are ideally his best spots when he plays for an extended period of time. He is excellent on the line and looping drives that are hit directly in front of him and often will come up with the spectacular catch. His arm is average but accurate and he never misses a cutoff man.

OVERALL:

Kaat: "Dwyer's value is his versatility in the outfield and as a pinch-hitter. He knows his role and does it better than anyone."

JACKIE GUTIERREZ
SS, No. 11
RR, 6'1", 175 lbs.
ML Svc: 3 years
Born: 6-27-60 in
Cartagena,
Columbia

HITTING, BASERUNNING, FIELDING:

Jackie Gutierrez is a high fastball hitter who is not particularly a threat at the plate. If he figures out a way to improve at the plate, he could win a job with someone.

He used to stand back off the plate and couldn't reach the outside pitch. He's still doesn't have a strong swing, even for a singles hitter.

He has excellent speed, but hasn't been on base enough to use it. He could be a stealing threat if he could get his butt to first base more.

Gutierrez's defensive ability is his strength. He has great range at shortstop and a strong arm. The knock against him in the field is that he doesn't always make the routine play. With Cal Ripken at shortstop, the Orioles gave Gutierrez trials at second and third base last year. All that's missing from him becoming a good player at those spots is experience.

OVERALL:

Kaat: "He can be a big league shortstop for somebody. He has to get over the feeling that, 'If I don't do it today, I'm going to be out of the lineup tomorrow.'"

FLOYD RAYFORD
3B/C, No. 6
RR, 5'10", 220 lbs.
ML Svc: 5 years
Born: 7-27-57 in
Memphis, TN

HITTING, BASERUNNING, FIELDING:

Which is the *real* Floyd Rayford? Is he the one who hit .306 with 18 homers in 1985, or the one who hit .176 with eight homers last year? The Orioles expect to find out this year.

Rayford injured his right thumb in spring training last year and it never healed properly. He also put on pounds and never took them off. Both hurt him at the plate.

Rayford is good with the high fastball. Low pitches--particularly the breaking ball--give him great trouble. He is an aggressive swinger who will strike out a lot. To improve, he has to be more patient and make more contact, which is no surprise.

Despite his build, Rayford is a deceptively quick runner. He has a good first step out of the batter's box and on the bases, but is not a basestealing threat.

Looking at Rayford's stocky build makes you think he'd be slow, but he has shown the quickness and agility to play third base and catch in the majors. After a solid 1985 season split between both positions, however, he slumped last year. The third base job was his, but 10 players eventually took a turn there and Rayford's 16 errors were the most on the team.

OVERALL:

Kaat: "Rayford isn't a defensive whiz, but he's better-than-average at third and catching. The key is if he's in shape. That's one thing that will sour a manager and management more than anything, and Rayford was not in shape last season."

JIM TRABER
1B/OF, No. 28
LL, 6'0", 194 lbs.
ML Svc: 1 year plus
Born: 12-26-61 in
Columbus, OH

HITTING, BASERUNNING, FIELDING:

Jim Traber was poised enough to sing the National Anthem before the game in which he made his major league debut in September 1984. He was a hit with the fans and got a hit off Oil Can Boyd in his second at-bat.

Traber is a lefthanded hitter who doesn't lack for confidence. He was called up when Eddie Murray was hurt last year and hit .342 with 10 home runs and 32 RBIs in his first 32 games with the Orioles. However, he batted only .147 with three homers and 12 RBIs in his last 33 games.

He is a good low-ball hitter, but pitchers mixed their pitches on him in the last six weeks and were successful.

Traber has below-average speed and is not a basestealing threat. He is not reckless, but he runs full tilt until he sees the stop sign.

He can play first base and is adequate in the outfield. He doesn't do anything wrong, but he's a step slow and is ideally suited to first base or designated hitter.

OVERALL:

Kaat: "He reminds me of a shorter version of Larry Sheets, only with a little more speed and he can sing."

BOSTON RED SOX

HITTING:

Tony Armas led the major leagues in home runs (43) and RBIs (123) in 1984, but injuries severely cut down his productivity over the past two seasons. His inabilty to come close to repeating his '84 figures eventually led to the Red Sox not exercising their option on his 1987 contract and releasing him (the buyout was $50,000) following the World Series last year.

In 1985, Armas was plagued with a torn thigh muscle that forced him to miss 48 games. He had only 23 homers and 64 RBIs that year and last season an ankle and thigh injury put him out of 31 games and lowered his productivity to 11 homers and 58 RBIs.

Armas has always been a low-fastball hitter who has trouble with hard inside pitches above the waist as well as with breaking balls from righthanders.

Rarely will Armas hit for average but he's always been dangerous with runners in scoring position, especially late in a game. He has always been a power hitter and RBI man.

BASERUNNING:

He is not much of a threat to steal anymore, although he's still an intelligent runner who knows when to take an extra base.

FIELDING:

Armas, always regarded as an outstanding defensive outfielder, has lost a step or two because of a succession of leg, knee and thigh injuries the last couple of years. But he can still do a decent job.

He has always had a strong throwing arm, which sometimes gets him into trouble when he tries to throw the ball all the way rather than hit the cutoff man.

**TONY ARMAS
CF, No. 20
RR, 6'1", 224 lbs.
ML Svc: 10 years
Born: 7-2-53 in
Anzoatequi,
Venezuela**

1986 STATISTICS

AVG	G	AB	R	H	2B	3B	HR	RBI	BB	SO	SB
.264	121	425	40	112	21	4	11	58	24	77	0

CAREER STATISTICS

AVG	G	AB	R	H	2B	3B	HR	RBI	BB	SO	SB
.251	1224	4513	542	1134	174	35	224	727	230	1055	16

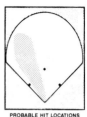

STRONG   STRONG

VS. RHP   VS. LHP   PROBABLE HIT LOCATIONS

OVERALL:

A popular player in Boston during his four years there, Armas might have been picked up by another club sooner had he not filed for free agency, which forced the team signing him to lose a number one draft choice. Had his agent waited until December 20th (the date players become unrestricted free agents if their former team doesn't tender them a contract), he would have been a free agent without costing a signing team a draft choice. The complications of dates and contracts might have tripped up Armas' 1987 season.

Kaat: "Armas will probably not be a factor as an everyday player again, but he still could be a valuable part-time player or designated hitter for some team. The experience and knowledge alone he would bring a club would be a plus."

BOSTON RED SOX

HITTING:

When he came up from Triple-A, Marty Barrett was faced with detractors who said he was in over his head, that he would never make it in the major leagues. He was slow, had no range, and would be overmatched at the plate by big league pitchers. He's made them all eat their words.

Barrett has developed into an outstanding contact hitter, which has made him the perfect number-two man in the Red Sox lineup behind Wade Boggs.

In addition to his ability to make contact, he is also good at hitting the high fastball.

Barrett takes a stance that has him turned slightly toward the first baseman. This enables him to handle all types of pitchers. Barrett slaps the ball around and loves to take the outside pitch and go to right field--which has done with success. And he is also able to take the inside pitch and pull it into left. Last year, he even powered four pitches out of the park.

Barrett is an excellent bunter and is the ideal number-two hitter in that he can handle the bat in hit-and-run situations. He rarely strikes out and constantly gets the bat on the ball, which provides excellent protection for the runner. Last season he fanned only 31 times in 690 plate appearances.

BASERUNNING:

Barrett does not have great speed but he picks his spots well. His judgment has allowed him to become a decent basestealer. Last season, he led the leadfoot Red Sox with 15 steals in 22 tries. He lulls opponents to sleep, then takes advantage. Barrett believes that he should be able to steal 20 bases successfully each year.

FIELDING:

Barrett is an adequate, hard-nosed, put-

MARTY BARRETT
2B, No. 17
RR, 5'10", 175 lbs.
ML Svc: 4 years
Born: 6-23-58 in
Arcadia, CA

1986 STATISTICS

AVG	G	AB	R	H	2B	3B	HR	RBI	BB	SO	SB
.286	158	625	94	179	39	4	4	60	65	31	15

CAREER STATISTICS

AVG	G	AB	R	H	2B	3B	HR	RBI	BB	SO	SB
.281	494	1696	216	476	89	8	12	163	166	108	27

  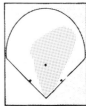

STRONG — VS. RHP STRONG — VS. LHP PROBABLE HIT LOCATIONS

your-face-in-the-dirt type of player. And by playing that way, he makes a lot of exceptional plays. He's not a very smooth or flashy type of second baseman, but he's a smart player who knows what's going on at all times, makes the plays he has to, and makes the double play pivot with the best of them.

OVERALL:

Barrett has made himself a winning player. He's the the team leader of the Red Sox infield and does many of the little things that go unnoticed yet help win ballgames.

Kaat: "When he got his chance to play, he made himself into one of the better second baseman in the league. His all-out intensity in every game makes him the player he is. He is one of those ballplayers who plays above the level of his skills."

BOSTON RED SOX

HITTING:

Don Baylor is the perfect designated hitter. He suffered an injury early in his career that cost him his throwing arm and thus took away his fielding game, but he's always been a dangerous clutch hitter and one of the better RBI men in the game.

Baylor cannot get around on the inside pitch as well he did in his younger days, but when he does connect, he sends towering home runs into the bleachers. Hitting the inside pitch is still his bread-and-butter.

Baylor stands straight up in the box and leans over the plate looking to pull. The result, of course, is that he gets hit a lot, sometimes too much. Opposing pitchers, knowing that Baylor will not not pull back from an inside buzzing are faced with a couple of interesting choices. In standing in so firmly, Baylor *owns* the inside part of the plate. So, on one hand, a pitcher might think, heck, why not just give it to him. It's safer to put this bruiser on first base than to take the chance of him ripping a double and surely driving in whoever is on base already. On the other hand, a pitcher who feels he would like to take home a scalp for the day, challenges Baylor by changing speeds and playing the inside/outside, high/low game with him. Whether Baylor or the pitcher wins is up to the chance of the moment. One thing is for sure, though: Baylor fears no pitcher. There are plenty of pitchers, however, who can't wait for him to retire.

BASERUNNING:

At one time Baylor could run--but no more. He's still very adept at breaking up the double play, as he has always gone into second base hard.

FIELDING:

Baylor will be used in left field or at first base only in an emergency. A poll around the league last year voted Baylor the worst first baseman in baseball. That's unfair. But he *is* strictly a hitter.

DON BAYLOR
DH, No. 25
RR, 6'1", 210 lbs.
ML Svc: 15 years
Born: 6-28-49 in
Austin, TX

1986 STATISTICS

AVG	G	AB	R	H	2B	3B	HR	RBI	BB	SO	SB
.238	160	585	93	139	23	1	31	94	62	111	3

CAREER STATISTICS

AVG	G	AB	R	H	2B	3B	HR	RBI	BB	SO	SB
.263	2072	7546	1141	1982	350	7	315	1179	726	966	280

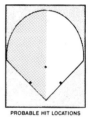

STRONG VS. RHP — STRONG VS. LHP — PROBABLE HIT LOCATIONS

OVERALL:

Aside from his run production, Baylor adds another dimension necessary for winning--attitude. Baylor is the type of player who *comes to play.* That expression is passed around baseball somewhat freely, but in his case it is true in its most literal sense. Baylor does not want to hear any excuses for a teammate who comes to the park to do otherwise. He is one of the most demanding players to play alongside. Last season, a description was made of the effect Baylor had on the Red Sox club: he transformed a club of twenty-five taxis into a team that rides one bus.

Kaat: "Don Baylor is going to be one of the key players if the Red Sox are to repeat this season. Championship ballclubs, with rare exception, share a common denominator: unity. He helped the Red Sox to develop that sense in 1986.

"I see no reason why he should not continue to provide the Sox with production as the DH this season, and perhaps even for several more."

BOSTON RED SOX

HITTING:

To date, Wade Boggs has earned: three major league batting championships in four years, four straight 200-hit seasons, 100 or more runs scored in four consecutive years, and an on-base percentage last season of .453.

Scouts constantly pay close attention to him, trying to pick up a weakness in his hitting. Thus far they've drawn blanks because he does not have any that are apparent.

Most good pitchers can neutralize hitters by getting ahead of them. Boggs is the exception to the rule. Rarely does he offer at the first pitch, and he's hit over .300 with two strikes on him.

He has never changed his Pete Rose-type of batting stance in which he crouches and looks the ball right into the catcher's glove.

BASERUNNING:

He's one of the quickest in the league at getting down the first base line but, overall, has below-average speed and is only an average runner. He runs hard and, occasionally, can hustle an extra base. He's not a good basestealer at all and is not called on to try very often. Last year he only attempted four and was caught each time.

FIELDING:

Boggs continues to improve as a fielder and, in the opinion of many, was a Gold Glove performer last year even though he wasn't voted one. He has worked as hard on his fielding as he has on his hitting. Almost daily, he is the first player on the field, and he takes extra fielding before batting practice begins.

WADE BOGGS
3B, No. 26
LR, 6'2", 197 lbs.
ML Svc: 5 years
Born: 6-15-58 in
Omaha, NE

1986 STATISTICS

AVG	G	AB	R	H	2B	3B	HR	RBI	BB	SO	SB
.357	149	580	107	207	47	2	8	71	105	44	0

CAREER STATISTICS

AVG	G	AB	R	H	2B	3B	HR	RBI	BB	SO	SB
.352	725	2778	474	978	178	17	32	322	417	206	9

  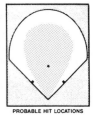

VS. RHP   VS. LHP   PROBABLE HIT LOCATIONS

OVERALL:

After signing his three-year contract prior to the '87 season, Boggs promised to come up with a secret weapon for this season. He was probably referring to power-hitting. He has always shown off his power in batting practice, but has never concentrated on that during a game. He has the ability to hit 20 or more home runs in a season; perhaps this is the year he turns on the switch.

Boggs can't miss having another outstanding hitting season and will be one of the premier infielders this year. He overcame a lot of personal tragedy last year.

Kaat: "Boggs is a tireless worker, and that will not only keep him the premier hitter in baseball but also make him even better. He's willing to work hard to improve his skills both at the plate, if that's possible, and in the field."

GOOD CONTROL

PITCHING:

Oil Can Boyd has won 43 games over the last three seasons, more than any other Red Sox pitcher. Yet he is only the third-best starter on the staff--which may be the best role for the high-strung 27-year-old right-hander.

Boyd won 16 games for the Red Sox in 1986, and that included a six-week stretch from July 9th through August 20th in which he didn't win a game. It was another turbulent year for The Can. He was suspended twice by the club in that stretch, once for walking out because he wasn't picked for the All-Star team and a second time after a brush with police. He was hospitalized for the second time since spring training for tests as well.

Stuff-wise, The Can has a vast and effective repertoire. His fastball is a bit above average but straight, meaning he has to have command of his breaking pitches to win. He has an above-average curveball and slider, along with a change-up. He can throw all his pitches from different angles and at any time in the count.

When he is pitching, Boyd is durable; he often pitches a full seven innings and will complete a good share of his starts. He won four games with three runs or less in support, and the Red Sox were shut out in three of his 10 losses. He hates to let a batter have a free pass to first. His control is excellent, and last year he issued only 1.89 walks per nine innings. Though he allowed a lot of home runs in 1986 (32), twenty of them were solos; ten of the remaining 12 came with only one runner aboard.

FIELDING:

Boyd is an excellent athlete who takes pride in being adept at all facets of the game. He is quick off the mound and handles the ball well. When he concentrates on baserunners, he holds them on well, and 47% of base thieves have been caught since he's been in the big leagues.

DENNIS BOYD
RHP, No. 23
RR, 6'1", 144 lbs.
ML Svc: 4 years
Born: 10-6-59 in
Meridian, MS

1986 STATISTICS

W	L	ERA	G	GS	CG	SV	IP	H	R	ER	BB	SO
16	10	3.78	30	30	10	0	214.1	222	99	90	45	129

CAREER STATISTICS

W	L	ERA	G	GS	CG	SV	IP	H	R	ER	BB	SO
47	44	3.85	112	105	85	0	791.1	816	376	339	190	462

OVERALL:

In 1985 he didn't win a game between the All-Star break and September while being depressed about being passed over for the All-Star team that year. Even so, Boyd could have won 20 games in 1985 had the bullpen not squandered five late-inning leads for him; and he could have won 19 last year had the bullpen not frittered away three more leads. A key for Boyd this year will be whether or not he lets losing his case in salary arbitration affect his pitching.

If The Can can lick his emotional problems and mature as a person, he can be a steady 16-18-game winner for the Red Sox, with the potential to win 20 some years. He has the proverbial rubber arm, never having had arm trouble, and is able to pitch a lot of innings despite his wispy frame.

Kaat: "Boyd has all the pitches and he can do about anything he wants to do with the baseball. And he has excellent control.

"It's an old cliche, but it applies to Boyd: If he could be intense without being tense, he could be an outstanding pitcher. But it's a big hurdle he has to overcome.

"I think it's refreshing to see a pitcher so emotional on the field--if he can harness that so it doesn't work against him. And most of the pressure this year will be on Clemens and Hurst, and that should help Boyd."

BOSTON RED SOX

HITTING:

There aren't many ballplayers who could have withstood the beating Bill Buckner has taken over the past two years.

There isn't a part of Buckner's 37-year-old body that escapes the aches and pains during the course of the year and, at times, it appears as though he has to use all his strength to pull his frame into the batter's box.

The years have not changed Buckner's style of hitting or his ability to hit. He continues to stand in the middle of the box in a slight crouch with the bat off his shoulder, and he's still almost as tough an out as he was early in his career.

Throw him a fastball and he's going to wind up either hitting it out of the park or getting on base. Last season, he drove in over 100 runs, hit 18 big ones and managed to maintain a .267 average.

Buckner is the type of a hitter who covers the strike zone very well. The breaking ball thrown down and away is about the only one he won't hit with authority. That, however, is true of most hitters if the pitcher gets it where he wants.

He has a great knack for tiring a pitcher by battling him. Buckner will foul off pitch after pitch--throwing his bat at balls if he has to. Then when the pitcher makes a mistake, he jumps on it.

Buckner is still one of the better clutch hitters in the game.

BASERUNNING:

His aggressive style at the plate carries over into his baserunning. Though his gams do not agree, Buckner still thinks he's in his early 20s. For the past two years, he has led the Red Sox in being thrown out on the bases. Late last year, with his bad ankles and bone spurs in both of his feet, he could barely move. He hopes off-season surgery will help loosen him up for the 1987 season.

FIELDING:

Buckner's bone spurs and bad ankles cut down on his range and can, at times, make

BILL BUCKNER
1B, No. 6
LL, 6'1", 182 lbs.
ML Svc: 17 years
Born: 12-14-49 in
Vallejo, CA

1986 STATISTICS

AVG	G	AB	R	H	2B	3B	HR	RBI	BB	SO	SB
.267	153	629	73	168	39	2	18	102	40	25	6

CAREER STATISTICS

AVG	G	AB	R	H	2B	3B	HR	RBI	BB	SO	SB
.292	2176	8424	1008	2464	462	46	164	1072	402	395	175

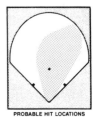

VS. RHP · VS. LHP · PROBABLE HIT LOCATIONS

him look awkward in the field. But he's a good defensive first baseman. His deficiencies are his limited range and a weak throwing arm.

OVERALL:

Buckner must ice down his hurting ankles two hours before a game, for an hour or so afterwards, and even at home in his spare time. He always gets a hotel room near the ice machine when the team travels on the road.

Buckner's error in Game Six in the 10th inning of the World Series last year has etched in the minds of many fans an image of him as a helpless wicket. He has been dealt an cruel blow by the hand of fate. He is one of the more hard-nosed of all major league ballplayers and is one of those players often referred to as a "throwback" type.

Hapless fans will ride him hard for that error; afficionados will not.

Kaat: "Bill will overcome whatever he has to in order to play this game. He has always done whatever was asked of him and has never used his injured legs as an excuse. He remains one of the biggest threats to a pitcher because he can hit one out of the park at any time."

PITCHING:

What can you do after you've done it all--except try to do it all again? Repeating--that's the dilemma facing Roger Clemens after a year in which he narrowly missed winning the unofficial Triple Crown of pitching (victories, strikeouts and ERA) and which he capped by winning the American League MVP and Cy Young awards.

The Scouting Report: 1986 reported Clemens had "the ability to be a 25-game winner," even though he was coming off shoulder surgery and had yet to pitch a full big league season. Pretty bold stuff, indeed, but Clemens did his part by fireballing his way to a 24-4 record in 1986.

Perhaps Clemens' most impressive feat was winning 14 times following Red Sox losses, halting potentially long losing streaks. There was the 14-game winning streak from the start of the season and, of course, the fabulous 20-strikeout, no-walk masterpiece against the Seattle Mariners in late April.

What Clemens does is more than just retire batters. He sends them down swinging. There weren't many batters who were able to catch up with his fastball last season (batters hit .195 against him): he struck out 10 or more batters in a game eight times.

If a batter is to get on base against Clemens, he is going to have to earn his way there. Clemens allowed fewer than nine baserunners per nine innings last year and averaged less than three walks per game.

Clemens has the best of both worlds: overpowering stuff and near-flawless control. And he can do it for nine innings. He recorded 10 complete games in 33 starts last season. He pitched into the seventh inning in 30 of his 33 starts and was pulled only once before the seventh.

Although he did show himself to be prone to the gopher ball last year, 13 of them were solos and the other eight came with only one runner on base.

Not only can Clemens rely on a fastball clocked as high as 97 MPH, he also possesses a forkball, slider and curveball--and he's not averse to throwing any of them in a tough situation.

ROGER CLEMENS
RHP, No. 21
RR, 6'4", 215 lbs.
ML Svc: 3 years
Born: 8-4-62 in
Dayton, OH

1986 STATISTICS

W	L	ERA	G	GS	CG	SV	IP	H	R	ER	BB	SO
24	4	2.48	33	33	10	0	254	179	77	70	67	238

CAREER STATISTICS

W	L	ERA	G	GS	CG	SV	IP	H	R	ER	BB	SO
40	13	3.15	69	68	18	0	485.2	408	182	170	133	438

FIELDING:

For a big man, Clemens is an adequate fielder. A slide step perfected in spring training last year improved his move to first base so drastically that after just four of 32 attempting basestealers were thrown out during his first two years, 14 of 22 runners were thrown out stealing in 1986, including such AL speedsters as John Cangelosi (twice), Gary Pettis, Brett Butler and Harold Reynolds.

OVERALL:

Clemens is not likely to rest on his 1986 laurels. His stamina seemed to suffer late last season, particularly in the ALCS and the World Series, when he was at the tail of a season during which he pitched the most innings of his pro career. With that first full year behind him, he should be stronger throughout 1987.

Kaat: "Clemens has the best fastball in the league and showed continued improvement with his breaking pitches last year. Confidence and control go hand in hand and he has both--and I'm not talking about control of pitches but control of himself on the mound.

"But he will have to improve in some way to do as well as he did last year, perhaps with better command of his breaking pitches. Don't look at the numbers this season, though: he could have a better year than he did in 1986 and only go 19-11. That's the way baseball is."

BOSTON RED SOX

PITCHING:

Steve Crawford is one of those versatile pitchers with the tools to become an outstanding pitcher as a starter or reliever. But the thing that has always held Steve Crawford back is his temperament. Crawford has two 90+ fastballs he can throw over the plate at will: a cross-seamer he can use for strikeouts and a hard sinker for grounders. The drawback is that he relies on those two pitches almost exclusively, and when he gets in a jam his solution is to try and throw harder rather than slow down his pace or mix in a curveball.

Crawford saved 12 games in 1985, most of them in the second half of the season. But when 1986 began and Bob Stanley was healthy, Crawford was relegated to set-up relief, generally coming into a game in the seventh inning to try and get the Red Sox to the ninth. In save situations he was only 4-for-8. He failed to hold four of 17 leads and one of four ties entrusted to him. He was only average at preventing inherited runners from scoring, stranding 63.4%.

Although he unintentionally walked only 1.89 batters per nine innings, the league hit .308 against him. First batters were 11-for-38 against him, although in close games (two runs or less either way) first batters were only 5-for-22. Four of the five homers he allowed came with the bases empty.

He started using a curveball as an off-speed pitch last season and it's a good one. But he needs to use it more in order to make it *and* his fastball more effective. Crawford has a powerful and durable arm, which enables him to pitch almost every day and as a starter, long reliever, or short reliever.

STEVE CRAWFORD
RHP, No. 28
RR, 6'5", 236 lbs.
ML Svc: 4 years
Born: 4-29-58 in
Pryor, OK

1986 STATISTICS

W	L	ERA	G	GS	CG	SV	IP	H	R	ER	BB	SO
0	2	3.92	40	0	0	4	57.1	69	29	25	19	32

CAREER STATISTICS

W	L	ERA	G	GS	CG	SV	IP	H	R	ER	BB	SO
14	12	3.87	144	16	2	17	309.1	365	162	133	94	152

FIELDING:

Crawford is an average fielder, especially for his size. He is good at holding runners on and few runners attempt to steal when he's pitching.

OVERALL:

If Crawford could ever learn to pitch instead of throw, he could be an effective pitcher in any role. He is aggressive and never gives in to a hitter.

Kaat: "Crawford did a good job last year for what the Red Sox askéd of him. Even though his stats may never be that great, he can be a staff-saver because he is always ready to pitch in any situation. If he's going to start or pitch to a batting order more than once, however, he has to come up with a better curveball or slider."

BOSTON RED SOX

HITTING:

A student of the late hitting specialist Charlie Lau, Dwight Evans has worked hard on applying the Lau fundamentals with Boston hitting coach Walter Hriniak. Evans has had good results.

When he first came into the league, Evans was strictly a high-fastball hitter. Now, however, after adopting the Lau-type stance-- front foot up on the toe while trying to hit everything up the middle--Evans is able to handle the low pitch much better.

He is the prototype streak hitter. When he is not hitting well, he can look more like Dale Evans than Dwight Evans but then go on a tear and be very difficult to get out. When he is hot, he is among the best, most effective hitters in the American League.

Evans continues, however, to be prone to chasing too many low breaking balls out of the strike zone. That results in his striking out more than he should. With his unusual stance, Evans commits himself early and, because he is up so high on his front foot, he has difficulty checking his swing. But he's a very dangerous hitter and a very productive one no matter where he's hitting in the order.

BASERUNNING:

Evans is no threat to steal. He's not fast, doesn't run the bases well and after having surgery on both knees will never be a threat as a basestealer.

FIELDING:

Evans has been one of the game's better right fielders for the past decade and a half. He has an outstanding throwing arm and a most accurate one.

Right field in Fenway Park is not the easiest position to play. The unusual curving wall

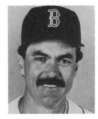

DWIGHT EVANS
RF, No. 24
RR, 6'3", 204 lbs.
ML Svc: 14 years
Born: 11-3-51 in
Santa Monica, CA

1986 STATISTICS

AVG	G	AB	R	H	2B	3B	HR	RBI	BB	SO	SB
.259	152	529	86	137	33	2	26	97	97	117	3

CAREER STATISTICS

AVG	G	AB	R	H	2B	3B	HR	RBI	BB	SO	SB
.268	1933	6661	1082	1785	361	57	291	949	989	1289	61

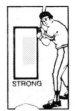

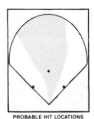

VS. RHP VS. LHP PROBABLE HIT LOCATIONS

down the line and the position of the sun during day games makes the right fielder work under unique and trying conditions.

Evans has adjusted to his corner of Fenway well, and no one in the league plays its quirks as well.

OVERALL:

Unless Evans suffers an injury which takes him out of the lineup for an extended period this season, the Red Sox, once again, will not have to worry about right field. And Evans will continue to do damage with the bat.

Kaat: "Evans has been around since 1972 but he keeps in good shape, is a tireless worker and should have a couple of more productive seasons left."

HITTING:

Just when Rich Gedman developed into an everyday catcher and attained All-Star status, he couldn't get together with the Red Sox on a contract and had to sit out until May 1st.

Gedman did not have as good a season at the plate in 1986 as he had the year before. Despite constantly working on his hitting and mechanics of hitting with coach Walter Hriniak, his average dropped from .295 to .258 last year, his home runs dropped from 18 to 16 and his RBIs went from 80 to 65.

The lefthanded Gedman still has the extremely wide open stance, keeps his head down as though he was hitting a golf ball, and releases the right hand from the bat as he swings. He still looks very bad when striking out but can turn on an inside pitch and pull it out of the park.

Like most lefthanders, he's a low-fastball hitter but, unlike most lefties, he does a pretty good job of handling the high pitch and usually gets his bat on that pitch.

Gedman has good power, and playing every day in Fenway Park, where opponents do not like to pitch lefthanders, should have worked to his advantage. But last year it did not--14 of his homers came on the road and he didn't hit any at home after July 4th.

Up-and-in or low-and-away is where pitchers try to work most hitters--and Gedman is no exception. Pitchers can change speeds on him with success because he does not handle that pitch very well.

BASERUNNING:

Gedman has no speed whatsoever and is not a good baserunner. He is thrown out too many times trying for an extra base he has no business attempting.

FIELDING:

Defensively, Gedman's 50% kill ratio was the highest percentage in the league last year (he was 44 of 88). He has a quick release, a great arm--very accurate--and you can't ask for much more.

He's developing into a good defensive

RICH GEDMAN
C, No. 10
LR, 6'0", 205 lbs.
ML Svc: 6 years
Born: 9-26-59 in
Worcester, MA

1986 STATISTICS

AVG	G	AB	R	H	2B	3B	HR	RBI	BB	SO	SB
.258	135	462	49	119	29	0	16	65	37	61	1

CAREER STATISTICS

AVG	G	AB	R	H	2B	3B	HR	RBI	BB	SO	SB
.273	656	2131	244	583	133	12	69	288	150	322	3

 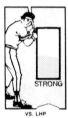 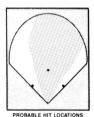

VS. RHP   VS. LHP   PROBABLE HIT LOCATIONS

catcher but sometimes gets lazy and is charged with too many passed balls. While he is not one of the best at calling a game, he has shown great improvement.

OVERALL:

Gedman does not have the reputation of a Bob Boone as a defensive catcher but he is very solid and very steady. As his club gains prominence, so will he. At this point in his career, he is the best catcher in the American League East at throwing out baserunners. He works hard to improve his hitting, has power and durability and would be a real asset to any ballclub.

Kaat: "If he's back with the Red Sox one of the challenges he faces is to handle the flack he gets from the fans because of his decision to turn down $2.65 million over three years. The money will probably become an issue with the people.

"His adeptness at throwing out attempting basestealers could be put to great use in the National League, where ballclubs run more than they do in the power-hitting AL East."

BOSTON RED SOX

HITTING:

Dave Henderson has been in the American League long enough to start becoming a more disciplined hitter. Perhaps having a full season under the tutelage of Red Sox hitting coach Walter Hriniak will help.

If Henderson was able to cut down on his big swing, he would strike out less often and hit for a higher average. Hriniak seems to have been able to get other hitters to do just that, and it would be a big plus for Henderson if he could adapt some of Hriniak's principles.

Henderson, who came to the Red Sox in mid-August last year, will also have the advantage of playing a full season in Fenway Park, which should help him to settle down at the plate.

He stands straight up in the box, has excellent power and can handle the fastball pitched either up and down. Too often, however, he tries to hit beyond his capabilities, and that results in him chasing too many bad pitches and striking out much more than he should.

When he gets behind in the count, Henderson is prone to chasing the breaking ball out of the strike zone. His big problem at the plate would seem to be trying to pull everything: this is where his hitting coach can be a big help this year.

BASERUNNING:

Henderson has decent speed but probably won't be allowed to use it much with the Red Sox, especially at Fenway Park. He is a reckless baserunner; that has hurt him in the past.

FIELDING:

Henderson is a good center fielder and has the speed that allows him to play shallow and go back and get balls. He has a better-than-average throwing arm and will be a plus in the field for the Sox.

OVERALL:

Henderson's day in the sun came last October. In Game 5 of the ALCS against California, the Red Sox were trailing 3-1 in the series. Down by one run with two out in the

DAVE HENDERSON
CF, No. 40
RR, 6'2", 212 lbs.
ML Svc: 6 years
Born: 7-21-58 in
Dos Palos, CA

1986 STATISTICS

AVG	G	AB	R	H	2B	3B	HR	RBI	BB	SO	SB
.265	139	388	59	103	22	4	15	47	39	110	2

CAREER STATISTICS

AVG	G	AB	R	H	2B	3B	HR	RBI	BB	SO	SB
.255	690	2174	285	555	117	12	80	274	186	454	26

VS. RHP   VS. LHP   PROBABLE HIT LOCATIONS

top of the ninth inning, the count ran up to one-and-two. Who is this guy, anyway? No-name Henderson had the hopes but likely not the confidence of the Red Sox fans...oh, but for Rice, Baylor or Boggs to be up now...low outside fastball--*CRACK!* In millions of slow-motion memories, the image of Dave Henderson's jubilation as that low fastball became Boston's highest moment is forever etched. The California demons tied it up in the bottom of the ninth, but in the top of the 11th with the bases loaded, Henderson now had the magic. His long sacrifice fly brought in the winning run. His heroics that day sealed him as beloved in the hearts of Boston's fans. The Red Sox' fate during the World Series in 1986 only slightly tarnishes the glitter of that day.

If the Red Sox are going to repeat as champions they will need a complete and very productive season from Dave Henderson. He has the chance to build on baseball's last taste of him.

Kaat: "At this point in Henderson's career, the time has come for him to be a productive player for an entire season. He's got the ability, speed and power to be a top player if he can discipline himself."

BOSTON RED SOX

PITCHING:

June 28, 1985, was the turning point in the career of Bruce Hurst. Although he had pitched well in streaks to that point in his career, the lefthander appeared to suffer from a lack of self-confidence. He had been rushed to the majors too soon and had paid the price; skeptics were beginning to believe he would never become a winning major league pitcher.

After being banished to the bullpen in June of 1985 (where he did not distinguish himself), Hurst was returned to the rotation on the 28th. He pitched seven innings of one-run ball with no walks and six strikeouts in a 6-1 Red Sox victory. Since then, he has blossomed.

By learning to throw his fastball inside and by mixing in his sweeping overhand curveball and a nasty forkball, Hurst was leading the American League in strikeouts late last May when he tore a groin muscle, which disabled him for six weeks. Were it not for the injury, he might have won 18-20 games and won the strikeout title.

Even the best pitchers in the league give up home runs to the opposition; a good pitcher bears down especially hard when there are runners on base. Hurst did just that last season: 16 of the 18 home runs he allowed occurred when the bases were empty. He allowed none in the pennant stretch (over his last 44 1/3 regular-season innings).

Hurst is at his best against righthanded hitters; in 1986, he was 6-0 in eight starts against lineups using exclusively righthanded hitters, a testament to his ability to buzz his fastball inside. Hurst threw four shutouts last year--all were in Fenway Park, with its famous left field wall looming behind third base. The Red Sox scored only nine runs in his eight losses.

FIELDING:

Hurst is a good fielder. His pickoff move, refined over the last three years (since 14 of 16 runners stole successfully against him in

BRUCE HURST
LHP, No. 47
LL, 6'3", 207 lbs.
ML Svc: 5 years
Born: 3-24-58 in
St. George, UT

1986 STATISTICS

W	L	ERA	G	GS	CG	SV	IP	H	R	ER	BB	SO
13	8	2.99	25	25	11	0	174.1	169	63	58	50	167

CAREER STATISTICS

W	L	ERA	G	GS	CG	SV	IP	H	R	ER	BB	SO
55	54	4.31	171	152	32	0	1003.2	1108	525	481	338	687

1983), is one of the best in baseball. Although his pickoffs dipped from 29 the previous two years to a mere trickle in 1986, he has put a complete halt to opponents' running games. Seven of 11 runners attempting to steal were caught last year and there were only three attempts after May 16.

OVERALL:

With an above-average fastball, one of the best curveballs in baseball, mastery of the forkball, and soaring confidence, Hurst is on the verge of establishing himself at age 29 as one of the premier lefthanders in baseball. He should win 18 to 20 games a season for the next few years.

Kaat: "Hurst proved to himself and other people he is right up there with the premier pitchers in the league. When you're a lefthander and has his control and his breaking ball, it's a tremendous advantage. A lot of righthanded hitters would rather hit off Clemens than off Hurst, I guarantee you.

"When you have spent so many years trying to prove you're better than a .500 pitcher and have the kind of year he did, it has to relax you. I would call him a Cy Young candidate in 1987."

BOSTON RED SOX

PITCHING:

How would you describe a player who had a 1.000 winning percentage, a 1.000 batting average and a 1.000 fielding percentage? The greatest player who ever lived, right? Well, lefthander Tim Lollar compiled those three figures for the Red Sox last season and nobody is calling him the greatest player who ever lived. The Red Sox wish they could just call him a *good* player someday.

For six years, baseball has been waiting for the 31-year-old Lollar to reach his potential. Except for a 16-9 season with a 3.13 ERA for San Diego in 1983, Lollar's career has been a never-ending struggle--mostly with his control. He has been tried as a starter, a middle reliever, and a special-situation reliever. He has thrived in none of those roles, and in the American League even his live bat is negated by the DH rule. So Lollar exists in limbo.

Lollar has a good arm, an above-average fastball, and good major league stuff. But Lollar, an All-American DH at Arkansas who did not become a full-time pitcher until he turned pro, has never been able to consistently get his pitches over the plate.

With his herky-jerky motion, he is caught in a vicious cycle: he needs to pitch to refine his control, but without contol the Red Sox won't let him pitch.

Stamina has always been a problem for Lollar as a starter. He has completed only nine of 131 major league starts. He was relegated to a mop-up role with the Red Sox most of last season. He pitched in 35% of the club's 66 losses and only 8% of their 95 victories. In the 23 losses in which Lollar appeared, the Red Sox were outscored by a whopping 233-136 margin, including seven games in which they allowed 10 or more runs.

Lollar is considered undependable in close games. Last year, he allowed a staggering 18.4 baserunners per nine innings pitched and walked 34 batters and hit three others in just 43 innings of work. The league hit .304 against him with seven homers. Lollar did all right with inherited runners, stranding 67% (24 of 36). But the first batters he faced upon

TIM LOLLAR
LHP, No. 48
LL, 6'3", 204 lbs.
ML Svc: 7 years
Born: 3-17-56 in
  Poplar Bluff, MO

1986 STATISTICS

W	L	ERA	G	GS	CG	SV	IP	H	R	ER	BB	SO
2	0	6.91	32	1	0	0	43	51	35	33	34	28

CAREER STATISTICS

W	L	ERA	G	GS	CG	SV	IP	H	R	ER	BB	SO
47	52	4.27	199	131	9	4	905.2	841	459	430	480	600

entering games hit .333 (8-for-24) with two homers, four sacrifice flies, two walks, one hit batter, and nine RBIs.

Lollar did, however, make one appearance as a pinch-hitter and responded with a single, and he takes regular hitting with the extra men in case he's needed in that role.

FIELDING:

Lollar is not a particularly agile fielder. He is poor for a lefthander at holding on runners. Basestealers were 4-for-4 against him last season.

OVERALL:

If Lollar could ever lick his control problems, he could be a consistent winner in the majors because his fastball and breaking pitches are all above average. Unless he can master control, however, he's always going to have trouble getting innings from his managers.

Kaat: "Lollar has always had a great arm, but outside of that one year in San Diego he has never developed into the pitcher people thought he should be. It comes down to one word: control.

"When he pitched a lot, his control and rhythm were better. But spot pitching does not help his control and, unfortunately, that is the only way the Red Sox can use him."

BOSTON RED SOX

PITCHING:

Injuries have kept Al Nipper from flashing the form which made him such an impressive pitcher as a rookie, when he was 11-6 with a 3.89 ERA for the Red Sox in 1984. If he can stay healthy, the 28-year-old righthander can become one of those rarities in this era of watered-down major league baseball: a fourth or fifth pitcher with a winning record.

Nipper has only an average major league fastball, so he has to depend on control and finesse. He has a good curveball and slider. He also throws a knuckleball; it could eventually become his best pitch.

Nipper was off to a good start in 1986. Although he was only 3-4 in mid-May, his ERA was 3.65, he had two complete games, and the Red Sox had scored only two runs in three of his losses. Then he suffered a deep spike wound above his right knee during a home plate collision with Texas' Larry Parrish, and it had to be repaired surgically, putting Nipper on the shelf for five weeks. Nipper rushed himself back to the rotation on June 25, in time to pitch and win perhaps the most crucial game of the season for the Red Sox last year. The Yankees had won the first two games of a series in Boston and were closing in when Nipper stopped them with seven gutty innings in a 5-4 Sox win. The Yankees never really threatened again.

Unfortunately for Nipper, he probably came back too soon. He struggled the rest of the year, although he did win one more important game in late July in Chicago when the Red Sox were suffering through a miserable 3-10 western swing. Nipper's ERA was 5.38, the league hit .290 against him, and he gave up 24 homers in 159 innings. Of those homers, 12 were solos and eight others came with one runner on base.

FIELDING:

Nipper is a hard worker who knows the

AL NIPPER
RHP, No. 49
RR, 6'0", 194 lbs.
ML Svc: 3 years
Born: 4-2-59 in San Diego, CA

1986 STATISTICS

W	L	ERA	G	GS	CG	SV	IP	H	R	ER	BB	SO
10	12	5.38	26	26	3	0	159	186	108	95	47	79

CAREER STATISTICS

W	L	ERA	G	GS	CG	SV	IP	H	R	ER	BB	SO
31	31	4.35	83	77	15	0	519.2	543	281	251	188	253

game. He is quick off the mound and knows what to do with the ball when he gets it. He is also good at making runners stop after taking their leads, which is vital for a pitcher who relies so much on off-speed pitches. Runners rarely get a good jump against him.

OVERALL:

When healthy, Nipper has the ability and poise to be a .500 or better pitcher. But he needs pinpoint control, to have all his pitches working, and to keep the ball down in the strike zone in order to be effective. If he masters the knuckleball, he could be a 14-15-game winner someday.

Kaat: "Nipper is a battling type of pitcher who can be a good fourth or fifth pitcher on any staff. When you have a pitching staff like Boston's, a guy who can give you a .500 season can be very, very valuable.

"If he can pitch on a regular basis, his control will return and will make him a better pitcher."

BOSTON RED SOX

HITTING:

Spike Owen was acquired in mid-August last year from Seattle to help the Red Sox in their drive to the pennant. Offensively, he didn't do well (.183), but he was not acquired for his bat.

Owen is a 5'10", 170-pound switch-hitter who tries to slap the ball around. Pitchers with above-average velocity on their fastballs can generally get the ball past him, and he's had his problems with off-speed pitches from the lefthand side of the plate. Owen hit for a higher average from the right side after the Sox made the trade for him.

In a lineup such as the one the Red Sox have, many baseball people feel that Owen could be a much more relaxed hitter than he was in Seattle.

FIELDING:

The old baseball cliche "makes all the routine plays" is true in the case of Owen. He's not going to look fancy but normally will handle anything he can get to. He looked bad at times right after the Sox picked him up, but that may have been because he was trying too hard to help a contending team.

BASERUNNING:

He is an alert baserunner with better-than-average speed, and if he had to he could steal bases. But the Red Sox are a team that does very little running--especially when playing at Fenway.

SPIKE OWEN
SS, No. 5
SR, 5'10", 165 lbs.
ML Svc: 4 years
Born: 4-19-61 in
Cleburne, TX

1986 STATISTICS

AVG	G	AB	R	H	2B	3B	HR	RBI	BB	SO	SB
.231	154	528	67	122	24	7	1	45	51	51	4

CAREER STATISTICS

AVG	G	AB	R	H	2B	3B	HR	RBI	BB	SO	SB
.235	504	1716	211	403	63	24	12	146	155	138	411

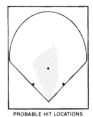

VS. RHP   VS. LHP   PROBABLE HIT LOCATIONS

OVERALL:

Owen was a good acquisition for the Red Sox last season, and unless a young phenom comes out of nowhere, a trade is made, or Glenn Hoffman makes a spectacular return, Owen will be a steady performer who will occasionally provide key hits. He'll be an asset.

Kaat: "Owen is perfectly suited to a team like the Red Sox: he gives them a sort of stability. He's steady and can provide the day-to-day consistency the team needs."

BOSTON RED SOX

HITTING:

Jim Rice bounced back from what he felt was an off year in 1985 (.291/27 homers/103 RBIs) to help the Red Sox to the American League pennant last season. In 1986, he hit .324 with 20 homers and 110 RBIs and finish third behind teammate Roger Clemens and the Yankees' Don Mattingly in MVP voting.

His .324 average was the second highest of his 12-year career (he hit .325 in 1979), the seventh time he's been over .300, the 11th time he hit at least 20 home runs (the strike year of '81 the only time he missed that figure), and the eighth time he's had 100+ RBIs.

With Rice, some things never change. He continues to use the stance that has brought him success in the past: deep in the batter's box and far off the plate. His attitude on hitting is also the same as ever: "I just try and go with the pitch and put the ball in play."

At one time, Rice was an impatient hitter who had trouble with the low breaking ball. But he's learned patience, and that has made him an even tougher out. He had a career high 62 walks while striking out only 78 times in over 700 plate appearances last year.

A pitcher who is able to change speeds may have some success with Rice. Rice is able to handle pitches most anywhere in the strike zone. But the ones high-and-tight and low-and-away give him, like every hitter who ever played, trouble.

BASERUNNING:

Rice is no threat on the bases. He was never fast and arthroscopic knee surgery after the 1985 season didn't help.

FIELDING:

Jim Rice has developed into a better-than-average left fielder, especially in Fenway Park. Like Ted Williams and Carl Yastrzemski before him, he's mastered the art of playing

JIM RICE
LF, No. 14
RR, 6'2", 217 lbs.
ML Svc: 13 years
Born: 3-8-53 in
Anderson, SC

1986 STATISTICS

AVG	G	AB	R	H	2B	3B	HR	RBI	BB	SO	SB
.324	157	618	98	200	39	2	20	110	62	78	0

CAREER STATISTICS

AVG	G	AB	R	H	2B	3B	HR	RBI	BB	SO	SB
.303	1790	7127	1104	2163	331	74	351	1289	564	1218	55

  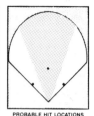

STRONG VS. RHP   STRONG VS. LHP   PROBABLE HIT LOCATIONS

the ball there. He's very adept at barehanding caroms and holding runners at first base. His throwing arm is below average, and that hurts him more in the larger parks of the league.

OVERALL:

Jim Rice will continue to be productive at the plate, especially since he now realizes he does not have to try to carry the offense of the entire team by himself. He's a feared hitter who is at his best when he is relaxed.

Kaat: "Jim is one of the most feared hitters in the game and he'll continue to wreak havoc when he steps to the plate. The addition of Don Baylor last season to the Red Sox helped take some of the pressure off Rice and enabled him to have a great season.

"His biggest challenge this year will be to stay within himself and not press to duplicate his numbers of last season. He only has to do what comes naturally, and the numbers will come."

BOSTON RED SOX

PITCHING:

In only his first full season as a short reliever, Calvin Schiraldi made great strides and came within one strike of saving what would have been the clinching game of the World Series for the Red Sox. The 24-year-old reliever, with a fastball in the low 90s, still needs more experience in the role, but he showed he was on the brink of stardom during the last two months of the season with the Red Sox.

Although Schiraldi possesses an outstanding fastball and a good slider, his niche may be short relief. Stamina has always been a problem for him as a pro (only nine complete games in 63 pro starts) and he starts to lose the velocity on his fastball in the middle innings.

He relied almost exclusively on his fastball with the Red Sox last season, and mixing in an occasional slider may keep batters from sitting on that fastball when they know he has to pitch to them.

Schiraldi posted nine saves in 12 opportunities and held 12 of 15 leads, although he did fail to hold two of four ties. He averaged 9.71 strikeouts per nine innings and only 2.29 unintentional walks, and the league hit only .201 against him.

One of the important skills a short reliever must develop is the ability to get the first batter out. In this regard, Schiraldi seems to run hot and cold. He is hot insofar as he can come in one day and blow that first batter away with a strikeout (he did so eight times last year), but runs cold as ice when the first batter knocks his pitch out of the park (that happened twice). Overall, the first batters he faced upon entering games were only 5-for-22 against him. He gave up five homers in 51 innings.

CALVIN SCHIRALDI
RHP, No. 31
RR, 6'4", 200 lbs.
ML Svc: 2 years
Born: 6-16-62 in
Houston, TX

1986 STATISTICS

W	L	ERA	G	GS	CG	SV	IP	H	R	ER	BB	SO
4	2	1.41	25	0	0	9	51	36	8	8	15	55

CAREER STATISTICS

W	L	ERA	G	GS	CG	SV	IP	H	R	ER	BB	SO
6	5	4.28	40	7	0	9	94.2	99	48	45	36	92

FIELDING:

Schiraldi tends to be a little lackadaisical as a fielder. He also needs work on holding runners. Basestealers were 5-for-6 against him last season.

OVERALL:

Kaat: "Schiraldi was a big surprise to most people last year. If he is used in the same role, he'll have to come up with some sort of breaking pitch because he doesn't try to finesse anybody and everybody knows what's coming.

"I think he also needs to be a little less passive in his approach to the game, although maybe that's what works best for him. When I think of short relievers, I think of Goose Gossage, Dave Righetti and even Dan Quisenberry, all of who take an aggressive approach to relief pitching."

PITCHING:

Although his record for the Red Sox was only 5-7, the acquisition of Tom Seaver at the end of June last year was the boost the club needed to assure itself of the American League East title. With their Big Three of Roger Clemens, Bruce Hurst and Oil Can Boyd, the Red Sox didn't need the aging Seaver to be their ace; all they needed from him was a solid, professional effort every time out. That's exactly what the 300-game winner gave them.

He averaged 6 1/3 innings per start for the Red Sox and gave up only eight homers in 104 1/3 innings while pitching half the time in one of baseball's smallest parks.

Seaver pitched better than his 1986 record indicates. The Red Sox scored three runs or less for him in all seven of his losses while he was in the game and they were shut out twice.

But Seaver proved he could still win the big games. Detroit was making a run at the Red Sox in August when Seaver started the first game of a four-game series at Tiger Stadium. The old grandmaster fired a five-hit, nine-strikeout complete game in a 6-1 Red Sox victory to blunt the Tigers' drive.

A late-season knee injury, which required arthroscopic surgery after the season, kept Seaver out of the ALCS and the World Series. Had he been available, manager John McNamara wouldn't have had to juggle his rotation and the Red Sox might have won the World Championship.

Once one of baseball's premier power pitchers, Seaver made the transition to a finesse pitcher several seasons ago with relative ease. Although he relies on excellent control to get by, he can still reach back and sneak a high fastball by a hitter on occasion. He still has a good curveball and changes speeds extremely well.

FIELDING:

Age has slowed him down somewhat, but Seaver won't mess up the balls he can reach. He was never particularly good at holding runners on base, and 14 of 18 thieves stole

TOM SEAVER
RHP, No. 41
RR, 6'1", 210 lbs.
ML Svc: 20 years
Born: 11-17-44 in
Fresno, CA

1986 STATISTICS

W	L	ERA	G	GS	CG	SV	IP	H	R	ER	BB	SO
7	13	4.03	28	28	2	0	176.1	180	83	79	56	103

CAREER STATISTICS

W	L	ERA	G	GS	CG	SV	IP	H	R	ER	BB	SO
311	205	2.86	656	647	234	0	4782.1	3971	1674	1521	1390	3640

successfully on him after he got to Boston, two of them even stealing on pitchouts.

OVERALL:

Seaver still has the cleverness to win after his best stuff has disappeared. He has always been one of the most cerebral of pitchers and relishes the mental battle between hitter and pitcher as much as any aspect of the game.

He can no longer be the ace of a staff, but, if healthy, he would nevertheless be a high-class and effective addition to a contending pitching staff in need of a fourth or fifth starter.

Seaver became a free agent after the '86 season, turning down a one-year, $600,000 offer from the Red Sox. He considered retirement, but could pitch again anytime this season if offers and interest fall into place.

Kaat: "The health of his knee and his back are the keys. If he can pitch, the only adjustment he'll have to make is being a spot-starter. He'll have to learn how to prepare himself to pitch every eight or 10 days instead of being in the regular rotation, but I think he could handle that.

"I enjoy watching him pitch now more than I did when he was 27 years old and it was always a mismatch with the hitters. He has learned to adjust over the years."

BOSTON RED SOX

PITCHING:

Although Bob Stanley has pitched in more games than any Red Sox pitcher in history and holds the club records for saves in a season and career and has performed whatever role the Red Sox have asked of him--starter, long relief, short relief--during his 10-year career, he has been the favorite whipping boy of Red Sox fans the last few years. Perhaps more than anything else, the booing by fans whenever he pitches has been the reason his effectiveness has diminished.

Stanley did a decent job in short relief before being displaced by Calvin Schiraldi during the final two months of the 1986 season. Stanley blew only five of 21 save opportunities, but 14 of his 16 saves came before the All-Star break. He held 30 of 35 leads but had trouble in tie games, failing to hold four of seven. He stranded 38 of 58 inherited baserunners (65.5%), which is about average for a relief pitcher.

Although the league hit .322 against him overall, Stanley was tough on first batters. The initial batters he faced upon entering games hit only .222 with 11 RBIs. He also induced three double plays and, although not known as a strikeout pitcher, struck out the first batter he faced 17 times. After April 20th, first batters hit only .169 against him. In close games (two runs or less either way), first batters were 7-for-32 against him with three RBIs.

Stanley still relies on a heavy sinker, although its velocity has dropped a little from its 90 MPH days. He has developed a decent slider in recent years. Last year he resurrected the palmball he used so effectively against lefthanded hitters a few years back, although he still has not gone back to throwing a spitter.

FIELDING:

Slow and not a gifted fielder, Stanley does

**BOB STANLEY
RHP, No. 46
RR, 6'4", 220 lbs.
ML Svc: 10 years
Born: 11-10-54 in
Portland, ME**

1986 STATISTICS

W	L	ERA	G	GS	CG	SV	IP	H	R	ER	BB	SO
6	6	4.37	66	1	0	16	82.1	109	48	40	22	54

CAREER STATISTICS

W	L	ERA	G	GS	CG	SV	IP	H	R	ER	BB	SO
100	76	3.84	503	65	17	123	1373.1	1468	606	526	374	537

work hard at it. His major flaw is losing his concentration on occasion and getting late to first base. He is very good at holding runners on base.

OVERALL:

One of the league's premier short relievers (33 saves) in 1983 and an outstanding long reliever in 1982 (12-7, 14 saves), Stanley may be cast in the role of a starter in 1987 for the first time since 1979, when he won 16 games. He was only a two-pitch pitcher back then, with a sinker and a change-up. With four pitches in his repertoire now, he may carve out a second career for himself in that role. Otherwise, a trade to another team may be the only way he'll regain his old form as one of the game's most versatile and durable pitchers.

Kaat: "Stanley was one of the outstanding relievers in the league, but not during the past few years. He has lost some velocity on that sinking fastball and he is still looking around for something effective against lefthanded hitters.

"Becoming a starter might make him a more relaxed pitcher, and all those other pitches might improve."

BOSTON RED SOX

PITCHING:

The Red Sox did not offer Sammy Stewart another contract after the 1986 season . . . and it could prove costly. Until he tore a muscle in his forearm at the end of May last year, Stewart was a vital link in the pitching chain and played a key role in getting the club into first place, where it remained the rest of the year.

Stewart was never used in a save situation but pitched in long relief. His job was to bail out faltering starters in the middle innings and keep the Red Sox, an outstanding late-inning, come-from-behind team, close. For the first two months of the '86 season, Stewart could be relied upon to get the Red Sox to the eighth or ninth inning, when Joe Sambito or Bob Stanley would take over. After he got hurt, however, Stewart missed eight weeks and was ineffective when he returned. Without Stewart, manager John McNamara was forced to go to Steve Crawford, Sambito and Stanley earlier than he wanted. And the more they had to pitch, the less effective they were.

If healthy, Stewart still possesses a fastball in the low 90s and a hard, wicked slider. Control has always been a problem for him, however. He walked more than six batters per nine innings last year. But with his 90 MPH heater, he is just wild enough to be intimidating.

FIELDING:

Stewart is not an adept fielder. He also has

SAMMY STEWART
RHP, No. 53
RR, 6'3", 208 lbs.
ML Svc: 8 years
Born: 10-28-54 in
Asheville, NC

1986 STATISTICS

W	L	ERA	G	GS	CG	SV	IP	H	R	ER	BB	SO
4	1	4.38	27	0	0	0	63.2	64	33	31	48	47

CAREER STATISTICS

W	L	ERA	G	GS	CG	SV	IP	H	R	ER	BB	SO
55	46	3.53	334	25	4	42	929.2	838	399	365	481	561

trouble holding runners on base because of his high kick and slow delivery.

OVERALL:

If he can make a full recovery from last year's injury, keep his weight down, and remain in shape, Stewart at age 32 can still be an effective and valuable middle-inning relief pitcher.

Kaat: "Stewart is durable and can pitch a lot of innings. He might have lost something from his fastball, however, and he has never been able to change speeds. His slider is almost as hard as his fastball, and if it isn't perfect it looks like a mediocre fastball to the hitters.

"He has the right temperament for a reliever, and at 32 he is not washed up."

BOSTON RED SOX

ELLIS BURKS
OF, No. 56
RR, 6'2", 175 lbs.
ML Svc: less than
one year
Born: 9-11-64 in
Vicksburg, MS

HITTING, BASERUNNING, FIELDING:

Ellis Burks has never played above the Double-A level but is one of the top prospects in the Red Sox system. He had his best professional season in 1986, when he hit .273 with 14 homers and 55 RBIs in his second season with the Double-A competition at New Britain.

He is regarded as an excellent defensive player, with speed and a strong arm. Those assets are enough to give him a good chance of seeing plenty of action this year. And if Dave Henderson has problems with his left knee, which underwent arthroscopic surgery, Burks could be the starting center fielder this year.

Those who have watched the 22-year-old since his first professional game at Elmira in 1983 have predicted he will eventually develop into an outstanding major leaguer.

There is some question as to whether he will be able to handle the good breaking pitches and change-ups at the major league level, but that's the case with most young prospects.

OVERALL:

The release of Tony Armas has accelerated the progress of this young prospect. He will be given a good look-see by Red Sox management, who would like to see their farm system's products playing successfully in Fenway Park.

WES GARDNER
RHP, No. 44
RR, 6'4", 185 lbs.
ML Svc: less than
one year
Born: 4-29-61 in
Benton, AK

PITCHING, FIELDING:

The key player for the Red Sox in the eight-player deal which sent Bob Ojeda to the Mets in 1985 was not Calvin Schiraldi but Wes Gardner. Although the Red Sox insisted both pitchers be included in the deal, they projected Schiraldi as a starter and Gardner as the savior in the bullpen. But Gardner came up with shoulder problems in spring training and after pitching just one inning in April was disabled for the year and underwent surgery (the same operation Roger Clemens had a year earlier).

Gardner had 53 saves in his last three seasons in the Mets' minor league system. He is basically a sinkerball pitcher with a 90 MPH fastball, but he can throw it upstairs when he needs a strikeout. He has a slider for a breaking pitch.

Gardner is considered a good fielder and decent at holding runners on base.

OVERALL:

If Gardner is healthy, he could wrest the short relief job from Calvin Schiraldi, or share it with him. That would also free Bob Stanley for duty as a long reliever or starter.

Kaat: 'If Gardner can do for the Red Sox what he did at the Triple-A level, he could really help their bullpen."

BOSTON RED SOX

GLENN HOFFMAN
SS, No. 18
RR, 6'2", 188 lbs.
ML Svc: 7 years
Born: 7-7-58 in
Orange, CA

HITTING, BASERUNNING, FIELDING:

Glenn Hoffman's best year at the plate was his rookie season of 1980 when, as a third baseman, he hit .285. Hoffman tore up his knee at the end of the 1983 season and lost his job to Jackie Gutierrez the following year but regained it last season. Then, misfortune bit again as he was struck down by what was finally diagnosed as a mild cardiac problem that sidelined him for all but a dozen games last season.

Hoffman always stood straight up in the batter's box and continues to do so. He has trouble with the low outside breaking ball and the high inside fastball.

He is a fairly big man at 6'2" and 195 lbs., but he has very little power.

Hoffman has never had much speed and is no threat to steal. Still, in the past, he has been a good baserunner. When Eddie Yost, the veteran third base coach, was with the team, he rated Hoffman as the best and smartest baserunner on the club. He knows when to try and take an extra base and is rarely thrown out.

Hoffman is an underrated shortstop. He is not flashy or spectacular and wasn't blessed with outstanding range. All he does is make the plays.

He has excellent hands and a strong, accurate arm. Rarely does he make a bad throw to first.

OVERALL:

If Hoffman is fully recovered from the cardiac condition, he could win back his old job this year. If is unable to play at 100%, it is likely that he'll provide excellent backup.

Kaat: "He's always been steady defensively but nothing sensational."

ED ROMERO
INF, No. 11
RR, 5'11", 150 lbs.
ML Svc: 6 years
Born: 12-9-57 in
Santurce, PR

HITTING, BASERUNNING, FIELDING:

Ed Romero is a high-fastball hitter with very little power. He's an aggressive free-swinger who could be a better hitter if he displayed a little more patience at the plate.

Like most players who do not get to play regularly, he has trouble with the sweeping breaking ball from righthanders and the high fastball from both right-and lefthanders.

He is a good baserunner but, like most of his teammates, has no speed.

Defensively, he does not have speed or range but handles everything he gets his hands on. He has a better-than-average arm and is accurate with his throws.

OVERALL:

Romero is one of the better utility players in baseball and it looks as though that's going to be his role again this year.

Kaat: "He can play three positions-- second, short, and third--and do a good job defensively at each. But don't look for much offense from him."

BOSTON RED SOX

JOE SAMBITO
LHP, No. 43
LL, 6'1", 190 lbs.
ML Svc: 10 years
Born: 6-28-52 in Brooklyn, NY

PITCHING, FIELDING:

Joe Sambito is a testament to just how misleading raw numbers can be when pertaining to relief pitchers. To look at Sambito's 4.84 ERA and the .298 batting average by opposing hitters and to dismiss his contributions as worthless would be a terrible injustice.

After being virtually written off following four years of trying to make a comeback from elbow surgery, Sambito was given a last shot by the Red Sox last year. He was a perfect 12-for-12 in save opportunities and squandered only two ties. He stranded a superb 81.3% of inherited baserunners. The first batters he faced upon entering games were only 10-for-51 against him with 11 strikeouts.

In close games (two runs or less either way) first batters were only 3-for-25 against him last year.

A power pitcher when he was with the Astros, Sambito adjusted well in becoming a finesse pitcher with the Red Sox last year, spotting his fastball and using his slider well. He worked on developing a screwball during the off-season to make him more effective against righthanded hitters.

Sambito is a good fielder and has his head in the game at all times.

OVERALL:

If Sambito can develop an effective screwball, he could get more innings and the chance to finish some games.

Kaat: "I thought he would never pitch in the big leagues again, so I have a lot of respect and admiration for him, especially because he was riding a good contract and could have walked away. In the AL East with all those tough lefthanded hitters, he could be a real help to the Red Sox."

JEFF SELLERS
RHP, No. 19
RR, 6'0", 181 lbs.
ML Svc: 1 year plus
Born: 5-11-64 in Compton, CA

PITCHING, FIELDING:

Jeff Sellers, a highly regarded 23-year-old righthanded prospect, has the unenviable task of trying to carve out a spot for himself in the rotation of the defending American League champions. Roger Clemens, Bruce Hurst, Oil Can Boyd and Al Nipper have spots locked up, but the departure of Tom Seaver to free agency has opened up a job for a fifth starter. Sellers will compete for that slot with Rob Woodward and perhaps Bob Stanley.

Sellers was 3-7 with a 4.94 ERA for the Red Sox in part-time duty last season. Consis-

tency was his biggest problem, particularly with his slider, which is his best pitch. At one moment he would give it a nasty break, but he had trouble throwing it the same way twice.

He does not have an overpowering fastball and he needs to find better control. He gives up too many walks and is prone to delivering a home run pitch with runners on base.

But Sellers does have a good make-up. He is aggressive and averaged six innings per start for the Red Sox.

Sellers is a decent fielder but needs to concentrate more on that aspect of his game. He also needs better concentration to hold runners closer to the base.

OVERALL:

If Sellers can find consistency with his slider and throw more strikes, he has a chance to develop into an effective major league pitcher.

BOSTON RED SOX

MARC SULLIVAN
C, No. 15
RR, 6'4", 213 lbs.
ML Svc: 2 years
Born: 7-25-58 in
Quincy, MA

HITTING, BASERUNNING, FIELDING:

Marc Sullivan has become an important cog in the Red Sox machine. He only appeared in 41 games last season, came to bat only 119 times and had just 23 hits.

Sullivan has the size and strength to be a power hitter. But he only displayed ability to hit the ball a long way in 1985, when he hammered out 15 home runs in 383 at-bats in the minors.

Last season, Sullivan did well by another means--getting hit by a pitch. He had two RBIs last season as the result of being hit with the bases loaded.

He is having trouble with big league breaking balls thrown low and away. While Sullivan has the ability to turn on an inside fastball, pitchers know that he can't hit breaking stuff, and rarely give him heat.

He works constantly with batting coach Walt Hriniak and has adopted the hitting coach's style of keeping his head down, trying to hit the pitch back up middle, and releasing the back hand from bat.

Sullivan has not had a chance to do much baserunning and it's probably just as well. Like most catchers, he's an extremely slow runner.

Sullivan came through the minor league system with the reputation as a good defensive catcher. As yet, however, he hasn't had much of a chance to show what he can do; he rarely has had the opportunity to play. Carlton Fisk was his boyhood idol and he has picked up many of Fisk's mannerisms, especially in the way he carries himself.

OVERALL:

Sullivan remains a mystery as a major league catcher. He's never had the opportunity to play regularly--and if you don't play, you can't hit. Defensively, he has a reputation of having a decent throwing arm but has had trouble holding onto pitches.

MIKE GREENWELL, OF, LR, 6'0", 189 lbs.
HITTING, BASERUNNING, FIELDING:
Mike Greenwell's first four hits when he got to the major leagues in 1985 were home runs, with the first two being game-winners. Much was expected of the lefthanded-hitting outfielder who had shown power in the minors with 16 homers in 1984 and 13 in 1985.

He has a good-looking swing but when hitting became a confused young man.

Combined with the fact he saw very limited action (35 at-bats, 11 hits, no homers), Greenwell experienced almost a lost year.

His baserunning speed is average and he's no basestealing threat.

Defensively, he is regarded as an adequate outfielder with an average arm.

OVERALL:
There are two hitting theories running around in Boston: one is the Ted Williams approach of pull-pull-pull. The other is that taught by Walt Hriniak whereby a hitter hits the ball where it is pitched and tries to spray to all fields. Some hitters adapt well to the latter, while others are strictly natural pull hitters who *can't* hit the other way even if the ball were teed up on the outside part of the part. It's possible that Greenwell is one of those hitters whose power is lost when he tries to hit to left field.

Greenwell is a lefthander all the way and as such, is likely to see some time at first base this season. He must, however, figure out a way to hit successfully in the major leagues.

JOHN MARZANO, C, RR, 5'11", 185 lbs.
HITTING, BASERUNNING, FIELDING:
The Red Sox number-one choice in the 1984 draft, John Marzano is the heir apparent to catcher Rich Gedman this year.

Marzano was invited to camp this spring as a non-roster player after just two seasons at the Double-A level in New Britain. But in their ideal scenario, the Red Sox would give him a year of Triple-A ball.

Marzano has the bat and the arm as well as the ability and confidence to catch at the major league level.

In his two seasons at New Britain, he hit .246 with four homers and 51 RBIs in 103 at-bats, then followed up with .283, 10 homers, 62 RBIs in 118 games.

OVERALL:
There are some observers who feel that Marzano has more potential than his numbers indicate. The supposition is that after his first season at Double-A, he became bored. He was too good for the competition there, but the Red Sox had Rich Gedman and had the luxury of not being forced to rush Marzano.

CALIFORNIA ANGELS

HITTING:

Bob Boone crossed the line between durability and miracle-worker in 1986 when, approaching age 39, he led American League catchers with 144 games. He comes closer to quarterbacking a game than any other current player, which is enough to make him invaluable. The emphasis he places on defense takes away from his bat but he remains a specialized force.

With his spread, rocking-chair stance, he's only concerned with making contact (one strikeout per 17 plate appearances). He can drive the high pitch hard up the middle, though his power is strictly limited to inside fastballs he can pull into the corner. Though he knows the strike zone so well he reacts with disbelief to any called strike, Boone isn't interested in waiting out walks.

Don't expect him to start many rallies; his average was by far the lowest of any American League regular with fewer than 40 strikeouts. He is infinitely more valuable with men on base, when his outs seldom fail to advance them. Boone is apt to throw his bat at an unmanageable pitch and dribble it perfectly behind the runner.

BASERUNNING:

The slowest man to first in baseball, feet down. Bob gets no jump out of the box at all but can accelerate to adaquate speed when trying for the extra base. He knows his limitations and will make the defense regret relaxing, such as when he scored from second base on a sacrifice fly in Comiskey Park last year.

FIELDING:

No one wraps up the package--calling the game and blocking pitches, making throws, distracting the offense--better than Boone, who cashes in on the full value of experience. Boone proves that the mechanics of throwing--a quick release and an accurate throwing arm--are as important as a strong arm. His is slightly above average, yet he is consistently among the league leaders in throwing out runners. Boone is never afraid to throw to any base, at any time, and turns

BOB BOONE
C, No. 8
RR, 6'2", 210 lbs.
ML Svc: 15 years
Born: 11-19-47 in San Diego, CA

1986 STATISTICS

AVG	G	AB	R	H	2B	3B	HR	RBI	BB	SO	SB
.222	144	442	48	98	12	2	7	49	43	30	1

CAREER STATISTICS

AVG	G	AB	R	H	2B	3B	HR	RBI	BB	SO	SB
.251	1843	5982	555	1501	252	24	96	702	533	497	32

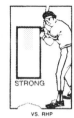  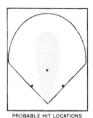

STRONG · VS. RHP   STRONG · VS. LHP   PROBABLE HIT LOCATIONS

even the most aggressive teams timid.

He has the total confidence of his pitching staff. Pitchers trust him to rate their stuff and go with what he considers to be working best. Boone is prone to overexposing a pitcher's key pitch and he gets burned occasionally.

Boone is such a cerebral catcher, he even managed to turn into a advantage his reputation for playing loose on plays at home. He mastered the art of faking out runners, standing relaxed at the plate, and at the last instant snatching the throw and tagging out the surprised runner.

OVERALL:

Boone's baseball intelligence more than compensates for any decline in his physical skills. He spends an inordinate amount of time on building up endurance. At his age, he is always under threat of a debilitating injury. But as long as he manages to avoid it, he remains an asset to a team in a pennant race.

Killebrew: "Boone is one of the outstanding veteran catchers in the American League. He's invaluable, particularly at handling young pitchers. He is an outstanding defensive catcher, even at his age."

CALIFORNIA ANGELS

PITCHING:

John Candelaria risked his left elbow last year for the Angels' title drive by returning to action a mere three months after his early-season surgery. As a result of putting too much stress on the still-weak joint, he ended the season beleaguered by tendinitis. The prognosis for 1987 depends on how he recovers from that sacrifice.

Significantly, Candelaria returned as a big winner last summer even though he lacked his best stuff. He got by on his famed control (which is as good as that of any southpaw in the league) and on his heart. The combination of control and guts makes him a feared and respected competitor.

Even in a weakened state, Candelaria still got his fastball into the upper 80s to low 90s. For a big man, he has an extremely fluid delivery and throws at a three-quarters angle that confounds lefty hitters, who regularly rate him their toughest foe. The first time Candelaria faced Kirk Gibson, he struck him out three times on nine pitches.

Candelaria gets his breaking ball over consistently, with a tight rotation and a late break. He'll use his slider to set up his main pitches. He likes to come in with curveballs to righthanders, setting up a fastball which tails away from them. His fastball has various gears: he'll make it sink when he needs a grounder, but can muster up a faster model that sails if he needs a strikeout.

He has a distinct advantage when hitters try to pull him. He's gotten more use out of his change-up of late--he now throws it even when he's behind in the count. Candelaria has confidence in all four of his pitches.

Candelaria is a fast, no-nonsense worker. In 1986, he retired the first batter of in the inning 69 out of 95 times. He doesn't like to waste pitches, which is one reason he has never been a top strikeout pitcher.

Unfortunately, each pitch now takes a definite toll on Candelaria's arm: he is at risk beyond the sixth inning. His days of surviving without his best stuff are over, and you can get a good read on him in the first couple of innings.

JOHN CANDELARIA
LHP, No. 45
LL, 6'6", 225 lbs.
ML Svc: 12 years
Born: 11-6-53 in
Brooklyn, NY

1986 STATISTICS

W	L	ERA	G	GS	CG	SV	IP	H	R	ER	BB	SO
10	2	2.55	16	16	1	0	91.2	68	30	26	26	81

CAREER STATISTICS

W	L	ERA	G	GS	CG	SV	IP	H	R	ER	BB	SO
141	89	3.11	350	300	47	15	2016.2	1876	775	698	477	1276

FIELDING:

Candelaria's move to first base is subpar for a lefthander. He has never really taken the time to develop it, being content to focus on the hitter.

He is a somewhat clumsy fielder but he always maintains his cool and will look to nail the lead runner at every opportunity.

OVERALL:

Prone to concentration lapses and periods of near-boredom, Candelaria in a sense has never reached the potential suggested by his no-hitter as a 22-year-old. But he ranks with the best in handling the big games.

In the equivalent of one full season with the Angels, he has a 17-5 record. The league batted a paltry .206 off him in 1986, injury or not. If a winter's rest cured his arm, he could be the American League's dominant lefty starter for a few more years.

Killebrew: "John is an excellent competitor. He has to answer the question of how he'll react to a recent string of injuries. He mixes all four pitches well and is one of the men you like to have on the mound with a big game on the line."

CALIFORNIA ANGELS

PITCHING:

Following years of struggle, Doug Corbett came back with a solid 1986 season. Responding to the frequent injuries of Donnie Moore, he saved 10 games in only 14 opportunities and also pitched well in long relief when asked to do so.

Yet, despite the Angels' need for relief, they let Corbett go after the season. So was his comeback an illusion? Not necessarily; after five seasons, the Angels tired of his day-to-day inconsistency. Corbett is a sinkerballer who must keep the ball down to survive; when he was bad last year, he was *horrible*. He allowed 11 homers in only 79 innings--a brutal ratio.

He has never been a hard thrower. Nor does he have a curve. What Corbett has always relied on is a herky-jerky sidearm motion that upsets batters' timing. When he feels really confident, he'll dabble with the slider and likes to throw lefthanders a mediocre change-up.

For the most part, however, Corbett earns his pay by keeping that sinker below the knees and making hitters beat it into the ground. The fewer pitches he must show a batter, the greater his chance to retire him. When he's outguessed, he has no premium stuff to fall back on.

Confidence, or lack of, has always been a big issue with Corbett. His ruination years ago began when his best pitches were hit for ground singles that led to a string of tough defeats. He changed his style in an effort to turn the tide and tried to punch people out. But throwing harder brought his pitches up, and they were, in turn, pummeled.

Corbett is a fast worker. For him, the faster, the better--because then he won't have much time to think.

He was particularly effective last season after isolating and eliminating a hitch in his delivery. He shortened his stride and the result was improved control.

FIELDING:

Corbett has an off-balance delivery, and

**DOUG CORBETT
RHP, No. 23
RR, 6'1", 185 lbs.
ML Svc: 7 years
Born: 11-4-52 in
Sarasota, FL**

1986 STATISTICS

W	L	ERA	G	GS	CG	SV	IP	H	R	ER	BB	SO
4	2	3.66	46	0	0	10	78.2	66	36	32	22	36

CAREER STATISTICS

W	L	ERA	G	GS	CG	SV	IP	H	R	ER	BB	SO
24	28	3.13	302	1	0	65	529	472	206	184	187	327

will often crumble to the ground after letting go of a pitch. This leads to an image of him being clumsy, and teams like to bunt on him.

But he has agile hands and a good glove and will snare most balls hit back to him. He makes a quick break to first and waits for the first baseman to call him off.

He is easily distracted by runners. He likes to throw to first base often, but there's nothing deceptive about his move.

OVERALL:

Corbett can be a head case. He'll pitch as well as a manager expects him to: he feeds off others' trust in him.

But he overcame several humbling seasons to post his best year since 1980-81 when, with the Twins, he ranked as the No. 2 reliever in the American League. He is still young enough (34) to enjoy a second career as a fireman.

Killebrew: "Corbett's a good competitor. He overcame a lot of professional and personal ups-and-downs to make a strong comeback in 1986. He can still reward a manager's faith in him."

CALIFORNIA ANGELS

HITTING:

The Angels openly tried to phase out Doug DeCinces last year. In the face of emotional and physical hardships--a separated left shoulder, his chronic back ailment--he responded with four-year highs in homers and RBIs. He proved anew his ability to decide games both with his bat and with his glove.

From his open stance, Doug lunges toward the plate on every pitch. As a result, he can be ruined by balls running in on his hands. But righties had better keep the ball down-and-in: he drives the away pitch well and has good opposite-field power if the ball is up in the strike zone.

DeCinces has sneaky power to the alleys; invariably, the balls carry farther than many expect them to when they leave the bat.

Since Doug is always alert for the pitch on the outside corner, pitchers have a hard time working on him. He doesn't have much patience in key situations and grows even more aggressive than usual. But it's a quality that has made him a feared clutch hitter, averaging 10 game-winning RBIs a year since 1980.

BASERUNNING:

DeCinces' lack of speed is most telling when he fails to beat out balls fielded in short left field by the shortstop. He'll seldom make a costly mistake on the bases, however, and will ignore his risky back to go into the base hard to break up a double play if it means saving a key out.

FIELDING:

It's ironic that Doug was made miserable in Baltimore by being constantly compared to Brooks Robinson--because he's become a Brooks clone in the field. He has little range but extremely quick reactions and the ability to make hard, accurate throws from any angle. No one has ever seen him throw the ball away after charging to barehand a bunt, for example.

He's stronger making the backhanded play

DOUG DeCINCES
3B, No. 11
RR, 6'2", 195 lbs.
ML Svc: 12 years
Born: 8-29-50 in
Burbank, CA

1986 STATISTICS

AVG	G	AB	R	H	2B	3B	HR	RBI	BB	SO	SB
.256	140	512	69	131	20	3	26	96	52	74	2

CAREER STATISTICS

AVG	G	AB	R	H	2B	3B	HR	RBI	BB	SO	SB
.261	1512	5347	712	1397	287	29	221	815	548	816	55

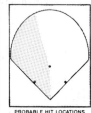

STRONG VS. RHP   STRONG VS. LHP   PROBABLE HIT LOCATIONS

to his right. Doug's only problems are a tendency to let up on easy plays, which results in throws to first in the dirt, and a distaste for holding his ground on tag plays. With his back condition, that's understandable. He was superior in many key departments to Gary Gaetti, the Gold Glove winner last year.

OVERALL:

DeCinces occasionally exhibits a whine streak. He tends to complain too much to anyone who'll listen but is able to quickly block out distractions and put his mind back on track. He is willing to take pressure off his teammates. He has the dedication to undergo the daily torturous conditioning that keeps his back loose and is rewarded by his continuing stature as a dangerous man with games on the line.

Killebrew: "He is one of the Angels' most productive veteran players. Doug has always had problems physically but somehow seems to overcome them. He is one of the better clutch hitters in the league."

GOOD CLUTCH HITTER

HITTING:

Brian Downing contradicts the belief that, to be played best, baseball must be played in a relaxed state. He's wound tight from the first pitch to the last, whether he is at the plate or in the field. Most of the time, he's giving pitchers the shakes: he ranks high on the list of hitters that pitchers least like to face with a game on the line.

From his unusual perspective--open stance, on the outer edge of the box--Downing can adjust to any pitch. But being a notorious guess hitter, he sets himself up for a specific pitch every at-bat. Righties give him trouble with sliders down-and-in but his longball power comes on the ones that slip up--19 of his 20 homers in 1986 were pulled to left field.

Downing is an oddity in that he consistently has better success against righthanders (42 points higher in 1986) and on the road. He'll often alter his stance and how he holds his hands, depending on how well he has been hitting and what he wants to accomplish. When the situation calls for it, he's excellent at going to right field behind the runner.

Gene Mauch is forever torn between taking advantage of Downing's power and his ability to find his way on base (386 walks the last five seasons). Thus, Downing is as apt to bat leadoff or sixth as No. 4. He is a crack clutchhitter best suited to the meat of the lineup.

In 1986, ten of his homers either gave the Angles a tie or put them ahead, and nine of them came in the seventh inning or later.

BASERUNNING:

Downing runs the way he does everything else: all-out. He has only average speed, but infielders had better not stay rooted in his tracks.

He won't take unnecessary chances on the bases, or force the defense. But he's smart--Mauch likes to start him on the hit-and-run.

FIELDING:

All one need know about Downing's dedication is that the former catcher has made himself into a record-setting outfielder, despite obvious physical limitations. Even

BRIAN DOWNING
LF, No. 5
RR, 5'10", 190 lbs.
ML Svc: 14 years
Born: 10-9-50 in
Los Angeles, CA

1986 STATISTICS

AVG	G	AB	R	H	2B	3B	HR	RBI	BB	SO	SB
.267	152	513	90	137	27	4	20	95	90	84	4

CAREER STATISTICS

AVG	G	AB	R	H	2B	3B	HR	RBI	BB	SO	SB
.266	1586	5201	763	1382	235	17	166	734	784	719	40

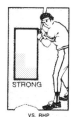

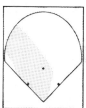

STRONG   STRONG

VS. RHP   VS. LHP   PROBABLE HIT LOCATIONS

now, he lacks instincts in left field but is aggressive enough to overcome almost any mistake.

He has trouble coming in for line drives (he often loses sight of them) or charging hits on the ground. Runners will consistently challenge his injury-weakened arm but he can still muster a long, accurate throw when it's needed. He'll never miss the cutoff man. And Downing has no fear of walls or railings.

OVERALL:

Through a new contract, the Angels made Downing feel wanted; he should be a more relaxed player this season as a result. He is too self-motivated for security to equal complacency in his case. At age 35, Downing set a career high in RBIs last year, indicative of his durable stature as one of the game's most dangerous and spirited performers.

Killebrew: "Brian has become one of the tougher hitters in the league. He has good power and reliably rises to the occasion. As one of the Angels' most veteran players, he'll now have a chance to show his leadership abilities."

CALIFORNIA ANGELS

PITCHING:

Chuck Finley began 1986 as a no-name and ended it as one of the American League's top pitching prospects. A fearless, hard-throwing 24-year-old, he has a versatility that confuses the Angels, who aren't sure of the best role for him. Once they decide, the next step could be stardom.

Finley made the toughest possible leap last spring. He started the season in Class-A ball and *just 10 games later was in California's bullpen!* Since his minor league experience had consisted of 27 games and 41 innings, manager Gene Mauch brought him along gingerly and kept him out of fire. Of the 25 games in which he appeared, the Angels lost 20.

That pace enabled Finley to gain confidence as the season wore on. By the end, he was challenging the toughest hitters with his 95 MPH fastball and had gained greater command of his new curveball.

Finley was signed as a one-pitch hurler and spent last spring learning a curve. His success with the new pitch in the minors earned him the quick promotion. He continued his education last winter, trying to work both a change-up and forkball into his repertoire.

He doesn't fool around on the mound and comes right at hitters with his strongest stuff from a three-quarters angle. The league hit him only for a .235 average in 1986, and lefthanders fared worse than that.

Chuck is a project. He's had some trouble fitting his lanky 6'7" frame into a comfortable delivery. As a result, he used the stretch exclusively last year. He spent winter ball developing a fluid windup, which should add 2-3 MPH to his already above-average fastball.

Chuck has a tendency to drop his arm into a cross-body delivery, and when he does that, his control suffers. When he comes over the top, he has much better command of all pitches.

His aggressive attitude is ideal for a late-inning fireman, as are the two pitches with which he can overpower hitters for brief stretches. The Angels may eventually want to work him into their rotation; in his longest stint last year, he blanked Kansas City on two

CHUCK FINLEY
LHP, No. 31
LL, 6'6", 220 lbs.
ML Svc: less than one year
Born: 11-26-62 in
Monroe, LA

1986 STATISTICS

W	L	ERA	G	GS	CG	SV	IP	H	R	ER	BB	SO
3	1	3.30	25	0	0	0	46.1	40	17	17	23	37

CAREER STATISTICS

W	L	ERA	G	GS	CG	SV	IP	H	R	ER	BB	SO
3	1	3.30	25	0	0	0	46.1	40	17	17	23	37

hits for 5 2/3 innings. But he'll need to perfect his two secondary pitches to become an effective starter.

FIELDING:

Finley is a good athlete for a big kid and reacts well to batted balls. He's not afraid to make an off-balance throw and he gives the first baseman a good target when he covers the bag.

He holds runners tight, but hasn't yet developed a dangerous pickoff move. As tall as he is, his natural stride is long, although he gets rid of the ball fast enough to keep runners from getting much of a jump.

OVERALL:

Finley joined the Angels as a wide-eyed innocent. Being used in all the right spots eased his transition. By the end of the year, he felt as if he belonged in the big leagues. Chalk that up to Gene Mauch.

The addition of a pair of off-speed pitches, such as the forkball and straight change-up, would make him an unwelcome sight to hitters. Whether it comes as a starter or reliever, Finley has a glowing future.

Killebrew: "Chuck really opened some eyes last year. He's just a big, raw kid who knows how to throw hard--and with surprising control. Give him time to learn how to pitch and he could really be something."

CALIFORNIA ANGELS

PITCHING:

When John Candelaria blew out his elbow in the first week of the 1986 season to leave the Angels without a lefthander on the staff, Terry Forster came to the rescue. Signed as a free agent following his spring release by Atlanta, he plugged the bullpen with his amazingly elastic arm.

Unfortunately, Forster also has an elastic stomach. When a July ankle injury left him on the disabled list, his legendary weight ballooned and the Angels were displeased enough to drop him off their post-season roster last year, even though they desperately could have used a veteran lefty in the playoffs. His post-season release ensued.

Forster can still be valuable to a contender. While his diet was intact--he stayed on a strict weight-control program during the first half of the season--his fastball occasionally moved back into the low 90s. His slider bends sharply away from lefthanders and is his out pitch. But he was hurt by his infamous competitive-ness--when he insisted on trying to overpower hitters, he was usually hit hard. He hardly ever threw his change-up last year.

Forster has one of the most remarkable arms around. It has already appeared in 614 big league games over 16 years, logging nine seasons of 40-plus games, but is still ready to go any time.

He tends to be his own biggest enemy. He allowed his demonstrative bouts with Gene Mauch over mound time to affect his concentration. Similarly, he couldn't shake off bad breaks. He became visibly upset on the mound and let rallies snowball.

FIELDING:

Forster can't go get the ball, but he'll snare every one hit within his reach. He has too

TERRY FORSTER
LHP, No. 51
LL, 6'4", 230 lbs.
ML Svc: 16 years
Born: 1-14-52 in
Sioux Falls, SD

1986 STATISTICS

W	L	ERA	G	GS	CG	SV	IP	H	R	ER	BB	SO
4	1	3.51	41	0	0	5	41	47	18	16	17	28

CAREER STATISTICS

W	L	ERA	G	GS	CG	SV	IP	H	R	ER	BB	SO
54	65	3.23	614	39	5	127	1105.1	1034	454	397	457	791

many mental lapses and, as unbelievable as it may be, this veteran *forgets* to break for first on grounders hit to the right side.

He lacks a threatening move to first. Big leads combined with his slow delivery make him an easy target for steals.

OVERALL:

In a situation that no longer calls on him to be the fireman, Forster can still be effective. Twenty of his 41 outings for the Angels lasted an inning or less.

His competitive fires continue to be fanned. An indication was how he suffered his severe ankle sprain--tripping over first base after covering for a crucial out in the 13th inning of the July 7 game in Milwaukee, which the Angels won in the 16th to take over permanent possession of first place (well, at least *that* time he remembered to cover first).

Killebrew: "Forster's conditioning is not going to impress anyone but the chef. But he is an admired competitor with a refreshing personality. He keeps the clubhouse loose and has a most unique and durable arm."

CALIFORNIA ANGELS

PITCHING:

Bill Fraser is the next candidate for quick, almost rushed, graduation from the Angels' farm system. He is given a strong chance this year of successfully following the route to stardom taken by Mike Witt and Kirk McCaskill.

Fraser, the club's top draft choice in June 1985, progressed in a hurry last year, starting in Class-A ball and winding up in California.

It isn't hard to figure out the reasons behind this fast advancement. He seems old beyond his 21 years, both physically and pitching-wise. Fraser already has command of the four basic pitches, a talent which is extremely rare in young hurlers. He mixes an above-average major league fastball and an outstanding forkball with a slider and change-up.

His control is also unusual for someone with so little pro experience. He shows a terrific walks-to-strikeout ratio (69:195) for his brief minor league career.

The Angels judged him ready after he responded to a late-summer jump into Triple-A with a 4-1 record, bringing his cumulative 1986 mark to 13-3. With Edmonton, in the offense-minded Pacific Coast League, he completed two of his six starts and walked only eight in 40 innings.

A product of a harsh New York City environment, Fraser is not easily intimidated. He already feels that he belongs in the majors and won't shy away from challenging big league hitters or coming inside to them.

FIELDING:

Many young pitching prospects concen-

BILL FRASER
RHP, No. 55
RR, 6'3", 200 lbs.
ML Svc: less than one year
Born: 5-26-64 in
New York, NY

1986 STATISTICS

W	L	ERA	G	GS	CG	SV	IP	H	R	ER	BB	SO
0	0	8.31	1	1	0	0	4.1	6	4	4	1	2

CAREER STATISTICS

W	L	ERA	G	GS	CG	SV	IP	H	R	ER	BB	SO
0	0	8.31	1	1	0	0	4.1	6	4	4	1	2

trate so intently on the batter that they have no time to think of anything else. Fraser is like that to a certain extent, but has the natural athletic skills to react to batted balls.

He has too much confidence in his ability to overpower batters to be distracted by baserunners. He needs a lot of work to develop a respectable move to first base.

OVERALL:

Without question, Fraser has the tools for big league success. He has all the necessary pitches and throws them with a fluid delivery.

All he needs are some big league innings under his belt. He figures to get them this season only if he can nail down the Angels' fifth-starter job. They wouldn't want to spoil him in their bullpen.

CALIFORNIA ANGELS

HITTING:

Playing close to home for the first time renewed this Los Angeles native's interest in being a productive performer. At age 36, George Hendrick made a strong, if streaky, comeback after being virtually a zero in 1985.

Hendrick can look confused striking out one minute, then hit a screaming line drive in his next at-bat. He remains a dangerous low-ball hitter, relying on strong wrists. It makes him effective against the split-finger fastballs that drive everyone else nuts.

He took to Gene Mauch's platoon arrangement, hitting far better against lefthanders last season (.293), with most of his power from that side as well. But Hendrick is too undisciplined a hitter to be much of an asset in Mauch's "Little Ball" strategy of playing for a run at a time. He has the power to belong in the heart of a lineup but his erratic efforts make that a risk.

He stands pretty far off the plate, and pitchers prey on him with outside stuff--especially since Hendrick consistently tries to pull the ball, which results in a lot of pop-ups and weak grounders to the left side.

BASERUNNING:

Is Hendrick a "lazy" runner, as his reputation goes? Mauch calls it being "inanimate." Maybe it's age. Whatever, he doesn't beat out a lot of balls it appears he should, including double play grounders on which he has a nagging habit of pulling up before he crosses the bag. He grounded into one double play every 26 at-bats, one of the highest incidences in the league.

Hendrick will run a lot of doubles into singles. He gives the impression whenever he's on base that he just wants to get off it. He'll avoid sliding at every opportunity, even standing up going home on close plays.

FIELDING:

Hendrick is a careless fielder, satisfied with making the basic play adequately--and

GEORGE HENDRICK
RF, No. 25
RR, 6'3", 195 lbs.
ML Svc: 16 years
Born: 10-18-49 in
  Los Angeles, CA

1986 STATISTICS

AVG	G	AB	R	H	2B	3B	HR	RBI	BB	SO	SB
.272	102	283	45	77	13	1	14	47	26	41	1

CAREER STATISTICS

AVG	G	AB	R	H	2B	3B	HR	RBI	BB	SO	SB
.281	1845	6584	892	1851	317	27	257	1042	528	933	58

  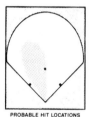

VS. RHP   VS. LHP   PROBABLE HIT LOCATIONS

occasionally unable to do even that. He's very adept at charging bloopers, but will often turn an easier play into a shoestring catch. He gets disoriented on balls hit over his head.

His arm is still very strong. Yet runners aware of his mental lapses will challenge him. But he can still make the difficult throw to second from the right field corner. He shies away from fences.

OVERALL:

Hendrick is extremely popular among his teammates, who probably appreciate his low-key approach. He can still be valuable as a platoon player but has reached the stage where he probably wouldn't play much if he weren't protected by a fat contract.

Killebrew: "Hendrick has reached the stage where being an everyday player is too demanding. Still, he's another one of those veterans whose experience makes him an asset to a club."

HITTING:

For a couple of years, Jack Howell has been one of the Angels' brightest prospects. He has proved to have outgrown the Pacific Coast League (where he has hit .373 and .359 the last two seasons). Being a lefthanded-hitting third baseman figured to make him very valuable. But the club's decision to re-sign Doug DeCinces forced Gene Mauch to try to seek a new position for Howell.

Wherever Howell plays, his bat can be a big asset. A late bloomer, he can be a 20-25 homer man while also hitting for average if he gets into 150 games. Jack has a smooth, level swing. At times, he seems to look for nothing but fastballs, leaving him vulnerable to off-speed stuff. With experience, he'll learn to hold back and drive breaking balls. He definitely has the bat speed needed to adjust to different pitches. Howell has had his troubles hitting in Anaheim Stadium (.154 in 136 at-bats over two years). This difficulty is the result of a "Fenway" swing, which he fell into while learning to take advantage of the Edmonton park's shallow left-field wall. A dividend is that he developed good power to left-center field. But to survive in the majors, he has to snap out of that habit and go back to hitting the ball to all fields.

BASERUNNING:

Howell has average major league speed. He is slow to accelerate but his fluid strides take him from first to third in a hurry. His intensity gets him into occasional trouble on the basepaths, where he sometimes loses sight of the runner in front of him.

Being a hard runner, and muscular, makes him a good bet on any bang-bang play: Jack is more likely to bowl over an infielder than to hook-slide his way around.

FIELDING:

Voted in 1984 as his minor league's top defensive third baseman and as the infielder with the best arm, Howell still looked raw in the field when he first joined the Angels. He had trouble going to his left and occasionally rushed himself into errors. He made dramatic

JACK HOWELL
INF, No. 16
LR, 6'0", 192 lbs.
ML Svc: 1 year plus
Born: 8-18-61 in Tucson, AZ

1986 STATISTICS

AVG	G	AB	R	H	2B	3B	HR	RBI	BB	SO	SB
.272	63	151	26	41	14	2	4	21	19	28	2

CAREER STATISTICS

AVG	G	AB	R	H	2B	3B	HR	RBI	BB	SO	SB
.236	106	288	45	68	18	2	9	39	35	61	3

VS. RHP

VS. LHP

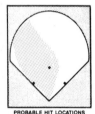

PROBABLE HIT LOCATIONS

improvement in 1986, when he was visibly more relaxed.

He owns a shortstop's arm and zings the ball across the infield on a line only two or three feet off the ground--an easy ball for the first baseman to handle. He reacts well to line drives hit over his head.

Few third basemen are candidates to be switched to the outfield. But Howell proved to be a versatile athlete when pressed into left field for seven games in 1986 and, indeed, that's where he may make his future home.

OVERALL:

Howell has waited quietly behind Doug DeCinces for two years. It remains to be seen how he'll take the disappointment of not having his patience rewarded and the realization he'll be 29 years old when DeCinces' new contract expires. Though the Angels have a vacancy at DH, Howell is too good an athlete to be wasted in that limited role.

Killebrew: "Jack has the potential to develop into a consistent power threat. As a lefthanded-hitting third baseman, he could have a very valuable future."

CALIFORNIA ANGELS

HITTING:

Ruppert Jones has had two virtually identical seasons back-to-back, making it easy to characterize what makes him an increasingly valuable role player. He's a streak hitter whose outs also come in bunches. But he always finds a way to get the job done and is one of the most efficient run producers in baseball.

Jones has a somewhat unorthodox, big swing, which he starts from his ear. So he feasts on high fastballs and is good at poking outside pitches to left. He is, therefore, best handled with low inside breaking balls, which force him to shorten his swing. With his natural pull swing, he is a good hit-and-run man.

For the second season in a row, he went into a horrendous second-half slump (.199). But also for the second straight season, 44% of his hits went for extra bases. The Angels batted him everywhere but No. 4 and No. 9; not being a clutch weapon (.196 with men in scoring position), but with a knack for getting on base and a nose for the plate makes him suitable for the top of the lineup.

BASERUNNING:

Jones is losing his speed faster than his hair. He isn't a threat to steal or leg out infield hits, yet he is an aggressive runner and fearless slider. His headfirst slide into Rich Gedman's shinguards to score the tying run in the ninth inning of the fifth playoff game last year typified his attitude.

He takes a good lead off first, as big as the pitcher will allow. At that point, he's already thinking of scoring: he scored a run per every 5.4 at-bats in 1986, possibly the best in the majors.

FIELDING:

Jones plays all three outfield positions and is best suited to right field, where he takes full advantage of being better at moving to his left.

RUPPERT JONES
RF, No. 13
LL, 5'10", 189 lbs.
ML Svc: 11 years
Born: 3-12-55 in Dallas, TX

1986 STATISTICS

AVG	G	AB	R	H	2B	3B	HR	RBI	BB	SO	SB
.229	126	393	73	90	21	3	17	49	64	87	10

CAREER STATISTICS

AVG	G	AB	R	H	2B	3B	HR	RBI	BB	SO	SB
.250	1246	4223	618	1056	207	36	139	551	541	812	141

  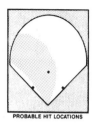

VS. RHP   VS. LHP   PROBABLE HIT LOCATIONS

His arm is up to that position's demands. He can fire a strike to second, but usually settles for relying on the cutoff man.

He is best at charging low line drives. Bloopers leave him indecisive and he tends to pull up on drives over his head and play even catchable balls off the wall.

OVERALL:

Jones could be even more valuable to the Angels in 1987, adding DH duty to his outfield versatility. He is a good influence on a team growing younger. It is no coincidence that he has played for teams that have won more than 90 games each of the last three years. It's hard to imagine a better fourth outfielder for a contender.

Killebrew: "Ruppert does everything well. He helped Detroit win in 1984, and the Angels also became winners with him. Veterans are supposed to know how to play; Jones also knows how to win."

CALIFORNIA ANGELS

HITTING:

A baby-faced youngster with a murderous bat, Wally Joyner was the toast of the American League's remarkable rookie class in 1986. He arrived with less hype than the others, but it would be untrue to say he snuck up on the league. Though he had no prior big league experience, most scouts spoke of him glowingly during spring training. He lived up to expectations and gave the Angels no chance to miss Rod Carew.

Joyner's keen eye and sharp reflexes enable him to hit the ball where it's pitched. He doesn't get fully around on a hard inside fastball but manages well enough to foul it off.

He adjusts marvelously for a young player: when a bruised shoulder late in the season prevented him from pulling the ball, his power suffered but not his average. Until then, Wally showed uncharacteristic power (16 homers by Memorial Day), the result of having discovered weight-training while playing winter ball in Puerto Rico.

Joyner had fantastic success on his first look at the league's pitchers--the better their reputation, the better he hit them. The league never did uncover any weaknesses in his hitting, though righties had their best luck pitching him up-and-away and lefties with fastballs in on the hands. But his swing is too smooth to leave any consistent holes.

He nearly always takes the first pitch. The combination of power plus average makes him the ideal No. 3 hitter, though Gene Mauch mainly used him in the second spot in the lineup.

BASERUNNING:

Wally is heavyset and carries what still looks like baby fat. His smooth strides make him seem faster than he really is. He won't run, except on the run-and-hit play.

He knows his way around the bases exceptionally well and will never surrender. He somehow avoided getting tagged on numerous rundowns or getting caught off base. Wally's instincts often prompt the defense into foolish mistakes.

WALLY JOYNER
1B, No. 21
LL, 6'2", 185 lbs.
ML Svc: 1 year
Born: 6-16-62 in
Atlanta, GA

1986 STATISTICS

AVG	G	AB	R	H	2B	3B	HR	RBI	BB	SO	SB
.290	154	593	82	172	27	3	22	100	57	58	5

CAREER STATISTICS

AVG	G	AB	R	H	2B	3B	HR	RBI	BB	SO	SB
.290	154	593	82	172	27	3	22	100	57	58	5

  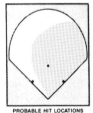

VS. RHP VS. LHP PROBABLE HIT LOCATIONS

FIELDING:

Joyner is extremely active in the field, ranging far behind the bag and often in front of the second baseman. His reflexes are tremendous; he reacts sure-handedly to bad hops, even to hard-hit balls caroming off the base.

He can throw with precision from anywhere on the field and dares to make the difficult throws. In situations with less than two outs and a man on first, he'll rarely settle for the automatic out at first. This gambling spirit gets him into occasional trouble but no one can fault his aggressive style.

OVERALL:

Killebrew: "To prove he wasn't a one-year phenomenon, Wally must overcome not only the sophomore jinx, but a debilitating blood infection that drained his power after the All-Star break. He'll also get fewer fat pitches without Reggie Jackson protecting him in the lineup."

GOOD CONTROL

PITCHING:

The Angels acquired Gary Lucas from Montreal last year to remedy their perrenial lack of quality lefthanded relieving. He took a while to deliver and did not make his first appearance until July 17th because of severe back problems. But he made the wait worthwhile by showing the promise of being able to recapture his glory days with the Padres in the early '80s.

Lucas has the sharp control managers love to bring out of the bullpen, as his six walks last year in 46 innings attest. He also relies on control for outs and gets hitters to go for pitches off the plate. He gets a tight break on his slider and a good drop on his sinker, but doesn't throw either hard enough to strike batters out.

Being forced to throw in a more upright position appeared to improve the break he gets on both of his key pitches. Lucas throws from a three-quarters position and is particularly effective against lefthanders when he is able to spot his breaking stuff on the outside part of the plate. After being used as a one- or two-batter specialist with the Expos, Lucas had surprising success in longer stints last year. That may be his role for Gene Mauch, who already has the hard-throwing lefty Chuck Finley for late-game duty.

Though Lucas has come back strong from early-season disablement for two straight years, his recurring back problems have cost him some flexibility. He can't warm up too quickly or too often in the bullpen. His outings have to be more predictable, hence he isn't qualified to be a closer.

FIELDING:

Lucas takes pride in his fielding and realizes

GARY LUCAS
LHP, No. 36
LL, 6'5", 200 lbs.
ML Svc: 7 years
Born: 11-8-54 in
Riverside, CA

1986 STATISTICS

W	L	ERA	G	GS	CG	SV	IP	H	R	ER	BB	SO
4	1	3.15	27	0	0	2	45.2	45	19	16	6	31

CAREER STATISTICS

W	L	ERA	G	GS	CG	SV	IP	H	R	ER	BB	SO
28	39	2.94	361	18	0	60	594.2	552	233	194	192	366

the importance of a pitcher who can protect the middle. Despite his trick back--which can go at any time--he leaps off the mound well.

He used to have an above-average move to first base, but will no longer stress his back by making many of those sudden throws.

OVERALL:

Except for a pitch that mysteriously slipped during the playoffs--hitting Rich Gedman and eventually turning into Boston's tying run in the pivotal fifth game--Lucas did a solid job last season.

The Angels were impressed enough to can Terry Forster and leave Lucas as the only veteran lefthander in their bullpen this year. He has a chance to prove wrong the people who say he's lost his nerve in tight spots--back permitting.

Killebrew: "After he missed more than half the season last year, Lucas did a better job than anyone had a right to expect. Lefthanded batters tend to stay loose in the batter's box when they see this big guy coming at them from their side."

CALIFORNIA ANGELS

PITCHING:

A one-time hockey pro who really hadn't logged many lifetime innings when he committed himself to a pitching career, Kirk McCaskill last year learned how good he could be. And he came very close to fulfilling his potential.

His new found confidence in his stuff was best reflected in strikeouts. As a rookie, he had played cat-and-mouse with hitters and seemed reluctant to challenge them. He grew more aggressive last year, however, and doubled his strikeouts in only 55 more innings. He fanned nine or more batters in a game 10 times last year, compared to only once in 1985.

McCaskill now ranks as a power pitcher with a fastball consistently in the upper 80s. It complements his tightly breaking curve. Alternating the fastball and curveball handcuffs batters. Manager Gene Mauch ranks his combination with Mike Witt's; but Kirk throws a harder curveball. His curve is more like a slurve--a curve/slider hybrid. Adding a change-up would make both pitches more effective.

McCaskill usually works the count to his advantage. He's a hard-nosed throwback. He'll brush hitters off the plate and is always willing to protect his own batters. In a jam, he keeps his poise and won't let hitters dictate his pitch selection.

He has learned not to get down because of a bad inning. He still lacks the experience to survive without his prime stuff. But when he has it, he tends to keep it through nine innings. He doesn't show signs of fatigue and absolutely hates to leave the mound, even arguing with Mauch for his right to stay in a game.

FIELDING:

Given his dual-sport background, McCaskill obviously is an excellent athlete. Sometimes, though, he tries to be too athletic. This results in an occasional

KIRK McCASKILL
RHP, No. 15
RR, 6'1", 190 lbs.
ML Svc: 2 years
Born: 4-9-61 in
Ontario, Canada

1986 STATISTICS												
W	L	ERA	G	GS	CG	SV	IP	H	R	ER	BB	SO
17	10	3.36	34	33	10	0	246.1	207	98	92	92	202

CAREER STATISTICS												
W	L	ERA	G	GS	CG	SV	IP	H	R	ER	BB	SO
29	22	3.94	64	62	16	0	436	396	203	191	156	304

bonehead throw to the wrong base. Except for this gambling instinct, he fields the middle as well as any pitcher in the league.

He has a strong move to first and in an obvious running situation is stubborn enough to overuse it. Along with his quick, compact delivery, the threat of his good move to first base disrupts the opposition's running game.

OVERALL:

McCaskill is a manager's delight: he is built for nine innings. He wouldn't mind if the entire bullpen called in sick on the days he pitches.

His 1986 development fulfilled the faith the Angels showed in his raw abilities even when he didn't have the minor league numbers to substantiate their hope. And it suggests a bright future.

Kirk is a viable threat to pitch a no-hitter or two one of these years. In his brief two-year career, he has already flirted with five of them, including two two-hitters and a one-hitter in 1986.

Killebrew: "Kirk has impressed a lot of people with his quick development. Not only is he hard to rattle, but he shows streaks of being a hard-nosed bulldog on the mound. He could take off and be a star pitcher for many years."

CALIFORNIA ANGELS

PITCHING:

Angels fans quickly fell out of love with Donnie Moore in 1986, one year removed from his club-record-setting 31-save season. Except for brief stretches, he wasn't the stopper he'd been the year before.

Aware of the need to justify his new three-year, $3 million contract, Moore put tremendous pressure on himself last year. He constantly pushed his arm beyond its capability. The result each time was injury, beginning with the sore shoulder he developed in spring camp by trying to throw too hard too soon.

The Angels countered that he had come to camp out of condition. All season, Moore raced to catch up. He lost.

Still, he led the staff with 21 saves. He never lost either his aggressiveness or his control, and there's no reason why he shouldn't bounce back strong this year.

The overhand thrower's biggest problem was that his weakened shoulder took too much off both his fastball and hard forkball--his two money pitches. He couldn't get as much movement on the heater as he mustered in the past, and as a result, he was forced to throw more breaking pitches. He threw a slurve (a combination of a curveball and a slider) and more change-ups than usual. As a direct result, he allowed 10 homers in only 53 innings, after having given up nine in 72 innings the year before.

Moore never lost the most important aspect of being a short reliever--bulldog determination. He continues to come right at batters, with the kind of marginal strikes they can't lay off. He'll knock them off the plate, protecting the outside corner where he rings up most of his strikeouts.

FIELDING:

Moore has a certain iciness about him and

DONNIE MOORE
RHP, No. 37
LR, 6'0", 185 lbs.
ML Svc: 9 years
Born: 2-13-54 in
Lubbock, TX

1986 STATISTICS

W	L	ERA	G	GS	CG	SV	IP	H	R	ER	BB	SO
4	5	2.97	49	0	0	21	72.2	60	28	24	22	53

CAREER STATISTICS

W	L	ERA	G	GS	CG	SV	IP	H	R	ER	BB	SO
36	36	3.64	375	4	0	80	601.1	626	279	224	169	379

it's never more evident than when he hustles to turn a difficult play into an easy one. He is stocky, but moves well and with outstanding quickness.

He is tough to steal against. He has a quick, all-arm move to first and makes it often. And he gets rid of the ball very quickly when he is pitching from the stretch.

OVERALL:

Moore survived a difficult season, right down to his hapless performance in the pivotal fifth game of the playoffs. A journeyman pitcher who suddenly struck it rich, Moore undoubtedly must consider complacency a factor in his off-key performance.

But he has the fierce pride and determination required to bounce back. Moore performs best with an incentive, and he now has one.

Killebrew: "Moore has been a great acquisition from the National League. He always comes in in the tough spots, and it's difficult to be consistent in that demanding role. But overall, he's done an excellent job for the Angels."

CALIFORNIA ANGELS

HITTING:

For years, Gary Pettis' defense and basestealing threats were enough compensation for his light bat. But he excited the Angels' brass with his improved, more assertive hitting late last season. Pettis hit .291 in September and kept going with a .346 playoff performance against Boston. It may have been the first glimpse of a late-blooming superstar.

Pettis is still more productive from the right side of the plate, but he packs more power as a lefty (10 of his 12 career homers have come off righthanders). The fight to shorten his swing goes on. He has struck out over 115 times every season; by contrast, he has never drawn more than 69 walks.

Pettis prefers fastballs over the plate, belt-high. Breaking balls on the outside fool him into meekly waving at the pitch. His regular swing has too much arc, and most of his strikeouts are on swinging third Ks. He doesn't look too confident at bat and umpires tend to take advantage of that by not giving him the close pitches.

BASERUNNING:

One of the fleetest, smoothest runners in the game, Pettis tears out of the box extremely well. On hits into the gaps, he becomes a blur between first and second. He has a habit of taking too wide a turn around bases, however.

Due to his sheer speed, Pettis hasn't had an incentive to learn the mechanics of stealing. He could afford to take a bigger lead; on most pickoff throws, he makes it back to the bag standing. He resumed sliding headfirst after a 1985 mishap at second briefly scared him away from it.

FIELDING:

Pettis earned his second consecutive Gold Glove in 1986. His defense is without weakness and he can be worth as much in the win column as a good starting pitcher. Purists say he plays too shallow, but that positioning allows him to grab potential hits and he has the speed to out-race any drive to the wall. He

GARY PETTIS
CF, No. 24
SR, 6'1", 160 lbs.
ML Svc: 4 years
Born: 4-3-58 in
Oakland, CA

1986 STATISTICS

AVG	G	AB	R	H	2B	3B	HR	RBI	BB	SO	SB
.258	154	539	93	139	23	4	5	58	69	132	50

CAREER STATISTICS

AVG	G	AB	R	H	2B	3B	HR	RBI	BB	SO	SB
.251	451	1469	247	369	46	21	12	126	198	389	162

  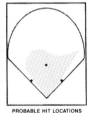

VS. RHP   VS. LHP   PROBABLE HIT LOCATIONS

gets a better jump to his left; it's not unusual to see him make catches in straightaway right.

Pettis' arm is only average but he has perfected the mechanics of throwing. He always fields the ball in ideal position to throw it. When he charges a hit, he seems to field and throw in the same motion. People frowned when Pettis turned to making basket catches last season, interpreting it as a hot-dog act. And two early-season collisions with Brian Downing made him visibly wall-shy.

OVERALL:

Some questioned Pettis' attitude when he began 1986 with both a defensive (four errors by mid-June matched his 1985 total) and basestealing (caught eight times in his first 17 attempts) slump. He proved them wrong by going on to have his best overall season.

Killebrew: "Gary has to rank among the top three or four center fielders in the American League. He has great range and does it all in the outfield. He is getting more patient at the plate and should continue to improve."

CALIFORNIA ANGELS

HITTING:

Dick Schofield made tremendous strides in 1986 and improved in every key department. It upset him that people were suprised by his production, as if they'd forgotten his glove-plus-power reputation as a prospect. When he first came up (1983), Schofield tried to hit the way he had in the minors--pull every pitch. He finally realized that playing with the big boys wasn't the same. Last year, Gene Mauch applauded every time he punched an outside breaking ball to right. Schofield now gives every indication he may yet fulfill his promise.

He became a more selective hitter last year, vastly improving his strikeouts-to-walks ratio (55:48). Only two years before, Schofield had more strikeouts than even hits. His increased selectivity helped his offense all around: he delivered the Angels' most important hit of the season, a two-out, ninth-inning grand slam that beat Detroit in late August.

He remains more comfortable swinging at fastballs and is a dead low-ball hitter, to the point of often looking bad chasing balls breaking into the dirt. His concentration in the batter's box still tends to lapse and pitchers who move the ball around have an easy time with him.

The Angels haven't found his proper place in the lineup, last year alternating him in the 2-6-7-8-9 spots. To profit from his speed, he would be most effective teamed with Gary Pettis, so he'll either become the permanent No. 2 hitter or replace Bob Boone as No. 9.

BASERUNNING:

Mauch's decision to use Schofield's legs as a weapon for the first time revealed one of the league's best-kept secrets: *this guy can run*. His stolen base percentage (23 of 28) was even better than Pettis'.

Even before getting a license to steal, Schofield was impressive on the bases. He has laudable smarts for a young player and no one in baseball has better sliding mechanics.

FIELDING:

Schofield led American League shortstops in fielding as a rookie (.982 in 1984), although

DICK SCHOFIELD
SS, No. 22
RR, 5'10", 176 lbs.
ML Svc: 4 years
Born: 11-21-62 in
Springfield, IL

1986 STATISTICS

AVG	G	AB	R	H	2B	3B	HR	RBI	BB	SO	SB
.249	139	458	67	114	17	6	13	57	48	55	23

CAREER STATISTICS

AVG	G	AB	R	H	2B	3B	HR	RBI	BB	SO	SB
.221	447	1350	160	298	48	12	28	123	122	212	39

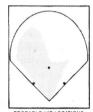

VS. RHP   VS. LHP   PROBABLE HIT LOCATIONS

no one talked about the balls he couldn't reach. He's much better and flashier now, with greater range both ways. In 1986, for the first time, he had no trouble connecting on the long throw from the hole. He has worked hard on getting rid of the ball more quickly.

Schofield is reliable on the difficult plays. Reacting to bad hops is a speciality. Most of his errors come on easy chances, a sure sign of flagging concentration. He reacts extremely well to pop-ups, often calling the left fielder off fouls down the line.

OVERALL:

Schofield continues to make steady year-to-year improvement, which is indicative of a potential star. His work habits have been criticized in the past, so it'll be interesting to see whether last year's success prompts a letdown in his attention to detail. A brief homer binge can ruin his swing for weeks.

Killebrew: "Schofield has proved he is one of the best defensive shortstops in the American League. He's improved with the bat and should do nothing but keep improving for the next several seasons."

CALIFORNIA ANGELS

PITCHING:

Don Sutton, the undisputed champion of year-to-year consistency, blazed through his 300th win in 1986 unlike any modern-day pitcher. He was one of the league's hottest pitchers during the second half of the season last year and enters his 22nd season with no indication that he may suddenly lose it all as a 42-year-old.

There's no secret to Sutton's longevity: as the arm ages, the mind gets sharper. And he is a master at outsmarting hitters by keeping them off-balance via changing speeds on all his pitches. He thrives on the pure competition between pitcher and hitter and is always searching for an angle or edge to beat the batter. It is this sense of keen competitiveness that enabled him to ring up over 100 strikeouts for the 21st consecutive year, extending his own major league record.

Sutton comes over the top with a big windup. Whatever he's lost off the fastball--and he'll rarely push it into the mid-80s these days--he more than makes up for with his breaking stuff. The curveball is his out pitch, effective when he can pinpoint it low on the outside corner. He has a slim margin of error; when he misses with it above the waist, he gets hit hard. He can throw the change-up over the plate anytime, but uses the slider only as a set-up pitch.

Sutton has become a second-through-sixth inning specialist. It usually takes him a while to get in gear, and he is a risk when he tires and starts getting the ball up. Hence, manager Gene Mauch has strictly enforced a 100-pitch-a-game limit on him.

Sutton has an amazing arm: he has missed only four starts throughout his career. Interestingly, hitters' complaints about Sutton's alleged doctoring of baseballs were less frequent last year than in the past. Perhaps it was their silent homage to this certain future Hall of Famer.

FIELDING:

Sutton is an alert fielder. He takes the approach of always expecting the ball to be hit back to him. Putting his entire body behind the pitch leaves him off-balance at the end of

DON SUTTON
RHP, No. 20
RR, 6'1", 190 lbs.
ML Svc: 21 years
Born: 4-2-45 in
Clio, AL

1986 STATISTICS

W	L	ERA	G	GS	CG	SV	IP	H	R	ER	BB	SO
15	11	3.74	34	34	3	0	207	192	93	86	49	116

CAREER STATISTICS

W	L	ERA	G	GS	CG	SV	IP	H	R	ER	BB	SO
310	239	3.19	723	706	177	5	5003	4402	1959	1776	1274	3431

the delivery but he rights himself quickly. He won't let down the first baseman and breaks to the bag on balls hit to the right side. He keeps a close watch on runners but will no longer sap his arm with too many pickoff throws. He leaves runners in the catcher's hands, and helps out his backstop by noticeably shortening his stride with runners on base.

OVERALL:

The time for Sutton to taper off is definitely here but there are no signs that he is ready to give in. It'll be interesting to see how he reacts to having reached all his career goals in 1986: not only the 300 wins, but also 700 starts and 5,000 innings.

Sutton recognizes his limitations. He pitches up to them and doesn't try to go beyond. His savvy is respected by his teammates and he has emerged as a helpful mentor to the Angels' young pitchers.

He brings an invaluable combination to big games: he is a callused veteran, unfazed by tough spots, with still enough stuff to get through them.

Killebrew: "Sutton is another veteran pitcher who has unlocked the secret of successful aging. For someone who doesn't rely on a low-stress trick pitch, like the knuckleball or forkball, he has remained remarkably consistent with no visible sign of a dropoff."

CALIFORNIA ANGELS

HITTING:

Devon White is an exciting prospect. For quick reference, he is often referred to as a *Gary Pettis with power*. He has the same physical gifts, with better batting instincts and more muscle. The Jamaica-born 24-year-old could give the Angels the majors' fastest outfield tandem.

White is a tremendous natural athlete. Scouts prefer comparing him to Willie Davis, the lanky former Dodger star. Unlike other speedsters who are taught to chop down on the ball, Devon has been encouraged to keep his standard swing. He doesn't seem to have any glaring holes and, once he gets to know the league, this natural righty will be a power threat from both sides.

Seeing more righthanded pitchers has made him, if anything, a better contact hitter from the left side. Right now, he definitely has more power from that side. He likes the ball out over the plate, above the thighs, but he has the wrists to fight off inside fastballs. During his first swing around the league, pitchers should feed him slow breaking stuff low-and-in.

BASERUNNING:

White doesn't get out of the box as well as he could, but he makes up for slow starts halfway down the line and explodes across the bag.

Still, his speed isn't fully appreciated until he's motoring from first to third or, better yet, running for a triple. He takes long strides and runs as fluidly as a well-oiled machine.

As a basestealing threat, he relies on sheer speed, without the science. White stole 188 bases while being brought along slowly in the minors, and is 9-for-9 in his brief major league exposure.

FIELDING:

White has to work a little more on charging

DEVON WHITE
OF, No. 30
SR, 6'1", 175 lbs.
ML Svc: less than one year
Born: 12-29-62 in
Kingston, JAM

1986 STATISTICS

AVG	G	AB	R	H	2B	3B	HR	RBI	BB	SO	SB
28	51	8	12	1	1	1	3	6	8	6	

CAREER STATISTICS

AVG	G	AB	R	H	2B	3B	HR	RBI	BB	SO	SB
49	58	15	13	1	1	1	3	7	11	9	

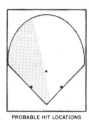

VS. RHP   VS. LHP   PROBABLE HIT LOCATIONS

balls. He sometimes takes too many steps before releasing a throw and occasionally gets his feet tangled. But his range has no limits and he will run into walls and through teammates to make the play. His arm is above average.

He is a born center fielder and would unquestionably play there on any other club. Two-time Gold Glove winner Pettis will nudge him to right, where some of White's talents will be wasted.

OVERALL:

If a couple of high-priced veterans weren't in his way, White would be a safe bet to play regularly in 1987. Young talents don't always take to part-time playing and full-time sitting, but White appears to have the dedication to turn it into a learning experience.

CALIFORNIA ANGELS

PITCHING:

For the last three years, Mike Witt has been one of the American League's pitching marvels. He has been durable, averaging 7½ innings over 103 starts. He has been successful, winning 48 games. At times, he has even been unhittable. Like last August, when he held the league to a .110 average while going 5-0. If he corrects the few remaining flaws in his game, this pitcher will be Hall of Fame material.

Witt throws over the top, mixing an excellent 90 MPH fastball with a wide-breaking curve. But he doesn't mix them often enough, occasionally becoming so enchanted with the breaking pitch he falls into a doomed "curve-rut." When he comes in with the heat, his curve freezes righthanded hitters. But he insists on curving power hitters and doesn't particularly like to pitch inside.

Witt has had a hard time mastering a true change-up and will scrap it for long stretches. He then uses a let-up curve as the change.

He sustains his speed well through nine innings. Yet the hard curve is his out pitch. It's good enough to get him through most games. In one outing against the Orioles last year, he threw 88 curves out of 102 pitches. Perhaps predictably, Cal Ripken beat him 2-1 by hitting one of them for a two-run homer.

He works relatively slowly, especially with men on base. Bad innings still tend to mushroom on him, although he has grown increasingly adept at working out of jams. And he is excellent at shaking off rocky innings and getting back on track.

FIELDING:

Witt has an average move to first base but he'll rarely throw there. To combat runners, he prefers to speed up his delivery. He has learned to pitch from the stretch without losing too much off his pitches.

Being big and lanky, he naturally has a hard

**MIKE WITT
RHP, No. 39
RR, 6'7", 192 lbs.
ML Svc: 6 years
Born: 7-20-60 in
Fullerton, CA**

1986 STATISTICS

W	L	ERA	G	GS	CG	SV	IP	H	R	ER	BB	SO
18	10	2.84	34	34	14	0	269	218	95	85	73	208

CAREER STATISTICS

W	L	ERA	G	GS	CG	SV	IP	H	R	ER	BB	SO
71	59	3.52	201	149	43	5	1229	1145	540	480	424	821

time reacting to hit balls. Oddly (since his delivery takes him in the opposite direction) he covers an amazing amount of ground to his right. But he is awful at fielding balls hit back to the mound; they freeze him, and he'll even dodge comebackers that should be easy to handle.

OVERALL:

Mike is a born power pitcher who tries to make himself into a control pitcher. He is a tremendous closer, partly because Gene Mauch hates to relieve him: Mauch reasons his stuff is so outstanding that hitters are always elated to see him go.

During his maturing seasons, Witt let veteran catcher Bob Boone guide him through games. With Boone gone, it'll be interesting to see how Witt fares with more decisions left up to him.

He is one of the majors' bright young aces and 1987 may see the 20-victory season that has been predicted for him since he broke in as a 20-year-old.

Killebrew: "Mike is a young veteran, with room for still more improvement, particularly in controlling his pitches. He has a great arm and an excellent curveball."

CALIFORNIA ANGELS

HITTING:

Butch Wynegar's offense has declined over each of the last three years, his average plummeting from a career high of .296 in 1983 to .267, then .223 and to a career low of .206 in 61 games last year.

Wynegar's season ended abruptly when he jumped the New York Yankees' unsteady ship on August 1st. He was placed on the restricted list for "physcial and mental fatigue."

Wynegar gets a new start with his trade to California, but the switch-hitter again must prove himself as a major league batter.

Wynegar is more of a home run threat from the right side of the plate. He usually gets his home runs on bad breaking balls.

Lefthanders do well against Wynegar by keeping the ball low-and-away. Righthanders must keep fastballs on the outside part of the plate. Wynegar's strength is the fastball down-and-in.

Whatever Wynegar hits is a bonus. He is valued for his skill behind the plate.

BASERUNNING:

Wynegar is extremely slow, even for a catcher. He runs the bases carefully and is aware of what he can do on the basepaths-- which is little.

FIELDING:

Entering 1986, Wynegar begins his 12th full major league season. That experience gives him an extensive knowledge of American League hitters and reassures his pitchers.

Wynegar is confident in his ability to call a game and to handle a staff. He became upset in New York when each of his last two managers with the Yankees, Billy Martin and Lou Piniella, berated him on the mound or in the dugout for his pitch selection. Wynegar balked at the intense approach of each man.

Wynegar has average throwing ability. Teams don't take liberties against him, but he can be run on.

OVERALL:

It is unclear what ailed Wynegar in 1986. He

BUTCH WYNEGAR
C, No. 27
SR, 6'1", 192 lbs.
ML Svc: 11 years
Born: 3-14-56 in
York, PA

1986 STATISTICS

AVG	G	AB	R	H	2B	3B	HR	RBI	BB	SO	SB
.206	61	194	19	40	4	1	7	29	30	21	0

CAREER STATISTICS

AVG	G	AB	R	H	2B	3B	HR	RBI	BB	SO	SB
.256	1343	4183	486	1069	170	14	64	493	609	408	10

  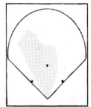

VS. RHP   VS. LHP   PROBABLE HIT LOCATIONS

underwent a battery of physical and psychological tests. Yankees sources said the catcher left the team because he was unsure whether he wanted to play baseball at all anymore--in New York or elsewhere. Wynegar later blamed his trouble on Martin, Piniella and the Yankees. The less-explosive Gene Mauch seems to be better-suited to a player such as Wynegar.

Actually, the abruptness of Wynegar's departure last season is not surprising. With the pressure to produce day in and day out in the arena of professional sports, one almost wonders why there aren't more cases such as Wynegar's. Though professional athletes are heavily compensated, sometimes, it appears, enough is enough.

Kaat: "Butch is a good, basic major league catcher. He's nothing exceptional, but certainly very capable.

"Wynegar has a knack for turning mistakes into game-breaking blows. He collected six game-winning RBIs last year despite his meager average. Wynegar can be counted on to make contact and is therefore a good hit-and-run man."

CALIFORNIA ANGELS

RAY CHADWICK
RHP, No. 48
RR, 6'2", 180 lbs.
ML Svc: 1 year
Born: 11-17-62 in
Durham, NC

PITCHING, FIELDING:

Last spring, Ray Chadwick was regarded as the brightest pitching prospect in the Angels' farm system and, appropriately, got the first in-season promotion. It was a disaster: unable to overcome some early bad luck, he found his efforts turning uglier and uglier. He's only 24 years old, but the question is whether he can reclaim his lost confidence and aggression.

A power pitcher who throws the four basic pitches (fastball, curveball, slider and change-up), Chadwick has the physical tools to be a big winner if he regains *trust* in his stuff (one of manager Gene Mauch's main beefs about young hurlers). Too often during his trial last season, Chadwick dreaded falling behind in the count and took a few feet off his fastball in aiming for strikes. He quickly learned that big league hitters pummel those fat ones. At full bore, he gets his fastball up into the low 90s.

A good athlete overall, Chadwick is quick off the mound. He isn't afraid of making low-percentage throws to cut down lead runners. He has a good move to first base but tends to make it too often, distracting him from the batter.

OVERALL:

Chadwick blew a golden opportunity last year and forced the Angels to re-evaluate his potential. But he is in a good situation to work himself back into the team's plans, though he'll have to do something spectacular to be noticed.

URBANO LUGO
RHP, No. 18
RR, 6'0", 190 lbs.
ML Svc: 1 year plus
Born: 8-12-62 in
Falcon, Venezuela

PITCHING, FIELDING:

Urbano Lugo's candidacy for a starting spot last year ended before it began, when a winter elbow injury required surgery. He gradually worked his way back into the majors and showed he's ready to mount a new bid by throwing a no-hitter in winter ball before the 1987 season.

An overhand pitcher, Lugo throws in the upper 80s but without much movement on the fastball. He continues to have trouble developing a good breaking pitch. He insists on relying on a sporadic forkball--when it's breaking well, he can be impressive. It's a good one, a true forkball as opposed to a split-finger fastball. But he throws it enough to make it predictable, which in turn makes it hittable.

He is a confident kid, yet too often avoids challenging hitters by trying to be too fine. Given his tendency to get wild, that is not the wisest approach.

Lugo seems to concentrate so much on pitching, he treats fielding the position as an afterthought. He'll handle the simple comebacker but will look disarrayed on more involved plays, as in bunt situations.

OVERALL:

Killebrew: "Lugo is still a young guy with a good arm. He needs to stay clear of injury. If he has a strong spring and can log a full season in the majors, there's no reason why he shouldn't win in double figures."

CALIFORNIA ANGELS

MARK McLEMORE
RHP, No. 28
SR, 5'11", 175 lbs.
ML Svc: less than one year
Born: 10-4-64 in San Diego, CA

HITTING, BASERUNNING, FIELDING:

Mark McLemore has been the jewel of California's farm system for years. The Angels have repeatedly rejected tempting offers to trade him, hoping to have a job available for him by the time he matures. Bobby Grich's retirement at the end of last season created that vacancy at second base.

McLemore is a switch-hitter who has more problems making contact from the left side, which keeps him from fully using his sprinter's speed. He has progressively improved as a hitter, though he doesn't have as much power as his solid build would indicate.

He has concentrated on developing speed as his chief weapon, and has averaged about 50 steals for each of his five minor league seasons. An intelligent runner with a thief's eye, he doesn't take long to get a read on pitchers.

His defensive range is tremendous and a strong arm allows him to nail runners from the edge of the outfield grass. The knock has been on his "hard" hands, and he spent the winter working on "softening" them by taking hundreds of grounders a day.

OVERALL:

McLemore has only a half-season of Triple-A experience and the Angels are leery about whether he's ready to assume a major league role. But they've been successful rushing along other position players. His speed should be enough of an asset until the rest of his game catches up.

DARRELL MILLER
C/OF, No. 32
RR, 6'2", 200 lbs.
ML Svc: 2 years
Born: 2-26-59 in Washington, D.C.

HITTING, BASERUNNING, FIELDING:

After spending the winter of 1985-86 refining his catching skills in hopes it would earn him a bigger role, Darrell Miller became a forgotten man in 1986. He was used chiefly as a late-inning defensive sub in the outfield, which did nothing to sharpen his batting eye.

He is a decent contact hitter for someone so aggressive and is dangerous with belt-high fastballs. Since he plays so infrequently, he can be kept off-balance with off-speed stuff anywhere in the strike zone. Being anxious, he'll chase pitches off the plate. In eight years of pro ball, Miller has exceeded 400 at-bats only twice, yet hit with consistent extra-base power both times.

Miller moves well for a big man and will sometimes be used to pinch-run. He slides hard; on double plays, fielders have to get rid of the ball in time to get out of his way.

He seems destined to spend his career floating from position to position. He handles many roles adaquately, making him valuable as a 24th man, but he doesn't perform well enough at any field position to start. As a catcher, he can be confused by the footwork and takes too long to release the ball. In the outfield, he has above-average range with an average arm.

OVERALL:

Killebrew: "Miller is a good defensive player and handles well the difficult shifts from catching to the outfield. He has good speed and needs only playing time to improve as a hitter."

JERRY NARRON
C, No. 34
LR, 6'3", 190 lbs.
ML Svc: 7 years
Born: 1-15-56 in
Goldsboro, NC

HITTING, BASERUNNING, FIELDING:

Not long ago, Jerry Narron showed the promise of becoming a dangerous lefthanded pinch-hitter with power--a modern-day Jerry Lynch. With the Angels, however, he hasn't had enough opportunities to get on a roll (11 pinch at-bats in 1986).

Narron is a lethal fastball hitter and he likes it down-and-in. Every at-bat, he's a sure bet to pull at least one drive into the corner, fair or foul. He goes up there hacking, gambling that he'll get his pitch. He's used almost exclusively against righties (only 3 at-bats against lefthanders in 1986), who have good luck with him by keeping the ball up-and-away. Narron will only go to the opposite field if he's fooled on the pitch.

On the bases, he just tries to keep out of others' way. Unless he's needed on defense, he'll always leave the game for a pinch-runner.

Narron is regarded a defensive liability and is used only in case of emergency. But he worked hard to improve his footwork last season and, as a result, his throwing greatly improved (he nailed 11 of 25 runners). He is weak on off-target pitches he has to go get, and on handling throws for plays at the plate.

OVERALL:

Narron showed defensive improvement at the right time, since Bob Boone's departure means the Angels may have to play him more. That should also help his offense by giving him more than an occasional at-bat.

Killebrew: "Jerry has the perfect make-up for being a dangerous pinch-hitter. He doesn't play much, but whenever he's needed he always seems to be ready. He is another of the Angels' key role players."

GUS POLIDOR
INF, No. 12
RR, 6'0", 170 lbs.
ML Svc: less than
one year
Born: 10-26-61 in
Caracas, VZ

HITTING, BASERUNNING, FIELDING:

This is a good year to keep an eye on Gus Polidor, who comes off two straight strong Triple-A seasons as a solid candidate for a big league reserve role.

Polidor's years of back problems seem to be behind him, as it were, and his pain-free play in 1986 justified the early reports on him. Polidor is a natural line drive hitter. He knows he's not strong enough to drive the ball deep and is satisfied with a top-hand swing. He'll struggle against the breaking pitch at first but, if his progress at Edmonton is any indication, he'll catch on quickly. He hit .300 last year and .285 the year before; his prior minor league high had been a meek .248.

He has below-average speed for a young middle infielder. He doesn't like to get physical on bang-bang plays on the basepaths.

Polidor's biggest assets on defense are his smooth hands. He belongs to an endless list of Latin Americans whose reflexes were honed on rock-strewn sandlot fields. A natural shortstop, he has handled shifts at third and second well. From second, he throws with a weird hitch, but the ball always gets there on time.

OVERALL:

Polidor is ideal for the all-around utility job handled in 1986 by Rick Burleson. If his line drive hitting becomes too hard to bench, he could emerge as a dark-horse starting candidate at second base.

CALIFORNIA ANGELS

MARK RYAL
1B, No. 6
LL, 6'0", 180 lbs.
ML Svc: *less than one year*
Born: *4-28-60 in Henrigetta, OK*

HITTING, BASERUNNING, FIELDING:

After lolling around in the minors for eight years, mostly in Kansas City's system, Mark Ryal exploded in 1986. He sustained the performance through a September trial with the Angels to force himself into their picture as a DH/fourth outfielder.

Ryal's Edmonton average (.340) was 55 points above his previous high and he also reached peaks in hits (163) and RBIs (84) last year. He generates good extra-base power with a controlled swing. He has overcome his biggest weakness, which had been a tendency to overswing. Last year, he struck out 65 fewer times in 89 more at-bats compared with the season before.

With no speed to speak of, the thick-legged Ryal is an overly cautious runner, never a threat to take two bases on any ball hit in front of him.

Despite his lack of speed, he is a quick outfielder. He gets a good jump on balls and has the reflexes necessary to make up for the times he tends to be too aggressive. He has a strong arm, good enough even for right field.

OVERALL:

It's easy to see what has held up Mark's progress. He doesn't have the eye-catching tools to make someone want to includue him in a starting outfield, and he lacks both the speed and the power a manager likes to have on the bench. At Edmonton he played first base; the added versatility makes him more valuable.

ROB WILFONG
2B, No. 9
LR, 6'1", 179 lbs.
ML Svc: *10 years*
Born: *9-1-53 in Pasadena, CA*

HITTING, BASERUNNING, FIELDING:

Wilfong had an opportunity to move in as California's regular second baseman last year but, despite a strong start, played himself back into a reserve role. Unfit for any other position, he has only limited value as a utilityman.

Rob unveiled a dramatically different stance in 1986, moving his arms away from his body in order to give him a better chance with breaking balls. As a result, he had good success against the lefthanders (.318) who used to own him. It also enhanced his power, with 27% of his hits going for extra bases. He basically remains a pull hitter and is often used to advance runners by hitting behind them.

Despite below-average speed, he is one of the best on the team in going from first to third. But he can no longer take full advantage of his peerless bunting ability.

What he lacks in range on defense he compensates for with savvy. He's not afraid to get dirty and excels at making the throw from the ground after a diving stop, though he is hampered by an awkward release.

OVERALL:

He is 33 years old and some feel Wilfong should still be given a full-time shot at the second base job this year. One of those in agreement is manager Gene Mauch, an old admirer. Wilfong is still capable of always steady--and sometimes spectacular--defense and can be a .270 hitter if he is kept in tune as a regular.

Killebrew: "Wilfong has fit into the Angels' scheme admirably. He is an ideal role player for Mauch. He remains an excellent bunter."

CHICAGO WHITE SOX

PITCHING:

The White Sox took a chance when they acquired Neil Allen prior to the 1986 season. After all, his potential was considered great with the New York Mets, good with the St. Louis Cardinals and suspect with the New York Yankees, the team from which the White Sox acquired him.

The Sox took his ever-present potential into consideration and also had to consider Allen's problems off the field. They didn't have high expectations, but Allen came through as the club's biggest surprise in 1986.

Best known as a relief pitcher, Allen initially was used out of the bullpen. When asked to work as a starter last year he proved his worth. Allen was injured late in the season but his 7-2 record overall gave him the best winning percentage on the staff.

Allen, who will be used exclusively as a starter this season, has always been known for his fastball, which he throws at 85-90 MPH. His control is above-average, especially since he took some of the break out of his curveball. When pitching in the National League, Allen's control was what got him into trouble.

Since he is now a starter, Allen has worked on the change-up, which has been a problem pitch throughout his career. He seems to have his confidence back after a successful stint as a starter and is good at keeping the ball down.

FIELDING:

Allen has a good move to first base, but if runners read him right, they can get a good jump because of his high leg kick.

He is a very good fielder who can cover the bunt or get over and cover first base.

NEIL ALLEN
RHP, No. 33
RR, 6'2", 190 lbs.
ML Svc: 8 years
Born: 1-24-58 in
Kansas City, KS

1986 STATISTICS

W	L	ERA	G	GS	CG	SV	IP	H	R	ER	BB	SO
7	2	3.82	22	17	2	0	113	101	50	48	38	57

CAREER STATISTICS

W	L	ERA	G	GS	CG	SV	IP	H	R	ER	BB	SO
53	58	3.63	367	46	7	75	797.2	759	356	322	344	499

OVERALL:

Allen's adjustment to the role of a starting pitcher still has the White Sox shaking their heads. It didn't cost them much to acquire his services, but he turned out to be quite a bargain.

The knock on Allen throughout his career has been his inability to consistently perform when called on. In his starting role, however, Allen was ready more often than not and forced himself into the starting rotation. After his success in '86, he is being counted on to deliver and maybe it's time he's ready to prove that the Cardinals didn't make a total mistake when they acquired him in exchage for a pretty good first baseman named Keith Hernandez.

Killebrew: "Allen was a big surprise last season. He used to pitch only in certain relief situations but proved he can also go as a starter, which he did very well. He's an excellent guy to have on your pitching staff. He should continue to pitch well if he can keep himself together."

CHICAGO WHITE SOX

HITTING:

Harold Baines has unwillingly developed the reputation of being a vastly underrated player. He won't say a word about the vast talent he has displayed to the rest of the American League over the past seven seasons; he'll just keep on putting up the good numbers.

If you want to talk about Baines, start with hitting. Not too many players can hit for average and power, but he has done it consistently since hitting the big time. As a matter of fact, Baines had what by his standards was an off-year in 1986. His .296 batting average was no problem, but his RBI total (88) was his lowest since 1981, when he played in only 82 games.

There was a time when Baines had to earn his bases off lefthanded pitchers, but not any longer. He thrives on inside pitches up in the strike zone and the majority of his home runs come on balls he is able to pull to right field. He has a rare talent in that he can adjust the length of his swing depending on the location of the pitch.

Baines is a legitimate power hitter, but he's built a .287 career average because he's a smart hitter who takes what a pitcher gives him. Pitch him outside and he'll go to left field. Few opponents challenge him down the middle. He has made great strides fighting off pitches that ride inside on his hands.

Baines has a classic swing and has quickly developed into one of the game's better hitters. He delivers in clutch situations and is not easy to strike out, like many of his peers with similar power stats. A perfect hitting specimen? No. He can't bunt.

BASERUNNING:

Watch Baines play the outfield and you'd probably figure him as a 20-40 stolen base man per year. Not so. Baines stole only two bases last season and that was his highest amount since 1983.

He is an average, non-aggressive baserunner and, obviously, not a threat to steal.

HAROLD BAINES
RF, No. 3
LL, 6'2", 189 lbs.
ML Svc: 7 years
Born: 3-15-59 in
Easton, MD

1986 STATISTICS

AVG	G	AB	R	H	2B	3B	HR	RBI	BB	SO	SB
.296	145	570	72	169	29	2	21	88	38	89	2

CAREER STATISTICS

AVG	G	AB	R	H	2B	3B	HR	RBI	BB	SO	SB
.287	992	3754	492	1077	182	38	140	589	263	539	29

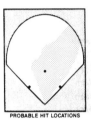

VS. RHP   VS. LHP   PROBABLE HIT LOCATIONS

FIELDING:

Baines has worked hard on his defensive play and it has paid off. Last season, he was the best right fielder in the American League West. His strength is not mobility, but his positioning--he knows where to be. As with his offensive abilities, his throwing arm is vastly underrated.

OVERALL:

Killebrew: "Baines is a rare player by today's standards. He is consistently among the best players in baseball and he leaves it at that. He enjoys playing the game and the fact that he is so good at it makes it just as enjoyable for those watching him.

"He is an outstanding hitter who just keeps getting better. He may not be a basestealer, but his overall game is as good as anybody's."

CHICAGO WHITE SOX

PITCHING:

Had Floyd Bannister received better offensive support last season, his 10-14 record would have at least been flip-flopped. He also went 10-14 in 1985, but he was a much better pitcher last year and showed signs of returning to the form that earned him a 30-21 combined mark in 1983-84.

Bannister always had a good mix of pitches, but was primarily known as a fastball specialist who knew how to pile up strikeouts.

That should change this season. Bannister has moved away from his straight over-the-top power delivery to more of a finesse style of pitching. He will throw more sinkers and sliders this season. Both pitches are thrown with considerable zip. He should be at his best against lefthanders looking to pull the ball. He has become very good at keeping the ball down and is not easy to take the ball out of the park on.

Bannister has also worked on his change-up, which he can throw at anytime for strikes.

He has developed a reputation as a hard-headed performer who is quick to shake off a sign. Bannister never did feel comfortable throwing the hard stuff over the inside corner. With his new style of keeping the ball down, he may not get as much criticism for letting hitters control the inside corner.

FIELDING:

Fielding is no problem for Bannister. He's not the quickest pitcher to come off the mound, but he gets to the ball and throws accurately to any base. He is good at getting over to first base and rarely makes an error.

Bannister has improved his move to first

FLOYD BANNISTER
LHP, No. 19
LL, 6'1", 193 lbs.
ML Svc: 10 years
Born: 6-10-55 in
Pierre, SD

1986 STATISTICS

W	L	ERA	G	GS	CG	SV	IP	H	R	ER	BB	SO
10	14	3.54	28	27	6	0	165.1	162	81	65	48	92

CAREER STATISTICS

W	L	ERA	G	GS	CG	SV	IP	H	R	ER	BB	SO
101	117	4.02	300	284	49	0	1832.1	1771	908	820	680	1405

and gets the ball over more quickly now than he used to. He is not much of a threat to catch a runner leaning, but he does a good job keeping them as close as possible.

OVERALL:

Bannister will still be primarily a power pitcher, but it should be interesting to see how well he throws out of more of a low-ball delivery.

His arm is sound and he can go the distance, as he proved last year by leading the staff with 6 complete games. His control has never been a problem and (much like the rest of the White Sox rotation) he would be a much better pitcher with some support.

Killebrew: "He has great stuff and could be a consistent winner. Maybe the element for Bannister is simply a matter of concentration, but good lefthanded starters are very hard to find. Southpaws will always be treated as prodigal sons."

CHICAGO WHITE SOX

HITTING:

The White Sox are ready. The question, however, is: *When will Daryl Boston be ready?*

Perhaps, six years in the minor leagues have prepared him for the rigors of playing center field on a regular bases, a role the White Sox anxiously expect him to fill this season.

Boston has the size and speed which helped him become the seventh player selected overall in the 1981 free-agent draft. He has been an outstanding player on all minor league levels but slow starts in the big leagues have plagued him.

He was handed a starting position before spring training began this year based not so much on his impressive minor league stats but on his big league performance at the end of the 1986 season.

At the plate, Boston has a big swing and can pull the ball to right as well hit outside deliveries to the opposite field. He is most effective hitting low pitches to left field or up the middle and has blazing speed which allows him to beat out infield grounders and reach first on bunts.

Like most young hitters, Boston has trouble with off-speed pitches and will reach for the breaking ball. He has abandoned the reckless swing which made him a prime strikeout candidate early in his career in favor of a more patient batting style.

BASERUNNING:

In a word, outstanding. Boston will become a basestealer to be reckoned with once he gets around the league and learns how to read opposing pitchers. He has amazing speed and a long stride. The former all-state high school quarterback goes in hard at second base.

FIELDING:

Looking for a flaw in Boston's game? Don't look at his defensive abilities. He covers as

DARYL BOSTON
CF, No. 8
LL, 6'3", 193 lbs.
ML Svc: 2 years
Born: 1-4-63 in
Cincinnati, OH

1986 STATISTICS

AVG	G	AB	R	H	2B	3B	HR	RBI	BB	SO	SB
.266	56	199	29	53	11	3	5	22	21	33	9

CAREER STATISTICS

AVG	G	AB	R	H	2B	3B	HR	RBI	BB	SO	SB
.233	186	514	57	120	27	5	8	40	39	97	23

  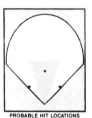

STRONG   STRONG

VS. RHP   VS. LHP   PROBABLE HIT LOCATIONS

much ground as anybody in center field and has a cannon for an arm. His speed allows him to play hitters short or deep without worrying about getting crossed up.

OVERALL:

The time has come for Boston to be successful in the major leagues. Because of his natural ability and minor league credentials, he won't be able to slide by as a marginal performer.

The White Sox have been very patient waiting for him to develop and expected him to take over center field last season. That didn't happen, though Boston showed enough flash when he was recalled late in the season to warrant another long look.

Killebrew: "He's the type of player that has all of the skills and he should develop into quite a major league player. He is young and still improving and he's got excellent speed. I know they are expecting a lot out of him."

CHICAGO WHITE SOX

HITTING:

The White Sox desperately want Ivan Calderon to be their starting left fielder this season. Whether or not Calderon feels the same way is another story. Acquired from the Seattle Mariners last season in a trade for Scott Bradley, Calderon failed to shake the enigmatic cloud which has followed him throughout his brief pro career.

The Sox are willing to wager that age and attitude can combine to help Calderon reach his potential. If not, the big outfielder may become another in a long line of minor league phenoms who never make the transition to the majors.

Injuries and a lengthy stint in Triple-A didn't help Chicago with its evaluation, but Calderon did show some spark when he made his way into the lineup.

Although he didn't always show them, Calderon has all the tools needed to be a power hitter. He is a devastating pull hitter who really tees off on pitches delivered up and over the plate. He is a swinger and can take a pitch off the plate to the opposite field.

Calderon will have to work on fighting off sliders and fastballs on the inside part of the plate, but he is capable of turning on them. A lot of pitchers have had success moving him off the plate and then throwing the out pitch off the plate.

Unless the situation absolutely calls for it, Calderon isn't going to bunt.

BASERUNNING:

Despite his bulk, Calderon has some speed and will occasionally take a chance at stealing a base. He needs to concentrate a bit more as a runner, but he'll gamble and is a scary sight to the pivot man attempting to turn two.

FIELDING:

Calderon has played all three outfield

IVAN CALDERON
LF, No. 22
RR, 6'1", 205 lbs.
ML Svc: 2 years
Born: 3-19-62 in
Fajaro, PR

1986 STATISTICS

AVG	G	AB	R	H	2B	3B	HR	RBI	BB	SO	SB
.250	50	164	16	41	7	1	2	15	9	39	3

CAREER STATISTICS

AVG	G	AB	R	H	2B	3B	HR	RBI	BB	SO	SB
.266	128	398	55	106	24	5	11	44	30	89	8

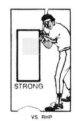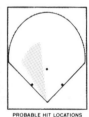

VS. RHP   VS. LHP   PROBABLE HIT LOCATIONS

positions but is best suited for left field, which is exactly where the White Sox have him penciled in. He has a good, if somewhat erratic arm, and is able to cover his turf.

OVERALL:

The White Sox have Harold Baines firmly implanted in right field, but need help in left and center. They will bend over backwards this year to make sure that Calderon gets the starting job in left field, but he will have to start producing there soon. His outlook on the game has reportedly improved, but only time will tell. A player with less potential would be long gone.

Killebrew: "Calderon needs to put it together this season. He has the ability to be a big hitter and that's what the White Sox are looking for."

CHICAGO WHITE SOX

HITTING:

If you were looking for some information on John Cangelosi in last year's White Sox media guide, join the crowd. The Bruce Springsteen look-alike had a nondescript past, but he made the most of the present.

Some how, some way, Cangelosi made the big jump from Double-A ball to the White Sox' starting lineup, although this rags-to-riches story hasn't been guaranteed a happy ending.

Cangelosi made it on sheer desire and hustle, but that does not a career make. Opposing pitchers were baffled by his crouched, open stance (a la Jose Cruz) and Cangelosi's name and the Rookie of the Year award became familiar topics despite the successes of California's Wally Joyner and Oakland's Jose Canseco.

But as midseason rolled around, Cangelosi started to collapse. A switch-hitter more dangerous batting lefthanded, Cangelosi fell apart at the plate. He started off strong because of his ability to punch the ball up the middle or to the opposite field, but in the heat of the summer, Cangelosi started popping the ball up and hitting lazy flies to the outfield.

Pitchers figured out that Cangelosi could hit the low fastball through the hole or chop it on the ground and beat the throw to first base. But when faced with off-speed pitches up over the strike zone, Cangelosi would bite and hit the ball in the air.

Cangelosi's playing time dropped off considerably as the season progressed, but he still has the skills that will make it hard to keep him out of the lineup. He is only 5'8" and much smaller than that in his unorthodox batting stance. With his baserunning ability, he needs to get on base anyway he can. He is a good bunter but could improve.

BASERUNNING:

Cangelosi made the major leagues as a basestealer and that won't change. Only Rickey Henderson did better in the American League last year, which is nothing to be ashamed of.

Much like the rest of his game, Cangelosi will challenge pitchers and catchers and he'll only get better with experience. He is

JOHN CANGELOSI
CF, No. 44
SL, 5'8", 150 lbs.
ML Svc: 1 year
Born: 3-19-63 in
Brooklyn, NY

1986 STATISTICS

AVG	G	AB	R	H	2B	3B	HR	RBI	BB	SO	SB
.235	137	438	65	103	16	3	2	32	71	61	50

CAREER STATISTICS

AVG	G	AB	R	H	2B	3B	HR	RBI	BB	SO	SB
.234	142	440	67	103	16	3	2	32	71	62	50

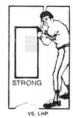
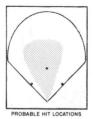

VS. RHP   VS. LHP   PROBABLE HIT LOCATIONS

extremely aggressive on the basepaths and will get picked off, but a sense of discomfort from the opposition becomes quickly evident when Cangelosi gets on base.

FIELDING:

With his great speed, Cangelosi can run down any ball that comes near him. He is especially skilled at robbing hitters expecting a double on balls hit into the gap on either side.

Cangelosi was not blessed with a great throwing arm, so he relies on his speed to compensate for that deficiency. He can be run on and baserunners are usually able to tag and take another base.

OVERALL:

Killebrew: "He needs work with the bat and in learning how to run the base paths. But he doesn't need to hit with power.

"He is a very exciting player to watch. He tailed off a bit last season after getting off to a great start, but I expect him to be a factor for the White Sox this year. He has excellent speed on the bases and he covers a lot of ground in the outfield."

CHICAGO WHITE SOX

PITCHING:

Over the course of the 1985 season, Joe Cowley pitched a no-hitter, tied an American League record by striking out the first seven batters he faced and led the Chicago White Sox in wins. This guy's a great pitcher, right?

Cowley could be, should be and just might be a pitcher destined for greatness, but the jury is still in conference. When he's on the top of his game batters can just forget it, but the big question throughout his career has been consistency. And attitude. If Cowley wants to win, he will. If he doesn't, he won't.

What makes Cowley an effective pitcher is his delivery. When he's on, his pitches look easy enough to hit--until they get to the plate. That is when his fastball suddenly picks up steam, his slider drops off the plate and his curveball breaks out of the strike zone.

In a way, Cowley is much like John Candelaria used to be when he was pitching for the Pittsburgh Pirates. If he can get through the first two or three innings, he'll earn his pay. But if he gets hit hard early, he gets rattled and takes an early shower.

When his breaking ball is sharp, he is very tough on righthanded hitters. He can also bring the fastball at close to 90 MPH. Along with the slider, Cowley has an above-average array of pitches and is right around the plate with all of them. Throughout his career, he has been a power pitcher with the rare ability to exhibit good control.

Cowley has sensed a need to add another dimension to his game and has been working on improving his change-up, which has been his major weak spot.

The White Sox are also hoping Cowley has worked on the mental aspect of pitching. He needs to concentrate before, after and during each of his outings if he is to be successful.

JOE COWLEY
RHP, No. 40
RR, 6'5", 210 lbs.
ML Svc: 4 years
Born: 8-15-58 in
Lexington, KY

1986 STATISTICS

W	L	ERA	G	GS	CG	SV	IP	H	R	ER	BB	SO
11	11	3.88	27	27	4	0	162.1	133	81	70	83	132

CAREER STATISTICS

W	L	ERA	G	GS	CG	SV	IP	H	R	ER	BB	SO
33	21	3.92	90	72	8	0	457.1	393	207	199	215	327

FIELDING:

For a righthanded pitcher supposedly at a disadvantage as a pickoff man, Cowley has done quite well. He has a quick, deceptive move and keeps runners close. He gets off the mound quickly and had developed the reputation as a good fielder, but was below average last season with the White Sox.

OVERALL:

Cowley tends to slide at times but is good enough to make up for it. He is a pitcher with winning potential, but he has to avoid the lapses that have plagued his career and demonstrate his ability over the long stretch.

He is a difficult player to manage but considering his talent, is worth the trouble.

Killebrew: "He pitched very well last season and seemed to thrive on throwing the big game. He needs to be more consistent, but all the signs point to him having a big year for the White Sox."

CHICAGO WHITE SOX

HITTING:

The White Sox were looking for an improvement out of Julio Cruz and, in a sense, they got it. Cruz improved on his .197 1985 average, but it is extremely doubtful that the .215 mark he produced last year is going to be good enough to earn him a starting job.

Cruz, an emotional player through much of his career, looked to be going through the motions again last season, his third disappointing year in a row since signing a big contract that runs through the 1989 season.

The switch-hitting Cruz started and finished slowly while showing brief flashes of his old self midway through the season. He remains most effective from the right side of the plate, but is no home run threat. He has a good eye, but has trouble with the curveball when hitting righthanded.

Cruz didn't get many chances against righthanded pitchers last season, but he is able to drive low pitches straight away. Although he is a free swinger out of a crouched stance from either side, Cruz has a sharp eye and isn't easily fooled. He is a capable bunter.

BASERUNNING:

Cruz has totally abandoned the aggressive base running style which made him of baseball's most feared base stealers in the late 1970's and early 80's. He still possesses above average speed but has lost his edge as a runner as his playing time has diminished.

FIELDING:

The strongest part of Cruz' game is his fielding. He easily covers ground to his right and left and still is able to turn the double play with a style not easily imitated. Should his troubles at the plate continue, the Sox would have no other choice than to sacrifice his

JULIO CRUZ
2B, No. 12
SR, 5'9", 180 lbs.
ML Svc: 9 years
Born: 12-2-54 in
Brooklyn, NY

1986 STATISTICS

AVG	G	AB	R	H	2B	3B	HR	RBI	BB	SO	SB
.215	81	209	38	45	2	0	0	19	42	28	7

CAREER STATISTICS

AVG	G	AB	R	H	2B	3B	HR	RBI	BB	SO	SB
.237	1156	3859	557	916	113	27	23	279	478	508	343

VS. RHP   VS. LHP   PROBABLE HIT LOCATIONS

fielding ability in favor of a player with better all-around skills.

OVERALL:

It appears the White Sox are ready and willing to live with Cruz' big contract, which means he'll remain a member of the team, but an inactive one at best. Cruz wouldn't be as noticeable in a lineup filled with proven hitters. Unfortunately for Cruz, the American League hasn't adopted the DF (designated fielder). Miracles do happen though and should Cruz play in 100 games or more and hit .250 or better, he'd be a candidate for Comeback Player of the Year. That's how rough his past three seasons have been.

Killebrew: "Once again, he's got to return to the form he had a couple years ago. He's proven that he can play the game and he plays hard."

CHICAGO WHITE SOX

PITCHING:

Joel Davis began last season as a pleasant surprise. Then he took a major league nosedive. The White Sox were very high on this young starter, and he opened the year pitching as though he believed in himself.

When the midseason point rolled around, however, Davis couldn't believe where he was headed. Davis was shuffled to Triple-A when it became apparent his control needed polish, but he didn't take the demotion happily. He was unimpressive in the minors and needs to refine his mental outlook if he hopes to make the team as the Number 5 starter.

Davis apparently worked on the mental aspects of his game in the off-season and on a change-up as well. He senses the need for an off-speed pitch, which could only improve his lively fastball and hard slider.

Pitching coach Dick Bosman and manager Jim Fregosi both went out of their way to give Davis a plug in spring training, because they realize the 6'5", 205-pounder may just be a proper attitude away from being a staff ace.

Davis was a mere 20 years old when he made his starting debut with the Sox in 1985, so patience would be a definite virtue with him. When he's on top of his game, his fastball and slider are brutal on righthanded batters. Adding a change-up to his arsenal will give him a boost against lefties, who pounded him last season.

JOEL DAVIS
RHP, No. 52
LR, 6'5", 205 lbs.
ML Svc: 1 year plus
Born: 1-30-65 in
Jacksonville, FL

1986 STATISTICS

W	L	ERA	G	GS	CG	SV	IP	H	R	ER	BB	SO
4	5	4.70	19	19	1	0	105.1	115	64	55	51	54

CAREER STATISTICS

W	L	ERA	G	GS	CG	SV	IP	H	R	ER	BB	SO
7	8	4.24	31	30	2	0	186.2	186	98	88	77	91

FIELDING:

Davis could use a little work on his fielding. His move to first base is particularly weak, which allowed runners to get big jumps off him.

OVERALL:

The White Sox are strong with starting pitching, but Davis just might force himself onto the staff. The big question with him is maturity, which is normal considering his age and rapid development. Davis feels he is a major league starter and he has the potential to develop in a good one before he's through.

Killebrew: "He started the season out very well and it looked as though he faltered after a while. There aren't too many starting pitchers younger than him and I think he'll develop into an outstanding prospect."

PITCHING:

Depending on who you believe, Jose DeLeon is either a diamond in the rough or a piece of fool's gold in the creek. He just may not be the highest quality diamond, but indications suggest that is the truer assessment.

Of course, that's exactly what the Pittsburgh Pirates were thinking before DeLeon had back-to-back records of 7-13 and 2-19 (yes, that's two-and-nineteen). With all of his ability, the word around the majors was that DeLeon was a great pitcher but was letting the Pirates' poor play get the best of him. He could never win with Pittsburgh, but watch out elsewhere.

The White Sox turned out to be the elsewhere and they got DeLeon for a good price: outfielder Bobby Bonilla in a straight-up swap. He arrived later in the season and made an immediate impact in the Sox' rotation. His 4-5 record was no gem, but a 2.96 ERA and flashes of dominance made him the club's best acquisition in quite a while.

DeLeon has the kind of arm most other pitchers dream of. His best pitch is the forkball and he throws it harder than anyone in baseball. It often is out of the strike zone, but hitters taking a rip at it will come up empty 90% of the time. His fastball augments his forkball and he can throw it at 90 MPH consistently.

DeLeon also has a good curveball and has worked on a slider in the off-season. His control is either on or off, usually on, but when it's not he gets into trouble. If he is struggling with the forkball, the rest of his game usually struggles as well.

FIELDING:

DeLeon needs some work on his fielding,

JOSE DeLEON
RHP, No. 26
RR, 6'3", 215 lbs.
ML Svc: 3 years
Born: 12-20-60 in
La Vega,
Dominican Republic

1986 STATISTICS

W	L	ERA	G	GS	CG	SV	IP	H	R	ER	BB	SO
5	8	3.87	22	14	1	1	95.1	66	46	41	59	79

CAREER STATISTICS

W	L	ERA	G	GS	CG	SV	IP	H	R	ER	BB	SO
21	43	3.87	98	82	10	4	558.1	426	261	240	287	499

but he showed a lot of improvement when he came over to the White Sox last year. His biggest problems are fielding bunts and covering first base.

OVERALL:

DeLeon is due for a big year. For some reason, he has never received offensive support--especially when he was with the Pirates--and the White Sox did little to change that trend. His attitude, specifically his confidence level, is a concern, but he has the talent to overcome anything.

Killebrew: "He seems to have been distracted at times, but he has the talent to be a big winner. Not many guys can throw the number of pitches he does as effectively. It still appears as though he has an awful lot going for him. He enters the 1987 season settled with the White Sox, and if he is ever to produce for a ballclub, now is the time."

CHICAGO WHITE SOX

PITCHING:

The big question on the subject of Rich Dotson isn't *Can he pitch?* It's *How's the shoulder?* An overdeveloped muscle in his throwing shoulder placed Dotson's career in jeopardy prior to the start of last season, but he made it through without missing a turn and now appears ready to return to the plateau he scaled in 1983, when he posted a sizzling record of 22-7.

Dotson was hardly in top form last season, as his 10-17 record and 5.48 ERA clearly indicates, he showed enough signs of his old self to be touted as the Sox' ace this year.

Dotson has had to abandon one of the best fastballs in baseball because of his injury, but he apparently has readjusted his thinking and changed his style completely. He has always been a great competitor, only now he will rely on a nasty curveball and newly-acquired slider to pick up wins.

Dotson appears to be completely recovered though, and has shown signs of bringing back the fastball. If he is able to put it all together, he just might exceed the lofty expectations the White Sox have already pinned on him.

Unlike the days of old, when he was one of the more challenging pitchers in baseball, Dotson has to rely on his new repertoire. When he gets in trouble, it's usually because his pitches sail away from him.

FIELDING:

Dotson has a deceptive move to first and is tough to run on despite his slow-paced delivery. He can field bunts but has trouble throwing to bases.

RICH DOTSON
RHP, No. 34
RR, 6'0", 204 lbs.
ML Svc: 8 years
Born: 1-10-59 in
Cincinnati, OH

1986 STATISTICS

W	L	ERA	G	GS	CG	SV	IP	H	R	ER	BB	SO
10	17	5.48	34	34	3	0	197	226	125	120	69	110

CAREER STATISTICS

W	L	ERA	G	GS	CG	SV	IP	H	R	ER	BB	SO
83	76	4.01	206	202	42	0	1295	1281	639	577	510	704

OVERALL:

Dotson's numbers were poor last year, but his uncommon shoulder injury was at first thought to be worse than the dreaded torn rotator cuff. He worked hard in the offseason to ensure another season like 1986 doesn't happen, and the White Sox are counting on his revival and leadership capabilities.

New pitching coach Dick Bosman is fully convinced that Dotson is ready to go, both physically and mentally.

Killebrew: "He has good command of everything he throws and he's never been afraid to challenge hitters.

"He's still trying to regain the form he had a couple years ago and I wouldn't be surprised if he did it. It's just a matter of whether or not his shoulder is healed and from what I've heard, he's completely recovered."

CHICAGO WHITE SOX

HITTING:

Carlton Fisk is still capable of providing the long ball and knocking in runs--but no longer on a daily basis. Extensive weight training has undoubtedly extended the 39-year-old veteran's career, but injuries and long stretches sitting on the bench took their toll on his offensive production in 1986.

Fisk played in only 125 games last season and his home run output fell from a career-high 37 in 1985 to 14. A rash of injuries, including a bruised wrist, a virus and a jammed thumb were responsible for keeping Fisk out of the lineup for a good chunk of the season, but he returns in good health this season.

Although he is nearing the end of a career that will merit Hall of Fame consideration, Fisk remains a strong line drive hitter who should play mainly against lefthanded pitchers this season. He can take a pitch down the middle and drive it with authority or take an outside pitch over the wall in right field.

An opposing pitcher's best bet would be to pitch Fisk on the inside half of the plate, although he won't hesitate to take first base compliments of the hit-by-pitch. A right-handed power pitcher with a rising fastball can get Fisk out.

BASERUNNING:

Fisk isn't going to challenge John Cangelosi for the team lead in stolen bases, but he rarely makes a mistake on the basepaths. As a former everyday catcher, Fisk learned baserunning techniques very well and hasn't forgotten them. Fisk did swipe two bases last season and may try to catch an opposing catcher off guard. He doesn't have the speed to beat out any infield grounders, but he still goes in hard at second when attempting to break up a double play.

FIELDING:

Much to his chagrin, Fisk was penciled in as

CARLTON FISK
C, No. 72
RR, 6'2", 235 lbs.
ML Svc: 16 years
Born: 12-26-47 in
Bellows Falls, VT

1986 STATISTICS

AVG	G	AB	R	H	2B	3B	HR	RBI	BB	SO	SB
.221	125	457	42	101	11	0	14	63	22	92	2

CAREER STATISTICS

AVG	G	AB	R	H	2B	3B	HR	RBI	BB	SO	SB
.271	1827	6521	1003	1767	316	42	281	977	619	1006	115

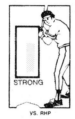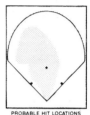

STRONG VS. RHP STRONG VS. LHP PROBABLE HIT LOCATIONS

the starting left fielder last year and, after 15 major league seasons as a catcher, wasn't able to adjust to the position. He will catch on a part-time basis this season and is excellent at handling young pitchers and blocking the plate. He has a good throwing arm.

OVERALL:

Fisk had trouble from the start last season. He strongly opposed being moved from behind the plate and got off badly both offensively and defensively. He missed 15 games with the virus and wasn't as strong physically for the rest of the season. The team desperately needs his bat in the lineup and it's up to Fisk to accept his new role as part-time player.

Killebrew: "It looks as though he got started on the wrong foot last year when he was playing in the outfield.

"He is still an excellent catcher and I suspect he'll catch a little and also play designated hitter."

CHICAGO WHITE SOX

HITTING:

Before the White Sox traded for Ozzie Guillen, they had a glaring need for an offensive threat in the top part of the batting order. They still do. Guillen's .250 batting average was cause for concern, but his most glaring shortcoming was his .265 on-base percentage. The fact that he led the Sox in games played (159) and at-bats (547) makes an improvement by Guillen even more important.

Guillen ripped up the league two seasons ago and was named the league's Rookie of the Year. His style of hitting was much the same as last year's, which goes to show that when you're a free swinger, sometimes you connect and sometimes you don't. He missed more last season as pitchers around the league fed him a steady diet of offspeed and breaking pitches.

To improve at the plate, Guillen, who started his pro career as a switch-hitter in the San Diego Padres chain, needs to be a bit more selective (he drew only 12 walks last season) and work on his concentration. When he puts the ball in play, it is usually line drives up the middle and he can take pitches on the outside part of the plate to left field.

He's coming off a subpar year, but still has plenty of potential at the plate. He didn't try to get on base by bunting quite as much in his sophomore season, but he is quite capable of doing it.

BASERUNNING:

Guillen is good at getting down the first-base line, but doesn't beat out many infield hits and is a good double play candidate because he hits the ball sharply. He has stolen only 15 bases in two seasons but has good speed and needs to learn how to avoid being picked off. He's a fun runner to watch and will often try to take an extra base.

OZZIE GUILLEN
SS, No. 13
LR, 5'11", 150 lbs.
ML Svc: 2 years
Born: 1-20-64 in
Oculare, Venezuela

1986 STATISTICS

AVG	G	AB	R	H	2B	3B	HR	RBI	BB	SO	SB
.250	159	547	58	137	19	4	2	47	12	52	8

CAREER STATISTICS

AVG	G	AB	R	H	2B	3B	HR	RBI	BB	SO	SB
.261	309	1038	129	271	40	13	3	80	24	88	15

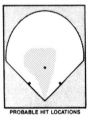

VS. RHP · VS. LHP · PROBABLE HIT LOCATIONS

FIELDING:

There aren't many shortstops in either league with better range than Guillen, but his 22 errors last season were way up from his club-record 13 in his rookie year. Guillen can go to his right or left to get a ball and is a strong double-play man. Throwing the ball on the run accounted for the bulk of his miscues.

OVERALL:

Guillen had an off year, but he still is a lock as the club's regular shortstop. Added concentration both offensively and defensively should help his game tremendously.

Killebrew: "He's going to get better as he plays more in the league. He's a lot of fun to watch and will probably be around for many, many years."

CHICAGO WHITE SOX

HITTING:

There are overachievers in major league baseball and then there is Jerry Hairston. The 13-year veteran has only turned in five complete seasons and is an afterthought defensively, but he still is an important contributor for the White Sox.

Although he played in only 11 games as an outfielder last season, Hairston was quite active in the role he has become quite skilled at filling: pinch-hitting. As a pinch-hitter, he finished sixth in the American League with a .304 average and has shown little signs of lost bat speed at age 35.

The switch-hitter is used primarily from the left side, where he is murder on pitches delivered up and over the plate. As a righthanded hitter he can take a high delivery straight away or hit a low, outside pitch to right field. He has better pop in his bat as a leftie.

Hairston has never been afraid to swing the bat, but was tough to strike out before last season. He is still a disciplined hitter who rarely is fooled by off-speed pitches. In addition, he has been around a while and doesn't fish for bad breaking balls.

He has never been a feared power hitter, but Hairston came through with five home runs last season in his limited role. When batting lefthanded, he is still strong enough to pull the right pitch out of the park.

BASERUNNING:

Hairston had good speed earlier in his career but hasn't been the same since suffering a knee injury when he ran into an outfield wall chasing down a fly ball in 1985. He is no stolen base threat and a single won't score him from second.

FIELDING:

Hairston has an adequate glove in the

JERRY HAIRSTON
PH/OF, No. 17
SR, 5'10", 190 lbs.
ML Svc: 11 years
Born: 2-16-52 in
Birmingham, AL

1986 STATISTICS

AVG	G	AB	R	H	2B	3B	HR	RBI	BB	SO	SB
.271	101	225	32	61	15	0	5	26	26	26	0

CAREER STATISTICS

AVG	G	AB	R	H	2B	3B	HR	RBI	BB	SO	SB
.260	788	1568	202	408	83	6	25	185	257	215	4

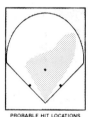

VS. RHP   VS. LHP   PROBABLE HIT LOCATIONS

outfield but his limited defensive play has taken a toll on his arm. His mobility is below-average.

OVERALL:

Hairston has "American League" written all over him. That would be bad news if Hairston was playing in the NL, but his current employer is quite aware of his value both as a pinch-hitter and designated hitter.

Killebrew: "He's an excellent pinch-hitter who gets the most out of his ability. He does a good job in the position he's put in and is a very tough out. Jerry is a knowledgable veteran and not ready to call it quits yet."

CHICAGO WHITE SOX

HITTING:

The White Sox weren't too thrilled with Ron Hassey's physical condition when a trade with the New York Yankees brought him over midway through last season. They had no complaints with his hitting, however.

A knee injury hampered Hassey's ability behind the plate, but he was a terror when standing beside it. Hassey hit a sizzling .353 in 49 games with the Sox while playing almost exclusively as a designated hitter.

Although he combined for only nine home runs last year with the Yankees and White Sox, Hassey has good power as a straight pull hitter. He is most effective hitting fastballs up and over the plate.

Pitchers have had the most success getting Hassey out on the straight change-up. He can also be set up with hard inside pitches followed by a curveball low and to the outside part of the plate.

Hassey has been around the game for a while and has become a disciplined hitter with a sharp eye at the plate. He should be a fixture in the lineup against righthanded mound opponents.

BASERUNNING:

When Hassey gets on base with the game on the line, look for a pinch-runner to replace him.

His speed has always been a detriment and is even worse following offseason arthroscopic knee surgery.

FIELDING:

Hassey successfully rehabilitated his knee following surgery, but it is very doubtful that he'll ever be 100% healthy for the rest of his career.

Ideally, the White Sox would like Hassey to

RON HASSEY
C, No. 25
LR, 6'2", 195 lbs.
ML Svc: 9 years
Born: 2-27-53 in
Tucson, AZ

1986 STATISTICS

AVG	G	AB	R	H	2B	3B	HR	RBI	BB	SO	SB
.323	113	341	45	110	25	1	9	49	46	27	1

CAREER STATISTICS

AVG	G	AB	R	H	2B	3B	HR	RBI	BB	SO	SB
.282	793	2331	249	658	121	7	50	322	274	235	10

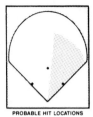

VS. RHP   VS. LHP   PROBABLE HIT LOCATIONS

catch 50 games this season and let Ron Karkovice and Carlton Fisk split the rest of the load. Hassey possesses an adequate throwing arm and calls a solid game.

OVERALL:

Hassey, much like Carlton Fisk, will be counted on for his offensive contributions this year on a team lacking in punch at the plate. He silenced critics quickly in 1986 with his quality hitting. Anything Hassey delivers as a catcher will be a bonus.

Killebrew: "As far as his catching goes, Hassey's reaction to his knee surgery will play a large part in how well he does this year.

"I really like him as a hitter. His success with the White Sox last year doesn't surprise me. He got the most out of a few at-bats."

CHICAGO WHITE SOX

HITTING:

Two years ago, according to popular thought, it was Donnie Hill's bat that stood between him and everyday play at the major league level. Hill has hushed such talk with a two-year average (.284) that ranked 20th among American League players after the '86 season.

Now people wonder about Hill's defensive shortcomings. Tony Phillips, who is a better all-around athlete, easily regained the second base job last spring, sending Hill to the bench despite his big year in 1985.

A switch-hitter, Hill is good from both sides. He hit .289 from the left and .275 from the right in 1986. He hadn't fared well as a righty in 1985, but improved by being more selective and spraying the ball more often.

Not uncommonly, this switch-hitter has two distinct styles. Hill is a low-ball hitter from the left and a high-ball hitter from the right. He drives the ball more often from the left side, but is not punchless from the right (eight doubles each way in '86). He feasts on pitches over the plate, so opponents often give him breaking balls away and then bust him inside with the fastball. Hill has developed a pretty good eye and is very good at the little game (bunting and executing the hit-and-run).

BASERUNNING:

Hill carried too much body weight last season, so his speed fell deeper into the medium range. He hustles on the basepaths, but rarely is able to take an extra base or steal.

FIELDING:

Hill lacks range, particularly toward the middle of the field. He compensated admirably in 1985, regularly diving to stop balls headed to the outfield. Last year, however, he played as if he didn't want to get his uniform dirty--it was rare to see him dive. He has become a sure-handed fielder.

Originally a shortstop, his arm is much

DONNIE HILL
2B, No. 15
SR, 5'10", 160 lbs.
ML Svc: 4 years
Born: 11-12-60 in
Pomona, CA

1986 STATISTICS

AVG	G	AB	R	H	2B	3B	HR	RBI	BB	SO	SB
.283	108	339	37	96	16	2	4	29	23	38	5

CAREER STATISTICS

AVG	G	AB	R	H	2B	3B	HR	RBI	BB	SO	SB
.273	357	1064	123	290	42	4	11	108	55	104	16

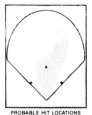

VS. RHP   VS. LHP   PROBABLE HIT LOCATIONS

stronger than most second basemen. He also played some third base last season and, after becoming acclimated, proved himself adequate.

OVERALL:

Hill welcomed the trade from Oakland because he had no chance of playing every day there. The White Sox see Hill as their regular second baseman, but if it doesn't work out for one reason or another, Hill must adjust his thinking. He was unhappy as a non-starter in Oakland, but his versatility and his uncanny knack of performing cold would ensure him 300-400 at-bats a year for many years.

Killebrew: "He's a good guy to have on a club because he can play more than one position and he comes off the bench so well. Also, being as good a switch-hitter as he is, that's a real plus. I like Donnie Hill a lot."

CHICAGO WHITE SOX

HITTING:

Tim Hulett proved he could deliver the long ball in 1986. Unfortunately, he has trouble hitting singles and doubles.

As the regular third baseman, Hulett will be expected to do more at the plate than he did last season. The White Sox aren't expecting him to hit .300, but they are hoping for something a little better than last year's .231 clip.

Hulett doesn't get cheated when it's his turn to bat and as a result, he is a frequent strikeout victim. He'll handle fastballs up and in, but has trouble with the breaking ball and off speed pitches, especially against righthanders.

The majority of Hulett's 17 home runs last season came on deliveries he was either able to pull or hit straight away. If he sees something he likes on the first pitch, he won't hesitate to take the bat off his shoulder.

BASERUNNING:

Hulett has decent speed but isn't a base-stealing threat. Fundamentally, he is a sound baserunner and effective at breaking up the double play.

FIELDING:

Hulett was expected to replace Julio Cruz as the starting second baseman, his natural position, but will hold down third base. His arm is strong enough to make the long throw from third, but he needs more time to adjust to the position. In splitting close to equal time at both positions last season, Hulett committed only four errors at second while making 11 at third.

He has shown the ability to keep the ball from getting down the line but needs more

TIM HULETT
INF, No. 32
RR, 6'0", 185 lbs.
ML Svc: 2 years
Born: 1-12-60 in
Springfield, IL

1986 STATISTICS

AVG	G	AB	R	H	2B	3B	HR	RBI	BB	SO	SB
.231	150	520	53	120	16	5	17	44	21	91	4

CAREER STATISTICS

AVG	G	AB	R	H	2B	3B	HR	RBI	BB	SO	SB
.245	305	927	106	227	35	9	22	81	52	176	11

STRONG

VS. RHP

STRONG

VS. LHP

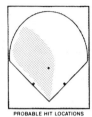

PROBABLE HIT LOCATIONS

work going to his left.

OVERALL:

Hulett emulated many power hitters last season by seemingly either hitting the ball a long way or striking out. He is still a young player and is expected to be a key contributer to the White Sox' future.

Hulett broke into the major leagues in 1985 with the reputation as a skilled defensive player, but has been affected by the switch from second to third base. Given time, his play in the field should improve markedly.

Killebrew: "He's got some pop in his bat for being a little guy. He's played different positions, but he's a solid defensive player and a key to the White Sox' future."

90+ FASTBALL

PITCHING:

Big Bob James will turn some heads this season. He's still got the beard, but much of his excess avoirdupois is missing. This is a critical year for the righthanded flame-thrower. He is coming off a knee injury that sidelined him for the second half of last season and figured the best way to get ready in the off-season was with exercise. And a better diet.

James entered training camp this season at 230 pounds, big by most standards, but 25 pounds lighter than his playing weight last season. His fastball hasn't lost anything though, and he can still let it fly at close to 95 MPH.

James doesn't expect to just walk back into his role as the club's stopper, but he is aiming to eventually return to his 1985 form, when he set a White Sox record with 32 saves. He will go with the same style: mainly fastballs with an occasional curveball. James has an excellent curve which prevents hitters from sitting back and waiting for the heat. However, he had some control problems with it last year, when he just never seemed to put it all together prior to the injury.

If he is able to recover from last season's knee injury, and all indications are that he already has, James will return to the intimidating style he became known for. He will move the ball all around and back any hitter off the plate.

FIELDING:

Even at his previous weight, James was a very good fielder for a player of his (former)

BOB JAMES
RHP, No. 43
RR, 6'4", 230 lbs.
ML Svc: 6 years
Born: 8-15- 58 in
Glendale, CA

1986 STATISTICS

W	L	ERA	G	GS	CG	SV	IP	H	R	ER	BB	SO
5	4	5.25	49	0	0	14	58.1	61	36	34	23	32

CAREER STATISTICS

W	L	ERA	G	GS	CG	SV	IP	H	R	ER	BB	SO
20	20	3.67	236	2	0	63	353.1	323	162	144	140	306

size and he got to the bag surprisingly quickly. His pickoff move to first is adequate at best and runners have been able to get good leads on him.

OVERALL:

James is a key member on this team, but has missed playing time in each of the last two seasons with injuries. He knows his career is starting to advance and worked unbelievably hard in the off-season to get himself into the best condition in years.

Should he come back successfully, the White Sox would have one of the better bullpens in the American League.

Killebrew: "He really wants to get back to the mound after missing so much of last season. If he's in shape and recovered from the knee injury, I really think he could become the dominant pitcher he once was.

"He is a tremendous competitor who wants the ball with the game on the line. His return would really give the White Sox a boost."

CHICAGO WHITE SOX

PITCHING:

Joel McKeon made the trip north following spring training in 1986, but his destination was Triple-A Buffalo rather than Comiskey Park. His stay in the minors was a short one though, and if his performance on the big league level was any indication, McKeon is here to stay.

McKeon fills a position vital to a team with pennant aspirations. He is the White Sox' lefthanded stopper and he did an outstanding job, going 3-1 with an ERA of 2.45. McKeon only picked up one save in 30 appearances, but was often called on only to retire a lefthanded batter.

McKeon's control needs some work, but he is an impressive looking power pitcher with a tough forkball to go along with a fastball clocked in the high 80s. He can throw either pitch for strikes. Against lefthanded batters, he keeps the ball low and tight and is very tough to hit. He has a quick delivery and makes it hard for the batter to pick up the ball early.

The big pitch McKeon has to gain confidence in is the curveball. He's got to be able to throw it for strikes, especially against righthanders. He is still a young pitcher with a solid arm and has worked hard to improve on that pitch.

FIELDING:

McKeon is very mobile off the mound and rarely is charged with an error. Despite his inexperience, he showed the ability to field the ball and get the ball away.

JOEL McKEON
LHP, No. 50
LL, 6'0", 185 lbs.
ML Svc: 1 year
Born: 2-25-63 in Covington, KY

1986 STATISTICS

W	L	ERA	G	GS	CG	SV	IP	H	R	ER	BB	SO
3	1	2.45	30	0	0	1	33	18	10	9	17	18

CAREER STATISTICS

W	L	ERA	G	GS	CG	SV	IP	H	R	ER	BB	SO
3	1	2.45	30	0	0	1	33	18	10	9	17	18

He has one of the better pickoff moves on the staff and because he gets the ball to the plate quickly, he's hard to steal against.

OVERALL:

Not too many baseball people outside of the White Sox know much about McKeon, probably because he came upon the scene quickly and unannounced. The club would be happy if McKeon turned in the same kind of season he did last year as a rookie. If he develops the curveball, his future is very bright.

Killebrew: "He's a good looking pitcher and gives the White Sox a reliable lefthander coming out of the bullpen. That's a tough role to fill, but he did an outstanding job for them last season."

CHICAGO WHITE SOX

HITTING:

Reid Nichols is somewhat like a second car. He doesn't get much use and that reflects on his performance. After six full seasons in the majors, Reid Nichols has failed to better his reputation as a steady utility player.

The biggest lag in Nichols' game is his hitting. When the White Sox acquired him in a trade for Tim Lollar late in 1985, he surprised everbody by hitting .297 in 51 games. A closer look reveals that Nichols played almost daily then, but he didn't last season and his average plummeted to .228 in a very limited role.

Unless he's an extremely late bloomer, Nichols won't get a shot at playing regularly, which will continue to take its toll on his offensive productivity. He has very little power and struggles against righthanded power pitchers. Breaking balls on the outside part of the plate also give him trouble.

Nichols is best as a singles hitter. He has a short stroke and is able to punch the ball up the middle. He doesn't bunt as much as he did earlier in his career (playing time has a lot to do with that), but he can lay the ball down and has the speed to beat the throw to first base.

BASERUNNING:

Nichols is good on the bases. Although he once swiped 66 bases in the minors, his effectiveness as a basestealer has tailed off considerably. He is muscle-pull prone, which doesn't help. When he is on base, Nichols plays it smart and rarely makes a mistake.

FIELDING:

Nichols has proven he can hit major league

REID NICHOLS
OF, No. 20
RR, 5'11", 172 lbs.
ML Svc: 6 years
Born: 8-5-58 in
Ocala, FL

1986 STATISTICS

AVG	G	AB	R	H	2B	3B	HR	RBI	BB	SO	SB
.228	74	136	9	31	4	0	2	18	11	23	5

CAREER STATISTICS

AVG	G	AB	R	H	2B	3B	HR	RBI	BB	SO	SB
.266	463	1013	134	269	55	6	18	111	85	136	25

pitching, but it's his fielding which earns the bulk of his pay. He can capably fill all three outfield positions and has consistently turned in high fielding percentages. He is fast enough to run down balls in center field and has a good enough arm to throw from any field. He hasn't played shortstop lately, but has a good glove and could fill in there as well.

OVERALL:

He is not thrilled with the way he is used, but he has a good attitude, likes the game and does the best he can.

Killebrew: "He is a good student of the game and is always hustling. He's quick in the outfield with a good, accurate arm. He does an excellent job with the way he is used."

PITCHING:

The biggest mistake of Bobby Thigpen's career just may prove to be last season's phenomenal success. How's that? It's like this. By making the jump from Double-A to the White Sox, Thigpen set a standard which will be difficult to match.

With normal righthanded ace Bob James out for most of the second-half last season with a sore arm, Thigpen quietly stepped in and posted a 2-0 record, 1.77 ERA and seven saves.

Prior to his sudden call to the big leagues last year, Thigpen was toiling away in the minors, where both is record and ERA were unimpressive. He worked as a starter in the minor leagues though he knew he was better suited for the bullpen.

Thigpen was able to make an impact with a big fastball that comes in at the knees. He also throws a cut fastball which looks a lot like a slider. He can throw consistently at 90 MPH, and when he improves mechanically, look for that heater to kick up to the 95 MPH range.

Thigpen is very tough on righthanded hitters and since he is able to keep the fastball and slider down, he keeps the baseball in the park. Though tall and lanky, he pitches with impressive control.

The most surprising thing about Thigpen's 1986 performance was his composure. He showed the ability to come into pressurized situations and retire the side.

Thigpen needs some work on his curveball to keep hitters off balance, but his delivery is effective and makes it hard for the batters to measure him.

BOBBY THIGPEN
RHP, No. 58
RR, 6'3", 195 lbs.
ML Svc: less than one year
Born: 7-17-63 in
La Grange, IL

1986 STATISTICS

W	L	ERA	G	GS	CG	SV	IP	H	R	ER	BB	SO
2	0	1.77	20	0	0	7	35.2	26	7	7	12	20

CAREER STATISTICS

W	L	ERA	G	GS	CG	SV	IP	H	R	ER	BB	SO
2	0	1.77	20	0	0	7	35.2	26	7	7	12	20

FIELDING:

Thigpen was flawless in the field during his first major league season. He is very good on the double play and has a good move to first base.

OVERALL:

If Bob James continues to struggle with arm injuries, Thigpen is slated to become the Sox' big gun out of the bullpen. If James is able to return to his form of old, Thigpen will help ease the workload.

The White Sox have their fingers crossed that last year was no fluke. He still qualifies as a rookie and is a strong candidate to be the best in the American League.

Killebrew: "He really came from out of nowhere last season. If Bob James comes back healthy, the White Sox will be surprisingly strong in the bullpen."

CHICAGO WHITE SOX

HITTING:

Greg Walker didn't get too many hands last season. He was too busy waiting for his own hand to heal. After missing a month early in the year with an injured wrist, Walker came back and hit the ball with more power than ever in his career, but he broke his right hand in on Aug. 3 and missed the rest of the season.

Walker racked up 13 home runs and 51 RBI in only 78 games as he began shoring up a perennial weakness by hitting lefthanders consistently and with power.

Walker had a long time to rehabilitate his injury and will again hit in the cleanup spot, where he began to feel comfortable last season.

His style of being a low fastball, first-ball hitter shouldn't change. Opposing pitchers will also remember to use every pitch in their repetoire when facing Walker.

Walker has the ability to hit both fastballs and breaking pitches straightaway. If pitched low, he take the ball out of the park or to either the right-center or left-center gaps.

Lefthanders still have the most success against Walker, who has trouble with breaking balls up and inside.

Walker is one of the smartest hitters in the game and the team's best hitter in clutch situations. He was originally hesitant to fill the role of cleanup hitter but has shown the ability to provide the long ball and drive in runs on a consistent basis.

BASERUNNING:

Walker never gets picked off base because he rarely tries to steal. Fundamentally, he is a solid baserunner.

FIELDING:

Walker's fielding has steadily improved and

GREG WALKER
1B, No. 29
LR, 6'3", 198 lbs.
ML Svc: 5 years
Born: 10-6-59 in
Douglas, GA

1986 STATISTICS

AVG	G	AB	R	H	2B	3B	HR	RBI	BB	SO	SB
.277	78	282	37	78	10	6	13	51	29	44	1

CAREER STATISTICS

AVG	G	AB	R	H	2B	3B	HR	RBI	BB	SO	SB
.275	506	1649	211	453	95	16	73	280	138	270	16

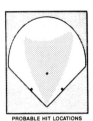

VS. RHP   VS. LHP   PROBABLE HIT LOCATIONS

last season's injury to his glove hand shouldn't hamper his progress. He is much better at flagging down balls hit to his left, but has a good glove overall.

OVERALL:

The loss of Walker for most of the season and the Sox' fifth-place finish were not a coincidence. Before being shelved for the year with a broken hand, Walker was headed for the best season of his career. If he is able to pick up where he left off last August, Walker will develop into one of the better players in the game.

Killebrew: "With the ability he has, he'll bounce right back. He's an outstanding hitter with very good form. I expect him to have a good year."

CHICAGO WHITE SOX

STEVE CARLTON
LHP, No. 32
LL, 6'5", 210 lbs.
ML Svc: 22 years
Born: 12-22-44 in
Miami, FL

PITCHING, FIELDING:

Steve Carlton, an old-timer himself, took a tip from a former colleague and is ready to put voluntary retirement on hold once again last year. Lefty started the 1986 season with the Philadelphia Phillies, was asked to leave, went to the San Francisco Giants, was asked to leave, and finished the year with the Chicago White Sox, who didn't ask him to return in 1987.

But over the course of his brief stint with the Sox, Hall of Famer Don Drysdale, a broadcaster for the team, picked up a flaw in Carlton's one-time flawless delivery and shared his discovery. Drysdale noticed that Carlton's follow-through was much more open than it ever had been, an adjustment was made, and Carlton is raring to start his 22nd major league season.

He was a combined 9-14 in '86, laughable by old Carlton standards, but he finished up the year strong enough to convince him to postpone retirement. Retirement is a notion this pitcher is not fond of.

Carlton's nasty slider is more a memory now, but his control is still there and his adjustment on his follow-through to the plate might put the Hall of Fame on hold a while longer.

Carlton's fielding has always been outstanding and is unlikely to change. He has an exceptional pickoff move.

OVERALL:

Carlton obviously doesn't want to quit the game. Maybe he knows something we don't.

Killebrew: "He's a guy who's always in excellent condition and he still has the capability and knowledge to be a winner. He doesn't have the great stuff anymore, but he knows how to pitch, of course."

BOB GIBSON
RHP, No. 40
RR, 6'0", 195 lbs.
ML Svc: 3 years
Born: 6-19-57 in
Philadelphia, PA

Only a couple of years ago, Bob Gibson was considered one of the Milwaukee Brewer's top pitching prospects. That didn't last long, however. When a new crop of strong young arms developed in the Brewers' farm system, Gibson's status slipped and he was left unprotected for the winter draft. The White Sox grabbed him.

Gibson's fastball used to be above average, but it has lost a little in the last few seasons.

His slider and curveball are just average and he lacks and effective change-up. He will rely on the fastball when he gets in trouble.

A lack of control has always been a problem for Gibson. He has a tendency to walk the first hitter he faces, which is the fastest way for a relief pitcher to get the hook.

An average fielder, Gibson has a quick move to first base, but doesn't throw over much. His delivery leaves him in a good position to field balls back to the mound.

OVERALL:

Although he has been used in most roles, Gibson is best suited as a long reliever. He also could be an effective spot starter, but he walks too many hitters to be successful in short relief.

CHICAGO WHITE SOX

RON KARKOVICE
C, No. 53
RR, 6'1", 215 lbs.
ML Svc: 1 year
Born: 8-8-63 in
Union, NJ

HITTING, BASERUNNING, FIELDING:

If Ron Karkovice was judged solely on his ability to hit major league pitching, odds are he'd still be in the minor leagues.

He's a big time player defensively, but the Sox are looking for him to come around at the plate if Karkovice is indeed to become their regular catcher for the next decade and beyond.

When he got his shot at the major leagues late last season, Karkovice struggled at the plate. He can take a pitch up and over the strike zone and pull it out of any park, but most pitchers opted for the inside slider and outside breaking ball, which often resulted in an easy out.

By shortening his stroke and becoming more selective at the plate, Karkovice would cut down his high strikeout ratio.

Karkovice is big and, as a catcher, isn't expected to be much of a threat on the basepaths. However, he has surprising speed and has been timed in 4.1 seconds to first base. Karkovice demonstrated outstanding defensive ability, particularly at throwing out attempting basestealers. He's not afraid to block the plate, but needs to cut down on passed balls. Batters who bunt the ball anywhere near him don't have a chance.

OVERALL:

Karkovice would probably still be in the minors if he were employed by most other teams. But the White Sox are thin at catcher and Karkovice needs to gain to gain confidence before being a good everyday player. He's got the arm and could develop into a good power hitter.

BRYAN LITTLE
INF, No. 47
SR, 5'10", 160 lbs.
ML Svc: 5 years
Born: 10-8-59 in
Houston, TX

HITTING, BASERUNNING, FIELDING:

Bryan Little was the Montreal Expos' starting shortstop in 1983. Now it's time for him to prove he can play in the American League.

Little, a switch-hitter with more skill from the left side, is coming off a season spent mostly in Class AAA with both the Yankees and Chicago White Sox. He only went to the plate 76 times in 1986 and if he's hoping for a longer stay, he'll have to fine-tune his bunting skills. He led the NL with 24 bunt hits while playing with the '83 Expos.

Little is a versatile infielder and can play second, shortstop and third. He was used exclusively at second base last season and is an excellent fielder with good range to either side. Little has a strong arm and is able to adjust his throws easily from any of the three positions. He has no trouble turning double plays. Little hasn't been a basestealing threat since the minor leagues but he is a smart runner.

OVERALL:

Killebrew: "He's a patient hitter and he knows the strike zone very well. He's versatile as an infielder and that makes him valuable in today's game."

CHICAGO WHITE SOX

STEVE LYONS
CF, No. 10
LR, 6'3", 192 lbs.
ML Svc: 2 years
Born: 6-3-60 in
Tacoma, WA

HITTING, BASERUNNING, FIELDING:

Steve Lyons came over in a trade from the Boston Red Sox with the reputation of being one of baseball's more flakier flakes who still wasn't able to hide the fact that he needs grooming at the plate.

A big player with an aggressive swing at the plate, Lyons can drive the hard stuff straight away but he needs to improve his stroke when the pitch is either breaking, off-speed or both. He showed some power earlier in his career but has become more of a gap hitter in the majors.

Lyons has good speed on the bases and can beat out a bunt to first. He'll steal a base on aggressiveness alone but will also get picked off for the same reason.

Defensively, Lyons is versatile. He can play all three outfield positions and has a good arm. Surprisingly, he got a look on the pitchers mound in the minor leagues. He can also play third base and shortstop.

OVERALL:

The White Sox were more interested in Lyons' glove when they acquired him from Boston last season. He has the potential to become a decent hitter, but is more effective as a late-inning defensive replacement.

Killebrew: "He's a good aggressive player who can help out in a lot of ways. You can put him in any outfield position and he'll get the job done. He's got some power and is able to deliver in any situation."

RUSS MORMAN
1B, No. 14
RR, 6'4", 215 lbs.
ML Svc: less than one year
Born: 4-28-62 in
Independence, MO

HITTING, BASERUNNING, FIELDING:

When regular first baseman Greg Walker was sidelined once and then twice last season, Russ Morman made the most of the opportunity. A young player with limited minor league experience, Morman stepped into the pressurized situation and rarely stumbled.

He is a classic power hitter who takes a big cut and looks for the fastball down the middle. He can pull the ball deep or hit with power straight away. As a righthanded hitting first baseman, Morman will give the White Sox the luxury of resting Greg Walker against overpowering lefthanded pitchers.

Despite his size, Morman is a very nimble baserunner. He won't break any records, but he can steal a base and is good in hit-and-run situations.

He is being projected as a future long ball hitter, but Morman has already arrived defensively. He has very soft hands at first base and could play the outfield and even third base in a pinch. Morman was guilty of only four errors in 372 chances at first last season and is very good at charging bunts and getting the ball to second on double plays.

OVERALL:

Morman was a prolific power hitter both in college (he led the NCAA with 105 RBIs at Wichita State in 1983) and the minor leagues. He got an early jump on the majors, but handled himself quite capably.

Killebrew: "It's easy to see that he's got the potential to be a very good power hitter in the major leagues. As he gets more playing time, he should only get better."

CHICAGO WHITE SOX

**JERRY ROYSTER
INF, No. 3
RR, 6'0", 165 lbs.
ML Svc: 11 years
Born: 10-18-52 in
Sacramento, CA**

HITTING, BASERUNNING, FIELDING:

His skills may have diminished somewhat, but Jerry Royster remains one of the more versatile players in the game. He can play at second or third base, shortstop or at any outfield position.

Royster probably was not used properly in San Diego, for he was seldom given a chance to show off his good speed. He is still capable of occasionally stealing a base and creating confusion on the basepaths and can beat out a bunt for a single. Royster also has surprising pop in his bat and can hit the home run ball.

He has a strong, strong throwing arm, but is subject to bouts of inconsistency. His glove seems to come and go, but he held his own last year despite being shuffled through the Padres' different position openings. He comes to the park ready to play and can be used in pinch-running situations.

OVERALL:

Royster is not a clutch hitter and not a pinch-hitter: it reduces his value somewhat because the market today is more geared to young and inexpensive backup talent. He is an upbeat player who is fundamentally sound.

Dierker: "Royster probably needs to hit for a higher average or walk more often to be effective offensively. He would fit into a backup role but he is not capable of starting at the major league level anymore."

CLEVELAND INDIANS

HITTING:

This may sound strange, but Andy Allanson's biggest problem at the plate is that he's 6'5"and weighs 215 pounds. Power hitter, right? Wrong.

The righthanded hitting Allanson is a spray hitter who goes to the opposite field extremely well. He did that just fine in his first 20 games with the Tribe after winning the No. 1 catcher's job in spring training last year as a rookie out of Double-A.

Then, however, this hefty rookie catcher started to hear the snickers: *How could a guy that big not hit home runs?* He took the snickers to heart.

After hitting .381 in his first 20 games, Allanson attempted to hit whatever home runs might be buried inside of him and tried to pull everything to left field. His average dropped like a stone in a well. The result was one home run June 23--in the Kingdome. Nothing after that.

The Seattle send-out is the only home run Allanson has hit in 1,163 professional at-bats. In the last 70 games of the season, he only hit .190 and lost his job to Chris Bando.

To compound the problem, Allanson went into a deep mental funk. For the second half of the season the intense young catcher didn't try to correct his mistakes. He simply didn't work in practice, choosing to sulk instead.

When he's in the groove, Allanson has good bat control. He beat out three bunt hits and had 11 sacrifice bunts last year.

BASERUNNING:

For a big man, Allanson can run well. He stole 10 bases in 1986 and was only thrown out once. That was the most steals by a Tribe catcher since 1937.

He is a good at taking a walking lead, lulling the pitcher to sleep and then breaking for second. Allanson is constantly looking to take the extra base and is good on the hit-and-run. Last year he hit seven doubles.

FIELDING:

Allanson made the Indians' big league roster last year because of his defense and ability to call a game. The Indians especially

ANDY ALLANSON
C, No. 6
RR, 6'5", 215 lbs.
ML Svc: 1 year
Born: 12-22-61 in Richmond, VA

1986 STATISTICS

AVG	G	AB	R	H	2B	3B	HR	RBI	BB	SO	SB
.225	101	293	30	66	7	3	1	29	14	36	10

CAREER STATISTICS

AVG	G	AB	R	H	2B	3B	HR	RBI	BB	SO	SB
.225	101	293	30	66	7	3	1	29	14	36	10

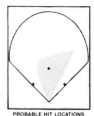

STRONG — VS. RHP STRONG — VS. LHP PROBABLE HIT LOCATIONS

liked the way he handled pitchers.

He has a rocket for an arm, but hasn't learned how to use it. Last year teams ran wild on him as 64 of 81 base runners successfully stole against him (a 21% kill ratio). While trying to throw those runners out, Allanson committed 15 of his 20 errors (those 20 errors were the most commited by a catcher in the majors last year).

The Indians didn't help his progress any by signing knuckleball pitchers Phil Niekro and Tom Candiotti. Allanson simply wasn't ready to catch them.

OVERALL:

The errors and his problems at the plate all collapsed on Allanson by midseason last year. Emotional and hot-headed behind the plate, the rookie seemed to run out of gas after the All-Star break.

Kaat: "Allanson is a better hitter when he sprays the ball around. But it wouldn't surprise me to see him start hitting more home runs now that he's been in the big leagues for a year. He's a good catcher with a good arm and I look for him to improve this season."

CLEVELAND INDIANS

PITCHING:

Last year Scott Bailes was a rookie pitcher who was squeezed and re-squeezed until there was nothing left in his left arm.

At the end of the 1985 Double-A season, the Indians invited him to their Instructional League camp in Florida. From there he went to winter ball and then to spring training with the big league club.

Bailes made the Indians out of spring training, but was not supposed to be a big factor on the club. Then Jamie Easterly went down with an ailing shoulder and neck and Bailes became the primary lefty out of the bullpen. Primary, *indeed*.

Bailes, a fastball/slider pitcher, made 51 relief appearances to go 9-7 with a 4.68 ERA and seven saves. From there, the Indians put him in the starting rotation, where he went 2-3 with a 5.26 ERA in 10 starts.

Somewhere in between, he came down with ulcers (caused by taking too many aspirins between appearances) and then, finally, his arm went *kaput!* The Indians didn't use him in the last two weeks of the season because Bailes couldn't lift his left arm anymore.

Plain and simple, Bailes burned out.

The Indians are split on how to use Bailes. Part of the front office feels he's better as a starter because he gets more rest, his slider is sharper and he can use his change-up. Others believe that he is more useful in the bullpen, where he can offer some relief to stopper Ernie Camacho in certain situations.

As a reliever, though, Bailes relies strictly on his fastball and slider. His fastball usually travels between 87-88 MPH, which is not overwhelming for a late-inning pitcher. Bailes also had major problems retiring the first hitter he faced and pitching with runners on base. Gradually, however, last year the rookie became more adept in key situations, though he never quite mastered the nuances of lefty vs. lefty matchups late in the game.

**SCOTT BAILES
LHP, No. 43
LL, 6'2", 175 lbs.
ML Svc: 1 year
Born: 12-18-61 in
Chillicothe, OH**

1986 STATISTICS

W	L	ERA	G	GS	CG	SV	IP	H	R	ER	BB	SO
10	10	4.95	62	10	0	7	112.2	123	70	62	43	60

CAREER STATISTICS

W	L	ERA	G	GS	CG	SV	IP	H	R	ER	BB	SO
10	10	4.95	62	10	0	7	112.2	123	70	62	43	60

FIELDING:

Bailes has a decent pickoff move to first-- that's good because he uses a big overhand delivery that gives runners a jump.

He is a good fielder but does have some problems on bunt plays. He covers first base well and is yet another Indian pitcher who got plenty of practice backing up third base and home plate.

OVERALL:

Bailes seems better suited as a starter than a reliever. He was 7-for-23 in save situations last year, and even for a rookie with a bad case of the shakes that's not a good record. As a starter, the somewhat frail Bailes could work with more rest and use a wider range of pitches.

Kaat: "It would help Bailes if the Indians indicated his role at the start of the season. He should be a quality starter for them and if they get in a jam, they know he's had success in the bullpen. But he should have the advantage of knowing what his primary role on the staff will be right from Day One."

CLEVELAND INDIANS

HITTING:

After his hitting ability virtually disappeared in 1985, this switch-hitting catcher saw his plate skills re-surface last year and he proved he could at least still put the bat on the baseball.

Bando hit .139 in 1985 and his future in the big leagues was very much in doubt. Last year he finished at .268 and even hit two home runs after suffering through the entire 1985 season without going deep once.

Like most switch-hitters, Bando is a high-ball hitter from the right side of the plate and a low-ball hitter from the left side. Although he played in only 92 games in 1986, he was able to maintain his patience at the plate (no small feat for a man whose big league life was on the line) and showed that he still knows the strike zone.

There are occasions, however, when he tends to take too many pitches. But overall, last year Bando appeared much more aggressive at the plate--much like the Bando of 1984 who hit .291 with 12 homers and 41 RBIs.

Hitting coach Bobby Bonds said Bando's re-emergence was due to an improved approach to the ball. Bonds said Bando was off-balance while striding into the pitch in 1985.

Bando felt his comeback in 1986 was in large part due to confidence in his ability to rebound. He hit the ball hard early and kept doing it the rest of the season.

Last year Bando also demonstrated good bat control. He was frequently called on to advance runners with sacrifice bunts and almost always came through.

BASERUNNING:

Bando is not a baserunning threat. Plain and simple, he's slow. He sometimes gets carried away, trying to stretch a single into a double, but in most cases he runs within his ability. He'll slide hard into second base to break up a double play.

FIELDING:

At 31, defense has become Bando's ticket in the big leagues.

CHRIS BANDO
C, No. 23
SR, 6'0", 195 lbs.
ML Svc: 5 years
Born: 2-4-56 in
**   Cleveland, OH**

1986 STATISTICS

AVG	G	AB	R	H	2B	3B	HR	RBI	BB	SO	SB
.268	92	254	28	68	9	0	2	26	22	49	0

CAREER STATISTICS

AVG	G	AB	R	H	2B	3B	HR	RBI	BB	SO	SB
.236	375	999	108	236	36	2	21	117	118	156	1

VS. RHP

VS. LHP

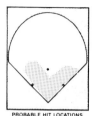

PROBABLE HIT LOCATIONS

He showed soft hands and good agility while chasing the knuckler last year. He also called a good game behind the plate--especially while working with the veteran's veteran, Phil Niekro.

Bando's arm is average, but he has a quick sidearm release. Still, he is not good at throwing out basestealers; last year his kill ratio was just 26%.

OVERALL:

The Indians seem intent on sticking with Allanson as their No. 1 catcher. However, Bando proved his worth last year by handling Niekro and Candiotti.

Bando also showed he can still contribute offensively. Now it is time for him to produce on a consistent level offensively *and* defensively. Since 1983, he's been stuck in a good year/bad year syndrome.

Kaat: "Two years ago, an awful lot was expected of Bando. Mentally, that's difficult for some players to handle. Now he seems to have a different outlook on things. He's valuable to the Indians in a lot of ways."

CLEVELAND INDIANS

HITTING:

Tony Bernazard is going to remember 1986 for a long time. It was a career year for the switch-hitting second baseman: he set all-time highs in average, home runs, RBIs, doubles and hits. Bernazard batted .338 righthanded with five homers and 21 RBIs. From the left side, he hit .287 with 12 homers and 52 RBIs. His improvement as a righthanded hitter was significant. Until last year, he'd only hit six career homers against lefthanded pitching.

Bernazard took another large step when he moved into the leadoff spot in late June. In 82 games as the Tribe's No. 1 hitter, he hit .299, scored 62 runs, hit 13 homers and drove in 51 RBIs. Four times Bernazard started games with a home run, twice he hit the game's first pitch out of the ballpark.

For most of his career, Bernazard has been a hitter required to do the little things: hit behind the runner, lay down a sacrifice bunt or draw a walk. When he took over the leadoff spot, he broke those chains and became a much more aggressive hitter.

Bernazard handles the low pitch very well from either side of the plate and knows the strike zone. At times, though, he is an overanxious hitter. Near the end of last season, he separated his shoulder swinging at a pitch.

He is a good bunter (six bunt hits last year) and sprays the ball around well. He is particularly effective dropping hits just inside the foul lines.

BASERUNNING:

Bernazard has good speed, but sometimes runs out of control. He stole 17 bases last year but was caught eight times. If the Indians asked him to steal more, he could.

Although not as fast as he once was, Bernazard still runs the bases well. He will go into second hard and always takes an aggressive lead off first, which makes him susceptible to the pickoff.

FIELDING:

Throughout his career, Bernazard has always been said to be an average to below-

TONY BERNAZARD
2B, No. 4
SR, 5'9", 160 lbs.
ML Svc: 7 years
Born: 8-24-56 in
Caguas, PR

1986 STATISTICS

AVG	G	AB	R	H	2B	3B	HR	RBI	BB	SO	SB
.301	146	562	88	169	28	4	17	73	53	77	17

CAREER STATISTICS

AVG	G	AB	R	H	2B	3B	HR	RBI	BB	SO	SB
.264	925	3181	450	841	151	28	61	342	355	502	94

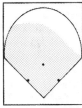

average second baseman. Last year, though, he made some startling plays in the field.

If it is possible for a professional ballplayer to improve defensively at the age of 30, then Bernazard did. He was especially effective going behind the bag for diving stops, although he did have problems moving to his left.

His pivot on the double play is average.

OVERALL:

Bernazard has made himself into a better player over the last two seasons. The vigorous weight-lifting program he started after the 1984 season has done wonders for him both offensively and defensively.

The question is, did Tony Bernazard have a career year in 1986 or is he capable of doing more?

Kaat: "He's an exciting player to watch because he is the kind of hitter who can ignite a lineup at the top of the order. If the Indians keep him at leadoff, he could give the club what Detroit has in Lou Whitaker and the Yankees have in Rickey Henderson: a leadoff hitter with speed who knows the strike zone and can hit with power."

CLEVELAND INDIANS

HITTING:

For some reason, Brett Butler stopped pulling the ball to right field in 1986. That fact, perhaps more than any other, led to a disappointing season for the center fielder on the heels of his best year ever in the big leagues.

In 1985, when Butler hit .311, he wore out the hole between first and second with one single after another. Last year pitchers kept the ball away from the little lefthander and he seemed to spend the whole season sending harmless flies to left field.

Hitting only .245 at the All-Star break, Butler lost his leadoff spot to Tony Bernazard and at one time was dropped to the seventh hole in the lineup. Gradually, he worked himself back to the No. 2 spot, but he never won his old spot back from the hot-hitting Bernazard.

Butler is a high-ball hitter but he often bites too quickly on fastballs inside. Discipline at the plate would help cut down his strikeouts, increase his walks and keep the ball on the ground--something he didn't do consistently last year.

Statistically, Butler turned a disasterous season into a respectable one by hitting .381 over the last 31 games to end the year at .278, 33 points below his 1985 average.

Still, he had his moments. Butler led the majors in triples with 14 and drove in a career-high 51 RBIs.

He also continued to use the bunt as an effective weapon. Butler beat out 24 bunt hits and has 73 since joining the Indians in 1984.

BASERUNNING:

Butler's stolen bases fell from 47 in 1985 to 32 last year. However, with Julio Franco, Joe Carter and Mel Hall hitting behind him, he really didn't have to run that much.

Still, Butler has a tendency to run wild: he was thrown out 15 times trying to steal.

His good speed allows him to turn singles into doubles and doubles into triples. He had 35 extra-base hits last year.

BRETT BUTLER
CF, No. 2
LL, 5'10", 160 lbs.
ML Svc: 5 years
Born: 6-15-57 in
Los Angeles, CA

1986 STATISTICS

AVG	G	AB	R	H	2B	3B	HR	RBI	BB	SO	SB
.278	161	587	92	163	17	14	4	51	70	65	32

CAREER STATISTICS

AVG	G	AB	R	H	2B	3B	HR	RBI	BB	SO	SB
.277	752	2695	442	747	95	53	17	198	317	277	200

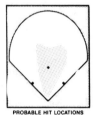

VS. RHP   VS. LHP   PROBABLE HIT LOCATIONS

FIELDING:

Butler plays a solid center field, although he is not as good a fielder now as he was in 1985 when he should have won the Gold Glove. He has committed only four errors in two years but last year he seemed to have trouble with balls hit deep in the gaps near the wall.

His arm is average but he can burn runners who blatantly try to challenge him.

OVERALL:

Kaat: "The real Brett Butler is somewhere between the 1985 version and the 1986 version. He is solid in center field and offensively can help a team at the top of the order with his bunting ability and speed.

"He could use more discipline at the plate, but he's a good little hitter. He plays a respectable center field--especially in Cleveland where there's not much room to have to cover."

90+ FASTBALL

PITCHING:

The fire returned to Ernie Camacho's fastball last season. After sitting out the 1985 season because of elbow surgery, Camacho came back to have his second 20-save season in the last three years.

Camacho is no mystery. He simply throws a tailing fastball that has been clocked as high as 97 MPH. Then he throws it again. And again and again.

Camacho is usually under strict orders not to experiment with anything fancy on the mound. He'd like to throw five or six different pitches if the Indians would let him, but in cutting down his assortment, he's found his first permanent home after eight seasons of seemingly endless baseball wandering.

Last year, though, he did throw one or two curveballs during each outing and found that it was usually an effective pitch. Batters reacted to it like a heart attack.

Last year Ernie came out smokin'--he saved six games in six opportunites. Then his right shoulder started hurting and he went on the disabled list. From that point on, he seemed reluctant to pitch when he was sore.

Camacho had 15 saves by the middle of August but managed only five during the balance of the season as the Indians went more and more to Frank Wills in tough situations. Still, Camacho is the first pitcher in Indians' history to have two 20-save seasons.

Jittery and high-strung on the mound, Camacho does not appear to be the fearsome reliever a team needs to close the door. But he pitched well with runners on base last year: only 17 of 55 inherited runners scored, and the first batters he faced had only a .255 batting average again him.

Still, strange things happen when he's on the mound. Camacho throws so hard that a lot of broken-bat and weird-hop hits result. Last year most of them seemed to find their way through the infield at the wrong time.

Camacho does not handle that kind of adversity well.

FIELDING:

Camacho is always in good position to field

ERNIE CAMACHO
RHP, No. 13
RR, 6'1", 180 lbs.
ML Svc: 4 years
Born: 2-1-56 in
Salinas, CA

1986 STATISTICS

W	L	ERA	G	GS	CG	SV	IP	H	R	ER	BB	SO
3	4	4.08	51	0	0	19	57.1	60	26	26	31	36

CAREER STATISTICS

W	L	ERA	G	GS	CG	SV	IP	H	R	ER	BB	SO
8	16	3.60	138	3	0	42	200	195	85	80	91	108

hard shots back to the mound. He gets off the mound cleanly and has decent accuracy throwing to any base.

He usually doesn't worry about using his pickoff move, choosing instead to concentrate on the hitter. He covers first base well.

OVERALL:

He is still badly scarred emotionally from the events of 1985. Camacho injured his elbow in the first week of the season and he felt that the Indians tried to rush him back. At the end of the year, he underwent another elbow operation that seemed to prove his belief that he really *was* hurt and not dogging it as some had suggested. The trauma was so great that Camacho had to see a psychologist before the start of the 1986 season.

Camacho has shown he can slam the door in a close game but he could definitely use some help from another hard thrower. The responsibility of being the team's No. 1 stopper does not rest easily on his shoulders.

Kaat: "He's a blower. Strictly a one-pitch pitcher. But after a few times around the league, that can catch up to him. He's *got* to improve his fastball. I don't mean he has to throw it harder, but he has to learn *how* to throw it: in and out, up and down."

CLEVELAND INDIANS

PITCHING:

An old man's pitch made young Tom Candiotti a big hit last year. He came out of nowhere to win 16 games and lead the American League in complete games using the knuckleball as his No. 1 pitch.

In 1985, the Milwaukee Brewers sent Candiotti to the minors so that he could perfect the knuckler. By the end of the year, the Brewers weren't impressed with his progress and Candiotti became a minor league free agent.

The Indians scouted him in Puerto Rico in the winter leagues, signed him to a Triple-A contract and brought him to spring training. At the end of spring training, they signed Phil Niekro, the master knuckleballer, partly to offer encouragement and counsel to Candiotti.

What makes Candiotti so effective is that the knuckler isn't his only pitch. He has a big-breaking curveball and an average to below-average fastball to go along with it. When thrown as part of the knuckleball plan, the fastball looks much faster and the curveball is a killer.

At the start of the 1986 season, Candiotti had control problems with the knuckler and was forced to throw the curve or fastball when he got behind in the count. By midseason he was using his secondary pitches to set up the knuckler --which he was now throwing at anytime in the count.

In just about every game last year, Candiotti had one bad stretch--usually in the early innings--when he couldn't throw the knuckler for strikes. The stretch would last about an inning and--if you don't know that this is just his *modus operandi*--it looks as though he's about to walk everybody in the ballpark.

Then his control would kick in and Candiotti would be almost unhittable.

He is a wire-to-wire pitcher. His first nine victories were all complete games and he finished 13-4 in his 17 complete games for the season.

Candiotti uses a three-quarters delivery. His biggest physical problem last year

TOM CANDIOTTI
RHP, No. 49
RR, 6'3", 205 lbs.
ML Svc: 2 years
Born: 8-31-57 in
*   Walnut Creek, CA*

1986 STATISTICS

W	L	ERA	G	GS	CG	SV	IP	H	R	ER	BB	SO
16	12	3.57	36	34	17	0	252.1	234	112	100	106	167

CAREER STATISTICS

W	L	ERA	G	GS	CG	SV	IP	H	R	ER	BB	SO
24	18	3.68	54	48	19	0	340.1	334	154	139	132	211

involved cracked finger nails: the touch of death for knuckleball pitchers.

FIELDING:

Candiotti fields his position well. Runners will steal on his knuckler but he has already learned to live with it and doesn't let the movements behind him upset his concentration.

He gets off the mound quickly and can make all the plays at first base. On a team that doesn't hold runners well, Candiotti had two pickoffs last year. His move is better than many baserunners expect.

OVERALL:

Niekro raves about Candiotti's potential. He's still learning the knuckler, but at age 29, it's not as though the clock is working against him.

Kaat: "If his loses his concentration or if his confidence deserts him, Candiotti would be susceptible to a loss of control.

"Many times, after a pitcher has had a big first year in the big leagues, he arrives at spring training feeling that he has earned the spot as kingpin of the staff. Mentally, unduly high expectations may make a pitcher try to do to much to live up to them. Candiotti needs to relax and concentrate on simply pitching well this year."

CLEVELAND INDIANS

HITTING:

In a year when Joe Carter did just about everything right, it was his hitting that made headlines. For the Indians, Carter's 1986 performance was the end of a two-year wait.

Concentrating on every at-bat, Carter led the majors in RBIs with 121, while hitting .302 with 29 homers, 29 stolen bases, 108 runs scored and 200 hits. Carter always had good bat control, but last year was the first time he consistently went to the opposite field with the outside pitch.

And he did it with power. A dead pull hitter when it comes to home runs, Carter also showed he could go deep the opposite way in 1986. When Carter came to the Indians along with Mel Hall and Don Schulze from the Chicago Cubs in the much-discussed trade involving Rick Sutcliffe in June of 1984, the Cubs said Carter couldn't hit a big league fastball.

Carter lived off fastballs--anywhere in the strike zone--last year. He also improved against the curveball, a pitch that had given him trouble during his first two years in Cleveland.

In 1986, Carter showed the ability to take over a game offensively. He had three five-hit games last year. At Fenway Park, he hit three home runs in one game.

In his first two seasons with the Indians, injuries had allowed Carter to show only flashes of his ability. Last year he stayed healthy and put together one of the best overall seasons in Indians' history.

Carter put together hitting streaks of 21 and 14 games and steered clear of slumps because of his bunting ability (he had four bunt hits last year) and his excellent speed to first on slow rollers.

BASERUNNING:

The man can flat-out run. He stole 29 bases and went into the last weekend of the season with a chance to go 30/30 (30 homers, 30 steals) but he fell just short of joining that elite group.

He was only thrown out seven times last year and at one point stole 13 bases in 14 attempts. Carter helped turn 13 of those

JOE CARTER
LF/1B, No. 30
RR, 6'3", 215 lbs.
ML Svc: 3 years
Born: 3-7-60 in
Oklahoma City, OK

1986 STATISTICS

AVG	G	AB	R	H	2B	3B	HR	RBI	BB	SO	SB
.302	162	663	108	200	36	9	29	121	31	95	29

CAREER STATISTICS

AVG	G	AB	R	H	2B	3B	HR	RBI	BB	SO	SB
.279	394	1447	210	404	70	11	57	222	68	238	56

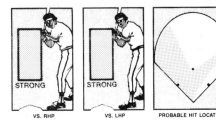

VS. RHP   VS. LHP   PROBABLE HIT LOCATIONS

steals into runs. He takes an aggressive lead off first and was picked off twice in 1986.

FIELDING:

Carter has played all three outfield positions but spent most of the second half of the season at first base. That seems like a waste of his athletic ability, but Carter has picked up the defensive requirements of that position quickly. He does not get out of synch--or psyche--playing the outfield one night and the infield the next.

At first base, he stretches well and picks balls out of the dirt. In the outfield, he goes to the fence with confidence and has good leaping ability. He had a little trouble coming in on ground balls in the outfield but that can be blamed on the fact that he really can't call one position home.

OVERALL:

Kaat: "As good a season as Joe Carter had last year, it appears as though it still wasn't his career year. He could be on the threshold of becoming one of the game's hottest players. He has do-it-all ability."

CLEVELAND INDIANS

HITTING:

Carmen Castillo is a mystery--one that may never be solved.

Over the last three years, Castillo has averaged a home run every 20.6 times at bat. Over the course of a full season, that offers the promise of a big year.

However, Castillo has never been given the playing .time necessary to see if he could produce those kinds of numbers. He's a platoon player facing mostly lefthanded pitchers. His defense is more than suspect in right field.

In addition to those handicaps, he's in an outfield that is already crowded with offensive talent in the forms of Joe Carter, Mel Hall and Cory Snyder. That's enough to frustrate any man or make him a full-time DH.

In time, the Indians might make Castillo their DH but currently that's a dead end, too. Andre Thornton, with two years left on a guaranteed contract, is the Tribe's man.

Castillo is powerfully built and has the most awesome swing on the Indians' roster. The big swing makes him an easy strikeout victim, although he cut it down last year and hit for a respectable .278 average.

Castillo loves low fastballs and can lose one in a hurry. He homered off Boston's Roger Clemens last season deep into the center field bleachers at Fenway. He does have problems with breaking balls, especially from righthanded pitchers.

He is no threat to bunt.

BASERUNNING:

Castillo has good speed on the bases but for some reason does not steal. He will go from first to third on a single to right field and can score from first on a double.

He doesn't take a very daring lead at first but will go into second hard to break up a double play when mood strikes him.

FIELDING:

Two years ago, Castillo put his own well-

CARMEN CASTILLO
RF, No. 8
RR, 6'1", 185 lbs.
ML Svc: 4 years
Born: 6-8-58 in
 San Pedro de Macoris,
  Dominican Republic

1986 STATISTICS

AVG	G	AB	R	H	2B	3B	HR	RBI	BB	SO	SB
.278	85	205	34	57	9	0	8	32	9	48	2

CAREER STATISTICS

AVG	G	AB	R	H	2B	3B	HR	RBI	BB	SO	SB
.254	309	756	117	192	29	4	32	107	51	142	7

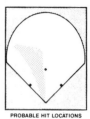

VS. RHP   VS. LHP   PROBABLE HIT LOCATIONS

being on the line every time he walked out to right field. Even routine flies were a struggle.

Last year his defense improved, although he made every catch as difficult as it could be. Once shy of the wall in right field, Castillo has no fear now.

At one time he had a powerful, although not always accurate throwing arm. A shoulder injury two years ago robbed him of some of that velocity.

OVERALL:

At 28, Castillo will probably never be an everyday player unless it's as a DH. Right now, his role is a bench player, to pinch-hit late in the game or play right field against certain lefthanders. He is also the Tribe's designated fighter when brawls erupt on the field.

Kaat: "Strictly an extra DH and power hitter off the bench. Defense is not in his game."

CLEVELAND INDIANS

HITTING:

Rick Dempsey has added power to his bat in recent years, reaching double figures in home runs each of the last three seasons. He has sacrificed in other areas, however. He struggled to keep his average above .200 last year, and his tendency to "swing from the heels" resulted in a strikeout once every 4.9 at-bats.

When he came up as a rookie 18 years ago, Dempsey had the ability to go the other way with the pitch. He hit with better control. Early in his career, he had his best success with pitches on the inside part of the plate. But he has a long swing and now pitchers can get the fastball inside on him much better than in the past.

Now, because of that long swing, he is better with the ball away from him. To his advantage, he's not predominantly a high or low ball hitter. He is a fastball hitter, though, and primarily a pull hitter. Breaking balls give him trouble, especially from righthanders.

BASERUNNING:

Dempsey has average speed for a catcher and is not a threat to steal. But he is aggressive on the basepaths.

He is adept at bunting and will use it at just the right time to get a base hit. He's also one of the most reliable players when it comes to moving the runner to second with a sacrifice bunt.

FIELDING:

Fielding is Dempsey's strong suit. Shoulder injuries have made his arm weaker than it once was, but that is not as big a factor in the AL East, where teams do not rely on running as much as in baseball's other divisions.

He is a good handler of pitchers, which is a big reason why the Indians signed him this year, and he can still field his position

RICK DEMPSEY
C, No. 24
RR, 6'0", 185 lbs.
ML Svc: 14 years
Born: 9-13-49 in
Fayetteville, TN

1986 STATISTICS

AVG	G	AB	R	H	2B	3B	HR	RBI	BB	SO	SB
.208	122	327	42	68	15	1	13	29	45	78	1

CAREER STATISTICS

AVG	G	AB	R	H	2B	3B	HR	RBI	BB	SO	SB
.238	1419	3949	438	939	183	12	78	380	466	575	17

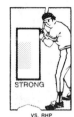

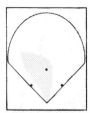

STRONG · VS. RHP   STRONG · VS. LHP   PROBABLE HIT LOCATIONS

aggressively and well.

OVERALL:

A funny story: Dempsey has always been known as a bit of a flake, and as a rookie that was especially true. Calvin Griffith, who was the Twins owner, didn't think Dempsey had the intelligence to be a catcher and suggested he try another position if he wanted to play in the majors. Dempsey's been catching in the big leagues now for 18 years.

Kaat: "If he catches behind Allanson or Bando, Dempsey will have to mentally adjust to the role of backup catcher. That could be a bigger thing for him to handle than many people realize. It might affect his throwing ability as well, because he won't get to use his arm as much everyday. That will be a challenge for him."

CLEVELAND INDIANS

PITCHING:

Jamie Easterly struggled last year from the minute the team left spring training. Bothered by a case of severe bursitis in his left shoulder and neck, Easterly went on the disabled list June 1 and didn't pitch again all season.

But even prior to his injury, Easterly had not done well. He worked in pain for the first two months of the season before he finally was forced to run up the white flag.

By that time, his fastball had dropped to between 79-83 MPH. Easterly usually throws his fastball and slider between 86-88 MPH. He was throwing batting-practice pitches but was too proud to admit it.

Even though the radar gun clearly indicated a drop in velocity, Easterly insisted again and again he could pitch. Finally, he gave in and returned to his hometown of Crockett, Texas, before the end of the season to begin rehabilitation.

When healthy, Easterly is a good situation pitcher. He can get a lefthander out when he has to and is versatile enough to go five innings as a spot-starter or to rescue the bullpen and pitch long relief.

He is a fast worker and uses a three-quarters to over-the-top motion. Easterly stands about 5'10", weighs 190 pounds and is the classic case of not being able to judge a book by its cover. Yes, he does resemble a beach ball but he is a beach ball with a nasty slider. That's his best pitch and when he's healthy and throwing well, it is tough to hit.

Easterly has had a good career with the Indians since coming to Cleveland in 1983. He is not the greatest pitcher in the world with the game on the line, however, and is definitely more of a set-up guy than anything else.

FIELDING:

Easterly is a good fielding pitcher and gets

**JAMIE EASTERLY
LHP, No. 36
LL, 5'10", 180 lbs.
ML Svc: 9 years
Born: 2-17-53 in
Houston, TX**

1986 STATISTICS

W	L	ERA	G	GS	CG	SV	IP	H	R	ER	BB	SO
0	2	7.64	13	0	0	0	17.2	27	16	15	12	9

CAREER STATISTICS

W	L	ERA	G	GS	CG	SV	IP	H	R	ER	BB	SO
22	32	4.62	314	36	0	14	581	637	343	298	306	328

off the mound quickly. He is especially good on bunts or slow rollers hit to the third-base side of the mound. He keeps runners fairly close with a decent move to first.

He will cover first base and catch a pop-up to the mound if no one else goes for it. He is not from the Alphonse-and-Gaston School of Fielding.

OVERALL:

This is an important season for Easterly. In late January, Easterly's shoulder was still bothering him. Last year the Tribe really missed him and Tom Waddell in the middle-to-long relief roles.

If he can't pitch again this season (this is his last year on a guaranteed contract), it will be twice as hard for him to come back in 1988. The Tribe loaded up on lefty relievers just in case Easterly can't pitch this year.

Kaat: "He's got to become a more aggressive pitcher. He tends to nibble too much and gets hurt. He has enough stuff to be a set-up man, though not enough to ever be a closer. He could use more control, but as a lefthander who can throw strikes, he's still a valuable commodity."

CLEVELAND INDIANS

HITTING:

Hitting is a game of adjustments. Julio Franco adjusted and hit for his highest average ever (.306) in the big leagues last season.

Franco--perhaps bitter over losing his salary arbitration case--started the season trying to hit home runs. He'd only hit six the year before but he kept trying to pull everything over the fence in left field.

For a contact hitter like Franco, that's an invitation to disaster. Finally, Franco saw the light and started hitting the ball through the middle and to right field. His average rose, but because of the slow start, Franco drove in only 74 runs compared to 90 in 1985.

Still, those are impressive numbers for a shortstop. Franco is now working on a string of three consecutive seasons in which he has 180 or more hits.

He is an aggressive, free-swinging hitter who can be fooled by breaking balls. Franco is a good high-ball hitter but most of the time he'll swing at anything close to the strike zone. Pitchers who try to sneak low strikes past him have come away sorry.

During the course of the season, Franco will give away several at-bats because of his aggressiveness. More discipline would make him an even better offensive player than he already is.

A hot-hitting Franco is essential to trigger the Indians' offense. That's why the Indians hit him No. 2 or No. 3 in the batting order for most of the season.

However, when he was still trying to hit home runs, he was dropped to the bottom of the order and sulked. He is a much more effective hitter higher in the order.

BASERUNNING:

As a rookie, Franco stole 32 bases. That number has gradually dwindled to the 10 he stole last season.

Franco is an avid weightlifter, which may account for his aversion to running. He also has knee and ankle problems. Still, he goes from first to third well, although he sometimes loafs to first on ground balls. If he has to, he'll slide hard into second to break up a double play.

JULIO FRANCO
SS, No. 14
RR, 6'0", 160 lbs.
ML Svc: 4 years
Born: 8-23-61 in
San Pedro de Macoris,
Dominican Republic

1986 STATISTICS

AVG	G	AB	R	H	2B	3B	HR	RBI	BB	SO	SB
.306	149	599	80	183	30	5	10	74	32	66	10

CAREER STATISTICS

AVG	G	AB	R	H	2B	3B	HR	RBI	BB	SO	SB
.288	634	2482	330	715	110	22	27	326	158	262	74

STRONG   STRONG

VS. RHP   VS. LHP   PROBABLE HIT LOCATIONS

FIELDING:

Franco showed the first signs of becoming an all-around shortstop last year when he cut his errors in half compared to 1985. Coming off two 36-error seasons in 1984 and 1985, Franco only made 18 last year.

The ordinary play has always been Franco's worst enemy. He goes to his left as well as any shortstop in the American League and he can make the stop in the hole, too, although he doesn't always have enough arm to make the play at first.

Last year, with the Indians playing better as a team, Franco seemed to improve in turn. His concentration was much better in the field than it had been in the past.

He rarely dives for balls, which frustrates some of his pitchers, and he is not a glutton for contact while making the double play relay.

OVERALL:

Kaat: "If the light ever goes on in Julio's head and tells him defense is as important as offense, he could be one of the top overall players in the game."

CLEVELAND INDIANS

HITTING:

Mel Hall came back in many ways last season.

First, he proved he could still play major league baseball after suffering serious injuries in an automobile accident in 1985. Not only did he play, but offensively he put together his best season ever. Playing strictly against righthanded pitchers, Hall set career highs in average, home runs, RBIs, runs and hits.

Hall yearns to play every day, but he has definite problems against lefthanded pitchers. His power numbers slipped dramatically after the All-Star break. In the last 63 games of the season he hit only one homer and went from July 21 to September 22 without going deep.

That may have been an after-effect of the accident, but Hall still maintained his average by concentrating on hitting through the middle. Hall likes fastballs and is a decent low-ball hitter. He is a sucker for off-speed stuff-- especially slow breaking balls on the outside corner.

He stands deep in the batter's box and last year opened his stance a little more than usual. Ideally, the Indians would like to bat him in the fifth position, but at the end of the year he was hitting cleanup in place of injured Andre Thornton.

He proved his worth coming off the bench as a pinch-hitter late in a game. Last year he hit .316 as a pinch-hitter with one homer and six RBIs. He hit .571 in bases-loaded situations.

BASERUNNING:

Hall has raw speed, but cannot be considered a basestealing threat. He goes from first to third with reckless abandon and showed no hesitancy on the basepaths following his accident.

He likes the headfirst slide into home plate whether it's a close play or not.

FIELDING:

Hall's play in left field definitely slipped last

MEL HALL
LF, No. 27
LL, 6'1", 185 lbs.
ML Svc: 4 years
Born: 9-16-60 in Lyons, NY

1986 STATISTICS

AVG	G	AB	R	H	2B	3B	HR	RBI	BB	SO	SB
.296	140	442	68	131	29	2	18	77	33	65	6

CAREER STATISTICS

AVG	G	AB	R	H	2B	3B	HR	RBI	BB	SO	SB
.281	440	1416	210	398	85	13	47	203	136	277	14

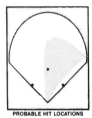

VS. RHP   VS. LHP   PROBABLE HIT LOCATIONS

season. The accident and nearly a year's inactivity cost Hall some flexibility and he often turned fly balls into high drama. Once in the Metrodome, he nearly got hit in the head after losing track of a fly ball in the roof.

Hall has decent speed going to the gap but the ball slicing toward the foul line gives him trouble. His arm has slipped to below-average at best. He is no threat to throw out anyone at home plate even on routine sacrifice flies to left.

OVERALL:

Offensively, Hall showed what he is capable of doing in 1986. An avid body builder, he must increase his stamina to play a full season in the field and at the plate in 1987.

Kaat: "He's a good-looking hitter, but if he doesn't win a starting position, he might cause problems on a club. He's the kind of player every pitcher would like to crease in the neck."

CLEVELAND INDIANS

HITTING:

Brook Jacoby is the essence of a streak hitter. When he's hot, he'll hit home runs in bunches. When he's not, Jacoby looks as though he's holding a bat for the first time in his life.

In the last two years, Jacoby has hit 37 home runs and driven in 167 runs. He's also struck out 257 times and set a club record with 137 strikeouts last year.

Pitchers rarely gave Jacoby anything on the inside part of the plate last year. He spent most of the season trying to go to right field and it proved to be a struggle.

In the second half of the season, he opened his stance more and started to pull the ball to left field with authority. Jacoby's power swing is to left, but last year five of his homers were to the opposite field.

He is a high-ball hitter, but pitchers threw high fastballs past him a lot last year. Change-ups and breaking balls give him trouble, too.

Jacoby could definitely use more patience. In his rookie year, he loved to swing at the first pitch. That tendency is still there, but is not as prevalant as it once was.

Jacoby has the right kind of temperament for a streaky power hitter. He never loses his cool no matter how good or bad he's going. He knows that no matter what, good times and bad times are bound to find a hitter.

The third baseman started the season batting fifth behind Andre Thornton. By the second part of the season, he was spending most of his time bouncing among the Nos. 6, 7 and 8 positions.

The lack of stability might have bothered some players, but not Jacoby. He had his best season ever average-wise last year and still managed to drive in 80 runs while spending most of his time at the bottom of the order.

He is not a good bunter and is seldom called on to do so.

BASERUNNING:

Jacoby's talents as a baserunner went backward last year. Hindered by back, knee and judgment problems, Jacoby hurt the Indians with poor baserunning several times.

His ability to go from first to third is

BROOK JACOBY
3B, No. 26
RR, 5'11", 175 lbs.
ML Svc: 3 years
Born: 11-23-59 in
**   Philadelphia, PA**

1986 STATISTICS
AVG	G	AB	R	H	2B	3B	HR	RBI	BB	SO	SB
.288	158	583	83	168	30	4	17	80	56	137	2

CAREER STATISTICS
AVG	G	AB	R	H	2B	3B	HR	RBI	BB	SO	SB
.275	460	1646	219	452	75	10	44	208	136	334	7

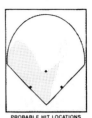

STRONG   STRONG   PROBABLE HIT LOCATIONS

VS. RHP   VS. LHP

questionable at best, but he always runs as hard as he can. The Indians like to use him as part of their double-steal combination.

FIELDING:

Jacoby made 25 errors at third last year-- second-most in the league--but may have become a better fielder in the process. In 1985 he had problems fielding bunts and balls to his right.

He made strides in both areas last year, although he still needs to improve. His range is limited--especially to the right--but Jacoby has never been afraid to throw his body in front of a ball.

He has a decent arm, and his throws seem to float to first and are easy to handle.

OVERALL:

He's on the verge of becoming one of the best third basemen in the American League.

Kaat: "Jacoby is a hard-working player who seems to get lost in the kind of lineup the Indians have. Very quietly, though, he's capable of putting up a lot of numbers at the end of the year."

CLEVELAND INDIANS

PITCHING:

Phil Niekro is a knuckleball pitcher. He always has been. And he always will be.

Yet during the early part of last season, Niekro kept going away from the knuckler. As is his history, Niekro got off to a poor start and was having control problems. In tight spots, he abandoned the knuckleball and threw a slider or a fastball.

When a pitcher is 47 years old and has won 300 games throwing the knuckler, turning a cold shoulder to the floater is not a good idea. The Indians urged Niekro to warm up again to his bread-and-butter pitch (catcher Chris Bando was especially insistent) and he eventually did. In the process, the elder statesman of pitching stabilized an odds-and-ends pitching staff and gave the Indians a consistent season.

Niekro has several pitches and is not afraid to use any of them. In his last start of the season against Minnesota, Knucksie pitched 6 1/3 innings, threw 76 pitches, allowed three earned runs and didn't throw a single knuckleball.

The 311-game winner is a fast worker. The only thing that slows him down is the time it takes his knuckleball to get to the plate. The knuckleball comes in three varieties: the slow one, the power pitch and the blooper knuckler.

Niekro relied a lot on the blooper version last year. He'd save it for certain spots--especially against big swingers--and then unload the high-arching, slow-motion pitch. It looks like a slo-pitch softball delivery.

Niekro's arm is still a marvelous piece of durable machinery. He was second on the team last year in complete games, innings pitched and ERA. He was third on the team in wins, starts and strikeouts.

Nothing upsets Niekro on the mound. Twenty-three years in the big leagues have shown him everything.

Even when his knuckler isn't dancing, Niekro can usually squeeze out five or six decent innings to keep his club close. However, if he has to make too many tough pitches early in a ballgame, that usually means a quick exit for Knucksie.

PHIL NIEKRO
RHP, No. 35
RR, 6'1", 193 lbs.
ML Svc: 22 years
Born: 4-1-39 in Blaine, OH

1986 STATISTICS

W	L	ERA	G	GS	CG	SV	IP	H	R	ER	BB	SO
11	11	4.32	34	32	5	0	210.1	241	126	101	95	81

CAREER STATISTICS

W	L	ERA	G	GS	CG	SV	IP	H	R	ER	BB	SO
311	261	3.27	838	690	243	29	5265	4881	2238	1915	1743	3278

FIELDING:

Niekro does not run wind sprints before games. He's too old for that.

But he does get off the mound quickly to field the frequent bunts he faces by hitters testing his ancient legs. His reflexes are still good. Every few days Niekro stands at second base and fields ground balls for about 20 minutes--he doesn't miss many.

The knuckleball gives basestealers an unfair advantage but Niekro has a quick move to first that keeps them honest. Some managers think Niekro balks whenever he throws to first but the umpires seldom agree.

Niekro does not get rattled with runners on base. In fact, he seems to pitch better.

OVERALL:

Niekro found a home in Cleveland last year. The Indians would be extremely happy if he produced the same kind of numbers this year.

Not only is he good in the clubhouse and can swap trade secrets with young knuckleballer Tom Candiotti, Niekro is versatile. Two of his wins came in relief last year.

Kaat: "As far as skills go, Phil can pitch until he's 60 years old. But he suffers from a bad back and it may cause him to give up the game long before the game gives up on him."

CLEVELAND INDIANS

HITTING:

It might be a mistake to mention hitting and Otis Nixon in the same sentence, but at least the switch-hitting outfielder has advanced beyond the days when he stepped to the plate with only two thoughts on his mind: *bunt* and *run*.

Last year Nixon collected 25 hits and only four were bunts. Why, he even had a five-game hitting streak and finished the season with four doubles and eight RBIs to give him a lusty 18 in three seasons with the Tribe.

He is a better hitter from the left side of the plate and last year proved he could at least get the ball out of the infield. When Nixon first broke in with the Indians (1984), the opposing third baseman could usually shake hands with him in anticipation of the bunt.

Nixon is strictly a slap hitter. He uses a big bat and chops down on the ball. He wants to put the ball on the ground and use his speed to reach base.

Otis only had 95 at-bats last year so when he got a chance to hit, he wasn't looking for a walk. With his speed, he could probably make himself more dangerous by drawing a few more walks, but his aggressiveness paid off last year when he hit .263, his highest average in the big leagues.

Nixon's production in the clutch improved in 1986. He hit .286 with runners in scoring position and was 2-for-4 with the bases loaded.

BASERUNNING:

Nixon has earned his spurs with the Indians for one reason: speed. Last year he scored 33 runs and almost half of them (16) came after he entered the game as a pinch-runner.

The Indians like to use him in the late innings in a tight ballgame. When he jogs out to replace a runner at first or second, it's no secret what's about to happen: Nixon is going to try to steal.

He had a career high 23 steals last year and was only caught six times. He eventually scored on 10 of those steals.

Nixon had stolen base streaks of six and nine straight during the season and five of his steals came at third base. Nixon doesn't

OTIS NIXON
OF, No. 20
SR, 6'2", 180 lbs.
ML Svc: 3 years
Born: 1-9-59 in
Evergreen, NC

1986 STATISTICS

AVG	G	AB	R	H	2B	3B	HR	RBI	BB	SO	SB
.263	105	95	33	25	4	1	0	8	13	12	23

CAREER STATISTICS

AVG	G	AB	R	H	2B	3B	HR	RBI	BB	SO	SB
.218	271	362	85	79	8	1	3	18	30	55	57

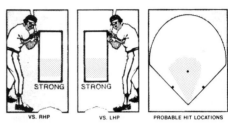

VS. RHP   VS. LHP   PROBABLE HIT LOCATIONS

waste time when he enters a game in a make-or-break situation. He usually runs on the first or second pitch.

FIELDING:

He is an adequate defensive replacement. Last year, he was often used to relieve Mel Hall in left field in the late innings when the score was close.

Nixon goes to the gap well and is not afraid of the fence. He has the speed necessary to make up for any judgmental mistakes, although he sometimes has trouble on balls he has to charge.

His best position is center field, but his arm is average and won't stop anybody from taking an extra base.

OVERALL:

Kaat: "Nixon fills his role on the Indians perfectly. He is a pinch-runner who can fly. His job is to steal bases, play late-inning defense and maybe pinch-hit once in a while.

"Whatever he does offensively is a plus-- running is his game. He needs to play every day to show whether or not he can hit."

CLEVELAND INDIANS

PITCHING:

The Indians never could figure out exactly what to do with Bryan Oelkers last year. This lefthander, who was Minnesota's No. 1 draft pick in 1982 (ahead of Dwight Gooden), baffled them. When Cleveland used him as a starter, he couldn't get past the fifth inning. When the Indians tried him as a short or long reliever, Oelkers' control unravelled at the wrong time. Last December, the Tribe dropped him from their 40-man roster.

Oelkers uses a big motion and his delivery is almost over the top. Hitters pick up the ball quickly on him. He has a good breaking ball, a pitch he has confidence in and does not hesitate to throw. His fastball is only decent.

Last season, the Indians were unable to place him and keep him in a designated role. After starting the season in the minors, he was called up to pitch in relief. Then when the Tribe had trouble with their fifth starter, Oelkers was given a chance to win the job there. When that didn't materialize, he was sent back to the bullpen. Still, he protected 11 of the 17 leads he inherited.

Oelkers never complained about bouncing from one spot on the staff to another. At one time, the Indians were carrying 11 pitchers on their staff and Oelkers was the only lefthander in the bullpen.

Oelkers earned his first major league win and save last year as he went 3-3. Late in the season, he seemed to find a groove as the first lefthander out of the pen to get a particular lefthanded batter out. In his last 10 appearances, he went 1-0 with a 3.38 ERA.

As a spot-starter, Oelkers runs out of gas around the fifth inning and the home runs start to fly.

In relief, Oelkers doesn't have much of a chance to use his off-speed pitches. He comes

BRYAN OELKERS
LHP, No. 33
LL, 6'3", 192 lbs.
ML Svc: one year
Born: 3-11-61 in
Zaragonza, Spain

1986 STATISTICS

W	L	ERA	G	GS	CG	SV	IP	H	R	ER	BB	SO
3	3	4.70	35	4	0	1	69	70	38	36	40	33

CAREER STATISTICS

W	L	ERA	G	GS	CG	SV	IP	H	R	ER	BB	SO
3	8	6.01	45	12	0	1	103.1	126	72	69	57	46

in throwing hard, but he often has trouble finding the strike zone. His strikeout to walk ratio (33:40) last year bears that out.

FIELDING:

Oelkers is an adequate enough fielder, though he may be a little off-balance after his follow-through. He will hustle to field balls hit in front of him and he covers first base well.

His big motion gives runners a chance to steal on him.

OVERALL:

This should be a big year for Oelkers. He must force himself onto the staff but he is going to have to pitch with better control in order to do it.

Kaat: "Oelkers is a curveball/fastball pitcher. He really can't be considered a starter and his only chance to make the club this year is as a reliever. He will have an edge inasmuch as he is a lefthander."

CLEVELAND INDIANS

PITCHING:

A forgotten pitcher in Minnesota, Ken Schrom took advantage of the Indians' potent offense last year and used his own experience to post his second-best season ever.

Schrom is not an overpowering pitcher. He is a control pitcher with a variety of pitches at his command. However, if his control is not true, home runs--*bunches of them*--are the end result. Last year Schrom allowed 34 homers and he couldn't use the Metrodome as an excuse. The one thing that got him off the hook time and time again was the Tribe's offense. A victim of poor offensive support in 1985 as a member of the Twins, Schrom was flooded with runs last year as a member of the Indians.

At one time, Schrom won eight consecutive decisions. In those eight wins, however, he allowed 13 home runs and 25 earned runs, but the Indians scored over six runs per game when he was on the mound.

Schrom's best pitch is probably his change-up, which he uses to set up his fastball and curveball. He is a deliberate worker who will change his pitching motion now and then to keep a batter off balance. Sometimes, however, he takes too much time between pitches.

He showed the ability to adjust last year. Schrom was 10-2 at the break and went to the All-Star game. But then he went into a slump when he didn't win a ballgame from the end of July to the beginning of September.

Pitching coach Jack Aker suggested that Schrom needed a new pitch to move hitters off the plate. He suggested Schrom use a cut fastball, which moves *in* on the hitter. Schrom used it and won three of his last four decisions.

Schrom did not have great success in the American League East last year, but he was 10-0 against the weaker western division (and only 4-7 in the Tribe's own neighborhood).

FIELDING:

Schrom is a well-conditioned athlete who

KEN SCHROM
RHP, No. 18
RR, 6'2", 195 lbs.
ML Svc: 5 years
Born: 11-23-54 in
Grangeville, ID

1986 STATISTICS

W	L	ERA	G	GS	CG	SV	IP	H	R	ER	BB	SO
14	7	4.54	34	33	3	0	206	217	118	104	49	87

CAREER STATISTICS

W	L	ERA	G	GS	CG	SV	IP	H	R	ER	BB	SO
45	38	4.46	144	108	18	1	746.1	778	409	370	263	311

gets off the mound quickly to field hits in front of him. Last year, though, he had trouble handling bunts.

He doesn't have much of a move to first and runners get a good jump on him because he's so locked in on home plate. His follow-through doesn't throw him off balance and he covers first well.

OVERALL:

Aided by the Indians' offense, he could continue to help Cleveland if he stays healthy and can avoid such hot and cold flashes that he showed last year. His greatest strengths are his experience and concentration. Still, he must cut down his hits to innings pitched ratio (more than one hit per inning last year) and has to improve against the AL East if the Indians are to be serious contenders.

Kaat: "Schrom is 32 years old but has only been in the major leagues for four seasons. Until last year, he had always been a .500 pitcher and there is no reason to think that trend won't continue.

"He's a blue-collar type pitcher. He has to work on getting ahead of hitters because most home runs come when a pitcher is working behind in the count."

CLEVELAND INDIANS

PITCHING:

A disturbing pattern has developed in the career of Don Schulze. Call it flameout, burnout or a lack of talent.

Whatever it is, it has put Schulze's career with the Indians on the line at the tender age of 24. In 1985, Schulze won his first three decisions. Then he spun into a seven-game losing streak and a trip to the minors.

Last year Schulze was 3-1 after his first seven starts. In his next seven starts, Schulze went 1-3 and earned a trip to the bullpen and then the disabled list with a sore shoulder.

When Schulze is on, he throws a hard sinker that can drop out of sight. His fastball can reach 90 MPH, but at 6'3" and 225 lbs., Schulze looks as though he should be able to throw harder.

During his 1986 slump, Schulze seemed to have trouble getting through a lineup the second time. His inability to remain effective for more than three innings forced the Indians to move him to the bullpen. But he injured his shoulder before the club got a good look at how he worked from the pen.

Schulze fights himself on the mound. When he doesn't get a call he wants from the umpire, an error is committed behind him or a batter hits a good pitch, he loses his composure in a flash. Afterward, Schulze tries too hard to compensate, throws too hard and the game begins to look more like batting practice.

Schulze is not afraid to throw inside. However, he needs work on his off-speed pitches.

He uses an over-the-top motion and a very compact wind-up and delivery. The Indians tinkered with his delivery late in the season to try and get more snap in his arm but Schulze didn't look comfortable with it.

DON SCHULZE
RHP, No. 37
RR, 6'3", 225 lbs.
ML Svc: 3 years
Born: 9-27-62 in
Roselle, IL

1986 STATISTICS

W	L	ERA	G	GS	CG	SV	IP	H	R	ER	BB	SO
4	4	5.00	19	13	1	0	84.2	88	48	47	34	33

CAREER STATISTICS

W	L	ERA	G	GS	CG	SV	IP	H	R	ER	BB	SO
11	21	5.46	62	49	4	0	281.2	348	191	171	88	119

FIELDING:

Schulze is an average fielder. A couple of years ago the Indians asked him to lose weight. He complied and now gets off the mound quickly.

When he follows through, he's in good position to field. He'll give the runner a look at first base but doesn't waste too many throws to the bag.

He covers first base well and learned the hard way how to cover home after being run down at the plate a couple of years ago by Milwaukee's Jim Gantner.

OVERALL:

Kaat: "Schulze still seems best-suited to be a starter, but if he makes the ballclub this season he will probably be used as a long reliever. The Indians removed him from their 40-man roster after last season.

"He's borderline when it comes to making the staff in 1986."

CLEVELAND INDIANS

HITTING:

The Indians waited until the middle of June last year to bring Cory Snyder to the big leagues. Based on what took place over the next four months, they may have waited too long.

How long? Well, the delay quite possibly cost Snyder the American League's Rookie of the Year Award.

The skinny righthanded hitter showed amazing power for someone who appears to be frail at 6'3" and 175 pounds. He finished second on the team with 24 home runs and 46 of his hits went for extra bases (*that's 41% of his total number of hits!*).

Snyder generates great bat speed and really turns on high fastballs and inside pitches. He has a natural home run swing but he can hit with power to the opposite field, too.

He is a free swinger who fanned 123 times in only 416 at-bats in 1986. Pitchers constantly struck him out with curveballs and sliders thrown low and away. However, he showed the ability to look terrible on one pitch and then hit the same pitch out of the ballpark later in the game.

Snyder has a large strike zone but it appears he is intimately familiar with every inch of it. He is also an intelligent hitter. With two strikes and a man on base, he has the ability to go to right field.

At the start, the Indians batted Snyder low in the order to relieve the pressure on him to produce too much too fast. Gradually, he moved into the fifth position behind Joe Carter.

BASERUNNING:

He has better-than-average speed, which is surprising for a player his size. In one game, he went from first to third twice on a pair of bunts.

He goes from first to third well and could steal more bases if asked. He does not go especially hard into second on double plays.

FIELDING:

Snyder appears to have the whole package:

CORY SNYDER
INF/RF, No. 28
RR, 6'3", 175 lbs.
ML Svc: less than one year
Born: 11-11-62 in
Englewood, CA

1986 STATISTICS

AVG	G	AB	R	H	2B	3B	HR	RBI	BB	SO	SB
.272	103	416	58	113	21	1	24	69	16	123	2

CAREER STATISTICS

AVG	G	AB	R	H	2B	3B	HR	RBI	BB	SO	SB
.272	103	416	58	113	21	1	24	69	16	123	2

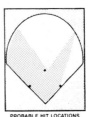

STRONG — VS. RHP STRONG — VS. LHP PROBABLE HIT LOCATIONS

versatility, power and a great arm. He played both right and left field as well as shortstop and third base last year. What's more, he played them all well.

Snyder's arm is his best attribute on defense. After starting the season at third in Triple-A, the Indians put him in right field and he barely missed a beat. Seldom is he out of position and his arm causes people to hold their breath on sacrifice flies to right.

At short and third, Snyder's arm seemed to freeze runners a foot or two from first. The Indians feel that his best positions (ranked from best to worst) are right field, short and third.

OVERALL:

Someday, Snyder could be the kind of player who dominates the league. Perhaps a 40-home-run man.

Kaat: "He's got great raw talent and is exceptionally quick on the inside pitch. If he plays right field, you'd have to rank him with Dave Winfield, Jesse Barfield and Dwight Evans as far as arm strength goes."

CLEVELAND INDIANS

PITCHING:

Greg Swindell's teammates took one look at his fresh plump face and his even plumper stomach and immediately nicknamed him "Flounder," after the fat fraternity pledge in the movie *Animal House*. They do not, however, kid about his ability to throw a baseball.

It took the 235-pound lefthander just over two months to leap from the University of Texas to the big leagues after the Indians made him the second player taken in the June draft last year. Along the way, Swindell stopped in Class A ball long enough to make three starts.

Swindell made his first big league start in late August last year against Boston and ended up a 24-5 loser in the worst loss in Indians' history. After that, things could only improve.

At one time, Swindell won four straight and five of his last six starts. For a rookie, he showed remarkable poise. The Indians feel that he was born to pitch.

He is a strikeout pitcher who gets the most out of his fastball through control and his ability to mix pitches. Swindell's best pitch is his fastball, which he throws in the high 80s. The thing that makes it so effective is his ability to throw it at the right time and in the right place.

He also throws a slider, but that pitch can damage a pitcher's arm in a hurry and it caused Swindell's elbow to swell last year. At the Tribe's Florida Instructional League after the season, pitching coach Jack Aker substituted a cut fastball for the slider and Swindell picked it up quickly.

Swindell's change-up is good now, but it will get better with work. He has an average curveball.

Unlike most rookie pitchers who just rear back and throw as hard as they can for as long as they can, Swindell "pitched" last year. He has no fear of throwing the change-up and knows how to set up a hitter.

He does not have the type of physique (ahem) normally associated with professional

GREG SWINDELL
LHP, No. 21
RL, 6'2", 225 lbs.
ML Svc: *less than one year*
Born: 1-2-65 in
Austin, TX

1986 STATISTICS

W	L	ERA	G	GS	CG	SV	IP	H	R	ER	BB	SO
5	2	4.23	9	9	1	0	61.2	57	35	29	15	46

CAREER STATISTICS

W	L	ERA	G	GS	CG	SV	IP	H	R	ER	BB	SO
5	2	4.23	9	9	1	0	61.2	57	35	29	15	46

athletes; in seven starts last year, he had one complete game and his ability to strike out batters decreases in the later innings. If he does not lose weight (as the Indians have instructed him to do), Swindell may become known as a five- or six-inning pitcher.

FIELDING:

In spite of his bulk, Swindell fields his position well. The biggest surprise is his good pickoff move. In his seven starts last year, Swindell's move led to one pickoff and four caught stealings--easily the best on the team.

He'll make all the plays at first and is usually in good position after his delivery to field balls in front of him .

OVERALL:

The Indians can't wait to see what Swindell will do over the course of a full season. If he keeps himself in condition, stays away from the slider and gains more control over his change-up and curve, they think he could become the ace of the staff.

Kaat: "Potentially, he could do for the Indians what Roger Clemens did for Boston. I'm not talking about winning 24 games, I'm talking about becoming the ace of their staff. He appears to be wise beyond his years when it comes to pitching ability."

GOOD CLUTCH HITTER

HITTING:

Hitting is what Pat Tabler does best. He proved that again last year when the Indians promoted rookie Cory Snyder from Triple-A.

In the shuffle that followed, Tabler not only lost his first base job to Joe Carter, but ended up on the disabled list with a thigh injury. When he returned, it was as a part-time player and Indians' manager Pat Corrales gave him this piece of advice:

"When you get a chance to play again, hit so I can't take you out," Corrales said.

Tabler's chance came late in July when Snyder twisted an ankle rounding third base. Tabler replaced him as a pinch-runner and went 2-for-2. He never stopped hitting or playing after that.

For the rest of the season Tabler hit .392 to finish with a .326 average--fourth highest in the American League last year. From July 21 to Sept. 1, Tabler hit .463 and raised his average from .258 to .332.

Tabler is a control-type hitter who likes high fastballs. He goes to right field extremely well but is not overly impressive when it comes to home runs (6) and RBIs (48).

The one thing that Tabler does do is hit with men in scoring position. Last year he led the team with a .306 average with runners in scoring position (38-for-124 with 42 RBIs). Although he only went 2-for-10 in bases-loaded situations, Tabler is still hitting a remarkable .533 in that category over his career (24-for-45 with 57 RBIs).

BASERUNNING:

Tabler has decent speed to first base but the thigh injury slowed him last year. He is no threat to steal but is successful on the delayed steal now and then. He does not clog the bases and will go hard into second to break up a double play.

FIELDING:

Tabler needs work on his defensive abilities at first base and he knows it. In 1985, he committed 14 errors. He lowered that to nine

PAT TABLER
1B, No. 10
RR, 6'2", 195 lbs.
ML Svc: 6 years
Born: 2-2-58 in
Hamilton, OH

1986 STATISTICS
AVG	G	AB	R	H	2B	3B	HR	RBI	BB	SO	SB
.326	130	473	61	154	29	2	6	48	29	75	3

CAREER STATISTICS
AVG	G	AB	R	H	2B	3B	HR	RBI	BB	SO	SB
.288	575	1966	250	566	98	16	29	252	178	301	8

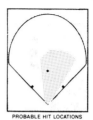

VS. RHP STRONG — VS. LHP STRONG — PROBABLE HIT LOCATIONS

last year but spent much of his time at DH in the second part of the season.

He can also play third and left field in a pinch.

OVERALL:

Tabler seems to be reaching his peak as a hitter. His .326 average last year was the highest in his four big league seasons.

The problem will be finding a place for him to play. A lot depends on how Andre Thornton, the Tribe's regular DH, responds to off-season knee surgery. As is normally the case, Tabler proved last year he is a much better hitter when he plays on an everyday basis.

Whether or not he could adjust to a part-time role and still be effective is questionable.

Kaat: "Pat is a typical AL East player. He is a guy who can hit well but is average in the field. Early in his career, he proved he could hit with men in scoring position. That's a great psychological advantage for him."

CLEVELAND INDIANS

HITTING:

Andre Thornton gambled in 1986. He won a little, but he may have lost more.

Thornton underwent surgery on his left knee during spring training in 1985. At the end of the season, he needed more surgery but elected not to go under the knife. He wanted to see if he could make it through 1986 without another operation.

It didn't work out that way. In late August he slid into second base at Fenway Park and the left knee snapped. He struggled through another month before pulling the plug on the season in late September in preparation for his fourth knee operation.

Thornton, a deadly low-ball hitter, still managed to hit 17 homers and drive in 66 runs. However, it's ironic that with the Indians' offense finally coming to bloom, the man who for so many years was the Tribe's offense couldn't contribute the way he wanted.

Now at age 38, Thornton's status as full-time DH will depend on how well he responds to surgery. The Indians have several DH candidates in waiting.

The man called Thunder is probably the Indians most disciplined hitter. His compact swing belies his power, although pitches on the outside corner give him trouble.

The righthanded Thornton is a pure pull hitter when it comes to power. When trying to keep the ball in play, he can go the opposite way, but Thornton doesn't get paid to hit behind the runner.

Thornton might be the Indians' most dangerous clutch hitter. He hit .417 (5-for-12) with a homer and six RBIs as a pinch-hitter and led the Indians in bases-loaded situations by going 4-for-5.

BASERUNNING:

Thornton came to the realization last year that he can no longer run the bases as he used to. His knees won't let him.

Even as a DH, Thornton delighted in taking the extra base, breaking up a double play and shocking the opposition by stealing a base. Last year, bad wheels and all, he still stole four bases.

ANDRE THORNTON
DH, No. 29
RR, 6'2", 205 lbs.
ML Svc: 13 years
Born: 8-13-49 in
Tuskegee, AL

1986 STATISTICS

AVG	G	AB	R	H	2B	3B	HR	RBI	BB	SO	SB
.229	120	401	49	92	14	0	17	66	65	67	4

CAREER STATISTICS

AVG	G	AB	R	H	2B	3B	HR	RBI	BB	SO	SB
.256	1529	5206	784	1332	242	22	253	890	866	826	47

  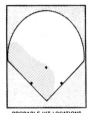

STRONG VS. RHP   STRONG VS. LHP   PROBABLE HIT LOCATIONS

Now that part of his game has all but eroded. Thornton was thrown out several times trying to stretch a single into a double last year and says he must adjust.

FIELDING:

At one time, Thornton was a solid first baseman but now the only time he wears a glove is to take grounders at third base and first during batting practice.

OVERALL:

Thornton is still a dangerous hitter. Now there is the kind of talent on the team to make sure pitchers can no longer pitch around him. The question remains, "Will his knees let him enjoy the last two years of his guaranteed contract?"

Kaat: "If Thornton is sound, it's a big boost for Cleveland. Many people are picking them to be contenders in the American League East this year. If they are, Thornton will be an important influence on a young club, most of whose players have never been in a pennant race before."

CLEVELAND INDIANS

PITCHING:

Perhaps more than any other absentee roster member, the Indians missed Tom Waddell last year. The club spent the entire season trying to fill holes at the bottom of their starting rotation and in middle relief--the kind of job opportunities a healthy Waddell would have grabbed in a New York minute.

Waddell underwent surgery on his pitching elbow late in the 1985 season. The operation was supposed to be minor, but it cost Waddell the entire 1986 season. He was sent to Triple-A twice on rehabilitation programs, but nothing worked.

It seemed Waddell was always "just a day or two" away from coming back. He'd be able to throw hard on the side every two or three days for a week, but then the pain and tingling sensation would return to the elbow and he was down again.

When healthy, Waddell is a fastball/slider pitcher. He'll top out at about 87 MPH, but he throws strikes and keeps the ball low.

He uses a herky-jerky three-quarters motion that makes it hard for the hitter to see the ball. Waddell hides the ball with his body and leg kick until very late in his delivery.

Waddell's versatility makes him attractive. In 1985 he had nine saves in 14 opportunities as a stopper. When he moved into the rotation, he won three straight and went 4-1 in nine starts for the year.

Not overpowering physically, Waddell is at his best when he works fast, keeps the ball down and throws strikes. However, when his control falters, the ball comes up and stays in

TOM WADDELL
RHP, No. 54
RR, 6'1", 190 lbs.
ML Svc: 3 years
Born: 9-17-58 in
**   Dundee, Scotland**

1986 STATISTICS

W	L	ERA	G	GS	CG	SV	IP	H	R	ER	BB	SO
--DID NOT PLAY--												

CAREER STATISTICS

W	L	ERA	G	GS	CG	SV	IP	H	R	ER	BB	SO
15	10	4.04	107	9	1	15	209.2	172	96	94	76	112

the strike zone. That results in a lot of home runs.

FIELDING:

Waddell is a decent fielder. He gets his share of comebackers and he's quick off the mound to field bunts and slow rollers.

His move to first is adequate, although his rather lengthy windup gives runners a good jump at first base.

OVERALL:

By late January, Waddell was still throwing at only 80%, according to the Indians. They entered spring training with the idea that they couldn't count on him and that any contribution he made would be a plus.

CLEVELAND INDIANS

PITCHING:

The Indians made Frank Wills make a difficult transformation last year. They asked him to switch roles: to go from a starter and/or long reliever to a stopper.

You see, Wills could always throw the ball through a brick wall--his fastball is just a little slower than Ernie Camacho's, which puts it in the 93-94 MPH range--controlling it, however, was his problem.

The Indians sent him to Triple-A to start the conversion to stopper. A shoulder injury set him back some, but the Indians brought him up in late July. It took a while, but by the end of the year the experiment was starting to show positive results.

In his last 10 appearances, Wills was 3-1 with three saves. He showed good control--a big plus--and had 15 strikeouts and issued only two walks. What's more, he showed the kind of temperament necessary for the late-inning role.

Much like Camacho, Wills is a one-trick pony when it comes to pitching. He throws his fastball and dares the batter to hit it.

He also has a change-up and curve, but seldom uses them in relief. He pitched well with men on base: only six of 32 inherited runners scored, and he protected 13 of 16 leads, while going 4-for-8 in save opportunities.

FIELDING:

Perhaps it was the pressure of pitching late in the ballgame. Or maybe Wills was just trying too hard. Whatever the cause, he looked awkward coming off the mound to field bunts. In one game against California, he came off the mound and slipped right on his butt.

Wills is no threat to pick anybody off base but he has a average move. He'll make the routine plays at first base.

FRANK WILLS
RHP, No. 43
RR, 6'2", 202 lbs.
ML Svc: 3 years
Born: 10-26-58 in
New Orleans, LA

1986 STATISTICS

W	L	ERA	G	GS	CG	SV	IP	H	R	ER	BB	SO
4	4	4.91	26	0	0	1	78.2	84	48	45	37	50

CAREER STATISTICS

W	L	ERA	G	GS	CG	SV	IP	H	R	ER	BB	SO
13	19	5.40	66	27	1	2	273.1	280	171	164	133	161

OVERALL:

Wills proved his mettle in a game against Toronto when he was hit by a wicked line drive on the bicep of his pitching arm. Even though he later revealed his arm was numb, he said it was all right so he could finish the game and earn the save.

But there were bad times, too. In a game against the Yankees, Wills walked weak-hitting Mike Fischlin to load the bases in the bottom of the ninth with the score tied to face Don Mattingly. Naturally, Mattingly singled home the winning run.

If he continues to improve, Wills could go a long way toward solidifying the Indians' bullpen. He could assume some of the pressure that Camacho has struggled with as the team's stopper and give the Indians one more option in a close ballgame.

Kaat: "For Wills to be effective, he must stay in control. When his control goes, he'll crash and burn quickly. He's a big guy and he throws hard. Today, more and more clubs are trying to find more than one stopper. He could be the complement to Ernie Camacho in the Indians' bullpen."

PITCHING:

Rich Yett is another faceless pitcher on the Indians' pitching staff. Cleveland seems to have dozens of no-name pitchers on their club--and just about all of them are former Minnesota Twins.

But remember *this kid's* name. Last year, the Indians pared their major league roster to the bone, but they left Rich Yett alone. That's because he does what the Indians like: he takes the ball whenever they ask and throws it hard.

Yett has an above-average fastball that can hit the low 90s on a good day. In his last start of the season, Yett shut out the playoff-bound California Angels on a complete-game four-hitter. For the pitching-poor Indians, that was enough to keep Yett in the front office's memory banks all winter.

Until last year, he had always been a starter. In 1986, Yett pitched in short, long and middle relief. When his knuckles weren't dragging on the ground, he even started three games. After being called up by the Indians from Triple-A, he was used almost exclusively in relief. Four of his five wins were earned out of the bullpen and his arm held up well.

As a reliever, Yett can get by on his hard stuff for an inning or two. However, if he's going to be a starter, he has to work on his curveball. In 78 2/3 innings last year, he allowed 84 hits, including 10 home runs.

New to relieving, Yett also had trouble entering games with runners on base. Twenty-two of the 48 runners he inherited scored. Unless he can overcome that, a stopper role is out of the question.

FIELDING:

Yett fields his position well. In 1985 he battled weight problems with the Twins, but he kept his weight under control last year.

RICH YETT
RHP, No. 42
RR, 6'1", 170 lbs.
ML Svc: one year plus
Born: 10-6-62 in
Pomona, CA

1986 STATISTICS

W	L	ERA	G	GS	CG	SV	IP	H	R	ER	BB	SO
5	3	5.15	39	3	1	1	78.2	84	48	45	37	50

CAREER STATISTICS

W	L	ERA	G	GS	CG	SV	IP	H	R	ER	BB	SO
5	3	5.24	40	4	1	1	79	85	49	46	39	50

His move to first base is nothing exceptional but he keeps runners honest. He gets off the mound in good shape and covers first well.

Yett is another Indian pitcher who got plenty of practice backing up third base and home plate, as his 5.15 ERA indicates.

OVERALL:

He had decent won-loss record last year for a rookie but now he must carve out a place for himself on the staff.

Yett could fit into the picture as an all-purpose pitcher--at least for a while until an opening occurs in the rotation.

Kaat: "He's got a good arm with a live fastball and good breaking stuff. If he can get control of his breaking ball, he could go either way: starter or reliever. At the end of last season, he was experimenting with a forkball or split-finger fastball that could be the change-of-pace pitch he needs.

"A lack of control was a major problem for Yett last year . . . he was either hot or cold. There was no in between."

CLEVELAND INDIANS

JOHN BUTCHER
RHP, No. 38
RR, 6'4", 190 lbs.
ML Svc: 7 years
Born: 3-8-57 in
Glendale, CA

PITCHING, FIELDING:

The best thing that happened to John Butcher in 1986 was that his fiancee bought him a Porsche for a wedding present. That should give you an indication of how his season went.

"Terrible" doesn't quite describe it for the control-type pitcher with the three-quarters delivery. Even a change of scenery and playing surface didn't help.

Butcher was 0-3 with a 6.30 ERA for the Minnesota Twins last year. The Indians obtained him in a deal for Neal Heaton thinking Butcher's sinker would slow down on its way through the natural grass at Cleveland Stadium as opposed to the Metrodome's artificial carpet. If anything, balls hit off his sinkerball seemed to travel faster in the grass.

With the Indians, Butcher was 1-5 with a 6.93 ERA. He allowed 86 hits in 50 2/3 innings.

Butcher had stopped throwing his best pitch--a sinking fastball--with the Twins and he never found it with the Indians. He went from the starting rotation to the bullpen to the disabled list.

In Cleveland, Butcher acted as if a bunted ball was a live grenade. Teams took pleasure in bunting on him and then watching the heavy-legged pitcher stumble after the ball.

He covers first base well and had a lot of practice backing up third base since he allowed 168 hits in 120 2/3 innings.

OVERALL:

Kaat: "I just don't see him as being a regular starter for any team this year. He has to get a lot of work to be sharp and he's going to have trouble getting that work."

DAVE CLARK
OF, No. 56
LR, 6'2", 198 lbs.
ML Svc: less than
one year
Born: 9-3-62 in
Tupelo, MS

HITTING, BASERUNNING, FIELDING:

Last year the Indians were looking for an extra lefthanded bat. They may have found one in September call-up Dave Clark.

Initially, Clark, who hit 19 homers in Triple-A, concentrated on simply making contact in the big leagues. The Indians weren't looking for a singles hitter. They wanted a lefthanded bat with some power to bring off the bench.

Clark, powerfully built at 6'2" and 198 pounds, finally showed them that with three homers and six RBIs in the last eight games of the season.

Clark has decent speed. He can go from first to third and will steal a base when he has to. He goes hard into second base to break up double plays.

Clark probably surprised the Indians more with his fielding than with anything else. They knew he could hit, but they didn't know he could play right field as well as he did.

He showed an average to above-average arm and came in on the ball very well, though he had some trouble going back to the fence.

OVERALL:

Clark didn't hurt his chances of making the club this year with his performance in 1986. His problems are an abundance of talented outfielders in front of him and whether or not the Indians will want to use a young player off the bench or have him play every day in the minors.

The fact that he hits lefthanded is a major advantage for this young slugger.

CLEVELAND INDIANS

DOUG JONES
RHP, No. 46
RR, 6'2", 190 lbs.
ML Svc: less than one year
Born: 6-24-57 in
 Covina, CA

PITCHING, FIELDING:

Last year Doug Jones kept turning the Triple-A International League on its ear. The Indians kept scratching their heads and calculating his numbers until they were forced to call him up in September for a serious look-- even if he was 29 and a career minor leaguer.

Jones had been pitching in the minors since 1978. It looked as if he'd stay there until 1985, when he came up with a screwball for the Tribe's Double-A team. The screwball baffled them in Triple-A last year and didn't do a bad job in the big leagues either.

Working in middle and short relief, Jones went 1-0 for the Tribe in 15 games. He is a trick pitcher who changes speeds on his fastball very well and throws a variety of breaking pitches--including the screwball.

He's the type of junkball pitcher who can be effective one time through a lineup. However, if a club sees him more than once in a series, he could be in trouble.

Jones uses a three-quarters motion and he seems to vary it.

Jones is an average fielder. He'll keep a runner close at first base but his pickoff move could use some work.

OVERALL:

Jones' showing late last season raised his value greatly in the organization. He could be the middle reliever the Indians' spent most of last season without.

DICKIE NOLES
RHP, No. 48
RR, 6'2", 190 lbs.
ML Svc: 7 years
Born: 11-19-56 in
 Charlotte, NC

PITCHING, FIELDING:

Dickie Noles made two impressions in the major leagues last year. The first came in spring training when he was hit on the left foot with a line drive. His foot hurt, but Noles kept pitching. He made the team and then it was discovered Noles' foot was really broken. Noles, it seemed, pitched through the pain because he really wanted to make the club.

The next impression came in a game against Detroit when the Indians were getting pounded. Noles, taking a beating to save the bullpen, nearly started a brawl by putting a number of Tigers on their haunches. The next day Detroit manager Sparky Anderson said Noles had "coconuts" for brains.

Noles was bothered by control problems last year. When his foot healed, he had no pop on his fastball and had to rely on a big-breaking curveball. It was his best pitch, but he hung it too often, allowing nine homers in only 54 2/3 innings.

Before getting hurt, he pitched well as a set-up man for short man Ernie Camacho. He will pitch inside all day long.

Noles is a decent fielder who comes off the mound hard and will make the play at first.

He has a big motion that gives baserunners a good jump.

OVERALL:

The Indians let Noles turn free agent last year but invited him to spring training. While the stats don't bear it out, observers feel that Noles can pitch in tight spots.

Last year was his first winning season (3-2) in the majors.

DETROIT TIGERS

HITTING:

Tom Brookens doesn't enjoy being labeled as a part-time player but, like it or not, his versatility perfectly fits that description.

If third baseman Darnell Coles needs a day of rest, Brookens is an adequate replacement. If shortstop Alan Trammell requires a day off, Brookens takes his place. If second baseman Lou Whitaker is benched against a certain lefthanded pitcher, Brookens appears in his stead. If the Tigers require a righthanded designated hitter, Brookens is often the choice. The little guy even caught five innings in an emergency two years ago.

His playing time is mostly limited to facing lefthanded pitchers. He handles the low fastball fairly well and his home run power is generated against breaking balls. Lefthanders pitch him away and ride fastballs up and in. He has a tendency to chase bad pitches when behind in the count.

On the rare occasions when Brookens faces righthanded pitching, he tends to go to the opposite field more frequently. Righthanders can handle him with high, tight fastballs and hard sliders away.

Brookens' offense picked up last season when he donned eyeglasses. His average rose from a high of .246 in the previous five seasons to .270.

BASERUNNING:

Brookens runs the bases intelligently, even though his speed doesn't stamp him as a stolen base threat. Sparky Anderson has repeatedly stated that Brookens never misses signs, which is important offensively and also defensively when he is stationed at third base and must relay bunt coverage to other infielders.

FIELDING:

Defensively, Brookens is more than

TOM BROOKENS
INF, No. 16
RR, 5'10", 170 lbs.
ML Svc: 8 years
Born: 8-10-53 in
Chambersburg, PA

1986 STATISTICS

AVG	G	AB	R	H	2B	3B	HR	RBI	BB	SO	SB
.270	98	281	42	76	11	2	3	25	20	42	11

CAREER STATISTICS

AVG	G	AB	R	H	2B	3B	HR	RBI	BB	SO	SB
.247	927	2658	324	657	124	30	48	300	179	416	74

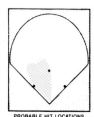

VS. RHP   VS. LHP   PROBABLE HIT LOCATIONS

adequate at third base and second base. His limited arm strength drops him a notch at shortstop. The majority of his mistakes stem from throwing errors.

OVERALL:

Brookens is a good utility player who can perform with the authority of a regular for a limited period of time. He's dedicated to winning and one of his strongest suits is his baseball insight.

Kaat: "Brookens is a very important player on the 24-man roster. He has accepted his part-time role and performs admirably because he prepares as if he's a regular. Brookens is well liked by his teammates; the Tigers do not suffer measurably with Brookens in the lineup."

DETROIT TIGERS

HITTING:

Darnell Coles went through almost as many managers during his three-year tenure with the Seattle Mariners as Dave Collins has during his vagabond major league career.

Injuries and conflicting managerial opinions have impeded Coles' progress. This youngster yearned for a legitimate chance to perform on an everyday basis. He received that opportunity in Detroit and delivered by joining Ray Boone and Eddie Yost as the only third basemen in Tiger history to hit as many as 20 home runs in one season.

The deal (in the winter of 1985 for pitcher Rich Monteleone) turned out to be a steal for the Tigers. Coles can play. He's relaxed and confident at the plate. He has quick hands and quick wrists that allow him to drive the inside fastball. His knowledge of the strike zone is improving, as is his ability to discipline himself at the plate.

Righthanders concentrate on working him down and away because it doesn't pay to bust him inside. Coles even sent a Roger Clemens' fastball sailing over the left field screen at Fenway Park last season. Lefthanders must change speeds and work him away. Anything that is thrown hard inside to Coles should be strictly cosmetic.

BASERUNNING:

Coles does not constitute a stolen base threat. Added experience will help him learn pitchers' moves better and enable him to improve his jump.

FIELDING:

Coles performed adequately at third base last year. He seems to have overcome his tendency to carry his offensive failures into the field. His footwork, however, requires improvement. He often tangles his feet, which results in throwing errors, but his reactions are quick enough to allow him to get straightened out in most cases. His arm is exceptionally strong, and he can excite a crowd with his throws from behind third base.

As he develops better work habits and a

DARNELL COLES
3B, No. 19
RR, 6'1", 185 lbs.
ML Svc: 2 years
Born: 6-22-62 in
San Bernardino, CA

1986 STATISTICS

AVG	G	AB	R	H	2B	3B	HR	RBI	BB	SO	SB
.273	142	521	67	142	30	2	20	86	45	84	6

CAREER STATISTICS

AVG	G	AB	R	H	2B	3B	HR	RBI	BB	SO	SB
.251	244	815	99	205	44	3	22	103	78	139	8

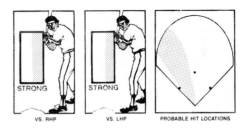

better knowledge of opposing hitters, Coles should become a better positional fielder. He does not always react well on bunts.

OVERALL:

Sparky Anderson handled Coles well last season by bringing him along slowly and surely. Anderson received assistance from batting instructor Vada Pinson, who was familiar with Coles from their joint days with the Mariners.

Coles will assume additional offensive responsibilities if Lance Parrish does not return to his role as a righthanded power hitter in the Tigers' lineup this season. Coles could wind up batting cleanup against lefthanded pitching.

Kaat: "The key to Coles' 1987 season will be for him to push himself to greater heights. Pitchers will pay attention to him following his successful 1986 campaign. He has become a marked man.

"He should improve in all areas with a year of experience under his belt."

DETROIT TIGERS

HITTING:

Darrell Evans is a rarity in professional baseball: he is an *everyday* performer at the age of 40. Evans is the type of hitter who continues, even at his age, to epitomize the emphasis placed on production via home runs in the Eastern Division of the American League.

Scouts wonder when Evans' bat will lose its pop. He had a terrible spring training in 1985 and yet ended the season with a league-leading 40 home runs. He started off slowly last season but finished with 29 homers, even though he batted only .215 after the All-Star break.

Few players in baseball ride the low, inside fastball out of the park more frequently than Evans. Dating back to his days with the Atlanta Braves and San Francisco Giants, he has handled that pitch as well as anyone.

Evans' knowledge of the strike zone accounts for his home runs. He's always a tough out because he is a selective hitter, and that makes him especially tough in the late innings when patience often results in a good pitch to drive. Evans is a student of hitting. He is adroit at detecting pitching patterns and is considered to be a guess hitter.

Pitchers most often have success challenging Evans early in the count, so that they avoid falling behind and being forced to throw cripple pitches. Lefthanders generally work Evans away with breaking pitches. Fastballs are usually waste pitches. Righthanders run fastballs up and in, or away, and change speeds frequently against Evans.

BASERUNNING:

Evans does not have good baserunning speed. He seldom grounds into double plays, however, because his uppercut swing often results in a lot of infield and outfield flies rather than DP grounders.

FIELDING:

No one in the American League plays a

DARRELL EVANS
DH/1B, No. 41
LR, 6'2", 205 lbs.
ML Svc: 16 years
Born: 5-26-47 in
Pasadena, CA

1986 STATISTICS

AVG	G	AB	R	H	2B	3B	HR	RBI	BB	SO	SB
.241	151	507	78	122	15	0	29	85	91	105	3

CAREER STATISTICS

AVG	G	AB	R	H	2B	3B	HR	RBI	BB	SO	SB
.251	2286	7761	1175	1947	294	35	347	1152	1380	1191	91

  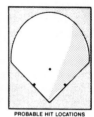

VS. RHP   VS. LHP   PROBABLE HIT LOCATIONS

deeper first base than Evans. That positioning allows him to maximize his range but also forces pitchers to cover first base on every ground ball hit to the right side. His astute knowledge of game situations offsets his physical limitations and provides the Tigers with a coach on the field.

OVERALL:

The years have been kind to Evans. His physical condition is good, in part because he plays a relatively injury-free position.

He continues to represent a home run threat and is well-suited to the short right field porch of Tiger Stadium.

Kaat: "A lot of the success Evans has had is relative to the lineup he hits in. Because he has got good hitters around him, he gets a lot of good pitches to hit. Once a pitcher gets behind in the count, it's Evans' game."

DETROIT TIGERS

HITTING:

The All-American boy is still striving to reach All-Star status. As time passes, Kirk Gibson's career might become a case of a player who never realized his advanced billing, which, in fairness to Gibson, was pretty lofty from the start. He was dubbed "The next Mickey Mantle" by Sparky Anderson when something like "The first Kirk Gibson" would have been more than adequate.

Gibson's blend of raw speed and power mark him as one of the most exciting and explosive players in the American League. He played last season at less than 100% after recovering from a severe ankle sprain he sustained in April.

Gibson handles low pitches extremely well and has home run power to all fields. He thrives on low, inside fastballs from righthanders but can be tied up by hard sliders thrown down and in. Above-average fastballs up-and-in tie him up and neutralize his quick bat. Lefthanders generally work Gibson away and are careful not to hang breaking pitches inside.

He has a tendency to open up his front shoulder as he swings the bat, which rotates his hips too quickly. When he does this, his whole body flies out of the proper alignment, and instead of striding *in* to the pitch, he ends up facing the first-base dugout. When he does this, Gibson is in for a prolonged slump. He would be well-advised to bunt and use his speed to limit those slumps, although an excessive reliance on bunting from Gibson would defuse the Tiger attack.

BASERUNNING:

Gibson is a great athlete with great speed and represents a legitimate stolen base threat. The Tigers shy away from running him too much because he is a big man (6'3", 215 lbs.) and tends to wear down if he runs too often.

Instinctively, Gibson is a good overall ballplayer and, as such, avoids falling into patterns when poised to attempt to steal a base. His competitive fires burn hot.

KIRK GIBSON
RF, No. 23
LL, 6'3", 215 lbs.
ML Svc: 7 years
Born: 5-28-57 in
Pontiac, MI

1986 STATISTICS

AVG	G	AB	R	H	2B	3B	HR	RBI	BB	SO	SB
.268	119	441	84	118	11	2	28	86	68	107	34

CAREER STATISTICS

AVG	G	AB	R	H	2B	3B	HR	RBI	BB	SO	SB
.275	765	2723	433	750	115	32	126	420	309	596	140

  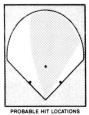

STRONG VS. RHP   STRONG VS. LHP   PROBABLE HIT LOCATIONS

FIELDING:

His speed is an asset defensively, although the Tigers were miffed for a period last season when he didn't utilize that speed to charge balls. Teams can consistently take an extra base on Gibson if he lays back on balls because his arm strength and accuracy are below average.

OVERALL:

Gibson is the fulcrum of the Tiger offense and an uplifting force in the clubhouse. The Tigers would like him to demonstrate more consistency, but his production speaks loudly.

Kaat: "He's a dynamite package capable of exploding and should be more relaxed this season after a 1985-86 winter of discontent when he was ignored as a premier free agent.

"Kirk is a potential MVP if he's back to full strength following his injury last year."

DETROIT TIGERS

HITTING:

With all due respect to Leo Durocher, nice guys *can* succeed in baseball. John Grubb proved that in 1986 when he batted .333 and slugged .590 in 210 at-bats as a platooned designated hitter.

Grubb's bat last year smoked to the point that he was elevated to the cleanup spot in the Tiger lineup against righthanded pitching after Lance Parrish was felled by injury at midseason.

Grubb wound up with 13 home runs and 51 RBIs, his highest totals in both departments since 1978.

His teammates call him "Papa Grubb" because of his age (38). Opposing pitchers, in a barely audible tone of voice, likely called him more than that. Grubb is one of the most disciplined part-time hitters in the league, which is a tribute to his work habits. He waits well on off-speed pitches and is seldom fooled by a pitch. By the same token, he has the quickness to rake low fastballs with his textbook swing. Grubb also has an uncanny ability to spoil high fastballs and keep his at-bat alive.

The acknowledged "book" on Grubb is to work him low and away, but the "book" lied last season when several of his home runs were struck to left-center field.

Grubb is comfortable in his part-time role and fully accepts his limited playing time. The Tigers are careful not to play him too much because he is vulnerable to injuries, which generally require a prolonged period to heal.

BASERUNNING:

Speed is not an asset for this part-timer. Grubb, like many players in the home run-conscious American League, is a station-to-station baserunner. He is not a threat to steal and does not command attention from opposing pitchers when he's on base.

FIELDING:

Grubb is an accomplished outfielder who

JOHN GRUBB
PH/OF, No. 30
LR, 6'3", 180 lbs.
ML Svc: 15 years
Born: 8-4-48 in
Richmond, VA

1986 STATISTICS

AVG	G	AB	R	H	2B	3B	HR	RBI	BB	SO	SB
.333	81	210	32	70	13	1	13	51	28	28	0

CAREER STATISTICS

AVG	G	AB	R	H	2B	3B	HR	RBI	BB	SO	SB
.280	1365	4040	444	1130	201	29	97	462	530	542	27

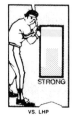

VS. LHP

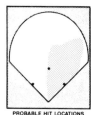

PROBABLE HIT LOCATIONS

rarely misjudges balls. His range and arm strength are limited, but he is a fundamentally sound outfielder. Grubb is not asked to play the outfield very often because of the risk of injury.

OVERALL:

Grubb will be hard-pressed to duplicate the numbers he produced in 1986 but he does seem to defy Father Time. He's a valuable property as a designated hitter or pinch-hitter, but Sparky Anderson must be careful to continue to reduce Grubb's potential for injury.

Kaat: "Grubb probably isn't capable of more than 300 at-bats over the course of a season, but you can bet that they will be quality at-bats.

"Grubb is an outstanding player coming off the bench, an asset to the Tigers as a veteran player comfortable in his role."

DETROIT TIGERS

HITTING:

This seems to be such a sad trend with the Braves: a once-promising hitter who blossomed briefly, then fell out. The characterization fits Terry Harper as snugly as anyone.

After many false starts, he appeared to arrive as an offensive ballplayer in 1985. But in 1986 he was inept at the plate, struggling with a sub-.200 batting average and no run production until he was finally benched by manager Chuck Tanner. He did not resurface until late season, when his swing appeared somewhat rejuvenated.

Harper is an intense person and this may hurt him as a hitter. His hitting success or failure seems to feed upon itself; good performances lead to more and better things, while bad performances lead to worse performances.

Harper is a strong hitter who, in good times, can handle almost all power pitches, can turn very effectively on the inside-corner offerings and can reach out and stroke low-and-away pitches to right field. In bad times, he can be made to look helpless by hard stuff on the fists or breaking stuff around the knees on the outside corner. He also will chase bad balls at times and, at other times, take perfectly hittable pitches for called strikes.

In general, he is basically a pull hitter who likes the fastball more than the breaking ball and he is a dangerous mistake hitter. Pitchers should be careful with him.

BASERUNNING:

Harper's speed appears to have declined from above-average to average. He is not the answer to the team's speed deficiency, although he may well recapture a spot in the starting outfield for 1987. Only rarely does his head appear not to be in the game and only rarely does he commit a blunder on the bases.

FIELDING:

Harper is a very competent outfielder. He is not dazzling, but he is solid. He has a strong

TERRY HARPER
LF, No. 19
RR, 6'1", 205 lbs.
ML Svc: 7 years
Born: 8-19-55 in
Douglasville, GA

1986 STATISTICS

AVG	G	AB	R	H	2B	3B	HR	RBI	BB	SO	SB
.257	106	265	26	68	12	0	8	30	29	39	3

CAREER STATISTICS

AVG	G	AB	R	H	2B	3B	HR	RBI	BB	SO	SB
.254	473	1337	135	339	49	5	32	163	128	229	36

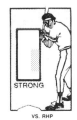  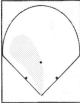

VS. RHP   VS. LHP   PROBABLE HIT LOCATIONS

enough arm, good enough range, good enough speed, good enough instincts. If Harper could have put the other components of his game together earlier in his career, he could have become an All-Star outfielder, because the defensive tools are there. These tools, in fact, are what kept the Braves attracted to him for so long.

OVERALL:

Most teams probably would have given up on Harper long before Atlanta did. Except for his impressive 1985 season, all of Harper's good numbers have come in the minor leagues. But he clearly has the tools to play in the big leagues and he'll have the opportunity in 1987 to show to the Tigers that he can--or can't--do.

Dierker: "Harper has his limitations, although he does show power and some things you like with the bat. He could be the kind of guy who could bounce back."

DETROIT TIGERS

HITTING:

Mike Heath would not want his career to be judged by the number of times he has been traded. Heath was sent from the Oakland A's to the St. Louis Cardinals for All-Star pitcher Joaquin Andujar in December of 1985. Eight months later he was sent unceremoniously to the Tigers for a fleeting first base prospect named Mike Laga.

Controversy has shadowed Heath in recent seasons. He was criticized in Oakland for his overall pitch selection and, in a specific instance, for failing to run out a ground ball in Detroit late in the 1985 season. The entire success of Heath's game, it has been suggested, depends on his temperament. He must be intense without being tense to realize the potential most scouts felt he brought to the major leagues.

Heath seems to fancy himself as a power hitter, which is an opinion no one else shares. He possesses the hitting ability to go to the opposite field and should use that ability to the fullest extent. He is considered a tough out when he sprays the ball around, but not when he concentrates on invisible power.

Lefthanders have maximum success against Heath when they work him hard inside. Righthanders ride fastballs up and in and then work breaking pitches away. If Heath is in a hitting groove, he'll go to the opposite field with the breaking pitches. If he's not in a good groove, he'll ground those breaking pitches harmlessly to the left side of the infield.

Heath frequently is a first-strike, fastball hitter.

BASERUNNING:

Heath possesses decent speed for a catcher. He is not a basestealing threat and his overexuberance on the basepaths is sometimes counterproductive, as he will run himself right into trouble.

FIELDING:

Heath is generally considered to have one of the strongest arms in baseball. He's an animated catcher who visits pitchers on the mound frequently during the course of a

MIKE HEATH
C, No. 8
RR, 5'11", 180 lbs.
ML Svc: 9 years
Born: 2-5-55 in
Tampa, FL

1986 STATISTICS

AVG	G	AB	R	H	2B	3B	HR	RBI	BB	SO	SB
.226	95	288	30	65	11	1	8	36	27	53	6

CAREER STATISTICS

AVG	G	AB	R	H	2B	3B	HR	RBI	BB	SO	SB
.248	853	2818	316	698	113	20	55	325	189	377	38

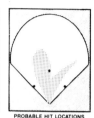

VS. RHP   VS. LHP   PROBABLE HIT LOCATIONS

game. The Tigers detected some minor mechanical flaws in his catching technique last season and assigned former All-Star catcher Bill Freehan to work with him during spring training this year.

Heath will require time to become familiar with the Tiger pitching staff and become comfortable with his role as their pilot. His hustle and quickness behind the plate are strong and highly desirable attributes, but if he doesn't accept his role as a part-time player, he could be a disruptive force as he expresses his discontent to a manager who won't have the inclination to listen.

OVERALL:

Heath's distasteful stint with the Cardinals did not enhance his career. His return to the American League could be a blessing--*if* he makes the most of a renewed opportunity.

Kaat: "He seemed comfortable with the Tigers during the final two months of last season and that's an important development considering the Tigers' uncertainty about the availability of a front-line catcher.

"Heath's best bet with the Tigers, however, remains as a part-time performer who has some defensive strengths."

DETROIT TIGERS

PITCHING:

Willie Hernandez was the toast of baseball in 1984. He came to the Tigers from the Philadelphia Phillies and led the club to a World Championship by featuring a screwball the American League was not familiar with.

The league is catching up with Hernandez, however. His effectiveness has diminished greatly, and Sparky Anderson is now talking about utilizing the now-trendy "bullpen by committee" in Detroit.

Last season, Hernandez tipped off his once-devastating screwball by rocking back farther in his delivery, giving he more attentive batters advance warning of its arrival. He also fell into a pattern where experienced opponents became aware of looking for the screwball with two strikes in the count.

Not surprisingly, Hernandez now is vulnerable to surrendering home runs. He yielded only six in 1984, but 13 in each of the past two seasons and all but one to righthanded hitters.

The Tigers harbor a fear. They wonder if Hernandez can pitch effectively at Tiger Stadium following a season during which Detroit fans got on his back. Hernandez is a sensitive person; he is vulnerable to constant booing. If it happens again this season, it could strip him of some motivation.

Hernandez's fastball remains a good pitch and an even better pitch if he can recapture his lost screwball. He enjoyed great success against righthanders in 1984 because the screwball deprived them of their power.

He continues to enjoy success against lefthanders for two reasons: he challenges them more frequently with his fastball and he drops down in his delivery at times, something he does not do to righthanded hitters.

WILLIE HERNANDEZ
LHP, No. 21
LL, 6'2", 185 lbs.
ML Svc: 10 years
Born: 11-14-54 in
Aguada, PR

1986 STATISTICS

W	L	ERA	G	GS	CG	SV	IP	H	R	ER	BB	SO
8	7	3.55	64	0	0	24	88.2	87	35	35	21	77

CAREER STATISTICS

W	L	ERA	G	GS	CG	SV	IP	H	R	ER	BB	SO
59	52	3.30	604	11	0	114	896	813	359	329	282	669

FIELDING:

Hernandez's fielding is not a strength. He is woefully weak at fielding bunts. His move to first base is below average but doesn't often come into play because he usually is used with the Tigers leading in the late innings when the opposition is not inclined to steal.

OVERALL:

A variance in pitching pattern would prove beneficial to Hernandez. Increased use of his fastball also would be helpful. That pitch has not yet deserted him.

Hernandez's success was built on his screwball. That's the pitch that made him famous. His fastball, however, remains his out pitch and he should pay attention to that fact.

Kaat: "The days of depending on one relief pitcher to close out games are over, but the Tigers must be mindful to give Hernandez enough work, within reason, or he'll lose his effectiveness."

DETROIT TIGERS

HITTING:

Baseball skills sometimes can vanish without the benefit of any logical explanation. Where have you gone, Larry Herndon?

Herndon belted 43 home runs and drove in 180 runs in 1982-83 after coming to Detroit from the San Francisco Giants. Over the last *three* years, however, he has accounted for 27 homers and 117 RBIs, a dismal decline in production.

There really was no explanation for his early productivity as a Tiger. He had never managed more than eight homers or 49 RBIs with the Giants--pitchers could knock the bat out of his hands with hard stuff inside. Herndon was a lamb if he couldn't extend his arms. American League pitchers apparently required two seasons to learn this fact. Accordingly, he has been pumped inside with a steady diet of fastballs, which has deprived him of his power alley to right-center field.

BASERUNNING:

Speed used to be one of Herndon's strengths, but knee problems have slowed him over the past two seasons. He is no longer a stolen base threat and his jump off first base is tediously slow.

FIELDING:

Herndon has developed into an above-average left fielder. He goes to the line well to limit doubles to singles. His arm is average in terms of strength and accuracy.

One fault of Herndon's is that he relies too heavily on center fielder Chet Lemon to chase down balls hit into the left field alley.

OVERALL:

Herndon has now been relegated from everyday status to a platoon role. His confidence has waned, along with his

LARRY HERNDON
LF, No. 31
RR, 6'3", 200 lbs.
ML Svc: 11 years
Born: 11-3-53 in
Sunflower, MS

1986 STATISTICS

AVG	G	AB	R	H	2B	3B	HR	RBI	BB	SO	SB
.247	106	283	33	70	13	1	8	37	27	40	2

CAREER STATISTICS

AVG	G	AB	R	H	2B	3B	HR	RBI	BB	SO	SB
.273	1372	4478	557	1222	168	74	94	483	307	721	91

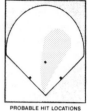

VS. RHP   VS. LHP   PROBABLE HIT LOCATIONS

offensive numbers. He has, at the age of 33, reached a crossroads of his career. He, seemingly, has not adjusted to his demotion at a time when advancing age means harder work and keen attention to work habits.

Most part-time players work on a part-time basis. Their skills diminish. Herndon must force himself to work harder and take extra batting practice so that he's prepared to play when called upon.

Kaat: "Herndon's redeeming feature is that he plays left field and bats righthanded. The Tigers are extremely short in both departments, and Herndon did manage to smack as many home runs (3) and drive in as many runs (12) last year as any pinch-hitter in club history.

"Herndon cannot be expected to return to everyday status. He is, in fact, in an annual struggle to extend his career. If he comes to grips with his role, he could be serviceable beyond this season."

DETROIT TIGERS

PITCHING:

Eric King was a throw-in when the Tigers acquired lefthanded pitcher Dave LaPoint from the San Francisco Giants following the 1985 season. Many people in the Giants' organization vehemently protested King's inclusion in the trade.

Those who protested were right.

LaPoint is gone. King is a reason for the Tigers to chortle over that deal.

The 22-year-old righthander began the 1986 season pitching in the minors. The Tigers summoned him to the big leagues in May, and he won 11 games as the club's first rookie pitcher to claim as many as 10 victories since Dave Rozema in 1977.

King is mature beyond his years. He is a power pitcher with a live arm and hard breaking pitches. He throws a slider and two fastballs, one that rides in to righthanded hitters and another that cuts away. The action on his ball, especially the fastball that cuts away, is so crisp that Tiger catchers often were handcuffed trying to catch him.

King, like teammate Frank Tanana, is not adverse to pitching inside to protect his territory. He enjoys running the ball in on righthanded hitters to the point that he practices knockdown pitches when warming up.

King's aggressiveness sets him apart from most young pitchers, who tend to be much more timid and in awe of their station. King does not yield to any hitter.

His success against the Baltimore Orioles last season is notable; he was 3-0 with one save versus the Birds in 1986. He allowed two runs in 26 innings while recording 23 strikeouts.

FIELDING:

King's fielding is below average. His footspeed is slow and he does not bounce off the mound quickly. He must learn to hold runners closer to first base but that should come with experience.

ERIC KING
RHP, No. 25
RR, 6'2", 180 lbs.
ML Svc: less than one year
Born: 4-10-64 in
** Oxnard, CA**

1986 STATISTICS

W	L	ERA	G	GS	CG	SV	IP	H	R	ER	BB	SO
11	4	3.51	33	16	3	3	138.1	108	54	54	63	79

CAREER STATISTICS

W	L	ERA	G	GS	CG	SV	IP	H	R	ER	BB	SO
11	4	3.51	33	16	3	3	138.1	108	54	54	63	79

OVERALL:

Sparky Anderson must decide how to best use this promising pitcher this season. The youngster was used as both a starter and a reliever in 1986. Anderson likes his power out of the bullpen and questions his ability to maintain concentration as a starter. Anderson expected to use King as a starter in spring training and return him to the bullpen only if some other young pitcher earned a spot in the starting rotation.

King's future excites the Tigers as much as that of any young pitcher they've had since Mark Fidrych. Anderson likes his maturity, but there are concerns: King must maintain his best pitching form and has a tendency to be overweight, and even if he is in good shape, no one knows how many innings he can pitch before he wears down. If King can manage to keep his waistline pared, he'll give himself an edge.

Kaat: "King can be effective out of the bullpen or in the starting rotation, but the Tigers need to spell out his role this year and stick with their decision."

DETROIT TIGERS

HITTING:

Chet Lemon is an enigma. He has the power to be a home run hitter and the speed to hit for average, but he seems to be caught in a mental trap somewhere between the two.

The result of riding the fence last season was that he did neither well and suffered a drastic reduction in both departments. Lemon's average plunged to .251, the lowest since his rookie season of 1976. His home run output dropped to 12, his lowest figure in five seasons. His RBIs were limited to 53, which represents three more than his lowest total since his rookie season. More alarming is the fact that one-half of the 30 home runs he has accounted for the past two seasons have been hit from September 1st to the end of the season--and everyone in baseball knows you *never* judge a player in the spring or the fall.

Pitchers, both lefthanders and right-handers, pound Lemon inside with fastballs. He even moved off the plate with very limited success in an attempt to handle that pitch. Instead, he gave third basemen and shortstops a good workout fielding all the harmless ground balls he hit while jamming himself.

Lemon is capable of driving with power the fastball that splits the plate in half, but so are a lot of other outfielders in a league blessed with home run hitters.

BASERUNNING:

Baserunning is not Lemon's strong suit, despite his above-average speed. His instincts are poor and he has stolen only two bases in the past two seasons. He also has a bad habit of diving headfirst into first base. That has produced more nagging injuries than base hits.

FIELDING:

Lemon's speed still stamps him as a good center fielder. He prides himself on his defense. His judgment on throws from the outfield has been questioned and he is prone

CHET LEMON
CF, No. 34
RR, 6'1", 190 lbs.
ML Svc: 11 years
Born: 2-12-55 in Jackson, MS

1986 STATISTICS

AVG	G	AB	R	H	2B	3B	HR	RBI	BB	SO	SB
.251	126	403	45	101	21	3	12	53	39	53	2

CAREER STATISTICS

AVG	G	AB	R	H	2B	3B	HR	RBI	BB	SO	SB
.277	1467	5150	747	1429	302	48	166	666	526	745	53

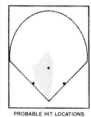

STRONG — VS. RHP   STRONG — VS. LHP   PROBABLE HIT LOCATIONS

to missing the cutoff man. Lemon rarely drops a ball he reaches, but seems to have lost half a stride. The jump he gets on balls is good. Unlike other good center fielders, however, he does not position himself shallow.

OVERALL:

Lemon must hit with extra-base power to justify his position in the Tigers' everyday lineup.

Motivation could be lacking in Lemon's case: he is signed through 1992. His skills are still there and he looms as a necessary righthanded bat in a lineup short on righthanded power. Any further lack of offensive production could result in a platoon system with Pat Sheridan.

Kaat: "Lemon is not a very good fundamental player. Like several other Tigers, if he's motivated, he has the ability to revert to his 1984 form. That's the manager's job."

ACE OF THE STAFF

PITCHING:

Jack Morris, a three-time All-Star, has never won a Cy Young Award or a Gold Glove.

All he has done is win more games (144) than any pitcher in baseball from 1979 to 1986. He is a modern day Jim Bunning, the pitcher-turned-politician who won 224 games and tossed no-hitters in each league only to be left outside Cooperstown's front door.

Morris is the type of pitcher any team would want as its ace (or so one would think). He has the fastball and slider to pitch with power and the split-finger fastball and change-up to keep opponents off stride. The four-pitch package allows Morris to win even when he doesn't have his best stuff. He surrendered 40 home runs in 1986, but 30 of the gophers were with the bases empty and 10 were offered with one runner on base. He gives the impression of being in command even when touched for a home run or two.

His dominance last season (18-4 following a 3-4 start) can be attributed to a greater reliance on his power pitches, which he used to challenge hitters. Morris made greater use of his slider than his split-finger fastball and usually had pinpoint control of his fastball, which he still considers to be his No. 1 pitch.

Morris is a manager's delight because he generally affords the bullpen a day of rest. He finished with 15 complete games last season, which was two more than the number finished by the entire staff of the New York Yankees, as many as the Texas Rangers and one less than the Toronto Blue Jays. Morris averaged 7.63 innings pitched for each of his 35 starting assignments. He's reliable, durable, intensely competitive and good.

FIELDING:

Morris' fielding skills are an asset. He probably is the best athlete among Tiger players. He's extremely quick and tough to bunt against. His first base coverage is without equal.

JACK MORRIS
RHP, No. 47
RR, 6'3", 200 lbs.
ML Svc: 9 years
Born: 5-16-55 in
St. Paul, MN

1986 STATISTICS

W	L	ERA	G	GS	CG	SV	IP	H	R	ER	BB	SO
21	8	3.27	35	35	15	0	267	229	105	97	82	223

CAREER STATISTICS

W	L	ERA	G	GS	CG	SV	IP	H	R	ER	BB	SO
144	94	3.57	302	280	110	0	2422.2	1895	910	842	754	1327

One weakness is his sometimes indifferent approach to baserunners. Morris has the ability and knowledge to hold runners close but his supreme confidence in retiring hitters and his ability to escape troublesome innings can result in the advancement of runners into scoring position on steals of second base.

OVERALL:

Morris has a hot temper, which is the byproduct of his competitive instincts. His fiery side has been counterproductive at times. Morris, approaching the age of 32, has begun to make strides to curb that temper, however.

Morris' high level of consistency has stamped him as the pitcher of this decade. His pride and desire to excel could be challenged this season after a winter of bickering with the Tiger front office over his free agent market value.

Kaat: "When you start predicting Cy Young candidates for 1987 you put Mike Witt, Teddy Higuera and Roger Clemens at the top, but you know Morris will be in the top five of almost every pitching category."

HITTING:

The perennial All-Star catcher is now entering a critical period in his distinguished career. Lance Parrish missed the final three months of last season with a congenital lower back condition which could jeopardize his future in baseball. Surgery was ruled out and Parrish made significant progress toward a full recovery by undergoing an extensive rehabilitation program over the winter.

It is a well-known fact that a healthy Parrish can put the hurt on opponents. He has slugged 142 home runs over the past five seasons, including 22 last year in only 327 at-bats.

He has the strength to flare inside fastballs thrown off the plate into the outfield for singles.

When he is behind in the count, Parrish is susceptible to outside breaking pitches from righthanders. Lefthanders change speeds more frequently against him because they don't have the advantage of throwing sliders and curves away from his power zone. The best approach is to get ahead in the count with fastballs away and then entice him to chase breaking pitches. He is, like most power hitters, prone to mechanical flaws that result in prolonged slumps.

Parrish is generally considered to be a pull hitter and has faced infield shifts from several clubs in recent years.

He is not a threat to bunt his way on by utilizing either footspeed or bat control. As a result, the defensive alignment of opposing infielders is rarely positioned at anything other than maximum depth.

BASERUNNING:

His speed on the basepaths is representative of the rate of motion which has come to be associated with players who assume the position of major league catcher.

FIELDING:

Parrish's defensive capabilities have earned him several Gold Glove awards. His 6'3", 220-pound frame provides his pitchers with a

**LANCE PARRISH
C, No. 13
RR, 6'3", 220 lbs.
ML Svc: 9 years
Born: 6-15-56 in
Clairton, PA**

1986 STATISTICS

AVG	G	AB	R	H	2B	3B	HR	RBI	BB	SO	SB
.257	91	327	53	84	6	1	22	62	39	83	0

CAREER STATISTICS

AVG	G	AB	R	H	2B	3B	HR	RBI	BB	SO	SB
.263	1146	4273	577	1123	201	23	212	700	335	847	22

  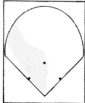

STRONG   STRONG   PROBABLE HIT LOCATIONS

VS. RHP   VS. LHP

good target. Parrish is mobile behind the plate and has an exceptionally quick release and a strong and accurate throwing arm. He is not adverse to making snap throws to first base in an attempt to pick off baserunners.

His status has grown over the years and he provides pitchers, especially young ones, with an added degree of confidence.

Many observers feel Parrish should adopt a second position, probably first base, to relieve his catching load and extend his career.

OVERALL:

A healthy Parrish is arguably the best catcher in baseball. At the age of 30, he is an offensive weapon at a defensive position. His off-season rehabilitation should allow Parrish to catch 120-130 games this year, and 500 at-bats will guarantee 25-30 home runs, which is rare among catchers.

Kaat: "Parrish's success in 1987 depends on his ability to stay healthy the entire season. If he's healthy, he ranks as one of the top catchers in baseball."

NEEDS ANOTHER PITCH

PITCHING:

Dan Petry was coasting to an outstanding career entering the 1986 season. He had, at the age of 27, posted 93 career victories. He had won 10 or more games for six consecutive seasons and seemed certain to reach 100 victories last year.

Instead, Petry enters 1987 faced with the biggest challenge of his career. He must rebound from surgery that removed four bone chips from his right elbow. Petry won only one of six decisions last season when he returned to the Tiger rotation following his midseason surgery. He finished with a 5-10 record and 4.66 ERA, well above his 3.49 career ERA entering the 1986 season.

Petry is still a young ballplayer and that, coupled with his strong desire to excel, is to his advantage as he begins his 1987 bid to regain his lost stature.

Petry has reached the stage in his career when he should develop a reliable off-speed pitch. He has survived very well on his fastball and slider in an era when starting pitchers with only two power pitches and no specialty weapons (such as a knuckleball) are a rare commodity.

Petry alternately has attempted to refine his curveball, split-finger fastball and straight change-up. He probably will concentrate on the change-up as his necessary off-speed delivery this year.

If Petry is able to develop an off-speed pitch effectively, he should be able to reduce the number of sliders he has to throw. His slider generally was considered to be among the best in the league, but it is a pitch that places tremendous strain on the elbow and could be considered an aggravation to his injury.

FIELDING:

Petry is an above-average fielder and is

DAN PETRY
RHP, No. 46
RR, 6'4", 200 lbs.
ML Svc: 8 years
Born: 11-13-58 in
Palo Alto, CA

1986 STATISTICS

W	L	ERA	G	GS	CG	SV		IP	H	R	ER	BB	SO
5	10	4.66	20	20	2	0		116	122	78	60	53	56

CAREER STATISTICS

W	L	ERA	G	GS	CG	SV		IP	H	R	ER	BB	SO
98	74	3.58	227	224	47	0		1504	1380	675	598	572	773

always in position to field any balls hit back to the mound. He gets off the mound well for someone his size and is not lethargic in covering first base.

His pickoff move to first base is above average. Opponents don't make a habit of attempting to steal against him.

OVERALL:

Petry's future as a pitcher hinges on a good performance this season. Many observers are skeptical about his chances to make a full recovery. His name was mentioned in trade talks several times during the off-season.

Kaat: "It is essential for Petry to develop an off-speed pitch to complement his fastball and slider. If he's comfortable in spring training with his rehabilitation and bounces back from his injury, he can again be a solid No. 2 starter."

DETROIT TIGERS

HITTING:

The Kansas City Royals released Pat Sheridan last spring because he had gained a reputation for being too laid back.

The Tigers, short on outfielders, liked his versatility (he can play all three outfield positions) and gambled that a new setting would provide Sheridan with a fresh outlook.

The jury is still out on the Tigers' move.

Sheridan is young enough at the age of 29 to make a marked improvement in his overall game. He handles low fastballs well from righthanders but is vulnerable to lefthanded pitching. He shows flashes of home run power but not enough to provide any promise as a home run hitter or justify his low batting average.

He must resist the temptation to aim shots at Tiger Stadium's short right field porch. The Tigers encouraged Sheridan to utilize the entire field of play and sent him to Harry Walker for hitting instruction this winter to improve his ability to make contact.

The bunt could be an offensive weapon for Sheridan, who hits from the left side of the plate and has good speed. He could emerge as a valuable contributor to the team's offense if he put the ball in play more often.

BASERUNNING:

If Sheridan was able to improve his on-base percentage, he would likely increase his stolen base totals. He stole nine bases in 11 attempts last season. Sparky Anderson is fond of that speed. It's up to Sheridan to put it to good use.

FIELDING:

Sheridan's defensive tools are above average, but they haven't had the opportunity to fully surface. His speed is an asset in the outfield, although he could charge balls harder than he does.

PAT SHERIDAN
RF, No. 15
LR, 6'3", 175 lbs.
ML Svc: 4 years
Born: 12-4-57 in
Ann Arbor, MI

1986 STATISTICS

AVG	G	AB	R	H	2B	3B	HR	RBI	BB	SO	SB
.237	98	236	41	56	9	1	6	19	21	57	9

CAREER STATISTICS

AVG	G	AB	R	H	2B	3B	HR	RBI	BB	SO	SB
.262	426	1257	166	329	54	9	24	125	105	251	42

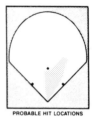

VS. RHP   VS. LHP   PROBABLE HIT LOCATIONS

Sheridan's arm strength is adequate. One drawback, however, is his release, which is slow. The slow release, combined with his timidity on charging balls, makes his average arm appear worse than it is.

OVERALL:

Sheridan is a project of the Tigers. Time is on his side and the Tigers have provided him with a second opportunity to realize his promise. If he can adjust to a part-time role and if his latent talent surfaces, he could make his mark at the major league level.

Kaat: "It will be interesting to see if a winter spent working with hitting coach Harry Walker has any positive influence on Sheridan. He has the size, strength and speed to be a good major league player, but so far he simply hasn't emerged."

PITCHING:

Frank Tanana used to rock-and-fire as a young pitching phenom for the California Angels. Back then, he could take the chill out of a California night with his flaming fastball.

That was years ago. Tanana passed through Texas in a stint with the Rangers and Boston with the Red Sox before he returned to his native Detroit without the fastball and sharp curve that froze hitters 10 years ago. Shoulder and elbow injuries have reduced Tanana to a pitching surgeon. His blazing fastball is now below average. The sharp bite is gone from his curveball. He relies greatly on control and the location of his pitches. Tanana must mix his assortment of pitches and the speed of each and use the entire width of home plate--black borders included--in order to be effective. His margin for error is slight.

The fastball is his purpose pitch. He'll waste it as often as not and also use it to move hitters off the plate. Tanana is not afraid to protect his territory by pitching inside. He turns the ball over frequently to righthanded hitters with his version of a screwball. His excellent control affords him the luxury of pitching around hitters.

Rhythm is important to Tanana. He prefers to work quickly, armed with the knowledge that he knows how to set up hitters. The less time he allows them to adjust, the more successful he can be. A comfortable, hitless day often is an opposing batter's lament.

Tanana's deceptive motion, which features an agonizingly slow delivery for someone who stands 6'3" and weights 195 pounds, is an asset. Tanana is especially tough on lefthanded hitters, and most clubs load up on righthanders when he's pitching.

FRANK TANANA
LHP, No. 26
LL, 6'3", 195 lbs.
ML Svc: 14 years
Born: 7-3-53 in
Detroit, MI

1986 STATISTICS

W	L	ERA	G	GS	CG	SV	IP	H	R	ER	BB	SO
12	9	4.16	32	31	3	0	188.1	196	95	87	65	119

CAREER STATISTICS

W	L	ERA	G	GS	CG	SV	IP	H	R	ER	BB	SO
159	153	3.39	408	392	123	0	2760	2596	1180	1041	772	1925

FIELDING:

Tanana has an average move to first base, but throws over repeatedly to hold runners close. He is above average as a fielder and gets off the mound well.

OVERALL:

Tanana has the ability to be an effective seven-inning pitcher. He relies heavily on his defense, especially the left side of the infield, because he no longer has the power pitches to record strikeouts in tough situations.

Kaat: "His success on any given day usually can be detected early. Tanana failed to get beyond the third inning in seven of his 31 starts in 1986.

"Tanana is the kind of guy who can do a good job for a contending team as a fourth or fifth starter."

DETROIT TIGERS

PITCHING:

Walt Terrell has been cast as trade bait during each of the two winters he has belonged to the Tigers. The club has resisted requests to send him elsewhere with good reason.

Terrell epitomizes the importance of a reliable No. 3 pitcher to a starting rotation. He has won 15 games in each of the past two seasons and is one of only 13 major league pitchers to accomplish that feat in 1985-86.

Quiet and unassuming, Terrell is durable if not overpowering or overly impressive. He generally provides the Tigers with seven or eight workmanlike innings each time he takes the mound and usually affords them the opportunity to emerge with a victory. Terrell relies heavily on a sinking fastball and slider, a limited combination from which he gets maximum results. The absence of an effective off-speed pitch accounts for his lack of consistency. He has a difficult time stringing together quality starts. A complementary third pitch could make a big difference in his overall effectiveness.

Terrell came to the Tigers with a reputation for throwing a good palmball. That pitch, however, seems to have slipped from his arsenal. He did use a knuckleball on occasion last season but doesn't have enough confidence in the pitch at this point of his career to use it on a consistent basis.

The sooner Terrell develops a third pitch, the better off he will be. He permitted only nine home runs in his first year in the American League after coming to Detroit from the New York Mets. That figure rose alarmingly to 30 last season.

Terrell sometimes has a tendency to be too fine with his pitches. He had more walks than strikeouts in 21 of 33 starts last season and walked five or more batters in six of those

WALT TERRELL
RHP, No. 35
LR, 6'2", 205 lbs.
ML Svc: 4 years
Born: 5-11-58 in
   Jeffersonville, IN

1986 STATISTICS

W	L	ERA	G	GS	CG	SV	IP	H	R	ER	BB	SO
15	12	4.56	34	33	9	0	219.1	199	116	110	98	93

CAREER STATISTICS

W	L	ERA	G	GS	CG	SV	IP	H	R	ER	BB	SO
49	45	3.88	125	123	21	0	818	797	391	353	372	404

starts, during which he suffered three of his 12 losses.

FIELDING:

Terrell, like most of the Tiger pitchers, has a three-quarters delivery. Terrell is slow afoot, but does an adequate job of fielding his position. His hold is average. However, his short leg kick during his delivery makes him difficult to steal against.

Opponents can bunt on Terrell, an offensive weapon that he detests.

OVERALL:

Kaat: "Terrell's strength is his durability. He thrives on competition and can be counted on to take his turn on a regular basis. It's possible that his sinker/slider pitching pattern is becoming too identifiable to opposing hitters.

"Terrell is valuable to a staff as a .500 pitcher. He's capable of better than that, however, if he adds a third pitch."

DETROIT TIGERS

PITCHING:

Mark Thurmond was a pleasant surprise for the Tigers after being acquired from the San Diego Padres at midseason last year. He won four of five decisions out of the bullpen as a lefthanded setup man for Willie Hernandez after working as a starter the majority of his time in San Diego. Thurmond is projected as a reliever this season, though the move doesn't seem to fit his personality.

The knock against him is that he lacks aggressiveness, which has come to be considered as an absolute must for any reliever. Thurmond has earned a reputation for being much too careful with his pitches and for working too slowly. He could take a cue from other successful relievers and pick up his pace. The results likely would be gratifying and his fielders would be more than appreciative.

Thurmond throws a fastball, curveball, slider and change-up. He is not overpowering and surrenders a lot of hits, but not many walks. He has decent command of all his pitches but is not particularly more effective against lefthanded hitters than righthanders. Thurmond requires a steady diet of work to be effective because he relies on his control and the ability to throw strikes in good locations.

If Thurmond is used sporadically, he will most likely lose his control. The bottom line will be bad outings. Thurmond walks a fine line between success and failure. Much of his success depends on good mechanics. He cannot compensate with power that does not exist. His mechanics require constant verbal reinforcement.

FIELDING:

Thurmond is an average fielder with a

MARK THURMOND
LHP, No. 40
LL, 6'0", 193 lbs.
ML Svc: 4 years
Born: 9-12-56 in
Houston, TX

1986 STATISTICS

W	L	ERA	G	GS	CG	SV	IP	H	R	ER	BB	SO
7	8	4.56	42	19	2	3	122.1	140	71	62	44	49

CAREER STATISTICS

W	L	ERA	G	GS	CG	SV	IP	H	R	ER	BB	SO
35	30	3.50	131	89	6	5	554.2	572	251	216	176	212

below-average hold for a lefthanded pitcher. His delivery is three-quarters and fluid, perhaps too fluid for someone who lacks power and does not brush back hitters.

OVERALL:

The Tigers long have sought an effective lefthanded middle reliever for their bullpen to force Eastern Division opponents laden with lefthanded bats to go to their bench. Bill Scherrer and then Chuck Cary were granted opportunities. Now the chance is being given to Thurmond.

Kaat: "Thurmond's effectiveness will go hand in hand with the amount of work he receives. Sparky Anderson must exercise patience because Thurmond probably will have his share of sub-par outings.

"If Thurmond can pick up his tempo, he could be a good middle reliever against predominantly lefthanded lineups."

DETROIT TIGERS

HITTING:

Several baseball observers believed Alan Trammell's career was in serious jeopary last spring. His right shoulder, which had required arthroscopic surgery following the World Championship season of 1984, was causing him pain.

Trammell overcame the pain and a slow start to finish with 21 home runs and a .277 batting average thereby re-establishing himself as a solid offensive shortstop.

The second-half rush that Trammell enjoyed last season was triggered by a minor adjustment in his batting stance. He spread his stance beginning on July 28 and proceeded to pound 14 of his 21 homers in the final nine weeks of the season.

His improved shoulder strength resulted from a program of extensive conditioning he underwent and also contributed to Trammell's surge last season. No longer did he wince and subconsciously exercise his shoulder as he had earlier in the season.

Trammell's primary offensive strength is his quickness on inside pitches, regardless whether they are pitched high or low in the strike zone. Few hitters handle the inside fastball with as much power as Trammell. Righthanders are most successful against him if they throw sliders away. Lefthanders must avoid breaking pitches inside, especially now that his spread stance is enabling him to wait longer on off-speed pitches.

His power and discipline are ideal for the Tigers in the No. 2 slot, from which he scored 107 runs and drove in 75. He probably could be an effective hit-and-run performer, but his extra-base power (61 extra-base hits in 574 at-bats) is too good to ask him to change his style of hitting.

BASERUNNING:

Trammell poses a stolen base threat but usually is asked to do so only in selected situations when the run he represents is meaningful. He is a knowledgeable base-runner and can be expected to take an extra base more often than not.

ALAN TRAMMELL
SS, No. 3
RR, 6'1", 175 lbs.
ML Svc: 9 years
Born: 2-21-58 in
    Garden Grove, CA

1986 STATISTICS

AVG	G	AB	R	H	2B	3B	HR	RBI	BB	SO	SB
.277	151	574	107	159	33	7	21	75	59	57	25

CAREER STATISTICS

AVG	G	AB	R	H	2B	3B	HR	RBI	BB	SO	SB
.281	1289	4631	702	1300	214	42	90	504	488	519	149

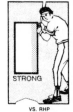

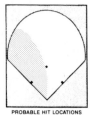

STRONG — VS. RHP   STRONG — VS. LHP   PROBABLE HIT LOCATIONS

FIELDING:

Trammell remains smooth and steady in the field, despite experiencing shoulder problems over the past two seasons. His quick delivery and accurate throwing arm allow him to compensate well for any remaining shoulder weakness.

He does seem hesitant at times to make snap throws while turning the double play.

OVERALL:

While Trammell's offensive production is substantial for his position, he probably will always perform in the shadow of his outstanding 1984 season, when he batted .314 and was named MVP of the World Series. It is highly unlikely that he will duplicate a season like that.

Kaat: "Trammell remains steady and devoted to the game. He has worked hard to overcome his shoulder ailment and is vital to the welfare of the Tigers. Trammell's pride drives him to excel.

"He is still a valuable player to the Tigers."

STRONG ARM

HITTING:

Few players in baseball can be so extraordinarily good on one day and so extraordinarily lackadaisical the next day as Lou Whitaker. The popular phrase "There's a .320 hitter lurking in that body" applies to him.

Whitaker, nonetheless, batted just .269 last season, even though he collected 20 home runs for the second consecutive season (21HR in 1985).

It has become apparent that Whitaker requires motivation to perform to his potential. Unfortunately, that motivation is too often absent. Whitaker's skills are abundant. He has speed, power and can hit for average. He probably should bunt more often. When he does lay one down, it often lacks explanation. Why, for example, should a lefthanded batter capable of hitting 20 home runs bunt against a righthanded pitcher at cozy Tiger Stadium when he represents the go-ahead run and isn't a legitimate stolen base threat?

Whitaker handles the low fastball extremely well. His quick wrists allow him to stay back in his stance and handle off-speed pitches much better than most hitters. That's one reason he should be a cinch .300 hitter.

His offensive discipline is as sporadic as his motivation. The two, in fact, go hand in hand.

Righthanders ride fastballs up and in and work off-speed pitches away in an attempt to escape Whitaker's power zone. Lefthanders generally work him away with success. His average against lefthanders, once exceptionally high, has dropped dramatically in the past two seasons.

BASERUNNING:

Whitaker could probably double his stolen base totals and could be asked to do so this season by manager Sparky Anderson. It is questionable whether Whitaker will be receptive to the idea, however.

FIELDING:

For years Whitaker has dazzled opponents with his defensive prowess. But last season he relinquished his Gold Glove to the Royal's second baseman Frank White. Perhaps the

LOU WHITAKER
2B, No. 1
LR, 5'11", 160 lbs.
ML Svc: 9 years
Born: 5-12-57 in
New York, NY

1986 STATISTICS

AVG	G	AB	R	H	2B	3B	HR	RBI	BB	SO	SB
.269	144	584	95	157	26	6	20	73	63	70	13

CAREER STATISTICS

AVG	G	AB	R	H	2B	3B	HR	RBI	BB	SO	SB
.280	1283	4704	725	1320	201	49	93	522	576	575	95

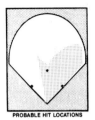

VS. RHP   VS. LHP   PROBABLE HIT LOCATIONS

Rawlings Co., which sponsors the Gold Glove awards, remembered that he refused to accept his 1985 award prior to a home game last season.

Whitaker still has the strongest arm of any American League second baseman. He is especially adept at ranging to his right and throwing across his body. His range on pop flies to right field and right-center field remains exceptional but he does not turn the double play with the same consistency he did earlier in his career, when he and Alan Trammell were considered to be the best DP combination in the American Leaue.

OVERALL:

Whitaker has potential that too often remains untapped. He has the wherewithal to be a more complete player than he has settled for. He doesn't take full advantage of his abilities. A judicious use of the bunt as an offensive weapon and a motivational fire are all that stand between Whitaker and stardom.

Kaat: "Lou's desire to perform at his optimum level will be a big factor in his success. The fact that this is the option year of his contract could provide him with the necessary push to produce."

DETROIT TIGERS

DAVE BERGMAN
1B/PH, No. 14
LL, 6'2", 190 lbs.
ML Svc: 11 years
Born: 6-6-53 in
Evanston, IL

HITTING, BASERUNNING, FIELDING:

Dave Bergman is a veteran player who has accepted his abbreviated role on the Tigers. The mere acceptance of his limited playing time has helped Bergman to succeed.

He remains a good lefthanded bat off the bench. Bergman is strictly a low fastball hitter, which suits him fine in a late-inning situation when pitchers must challenge hitters. His experience has given him an awareness of adjusting to situations. He has the patience and power to deliver home runs and the bat control to advance runners.

Bergman is average on the basepaths and does not represent a threat to steal.

He is capable of filling in at first base where his experience is beneficial. Bergman also is capable of playing in left field or right field in an emergency.

OVERALL:

One of Bergman's strongest attributes is his baseball knowledge and even temperament. He has helped many Tigers prepare for and adjust to their roles.

Kaat: "Bergman will never receive the opportunity to play full-time, but is a positive influence in the clubhouse and dugout. Bergman is a useful player; he doesn't always hit the ball hard, but he puts his bat on the ball.

"He remains one of the few links to a 1984 bench that contributed heavily to the Tigers' World Championship."

DWIGHT LOWRY
C, No. 12
LR, 6'3", 210 lbs.
ML Svc: 1 year
Born: 10-23-57 in
Robeson Co., NC

HITTING, BASERUNNING, FIELDING:

The Tigers asked Dwight Lowry to consider a coaching position last spring. Lowry said he preferred to pursue his major league career.

The undaunted Tigers then asked Lowry to consider a job as player/coach. He remained firm.

The Tigers are grateful.

Lowry handles low fastballs reasonably well, but is susceptible to fastballs upstairs and off-speed pitches. He must learn to wait longer before committing himself to pitches and can improve the quickness of his bat speed.

Lowry is a slow runner in the style of most catchers; his baserunning is not a deciding factor in the game.

Lowry now looms as a platoon catcher for Detroit, and the Tiger pitching staff isn't complaining. Lowry receives high marks for his abilities as a receiver. His arm is average in terms of strength and accuracy, but his intelligence and catching fundamentals are superior.

Lowry works well with pitchers and is a student of opposing hitters. He is able to maximize the effectiveness of a staff which has the utmost confidence in his abilities.

OVERALL:

Lowry brings out the best in Tiger pitchers. His ability to do that cannot be underestimated as the club enters the 1987 season leaning heavily on pitching for its success. He is more than capable in his role as a platooned catcher.

Kaat: "Lowry is a student of the game who works well with his pitchers. The confidence he brings out in them is one of those intangible fact

HITTING:

Steve Balboni was on his way to his greatest offensive season until a back problem ended his season a month early. Balboni was sidelined with a ruptured disk and a bulging disk but the injury did not necessitate off-season surgery.

Balboni has been the Royals' top power hitter for the last three seasons; last year, he hit 29 homers and drove in 88 runs in 138 games. Yet, once again, his strikeouts were too high and his batting average was too low. Balboni's biggest need is to lay off the high and inside fastball. He also gets caught far too often chasing the breaking ball outside the strike zone.

Yet, when Balboni is on a streak, he can be terrorize any pitcher who makes a mistake. But when Balboni is into one of his slumps, he can not hit a thing.

Balboni is a dead pull hitter. And he's so powerful that even when his body is moving too quickly in the strike zone, he's able to drive the ball because he can keep his hands back.

BASERUNNING:

Balboni never will be a threat to steal a base, but for a man his size, he has surprising speed out of the box. More than once last season, he caught lackadaisical fielders off guard and obtained infield hits.

FIELDING:

Perhaps it was because of his ailing back, but whatever the reason, Balboni regressed as a fielder last season. He simply did not get down as well as he has in the past. He has decent range to his left, but he is very limited to his right. Balboni has had a lot of trouble on throws to second base in recent years, but in that regard, improved dramatically last season. Instead of stopping to think about the

STEVE BALBONI
1B, No. 45
RR, 6'3", 225 lbs.
ML Svc: 4 years
Born: 1-16-57 in
Brockton, MA

1986 STATISTICS

AVG	G	AB	R	H	2B	3B	HR	RBI	BB	SO	SB
.229	138	512	54	117	25	1	29	88	43	146	0

CAREER STATISTICS

AVG	G	AB	R	H	2B	3B	HR	RBI	BB	SO	SB
.235	493	1750	204	412	81	7	100	276	155	512	1

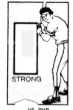

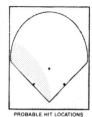

STRONG VS. RHP   STRONG VS. LHP   PROBABLE HIT LOCATIONS

throw, it appeared to be instinctive last season. Balboni's best defensive attribute is his ability to scoop balls out of the dirt.

OVERALL:

Balboni was not offered a contract in the off-season because of his back injury. Yet, he was expected to be signed by the Royals who desperately need his power. Although he strikes out far too often to be a cleanup hitter, he's quite valuable to the Royals as a No. 6 or No. 7 hitter.

Killebrew: "Here's a guy who needs to be more selective at the plate. But he's done a pretty god job in a tough ballpark for him to hit in. He has outstanding power and he could could be a 40-home run hitter somewhere else. If he could be more selective, and get a more compact swing, he could be very, very valuable."

HITTING:

Juan Beniquez has become a better hitter over the years, as hitting over .300 the last four years will attest.

He has grown fat off his ability to hit lefthanded pitching. No matter who they are or what they throw, Beniquez can hit a pitch from a southpaw anywhere. He'll use the whole park. Beniquez is not quite as good off righthanders because he's a bit of a wild swinger and he misses the breaking balls.

Beniquez is a good man to have as a righthanded bat on the bench. He's an excellent pinch-hitter and is aggressive at the plate, but he will draw his share of walks.

He has continued to improve himself at the plate; he has probably not peaked yet.

BASERUNNING:

Beniquez has slowed down over the years, but he still has good speed. He's not much of a basestealing threat anymore, but he can still get from first to third base in good time on a base hit and has good instincts.

He's not going to bunt for many base hits. He's up at the plate to swing.

FIELDING:

Originally a shortstop, Beniquez moved to the outfield soon after he reached the majors and became a good outfielder. He can play all three positions, but because his arm is not what it once was, he has played mostly in left field over the last few years.

He can fill in at first base and third base or even shortstop if he had to. He is adequate at the corners, but hasn't played enough at

JUAN BENIQUEZ
OF/DH, No. 12
RR, 5'11", 175 lbs.
ML Svc: 14 years
Born: 5-13-50 in
San Sebastian, PR

1986 STATISTICS

AVG	G	AB	R	H	2B	3B	HR	RBI	BB	SO	SB
.300	113	343	48	103	15	0	6	36	40	49	2

CAREER STATISTICS

AVG	G	AB	R	H	2B	3B	HR	RBI	BB	SO	SB
.275	1377	4338	581	1193	176	29	70	421	325	503	104

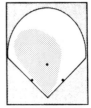

VS. RHP   VS. LHP   PROBABLE HIT LOCATIONS

shortstop in recent years to stay there any length of time.

OVERALL:

Beniquez has the kind of ability that may fit in well as a power outfielder with the Royals. The Orioles were loaded with his type of player, but Kansas City could be the right situation for him.

Kaat: "I always thought Beniquez could have been a heckuva ballplayer, but he's been a platoon player for much of his career. He so always seemed to be content with himself. He needs motivation, and the Royals may provide that with a chance to play more."

KANSAS CITY ROYALS

PITCHING:

Buddy Black was banished to the bullpen last season with the return of Dennis Leonard, and performed adequately. It was not until Black learned to accept his role that he began to pitch well again.

Black, who was 17-12 with a 3.12 ERA just two years ago, suddenly has lost confidence. Last year he challenged hitters infrequently and struggled with righthanded hitters. He has three pitches--fastball, curveball and slider--that he's not afraid to use, but far too often in key situations last year he gave up the home run ball. Black's fastball, which once was consistently in the upper 80s, has dropped off in velocity and he's beginning to experiment with a sidearm fastball. Black still has a tendency to leave the ball over the middle of the plate too often--particularly when he gets in trouble.

Black dearly wants to become a starter again, after losing his role after just four starts last season. But for now, he's the Royals' only lefty in the bullpen and the Royals were impressed with the way he finished the season. In the last six weeks, Black allowed just four earned runs in 25 innings for a 1.44 ERA. Perhaps it took him that long just to adjust to the idea that would no longer be a starter.

FIELDING:

Black is one of the best athletes on the team and has no fielding problems. He also has an

BUDDY BLACK
LHP, No. 40
LL, 6'2", 180 lbs.
ML Svc: 5 years
Born: 6-30-57 in
San Mateo, CA

1986 STATISTICS

W	L	ERA	G	GS	CG	SV	IP	H	R	ER	BB	SO
5	10	3.20	56	4	0	9	121	100	49	43	43	68

CAREER STATISTICS

W	L	ERA	G	GS	CG	SV	IP	H	R	ER	BB	SO
46	50	3.71	172	109	16	9	834.1	795	382	344	246	428

excellent pickoff move, which fooled the umpires so much in his rookie season that he was called for seven balks before they accepted it as his natural move.

OVERALL:

The key to Black's success may be finding out his role early in 1987. He's scheduled again for the bullpen, but if the Royals can find another lefthander to replace him, the Royals foresee him becoming a starter again.

Killebrew: "He throws in the high 80s, he's got a good breaking pitch and he throws strikes. He seems to throw well in the big games. I think if he can work on challenging the righthanded hitters, he'd really help himself."

HITTING:

As his own greatest critic, George Brett felt embarrassed by his 1986 season. It began with a slew of walks (21 in the first 13 games, including five intentionally) and ended with him missing 23 of the last 31 games with a right shoulder injury.

Besides the shoulder injury, which caused him to miss a total of 38 games, perhaps the walks were the biggest contributor to Brett's off season last year that resulted in a .290 batting average with 16 homers and 73 RBIs. The walks threw off Brett's timing and his .318 batting average on April 14 (7-for-22) plummeted to .226 (12-for-53) by April 29 and he wasn't able to recover until June. Then, after hitting .355 in June, Brett injured his shoulder and he was never really able to bounce back. The injury required off-season surgery; torn cartilage and a piece of his clavicle were removed.

Brett is acknowledged as one of the premier hitters in the game and can use all fields equally well. He's an excellent fastball hitter and over the years has become as adept at hitting breaking balls.

Perhaps Brett's greatest strength is that he's able to adapt to what is pitched and knows what pitches he can drive. He has excellent discipline at the plate but he'll swing at pitches that are not in the strike zone if he feels he can drive them. In fact, the bulk of his home runs hit to left field occur on pitches up and out of the strike zone.

Brett's primary weakness is the hard slider. Yet he can hit lefthanders and righthanders with equal power and average. He has a picture-perfect swing, keeping his weight on his back foot and gliding through the ball. When in a slump, Brett returns to a basic, proven theory of hitting: stay back and wait on the ball.

BASERUNNING:

In three attempts Brett stole just one base last season. He has slightly below-average speed (he goes from home to first in 4.3 seconds), but he's a smart baserunner. Brett's problem, which has haunted him throughout his career, is just remaining healthy. With his history, the Royals aren't anxious to send their star down the basepaths risking another injury.

GEORGE BRETT
3B, No. 5
LR, 6'0", 195 lbs.
ML Svc: 14 years
Born: 5-15-53 in
Glendale, WV

1986 STATISTICS

AVG	G	AB	R	H	2B	3B	HR	RBI	BB	SO	SB
.290	124	441	70	128	28	4	16	73	80	45	1

CAREER STATISTICS

AVG	G	AB	R	H	2B	3B	HR	RBI	BB	SO	SB
.314	1741	6675	1072	2095	428	112	209	1050	695	488	141

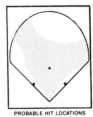

STRONG STRONG

VS. RHP   VS. LHP   PROBABLE HIT LOCATIONS

FIELDING:

Brett did not report to camp in 1986 in the same good shape as the year before and it showed in the loss of a little range. Balls that he snagged in 1985 when he won his first Gold Glove award, suddenly were getting by him. He goes to his left better each year, but backhanding balls stills remains a problem. Perhaps with his off-season shoulder surgery and improved conditioning, Brett will regain his lost step.

OVERALL:

The key simply is for Brett to remain healthy. He again embarked on a rigorous off-season conditioning program, which proved so successful for the 1985 season when he hit .335 with 30 homers and 112 RBIs. Also, Brett has history in his favor. In the three previous seasons Brett hit below .300, he returned the following season to hit at least .308.

Killebrew: "What the heck can you say about this guy that already hasn't been said? If he can stay away from injuries, he'll have another good year. The numbers he puts up strictly depend on if he stays healthy."

KANSAS CITY ROYALS

PITCHING:

Steve Farr perhaps was the biggest surprise on the Royals' pitching staff this season. Who would have guessed at the beginning of the season that Farr would be the Royals' ace in the bullpen?

Farr, who was working in construction just a couple of years ago, was the Royals' top reliever with an 8-4 record and 3.13 ERA. He made a challenge for the All-Star game with a 6-1 record and four saves. Yet, the innings Farr was required to pitch because of Dan Quisenberry's collapse finally caught up to him. His arm became tired in August and when September rolled around, he was able to pitch only 8.2 innings.

Farr has only an average fastball but he uses it effectively. He'll set up batters with his breaking pitches--mostly sliders--and then strike them out with his 85 MPH fastball. Farr has four pitches--fastball, curveball, slider and change-up--but his slider is his biggest weapon. His slider is not exceptionally fast, but it breaks hard.

Farr is extremely valuable because of his resiliency. He can pitch five days a week. And although middle relief is his best role, he proved this past season he can pitch in the late innings if needed. His biggest problem is that he lacks a power pitch. When he falls behind hitters, he does not have a power pitch to challenge them with.

FIELDING:

Farr will not pick anyone off base with his

STEVE FARR
RHP, No. 26
RR, 5'11", 190 lbs.
ML Svc: 2 years
Born: 12-12-56 in
Cheverly, MD

1986 STATISTICS

W	L	ERA	G	GS	CG	SV	IP	H	R	ER	BB	SO
8	4	3.13	56	0	0	8	109.1	90	39	38	39	83

CAREER STATISTICS

W	L	ERA	G	GS	CG	SV	IP	H	R	ER	BB	SO
13	16	3.76	103	19	0	10	263	230	115	110	105	202

move toward first. He has a very deliberate motion and baserunners love to take off with Farr on the mound. He's an adequate fielder and will attempt to throw out the lead runner on most occasions.

OVERALL:

Farr still is an unproven commodity. Although he had an exceptional year in 1986, he still must prove one more time that he's for real.

Killebrew: "They used him in a lot of situations where you thought they'd use Quiz, so you know the Royals like him. I think, right now, Farr is pitching the best that he can and is in his prime."

KANSAS CITY ROYALS

PITCHING:

Mark Gubicza was the Royals' best pitcher by the season's conclusion after being their worst at the season's beginning. After opening the season with an 0-4 record and 7.27 ERA, Gubicza ended the season by winning five straight decisions and nine of his last 10 with an ERA of 3.35.

Gubicza is a pure power pitcher. He has a 94 MPH fastball and his slider is clocked consistently between 83-87 MPH. Most impressively, Gubicza rarely tires before the eighth inning. On a hot August afternoon against the New York Yankees last season, he threw a six-hit shutout and his fastball still was being clocked at 90 MPH in the ninth inning. If he can develop a change-up, Gubicza has a legitimate chance to be a 20-game winner.

The main ingredient holding back Gubicza is his control. He walked a whopping 84 batters in 180.2 innings last season and had 77 walks in 177 innings the previous year. But Gubicza appears to be maturing and in the last month of the season, he cut down his walks to 14 in his final six starts.

FIELDING:

Gubicza has a big motion that allows baserunners to get a big jump but he keeps them honest with a quick move to first base. His biggest trouble is that he pitches with so

**MARK GUBICZA
RHP, No. 23
RR, 6'5", 210 lbs.
ML Svc: 3 years
Born: 8-14-62 in
    Philadelphia, PA**

1986 STATISTICS

W	L	ERA	G	GS	CG	SV	IP	H	R	ER	BB	SO
12	6	3.64	35	24	3	0	180.2	155	77	73	84	118

CAREER STATISTICS

W	L	ERA	G	GS	CG	SV	IP	H	R	ER	BB	SO
36	30	3.92	93	81	7	0	547	487	255	238	204	328

much force, he falls off the mound with little control of his body. He's agile however and is able to limit the number of bunt attempts against him.

OVERALL:

If Gubicza can ever settle down early in a season, he could easily be capable of winning 20. Although his control remains his biggest albatross, he's maturing more quickly than teammates Bret Saberhagen or Danny Jackson.

Killebrew: "Now *here's* a guy I really like. He needs to improve his off-speed breaking stuff but his fastball really moves and it'll break on occasion. His only real problem is that he's wild, but he's going to get better."

KANSAS CITY ROYALS

PITCHING:

Danny Jackson is the biggest enigma on the Royals' pitching staff. He has a fastball that is consistently in the 88-91 MPH range and which is perhaps the liveliest of any lefthander's in the major leagues. He has a hard, wicked slider that breaks at the knees. And his overall makeup is as good as any lefthander in the American League.

So what gives? Why does Jackson possess an abundance of talent and yet has never won more than 14 games in any season?

The answer is pure and simple: immaturity. Jackson lacks the proper temperament to be a 20-game winner and until he does, he'll only be frustrated throughout his career. *Jackson has got to overcome his temper.* He cannot continue to allow the little things in baseball to rattle him. Far too often, Jackson will become unnerved at the sight of an error. Or he'll become increasingly angry every inning the Royals are unable to score. And when his anger rises, his concentrations drops. Soon, his game falls apart and Jackson is back in the clubhouse throwing a fit.

Perhaps, though, this will be the season Jackson regroups. Detroit Tigers manager Sparky Anderson predicts he'll be the best lefthander in the American League this season. Others say 20 victories are right around the corner. If Jackson can establish his change-up to go along with fastball and slider and his temper can be controlled, this may indeed be Jackson's season.

FIELDING:

Jackson is the worst-fielding pitcher on the

**DANNY JACKSON
LHP, No. 25
RL, 6'0", 190 lbs.
ML Svc: 4 years
Born: 1-5-62 in
San Antonio, TX**

1986 STATISTICS

W	L	ERA	G	GS	CG	SV	IP	H	R	ER	BB	SO
11	12	.3.20	32	27	4	1	185.2	177	83	66	79	115

CAREER STATISTICS

W	L	ERA	G	GS	CG	SV	IP	H	R	ER	BB	SO
28	31	3.54	83	73	9	1	488.2	496	230	192	196	278

team and among the worst in the league. He comes off the mound so hard, that he seldom is in control of his body. Jackson has only an average throw to first base, so he must throw there often to keep runners close. Runners are able to get an extra jump on him after studying his delivery.

OVERALL:

This season perhaps will determine if Jackson will ever live to his billing of becoming one of the best lefthanders in the game.

Killebrew: "Danny has often shown the potential for stardom but seldom has he shown any consistency. There are a lot of people in baseball who are very high on him and feel that he is just a bit young yet but is going to get better. I really don't see any weaknesses with his pitching."

KANSAS CITY ROYALS

HITTING:

Mike Kingery, who grew up playing baseball with football goal posts in the outfield, is beginning to mature as a player.

Although Kingery never will hit for power, he figures to have a solid career as a platoon lefthanded hitting outfielder. Kingery is a line-drive, straightaway hitter who'll usually hit balls to dead center or left-center field.

Kingery loves the fastball over the middle or outside part of the plate. He has considerable trouble, however, with outside breaking balls and those low and away. Lefthanded pitchers give him fits, and it's questionable whether he'll ever be able to hit them.

Kingery still needs to learn to become more disciplined at the plate. He'll often chase balls out of the strike zone, which was evidenced by his 30 strikeouts in 209 at-bats. That's far too many strikeouts for a player who had just three home runs and 14 RBIs last season.

BASERUNNING:

Kingery has good speed, which is complemented well by his excellent hustle. He runs the bases exceptionally well, but must learn how to read the pitcher. He stole seven bases last season and was caught three times.

FIELDING:

Kingery is an exceptional outfielder and easily had the strongest arm among the Royals' outfielders last season. He has great range to his right and left and figures only to improve with maturity.

Not only does Kingery have a deceptively strong arm, it is also highly accurate.

MIKE KINGERY
RF, No. 27
LL, 6'0", 180 lbs.
ML Svc: less than one year
Born: 3-29-61 in
St. James, MN

1986 STATISTICS

AVG	G	AB	R	H	2B	3B	HR	RBI	BB	SO	SB
.258	62	209	25	54	8	5	3	14	12	30	7

CAREER STATISTICS

AVG	G	AB	R	H	2B	3B	HR	RBI	BB	SO	SB
.258	62	209	25	54	8	5	3	14	12	30	7

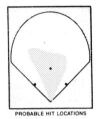

VS. RHP   VS. LHP   PROBABLE HIT LOCATIONS

Baserunners take a huge risk when they attempt to take an extra base on Kingery. He takes as much delight in throwing out runners as he does hitting.

OVERALL:

Kingery could be a consistent .270-.280 hitter in this game for many years to come. Whatever he lacks in physical ability, he overcomes with his driving desire and hustle. Clearly, it's easy to see why he's a favorite among fans and management.

Killebrew: 'He looks like a good, consistent player. He is a fun player to watch, despite his lack of power."

KANSAS CITY ROYALS

PITCHING:

Charlie Leibrandt was yet another mystery man for the Royals' in 1986. After posting a 4-0 record with a 3.37 ERA in April, Leibrandt went an entire month without winning a game. And not until his last three starts of the season was he ever able to win three in a row again.

Leibrandt's inconsistency can be blamed on his erratic screwball. The pitch that was so effective for him in 1985, enabling him to compile a 17-9 record and 2.69 ERA then, abandoned him last season. And when Leibrandt's control is not precise, he's just a very average pitcher.

Leibrandt's control problems resulted in a barrage of walks. He walked six in his first start of the season and had 28 in his first nine starts. Even when he wasn't walking hitters, he usually was falling behind them. And because his fastball is average (only 83-84 MPH), Leibrandt's pitches often became a hitter's delight.

Yet, despite Leibrandt's control problems, he continued to pitch when he was needed. He did not miss a start for the second straight season and he led the Royals in wins, innings, complete games and starts. Leibrandt has never had any arm problems and should be around for at least another two seasons.

FIELDING:

Leibrandt is the best fielding pitcher on the

CHARLIE LEIBRANDT
LHP, No. 37
RL, 6'3", 200 lbs.
ML Svc: 7 years
Born: 10-4-56 in
Chicago, IL

1986 STATISTICS

W	L	ERA	G	GS	CG	SV	IP	H	R	ER	BB	SO
14	11	4.09	35	34	8	0	231.1	238	112	105	63	108

CAREER STATISTICS

W	L	ERA	G	GS	CG	SV	IP	H	R	ER	BB	SO
58	44	3.77	173	132	22	2	928.1	979	429	389	288	375

Royals after Bret Saberhagen. He's not particularly adept at holding runners on base but he has a good move to first. His trouble is that his delivery is slow, which often allows runners to get a good jump.

OVERALL:

If Leibrandt locates his pinpoint control, there's no reason he shouldn't win 16 to 18 games again. For a fourth starter, there are few better in baseball.

Killebrew: "Leibrandt looked like the same pitcher in 1986 as he was the year before--he's very consistent. One of the things I like about him is that he can throw a breaking ball when he's behind in the count. And maybe most important, he's not afraid to throw inside to a righthander."

KANSAS CITY ROYALS

PITCHING:

What happened here? Dan Quisenberry, the man who led the Qmerican League in saves each of the last four seasons (averaging 40 saves in those seasons) finished 1986 with a career-low 12 saves.

Everything seemed to go wrong with Quisenberry last year. For the first time since 1980, he lost his control and walked 24 batters in just 81.1 innings. Not since 1980 had his ERA ever been above 2.77. Quiz has had his ups and downs before, but *never, ever* did he experience a season such as this.

Quisenberry was not doing any different mechanically, but for some unknown reason, his bread-and-butter pitches suddenly abandoned him. Over the years, his classic submarine pitch has had hitters swinging in the dirt. Now they were hanging over the middle of the plate. His pinpoint control resulted in far too many walks.

And for the first time in his career, the Royals simply lost faith in him. His decline began May 5 against the Cleveland Indians when he gave up four hits and two runs (one earned) in 1.1 innings and got the loss. One week later, the Royals almost blew a 6-1 lead in the eighth inning when Quisenberry could not retire a single batter in the eighth inning and was charged with three earned runs. He then sat and sat, only pitching when the game was not on the line. In fact, after his third save of the season April 20, Quisenberry did not record another until June 4. And he finished the season with just four saves after the All-Star break.

Quisenberry admitted to being embarrassed by his performance and perhaps pressing led to his control problems. But no one ever discovered the true reason why Quisenberry's sinker was thrown at the hitter's belt and only dropped to the knees. Even his curveball was up far too much.

Looking to this season, the Royals and Quisenberry are confident of his return. He has no arm problems ("How can you hurt that arm, with the stuff he throws?" asked one

DAN QUISENBERRY
RHP, No. 29
RR, 6'2", 180 lbs.
ML Svc: 7 years
Born: 2-7-53 in
 Santa Monica, CA

1986 STATISTICS

W	L	ERA	G	GS	CG	SV	IP	H	R	ER	BB	SO
3	7	2.77	62	0	0	12	81.1	92	30	25	24	36

CAREER STATISTICS

W	L	ERA	G	GS	CG	SV	IP	H	R	ER	BB	SO
47	42	2.51	506	0	0	229	845.1	839	267	236	124	295

scout, referring to Quisenberry's 77-80 MPH fastball.) Perhaps the most important ingredient that Quisenberry needs to be successful again is just plain work. For him to be effective, he needs to pitch 3-4 days a week. Yet last season he often went four days without even throwing.

FIELDING:

Quisenberry is excellent coming off the mound in proper fielding position. He also can hold runners on first base by throwing over frequently without losing concentration. He's not afraid of trying to throw out the lead runner and often is successful.

OVERALL:

Time will tell if 1986 was just an off season for Quisenberry or if it was the beginning of the decline of his career. If his sinker and slider fail him again, Quisenberry could find himself in deep trouble.

Killebrew: "I think it's tough for a reliever to be effective for as many years as Quiz has been. It's very difficult for him to be consistently so good year after year. Last year, he just wasn't as effective. But I think he's entitled to an off year once in a while."

PITCHING:

Just one year after winning virtually every conceivable award available to a pitcher, Bret Saberhagen fell flat on his face in 1986. Not only did Saberhagen finish the season with a 7-12 record and 4.15 ERA but he went the entire season without winning two starts consecutively.

Although many reasons have been bantered about for his demise, the common sentiment is that Saberhagen's success simply overwhelmed him. He was not ready for the barrage of banquet circuit stops that filled his off-season, which did not allow him the time to even consider working out. When it was time for spring training, he was simply not prepared. The result was a sore shoulder that occurred midway through spring training, and which eventually sidelined him for three weeks in August. By the time the Royals curtailed his off-the-field activities-- which came to a head in May when they spotted him on the field filming a car commercial just hours before he was scheduled to pitch--the damage already had been done.

Yet, the good news for Saberhagen is that his pitches never really left him, only his concentration. Saberhagen still has a 90-92 MPH fastball, an excellent curveball and one of the best change-ups in the league.

Saberhagen's problem last year was that he just lost his pinpoint control, which is blamed on his off-the-field activities. And once he fell behind on hitters, they were awaiting his fastball. For the first time in his life, Saberagen's confidence had eroded. "What I saw was anxiety and frustration that I had never seen before," said Bob Saberhagen, Bret's father. "I guess looking back, I saw fear in him for the first time of my life."

Yet, the Royals fully expect Saberhagen to

BRET SABERHAGEN
RHP, No. 31
RR, 6'1", 160 lbs.
ML Svc: 3 years
Born: 4-11-64 in
**   Chicago Heights, IL**

1986 STATISTICS

W	L	ERA	G	GS	CG	SV	IP	H	R	ER	BB	SO
7	12	4.15	30	25	4	0	156	165	77	72	29	112

CAREER STATISTICS

W	L	ERA	G	GS	CG	SV	IP	H	R	ER	BB	SO
37	29	3.41	100	75	16	1	549	514	227	208	103	343

return to the Saberhagen of 1985. He committed himself to a vigorous off-season conditioning program during the winter and most important, he came to an understanding of what went wrong in 1986.

FIELDING:

Saberhagen is the Royals' best fielding pitcher and one of the best in the league. His quick move to first prevents baserunners from establishing much of a lead. He also has quick reflexes off the mound and can move as well to his left as his right.

OVERALL:

Time will tell if 1986 was just an off year or whether 1985 was a fluke. Few, if any, however, believe it was the latter.

Killebrew: "The guy was a mystery. He just had an off year and no one really knows why. He's got good stuff and he's very poised--and he is almost sneaky on the mound. I expect him to come back and have a fine year."

KANSAS CITY ROYALS

HITTING:

After a knee injury forced Lonnie Smith to miss 24 games in the first two months of the 1986 season, he went into a tear the final two months. Beginning on August 10th when he was batting .246, Smith hit safely in 30 of 34 games, hitting .420 (60-for-143). Smith finished the season with a .287 batting average--his highest since 1983.

Smith is an inside-out hitter. He's a first-ball, fastball hitter, but he's become a decent breaking ball hitter. He loves the fastball over the middle or outside part of the plate. Sliders, however, leave him in a funk. Perhaps Smith's greatest difficulty at the plate is that he pays little attention to who's pitching and does not study opposing pitchers' habits.

Smith is an excellent hit-and-run man and always keeps the infield on its toes with frequent bunt attempts.

BASERUNNING:

Smith makes things happen on the basepaths. He's a rugged competitor and is unafraid to barrel into the opposing second baseman to break up a double play.

He has great baserunning instincts and always seems to know when to take the extra base. He still has great speed--from home to first in 4.05 seconds from the right side of the plate--and unlike teammate Willie Wilson, he is not afraid to use it.

FIELDING:

With Smith in the outfield, everything is an adventure. He does not know how to go back on balls and frequently loses his footing when he does. Because of this weakness, Smith plays so deep in left field that often he's left diving for routine fly balls.

Smith's arm is as erratic as his fielding. Although he'll get a good jump on balls hit to his left and right and gets rid of the ball

LONNIE SMITH
LF, No. 21
RR, 5'9", 170 lbs.
ML Svc: 9 years
Born: 12-22-55 in Chicago, IL

1986 STATISTICS

AVG	G	AB	R	H	2B	3B	HR	RBI	BB	SO	SB
.287	134	508	80	146	25	7	8	44	46	78	26

CAREER STATISTICS

AVG	G	AB	R	H	2B	3B	HR	RBI	BB	SO	SB
.291	909	3148	571	915	166	37	41	289	326	458	299

 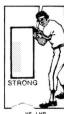 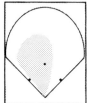

STRONG   STRONG

VS. RHP   VS. LHP   PROBABLE HIT LOCATIONS

quickly, his accuracy leaves much to be desired.

Smith's defensive skills, or rather lack of them, may have signaled the end of his left field days. He's expected to become a designated hitter for the duration of his career.

OVERALL:

Smith's value is underestimated. He can quickly ignite an offense and when he is in a hitting streak, can be responsible for a few runs a game. Unfortunately, so can his defense.

Killebrew: "Lonnie has trouble with the breaking stuff and offspeed stuff. He's not very selective at the plate, either. But he's got good speed, is aggressive on the bases and still has a lot of value."

KANSAS CITY ROYALS

HITTING:

Simply put, Jim Sundberg's 1986 season was dismal. Not only did Sundberg hit a mere .212, but his ratio of throwing out basestealers was little better: 36% (31 of 86). Perhaps the only gratifying aspect of his season was that he was able to sign a two-year contract for about $1.4 million before his game collapsed.

Sundberg is having more and more difficulty with the breaking ball. And now, perhaps because of his age, pitchers are finding an easy time of throwing fastballs right by him. Sundberg, primarily a pull hitter in the past, has learned to use the whole field over the past two seasons, particularly in right-center field. But still, lefthanders came in often with fastballs to strike him out and righthanders get him out with breaking balls. The result of their strategy last year was a career-high 91 strikeouts, 24 more than he had a year ago.

Although Sundberg never will be mistaken for a power hitter, he hit a career-high 12 home runs last season and now has hit 22 in the last two years. He'll surprise opposing pitchers who make the mistake of leaving fastballs over the middle of the plate. Yet, the Royals gladly would trade his new-found power for a higher batting average. His .212 batting average was his second-lowest since 1975.

One way the Royals will try to improve his proficiency is by resting him more often this season. He played in 140 games last season and the Royals feel he no longer can handle the workload.

BASERUNNING:

Sundberg actually stole a base last season-- his first in two years--but his speed is only average for a catcher. Although he's an excellent baserunner and knows exactly when he can get an extra base, he is awfully slow running to first. Yet, Sundberg pushes himself hard and never will get thrown out because of lazy running.

FIELDING:

Sundberg, who's third among active

JIM SUNDBERG
C, No. 8
RR, 6'0", 195 lbs.
ML Svc: 13 years
Born: 5-18-51 in
Galesburg, IL

1986 STATISTICS

AVG	G	AB	R	H	2B	3B	HR	RBI	BB	SO	SB
.212	140	429	41	91	9	1	12	42	57	91	1

CAREER STATISTICS

AVG	G	AB	R	H	2B	3B	HR	RBI	BB	SO	SB
.250	1763	5590	578	1395	229	44	83	579	642	911	20

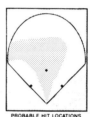

VS. RHP   VS. LHP   PROBABLE HIT LOCATIONS

catchers in games caught, is the only catcher to win six Gold Gloves. He again led all American League catchers last year with just four errors.

Yet, although Sundberg once had one of the best arms in the game, his arm strength has dropped off dramatically as of late. Only his footwork allows him to compensate for his weak arm and long windup.

OVERALL:

Only Sundberg's big contract prevented the Royals from searching for a catcher in the off-season. Although he's still in excellent physical shape, the Royals fear that his time is near.

Killebrew: "I still think he's got some good years left in him. He's been very important to that pitching staff. Good, experienced catchers like Sundberg are at a premium and hard to find."

HITTING:

Skeptics wondered if Danny Tartabull's power-heroics at the minor league level would carry over into the big leagues. The answer was an emphatic yes! as Tartabull slammed 25 home runs in his rookie season.

The ball literally jumps off his bat when he gets all of it, and there isn't a ballpark that has been constructed that can keep his most mammoth shots from reaching the seats.

But he also has to learn to cut down on his swing when the situation dictates it. That is part of the reason he had only six game-winning RBIs a year ago, far too few for a guy who drives in 96 runs. He hits the ball in the air a lot, obviously, and yet he had only three sacrifice flies all season.

Pitchers can take advantage of his aggressive style at the plate and get him out with low breaking pitches. He's an excellent fastball hitter, and when he does go to the opposite field he has enough power to hit the ball out of the park.

BASERUNNING:

Tartabull is not fast but will become a better baserunner as he gets more experience. He stole four bases and was caught eight times in his rookie season. He needs to study outfielder's arms more so he can advance a base more when the extra base can be taken.

FIELDING:

Tartabull probably found his permanent home in the field when the Mariners shifted him from second base to right field last year. There isn't as much pressure there, and although he's far from being a skilled outfielder, he showed much improvement.

DANNY TARTABULL
RF, No. 38
RR, 6'1", 185 lbs.
ML Svc: 1 year plus
Born: 10-20-62 in
San Juan, PR

1986 STATISTICS

AVG	G	AB	R	H	2B	3B	HR	RBI	BB	SO	SB
.270	137	511	76	138	25	6	25	96	61	157	4

CAREER STATISTICS

AVG	G	AB	R	H	2B	3B	HR	RBI	BB	SO	SB
.277	166	592	87	164	32	7	28	110	71	174	5

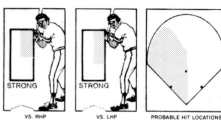

VS. RHP   VS. LHP   PROBABLE HIT LOCATIONS

He has a cannon for an arm so it isn't wise to challenge him.

OVERALL:

He could be a star if he stays in the outfield. Moving him back to the infield would be a mistake because that takes away from his strength--his bat.

Killebrew: "Tartabull was one of the most impressive-looking rookies in the American League last season and it will be interesting to see how he adjusts to hitting in a bigger ballpark. Royals Stadium is anything but a home run hitter's park and it will hurt him if he gets frustrated because long drives are caught at the fences."

KANSAS CITY ROYALS

HITTING:

Frank White is defying the laws of old age. Instead of regressing, White is actually improving with age. At the age of 36, White had the finest season of his 13-year career last year.

White merely equalled his career high of 22 home runs, drove in a career high 84 runs and hit .272, 14 points above his career average. And, oh yeah, he won his seventh Gold Glove.

White, who is engrossed in a strenuous off-season weight-training program, has become much stronger in recent years. White's new-found strength is evidenced by his 61 homers over the last three seasons. In his previous 10 seasons, he had hit only 68 homers.

White has powerful wrists and has become an excellent high fastball hitter. He's become primarily a pull hitter, but occasionally will go to right-center field.

White's weakness, as pitchers have found, is his habit of chasing curveballs away. Righthanders and lefties alike throw him plenty of breaking balls away from him.

BASERUNNING:

White stole just four bases last season, equalling his lowest total since his rookie season. He'll occasionally catch pitchers off guard and attempt to steal, but he was caught stealing as many times as he was successful last season. White also will bunt when the opposing third baseman is playing deep.

FIELDING:

After winning six consecutive Gold Gloves from 1976-1982, White won his seventh last season. He has lost a couple of steps to his right, but he's still considered one of the best

**FRANK WHITE
2B, No. 20
RR, 5'11", 175 lbs.
ML Svc: 14 years
Born: 9-4-50 in
Greenville, MS**

1986 STATISTICS

AVG	G	AB	R	H	2B	3B	HR	RBI	BB	SO	SB
.272	151	566	76	154	37	3	22	84	43	88	4

CAREER STATISTICS

AVG	G	AB	R	H	2B	3B	HR	RBI	BB	SO	SB
.260	1803	6100	743	1583	314	53	131	693	300	798	166

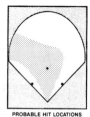

STRONG — VS. RHP   STRONG — VS. LHP   PROBABLE HIT LOCATIONS

in the game going to his left and takes up the slack left between first and second base left by Steve Balboni.

White's greatest strength, however, may be his experience and knowledge that allows him to position himself almost perfectly each time. White also has a strong arm and can turn the double play with the best of them.

OVERALL:

Killebrew: "Here's a guy who still has great range at second base and he can make the double play as well as anyone. The Royals have not had to worry about second base ever since he took it over. Frank should have several more good years and if he keeps playing like he is, he definitely has a chance at the Hall of Fame."

KANSAS CITY ROYALS

HITTING:

Perhaps it's only a coincidence, but Willie Wilson's game has drastically slipped since he signed a lifetime contract that guarantees him $1 million a year through 1989, with options through 1994.

Wilson hit just .269 last season, the second-lowest batting average of his major league career. And after hitting just .278 in 1985, Wilson's lifetime batting average has dipped to below .300 for the first time this decade.

Inexplicably, Wilson has virtually abandoned his bunting game, quit being a contact hitter, and now is swinging for the fences. Also, he equalled the lowest stolen base total of his career last season with 34. This is not what the Royals have in mind for their center fielder.

If he just learned to bunt and would settle for slapping singles into the outfield, he could still be a .300-.310 hitter. Yet, for the past two seasons, he seems obsessed with trying to hit for the fences. Sure, he hit nine home runs last season, one more than his combined lifetime total, but he also struck out 97 times last season and 191 times in his last two seasons. That's hardly the productivity the Royals are looking for from their leadoff hitter.

Wilson is an excellent low fastball hitter from the left side of the plate. He likes it up and over the plate from the right side. He has learned to drive the ball from the left side and has abandoned the lightweight bat he always used from the left side. He also no longer is susceptible to inside fastballs from the left side. Still, Wilson has more power from the right side of the plate.

Wilson has problems with the breaking ball, particularly the good curveball and slider. Pitchers also have learned that Wilson has a bad habit of chasing the high fastball.

BASERUNNING:

Wilson is one of the premier baserunners in the game, but he appears to have lost his initiative. He'll occasionally attempt to steal a base in late-inning situations, but really shows little indication that he even wants to steal.

FIELDING:

Wilson remains one of the premier center

WILLIE WILSON
CF, No. 6
SR, 6'3", 195 lbs.
ML Svc: 11 years
Born: 7-9-55 in
Montgomery, AL

1986 STATISTICS

AVG	G	AB	R	H	2B	3B	HR	RBI	BB	SO	SB
.269	156	631	77	170	20	7	9	44	31	97	34

CAREER STATISTICS

AVG	G	AB	R	H	2B	3B	HR	RBI	BB	SO	SB
.297	1267	4908	775	1457	176	97	30	357	249	661	470

  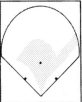

VS. RHP — STRONG | VS. LHP — STRONG | PROBABLE HIT LOCATIONS

fielders in baseball, and his range is as good as anyone in the game. He gets an excellent jump on balls hit to his right and left and has excellent leaping ability. He also has no fear of fences.

Wilson's problem is his arm. It's one of the weakest in the game and it's getting worse. Even fly balls hit to the shallowest part of center field can become sacrifice flies. Still, his speed allows him to compensate for some of his arm deficiencies and he often cuts off balls that would normally roll to the fence.

OVERALL:

This figures to be pivotal year in Wilson's career. If he has another bad year at the plate, he may find himself at the bottom of the batting order during his remaining years. He must regain his discipline at the plate, or it will be another long year.

Killebrew: "Here's a guy who when he came up to the Royals, I thought would never make it as a hitter. But now that he's made it, he has to learn to be patient. His problem is that because of his speed, pitchers pitch him more carefully than most others because they need to keep him off the bases."

KANSAS CITY ROYALS

BUDDY BIANCALANA
SS, No. 1
SR, 5'11", 160 lbs.
ML Svc: 3 years
Born: 2-2-60 in
Larkspur, CA

HITTING, BASERUNNING, FIELDING:

Buddy Biancalana, the hero of the 1985 World Series, became just another light-hitting shorstop last season. Although Biancalana raised his batting average from from .188 in 1985 to .242 last season, he hardly is an offensive threat. Biancalana drove in eight runs last season and now has a grand total of 23 in his three major league seasons.

Biancalana has tremendous difficulties just handling the fastball. Anything that's thrown faster than 87 MPH, forget it, Biancalana doesn't have a chance. Biancalana can not drive the ball out of the ballpark and must learn to stay within himself. Perhaps most exasperating to the Royals is that oftentimes Biancalana is not even ready to swing when the pitcher starts his delivery.

Biancalana has above-average speed, he makes it to first in 4.1 seconds from the left side of the plate. He stole a career high five bases last season, but yet, he's not a smart baserunner and seldom gets a big lead.

Biancalana is one of the better shortstops in the league and he has a strong arm. He's excellent on artificial turf and goes to his left quite well. If not for his defensive ability, he wouldn't even be in the big leagues.

OVERALL:

Killebrew: "Buddy's a good defensive player, he just lacks consistency at the plate. I think the Royals would like to use him as a utility player, not as a starter."

BO JACKSON
RF, No. 16
RR, 6'1", 222 lbs.
ML Svc: less than one
year
Born: 11-30-62 in
Bessemer, AL

HITTING, BASERUNNING, FIELDING:

Certainly, no one on the Royals possesses greater athletic abilities than Bo Jackson. He perhaps is the fastest player in the game out of the box with his 3.62-second sprint from the plate. He already has the best arm among the Royals' outfielders. He has already hit the longest home run in Royals Stadium history: a 475-foot shot against the Seattle Mariners last year. The only ingredient he lacks is experience.

Jackson had played in only 89 collegiate games before joining the Royals, and lacks the fundamentals of baseball. His fielding is atrocious, his arm is erratic and he's undisciplined at the plate. Yet, no one expected him to progress as rapidly as he did last year in such a short time. After an awful start at Double-A, Jackson hit .338 in the final 40 games and lifted his average to .277 (51-for-184).

Jackson is a more disciplined hitter than the Royals originally anticipated. He consistently laid off the breaking balls, although he did have a tendency to chase high fastballs. He's a dead fastball hitter and has power to all fields.

Now, he must learn to read the pitchers--he also must learn how to use his blazing speed. Still, once he learns the game, scouts predict that he could be the first player in baseball to hit 50 homers and steal 50 bases in one season.

OVERALL:

Killebrew: "I think he's the kind of guy that they should put in there and just let him play. I'm impressed by his arm, his outstanding speed and his outstanding power. But it's hard to tell what he can do unless he's thrown out there for all to see."

***RUDY LAW
CF, No. 23
LL, 6'2", 176 lbs.
ML Svc: 7 years
Born: 10-7-56 in
Waco, TX***

HITTING, BASERUNNING, FIELDING:

Rudy Law proved to be a valuable asset to the Royals last season but then was felled by a minor cartilage tear to his left knee that all but ended his season in July.

After two consecutive off seasons when he hit .251 and .259, Law bounced back with his new ballclub. He was hitting .300 as late as June 8. But Law slipped on the wet turf a couple of days later and arthroscopic surgery was prescribed in July. Still, Law defied the critics who said he was washed up.

Law was used mostly as a platoon player in right field and primarily faced only righthanded pitching. He likes the inside fastball but has all kinds of trouble with hard sliders and curveballs that break inside. He's pretty much a spray hitter who tries to find the gaps in the outfield.

Law still has plenty of speed: his time to first is 4.0 seconds from the left side of the plate. Yet, after his injury, he was two-tenths of a second slower. Law is a smart baserunner and often will get a good jump off the pitcher.

Although he was used mostly in right field last season, he's expected this year to play in left. His arm is too weak for him to play in right field but he's adequate in left.

OVERALL:

Killebrew: "A lot of clubs were sorry they didn't pick him up after they saw what he did with the Royals. He's a good hitter, a good fielder, has good speed and is just good to have around. The kind of year he has this season depends on how he bounces back from his injury."

***HAL McRAE
DH, No. 11
RR, 5'11", 185 lbs.
ML Svc: 18 years
Born: 7-10-45 in
Avon Park, FL***

HITTING, BASERUNNING, FIELDING:

Finally, age has caught up with 41-year-old Hal McRae. Although he'll be a player/coach with the Royals this season, the bulk of his work will be as a hitting instructor. He'll likely only be used as a pinch-hitter.

McRae, who still hit .252 with seven homers and 37 RBIs last season, can be an effective bat off the bench. He's primarily a fastball hitter but still has the ability to drive a breaking ball. He'll make the pitcher throw him the first strike and if he gets ahead in the count, he'll open up his stance and try to drive a pitch.

McRae (who's been playing professionally before man first set foot on the moon) no longer has any speed left. It's impossible for him to steal a base, let alone beat out an infield single. He also has not played a game in the field in the last four years.

Yet, McRae's leadership is invaluable. While George Brett is the Royals' leader on the field, McRae is King of the Clubhouse. He's held in reverence by his teammates, who constantly seek his advice.

OVERALL:

The Royals finished 13th offensively in each of the last two seasons and batted a pitiful .252 last season. With McRae's leadership and guidance, the Royals' front-office is anticipating instant improvement.

Killebrew: "He's the best designated hitter I've ever seen. He seems to have that mental outlook necessary for that role; you have to keep yourself in the game mentally, which he constantly does."

KANSAS CITY ROYALS

JORGE ORTA
DH/OF, No. 3
LR, 5'10", 175 lbs.
ML Svc: 15 years
Born: 11-26-50 in
Mazatlan, Mexico

leave him chasing breaking balls away from him. A line drive hitter, Orta has a short, quick stroke and good bat control.

Orta did not steal a base last season and has only three in the last five years. He's not an aggressive baserunner, but will break up the double play.

Orta has not played a field position in two seasons.

HITTING, BASERUNNING, FIELDING:

Jorge Orta remains one of the best lefthanded pinch-hitters in the league. He's a part-time designated hitter, who has adjusted well to his role.

Orta hit .277 with 46 RBIs in 106 games last season and is one of the best low fastball hitters in baseball. Pitchers will exploit his weakness by throwing fastballs up-and-in or

OVERALL:

Orta is a threat off the bench and can be used as a part-time designated hitter. His physical stamina allows him to remain effective in this game.

Killebrew: "Everyone respects Jorge and although he's getting older, he still keeps himself in good shape and is valuable to the team. He's a perfect situation-type player."

GREG PRYOR
3B, No. 4
RR, 6'0", 185 lbs.
ML Svc: 8 years
Born: 10-2-49 in
Marietta, OH

located, will leave Pryor swinging in vain. Even as a utility player, Pryor's only asset is his experience. He has a strong arm, but his fielding prowess has deteriorated.

Pryor can play shortstop and at second base in emergencies, but his skills are limited at each position. His biggest feat last season was that he stole one base, one more than he stole in his three previous seasons.

HITTING, BASERUNNING, FIELDING:

Greg Pryor has slipped drastically in all phases of the game. One member of the Royals' front office said: "If he makes the team, we're in trouble."

Pryor hit a career-low .170 (19-for-112) last season and made six errors in his limited playing time. Pryor filled in when George Brett was disabled with a shoulder injury, but unlike 1984 when he was an adequate replacement, he flopped miserably last year.

A good fastball, no matter where it's

OVERALL:

It's likely that Pryor will find himself without a team this year. Although he still has a guaranteed contract for 1987, the Royals have shown no interest in retaining him and instead have offered him a minor league coaching job which Pryor refused.

Killebrew: "He does a pretty good job filling in at times. He knows what his role is and he's a veteran-type player who's played on winning ballclubs. That may a good enough reason to keep him around."

KANSAS CITY ROYALS

JAMIE QUIRK
C, No. 18
LR, 6'4", 200 lbs.
ML Svc: 10 years
Born: 10-22-54 in
Whittier, CA

HITTING, BASERUNNING, FIELDING:

Jamie Quirk still has a valuable arm, evidenced by his ability to throw out 18 of 30 baserunners last season, but all other facets of his game are limited.

Quirk, a lefthander hitter with a little power, is strictly a fastball hitter. He appears lost with sliders and breaking balls. Defensively, Quirk can play three positions: catcher, third base and first base. Yet, he has trouble at all three and his career could be in jeopardy. His best attribute is that he has

accepted his role as a part-time player and can be a decent bat off the bench.

As a catcher (where Quirk filled in for Sundberg), he had trouble locating pop-ups and rarely would prevent any wild pitches. He does have a quick release with an accurate arm, however, and this perhaps allows him to remain in the majors as a backup catcher.

OVERALL:

Quirk, who's facing the end of his career, must have a strong spring training just to make the team. He has limited value as a player, but yet, the Royals may find room for him in their organization as a coach.

Killebrew: "What I like about Jamie is that he's a good guy to have on a ballclub and he can play a lot of positions. The thing that surprises me is that he's more than adequate and he's a good utility player. He's the type of guy I'd like on my ballclub."

ANGEL SALAZAR
SS, No. 2
RR, 6'0", 190 lbs.
ML Svc: 2 years
Born: 11-4-61 in
Anzoategui,
Venezuela

HITTING, BASERUNNING, FIELDING:

Angel Salazar hit .245 and drove in 24 runs last season, the most by a Royals shortstop in years. Yet, the Royals believe there's an abundance of room for improvement.

Salazar stands far too deep and away from the plate. Because of the way he positions himself at the plate, he doesn't have a chance at breaking balls away. Salazar is most adept at hitting the fastball or the hanging breaking

ball. He's an opposite field hitter with little power, but he has the knack of hitting the ball into the gaps.

He's an above-average baserunner, with 4.1 speed down to first base from the right side. He's also unafraid of breaking up the double play.

Defensively, Salazar has one of the finest arms on the team. He's excellent going to his right but has limited range to his left. Salazar's biggest problem appears to be his stamina. As the season progresses, he tends to run out of gas. The Royals attribute this to playing winter ball and believe Salazar would be much more fresh if he rested all winter.

OVERALL:

There's no reason why Salazar shouldn't win the starting shortstop job on the team this year, but he must become much more consistent in order to do so.

KANSAS CITY ROYALS

KEVIN SEITZER
OF/INF, No. 33
RR, 5'11", 180 lbs.
**ML Svc: less than
one year**
**Born: 3-26-62 in
Springfield, IL**

HITTING, BASERUNNING, FIELDING:

Kevin Seitzer figures to have a bright future at the plate with the potential to be a consistent .300 hitter. He hit .319 with 13 homers and 74 RBIs at the Royals' Triple-A club and then hit .323 with two homers and 11 RBIs in the final month of the season with the Royals.

Surprisingly, he is a very disciplined and patient hitter for his age (25). He walked 19 times in just 115 plate appearances with the Royals last season. He's a good fastball hitter and is excellent at hitting behind the runner. He'll often hit the breaking ball to right-center field and has learned to turn on an inside pitch. He has the most difficulty with the hard slider thrown down-and-away.

Seitzer is a smart baserunner and has acceptable speed from the right side (4.2 seconds to first).

Defensively, Seitzer is a below-average outfielder with an average arm. He still lacks the proper instincts in the outfield and has problems judging the ball. Yet, he's capable of playing third base and first base.

OVERALL:

Seitzer is capable of hitting .300 with 15-18 homers and 75-80 RBIs. He just may be the biggest surprise on the Royals' team this season. If he can maintain his discipline at the plate, he should become the first regular developed by the Royals farm system since Willie Wilson.

MILWAUKEE BREWERS

HITTING:

Glenn Braggs looks as though he could play tight end for the New York Giants. *He's huge.* Teammate Dan Plesac calls him a "manster" (half man/half monster). Although Braggs does only nominal work with weights, his body ripples with powerful muscles that scouts predict will generate tremendous major league power someday.

But Braggs isn't just strong: he has good speed and a strong throwing arm. He has all the tools necessary to become a tremendous baseball player.

He generates awesome power with his quick, tight swing but sometimes causes problems for himself by trying to lift pitches down in the strike zone. Breaking balls can give him problems.

Braggs joined the Brewers at midseason last year after batting .360 with 15 homers and 75 RBIs for Vancouver of the Pacific Coast League. Although he was hitting the ball hard when he first arrived in the major leagues, Braggs wasn't hitting for a high average. In an attempt to correct his stroke, he made improper adjustments in his swing. Instead of the nice compact swing he was using, he started chasing pitches out of the strike zone and his average suffered further.

With a half season in the major leagues behind him, Braggs should be more comfortable this season and play up to the potential everyone has predicted for him.

BASERUNNING:

Because of his excellent speed, Braggs is capable of stealing 20-25 bases a season. Because he will eventually wind up in a power slot in the batting order, he may not be called on to run that often this season, however. But if it looks as though his hitting is consistent, Trebelhorn may turn Braggs loose on the bases. If that occurs at some point--this season or is subsequent ones--Braggs could run his way into the 20/20 club (SB/HR).

FIELDING:

Braggs has a strong arm but he still has to

GLENN BRAGGS
OF, No. 26
RR, 6'3", 210 lbs.
ML Svc: 1 year
Born: 10-17-62 in
San Bernadino, CA

1986 STATISTICS

AVG	G	AB	R	H	2B	3B	HR	RBI	BB	SO	SB
.237	58	215	19	51	8	2	4	18	11	47	1

CAREER STATISTICS

AVG	G	AB	R	H	2B	3B	HR	RBI	BB	SO	SB
.237	58	215	19	51	8	2	4	18	11	47	1

  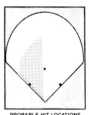

VS. RHP   VS. LHP   PROBABLE HIT LOCATIONS

learn to control it. With his speed and strong arm, he should be a good outfielder but he had problems judging fly balls in left field last season.

He had been a right fielder and center fielder in the minor leagues and appeared to have problems adjusting to the new position in left.

OVERALL:

Braggs has all the qualities to be a star player. He has been compared to a young Don Baylor but with better defensive ability. Braggs has the potential to be a good player for a long time--all he is missing is the experience.

Kaat: "He's been called one of the best-looking players scouts have seen in years and years. If this guy gets a chance to play every day, there's a chance people are going to hear a lot about him in a hurry. He's that good."

POWER POTENTIAL

HITTING:

Greg Brock got his wish over the winter: escape from Los Angeles.

Although Brock was demonstrably a better offensive player in each of the four seasons since he took over for Steve Garvey at first base, Dodger fans never forgave his relative lack of charisma and his inconsistency.

Brock hit 71 homers for the Dodgers, yet most seemed to come after games were decided. Say what you will about game-winning RBIs, but something's amiss when a hitter collects only 14 of them in four years while batting in the middle of the Dodger lineup. (Why, even Bill Russell had 15 in the same span.)

Dodger management advertised him as the next Duke Snider after he hit 44 homers at Triple-A in 1982, but such great expectations only weighed down Brock, who is more of a quiet, businesslike player than the hype considered.

The new expectation is that Brock will find himself, as Candy Maldonado did upon leaving the Dodger pressure-cooker, and put together some 30-homer seasons in the American League. Milwaukee, which gave up Tim Leary and a minor leaguer to get a replacement for Cecil Cooper, gains a lefthanded-hitting Rob Deer type: low average, lots of power, lots of walks, lots of strikeouts.

Brock is a high-ball hitter who likes to pull everything. He has trouble with off-speed pitches, fastballs that jam him, and lefthanders in general. He hit .102 in limited action against lefties in 1986, but platooning hurts his confidence.

The Dodgers wanted Brock to be more aggressive--just swing at more pitches--and go to left field more often. These are things the Brewers will no doubt want from this potentially fine hitter as well.

BASERUNNING:

Brock is a slow runner and is getting ˌslower. He needed arthroscopic surgery last June to remove bone chips from his left knee,

GREG BROCK
1B, No. 9
LR, 6'3", 205 lbs.
ML Svc: 4 years
Born: 6-14-57 in
**   McMinnville, OR**

1986 STATISTICS

AVG	G	AB	R	H	2B	3B	HR	RBI	BB	SO	SB
.234	115	325	33	76	13	0	16	52	37	60	2

CAREER STATISTICS

AVG	G	AB	R	H	2B	3B	HR	RBI	BB	SO	SB
.233	496	1506	195	351	53	2	71	219	214	255	19

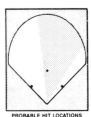

VS. RHP   VS. LHP   PROBABLE HIT LOCATIONS

which had undergone a major reconstruction in high school.

FIELDING:

Though he's no Garvey when it comes to scooping low throws, Brock is a good first baseman. Few cheat as well as he does by coming off the bag inches ahead of the ball.

OVERALL:

With Franklin Stubbs and others looking over Brock's shoulder at first--and the player himself requesting a trade--the Dodger front office made the obvious move. Al Campanis will be faulted if Brock, who'll be 30 in June, hits his stride in Milwaukee. But that's a chance the LA vice president has chosen to take.

Dierker: "Brock has great raw power and can hit the ball out of the ballpark anywhere. He's always dangerous, but not consistently so."

MILWAUKEE BREWERS

HITTING:

Rick Cerone's defense keeps him in the game. When he first came into the majors (1976), he was *all* defense and had a tremendous throwing arm. Then in 1980 while with the New York Yankees, he developed into what appeared to be a dangerous hitter. But just as quickly, his offensive momentum swung back the other way.

Cerone has lost a lot of his bat speed and has really declined as a hitter in recent years. He used to be quick to get around on an inside pitch but the only pitches he seems to hit now are out over the plate. That tells you that his quickness is gone.

He is a straightaway hitter and will often go to center or right-center field. Pitchers should keep the ball down-and-in. Although he can be overpowered, it's best to mix up the offerings sent to Cerone.

Not a big power hitter, he's still capable of hitting an occasional home run.

BASERUNNING:

There's no advantage whatsoever having Cerone on base. He is no basestealing threat and his instincts on base are not especially good, probably because he has never been called on to run.

FIELDING:

Catching is Cerone's strong suit. Although his arm is not what it once was, he still throws well and runners can't take liberties with him. He handles pitchers very well. He has enough experience that pitchers automatically have confidence in him. That can be a big help.

Cerone is aggressive with his pitchers and is not timid about telling them how he'd like to work a ball game. For the most part, that kind

RICK CERONE
C, No. 11
RR, 5'11", 195 lbs.
ML Svc: 10 years
Born: 5-19-54 in
Newark, NJ

1986 STATISTICS
AVG	G	AB	R	H	2B	3B	HR	RBI	BB	SO	SB
.259	68	216	22	56	14	0	4	18	15	28	1

CAREER STATISTICS
AVG	G	AB	R	H	2B	3B	HR	RBI	BB	SO	SB
.228	858	2916	266	665	126	12	43	304	198	290	4

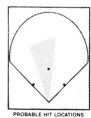

VS. RHP   VS. LHP   PROBABLE HIT LOCATIONS

of decisiveness is what a staff prefers.

OVERALL:

Rick Cerone's moment of glory was clearly in 1980 with the Yankees. He gained a degree of fame from his stay in New York, but if he had spent those seasons with a less highly profiled club than New York, expectations for him would have been much less grand.

Kaat: "Cerone will probably not play regularly anymore but is still a valuable backup catcher. He worked very well with the Milwaukee Brewers' young pitching staff last season and his knowledge of the game and the hitters will help his pitchers and other catchers as well."

MILWAUKEE BREWERS

PITCHING:

Mark Clear got things under control last season and had an impressive year for the Brewers. After the Boston Red Sox gave up on him because of his lack of control, then-Brewers manager George Bamberger made Clear his bullpen stopper. Clear responded to the regular work with some excellent numbers and a very good walks-to-strikeouts ratio.

Clear has always had the reputation of having one of the best curveballs in the major leagues. When he can control it, he is almost unhittable--but his key to success is throwing strikes. That's not easy to do with a big curveball like Clear's.

His fastball is above average and he has to use it to set up the breaking ball. If his breaking ball isn't working, however, hitters can sit on his fastball and his heater isn't hot enough to last long against big league hitters. He can't be a one-pitch pitcher. When he is behind in the count, look for the fastball.

Clear worked from the hole often but managed to throw strikes when he needed them in his first season with the Brewers. He teamed with rookie Dan Plesac to give the Brewers an excellent righty/lefty bullpen combination.

His delivery is a little awkward and unconventional. He has gone away from a high kick to keep runners from stealing at will.

FIELDING:

Clear does not appear to be a good athlete

MARK CLEAR
RHP, No. 25
RR, 6'4", 215 lbs.
ML Svc: 8 years
Born: 5-27-56 in
Los Angeles, CA

1986 STATISTICS

W	L	ERA	G	GS	CG	SV	IP	H	R	ER	BB	SO
5	5	2.20	59	0	0	16	73.2	53	23	18	36	85

CAREER STATISTICS

W	L	ERA	G	GS	CG	SV	IP	H	R	ER	BB	SO
62	44	3.80	394	0	0	77	689.1	576	332	291	469	691

and has his problems defensively. Hitters can bunt on him because his reactions are slow and he has trouble bending down and picking up the ball.

OVERALL:

Although Dan Plesac is liable to move ahead of him as the Brewers' No. 1 short reliever, Clear could have another good year if his control problems are behind him. He is durable and can pitch several days in a row.

Kaat: "After his ups and downs in Boston, the change of scenery appeared to be a boost to his career.

"Even though he had a good season in 1986, Clear has to continue to improve on his control. If he does that, he can be a valuable member of the Brewers' bullpen."

MILWAUKEE BREWERS

HITTING:

At one time, Cecil Cooper was certainly in a class by himself. Three years ago, he was one of the best hitters in baseball, hitting .300 or better for six straight seasons. There are many who continue to expect him to hit .352 (as he did in 1980) every year but that is as unrealistic as could be.

He continues to be a legitimate threat at the plate, however. Cooper got off to a slow start last season after undergoing elbow surgery during the '85-86 off-season but he still finished second on the team in RBIs.

Cooper's big-power output disappeared three seasons ago but he still has enough slugs in him that a pitcher can never become complacent.

He bats from a deep crouch and a wide-open stance. He's a good low fastball hitter but can still get his bat on the high pitch. He waits long enough and doesn't get way out front, so he doesn't get fooled too often on breaking stuff. The best bet is to feed him fastballs up-and-in.

BASERUNNING:

Cooper has enough speed to steal a few more bases than he does, but rarely will attempt to do so, and is only an average baserunner. He doesn't slide hard and doesn't run hard on balls that appear to be routine outs, something that has embarrassed him a few times when an outfielder has dropped a ball and Cooper was unable to take an extra base.

FIELDING:

Cooper still looks pretty slick at first base but his range isn't what it used to be. He is scheduled to be a designated hitter most of the time this season. He digs low throws out of the dirt as well as anyone.

CECIL COOPER
1B, No. 15
LL, 6'2", 190 lbs.
ML Svc: 16 years
Born: 12-20-49 in Brenham, TX

1986 STATISTICS

AVG	G	AB	R	H	2B	3B	HR	RBI	BB	SO	SB
.258	134	542	46	140	24	1	12	75	41	87	1

CAREER STATISTICS

AVG	G	AB	R	H	2B	3B	HR	RBI	BB	SO	SB
.300	1833	7099	987	2130	402	47	235	1089	431	860	88

  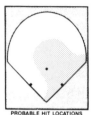

VS. RHP   VS. LHP   PROBABLE HIT LOCATIONS

OVERALL:

Cooper is still an offensive threat and should continue to be a productive player for several more years. A lot of his problems early last year were a result of his late start caused by his elbow surgery. Now that he's healthy again, he can be expected to have another Cecil Cooper-type year.

Kaat: "He's getting to the age where he will be used mostly as a DH, however, and most of his contributions will be on offense. At this stage in a player's career, production often depends on the individual's motivation to prove that he can still be a quality player. If Cecil has the drive, I think he can still produce. He still has the ability to be a very good player for some time."

MILWAUKEE BREWERS

HITTING:

Rob Deer finally got his chance last year and definitely took advantage of it. After spending seven seasons in the minor leagues and sitting on the bench most of 1985 for the San Francisco Giants, Deer was traded to the Brewers for two minor league pitchers. With the Brewers, he was told, "Here's a job, we're going to see what you can do with it for a year."

Deer struck out a lot, just as everybody had always said he would, but he hit 33 home runs and drove in 86 runs. The deal turned out to be a bargain for the Brewers, their first in a while.

Deer has as much strength as anybody in the major leagues. In his first game as a Brewer, it was almost as though he was looking to take revenge on the ball for all of his years in the minors--his home run was shot over the roof in Chicago's Comiskey Park.

If Deer is allowed to get his arms extended on a fat pitch, it is gone-gone-gone. Pitchers *can't* give him anything out over the plate. They have to try to get ahead of him, then bust a fastball up-and-in or get him to chase a breaking ball out of the strike zone. He can hit the low fastball.

BASERUNNING:

Deer has good speed for someone his size but he's no threat on the basepaths. His specialty is circling the bases four at a time.

FIELDING:

Deer is a hard worker and an aggressive outfielder whose hustle makes up for his defensive shortcomings. Playing more and more will make him better but he will never be a Gold Glove candidate. He has an extremely strong arm and covers a lot of ground for a player as large as he is.

OVERALL:

Pitchers are obviously going to have to take him more seriously next season. Deer will

ROB DEER
OF/DH, No. 45
RR, 6'3", 210 lbs.
ML Svc: 2 years
Born: 9-29-60 in
Orange, CA

1986 STATISTICS

AVG	G	AB	R	H	2B	3B	HR	RBI	BB	SO	SB
.232	134	466	75	108	17	3	33	86	72	179	5

CAREER STATISTICS

AVG	G	AB	R	H	2B	3B	HR	RBI	BB	SO	SB
.218	225	652	102	142	22	4	44	109	102	260	6

  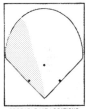

STRONG — VS. RHP   STRONG — VS. LHP   PROBABLE HIT LOCATIONS

have to prove himself all over by becoming an even better hitter this season. Deer will never be a high-average hitter but his enormous power potential makes up for it. His biggest problem will be cutting down on the strikeouts.

Deer is a hard-nosed, aggressive player who had to work hard to attain his success last season. If determination is the key, he should prove that 1986 was no fluke and have several successful seasons.

Kaat: "When Deer was in the National League, the book on him was if he hits it, it's going out anywhere--but he won't hit it often. He showed in 1986 that he could hit enough to be productive.

"I've always used the expression, 'A guy's got to get *better* to be just as good as he was the year before.' That's the key with a player such as Rob Deer: to see if he can cut down on his strikeouts and maybe be more selective to make himself a better hitter.

"If he continues to work hard and improve, he should be a real find for the Brewers, and they didn't have to give up much to get him. He's been a real steal."

MILWAUKEE BREWERS

HITTING:

Former Brewer manager George Bamberger referred to Jim Gantner as "the glue that holds the Milwaukee Brewers together." Current manager Tom Trebelhorn calls him "the captain of the infield."

Gantner is a hard-nosed player who will do anything to win, whether it's risking his health to turn a double play or kicking the ball out of a shortstop's glove on a hard slide into second base.

As a hitter, the first thing that makes him different than most lefthanded hitters is he's a high fastball hitter. Gantner is an aggressive hitter, making it extra important for a pitcher to get ahead of him. When Gantner is behind in the count, he will start chasing bad pitches.

Lefthanders should feed him breaking balls down and away. Righthanders can throw him low fastballs.

He doesn't have much power, although he will knock one out of the park every now and then. Because of his lack of power, he should bunt more often than he does because he has good speed and would be able to leg out a few hits. He also has a tendency to try to pull the ball too often instead of trying to use the whole field by going with the pitch.

He usually hits seventh to ninth in the order but he could be an ideal No. 2 hitter. He has the speed to hit high in the order, and being a lefthanded hitter, he would have a good chance to hit one into the hole on the right side of the infield with a man on first base.

BASERUNNING:

Gantner has the speed to steal a few bases but doesn't run very often, perhaps because he usually bats down deep in the order. He runs the bases wisely and will take the extra base when he sees the opportuntiy.

FIELDING:

As a fielder, Ganter can often look

JIM GANTNER
2B, No. 17
LR, 5'11", 175 lbs.
ML Svc: 9 years
Born: 1-5-54 in Eden, WI

1986 STATISTICS

AVG	G	AB	R	H	2B	3B	HR	RBI	BB	SO	SB
.274	139	497	58	136	25	1	7	38	26	50	13

CAREER STATISTICS

AVG	G	AB	R	H	2B	3B	HR	RBI	BB	SO	SB
.275	1120	3871	450	1066	155	23	40	367	241	326	63

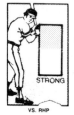  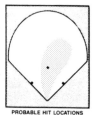

awkward--but he gets the job done. Gantner's style is reminiscent of one-time short-stop/now San Diego manager Larry Bowa: Bowa didn't do the job gracefully but did it as well as anyone.

Gantner, because of his tenacity and aggressiveness, will dive or do anything to stop the ball. He has a good arm, good quickness and turns the double play very well.

OVERALL:

Gantner isn't very big but ballplayers respect him for the way he plays.

Kaat: "He's a good defensive player and a tough hitter, although he could make better use of his good speed. He has been a fine player for the Brewers for years and the fans respect his effort. He should continue to be a valuable big leaguer for several more seasons."

ACE OF THE STAFF

PITCHING:

Teddy Higuera has only been in the major leagues for two seasons but he already has moved into the elite among American League pitchers. After winning 15 games as a rookie, Higuera came back in 1986 to become just the third 20-game winner in the Brewers' history.

Higuera's fastball is a "live" one and good enough for him to win with its explosiveness alone. But Higuera has secured himself for the future with more: he also throws a good slider and a change-up that breaks like a screwball. When he first entered the majors, he also threw a screwball and curveball but ditched them when he found he could exact success with simply the fastball, slider and change-up.

Higuera releases his 90 MPH fastball from a three-quarters delivery. His delivery is smooth and his rhythm is consistent. Despite the smooth motion, he hides the ball well. He's a very fast worker who doesn't waste time between pitches. His control is good and he moves the ball around the plate well, slicing in and out of the hitter's strength.

Higuera is a good closer, a trait a lot of good pitchers have. Like fellow southpaw Fernando Valenzuela, if you don't get him early, you don't get him. Once Higuera gets his rhythm and goes through the batting order once, he gets better. His fastball still clocks in the high-80s in the eighth and ninth innings.

FIELDING:

He doesn't have an outstanding pickoff move but his motion makes baserunners pay attention. His delivery puts him in excellent position to field a ball and his defense is excellent. He did not commit an error last

TEDDY HIGUERA
LHP, No. 49
SL, 5'10", 178 lbs.
ML Svc: 2 years
Born: 11-9-58 in
** Los Mochis, Mexico**

1986 STATISTICS

W	L	ERA	G	GS	CG	SV	IP	H	R	ER	BB	SO
20	11	2.79	34	34	15	0	248.1	226	84	77	74	207

CAREER STATISTICS

W	L	ERA	G	GS	CG	SV	IP	H	R	ER	BB	SO
35	19	3.30	66	64	22	0	460.2	412	189	169	137	334

season--and he pitched an awful lot of innings.

OVERALL:

One of the keys to Higuera's success was making him a three-pitch instead of five-pitch pitcher in his rookie season. By shelving two pitches, he was forced to perfect his fastball--and, boy, did he ever. He's easily the best of a lot of talented young pitchers on the Brewers' staff.

His only problem has been the English language but he's been studying the language and has made great progress there too.

Anytime a team gets their mitts on a lefthander with good control who can make the ball run away from lefthanded hitters, the front office lights up the cigars, kicks backs contentedly and waits for a pennant.

Kaat: "This isn't going out on a limb by any means, but I'd have to put him up there as a leading Cy Young candidate for this season. Coming off a great rookie year and putting together a year like he did last year, he should have a world of confidence going into 1987."

MILWAUKEE BREWERS

PITCHING:

After years of bouncing around from team to team, John Henry Johnson's road to survival led him to Milwaukee last season. The results were encouraging for both Johnson and the Brewers. Used as a long reliever and set-up man after he was called up from the minors at midseason, Johnson fit in well with closers Dan Plesac and Mark Clear.

Johnson's success was because he began to throw the split-finger fastball successfully. The new pitch could keep him in the big leagues. Four or five years ago he was a hard thrower, but Johnson doesn't have the stuff he did back then. Before he added the split-finger pitch, Johnson never had any kind of outstanding breaking ball.

Johnson's straight up-and-down style of delivery causes some problems for him; he should try to develop more rhythm and smoothness. A more fluid motion would help him to maintain control, something which has been a problem for him in the past.

Johnson's health also has been a factor impeding his career. Over the years, he has been on the disabled list too often.

FIELDING:

Johnson always has been a below-average fielder. His pitching motion leaves him in a bad position to field balls hit back to the

JOHN HENRY JOHNSON
LHP, No. 34
LL, 6'2", 210 lbs.
ML Svc: 7 years
Born: 8-21-56 in Houston, TX

1986 STATISTICS

W	L	ERA	G	GS	CG	SV	IP	H	R	ER	BB	SO
2	1	2.66	19	0	0	1	44	43	15	13	10	42

CAREER STATISTICS

W	L	ERA	G	GS	CG	SV	IP	H	R	ER	BB	SO
26	32	3.64	204	59	9	9	576.1	543	264	233	232	389

mound. His move to first base is not exceptional.

OVERALL:

Johnson has been scuffling for years just to stay in the major leagues and this could be his last chance. His fastball has lost a lot and he desperately needed to add the extra pitch just to survive.

Kaat: "Johnson would not be a good short man, though he might become important to the Brewers' staff as a set-up man if he is able to maintain control of the split-finger fastball. It is, however, a very tough pitch to keep on track."

MILWAUKEE BREWERS

HITTING:

Rick Manning has always been an outstanding defensive player but a disappointment as a hitter. Used in the unfamiliar role as a backup outfielder in 1986, Manning ended up playing a valuable role for the Brewers. Although he's still relatively young (in *real* life), the role of fifth or sixth outfielder could be one he will have to become accustomed to.

Manning doesn't have much power and doesn't take advantage of his speed. With his speed and athletic ability, he should be a better hitter. He tends to try to pull the ball too often and doesn't bunt for a hit.

Manning hits from a closed stance deep in the box and never appeared to be a very disciplined hitter last year. He handles high pitches better than low ones, which is a bonus for a lefthanded hitter.

He will chase breaking balls thrown down-and-away from a lefthander. Righthanders should pitch him down-and-away but they can get by with breaking balls down in the strike zone.

BASERUNNING:

Manning has good speed and has stolen as many as 30 bases in one season as a major leaguer (1979 with Cleveland). If the Brewers play more of a running game this season under new manager Tom Trebelhorn, Manning might, once again, become more of a basestealing threat. He has enough speed to be stealing more than he has in the last few seasons.

FIELDING:

Manning is a talented defensive player and can run down a ball in center field as well as anybody. Defensively, he is one of the most underrated outfielders in the American

RICK MANNING
OF, No. 28
LR, 6'1", 180 lbs.
ML Svc: 12 years
Born: 9-2-54 in
Niagara Falls, NY

1986 STATISTICS

AVG	G	AB	R	H	2B	3B	HR	RBI	BB	SO	SB
.254	89	205	31	52	7	3	8	27	17	20	5

CAREER STATISTICS

AVG	G	AB	R	H	2B	3B	HR	RBI	BB	SO	SB
.258	1458	5134	643	1323	182	42	56	445	459	598	164

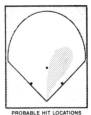

VS. RHP   VS. LHP   PROBABLE HIT LOCATIONS

League.

He plays a very shallow center field, probably because he started his career in Cleveland, which has a short center field. His arm is only average.

OVERALL:

Manning's career appears to be on a downward slide and he isn't likely to ever be a regular player again. He has never lived up to his potential.

Kaat: "He's going to have to accept a backup role but a guy like Manning, who is a good defensive player and has speed, should have value. If the Brewers were a more powerful slugging team, Manning might have a better chance at playing every day because they could 'hide' his offensive deficiencies."

HITTING:

Paul Molitor is the kind of player for the Milwaukee Brewers as Rickey Henderson is for the New York Yankees. Now hold on . . . no, Molitor doesn't have anything close to Henderson's blazing speed and won't steal monstrous numbers of bases, *but*, like Henderson, Molitor can beat you in a lot of ways. He can hit for power. He's got speed. He can bunt. Molitor is a well-skilled offensive player and if the Brewers are going to click at all this season, look at Molitor's numbers to see how the club is going.

He has bounced back from the surgery he underwent in 1984 to replace a tendon in his right elbow and appears to have the same approach to hitting as he did when he helped the Brewers win the American League pennant in 1982. In 1986, however, there was a new injury--one of the many that have plagued Molitor throughout his career. This time, he missed a considerable number of games last season with a torn hamstring muscle. A healthy Molitor is important for the Brewers.

Molitor is an excellent leadoff hitter. He makes good contact and hits to all fields with occasional power. He is also an excellent bunter and will bunt for a base hit.

Hitting from a slightly closed stance, Molitor is up there ready to swing: he doesn't wait for a pitcher to send him something down the middle of the plate. If the first pitch looks good, Molitor is going to go after it. He likes the ball up and over the plate, so it's best to give him breaking balls down and away.

BASERUNNING:

Molitor is a very aggressive baserunner with good speed. He probably has the best instincts on the bases of any Brewers player. He likes to challenge outfielders and is always a threat to go for the extra base. As a basestealer, he picks his situations well and has a very high success ratio (last year, Molitor stole successfully in 80% of his attempts).

PAUL MOLITOR
3B/OF, No. 4
RR, 6'0", 175 lbs.
ML Svc: 9 years
Born: 8-22-56 in
St. Paul, MN

1986 STATISTICS

AVG	G	AB	R	H	2B	3B	HR	RBI	BB	SO	SB
.281	105	437	62	123	24	6	9	55	40	81	20

CAREER STATISTICS

AVG	G	AB	R	H	2B	3B	HR	RBI	BB	SO	SB
.291	1010	4139	676	1203	200	45	79	390	364	515	231

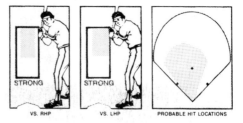

FIELDING:

He has good quickness and although you don't look at him as a Gold Glove candidate, Molitor is an adequate third baseman. Last season, it appeared as though his throwing was unaffected by his elbow surgery.

OVERALL:

Molitor is an exciting ballplayer who is a lot of fun to watch. He was nicknamed "The Ignitor" early in his career--and the name fits. He makes the Brewers' offense go. His biggest problem has been his health. Since joining the Brewers in 1978, however, he has had only one injury-free season.

Kaat: "When he's healthy, he is a very important player to the Brewers offensively and defensively. He plays hard all the time and can do a lot of things to beat you.

"He's still young and there's no reason he shouldn't have several quality seasons left in him. He's a key player to the Brewers, no question about that."

MILWAUKEE BREWERS

HITTING:

After more than 13 seasons in a Milwaukee Brewers' uniform, Charlie Moore gave way to the team's youth movement at the end of last season and became a free agent. He is still a handy guy to have around because of his versatility.

Although he has been a catcher for most of his career, Moore spent two full seasons in the outfield and has even been used in the infield on occasion. He's not an everyday player anymore but because of his many talents, he is the type of player who could be especially valuable to a club looking to fill that 24th roster spot.

Moore isn't a power hitter but makes good contact and would be a good No. 2 hitter. He has the ability to go to right field, has good bat control and is a very good bunter. Moore is a hitter who gives a pitcher a fight--he refuses to be cheated at the plate.·

He hits from a slightly open, semi-crouched stance and hits the low fastball well. He will swing at the first pitch. Pitchers are able to change speeds on him and give him a lot of off-speed stuff and breaking balls because he is an aggressive hitter. Moore has never been a big run-producer but he can hit in the clutch and is a good pinch-hitter.

BASERUNNING:

Moore isn't a big basestealing threat but he has good instincts because of his experience. The Brewers often used him as a pinch-runner. He knows when to go for the extra base and has good speed for a catcher. He slides hard and will break up the double play.

FIELDING:

Moore isn't an exceptional catcher, probably because he has never played the position every day but he is a capable backstop. He throws well and did an excellent job handling the Brewers' young pitchers last

CHARLIE MOORE
C, No. 22
RR, 5'11", 180 lbs.
ML Svc: 13 years
Born: 6-21-53 in
Birmingham, AL

1986 STATISTICS

AVG	G	AB	R	H	2B	3B	HR	RBI	BB	SO	SB
.260	80	235	24	61	12	3	3	39	21	38	5

CAREER STATISTICS

AVG	G	AB	R	H	2B	3B	HR	RBI	BB	SO	SB
.262	1283	3926	441	1029	177	42	35	401	333	458	51

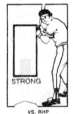

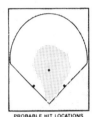

STRONG   STRONG

VS. RHP   VS. LHP   PROBABLE HIT LOCATIONS

year.

As an outfielder, Moore is very good. He is quick and has an outstanding arm. In the outfield, he is always diving, making every effort to catch a ball, possibly a carry-over from his experience behind the plate.

OVERALL:

Although he is getting to an age where he can no longer play every day, Moore is a very valuable player to have around because of his versatility. He can catch, play the outfield, pinch-hit, pinch-run or even fill in at second or third base. There aren't too many players around as versatile as Moore.

Kaat: "Charlie is an aggressive player who always plays hard. He provides a veteran's demeanor and, from a manager's standpoint, you know that you can signal for him off the bench for just about any assignment."

MILWAUKEE BREWERS

PITCHING:

When Juan Nieves joined the Brewers in 1986, everybody expected a lot from the then-21-year-old lefthander. And why not? Nieves had never known anything but success. As a high school star at Avon (Conn.) Old Farms Prep School, Nieves posted a 19-1 record. In three seasons in the minor leagues, he won 33 and lost only 9 while compiling a 3.19 ERA.

The major leagues didn't prove to be much more difficult at the start. He had a 10-4 record by the end of July last year and seemed like a strong candidate for Rookie of the Year honors.

After July, however, Nieves struggled for the first time in his life. He lost eight consecutive games and didn't win again until he was the winner in relief in the last game of the season. It was a learning experience for the young pitcher and might turn out to be more valuable than all of his previous successes.

No one questions Nieves' potential. He has a good live fastball, but must continue to work to develop his breaking ball. The lack of a real good breaking pitch is not unusual for a young pitcher. At times, Nieves has a tendency to try to overthrow his fastball. That, too, is not uncommon in rookie pitchers.

What is promising for this young pitcher is that he has good mechanics, with a delivery on the upright side. He pitches from three-quarters to straight overhand.

He also has maturity on his side. He is very poised for such a young player and takes a good mental approach to the game. Despite his bad second half of the season, he should benefit from the experience he gained pitching in the major leagues every fifth day.

FIELDING:

Nieves' pickoff move is adequate for a

JUAN NIEVES
LHP, No. 30
LL, 6'3", 175 lbs.
ML Svc: 1 year
Born: 1-5-65 in
Santurce, PR

1986 STATISTICS

W	L	ERA	G	GS	CG	SV	IP	H	R	ER	BB	SO
11	12	4.97	35	33	4	0	184.2	224	124	102	77	116

CAREER STATISTICS

W	L	ERA	G	GS	CG	SV	IP	H	R	ER	BB	SO
11	12	4.97	35	33	4	0	184.2	224	124	102	77	116

lefthander. His delivery leaves him in good position to field a ball and he plays his position well.

OVERALL:

Nieves is one of the better young prospects in the league. He still has to master a breaking ball, but his fastball is in the 90s. With his age and his live arm, there's no limit to his potential.

Kaat: "The confidence factor is important with young pitchers. They have to have the ability to start fresh and to put past mistakes behind them in order to progress. Nieves should go into 1987 with a comfortable feeling. He did prove he could win in the major leagues.

"He should be able to relate easily to the Brewers' other young, successful pitchers, Teddy Higuera and Dan Plesac, and know that he can do the same thing that they did last year."

MILWAUKEE BREWERS

GOOD CONTROL

PITCHING:

After pitching in Double-A in 1985, Dan Plesac wasn't expected to be ready for the major leagues in 1986. The Brewers expected him to need a full year in Triple-A to work on his command. In the minors, he worked from behind in the count too often. A few days of spring training was all then-Brewers manager George Bamberger needed to decide that Plesac was ready.

Always a starter in the minor leagues, Plesac went into the Brewers' bullpen for what was supposed to be just long enough for him to get his feet wet, then move into the rotation. He was so impressive as a reliever that he became the team's lefthanded stopper.

Plesac has a live arm and his fastball is one of the best in baseball. He also throws a slider but doesn't often throw the change-up he used in the minor leagues since he has been tagged as a short man.

Despite his problems in the minor leagues, Plesac's control was excellent last season. When he's behind in the count, he will come in with his fastball--but it's an outstanding one and he can get away with it.

Plesac has a nice, smooth delivery, which is important because he might appear in as many as 60 games a year. There's no strain placed on his arm because his is a delivery that has no mechanical problems.

He has great poise on the mound and goes right after hitters. He's intelligent and aggressive, and although he's still learning to pitch out of the bullpen, he's already an outstanding reliever.

FIELDING:

Plesac keeps the runners close. He fields

DAN PLESAC
LHP, No. 37
LL, 6'5", 210 lbs.
ML Svc: 1 year
Born: 2-4-62 in
Gary, IN

1986 STATISTICS

W	L	ERA	G	GS	CG	SV	IP	H	R	ER	BB	SO
10	7	2.97	51	0	0	14	91	81	34	30	29	75

CAREER STATISTICS

W	L	ERA	G	GS	CG	SV	IP	H	R	ER	BB	SO
10	7	2.97	51	0	0	14	91	81	34	30	29	75

his position well and has good hands. He appears to be a good athlete.

OVERALL:

Plesac is the rare type of pitcher who could be successful as either a starter or a reliever. It's important to establish his role on the staff early and not change it. Right now, it appears the Brewers' plans are for him to remain in short relief. He has the makeup and the arm to be one of the very best.

Kaat: "For a youngster to come in and be successful as a short reliever is remarkable. Plesac has the ability to be one of the top short relievers in the league. He should be to the Brewers what Dave Righetti is to the Yankees.

"A pitcher has to have the right mentality to be a short reliever: *he has to really like it.* Plesac seems to be perfect for the role."

MILWAUKEE BREWERS

HITTING:

Unlike most shortstops, Ernest Riles is in the major leagues because of his ability to swing a bat, not because of his defense. Even though his numbers last year were down from his rookie season in 1985, Riles is a good-looking young hitter who sprays the ball all over the field. As a shortstop, he still has a lot to learn.

Riles hasn't shown a lot of power but does have streaks where he will hit two or three home runs in a short period of time. He's a good clutch hitter because of his ability to make contact. One of the best aspects of Riles' hitting is that even when he has two strikes on him, he makes good contact. He has a good idea of the strike zone and won't chase too many pitches even when far behind in the count.

Riles is a low fastball hitter and lefthanders should throw him fastballs up-and-in and breaking balls down-and-away. Righthanders can throw him fastballs in on the belt and breaking balls in the dirt. You don't want to throw him breaking balls down and in the strike zone because that's where his power is.

He has good speed and is a capable bunter but doesn't bunt for a hit.

BASERUNNING:

Riles has good speed but hasn't run much since coming up to the major leagues. He could benefit from new manager Tom Trebelhorn's style of play, which should have the Brewers running more. At this point, Riles is not an aggressive baserunner.

FIELDING:

Riles is only an average shortstop and has a lot of improvements to make in several areas. He plays his position "defensively," when, as the shortstop, he should be much more aggressive. His arm is only adequate and he doesn't make the play in the hole very well.

Riles also has the tendency to play hitters too deep and will often make an easy, relaxed throw to first base instead of throwing hard

ERNEST RILES
SS, No. 1
LR, 6'1", 180 lbs.
ML Svc: 2 years
Born: 10-2-60 in
Whigham, GA

1986 STATISTICS

AVG	G	AB	R	H	2B	3B	HR	RBI	BB	SO	SB
.252	145	524	69	132	24	2	9	47	53	80	7

CAREER STATISTICS

AVG	G	AB	R	H	2B	3B	HR	RBI	BB	SO	SB
.267	261	972	123	260	36	9	14	92	89	134	9

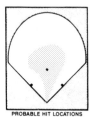

VS. RHP — VS. LHP — PROBABLE HIT LOCATIONS

and fast: he takes his time getting rid of the ball.

OVERALL:

In his first two big league seasons, Riles has impressed people, proving he can be a solid major league player. He's much better offensively than defensively, but his defense should improve with experience. He's still young and if he gets to continue to play every day, he could get better with age and experience.

Kaat: "He has been a shortstop for most of his career but with his arm and limited range, he might be a better third baseman. To be a good player defensively, a guy has to work at it. Riles needs the chance to keep playing in order to have the chance to smooth out his rough edges and become more confident.

"If the Brewers go to a running game this season, it would help Riles to tie his overall game together."

MILWAUKEE BREWERS

HITTING:

Bill Schroeder was supposed to be the Milwaukee Brewers' regular catcher last year, but for the second consecutive season, he spent a lot of time watching a teammate do most of the catching.

After playing in only 53 games in 1985 because of elbow injuries, Schroeder opened the 1986 season on the disabled list after undergoing elbow surgery in September 1985. When he was finally ready to play (two weeks into the season), his job had been taken over by the platoon combination of veteran catchers Charlie Moore and Rick Cerone. Schroeder had lost the first-string catcher's job for the rest of the year.

Schroeder appeared in only 64 games last season--just 35 of which found him behind the plate. The inactivity didn't help him at the plate. A free-swinger who hits from an extremely wide, closed stance, Schroeder doesn't have the ability to adjust to hitting once every five or six days.

When he played regularly in the past, Schroeder put together some torrid streaks, hitting home runs in bunches, but he has to be in the lineup regularly or he looks lost as a hitter.

Basically a pull hitter, Schroeder has shown some power to right-center field. He drives the belt-high fastball well enough but has trouble with breaking balls and off-speed pitches. He strikes out too often. Pitchers can jam him to keep him from extending his arms for that big swing.

BASERUNNING:

Schroeder is a very slow runner and is no threat to steal or take an extra base. The opposition can ignore him when he's on first base--he's not going anywhere.

FIELDING:

With his arm still shy of 100% after the elbow surgery last year, Schroeder did not throw well at all last season. He's not quick behind the plate and is an average catcher defensively. He is intelligent and calls a good

BILL SCHROEDER
C, No. 21
RR, 6'2", 200 lbs.
ML Svc: 4 years
Born: 9-7-58 in
Baltimore, MD

1986 STATISTICS

AVG	G	AB	R	H	2B	3B	HR	RBI	BB	SO	SB
.212	64	217	32	46	14	0	7	19	9	59	1

CAREER STATISTICS

AVG	G	AB	R	H	2B	3B	HR	RBI	BB	SO	SB
.231	201	694	86	160	30	1	32	76	32	197	1

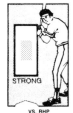 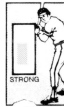 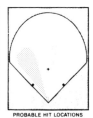

VS. RHP   VS. LHP   PROBABLE HIT LOCATIONS

game, however, and pitchers like throwing to him. He takes charge behind the plate and doesn't hesitate to get on a pitcher when it's necessary to prod maximum performance.

OVERALL:

Schroeder's power potential could make him a valuable player for the Brewers, who have been looking for more offensive punch for the last three years, but he has to play more often to be productive. His inactivity over the past two seasons has slowed the progress he was hoping to make in his major league career and he's getting to an age where he is going to have to establish himself soon.

Kaat: "He will never hit for a high average and will always strike out a lot but Schroeder looks as though he has the potential to hit 20-25 home runs if he plays every day.

"The condition of his elbow is still a big question mark; runners will undoubtedly test his throwing arm early in the season to see if he can nail them."

MILWAUKEE BREWERS

PITCHING:

Pete Vuckovich was thought to have finally surrendered to the aching shoulder that had bothered him since he won the Cy Young Award in 1982 when he announced his retirement near the end of spring training 1986. But Vuckovich is no quitter.

He ended his brief retirement near the end of July and pitched very well for the Brewers' Vancouver farm club. Called up to the major leagues in September, he pitched impressively and appeared to have no problems with his shoulder.

He doesn't have to prove he can pitch. He just has to prove to everyone--including himself--that his shoulder can *hold up* for an entire season.

Vuckovich hasn't pitched many innings since 1982, but if his comeback is a success, he shouldn't look much different from the Vuckovich who helped the Brewers win their only pennant.

He never was a hard thrower, but he can make a baseball do a lot of different things. Vuckovich is a student of the mechanics of the ball's flight and he can make his pitches sink, slide and change speeds. He throws fastballs, slurves, change-ups and an occasional knuckleball. He has also been suspected of loading one up on occasion. He throws all of his pitches at different speeds and from different locations. There isn't anything he wouldn't try to get a hitter out.

Vuckovich's delivery is part of his arsenal. He has a herky-jerky motion that he uses effectively to deceive hitters. His huge, floppy uniform shirt serves a purpose, too--to distract the concentration of the hitter.

FIELDING:

For a big guy, Vuckovich moves better than most people give him credit for. He has a

PETE VUCKOVICH
RHP, No. 50
RR, 6'4", 220 lbs.
ML Svc: 10 years
Born: 10-27-52 in
Johnstown, PA

1986 STATISTICS

W	L	ERA	G	GS	CG	SV	IP	H	R	ER	BB	SO
2	4	3.06	6	6	0	0	32.1	33	18	11	11	12

CAREER STATISTICS

W	L	ERA	G	GS	CG	SV	IP	H	R	ER	BB	SO
93	69	3.66	286	186	38	10	1454.1	1474	665	592	545	882

quick move to first and the ability to hold runners on first base and to unload to home quickly.

OVERALL:

The condition of Vuckovich's shoulder is still a nagging question. If he is able to pitch for an entire season, there is no reason he shouldn't be successful. He's an extremely smart pitcher and would add a lot to the Brewers' young pitching staff.

Kaat: "His competetive spirit is as important as anything he throws. Vuckovich doesn't want to be beaten by anyone or anything--including a serious shoulder injury. He has an immense desire to bounce back and prove he can still pitch.

"Sometimes a pitcher such as Pete Vuckovich--even if he has only a .500 season-- can be an important member of the staff just by taking the ball every four or five days and giving them the innings. His determination to return to pitch at the major league level should serve as a positive influence on the younger pitchers."

MILWAUKEE BREWERS

PITCHING:

The 1986 season was a real learning experience for Bill Wegman. Trying to win in the major leagues, he found out, is not an easy way to make a living. Still, the tall righthander pitched better in his rookie season than his 5-12 record indicates. He was not involved in the decision in 15 of his starts, but the Brewers went on to win nine of those games.

The fastball is Wegman's best pitch. He doesn't throw in the 90s like teammates Dan Plesac and Juan Nieves, the Brewers' more publicized rookies last season, so Wegman has to rely on spotting his pitches in order to be effective. Wegman has to keep the ball down in the strike zone to be successful.

Wegman will never rack up a bevy of Ks, so he has to depend on a pitcher's best friend--the ground ball. And he will induce them because he throws a good slider (although he has been inconsistent with his control). His third pitch is a change-up that he uses effectively.

Wegman has a nice, smooth delivery and a live arm. He has the talent to be effective, although he doesn't seem to challenge hitters enough.

FIELDING:

Wegman is a good athlete who played in the infield at times in college and actually thought he had been drafted as a third baseman. His athletic ability serves him well defensively. He has a quick move to first base and will use it. He has good reflexes on balls hit back to the mound and has a good knowledge of fielding fundamentals.

OVERALL:

Wegman is one of the hardest workers in

**BILL WEGMAN
RHP, No. 46
RR, 6'5", 200 lbs.
ML Svc: 1 year plus
Born: 12-19-62 in
Cincinnati, OH**

1986 STATISTICS

W	L	ERA	G	GS	CG	SV	IP	H	R	ER	BB	SO
5	12	5.13	35	32	0	0	198.1	217	120	113	43	82

CAREER STATISTICS

W	L	ERA	G	GS	CG	SV	IP	H	R	ER	BB	SO
7	12	5.00	38	35	0	0	216	234	128	120	46	88

the Brewers' organization. He's young, and if desire has anything to do with it, he will be successful.

He has been used mainly as a starter, but is durable and strong enough to pitch out of the bullpen. He could fill almost any role. He could start, pitch short or long relief or be used as a spot starter and reliever. Although he was in the starting rotation for most of the 1986 season, his role this year might be as a fifth starter who could be used out of the bullpen a lot.

Kaat: "I think that Wegman is kind of a sleeper-type of pitcher. He hasn't had the rave reviews that Nieves, Plesac and Higuera received last year, but he has pitched some good ballgames. He's still inconsistent at times and if he wants to share any of the headlines with his fellow pitchers, he has to begin to challenge hitters all the time."

MILWAUKEE BREWERS

HITTING:

Robin Yount had quite a year in 1986. The Brewers' transplanted shortstop led the team in batting and became a better-than-average center fielder in just his second season in the outfield. Still, Yount wasn't anywhere near the player he was before a shoulder injury that needed surgery after the 1984 and '85 seasons. The shoulder is improving and if it gets back to full strength you can expect Yount to once again be one of the better players in the game.

Yount is a very disciplined hitter with good power, although the surgery has robbed him of some of his slugging ability. He hits pitches down in the strike zone well and has the ability to take a pitch down and over the plate to right-center field with power.

Lefthanders should throw him fastballs up-and-in and righthanders can get him to chase breaking balls. Pitchers should try to keep everything on the outside half of the plate.

Normally, Yount drives in a lot of runs for a No. 2 hitter but the shoulder problem has cut down on his ability to drive in runs. Despite his high average, he was not a very productive hitter in 1986.

He has good speed and can beat out an infield hit but doesn't bunt for a hit.

BASERUNNING:

Although Yount is always a threat to steal, the Brewers have never taken advantage of his speed. He can go from first to third and knows when to do it. Even though he has not often been called upon to utilize it, his baserunning instinct is excellent.

FIELDING:

Yount, who was an outstanding shortstop before his sore shoulder forced him to move to the outfield, easily adjusted to his new position. His good speed and quickness help him race to reach a lot of balls hit to center field. He covers a lot of ground and charges balls with the same aggressive approach that he used when he was a shortstop.

Yount's poor throwing arm hurts him and the Brewers. Although it got stronger as the

ROBIN YOUNT
CF, No. 19
RR, 6'0", 180 lbs.
ML Svc: 13 years
Born: 9-16-55 in
Danville, IL

1986 STATISTICS

AVG	G	AB	R	H	2B	3B	HR	RBI	BB	SO	SB
.312	140	522	82	163	31	7	9	46	62	73	14

CAREER STATISTICS

AVG	G	AB	R	H	2B	3B	HR	RBI	BB	SO	SB
.283	1811	7137	1043	2019	380	82	153	827	535	780	166

  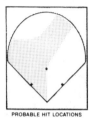

STRONG VS. RHP — STRONG VS. LHP — PROBABLE HIT LOCATIONS

season progressed, even the slowest runners in the league were still able to take liberties on balls hit to center field.

OVERALL:

Yount became one of the youngest players in history to reach 2,000 hits last season and has plenty of time to record some impressive statistics before his playing career is through, especially if his shoulder continues to improve. Despite his injury, he's still one of the top players in the American League. Along with third baseman Paul Molitor, Yount is a key player for this club. With both of them healthy and in the lineup every day, the Brewers could climb a few rungs in the standings this year.

Kaat: "It's taken a year or so for Robin to get back in the groove of playing well because of his injury. It wouuldn't surprise me now, however, to see him have the same kind of year he had back in 1982, when he was the Most Valuable Player. When Yount is 100% physically, you have to consider him as good as anyone."

MILWAUKEE BREWERS

MIKE BIRKBECK
RHP, No. 55
RR, 6'2", 185 lbs.
ML Svc: less than one year
Born: 3-10-61 in
  Orrville, OH

PITCHING, FIELDING:

Mike Birkbeck is one of the many talented pitching prospects in the Brewers' system. An outstanding first half in the Pacific Coast League earned him a promotion to the major leagues last July, but a slow-healing blister on his pitching hand kept him from showing what he could really do.

Birkbeck has a good fastball, but his best pitch is an outstanding breaking ball. He threw it to Reggie Jackson in spring training in 1986, prompting the Angels' slugger to comment, "That's not a spring training breaking ball. That's a July breaking ball."

The breaking ball is hard to get over the plate for any pitcher--never mind a rookie pitcher--so Birkbeck has to hit his spots with his fastball, which is not overpowering. He started throwing a slider late in the season and used it effectively.

Birkbeck has a good pickoff move and is a good-to-excellent fielder.

OVERALL:

Birkbeck has had a lot of success in the minor leagues and has a chance to be the Brewers' fourth or fifth starter this season. The addition of the slider has been a big help and when he has control of his great breaking ball, it looks as though he is going to be very tough.

BRYAN CLUTTERBUCK
RHP, No. 48
RR, 6'4", 225 lbs.
ML Svc: less than one
  year
Born: 12-17-59 in
  Detroit, MI

PITCHING, FIELDING:

It took five-and-a-half years of hard work for Bryan Clutterbuck to make it to the major leagues. When he got there, a weight problem almost wasted all of that hard work.

He has an above-average fastball and a good change-up. When he doesn't use the change-up, he gets hit hard. He throws a slider that doesn't break much.

Clutterbuck has an average-to-good pickoff move. He fields his position well for someone his size.

OVERALL:

Clutterbuck doesn't have as much natural ability as the Brewers' other young pitchers, but he impressed former Brewers manager George Bamberger with his bulldog nature. He wasn't afraid to go right after hitters in some sticky situations when he made his first appearance in a spring training game. A tendency to put on weight is his biggest problem.

Clutterbuck has been used as a starter and in relief. He is best suited for middle relief, but he could pitch in short relief if called on to do so.

MILWAUKEE BREWERS

BILLY JOE ROBIDOUX
1B, No. 13
LR, 6'1", 200 lbs.
ML Svc: 1 year plus
Born: 1-13-64 in
Ware, MA

HITTING, BASERUNNING, FIELDING:

The Brewers handed Billy Jo Robidoux the starting first baseman's job last season when Cecil Cooper opened the season on the disabled list. Robidoux took advantage of that opportunity and was batting over .300 and leading the team in RBIs after six weeks. Then he injured his knee and spent most of the season on the disabled list.

When he did return to the lineup, he had weight problems and didn't look like the same hitter. When he is hitting well, he is balanced at the plate, has a short stroke and gets a good look at the ball. Robidoux doesn't have a lot of power but makes good contact. He can take the pitch up-and-away and take it to the opposite field. A good-looking young hitter, Robidoux likes to hit fastballs but doesn't appear to get fooled badly on breaking pitches.

Not blessed with great speed, Robidoux is no threat on the bases. His lack of running speed may ultimately rob him of potential base hits.

Robidoux has adequate defensive skills although his range and movement are nothing special. He is not regarded as a defensive wizard but will come to be known for his offense.

OVERALL:

Robidoux is still young and needs to play and going back to Triple-A to get his bat back on track might not hurt. If he gets off to a good start in the minors, he looks like a player who will figure in the Brewers' plans--maybe before the 1987 season is over.

DALE SVEUM
3B, No. 27
SF, 6'3", 185 lbs.
ML Svc: less than one year
Born: 11-23-63 in
Richmond, CA

HITTING, BASERUNNING, FIELDING:

Dale Sveum is considered one of the best athletes in the Brewers' organization and was a highly recruited quarterback before the Brewers made him their first-round draft choice in 1982.

A switch-hitter, Sveum hits for a better average when batting lefthanded. Either way, he's a contact hitter who uses the whole field. He has never been a high-average hitter but hits well with runners in scoring position. He shows occasional power, coming mostly from the left side.

Sveum got off to a quick start last year after joining the Brewers and was batting over .350 after his first month. When pitchers started feeding him more breaking balls, his average dropped, especially from the right side.

Sveum has average speed but has never been a big basestealer.

Always an outstanding defensive player in the minor leagues, Sveum got a case of the yips and had trouble handling anything at all last year. He finished the season with a team high of 30 errors in just 91 games. He should field better than that.

Originally a shortstop, Sveum was moved to third base in the minor leagues. He has a strong arm, but not great quickness or range in the infield.

OVERALL:

Sveum is expected to be used as a utility player with the Brewers. Although he spent most of his defensive time at third base in his rookie season, he played well at shortstop and second base when he was asked to fill in. If he can overcome the defensive problems that plagued him in his rookie year, Sveum has enough athletic ability to become a good player.

MINNESOTA TWINS

KEITH ATHERTON
RHP, No. 22
RR, 6'4", 200 lbs.
ML Svc: 4 years
Born: 2-19-59 in
Matthews, VA

PITCHING:

Oakland gave up on Keith Atherton last year. The Twins picked him up one month into the season, and found that they had a stopper who was effective for a couple of months and finished the season with a team and personal high of 10 saves. He enjoyed the challenge of being the terminator instead of the set-up man, although the Twins don't plan on him continuing in a game-saving role on a regular basis this season.

Atherton is primarily a power pitcher and throws a fastball and a slider. He can keep batters from digging in with an off-speed pitch that acts like a screwball. Also, Atherton began to experiment with a submarine delivery toward the end of last season, a project he sounded determined to continue in 1987. That's a good idea because Atherton's career pattern has been to pitch well in streaks and then falter, a pattern that could be broken if he has more tricks to rely on.

Atherton can be especially tough on righthanded batters and almost seems to benefit from little bouts of wildness. Walking a batter or two serves a purpose if it keeps opponents from getting too comfortable at the plate. He needs to do little things to keep the rest of the league from catching up with him.

Atherton seems to have a rubber arm, which allows him to throw a couple of innings on consecutive days without losing anything from his fastball. His heater is usually clocked in the high 80s.

In fact, Atherton felt that a big problem he had when he was with the A's was an inconsistent pattern of use. Infrequent appearances were a thing of the past once he came to Minnesota--the Twins had the highest ERA in the majors last year and needed all the help they could get.

FIELDING:

Atherton is a tiger who prefers challenging

a batter to worrying too much about runners on base. He gets away with that because of a speedy delivery that keeps his catchers happy. His move to first is nothing special, anyway. Atherton fields his position well.

OVERALL:

Atherton found that it was hard to get pumped up to pitch when he was with Oakland because he wasn't being used often in situations where the game was on the line. He may need to realize that every bullpen needs an effective set-up man. At the same time, with the unsettled nature of the Minnesota bullpen, he may again be the guy called upon to get the final out in a one-run game. Atherton's also a good fit in Minnesota because, for gosh sakes, he's the father of twins. (So is Roy Smalley, in case you were wondering.)

Killebrew: "Keith worked on using more than just his fastball last year, a change from the past that seemed to help because he needs to be more than a one-pitch pitcher. Anything he can master that will vary his game will help."

1986 STATISTICS

W	L	ERA	G	GS	CG	SV	IP	H	R	ER	BB	SO
6	10	4.08	60	0	0	10	97	100	47	44	46	67

CAREER STATISTICS

W	L	ERA	G	GS	CG	SV	IP	H	R	ER	BB	SO
19	28	3.97	202	0	0	19	374	352	171	165	149	242

MINNESOTA TWINS

PITCHING:

Only nine major league pitchers won more games than Bert Blyleven did last year and, with the exception of Milwaukee Brewers lefty Ted Higuera and the Los Angeles Dodgers' Fernando Valenzuela, all the others played on teams with winning records. So winning 17 games for the Twins was not an accomplishment to be taken lightly despite the fact that Blyleven's ERA was over 4.00 for only the second time in his distinguished career. There was a spell during July and August when Blyleven was as tough a pitcher as there was in the American League.

What many people will remember about 1986, however, was that Blyleven set a record by giving up 50 home runs--breaking the old mark of 46 set by Hall of Famer Robin Roberts. There are a lot of good pitchers with a history of allowing lots of homers and the trick to survival is to make sure no one's on base when they occur. When Blyleven does that, he's able to win.

In order to be on top of his game, Blyleven must make a conscious effort to keep hitters from digging in. That he walked only 58 batters in 271 2/3 innings suggests he should pitch inside more often. If Blyleven can make a batter wary, he can own the outside part of the plate, all the more because his curveball is among the sharpest that's ever been thrown. When he's on top of his game, Blyleven also can throw an 89 MPH fastball that helps to set up the curve.

Blyleven did some work with a new pitch, a palmball that had action similar to a knuckler. He'd trot out the super-slow offering once in a while and, in its proper place, the pitch can be an effective addition to his repertoire. He also needs to guard against throwing a "batting practice fastball"--a fastball with something taken off--so often that opponents are waiting for it. He also has a pattern of having one bad inning per game. On his best days, opponents don't have a clue as to what's coming next, and a double-digit strikeout total is common.

Blyleven can adjust when he's having problems, as is apparent by the fact he's

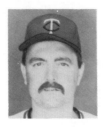

BERT BLYLEVEN
RHP, No. 28
RR, 6'3", 205 lbs.
ML Svc: 17 years
Born: 4-6-51 in
Zeist, Holland

1986 STATISTICS

W	L	ERA	G	GS	CG	SV	IP	H	R	ER	BB	SO
17	14	4.01	36	36	16	0	271.2	262	134	121	58	215

CAREER STATISTICS

W	L	ERA	G	GS	CG	SV	IP	H	R	ER	BB	SO
229	197	3.08	541	535	216	0	3989	3605	1532	1365	1072	3090

pitched 40 complete games over the last two seasons. He's a fierce competitor who takes losing harder than most players. Unfortunately, playing for second-division teams most of his career has given him more practice at defeat than he would care to remember--and makes his 229 lifetime victories that much more impressive.

FIELDING:

Blyleven needs to pay a lot of attention to base runners because his move to first is average and Twins catchers haven't shown much ability to compensate. He handles balls hit back to him quite well but doesn't always cover as quickly as he should on grounders hit toward first base.

OVERALL:

The Twins acquired Blyleven with the idea that he'd put them on the verge of pennant contention. While it hasn't worked out that way, Blyleven remains a threat to win 20 games and gives no indication that the end of his already lengthy career is imminent.

Killebrew: "Bert continues to win a lot of games while playing for struggling teams. He's remarkably durable and would be valuable for no other reason than he's always a complete-game threat. But he also does much more."

MINNESOTA TWINS

HITTING:

Maybe too much has been expected from Tom Brunansky. Since getting him from the Angels five years ago, Minnesota fans have patiently waited for him to bat .300 and hit 40 home runs. It could well be that lofty goals such as those are simply out of his reach and that he'll only hurt himself by trying for them.

But is there any shame in having a guy who can hit 25 home runs without anyone giving it a second thought? The improvement of other Twins players, most notably Kirby Puckett and Gary Gaetti, could help Brunansky because it could allow him to be dropped in the batting order--from fourth to sixth, let's say. Such a move might put less pressure on him, and Brunansky seems to play better in a relaxed frame of mind.

Brunansky knows his weaknesses: his swing sometimes is too long and he chases too many breaking balls that veer out of the strike zone. There have been streaks when he's managed to shorten his swing with two strikes, stretches in which his average rises and people have visions of stardom.

Batting righthanded in the Metrodome also costs him several home runs every season on fly balls that would leave the park if hit to right-center field. Pulled to left-center as most are, however, they are frustrating fly outs. They seem to come in bunches and appear to frustrate Brunansky as much as anything else.

It would be unwise to speculate on Brunansky's future and one needs to look only as far as teammate Gaetti to see why. Just when most people had cubbyholed him as a sometime slugger who'd always fall short in average and RBIs, Gaetti came up with the best season of his career. You never know.

BASERUNNING:

Brunansky's one bad habit is that, as an after-effect of his hard swing, he is very slow out of the batter's box. He seems to ground into double plays when it would be reasonable to expect him to beat the relay to first.

On the other hand, despite his limited speed, Brunansky has become a very good basestealer. He had 12 in 16 attempts last

TOM BRUNANSKY
RF, No. 24
RR, 6'4", 211 lbs.
ML Svc: 5 years
Born: 8-20-60 in West Covina, CA

1986 STATISTICS

AVG	G	AB	R	H	2B	3B	HR	RBI	BB	SO	SB
.256	157	593	69	152	27	1	23	75	53	98	12

CAREER STATISTICS

AVG	G	AB	R	H	2B	3B	HR	RBI	BB	SO	SB
.248	758	2765	369	687	130	11	133	384	321	484	25

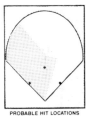

VS. RHP   VS. LHP   PROBABLE HIT LOCATIONS

year, mostly by reading the pitcher and getting a good jump.

FIELDING:

There was a time when Brunansky was considered to have one of the best arms in the league. That is no longer true. Brunansky doesn't get rid of the ball as quickly as he used to and his throws sometimes lack zip. His arm is accurate, however, and opponents can't take too many liberties--especially on turf. He's also unafraid to take on the outfield wall, the surest sign that his shortcomings aren't caused by lack of effort.

OVERALL:

If the Twins don't expect too much from Brunansky, maybe he'll surprise them by producing more than expected.

Killebrew: "The challenge for Brunansky is whether he can hit for a higher average, .280 or so, and still keep hitting home runs. To achieve that goal, he'll need to avoid the extended slumps that have plagued him in the past."

MINNESOTA TWINS

HITTING:

The pattern to Randy Bush's career is that the more he plays, the better he hits--within the confines of being a platoon player, that is. His batting average last year, .269, was the highest of a 4½-year career during which Bush has gone from being strictly a designated hitter to getting most of his playing time in the outfield.

On a solid team, Bush would be the ideal fourth outfielder/DH/pinch-hitter--the sort of guy who would get his 350 at-bats while performing several jobs. In indfof the last three seasons, Bush has been the best pinch-hitter in the American League. Last year, he had a .433 average (13-for-30) in those situations with a .469 on-base percentage and .700 slugging percentage. Bush knows what to watch for from an opposing pitcher and how to react to what he sees.

Bush is primarily a pull hitter but has taken to going with the pitch more often than in the past. Inside fastballs are his favorite pitch and breaking balls a constant nemesis. The Twins have always found someone in spring training to give Bush a challenge for his place on the roster and every year he outlasts the competition and does something to improve himself.

BASERUNNING:

Put Bush on the front end of a hit-and-run and he'll get from first to third reasonably well once he shifts into high gear, which seems to take him a little longer than most others. And if a pitcher isn't paying attention, Bush isn't above trying to steal. He's one of the Twins smart-but-limited runners.

FIELDING:

Bush got the chance to play left field when Mickey Hatcher lost that full-time job. Bush can also play first base in an emergency. His outfield skills are marginal. Having Kirby

RANDY BUSH
DH/LF, No. 25
LL, 6'1", 186 lbs.
ML Svc: 5 years
Born: 10-5-58 in
Dover, DE

1986 STATISTICS

AVG	G	AB	R	H	2B	3B	HR	RBI	BB	SO	SB
.269	130	357	50	96	19	7	7	45	40	63	5

CAREER STATISTICS

AVG	G	AB	R	H	2B	3B	HR	RBI	BB	SO	SB
.246	519	1394	178	343	79	15	43	192	137	232	9

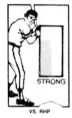

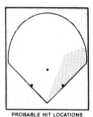

VS. RHP VS. LHP PROBABLE HIT LOCATIONS

Puckett playing center cuts down on the range that's required of him, and his arm, at best, is average. That the Twins are still looking for a regular left fielder is probably the best commentary.

OVERALL:

If Bush had a tattoo on his arm, it would probably say: "110%". More than his ability, his work habits are what make him a respected player and he seems to have a place on the Twins roster that's beyond question. Becoming more versatile has made him more valuable.

Killebrew: "Randy had made the most of his ability and made it clear that he intends to stay in the majors even if he's not the flashiest guy around. The Twins have been looking for guys who could take his place on the roster and Bush has met every challenge."

MINNESOTA TWINS

PITCHING:

George Frazier has the heart and soul of a 30-save pitcher. Now, if only his body would cooperate. Even when he's pitching well, Frazier has a tendency toward wildness and knows that the main thing keeping him from being successful are the 2-and-0 and 3-and-1 counts that mar his effective appearances.

The final seven weeks of last season, after Frazier's trade from the Chicago Cubs to the Twins, provided some turnaround in his fortunes. He notched six saves for his new team, which put him second in that department to Keith Atherton. It also was one more save than in his entire 2 1/3-season tenure with the Chicago Cubs, a span in which he established himself as one of the least favorite players of popular announcer Harry Caray. A 6.39 ERA, which Frazier compiled in 1985, will do that to a pitcher.

Frazier's best pitch is a split-finger fastball, and the strikeouts pile up when it's working well. (He had 25 Ks in 26 2/3 innings for the Twins last year and, despite his problems with the Cubs, had 41 in 51 2/3 innings while pitching for them.)

The split-finger pitch is, however, difficult to control, and Frazier can get into trouble when it isn't working and when he ditches it in favor of his other pitches. For some reason, he's had more success pitching in the American League (with the Yankees, Cleveland and the Twins) than for the Cubs and St. Louis in the NL.

GEORGE FRAZIER
RHP, No. 39
RR, 6'5", 205 lbs.
ML Svc: 9 years
Born: 10-13-54 in
Oklahoma City, OK

1986 STATISTICS

W	L	ERA	G	GS	CG	SV	IP	H	R	ER	BB	SO
3	5	5.06	50	0	0	6	78.1	86	49	44	50	66

CAREER STATISTICS

W	L	ERA	G	GS	CG	SV	IP	H	R	ER	BB	SO
30	38	4.09	361	0	0	27	594.2	576	300	270	262	391

FIELDING:

Frazier has both a quick delivery and a good move to first base. As might be expected from someone who had college scholarship offers in three sports--he chose to play baseball at Oklahoma--Frazier is agile and fields his position well. He has a reputation for being fundamentally sound, making the right move in situations that require quick thinking.

Killebrew: "It was obvious that Frazier benefited from being traded last year. The Twins are hoping that he can regain the form that made him an effective part of the Yankees bullpen in 1982 and 1983."

MINNESOTA TWINS

HITTING:

Now, a quick look back to the THE SCOUTING REPORT: 1986, "As long as the Twins don't expect too much from Gaetti, he will provide them with enough power to be a useful everyday player. To expect him to hit .300 or drive in 100 runs is unrealistic."

Guess who had 108 RBIs last year? Guess who batted .287? Guess who was third in the American League with 34 home runs? The answer to all of those questions is none other than Gary Gaetti, who established himself as the best third baseman in the American League--for 1986, at least. It's hard to believe that in 1984, when the Twins were battling for the division title until the last weekend of the season, Gaetti had only five homers.

Gaetti is coy about the reasons for his fantastic season last year. He had the good sense not to spend much time gloating about his individual accomplishments while the Twins were battling to keep from finishing last in the American League West. The temptation must have certainly been there because he'd gone to salary arbitration in February and lost his case.

It seemed that Gaetti became a more astute hitter last season. He approached each at-bat with a set objective depending on the game situation. There were times when he swung for the fences with two strikes and others when he knew from the start that getting on base was as important as trotting around them. Now, it's harder for a pitcher to guess along with Gaetti and his maturity may make him Minnesota's cleanup hitter for years to come.

BASERUNNING:

The good news for the Twins was that Gaetti set another career high with 14 stolen bases. The bad news was that he was thrown out 15 times. He isn't blessed with a lot of speed and would be more valuable if he stole 10 bases in 15 tries. Gaetti has taken out more second basemen with a hard slide and treats catchers with the same abandon.

There are occasions when Gaetti is not as quick as he should be getting out of the batter's box.

GARY GAETTI
3B, No. 8
RR, 6'0", 184 lbs.
ML Svc: 5 years
Born: 8-19-58 in
Centralia, IL

1986 STATISTICS

AVG	G	AB	R	H	2B	3B	HR	RBI	BB	SO	SB
.287	157	596	91	171	34	1	34	108	52	108	14

CAREER STATISTICS

AVG	G	AB	R	H	2B	3B	HR	RBI	BB	SO	SB
.254	790	2862	361	728	149	12	107	401	224	512	45

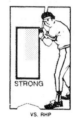

STRONG

VS. RHP

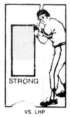

STRONG

VS. LHP

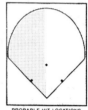

PROBABLE HIT LOCATIONS

FIELDING:

The Twins always contended that Gaetti was among the better third basemen in baseball, and his efforts finally received outside recognition: he won the Gold Glove for his position in 1986.

His biggest improvement in 1986 was the accuracy of his throws. In prior seasons, Gaetti would go through streaks where the ball would sail on him--and beyond the helpless first baseman. His range toward the foul line is outstanding.

OVERALL:

Gaetti is among the hardest working and most popular Twins players, a leader by example who can also be vocal when a situation calls for such behavior.

Killebrew: "Gaetti had a better 1986 season than anyone could have expected and it didn't look like a fluke. Gary had always tried things to improve his game and has hit upon some answers that make his future an exciting one. He's proof that hard work pays off."

MINNESOTA TWINS

HITTING:

Toward the end of last season, Greg Gagne appeared to make progress at the plate. He cut down on his big swing that resulted in too many strikeouts (108, tying him with Gary Gaetti for the team high) and improving his average enough to establish himself, beyond much doubt, as the Twins No. 1 shortstop. The latter matter had been open to debate coming into last season.

For a slender guy, Gagne is deceptively strong. He smacked a couple of long home runs and also had two inside-the-park homers, both in the same game, to finish the season with 12 (up from two in 1985). He is fast enough to take advantage of artificial surfaces and doesn't need much help to turn an apparent single into a double. He needs to take better advantage of his physical gifts and learn how to bunt more effectively. Gagne grounded into just four double plays, one per 118 at-bats.

Gagne made some improvement last year at hitting breaking pitches, although he still needs more work in this area. The Twins have toyed with batting him leadoff but he seems to be a logical fit for the No. 9 spot. By batting him so low in the order, the opposition is likely not to expect him to bat .300, and those at the top of the order can move him around the bases.

BASERUNNING:

Gagne is one of the fastest Twins and possibly the best at going from first to third on a single. He stole 12 bases last year but needs to learn to be a more effective basestealer; he was thrown out 10 times last year. Pitchers must pay attention to him.

FIELDING:

A former teammate who also played with him in the low minors once said that Gagne had about the worst glove he ever saw. In

GREG GAGNE
3B/SS, No. 31
RR, 5'11", 185 lbs.
ML Svc: 2 years
Born: 11-12-61 in
Fall River, MA

1986 STATISTICS

AVG	G	AB	R	H	2B	3B	HR	RBI	BB	SO	SB
.250	156	472	63	118	22	6	12	54	30	108	12

CAREER STATISTICS

AVG	G	AB	R	H	2B	3B	HR	RBI	BB	SO	SB
.236	282	793	102	187	38	9	14	80	50	171	22

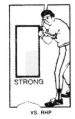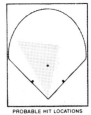

VS. RHP   VS. LHP   PROBABLE HIT LOCATIONS

spite of leading American League shortstops with 26 errors last year, he made some progress. Gagne has an extremely quick first step and excellent range, which gives him the chance to make flashy plays.

Grabbing the ball, though, is another story- -and one that needs work to make him a complete defensive player.

OVERALL:

Through tedious therapy, Gagne has conquered the lower-back problems that hindered him in the past. He appears set as the regular shortstop.

Killebrew: "Gagne made some improvements from his rookie season both at the plate and in the field. In the process, he has established himself as the Twins regular shortstop. Some of his errors come after fielding balls that other shortstops couldn't get to."

MINNESOTA TWINS

HITTING:

The first five weeks of last season was a nightmare for Mickey Hatcher because his batting touch, his main contribution to the Twins for several years, took an extended vacation. He was batting under .100, feuding with the manager and spending more time than ever before watching from the bench. Hatcher was a most unhappy fellow.

Then, the hits began falling again and, by the end of the season, Hatcher's statistics had worked their way back to respectability and there was talk that he'd get a shot at playing on a more regular basis in 1987.

Hatcher is a contact hitter who, in his enthusiasm to swing the bat, has never bothered much to learn the strike zone. He can send an outside pitch into the right field corner almost as easily as some people can drive a fastball up the middle, back over the pitcher's head. He has only one strikeout for every 14 career at-bats. Of course, Hatcher didn't draw his 100th career walk until last season, either.

Low pitches, especially breaking pitches, seem to give Hatcher the most trouble. Even when he is swinging well, Hatcher isn't a pretty hitter--certainly not the sort to be featured in any how-to films for aspiring Little Leaguers. To his credit, Hatcher has begun paying more attention to conditioning and he stayed free of the nuisance injuries that hounded him through much of 1985.

BASERUNNING:

Hatcher stole as many bases in 1986 as he did in the previous four years combined: two. One of them came when he went from second to third while the second baseman was elsewhere and the pitcher could do nothing but watch. Hatcher is slow enough that infielders have a second chance to throw him out. He'll break up a double play if the second baseman still has the ball when Hatcher arrives.

FIELDING:

There's no such thing as a routine fly with

MICKEY HATCHER
LF, No. 9
RR, 6'2", 199 lbs.
ML Svc: 8 years
Born: 3-15-55 in
    Cleveland, OH

1986 STATISTICS

AVG	G	AB	R	H	2B	3B	HR	RBI	BB	SO	SB
.278	115	317	40	88	13	3	3	32	20	26	3

CAREER STATISTICS

AVG	G	AB	R	H	2B	3B	HR	RBI	BB	SO	SB
.281	762	2543	269	715	133	16	28	270	119	182	9

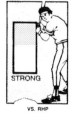
STRONG
VS. RHP

STRONG
VS. LHP

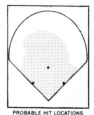
PROBABLE HIT LOCATIONS

Hatcher in left field. He makes most plays but sometimes in a fashion that's hard on the nerves. Hatcher's range is limited and his arm is mediocre. Opponents often will attempt to take an extra base against him and every now and then he'll surprise them with a throw reminiscent of the young Mickey Hatcher.

OVERALL:

Hatcher wants to be Minnesota's regular left fielder. The Twins would like to find someone with more speed and better defensive skills. If their younger players don't come through and Hatcher has an impressive exhibition season, look for him to make a comeback. This year is especially important because it's the last guaranteed season on his contract, which has options for 1988 and 1989.

Killebrew: "Still a crowd favorite, Hatcher is a solid offensive player who can bat his way into the lineup on a regular basis. Even if he doesn't play every day, it has to be nice for the Twins to know they have a .280 hitter on the bench who can hit line drives in his sleep."

MINNESOTA TWINS

HITTING:

The battle continues to rage within Kent Hrbek. Should he concentrate on hitting all the home runs that he can while letting his average fall where it may? Or should he make the most of his natural talent, concentrating on his batting average with a virtual guarantee of still swatting about 20 homers? Hrbek's approach has changed throughout his five-year career.

For a chunk of 1986, he was able to do both: hit for average *and* hit for power. Hrbek was among the American League batting leaders at midseason while showing a lot of power with his wide-open batting stance that reminded some people of Oscar Gamble. Then Hrbek slumped. He finished with the lowest batting average of his career (.267) and a personal home run high (29). For the first time in three seasons, he didn't lead the club in RBIs.

Last season, he was bothered by a sore shoulder and sore knee--which are chronic problems--and also was kept out of the lineup for a couple of weeks by an injured wrist. Some of Hrbek's health problems have been blamed on the extra weight he carries. He weighed 218 pounds as a rookie but neared the 250 mark for parts of last year. Manager Tom Kelly discussed that subject with Hrbek at the end of the season and is hopeful Hrbek will pay more attention to conditioning.

Among the things that makes Hrbek so valuable is his ability to hit lefthanded pitchers almost as well as righties. Once he got used to it, the open stance allowed him a better view of the ball, and a hot Hrbek will hit any pitcher at any time to any part of the ballpark. The slumping model will hit a lot of topspin grounders and pop-ups to the second baseman.

BASERUNNING:

Next to the potential for injury, Hrbek's extra weight also hurts him most on the bases. He is a smart runner but has slowed appreciably over the years and doesn't have the speed to match his instincts. After an inside-the-park homer a few years back, Hrbek needed oxygen before he could return

KENT HRBEK
1B, No. 14
LR, 6'4", 235 lbs.
ML Svc: 6 years
Born: 5-21-60 in
   Minneapolis, MN

1986 STATISTICS

AVG	G	AB	R	H	2B	3B	HR	RBI	BB	SO	SB
.267	149	550	85	147	27	1	29	91	71	81	2

CAREER STATISTICS

AVG	G	AB	R	H	2B	3B	HR	RBI	BB	SO	SB
.289	761	2816	405	815	156	15	117	474	319	415	11

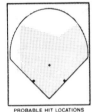

VS. RHP   VS. LHP   PROBABLE HIT LOCATIONS

to the field.

FIELDING:

Hrbek is a better fielder than most people are willing to believe. To watch him on a daily basis means seeing him make diving stops that betray his size and start 3-6-3 double plays as well as anyone in the majors. There does seem to be a correlation between his hitting slumps and botching routine plays in the field.

OVERALL:

Even though he's been reluctant to acknowledge how important he is to the Twins, how Hrbek goes is among the most important Minnesota barometers.

Killebrew: "What would pass as a good year for most players is below what Kent is capable of doing. That's how much talent he has. It's superstar potential. Kent seems to realize that carrying extra weight is a problem and wants to do something about it this year. We'll see."

MINNESOTA TWINS

HITTING:

The Twins are no longer waiting for Laudner to bust out and become their regular catcher. That may be the best thing for all concerned because, given a role to fill, he can make an acceptable contribution. Laudner can hit for some power and for reasonable average against lefthanded pitchers.

His main problem has been contact. Laudner is one of those rare players who has the dubious distinction of having more strikeouts than hits over the course of his career. Whiffs currently hold a 319-to-256 edge.

The most troublesome thing for Laudner is finding the patience to get ahead in the count, which would also put him in better position to get the fastballs that he can send over the fence. But he falls behind too often and hasn't learned to strive for contact when the count reaches two strikes. Too often, Laudner seems to be fighting himself.

As might be expected, Laudner doesn't bunt well and rarely hits to the opposite field. He gets hurt in the Metrodome because left-center field is the deepest part of the playing field and, as if he didn't already have enough troubles, some of his well-hit fly balls are nothing but lengthy outs.

BASERUNNING:

Put it this way: don't look for Laudner to come off the bench as a pinch-runner. When you don't hit, you don't get much chance to improve at running the bases.

FIELDING:

Of the three Twins catchers, Laudner has skills behind the plate that are better than Mark Salas' and not as solid as Jeff Reed's.

TIM LAUDNER
C, No. 15
RR, 6'3", 208 lbs.
ML Svc: 5 years
Born: 6-7-58 in
Mason City, IA

1986 STATISTICS
AVG	G	AB	R	H	2B	3B	HR	RBI	BB	SO	SB
.244	76	193	21	47	10	0	10	29	24	56	1

CAREER STATISTICS
AVG	G	AB	R	H	2B	3B	HR	RBI	BB	SO	SB
.225	404	1136	129	256	61	2	42	139	106	319	1

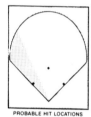

VS. RHP — STRONG   VS. LHP — STRONG   PROBABLE HIT LOCATIONS

Laudner has worked hard enough over the years to go from a poor defensive catcher with a poor arm and limited mobility to an acceptable one. His arm is erratic. Laudner seems to enjoy the challenge of thinking along with opposing batters.

OVERALL:

Laudner seems destined to be a player who will be dependable within limits and sometimes even pretty valuable.

Killebrew: "Laudner seems to have found a niche as a platoon catcher and hits lefthanded pitching pretty well. He'll probably always be a homer-or-strikeout kind of player who will perform capably behind the plate."

HITTING:

Though he has shown flashes of solid offense and even got a brief shot at batting leadoff (last year), instead of Kirby Puckett, Lombardozzi suffered from a weak bat that seemed to drag as the season wore on. Playing in 156 games can do that to a rookie.

Last year, Lombardozzi could be fooled by good pitches, and he chased bad ones. There were times when he seemed to be totally overmatched at the plate. But that performance wasn't entirely unexpected: Lombardozzi wasn't much of an offensive threat in his two years of Triple-A service. He was awarded the regular job at second base last spring without much contest because of his good fielding skills.

He showed some power in the minors, but the Twins want him to work on being a hitter who can go with the pitch and take advantage of the Metrodome turf. His bunting skills need work, especially because Lombardozzi has the speed to catch opponents by surprise.

Lombardozzi has a good batting eye, witness the 52 walks that at least made his on-base percentage respectable, and has enough potential not to be considered an automatic out. His problems at the plate were comparable to what Greg Gagne went through as a rookie in 1985--and Gagne improved his average to .250 last year.

BASERUNNING:

Despite having good speed, Lombardozzi has not emerged as a threat to steal bases and managed only three in four attempts in 1986. The Twins would like to see him improve that part of his game and feel he should eventually be able to steal 15-20 bases in a season.

FIELDING:

As a second baseman, Lombardozzi does everything well. He turns double plays with flair, has excellent range and picked up some of the positioning skills that enhanced his other strengths. He made only six errors in

STEVE LOMBARDOZZI
2B, No. 4
RR, 6'0", 175 lbs.
ML Svc: 2 years
Born: 4-26-60 in
Malden, MA

1986 STATISTICS

AVG	G	AB	R	H	2B	3B	HR	RBI	BB	SO	SB
.227	156	453	53	103	20	5	8	33	52	76	3

CAREER STATISTICS

AVG	G	AB	R	H	2B	3B	HR	RBI	BB	SO	SB
.243	184	507	63	123	24	6	8	39	58	82	6

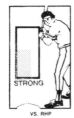  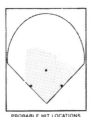

STRONG STRONG PROBABLE HIT LOCATIONS

VS. RHP   VS. LHP

702 chances, leading American League second basemen with a .991 percentage. Obviously, he was able to keep his problems at the plate from disturbing him in the field. Lombardozzi and Gagne may mature into one of the league's elite double play combinations.

OVERALL:

It's fantasy to expect Lombardozzi to hit as well as he fields. The Twins should settle for improvement with the bat and continued quality with the glove. They don't miss Tim Teufel.

Killebrew: "The Twins needed better defense from their second baseman and Steve certainly filled the bill last year. He's a heady player, a future Gold Glove winner. He does need to work on his offense to try to figure out a way to keep the tired bat that hindered him during the final part of last season from returning."

MINNESOTA TWINS

PITCHING:

The Twins are hoping that Mark Portugal is past the stage of shuttling between the majors and minors. For that matter, so does Portugal. He was in Minnesota for most of last season and showed signs that he could be an excellent pitcher. At other times in 1986, however, he was a struggling rookie haunted by mistakes he could get away with only as a pitcher for the Toledo Mud Hens.

Portugal has a confident demeanor and has been accused more than once of crossing the line into being outwardly cocky. It's a charge to which he'll plead guilty without caring what anyone thinks. The attitude looks good when he's pitching well. New manager Tom Kelly likes Portugal enough that he's considering using him in a stopper's role out of the bullpen, a space opened up by last summer's trade of Ron Davis. Portugal has expressed enthusiasm with the idea.

One reason for the move is that, when he was a starter, Portugal seemed to throw hard for a few innings and then relied on breaking pitches more as the game progressed. He also has a very good change-up, which is his out pitch. Kelly is intrigued by Portugal's potential for keeping batters off balance with his breaking pitch and change-up.

Nevertheless, Portugal will have to improve his control somewhat. He has averaged about one walk for every two innings through his professional career, a ratio that's too high for a reliever. On his good days, Portugal can throw several consecutive change-ups and twist batters in knots of frustration. There's been some question about Portugal's stamina; he seemed to tire markedly in the fifth or sixth inning of several starts last year, and bullpen work would keep that question from arising.

FIELDING:

Portugal has an excellent pickoff move, the

MARK PORTUGAL
RHP, No. 36
RR, 6'0", 190 lbs.
ML Svc: 1 year plus
Born: 10-30-62 in
Los Angeles, CA

1986 STATISTICS

W	L	ERA	G	GS	CG	SV	IP	H	R	ER	BB	SO
6	10	4.31	27	15	3	1	112.2	112	56	54	50	67

CAREER STATISTICS

W	L	ERA	G	GS	CG	SV	IP	H	R	ER	BB	SO
7	13	4.53	33	19	3	1	137	136	72	69	64	79

best on the Twins, perhaps. Probably because he was a rookie and such things have to be seen before they are believed, he picked off several runners last year who didn't have a chance of returning to their base.

He has some problems getting squared around to field grounders, a problem that Portugal shares with many Twins pitchers.

OVERALL:

If Portugal can be a reliable stopper for the Twins this season, he would be far more valuable than anyone could have anticipated. When a team is coming off a sixth-place finish, as this club is, such an experiment is totally within reason. Portugal could also end up as a member of the starting rotation.

Killebrew: "Portugal is in the process of finding his role in the majors. He should be flattered that the manager has enough confidence in him to offer the stopper's role. Even if that doesn't work, there's no reason he can't settle into a spot in the starting rotation."

MINNESOTA TWINS

HITTING:

As last season wore on, Puckett was one of the few valid reasons that Twins fans had for watching their team. He battled Wade Boggs and Don Mattingly for the American League batting title before tailing off and finishing third. Also, after hitting only four home runs in his first two seasons, Puckett took advantage of his tremendous strength and smacked 31 of them.

In sum, it was a thoroughly awesome season for Kirby Puckett. Awesome enough that he finished sixth in Most Valuable Player voting, the highest finish for a player in the AL West, even though his main value to the Twins was in allowing them to finish in sixth place instead of last.

What happened? Puckett, who modestly gave much of the credit for his success to hitting instructor Tony Oliva, decided that he was no longer satisfied with grounding singles between the first and second basemen. Last year he became a line drive hitter who didn't need to swing for the fences to clear them. Puckett led the league in homers for much of the first month of the season, as if opposing pitchers couldn't believe the reports they were getting from their advance scouts and insisted on trying to blaze fastballs past him. Eventually, they learned.

A speedster desite his chunky frame, Puckett still was able to beat out infield hits and could work his way out of slumps by redoubling his efforts to make contact. He doesn't need much help to take an extra base and keeps opposing third basemen wary with his bunting ability.

His only weakness at the plate is that he doesn't draw enough walks, especially for someone who's only 5'8". Puckett had only 34 walks last year, a flaw that won't be as noticeable if the Twins find another leadoff batter and are able to move him lower in the batting order to take advantage of his power.

BASERUNNING:

The Twins have hoped that Puckett would become one of the top basestealers in the league, but he's fallen short of that goal. He concentrated on that skill last spring, but his

KIRBY PUCKETT
CF, No. 34
RR, 5'8", 185 lbs.
ML Svc: 3 years
Born: 3-14-61 in Chicago, IL

1986 STATISTICS

AVG	G	AB	R	H	2B	3B	HR	RBI	BB	SO	SB
.328	161	680	119	223	37	6	31	96	34	99	20

CAREER STATISTICS

AVG	G	AB	R	H	2B	3B	HR	RBI	BB	SO	SB
.304	450	1928	262	587	78	24	35	201	91	255	55

  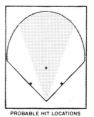

VS. RHP   VS. LHP   PROBABLE HIT LOCATIONS

season total was 20, one less than in 1985. He'd been thinking about 40.

FIELDING:

Oh, yeah, Puckett also won a Gold Glove for the first time in his career even though his 1986 assist total, eight, was less than half that of the previous season. He won the coveted award because, after two seasons in which opponents didn't take his arm seriously, they finally thought better of taking an extra base.

His range is such that the Twins have been able to use slow-footed left fielders without worrying about balls going into the gap. The most spectacular part of Puckett's defensive package is his ability to reach well above the wall in center field to rob opponents of home runs, a trick he pulls off several times every season.

OVERALL:

Killebrew: "Puckett exploded last season, hitting with more power than anyone could have imagined while maintaining all the other facets of his game."

MINNESOTA TWINS

PITCHING:

Jeff Reardon's 1986 numbers were worthy of this top-notch stopper: of 28 runners he inherited on entering a game, only four scored, and in 47 save opportunities, Reardon succeeded 35 times. If he had had a better second half (Reardon blew five leads in July alone), he would have won his second consecutive Rolaids *Relief Man of the Year* award as the National League's top reliever.

Reardon's midseason slump is becoming a pattern, perhaps because his arm suffers from overuse in the first half. Although Reardon discarded his sidearm curveball in 1985 because it hurt his elbow, he still had twinges here and there from the hard, overhand slider he developed as a replacement.

From the middle of June through the middle of August, Reardon managed just nine saves, an 0-4 record and a 6.04 ERA. He also got himself into hot water with some comments at the All-Star game about the Montreal fans, whom he described as "terrible" and "aggravating." He added that it wouldn't bother him if the Expos traded him.

The incident quickly blew over, as Reardon won most of the fans back with his crackling fastball (in the low 90s) and devastating curveball, which Reardon isn't afraid to throw when he's behind in the count.

Perhaps because of his increasingly tender elbow, Reardon's fastball wasn't nearly as overpowering in the second half, and it got the righthander into home run trouble. Batters slammed 12 homers against Reardon in 89 innings, about six more than he normally yields.

FIELDING, HITTING, BASERUNNING:

Reardon's delivery usually leaves him out of position to reach sharply hit balls back to the mound. He suffers from a periodically stiff back and when he is ailing, it shows in his awkward fielding movements.

As a short reliever, Reardon doesn't get much chance to hit or to run the bases, which

**JEFF REARDON
RHP, No. 41
RR, 6'0", 200 lbs.
ML Svc: 8 years
Born: 10-1-55 in
Dalton, MA**

1986 STATISTICS

W	L	ERA	G	GS	CG	SV	IP	H	R	ER	BB	SO
7	9	3.94	62	0	0	35	89	83	42	39	26	67

CAREER STATISTICS

W	L	ERA	G	GS	CG	SV	IP	H	R	ER	BB	SO
42	46	2.80	456	0	0	162	665.2	551	226	207	246	537

is good because he is not good at either. He could especially use some work on his bunting because there are times that manager Buck Rodgers likes to use him as early as the seventh inning, sometimes giving him a key at-bat with a runner aboard who needs advancing.

OVERALL:

It appeared almost inevitable that Reardon would play this year for a team other than the Montreal Expos. He will begin the season with a new team and will, hopefully, be off to a fresh start with new fans.

At age 31, he is now at his peak value. While Reardon is not especially old for a reliever, it must be noted that he has made a lot of appearances and pitched a lot of innings over the past few seasons. The wear and tear on his arm may begin to show soon.

There is little doubt that he is a dominant reliever. His new manager will have to resist the temptation to get him into a game too early; Reardon should be strictly a ninth-inning pitcher in a save situation.

Rooker: "Reardon is using the slider more these days, but he still lives and dies with the heat. He needs the help of his set-up men to share the late-innings load with him."

MINNESOTA TWINS

HITTING:

Mark Salas surprised everyone, himself included, by batting .300 as a rookie in 1985, but came back last year to suffer through a mediocre season, struggling from start to finish. Salas needs to get off well early to reestablish himself as Minnesota's regular catcher against righthanded pitching.

Salas seemed to be caught between two philosophies in 1986. There were times when he wanted to pull every pitch to right field and others when he showed off a smooth stroke and the ability to hit a pitcher's best offering. He did neither well, batting only .233 with eight home runs in 91 games. In fact, he may not figure in team plans as much as the other lefthanded batting catcher, Jeff Reed.

When sharp, Salas has a quick and compact swing from which home runs should come as natural extensions of the line singles and doubles to the gap in right-center. Playing in the Metrodome allows him the opportunity to bombard the shallow wall in right when he's on a roll. That's another reason it's silly to think of him as a slugger.

Salas is a stoic sort of guy, a catcher with the heart of an offensive lineman who's willing to play through pain. He did spend time on the disabled list last summer with a toe injury that bothered him for months before he let anyone know how much pain he was suffering. Concerned with his status as a youngster who needs to prove himself, Salas took advantage of his big chance to play, and didn't let anything keep him out of the lineup and didn't let on about an assortment of aches until the end of the season.

BASERUNNING:

Chug-chug-chug. Salas stole three bases last season, which was three more than he had as a rookie. He runs the bases hard and intelligently, which unfortunately doesn't make up for his lack of speed. Second baseman don't relish meeting him when

MARK SALAS
C, No. 12
LR, 6'0", 205 lbs.
ML Svc: 2 years
Born: 3-8-61 in
Montebello, CA

1986 STATISTICS

AVG	G	AB	R	H	2B	3B	HR	RBI	BB	SO	SB
.233	91	258	28	60	7	4	8	33	18	32	3

CAREER STATISTICS

AVG	G	AB	R	H	2B	3B	HR	RBI	BB	SO	SB
.266	225	638	80	170	28	9	17	75	36	72	3

  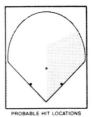

VS. RHP   VS. LHP   PROBABLE HIT LOCATIONS

turning a double play.

FIELDING:

Salas tries hard and his bad toe limited his mobility last season; that was the main reason he finally 'fessed up and had surgery for removal of a painful bone spur. Still, Salas doesn't have soft hands and has trouble with balls that other catchers handle cleanly. He was called for interference three times last season, including twice in one game at Seattle. His arm is below average.

OVERALL:

Killebrew: "This season should go a long way toward determining Salas' future with the Twins, who'd love to see Mark play as well as he did in 1985. But because he bats lefthanded, there should always be some interest in him regardless of what happens."

MINNESOTA TWINS

HITTING:

Roy Smalley would be the first one to admit that he has employed a more cerebral approach to hitting than most major leaguers. His natural skills wouldn't have gotten him very far. Having evolved into a hitting specialist who rarely gets a chance in the field, it's easy to forget that Smalley came to the majors with a reputation for slick fielding and sickly batting; he was a singles hitter who struck out too much.

Now, however, Smalley's best weapons are power and a batting eye good enough to draw more walks than most of his teammates. In fact, his mediocre batting average was boosted to a respectable .342 on-base percentage because he drew 68 walks, second highest total on the Twins. He sometimes seems to have a better eye than the home plate umpire, which can surface as a problem when a strike is called on a pitch that Smalley has found unworthy.

Despite being a switch-hitter, Smalley's main role at this stage of his career is as a designated hitter against righthanded pitching. During his seasons with the Yankees (1982-1984), it was decided that he swung the bat much better from the left side, which curtailed his improvement as a righthanded hitter. When Ray Miller took over as manager of the Twins in June 1985, he too was loathe to bat Smalley from the right. Smalley contends that those skills suffered because he didn't get enough chances, instead of vice versa. Whatever the case may be, Smalley now is much more dangerous from the left.

Smalley is an excellent low fastball hitter who is overmatched against only the hardest throwers. He seems to concentrate harder with each pitch thrown to him, and the result has been several lengthy and memorable at-bats against pitchers who are forced to resort to all their tricks in order to retire him.

Because he is a pull hitter from the left side of the plate, the Metrodome is a good place for Smalley to hit, although his lack of power holds some of the balls that he hits off the right-field wall to singles.

ROY SMALLEY
SS, No. 5
SR, 6'1", 182 lbs.
ML Svc: 12 years
Born: 10-25-52 in
Los Angeles, CA

1986 STATISTICS

AVG	G	AB	R	H	2B	3B	HR	RBI	BB	SO	SB
.246	143	459	59	113	20	4	20	57	68	80	1

CAREER STATISTICS

AVG	G	AB	R	H	2B	3B	HR	RBI	BB	SO	SB
.256	1543	5348	713	1369	228	24	155	660	734	856	25

VS. RHP   VS. LHP   PROBABLE HIT LOCATIONS

BASERUNNING:

Smalley looks as though he should be a reasonably fast runner. He isn't. Unless he knows that an extra base is there to be taken, Smalley is a one-base-at-a-time runner and is smart enough to stay within that limitation.

FIELDING:

Even when he set a record for chances by a shortstop (since broken), Smalley didn't have much range. He made up for that shortcoming by knowing opposing batters as well as anyone.

Now, his range is minimal and because Smalley doesn't play the field much, that sixth sense has been lost. But his arm still is strong and he is a capable backup to Gary Gaetti at third base. Smalley is also able to play at first base in a pinch.

OVERALL:

Killebrew: "Smalley's main value is as a hitter, and he works hard on those skills. Anyone who can hit 20 home runs in a season performs a vital function."

MINNESOTA TWINS

PITCHING:

Mike Smithson is one of those pitchers who always seems to be pitching a smidgen below the level of which he's capable. He's been a .500 pitcher in his three seasons with the Twins--two games over .500, actually--and he has never been able to pitch well for an extended period of time. The pattern has been for him to win a couple, lose a couple and come out even in the end.

Last year was Smithson's worst with the Twins. After not missing a start because of injury or ineptitude, he was bothered by a strained elbow and removed from the rotation for a spell because he wasn't getting anyone out. Smithson was especially bothered by the latter.

By his appearance--the former University of Tennessee basketball player is the tallest player in the majors--one would expect Smithson to be an overpowering pitcher. He isn't. His fastball is slightly above average and Smithson needs to have his slider working in order to win. There have been times when he's been unable to control that pitch, unable to keep it in or near the strike zone, and has been forced to rely on only a fastball and a change-up. When that happens, the bullpen had better get ready. Smithson suffered more early knockouts, before the third inning, than any other Minnesota pitcher.

At his best, Smithson works inside to righthanders, setting them up to be finished off with a slider. He throws two variations on the pitch, one that has a tight break and serves to keep opponents off-balance and another that resembles a curve and is designed to fool them completely. When Smithson is able to strike out a significant number of batters, the latter type of slider seems to be the reason.

Smithson usually isn't bashful about staking his claim to home plate. Even though he has very good control, he was second in the majors with 14 hit-batsmen last year and led with 15 the season before. He was ejected from a game against Detroit after hitting three Tigers. Smithson doesn't lack for guts. But

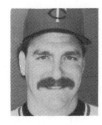

MIKE SMITHSON
RHP, No. 48
LR, 6'8", 215 lbs.
ML Svc: 5 years
Born: 1-21-55 in
Centerville, TN

1986 STATISTICS

W	L	ERA	G	GS	CG	SV	IP	H	R	ER	BB	SO
13	14	4.77	34	33	8	0	198	234	123	105	57	114

CAREER STATISTICS

W	L	ERA	G	GS	CG	SV	IP	H	R	ER	BB	SO
56	59	4.19	148	147	39	0	977	1028	498	455	273	544

then, how many guys are going to run uphill to battle someone who stands 6'8"?

FIELDING:

It takes a long time for Smithson to deliver the ball, meaning he has to pay extra attention to runners on first base. He's pretty easy to steal against. Smithson has soft hands and good range from the mound, strengths he shows off well when fielding bunts.

He does have a hard time with come-backers, in part because of his height and in part because of a harrowing incident in 1984 when he was struck in the neck by a Jim Gantner line drive. Smithson admits that he still flinches when a ball is zapped back toward him.

OVERALL:

It's probably more realistic to consider him a workmanlike pitcher who will have good days and bad than to expect him to become a 20-game winner. Getting through the first couple of innings is especially important.

Killebrew: "Mike will always be fighting battles with his mechanics, and the question is how long can he keep them under control? For weeks or months? If he finds a groove, he'll be dangerous."

PITCHING:

Though Frank Viola has shown flashes of great potential, he hasn't yet reached the plateau of excellence the Twins have been expecting. He seems to make progress in some areas while at the same time suffering setbacks in others. There are those who would argue that Viola should tune out everything going on around him and let his talent carry the load. Instead, Viola sometimes is too easily distracted.

In the past, a bad play in the field or a call that went against him seemed to rattle Viola to the point that he'd allow hits to batters who'd previously been unable to touch him. He made some progress on that front last year, but also seemed to be bothered more by baserunners. He would pitch a couple of strong innings, and then, at the first sign on trouble, his rhythm would be thrown off. Sometimes, with a runner or two on base, Viola would slow the game's pace to a crawl.

There is a school of thought that believes that if Viola can learn to handle the mental part of pitching, he will be able to put together the overwhelming sort of season that has so far eluded him.

The lefthander throws all four pitches: fastball, curveball, change-up and slider. He has outings when all are working, and when that happens, batters had better beware. He does have a knack for figuring out which pitches are his most effective on any given day and not forcing the ones that are taking the day off. The fastball and change-up (which, for him, acts like a screwball) are his No. 1 and 2 out pitches.

His fastball has been clocked at 91-92 MPH, especially in the early innings, and some people have suggested that Viola may be better suited to relief, in the manner of Dave Righetti. Of course, a reliever distracted by baserunners is a reliever doomed to fail.

Viola's preference is to start and to pitch with only three days rest as often as possible. He feels as though he has better command pitching on that schedule. He was bothered when the Twins used a five-man rotation when off days sometimes gave him five or six

**FRANK VIOLA
LHP, No. 16
LL, 6'4", 209 lbs.
ML Svc: 5 years
Born: 4-19-60 in
Hempstead, NY**

1986 STATISTICS

W	L	ERA	G	GS	CG	SV	IP	H	R	ER	BB	SO
16	13	4.51	37	37	7	0	245.2	257	136	123	83	191

CAREER STATISTICS

W	L	ERA	G	GS	CG	SV	IP	H	R	ER	BB	SO
63	64	4.38	165	164	33	0	1090	1138	591	530	354	686

days of rest between starts.

One good gauge of Viola's effectiveness is the number of pitches that he throws. He isn't one to recover from a shaky start, and if he has thrown 70 pitches or so through the first four innings, falling behind in the count and pitching into trouble, chances are he'll be ripe for picking as the game progresses.

FIELDING:

Viola has a good move to first that tends to startle unsuspecting runners; basestealers have trouble getting a good jump. His fielding is slightly above average: Viola is better at covering first base than he is at fielding ground balls. He's tall and sometimes doesn't get down fast enough on balls hit near him.

OVERALL:

When other teams conduct trade talks with the Twins, Viola is the pitcher they most covet. The Twins haven't seriously considered trading him and are hoping he can put together the sort of spectacular season that's put him in such demand.

Killebrew: "Viola is still on the brink of excellence. He has all the tools to win more than 20 games--it's a question of harnessing all of his abilities. The most important adjustments for him to make are mental ones."

MINNESOTA TWINS

HITTING:

Washington's strengths are not those of your typical utility infielder. Many of that breed are lucky if their batting average exceeds their weight, and stick around because of their defensive skills. The biggest contribution Washington can make is with his bat; he comes off the bench for a couple of days to replace a slumping or injured regular.

As much as it hurts not to be considered as a regular, Washington has always handled his situation with professional cool and has never let his anguish affect his ability. Because it took him so long to make the majors (11 years), the Twins have always wanted to give younger players a longer look.

Because the Twins had set middle infielders for the first time in several years, Washington got fewer at-bats last year than in any previous season with the Twins and also spent two stints in the minors. The lack of playing time sometimes translated into a lack of calm at the plate as, keyed up at getting a chance, Washington would swing at bad pitches. He did have several big games and four of his 19 hits were home runs.

Washington has always chased pitches outside of the strike zone, especially those up and away, but he hammers pitches that aren't far enough outside. He also seems to generate most of his power to right-center field. His speed allows him to take advantage of artificial turf and, when he's been playing enough to get into a groove, Washington is a good choice for the hit-and-run.

BASERUNNING:

Even though he'll be 35 years old this season, Washington still is among the fastest runners on the Twins. Whether that should be considered a point in his favor or a demerit against the team is open for debate. He's quick out of the batter's box and gets a good jump on the bases.

FIELDING:

Washington will play anywhere he's asked

RON WASHINGTON
INF, No. 38
RR, 5'11", 169 lbs.
ML Svc: 6 years
Born: 4-29-52 in
New Orleans, LA

1986 STATISTICS

AVG	G	AB	R	H	2B	3B	HR	RBI	BB	SO	SB
.257	48	74	15	19	3	0	4	11	3	21	1

CAREER STATISTICS

AVG	G	AB	R	H	2B	3B	HR	RBI	BB	SO	SB
.266	462	1277	152	340	47	19	17	119	55	212	25

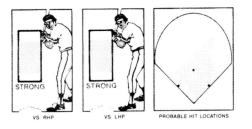

VS. RHP   VS. LHP   PROBABLE HIT LOCATIONS

and the Twins have considered him both an emergency outfielder and catcher, positions he played in the minors. He's best at second base and acceptable at shortstop. Washington's range and arm are pretty good. The same praise can't be offered about his hands.

OVERALL:

Just because Washington has spent considerable time on the bench doesn't mean he's been idle. He absorbs things that other people miss, and is the sort of player who ought to get a chance to coach or manage when his playing career ends.

Killebrew: "Washington is rarely an easy out and provides an offensive spark off the bench. His fielding suffers more than his hitting from the lack of playing time."

ALLAN ANDERSON
LHP, No. 49
LL, 5'11", 169 lbs.
ML Svc: 1 year
Born: 1-7-64 in
Lancaster, OH

PITCHING, FIELDING:

After pitching 10 strong innings in his midseason major league debut and a three-hitter against the White Sox in his third career start, Anderson began having problems that plagued him for the rest of the season.

They were the sort of mistakes that shouldn't have been unexpected from a pitcher just two years out of Double-A and four years out of high school. Too many of Anderson's pitches were up in the strike zone and he rarely was able to get into a groove that lasted for more than a couple of innings. Batters seemed to figure him out after facing him once or twice, and Anderson ended up coming out of the bullpen as often as he started, which was hardly a boost for his confidence. Anderson would have been better served by a full season in the minors.

When he's on his game, Anderson is adept at mixing up pitches that appear more hittable than they really are and at getting batters to swing at pitches that end up in the dirt. His fastball is usually clocked in the 86-88 MPH range and he knows better than to think of himself as overpowering.

Anderson fields his position fairly well and took an interest in keeping runners close to first base.

OVERALL:

With Mark Portugal perhaps headed for the bullpen this year, Anderson is the main candidate to be the fifth starter in the rotation. How much he learned by spending a half-season in the majors, pitching sporadically and inconsistently, will be revealed.

BILLY BEANE
OF, No. 20
RR, 6'4", 195 lbs.
ML Svc: 1 year plus
Born: 3-29-62 in
Orlando, FL

HITTING, BASERUNNING, FIELDING:

The Twins thought they were getting a "can't miss" player when the New York Mets traded Billy Beane to Minnesota last January. They figured on him becoming their starting left fielder, a position the Twins have been trying to fill to their satisfaction for the last couple of years.

Beane turned out to be a disappointment both at the plate and in the field. He struggled to raise his average above .200--making contact was his biggest problem--and proved to be a sub-standard fielder. A midseason demotion to the minors didn't seem to help.

At the plate, Beane was unable to resist pitches outside of the strike zone, especially high ones. His strikeout pace was such that if Beane had gotten 550 at-bats, he would have struck out 162 times. Because he spent six minor league seasons in the Mets organization, and had similar problems making contact, there is reasonable doubt whether he'll ever make much improvement.

Especially disppointing was Beane's arm, which was thought to be above average and turned out to be anything but. However it happened (Twins officials blamed a spring training shoulder injury that put him on the disabled list for the first few weeks of the season), runners found they could advance on Beane without much difficulty.

OVERALL:

Beane will probably get one more chance to show what he can do before the Twins give up on him. In 1980, when the Mets had the first choice in the amateur free agent draft, there was some debate whether to take Beane or another hot prospect. They selected the other: Darryl Strawberry.

TOM NIETO
C, No. 23
RR, 6'1", 205 lbs.
ML Svc: 2 years
Born: 10-27-60 in
Downey, CA

HITTING, BASERUNNING, FIELDING:

It was an unsettled year for Tom Nieto in 1986. It seemed that whenever he wasn't being optioned to or recalled from the minors, he was injured. At first, it was an injured middle finger and then a strained right elbow toward the end of the season.

The unsettled season may have been a contributing factor to Nieto's .200 batting average. Like Dann Bilardello, Nieto had a chance to earn some high marks with Mike Fitzgerald out of action. Although he was designated as the number one catcher to start the season, Nieto wasn't able to establish himself.

Nieto likes the ball in from lefthanders and away when facing righthanders. He'll hit the odd homer, but he does not really have too much extra-base power.

Speed isn't among Nieto's assets, but he is always hustling on the bases. His arm could best be termed as "so-so" and there is the added concern that his elbow problems last season could become chronic.

OVERALL:

Rooker: "Tom calls a good game and he handles pitchers well. He does not have all the raw talent in the world but he gets the most out of what he has."

NEW YORK YANKEES

PITCHING:

As successful as Ron Guidry has been, it was difficult for the Yankees and other teams this winter to determine his future value. Perhaps as a result of this confusion, the Yankees were unable to reach agreement on a new contract with Guidry and lost negotiating rights to their long time ace until May 1st.

Guidry hurt his value in 1986, when he suffered only his second losing record in 10 seasons and failed to win in double figures for the first time.

Guidry, who once relied on "Louisiana Lightning"--a crackling fastball and a wicked slider--continues to be in a period of adjustment.

The key to his season is whether he will be able to begin his season with a clear plan: he must decide what kind of pitcher he is going to be. Will he go right at hitters with his slider the way he used to or throw more curveballs from now on?

The lefthander is at the point where he must drastically reduce use of his once-devastating slider. The snap on a pitcher's slider is the first thing to go and Guidry's slider has dropped off tremendously. He was hurt badly last year by throwing flat sliders.

Guidry's time would be well spent in developing his curveball. He can be very successful with a slow curve to complement his fastball.

Guidry must recognize, though, that his fastball will never be what it once was. Still, he has an above-average major league fastball, often clocking in the high-80s. Occasionally, he can reach back for heat in the low-90s.

Guidry may find that since his workload diminished in 1986, his arm will bounce back better this year. There is the chance he will have an improved fastball in 1987.

FIELDING:

Guidry is a deserving Gold Glove-winner.

***RON GUIDRY
LHP, No. 49
LL, 5'11", 157 lbs.
ML Svc: 12 years
Born: 8-28-50 in
Lafayette, LA***

1986 STATISTICS

W	L	ERA	G	GS	CG	SV	IP	H	R	ER	BB	SO
9	12	3.98	30	30	5	0	192.1	202	94	85	38	140

CAREER STATISTICS

W	L	ERA	G	GS	CG	SV	IP	H	R	ER	BB	SO
163	80	3.24	334	296	93	4	2219.1	2030	875	800	580	1650

He still possesses cat-quick reflexes. The first few steps off the mound are critical for any pitcher. Guidry's motion, which he's said he wouldn't trade with anyone's, leaves him in perfect fielding position and he covers ground better than any other pitcher in the league (though Yankee newcomer Rick Rhoden is pretty good).

Guidry's pickoff move is not good considering the lefthander's athletic ability. He did not have to devote time to his pickoff when he broke into the majors a decade ago-- Guidry didn't face many baserunners then.

OVERALL:

Guidry pitched better in 1986 than his record indicates. With any luck, he could have been a .500 pitcher at least. He has rebounded before from subpar efforts, going from 10-11 in 1984 to 22-6 a year later.

Kaat: "Guidry is a very proud pitcher and when one considers his motivation this season after failing to reach terms with the Yankees last year, you have to predict he will bounce back for a pretty successful 1987."

EXCELLENT SPEED

HITTING:

Rickey Henderson was not as effective in 1986 as he had been in the past. His average dipped from .314 in 1985 to a career-low .263 last year. His on-base percentage plunged from .419 to .358.

Henderson's greatest value as a leadoff hitter is his ability to get aboard and make things happen. But last season, he seemed to lose sight of that. And that's dangerous. He appeared to change his pattern from a player content to hit for high average to more of a middle-of-the-order power hitter.

Righthanders stand their best chance against Henderson by depending on breaking balls low and away. For lefthanders, the best combination is fastballs low and away and breaking balls in the dirt.

Henderson walks often. He has a good eye and presents a difficult strike zone due to his extreme crouch . He is a small target to begin with but his crouch gives him about a 10" strike zone. Henderson, who always snipes at the umpires, had more trouble with them than usual in 1986. The debate concerned whether Henderson's strike zone is defined by the time he enters his crouch or when he uncoils himself to swing. Calls against him were inconsistent, but he was unable to ignore the problem.

BASERUNNING:

Henderson has learned more about his craft since his record-setting running of 1982, when he stole 130 bases to break Lou Brock's record of 118. He reads pitchers better now than most suspect.

Pitchers and catchers can best handle Henderson by ignoring him--they can't stop him anyway. Pitchers should save their pickoff throws until later in the game, when it matters most. When Henderson knows he has the pitcher's attention, it *inspires* him to run. He also is given to taunting the man on the mound, unsettling him and stealing his attention away from the batter.

If Henderson doesn't steal with a dusty, headfirst slide, he fulfills his mission by causing the pitcher to balk, uncork a wild pitch or make a bad pitch.

RICKEY HENDERSON
CF, No. 24
RL, 5'10", 195 lbs.
ML Svc: 8 years
Born: 12-25-58 in
Chicago, IL

1986 STATISTICS

AVG	G	AB	R	H	2B	3B	HR	RBI	BB	SO	SB
.263	153	608	130	160	31	5	28	74	89	81	87

CAREER STATISTICS

AVG	G	AB	R	H	2B	3B	HR	RBI	BB	SO	SB
.290	1087	4071	862	1182	188	39	103	417	708	562	660

  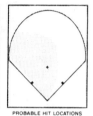

STRONG   STRONG

VS. RHP   VS. LHP   PROBABLE HIT LOCATIONS

FIELDING:

Henderson should be an exceptional center fielder. He isn't. He has trouble judging balls and relies on his speed to overcome these lapses. Most of the time it works; sometimes it doesn't and he is guilty of a game-breaking gaffe.

Henderson alone can determine if he will improve as a center fielder. It's simply a matter of hard work. Henderson has one deficiency that will never change, however: a weak arm. Runners can go from first to third on him. He will regularly throw to the wrong base, making a bad situation worse.

Henderson should consider playing a more shallow center field. With his speed, he could still retreat in time to cover Yankee Stadium's vast center field.

OVERALL:

Kaat: "Henderson could be better. Where much is given, much is expected. He has the potential to be the best offensive threat in baseball. He can completely change the complexion of the game in almost any way he wants."

NEW YORK YANKEES

PITCHING:

The next manager or pitching coach who succeeds in solving the riddle of Charles Hudson will be the first.

He is a pitcher with better-than-average stuff: a 93 MPH fastball, a good hard slider, and a change-up that could be effective if he used it more and put it in the right location when he did. But he doesn't. And he doesn't win.

Hudson is a young veteran who has been a sub-.500 pitcher for three seasons. Last season, he managed to pitch his way out of a job on the Philadelphia pitching staff which was desperate for help.

He cannot complete what he starts; worse still, he can barely make it to the sixth or seventh inning. In late August last year, he was banished to the bullpen. He gives up hit after hit after hit and at times, home run after home run. At one point last season when he was still in the starting rotation, he went six weeks between victories.

FIELDING, HITTING, BASERUNNING:

Hudson is a decent fielder but because he has a poor move to first, baserunners looking to steal can have their way with him.

He is a horrible hitter and his poor judgment of the strike zone prevents him from drawing walks. Because he rarely gets on base, he does not often get the opportunity to show off his good running speed.

OVERALL:

Hudson's problems have nothing to do with the calibre of his stuff or the physical condition of his arm. Hudson cannot

CHARLIE HUDSON
RHP, No. 49
RR, 6'3", 185 lbs.
ML Svc: 4 years
Born: 3-16-59 in
Ennis, TX

1986 STATISTICS

W	L	ERA	G	GS	CG	SV	IP	H	R	ER	BB	SO
7	10	4.94	33	23	0	0	144	165	87	79	58	82

CAREER STATISTICS

W	L	ERA	G	GS	CG	SV	IP	H	R	ER	BB	SO
32	42	3.98	127	105	7	0	680	692	353	301	237	399

concentrate for more than a few innings at a time. Two-strike hits, two-out rallies and coughing up leads have become trademarks of a Charles Hudson performance.

Driven to frustration last season, Claude Osteen, the Phillies' pitching coach, went so far as to challenge Hudson's desire to pitch. Osteen was trying to light a fire under Hudson with the criticism. But that such a charge would be made was a stunning indictment of a pitcher. And it pointed out that at least part of Hudson's problem had to do with motivation. Hudson was at his best when he was trying to prove someone wrong. Unfortunately, and this may speak more for Hudson as a major leaguer than any other comment, Hudson is only able to manufacture intensity when his job is on the line.

Rooker: "Hudson has gone backward since his rookie year. That's too bad because physically he has the tools. Whenever you see a young pitcher regress, you wonder if he is stubborn, or if he is incapable of learning from his mistakes."

NEW YORK YANKEES

HITTING:

Last year, Don Mattingly narrowly missed his second American League batting championship last year in three full years as a major leaguer, achieving a glittering .352 average. He was runner-up to Boston pitching ace Roger Clemens in a bid for a second consecutive Most Valuable Player Award.

What makes Mattingly a superior offensive player is his ability to hit for average and "do damage," as he puts it. But Mattingly *can* be pitched to. The most important task for pitchers is to get ahead in the count. Mattingly takes a lot of first pitches to get a feel for the at-bat and what his opponent has on that particular day. He varies his placement in the batter's box, standing up farther against pitchers who can't throw the ball by him.

Not surprisingly, Mattingly is painstaking in his analysis of pitchers and is well prepared mentally for what a pitcher's game plan might be. Still, he claims to have trouble picking up the flight of a good change-up.

Pitchers should gamble with fastballs early, hoping to get ahead. The deeper the count goes, the more dangerous Mattingly becomes. This is true of all great hitters.

The book on Mattingly is to go up-and-away with fastballs, which is an area generally avoided when facing top hitters. In Mattingly's case, up-and-away is his only vulnerable zone.

When Mattingly is not in a groove, he will swipe at the pitch up-and-away and send lazy fly balls to left field (most of his left-field attempts are fly balls). When he is hot, the same pitch will be laced into the gap or down the left-field line.

Mattingly adjusts to situations and will pull the inside fastball into the upper deck if the Yankees need a home run.

BASERUNNING:

Running the bases is the one aspect Mattingly does not have a feel for. His instinct is not what it should be and serves only to magnify his lack of speed.

FIELDING:

Earlier this year, Keith Hernandez said that

DON MATTINGLY
1B, No. 23
LL, 6'0", 175 lbs.
ML Svc: 4 years
Born: 4-20-61 in
Evansville, IN

1986 STATISTICS

AVG	G	AB	R	H	2B	3B	HR	RBI	BB	SO	SB
.352	162	677	117	238	53	2	31	113	53	25	0

CAREER STATISTICS

AVG	G	AB	R	H	2B	3B	HR	RBI	BB	SO	SB
.332	572	2223	349	737	160	11	93	401	171	141	3

  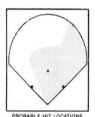

VS. RHP   VS. LHP   PROBABLE HIT LOCATIONS

Don Mattingly was the best first baseman in New York. Well, that should be it, right?

Rate them one and one. Mattingly is unequalled in his ability to pursue pop-ups, which is odd because he lacks speed. Somehow, Mattingly compensates by anticipating where the ball will land and making near-impossible plays look easy.

Mattingly and Hernandez are both exceptional at turning the 3-6-3 double play. However, nobody converges on bunts with the suddenness and skill of Hernandez, although Mattingly has markedly improved this skill.

How?

By watching Hernandez, Mattingly said.

Rate them gracious and more gracious.

OVERALL:

Kaat: "He follows the weight-shift theory of Charlie Lau and says that the shift has enabled him to give the ball enough backspin to hit it out of the park.

"There is growing sentiment to declare Don Mattingly the best player in the game. His peers already did so in a poll conducted by *The New York Times* last year. "

NEW YORK YANKEES

PITCHING:

Joe Niekro's future was thrown into doubt when it was revealed last September that he had been pitching with shoulder problems for much of the 1986 season. He was diagnosed as having a "fraying" of the rotator cuff, a condition that might almost be expected in someone who has labored more than 3,400 innings in his career.

Niekro's physical problems culminated a nightmarish first season with the Yankees. He was devastated when his older brother, Phil, was cut loose in spring training. Such disappointment is no excuse for poor performance, but Joe's reaction was only human.

Joe is more of a fastball/slider pitcher than Phil, but both depend on the darting, dancing knuckleball they learned from their father in the backyard. Joe developed the pitch even more when he realized the fastball/slider combination wasn't enough to keep him in the majors.

Joe had trouble controlling the knuckleball last summer and this may well have been related to his physical problems. He is a smart, veteran pitcher, a gamer who never admitted to a serious problem until it was impossible for him to throw anymore.

FIELDING:

Niekro was aided during his time in Houston by Astroturf, which provides truer hops and more time for fielders to make their throws. Niekro is an adequate fielder on

JOE NIEKRO
RHP, No. 39
RR, 6'1", 195 lbs.
ML Svc: 21 years
Born: 11-7-44 in
   Martins Ferry, OH

1986 STATISTICS

W	L	ERA	G	GS	CG	SV	IP	H	R	ER	BB	SO
9	10	4.87	25	25	0	0	125.2	139	84	68	63	59

CAREER STATISTICS

W	L	ERA	G	GS	CG	SV	IP	H	R	ER	BB	SO
213	190	3.50	670	472	106	14	3426	3295	1506	1331	1189	1656

natural grass. He has slowed a bit, but he remains effective at fielding what comes his way.

Niekro's pickoff move is good for a righthander. For a knuckleballer, of course, this is essential because the butterfly pitch seems to take forever before it floats into the catcher's glove. Niekro has worked on this aspect and he prevents runners from taking liberties.

OVERALL:

Kaat: "Niekro's success or failure is all related to his physical condition. If Joe is healthy, you can throw the age factor out the window because knuckleballers can pitch for a long, long time."

NEW YORK YANKEES

HITTING:

If Mike Pagliarulo felt a certain emptiness after his 1986 season, it was understandable. For a batter who ranked among the American League home run leaders and clouted 21 homers before the All-Star break, Pagliarulo's faltering finish last season was distressing. Pagliarulo ended the year with 28 home runs-- but only *one* was hit after August 24th. He produced only three of his 71 RBIs after that date.

It's possible that Pagliarulo may be too hard a worker for his own good. This is a player who (at lease once) took batting practice *after* a game and who has to be discouraged by coaches from taking so many extra cuts in the batting cage.

Pagliarulo is a typical power hitter, which is to say he is a streaky one. When he is slumping, he becomes more undisciplined and his aggressiveness leads him to chase pitches not close to the strike zone. When he is going well, he shows much more patience at the plate and lays off bad pitches.

Pagliarulo is an exceptional fastball hitter who still has trouble with breaking balls, particularly when dealt by southpaws.

Lefthanders have a fairly easy time against Pagliarulo by keeping the breaking ball down-and-away and firing fastballs up-and-in. Pagliarulo will hang in there against the fastball in tight--this led him to be hit by a fastball from Oakland's Curt Young in a frightening accident last year--but he can be jammed.

Pagliarulo can only solve his problems against lefthanders by seeing them on a regular basis. When he plays *every day*, observers can see the confidence he feels as he strides purposefully to the plate.

BASERUNNING:

Baserunning is not one of Pagliarulo's assets. He does not have good speed and there are too many times when he runs himself into outs or bad plays by making fundamental baserunning mistakes.

FIELDING:

The Yankee players barked last season

MIKE PAGLIARULO
3B, No. 12
LR, 6'2", 195 lbs.
ML Svc: 3 years
Born: 3-15-60 in Medford, MA

1986 STATISTICS

AVG	G	AB	R	H	2B	3B	HR	RBI	BB	SO	SB
.238	149	504	71	120	24	3	28	71	54	120	4

CAREER STATISTICS

AVG	G	AB	R	H	2B	3B	HR	RBI	BB	SO	SB
.238	555	1085	150	259	55	8	54	167	114	252	4

VS. RHP

VS. LHP

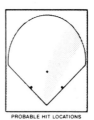

PROBABLE HIT LOCATIONS

about the uneven quality of the Yankee infield (in fact, the infield has been re-surfaced for this season). The poor condition of his home field may have played a factor in Pagliarulo's poor defense last season. He lacked rhythm in the field and never looked comfortable on a consistent basis.

The field conditions notwithstanding, Pagliarulo's lateral movement could be improved. He compensates for a lack of mobility, however, with a great deal of intensity. He will dive and scratch to come up with smashes that might scoot by a less determined fielder and he makes strong throws.

OVERALL:

Pagliarulo has reached the stage now where he must develop a better workout pattern. There is absolutely no doubt that Pagliarulo works hard; what he needs to do now is to work *smarter*.

Kaat: "Mike is a good major league third baseman who is going to get better. He's got the good reactions, the strong arm and the desire to succeed."

HITTING:

Dan Pasqua has the ability to provide a ballclub with a total offensive package. Because of his short, quick stroke, Pasqua can hit for a high average and he has as much power as anybody on the Yankees. In fact, he has as much power as anybody in the American League. Last season, fans came out to the ballpark early to watch Oakland slugger Jose Canseco take batting practice but Pasqua stages a show worth watching, too.

Pasqua is a low fastball hitter but his short stroke gives him the ability to connect on breaking balls as well. Pasqua can be waiting on the fastball and still adjust in time to make contact with an off-speed pitch.

Even with all of the Yankees' punch, the young slugger should be batting cleanup against righthanders, no lower than fifth or sixth against lefthanders. He will have moments when he looks bad against southpaws. But the more he sees them, the more he will hit them. In exchange for his extraordinary Yankee Stadium power the Yankees must come to accept Pasqua's frequent strikeouts.

When pitchers are able to get ahead in the count, Pasqua will chase bad pitches, including breaking balls in the dirt. Pitchers can then send him back to the dugout with good, high fastballs.

BASERUNNING:

Pasqua has ordinary speed but is a liability on the basepaths because he is not always alert to what is happening around him. There have been occasions when he has forgotten the number of outs in an inning. At other times, he misses opportunities to advance.

FIELDING:

Pasqua came to the majors with a reputation as a below-average fielder. It's a bad rap. He has a low-key personality and sometimes plays the outfield almost sluggishly but his defensive ability is not lacking.

**DAN PASQUA
LF/DH, No. 21
LL, 6'0", 205 lbs.
ML Svc: 2 years
Born: 10-17-61 in
Yonkers, NY**

1986 STATISTICS

AVG	G	AB	R	H	2B	3B	HR	RBI	BB	SO	SB
.293	102	280	44	82	17	0	16	45	47	78	2

CAREER STATISTICS

AVG	G	AB	R	H	2B	3B	HR	RBI	BB	SO	SB
.264	162	428	61	113	20	1	25	70	63	116	2

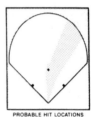

VS. RHP   VS. LHP   PROBABLE HIT LOCATIONS

Pasqua gets a good jump on most balls, overcoming his lack of speed, and has an above-average arm once he makes the catch. He is more than adequate in left field in Yankee Stadium.

OVERALL:

Pasqua needs additional playing time and a shot of confidence from the Yankees. Last spring training, Pasqua felt pressured to make a big early showing. That stress, combined with the death of his mother, led to a terrible spring that landed him in Triple-A Columbus for the first month of the season.

The Yankees, while expressing a commitment to Pasqua, have constantly acquired players who pose a threat to his status as a regular. The time has come for him to play every day.

Kaat: "If the Yankees pencil in Pasqua as their left fielder and leave him alone, they will be amazed at the numbers he will have for average, home runs and RBIs."

NEW YORK YANKEES

HITTING:

In a game of slumps and streaks, Willie Randolph's overall consistency is unusual. Consider his averages the last five years: .280, .279, .287, .276 and .276. There are precious few major leaguers who can claim that kind of even keel.

Then again, those marks are not surprising considering Randolph's patience and good judgment at the plate. Those qualities make Randolph an ideal No. 2 hitter behind leadoff man and stolen base king Rickey Henderson.

Perhaps due to his experience as a No. 2 hitter, Randolph is able to go to the opposite field and, while not a home run threat, he possesses surprising power to right-center field.

Pitchers don't want to throw too many breaking balls to Randolph for fear of falling behind in the count. The deeper the count gets, the better a hitter Randolph becomes.

As a general pattern, pitchers should go either high and tight on Randolph or low and away. He will drive anything that stays out over the plate to right-center and frequently finds the gaps in right- and left-center field for doubles.

Randolph's ability seems to diminish with men on base, however. He is not a good clutch hitter.

BASERUNNING:

Randolph is always alert and has good instincts. He can still steal a base in a key spot and keeps himself in excellent physical condition. He plays the game hard and stays away from baserunning blunders.

FIELDING:

Randolph had his troubles the first half of last season and his overall defense was not as sharp as in previous years.

Randolph has long complained about the quality of the infield at Yankee Stadium, citing, among other things, that it is not level. That may be so, but it cannot be used as an excuse--even for this veteran.

Randolph has lost some range, but his hand-eye coordination remains excellent. He

WILLIE RANDOLPH
2B, No. 30
RR, 5'11", 166 lbs.
ML Svc: 12 years
Born: 7-6-54 in
Holly Hill, SC

1986 STATISTICS

AVG	G	AB	R	H	2B	3B	HR	RBI	BB	SO	SB
.276	141	492	76	136	15	2	5	50	94	49	15

CAREER STATISTICS

AVG	G	AB	R	H	2B	3B	HR	RBI	BB	SO	SB
.274	1494	5511	897	1511	216	55	39	451	874	447	233

  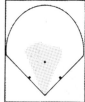

STRONG — VS. RHP | STRONG — VS. LHP | PROBABLE HIT LOCATIONS

makes backhand grabs behind the bag on choppers that would elude other second basemen.

Manager Lou Piniella gets no argument when he claims Randolph turns the double play better than anyone else. Randolph does not lose an instant in getting rid of the ball and takes whatever punishment the baserunner might inflict in order to make his relay throw.

Randolph has been forced to work with a series of shortstops in recent years and adjusts with relative ease to the quirks of each.

OVERALL:

The Yankees continue to treat their best players with negotiations that go down to the wire when it would show considerably more savoir faire to handle matters in a timely fashion. Last season, they signed co-captain Randolph as a free agent to a two-year contract on the last day possible. His signing is a decision they will not regret.

Kaat: "Randolph is the last remaining everyday player from the Yankees' last world championship team in 1978, which is no fluke. He has the steadiness desired in a champion.

NEW YORK YANKEES

PITCHING:

The Yankees have always thought highly of Dennis Rasmussen's ability, so much so, in fact, that they acquired him twice through trades. The tall lefthander finally proved them right in 1986, his first full major league season.

What was it that transformed Rasmussen, who spent much of the 1985 campaign in Triple-A? Part of the answer lies in the Yankees' decision to change managers, going from Billy Martin to Lou Piniella. Martin felt Rasmussen was too timid and the youngster could do nothing to please the fiery former-former-former-former manager. Piniella's arrival represented a second chance for Rasmussen to prove himself.

Rasmussen's biggest problems were his lack of confidence and aggressiveness. He was a defensive pitcher even at the start of the 1986 campaign, nibbling at the plate and generally making his craft into more of a chore than it has to be for someone of his ability.

The once-gawky Rasmussen has developed a big, slow, easy motion. At 6'7", he has an advantage over hitters simply because his high release point causes the ball to come at the hitters at such a sharp angle.

His fastball generally falls in the 85-88 MPH range and is actually much livelier than it appears to be from the stands or the dugout.

He also throws a sharp curveball to complement his fastball. His curve is a good one--big and slow--but he threw it less often last year than in the past to make way for more fastballs. It was a good decision. Rasmussen didn't seem to realize until last year how effective his fastball can be.

Even with as many strides as he made in 1986, Rasmussen can still become a more aggressive pitcher. He must look to polish off hitters faster and will do so if he simply attacks them with his good stuff rather than going into deep counts on countless batters.

Rasmussen dug himself into holes in late innings last year by being too cautious and becoming his own worst enemy by issuing too many walks. He was unable to give the Yankees the complete games they needed from him and cost himself several victories by creating rallies the bullpen did not stamp out.

DENNIS RASMUSSEN
LHP, No. 45
LL, 6'7", 225 lbs.
ML Svc: 2 years
Born: 4-18-59 in
**   Los Angeles, CA**

1986 STATISTICS

W	L	ERA	G	GS	CG	SV	IP	H	R	ER	BB	SO
18	6	3.88	31	31	3	0	202	160	91	87	74	131

CAREER STATISTICS

W	L	ERA	G	GS	CG	SV	IP	H	R	ER	BB	SO
30	17	4.06	81	72	3	0	465	394	231	210	184	317

FIELDING:

Rasmussen has good athletic ability, but he does not possess the quickness that could be expected of a smaller man--all of which leaves him as an adequate fielder.

There is an amount of deception in Rasmussen's pickoff move. He throws over far too much, however, often in meaningless situations. His persistence is rewarded sometimes, but he could catch the same number of runners with fewer throws over to first base. Rasmussen must realize that the more the runners see his move, the better they read it and the more vulnerable he becomes to the stolen base.

OVERALL:

Rasmussen was one of the biggest surprises in baseball last season. Many think he will suffer an equally startling fall in 1987, believing that last year's performance was a fluke. Rasmussen needs another big season before he can be regarded as an established winner.

Kaat: "Anytime a pitcher has a season like Rasmussen had in 1986, he must understand that he will have to be *better* the next year to be as good as he just was. For some pitchers, this means adding a pitch. For some, it means changing speeds more. In Dennis' case, it's convincing himself he can be even more aggressive than he was last year."

NEW YORK YANKEES

PITCHING:

Rick Rhoden had a tempestuous 1986 season. Early last year, he demanded a trade but didn't get it. Then he decided that the new Pirate atmosphere was to his liking and quieted down. Throughout the season, he was the topic of rumors and was accused of scuffing the ball. Yet he managed so well that until he lost his final six decisions, Rhoden was one of the top three candidates for the Cy Young Award with a 15-6 record and a 2.84 ERA (he finished at 15-12).

Rhoden has it all on the mound: a good fastball, curveball, slider and change-up. He also has outstanding control and is a smart pitcher who learned a great deal about the "art" of pitching from Don Sutton while with the Dodgers.

He uses his slider as his out pitch. Rhoden is a control pitcher who won't issue many walks although hitters will get their fair share of hits off him. However, he bears down with runners on base and can finish off a batter for the crucial third out.

Rhoden is a workhorse pitcher who will pitch a lot of innings. He is a perfectionist who likes to finish what he starts. Last season, he recorded 12 complete games, the most by a Pirate pitcher in more than a decade.

FIELDING:

The Yankees are getting another infielder in Rhoden; he was one of the National League's best fielding pitchers. He anticipates and moves on bunts well, covers first base quickly and always keeps his head in the game.

He has made only five errors in his career and led all National League pitchers in fielding last year by not making an error in 66 chances. He has not made an error in his last 79 games.

Rhoden also has an outstanding pickoff move and picked six runners off base last year.

RICK RHODEN
RHP, No. 29
RR, 6'4", 203 lbs.
ML Svc: 12 years
Born: 5-16-53 in
Boynton Beach, FL

1986 STATISTICS

W	L	ERA	G	GS	CG	SV	IP	H	R	ER	BB	SO
15	12	2.84	34	34	12	0	253.2	211	82	80	76	159

CAREER STATISTICS

W	L	ERA	G	GS	CG	SV	IP	H	R	ER	BB	SO
121	97	3.48	333	304	60	1	2118	2108	903	818	643	1177

OVERALL:

Rhoden is a tough pitcher who has pitched well for teams with little chance to be in contention. With the exception of the 1983 season when the Pirates finished in second place in the National League East (six games behind Philadelphia), the Bucs were woeful during Rhoden's eight seasons with the club. His Pirate record is 79-73.

He *has* to be excited about pitching in the spotlight and for a contender. But his success is not entirely up to him. Even assuming that the Yankees give him offensive support, he will still need the advantage of an experienced catcher to steer him around the American League batters. A peaceful relationship with owner George Steinbrenner would be another advantage--though it is unlikely to occur if things go awry. And Rhoden will need to maintain the mental advantage he gains from the allegations that he scuffs the ball. Does Rick Rhoden scuff the ball? At times, he probably does. He has denied it and no evidence has proven otherwise.

Rooker: "With the addition of Rhoden to the pitching staff, the Yankees are getting that quality starter they have needed for several seasons. With the help of the Yankee artillery of sluggers, Rhoden is capable of having an 18-win season. That would have been enough to put the Yankees into the playoffs last season."

NEW YORK YANKEES

PITCHING:

Dave Righetti was a man on a mission last season, out to prove to anyone who continued to consider him as a possible starter that he could be an outstanding reliever.

Now, after he broke the major league record with 46 saves last year, there is no question that Righetti, remembered forever for his no-hitter against Boston on July 4, 1983, has settled in as one of the games' premier relievers.

Righetti has all the qualities sought in a reliever. He has the right temperament. He is able to recover from a big home run or a bad outing. He has endured horrible slumps in the early part of the last two seasons and kept his head, even if others about him were losing theirs.

He cares about doing well, a point he made emphatically by heaving a ball over the right field wall at Toronto's Exhibition Stadium after a home run capped an improbable rally against him. Manager Lou Piniella exulted in the attitude Righetti's throw reflected. (Press box onlookers agreed it was the best throw he had made all night.)

Most nights, such displays of temper aren't necessary for Righetti. He causes batters to fling helmets and bats in disgust after losing a fight with his fastball. When people refer to a "live major league fastball," they're talking about the type that Righetti throws regularly.

That pitch, which zips along in the high-80s/low-90s, is what all the hitters talk about. The ball explodes as it reaches the plate. Give Righetti the added benefit of late-afternoon shadows and it's lights out.

Righetti has a good slider and he's working on an off-speed pitch to further annoy big league batters. He realizes that success in the major leagues requires constant adjustments and the refining of skills.

FIELDING:

As good an athlete as Righetti is, he should be a better fielder. His delivery leaves him far off to the third-base side. He must work harder at getting himself back into a good

***DAVE RIGHETTI
LHP, No. 19
LL, 6'3", 198 lbs.
ML Svc: 6 years
Born: 11-29-58 in
San Jose, CA***

1986 STATISTICS

W	L	ERA	G	GS	CG	SV	IP	H	R	ER	BB	SO
8	8	2.45	74	0	0	46	106.2	88	31	29	35	83

CAREER STATISTICS

W	L	ERA	G	GS	CG	SV	IP	H	R	ER	BB	SO
58	44	3.01	294	76	13	107	832	697	312	278	340	699

fielding position after his delivery.

Righetti occasionally makes a spectacular stop behind his back. More often, though, balls he should at least deflect roll harmlessly up the middle for rally-starting singles.

Righetti's pickoff move is average, if not below-average. His concentration remains on the plate. He is so confident in his ability to retire the batter that baserunners become almost trivial.

OVERALL:

It is unlikely that Righetti will surpass his own saves record this season. He could have a significant falloff, however, and still have as good a year. Saves for a reliever can be like steals for a baserunner: situation means everything.

Kaat: "Righetti has made the mental adjustment to being a reliever. He wants to keep thoughts about starting out of his mind. At this stage in his career, a return to the rotation should be out of the question.

"In his desire to protect a Yankee lead last year, rookie manager Lou Piniella often went as fast as he could to get Righetti to the mound. Short relievers should not be brought into the game until at least the eighth inning, but Righetti often pitched in the seventh inning last year. Dave tends to throw a lot of pitches in an inning and it's possible that the number of innings he pitched last season could have strained his arm for 1987."

NEW YORK YANKEES

PITCHING:

For two years, Ron Romanick was the classic case of a young pitcher succeeding without overpowering heat. In 1986, he turned into a case study in self-destruction.

Romanick had been a winner by making batters hit *his* pitch. A string of bad breaks made him lose his confidence and he began to overthrow, trying to retire everyone by himself. Next thing he knew, he was in the minors and was all but forgotten.

Whatever the reason, Romanick was truly terrible by the time the Angels gave up on him. He had become possibly the worst starter in a regular rotation in the majors. He won only six of his last 28 starts.

Yet, he can still be the same pitcher who stood 13-4 at one point in 1985. Maybe even better: his arm has gradually regained strength from an early 1980s injury and his fastball now is better than it was when he broke into the big leagues--in the upper 80s.

Now, however, Romanick must regain the confidence to throw his pitches inside. He has to do so to move batters off the plate so he can get them to chase his slow curveball, which is most effective when thrown outside. He has to learn to again trust his defense; he'll never be one to blow people away. He has struck out only 60 in his last 155 innings.

Coming out of the same overhand delivery as his other pitches is a terrific change-up. When he is in groove, Romanick gets many of his strikeouts with it. But he must mix all four of his pitches, which include a slider, to win.

He is a spunky kid, almost arrogant. With that personality, regaining confidence should come easy once he gets over the hump. Obviously, he'd like nothing more than to prove the Angels made a big mistake.

FIELDING:

Romanick tends to be clumsy, a portrait of the pitcher-as-a-nonathlete stereotype. He lands in good position to field balls but

RON ROMANICK
RHP, No. 10
RR, 6'4", 203 lbs.
ML Svc: 3 years
Born: 11-6-60 in
Burley, ID

1986 STATISTICS

W	L	ERA	G	GS	CG	SV	IP	H	R	ER	BB	SO
5	8	5.50	18	18	1	0	106.1	124	68	65	44	38

CAREER STATISTICS

W	L	ERA	G	GS	CG	SV	IP	H	R	ER	BB	SO
31	29	4.24	82	82	15	0	531	574	276	250	167	189

sometimes doesn't know what to do with them. He tends to get a late break to first on grounders and will turn many of the easier plays into bang-bang affairs.

To make up for a somewhat slow and stretched delivery, he'll frequently throw to first base. But his move is only adequate. He was one of the easier Angels pitchers to steal on in 1986.

OVERALL:

One of the raps against Romanick was that success swelled his head. He supposedly grew less dedicated and more drawn to the bright lights. If that's the case, being in New York won't help that attraction to distraction.

But he also offers the classic case of someone who could benefit from a change of scenery. He has always pitched well in Yankee Stadium. His 1986 problems may prove to be only a brief interruption in a long career.

Killebrew: "Ron is young enough to overcome his recent ups-and-downs. If new scenery renews his confidence, he can still be a successful major league pitcher."

NEW YORK YANKEES

HITTING:

Joel Skinner's lack of offensive punch stands in the way of his ability to establish himself as a front-line major league catcher.

The Yankees acquired the son of Atlanta Braves coach Bob Skinner as part of a six-player trade with the Chicago White Sox at midseason last year. In doing so, they gambled that everyday play and the tutelage of Lou Piniella, a noted batting instructor before he became manager, would spark Skinner's offense.

It appears the gamble may pay off. Last year, Skinner reduced his long, looping swing and became more of a contact hitter under the guidance of Piniella and focused his attention on driving the ball through the middle of the diamond.

Skinner batted .259 in 54 games with New York compared to .201 in 60 games with the White Sox. Given the offensive firepower surrounding Skinner, the catcher won't need to produce much more than that with the Yankees.

Skinner still strikes out much too often, however. He has trouble with the slider low-and-away against righthanded pitchers. Like many righthanded batters who have reached the majors recently, Skinner can drive the low fastball.

Skinner does not have Yankee Stadium power and should continue making the adjustments necessary to become more of a contact hitter. For Skinner, hitting will always be secondary because his defensive skills can mean so much to a club.

BASERUNNING:

Skinner is a typical catcher--painfully slow. He is not a threat to steal and generally advances one base at a time.

FIELDING:

Defensively, Skinner compares with the finest catchers in the league with his strong arm and quick release. Not many teams will test the young catcher.

Skinner needs to learn the Yankees pitchers and begin working with them, which

JOEL SKINNER
C, No. 22
RR, 6'4", 204 lbs.
ML Svc: 2 years
Born: 2-21-61 in
La Jolla, CA

1986 STATISTICS

AVG	G	AB	R	H	2B	3B	HR	RBI	BB	SO	SB
.232	114	315	23	73	9	1	5	37	16	83	1

CAREER STATISTICS

AVG	G	AB	R	H	2B	3B	HR	RBI	BB	SO	SB
.240	185	450	38	108	15	2	6	46	28	116	2

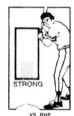

VS. RHP

VS. LHP

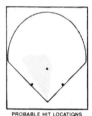

PROBABLE HIT LOCATIONS

seems to be a lost art for many catchers these days.

Skinner couldn't be expected in half a season to learn the strengths and weaknesses of his pitchers or to win their confidence. Skinner's task is made more difficult by the constant flux in a problem-filled staff. If the Yankees can improve on last year's 4.11 ERA this season, Skinner should get some of the credit.

OVERALL:

The Yankees aren't known for taking a chance on young, unproven players, but they are so impressed with Skinner's basic tools they believe he can play a significant role for them.

Still, if Skinner has a string of poor games defensively or slumps at the plate, the Yankees' patience could run out quickly. With the Yankees, pressure to perform comes immediately.

Kaat: "Skinner needs to be told in spring training, 'This is your job and that's it.' If he is given that confidence, he will get better and better."

NEW YORK YANKEES

PITCHING:

When Bob Tewksbury accompanied the Yankees north out of spring training to start the 1986 season, he became the first Yankee rookie pitcher to do so since Mike Griffin in 1980.

But Tewksbury never pitched like a rookie. As much a cliche as it may sound, Tewksbury knows how to pitch. He has a feel for his art, approaches hitters intelligently and maintains his poise on the mound.

These qualities compensate for an assortment of pitches that form only an adequate repertoire.

He throws an average major league fastball with just enough zip to get by. The pitch is potent enough for Tewksbury, however, because of his outstanding control. This righthander's location is excellent no matter what he throws.

Tewksbury's curveball is only fair. He is better off using a slider that consistently breaks well for him.

Tewksbury has an even temperament on the mound and is fearless. Unlike many young pitchers, he recognizes the need to keep batters off balance by going inside and does so willingly.

This got him into trouble in one of his first major league starts, in Kansas City against the Royals. Veteran Willie Wilson charged the mound after he was struck by an 0-2 pitch. The rookie's reaction?

"Why would I want to hit you?" Tewksbury yelled at Wilson. "You're an instant out."

Tewksbury puts the ball in play and lets his fielders help him. Although he permits many hits, he rarely walks anybody and avoids giving up the big home run.

His confidence and concentration almost appear to be better when he's in a jam than at the start of an inning. He has a knack for making the one pitch needed to escape a predicament. When he fails, it is because he has overthrown or otherwise tried to exceed his capabilities.

BOB TEWKSBURY
RHP, No.
RR, 6'4", 180 lbs.
ML Svc: 1 year
Born: 11-30-60 in Concord, NH

1986 STATISTICS												
W	L	ERA	G	GS	CG	SV	IP	H	R	ER	BB	SO
9	5	3.31	23	23	2	0	130.1	144	58	48	31	49

CAREER STATISTICS												
W	L	ERA	G	GS	CG	SV	IP	H	R	ER	BB	SO
9	5	3.31	23	23	2	0	130.1	144	58	48	31	49

FIELDING:

Tewksbury has the reflexes necessary to be a good fielder. He is always alert and is willing to dive or do whatever it takes to stop a ball another pitcher might let skip by. He appears to have put quite a bit of time into his pickoff move. The key for a righthander is quick feet--and Tewksbury's got 'em.

OVERALL:

For whatever reason, Tewksbury never gained the confidence of manager Lou Piniella last year. The condition of Tewksbury's arm is a constant concern. He suffered a major setback because of an injury in the minor leagues and missed a few turns with tendinitis in 1986.

Despite a strong start and finish in 1986, Tewksbury must convince the Yankees that he is capable of winning in the major leagues. The Yankees and Piniella may have to learn to be more patient with this righthander, who will not overpower anyone.

Kaat: "The key for Tewksbury will be his durability. If he is mentally tough enough and physically healthy, he should have a big season for the Yankees this year."

NEW YORK YANKEES

HITTING:

Those who enjoy watching Wayne Tolleson's determined effort would like to be wrong, but it is doubtful whether Tolleson can remain productive as an everyday player in a draining 162-game season.

When Tolleson is fresh, he is the kind of offensive player a manager loves to have. He usually hits toward the bottom of the order, which is where he belongs with the high-powered Yankees, but he manages to get his share of hits.

Pitchers can dispatch with Tolleson when they go at him with their basic hard stuff and stay away from an assortment of breaking balls. Tolleson will eat up any breaking ball down-and-in. Pitchers shouldn't get fancy with him because he has a short strike zone and a good eye.

Tolleson was a streaky hitter as a regular with the Yankees last year, perhaps a reflection of the physical highs and lows he might feel over the course of the season more than another player. If the Yankees are going to try Tolleson on an everyday basis, they will require a strong backup.

BASERUNNING:

Tolleson has good speed and will steal his share of bases. The most impressive things about Tolleson as a baserunner are his aggressiveness and his instincts.

An example: Tolleson made a key play in a Yankees victory over Cleveland last year when, sensing that the ball would reach the outfielder slowly through the Yankee Stadium grass, he turned a ground single into a double.

FIELDING:

Tolleson lacks the fluidity and grace of Toronto's Tony Fernandez or the strength of Baltimore's Cal Ripken. Of course, they are All-Star shortstops while Tolleson, in spite of his tenacity, is average.

He prides himself on his ability to consistently make the routine play and stay

WAYNE TOLLESON
SS, No. 2
SR, 5'9", 160 lbs.
ML Svc: 5 years
Born: 11-22-55 in Spartanburg, SC

1986 STATISTICS

AVG	G	AB	R	H	2B	3B	HR	RBI	BB	SO	SB
.265	141	475	61	126	16	5	3	43	52	76	17

CAREER STATISTICS

AVG	G	AB	R	H	2B	3B	HR	RBI	BB	SO	SB
.255	568	1700	217	433	48	14	7	93	146	256	96

VS. RHP   VS. LHP   PROBABLE HIT LOCATIONS

away from glaring errors. He will occasionally make a flashy play. Tolleson will sacrifice his body when he has to to keep a ball from rolling through.

Since Tolleson's arm is not exceptional, second base is actually his best position. But the Yankees have no need for him at that position, which has been manned by Willie Randolph since 1976.

OVERALL:

The Yankees had been interested in Tolleson for some time before finally acquiring him as part of a six-player trade with the Chicago White Sox on July 29. They view him as an offensive sparkplug, like his versatility and hope his desire can be infectious.

Kaat: "I'd like to see Tolleson do for the Yankees what Wally Backman did for the Mets: become a popular player who does not have tremendous ability but is important to the ballclub for his intensity and determination."

NEW YORK YANKEES

HITTING:

When Claudell Washington first came to the major leagues (with Oakland in 1974), his raw talent created considerable excitement. Here, everyone in baseball said, was a player with a lot of potential.

They said the same thing when Texas acquired him in 1977, when the Chicago White Sox obtained him in 1978, when the New York Mets picked him up in 1980, and when he moved on to Atlanta in 1981. The Yankees represent Washington's sixth stop in the majors in twelve years and the travelling man can no longer be described in terms of potential. At this point, Washington's career is more appropriately described as "stymied by wasted ability."

All of Washington's skills have deteriorated. As a hitter, he has lost some of his discipline. He can still pull a fat fastball out of the park but pitchers who jump ahead of him in the count with fastballs can polish him off with breaking balls in the dirt.

The Yankees plan to use Washington, who they obtained in June of last year, as a designated hitter and pinch-hitter this season. Washington has insisted he can handle the mental preparation necessary to fill that limited role. It remains to be seen.

BASERUNNING:

Although Washington still has fine speed, he does not get as much out of his baserunning as he could. Washington is not careless on the basepaths. With his ability, though, more daring and aggressiveness would be desirable.

FIELDING:

Washington is only adequate as a fielder. At one time, he possessed great speed and a

CLAUDELL WASHINGTON
LF, No. 15
LL, 6'2", 195 lbs.
ML Svc: 12 years
Born: 8-31-54 in
Los Angeles, CA

1986 STATISTICS

AVG	G	AB	R	H	2B	3B	HR	RBI	BB	SO	SB
.254	94	272	36	69	16	0	11	30	21	59	10

CAREER STATISTICS

AVG	G	AB	R	H	2B	3B	HR	RBI	BB	SO	SB
.278	1529	5488	762	1524	275	61	130	665	446	976	270

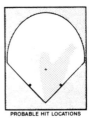

VS. RHP   VS. LHP   PROBABLE HIT LOCATIONS

good arm. He has declined dramatically in both aspects. This player simply has not applied himself.

Washington is versatile (he is capable of playing all three outfield positions) and delights in spelling Rickey Henderson in center field. In watching Washington play any field position, however, there is the feeling that looping singles that plop in front of him would be caught if he was tapping all of his resources.

OVERALL:

Kaat: "Washington still has some value, especially in the American League as a designated hitter and pinch-hitter. I don't see him as an everyday player."

NEW YORK YANKEES

HITTING:

Dave Winfield's problems in New York worsened in 1986 and resulted in the worst average of his career (.262). He did surpass 100 RBIs for the fifth straight year but, everything considered, it was a season Winfield would prefer to put behind him.

Winfield has been burdened by too-high expectations since he signed a 10-year, $23-million Yankees contract as a free agent in December 1980. The contract is so lavish even the hard working, talented Winfield can't hope to justify it.

Winfield further suffers from the demands of insatiable owner George Steinbrenner, who has dubbed him "Mr. May." Steinbrenner continues to smear Winfield by reminding anyone who will listen that Winfield is not the clutch player Reggie Jackson, "Mr. October," was for the Yankees.

All of this leads Winfield to try to do more than his capabilities will allow. Some observers watched the overeager Winfield take futile swings last year and suggested that age was beginning to overtake him. Not so. Winfield's ability is the same as it has always been.

Winfield has never been a disciplined hitter. He looks to pull pitches instead of being content with hitting the ball hard someplace.

The book on Winfield doesn't change. He will chase breaking balls thrown low-and-away. It is essential to keep him from extending his long and powerful arms. Pitchers must establish the fastball inside. Winfield will not back off of the plate, but he will hit the dirt quickly at anything that comes close.

BASERUNNING:

Winfield has excellent instincts on the basepaths and is always opportunistic. He generates great speed with his long, powerful strides once he's underway.

FIELDING:

It is when playing right field that Winfield's great athletic ability really shines. He makes

DAVE WINFIELD
RF, No. 31
RR, 6'6", 220 lbs.
ML Svc: 14 years
Born: 10-3-51 in
St. Paul, MN

1986 STATISTICS

AVG	G	AB	R	H	2B	3B	HR	RBI	BB	SO	SB
.262	154	565	90	148	31	5	24	104	77	106	6

CAREER STATISTICS

AVG	G	AB	R	H	2B	3B	HR	RBI	BB	SO	SB
.286	1964	7287	1135	2083	353	71	305	1234	791	1040	195

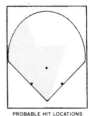

STRONG   STRONG
VS. RHP   VS. LHP   PROBABLE HIT LOCATIONS

more remarkable plays in one season than many outfielders make in a career. He has an uncanny sense for where the fence is and his timing is unbelievable. His 6'6" stature and experience as a collegiate basketball player at Minnesota contribute to his success.

Winfield's arm ranks at the top of the class among outfielders. He will show off his arm in meaningless situations, but it serves a purpose: runners are subsequently discouraged from testing him.

He also has played left field and appears better suited there, in spacious Yankee Stadium, where his arm can be more of a factor.

OVERALL:

Kaat: "Winfield is the opposite of Don Mattingly. While Mattingly is a good athlete who is a great baseball player, Winfield is a great athlete who is a good baseball player.

"Dave is a star in New York but he will never be great the way people expect him to be. He will never have the kind of numbers Mattingly puts up."

NEW YORK YANKEES

PAT CLEMENTS
LHP, No. 15
RL, 6'0", 180 lbs.
ML Svc: 2 years
Born: 2-2-62 in
McCloud, CA

PITCHING, FIELDING:

Pat Clements' biggest problem at this point is his lack of confidence. He does not feel secure in his role, and without that aplomb, he will never improve.

He doesn't have the ability to bear down to get tough hitters out. In his relief role, *every* hitter he faces is a tough hitter. He walks many lefthanded hitters he should have struck out. He does not have the big stopper's mental makeup.

Clements is a control pitcher with a decent curveball. Some of his problems might be traced to his delivery. His leg kick is small, so much so, in fact, that a hitter quickly feels comfortable facing him. He might do well with a higher leg kick in the fashion of the Mets' Bobby Ojeda, who fools hitters with his delivery. Clements needs a little more deception to be effective.

He is a good fielder but must improve his move to first base. He gets off the mound well to field bunts and cover first base.

OVERALL:

Rooker: "Clements appeared in 92 games during his season and a half in the National League. He wasn't able to record any victories and managed only four saves. He is a lefthanded pitcher who has trouble getting lefthanded hitters out."

JUAN ESPINO
C, No. 58
RR, 6'1", 190 lbs.
ML Svc: 1 year plus
Born: 3-16-56 in
Bonao,
Dominican Republic

HITTING, BASERUNNING, FIELDING:

Juan Espino can be valuable to an organization because he has the temperament and enough ability to be a backup major league catcher. If necessary, the hardworking, likeable Espino can do at least an adequate job as a starter on a short-term basis.

Espino is a fastball hitter who has trouble with good breaking pitches. He is aggressive at the plate and confident in his ability to hit major league pitching.

Espino, like most catchers, does not provide the club with any speed.

The Yankees have long appreciated Espino for his strong throwing arm and his willingness to fill a role, whatever and wherever that role may be. Espino is competent in his handling of pitchers, although his pitch selection has been questioned from time to time. No manager can stay mad at him for long, though, because Espino is such an easy-going guy.

OVERALL:

Kaat: "Juan's best bet is to be a backup catcher with the Yankees, No. 2 or 3, depending on how many they carry."

CECILIO GUANTE
RHP, No. 47
RR, 6'3", 205 lbs.
ML Svc: 4 years
Born: 2-2-60 in
 Jacagua,
 Domincan Republic

PITCHING, FIELDING:

Cecilio Guante is a power pitcher. Make that power *thrower*. He is not a pitcher. Guante just comes at the hitter with a 90+ fastball and dares the batter to hit his pitch. Somehow, in close games, hitters often do just that.

Guante can be extremely tough on righthanded hitters because in his delivery he comes at them from all angles with his fastball and slider.

As American League hitters will soon discover, Guante can be unsettling to face because, aside from the difficulty of hitting his blazing fastball, they simply can't trust him. In many outings, Guante does not have good control, and if *he* doesn't know where that fastball is going, how can a hitter be sure? Mike Schmidt of the Phillies seldom got a hit off Guante.

The Pirates tried to use him as a stopper last season but the only thing he stopped was Pirate winning streaks. The Yankees have slated him to pitch in long relief in 1987.

Guante is a poor fielder. He has trouble on bunt plays and on balls hit back at him. He does not have a good move to first base, but since he is among the quickest of the league's pitchers in going to the plate, he is difficult to steal against.

OVERALL:

Rooker: "Guante could be one of the best stoppers in the league but he has been unreceptive to learning from his past mistakes. He had better get it together this year because New York fans are a tough crowd.

"If he could throw 50% more strikes he'd be five times more effective."

TOMMY JOHN
LHP, No. 25
RL, 6'3", 200 lbs.
ML Svc: 23 years
Born: 5-22-43 in
 Terre Haute, IN

PITCHING, FIELDING:

Tommy John experienced a mixed blessing in 1986. The 264-game winner showed he can still pitch *when he is healthy.* John's arm remains strong. But last season, he lost several turns in the rotation because of a strained lower back, a strained Achilles tendon and a broken left thumb suffered when he slipped off a bullpen mound in Oakland late in the season.

He hasn't lost his ability to make the ball sink and batters are still hammering that deceptive sinker into the ground for rally-squashing double plays.

After John gets ahead in the count with the sinker, he is able to come back with another at a different speed. John's second-best pitch is a sweeping curve.

John has difficulty fielding his position now. He has lost his quickness to age and injuries. It appears to be a strain for him merely to cover first base. Teams will test and torment him with bunts.

John is cagey and knows how to keep baserunners off balance. He does not throw over a lot, but will let loose with his best pickoff move at the perfect moment.

OVERALL:

He has developed a strong, if unlikely, ally in owner George Steinbrenner, who induced John to come to spring training this year with a $300,000 contract guaranteed whether he makes the staff or not.

Kaat: "With his experience, the lefthander has mastered the art of setting up hitters. I wouldn't bet against Tommy John being an effective starter even this year. The key is whether he can avoid injuries over a complete season. He didn't prove last year that he can, however."

NEW YORK YANKEES

RON KITTLE
DH/OF, No. 42
RR, 6'4", 212 lbs.
ML Svc: 5 years
Born: 1-5-58 in
Gary, IN

HITTING, BASERUNNING, FIELDING:

When Ron Kittle won Rookie of the Year honors and powered the Chicago White Sox to the American League West title in 1983, it appeared he might develop into one of the great home run hitters of his time. Kittle still clouts home runs but as an overall hitter, he is sorely lacking. He is finding out that, for any hitter who does not improve, the pitchers catch up to you.

Pitchers caught up to Kittle by learning he can be overpowered by high fastballs. He sees one after another and swings through them, producing an inordinate number of strike-outs, even for a slugger.

With his raw strength, it's a shame Kittle has not put in the time to make adjustments and get better at the plate.

Kittle is slow and does not help his cause with his limited ability as a baserunner.

As an outfielder, he never covered much ground. To make matters worse, a collision with Comiskey Park's left-field wall in April 1985 caused a shoulder injury that still hampers his throwing.

OVERALL:

Kaat: "His tremendous power puts 35-40 home runs within his reach if he is used as an everyday designated hitter. This is unlikely, however, because most teams are going to become frustrated with his rally-silencing strikeouts. Kittle is out of place with the Yankees, who can generate power at other positions."

BOBBY MEACHAM
SS, No. 20
SR, 6'1", 180 lbs.
ML Svc: 3 years
Born: 8-25-60 in
Los Angeles, CA

HITTING, BASERUNNING, FIELDING:

In one nightmarish season, Bobby Meacham went from the Yankees' starting shortstop to a player who may soon be fighting for his professional baseball life.

It seems the faltering career of Meacham lies in both his own hands and in his handling by the Yankees.

Manager Lou Piniella has acknowledged making mistakes in his handling of the gentle, soft-spoken shortstop. When Meacham was returned to Columbus in June last year, he was told to work on his fielding. But Meacham quickly found himself placed at an unfamiliar position: second base.

Meacham lost his confidence as a fielder. There were times he appeared almost to be hoping the ball would not come his way. No play in 1986 was routine for him.

Insiders say that Meacham never did his part to work and resisted instruction in spring training. It is up to Meacham to show he has a positive attitude and is willing to work on his throwing and catching skills.

Those abilities are essential for Meacham because major league pitchers with good stuff just about knock the bat out of his hands. Meacham lacks patience and will swing at terrible pitches. He will have a good day once in a while, but never pieces together near a streak.

Despite good speed, Meacham can be an unhappy adventure on the bases. He once lost a home run at Texas' Arlington Stadium because he passed the baserunner ahead of him. That's dumb.

OVERALL:

Kaat: "Time could be running out on Meacham. You don't get that many chances in this game. If he doesn't improve his defensive skills, he won't be around for long."

NEW YORK YANKEES

ROD SCURRY
LHP, No. 28
LL, 6'2", 195 lbs.
ML Svc: 7 years
Born: 3-17-56 in
Sacramento, CA

PITCHING, FIELDING:

Despite ability that could make him an outstanding reliever, Rod Scurry has never become a consistent major leaguer. His off-field problems of cocaine and alcohol abuse have been well-documented. He never appears to be in great physical condition and he has a laid back, almost sleepy, appearance on the mound that mirrors his low-key personality.

A first-round draft choice of the Pittsburgh Pirates in June 1974, Scurry's career remains alive because he has a curveball/fastball combination that can overpower lefthanded batters. Give Scurry an 0-2 count on a lefthanded batter and he's practically untouchable.

The key for Scurry is getting ahead in the count. Although the curve is clearly his best pitch, he would do well to gamble with his fastball early, looking to get ahead with that. He can then finish with the curve, which the batter is likely to chase if he's behind in the count.

Scurry often digs a hole when he does not have command of the curve and is forced to come in with the anticipated fastball.

Scurry has slow reflexes and is not a good fielder. His pickoff move is not good, either.

OVERALL:

Kaat: "If he puts a little more into his craft, becomes a better fielder and works on his control, he's got the ability to be whatever any club wants in a lefthanded reliever. He's got to apply himself and he knows that."

BOB SHIRLEY
LHP, No. 29
RL, 6'0", 180 lbs.
ML Svc: 10 years
Born: 6-25-54 in
Cushing, OK

PITCHING, FIELDING:

On every 10-man staff, there are starters, middle relievers, short relievers and--if a team is lucky--one pitcher who can do all of those things. That's where Bob Shirley fits in with the New York Yankees.

Shirley has the willingness to pitch in any capacity and is blessed with the arm to fill any need, although the workload can take its toll. The lefthander struggled due to a tired arm in the middle part of the 1986 season.

None of Shirley's pitches is exceptional but his repertoire is extensive enough that he can enter at any stage of the game and be effective. On occasion, Shirley's mental toughness allows him to be a game-saver, although this is hardly his best role. He has a knack for walking or surrendering a hit to the first batter or two he faces.

Shirley makes up for lack of velocity on his fastball, which averages in the mid-80s, with good movement. He owns a good curveball and an average slider.

Shirley is below average as a fielder; his pickoff move is only average.

He does have the penchant for the bizarre play, snagging smashes behind his back or through his legs. Once, he turned a double play on a line drive hit with such force it almost knocked him over.

OVERALL:

Shirley is a character in the clubhouse. He is popular wherever he plays and fits in immediately. His exploits help keep the club loose.

Kaat: "If Shirley was with a club that could give him one role and let him stick to it, he would be better off. He would be successful in that role."

NEW YORK YANKEES

TIM STODDARD
RHP, No. 43
RR, 6'7", 250 lbs.
ML Svc: 8 years
Born: 1-24-53 in
East Chicago, IN

PITCHING, FIELDING:

Tim Stoddard got new life when the New York Yankees acquired him from San Diego for Ed Whitson, a righthander who had become fearful about pitching at Yankee Stadium and *being* in New York. The Yankees would have dealt Whitson and his fat contract for no one and considered it a steal. That they received Stoddard proved to be more of a plus than they anticipated.

Stoddard had fallen out of favor in San Diego and was used infrequently, a situation that upset him and made it impossible for him to have good control when he was called upon. With the Yankees desperate for relief help, the hard-thrower got the work he needed and responded by firing strikes and getting outs.

Stoddard has the aggressiveness desired in a reliever. He throws fastball after good fastball and, less frequently, a slider. He doesn't change speeds much, but few relievers do.

Stoddard doesn't care about wins or saves. He only asks for a role on the staff and the opportunity to contribute.

Stoddard is a huge man who has difficulty moving well on the diamond. Still, he has good enough athletic ability to do an adequate job as a fielder in most instances.

Stoddard focuses all of his attention on the batter and is not distracted by baserunners. He does not throw over often. American League players will have to reacquaint themselves with his pickoff move.

Kaat: "Stoddard needs to find the right team and perhaps a patient manager. If the Yankees are that team, Stoddard could be an effective set-up man for stopper Dave Righetti."

GARY WARD
LF, No. 32
RR, 6'2", 202 lbs.
ML Svc: 6 years
Born: 12-6-53 in
Los Angeles, CA

HITTING, BASERUNNING, FIELDING:

Gary Ward went to arbitration before last season and lost. One of the major points brought out in the hearing was that his batting average could have been higher.

So Ward spent most of last season punching singles to right. It improved his average, all right, but he hit only five homers. The Rangers let him become a free agent and he was subsequently signed by the Yankees, who plan to platoon him in left field.

Ward likes the ball out over the plate. When he's thinking home run, he can drive a breaking ball if he is looking for it or homer to right on a fastball outside. He seems to have the most trouble handling low sliders.

He is a good, experienced baserunner and although he doesn't always look graceful in the outfield, he usually gets the job done.

OVERALL:

Last season, Ward's father passed away early in the season, his wife experienced a complicated pregnancy, and one morning in September he awoke with great pain caused by an abdominal blockage. His off-the-field worries prevented him from ever being able to get into a decent hitting groove.

OAKLAND A's

JOAQUIN ANDUJAR
RHP, No. 47
SR, 6'0", 180 lbs.
ML Svc: 11 years
Born: 12-21-52 in
San Pedro de Macoris,
Dominican Republic

PITCHING:

Because of his strong finish last season, Joaquin Andujar restored all of the hope Oakland held for him coming into the 1986 season. The hard-throwing righthander went 5-1 with six complete games in his last nine starts, thus easing the concern caused by an injury-filled first half and all of his idiosyncracies.

Among other bizarre incidents (which have come to be considered normal where Andujar is concerned), Andujar threatened to retire last season because he believed there was an umpiring conspiracy against him. He also spoke of demanding a trade if the A's didn't renegotiate his contract. In both cases, he quickly forgot his allegations.

On the mound, Andujar is no mystery. His only trick involves his release point. He may come at the hitter from over the top, three-quarters or sidearm. In any case, he will come at you *hard*. His fastball runs 88-90 MPH and he throws it regularly for six or seven innings. Off-speed stuff is a rarity for him; a change-up simply doesn't fit Andujar's style. He does have a slider and he gets by with two pitches because both have so much movement.

If he is struggling or tiring, Andujar will try for location. It is when he misses that the home runs come.

Smart and solid, Andujar never beats himself with walks or errors. But his temperament can work against him at times; his season-long suspicion that umpires were retaliating for the Denkinger Affair (World Series, Game 7, 1985--how could anyone forget?) led to great frustration and occasional lapses in Andujar's concentration last year.

1986 STATISTICS

W	L	ERA	G	GS	CG	SV	IP	H	R	ER	BB	SO
12	7	3.82	28	26	7	1	155.1	139	70	66	56	72

CAREER STATISTICS

W	L	ERA	G	GS	CG	SV	IP	H	R	ER	BB	SO
122	108	3.49	369	282	67	9	2014.1	1859	869	781	684	965

FIELDING:

Defensively, Andujar is among the best pitchers in the league. His pickoff move is extraordinarily quick and he isn't afraid to gun the ball to first, or any other base, for that matter. Fast is the only speed he knows.

His delivery leaves him in textbook position, legs and torso square to the plate and hands in a good fielding position. He's got a golden glove, even if nobody's ever awarded him one.

OVERALL:

The key to a successful Andujar is keeping him healthy and happy. Manager Tony LaRussa's arrival may have been the tonic for him last year. When things are going well, he is far more tolerant and tolerable.

Killebrew: "Leg problems and elbow pain hampered him most of last season. He's a proven big winner, so if he stays 'OK physically, there is little doubt that he could be a winner for this ballclub."

OAKLAND A's

HITTING:

No mortal could have lived up to the mountainous hype that preceded Jose Canseco's rookie season, but few will come as close as Canseco did in 1986. Until the final weeks of the season, Canseco was threatening to become the first rookie ever to lead a league in home runs and RBIs. He finished fourth in homers and second in RBIs.

Rookie of the Year voters could not overlook that, so they overlooked California's Wally Joyner, who out-hit Canseco by 50 points and clearly had a better all-around season.

An 0-for-40 drought (the longest in the majors last year) ending in mid-August and his 175 strikeouts took some of the shine off Canseco's season. Pitchers kept adjusting their approach to Canseco, and there were times when they always seemed to be one step ahead of him. Pitchers found that their greatest success came when they changed speeds and kept Canseco off balance. Breaking balls on the outside corner also gave him trouble, partly because of his exaggeratedly open stance.

Two years of weight-lifting have left Canseco with a Bunyanesque build and the power to match. Most telling: thirteen of his first 25 homers were to center field or right.

He handled himself well in a difficult situation; in addition to enduring the preseason hype, he felt umpires were going heavy on the rookie treatment. He expected that they would have a big strike zone for him but felt that they were picking on him more than any other rookie. He showed himself to be tough in the clutch; before the All-Star break, he batted .337 with men in scoring position.

His bat speed is such that long slumps seemed impossible; ground balls move through the infield before fielders can reach them. In fact, it was late July before Canseco went more than three games without a hit.

BASERUNNING:

Canseco moves exceptionally well for a big man. He stole 15 bases in 22 attempts last year. He has a graceful running motion that is

JOSE CANSECO
LF, No. 33
RR, 6'3", 210 lbs.
ML Svc: 1 year plus
Born: 7-2-64 in
Havana, Cuba

1986 STATISTICS

AVG	G	AB	R	H	2B	3B	HR	RBI	BB	SO	SB
.240	157	600	85	144	29	1	33	117	65	175	15

CAREER STATISTICS

AVG	G	AB	R	H	2B	3B	HR	RBI	BB	SO	SB
.249	186	696	101	173	32	1	38	130	69	206	16

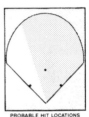

STRONG — VS. RHP   STRONG — VS. LHP   PROBABLE HIT LOCATIONS

often mistaken for a lack of hustle. Sometimes there is no mistake--he occasionally needs to be pushed.

FIELDING:

The A's would be best-advised to push Canseco defensively. He has all the makings of a great outfielder and, thus, has a legitimate chance of becoming one of the greatest players ever. He has good speed and a great arm, but he has yet to take a serious interest in the defensive part of his game. So his throwing is erratic and he tied for the league lead in outfield errors (14) last year, many of them dropped fly balls.

OVERALL:

Killebrew: "You know there's something here when fans come out to the ballpark early to watch him take batting practice. The first time I saw Canseco play was in Idaho Falls in 1982. He was a tall, skinny kid and weighed about 160 pounds. I've never seen anybody undergo a more dramatic physical change. He has as much power now as anybody in the game."

OAKLAND A's

HITTING:

Ron Cey continued to demonstrate his power swing last season despite being relegated to a more limited playing role than at any other point in his career. He has always been a fastball hitter who tries to pull everything, but Cey made a concerted effort to go to the opposite field in 1986 and managed to belt a few home runs to right field · as a result.

As they become older, many hitters become conscious of the speed of their swing and begin to fear their reflexes are slowing down. As a result, a hitter such as Cey over-prepares for the 90 MPH fastball and leaves himself vulnerable to the breaking ball by being unable to check himself quickly enough. Cubs hitting coach Billy Williams worked with Cey on convincing him that his reflexes are still there and to trust his own ability to adjust.

Both lefthanded and righthanded pitchers successfully pitch Cey away with breaking pitches and up-and-in with hard stuff. Cey has lost his clutch-hitting ability over the past three seasons. His home runs are all too often hit when the game's victor has already been decided. He is still, however, one of the strongest men in the game and is capable of 25-30 homers if allowed a proportionate number of at-bats.

BASERUNNING:

Cey has always been slow and his advancing age and the occurrence of nagging injuries make his movements look robot-like on the bases. He has trouble scoring from second on a single.

FIELDING:

His lack of range, and not his inability to make the routine play, makes Cey a defensive liability. He does not have a strong arm, yet he very often plays too deep at third base. His positioning leaves him especially vulnerable

RON CEY
3B, No. 10
RR, 5'9", 185 lbs.
ML Svc: 14 years
Born: 2-15-48 in Tacoma, WA

1986 STATISTICS

AVG	G	AB	R	H	2B	3B	HR	RBI	BB	SO	SB
.273	97	256	42	70	21	0	13	36	44	66	0

CAREER STATISTICS

AVG	G	AB	R	H	2B	3B	HR	RBI	BB	SO	SB
.261	2028	7058	965	1845	322	21	312	1128	990	1203	24

  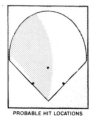

VS. RHP   VS. LHP   PROBABLE HIT LOCATIONS

to the bunt and its more adept and mercurial practitioners can almost be assured of a base hit when they lay one down. He seldom dives for balls to his left.

OVERALL:

Cey takes great pride in the fact that he is one of only a handful of big league third basemen to slug 300 home runs or more in his career, but at this point, it is undeniable that his overall game has suffered with age.

Rooker: "Cey has been at the crossroads for about three seasons. He has had productive seasons with the Los Angeles Dodgers and the Cubs, but may have his brightest future in the American League as a designated hitter.

"He is a hardworking athlete who keeps himself in the best possible shape all year-round, but weights and conditioning cannot stop time's erosion of the precise reactions necessary for this game."

OAKLAND A's

PITCHING:

Chris Codiroli finds himself in a familiar position this year: he must prove himself. Coming off elbow surgery, which ended his season in late June last year, the righthander came back healthy and, more important, proved himself worthy to new manager Tony LaRussa.

One of those skinny guys (160 pounds) with a whip-like arm, Codiroli can throw the fastball past big league batters. However, his velocity often drops into the mid-80s after the first run through the order, and, has to bear down the second time around.

Codiroli has two other pitches--a sinker and a slider--but he'll leave all of them high in the strike zone if he's tired. His home run ratio (one every 24 at-bats) was worst on the staff last year and his walks were up.

The slider, if it's working, eliminates most problems. Codiroli throws it with a three-quarters delivery and it's almost as tough on lefties as it is on righties. His best games come when the slider is in top form. Codiroli really could benefit by a better off-speed pitch.

There is a growing sentiment that Codiroli will never be better than a .500 pitcher. His stuff is better than that, but his career record (38-40) isn't.

FIELDING:

Codiroli prefers to think of himself as a jinxed pitcher, one often victimized by his offense, his defense or his bullpen. There's some validity to that, though it's not

CHRIS CODIROLI
RHP, No. 23
RR, 6'1", 160 lbs.
ML Svc: 4 years
Born: 3-26-58 in Oxnard, CA

1986 STATISTICS

W	L	ERA	G	GS	CG	SV	IP	H	R	ER	BB	SO
5	8	4.03	16	16	1	0	91.2	91	54	41	38	43

CAREER STATISTICS

W	L	ERA	G	GS	CG	SV	IP	H	R	ER	BB	SO
38	40	4.59	121	101	13	2	629.1	654	369	321	26	288

uncommon to see Codiroli play the leading role in his demise. He is one of the worst fielders in the game, and when he does manage to corral a ball, there is still the matter of throwing it. He has more errors (9) over two seasons than any other starter in the American League.

He is a poor athlete with a great arm.

OVERALL:

If Codiroli doesn't win a spot in the rotation this year, the A's will probably try to move him elsewhere. He has some value in the trade market (if he's healthy, that is) and his previous exiles to the Oakland bullpen have been met with resistance and ineffectiveness.

Killebrew: "The thing you've got to like about Codiroli is his competitiveness. He is a battler out there and doesn't like to let the hitter have an inch."

OAKLAND A's

HITTING:

Just one look, that's all it takes to believe Mike Davis can be a star, maybe a superstar. Long, lean and muscular, Davis is a splendid athlete. However, time is running out. Davis will be 28 years old in June and he has yet to meet expectations. He came close in 1985 (.287, 24HRs and 82 RBIs), but slipped in 1986. Batting .236 just before the break, Davis reached respectability by hitting .293 the rest of the way.

Like most lefthanders, Davis is a low-ball hitter. He likes the ball over the plate and he looks for pitchers to open with a fastball. They were doing a lot of that in April of '85, and Davis feasted, hitting nine homers and batting .325. Since then, pitchers have opted to jam Davis or feed him off-speed pitches away. Davis often will chase pitches out of the strike zone, lunging to the outside corner but seldom taking those pitches to left field. Davis is constantly reminding himself to be patient; you will frequently see Davis step out of the box and tell himself to relax.

At times, under both managerial regimes in '86, Davis found himself on the bench when the A's faced a lefthander. He insists he's an everyday player and did something to prove it (.299 vs. lefties last year).

BASERUNNING:

If Bob Uecker can joke about running a school for aspiring young catchers, Davis can joke about having one for baserunners. He was picked off four times last year, including once at second and once at third--and this was an *improvement* from 1985.

Physically, there is no problem. Davis has a sprinter's build and goes from first to third easily. He has finally gained a grip of the nuances of basestealing and was 27-for-31 in that department.

MIKE DAVIS
RF, No. 16
LL, 6'3", 185 lbs.
ML Svc: 7 years
Born: 6-11-59 in
San Diego, CA

1986 STATISTICS

AVG	G	AB	R	H	2B	3B	HR	RBI	BB	SO	SB
.268	142	489	77	131	28	3	19	55	34	91	27

CAREER STATISTICS

AVG	G	AB	R	H	2B	3B	HR	RBI	BB	SO	SB
.268	649	2051	300	549	111	12	62	263	153	356	102

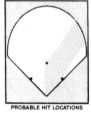

VS. RHP — STRONG   VS. LHP — STRONG   PROBABLE HIT LOCATIONS

FIELDING:

Davis has become a big play outfielder, but he still has trouble with fundamental things like establishing the proper angle on balls to the alley. He's short on instinct, so he often throws to the wrong base. His speed and his arm are well above average, however.

OVERALL:

There is no reason for Davis not to have a big year, but that's nothing that hasn't been said before. His strong second-half made a fan of Tony LaRussa, and that may help. Davis too often has felt the pressures of superstar potential.

Killebrew: "He's come a long way since those days as a skinny kid--and not just physically. He's really matured as a player. I don't think he'll do anything except continue to improve."

OAKLAND A's

HITTING:

If Alfredo Griffin had spent the last few seasons in New York (rather than in media outposts like Toronto and Oakland), he would be starting his third straight All-Star Game this July in Oakland.

As it is, Griffin has been on the All-Star team only once in his career (1984) and that selection was not so much an honor as it was a story; Griffin had come to watch the game as a guest of Damaso Garcia and was at the workout when Alan Trammell's sore arm left only one shortstop on the American League roster. Griffin had never had an All-Star year at the plate, except in 1979 when he won Rookie of the Year with a .287 average.

Suddenly, though, Griffin has emerged as an All-Star hitter. After five weak years (.241 composite), he has put together seasons of .270 and .285 and increased his run production by more than 25%.

How? For Griffin, the biggest key has been patience. He still doesn't have a lot of it, but he used to have *none* (he set a major league record in '84 by walking only four times in 423 trips). Consequently, he has been seeing more strikes. And Griffin can hit anything in the strike zone, from either side of the plate. He has a low-ball preference from both sides. He is best from the left (.301 to .254), mostly because he is so adept at taking fastballs and outside breaking balls to left field. What little power he has comes from the left side too.

Griffin will almost always make contact (he is the toughest to strike out among the A's). He's an excellent drag bunter who loves doing it with a man at third.

BASERUNNING:

Griffin has endeared himself to A's fans with a hustling, gambling style on the basepaths. Item: Griffin scores from second--on a walk (for details, see Mike Moore and Bob Kearney, the Seattle batterymen who momentarily fell asleep that night). Griffin further disrupts with a herky-jerky running motion. Last season, he had his career-high for stolen bases. Still, he has never really been able to read pitchers. He was caught stealing 16 times last year, a figure he had seen thrice previously.

ALFREDO GRIFFIN
SS, No. 3
SR, 5'11", 165 lbs.
ML Svc: 9 years
Born: 3-6-57 in
**   Santo Domingo,**
**   Dominican Republic**

1986 STATISTICS

AVG	G	AB	R	H	2B	3B	HR	RBI	BB	SO	SB
.285	162	594	74	169	23	6	4	50	35	52	33

CAREER STATISTICS

AVG	G	AB	R	H	2B	3B	HR	RBI	BB	SO	SB
.257	1228	4408	501	1133	160	63	19	335	194	390	135

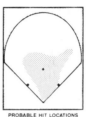

STRONG — VS. RHP   STRONG — VS. LHP   PROBABLE HIT LOCATIONS

FIELDING:

The most telling statement about Griffin's play afield was made by league managers, who voted him a Gold Glove in 1985 despite 30 errors (the second highest total in the league). Griffin has exceptional range to the hole and up the middle. Most of his errors come on the throw and many can be traced to his chronically sore right elbow.

OVERALL:

Strictly speaking, Griffin is Oakland's most valuable player. Without him, the A's go nowhere. The fear is not in his performance, but in his health; his medical problems ran the gamut last year and the elbow is a constant concern.

Killebrew: "He sure looks as though he enjoys the game. He has played the full 162 games four times in the last five years and he has a streak close to 400 straight games.

"He has given the A's everything he's got and has always been one of their brightest stars."

OAKLAND A's

PITCHING:

Moose Haas was on track to a dream season in 1986. The way it ended, however, surprised no one--least of all the people in Milwaukee. The Brewers had traded him to Oakland near the end of spring training, primarily because something always seemed to keep him from taking his share of innings.

For a while, though, Haas made the Brewers look so bad: he won his first six starts (including one at Milwaukee) and was 7-1 when his right shoulder stiffened up in late May at New York. The condition was later diagnosed as bursitis and Haas made only three more starts the rest of the season, going 10 weeks without at one point.

On the mound, Haas did little different from previous years. He was essentially the same pitcher who won only nine games in 1984 and eight games in '85. What made a difference for him in Oakland, however, was his bullpen, his defense and, most of all, his new club's offense. In his 12 starts, the A's scored 89 runs (7.4 per start). It's hard to lose with *that* many runs scored for you.

Haas disputes the notion that he was once a power pitcher. There is no argument now. A major arm injury in 1978 and, perhaps, his planned weight loss (from 190 to 165) in 1984 has left his fastball in the low 80s. Still, he sets hitters up well enough to sneak a third strike past them on occasion. He was averaging four strikeouts per game before the bursitis set in.

Haas' game plan, however, is to let batters put the ball in play. They often get only a piece of it.

He has a good break on his slider and m:od movement on his sinker. His change-up, which was his key pitch in his injury-shortened 13-3 season in 1983, still serves him well. Back then, he named it "The Dead Fish." The action he puts on the pitch makes it flop down through the strike zone.

Haas is always around the plate, and he moves his pitches in and out and up and down. He has great command of them: since 1978, he has averaged only slightly more than two walks per nine innings. He has become a pretty fast worker, and that complements his

MOOSE HAAS
RHP, No. 30
RR, 6'0", 170 lbs.
ML Svc: 10 years
Born: 4-22-56 in
Baltimore, MD

1986 STATISTICS

W	L	ERA	G	GS	CG	SV	IP	H	R	ER	BB	SO
7	2	2.74	12	12	1	0	72.1	58	23	22	19	40

CAREER STATISTICS

W	L	ERA	G	GS	CG	SV	IP	H	R	ER	BB	SO
98	81	3.97	257	243	56	2	1614.2	1660	777	712	427	840

game plan. The A's erred in only two of Haas' games.

FIELDING:

Haas is a good athlete. Magic and the martial art Tae Kwon Do are among his many interesting hobbies and he has achieved a high level of proficiency in each.

Defensively, he has a tendency to be overly wary of runners at first. At times, he will make repeated lobs to first. The effect on Haas' concentration is arguable. The effect on crowds outside Oakland is not--they heartily boo his attempts to pick off the runner at first base.

OVERALL:

Haas came to the majors with the tag of potential 20-game winner. He's never come closer than 16, but his new team and his home park make that a reasonable expectation. The A's didn't doubt the validity of Haas' injury (as Milwaukee had taken practice of doing), but as an incentive to good health, the A's have packed Haas' contract with bonuses for innings pitched.

Killebrew: "He's always been a guy who's around the plate and he knows how to pitch. If he's able to pitch enough, he could be a big winner."

OAKLAND A's

PITCHING:

Jay Howell's troubles started on one of the first days of spring training. He suffered a stress fracture of his right heel while covering first base during a fielding drill. That kept him from throwing for six weeks. May would bring a sore arm and two stays on the disabled list. In all, Howell missed 45 games last year because of tendinitis in his right elbow and forearm. In September, he missed 10 more with a strange virus that made him weak and shaky.

Unlike 1985, when he was a mound Rambo, Howell had precious few moments in '86 and disaster was always close behind. Typical of his season: one game after fanning five of six Mariners to preserve a 1-0 victory, Howell blew an eighth-inning lead and then a ninth-inning tie to finish April with a 4.91 ERA.

Howell's fastball--a 90 MPH howitzer delivered in a big overhand motion--rarely exploded last year the way it had in '85. Strikeouts came less frequently, too; even during his best stretch (14 consecutive scoreless outings in July-August), his strikeouts were down. His walks were up, mainly because he couldn't throw his curveball for strikes. That had been a big key in '85; knowing Howell could throw the curveball for strikes kept batters from focusing all their energy on his fastball. The league didn't hit Howell any better in 1986 (.262, up from .261) than in 1985, but his ERA rose 53 percentage points and moved beyond the range of respectability for a closer.

Some suspect Howell will never be as consistently overpowering as he was in 1984

JAY HOWELL
RHP, No. 50
RR, 6'3", 205 lbs.
ML Svc: 6 years
Born: 11-26-55 in Miami, FL

1986 STATISTICS

W	L	ERA	G	GS	CG	SV	IP	H	R	ER	BB	SO
3	6	3.38	38	0	0	16	53.1	53	23	20	23	42

CAREER STATISTICS

W	L	ERA	G	GS	CG	SV	IP	H	R	ER	BB	SO
26	26	3.97	202	21	2	52	390.1	399	184	172	146	312

and most of '85.

FIELDING:

Howell has pitched in 101 games for the A's and has yet to make an error. The rest of his defensive game is solid, but not at all extraordinary.

OVERALL:

Oh, for an injury-free spring! Howell barely threw in the '85 camp because of a sore arm. The A's got him some help by trading for Gene Nelson. However, they would strongly prefer that Howell stay healthy. The plan does not include push-ups and varied other boot-camp activities, as it did last spring. The push-ups likely contributed to Howell's arm problems and he seems to be a more effective pitcher when he's heavy.

OAKLAND A's

HITTING:

Reggie surprised a lot of people last year with his willingness, and ability, to adapt to being 40 years old. Until the experiment began to bore him, he cut down on his swing and became a more of a contact hitter and carried a .300 average into July. He was patient at the plate, drawing more walks (92) than in any season since 1969. Reggie's positive adjustments enabled him to produce enough to earn a farewell contract.

Jackson no longer wastes an entire at-bat looking for a low inside pitch he can pull. He is willing to slap pitches away into left for singles, which leaves him still able to adjust and drive balls to center field, where most of his power now is concentrated. Off-speed pitches ruin his timing, and as a result he's become less effective deep in the count.

He can't touch a breaking ball on the outside corner from lefthanders, mainly because he sees so few of them (71 at-bats against LHP last season, with no homers).

Reggie no longer means *clutch*. Last year, he managed only a .225 average with men in scoring position. But he remains in superb condition and is still a threat to explode any time, as he did by slugging seven homers last September during the Angels' pennant stretch.

BASERUNNING:

Since he has been limited to being a platooned DH, running the bases is as close as Jackson comes to feeling like a complete ballplayer. It shows in his behavior, as he is prone to run amok, aware of the chance to motivate the team with the unexpected.

Too often, though, he is like a runaway Mack truck, ignoring coaches and taking rash gambles. Considering his kamikaze landings, it's amazing he hasn't been seriously injured while sliding.

A tribute to his professional pride, in California he was always one of the fastest men down the line to first. He runs all-out, as evidenced by the fact he grounded into only 14 double plays last season.

REGGIE JACKSON
DH, No. 44
LL, 6'0", 208 lbs.
ML Svc: 20 years
Born: 5-18-46 in
Wyncote, PA

1986 STATISTICS

AVG	G	AB	R	H	2B	3B	HR	RBI	BB	SO	SB
.241	132	419	65	101	12	2	18	58	92	115	1

CAREER STATISTICS

AVG	G	AB	R	H	2B	3B	HR	RBI	BB	SO	SB
.263	2705	9528	1509	2510	449	48	548	1659	1343	2500	226

  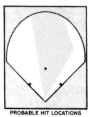

VS. RHP VS. LHP PROBABLE HIT LOCATIONS

FIELDING:

Basically, Jackson no longer need worry about his ability as a fielder. He made only four outfield appearances last year. But he still enjoys the involvement of playing defense and can play it aggressively. But only in an emergency, please.

OVERALL:

As a player, Jackson at this stage would be more valuable if he were a better pinch-hitter. But he has never been effective off the bench, since he usually needs a couple of at-bats to adjust to pitchers. His presence can stimulate a winning atmosphere, but it can also divide a losing clubhouse.

Killebrew: "Reggie's been a winner everywhere. He's been one of the American League's greatest assets for two decades. He tried to overplay last year because he wanted to win so much. Nonetheless, he still has another outstanding year left in him."

OAKLAND A's

HITTING:

Young Stanley Javier made two visits to Oakland in 1986 and at no time did he show himself to be capable of hitting big league pitching. The 20-year-old son of former St. Louis Cardinal Julian Javier came up when Dwayne Murphy went down with a disk problem and batted .185 in 34 games. The A's brought him back in September and he batted .229 in nine games.

Javier is a switch-hitter who has problems as a lefty with the inside pitch and as a righty with the outside pitch. He was frequently overpowered by righthanded pitchers, fanning 18 times in 64 at-bats. He was more apt to make contact from the right side, but not for hits: he batted .160 righthanded and .234 lefthanded. Javier sprays the ball to all fields. The A's would like to see him pull the ball more often.

It may just be a matter of confidence and adjustment for Javier. He was an excellent leadoff hitter at Triple-A (.327), even after his first trip to Oakland, and he had a big winter in the Dominican Republic, hitting close to .400 and winning the batting crown.

BASERUNNING:

He's fast: Javier stole 61 bases at Double-A in 1985 and was 8-for-8 with the A's last year. He wasn't on the bases enough to reveal much else, however.

FIELDING:

If nothing else, Javier showed on his first visit that he could play the field. He ran down balls in the gaps, handled balls over his head fairly well and unveiled an exceptionally

STAN JAVIER
OF, No. 28
SR, 6'0", 180 lbs.
ML Svc: 1 year
Born: 9-1-65 in
**   San Pedro de Macoris,**
**   Dominican Republic**

1986 STATISTICS

AVG	G	AB	R	H	2B	3B	HR	RBI	BB	SO	SB
.202	59	114	13	23	8	0	0	8	16	27	8

CAREER STATISTICS

AVG	G	AB	R	H	2B	3B	HR	RBI	BB	SO	SB
.198	66	121	14	24	8	0	0	8	16	28	8

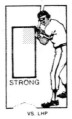
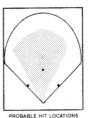

VS. RHP   VS. LHP   PROBABLE HIT LOCATIONS

strong arm. He also showed some moxie for a young rookie, taking rein (albeit a loose rein) of the outfield after Murphy's injury brought instant chaos to the group. The defensive part of Javier's game is already at a big league level and he should get even better as he gains knowledge of the league's hitters.

OVERALL:

He's ready to contribute as an extra man--if the A's are willing to risk his development. He should spend some more time at Triple-A, playing every day and building his confidence as a hitter.

OAKLAND A's

HITTING:

When the A's decided to re-sign Dave Kingman for the 1986 season, their rationale was that 30 homers and 91 RBIs were too much to cast aside. Kingman bettered those numbers in '86 (35 homers and 94 RBIs) but guess what? The A's cast him aside anyway, choosing not to offer him a contract for 1987. Money was not the deciding factor. The A's were looking for two things Kingman absolutely cannot provide: leadership and hits.

In his 15-year career, Kingman has never spent more than three seasons with the same team and it's always the same old story. His first season is a honeymoon, on the field and with the media. The second season marks a decline in both areas. And the third season? Kingman batted .210 in 1986 (down 58 points from his first year in Oakland), put together the worst on-base percentage (.255) in the majors and immersed himself in controversy by sending a live rat to a Bay Area reporter in the press box at Kansas City. Some say the decision to dump Kingman was made that night by team ownership, but Kingman's on-field performance was dubious enough anyway.

Kingman is free-swinger with a big uppercut. He likes the ball down and his ultimate preference is down-and-in, as Bobby Witt learned one June night in Texas. The Ranger rookie put a 90 MPH fastball in that vicinity, and Kingman drove it deep into the black sky. A high fastball will beat Kingman if thrown at the right time, but breaking balls are much safer. He is extremely vulnerable to pitches on the outside corner and is prone to chasing ones wide of the strike zone.

He developed an attraction to the ambush bunt last year and, for a while, was picking his spots well.

BASERUNNING:

Kingman is a smart baserunner, but that only goes so far when you're slow and getting slower. It's pretty much station-to-station with him, but he will surprise when teams

DAVE KINGMAN
DH, No. 26
RR, 6'6", 215 lbs.
ML Svc: 16 years
Born: 12-21-48 in
Pendleton, OR

1986 STATISTICS

AVG	G	AB	R	H	2B	3B	HR	RBI	BB	SO	SB
.210	144	561	70	118	19	0	35	94	33	126	3

CAREER STATISTICS

AVG	G	AB	R	H	2B	3B	HR	RBI	BB	SO	SB
.236	1941	6677	901	1575	240	25	442	1210	608	1816	85

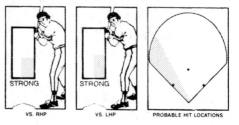

VS. RHP   VS. LHP   PROBABLE HIT LOCATIONS

aren't careful.

FIELDING:

Believe it or not, Kingman was Oakland's Opening Day first baseman in 1986. He made two fielding errors that day and never returned to the position after a second (and less eventful) start in mid-April. Nor will he. It would be wise to pack the glove away forever.

OVERALL:

Kingman can still hit home runs and, in a place like the Seattle Kingdome, he could make history. In the Kingdome, Kingman's career numbers project to 51 homers and 119 RBIs for a full season--and that doesn't count road games.

Killebrew: "Nobody has more power. He can go on a streak that will carry a team for a long time. If he gets enough at-bats, you know he's going to put some numbers on the board. You know he's going to hit home runs and drive in runs."

OAKLAND A's

HITTING:

Whatever the numbers, Carney Lansford's 1986 season must be judged a success because he did not suffer a serious injury. He managed to get through through a full season for only the second time in five years.

But real success to Lansford is batting .300, something he did for four straight years until 1985. He fell short of the mark again in '86, but he hit 19 homers last year, tying his career high. Though Lansford has no explanation for his power exhibition last year, there seems to have been a trade-off between average and power. In 1985, when the string ended with a .277 average, Lansford was on pace to a 20-homer season. Of course, a broken wrist took care of that.

Lansford is an excellent contact hitter who can spray line drives to any field. He likes the ball over the plate. He's primarily a fastball hitter, but he can hit the breaking ball with authority. Pitchers try to keep the ball away from him; Lansford counters with a one-armed, lunging swing that he has been practicing since his years in Boston. There is no set way to pitch Lansford because he always adjusts. He's patient and selective, though he some times seems to lose those qualities in key situations.

No Oakland hitter has more respect around the league than Lansford. As an example, in the ninth inning of a tie game last year, Royals Manager Dick Howser walked Lansford and decided to take his chances against rookie slugging sensastion Jose Canseco.

BASERUNNING:

Lansford is not fast, but he is aggressive and sneaky on the bases. He stole 16 bases last year, his highest total since 1979. He does not foul up. Like every part of his game, this part is solid if unspectacular.

FIELDING:

Lansford was rankled when the A's first

CARNEY LANSFORD
3B, No. 4
RR, 6'2", 195 lbs.
ML Svc: 9 years
Born: 2-7-57 in
San Jose, CA

1986 STATISTICS

AVG	G	AB	R	H	2B	3B	HR	RBI	BB	SO	SB
.284	151	591	80	168	16	4	19	72	39	51	16

CAREER STATISTICS

AVG	G	AB	R	H	2B	3B	HR	RBI	BB	SO	SB
.292	1139	4478	634	1307	212	30	113	563	319	524	108

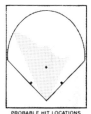

STRONG STRONG PROBABLE HIT LOCATIONS

VS. RHP VS. LHP

mentioned the possibility of him doing some time at first base. But he played it solidly and came to like it. Despite playing 60 games at a foreign position, Lansford made only six errors in 160 games last year.

Ultimately, he will become a full-time first baseman, because his range is small and his arm is often sore. At third, he has an annoying habit of checking the seams before he throws the ball.

OVERALL:

Lansford is quietly intense and takes losing hard. He became something of a leader last year when Dwayne Murphy was injured and the team was crashing. On the field, Lansford has had to play too great a role for the A's to be successful. He cannot carry a team, but he can do most anything short of that.

Killebrew: "The main thing with Carney is that he has to remain healthy. If he does, you can count on him having a good year, because he such a good, solid hitter. He'll do well defensively, too, no matter which position he's at."

OAKLAND A's

HITTING:

Mark McGwire's future seemed to be merging with the present last summer. For a few wonderful days in late August, McGwire's presence in the 1987 Opening Day lineup was almost guaranteed.

Now, after an off-season that included his unapproved departure from winter ball and Oakland's acquisition of Ron Cey, McGwire will be hard-pressed to make the early April party.

The excitement about McGwire was already in recession at the end of the season. By September, it was known that the holes in McGwire's bat and glove still might be too big for the big leagues. McGwire struck out 18 times in 57 tries for the A's last season and he went 6-for-39 after a wild start: three days after he became the ninth member of the 1984 Olympic team to reach the big leagues, McGwire became one of the only players in history to homer to dead center at Tiger Stadium.

Some members of the Oakland organization think McGwire could be the next Mike Schmidt. McGwire hits the ball hard to all fields; in addition to his 26 homers last season, he had 37 doubles (and he does not run well).

He has a good idea of the strike zone, but his lack of patience sometimes provokes him to chase the outside pitch. McGwire likes the ball pitched high in the strike zone. The big swing hurts him most often on breaking balls and off-speed stuff. It is best to keep the heat off the plate.

FIELDING:

McGwire made six errors in 36 chances for Oakland, the second-worst fielding percentage (.833) in the league among players with 10 or more games. (OK, the answer is Baltimore's Rex Hudler, who handled only five chances all year and erred on the one of them for a .800 percentage.)

MARK McGWIRE
3B, No. 25
RR, 6'5", 215 lbs.
ML Svc: less than one year
Born: 10-1-63 in
Pomona, CA

1986 STATISTICS
AVG	G	AB	R	H	2B	3B	HR	RBI	BB	SO	SB
.189	18	53	10	10	1	0	3	9	4	18	0

CAREER STATISTICS
AVG	G	AB	R	H	2B	3B	HR	RBI	BB	SO	SB
.189	18	53	10	10	1	0	3	9	4	18	0

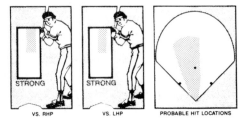

VS. RHP   VS. LHP   PROBABLE HIT LOCATIONS

Actually, the hole is not in McGwire's glove. Most of his errors come on the throw, and that probably stems from having moved from first base just two years ago. Thinking that practice makes better, the A's sent McGwire to winter ball after the '86 season ended; he came home quickly--against Oakland's wishes--and returned with only bad stats.

OVERALL:

Manager Tony LaRussa won't penalize McGwire for leaving winter ball, but the acquisition of Ron Cey makes McGwire's chances of making the club less definite.

Killebrew: "It is hard to overlook the fact that McGwire has a penchant for big hits--his 10 hits produced 16 runs--and there's no better way to win friends and influence managers than that."

OAKLAND A's

HITTING:

Maybe it wasn't such a great thing that Dwayne Murphy hit 33 home runs in 1984. Murphy hasn't come close to that since--and it's not for a lack of trying. He has fallen in love with the long ball, and that single-mindedness has hurt his game.

Since '84, Murphy has hit only 29 homers and, more disconcerting to him, driven in only 98 runs. A serious back condition (a herniated disk) cost him 50 games last year, but his RBI total has suffered mostly from a lack of hits.

Murphy has never been one to hit for average, but his home run obsession has forced him away from things like the drag bunt and opposite field hitting. Occasionally, he'll slap an off-speed pitch to left field, but he's not satisfied with such hits and will take them only in dire circumstances.

Murphy has become a free-swinger and pitchers exploit his big stroke. Righthanders jam him with fastballs. Murphy can't get the fat of the bat on the ball, which leads to a preponderance of routine grounders to second base. Lefthanders like to fool Murphy with breaking balls and they usually do; Murphy hit .229 against lefties in '86, and that was an improvement from '85.

BASERUNNING:

There was a time when Murphy could run (he stole 26 bases in 1982), but chronic foot problems have forced him to shelve this part of his game. However, he still has some speed and, mixed with his smarts, he is able to take advantage of certain situations.

FIELDING:

Murphy's tools have eroded badly and yet he remains among the game's finest outfielders. His deep knowledge of opposing hitters compensates for his loss of speed. His arm, once a rifle, has now become terribly weak, but he counters that with a super-quick release and accuracy. He still plays as shallow

DWAYNE MURPHY
CF, No. 21
LR, 6'1", 185 lbs.
ML Svc: 9 years
Born: 3-18-55 in
Merced, CA

1986 STATISTICS

AVG	G	AB	R	H	2B	3B	HR	RBI	BB	SO	SB
.252	98	329	50	83	10	3	9	39	56	80	3

CAREER STATISTICS

AVG	G	AB	R	H	2B	3B	HR	RBI	BB	SO	SB
.248	1131	3828	575	948	121	20	145	528	636	822	95

  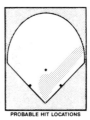

VS. RHP — STRONG   VS. LHP — STRONG   PROBABLE HIT LOCATIONS

as anybody in the league and he still gets to almost everything hit over his head. The time he missed with the back injury kept him from winning his seventh straight Gold Glove last year.

OVERALL:

For years Murphy has been the team's one steadying influence; while he was in traction last year, the A's went 17-40 and fell from second place to last. However, his offensive problems and the development of Stan Javier could relegate Murphy to a platoon system in center field.

Killebrew: "Even now, I think he's one of the four best center fielders in the league. As far as the top spot, it's a toss-up between him, Puckett, Pettis and Henderson.

"As a hitter, it seems as though he's got it in his mind that he's going to swing and, as a result, he's not as selective as he could be."

OAKLAND A's

PITCHING:

Gene Nelson has filled a variety of roles with a variety of teams in his major league career and has developed the reputation as being an overachiever. He has average stuff and relies on smarts and savvy for success.

Nelson has been a starter when called on, but is best suited to long relief. Nelson is more comfortable facing righthanded batters. His fastball is deceptive (in the mid-80s) and he can also throw the split-finger fastball and sinker.

Lefthanders can hit him hard if they wait on his fastball. Nelson's change-up can catch a batter off-guard, but his curveball has never been a strength and he doesn't throw enough strikes with it. Nelson is fine in long relief, but gets noticeably tired and that's why he never found success as a starting pitcher.

He is very crafty at his trade, especially at going after batters he thinks he can get out. But he needs to be watched closely when runners get on base. He has the ability to work out of jams but can get rattled which leads to him getting hit hard.

Nelson is good at avoiding the gopher ball, especially against righthanders, and his strikeouts-to-walks ratio has always been outstanding.

FIELDING:

Nelson has usually been a decent fielder

GENE NELSON
RHP, No. 30
RR, 6'0", 175 lbs.
ML Svc: 6 years
Born: 12-3-60 in
Tampa, FL

1986 STATISTICS

W	L	ERA	G	GS	CG	SV	IP	H	R	ER	BB	SO
6	6	3.85	54	1	0	6	114.2	118	52	49	41	70

CAREER STATISTICS

W	L	ERA	G	GS	CG	SV	IP	H	R	ER	BB	SO
28	34	4.54	160	59	6	10	529.2	545	287	267	229	305

but was especially sharp last season. He worked on his follow-through coming off the mound; he can make the throw to any base.

He has a quick move to first base for a righthander and is good at covering the bag.

OVERALL:

Nelson is a reliable long relief pitcher who may never be a superstar, but he's a quality major leaguer. His stamina isn't really a factor as long as he's not starting.

Killebrew: "He's been around the game for a while and is good at working in long relief. He gives his all to the game."

OAKLAND A's

HITTING:

Rob Nelson had only a fair chance of making the Oakland A's major league roster in 1986--until Bruce Bochte decided to retire last winter. Now Nelson stands as the most qualified candidate at first base--and the A's should find that a bit worrisome, given Nelson's gross lack of experience.

Little can be told from Nelson's visit to Oakland last September; he played in only two games at first base and stepped to the plate just nine times. His minor league stats are interesting, however. At the Double-A level, he was a power hitter (32 home runs during the 1985 season) who, in the typical style of sluggers, hit for a low batting average (.232). Promoted to Triple-A for the 1986 run, Nelson seemed to adjust well to the league's more advanced pitchers and lifted his average by 50 points. Perhaps as an effect of making better contact, his power output suffered, as he hit just 20 home runs in the minors last year.

Nelson has a pretty lefthanded swing. But it has a big hole in it--he strikes out too much (395 Ks over the last three years). He is a fastball hitter with much to learn about breaking balls and off-speed pitches. Overall, he also lacks patience at the plate. Fastball pitchers can get him up-and-away, but he will feast on offerings from the waist down.

His performance in the minors against lefties was encouraging.

BASERUNNING:

As a baserunner, Nelson is painfully slow. He is a big man who has the smarts, but not the speed, to take an extra base. His doubles have to go to the gaps.

FIELDING:

As a first base prospect, Nelson appears to have good hands and a better-than-average arm. But his range is seriously limited,

ROB NELSON
1B, No. 49
LL, 6'4", 215 lbs.
ML Svc: *less than one year*
Born: *5-17-64 in Pasadena, CA*

1986 STATISTICS

AVG	G	AB	R	H	2B	3B	HR	RBI	BB	SO	SB
.222	5	9	1	2	1	0	0	0	1	4	0

CAREER STATISTICS

AVG	G	AB	R	H	2B	3B	HR	RBI	BB	SO	SB
.222	5	9	1	2	1	0	0	0	1	4	0

VS. RHP

VS. LHP

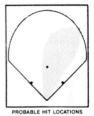
PROBABLE HIT LOCATIONS

particularly to his right. He will be able to get to most balls hit near him, but is not likely to stop those lefthanded shots headed to right field.

His size makes him an excellent target for throws from the infield. Nelson seems fairly adept at scooping throws out of the dirt.

OVERALL:

The A's sent Nelson to winter ball in the hope that he would allay one of their concerns: first base. Instead, he batted below expectations and had only two homers in his first 61 at-bats.

The acquisition of Ron Cey cuts the A's some slack. If Nelson can't make it, Carney Lansford will move to first base this season full-time with Cey and others taking over at third base. Another trade is not out of the question.

OAKLAND A's

PITCHING:

Steve Ontiveros is excellent fodder for those who believe in the sophomore jinx. As a rookie in 1985, Ontiveros pitched 56 innings before his ERA reached 1.00 and, even after some September carnage, American League hitters finished with only a .174 batting average against him, the best in the league. Last year, Ontiveros got hit at a .265 clip and by June 3, he had given up twice as many homers (8) as he had in all of '85.

Those who don't buy the jinx theory attribute Ontiveros' crash to the condition of his arm and the condition of the Oakland bullpen for much of the season. Injuries to Jay Howell and others put the bullpen in an almost-constant state of chaos. Ontiveros spent much time out of his customary role as a set-up man and did not react well to his necessity-induced promotion into Howell's job as stopper. That situation probably won't repeat itself in '86, but what about Ontiveros' arm problems? He had shoulder pain early and late, missing six weeks after the All-Star break.

When he's feeling just right, Ontiveros can beat hitters all day with just two pitches, a fastball and a slider. Trouble is, there are so many times when he doesn't feel just right. The A's feel he has much to learn about pitching effectively under less-than-ideal circumstances.

Ontiveros usually comes overhand, though he will drop to a three-quarters delivery at times. His fastball falls into the sneaky-fast category. Because of his size and his fluid delivery, it's a surprise to see consistent clockings in the upper 80s. His slider breaks sharply and is most effective against righthanded hitters. He can beat them with that or use it to set up his fastball, which he isn't afraid to bring in on the batter's hands.

STEVE ONTIVEROS
RHP, No. 53
RR, 6'0", 180 lbs.
ML Svc: 2 years
Born: 3-5-61 in
Tularosa, NM

1986 STATISTICS

W	L	ERA	G	GS	CG	SV	IP	H	R	ER	BB	SO
2	2	4.71	46	0	0	10	72.2	72	40	38	25	54

CAREER STATISTICS

W	L	ERA	G	GS	CG	SV	IP	H	R	ER	BB	SO
3	5	3.30	85	0	0	18	147.1	117	57	54	44	90

He is best when he stays around the corners and keeps the ball down. Oftentimes in '86, he could do neither.

FIELDING:

He is another Karate Kid (along with Moose Haas and Dave Stewart), so there is no questioning Ontiveros' quality as an athlete. He shows good quickness and good hands and is a fundamentally sound defensive player.

OVERALL:

At this time a year ago, Ontiveros loomed as a perennial and vital cog in the Oakland system. Now, with durable Gene Nelson and, possibly, Dave Stewart, joining the bullpen, Ontiveros may become expendable. He'll need to show some things in spring to keep his job as Jay Howell's set-up man.

Killebrew: "He had some troubles last year, but he's a pitcher with good stuff. He's also a real competitor. He knows how to finish a hitter off."

OAKLAND A's

HITTING:

As June approached last season, Tony Phillips was the right choice for the American League All-Star team. The voting public didn't agree, however, and in the end they were right. Batting .345 in late May, Phillips went into an incredible tailspin and was at home with a .259 average when the All-Star Game came on TV. Phillips had shown little sign of recovery when his season ended with a leg injury in mid-August.

Phillips now has had three near-full seasons with the A's and, much to their disappointment, his composite for that time is a .257 average. Neither that nor the little switch-hitter's problems from the left side of the plate will evoke thoughts of making Phillips a platoon player, however: he is Oakland's most legitimate leadoff hitter.

Despite his inadequacies, he had a productive debut in that role; he was among the league leaders in runs until shortly before his injury; he also had 52 RBIs.

Phillips continues to be a much better hitter from the right side (.321, compared to .228 from the left). Much of his problem as a righthanded hitter stems from a desire to do too much. During the bad times last year, he started uppercutting his swing, and the result was a lot of fly balls. This also fed his strikeout total (82), which is too high for a leadoff hitter with his power.

BASERUNNING:

Phillips is exceptionally quick and seems to have the tools of a big basestealer. But he isn't one. He got 15 last year, but he also got caught 10 times. He doesn't read pitchers well, though that probably can be traced to his inactivity the last two seasons. Also, his foot injury may have held him back, physically and/or mentally.

FIELDING:

Phillips has cut down on his errors, but his .976 fielding percentage in 1986 still ranked second-to-last among the league's regular second basemen (Willie Randolph, at .972, was last). Phillips has excellent range in all

TONY PHILLIPS
2B, No. 2
SR, 5'10", 160 lbs.
ML Svc: 4 years
Born: 11-9-59 in Atlanta, GA

1986 STATISTICS

AVG	G	AB	R	H	2B	3B	HR	RBI	BB	SO	SB
.256	118	441	76	113	14	5	5	52	76	82	15

CAREER STATISTICS

AVG	G	AB	R	H	2B	3B	HR	RBI	BB	SO	SB
.257	502	1546	226	397	64	15	17	149	191	298	46

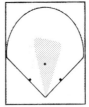

VS. RHP   VS. LHP   PROBABLE HIT LOCATIONS

directions, making him and Alfredo Griffin an exciting middle-infield combo.

They are less impressive as a double play combo; the A's turned only 120 double plays last year, easily the worst mark in the league. Phillips' absence surely had some part in that, but not all. He needs work on making the pivot and, again, his inactivity and his foot injury may have affected him in this regard.

OVERALL:

Phillips still hasn't played a full season at second base; it is possible that a 162-game stint there would improve him naturally.

Killebrew: "At the plate, Phillips needs practice. He should be content to make contact and stop swinging for extra bases. If he remains healthy, this will be a telling year for him.

"Last year was his first opportunity as a leadoff hitter. It takes time for some players to adjust to a specific role in the lineup; I think his experience at hitting No. 1 will pay off this season in his overall hitting."

OAKLAND A's

PITCHING:

The A's broke a promise to themselves last May when they began using Jose Rijo in relief. Shuttling the talented, but easily affected, righthander from the rotation was seen as the Yankees' big mistake in 1984. But the A's saw no better choice than to put Rijo in the bullpen *both times* relief ace Jay Howell went down with arm problems.

As a result of the A's indiscretion, the worst-possible scenario was realized: Rijo was a bust in the bullpen (0-4, 8.53 ERA), and the psychological fallout retarded his development for the rest of the season.

Rijo is experiencing all the problems of a young and overpowering pitcher. He is wild and not wise. The wildness lessened after the arrival last season of new pitching coach Dave Duncan. Rijo's three-quarters delivery was adjusted and his release point became more consistent. He still has a tendency to rush his pitches and his knowledge of pitching is elementary, at best. Too often, he ignores his fastball and tries to get cute with the slider. And equally as often, his second-best pitch gets beat.

Rijo is sometime able to overcome all shortcomings, however, because of a blazing fastball (89-92 MPH) that can last the full nine innings at just about peak velocity. He also has a great slider; it was the key pitch in his 16-strikeout performance at Seattle last April. He was working on a change-up, but increased levels of command and confidence are needed before it becomes a useful pitch.

Rijo shows a disturbing proficiency for allowing runs immediately after getting some. He readily admits to frequent lapses in concentration.

FIELDING:

Rijo has a good move to first base, primarily

JOSE RIJO
RHP, No. 38
RR, 6'2", 195 lbs.
ML Svc: 2 years
Born: 5-13-65 in
San Cristobal,
Dominican Republic

1986 STATISTICS

W	L	ERA	G	GS	CG	SV	IP	H	R	ER	BB	SO
9	11	4.65	39	26	4	1	193.2	172	116	100	108	176

CAREER STATISTICS

W	L	ERA	G	GS	CG	SV	IP	H	R	ER	BB	SO
17	23	4.45	75	40	4	3	319.2	303	182	158	169	288

due to the many hours he spends with Andujar, his self-appointed mentor. Rijo also has heard a lot of advice about his follow-through, because it kills him on almost every ball hit to the mound. He lands so far off to the right and his posture is so torqued that he's unable to stop any ball not hit near his glove. The problem is, fixing this has been said to have an effect on his velocity--and that's a no-no with this fireballer.

OVERALL:

One gets the feeling Rijo might always be an all-or-nothing pitcher, a guy who'll fan 16 one night and **walk eight** another. But youth and vast potential **dem**and patience and the A's are trying.

Killebrew: "He's young. He needs improvement on his control. With the stuff he has, he could throw a perfect game, but he has to get the ball over the plate. He needs to realize how many hitters *can't* hit his fastball--and who they are."

OAKLAND A's

PITCHING:

The story of Dave Stewart's 1986 season is best told by two scenes. In May, he was out on the streets, job-hunting after being released by the Phillies. In December, he was signing a multi-year contract, the first for an Oakland player since 1983.

How was it that Stewart, winless for 22 months, went into the final four weeks with a 9-1 record in only 12 starts ? He developed a new pitch. Actually, the forkball had been in Stewart's repertoire for some time. He just didn't use it, for lack of confidence in the pitch and for love of the fastball.

After first attributing his turnaround to a long-awaited change in luck, Stewart credited pitching coach Dave Duncan for talking him into employing the forkball. Fact: Stewart was 0-0 with a 4.85 ERA before Duncan arrived with now-Oakland manager Tony LaRussa in July. He was 9-5 with a 3.46 ERA after their arrival. Some of that is merely a reflection of use. Stewart saw little meaningful action in the pre-LaRussa days, but won over the new regime with an emergency-start victory over Roger Clemens at Fenway in LaRussa's first game.

The forkball gives Stewart a change-up to mix in with his fastball. His is an underrated fastball. Batters had been sitting on it and hitting it for so long that nobody seemed to care anymore that Stewart can throw 90 MPH for as many as seven innings. Stewart also has a respectable slider and a curveball. When he's tired or struggling, he's likely to mix in all four pitches. He's still most apt to go with the heat when he needs a strike.

Stewart can start or relieve. He pitched in both roles last year and expresses no preference. With Vida Blue now joining the rotation, the A's may put Stewart back in the bullpen. He likes a lot of innings and is able to pitch three days in a row.

FIELDING:

Stewart's muscular build precludes any

DAVE STEWART
RHP, No. 34
RR, 6'2", 200 lbs.
ML Svc: 6 years
Born: 2-19-57 in
Oakland, CA

1986 STATISTICS

W	L	ERA	G	GS	CG	SV	IP	H	R	ER	BB	SO
9	5	3.74	29	17	4	0	149.1	137	67	62	65	102

CAREER STATISTICS

W	L	ERA	G	GS	CG	SV	IP	H	R	ER	BB	SO
39	40	3.90	235	72	9	19	749.1	711	356	325	302	473

questions about his athletic ability. But, for proof, we give an example of his Tae Kwon Do proficiency (July 1, 1986): Cleveland manager charges the mound. Stewart comes to meet him. Corrales attempts a karate kick. Stewart stops the kick by catching his foot with one hand and delivers a right cross that drops Corrales to the ground. End of discussion.

With a (baseball) glove, Stewart is only slightly less impressive: cat-like quickness on comebackers and tough to burn with a bunt out front. Strangely, his only error of the year cost him victory No. 10 on the second-to-last day of the season.

OVERALL:

Stewart went 0-4 with a 4.62 ERA in the final four weeks of 1986, so the hardcore skeptics remain. The A's believe they saw the real Stewart in July and August.

Killebrew: "Here's a guy who finally matured and, with that new pitch, you've got to think he's could have another solid year for the A's."

OAKLAND A's

HITTING:

Now Mickey Tettleton *really* knows how Mike Heath felt. All during the 1985 season, Tettleton spoke sympathetically of Heath, whose job was slowly but so surely being taken away. It was being given to Tettleton. These are the fruits of Mickey's first season as Oakland's regular catcher: the A's spent the winter talking to Rich Gedman and talking about Terry Steinbach, a Double-A slugger who had been a third baseman only 18 months earlier.

The A's didn't ask Tettleton to hit much in '86--and he didn't. Aside from a six-week stretch in late summer, Tettleton batted .179 for the season. The stretch (.253) was more in line with expectations and, in one regard, beyond them (8 homers in 71 at-bats).

By the same token, the A's didn't meet Tettleton's expectations; by the 10th game, he was already being platooned with Bill Bathe, and the A's would later fall temporarily in love with Jerry Willard, letting Tettleton sit on the disabled list for five weeks with a foot injury that healed in half that time.

Tettleton is a switch-hitter who is much better from the right side (.262) than the left (.165). Impressively built, he looks to have more power as a lefty, but he showed it more from the right side in 1986. Like most lefties, he's a low-ball hitter. As a righty, he likes pitches up and over the plate. He strikes out (both ways) far too often. He's vulnerable to breaking balls and hard stuff away. The fastball can beat him, but it's best not to open with one in the strike zone.

Tettleton has an excellent eye; despite his weak average, he ranked a close third (behind Ernie Whitt and Lance Parrish) among league catchers in on-base percentage last year.

BASERUNNING:

Tettleton has better-than-average speed for a catcher and was either smart enough or quick enough to be 7-for-8 on steal attempts. However, he blundered on the bases occasionally, and most times it seemed due to a failure to anticipate the situation.

MICKEY TETTLETON
C, No. 6
SR, 6'2", 200 lbs.
ML Svc: 3 years
Born: 9-16-60 in
   Oklahoma City, OK

1986 STATISTICS

AVG	G	AB	R	H	2B	3B	HR	RBI	BB	SO	SB
.204	90	211	26	43	9	0	10	35	39	51	7

CAREER STATISTICS

AVG	G	AB	R	H	2B	3B	HR	RBI	BB	SO	SB
.242	223	542	68	131	27	2	15	60	83	144	9

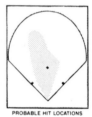

VS. RHP   VS. LHP   PROBABLE HIT LOCATIONS

FIELDING:

Defense was the one thing the A's were counting on from Tettleton--and they didn't get that either. Tettleton had 11 passed balls and eight errors in 89 games in 1986. Moreover, some of the pitchers who had favored him in '85 began to think less of him as a receiver and game caller.

Tettleton has a strong arm: he threw out basestealers at a respectable 30% clip last season.

OVERALL:

His stock has dropped drastically. He may start the season as the No. 1 catcher, but don't be surprised if he doesn't finish it that way.

Killebrew: "The main thing with him, I think, is he needs to play and gain experience. Some players need long stretches of playing time to get into a comfortable groove. But at the major league level, a club with that kind of time to offer is hard to find."

OAKLAND A's

PITCHING:

Curt Young's resurrection in 1986 was as unexpected as the A's having the worst record in baseball on July 4. No other team in baseball came close to their Independance Day mark of 30-50--not even the Pittsburgh Pirates.

After a promising rookie year in 1984, there were whispers that Young had the potential to win 18 games in '85. The lefthander fell 18 short of that dream that year and the only thing that hurt more than a winless season was his tendinitis-ravaged shoulder.

It was such a bad year (a 7.24 ERA and 15 HRs in only 46 innings) that Young's confidence still hadn't recovered by spring training of 1986, when he found himself in Triple-A.

Ironically, Young almost got his 18 last year, winning four for Tacoma and 13 more for Oakland after the first wave of A's injuries prompted his recall in early May.

Young's arm was finally healthy and had much to do with his comeback last year. But more than anything else, it was the development of a new pitch--a change-up--that transformed this spring training roster cut into the team leader in wins and innings pitched (198).

Young's fastball is average at best (83-86 MPH), but it has some movement, and sometimes sinks. His overhand curveball, which served as his out pitch in '84, also found its way back into the strike zone last year. The addition of the change-up made both the fastball and the curveball more effective.

Young turns his change-up over, which makes it especially tough on righthanded hitters, as it breaks down and away from them. As a result, righties did not savage him last season as they had in '85 (when they hit .331 and slugged .690). Lefties didn't have much luck either; Young held the league to a

CURT YOUNG
LHP, No. 29
RL, 6'1", 175 lbs.
ML Svc: 3 years
Born: 10-18-59 in
Saginaw, MI

1986 STATISTICS

W	L	ERA	G	GS	CG	SV	IP	H	R	ER	BB	SO
13	9	3.45	29	27	5	0	198	176	88	76	57	116

CAREER STATISTICS

W	L	ERA	G	GS	CG	SV	IP	H	R	ER	BB	SO
22	18	4.43	76	53	7	0	361.2	368	196	178	115	181

.236 batting average.

Young is a gritty competitor (he was an all-conference quarterback in high school), but he is also smart enough (a business major at Central Michigan) to know he can't challenge many hitters. His game is to fool them.

If he is going to have any kind of longevity in this game, however, he needs to become stronger; he tires regularly and he wore down badly near the end of the season, though he finished with a (tainted) one-hitter.

FIELDING:

Young's move to first base is mediocre, but being a lefty, he is rarely taken advantage of by baserunners. He is a solid fielder who rarely causes himself problems.

OVERALL:

Clearly, he is back on track. Whispers of 18-win seasons and a 200-win career (former teammate Don Sutton predicted that early in 1985) are no longer being met with snickers.

Killebrew: "I think the only thing keeping Curt Young from being a big winner is time."

OAKLAND A's

MIKE GALLEGO
INF, No. 9
RR, 5'8", 160 lbs.
ML Svc: one year
Born: 10-31-60 in
Whittier, CA

HITTING, BASERUNNING, FIELDING:

It's difficult to say which is a bigger problem for Mike Gallego: his bat or the organization's doubts about his bat. The little pepperpot hadn't hit better than .243 since leaving the Class-A level in 1981, so last year's showing at Tacoma (.275) and Oakland (.270 in September) won only a few converts, if any.

Gallego has serious trouble with the outside pitch and he is only somewhat better with offerings on the inside half of the plate. He is not good at off-speed or breaking pitches, although he can handle big league fastballs. He will hit to the opposite field. Fastball-hitting is not enough to maintain employment in the majors, however.

A heady player with a minuscule strike zone, he should draw more walks than he does. His lack of patience may coincide with his desire to prove himself as a major league hitter, because he has shown much more patience in the minors.

It is Gallego's defensive skills that continue to merit consideration. Given the chance to play second base regularly, he might come to be recognized as one of the best defensive players in the game. He is sure-handed (he has made only two errors in 228 chances in the majors) and has exceptional range in all directions. His lack of really good arm strength can be a problem when he plays at shortstop, but he has no problems when he is at second base or third.

OVERALL:

Gallego is the best bet to replace Donnie Hill as the A's utility infielder this season. The big chance he's been waiting for will come if injury visits Tony Phillips for a third straight year.

ERIC PLUNK
RHP, No. 51
RR, 6'5", 210 lbs.
ML Svc: 1 year
Born: 9-3-63 in
Wilmington, CA

PITCHING, FIELDING:

Eric Plunk came to the majors with little experience (17 games) at the Triple-A level, and the awkward righthander found the step too big to make. He could become the second washout from the 1984 Rickey Henderson trade (joining Tim Birtsas) and he'll likely be pitching alongside Birtsas at Triple-A this season. But the A's aren't giving up on Plunk. It's tough to give up on a 23-year-old who throws 90 MPH.

Plunk is a fastball pitcher. He has nothing else, though he has begun work on a curveball and a slider. Plunk was clocked as high as 93 MPH last season and he is usually in the 89-93 range. He can maintain that velocity into the late innings, if he can get that far. A mechanical mess (probably due to his size), Plunk often can't find the plate. He had 79 walks in 15 starts in 1986 and, overall, he averaged nearly eight walks per nine innings. He had the same problem at Triple-A (33 walks in 32 2/3 innings).

He is not a bad fielder for a big man and he may get better when he becomes accustomed to his body; he has filled out considerably in the last 18 months. He has a surprisingly quick move to first base.

OVERALL:

The A's don't believe he's anywhere near his potential. He could end up as a short reliever someday.

OAKLAND A's

DAVE VON OHLEN
LHP, No. 57
LL, 6'2", 200 lbs.
ML Svc: 4 years
Born: 10-25-58 in
Flushing, NY

PITCHING, FIELDING:

Barring a rush from many relievers who have already tried and failed, Dave Von Ohlen will get the call when a lefthanded hitter steps in against Oakland this year. Recalled from Triple-A at midseason last year, Von Ohlen stuck around by getting lefthanded batters out. He held them to a .207 average and gave up nothing more than singles. Against righties, it's a far different story: they hit .387 against him last year.

Von Ohlen's No. 1 pitch is the curveball. It's a big, slow bender, delivered with a big, slow overhand motion. His fastball is not special, so Von Ohlen's trouble comes when he can't throw the curve for strikes.

Von Ohlen didn't have much chance to reveal any defensive strengths or weaknesses last year: he faced more than three batters in only five of his 24 outings. As was the case during his brief stint with St. Louis and Cleveland, he made little impression.

OVERALL:

The A's have been looking for a quality lefthanded reliever for years. They're not sure Von Ohlen's the answer, but he will keep the job unless offseason acquisition, Carlos Diaz, finds the stuff he lost after the Mets traded him to the Dodgers in '86. Von Ohlen will get less of a challenge from Bill Krueger and Dave Leiper.

TERRY STEINBACH
C, No. 36
RR, 6'1", 195 lbs.
ML Svc: less than one year
Born: 3-2-62 in
New Ulm, MN

HITTING, BASERUNNING, FIELDING:

Terry Steinbach had shown a live bat for three years in the minors (a .291 composite), but even the A's were surprised by his numbers last year at Double-A. Steinbach batted .327, hit 24 homers and broke Steve Balboni's Southern League record for RBIs with 132. Then he barged into Oakland; a September recall, he homered in his first big league plate appearance.

Nevertheless, the A's don't foresee Steinbach as more than a 15-homer man in the majors, but they believe they can groom him into a highly productive hitter. Steinbach is an aggressive hitter who consistently drives balls to the gaps for extra bases (33 doubles at Double-A). He prefers pitches up in the strike zone, but showed he could hit low strikes equally well. He has a good eye and is a patient--which is why he is not being viewed as strictly a power-potential prospect.

Like most young hitters, Steinbach is at his best against fastball pitchers. But the A's are encouraged because he has shown little trouble hitting breaking balls. Righthanders found some success pitching down-and-in.

As a baserunner, Steinbach is smart and aggressive on the double play. His smarts make up for his lack of speed.

Last season was Steinbach's first full season as a catcher. Drafted as a third baseman, he spent some time behind the plate in '85 before moving there full time in '86. Naturally, he needs to develop his skills, primarily as a receiver. His arm is decent and accurate. He fared well against basestealers last year, but that was working two steps below the major league level.

OVERALL:

The A's are hoping Steinbach can help their catching situation this season. Though his bat seems ready for the big time, the A's may be asking for too much.

OAKLAND A's

JERRY WILLARD
C, No. 7
LR, 6'2", 196 lbs.
ML Svc: 3 years
Born: 3-14-60 in
Oxnard, CA

HITTING, BASERUNNING, FIELDING:

Here's everything you need to know about Jerry Willard as a catcher: he hit .267 last season and the A's dumped him off the 40-man roster. Cleveland dumped him last spring, after Willard had hit .269. The rap is that Willard can't do anything but hit, and he's not *that* great a hitter. He's cut down on his swing a bit, but the breaking balls and off-speed stuff still kill him. He's a dead pull hitter with lots of pop--if the ball is straight and on the inner half of the plate.

Like most catchers, Willard is slow, exceptionally so. A memorable night: in Tony LaRussa's debut as manager, Willard twice failed to score from second base on singles by Jose Canseco and LaRussa altered his batting order the next day so that Canseco would have less chance of coming to the plate with Willard on base.

Behind the plate, Willard does a fair job of receiving but his lack of agility hurts him. He once had the reputation of being a strong thrower, but his numbers last year didn't show it. Willard threw out only six of 42 basestealers.

OVERALL:

His bat may be enough to keep him around the game for some years.

SEATTLE MARINERS

PITCHING:

Scott Bankhead displayed signs of brilliance in his first major league season last year, but he still must prove his arm can withstand the wear and tear of an entire season.

Bankhead, who's just 5'10" and 160 pounds, made his major league debut in late May last year by pitching four shutout innings in the Royals' 2-1, 17-inning victory over the Chicago White Sox. He won his first three appearances, but then his collapse began. He lost four straight decisions and never again was able to put a streak together. More alarming, he began experiencing soreness in his arm. He gave up five earned runs in three of four starts in August. Then, after lasting just 4.2 innings September 5th against the Texas Rangers and giving up seven hits and five earned runs, Bankhead did not start a game for the rest of the season.

Thus, the biggest question regarding Bankhead with his new team is his stamina. Bankhead began the season throwing an 88-89 MPH fastball but by the season's conclusion, it had diminished to 83-84 MPH. Bankhead's best pitch is a backdoor slider, which will break in and hard on the hitter instead of away from him. His change-up, however, is below-average and is a pitch that Bankhead needs to refine.

Bankhead is not expected ever to be a consistent 20-game winner, but it wouldn't surprise anyone if he consistently won 15-17 games a season. The biggest adjustment he may need to make is reducing the number of home run pitches, expecially considering where he'll be pitching most of this season. Bankhead allowed 14 homers in just 121 innings last season.

SCOTT BANKHEAD
RHP, No. 28
RR, 5'10", 175 lbs.
ML Svc: less than one year
Born: 7-31-63 in Raleigh, NC

1986 STATISTICS

W	L	ERA	G	GS	CG	SV	IP	H	R	ER	BB	SO
8	9	4.61	24	17	0	0	121	121	66	62	37	94

CAREER STATISTICS

W	L	ERA	G	GS	CG	SV	IP	H	R	ER	BB	SO
8	9	4.61	24	17	0	0	121	121	66	62	37	94

FIELDING:

Bankhead gets off the mound well and is an adept fielder. Seldom will any hitter attempt to bunt against him. His delivery is not particularly quick, but he takes great pains at keeping runners close to first. With experience, Bankhead should be one of the better fielding pitchers in the league.

OVERALL:

The biggest question concerning Bankhead is his stamina. Can he last an entire season? Will he be able to survive the Kingdome? Bankhead's best attribute may be his maturity and pitching for the Mariners this season, he needs all of the help he can get.

Killebrew: "I'm impressed with him--he shows me a lot of poise. He has a good fastball, good control and decent breaking stuff. Mechanically, he has all of the tools, and he's got a chance to be a real fine pitcher."

PITCHING:

Off-season elbow surgery makes Karl Best a major question mark for 1987. He spent more time on the disabled list last season than on the mound, appearing in just 26 games.

With a shoulder injury to cut short his rookie season two summers ago, Best is becoming a disaster waiting to happen. Maybe this will be the year that he can stay 100% fit.

Best has two pitches that are major league calibre--a fastball and a slider--and that makes him an excellent late inning relief candidate. That is his favorite role, to be sure, and he has the mental makeup to be a good one.

He backs down to no one and when his control is sharp, Best can be a terrific closer. At the end of the '85 season, he had a string of six straight appearances covering 12 innings that he didn't allow an earned run, picking up saves in all four of his save opportunities.

Best's control was one of his main strengths two years ago--six walks and 32 strikeouts in 32 1/3 innings--but not last summer when he walked 21 and struck out 23 in 35 2/3 innings.

He has a tendency to get down on himself when he doesn't do well and probably lets things bother him more than he should. He prefers short relief to long or middle relief and it bugs him when he's shoved into middle or long relief. He has to be patient and wait for his opportunity--and then jump at it.

FIELDING:

An excellent athlete, Best handles himself well with runners on base. He isn't bashful about letting them know he's there, and has a

KARL BEST
RHP, No. 39
RR, 6'4", 210 lbs.
ML Svc: 2 years
Born: 3-6-59 in
Aberdeen, WA

1986 STATISTICS

W	L	ERA	G	GS	CG	SV	IP	H	R	ER	BB	SO
2	3	4.04	26	0	0	1	35.2	35	19	16	21	23

CAREER STATISTICS

W	L	ERA	G	GS	CG	SV	IP	H	R	ER	BB	SO
5	6	3.74	50	0	0	5	79.1	81	39	33	32	64

very good pickoff throw. It will get better the more he gets to pitch. Focusing on the batter and the runner never has been a problem for Best.

His short, compact delivery prevents runners from getting a good jump. Best also finishes in a strong position which enables him to field anything hit up the middle.

OVERALL:

Some day Karl Best could emerge as one of the league's top stoppers, but it is going to take him a while to recover from the aches and pains of 1986. If he can be patient, good things could happen. If he becomes impatient and discouraged, bad things will happen.

Killebrew: "He's a power pitcher who throws over the top. He doesn't use a curveball much, but he doesn't need one in his role. He has an excellent fastball and is the prototype for a short reliever."

GOOD CLUTCH HITTER

HITTING:

One year after establishing himself as a power hitter, Phil Bradley became more of a contact hitter who uses all fields. Pitchers who had been getting him out by keeping the ball away from him found themselves watching line drives fall into the right-center field power alley.

Bradley is one of the hardest workers on the club both offensively and defensively. He will spend time before each game sitting on the bench watching the opposition take batting practice. A perfectionist, Bradley will spend hours upon hours working on his batting stroke, trying to correct any weaknesses he might have.

A perennial .300 hitter--he batted .310 last year after a horrendous start--he is unquestionably the best overall hitter on the club.

Former batting coach Deron Johnson worked well with Bradley and it will be interesting to see how Bradley adjusts to a new batting coach (Bobby Tolan) this year.

Bradley is a guy who will try any number of stances to get into a solid hitting groove. A heady player, Bradley will not hesitate to lay down a bunt if he sees the third baseman playing behind the bag. He has excellent speed.

BASERUNNING:

When a pitcher doesn't pay enough attention to Bradley, a stolen base usually is the result. Bradley swiped 21 bases last year and was caught stealing 12 times. He studies pitchers and their pickoff moves, gets a good lead and is aggressive. He also is extremely intelligent and rarely runs himself into an out.

FIELDING:

He made only one error last year and that says it all about his defense in left field. Although he easily could be a good center fielder, Bradley prefers left field and he's at

PHIL BRADLEY
OF, No. 29
RR, 6'0", 178 lbs.
ML Svc: 3 years
Born: 3-11-59 in
Bloomington, IN

1986 STATISTICS

AVG	G	AB	R	H	2B	3B	HR	RBI	BB	SO	SB
.310	143	526	88	163	27	4	12	50	77	134	21

CAREER STATISTICS

AVG	G	AB	R	H	2B	3B	HR	RBI	BB	SO	SB
.302	449	1556	245	470	74	16	38	167	174	329	67

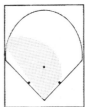

VS. RHP   VS. LHP   PROBABLE HIT LOCATIONS

home there.

He goes to his left especially well, running down balls that have extra-base hit written all over them, and he's not afraid to battle the fence to make the catch. He has a good arm and his throws usually are on the money-- whether it's to a base or the cutoff man. He has nailed many a baserunner who was trying to stretch a single into a double on balls hit down the left field line.

OVERALL:

Phil Bradley definitely is All-Star material. He's a quiet leader on the team, not a rah-rah type. His actions speak loudly enough.

Killebrew: "Bradley gets as much out of his ability as anyone. He's a hard worker and does a good job in the outfield and at the plate. He became a different kind of hitter last year, but he's still a guy you have to be very careful with. He's a good clutch hitter."

SEATTLE MARINERS

HITTING:

The first time he stepped into a batter's box in the major leagues, Mickey Brantley promptly delivered a game-opening triple. But there weren't many base hits after that and he has a ways to go to match some impressive minor league statistics.

Despite missing the final 1½ months of the Pacific Coast League season, Brantley still led the league with 30 homers last season and it is that power that impresses the Mariners no end.

Major league breaking pitches gave him fits and he finished with a .196 average in 27 games last summer. A 2-for-25 start after being recalled from the minors sapped his confidence and he never fully recovered although he did have one impressive stretch when he went 10-for-29.

Brantley averaged one strikeout every five at-bats but should be able to improve once he gets accustomed to the pitchers.

A good fastball hitter, Brantley needs a lot of work on hitting curves and sliders. A pull hitter, outside breaking pitches are his nemesis.

BASERUNNING:

Brantley is a little hesitant on the bases and has yet to utilize his speed, which isn't bad. He attempted just two stolen bases last season and he can do much better.

FIELDING:

A run-in with a wall when he was in the minors two years ago resulted in a shoulder injury that required surgery. He still hasn't fully recovered and his throwing is suspect. Despite the experience, Brantley is not gun-

MICKEY BRANTLEY
OF, No. 19
RR, 5'10", 185 lbs.
ML Svc: 1 year
Born: 6-17-61 in
Catskill, NY

1986 STATISTICS

AVG	G	AB	R	H	2B	3B	HR	RBI	BB	SO	SB
.196	27	102	12	20	3	2	3	7	10	21	1

CAREER STATISTICS

AVG	G	AB	R	H	2B	3B	HR	RBI	BB	SO	SB
.196	27	102	12	20	3	2	3	7	10	21	1

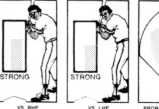

VS. RHP   VS. LHP

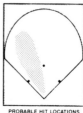

PROBABLE HIT LOCATIONS

shy about making mad dashes toward the fences and catches what he can get his glove on.

OVERALL:

Brantley's determination never has been questioned and the Mariners feel he has a bright future.

Killebrew: "Brantley is a guy who's had success in the minor leagues but needs more major league experience to realize his full potential. He has a lot of power but needs to get a better idea of the strike zone. Pitchers can get him out by keeping the ball down and away from him. Don't pitch him inside, though, or you're asking for trouble."

SEATTLE MARINERS

HITTING:

A strange thing has happened to Alvin Davis since he burst upon the major leagues and won Rookie of the Year honors in the American League. His power production has gone down each of the last two years.

Regarded as a present and future star of the league when he batted .284 with 27 homers and 116 RBIs as a rookie, Davis is now struggling to return to that early form. Pitchers have adjusted to him faster than he has adjusted to the way he is being pitched. His .271 average last year marked a professional low for the quiet, likable first baseman/designated hitter.

Basically a pull hitter, Davis has worked on going to the opposite field and with his power, he can hit an outside pitch a long ways. That is especially important in the Kingdome with its short fences.

Davis has an excellent eye and in just three seasons ranks No. 3 on the Mariners' all-time walk list with 263, 97 behind leader Julio Cruz.

On a team loaded with guys who strike out a lot, Davis doesn't fit in. He was the only regular who struck out fewer times (68) than he walked (76) a year ago when the team set an American League strikeout record.

BASERUNNING:

Speed is not one of Davis' strong suits but his intelligence is. He didn't steal a base last year and was caught three times. But he is capable of taking an extra base when the defense pays little attention to him. He grounded into 11 doubles plays a year ago.

FIELDING:

Never a great fielder, Davis regressed even more last season when he committed 14 errors, far too many for a first baseman. His defense got so spotty, in fact, that he spent much of the second half of the season as the Mariners' designated hitter.

ALVIN DAVIS
1B, No. 21
LR, 6'1", 190 lbs.
ML Svc: 3 years
Born: 9-9-60 in
Riverside, CA

1986 STATISTICS

AVG	G	AB	R	H	2B	3B	HR	RBI	BB	SO	SB
.271	135	479	66	130	18	1	18	72	76	68	0

CAREER STATISTICS

AVG	G	AB	R	H	2B	3B	HR	RBI	BB	SO	SB
.281	442	1624	224	457	85	5	63	266	263	217	6

His range is limited and he is especially weak in going to his left, which is his glove-handed side. He does have a strong arm and makes accurate throws.

OVERALL:

Unless his defense improves appreciably, Davis may become a full-time designated hitter before his time. With his offensive capabilities, it is tough to keep him out of the lineup, but on a team trying to build sucess around pitching and defense, having him at first base is a liability.

Killebrew: "Davis' average went down last season, but he's a solid hitter with a lot of power. He should hit more than 20 homers every season because he plays half of his games in the Kingdome. I don't see many weaknesses in his bat. He can hit the fastball and breaking pitches equally well."

SEATTLE MARINERS

HITTING:

No matter how much he plays, Bob Kearney seems to be a player who will give you around six home runs a season and around 30 runs batted in.

Although he had only 204 at-bats last season--the fewest in his four major league seasons--Kearney still managed to hit six homers (his career high is eight) and drive in 25 runs (his career high is 43).

Kearney likes to pull the ball and stands so far away from the plate that pitchers work him inside and then go outside to finish him off.

Last year, Kearney worked harder on hitting the ball to right field, especially in situations when he was behind in the count.

Pitchers who make a mistake inside on him pay for it. His favorite pitch is the high fastball over the inside part of the plate.

Kearney is not one to let a hittable pitch go by, even if it's a little bit out of the strike zone.

BASERUNNING:

Kearney won't win a game with his speed on the bases, but he won't lose you one by making stupid mistakes. He is a player who isn't afraid to make contact if someone is in his way, which may be a way to dish out some of the punishment he has taken behind the plate.

FIELDING:

If Kearney could produce offensively the way he does defensively, he would be a starter every year. His arm is strong and accurate. Last season he gunned down 45% (32 of 71) of the would-be basestealers when he was able to make a throw and was 32 of 77 (42%) overall.

The rap on him is that he can't call a good game, but there weren't as many complaints during the second half of the season when he did most of the catching while Steve Yeager sat. Mark Langston, who led the league in strikeouts, would rather pitch to Kearney and he wasn't alone.

BOB KEARNEY
C, No. 11
RR, 6'0", 185 lbs.
ML Svc: 4 years
Born: 10-3-56 in
San Antonio, TX

1986 STATISTICS

AVG	G	AB	R	H	2B	3B	HR	RBI	BB	SO	SB
.240	81	204	23	49	10	0	6	25	12	35	0

CAREER STATISTICS

AVG	G	AB	R	H	2B	3B	HR	RBI	BB	SO	SB
.235	455	1309	126	308	62	2	27	132	66	226	9

  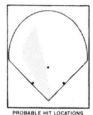

VS. RHP   VS. LHP   PROBABLE HIT LOCATIONS

Few catchers in the league are better at blocking home plate, although Kearney does get himself in trouble when he's so intent on blocking the runner, he doesn't keep his eye on the baseball. He made five errors last season, two more than in '85 when he was a first-stringer.

OVERALL:

Kearney adjusted well to losing his regular-player status to Steve Yeager. He didn't mope, complain or ask to be traded. He figures to be No. 2 again this season, but not to Yeager. Young Dave Valle, who offers more offense, is ticketed as the No. 1 catcher.

Killebrew: "Kearney is a high fastball hitter who likes the first pitch. Pitchers try to keep the fastball away and throw him breaking stuff. He's become a better hitter through hard work.

"He doesn't seem to pull the ball as much as he used to do, but he is just an excellent defensive catcher. I don't believe that he is an everyday catcher, but he is a valuable backup.'

SEATTLE MARINERS

PITCHING:

When it looked as though the major leagues had perhaps seen the last of Pete Ladd, he reappeared in the great Northwest. Released by the Milwaukee Brewers after four up-and-down seasons, Ladd came on to give Seattle some stellar middle- and late-inning relief in 1986.

The six saves he recorded were the most for him since he saved 25 games for the Brewers in 1983.

Determination is one of Ladd's chief characteristics. There isn't a batter in the league that Ladd doesn't think he can retire. His bread-and-butter pitch is his fastball. He also has a slider and a curveball.

Ineffective when he tries to overpower batters, Ladd must work hitters in and out or up and down. He's able to do this because control is one of his strongest suits. Ladd walked just 19 batters in 80 innings last season while striking out 59. Seldom does he come into a game and not have good control.

The more work Ladd gets, the better he is. He is not the type of pitcher a manager wants to leave in the bullpen for five or six days in a row. Ladd is a valuable member of a bullpen because he can pitch in long relief or short relief or be the set-up man for the closer.

Ladd is valuable to a manager for another, very important reason: he doesn't complain about anything. He is happy just to be a major league ballplayer.

FIELDING:

Because of his size, Ladd is not a gazelle in

PETE LADD
RHP, No. 46
RR, 6'3", 240 lbs.
ML Svc: 4 years
Born: 7-17-56 in
Portland, ME

1986 STATISTICS

W	L	ERA	G	GS	CG	SV	IP	H	R	ER	BB	SO
8	6	3.82	52	0	0	6	70.2	69	33	30	18	53

CAREER STATISTICS

W	L	ERA	G	GS	CG	SV	IP	H	R	ER	BB	SO
17	23	4.14	205	1	0	39	287	275	147	132	96	209

the field and at times has difficulty making plays on balls hit back up the middle. He has a tendency to fall off to his left after his delivery.

OVERALL:

Once considered by the Brewers as washed up, Ladd came back in a big way a year ago. He may never fill the role as a late-inning stopper again, but his attitude is such that it doesn't matter, as long as he gets to pitch in the big leagues.

Killebrew: "Pete has a good fastball, good control and can do a lot of things for a pitching staff. He does an excellent job and a lot of work doesn't seem to bother him, mentally or physically. He is most successful when he keeps the ball down."

SEATTLE MARINERS

PITCHING:

Once he gets his control down, Mark Langston could be one of the best lefthanders in the game. He has an excellent fastball that moves and is usually in the 91-92 MPH range, a nasty curveball and a slider that busts in sharply against righthanded batters and away from lefthanders.

But Langston has a tendency to lose his control and will throw eight (or even more) consecutive balls which gets him into immediate trouble. His fastball can pull him out of a jam in a hurry, but that doesn't always happen.

Because he is prone to wild streaks, he doesn't always get the calls from umpires on borderline pitches.

Langston led the American League in strikeouts last season with 245 but also walked 123 in 239 1/3 innings. He also uncorked a club high 10 wild pitches. His single-game strikeout high was 15, which also was a club record.

Langston primarily is an over-the-top pitcher, but occasionally will go sidearm against lefthanded batters.

He is capable of going on a hot streak, as he did last June and July when he rattled off four straight wins and drew some All-Star Game consideration.

One of his faults is letting things like a botched play bother him. But he made positive strides during the course of the season to correct that. Still only 26 years of age, Langston has yet to reach his peak years.

FIELDING:

Langston's pickoff move to first base is just average for a lefthander, and he has a tendency to make wild throws when he throws to first without using a leg-kick.

MARK LANGSTON
LHP, No. 12
RL, 6'2", 180 lbs.
ML Svc: 3 years
Born: 8-20-60 in
San Diego, CA

1986 STATISTICS

W	L	ERA	G	GS	CG	SV	IP	H	R	ER	BB	SO
12	14	4.85	37	36	9	0	239.1	234	142	129	123	245

CAREER STATISTICS

W	L	ERA	G	GS	CG	SV	IP	H	R	ER	BB	SO
36	38	4.43	96	93	16	0	591	544	326	291	332	521

His follow-through is smooth and he winds up in a good position to make the plays on balls hit back through the middle. Rarely does he not cover first base when he should.

OVERALL:

There is no good reason, except for injury, why Langston shouldn't emerge as a big winner. All he needs is to improve his concentration and mental toughness.

The elbow injury that ruined his second major league season (1985) is a thing of the past and he had a perfectly healthy '86 season, making a career-high 36 starts.

Pitching in the Kingdome is not conducive to having a low earned run average, but his 4.85 ERA was higher than it should be for a pitcher of his outstanding ability.

Killebrew: "I think he's one of the best young pitchers in the American League, no question about it. He has an outstanding fastball. There had been some concern about his arm, but he led the league in strikeouts last year, so certainly those doubts must be dismissed."

SEATTLE MARINERS

PITCHING:

Talk about enigmas. Just when the Mariners thought they had one of the best starting pitchers in the American League, something happened. Mike Moore, a 17-10 pitcher in 1985, became a 11-13 hurler in '86 and most baseball people were at a loss to explain what went wrong.

The first pitch Moore threw in the 1986 season was hit into the seats for a home run and that was a harbinger of things to come. He surrendered a career-high 28 homers and his 4.30 ERA was nearly one run a game higher than the previous season.

His problem was a lack of location. He is not an overpowering pitcher (146 strikeouts in 266 innings) and needs to move the ball around. Two years ago he walked 70 batters in 247 innings and last season walked 94 in 266 innings.

He should pitch inside more--especially to righthanded hitters--and also change speeds, particularly when he gets into a jam.

When Moore moves the ball around, he's tough. His fastball has natural movement and he has a devilish sinker. It is important for Moore to get his hits-per-innings-pitched ratio more in line.

When he won 17 games in 1985, he allowed 230 hits in 247 innings. A year ago, he allowed 279 hits in 266 innings with basically the same kind of stuff. He simply didn't have the same kind of location and didn't pitch inside enough to either right or lefthanded hitters.

Some have questioned his killer instinct and cite its absence as the reason he lost leads in the late innings last year. The bullpen was little help to him a year ago. Ten times he left a game with a lead, only to end up with a loss or no decision.

FIELDING:

The tall, lanky righthander has a deliberate move to the plate, but is good at holding

MIKE MOORE
RHP, No. 25
RR, 6'4", 205 lbs.
ML Svc: 5 years
Born: 11-26-59 in Eakly, OK

1986 STATISTICS

W	L	ERA	G	GS	CG	SV	IP	H	R	ER	BB	SO
11	13	4.30	38	37	11	1	266	279	141	127	94	146

CAREER STATISTICS

W	L	ERA	G	GS	CG	SV	IP	H	R	ER	BB	SO
48	62	4.44	157	152	35	1	997.1	1034	534	492	388	640

baserunners close to the base. His pickoff moves is the best on the staff among righthanders and he rarely gets burned by the stolen base. Seldom does he make a bad pickoff throw. He fields his position well.

OVERALL:

Moore, the nation's No. 1 draft pick in 1981, has yet to live up to the expectations. He has barely scratched the surface of his ability, and he needs to be more of a bulldog on the mound. If he could become more tenacious, especially with a late inning lead (as Jack Morris does), there is no question that he could be a big winner.

Killebrew: "Here is a guy who had a bad year in '84, a good one in '85 and then reverted last season. He seems to be on the verge of becoming an excellent pitcher and big winner in this league.

"He is the type of pitcher who has the stuff it takes to win, but something is holding him back. He should win 17 games every year. He's one of the few guys who can throw in the 90s for an entire game."

SEATTLE MARINERS

PITCHING:

There is good news and bad news when discussing Mike Morgan and his 1986 season. He won a career-high 11 games for the Mariners last year . . . but he also lost a career-high 17 games.

It has been nine years since Morgan stepped off a Las Vegas, Nevada high school pitching mound into the major leagues with the Oakland A's. Until last season, his big league win total was 10, so more than doubling that in one season is encouraging.

Still, there is a lot of room for improvement. Perhaps his biggest gain a year ago was his ability to block things out of his mind and concentrate on the hitter. In the past, his mind had a tendency to wander. Getting ahead of hitters--something he has to do to be effective--came easier last year. But all too often he would try to make the perfect pitch and get himself into trouble.

Morgan still lacks the confidence it takes to be a consistent winner in the major leagues.

His control wasn't bad, although he walked 86 batters in 216 1/3 innings. When he got too nitpicky and tried to nip the corners, he got into trouble.

Morgan has a good, if not overpowering fastball that moves well. He also has a good slider and curveball. But he needs a better off-speed pitch and should establish himself better with inside pitches. He needs to move the ball around, but not so much that he loses his aggressiveness.

FIELDING:

There are too many times when Morgan forgets to cover first base on balls hit to the

MIKE MORGAN
RHP, No. 35
RR, 6'2", 185 lbs.
ML Svc: 5 years
Born: 10-8-59 in
Tulare, CA

1986 STATISTICS

W	L	ERA	G	GS	CG	SV	IP	H	R	ER	BB	SO
11	17	4.53	37	33	9	1	216.1	243	122	109	86	116

CAREER STATISTICS

W	L	ERA	G	GS	CG	SV	IP	H	R	ER	BB	SO
21	45	4.92	101	78	14	1	506.1	590	302	277	237	228

right side. That is inexcusable, considering how much time is spent in spring training practicing that. His pickoff move is so-so, but he has a compact motion when going to the plate so runners don't get a particularly good jump.

OVERALL:

Morgan may never be a big winner in the major leagues or someone a manager can count on for 10-15 wins a season. But he should be a .500 pitcher at worst and a valuable member of a starting staff.

Killebrew: "I've always been impressed with him. I think he has outstanding stuff. He looks like a guy who's capable of being a big winner, but for some reason hasn't been. I think he can reverse the 11-17 record he had last season."

SEATTLE MARINERS

PITCHING:

Edwin Nunez appeared ready to step into the role as the late inning stopper for the Mariners last summer, but one of those easily forgettable seasons came his way instead.

Transformed into a reliever two years ago, the big righthander went to spring training with the stopper role in his back pocket. But he suffered recurring groin injuries and his coming-out party had to be put on hold for at least another year.

If one were to feed information into a computer to come up with the perfect late-inning relief pitcher, it would spit out someone like Nunez. He is big, strong and has nerves of steel. He can pitch three or four days in a row without big concern.

Cranking out 90+ fastballs is simple stuff for Nunez and hitters would be wise not to dig in against him. He will come inside in a hurry.

Nunez is especially tough on righthanded hitters because he throws anywhere from over-the-top to sidearm. His fastball moves and he also has a sharp-breaking slider, change-up and curveball (which he doesn't use very often).

Questions linger about his health. Groin and then a shoulder problem (tendinitis) limited Nunez to 25 appearances last season and only two of his appearances were in save situations. He saved neither and his only victory of the season came in a starting role.

Mentally, Nunez appears to be better suited to be a short reliever because his concentration is much better in tight situations. He also goes after hitters much more when coming out of the bullpen as he doesn't have the luxury of nibbling at the corners.

FIELDING:

A big guy who throws the ball hard, Nunez

EDWIN NUNEZ
RHP, No. 30
RR, 6'5", 235 lbs.
ML Svc: 3 years
Born: 5-27-63 in
Humacao, PR

1986 STATISTICS

W	L	ERA	G	GS	CG	SV	IP	H	R	ER	BB	SO
1	2	5.82	14	1	0	0	21.2	25	15	14	5	17

CAREER STATISTICS

W	L	ERA	G	GS	CG	SV	IP	H	R	ER	BB	SO
11	13	3.75	143	11	0	23	252	235	116	105	98	194

is subject to fielding breakdowns once he delivers the ball. He falls off to the left side of the mound which prevents him from being in ideal position to field grounders hit up the middle or slightly to the right of the mound.

His ability to hold runners close to the base is good. He has a quick-step, hard-throw move to first base and one of his biggest thrills is picking runners off base.

OVERALL:

Still only 24 years of age, Nunez has yet to reach his prime. He has a little over three years of big league experience now and should be ready to emerge as a star--if he's going to become one.

Killebrew: "He tries to power-pitch his way through and has displayed good control. He throws up in the strike zone, but with the stuff he has he can get away with it. Nunez is an ideal short man in the bullpen. He's a strong kid who throws strikes. He should improve."

SEATTLE MARINERS

HITTING:

Throughout his career, Ken Phelps has had a good idea of where the strike zone is and where the seats are. He walks a lot and also homers a lot.

Last year, the lefthander hit a home run every 14.2 at-bats and equalled his career-high with 24 easy trips around the bases. He also led the Mariners in walks with 88.

But one of the knocks on Phelps is that his home runs seem to come when no one is on base. Despite his home runs, Phelps was responsible for driving in just 64. For his power and position in the lineup, he should drive in more than that.

Phelps is a power hitter who can be overpowered by a power pitcher. He struck out 96 times last year in 434 at-bats (once every 4.7 plate appearances).

He is an excellent breaking-ball hitter, and when a pitcher hangs a pitch, that pitcher ends up hanging his head as the ball sails into the seats.

Because he has such a good idea of the strike zone, Phelps is able to wait on a pitch and go the opposite way with it. He has worked hard to develop that trait in the Kingdome, where long fly balls to left field end up in the seats.

BASERUNNING:

If you want speed on the bases, don't dial Phelps' number. He is slower than slow, but surprisingly doesn't ground into a lot of double plays. He hit into only four DPs last season, mainly because most of the balls he hits are in the air.

FIELDING:

Used on a part-time basis at first base a

KEN PHELPS
DH, No. 44
LL, 6'1", 204 lbs.
ML Svc: 5 years
Born: 8-6-54 in Seattle, WA

1986 STATISTICS

AVG	G	AB	R	H	2B	3B	HR	RBI	BB	SO	SB
.247	125	344	69	85	16	4	24	64	88	96	2

CAREER STATISTICS

AVG	G	AB	R	H	2B	3B	HR	RBI	BB	SO	SB
.235	371	911	150	214	32	6	64	156	187	245	7

VS. RHP   VS. LHP   PROBABLE HIT LOCATIONS

year ago, Phelps showed that his future is as a designated hitter. He committed nine errors in his limited exposure at the position. His range is terrible. Because of his soft hands, he is best at scooping up low throws.

OVERALL:

Phelps hasn't gotten the recognition or the playing time he thinks he deserves. Accepting the role as part-time DH (sitting against most lefthanders) hasn't been easy for the muscular Phelps.

Killebrew: "For someone who doesn't get an awful lot of playing time, he does an outstanding job. The Mariners get a lot of mileage out of him."

SEATTLE MARINERS

HITTING:

Jim Presley demonstrated that he is no flash in the pan by putting together a second consecutive productive season.

Even though American League pitchers had the opportunity to get a good "book" on him last year, Presley was not to be understood at first read. He hit 27 home runs (one less than his rookie season and 23 more than the previous year) and drove in 107 runs. He was the Mariners' representative in the All-Star game.

He is a free-swinger and, as might be expected, strikes out a lot. He set a club record with 172 strikeouts last season, which was 100 more than the previous year.

Presley has the ability to fight off inside pitches and if the pitcher doesn't get it inside enough, Presley makes him pay for it.

He loves to be at the plate in a game winning situation. He led the team in game-winning RBIs with 13, *two* coming on extra-inning grand slams.

A streaky hitter, Presley can be a one-man wrecking crew when he is hot. Last year, he went on a 33-game hitting streak from June 2 through July 6 when he hit 12 homers and drove in 33 runs. But he also can go into a rut, like the 3-for-42 drought he had at season's end.

BASERUNNING:

He has below-average speed and is pretty much a station-to-station baserunner, especially in the Kingdome where the outfielders are so close. He plays hard and is aggressive, not afraid to mix it up with a hard slide into a base.

FIELDING:

While his bat remained about the same as his first full season, Presley's defense improved by leaps and bounds. Hard work turned him into an excellent defender and he can go to his right or left with equal deftness. He also has a strong arm and is accurate most

JIM PRESLEY
3B, No. 17
RR, 6'1", 185 lbs.
ML Svc: 3 years
Born: 10-23-61 in
Pensacola, FL

1986 STATISTICS

AVG	G	AB	R	H	2B	3B	HR	RBI	BB	SO	SB
.265	155	616	83	163	33	4	27	107	32	172	0

CAREER STATISTICS

AVG	G	AB	R	H	2B	3B	HR	RBI	BB	SO	SB
.262	380	1437	181	377	78	6	65	227	82	335	3

  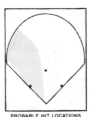

STRONG   STRONG   PROBABLE HIT LOCATIONS

VS. RHP   VS. LHP

of the time.

He does run into trouble when he charges bunts or choppers down the line, bare-handing the ball when he has time to glove it and make the throw.

OVERALL:

The Mariners turned down a Presley-for-Storm Davis trade two winters ago--and the M's are so happy they did. Third base had been just one of the year to year problems for the franchise, but Presley figures to be a fixture there for a long time.

Killebrew: "This guy is one of the best young hitters in the game. He's just outstanding. He's young and as he gets more experience, he will become more selective at the plate and cut down on his strikeouts. He'll always strike out a lot, but the main thing with Jim is he has to be a better judge of what to take and what to go for."

SEATTLE MARINERS

HITTING:

If Rey Quinones weighed five pounds more, he wouldn't have hit his weight for the Mariners after being acquired from the Boston Red Sox late last summer. The 185-pound shortstop batted .189 in 36 games with Seattle.

But those who have seen him develop, say this youngster (23 years old) will someday be a good major league hitter. Ted Williams, in fact, believes that if the Mariners leave him alone, he'll be productive.

Former Mariners hitting coach Deron Johnson worked overtime trying to get Quinones out of the habit of wanting to pull everything. And Quinones never felt comfortable about it.

When he would try to hit the ball to right field, he would either pop it up or ground it weakly to the right side of the infield and become discouraged.

Because of his pull-everything approach to hitting (no wonder Ted Williams likes him), pitchers are able to get him out rather easily with outside pitches, especially righthanders.

Quinones can handle anything on the inside part of the plate.

BASERUNNING:

Quinones is not a speed burner and seldom even tries to steal a base. He was 1-for-2 in stolen base attempts for the Mariners, but didn't ground into any double plays. He will take the extra base if the outfield gets lazy and for a young player, he doesn't run himself into many outs.

FIELDING:

Fielding is Quinones' forte. He has more range than any shortstop the Mariners ever have had. He is especially good at going to his left and charging the ball.

He has a strong arm although he seems to

REY QUINONEZ
SS, No. 51
RR, 5'11", 185 lbs.
ML Svc: 1 year
Born: 11-11-63 in
Rio Piedras, PR

1986 STATISTICS

AVG	G	AB	R	H	2B	3B	HR	RBI	BB	SO	SB
.218	98	312	32	68	16	1	2	22	24	57	4

CAREER STATISTICS

AVG	G	AB	R	H	2B	3B	HR	RBI	BB	SO	SB
.218	98	312	32	68	16	1	2	22	24	57	4

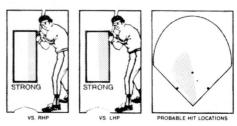

VS. RHP   VS. LHP   PROBABLE HIT LOCATIONS

have trouble when he falls into a nonchalant mode. He has to learn to bear down just as hard on routine plays as he does on the difficult plays. He made nine errors in 36 games and most were on routine plays.

OVERALL:

The Mariners think Quinones is going to be their regular shortstop for many years to come. He has showed a willingness to work hard and he needs experience more than anything else. Playing most of his games on artificial surface should be a big help defensively.

Killebrew: "There is no question about Quinones' defensive ability but he *has* to be more consistent at the plate. He has trouble with outside breaking pitches because he tries to pull everything. If he learns to use all fields, I think he'll improve a lot."

SEATTLE MARINERS

HITTING:

When you play as infrequently as Domingo Ramos does, finding a hitting groove is next to impossible. But when he does get a chance to hit, Ramos does not allow himself to get cheated at the plate.

If the first pitch he sees is close to the strike zone, he'll take a swipe at it. He is not one to wait around for a walk, although he has a pronounced crouch at the plate which enables him to get a good look at the pitch.

Ramos is aggressive and will try to hit the ball where it is pitched. He uses all fields.

Pitchers have the most success against him by pitching him inside with hard stuff and then teasing him with breaking pitches on the outside part of the plate.

Although he has been a good bunter most of his career, Ramos has gotten away from laying the ball down, probably because he no longer feels comfortable or confident since he hasn't had a chance to practice in game situations.

BASERUNNING:

Basically, Ramos is a station-to-station baserunner who rarely tries to steal a base. He should be more aggressive than he is, especially when going from first to third on a ball hit to right field.

FIELDING:

Ramos has been the Mariners' utility infielder for the last four years and, in fact, is the senior member of the club. The reason for his longevity: versatility. He can play any of the four infield positions and can also catch. In the days of the 24-man roster, protean players are important and Ramos is a prime example of how versatility can keep you in the big leagues.

DOMINGO RAMOS
INF, No. 3
RR, 5'10", 154 lbs.
ML Svc: 5 years
Born: 3-29-58 in
Santiago,
Dominican Republic

1986 STATISTICS

AVG	G	AB	R	H	2B	3B	HR	RBI	BB	SO	SB
.182	49	99	8	18	2	0	0	5	8	13	0

CAREER STATISTICS

AVG	G	AB	R	H	2B	3B	HR	RBI	BB	SO	SB
.209	250	517	50	108	16	0	3	33	42	67	5

VS. RHP   VS. LHP   PROBABLE HIT LOCATIONS

His best position is third base, but he plays more often at shortstop for the Mariners than any other position. He has a strong arm and is able to make an accurate throw to first from deep shortstop without much trouble. His range, however, is not good.

OVERALL:

Ramos is quiet and goes about his work without fanfare. He has shown that he is not an everyday player, but at the same time he has also shown that there is always a place for a player with his chameleon-like qualities.

Killebrew: "When he gets to play, he plays hard; and when he doesn't get to play, he continues to work hard. He has an excellent attitude, and a utility player definitely needs that."

SEATTLE MARINERS

HITTING:

Harold Reynolds received his first real shot at making it as a major league second baseman soon after Dick Williams became the Mariners manager. A steady .300 hitter in all of his minor league seasons, Reynolds had difficulty keeping his average much above the .200 mark last year against big league pitching and he needs to improve.

His main asset is his legs. He is quick and even though it is more difficult to get bunt singles on artificial surfaces, the Mariners think that for Reynolds to become more of an offensive factor, he has to work harder on his drag-bunting techniques.

A switch-hitter, he is more consistent batting righthanded, but he is more pesky as a lefthander because of his speed. He also sprays the ball around better batting from the left side.

He was the second-most difficult Mariner to strike out with 42 in 445 at-bats. But he should walk more than the 29 times he did a year ago.

BASERUNNING:

Reynolds can make things happen on the bases and Williams likes to use speed. Reynolds led the club in stolen bases with 30 and was caught 12 times. Once he can get his average up to around .250, there is no reason the speedster can't swipe 50 or more bases. He's aggressive and intelligent on the basepaths and will get better as he gets more experience.

FIELDING:

In the field, Reynolds is solid as a rock. He makes the routine and sensational play game after game and is especially adept at turning

HAROLD REYNOLDS
2B, No. 19
SR, 5'11', 165 lbs.
ML Svc: 2 years
Born: 11-26-60 in
Eugene, OR

1986 STATISTICS

AVG	G	AB	R	H	2B	3B	HR	RBI	BB	SO	SB
.222	126	445	46	99	19	4	1	25	29	42	30

CAREER STATISTICS

AVG	G	AB	R	H	2B	3B	HR	RBI	BB	SO	SB
.209	222	618	72	129	26	6	1	32	48	66	34

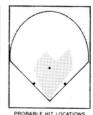

STRONG   STRONG

VS. RHP   VS. LHP   PROBABLE HIT LOCATIONS

the double play. He has a strong relay throw to first and oncharging baserunners don't seem to bother him. His pivot is quick and sure.

OVERALL:

It was his defense that kept Reynolds in the lineup but he still needs a lot of work with his bat to insure his major league future.

Killebrew: "He's a low-ball hitter batting lefthanded and is a high-ball hitter batting right, just like most switch-hitters. He has to use his speed more by laying down the ball more than he has in the past. I think his batting average will go up when he learns to use his speed."

SEATTLE MARINERS

PITCHING:

A control type righthander, Mike Trujillo has the ability to be a solid long relief specialist or spot-starter. Rescued from the Boston Red Sox farm system last summer, Trujillo pitched better than the Mariners ever expected.

His forte is moving the ball around and keeping the hitters off-balance. He won't blow anyone away, but he'll seldom throw two pitches in the same place.

He has a mediocre fastball, adequate slider and curveball and a change-up that makes his fastball look better than it actually is. When he mixes them all together, he's tough to beat, as evidenced by the one-hitter he threw at Kansas City late in the season in one of his rare starts.

To be most effective, Trujillo has to keep the ball down in the strike zone. When he gets his pitches above the belt, he gets belted and pitching in the Kingdome, it isn't wise to give up a lot of fly balls.

His forte is going to be as a long reliever or spot-starter, something every team needs.

With little major league experience, Trujillo obviously has a lot to learn about the hitters. But he seems to be a fast learner and that can only help him.

FIELDING:

Trujillo has only an average pickoff move to first base, but his compact and quick delivery

MIKE TRUJILLO
RHP, No. 43
RR, 6'1", 180 lbs.
ML Svc: 2 years
Born: 1-12-60 in
Denver, CO

1986 STATISTICS

W	L	ERA	G	GS	CG	SV	IP	H	R	ER	BB	SO
3	2	3.26	14	4	1	1	47	39	17	17	21	23

CAREER STATISTICS

W	L	ERA	G	GS	CG	SV	IP	H	R	ER	BB	SO
7	6	4.26	41	11	2	2	131	151	72	62	44	42

to the plate makes it more difficult to steal a base off him. A good athlete, he can field comebackers well and he seldom is caught not covering a base.

OVERALL:

Not blessed with outstanding, can't-lose type of stuff, Trujillo nonetheless is an effective pitcher because he pitches instead of throws.

Killebrew: "When he spots the ball and keeps his pitches below the belt, he's very effective. He has a good attitude."

HITTING:

Slowly but surely, Dave Valle has been developing into a candidate for the job of being the No. 1 catcher. This may be his year. His bat appears to have caught up with his work behind the plate, and Valle is expected to put in a lot of time calling pitches this summer.

A second-round draft pick in 1978, Valle never was a .300 hitter or much of a power hitter, either. His career high had been 12 homers.

But last year at Calgary, Valle not only hit for power (21 homers) but also for average (.312). He did the same for Seattle, batting .340 with five HRs in 22 games.

That was impressive enough to have manager Dick Williams say Valle most likely would be his regular catcher this season.

That is not to say he will hit .300 or homer 25 times. Pitchers can get him out with breaking balls away, although Valle is much more disciplined at the plate and doesn't chase pitches the way he used to. He has a good power stroke and can hit the ball a good distance the opposite way.

BASERUNNING:

Valle is smart, but not fast, on the basepaths. He will not dazzle you with his ability to go from first to third on anything hit to right or center fields, but he won't foolishly try it, either.

FIELDING:

Defensively, he's not as good as teammate Bob Kearney, but he isn't far behind. He has a good, strong throwing arm and excellent mechanics behind the plate. He blocks balls in the dirt well and now it's a matter of getting

DAVE VALLE
C, No. 5
RR, 6'2", 200 lbs.
ML Svc: 2 years
Born: 10-30-60 in
Bayside, NY

1986 STATISTICS

AVG	G	AB	R	H	2B	3B	HR	RBI	BB	SO	SB
.340	22	53	10	18	3	0	5	15	7	7	0

CAREER STATISTICS

AVG	G	AB	R	H	2B	3B	HR	RBI	BB	SO	SB
.247	66	150	16	37	5	0	6	23	9	29	20

STRONG STRONG

VS. RHP   VS. LHP   PROBABLE HIT LOCATIONS

the confidence of the pitchers before he really blossoms. The Mariners tell you that he also calls a good game.

OVERALL:

Valle is finally going to get the chance he's been longing for--a shot at being No. 1. At 26 years of age, he is just reaching his peak years, and if last year wasn't a fluke, he could be around for a long time.

Killebrew: "The only question about Valle is his hitting at the major league level. He's an excellent defensive catcher and will be given every chance to become the team's No. 1 catcher this year. If he stays away from injuries, he could be the regular catcher for several years. He's a strong kid capable of hitting 20 to 25 home runs a year."

SEATTLE MARINERS

SCOTT BRADLEY
C, No. 22
LR, 5'11", 185 lbs.
ML Svc: 1 year plus
Born: 3-22-60 in
Essex Falls, NJ

HITTING, BASERUNNING, FIELDING:

Scott Bradley made the most of his first real opportunity to make a name for himself in the major leagues last year. He didn't get that kind of chance in either of his previous stints with the Yankees and the White Sox.

A pesky hitter, Bradley will get a good at-bat practically every time he steps into the batter's box. He struck out only seven times in 217 at-bats after coming to Seattle from the White Sox organization.

He is probably too much of a pull hitter and needs to go to the opposite field more often than he does. He grounded into 12 double plays last year, primarily because he tried to pull pitches on the outside part of the plate.

His power is not outstanding, but last year he delivered a pinch-hit home run twice. Bradley is a good low-ball hitter who rarely chases a bad pitch. He doesn't walk much, but is a tough out.

He doesn't have a lot of speed, which is reflected in the number of DPs he hit into. But he's smart and will take an extra base if the outfielder is slow getting the ball back to the infield.

Defensively, Bradley is good at knocking down pitches but has to improve on his release to be considered a good defensive catcher. His arm is not strong so his release is that much more important.

OVERALL:

He is a good pinch-hitter and a superb human being who adds a lot of class to the clubhouse.

Killebrew: "Bradley is not a top-notch defensive player and needs some improvement, but he puts the ball in play, and when you can do that, good things will happen."

STEVE FIREOVID
RHP, No. 47
SR, 6'2", 195 lbs.
ML Svc: 2 years
Born: 6-6-57 in
Bryan, OH

PITCHING, FIELDING:

Although he has a better-than-average fastball, Steve Fireovid's best pitch is a slider so he needs excellent location.

At 28 years of age, Fireovid should be entering the prime of his career. But he still doesn't have enough major league experience to be considered dependable. He needs better command of his pitches.

An original draft choice (seventh round) by the San Diego Padres in 1978, he has bounced around the minor leagues and Seattle is his fourth organization.

Fireovid showed good control last year with four walks in 20 innings for the Mariners.

He has only an average move to first base and his fielding is adequate.

OVERALL:

Chances are, Fireovid will never be more than the ninth or 10th pitcher on a pitching staff. At 28 years of age he has yet to find solid ground at the major league level.

Killebrew: "Fireovid is another pitcher who has bounced around and still is trying to get established in the major leagues. He has pretty good pitches, but he needs more consistency."

SEATTLE MARINERS

MARK HUISMANN
RHP, No. 28
RR, 6'3", 195 lbs.
ML Svc: 3 years
Born: 5-11-58 in
Lincoln, NE

PITCHING, FIELDING:

A sinker/slider pitcher, Mark Huismann is most effective when he spots the ball and never leaves it upstairs. With a fastball that reaches only into the low- to mid-80s, the righthander gets hurt bad--as in the long ball--when his location is somewhere above the belt.

He has a reputation of doctoring baseballs. His control is good (19 walks in 80 innings last season) but his penchant for giving up home runs haunts him. Huismann allowed 18 homers in those 80 innings and that's not what a manager likes to see in a reliever.

Huismann has a below-average move to first base although his motion is compact enough so that runners don't get exceptional jumps off him. He is not a good fielder.

OVERALL:

Huismann doesn't have a lot of raw talent, but he has the ability to pitch several days in a row without physical repercussions. He will have a battle on his hands to stay in the major leagues.

Killebrew: "Huismann is not going to dazzle you with his stuff, but if he keeps the ball down and moves it around, he can be effective. He's probably best suited as a long reliever."

JOHN MOSES
CF, No. 26
SL, 5'10", 170 lbs.
ML Svc: 2 years
Born: 8-9-57 in
Los Angeles, CA

HITTING, BASERUNNING, FIELDING:

John Moses gets a lot of mileage out of hard work and paying attention. He has made himself into a solid player.

A switch-hitter, Moses uses all fields regardless which side of the plate he hits from. He has more power batting righthanded, but to be more successful he has to use his tremendous speed to better advantage. He should bunt more than he does.

Moses strikes out more than a so-called contact hitter should, and if he walked more he could be the leadoff hitter the Mariners need. He hits fastballs better than breaking pitches, but a pitcher can get him out with high hard stuff. He isn't disciplined enough to lay off those pitches.

Moses set personal highs in every offensive category last summer when he got his first real shot, including stealing 25 bases, but he was caught 18 times and that is not a good ratio for someone with his kind of speed. The bases he did swipe were primarily because of his speed, not because he got a good jump on the pitcher.

Although small in stature, Moses stands tall as a center fielder. His outstanding speed enables him to catch or cut off balls in the power alleys. He will run into a wall if he has to to make a catch. He is much better at going back on a ball than coming in.

OVERALL:

Killebrew: "Moses is at the point in his career where he will have to battle for a job in spring training and then work hard and maintain a good attitude during the course of the season. He can't afford to get frustrated."

SEATTLE MARINERS

DENNIS POWELL
LHP, No. 48
LL, 6'3", 200 lbs.
ML Svc: 1 year
Born: 8-13-63 in
Detroit, MI

PITCHING, FIELDING:

For a guy who went 9-0 in the minors the season before, Dennis Powell displayed extreme inconsistency in 1986 before undergoing elbow surgery to remove bone chips. At his best, he shut out the Reds for 7 1/3 innings on three singles in August. At his worst, he gave up five runs without retiring a Giants batter in an April start.

When he was "on," Powell, 23, impressed Dodger coaches with his confidence in starting batters with curveballs, sliders and off-speed pitches. The trouble came when he couldn't throw those pitches for strikes and batters could sit on his fastball, which is average at best.

An excellent athlete, Powell chased down batting-practice fly balls better than most Dodger outfielders. That may pay off in the Kingdome, where pitchers often feel their backs are against the wall.

OVERALL:

The trade to Seattle from the Dodgers might not be a good move for this young pitcher. Powell's development could suffer in the less forgiving Kingdome, without an experienced catcher like Mike Scioscia to guide him through his learning process.

Many in the Dodgers organization hoped Powell would be given an extended shot at the fifth spot in the starting rotation this season. With the Mariners, he should get his chance.

JERRY REED
RHP, No. 31
RR, 6'1", 190 lbs.
ML Svc: 2 years
Born: 10-8-55 in
Bryson City, NC

PITCHING, FIELDING:

Jerry Reed is 30 years old and has yet to spend an entire season in the major leagues. He has accumulated a lot of bonus miles on airplanes over the years, but landing on his feet in a big league ballpark hasn't happened.

Versatility isn't a problem: he can start or relieve. He has only average ability, but was getting the most out of it last summer in Seattle before a line drive slammed off his right wrist, broke it and ended his season prematurely.

To be effective, Reed has to move the ball around, stay away from the middle of the plate and count on his defense doing the job behind him. He's not a strikeout pitcher (16Ks in 34 2/3 innings), and his control could be better.

Because he is able to spot the ball, Reed is not prone to give up a lot of home runs. He was one of only two Mariners pitchers who pitched at least 30 innings last year and didn't allow a home run.

As a fielder, Reed has an acceptable move to first base and he has a solid finish when he throws to the plate.

OVERALL:

If some of the trades the Mariners made during the winter strengthen the staff as much as they hope it will, Reed could be on the outside looking in. He is getting the most out of his ability and he certainly tries hard without complaining.

Killebrew: "Reed is a journeyman pitcher who has to be considered a question mark because of the broken wrist he suffered last season. I like his attitude and work habits and he seems to be getting the most out of his ability.'

SEATTLE MARINERS

BILLY SWIFT
RHP, No. 18
RR, 6'0", 180 lbs.
ML Svc: 2 years
Born: 10-27-61 in
South Portland, ME

PITCHING, FIELDING:

The story of Billy Swift's baseball life is: one step forward, two steps back. The young righthander has been rushed to the major leagues two straight seasons and more than anything else, needs to spend one full season in the minor leagues to get his feet back on the ground.

He has four quality pitches, but has to develop an off-speed pitch before he becomes a consistent winner and also must move the ball around more. He is capable of going 4-5 innings without getting hit and then all of a sudden will get lit up. He has yet to learn how to adjust when he gets into a jam and all too often will turn defensive, nibble at the corners and only get into deeper trouble.

Swift also has a tendency to fall into the habit of "short-arming" the ball.

Once he throws the ball, Swift is in good position to field it and make the play to any base. He is a good athlete, but sometimes fails to get over and cover first base the way he has to.

OVERALL:

Some day down the road, Swift is going to be a big winner. All he needs is more experience and confidence. He can throw now, but he still has to learn how to *pitch* and when you have to learn in the major leagues, that is tough.

Killebrew: "He's a young guy who has four pitches with especially good rotation on his breaking balls. His fastball has some movement but he has to spot it to be successful. He needs to be more consistent, but with experience he's going to be much better."

TEXAS RANGERS

HITTING:

Steve Buechele made progress last year at being known for something other than rooming with John Elway at Stanford.

Entering the 1986 season, manager Bobby Valentine said loudly and often that Buechele would be his starting third baseman, no matter what. There were a lot of baseball people who thought that Valentine was crazy. After all, Buechele was a guy who had batted just .219 after being called up the year before.

But Buechele came through with a solid season and showed some power. And, at age 25 with a full major league season behind him, the Rangers now expect him to get even better.

Buechele likes the ball out over the plate, and the pitchers who had the most success against him were the ones who mixed up their pitches and moved the ball around the strike zone, unsettling him in the batter's box.

He is constantly fiddling with his stance and goes into slumps when he thinks too much about his mechanics. He needs to get in a good groove and let his natural talent take over.

He has pretty good bat control for a hitter with the power to hit 20 homers. He needs to lift his average this year, however, in order to help the team more.

BASERUNNING:

Buechele is not the fastest runner on the team, but he makes up for it by playing it smart. He will take an extra base, but rarely gets thrown out trying to do it.

FIELDING:

Buechele occasionally makes acrobatic fielding plays that remind the Rangers of six-time Gold Glover Buddy Bell, the man he replaced at third base. Buechele still is not as

STEVE BUECHELE
3B, No. 22
RR, 6'2", 190 lbs.
ML Svc: 1 year plus
Born: 9-26-61 in
Lancaster, CA

1986 STATISTICS

AVG	G	AB	R	H	2B	3B	HR	RBI	BB	SO	SB
.243	153	461	54	112	19	2	18	54	35	98	5

CAREER STATISTICS

AVG	G	AB	R	H	2B	3B	HR	RBI	BB	SO	SB
.235	222	680	76	160	25	5	24	75	49	136	8

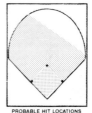

STRONG   STRONG

VS. RHP   VS. LHP   PROBABLE HIT LOCATIONS

consistent as Bell was, however.

He has a strong arm and can make an accurate throw while off-balance. He increased his value to the team by playing 30 games at second base last year and even started one game in the outfield.

OVERALL:

Valentine loves Buechele's poise and ability to produce in pressure situations. He has tremendous confidence in himself and is quietly developing into a team leader.

Killebrew: "As Buddy Bell's replacement at third base, Buechele was in a tough spot. He seems to have cut his own niche, however, and has overcome whatever comparisons were made to Bell. He's a good worker and, with more experience, he's bound to improve."

TEXAS RANGERS

PITCHING:

When last season started, Rangers righthander Edwin Correa was 20 years old, the youngest player in the major leagues.

But you'd never have known it by the way he pitched.

Correa showed unusual poise and unexpected command of his pitches and, despite a midseason slump that was probably related to pitching through the previous winter in Puerto Rico, came on strong at the end of the season. He is considered one of the Rangers' bright young hopes for the future.

Correa is a fast worker. Early in the season hitters tried stepping out of the box to disturb his rhythm, but it didn't work.

He is a power pitcher with an above-average fastball, but he uses it to set up his out pitch, a terrific change-up.

He hides the ball well during his windup and then delivers his pitches straight overhand from a herky-jerky motion.

In the second half of the season he began using his curve more, which increased his effectiveness.

Correa doesn't exhibit his emotions outwardly but holds his frustrations in. That was particularly evident during his slump, when he fretted privately that he didn't think the Rangers' catchers were calling a good game when he pitched.

Correa was impressive enough that, during the offseason, the Rangers agreed that he could honor his Seventh Day Adventist religion by not pitching Friday nights or Saturday afternoons.

And it didn't hurt that Texas is also interested in signing his 16-year-old brother, Ranser, when he becomes eligible this summer.

ED CORREA
RHP, No. 18
RR, 6'2", 192 lbs.
ML Svc: 1 year plus
Born: 4-29-66 in
Hato Rey, PR

1986 STATISTICS

W	L	ERA	G	GS	CG	SV	IP	H	R	ER	BB	SO
12	14	4.23	32	32	4	0	202.1	167	102	95	126	189

CAREER STATISTICS

W	L	ERA	G	GS	CG	SV	IP	H	R	ER	BB	SO
13	14	4.36	37	33	4	0	212.2	178	111	103	137	199

FIELDING:

Correa is highly intelligent and that carries over to the way he handles himself on the mound. He is mechanically sound and usually makes the correct play. He needs to improve his move to first and become more aware of runners on base.

OVERALL:

In addition to all his physical skills, Correa is a fierce competitor. He seems to be at best when a runner gets to third and he has to reach back for something extra to keep the run from scoring.

As he gains experience and is able to use the same intensity to keep runners off base in the first place, he should do nothing but continue to get better."

TEXAS RANGERS

HITTING:

When the Rangers swung a big deal with the Chicago White Sox before last season, Edwin Correa was the thrower the Rangers really wanted; Scott Fletcher was almost a throw-in.

But instead of replacing one feisty little role player (Wayne Tolleson) with another, Texas ended up finding an everyday shortstop in Scott Fletcher.

Surprising everybody but himself, Fletcher blossomed into a legitimate star last year. As a result, the Rangers rewarded him with the first two-year contract they've given out in more than a year.

Now, however, the onus is on Fletcher to prove that it wasn't a one-year fluke.

He, for one, is sure that he isn't. Never comfortable with the thought of spending his career as utility player, Fletcher may have unlocked the secret to success last season. He says that he finally grasped the concept of weight transfer during his swing and that it has made all the difference for him.

Fletcher designed a workout for himself by taking and rearranging an idea from Rangers' pitching coach Tom House (House is an innovative coach and exercises his pitchers by having them toss footballs to develop fluid motion). Fletcher took to using a fungo bat to hit soft tosses. This "underloading" theory seems to have helped Fletcher improve his bat speed and generate power.

He's a good fastball hitter who can have trouble with breaking stuff. He can bunt and although he doesn't have home run power, he showed that he can drive the ball into the gaps for extra bases.

BASERUNNING:

Fletcher has slightly-above-average speed but was successful on barely half his stolen base attempts last year. He is aggressive almost to the point of being reckless on the basepaths and will sacrifice his body to break up the double play.

FIELDING:

Fletcher is now considered the Rangers'

SCOTT FLETCHER
SS/2B, No. 1
RR, 5'11", 173 lbs.
ML Svc: 5 years
Born: 7-30-58 in
*   Ft. Walton Beach, FL*

1986 STATISTICS

AVG	G	AB	R	H	2B	3B	HR	RBI	BB	SO	SB
.300	147	530	82	159	34	5	3	50	47	59	12

CAREER STATISTICS

AVG	G	AB	R	H	2B	3B	HR	RBI	BB	SO	SB
.263	559	1619	218	426	75	14	11	149	163	183	32

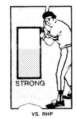

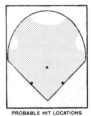

STRONG   STRONG

VS. RHP   VS. LHP   PROBABLE HIT LOCATIONS

starting shortstop, but last year he also proved he can play second base and third base if needed. That versatility gives Bobby Valentine some added maneuverability--and the strategy-minded skipper likes that.

Fletcher isn't afraid to get his uniform dirty diving for a ground ball. He has good range and a good arm.

OVERALL:

Off the field, Fletcher looks like a mild-mannered college professor. *On the field,* however, he's a gutsy, all-out player who now must show he's more than a one-year flash. Several Rangers believed that he deserved to be on the All-Star team last season and were upset when he wasn't included.

Killebrew: "Fletcher was certainly a good acquisition for Texas. He knows how to handle the bat. He's a very competitive guy who has taught himself to be an everyday player through determination and hard work."

TEXAS RANGERS

PITCHING:

After the first time he watched Rangers righthander Jose Guzman pitch, Baltimore Orioles manager Earl Weaver was moved to say: "He must have learned to pitch in heaven."

Well, not likely--Guzman's 1986 performance was considerably more down to earth in his first full big league season. He didn't measure up to the lofty expectations the Rangers had for him entering last season.

When Charlie Hough hurt his thumb during spring training last year, Guzman got the tag as the Rangers' Opening Day starter. That might have been the highlight of Guzman's season; he was ineffective for much of the season.

Part of the reason might have been that Guzman's arm was tired. Including the Puerto Rico Winter League, he had pitched over 350 innings in the 12 months prior to the season. The Rangers were careful to see that Guzman took most of last winter off.

When he's right, Guzman keeps everything down. He has an above average fastball with a natural sinking action that tails away from righthanded hitters.

He also has a good curveball that breaks sharply downward and a decent slider.

Whether because of physical or mental fatigue, Guzman too often got his pitches up in the strike zone last year, and when he did he was hit hard.

The Rangers are hoping that a renewed emphasis on mechanics and a winter of rest are all that Guzman needs to snap back to the form that so impressed Earl Weaver.

FIELDING::

Guzman remains well balanced after his

JOSE GUZMAN
RHP, No. 23
RR, 6'3", 185 lbs.
ML Svc: 1 year plus
Born: 4-9-63 in
**   Santa Isabel, PR**

1986 STATISTICS												
W	L	ERA	G	GS	CG	SV	IP	H	R	ER	BB	SO
9	15	4.54	29	29	2	0	172.1	199	101	87	60	87

CAREER STATISTICS												
W	L	ERA	G	GS	CG	SV	IP	H	R	ER	BB	SO
12	17	4.26	34	34	2	0	205	126	114	97	74	111

follow-through and, as a result, gets off the mound quickly to make fielding plays or cover first base. The Rangers have been trying to bring their young pitchers along one step at a time. All have been told to concentrate on the batter and not worry about the runner. So Guzman, like most of the other young Texas pitchers, does not do a very good job of holding runners.

OVERALL:

The Rangers haven't given up on Guzman, but the pressure is on him to prove that 1986 was simply an off season, not the norm. If he doesn't, it's uncertain that Guzman will get another chance. The Rangers appear to be loaded with talented arms. Guzman is in a position where he has to prove himself all over again.

Killebrew: "Jose is going to have to prove that he has something going for him in order to hold onto his spot in the starting rotation this season."

TEXAS RANGERS

PITCHING:

Two years ago, Rangers reliever Greg Harris attracted a lot of media attention because he could throw a baseball with either arm. Last season, the Rangers wished he could be a little more consistent with his right one, the one he uses in games.

Harris tried to make the transition from middle to short relief, but was not successful. He was inconsistent. He had total 20 saves last year, but only five of them came after July 4th.

Harris' best pitch is his curveball. He throws it most of the time, even when he's behind in the count. Harris can be effective only when he is throwing the curveball over for strikes. When he cannot do that, his backup pitches are too weak to carry him through. It's just about that simple.

He has a pretty good fastball and a slider which he uses to set up his curveball. While his fastball has good velocity, it doesn't move that much.

For a pitcher who throws so much breaking stuff, he's pretty durable. But he loses effectiveness if he tries to pitch three days in a row, which limits his effectiveness if used as a short man.

He throws his curveball from over the top. His major problem last year was that he went through periods in which he couldn't throw strikes.

FIELDING:

Harris has a pretty good move to first. He

GREG HARRIS
RHP, No. 27
SR, 6'0", 175 lbs.
ML Svc: 5 years
Born: 11-2-55 in
Lynwood, CA

1986 STATISTICS

W	L	ERA	G	GS	CG	SV	IP	H	R	ER	BB	SO
10	8	2.83	73	0	0	20	111.1	103	40	35	42	95

CAREER STATISTICS

W	L	ERA	G	GS	CG	SV	IP	H	R	ER	BB	SO
22	25	3.42	216	25	1	36	440	378	188	167	178	373

isn't exceptionally quick getting off the mound, but makes up for that by being in good fielding position at the end of his follow-through.

OVERALL:

If Harris can regain the consistency he had in 1985, he can be an important part of the Rangers bullpen. If some of the young righthanders emerge, he will probably go back to being used in long to middle relief, a role he seems to feel more comfortable in.

Killebrew: "He is going to have to one of two things: figure out how to throw the curveball consistently for strikes or develop another pitch. He has good concentration and his curve is outstanding--*when* he gets it over the plate."

TEXAS RANGERS

PITCHING:

Traditionally, Charlie Hough is a slow starter. Slow start, ok. But last year was *ridiculous.* Late in spring training he shook hands with an old friend . . . and broke his right pinkie finger.

As usual, Hough didn't let it throw him. In fact, before the season was over he made the All-Star team for the first time and won a career-high 17 games.

Nothing seems to bother Hough. After a game in which he has been hit hard, his usual summation is a straightforward "I stunk."

He doesn't stink too often, however. Hough has been the Rangers' most consistent starter since 1982 and has been named the team's Pitcher of the Year four seasons in a row. And the Rangers expect him to be a consistent winner for them for many more years.

It's said that knuckleball pitchers only get better with age and, if that's true, Hough's best could still be ahead of him.

Like most pitchers who throw the knuckler--and there are only a handful of them in the majors--Hough lives and dies by his pet pitch. And like the others, he hits streaks when the pitch simply won't behave.

Hough normally doesn't have a problem with his pitch not breaking and allowing hitters to tee off. Rather, he gets hurt when the knuckler breaks too much and he can't keep it in the strike zone.

When that happens, Hough has to come in with his fastball or slider. While those pitches are effective when he's getting his knuckler across and can use them as he wants, the hitters have the big edge when they know he *has* to throw them.

Hough is considered an extra pitching coach on the field. He is a real student of the game, with aspirations to be a manager or general manager when his playing career is over. But all indications are that won't be for many years.

CHARLIE HOUGH
RHP, No. 49
RR, 6'2", 190 lbs.
ML Svc: 17 years
Born: 1-5-48 in
Honolulu, HI

1986 STATISTICS

W	L	ERA	G	GS	CG	SV	IP	H	R	ER	BB	SO
17	10	3.79	33	33	7	0	230.1	188	115	97	89	146

CAREER STATISTICS

W	L	ERA	G	GS	CG	SV	IP	H	R	ER	BB	SO
131	115	3.54	609	193	65	61	2168.2	1838	963	854	918	1383

FIELDING::

Hough has an outstanding pickoff move to first. It borders on being a balk. In fact, he started using the move after he noticed that American League umpires allowed it, something NL umps didn't (Hough pitched in the National League from 1970 -1980).

He is not a great natural athlete, but is almost always in the right place at the right time. He rarely makes the wrong play because of a lack of concentration.

OVERALL:

Hough is a hard worker who presents a good example for the Rangers' young staff. He is a consummate professional.

Killebrew: "Charlie is a great competitor with outstanding concentration. He got off to a late start last year because of his thumb, but he really showed what he could do by coming back so strong thereafter. He is one of the fortunate pitchers who has control of his knuckleball more often than not and, because that pitch is so easy on the arm he can pitch almost as long as he wants to."

TEXAS RANGERS

HITTING:

There were those who thought the Rangers were taking a big gamble when they decided to make Pete Incaviglia their everyday right fielder and cleanup hitter last year. After all, he didn't have a single inning of professional experience.

Well, the gamble paid off and Texas hit the jackpot.

Incaviglia led the Rangers in homers and helped solidify the middle of their batting order in his debut campaign.

From the start, Incaviglia showed the ability to take an outside pitch up the middle or to right field, although as the season wore on, he did that less often.

He is a free-swinger who strikes out far too often. Although he claims it doesn't bother him ("An out is an out."), the Rangers will be trying to help him be a little more selective at the plate this season without dampening his natural exuberance.

Incaviglia can look bad at the plate, but when he gets *his* pitch--a waist-high fastball-- look out. He would hit even more homers if he pulled the ball consistently, but the Rangers are reluctant to tamper too much with his swing.

He went through some deep slumps last year and eventually was moved down in the batting order to take the pressure off him, but he is a youngster with a tremendous amount of confidence and never got down on himself.

BASERUNNING:

What Incaviglia lacks in speed, he makes up for in hustle and determination on the basepaths. He is a hard-nosed player who will break up a double play and doesn't take unnecessary chances.

FIELDING:

For the first six weeks of his rookie season, Incaviglia had severe problems in the outfield. But after making a diving catch at Fenway Park in mid-May, he seemed to become more comfortable in the outfield and his rating was raised to "adequate" for the rest of the year.

PETE INCAVIGLIA
RF, No. 29
RR, 6'1", 220 lbs.
ML Svc: 1 year
Born: 4-2-64 in
Pebble Beach, CA

1986 STATISTICS

AVG	G	AB	R	H	2B	3B	HR	RBI	BB	SO	SB
.250	153	540	82	135	21	2	30	88	55	185	3

CAREER STATISTICS

AVG	G	AB	R	H	2B	3B	HR	RBI	BB	SO	SB
.250	153	540	82	135	21	2	30	88	55	185	3

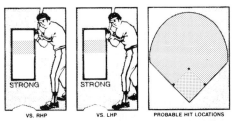

The Rangers plan to move him to left field this season.

OVERALL:

Incaviglia came to the majors last season with a well-deserved reputation as an arrogant, very challenging type of hitter. During spring training, it appeared as though his roguishness would continue. But once the season began, Incaviglia became almost docile. He was clean-cut and clean-shaven and accepted called strikes peacefully. He was also in a slump. After a talk with Valentine, who urged him to just be his same old self and worry about hitting the baseball, Incaviglia allowed his stubble to return, didn't worry about tucking his shirt in--and coincidentally or not--began to hit the heck out the ball and chew out the umps. Ranger fans loved it; the umpires did not.

Killebrew: "As a power hitter, he is a sure bet to continue to strike out a lot. But a manager can learn to live with that as long as the home runs keep coming. The thing that I like about Incaviglia is that he has good power to all fields. He can do the job and he drives in big runs."

TEXAS RANGERS

PITCHING:

Mike Mason feels left out of the Rangers youth movement. He's 28 years old, an age at which he should just be entering the best years of his career. But has let it be known he wants to be traded.

For starters, Mason would like to be in the rotation. The Rangers won't guarantee him a regular turn in the rotation, however.

Mason got off to a hot start last season, especially after he went to a more compact windup and became more aggressive on the mound.

After going on the disabled list, though, he found himself in the bullpen. The final straw came in September when Mason got a start, took a one-hitter and a lead into the fifth and was taken out of the game. His reliever gave up two homers, the Rangers lost, and Mason blasted manager Bobby Valentine after the game.

Mason throws an above-average fastball and a good curveball from a three-quarters delivery. His curveball breaks sharply and he will use it when he's behind in the count or needs a ground ball. Until last year, Mason did not have a lot of confidence in his curveball. But in May, he struck out Kansas City's George Brett three times in one game--by throwing his curveball.

He spots his fastball on the corners, using sinkers and sliders as his out pitches. He has also developed an excellent change-up. Another area in which he's improved over the past few seasons is changing speeds off his fastball and moving the ball around within the strike zone.

He has good control of his pitches and is effective turning the ball over against righthanded hitters. He exhibits a lot of poise on the mound. It's his poise off the mound,

MIKE MASON
LHP, No. 16
LL, 6'2", 195 lbs.
ML Svc: 3 years
Born: 11-21-58 in
Faribault, MN

1986 STATISTICS

W	L	ERA	G	GS	CG	SV	IP	H	R	ER	BB	SO
7	3	4.33	27	22	2	0	135	135	71	65	56	85

CAREER STATISTICS

W	L	ERA	G	GS	CG	SV	IP	H	R	ER	BB	SO
25	35	4.31	110	80	7	0	532	537	282	255	195	307

however, that occasionally gets him in trouble.

FIELDING:

Mason is quick getting off the mound to field bunts and is fundamentally sound getting over to cover first base. He does not have a great move to first, however, especially for a lefthander. He has a fairy slow delivery to the plate and, as a result, needs to pay more attention to holding runners close to first.

OVERALL:

Mason is at a turning point of his Rangers career. He has to put his past differences behind him and concentrate on getting hitters out no matter what role he's used in.

Killebrew: "He knows how to pitch and his off-season conditioning program should add durability, which has been a problem for him in the past. Because he's lefthanded, he may get his chance to start this year. He has a nice, easy delivery."

TEXAS RANGERS

HITTING:

Manager Bobby Valentine would like Oddibe McDowell to be the player he himself never was. McDowell is small but has big talent: he has speed, power and the ability to do a lot of things on a baseball field. Valentine was the same kind of prospect until he shattered his leg running into an outfield wall in 1973.

"He's my favorite, if I'm allowed to have one," Valentine is fond of saying.

At the plate, McDowell is a nice combination of speed and power. He was one of only seven players in the majors last season to hit at least 15 homers and steal at least 30 bases. He can also bunt for a hit when the situation calls for it.

While his power-hitting ability is a nice touch for a leadoff hitter, McDowell nevertheless has two major deficiencies as a No. 1 hitter. He strikes out too much and he doesn't walk enough. McDowell is improving in both categories, but if he is unable to develop the kind of good eye needed for his spot in the lineup, his future may lie in batting farther down in the order.

McDowell is a fairly tough out, but he can be fooled with off-speed stuff. He can hit a fastball out over the plate a long way. He could raise his average if he learned to go the other way with pitches on the outside part of the plate.

BASERUNNING:

McDowell is an above-average runner who will be even more dangerous when he becomes familiar with pitchers' pickoff moves. He is one of those rare runners who seems to be able to kick himself into a higher gear when he smells an extra base.

FIELDING:

McDowell plays a shallow center field--his positioning allows him to reach many balls that might otherwise fall in for singles, but occasionally it also allows flies to get over his head for extra bases. The installation of a wraparound-style scoreboard at Arlington Stadium in 1984 created a unique wind condition which especially affects the center

ODDIBE McDOWELL
CF, No. 0
LL, 5'9", 160 lbs.
ML Svc: 2 years
Born: 8-25-62 in
Hollywood, FL

1986 STATISTICS

AVG	G	AB	R	H	2B	3B	HR	RBI	BB	SO	SB
.266	154	572	105	152	24	7	18	49	65	112	33

CAREER STATISTICS

AVG	G	AB	R	H	2B	3B	HR	RBI	BB	SO	SB
.255	265	978	168	249	38	12	36	91	101	197	58

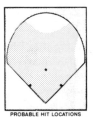

STRONG VS. RHP STRONG VS. LHP PROBABLE HIT LOCATIONS

fielder. For most of the summer, a prairie wind blows in from right field and around the private boxes high above home plate and is forced back into the outfield from straight-away toward right. This provides an advantage to the hitter as the wind will clearly lift a warning-track fly ball over the fence for a home run. If a center fielder is playing shallow, as McDowell does, he will spend more time backpedaling at Arlington than he would anywhere else.

OVERALL:

McDowell is something of a mystery figure for the Rangers. Last year, he set a club record for runs scored, but some in the organization continue to feel that he is not yet producing to his maximum potential. Last season, Valentine publicly chastised him for missing a voluntary post-All-Star Game workout and then striking out three times in the first game after the break.

Killebrew: "For a player without much physical size, McDowell shows pretty good power. If the club sticks with him and he applies himself, he could develop into a really bright spot on this evolving club."

PITCHING:

Dale Mohorcic thought his last chance of making the major leagues had passed a few spring trainings ago when Pittsburgh Pirates manager Chuck Tanner called him in to tell him that, once again, he was being sent to the minors. "Lefty, we're going to have to send you down," Tanner said, patting him consolingly on the back.

Since borderline lefthanders generally get the call before a righty, Mohorcic figured he didn't have much of a future.

He was wrong.

The Rangers brought him up at midseason last year, and Dale Mohorcic made his first major league appearance at age the age of 30. Before the season was over, he tied a major league record by appearing in 13 consecutive games.

Mohorcic has two outstanding attributes. He has a rubber arm which allows him to pitch almost every day. And he has developed an outstanding sinker, which allows him to deliver ground balls almost on demand.

His other pitches (fastball, curveball, slider) are only average, but he has the ability to change speeds with them and moves them around so he doesn't get hurt. He keeps batters off balance, but when he needs an out --he goes to the sinker.

Another of his attributes, one whose effect will never show up in his ERA or strikeouts, is that he has no visible emotion on the mound. Oftentimes, a batter wants to see a pitcher grimace and struggle, but Mohorcic spent so many offseasons working as a bouncer in a bar and driving trucks loaded with propane gas tanks, he's tough to scare. He also knows how to make a living outside of baseball and is able to keep the importance of a baseball game in perspective.

DALE MOHORCIC
RHP, No. 34
RR, 6'3", 220 lbs.
ML Svc: less than one year
Born: 1-25-56 in
Cleveland, OH

1986 STATISTICS

W	L	ERA	G	GS	CG	SV	IP	H	R	ER	BB	SO
2	4	2.51	58	0	0	7	79	86	25	22	15	29

CAREER STATISTICS

W	L	ERA	G	GS	CG	SV	IP	H	R	ER	BB	SO
2	4	2.51	58	0	0	7	79	86	25	22	15	29

FIELDING:

Defensively, Mohorcic does not have great mobility, but he is fundamentally sound. His follow-through leaves him in a good position to get off the mound to make a play or cover first. His pickoff move is decent and he is aware of the runners on first.

OVERALL:

Mohorcic will be effective as long as he can throw an effective sinker. And while it's hard to imagine that he can improve much at his age, some scouts think he was the best pitcher in the Dominican Republic Winter League this past season.

Killebrew: "He did an outstanding job in 1986. He pitched a lot of innings, kept the ball down and had good control. A manager can't ask too much more than that."

TEXAS RANGERS

HITTING:

Pete O'Brien enjoyed a great year in 1986. The problem was that he couldn't really enjoy it. A divorce before the season started was followed by the death of his father. But if it bothered him, he didn't let it show during the games.

He led the Rangers in several offensive categories last year and matured as a clubhouse leader in the process, gaining increased respect from his teammates.

O'Brien is the type of confident hitter who is not afraid to swing at the first pitch--especially if he sees a fastball. He is becoming a better pull hitter than he has been in the past and is learning to be more selective at the plate. Pitchers must try to keep everything down on him; if they get it up, he'll jump on it. He still reaches for pitches out over the plate.

O'Brien's major improvement last year came against lefthanded pitching. He batted .309 against southpaws after hitting just .225 against them in 1985.

He has a classic swing and is a great believer in himself. He is one of those hitters who can carry a team when he is hot, and his cold streaks are becoming less frequent and less severe.

BASERUNNING:

O'Brien has average speed and can't be considered a threat to steal. He is an aggressive runner when he gets on base, however, and isn't afraid to break up a double play or try to take an extra base.

FIELDING:

There are those who think O'Brien has Gold Glove potential, although he still occasionally makes errors that seem to stem from lack of concentration.

He is as good as Yankee first baseman Don Mattingly at turning the 3-6-3 double play. O'Brien has good range (especially to his right) and can play in close when the situation

PETE O'BRIEN
1B, No. 9
LL, 6'1", 198 lbs.
ML Svc: 4 years
Born: 2-9-58 in
Santa Monica, CA

1986 STATISTICS

AVG	G	AB	R	H	2B	3B	HR	RBI	BB	SO	SB
.290	156	551	86	160	23	3	23	90	87	66	4

CAREER STATISTICS

AVG	G	AB	R	H	2B	3B	HR	RBI	BB	SO	SB
.269	631	2235	278	602	111	14	75	328	273	239	18

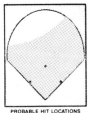

VS. RHP VS. LHP PROBABLE HIT LOCATIONS

calls for it because he doesn't flinch at sharply hit grounders.

OVERALL:

For most of last season, O'Brien hit in the number three spot in the order, with rookie powerhouse Pete Incaviglia right behind him, and Larry Parrish batting No. 6. The trio made for a very tough middle of the order; pitchers were lucky to get through them safely.

O'Brien is a keystone to the Rangers future, an emerging leader with a great attitude and plenty of physical talent.

Killebrew: "Pete is one of the guys I really like. He is one of the better hitters in the American League. He's the type of hitter who can bug a pitcher because the pitcher has to pitch him carefully or work around him.

"And I think he'll do nothing but improve."

TEXAS RANGERS

HITTING:

As the Rangers were making plans for their 1986 season, they were justifiably concerned about Larry Parrish. He was coming off arthroscopic surgery and no one was quite sure how well the healing process was coming along. And he was in opposition to the Rangers' desire to make him the everyday designated hitter.

The team was concerned enough to decline to negotiate an extension on Parrish's contract. That made him unhappy and made the team even more concerned.

But Parrish put all that behind him once the season started. His offense was a major reason the Rangers were the most improved team in baseball in 1986. Parrish hit for average and for power, drove in big runs and counseled the Rangers' plethora of younger players--especially the rookie slugger, Pete Incaviglia.

Parrish can be made to look foolish by off-speed stuff low and outside. But he doesn't let one bad swing carry over to the next pitch. He looks for a fastball on the first pitch. Pitchers have to move the ball around and vary speeds to try to keep him off-balance if they are going to stand a chance of sending him back to the dugout.

His 1986 numbers would have been even better if he hadn't missed a month of the season with a pulled muscle in his side.

BASERUNNING:

Parrish has decent speed for a big man, especially considering he wears a brace to protect his left knee. He is a conservative runner who usually doesn't try for an extra base unless he's certain he can make it. His pre-season knee surgery did not affect his running to any noticeable degree.

LARRY PARRISH
DH/RF, No. 15
RR, 6'3", 215 lbs.
ML Svc: 13 years
Born: 11-10-53 in
Winter Haven, FL

1986 STATISTICS

AVG	G	AB	R	H	2B	3B	HR	RBI	BB	SO	SB
.276	129	464	67	128	22	1	28	94	52	114	3

CAREER STATISTICS

AVG	G	AB	R	H	2B	3B	HR	RBI	BB	SO	SB
.266	1619	5829	739	1552	324	31	210	840	452	1094	27

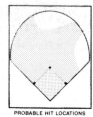

STRONG   STRONG

VS. RHP   VS. LHP   PROBABLE HIT LOCATIONS

FIELDING:

After starting his career as a third baseman for the Montreal Expos, Parrish played right field almost exclusively after joining the Rangers in 1982. That changed last year when he was the DH, but he did play 30 games at third base in 1986 and handled himself well, especially on grass. He has a strong, accurate arm.

OVERALL:

Killebrew: "Parrish is the kind of hitter who can carry a team for a week or more. He's a streaky hitter who is getting more consistent and may be in the prime of his career. He is a smart hitter, and pitchers must be careful never to pitch him the same way twice."

TEXAS RANGERS

HITTING:

When scouts and longtime baseball people watch Ruben Sierra, almost all make the same claim: This kid can be as good as Roberto Clemente.

That kind of talk pleases Sierra. Like the late Pirate Hall of Famer, Sierra is from Puerto Rico. And he developed his game at the Roberto Clemente Sports City, which is located outside San Juan.

Sierra has tremendous, if occasionally untamed, talent. He's just 21 years old and, with a half-season of major league experience behind him, may be ready to take his place this year as one of the best outfielders in the American League.

Before he does that, however, he is going to have to earn his spot in the lineup. He needs to improve his knowledge of the strike zone: he now chases too many bad pitches. Good breaking stuff gives him some problems, but he can handle most anything in his zone which is up and in.

Nobody doubts his physical ability. The Rangers will watch carefully to see that the language barrier (Sierra speaks very little English), his innate shyness and life in the big league fast lane don't keep him from developing into a top player.

BASERUNNING:

Sierra has above-average speed, but won't be a real threat to steal until he learns pitchers' moves better. He will take an extra base and is likely to become more aggressive as his confidence increases.

FIELDING:

Sierra played mostly in left field last year, but the Rangers plan to move him to right in 1986 to take advantage of his superior arm.

RUBEN SIERRA
OF, No. 3
SR, 6'1", 175 lbs.
ML Svc: 1 year
Born: 10-6-65 in
   Rio Piedras, PR

1986 STATISTICS

AVG	G	AB	R	H	2B	3B	HR	RBI	BB	SO	SB
.264	113	382	50	101	13	10	16	55	22	65	7

CAREER STATISTICS

AVG	G	AB	R	H	2B	3B	HR	RBI	BB	SO	SB
.264	113	382	50	101	13	10	16	55	22	65	7

VS. RHP   VS. LHP   PROBABLE HIT LOCATIONS

He gets a good jump on fly balls and can cover a lot of ground.

Defensively, he is fundamentally sound, and showed surprisingly good judgment in the field for a rookie.

OVERALL:

Because they feel that Sierra has the potential to be a star for many years, the Rangers hope he will be able to keep a good perspective. If he continues to work hard, there's no telling how good he can be.

Killebrew: "This guy is already one of the better young outfielders in the American League. He's just outstanding and, like so many of these young Rangers, should only improve with experience."

TEXAS RANGERS

HITTING:

The Rangers asked Don Slaught to do something last year he'd never done before: hit home runs.

All Slaught did was set team records for homers and runs batted in by a catcher, and he did it despite missing six weeks of the season after being hit in the face by a pitch from Boston's Oil Can Boyd on May 17th.

He improved his power last year simply by turning more on inside pitches instead of settling for lining a single.

This year Slaught will attempt to add physical strength. His arms and upper body are noticeably bulked up after an offseason of weight work.

He looks for a high fastball, so he can sometimes be caught on breaking balls away--especially now that's he's conscious of trying to pull the ball. He is, however, an excellent hit-and-run man with good concentration at the plate.

He didn't hit quite as well after coming back from the injury, but he's a tough player who could be primed for a big season.

BASERUNNING:

Slaught is a pretty good runner . . . for a catcher. He isn't a threat to steal, but he was successful in three of four attempts last year. He can bunt and his aggressive style of play carries over onto the basepaths.

FIELDING:

Some Rangers pitchers grumbled about Slaught's pitch selection, and that's an area the Rangers have been working on with him.

On the other hand, Rangers pitchers didn't do much to help Slaught. Opposing runners were highly successful stealing against him, but that was mostly because, in general, the young Texas pitchers didn't do a good job of holding them on base.

All in all, he's a good receiver who has improved his mechanics behind the plate and has shown an ability to catch Charlie Hough's knuckleball.

DON SLAUGHT
C, No. 4
RR, 6'1", 190 lbs.
ML Svc: 4 years
Born: 9-11-58 in
Long Beach, CA

1986 STATISTICS

AVG	G	AB	R	H	2B	3B	HR	RBI	BB	SO	SB
.264	95	314	39	83	17	1	13	46	16	59	3

CAREER STATISTICS

AVG	G	AB	R	H	2B	3B	HR	RBI	BB	SO	SB
.278	447	1457	156	405	80	13	28	159	76	194	11

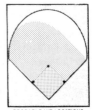

STRONG   STRONG   PROBABLE HIT LOCATIONS
VS. RHP   VS. LHP

OVERALL:

The Rangers will be looking for continued improvement from Slaught, both offensively and defensively. He's only 28, so he could still have several productive years ahead of him. Injuries have been a problem the last couple years, so he needs to show he can play a full season.

When he was hit in the face by Boyd's pitch, the Rangers held their breath as he went down in a heap. When he returned to the lineup seven weeks later, Slaught protected his face by wearing a helmet with a plexiglass shield over the jaw. At one point, Slaught believed that wearing the helmet was actually helping him to concentrate and thought he would wear it for the rest of his career. He changed his mind, however after a few weeks and ditched the helmet in August when he was in the midst of a slump.

Killebrew: "The big thing to worry about with Slaught is his possible fear about getting hit in the face again, but he's the type who can overcome that. I'd call him a leader on the ballclub with an aggressive attitude. He's a little rough around the edges, but he comes to play."

TEXAS RANGERS

PITCHING:

Mitch Williams' life is uncomplicated. It consists of driving his hot new car, going on dates and watching television--and pitching. He says his favorite fare on TV is videotapes of himself pitching.

And his pitching style is similarly straightforward. He throws fastballs. The batter must see if he can hit it.

Until this year, hitters rarely had a chance. He was a walking example of the old joke about the pitcher who could throw a baseball through a brick wall, except you never knew which wall.

While his control still is far from good (Baltimore manager Earl Weaver called him "dangerous" after one game last year when Williams hit three Orioles batters with pitches in one game), he has worked on it to at least make it "adequate."

He throws a curveball and a slider, but relies mostly on his fastball. Rangers pitching coach Tom House, who has known Williams since the youngster was 16, decided one solution was to change him from a starter to a reliever and make sure he got into the game three or four times a week.

It seems to have worked. Williams is a bit of a high strung pitcher, but frequent work seems to have calmed him down somewhat.

FIELDING:

Williams' follow-through carries him far to the third base side of the mound, so he has

MITCH WILLIAMS
LHP, No. 28
LL, 6'4", 200 lbs.
ML Svc: 1 year
Born: 11-17-64 in
Santa Ana, CA

1986 STATISTICS

W	L	ERA	G	GS	CG	SV	IP	H	R	ER	BB	SO
8	6	3.58	80	0	0	8	98	69	39	39	79	90

CAREER STATISTICS

W	L	ERA	G	GS	CG	SV	IP	H	R	ER	BB	SO
8	6	3.58	80	0	0	8	98	69	39	39	79	90

trouble covering first base on a ball hit to the right side of the infield. He has bad knees, which makes it difficult for him to bounce off the mound to field bunts. He concentrates on the batter instead of the runner, which allows runners to get a good jump for second. He needs to to both improve his pickoff move and remember to use it.

OVERALL:

Williams is an intense competitor, who gets visibly upset when he is taken out of a game. He has one of the better arms in the American League. He had a good rookie season. As he gains maturity, more control and a wider array of pitches, he could get even better.

TEXAS RANGERS

PITCHING:

The rookie season of the pitcher who the Rangers think can be as good as Roger Clemens someday soon is best described by a permutation of the name of a water amusement park near Arlington Stadium:

Witt 'N Wild.

Bobby Witt hadn't won a professional game before making the Rangers out of spring training. And in the first part of the season, he was spectacularly inconsistent. Walks and wild pitches competed with strikeouts in accounts of Witt's outings.

On one particularly memorable afternoon in Milwaukee, Witt left the game after five innings with a no-hitter going--he had also struck out 10, walked eight and thrown four wild pitches.

Witt lost a lot of games early, but he never lost was his sense of humor. Following his last start before the All-Star game, a reporter asked Witt idly what was up.

"My earned run average," he replied with a smile.

The Rangers were determined that they would resist any pressure to send Witt down as long as he didn't lose confidence in himself. Their confidence in Witt was rewarded at the end of the season.

Texas won the last 12 games Witt started, and he got the decision in seven of them.

Witt has more tools than a hardware store. The only thing missing was an ability to throw strikes.

His fastball is one of the best in the American League. He also has a sharp-breaking curve and a slider and can change speeds off all his pitches.

Control has apparently been a mental rather than a physical problem. He had no trouble throwing strikes in the relaxed atmosphere of spring training, when he was

BOBBY WITT
RHP, No. 48
RR, 6'2", 200 lbs.
ML Svc: 1 year
Born: 5-11-64 in
Arlington, VA

1986 STATISTICS

W	L	ERA	G	GS	CG	SV	IP	H	R	ER	BB	SO
11	9	5.48	31	31	0	0	157.2	130	104	96	143	174

CAREER STATISTICS

W	L	ERA	G	GS	CG	SV	IP	H	R	ER	BB	SO
11	9	5.48	31	31	0	0	157.2	130	104	96	143	174

almost unhittable, but he began to have trouble once the season opened before big crowds in games that counted.

Once he got over that, he became almost dominant. The Rangers are counting on him picking up right where he left off.

FIELDING:

Witt finishes his follow-through squared to the plate and can go to his right or left equally well. He does a good job of getting over to cover first base. He doesn't pay a lot of attention to runners on base, and eventually will need to develop a pickoff move.

OVERALL:

There doesn't seem to be any limit to how good Witt can become. The Rangers use comparisons to such stars as Roger Clemens and Sandy Koufax, but Witt seems to have the ability not to put pressure on himself. He gave Texas an exciting glimpse of what his future might be in the last couple months of the season, but he still has to prove he can do it consistently over the long haul.

TEXAS RANGERS

KEVIN BROWN
RHP, No. 43
RR, 6'4", 195 lbs.
ML Svc: less than one year
Born: 3-14-65 in
McIntyre, GA

PITCHING, FIELDING:

The Rangers continued their emphasis on acquiring pitching in last June's draft, selecting righthander Kevin Brown in the first round.

Brown didn't get off to a great start, however. His contract negotiations were prolonged and when he finally did report to the club, he had to undergo minor surgery to remove a cyst from his neck.

The surgery left him physically weak for the rest of the season.

To make up for lost time and to help him to fulfill his promise, Rangers pitching coach Tom House went to the Florida Instructional League last winter to work with Brown. He came away impressed.

Brown has a fastball that zips in at over 90 MPH and a good, sharp curveball. House says Brown is more mechanically sound than almost any young pitcher he has ever seen.

If Brown has a fault it's that he sometimes appears to lack competitiveness, although it is possible that his aggressiveness simply hasn't been seen at the big league level yet: he barely pitched after the Rangers called him up in September.

Brown is a good athlete who can make the plays coming off the mound. Like many young pitchers who dominated at ealier levels of competition, he sometimes forgets to hold runners on base.

OVERALL:

The Rangers think that Brown has a chance to make the starting rotation out of spring training this year despite his lack of pro experience. He has all the physical tools, and now just needs to demonstrate he has the mental toughness to pitch at the major league level.

MIKE LOYND
RHP, No. 46
RR, 6'4", 210 lbs.
ML Svc: less than 1 year
Born: 3-23-64 in
St. Louis, MO

PITCHING, FIELDING:

After he gets a batter out, Mike Loynd does everything on the mound but snap his fingers, shuffle his feet and sing doo-wa-diddy-diddy-dum-diddy-do.

The Rangers called him up after only five Double-A appearances last year because they liked his enthusiasm. But hitters hate those kind of antics because it looks as though the pitcher is showing them up (by the same token, pitchers hate jubilant home run trots). The Rangers now realize that Loynd will have to temper his enthusiasm to be successful in the long run.

There probably isn't a pitcher in baseball today who gets more out of his natural ability than Loynd. He wasn't picked until the seventh round of last year's draft because he does not have much velocity on his fastball. What he does do, however, is throw his curveball for strikes in any situation. He keeps the ball down, changes speeds and moves the ball around in the strike zone.

He is an intense competitor who avidly reads anything about pitching he can find. He has developed his own training routine, which includes warming up with a weighted baseball in the bullpen before his starts.

Loynd beat the Cleveland Indians in his first start last year, but was increasingly ineffective in each succeeding appearance. His confidence waned and he was eventually sent to the bullpen.

OVERALL:

Loynd has talent and a history of being a winner. He is in danger of getting overlooked in a crowded Rangers pitching picture, but it would be a mistake to count him out based on the mixed results of his rookie season.

TEXAS RANGERS

TOM PACIOREK
PH/INF, No. 44
RR, 6'4", 204 lbs.
ML Svc: 14 years
Born: 11-2-46 in
Detroit, MI

HITTING, BASERUNNING, FIELDING:

Tom Paciorek and Bobby Valentine came up through the Los Angeles Dodgers system together and are fast friends. So it wasn't a shock when the Rangers signed Paciorek, and there's even heavy speculation he'll be a coach for Valentine when his playing days are over.

In the meantime, though, Paciorek is a valuable role player for Texas.

He is not afraid to swing at the first pitch. He lacks power but is a good contact hitter. One thing that hurt him last year is that many of his soft line drives carried to the outfielders in windy Arlington Stadium instead of falling in front of them for hits.

Paciorek began to hit the ball more consistently after a midseason adjustment in his stance, in which he exaggerated his crouch. That helped him see the ball better and reminded him to just try to make contact. He uses the whole field and doesn't strike out much.

At 40, he is no threat to steal. But he is a smart baserunner who doesn't make many mistakes.

He played first base and the outfield as well as designated hitter last year, and handled himself well in the field.

OVERALL:

Killebrew: "For a young club such as the Rangers, the influence of a knowledgeable veteran around the clubhouse can be an intangible ingredient toward an overall winning attitude. Paciorek is the kind of player who provides a positive influence on young players eager to learn."

GENO PETRALLI
C, No. 12
SR, 6'1", 180 lbs.
ML Svc: 2 years
Born: 9-25-59 in
Sacramento, CA

HITTING, BASERUNNING, FIELDING:

After being released by the Cleveland Indians' Triple-A team last year, Geno Petralli didn't figure to have much of a future in baseball. After all, the Indians are still looking for catching.

But Petralli has worked hard and it has paid off. He has completely revamped his mechanics behind the plate and has turned himself into a pretty good catcher.

Put in the right spots, Petralli is not a bad hitter. He drove in several big runs for Texas last year, most memorably an eighth-inning, two-run homer off Boston's Roger Clemens to tie a Monday Night Baseball game in late August.

Petralli is primarily a low fastball hitter from the left side, which is where he takes most of his at-bats. When he bats righthanded, he prefers the pitches thrown high in the strike zone.

As a baserunner, he has fair speed for a catcher.

He started his career as an infielder, and this kind of versatility adds to manager Bobby Valentine's ability to plan for manuevers in the late innings.

OVERALL:

Petralli has a good sense of humor and keeps the team loose with his impersonations of third base coach Tim Foli. But he is a hard worker and intense when the game starts.

Killebrew: "He is not as consistent as he should be at the plate. He is not going to be a power hitter, and so he must establish himself as more of a contact hitter."

***DARRELL PORTER
C, No. 17
LR, 6'1", 200 lbs.
ML Svc: 14 years
Born: 1-17-52 in
Joplin, MO***

HITTING, BASERUNNING, FIELDING:

When the Rangers signed Darrell Porter to a free agent contract before last season, a lot of people wondered why. After all, Porter hadn't had a big season in years and the Rangers had said they were going to shy away from the free agent market.

But Porter came in and did almost exactly what the Rangers hoped he would do. Manager Bobby Valentine picked Porter's spots carefully, usually putting him in against righthanded pitchers who had better fastballs than breaking stuff.

And Porter, catching and playing designated hitter, responded to the strategy by hitting a home run for every 12.9 at-bats, the best ratio in the American League in 1986 among players who hit at least 10 homers.

The one thing that Porter was unable to do was stay healthy. When Don Slaught was lost for nearly two months, the Rangers expected Porter to handle the bulk of the catching. But two weeks later, he suffered a non-displaced fracture of his lower right leg and went on the disabled list.

At 35, Porter is still a decent runner. He can handle himself behind the plate and calls a good game, although he did have problems catching Charlie Hough's knuckleball at times.

OVERALL:

Killebrew: "He's one of those veteran players it is good to have on a ballclub. He has pretty good power and can do the job, especially if he doesn't have to play too much."

***JEFF RUSSELL
RHP, No. 40
RR, 6'4", 195 lbs.
ML Svc: 3 years
Born: 9-2-61 in
Cincinnati, OH***

PITCHING, FIELDING:

Just when it looked as though the Rangers would get nothing from the Buddy Bell trade, Jeff Russell showed signs of finally realizing his potential.

He's always had a good fastball but never really knew *how* to pitch. Now, however, he sets up hitters carefully instead of simply trying to throw his fastball past major league hitters.

After being brought up from the minors at midseason last year, Russell showed the ability to use his curveball to set up his fastball and slider. As a result, the Rangers have switched Russell from a starter to reliever.

He has adequate control for a power pitcher but still isn't as consistent getting batters out as he needs to be. He is, however, improving.

A good athlete, Russell does all the mechanical things necessary to be considered a good fielder. Like most of the Rangers pitchers, he needs to improve his move to first and to concentrate more on holding runners on base.

OVERALL:

Russell is a highly competitive individual. He may be just coming into his own, but his previous teams have thought that and been disappointed. This is a pivotal year for his career.

Killebrew: "He has al the tools, but consistency is a problem. He's a young guy with a great arm who still looks to me like he could be a starter."

TEXAS RANGERS

MIKE STANLEY
C, No. 62
RR, 6'1", 185 lbs.
ML Svc: *less than*
one year
Born: 6-25-63 in
Ft. Lauderdale, FL

HITTING, BASERUNNING, FIELDING:

On the knob of his bats, Mike Stanley writes: TPTM. It means "This pitch, this moment" and it reminds him to concentrate on every pitch.

It works for him.

With less than two years of professional experience, Stanley is considered to have a good chance to make the Rangers this spring after the club got a good enough look at him during two short stints with Texas last year.

He has uncommon patience at the plate for a young hitter. He prefers fastballs pitched inside, but isn't intimidated by breaking stuff and will go to right field with off-speed stuff.

He doesn't have a lot of power, but could develop it as he gets older and stronger. Right now he is a line drive hitter who uses the whole field.

He has the tools to become an outstanding catcher. Pitchers love to throw to him. He can also play the outfield and, in a pinch, third base. He has average speed.

He spent the winter in the Dominican Republic working on his game and it could pay off right away for him.

OVERALL:

Stanley is kind of a surprise, since he wasn't drafted out of the University of Florida until the 16th round.

CURTIS WILKERSON
SS/2B, No. 19
SR, 5'9", 158 lbs.
ML Svc: 3 years
Born: 4-26-61 in
Petersburg, VA

HITTING, BASERUNNING, FIELDING:

Curtis Wilkerson was the Rangers' Rookie of the Year in 1984. That says more about the rookies that played for Texas in 1984 than it does about Wilkerson.

He was handed the Rangers' starting shortstop position in spring training last year, but couldn't hold it. Over the offseason, the Rangers quietly tried to trade him.

A switch-hitter, Wilkerson is a high fastball hitter righthanded and prefers low pitches lefthanded. He's a better hitter lefthanded and most of what little power he has comes from that side, too. He prefers fastballs. He can bunt.

He gained about 20 pounds two years ago and doesn't have the kind of speed that is ideal for a middle infielder. He has pretty good range in the field, but makes errors on routine plays because of concentration lapses.

OVERALL:

Wilkerson has some talent, but probably needs a change of scenery to show it.

Killebrew: "He needs to learn to be more selective at the plate, to hit with more consistency and not strike out so much."

TORONTO BLUE JAYS

HITTING:

Last season, Jesse Barfield was asked by new manager Jimy Williams to bat higher in the lineup than his traditional No. 8 spot in the order. The intention behind the rookie manager's move was to elicit more "damage" from Barfield. "Damage" in baseball is . . . you know, trouble, home runs, game-winners, that sort of thing.

In 1986, Barfield led the major leagues with 40 home runs, shared the club lead in RBIs with 108, was second in the American League league in extra-base hits with 77 and set a Blue Jay record in slugging percentage, at .559. *That's damage.*

Barfield is primarily a fastball hitter. Though he prefers the pitch between his waist and knees or the inside heater, he was successful last year on just about any type of fastball he was shown. Hanging breaking balls--especially when they were pitched up-and-in--were never seen again.

Last year, Barfield seemed to be waiting on the ball better and seeing it longer than he had in the past.

Righthanders try to get the slider and curveball low-and-away or jam him with a fastball thrown up-and-in. Lefthanders can give him trouble with the slider down-and-in, the fastball up-and-in, or if they change speeds to interrupt his rhythm.

He has learned that he does not have to pull everything in order to hit home runs. In 1986, he hit roughly a quarter of his home runs to center and right-center field last year, though for the most part, Barfield remains a pull hitter.

He still strikes out a lot and is not a good hitter with runners in scoring position (.288 in 1986).

His average fell off in the final months of the season (he hit just .226 from September on), but 10 of his last 26 hits were home runs.

Although Barfield has always hit best at Exhibition Stadium, he had 24 home runs on the road last year. By far, most of his home runs (31) and RBIs (82) were against righthanded pitching.

BASERUNNING:

Last year, Barfield didn't try to run much, and his stolen base total dropped from 22 the

JESSE BARFIELD
RF, No. 29
RR, 6'1", 200 lbs.
ML Svc: 5 years
Born: 10-29-59 in
Joliet, IL

1986 STATISTICS

AVG	G	AB	R	H	2B	3B	HR	RBI	BB	SO	SB
.289	158	589	107	170	35	2	40	108	69	146	8

CAREER STATISTICS

AVG	G	AB	R	H	2B	3B	HR	RBI	BB	SO	SB
.273	715	2325	371	634	112	19	128	376	238	578	45

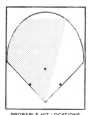

STRONG   STRONG

VS. RHP   VS. LHP   PROBABLE HIT LOCATIONS

year before to just 8 last season. He gets out of the box quickly and shows good judgment as a baserunner.

FIELDING:

An excellent right fielder, Barfield won his first Gold Glove last year. He has the best right-field arm in the American League. He led the league in outfield assists (20) for the second year in a row. He notches assists not because runners are testing him, no, the word has long been out on the strength of his arm, but because he nails so many runners at the plate and in two-out situations when the runners are going.

He goes well both to his left and right, and will make catches against the fence or sliding while coming in to greet the ball.

OVERALL:

Kaat: "His 1986 success against right-handed pitching could have been because he concentrated so much better at the plate last year--or simply because he saw so many righthanders that he figured them out. Harmon Killebrew hit more homers off righthanders during his career because, he said, he saw the ball better against them."

TORONTO BLUE JAYS

HITTING:

George Bell is a strong and aggressive hitter who doesn't strike out much--in spite of himself. He uses the type of big swing that causes mosthitters to whiff away, Bell manages to hit well.

He's neither a patient nor selective hitter, as in the style of Tony Oliva. If Bell sees it and it looks good, he's going to hack at it. If he tried to be more selective, it might take away from his overall hitting ability.

Bell is a good fastball hitter and he likes the ball up in the strike zone, but if a pitcher thinks that Bell won't sweep the plate on a low pitch, he had better think again.

Righthanders try to tease him with off-speed stuff thrown low-and-away and then bust the fastball up-and-in. Lefthanders give him the fastball up-and-in and change speeds.

He has become more of a pull hitter now than he was when he first came up from the minors (1981), though he would be well served at this point in his career if he learned to go with the outside pitch to the opposite field more often.

Bell continues to become a better hitter, year after year. He increased his home run and RBI output last year and recorded his best overall average, despite an 0-for-26 slump in May and another dive in the final two weeks. He also ranked third in the league in total bases and extra-base hits, fourth in slugging percentage and shared the league lead with 15 game-winning RBIs last year.

He wants to play every day, and he plays hard, despite ongoing problems with a sore knee and sore shoulder.

A great competitor, Bell belted .325 with runners in scoring position last year and was the Jays' best hitter at home (.327). He continues to hit for more power off righthanders (21 home runs in '86).

He has never had a sacrifice bunt in his major league career.

BASERUNNING:

Last year, Bell didn't try to steal much. But that's probably a good thing: he is not a good heads-up baserunner. He is a very "macho" type of player and is liable to do anything on

GEORGE BELL
LF, No. 11
RR, 6'1", 194 lbs.
ML Svc: 5 years
Born: 10-21-59 in
San Pedro de Macoris,
Dominican Republic

1986 STATISTICS

AVG	G	AB	R	H	2B	3B	HR	RBI	BB	SO	SB
.309	159	641	101	198	38	6	31	108	41	62	7

CAREER STATISTICS

AVG	G	AB	R	H	2B	3B	HR	RBI	BB	SO	SB
.287	574	2129	297	610	112	21	92	319	117	282	43

  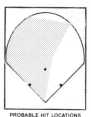

VS. RHP   VS. LHP   PROBABLE HIT LOCATIONS

the bases. He runs through signs and is as unharnessed on the bases as he is at the plate.

FIELDING:

Bell is not an aggressive fielder. He does not challenge the fences to make a catch.

His arm is strong and underrated and he hits the cutoff man well, however. He had nine outfield assists in one span of 15 games in August, and totalled 17 for the year, second in the league only to Jesse Barfield.

OVERALL:

Bell and Barfield feed off each other in a friendly offensive competition, which can bring out the best in both of them. Bell also keeps a close eye on the boxscores of the National League, watching fellow Dominican slugger Pedro Guerrero of the Dodgers, keeping tabs on the Los Angeles outfielder.

Kaat: "I look for Bell to continue to improve and can see him hitting in the .325-.330 range in the not-too-distant future. He's definitely one of the best hitters in the league, and he loves the challenge of the battle with the pitcher."

TORONTO BLUE JAYS

PITCHING:

Bill Caudill has always been a power pitcher, but it seems as though somebody pulled the plug on his power in the last two years. He doesn't have his 90 MPH fastball anymore. The years of answering the eighth- and ninth-inning bell 65-70 times a season may finally have taken their toll on Caudill's arm.

Caudill began the 1986 on the disabled list with tendinitis and when he returned to the roster, he found that his stuff could not compete with that of Mark Eichhorn or Tom Henke.

He has not yet come up with a quality breaking pitch that can sneak under a big league hitter's bat and so he is at the mercy of his fastball. And that does not bode well for him at this point.

After getting 88 saves in three seasons (1982-84), Caudill's figures crashed to 14 saves in 1985 and almost didn't even exist at just two SVs last year.

In an effort to help himself, he did a good job in trimming his weight prior to last season and he managed to keep it off.

FIELDING:

Caudill has always had a problem with holding runners close. He worked on that prior to the '85 season but blamed the changes in his delivery for some of his subsequent problems. He is slow in coming to the plate and runners take advantage of him,

BILL CAUDILL
RHP, No. 36
RR, 6'1", 225 lbs.
ML Svc: 8 years
Born: 7-13-56 in
**   Santa Monica, CA**

1986 STATISTICS

W	L	ERA	G	GS	CG	SV	IP	H	R	ER	BB	SO
2	4	6.19	40	0	0	2	36.1	36	25	25	17	32

CAREER STATISTICS

W	L	ERA	G	GS	CG	SV	IP	H	R	ER	BB	SO
35	52	3.62	439	24	0	105	659.1	577	289	265	287	612

although his move to first base is decent.

OVERALL:

Caudill has either to find the warmth of his heater or come up with something new. The Blue Jays don't want to have to eat the two remaining years on his guaranteed contract which is a hard to digest $2½ million.

Kaat: "The word is that he has been working to develop a change-up. He has to develop some kind of breaking ball or off-speed pitch to make his fastball look better.

"Young pitchers can't stand still and neither can veterans. Caudill is challenging for his job in the bullpen and he is going to have a rough go of it."

TORONTO BLUE JAYS

PITCHING:

The Blue Jays made some changes in John Cerutti's mechanics last season when he was with their Triple-A club. They made him abandon his windup. This helped his control and got him promoted to the Jays in mid-May last year.

Cerutti is not overpowering, but he has a decent fastball, much like Jimmy Key. He has a good change-up and he is working on his breaking pitches.

He is strong and was able to work effectively either as a starter (7-4 in 20 games) or in relief (2-0 in 14 appearances).

A lefthanded pitcher who can throw strikes and challenge the hitters can stick around a long time--and that's what it appears this southpaw might do.

If he has a fault, it was the 25 home runs he allowed in 145 innings. But he pitched well on the road (7-3) and he had a great record against the tough AL East (7-1).

FIELDING:

Cerutti is an average fielder with an ordinary move to first base. This year, he ought to work to make his pickoff move better.

OVERALL:

His follow-through motion tends to leave

JOHN CERUTTI
LHP, No. 55
LL, 6'2", 195 lbs.
ML Svc: 1 year
Born: 4-28-60 in
Albany, NY

1986 STATISTICS

W	L	ERA	G	GS	CG	SV	IP	H	R	ER	BB	SO
9	4	4.15	34	20	2	1	145.1	150	73	67	47	89

CAREER STATISTICS

W	L	ERA	G	GS	CG	SV	IP	H	R	ER	BB	SO
9	6	4.20	38	21	2	1	152	160	80	71	51	94

him upright which makes it harder for him to keep the ball down consistently. He is still young and does not have enough experience to win on days when he doesn't have his best stuff. He is strong and he is able to go nine innings regularly.

Kaat: "He could be a number four or five starter, but his ability to start or relieve makes him especially valuable. He needs to improve his breaking ball and keep it down. If I were him, I would pay a lot of attention to Jimmy Key for tips."

TORONTO BLUE JAYS

PITCHING:

One of the three survivors from the Blue Jays' original expansion draft (Ernie Whitt and Garth Iorg, the others), Jim Clancy is the senior man in point of service.

Back in 1980, it was generally believed that Clancy was the type of pitcher "to build a franchise around." But a series of injuries have prevented him from fulfilling those extraordinary expectations. Last year he became the first Blue Jay to win 100 games-- but it took him 10 major league seasons to do it.

He was the Jays' most consistent starter in 1986 and his record would be even better except he lost his last seven starts, which included back-to-back complete game losses (2-1 in Detroit and 2-0 in Boston).

Clancy is still basically a power pitcher. He relies on his fastball, which he throws in the 88-91 MPH range. He also has an excellent slider. His curveball was better last year than it has been in the past; he was throwing it over the plate more consistently. The confidence he had in his curveball showed in the frequency of its offering last year. It makes his other pitches much more effective.

For some time, he had been working to develop a forkball to substitute for a change-up and surprised a lot of hitters last year because they didn't know he had one.

He has been around long enough to know how to get by on his fastball until his slider comes around. When he gets behind in the count, he will challenge the hitter with the fastball. He throws the fastball up-and-in to a righthanded hitter.

Clancy is a streaky pitcher. His ERA balloons because he has a tendency to get hit hard early in games when he does not have his good control. He will come back in the next

JIM CLANCY
RHP, No. 18
RR, 6'4", 218 lbs.
ML Svc: 10 years
Born: 12-18-55 in Chicago, IL

1986 STATISTICS

W	L	ERA	G	GS	CG	SV	IP	H	R	ER	BB	SO
14	14	3.94	34	34	6	0	219.1	202	100	96	63	126

CAREER STATISTICS

W	L	ERA	G	GS	CG	SV	IP	H	R	ER	BB	SO
102	116	4.13	279	277	64	0	1768.1	1744	895	812	687	939

outing and hold the opposition to just a run or two. He always seems to be more successful against teams under .500 (6-8 in 1986). In July, he was 5-0 but went 0-7 in his last seven starts.

FIELDING:

He is not agile for his size, but he got better in fielding hard-hit balls back up the middle last year. He is an ordinary fielder but is getting better at going over to cover first base.

OVERALL:

Kaat: "We have been waiting for him to have that really big year. Possibly it relates to motivation, but he has had more than his share of physical problems.

"He is still young enough and strong enough to be a solid number three man in the rotation and capable of pitching complete games. If he changes speeds more and gets his breaking pitches over, he is capable of posting a higher number of wins."

TORONTO BLUE JAYS

PITCHING:

In a season when the American League was loaded will brilliant rookie hitters like Jose Canseco and Pete Incaviglia, pitcher Mark Eichhorn did not get the recognition he merited until the final statistics spotlighted the brilliance of his first-year performance.

He only missed winning the ERA title because he came up five innings short of qualifying: he had the misfortune of spending 16 days on the disabled list after he got spiked while covering first base in June.

A non-roster invitee to spring training last year, Eichhorn got his chance to earn a spot on the staff because Bill Caudill started the season on the disabled list. Thereafter, Eichhorn got lots of work because of the inconsistency of Dennis Lamp (who, if doing well, would have been the set-up man for Tom Henke).

Eichhorn allowed only one baserunner per inning and he averaged 6.02 hits per nine innings, while striking out 9.52 over nine innings pitched.

He has a good fastball, which is made even better by a fantastsic change-up and a slider that breaks away from righthand hitters like a frisbee.

Normally hitters argue about how hard a pitcher throws but in Eichhorn's case, the opposite is true. Even the most veteran hitters say they have never seen a major league pitcher throw a pitch as *slow* as Eichhorn does.

He was murder against the big righthanded power hitters but did experience more difficulty with lefthanded batters last season.

Frequently, Eichhorn worked three or loul innings and his longest outing was six innings against Seattle, in which he struck out a season high of eight batters.

He is striving to improve his control--he hit seven batters in 1986 because there was so much movement on his breaking pitch.

Some observers speculated that the young pitcher would have trouble in the second half of the season after the hitters had seen him, but from the way Eichhorn pitched during the second go-round, the hitters are going to need to take a few more peeks.

MARK EICHHORN
RHP, No. 38
RR, 6'3", 200 lbs.
ML Svc: 1 year
Born: 11-21-60 in
San Jose, CA

1986 STATISTICS

W	L	ERA	G	GS	CG	SV	IP	H	R	ER	BB	SO
14	6	1.72	69	0	0	10	157	105	32	30	45	166

CAREER STATISTICS

W	L	ERA	G	GS	CG	SV	IP	H	R	ER	BB	SO
14	9	2.45	76	7	0	10	195	145	60	53	59	182

His only letdown came after coming off the disabled list, when in seven appearances, he gave up 10 earned runs in 19 innings before he found his groove again.

He was a starting pitcher in 1983, but he injured his shoulder and it has taken him two years to come back. As a result of the injury, Eichhorn was forced to change his style of delivery and now throws sidearm. He uses a herky-jerky motion and literally *jumps to his right* at the end of his delivery.

FIELDING:

He falls off the mound toward the third base side, which makes it harder for him to field balls hit back to him but he didn't really have difficulty in fielding his position or covering first base. He has an average move to first base and does a good job of holding runners on base.

OVERALL:

Eichhorn enters the 1987 season with considerable confidence as a result of his outstanding rookie season. He now can work on developing something to neutralize lefthanded hitters.

Kaat: "He has an awful lot going for him because of his unusual motion. I wouldn't be surprised if he became the No. 1 man in the bullpen ahead of Tom Henke this year. Certainly with his slow stuff and Henke's power, they complement one another well and make an effective duo."

TORONTO BLUE JAYS

HITTING:

Teammates call him "Mr. Gadget" because of all his exercise gimmicks, but last year, Tony Fernandez's gadgeteering paid off. A bone was broken in his left hand late in the 1983 season and subsequently hampered his power-hitting ability from the right side of the plate. But his tireless exercising renewed his strength and fans got to see the other side of Tony Fernandez last season--the power side of his game as a righthanded hitter.

Now he hits equally well from both sides of the plate and actually was more productive against lefthanded pitching last year. He went to a lighter bat when hitting righthanded a (he uses a 32 oz. bat when lefthanded and a 31 oz. model as a righthander) to get more bat control. He also worked on his weight shift and getting his hands moving through his swing faster.

After being moved to the leadoff spot in early June, he thrived on it and totalled 213 hits last season which led all major league shortstops and for as far as official records are kept by position, a baseball record.

Fernandez stands square to the plate, with his knees slightly bent, and holds the bat high. As is characteristic of switch-hitters, he is a low-ball hitter from the left side but likes the ball up from the right side. Batting left, Fernandez will occasionally try to push the ball past the mound for a hit; he is an excellent bunter.

He batted .328 with runners in scoring position last year. He was not in the starting lineup only once, but he won that game with his first major league pinch-hit. He struck out more often last season than in the past but he is, overall, a much more disciplined hitter than most Latin ballplayers.

BASERUNNING:

Though he naturally gets a better break from the box as a lefthanded hitter, Fernandez dashes very well from the right side, too. He is an excellent baserunner and stole 25 bases last year. He could take well over 35 bases this season if he remains in the leadoff spot.

TONY FERNANDEZ
SS, No. 1
SR, 6'2", 165 lbs.
ML Svc: 3 years
Born: 8-6-62 in
  San Pedro de Macoris,
  Dominican Republic

1986 STATISTICS

AVG	G	AB	R	H	2B	3B	HR	RBI	BB	SO	SB
.310	163	687	91	213	33	9	10	65	27	52	25

CAREER STATISTICS

AVG	G	AB	R	H	2B	3B	HR	RBI	BB	SO	SB
.295	427	1518	196	448	70	23	15	137	89	110	43

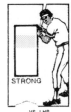
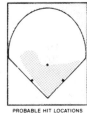

STRONG   STRONG

VS. RHP   VS. LHP   PROBABLE HIT LOCATIONS

FIELDING:

As evidenced by his first Gold Glove last year, Fernandez is the best shortstop in the American League. His fielding is at times as dramatic and theatrical as any of baseball's best infielders.

He cut down on his errors last year by not trying to make a throw on everything he came up with. He has a great flip throw and can get something on it even when he is off-balance. He makes the play in the hole as well as anyone and is also adept at charging the slow roller. His range to his left is exceptional.

OVERALL:

Physically, Fernandez is not built like a Cal Ripken, but he has the same kind of stamina and has played in 327 consecutive games entering the 1987 season.

Kaat: "One of the reasons why Ozzie Smith is so good is because he never gets careless on a routine play. But Fernandez is still young and has so much natural ability, that I think he is sometimes he is guilty of not paying as much attention as he should to the 'easy' or routine plays."

TORONTO BLUE JAYS

HITTING:

Kelly Gruber just needs some more time in the big leagues. He is a good fastball hitter, but will probably have to adjust to big league heaters and the plethora of professional breaking pitches he will see in the American League.

Pitchers are going to bust the fastball up-and-in on him to try to get ahead in the count as quickly as they can against this power-hitting rookie. Once ahead, they are going to taunt him with the breaking ball away.

In the beginning, it is hard to say who will have the edge: the pitcher or Gruber. He is a good fastball hitter and has shown nice power at the Triple-A level, twice having hit 21 home runs in a season (1984 and '85). It is not going to be easy to blow the fastball right by him--he pulls a lot of them foul.

He has not shown himself to be a selective hitter and in all likelihood, will amass a ton of Ks this season. He needs to work on his weight shift to enable to wait on pitches better.

BASERUNNING:

He gets out of the box quickly and has good speed. An excellent baserunner, Gruber had 20 stolen bases in Triple-A in 1985. His good speed is one of his greatest assets; if he continues to progress at the major league level as expected, it is not unreasonable to think that he could join the 20/20 club very soon (HR/SB).

FIELDING:

The Jays are hoping that he will be good enough at third base to enable them to retire their hot corner platoon system which has been in effect for several seasons.

Gruber shows excellent range and has a strong arm, although he needs to work on being more accurate with his throws.

KELLY GRUBER
3B, No. 17
RR, 6'0", 180 lbs.
ML Svc: 2 years
Born: 2-26-62 in Houston, TX

1986 STATISTICS

AVG	G	AB	R	H	2B	3B	HR	RBI	BB	SO	SB
.196	87	143	20	28	4	1	5	15	5	27	2

CAREER STATISTICS

AVG	G	AB	R	H	2B	3B	HR	RBI	BB	SO	SB
.186	107	172	21	32	4	1	6	18	5	35	2

STRONG

VS. RHP

STRONG

VS. LHP

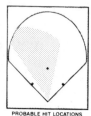

PROBABLE HIT LOCATIONS

OVERALL:

Like many young bucks who come up from the minors, Gruber was an everyday Triple-A player who had to adjust to sitting on the bench in the majors. He did so well. He is 25 years old and the time has now come to find out if he can play in the major leagues.

Kaat: "His reputation as a great prospect preceeds him. The league has not had a good look at him yet; it seems that he needs to get some time in playing everyday in order to show everyone if he can really cut loose and run and hit the way Toronto is predicting.

"The Blue Jays' farm system has been impressive, so you know they're not blowing smoke. This rookie has got something to watch. He may turn out to be this season's big eye-opener."

TORONTO BLUE JAYS

PITCHING:

Last year, the Blue Jays made some alterations in Joe Johnson's mechanics and tightened up his delivery. But so what if he did not appear to have the same fastball in Toronto that he had in Atlanta? Not really a power pitcher, he throws a good sinking fastball in the 80s range and uses a three-quarters delivery.

His best pitch is a sinkerball which he must keep down in order to be effective. He did a good job of that with the Blue Jays. The sinker gives the infielders a good workout, and when Johnson is throwing it well, he will not have to pitch his way out of big-hit innings. Last year, he surrendered only three home runs.

Johnson will never strike out a lot of batters and most will get a piece of the ball at some point, but he has good control and hitters are going to have to earn their own way to first base.

He will challenge the hitters and come inside as he did in September when he beat the Boston Red Sox the first time he faced them--and that's when they were in their stretch drive.

On thing you've got to like about Johnson: he was 4-0 against the contending teams in the American League East. His record might have been even better if the bullpen had not let a couple of leads slip away.

FIELDING:

Johnson is an average fielder and about average in his move to first base and in holding runners.

JOE JOHNSON
RHP, No. 33
RR, 6'2", 195 lbs.
ML Svc: less than one year
Born: 10-30-61 in Brookline, MA

1986 STATISTICS

W	L	ERA	G	GS	CG	SV	IP	H	R	ER	BB	SO
7	2	3.89	16	15	0	0	88	94	39	38	22	39

CAREER STATISTICS

W	L	ERA	G	GS	CG	SV	IP	H	R	ER	BB	SO
11	6	3.99	31	29	1	0	173.2	189	83	77	46	73

OVERALL:

He was only with the Blue Jays for half a season after his trade from Atlanta. The American League only got a fast look at him last year.

He recorded no complete games and physically, may not be able to pitch nine innnings. However, once he learns the American League, this could change. There is not as much premium on going nine as there used to be and the Blue Jays have an excellent bullpen.

Kaat: "Johnson is right behind Key, Clancy and Stieb in the Blue Jays rotation and his success in half a season indicates a good future.

"You've got to show major league hitters you can throw strikes with a breaking ball when you are behind 2-0 and 3-1 in the count. Johnson is not afraid to challenge hitters and he changes speeds well. All he needs is a little better control of his breaking pitches."

TORONTO BLUE JAYS

PITCHING:

Oh man, did Jimmy Key get off to a bad start last year.

It took an awful lot of guts for him to work his way out it and an awful lot of confidence from his manager. In his first six starts batters thought of him as Santa Claus. He had a not-so-merry 13.75 ERA and an 0-3 record.

Key gets in trouble when he can't get the ball where he wants it--and that doesn't mean just for strikes. A pitcher's control has to be good enough to enable him to pitch *anywhere*: his inability to pitch to locations accounted for the 24 home runs he served up last year.

Key does change speeds well. He throws a big curveball and a slider with a good drop on it. He will throw his change-up to good advantage. He thinks of himself as a breaking-ball pitcher, but his fastball (85-87 MPH) is still his best pitch. The heater is the pitch he uses when hself as a breaking-ball pitcher, but his fastball (85-87 MPH) is still his best pitch. The heater is the pitch he uses when he is behind in the count.

He has a great deal of poise and is unflappable in a big game. He had the best record on the team away from Exhibition Stadium last season (7-2) and also was the Blue Jays' best pitcher against the American League's top teams; against pennant contenders (those with of .500 or better), Key was 10-4 in 1986.

He finished **strong**. He ended the season with a string of 19 scoreless innings in Boston and New York. If he can build on that, he will be among the top lefthanders in the league.

FIELDING:

Key has just an ordinary move to first base. He has improved his move somewhat since

JIMMY KEY
LHP, No. 22
RL, 6'1", 185 lbs.
ML Svc: 3 years
Born: 4-22-61 in
Huntsville, AL

1986 STATISTICS

W	L	ERA	G	GS	CG	SV	IP	H	R	ER	BB	SO
14	11	3.57	36	35	4	0	232	222	98	92	74	141

CAREER STATISTICS

W	L	ERA	G	GS	CG	SV	IP	H	R	ER	BB	SO
32	22	3.47	134	67	7	10	506.2	480	212	195	156	270

he first came into the league, but he is still guilty of ignoring runners on base.

An outstanding fielder, Key is a good overall athlete. He is quick off the mound in fielding bunts or in getting over to cover first base. He is also good at handling hard-hit balls up the middle.

OVERALL:

He showed tremedous heart by pitching his way back from his horrendous start last year. He will become even more successful the longer he is in the league. He is a hard-worker and spends time making his pitches even better.

Kaat: "I don't put much stock in velocity. I am more interested in movement and he has an outstanding curveball. Key has learned to throw inside more than he did in his first season as a starter--and that's very important if you want to establish yourself as a pitcher to be taken seriously.

"He is still on the rise and I look for him to be one of the top half dozen lefthanders in the league."

TORONTO BLUE JAYS

PITCHING:

After a season when everything went right (11-0 in 1985) everything went wrong for Dennis Lamp.

Basically a two-pitch pitcher, Lamp throws just the sinker and the slider. Both of his pitches are almost the same speed--in the upper 80s MPH.

He is a control type of pitcher and long relief seems to be his best spot. He does not have the temperament or the stuff to be a short man. He seemed very well-suited to the obscurity of middle relief in 1985, but that was the Jays' big year all around.

He doesn't pitch inside much, preferring to try to keep the ball down and away. He had a lot of difficulty last season in keeping the ball down.

His motion is herky-jerky which makes it tough for the hitter to pick up the ball.

When he gets behind in the count, he goes to the sinking fastball.

Lamp can start in an emergency and did so twice last year.

Last season, he gave up runs in seven of his first eight appearances and 11 of his first 14. As a result, he did not get the work he needs to be effective. In September, he went through a stretch of 26 days without being used. He was so disturbed by his lack of work that he filed a grievance against the Blue Jays for not using him. Continuing his 1986 jinx, he lost.

FIELDING:

He has a good move to first base and will

DENNIS LAMP
RHP, No. 53
RR, 6'3", 215 lbs.
ML Svc: 10 years
Born: 9-23-52 in
Los Angeles, CA

1986 STATISTICS

W	L	ERA	G	GS	CG	SV	IP	H	R	ER	BB	SO
2	6	5.05	40	2	0	2	73	93	50	41	23	30

CAREER STATISTICS

W	L	ERA	G	GS	CG	SV	IP	H	R	ER	BB	SO
74	76	3.90	396	157	21	33	1353.2	1464	670	587	411	590

throw over frequently to hold the runner. He is an average fielder but is always ready to try for the double play on balls hit back to him.

OVERALL:

One of his assets is his experience in all phases of pitching: starting, middle or long relief. He thrives on work.

Kaat: "Because of his sinker, one might argue that he is better suited to pitching on grass than artificial turf. I think it is more a matter of confidence with Lamp than surface, however--it doesn't matter if you are pitching on Interstate 95 or on quicksand if you have your confidence."

TORONTO BLUE JAYS

PITCHING:

Before Gary Lavelle had the "Tommy John surgery" performed last April by Dr. Frank Jobe, he was a power pitcher with an outstanding slider. He used to throw in the 85-89 MPH range and use a three-quarters delivery, dropping down occasionally to throw sidearm.

He made 69 appearances in 1985, despite being bothered off and on all season by his ailing elbow.

After ten years as one of the premier lefty relievers in the National League, Lavelle knows his role. He cannot afford to let the batter's take even one inch of the plate away from him and will not hesitate to pitch inside.

His strength is his ability to get lefthanded hitters out.

FIELDING:

He has a high leg kick and a slow delivery to the plate, which makes him an easy pitcher to attempt a stolen base against. He is not particularly agile. He has an average move to first and he covers first base quickly.

OVERALL:

Lavelle's return could have a positive effect

**GARY LAVELLE
LHP, No. 46
RL, 6'1", 217 lbs.
ML Svc: 12 years
Born: 1-3-49 in
Scranton, PA**

1986 STATISTICS

W	L	ERA	G	GS	CG	SV	IP	H	R	ER	BB	SO
--DID NOT PLAY--												

CAREER STATISTICS

W	L	ERA	G	GS	CG	SV	IP	H	R	ER	BB	SO
78	74	2.84	716	3	0	135	1053.1	964	389	332	418	746

on the whole pitching staff. He is an ideal candidate to serve as a complement to Mark Eichhorn and Tom Henke.

Kaat: "It is absolutely imperative for a club to have a lefthander in the bullpen--especially one with experience. Against the highly experienced American League East teams such as the Yankees, who can send up a parade of lefthanded hitters, a staff without a southpaw is going to be in deep trouble.

"I know Lavelle is motivated to prove something to himself after he had to sit out the 1986 season. The factor to watch as he attempts his comeback will be whether he can maintain his control."

TORONTO BLUE JAYS

RICK LEACH
DH, No. 9
LL, 6'0", 195 lbs.
ML Svc: 5 years
Born: 5-4-57 in
Ann Arbor, MI

HITTING:

Rick Leach has made the mental adjustment to accepting his role, which is coming off the bench as a pinch-hitter, occasionally playing the outfield or DHing.

A good low-ball hitter, Leach drove the ball better last year than ever before after batting coach Cito Gaston made some changes to get Leach's bat moving. When he used to hit from a standstill stance and his best shot was to the warning track. While he is not going to become a powerhouse-type of hitter, it does appear that his new, looser stance has increased his ability to hit the ball farther than he was able to in the past.

Righthanders try to get him out with off-speed stuff and fastballs up-and-in. He's a patient hitter with a good idea of the strike zone and he'll go the other way on an outside pitch.

He shared the team lead in pinch-hits with 10 last year. He drove in 39 runs off righthanded pitching, only two less than Willie Upshaw in far less at-bats.

BASERUNNING:

He doesn't have much speed on the bases and doesn't try to steal.

FIELDING:

Leach was a center fielder in college ball and can still cover ground when he plays the outfield (usually in right field) despite his lack of speed.

He is an excellent defensive first baseman.

1986 STATISTICS

AVG	G	AB	R	H	2B	3B	HR	RBI	BB	SO	SB
.309	110	246	35	76	14	1	5	39	13	24	0

CAREER STATISTICS

AVG	G	AB	R	H	2B	3B	HR	RBI	BB	SO	SB
.259	426	877	102	227	47	7	12	96	113	112	6

  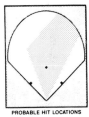

VS. RHP   VS. LHP   PROBABLE HIT LOCATIONS

OVERALL:

After battling back from almost being eliminated from the game, Leach's confidence factor should be up after last year. He was a standout football player at the University of Michigan (1974-78) and his overall athletic talent has helped him along the way.

Kaat: "I would have to expect that Rick is going to hit with more power this year because he should have confidence in his corner now. So much of this game is tied in with how much a player *believes* he can accomplish. When you are struggling, you swing defensively and rarely do much good.

TORONTO BLUE JAYS

PITCHING:

Craig McMurtry was a complete mystery to the Braves. They could not figure out why he was unable to return to the form he showed in 1983, when as a rookie, he won 15 games and lost only nine.

At this point, it is beginning to look like McMurtry will never recapture that form. The biggest differences appear to be that McMurtry lacks the control and the confidence that distinguished him as a rookie. Unless he finds the control, the confidence probably will never return.

McMurtry has a 90+ MPH fastball, but it is not an overpowering, moving fastball most of the time. His breaking pitches are good but not extraordinary. To be effective with any of his pitches, McMurtry must get them low in the strike zone and he has not done that consistently in the past few years. He has been particularly hurt with mistakes on high breaking balls.

A righthander without great movement on his fastball and with basically only two pitches, McMurtry can win only with precise control. The Blue Jays are hoping that he finds the groove again.

FIELDING:

McMurtry is a tall, lanky pitcher who has good athletic skills. He has a technically sound delivery and has no problem fielding his position. His pickoff move is decent.

CRAIG McMURTRY
RHP, No. 29
RR, 6'5", 192 lbs.
ML Svc: 4 years
Born: 11-5-59 in
Temple, TX

1986 STATISTICS

W	L	ERA	G	GS	CG	SV	IP	H	R	ER	BB	SO
1	6	4.74	37	5	0	0	79.2	82	46	42	43	50

CAREER STATISTICS

W	L	ERA	G	GS	CG	SV	IP	H	R	ER	BB	SO
25	35	4.06	127	76	6	1	532.2	526	268	240	260	282

OVERALL:

Three seasons have passed since his rookie year. Finally, the Braves gave up on McMurtry. He has the opportunity to begin anew in Toronto. He will have to earn a spot in the starting rotation by pitching with good control. But in order to do that, he is going to have to maintain his confidence.

Because the hitters of the American League have never faced McMurtry before, he might have the edge during the first go-round. After that, however, unless he gets it together, 1987 could be another bust season for him.

Dierker: "He's going to have to show something right from spring training or he will find himself working out of the bullpen--or in the minors."

TORONTO BLUE JAYS

HITTING:

Lloyd Moseby hit a career-high 21 home runs last season. His batting average was lower than in previous years. However, this was not a result of his increased power, but from slumps caused by a bad back in September and a viral infection in July.

Moseby is more of a high fastball hitter than most lefthanded hitters tend to be. Righthanders try to pitch him low-and-away and then come up-and-in. He had a better average and more homers (15) off righties last year, although he has always had his share of hits off lefthanders.

Blue Jays' batting coach Cito Gaston worked with Moseby last season to correct a flaw in his swing: Moseby was turning his upper body and not using the proper weight shift as he strode into a pitch. The correction led to more of a closed stance in 1986. He now stands deep in the box, square to the plate, with his legs spread wide.

Still, Moseby doesn't hit as much to the opposite field as he could. He's got the strength and quickness to take the high fastball and go the other way. He has the ability to cover both halves of the strike zone and should be able to hit for a better average.

Moseby does not take advantage of his speed as much as he should. He's an excellent bunter and should attempt to use it to get on base more often.

BASERUNNING:

Baserunning is a big part of Moseby's game. He gets out of the box quickly, takes a good lead and draws a lot of attemped pickoff throws from the mound.

The headfirst slide is his specialty and Moseby has perfected the skill to the point where he is able to bounce up quickly and take the extra-base on a poor throw. He led the team with 32 steals last year and more importantly he gets the big steals, the kind that put a runner into scoring position when the team needs it.

FIELDING:

Moseby's defensive prowess is right up

LLOYD MOSEBY
CF, No. 15
LR, 6'3", 205 lbs.
ML Svc: 7 years
Born: 11-5-59 in
Portland, AR

1986 STATISTICS

AVG	G	AB	R	H	2B	3B	HR	RBI	BB	SO	SB
.253	152	589	89	149	24	5	21	86	64	122	32

CAREER STATISTICS

AVG	G	AB	R	H	2B	3B	HR	RBI	BB	SO	SB
.261	974	3558	513	928	173	46	102	471	351	697	161

VS. RHP

VS. LHP

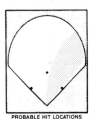

PROBABLE HIT LOCATIONS

there with the top center fielders in the league in terms of his range. He cuts off the balls in the alleys--a talent greatly needed in ballparks with artificial surface. His arm is average in terms of strength and accuracy.

He is equally good at coming in, making the sliding catch, and going back to the wall for the ball, though last season was not his best defensive year. It appeared that some balls fell in front of him which might have been charged and caught earlier.

OVERALL:

The Blue Jays' outfield is among the best in baseball. Moseby is currently rated No. 3 of the three; there is considerable competition among all of them--Bell, Barfield and Moseby-- to be the best one.

Kaat: "I wouldn't be surprised if he made up his mind to be a table setter for Barfield and Bell, he could lead the league in scoring runs. He's capable of raising his average back to where it was in '83-84 (.280)."

TORONTO BLUE JAYS

HITTING:

Rance Mulliniks worked on an off-season weight training program before the start of the 1986 season. For four months, he worked out four times a week to build up his strength. His program seemed to pay off--he had already hit a career-high 11 home runs before a problem with his lower back put him on the disabled list for a month shortly after the All-Star break. And when Mulliniks came back to the lineup, the home runs did not. He never hit another one last year.

Mulliniks is a low fastball hitter with an excellent idea of what he wants to do at the plate. He's a real student of hitting and a very disciplined one. He is capable of pulling the ball one time and then go the opposite way in his next at-bat if he gets pitched outside.

Righthanded pitchers try to change speeds on him and work on him with breaking stuff.

Mulliniks is a good clutch hitter, and though his 1986 numbers as a pinch-hitter were not good, he did hit well with runners in scoring position.

He is comfortable with his role as a platoon player, which makes him more useful to a manager.

BASERUNNING:

He gets out of the batter's box quickly, but his good dash is not put to much use; as he has no speed. He is a good baserunner, but he doesn't steal.

FIELDING:

Mulliniks has worked hard to become a solid defensive player, although his back problems hampered him last year before he

RANCE MULLINIKS
3B, No. 5
LR, 6'0", 170 lbs.
ML Svc: 9 years
Born: 1-15-56 in Tulare, CA

1986 STATISTICS

AVG	G	AB	R	H	2B	3B	HR	RBI	BB	SO	SB
.259	117	348	50	90	22	0	11	45	43	60	1

CAREER STATISTICS

AVG	G	AB	R	H	2B	3B	HR	RBI	BB	SO	SB
.268	822	2288	295	614	150	12	43	273	267	339	11

  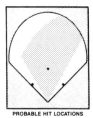

| VS. RHP | VS. LHP | PROBABLE HIT LOCATIONS |

went on the DL. He moves well to both his left and right. He has a shortstop's arm and his throws are usually accurate.

OVERALL:

Mulliniks is an underrated player who has a lot of value even if youngster Kelly Gruber becomes the regular third baseman this year.

Kaat: "Rance is the kind of player who provides his club with a good insurance policy. He has a good head for the game--he's steady in everything he does.

"He can continue to be a productive player if used in the role of DH or pinch-hitter."

TORONTO BLUE JAYS

PITCHING:

After leading the league in ERA in 1985, and with the best ERA of any starter in the league over a three-year period (1983-85), Dave Stieb's ERA jumped to 4.74 last year. He produced only seven wins, his lowest total since he won eight in less than a full season in his rookie year.

Stieb is one of the game's most intense competitors--to a fault. He wants to pitch a no-hitter every time he takes the ball and he seems to believe that it's possible.

Stieb is a power pitcher and throws from a compact three-quarters delivery. He continues to throw his fastball with good velocity (in the 90-91 MPH range).

Stieb's devastating pitch is his slider. When right, it's got a beautiful, natural drop that makes it almost impossible to hit. But a hanging slider--even one sent from the hand of Stieb--is a hitter's delight, and that's what he offered all too often last year. He needed to concentrate on pitching low, low in the strike zone, and to forget about moving in and out until he could correct himself. But he was unable to get his pitches down until late in the season.

His problems really started in the second half of the 1985 season. Then, he blamed his ineffectiveness on mechanics. It wasn't until the second half of the 1986 season that he became fine-tuned and found a consistent release point for his slider. He won more games in September (4-2 and 2.45 ERA) than he did in the first half last year (2-9, 5.80 ERA).

At times last season, he seemed to rely more on a curveball than on his hard slider.

He has always been one of the quickest workers in the league, but last year, he appeared more tentative. At times, it looked as though he was puzzled by what was happening to him.

Because he always feels as though he can beat any hitter with his best stuff, Stieb gets hurt on a lot of two-strike counts.

FIELDING:

He has always been among the best

DAVE STIEB
RHP, No. 37
RR, 6'1", 195 lbs.
ML Svc: 8 years
Born: 7-22-57 in
Santa Ana, CA

1986 STATISTICS

W	L	ERA	G	GS	CG	SV	IP	H	R	ER	BB	SO
7	12	4.74	37	34	1	1	205	239	128	108	87	127

CAREER STATISTICS

W	L	ERA	G	GS	CG	SV	IP	H	R	ER	BB	SO
102	92	3.34	259	254	85	1	1859.1	1673	773	690	631	1069

fielding-pitchers in the league, but last season, this aspect of his game showed wear and tear. He did not eat up comebackers with the same vigor of his better days.

He has an excellent move to first base and holds runners tight.

OVERALL:

As unbelievable as it is, Stieb was converted from an outfielder to a pitcher only nine years ago, in 1978. His transition at the age of 21 is especially noteworthy now as his lack of mechanical training is beginning to show. In short, he is not a "professional" pitcher in the same sense that craftsmen like Tom Seaver or Tommy John are. They have the background to be able to "right" themselves, but with no history of clinks and glitches, Stieb is struggling to repair a gift that has always been natural.

For the past two seasons, he has complained of shoulder ailments and an examination last December did reveal some calcification which may require surgery after the 1987 season.

Kaat: "He needs to go back to his upbeat tempo and aggressive frame of mind. He has to ask himself if mentally and physically he is going to have to change his method of pitching. He has never been the winner he should be considering his stuff. The type of stuff he threw last season was not the same as he had when he led the league in ERA."

TORONTO BLUE JAYS

HITTING:

Willie Upshaw's job is in jeopardy. In 1986, for the third consecutive year, his average, power and run production declined. His trouble started at midseason of 1984 when he suffered a wrist injury while swinging the bat and since then he has made numerous adjustments in his batting style.

Upshaw got off to a bad start in '85 when he sacrificed power in an attempt to raise his batting average. He stopped pulling everything and began to hit often to the opposite field. But last season, he couldn't pull the trigger even when he was pitched inside. He had only two home runs at the All-Star break. As he worked to develop the ability to go with the outside pitch to the opposite field, he lost the ability to pull the inside pitch. When he got pitched inside, he was not capable of handling it.

He's a line drive hitter who is capable of hitting the ball out of the park. He likes the low fastball.

He has always hit lefthanders well and, until last year, did so with power.

Righthanders work him up-and-in and with breaking balls away. Lefthanders throw the fastball away and also use a sweeping breaking ball.

He is a patient hitter with a good idea of the strike zone and had a career-high of 78 walks last year.

BASERUNNING:

Upshaw is quick out of the batter's box and runs well. He's got the green light and took full advantage of it (perhaps in an attempt to salvage what he could to help his club by stealing bases). He had a career high 23 steals last year and was thrown out only five times.

FIELDING:

He's an excellent fielder with good range. He goes to his right well to make the force play at second. Before it was replaced before the 1985 season, the carpet at Exhibition Stadium was especially worn around first base. More than any other position player,

WILLIE UPSHAW
1B, No. 26
LL, 6'0", 192 lbs.
ML Svc: 8 years
Born: 4-27-57 in
Blanco, TX

1986 STATISTICS

AVG	G	AB	R	H	2B	3B	HR	RBI	BB	SO	SB
.251	155	573	85	144	28	6	9	60	78	87	23

CAREER STATISTICS

AVG	G	AB	R	H	2B	3B	HR	RBI	BB	SO	SB
.268	1065	3198	470	857	155	38	97	420	332	616	66

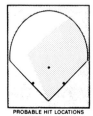

VS. RHP / VS. LHP / PROBABLE HIT LOCATIONS

Upshaw's fielding was affected by the poor surface; when the new carpet was installed, Upshaw's fielding picked right up.

Normally he doesn't take his failures at the plate into the field, but was charged with three errors in one inning in a game in Boston last year.

OVERALL:

Kaat: "There have been suggestions that working with weights has got Upshaw all tied up at the plate. I don't think weight training is harmful if it is combined with stretching at the same time to maintain flexibility.

"Upshaw may have been pressing last year. And if he was not as relaxed as he should have been at the plate, he may have been gripping the bat too tightly. A batter must have a loose grip, just like a pitcher who, if he grips the ball too tightly, doesn't get as much on it.

"This is an important year for him. If he tries to repeat his 27-homer year (1983), he could be making a mistake. He must try to be intense without being tense."

TORONTO BLUE JAYS

HITTING:

Ernie Whitt got off to a slow start last year. He was troubled by a lower-back ailment and though he did not feel as though it was serious enough to force him to the DL, the Jays overruled because it was too early in the season to take an unnecessary gamble with such an important player.

He had a poor first half, and at the All-Star break had hit just .235 with eight home runs. After the All-Star break, however, the veteran catcher hit .303 to finish with a career high .268 average.

Whitt is a good low fastball hitter who is strictly a pull hitter. He tries to lay off the high fastball, but at times he goes after it, and if bat meets ball, Whitt will crush the pitch.

Since early in the 1981 season, Whitt has been platooned with Buck Martinez at catcher. Whitt has been used almost exclusively against righthanded pitching. Righthanders try to get him out with breaking balls and change-ups, thrown either down-and-in or away.

When he does face a southpaw, he has trouble with the breaking ball. He's not a high-average hitter, but he has good home run potential.

As Toronto is not traditionally of the American League's foremost preservers of the little maneuver known as the "bunt," it is a somewhat dubious distinction that Whitt is the best bunter on the team.

BASERUNNING:

He has below-average speed and is slow leaving the batter's box. He will slide hard to break up the double play. Whitt is not a threat to steal, but he runs the bases alertly and has been around long enough to know when to go and when not to take foolish gambles.

FIELDING:

He doesn't throw out a high percentage of runners (last year, he threw out 26 of 82 attempting thieves for a 31.7% kill ratio).

ERNIE WHITT
C, No. 12
LR, 6'2", 200 lbs.
ML Svc: 9 years
Born: 6-13-52 in Detroit, MI

1986 STATISTICS
AVG	G	AB	R	H	2B	3B	HR	RBI	BB	SO	SB
.268	131	395	48	106	19	2	16	56	35	39	0

CAREER STATISTICS
AVG	G	AB	R	H	2B	3B	HR	RBI	BB	SO	SB
.248	835	2303	266	571	107	11	86	323	248	312	13

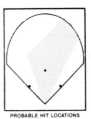

VS. RHP   VS. LHP   PROBABLE HIT LOCATIONS

Sometimes he hurries his throw which leads to inaccuracy.

Whitt is good at chasing down foul pop-ups and at slow-rolling bunts.

He shows good judgment in handling throws at the plate. He handles the long, line-drive throws from outfield sharpshooters Bell and Barfield very well, having worked successfully with them for several seasons. He goes out to get the short throws and can spin to sweep the runner at the plate more often than not.

OVERALL:

His strength is his experience in handling the Jays' pitching staff. He calls a good game and he has their confidence.

Kaat: "Ernie is at the peak of his game, and as such, he is not likely to improve any more at this stage of his career. He's steady and should be playing for several more years until somebody younger or better comes along."

TORONTO BLUE JAYS

CECIL FIELDER
DH, No. 23
RR, 6'3", 217 lbs.
ML Svc: 1 year plus
Born: 9-21-63 in
Los Angeles, CA

HITTING, BASERUNNING, FIELDING:

A big, strong righthanded hitter, Cecil Fielder came within one home run of equalling the league record in winter ball in Venezuela this year. He hit 19 of them and also led the league in RBIs.

Fielder was with the Jays in the second half of the '85 season, playing first base against lefthanded pitching. He had a good spring in '86 and opened the season as the club's designated hitter, but then lost the job to veteran Cliff Johnson.

Fielder is a low-ball hitter who drives the ball into the alleys from left- to right-center. He likes the ball out over the plate. Lefthanded pitchers try to jam Fielder up-and-in, then tease him with breaking pitches away. But don't make any mistakes or Fielder will send them out of the park.

He is only 23 years old; he is learning discipline at the plate--not just on balls and strikes--but also with the knife and fork: he tends to be overweight.

Fielder will get a chance to become the DH, either on a regular basis or in a platoon arrangement this year. If he is platooned, he would start against southpaws.

He is slow out of the batter's box, and doesn't run well. He has no speed and is no threat on the bases.

Fielder is not much of a fielder, though it would make for great copy if he were. He has good hands, but his range is limited.

OVERALL:

Coming off a big winter in Venezuela, Fielder's confidence level should be way up. He's a threat with the bat, and his best shot will be as DH. There are enough big bats in the Jays' lineup to take a lot of pressure off him.

TOM FILER
RHP, No. 49
RR, 6'1", 198 lbs.
ML Svc: 2 years
Born: 12-1-56 in
Philadelphia, PA

PITCHING, FIELDING:

Tom Filer finally got an opportunity to prove he could pitch in the major leagues in the 1985 season. Then, he went 7-0 in nine starts before a tender elbow put him on the sidelines. Last year when his elbow bothered him in spring training, he underwent surgery and sat out the entire season.

Filer has always had a good curveball, which he mixed with a slider, change-up and fastball.

Even if surgery should take some of the zing out of his fastball and the sharpness out of his slider, Filer is a pitcher who knows how to pitch; he can get by with changing speeds and with good control.

He has just an average move to first but throws over frequently to hold the runners close. He is a good athlete and his delivery leaves him in good position to field the ball. He does a good job of covering first base.

OVERALL:

Entering spring training, he is a non-roster player and must prove that he is physically sound in order to have any shot at all of making the club. He could be used either in long relief or as a spot-starter or the fifth starter. Filer's chances of making the club may depend on whether the Jays can make a deal for another lefthander.

Kaat: "His best asset is that he knows how to pitch. Before his elbow surgery, Filer had command of his breaking pitches. Now, who knows?"

MANNY LEE
SS, No. 4
SR, 5'9", 151 lbs.
ML Svc: *less than one year*
Born: 6-17-65 in SP de Macoris, Dominican Republic

HITTING, BASERUNNING, FIELDING:

Before his strong showing at the plate last August, Manny Lee looked as though he might be just a good field/no hit shortstop. But he did well and finished in the Top Ten in hitting over this past winter playing in the Dominican League.

Lee seemed to be making better contact and hit the ball more sharply than he had in his previous major league stint. He is a switch-hitter with more power batting as a righthanded hitter, but last year, he even hit one out batting lefthanded. Overall, Lee hits for a better average from the left side.

He's small (151 pounds) and a lot of pitchers are going to try to blow the fastball by him. He still gets fooled at times by breaking pitches.

He needs to work on making his hands stronger and is taking a page from teammate Tony Fernandez's book by using assorted exercises to help himself to improve his strength.

He has good speed, although he hasn't had much opportunity to show it. He did steal 24 bases in Class-A in 1984.

The Jays used him at second base, subbing for Damaso Garcia, last season. Lee showed great range and seems to be able to turn the double play well.

His regular position is shortstop and the Blue Jays think he might be the second-best shortstop in the league defensively, behind Tony Fernandez.

OVERALL:

Lee's excellent glove, good range and his quickness are going to get him a job somewhere. He led his Class-A league in hitting and after a strong showing in winter ball before the start of the 1987 season. He has a good shot to earn the starting job at second base this year.

THE
NATIONAL LEAGUE

ATLANTA BRAVES

PITCHING:

Three days before the All-Star break last season, the Braves were just one game out of first place in the NL West and general manager Bobby Cox thought maybe the team could win the division if it had more experience on the pitching staff. So he dealt young pitchers Duane Ward and Joe Johnson to Toronto for veteran pitchers Jim Acker and Doyle Alexander.

The Braves, no direct result of the performances of Acker and Alexander, went into a tailspin and were soon out of the race. And now it is unclear where Acker, who pitched decently but not spectacularly, fits into the team's future.

He appears to be better suited to relief than starting. He is a fastball/slider pitcher and when he has good control of the pitches, they are above-average. He throws hard and has a good, sharp-breaking ball. On a given night, he can appear very impressive out of the bullpen and really shut down a game in the middle innings. But as a starter, he does not appear to have the consistent breaking ball that is necessary for that role. When he starts, the hitters seem able to wait on the hard stuff and when he makes a mistake they hit it.

Because he is basically a two-pitch pitcher, Acker appears better suited for relief. But the Braves' shortage of starters might force him in the other direction.

FIELDING, HITTING, BASERUNNING:

Acker is a good athlete who, consequently, is a good fielder. He holds runners on base well, a necessity for a relief pitcher and plays bunts with confidence and decisiveness in clutch situations.

He is a non-entity as a hitter, the product of

JIM ACKER
RHP, No. 31
RR, 6'2", 210 lbs.
ML Svc: 4 years
Born: 9-24-58 in Freer, TX

1986 STATISTICS

W	L	ERA	G	GS	CG	SV	IP	H	R	ER	BB	SO
5	12	4.00	44	19	0	0	155	163	51	69	48	69

CAREER STATISTICS

W	L	ERA	G	GS	CG	SV	IP	H	R	ER	BB	SO
20	20	3.99	175	27	0	12	411	431	177	182	154	188

several years' inactivity in the American League. But if he is used as a middle reliever, he'll bat only slightly more often in the NL than he did in the American League. His baserunning skills are a non-factor, too, although again he is a good athlete who runs better than some.

OVERALL:

The Johnson/Ward for Acker/Alexander deal can be better assessed in several years, when it is determined how good the younger pitchers will be.

Dierker: "For now, the Braves at least have a serviceable arm which should be of some benefit to a very thin pitching staff. If the staff falls together as the Braves would like, a young pitcher will emerge to claim a spot in the starting rotation, freeing Acker for middle relief. There, he would be a set-up man for short relievers Gene Garber and Paul Assenmacher. My best bet is that Acker will be working out of the bullpen in 1987."

ATLANTA BRAVES

PITCHING:

Doyle Alexander's career has been one of many twists and turns and there has been a contract squabble around many of them. But there has been one constant: Alexander has always pitched his best for Bobby Cox, first when Cox was manager of the Braves and later when Cox was manager of the Toronto Blue Jays. Last season Cox and Alexander were reunited in Atlanta, albeit with Cox as general manager this time.

Alexander was a welcomed, dependable addition to the Braves' starting rotation in the second half of last season. Alexander is a seasoned, crafty pitcher known by fans and critics alike as a junkballer. He pitches with his mind more than his arm.

He nibbles at the corners. He changes speeds, no two pitches coming in at precisely the same velocity or from precisely the same angle. He throws a lot of breaking balls and off-speed pitches, turning the fastball over a little bit and keeping it on the corners.

He cannot pitch successfully when his control is anything less than flawless. Walks hurt him, but he is hurt even more when he throws the ball down the middle of the plate. Any big league hitter can hit him if his pitches are down the middle. Location is everything.

FIELDING, HITTING, BASERUNNING:

Alexander needs every advantage he can get to win and he knows it. Thus, he rarely hurts himself. He works hard at his fielding and it shows. He almost never is late covering first base or getting off the mound. He follows through in a good fielding position. An Alexander error on the mound is rare.

He is not as efficient as a hitter, however.

DOYLE ALEXANDER
RHP, No. 37
RR, 6'3", 200 lbs.
ML Svc: 16 years
Born: 9-4-50 in
 Cordova, AL

1986 STATISTICS

W	L	ERA	G	GS	CG	SV	IP	H	R	ER	BB	SO
11	10	4.14	34	34	5	0	228.1	255	114	105	37	139

CAREER STATISTICS

W	L	ERA	G	GS	CG	SV	IP	H	R	ER	BB	SO
160	135	3.71	467	370	82	3	2708.1	2693	1228	1117	803	1199

He seems to enjoy taking his cuts and he does work at batting practice. But he generally looks helpless at the plate. He wanders more than he runs on the bases.

OVERALL:

Alexander was a free agent this winter and the Braves failed to re-sign him. He is an important part of the Braves pitching puzzle, not because he is a known commodity whom the Braves can count on for 20 wins, but because he is a seasoned pitcher who they count of for a lot of innings. The Braves figure Alexander will keep them in the game and if the offense and bullpen come through, they will have a chance to win. At this point, that's about all the Braves can hope for from their starters.

Dierker: "Doyle is a good pitcher and a good competitor. If he has a good year this season, it would really help the Braves. He is capable, but not so talented that he is not capable of an off year."

ATLANTA BRAVES

PITCHING:

When the Braves attempted to talk trade during the off-season, they found few of their players--and, frankly, only two of their pitchers--in demand. One was Paul Assenmacher. (The other: Zane Smith.)

Assenmacher made the Braves' staff as a rookie last spring and got off to an impressive start out of the bullpen. However, he faded somewhat, presumably because of a heavy workload for which he might not have been physically prepared. The Braves and other teams believe Assenmacher has the potential to become one of the league's top lefthanded short relievers.

Assenmacher, tall and lanky, is nasty on lefthanded hitters with his crossfire/sidearm motion. He has an exceptional breaking ball that is his best pitch; it also adds to the effectiveness of a fastball that looks quicker than it is. But his fastball would not sustain him in the major leagues on its own merits; he must spot it well to use it effectively. His breaking ball also has a bite to it, and when he is right he can give righthanded hitters trouble as well.

But at other times he can have great trouble with righthanded hitters, and this shortcoming is the biggest obstacle standing between Assenmacher and a distinguished career as a big league relief pitcher. It remains to be seen if he overcomes it. Right now he has great difficulty against righties when he is not getting the fastball on the corner and having trouble getting the breaking ball over. He is much more consistent against lefthanded hitters.

FIELDING, HITTING, BASERUNNING:

Assenmacher makes use of his advantage of being a lefthander, in holding runners on

PAUL ASSENMACHER
LHP, No. 30
LL, 6'3", 200 lbs.
ML Svc: one year
Born: 12-10-60 in Detroit, MI

1986 STATISTICS

W	L	ERA	G	GS	CG	SV	IP	H	R	ER	BB	SO
7	3	2.50	61	0	0	7	68.1	61	23	19	26	56

CAREER STATISTICS

W	L	ERA	G	GS	CG	SV	IP	H	R	ER	BB	SO
7	3	2.50	61	0	0	7	68.1	61	23	19	26	56

base. He follows through from his delivery in good fielding position and there is no indication he'll hurt himself defensively.

As a hitter and baserunner, he really isn't a factor since he's a short-stint relief pitcher who rarely would bat for himself. But for the record, he doesn't appear to have a clue with the bat.

OVERALL:

Assenmacher definitely is an asset to the Braves' bullpen, as he would be to any major league bullpen.

Dierker: "The question now is how valuable Assenmacher will be. Will he be only a role player whose primary purpose is to get out one or two lefthanded hitters and then turn the game over to the main guy in the bullpen? Or will he become the main guy, the closer who finishes the task against both left- and righthanded hitters? The 1987 season should provide the answer."

ATLANTA BRAVES

HITTING:

It seems so long ago (it was 1983, actually) when Bruce Benedict looked like a significant offensive threat. In 1983, as the Braves' starting catcher, he hit .300 for much of the season before finishing at .298. He hit .300 from July on, .328 with runners in scoring position, .338 at home, and he set career highs in games, hits, runs and walks. Now back to the present . . .

Benedict, now a 31-year-old backup catcher, only fleetingly resembles the hitter of 1983. He was never that hitter before or after. No one can explain the difference.

At this point, Benedict is a below-average major league hitter. He is a pull hitter, but in his case, that is a disadvantage. He does not have the power to benefit from pull hitting but he has the predictability that allows defenses to bunch up against him. He also lacks the speed to beat out many hits. He can be overpowered with power pitches and he can be befuddled with breaking pitches.

Say this, however, for Benedict as a hitter: he is tough from the standpoint of battling a pitcher. He'll foul the ball off, take the excruciatingly close ball, do his best to work the pitcher for a walk. Consequently, his on-base percentage is generally disproportionately high in relation to his batting average.

BASERUNNING:

Benedict's lack of speed has long been an internal joke among the Braves, as well as among the personable catcher's many friends around the league. Benedict simply does not have the speed to beat out infield hits, to steal a base, to score from second on anything other than the purest of RBI hits. He is perhaps a typical catcher on the bases, clogging up the bases for a team woefully short on speed anyway.

Benedict is an intelligent baseball player and just as he battles a pitcher for whatever advantage he can muster, he is a thinking man's baserunner. He rarely will attempt something beyond his ability, and thus he rarely makes an unnecessary out on the bases.

BRUCE BENEDICT
C, No. 20
RR, 6'2", 195 lbs.
ML Svc: 8 years
Born: 8-18-55 in
Birmingham, AL

1986 STATISTICS

AVG	G	AB	R	H	2B	3B	HR	RBI	BB	SO	SB
.225	64	160	11	36	10	1	0	13	15	10	1

CAREER STATISTICS

AVG	G	AB	R	H	2B	3B	HR	RBI	BB	SO	SB
.249	789	2387	187	594	87	6	16	230	269	192	12

  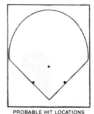

STRONG — VS. RHP   STRONG — VS. LHP   PROBABLE HIT LOCATIONS

FIELDING:

Pitchers like to work with Benedict. He calls a good game, has a take-charge attitude and has been around long enough to know the hitters' strengths and weaknesses. Indeed, he can quarterback a team from behind the plate.

But aside from these assets, which are largely intangible, Benedict is an average defensive player. His fielding is average in terms of handling pitches (by saving wild pitches, for example) and receiving the ball. His throwing has deteriorated much as his hitting has done.

There was a time when Benedict threw out as many baserunners as any of the league's top catchers. But, for whatever reason, that didn't last long. His mechanics often seem confused, and his throws often are errant.

OVERALL:

Dierker: "The Braves still haven't solved their catching problems, so it is possible Benedict will work his way into more playing time once again. He is a good backup catcher in that he is a competitor. But overall, he is not a good defensive catcher."

ATLANTA BRAVES

PITCHING:

The Braves have not given up on Jeff Dedmon, but they don't talk quite as frequently or loudly any more about the great relief pitcher he will become. He has the pitches to be a top-flight reliever and the Braves for the past three years have hyped him for the role. But curiously, they've never really given him a shot at it and in the limited roles he has been given, Dedmon has been only marginally successful.

He now is seen as an all-purpose pitcher who can be valuable to a staff as an 8th, 9th or 10th member. He is principally a middle and short reliever, but he also can be used as a long reliever and, if necessary, a spot starter.

His best pitch is a knuckle-curve. He has an average to slightly above-average fastball, but he needs to have it move to be effective. Sometimes it comes in straight and this, of course, leads to trouble. The keys for Dedmon are to get movement on his fastball and to get his breaking ball over the plate. He has been plagued by erratic control.

Dedmon seems to have a good idea of how to pitch, how to move the ball around, how to set up hitters. But he can execute what he knows only if he gets the ball where he wants it. It still isn't too late for Dedmon to blossom.

FIELDING, HITTING, BASERUNNING:

Dedmon is a good fielder. He is very quick on the mound and he makes decisive plays when there are runners on base and options with the ball. He could use a little work on his pickoff move.

JEFF DEDMON
RHP, No. 49
LR, 6'2", 200 lbs.
ML Svc: 3 years
Born: 3-4-60 in Torrance, CA

1986 STATISTICS

W	L	ERA	G	GS	CG	SV	IP	H	R	ER	BB	SO
6	6	2.98	57	0	0	3	99.2	90	43	33	39	58

CAREER STATISTICS

W	L	ERA	G	GS	CG	SV	IP	H	R	ER	BB	SO
16	12	3.72	176	0	0	7	270.2	270	140	112	123	153

Dedmon has had little exposure as a hitter or baserunner in the major leagues. He appears to take a pretty good swing, but he usually is overmatched at the plate.

OVERALL:

Dedmon probably will make the Braves' pitching staff again in 1987, which could be a decisive year in his career. If he doesn't solidify his status, the Braves probably will try to move him and turn to another young pitcher.

Dierker: "With Bruce Sutter's continued arm problems and a thin pitching staff from top to bottom, the Braves certainly will give Dedmon the opportunity to make it. He is an all-purpose pitcher who I think could start, pitch mid-relief or pitch short-relief."

ATLANTA BRAVES

PITCHING:

If his form holds, Gene Garber will not have another outstanding season until 1990.

Garber had a tremendous season out of the Braves' bullpen in 1978, then had three lesser seasons, then was outstanding again in 1982, then had three lesser seasons, then was outstanding again in 1986. If the one-on, three-off trend holds, he'll not match his 1986 numbers in any of the next three seasons before finding the groove again at the start of the next decade.

Not that Garber has been without his good streaks during the three-year stretches between outstanding seasons. But, as a Brave, Garber has been consistent only in '78, '82 and '86.

He was the Braves' No. 1 relief pitcher last season, picking up the slack when it becme clear Bruce Sutter was not up to the task. Garber is a thinking man's pitcher, his success or failure hinging completely on outthinking and outmaneuvering the hitter.

Every Garber pitch is targeted for a specific part of the plate, usually one corner or the other, and every Garber pitch has something a little different from the last one on it. His best pitch is the change-up, which during his good years may be the very best change-up in the game. He also throws a slider, a sinking fastball, a curveball, an occasional screwball and other pitches that are combinations of the above.

He pitches with a sidearm delivery, sometimes three-quarters, sometimes almost submarine. He has a unique motion in that he turns his back to the batter briefly. The sidearm delivery makes his change-up particularly difficult on righthanded batters,

GENE GARBER
RHP, No. 26
RR, 5'10", 172 lbs.
ML Svc: 14 years
Born: 11-13-47 in
Lancaster, PA

1986 STATISTICS

W	L	ERA	G	GS	CG	SV	IP	H	R	ER	BB	SO
5	5	2.54	61	0	0	24	78		76	23	22	20	56

CAREER STATISTICS

W	L	ERA	G	GS	CG	SV	IP	H	R	ER	BB	SO
88	99	3.29	843	9	4	194	1393.1	1335	595	509	403	869

who cannot pick up the path of the ball. He also spots his slider well and, perhaps above all, is the ultimate competitor.

FIELDING, HITTING, BASERUNNING:

Garber works hard at all facets of the game and is a good fielder. He attacks the batted or bunted ball and knows what to do with it. He likes to hit, but isn't any kind of threat at the plate. As a short relief specialist, he rarely bats and almost never runs the bases.

OVERALL:

Dierker: "Based on his performance last season, Sutter's continued unavailability and the state of the rest of the bullpen, Garber enters the 1987 season as the Braves' No. 1 relief pitcher. They can only hope that he puts together back-to-back sterling seasons for the first time ever."

ATLANTA BRAVES

HITTING:

When you put a bat in Damaso Garcia's hands, you're in for a show. He will swing at *anything*.

Garcia hates the base on balls and last season only suffered through 13 of them. Although he has many of the qualities needed of a good leadoff hitter, his inability to show any kind of patience at the plate forced the Blue Jays snatched him from the No. 1 spot and made him hit down at the No. 9 position last year. At first, Garcia did not complain. But then, he screamed because he felt that *anybody* could hit ninth.

Nonetheless, that's where he stayed.

Just because he's got ants in his pants as a hitter, pitchers should not get the impression that Garcia is easy to strike out: he is not. One way or the other, he will usually get a piece of a pitch. He's an excellent bunter and will bunt his way on base.

He is a better high-ball hitter than he is against pitches thrown below his waist, but because he wants so badly to hit the ball, Garcia has been known to go after a nasty low pitch and rifle it into right field.

As one might expect, Garcia loves the first-pitch fastball. The key for a pitcher against this anxious hitter is to play on Garcia's emotions as he becomes even more quick to commit himself as he falls further behind in the count. If a pitcher gambles and gets a strike on him with the first pitch, Garcia will chase almost anything after that.

Pitchers change speeds on him and give him trouble with the breaking ball pitched away. Garcia is continually changing stances but usually has his feet close together with his toes pointing in.

BASERUNNING:

Garcia is in motion as he strides into the pitch and gets out of the box quickly. He takes a big lead off first base and commands a lot of attention from the pitcher. He was still smarting from the effects of a sore knee suffered while turning a double play at the end of the 1985 season (see FIELDING below). He didn't attempt to steal as frequently last season as he has in the past.

DAMASO GARCIA
2B, No. 7
RR, 6'0", 183 lbs.
ML Svc: 9 years
Born: 2-7-57 in
Moca,
Dominican Republic

1986 STATISTICS

AVG	G	AB	R	H	2B	3B	HR	RBI	BB	SO	SB
.281	122	424	57	119	22	0	6	46	13	32	9

CAREER STATISTICS

AVG	G	AB	R	H	2B	3B	HR	RBI	BB	SO	SB
.286	931	3651	461	1046	173	26	32	301	115	292	197

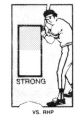

STRONG   STRONG   PROBABLE HIT LOCATIONS

VS. RHP   VS. LHP

Last year, Garcia was thrown out stealing third base for the first time in five seasons (he had been successful 24 consecutive times). Garcia is a good baserunner who is fast enough to score on almost anything.

FIELDING:

Plagued by a sore right shoulder all season he required several cortisone shots but got a clean bill of health from doctors after the season.

When he's right, Garcia is among the best second baseman in the league. He makes the double play with the best of them (when Rickey Henderson displaced him on the DP last year, it was Garcia's first up-ending since he's been in the major leagues!)

OVERALL:

Garcia is a player who can help his team in a lot of ways. He gets on base, he runs when he gets there and he can field. The only thing he doesn't do is hit home runs.

Kaat: "His success hinges on his attitude. This change of scenery might be great for Garcia. He should have the motivation to push him to a big year this season. He's capable of getting 200 hits in a season."

HITTING:

One of the interesting developments with the 1986 Braves was the midseason acquisition of Ken Griffey from the New York Yankees (for Claudell Washington and Paul Zuvella) and Griffey's strong offensive showing after joining the Braves. For some reason, he showed more long-ball power than he did when he was with the Cincinnati Reds at the peak of his career.

The Braves were sufficiently impressed with Griffey that they will enter the 1987 season with him entrenched in left field and in the heart of the batting order. The Braves hope he can hit 20 to 25 home runs, drive in 80 to 90 runs, hit .280 or so. It is asking a lot for his age (37), but he showed a quick bat last season.

He hits the ball all over the park, and did not fall into any predictable pattern that would aid a battery to determine a surefire strategy of pitching to him.

He also can handle the ball in all parts of the strike zone, although he is toughest on waist-high, inside pitches and weakest on low, away breaking pitches.

He should benefit from the dimensions of Atlanta-Fulton County Stadium and should fit in nicely with Bob Horner and Dale Murphy in the batting order.

BASERUNNING:

When with Cincinnati, Griffey was a legitimate basestealing threat, if not a speed demon. Age has changed that, inevitably. But Griffey still does not clog up the bases as badly as many of his younger teammates and he is an intelligent baserunner. He gets out of the box swiftly and anticipates well, and he rarely runs himself into an out.

FIELDING:

He is no better than average at this point and the Braves will have to recognize that and limit his duty to left field. His arm has slipped to below-average status and his range has slipped to average. As he proved in 1985 while he was still with the Yankees, he can pull off the spectacular catch on occasion. His wall-

KEN GRIFFEY
LF, No. 22
LL, 6'0", 200 lbs.
ML Svc: 14 years
Born: 4-10-50 in
Donora, PA

1986 STATISTICS

AVG	G	AB	R	H	2B	3B	HR	RBI	BB	SO	SB
.306	139	490	69	150	22	3	21	58	35	67	14

CAREER STATISTICS

AVG	G	AB	R	H	2B	3B	HR	RBI	BB	SO	SB
.300	1678	6126	983	1839	315	73	121	707	600	650	188

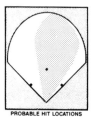

VS. RHP — STRONG   VS. LHP — STRONG   PROBABLE HIT LOCATIONS

climbing made while he was stretched clear into the fourth row of seats to rob Boston's Marty Barrett of a home run at Yankee Stadium drew cheers in the Bronx.

He always keeps his head in the game and he seems to know the tendencies of the hitters well enough to make adjustments that are worth a step or two. Still, he will have to hit to be an asset.

OVERALL:

A front-line contender probably would pick up a Ken Griffey-type player as a fourth outfielder at this point in his career. But the Braves are not a front-line contender and they are happy with Griffey as a starting outfielder and integral part of their offensive plan for 1987. His bat could slow down at any time given his age, but there is no guarantee that it'll be this year or even next year.

Dierker: "He is still a good, solid hitter and he should be an asset to Atlanta's lineup. If they choose to use him in the top of the lineup, he will also deliver with a good on-base percentage, although not as good as he used to have with the Reds."

ATLANTA BRAVES

HITTING:

The saga continues.

Ever since Bob Horner jumped directly from the Arizona State University campus to the Braves' starting lineup in 1978--and homered in his first game--learned people around baseball have fantasized about the type of numbers Horner would put up some year. Forty home runs, or maybe 50, they have said. One hundred twenty RBIs, maybe 140, they have suggested. A .320 batting average, maybe much higher, they have thought. Long ago, the count was lost on how many baseball people have looked at Horner and said, publicly or privately, "That guy could win the Triple Crown."

None of that has happened. After all these years, Horner still hasn't had that phenomenal season forecast for him, much less sustained that level for a number of years.

But this is not to say Horner is not a productive big league hitter, just to say that the Braves were having a hard time deciding whether to keep paying him $1.5 million a year.

Horner is the classic streak hitter, a virtually unstoppable force when he's hot and feeling good at the plate. He is an almost precise mistake hitter, who jumps all over a pitch up and over the inside part of the plate. But he also is a notoriously slow starter: his career batting average for the month of April is .187.

Horner is a pull hitter and the pitchers' best chance against him is to keep the ball down and away. He should be played to pull on the infield but not as much in the outfield. You can put a shift on him in the infield to try to force him to hit the other way, and he will try to do that if you try to keep him in the ballpark.

BASERUNNING:

Slow . . . slow out of the box . . . slow as he moves around the bases . . . so slow, that any battery who pays attention to him is kidding themselves.

FIELDING:

A second baseman in college (imagine

BOB HORNER
1B, No. 11
RR, 6'1", 215 lbs.
ML Svc: 9 years
Born: 8-6-57 in
Junction City, KS

1986 STATISTICS
AVG	G	AB	R	H	2B	3B	HR	RBI	BB	SO	SB
.273	141	517	70	141	22	0	27	87	52	72	1

CAREER STATISTICS
AVG	G	AB	R	H	2B	3B	HR	RBI	BB	SO	SB
.278	960	3571	545	994	160	7	215	652	337	489	14

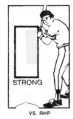

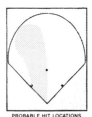

VS. RHP · VS. LHP · PROBABLE HIT LOCATIONS

that!) Horner arrived in Atlanta as a third baseman. He had sure hands and a reliable arm, but absolutely no range. He now is a first baseman.

Despite the lack of range, he has become a respectable first baseman, albeit not in the top class of the league. He is mentally in the game at all times, doesn't make mistakes, doesn't botch the balls he can reach and seems to pick throws out of the dirt most of the time.

OVERALL:

Horner's career has been marked by weight and injury problems. But he has kept his weight under control the last four years (he has never exceeded 215 pounds, as required by a weight clause in his contract) and has been less injury-prone in the last two years.

Dierker: "Obviously, Bob is one of the best power hitters in the National League but everyone is still waiting for him to have that season that will prove he is among the tops."

ATLANTA BRAVES

HITTING:

Glenn Hubbard's performance of the past five seasons mirrors that of the team: a high in 1982 and 1983 (when the Braves won one division title and contended for another). After that, however, both Hubbard and the team have been in a steady decline. His fadeaway has been most pronounced at the plate.

Despite his size, at times, Hubbard can flash some surprising power. Over the past few seasons, however, those flashes have become more infrequent. He will hit a mistake, but good, well-crafted pitching will get him out.

He likes the ball up and out over the plate and he is particularly troubled by breaking balls down-and-away or hard stuff low-and-in.

He can hit to all fields, but most often pulls the ball or hits up the middle.

Hubbard always considered his offensive talents secondary to his defense, but now his hitting has fallen to the point where the Braves are reconsidering his spot in the starting lineup. On a team that, contrary to its big-bopper image, is suffering from a lack of offense, Hubbard is part of the problem.

BASERUNNING:

Even the little guys on this team like Hubbard are slow. He is not a basestealing threat, not a threat to bunt for a hit or to beat out a ground ball, not a threat to score on a shallow fly ball or to take an extra base very often.

But he does have one thing going for him as a baserunner: he is tough, which means he'll run in as hard as anyone when it's time to attempt breaking up a double play.

FIELDING:

He is, first and foremost, a competitor. Nothing scares him, certainly not a wicked ground ball or a hard-charging baserunner.

When he came into the league, Hubbard impressed everyone with his ability to turn the double play and he still turns it as well as

GLENN HUBBARD
2B, No. 17
RR, 5'7", 169 lbs.
ML Svc: 8 years
Born: 9-25-57 in
 Hahn AFB, Germany

1986 STATISTICS

AVG	G	AB	R	H	2B	3B	HR	RBI	BB	SO	SB
.230	143	408	42	94	16	1	4	36	66	74	3

CAREER STATISTICS

AVG	G	AB	R	H	2B	3B	HR	RBI	BB	SO	SB
.242	1055	3573	429	866	163	18	59	365	410	513	31

STRONG

VS. RHP

STRONG

VS. LHP

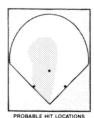

PROBABLE HIT LOCATIONS

anyone in the league. But those qualities-- toughness and efficiency at turning the double play--pretty much cover his defensive strengths.

His range is no better than average, either to his left or right. He has good hands, although he seems to boot more balls than he used to two or three years ago.

OVERALL:

Hubbard is at (or nearing) a crossroads in his career. He needs a strong spring training and a strong 1987 season to keep himself entrenched as the Braves' starting second baseman. Otherwise, he might lapse into utilityman status for the balance of his career, whether with the Braves or another team.

Dierker: "Despite his real good hands, unless he can pick up the pace with the bat, he will not be considered among the league's top second baseman. That is a dropoff for Glenn, because a few years ago he was right up there with the best of them."

ATLANTA BRAVES

PITCHING:

Rick Mahler did not have a good season in 1986 and the Braves have turned lukewarm on his future role with the team. In fact, they offered him to Montreal for relief pitcher Tim Burke at the winter meetings but were put on hold while the Expos attempted to do better for Burke.

Mahler is much the same kind of pitcher as teammate and friend Doyle Alexander: a thinker, not a thrower. He is a nibbler, not a challenger.

Mahler rarely throws a pure fastball; if he throws a fastball at all, he turns it over and shoots for a corner. His primary pitch is a big, slow curveball. When Mahler has it working, he can make hitters look helpless by mixing this pitch with a change-up, a forkball, an occasional slider and screwball, even a once-in-a-while knuckleball.

Location is everything with Mahler; just throwing strikes is not enough. In fact, Mahler often pitches from behind in the count, but doesn't mind throwing breaking balls on 2-1, 3-1 and 3-2 counts.

He is a streak pitcher and a fast starter. When he's in a groove, he can put together strings of five or six sterling games but he also can go in the other direction and get rocked for five or six games consecutively. Mahler normally pitches his best early in the season; in fact, three of his five career shutouts have been in Opening Day starts.

FIELDING, HITTING, BASERUNNING:

Because of the lack of velocity on his pitches, Mahler does not have great success at deterring basestealers. He has an average move to first base and does devote a lot of attention to making throws over to first base.

RICK MAHLER
RHP, No. 42
RR, 6'1", 202 lbs.
ML Svc: 6 years
Born: 8-5-53 in Austin, TX

1986 STATISTICS

W	L	ERA	G	GS	CG	SV	IP	H	R	ER	BB	SO
14	18	4.88	39	39	7	0	237.2	283	139	129	95	137

CAREER STATISTICS

W	L	ERA	G	GS	CG	SV	IP	H	R	ER	BB	SO
61	59	3.85	216	154	28	2	1084	1132	512	464	361	529

One of the more interesting components of Mahler's game is his hitting ability. He is one of the better hitting pitchers in the game and surely gets as much pleasure out of taking his cuts as anyone. He can hit high fastballs on the line for singles and doubles, and he also has had a lot of success by hammering off-speed pitches with his unorthodox swing.

As a baserunner, Mahler is nothing distinctive. He is slow afoot and generally gets out of the box slowly because he likes to watch his hits.

OVERALL:

The Braves are not exactly enthralled with Mahler at the moment, as witnessed by their willingness to deal him during the winter.

Dierker: "If Rick remains with the Braves, he almost certainly will be a member of their starting rotation in 1987, probably joining fellow junkballer Doyle Alexander, lefthander Zane Smith, righthander David Palmer and a fifth starter yet to be determined."

ATLANTA BRAVES

HITTING:

Dale Murphy is simply one of the best hitters in baseball. He also has become a consistent hitter, year after year. With him, the difference in his best seasons and off seasons is only a matter of degree. Last season would be classified as an off-season by Murphy standards.

He is--and has always been--a very streaky hitter, even more so than teammate Bob Horner. But he is consistent in this respect: he always has about the same number of streaks, good and bad, from one season to the next. When he is on a hot streak, pitchers would be well-advised to throw him nothing to hit: just walk him or force him to chase a bad pitch. He has no weakness when he is on one of his tears. He'll hit the outside-corner pitch; he'll hit the pitch in the dirt; he'll turn on the inside pitch; he can hit curveballs off his ankle; he can hit the ball out of any part of any park.

At other, more mortal times, Murphy struggles. At these times, he appears confused at the plate and is vulnerable to low-and-away breaking pitches, good curveballs, even high fastballs at times. It is very important to have a current scouting report on Murphy going into every series because his hitting habits change so radically from streak to slump. At times, you just go after him, and at other times you just don't let him have anything to hit at all.

BASERUNNING:

Just four seasons ago, Murphy was capable of stealing 30 bases. Now he has lost a couple of steps and probably won't steal more than seven or eight bases in 1987. These steals generally will come against pitchers with weak moves to first base or in surprising situations where the pitcher and/or catcher do not expect him to run.

He gets out of the box quickly, makes early commitments on whether to take an extra base and slides aggressively.

FIELDING:

Murphy has become a perennial Gold Glove winner but his defense actually has slipped a little in the last couple of years. At one time, both his arm and his range were far above average for a center fielder. Now, they

DALE MURPHY
CF, No. 3
RR, 6'4", 215 lbs.
ML Svc: 9 years
Born: 3-12-56 in Portland, OR

1986 STATISTICS

AVG	G	AB	R	H	2B	3B	HR	RBI	BB	SO	SB
.265	160	614	89	163	29	7	29	83	75	141	7

CAREER STATISTICS

AVG	G	AB	R	H	2B	3B	HR	RBI	BB	SO	SB
.277	1360	5017	813	1388	214	32	266	822	617	1094	129

STRONG VS. RHP — STRONG VS. LHP

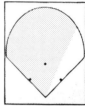

PROBABLE HIT LOCATIONS

are no better than average. The Braves possibly would be well-served to move him to right field and install a center fielder with more range.

This is not to say Murphy has become a liability in the field, just that he isn't the force he once was. His arm still commands respect, and he still reacts well enough to the batted ball to cover sufficient ground. He is a quarterback in the outfield.

OVERALL:

Occasionally there are whispers that the Braves should trade Murphy for a package of younger players. But they resist. The Braves know that both Murphy and Horner, once the young anchors of an ultra-promising team, are now the not-so-young anchors of an underachieving team. To have two such commodities at the same time and win nothing more than one division championship (1982) would be a real waste. That may be the Braves' plight.

Dierker: "He is one of the game's top players. Overall, the Braves might be better with him in right field and a center fielder who can go get it better than Murphy can at this stage."

ATLANTA BRAVES

HITTING:

Ken Oberkfell was one of the few pleasant surprises on the 1986 Braves. Lightly regarded--the Braves had considered trading him away in spring training--Oberkfell became an integral part of the Braves' offense, such as it was.

Oberkfell has a good idea of the strike zone and draws a lot of walks. He hits for a good average and gets on base a lot. He does not, however, have good power, and that is a drawback for his position (third base). Despite his ability to hit for average and his good eye, he does not exactly terrorize pitchers, partly because of his lack of power and partly because he does not seem to rise to the occasion in many clutch situations.

A lefthanded hitter, he has the somewhat unusul quality of being a good high-ball hitter. His weakness is the low-and-away pitch. He can get around on the inside pitch, so you will see pitchers who are most familiar with him feeding him a steady diet of low-and-away, low-and-away, low-and-away.

BASERUNNING:

He never had good speed, and in fact his speed has diminished since he first came into the league. He has gained some weight and become larger through his upper body in the past few years, consequently losing a step or two.

Like Bob Horner, Oberkfell has a weight clause in his contract. Horner got an extra $100,00 per season if he weighed in at 215 pounds or less before every Friday home game; Oberkfell gets an extra $50,000 per season if he does the same.

FIELDING:

Oberkfell has good sure hands and an accurate arm. He is not the kind of guy who is going to make a lot of spectacular plays at

KEN OBERKFELL
3B, No. 24
LR, 6'1", 210 lbs.
ML Svc: 9 years
Born: 5-4-56 in
Maryville, IL

1986 STATISTICS

AVG	G	AB	R	H	2B	3B	HR	RBI	BB	SO	SB
.270	151	503	62	136	24	3	5	48	83	40	7

CAREER STATISTICS

AVG	G	AB	R	H	2B	3B	HR	RBI	BB	SO	SB
.283	1059	3423	408	970	169	36	20	303	414	253	54

  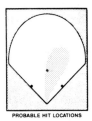

VS. RHP   VS. LHP   PROBABLE HIT LOCATIONS

third base, but he is the kind of guy who you begin to appreciate defensively after watching him day after day.

He won't botch the easy play, has range somewhere between a Brooks Robinson and a Bob Horner, and throws accurately.

OVERALL:

The Braves seem somewhat ambivalent about whether Oberkfell is a short- or long-term solution at third base. Most teams would prefer more power from the position.

Dierker: "A lot of observers wonder why the Braves don't move Oberkfell to second base, Horner back to third and play Gerald Perry at first base. But the Braves' answer is that Horner is much better suited for first base and that Oberkfell is not suited to be an everyday second baseman. So he figures to remain their starting third baseman in 1987."

ATLANTA BRAVES

PITCHING:

Ed Olwine is probably never going to be a big star in the major leagues, but he was a surprising contributor to the Braves' staff last season. He showed enough that the Braves have to figure he'll be in their bullpen when the 1987 season opens.

A veteran minor leaguer, Olwine has not been a highly touted or anxiously awaited prospect because he does not throw hard. But he has a good off-speed pitch, a good breaking ball and good control. And perhaps most significantly, he demonstrated last season that he can pitch at the major league level without getting rattled. That alone makes him an asset in a thin bullpen.

He wasn't afraid to use his fastball last season, although it's far from a great big league fastball, and he got some outs with it. He moves it around the plate very well and he mixes it up with his other pitches.

FIELDING, HITTING, BASERUNNING:

He does a good job holding runners on base and he does not get rattled as a fielder any more than as a pitcher. He is another of those role-player relief pitchers who seldom get an opportunity to hit.

OVERALL:

Olwine is the kind of pitcher who can help a

ED OLWINE
LHP, No. 31
RL, 6'2", 170 lbs.
ML Svc: *less than one year*
Born: 5-28-58 in
  Greenville, OH

1986 STATISTICS
W	L	ERA	G	GS	CG	SV	IP	H	R	ER	BB	SO
0	0	3.40	37	9	0	1	47.2	35	20	18	17	37

CAREER STATISTICS
W	L	ERA	G	GS	CG	SV	IP	H	R	ER	BB	SO
0	0	3.40	37	9	0	1	47.2	35	20	18	17	37

team if it identifies a role for him, clearly defines it and holds to it. In his case, his value probably is as a long to middle reliever who pitches an inning or two here and there, hopefully keeping the game from getting out of hand. Or he possibly could be a middle-to-late-inning set-up man for the closer.

Dierker: "Olwine showed enough last season to make the Braves think of him as a major league pitcher instead of as a minor league journeyman.

"He had to be a pleasant surprise for the Braves last year and I think they would have to look at him as a guy who'll help them in 1987."

PITCHING:

The time has arrived for Randy O'Neal to make a significant contribution. The Braves could be his last chance.

O'Neal was the winning pitcher when the Tigers clinched the Eastern Division championship in 1984. He worked six shutout innings against the Milwaukee Brewers on that September evening, and Tiger brass projected him as a future member of the starting rotation.

O'Neal has been afforded that opportunity during each of the past two seasons, but he has not capitalized on his chances. The consensus of Tiger brass was that O'Neal lacks heart.

In fairness to O'Neal, what he lacks is an assortment of pitches. O'Neal's best two pitches--an above-average sinking fastball and an outstanding split-finger fastball--are similar in action, if not speed.

O'Neal attempted to make greater use of his slider last season, but he is not able to throw it as consistently well as is required of an effective starting pitcher.

The inconsistency of his slider left him clinging to his two primary pitches last year. He had a tendency to be too clever and, subsequently, lost his aggressiveness and control.

O'Neal seems much more suited to a middle relief role because of the limited assortment of his pitches and the quality of his split-finger fastball.

FIELDING, HITTING, BASERUNNING:

O'Neal's fielding is average and he sometimes is slow coming off the mound. His awareness of game situations can be lacking. This tendency perhaps stems from his fervent desire to be a starter and his reluctance to

**RANDY O'NEAL
RHP, No. 49
RR, 6'2", 195 lbs.
ML Svc: 2 years
Born: 8-30-60 in
Ashland, KY**

1986 STATISTICS

W	L	ERA	G	GS	CG	SV	IP	H	R	ER	BB	SO
3	7	4.33	37	11	1	2	122.2	121	69	59	44	68

CAREER STATISTICS

W	L	ERA	G	GS	CG	SV	IP	H	R	ER	BB	SO
10	13	3.82	69	26	1	3	235.2	219	118	100	86	132

work out of the bullpen.

Opponents will run on O'Neal because of his slow delivery.

His abilities as a hitter or baserunner are unknown at the major league level as he has pitched in the American League exclusively.

OVERALL:

This season is important to O'Neal's improvement as a major league pitcher. He is being given the opportunity to prove himself to a new team in a new league.

In his brief career, he has enjoyed limited success, but has not been able to demonstrate any degree of consistency. It is essential for O'Neal to be slotted into a middle relief role and equally important for him to accept that role. Otherwise, success could escape him.

Kaat: "While he was with the Tigers, O'Neal was caught in the middle as a starter one day and reliever the next. He has a tendency to throw more than pitch and should work out of the bullpen where he can go at hitters with his split-finger fastball."

ATLANTA BRAVES

PITCHING:

The big news on David Palmer last season was not how he pitched, which was very well thank you, but that he stayed injury-free. His career had been a succession of injuries and his stock had fallen to the point that the Braves were able to sign him uncontestedly as a free agent to a one-year contract. But Palmer stayed healthy in 1986, stayed in the Braves' starting rotation all season and made a significant contribution. The Braves again look to Palmer as a member of their starting rotation for 1987.

He pitched more innings in 1986 than in any other year of his career. And he showed the tools of a good front-line pitcher: a strong fastball, a good slider, an outstanding curveball and a great competitive quality.

His best pitch is a fastball which he cuts, making it act like a slider. This pitch looks like it would be hard on a pitcher's arm, perhaps explaining Palmer's history of injury problems.

Palmer did have control problems in 1986 (perhaps from rustiness) and those problems kept him from putting together a truly outstanding season. The Braves hope his control will be better this season. If it is, and if he remains injury-free, he might become the needed ace of the Braves' starting rotation.

FIELDING, HITTING, BASERUNNING:

Palmer does a pretty good job of holding runners on base, but it is essential that he concentrate even more on holding runners because the Braves' catchers are not a strong-armed lot. Palmer fields his position adequately and keeps his head in the game at all times.

DAVID PALMER
RHP, No. 46
RR, 6'1", 205 lbs.
ML Svc: 8 years
Born: 10-19-57 in
Glens Falls, NY

1986 STATISTICS

W	L	ERA	G	GS	CG	SV	IP	H	R	ER	BB	SO
11	10	3.65	35	35	2	0	209.2	181	98	85	102	170

CAREER STATISTICS

W	L	ERA	G	GS	CG	SV	IP	H	R	ER	BB	SO
49	36	3.36	157	121	9	2	787.1	713	235	294	311	540

He looks like he knows what's doing with a bat in his hands and if a pitcher makes a mistake, he can cash in. He runs the bases like a pitcher.

OVERALL:

The Braves made a rare free-agent "steal" when they signed Palmer. It remains to be seen whether he'll be healthy over the long term, but they got their money's worth out of him last season. And there is really no reason other than injuries why Palmer shouldn't be a significant part of the Braves' pitching staff for the next few years. If his arm feels good in spring training, it is realistic to expect that his confidence would be bolstered and he might get into a groove.

Dierker: "I think if the Braves had been a winning team last year he would have been a real fine starter for them, but sometimes it's hard to overcome a losing atmosphere."

ATLANTA BRAVES

HITTING:

Rafael Ramirez is yet another case study that provides insight into why the Braves did not progress from their 1982 division championship. Ramirez was a starter on that team, a good offensive player who, although erratic defensively, figured only to get better. He has not improved on defense and probably has regressed on offense.

As a batter, he is undisciplined, swinging at everything and drawing few walks. A pitcher can get him out by simply not throwing strikes. He will eventually swing at bad pitches, and this kind of information circulates among the pitching fraternity pretty fast.

He does have a quick bat and a little power. He can hit to all fields, although he principally is a pull hitter; he likes the ball waist-high or lower over the middle or outer portion of the plate. But he will not become a good hitter until he becomes more selective at the plate and there are fewer and fewer people who expect him ever to do that. Ramirez, a native of the Dominican Republic, has never apologized for his free-swinging ways. "A walk," he likes to say, "won't get you off the island." But his lack of selectivity apparently will cost him a spot in the Braves' starting lineup.

BASERUNNING:

On most teams, Ramirez's speed would be considered average to below-average: certainly nothing special. But on the slow-footed Braves team, Ramirez's speed is substantially above-average. He is about as close as the Braves get to having a basestealing threat and he is capable of occasionally taking an extra base, beating out a bunt or an infield hit, scoring on a shallow fly ball, etc. The Braves will take whatever baserunning skill they can get.

FIELDING:

For several seasons, the Braves dismissed Ramirez's high error totals by pointing out his youth and inexperience and stating confidently that he would improve. The club believed that he would become the next Dave

RAFAEL RAMIREZ
SS, No. 16
RR, 5'11", 190 lbs.
ML Svc: 6 years
Born: 2-18-59 in
San Pedro de Macoris,
Dominican Republic

1986 STATISTICS

AVG	G	AB	R	H	2B	3B	HR	RBI	BB	SO	SB
.240	134	496	57	119	21	1	8	33	21	60	19

CAREER STATISTICS

AVG	G	AB	R	H	2B	3B	HR	RBI	BB	SO	SB
.263	871	3358	365	882	127	21	36	280	165	370	87

  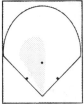

STRONG   STRONG

VS. RHP   VS. LHP   PROBABLE HIT LOCATIONS

Concepcion. It never happened.

No longer young or inexperienced by baseball standards, Ramirez remains as erratic as ever on defense.

He does have extraordinary range, but it is completely unpredictable what he will do with the ball when he reaches it. Sometimes he drops it . . . sometimes he kicks it . . . oftentimes he throws it away. Compounding the deficiency, Ramirez also is erratic on the routine, directly-to-him plays. He does turn the double play well and, in this regard, makes a fine combination with Hubbard.

OVERALL:

The bottom line is that the Braves have just about had enough of Ramirez as their starting shortstop. They no longer think he will improve as a defensive player and they feel he has leveled off as an offensive player. The result: young Andres Thomas most likely will start at shortstop on opening day 1987 for the Atlanta Braves.

Dierker: "He has never become the player that the Braves thought he could become. He seems to have a lack of mental discipline both as a fielder and at the plate."

ATLANTA BRAVES

HITTING:

Ted Simmons is not the All-Star player of his younger days, but he can still strike fear in an opposing pitcher when he wanders to the plate in a crucial late-game situation as a pinch-hitter. He got off to a strong start off the Braves' bench last season, tapered off slightly, then reignited toward the close of the season. He'll be back in 1987 for the same role, which is largely as a pinch-hitter.

Simmons appears to have lost some of his power but he knows all of the pitchers and is a threat to empty the bases with a line drive to the gaps at any time. He can hit from either side of the plate, doubling his value as a force on the bench in the late innings. He is particularly valuable in situations where there are two pitchers warming up in the bullpen, a lefty and righty. He still hits well from both sides of the plate.

He would not have stayed in the big leagues this long if there were a surefire way to get him out. He likes the ball out and over the plate, and he handles both hard and breaking pitches.

BASERUNNING:

Simmons never had blazing speed and the combination of his advancing age and all those innings behind the plate has slowed him. He is basically a non-factor as a baserunner for the Braves. If he gets a pinch-hit in a situation where he is the winning or tying run on base, the Braves generally use a pinch-runner for him. This can serve to deplete a bench, so it is one disadvantage to Simmons as a pinch-hitter.

FIELDING:

Simmons' defensive skills are not sufficient for him to be an everyday player. A catcher for most of his career, he now is only an average to below-average receiver with an average to below-average arm. But he will take his turn behind the plate when called

TED SIMMONS
C, No. 23
SR, 6'0", 200 lbs.
ML Svc: 17 years
Born: 8-9-49 in
Highland Park, MI

1986 STATISTICS
AVG	G	AB	R	H	2B	3B	HR	RBI	BB	SO	SB
.252	76	127	14	32	5	0	4	25	12	14	1

CAREER STATISTICS
AVG	G	AB	R	H	2B	3B	HR	RBI	BB	SO	SB
.286	2305	8396	1048	2402	469	47	242	1348	819	662	20

  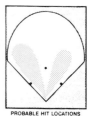

VS. RHP   VS. LHP   PROBABLE HIT LOCATIONS

upon and do a respectable job.

The Braves will also work him some at third base this season, more for emergency duty than anything else. He will get some innings at first, particularly when manager Chuck Tanner urgently wants to get Simmons four at-bats in a game against a particular pitcher.

OVERALL:

He is an expensive, but valuable, person on the Braves' bench. His value to the team is actually two-fold: as a pinch-hitter and as a motivational force in the clubhouse. He became something of a team leader last season, coining the nickname "Bomb Squad" for the Braves' reserves and helping keep the team's morale relatively high considering its low position in the standings.

Dierker: "Ted is a good guy to have on a ballclub if you can afford to have a guy with that high a salary on the bench."

ATLANTA BRAVES

PITCHING:

Zane Smith is the most marketable pitcher on the Braves' staff and, outside of Dale Murphy, the most marketable player on the team. Every time the Braves opened trade negotiations this past winter, the other party wanted Smith. The Braves wanted badly to acquire center fielder Brett Butler from Cleveland, but resisted parting with Smith to do so.

The interest in Smith is not surprising, for he is a young, classy, lefthanded starting pitcher with great stuff and even greater potential. But it should not be forgotten that he struggled colossally in the second half of the 1986 season and even was bounced out of the Braves' starting rotation at one point. The Braves don't know why Smith encountered such problems after a very strong start, but other teams' interest in him reinforced the Braves' belief that he'll be OK.

They are counting on him as an integral part of the starting pitching rotation this season--and they need him *badly*.

But given all his potential, he still needs to develop another pitch. He is a fastball/slider pitcher and when his control is not good, a righthanded batter can take advantage of him. For Smith to have any sustained success, he is going to have to find a way to handle righthanded hitters consistently, even on those inevitable occasions when his control is off.

Obviously, opposing teams have good enough scouting reports to know to stack the lineup with righthanded hitters when Smith is pitching.

He throws from a sidearm position, seems to have good maturity on the mound and seems to relish challenging hitters. His fastball and slider have good velocity and good movement. A first-rate change-up would automatically make him a big winner.

ZANE SMITH
LHP, No. 34
LL, 6'2", 195 lbs.
ML Svc: 2 years
Born: 12-28-60 in
Madison, WI

1986 STATISTICS

W	L	ERA	G	GS	CG	SV	IP	H	R	ER	BB	SO
8	16	4.05	38	32	3	1	204.2	209	109	92	105	139

CAREER STATISTICS

W	L	ERA	G	GS	CG	SV	IP	H	R	ER	BB	SO
18	26	3.85	83	53	5	1	371.2	360	186	159	198	240

FIELDING, HITTING, BASERUNNING:

Because he is a lefthander, Smith doesn't have to worry quite as much as some of the Braves' pitchers about bases being stolen on him. He does a good job of watching baserunners and his pickoff move is well developed. He fields his position adequately. As for his hitting, if the pitcher makes a mistake he'll sometimes cash in.

OVERALL:

The Braves desperately need Smith to come through. The team has not produced a quality lefthanded pitcher since it moved to Atlanta in 1966 and Smith is as good a candidate as it has had to break that drought. The 1987 season probably will reveal whether Smith is going to make it big.

Dierker: "Because he basically has two good pitches and sometimes has trouble against righthanded lineups, it might be better for him to come out of the bullpen, if the Braves could come up with another starter. Either that, or he'll need to come up with a better off-speed pitch. But the fastball is good and so is the slider."

ATLANTA BRAVES

PITCHING:

The most immediate question with Bruce Sutter is *when he will pitch again.*

Sutter underwent shoulder surgery after the 1985 season, attempted a quick comeback, developed more shoulder problems and late last season heard the words pitchers dread most: torn rotator cuff. Sutter fully expects to pitch again and the doctors and the Braves' front office share that expectation. But the Braves do not know when or, more importantly, *whether* he'll pitch like the Sutter of old.

For now, the Braves cannot count on Sutter as they structure their pitching staff for the start of spring training. They must look to Gene Garber as the stopper in the bullpen and simply wait and see on Sutter.

If Sutter is healthy and back to his old form, everyone knows what the Braves have in him: one of the very best relief pitchers of all time, a pitcher who saved 45 games for the St. Louis Cardinals in 1984.

Sutter's special pitch, of course, is the split-finger fastball, a devastating offering that drops dramatically. It often winds up out of the strike zone, but that is long after the batter has committed himself.

But the question now is when Sutter's shoulder will allow him to throw the very special pitch again. And whether the pitch will still be as special.

FIELDING, HITTING, BASERUNNING:

Sutter has pitched hundreds of innings in the most pressure-packed situations imaginable and nothing rattles him. He is a master of all the details of late-inning baseball, including holding runners on base and making

BRUCE SUTTER
RHP, No. 40
RR, 6'2", 190 lbs.
ML Svc: 11 years
Born: 1-8-53 in
Lancaster, PA

1986 STATISTICS

W	L	ERA	G	GS	CG	SV	IP	H	R	ER	BB	SO
2	0	4.34	16	0	0	3	18.2	17	9	9	9	16

CAREER STATISTICS

W	L	ERA	G	GS	CG	SV	IP	H	R	ER	BB	SO
67	67	2.75	623	0	0	286	995.2	830	344	304	298	821

the gutsy throw to the lead base on sacrifice bunt attempts. He does not beat himelf in the field.

As a short relief specialist, Sutter very rarely gets an at-bat and when he does, it almost always is against the opposing team's top relief pitcher. So the result is normally a strikeout.

OVERALL:

Last year, the Braves may have expected too much too quickly from Sutter, considering that he had undergone off-season surgery. This year, they are taking the opposite approach.

Dierker: "Sutter's future is one of baseball's biggest question marks. Everyone knows how good he can be when he is right, but even if he were back to 100% this season, it's hard to determine how many opportunities he will have to save games for this team.

"Everyone is wishing him the best, but who knows?"

ATLANTA BRAVES

HITTING:

The Braves are very high on Andres Thomas right now, just as they were very high on Rafael Ramirez a few years ago. Thomas made the team unexpectedly in spring training last year and made a strong impression with his bat in the first half of the season. His second-half work with the bat, although still encouraging, was more in line with his status of a raw rookie.

In Thomas, the Braves see the potential to hit .300, a good number of extra-base hits (if not home runs) and a good number of RBIs. They see, in short, exactly what they saw in Ramirez a few years ago.

Thomas, like Ramirez, swings at far too many bad pitches and works pitchers for far too few walks. Thomas has not had enough exposure to big league pitching for a binding assessment on his long-term strengths and weaknesses, but he has appeared to be most vulnerable to crafty breaking balls, particularly low and away, and most adept at hitting power pitches over the inside portion of the strike zone, waist-high and lower.

But to be any kind of consistent success as a hitter, Thomas will have to take more pitches, accept more walks and force pitchers to throw him his pitch.

BASERUNNING:

Like Ramirez, Thomas has decent speed, which is downright exceptional on this team. He does not have the type of speed that makes him an automatic basestealing threat, but he could develop into a runner capable of stealing 20 to 30 bases a year if he works at it, learns the pitchers and hits .280 or above.

Meanwhile, Thomas at least is capable of making a few things happen for the Braves on the bases. He is one of their few players capable of going first to third, or capable of scoring from first base on a short double. But he also has shown a rookie tendency of making mistakes on the bases that result in unnecessary outs.

FIELDING:

In the first half of last season, Thomas

ANDRES THOMAS
SS, No. 14
RR, 6'1", 185 lbs.
ML Svc: 1 year plus
Born: 11-10-63 in
** Boca Chica,**
**   Dominican Republic**

1986 STATISTICS

AVG	G	AB	R	H	2B	3B	HR	RBI	BB	SO	SB
.251	102	323	26	81	17	2	6	32	8	49	4

CAREER STATISTICS

AVG	G	AB	R	H	2B	3B	HR	RBI	BB	SO	SB
.252	117	341	32	86	17	2	6	34	8	51	4

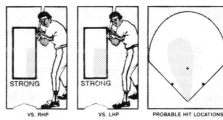

VS. RHP   VS. LHP   PROBABLE HIT LOCATIONS

displayed some simply dazzling abilities in the field, conjuring up comparisons not only with Davey Concepcion in his prime but with Ozzie Smith. In the second half, Thomas showed the flip side of his defense: too many mistakes on easy plays. But if he gets over that hurdle, which Ramirez never cleared, he can become a front-line shortstop (an All-Star, even) for the Braves.

Thomas has exceptional range, good hands and a good arm. He needs only to concentrate and learn.

OVERALL:

The best off-season bet was that Thomas would start the 1987 season at shortstop for the Braves. The qualifications for the everyday spot are modest: he must simply hit and field better than Ramirez to keep the job. The Braves' brass will certainly be pulling for him.

Dierker: "Thomas is young and last season, swung at bad pitches and played without the mental discipline you would like to have in a middle infielder. He still has the chance to improve and become a good one."

ATLANTA BRAVES

HITTING:

When Bobby Cox took over as general manager of the Braves following the 1985 season, he felt a need to strengthen the team at the catcher's position. He wanted a catcher who would stabilize the position while also bolstering the team's offense. And Cox felt satisfied that his objectives had been achieved when he traded relief pitcher Steve Bedrosian and young outfielder Milt Thompson to Philadelphia for Ozzie Virgil.

After one season, Cox still hopes the trade will work out to the Braves' benefit. But the jury very definitely is still out.

The Braves expected Virgil to make a much more significant offensive impact than he did; in fact, he labored just to get his average to the .200 level. Both Cox and Virgil are at a loss to explain that performance, but both predict a much better 1987 season. "I just know he'll hit 25 home runs," Cox says.

Virgil has a lot of raw power and should benefit from playing half his games in cozy Atlanta-Fulton County Stadium. He is a mistake hitter, but last season he missed more mistake pitches than is characteristic of him.

A good pitcher can get him out with good pitches and probably always will be able to, but when Virgil is having a good year, he won't miss many mistakes. "Mistakes," of course, are pitches up and over the plate, breaking balls that hang and invite attack, pitches that invade Virgil's power zone.

BASERUNNING:

What can be said? He's a catcher.

And like the stereotypical catcher, he is slow. He gets out of the batter's box slowly, is a one-base-at-a-time type of runner, scores only laboriously on almost anything. He is easily doubled up on ground balls to the infield and can clog up the bases, although the Braves, devoid of team speed, rarely if ever have a speedster on base behind him anyway.

FIELDING:

He is slightly below-average in receiving the

OZZIE VIRGIL
C, No. 9
RR, 6'1", 205 lbs.
ML Svc: 5 years
Born: 12-7-56 in
Mayaguez, PR

1986 STATISTICS

AVG	G	AB	R	H	2B	3B	HR	RBI	BB	SO	SB
.223	114	359	45	80	9	0	15	48	63	73	1

CAREER STATISTICS

AVG	G	AB	R	H	2B	3B	HR	RBI	BB	SO	SB
.240	497	1493	176	359	60	5	61	202	175	312	2

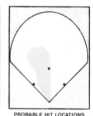

VS. RHP — STRONG   VS. LHP — STRONG   PROBABLE HIT LOCATIONS

ball and only average in throwing it. But he can improve.

He has the size, the strength, the arm and the disposition to become a good, well-rounded catcher in the big leagues. He needs improvement from the Braves' pitchers in holding runners on base and improvement from the middle infielders in applying tags. He also needs to accelerate his release and get a little more velocity and accuracy on his throws.

OVERALL:

The Braves are not giving up on Virgil. In fact, they know he is the best and perhaps only immediate hope for them at catcher. They can only fantasize that, in 1987, he will blossom into what they traded for: a home run, RBI hitter who also takes command of the game behind the plate, calls good pitches and throws out runners.

Dierker: "He has a lot more upward potential than either Simmons or Benedict, although he is not a youngster anymore. I don't think he is a good catcher yet, probably average at best."

ATLANTA BRAVES

CHUCK CARY
LHP, No. 43
LL, 6'4", 210 lbs.
ML Svc: 1 year
Born: 3-3-60 in
Whittier, CA

PITCHING, FIELDING:

The stock of Chuck Cary fell more in 1986 than that of any other Tiger pitcher.

The 26-year-old lefthander raised expectations in the final month of 1985 with his lively fastball and split-finger fastball. Cary was originally projected as a lefthanded bullpen complement to Willie Hernandez and opened the 1986 season with the Tigers. But he fell victim to a couple of nagging injuries and fell out of favor because of an absence of control.

Cary was dispatched to the minors and told to work on his breaking pitches. His heart was not in the assignment, however, and, even though he was recalled in September, he did not appear in a game after the first week. That does not bode well for his future as a Tiger.

Cary must commit himself to good work habits if he's going to have a major league career. He does possess good tools. The development of a breaking pitch would be to his advantage, although his fastball and split-finger fastball are satisfactory enough in a relief role.

Cary's control needs to be sharpened. His pitch location requires refinement. He is essentially a thrower--not a pitcher--at this stage of his career.

OVERALL:

Cary will have to work hard to return to favor and find a role in the major leagues. He must react positively to the minor league assignment he might receive. He can climb the ladder back if he applies himself.

Kaat: "Cary is lefthanded and that's a big advantage--southpaws are always treated with more patience than righthanded strugglers. His future seems to be in his own hands."

DARRYL MOTLEY
RF, No. 24
RR, 5'9", 196 lbs.
ML Svc: 5 years
Born: 1-21-60 in
Muskogee, OK

HITTING, BASERUNNING, FIELDING:

Darryl Motley has become an enigma. He was scheduled to be a permanent fixture in right field for the Kansas City Royals last season but now finds himself with the Braves battling for a spot in right field. Motley was totally lost last season. He blundered along and hit .203 in 72 games with the Royals, spent a few weeks in the minor leagues, and finally was traded to Atlanta the last two weeks of the season.

Motley has above-average speed but is not a smart baserunner. He does not read pitchers well and does not get a good jump. Far too often, he winds up getting picked off. He's also an above-average fielder and has a strong arm for a left fielder (and average for a right fielder). Yet, he often finds himself at a disadvantage by not anticipating what the runners will do.

OVERALL:

Motley has the physical skills to be a legitimate major league player but he needs to find his confidence. Unless someone can help Motley regain his confidence, his major league career may be short-lived.

Killebrew: "He needs to be more selective at the plate. He runs pretty well; he's a good defensive player but he's lacking something. Still, he has a good chance to improve and I like his chances."

CHICAGO CUBS

HITTING:

One of the game's top pinch-hitters, Thad Bosley still wants to play everyday. Ironically, his desire to play might be what's keeping Bosley on top of his game as a pinch-hitter, and his success a a pinch-hitter keeps him in that role. Bosley led the majors in pinch-hits with 20 in 1985 and set a Cubs record in that category as well.

Bosley does not bat often against lefthanded pitching. He loves the ball from the middle of the plate in. Bosley is basically a line drive hitter though he is capable of hitting for power.

Bosley hit .275 in just 120 at-bats last year. Only six of his 33 hits were for extra bases. He knows the strike zone and his strikeout-to-walk ratio has been good.

BASERUNNING:

Bosley has fine speed on the bases but rarely has a chance to display it because he is generally brought into the game as a pinch-hitter when the team is trailing. He stole three bases last season. In 1976, he stole 90 bases while in the minors.

FIELDING:

The biggest rap against Bosley by the Cubs' management in deciding against making him a regular starter is his lack of defense. This in spite of the less-than-dazzling defensive abilities of the 1986 Cubs outfield.

Bosley has an average arm and makes the routine plays well. Playing sporadically in any of the three outfield positions is a difficult

THAD BOSLEY
OF, No. 27
LL, 6'3", 175 lbs.
ML Svc: 7 years
Born: 9-17-56 in
Oceanside, CA

1986 STATISTICS

AVG	G	AB	R	H	2B	3B	HR	RBI	BB	SO	SB
.275	87	120	15	33	4	1	1	9	18	24	3

CAREER STATISTICS

AVG	G	AB	R	H	2B	3B	HR	RBI	BB	SO	SB
.277	587	1276	152	353	37	11	17	121	119	213	43

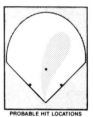

VS. RHP — VS. LHP — PROBABLE HIT LOCATIONS

task, at best.

OVERALL:

Despite his disdain for a restricted pinch-hitting role, Bosley wants to contribute to a winning cause more than anything else. If the Cubs are winning and Bosley is used strictly as a pinch-hitter, he can live with the situation.

Rooker: "Bosley's well-disciplined approach to the game, on and off the field, makes him an asset. At age 30, Bosley is at the stage of his career during which he should be hitting his stride as an overall performer."

CHICAGO CUBS

HITTING:

There has been no sound replacement for catcher Jody Davis for five years and *that* has been Davis' undoing. Davis won the starting catcher's job in spring training of 1982 and has been the Cubs' backstop ever since.

The domino effect of a slumping middle of the batting order last season engulfed Davis, who takes too many hittable pitches and sacrifices too much of the outer part of the plate with less than two strikes. Davis loves to uppercut pitches that are pitched down-and-in. Both left- and righthanded pitchers concentrate on pitching him away.

Davis would be more difficult to defense if he went more to the opposite field with less than two strikes. He is learning to do a better job of hitting balls into the gaps in larger parks on the road.

As an effect of the wear and tear on Davis' body, he traditionally demonstrates a "tired bat" after the All-Star break. He doesn't swing as aggressively as in the first half and is simply not a well-tuned hitter in the later months.

BASERUNNING:

He is the team's slowest runner and a liability on the bases, forcing automatic hit-and-run strategy to move him from first to third on a single. The absence of a backup catcher takes away the option of pinch-running for Davis.

FIELDING:

Cubs bullpen coach Johnny Oates deserves credit for the club's improvement at holding runners on base as well as for Davis' progress in the mechanics of his release. Oates has worked with the pitching staff to shorten their trademark long stretches and high leg kicks and with Davis to enable him to get rid of the ball more quickly.

Davis threw out the most baserunners of his career last season, racking up a 45% kill ratio (78-for-173 plus nine assists on pickoff attempts). Davis has a strong, accurate arm and in 1986 also showed more confidence in his pickoff throws to all bases.

Unhappy with Davis' pitch selection--and much to Davis' chagrin--Oates called the pitches from the dugout during the last month or so of the 1986 season. Too many "fat" pitches were being thrown and the staff was

JODY DAVIS
C, No. 7
RR, 6'3", 210 lbs.
ML Svc: 6 years
Born: 11-12-56 in
Gainesville, GA

1986 STATISTICS

AVG	G	AB	R	H	2B	3B	HR	RBI	BB	SO	SB
.250	148	528	61	132	27	2	21	74	41	110	0

CAREER STATISTICS

AVG	G	AB	R	H	2B	3B	HR	RBI	BB	SO	SB
.254	777	2641	274	671	138	9	97	383	226	505	6

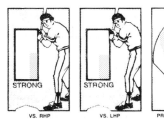

not taking command by brushing back hitters. The Cubs want Davis to take charge of the staff more and not allow them to shake off his signals unchallenged.

The demands of catching everyday wear Davis out and are statistically indicated by the number of late-season passed balls he allows.

OVERALL:

The strain from catching everyday in the majors was made alarmingly clear last season when then-Yankee catcher Butch Wynegar suffered what amounted to a nervous breakdown. While neither a correlation nor a prediction is being made here, Wynegar's situation should serve to underscore what has become an urgent need to rest Davis and to allow him to catch only the 135 games he has requested.

Rooker: "The only real backup Davis ever had was Steve Lake, who has since been traded to St. Louis. Defensively, Lake was an excellent alternative, but offensively, the Cubs wanted more. At this point, however, the Cubs have no suitable backup and Davis is an everyday catcher who is showing the strain."

CHICAGO CUBS

HITTING:

Like the Cubs as a whole, Bob Dernier has gone from the penthouse to the outhouse in three short seasons. In 1984, he was a key player on the Cubs team that captured the National League East pennant. But in 1986, Dernier was one of this woeful club's biggest disappointments.

Dernier is the leadoff hitter, yet at .225 he had one of the club's lowest batting averages and on-base percentages (.273). The biggest criticisms of Dernier were that he failed to bunt, failed to try to go to the opposite field and failed to coax more walks by becoming more patient at the plate. When he gets ahead in the count to 3-1 or 3-2, he knows a fastball is probably coming and will swing rather than try to work the walk to get on base.

Dernier has become a more selfish player than he has been in the past and considers a bunt as giving up an at-bat. He tries to pull everything in disregard to the game's situation and won't swing down on the ball to drive ground balls through the infield.

He has problems handling pitches in or away, especially breaking pitches. He is a line drive hitter who would do better on artificial surfaces if he concentrated more on hitting down on the ball. He seems to feel that he has a power stroke; in his failure to swing down on the ball, he hits weak fly-ball outs. If he would go the other way with pitches, he could raise his average 10-20 points.

He should bunt at least once a game.

BASERUNNING:

Dernier could steal 50-60 bases a season with his outright speed alone, but he can't steal if he ain't on base. He is excellent at going from first to third on base hits but he tends to run with his head down, missing signals from the third base coach.

FIELDING:

Dernier is one of the best defensive center fielders in the game as far as running the ball down in the gaps is concerned. A shoulder

BOB DERNIER
CF, No. 20
RR, 6'0", 165 lbs.
ML Svc: 5 years
Born: 1-5-57 in
**   Kansas City, MO**

1986 STATISTICS

AVG	G	AB	R	H	2B	3B	HR	RBI	BB	SO	SB
.225	108	324	32	73	14	1	4	18	22	41	27

CAREER STATISTICS

AVG	G	AB	R	H	2B	3B	HR	RBI	BB	SO	SB
.254	636	1931	291	491	80	11	13	108	180	235	185

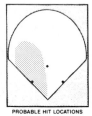

VS. RHP   VS. LHP   PROBABLE HIT LOCATIONS

injury last season further restricted his already very average throwing arm. He needs to work on charging ground balls. He takes charge in the outfield in compensation for the slower veterans who have been flanking him.

OVERALL:

This will be an important season in the career of Dernier, whose big league ability is still questionable despite a fine 1984 campaign. A foot injury in 1985 and a shoulder problem last season have totally disrupted his game.

Rooker: "If Dernier can stay healthy this year, he could help make things happen for the Cubs. In recent seasons, he has not stayed within himself at the plate. Sometimes he tries to do too much, and at other times, he tries to do things his club doesn't need. Gene Michael's managerial demands will probably mean that Dernier will have to do some of the 'little things,' such as bunting and hitting ground balls more this year."

CHICAGO CUBS

HITTING:

Despite just two years of major league experience, Shawon Dunston has already earned the reputation as a notorious free-swinger. With improved discipline at the plate, Dunston could emerge as a high-average hitter with substantial power. His 17 home runs last year were the most by a Cubs shortstop since Hall of Famer Ernie Banks slugged 29 in 1961.

Dunston is an extremely demonstrative (and sometimes overly dramatic) player and is constantly fidgeting in and out of the batter's box. He guesses at pitches when he is ahead in the count and as a result, lunges after level pitches. Dunston has improved at handling pitches up-and-in in the strike zone as he continues to stand on top of the plate.

Dunston needs to improve his bunting technique, which could lift his average considerably because of his outstanding speed and hustling approach.

Among the league-leaders in doubles last year, Dunston is primarily a pull hitter but can drive the ball to all fields. He could hit 25 homers or more a season if he was stronger. Dunston hits notably better when positioned high in the batting order, either as leadoff or in the No. 2 spot.

BASERUNNING:

Dunston has fine speed and could become a big basestealer in the future. He hustles to first on every ball hit, including ground outs back to the mound. He advances from first to third as well as any player.

He runs with his head down and as a result, misses signs from the third base coach. He has run through stop signs directly into game-ending plays. He must concentrate on game situations and weigh his chances for success more carefully.

FIELDING:

Unquestionably, Dunston has the strongest arm among National League shortstops. Dunston is deadly with his throws from deep in the hole. His relay throws from short left field to the plate are lethal for opposing baserunners.

Dunston committed a team-high of 32

SHAWON DUNSTON
SS, No. 12
RR, 6'1", 175 lbs.
ML Svc: 2 years
Born: 3-21-63 in
Brooklyn, NY

1986 STATISTICS

AVG	G	AB	R	H	2B	3B	HR	RBI	BB	SO	SB
.250	150	581	66	145	36	3	17	68	21	114	13

CAREER STATISTICS

AVG	G	AB	R	H	2B	3B	HR	RBI	BB	SO	SB
.253	224	831	106	210	48	7	21	86	40	156	24

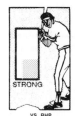  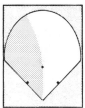

VS. RHP   VS. LHP   PROBABLE HIT LOCATIONS

errors, at least 10 of which came on needless throws to first base after the runner would have had the play beat out for a hit anyway.

He needs to work on his double play pivot technique. When covering the bag, he receives the ball and, in a flamboyant but fundamentally poor move, tries to leap over the runner instead of moving laterally away to make a clean throw. His throws made from his leap are often wild. He suffered several hand and wrist injuries on tag plays last year because of his bad technique.

OVERALL:

Dunston proved himself in 1986 to be an exceptional big league prospect after his shaky debut in 1985 as Larry Bowa's backup.

Rooker: "Dunston has great tools and could become one of the best *if* he matures properly. His mechanics at second base need help but the positive influence of Sandberg has already been seen with Shawon.

"Gene Michael will be managing the Cubs from start to finish this season and his take-charge, make no excuses and play baseball approach should expedite Dunston's maturity as a ballplayer."

CHICAGO CUBS

HITTING:

Leon Durham, the Cubs' only lefthanded power hitter last season, has not fulfilled the club's expectations of him. Several seasons ago, the Cubs envisioned Durham becoming a Dave Parker-type of player, a driving offensive force, consistent and dedicated. That has not happened.

The Cubs have spent a considerable amount of time working with Durham to get him to adjust his batting stance to keep up with crafty pitchers who have been adjusting to him. Durham has been an almost stoic hitter, looking for just one pitch--the high, outside fastball--in order to maximize his power by extending his arms. Continually fouling inside pitches off the handle of the bat, he has traditionally broken dozens of bats a month. He failed to make an adjustment in his batting stance until late last year, when hitting coach Billy Williams succeeded in moving him away from the plate in order to handle the inside pitch.

Durham is a gap type of hitter with power to all fields. Lefthanders must pitch him inside with hard stuff and breaking balls away. Righthanded pitchers must try to come up-and-in with fastballs and down with breaking pitches.

BASERUNNING:

Durham is a better-than-average base-runner but leg injuries (mostly hamstring pulls) in the past have made him increasingly tentative. He has a tendency to arrive at training camp between 10-15 lbs. overweight, which makes him more of a liability than usual on the basepaths until he gets in shape by midseason.

FIELDING:

Durham makes the flip on the first baseman-to-pitcher play as well as anyone in the league, with the exception of the Mets' Keith Hernandez. He has good range and a good throwing arm for the difficult 3-6-3 double play.

LEON DURHAM
1B, No. 10
LL, 6'2", 210 lbs.
ML Svc: 7 years
Born: 7-31-57 in
Cincinnati, OH

1986 STATISTICS

AVG	G	AB	R	H	2B	3B	HR	RBI	BB	SO	SB
.262	141	484	66	127	18	7	20	65	67	98	8

CAREER STATISTICS

AVG	G	AB	R	H	2B	3B	HR	RBI	BB	SO	SB
.281	862	3006	436	844	160	38	116	458	377	551	104

  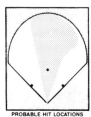

VS. RHP — STRONG   VS. LHP — STRONG   PROBABLE HIT LOCATIONS

OVERALL:

A series of personal problems, including the death of his half-brother, proved distracting to Durham last season. Still, the Cubs have questioned Durham's intensity to perform at optimum level on a day-to-day basis, citing what they consider to be his wanting too much rest for minor injuries. Last season, they threatened to put him on the disabled list twice after hand and shoulder injuries kept him out of the lineup a few days. In both instances, Durham returned to action shortly thereafter.

Despite his lack of production in the past, Durham is being counted on to come through more in clutch RBI situations this season.

Rooker: "Leon was glad to get back to playing at first base, which is really his natural position, a few seasons ago. By now, he should be able to concentrate more on his hitting and should have a better RBI year this season. Coach Billy Williams has been a big help to Durham."

CHICAGO CUBS

PITCHING:

One of the game's best control pitchers, Dennis Eckersley nonetheless fell on hard times along with his Cubs teammates last season. Eckersley struck out 137 and walked only 43 in 201 innings last season. But he gave up a team-high 21 homers (along with Scott Sanderson) and 226 hits. He had only one complete game in 33 starts.

Eckersley would be more effective if he used more of the inside of the plate. His three-quarters-to-sidearm delivery makes him very tough on righthanded hitters.

A tough competitor, Eckersley's "Give me the ball" motto makes him the type of pitcher who sets an enthusiastic tone for the staff. He could still win between 15-20 games with sufficient offensive support.

He fashions an above-average fastball with an average curveball and slider.

After spending 10 years in the American League with Cleveland and Boston, Eckersley has made the transition to the National League after a 1984 trade. He tossed a no-hitter in 1977 against California when he was a member of the Indians.

FIELDING, HITTING, BASERUNNING:

Eckersley is an average fielder. His high leg kick on his delivery allows many runners to get a jump. Not known for his hitting, Eckersley surprised a few opposing teams (and himself, too) with a couple of key homers

DENNIS ECKERSLEY
RHP, No. 43
RR, 6'2", 190 lbs.
ML Svc: 12 years
Born: 10-3-54 in
Oakland, CA

1986 STATISTICS

W	L	ERA	G	GS	CG	SV	IP	H	R	ER	BB	SO
6	11	4.57	33	32	1	0	201	226	109	102	43	137

CAREER STATISTICS

W	L	ERA	G	GS	CG	SV	IP	H	R	ER	BB	SO
151	136	3.67	376	359	100	3	2496	2401	1101	1018	624	1627

and game-winning hits in 1986. He is an average baserunner for a pitcher.

OVERALL:

Perhaps the guttiest pitcher on the Cubs' staff the past two seasons, Eckersley was truly embarrassed by his 1986 numbers and vows to correct them next season. His success on the mound will likely correspond with the offensive support he receives since he seldom gets himself into jams with control problems.

Rooker: "Dennis is a very important pitcher in the Cubs' rotation. He could have another 20-wins season if the rest of the club would give him some run support."

CHICAGO CUBS

PITCHING:

One of the Cubs' most pleasant surprises last season, Dave Gumpert emerged as a rather consistent bullpen performer. A career minor leaguer, the 28-year-old Gumpert proved a good set-up man for Lee Smith. He was used to get the team over the hump of the six and seventh innings.

While he doesn't sport any one outstanding pitch, Gumpert thrives on good control and an adequate sinker. He has an above-average fastball (which can reach close to 90 MPH) and a decent slider and has been working to develop something off-speed.

Gumpert has an explosive delivery in that he pushes off the mound well and puts his whole body behind his pitches. He could become more intimidating if he used his physical size as well as his good velocity to his advantage and took the inside part of the plate for himself more often. Hampered by arm and shoulder troubles over the past few seasons, Gumpert's main concern is his health. Yet he thrives on being used on a regular basis and his arm seems to bounce back after frequent appearances.

Gumpert gave up a hit per inning pitched last year, but he had a good strikeout-to-walk (45:28) ratio. When his sinker is working well, Gumpert induces ground ball outs and double play balls to quell rallies.

FIELDING, HITTING, BASERUNNING:

Accustomed to entering the game in trouble situations, Gumpert holds runners on

DAVE GUMPERT
RHP, No. 45
RR, 6'1", 190 lbs.
ML Svc: 2 years
Born: 5-5-58 in
 South Haven, MI

1986 STATISTICS

W	L	ERA	G	GS	CG	SV	IP	H	R	ER	BB	SO
2	0	4.37	38	0	0	2	59.2	60	32	29	28	45

CAREER STATISTICS

W	L	ERA	G	GS	CG	SV	IP	H	R	ER	BB	SO
3	2	4.03	78	1	0	5	116	122	61	52	44	63

well and does an average job of fielding his position.

He does not get to bat much in his role as reliever, and that's a good thing. He struck out four times in five at-bats last year.

OVERALL:

Forced into steady action when incumbent Cub relievers faltered early last year, Gumpert took advantage of his opportunity and could develop into the type of middle reliever the Cubs can build around in 1987.

Rooker: "Cubs manager Gene Michael likes Gumpert's control and his willingness to go right after hitters instead of nibbling at the corners. He will probably never become one of the 'brand-name' relievers in the game, but he might have found his niche as a set-up man."

CHICAGO CUBS

PITCHING:

Ed Lynch was a member of the Mets' organization from 1979 until May of last year, when he was deprived of the opportunity to be a part of their eventual world championship season but given the chance to crack the Cubs' starting rotation.

Until the September roster swelled with young pitchers the Cubs wanted to get a look at, Lynch was able to pitch well enough to become a regular member of the Cubs' starting rotation. In September, Lynch was being used mostly in middle relief.

Lynch is a control pitcher who throws both a sinker and a slider--both of which are very good pitches. He throws an average major league fastball that comes in at around 86 MPH. His strength lies in the control of his pitches and his ability to keep the ball down-- an absolute *must* at Wrigley Field. His sinker doesn't have the kind of drop that makes batters swing wildly high, but he places it low enough in the strike zone that when they get a piece of it, it stays on the ground and often heads directly to the Cubs' steady infielders, Ryne Sandberg and Shawon Dunston.

Lynch is not a strikeout pitcher and will give up a lot of hits (last year, he averaged more than a hit per inning).But batters have to earn their way on base against Lynch because when he has his control, he is not going to issue many free passes. His stingy total of 23 walks issued generally kept him out of trouble last year.

His three-quarters motion is a smooth one and is not prone to mechanical flaws.

FIELDING, HITTING, BASERUNNING:

Lynch is tall and can look awkward coming off the mound, but he does an adequate job of

ED LYNCH
RHP, No. 37
RR, 6'5", 207 lbs.
ML Svc: 6 years
Born: 2-25-56 in Brooklyn, NY

1986 STATISTICS

W	L	ERA	G	GS	CG	SV	IP	H	R	ER	BB	SO
7	5	3.73	24	13	1	0	101.1	107	48	42	23	58

CAREER STATISTICS

W	L	ERA	G	GS	CG	SV	IP	H	R	ER	BB	SO
45	45	3.82	190	111	8	4	829.1	920	396	352	181	316

fielding his position. He can be counted on to execute good throws to the proper base on sacrifice bunt attempts and he also holds runners on base well.

As a hitter, Lynch is not a threat but he is a good bunter. His baserunning technique is not worthy of filming for clinics.

OVERALL:

Lynch seems to have become a stronger pitcher over the past two years. He was a steadying influence on a shaky Cubs staff in 1986. He knows his limitations and no longer tries to overpower hitters. The Cubs could see him develop into a reliable fifth starter.

Rooker: "Although he might experiment with a new pitch in the spring, Lynch is at the point of his career during which he will stick with his known strong points. Pitching at tiny Wrigley Field last season, Lynch learned that he could keep the ball down and be effective. He is an intelligent athlete who will get the most out of his talents."

HITTING:

Just when baseball was ready to write off Gary Matthews, the veteran left fielder rebounded in the second half of the 1986 season to raise his average to a respectable .259 with a team-high 21 home runs.

Matthews generally likes the ball up from a righthanded pitcher and down-and-in from a lefthander. He is a better fastball hitter than he is a breaking ball hitter.

He has become exceptionally patient at the plate and draws an inordinate percentage of walks. In 1986 Matthews ranked second on the team in walks with 60 despite having only 370 at-bats. Contrastly, Matthews remains a very aggressive swinger with the ability to hit with power to all fields. Matthews, who will turn 37 years old around the All-Star break, is far more effective when he is allowed to play at least three or four times a week. He proved ineffective in a pinch-hitting role early last year.

BASERUNNING:

Matthews remains an aggressive base-runner but he has slowed down considerably because of knee surgery, added weight and advanced age. He will still slide into second with his spikes up to break up a double play, but Matthews is less likely to take the extra base at this stage of his career.

FIELDING:

A notoriously shaky fielder, Matthews has worked hard to become adequate defensively. He has an average arm but his lack of defensive instincts are often accentuated. Matthews must have an excellent--and healthy--defensive center fielder such as Bob

GARY MATTHEWS
OF, No. 36
RR, 6'3", 205 lbs.
ML Svc: 14 years
Born: 7-5-50 in
*   San Fernando, CA*

1986 STATISTICS

AVG	G	AB	R	H	2B	3B	HR	RBI	BB	SO	SB
.259	123	370	49	96	16	1	21	46	60	59	3

CAREER STATISTICS

AVG	G	AB	R	H	2B	3B	HR	RBI	BB	SO	SB
.282	1944	6986	1070	1972	315	51	231	955	921	1092	183

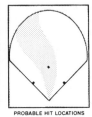

VS. RHP   VS. LHP   PROBABLE HIT LOCATIONS

Dernier to make him look respectable. Matthews' lack of range and dependability on routine plays make him a defensive risk.

OVERALL:

Matthews' strong suits are his offensive ability and his take-charge leadership qualities. But those assets are lost on a fifth-place ballclub as the Cubs were in 1986.

Rooker: "His home run power will probably keep him around a few more seasons, though he really should start to hit the other way soon. Gary is a gung-ho type of leader and could be valuable to an American League ballclub as a designated hitter or on a contending team in the National League."

CHICAGO CUBS

HITTING:

Although his power is to left field, Keith Moreland has learned to hit to all fields effectively. Other than his occasional tendency to chase the high fastball, Moreland has a sound swing and a good knowledge of the strike zone. Lefthanded pitchers try to pitch him inside, but they have become reluctant to try that approach at Wrigley Field. Righthanders try to work him in and out.

Moreland has been the Cubs' top clutch hitter the past several seasons, thriving on game situations and RBI opportunities. He is one of the game's better two-strike hitters because of his ability to go to the opposite field.

Moreland is an excellent fastball hitter.

Like that of many of his teammates, Moreland's home run production fell off last year. His batting average fell nearly 20 points off his career mark and 36 points off his 1985 standard. But he matched his 1985 total of 30 doubles last season.

Moreland batted cleanup most of last season, out of default. He would probably be more effective batting fifth or sixth.

BASERUNNING:

Moreland almost rivals Jody Davis for the dubious distinction of being the slowest Cubs player. He stole only three bases in nine attempts last season after swiping a career-high 12 bases in 1985. Although he is generally a fierce competitor, Moreland has a tendency to run at half-speed to first base on ground outs.

Moreland was embarrassed late last season by being thrown out at first base by Phillies right fielder Glenn Wilson after an apparent base hit (partial credit must go to Wilson's arm). Moreland would be able to reach superstar status if he had good foot speed. He is a gutty performer who is willing to slide in hard to break up a double play or force a collision on a close play at the plate.

FIELDING:

Considered to be a jack-of-many-positions

KEITH MORELAND
RF, No. 6
RR, 6'0", 200 lbs.
ML Svc: 8 years
Born: 5-2-54 in Dallas, TX

1986 STATISTICS

AVG	G	AB	R	H	2B	3B	HR	RBI	BB	SO	SB
.271	156	586	72	159	30	0	12	79	53	48	3

CAREER STATISTICS

AVG	G	AB	R	H	2B	3B	HR	RBI	BB	SO	SB
.286	887	3082	363	880	142	13	83	477	295	353	20

VS. RHP   VS. LHP   PROBABLE HIT LOCATIONS

but a master of none, Moreland will be given an opportunity to start at third base this season. He has felt most comfortable as a right fielder, but his lack of speed and range have been a liability there. Moreland can also adequately serve as a backup catcher and first baseman. He has a better-than-average arm and he is aggressive defensively. He committed nine errors last season (five of which came while he was experimenting with playing at third base).

OVERALL:

Moreland just signed a three-year contract averaging nearly $1.3 million a year although his statistics have not been in the superstar range.

Rooker: "Keith is generally a consistent player offensively and defensively, but will be put to a big test this season to see if he can provide adequate defense at third base and still maintain his offensive contributions.

"Last season, he reported to spring training overweight. He will have to aviod carrying excess baggage this year, especially if he is going to play at third base."

CHICAGO CUBS

PITCHING:

Perhaps the saddest commentary on the Cubs' woeful pitching performances of 1986 was the fact that rookie Jamie Moyer, who was called up from the minors at midseason, wound up with the most victories among the starters with seven.

Scott Sanderson won nine games, but three of those came in a relief role late in the season. The staff's lack of a 10-game winner marked the first time in the history of the Cubs that they didn't have at least one pitcher in double figures.

Control problems, especially in the first two or three innings, have been Moyer's undoing. When he does not have his control in a particular outing, he gets behind in the count, issues walks, then tries to correct this by putting the ball down the middle of the plate-- and watches batters tee off. When things start to unravel, Moyer begins to lose confidence in his best pitches, which are off-speed pitches, and strays from his game-plan. His fastball is not a major league pitch.

However, since he thrives on off-speed pitches, Moyer's fastball can sometimes be sneaky, especially when he keeps it in on the fists of righthanded hitters. When he was most effective last year, the slightly built lefthander managed to keep hitters off balance with a deceiving change-up.

The highlight of Moyer's season was a brilliant one-hit performance against the Montreal Expos in August.

FIELDING, HITTING, BASERUNNING:

Moyer has a tendency to get rattled, especially early in the game, if his control falters. Runners can take advantage of his divided attention by getting the jump on him. He does have a decent pickoff move and he is an average fielder .

JAMIE MOYER
LHP, No. 49
LL, 6'1", 170 lbs.
ML Svc: less than one year
Born: 11-18-62 in
Sellersville, PA

1986 STATISTICS

W	L	ERA	G	GS	CG	SV	IP	H	R	ER	BB	SO
7	4	5.05	16	16	1	0	87.1	107	52	49	42	45

CAREER STATISTICS

W	L	ERA	G	GS	CG	SV	IP	H	R	ER	BB	SO
7	4	5.05	16	16	1	0	87.1	107	52	49	42	45

Moyer executes the sacrifice bunt well and makes decent contact as a hitter.

OVERALL:

Moyer is young and was a bit in awe of the majors last season. He is an enthusiastic rookie who, unlike many players, wants to learn and study more about his opponents. He spends time in the dugout taking notes and watching the master pitchers of the league work their magic. He is very receptive to coaching and to the advice of veteran pitchers. Moyer could develop into a 10- to 15-game winner.

Rooker: "Like John Tudor, Moyer is a change-up pitcher. But unlike the Cardinals' ace, he does throw his change-up with a lot of velocity. He will have to move the ball around more to be effective.

"After a year in the big leagues, Moyer may need to develop another pitch to complement his excellent change-up. Not a big strikeout pitcher, Moyer needs to cut down on his walks to become a steady winner."

CHICAGO CUBS

HITTING:

In his first season with the Cubs last year, veteran outfielder Jerry Mumphrey led the club in hitting with a .304 average, in spite of being limited to a part-time role. A switch-hitter, Mumphrey has hit better from his left side throughout his career. With all of the problems the Cubs had in 1986, it is surprising Mumphrey didn't have an opportunity to play more.

Mumphrey continues to have a quick bat and he sprays the ball to all fields. He has occasional pop in his bat but is not a big home run hitter. He covers the strike zone well, making it difficult to strike him out. Mumphrey was more effective on artificial surfaces as a younger player because of his ability to swing down on the ball and send sharply hit shots through the fast surface. But his chronically sore knees and advanced age now make him less of a threat to beat out infield hits.

BASERUNNING:

Once a major threat on the basepaths, Mumphrey stole only two bases in five attempts last season. He once stole 52 bases for San Diego in 1980. Mumphrey is still a savvy baserunner, however, and is efficient in hit-and-run situations.

FIELDING:

Never known for having excellent hands or the best instincts in the outfield, Mumphrey performs best in right field. His decreased mobility because of the knee injuries make him ineffective in center field. He has an average arm and needs to play one position on a fairly regular basis to make his best

JERRY MUMPHREY
CF, No. 22
SR, 6'2", 200 lbs.
ML Svc: 11 years
Born: 9-9-52 in Tyler, TX

1986 STATISTICS

AVG	G	AB	R	H	2B	3B	HR	RBI	BB	SO	SB
.304	111	309	37	94	11	2	5	32	26	45	2

CAREER STATISTICS

AVG	G	AB	R	H	2B	3B	HR	RBI	BB	SO	SB
.288	1404	4618	616	1330	196	53	57	522	436	625	172

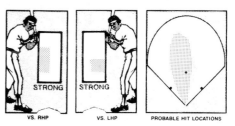

VS. RHP   VS. LHP   PROBABLE HIT LOCATIONS

contribution.

OVERALL:

Mumphrey has played for five teams in the majors and although he has been a full-time starter only sporadically, his ability to get the bat on the ball, hit doubles and show occasional power make him an important player for any club.

Rooker: "Above all else, the 34-year-old, 11-year major league veteran can still hit. He is a career .288 hitter and a professional player who brings a lot of experience to the bench. He has been through a lot in his career and takes the ups as well as the downs."

CHICAGO CUBS

HITTING:

Ryne Sandberg is one of the game's most consistent hitters both for average and for power. For the most part, he is a pull hitter. But Sandberg is very conscious of game situations and hits to the opposite field if it will benefit the team.

If pitchers can't get the breaking ball over against Sandberg, forget it. He sits on the fastball or hard slider when he is ahead in the count.

With his good speed, Sandberg could bunt more often than he does, but the 1986 Cubs rarely needed a sacrifice bunt and looked to Sandberg to supply them with much-needed run production. In search of the long ball, the Cubs decided to sacrifice his ability to hit doubles and triples, and juggled him in the batting order from the No. 2 spot to No. 3 to cleanup.

Sandberg eats up lefthanded pitching and is a strong gap hitter. He avoided his traditionally atrocious start at the plate last season in large part because he tried to concentrate more on swinging down at the pitch and on going with the pitch instead of pulling everything. In doing so, he sacrificed his usual hot streaks in the hot months and his home run total was his lowest in three years.

BASERUNNING:

He has excellent baserunning instincts both when trying to steal a base or when going from first to third on a single. Over the past two seasons, Sandberg has stolen home three times and has proven to be an expert at the delayed steal.

Last season, Sandberg became the first Cub to steal 30 or more bases in five straight years since Frank Chance did it in 1906-1910.

FIELDING:

Without peer as a defensive second baseman, Sandberg set a major league record for fielding percentage in 1986. His five errors tied Pittsburgh's Johnny Ray for the fewest miscues by a second baseman in a season. Sandberg had three errorless streaks of 36 games or more. Incredibly, he made no errors on artificial turf during the regular season. (His only artificial surface error during 1986

RYNE SANDBERG
2B, No. 23
RR, 6'2", 180 lbs.
ML Svc: 5 years
Born: 9-18-59 in
Spokane, WA

1986 STATISTICS
AVG	G	AB	R	H	2B	3B	HR	RBI	BB	SO	SB
.284	154	627	68	178	28	5	14	76	46	79	34

CAREER STATISTICS
AVG	G	AB	R	H	2B	3B	HR	RBI	BB	SO	SB
.287	790	3146	494	902	153	39	74	345	242	447	189

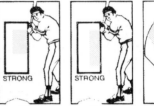

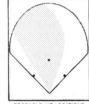

VS. RHP   VS. LHP   PROBABLE HIT LOCATIONS

was a tough but accurate call during the All-Star Game at the Astrodome.)

He has excellent range and the knack of making difficult plays look routine. Sandberg's brilliance is never more evident than in his artistry at backhanding shots behind second base, turning his body and firing the ball with a skimming bounce to first base. Sandberg's arm is not very strong but he is very accurate with his throws and has a quick release.

By his example of consistency, he has been a steadying influence on young shortstop Shawon Dunston.

OVERALL:

A quiet leader, Sandberg is a study in concentration and discipline. He is the type of player whose defensive skills and consistent offensive contributions will be better appreciated at the end of his career.

Rooker: "Like Mike Schmidt, Sandberg can do anything he wants in this game. If the other Cubs hitters start supporting him by getting on base and providing power, he could have his .300 season with 30 homers, 30 stolen bases and 100 RBIs anytime now."

CHICAGO CUBS

PITCHING:

A starting pitcher since 1980, righthander Scott Sanderson endured the personal humiliation of being taken out of the rotation late last season and proceeded to become the Cubs' most efficient middle reliever.

He has an above-average overhand fastball and curveball. And he is becoming more reliant on a change-up as an "out" pitch. Sanderson has a better fastball than he sometimes gives himself credit for and he works the ball around the strike zone well.

He gave up 21 home runs in 1986, matching Eckersley for the team high. When Sanderson gives up a home run, it is because he has not placed the ball well, delivering a high fastball when he was ahead in the count rather than challenging the hitters and throwing inside.

Sanderson nearly matched the control efficiency of teammate Dennis Eckersley, fanning 124 and walking 37 in 169 2/3 innings. But he practically allowed a hit an inning and completed only one game.

Notorious for working slowly, Sanderson has lulled his teammates into not concentrating on defense when he is on the mound.

FIELDING, HITTING, BASERUNNING:

Because of his persistently bad back, Sanderson is not wont to pounce on a bunt or dribbler down the line. His high kick and purposeful delivery give baserunners the edge on steal attempts.

Sanderson is not a good hitter and is often instructed before he enters the batter's box not to swing. He is a fairly good bunter but not

SCOTT SANDERSON
RHP, No. 21
RR, 6'5", 200 lbs.
ML Svc: 8 years
Born: 7-22-56 in
Dearborn, MI

1986 STATISTICS

W	L	ERA	G	GS	CG	SV	IP	H	R	ER	BB	SO
9	11	4.19	37	28	1	1	169.2	165	85	79	37	124

CAREER STATISTICS

W	L	ERA	G	GS	CG	SV	IP	H	R	ER	BB	SO
78	69	3.40	229	207	30	3	1313.2	1243	551	497	328	883

a good baserunner.

OVERALL:

Sanderson was virtually injury-free last year for the first time in several seasons. But persistent back spasms will likely be a recurrent problem.

Sanderson was 16-11 in 1980 as a member of the Montreal Expos, but since then has been just barely over .500.

Rooker: "Several circumstances need to come into play this season for Sanderson to have the outstanding year many have been predicting for him since he entered the league. Remaining healthy is the most significant factor since he shows all the raw talent necessary to win. And the Cubs have to start producing runs for him: the team has scored an average of two runs or less in his losses over the last three years."

CHICAGO CUBS

PITCHING:

The first National League pitcher to save 30 or more games in three consecutive seasons, Lee Smith saved 31 games in 1986 to pace the Cubs' struggling bullpen last season. Smith also tied for the club lead in wins with nine, therefore figuring in 40 of the club's 70 wins, or 57%. The Cubs finished last in the league with a cumulative 4.49 ERA, but Smith's 3.09 ERA was the stingiest on the team.

Smith is a power pitcher who is one of the most feared in the league. He continues to blow hitters away and averaged more than a strikeout per inning last year.

Nonetheless, Smith is not the totally dominant pitcher he could be. The biggest criticism of the imposing righthander is that he fails to work the inside part of the plate enough to accentuate his 95+ MPH fastball. Smith has a three-quarters delivery and throws a rising fastball, slider and cut fastball. Utilizing the inside of the plate would totally devastate batters who are basically sitting back on their heels to try to time his fastball. Oddly, the "little guys" who just want to make contact seem to give Smith the most trouble as they wait for the eventual fastball that will come in as though from a pitching machine.

One of the attributes that may be holding Smith back from becoming as awesome a reliever as, say, Rich Gossage in his heyday, is the lack of an unwavering "killer instinct." Smith has a tendency to get behind in the count often and walked 42 batters last season. He needs to become more aggressive when going in for the kill--especially when he gets ahead in the count.

Smith worked on an off-speed pitch during spring training in 1986, but seemed to lack the confidence to throw it once the season began.

LEE SMITH
RHP, No. 46
RR, 6'6", 235 lbs.
ML Svc: 6 years
Born: 12-4-57 in
Jamestown, LA

1986 STATISTICS

W	L	ERA	G	GS	CG	SV	IP	H	R	ER	BB	SO
9	9	3.09	66	0	0	31	90.1	69	32	31	42	93

CAREER STATISTICS

W	L	ERA	G	GS	CG	SV	IP	H	R	ER	BB	SO
36	41	2.89	396	6	0	144	598.1	507	210	192	232	548

FIELDING, HITTING, BASERUNNING:

Smith is an average fielder whose enormous size and awkward positioning after his delivery make him vulnerable to the bunt and to balls hit to the left of the mound. He is a poor hitter because he is seldom in the game long enough to bat, but has the raw strength to hit the ball a long way.

Smith holds baserunners close but often makes errant pickoff throws to first.

OVERALL:

Smith's sore left knee hampered him at the end of the season but he avoided off-season arthroscopic surgery when doctors concluded there was no ligament or tendon tear.

Rooker: "Smith could cross the sometimes nebulous line from star to superstar by perfecting a few raw edges. Still young and strong, Smith needs to refine the control of his slider and to develop an off-speed pitch if he wants to completely dominate the league."

CHICAGO CUBS

PITCHING:

From the ecstacy of a 16-1, Cy Young Award season in 1984, Rick Sutcliffe sank to an agonizing 5-14 campaign for the Cubs in 1986. Hamstring and shoulder injuries put Sutcliffe on the disabled list three times in 1985 and his injury-plagued follow-up season to the Cy Young Award further fueled the flames of the legend known as the Cy Young jinx. The effects of the '85 injuries seemed to linger into last season and Sutcliffe did not appear to be pitching as though he was fully recovered.

He pitches using a three-quarters delivery and when right, thrives on a better-than-average fastball and pinpoint control of his slider. Last year, however, Sutcliffe walked a team-high 96 batters in 176 2/3 innings.

More damaging than the walks he issued, however, were the hitters who took advantage of getting ahead in the count by stroking hits off Sutcliffe. Opposing hitters said they noticed a big difference in Sutcliffe's offerings in 1986. They noted that they were lucky to get one hittable pitch in four at-bats in 1984, whereas they generally got at least one hittable pitch during each at-bat in 1986.

The Sutcliffe fastball that was clocked in the low-90 MPH two or three years ago slipped into the mid- to high-80s last season. There are games when his fastball will be clocked at 90 MPH in the first inning or two, but then drops down into the 80s. His lack of arm strength makes it doubtful that he will be pitching at 90 MPH consistently--his arm just won't do it. His slider that hit the corners in past seasons sailed high and wide of the plate in 1986.

Sutcliffe did suffer from recurring tendinitis late in the season which tangibly restricted his velocity.

FIELDING, HITTING, BASERUNNING:

Sutcliffe is a good all-around athlete and fields his position well. But his 1985 hamstring injury has slowed his ability to get off the mound as quickly as he needs to. His

RICK SUTCLIFFE
RHP, No. 40
LR, 6'7", 215 lbs.
ML Svc: 9 years
Born: 6-21-56 in Independence, MO

1986 STATISTICS

W	L	ERA	G	GS	CG	SV	IP	H	R	ER	BB	SO
5	14	4.64	28	27	4	0	176.2	166	92	91	96	122

CAREER STATISTICS

W	L	ERA	G	GS	CG	SV	IP	H	R	ER	BB	SO
86	68	3.84	251	191	41	6	1416.2	1328	669	605	599	934

deliberate delivery (his left leg lifts up in almost two separate moves) does not help his ability to hold runners on base. When runners are on base, Sutcliffe can slow the game down to a snail's pace by taking a lot of time between pitches.

Sutcliffe is a good enough hitter to be used as a pinch-hitter; he hits for power and takes a ferocious cut. He is a slow baserunner as a result of the old leg injury but still slides aggressively if he thinks it will help the team.

OVERALL:

Sutcliffe really hasn't been the same since tearing his hamstring on May 19, 1985, in Atlanta. Experts say it generally takes more than one season for a pitcher to rebound from a serious injury and regain the strength and rhythm that are requisite for a winning effort.

Rooker: "Even at his healthiest, Sutcliffe was not regarded as a power pitcher. He has a little delay in his delivery and that is part of his secret; he was also able to thrive on the average of nearly six runs a game that the Cubs provided in his 16 wins in 1984. It wouldn't hurt him to receive that kind of offensive support again.

"Sutcliffe has an excellent attitude and good work ethic that should pay off in dramatically better numbers this season."

CHICAGO CUBS

PITCHING:

Steve Trout is an enigmatic lefthander with an exceptional sinker. Control problems, particularly in the second half of last season, proved to be his undoing as he was eventually taken out of the starting rotation.

Trout has developed a good change-up but needs to gain control of his slider in order to get ahead of hitters. Manager Gene Michael looked at films of Trout taken in 1984 and, in comparing them with the 1986 Trout, spotted mechanical flaws relating to Trout's rhythm. Nevertheless, Trout was unable to get the old 1984 motion back. Too bad; it won him a career high of 13 games.

When he is most effective, Trout induces ground ball outs with his "heavy" sinker and tantalizing off-speed pitch. He is working on pitching on the inside of the plate to righthanded batters because they learned to take him to the opposite field late in the year with the outside pitches.

Trout is renowned for his lapses in concentration on the mound and new Cubs pitching coach Herm Starrette will have his hands full trying to replace the fired Billy Connors. Connors was a self-styled surrogate father and psychologist for the emotional Trout.

FIELDING, HITTING, BASERUNNING:

Trout has improved his fielding after years of floundering, but still tends to get flustered easily with runners on base. Off-balance pickoff throws still occur too often.

Although Trout may have the worst batting stance and swing in the league, he amazingly makes contact fairly often and occasionally lines a base hit. Once he gets on base, though,

STEVE TROUT
LHP, No. 34
LL, 6'4", 189 lbs.
ML Svc: 8 years
Born: 7-30-57 in
Detroit, MI

1986 STATISTICS

W	L	ERA	G	GS	CG	SV	IP	H	R	ER	BB	SO
5	7	4.75	37	25	0	0	161	184	88	85	78	69

CAREER STATISTICS

W	L	ERA	G	GS	CG	SV	IP	H	R	ER	BB	SO
74	75	3.94	242	200	29	4	1294	413	648	567	466	566

it is a different story. He has a very slow, loping stride and often touches the outfield grass while circling the bases.

OVERALL:

Trout has always been a non-traditional type of pitcher. He engages in his own style of meditation before games he is to pitch and follows a course of vitamins and nutrition that is highly specialized. He is a pitcher who is looking to pitch on his own terms.

Trout suffers from a chronic elbow problem which is the result of throwing the sinkerball. It is a major soure of concern for the Cubs.

Rooker: "Trout's sinkerball induces a lot of ground balls. Last season, he pitched batters into grounding into a team-high of 19 double plays. Because of the thickness of the grass at Wrigley Field and the sure-handed fielding of Sandberg and Dunston, Trout is assured of doing well when his sinker is working well."

CHICAGO CUBS

RON DAVIS
RHP, No. 39
RR, 6'4", 205 lbs.
ML Svc: 8 years
Born: 8-6-55 in
Houston, TX

PITCHING, FIELDING, HITTING, BASERUNNING:

Once regarded as one of the premier relievers in the game, righthander Ron Davis was dealt to the Cubs from the Minnesota Twins late last season. Davis still throws around 90 MPH but he needs better control of his slider and could use another pitch.

His inability to put hitters away after getting ahead in the count has been a problem for Davis in recent years.

Davis is not good at holding runners on base and he is a below-average fielder.

He was used as both a middle reliever and set-up man for ace Lee Smith last season. A stricter definition of his role could help Davis.

OVERALL:

Davis seems to have good movement on his fastball and breaking pitch, but the cold facts are that he was 0-2 with a 7.65 earned run average with the Cubs.

Rooker: "He seemed to lose confidence after pitching in the confining "HomerDome" of Minnesota and cozy Wrigley Field doesn't do much to reassure a pitcher."

FRANK DiPINO
LHP, No. 33
LL, 6'0", 180 lbs.
ML Svc: 5 years
Born: 10-22-56 in
Syracuse, NY

PITCHING, FIELDING, HITTING, BASERUNNING:

Acquired by the Cubs in a late-season trade with Houston for Davey Lopes, veteran lefthanded reliever Frank DiPino struggled after a good start in 1986. DiPino still throws hard but his fastball doesn't have the old movement it once had. A lack of control (which means getting behind in the count) seems to be DiPino's biggest problem and that can be murder for a southpaw in Wrigley Field.

He has good control of his body and fields his position well. DiPino throws three-quarters overhand and he has an average move to first base. He takes a good cut with the bat and is a decent baserunner.

OVERALL:

Because of the Cubs' abysmal 1986 season, DiPino was forced into several untenable situations, facing the likes of righthanded slugger Mike Schmidt in the ninth inning, for example.

Rooker: "To be effective, DiPino must be spotted in one- or two-inning relief stints primarily against lefthanded hitting. He is a good competitor and still shows good stuff. If he can get his control back this season, he could boost the Cubs' bullpen."

CHICAGO CUBS

TERRY FRANCONA
INF, No. 16
LL, 6'0", 175 lbs.
ML Svc: 6 years
Born: 4-22-59 in
Aberdeen, SD

HITTING, BASERUNNING, FIELDING:

Three years ago, Terry Francona was beginning to emerge as one of the league's best hitters for average, but he has since suffered two major knee injuries and has been consigned to part-time duty as a pinch-hitter and role player.

Francona does not have much power but is tough to pitch to. He hits the low inside fastball to all fields and is a line drive type of hitter. He is an excellent two-strike hitter but his lack of foot speed due to knee surgery limits his effectiveness. He was used primarily as a pinch-hitter by the Cubs last season but also saw limited duty at first base and in the outfield.

Francona's ability to run straight ahead is not nearly as impaired as is his lateral mobility; as a result, he has difficulty turning the corners on the bases.

Defensively, first base is Francona's best position but his lack of power makes it unwise to play him there on a long-term basis. He is a good fundamental player with good hands and an adequate arm.

OVERALL:

Rooker: "Francona's positive attitude, discipline and strong will to succeed make up for a multitude of physical liabilities. He is still young and willing to work hard to regain the surgery-sapped strength in his ailing knees. He should be a positive addition to any team that can utilize his skills to the fullest."

GUY HOFFMAN
LHP, No. 30
LL, 5'9", 175 lbs.
ML Svc: 2 years
Born: 7-9-56 in
Ottawa, IL

PITCHING, FIELDING,
HITTING, BASERUNNING:

A career minor leaguer, lefthander Guy Hoffman seemed to find his niche with the Cubs last season, winning his last four decisions to finish with a 6-2 record.

Because of a tender elbow that kept him out of action in 1985, Hoffman is much better as a starting pitcher. He was a starter when Jim Frey was manager in the beginning of last season, but when Gene Michael took the reins, Hoffman was out of the rotation. The lefthander got ripped. His arm needs at least four days' rest between appearances to be most effective.

Hoffman is a control pitcher with a good curveball and change-up. He has a sneaky fastball but it has to be spotted on the corners or down to be effective.

He does not throw hard and is physically small, so there is the tendency to write him off as a bad major league prospect. He is used to being sent back and forth between the minors and the big leagues and last season was no exception.

Hoffman is an average fielder but he needs to improve on holding runners close. He is an average hitting pitcher but needs to improve on his bunting technique. Hoffman is a pretty good baserunner.

OVERALL:

Because of his physical limitations, Hoffman must be used properly to extract the best results from him. Despite his age, Hoffman has limited big league experience and is still hungry to earn a spot on a big league roster. His 1986 performance has earned him a good long look in 1987.

CHICAGO CUBS

DAVID MARTINEZ
CF, No. 1
LL, 5'10", 150 lbs.
ML Svc: 1 year
Born: 9-26-64 in
New York, NY

HITTING, BASERUNNING, FIELDING:

Considered one of the top young prospects in the Cubs' organization, David Martinez was a disappointment in his first big league stint last season. He hit only .139 in 108 at-bats, but at the age of 22, Martinez will be given many more looks.

A spray hitter with some power, Martinez's swing reminds scouts of Houston All-Star Jose Cruz. But Martinez needs to relax at the plate and make adjustments. He has problems with the breaking pitch. He likes fastballs down-and-in.

With improved confidence and success at the plate will come more productivity on the bases, where Martinez excelled in the minors. He needs time to learn the pitchers' moves to first to avoid being picked off and getting poor jumps on steal attempts.

Martinez has a strong arm and could emerge as the Cubs' center fielder or right fielder of the future. He moves back on the ball well and displays exceptional range in center field.

OVERALL:

Rooker: "Martinez has shown too much raw talent in the minors to be discounted because of a poor showing in 1986. He is very coachable and is intent on making it in the big leagues. Like most young players, it is important for Martinez to get off to a fine start offensively this season."

CHRIS SPEIER
SS, No. 28
RR, 6'1", 180 lbs.
ML Svc: 16 years
Born: 6-28-50 in
Alameda, CA

HITTING, BASERUNNING, FIELDING:

Chris Speier is that rare major league player who has graciously accepted his relegation to a utility role after several years as a starting shortstop.

Speier helped the Cubs last season with timely hitting and occasional pop in his bat. He is a contact hitter who pulls the fastball. He is a good situation hitter. Speier works hard to keep himself in shape and practices fundamentals such as bunting and hitting to the opposite field to advance runners.

Speier relies more on guile than foot speed to get the job done on the basepaths. Although he has been used occasionally as a pinch-runner, Speier is not a real burner.

Speier provides better-than-average defense as a fill-in at shortstop, second base or at third. He has average range and only a fair arm but continues to execute the double play and other routine plays with precision. Willing to do whatever is necessary to help his club, Speier is even willing to learn how to catch--if it comes to that.

OVERALL:

Rooker: "Speier's value to a ballclub is accentuated by the limitations of the 24-man roster. His ability to play any infield position and remain a proficient contact hitter should ensure him a place on a big league club. His excellent attitude and workmanlike habits generally rub off on younger teammates."

CHICAGO CUBS

MANNY TRILLO
INF, No. 19
RR, 6'1", 164 lbs.
ML Svc: 13 years
Born: 12-25-50 in
Caritito, Venezuela

HITTING, BASERUNNING, FIELDING:

One of the game's all-time proficient second basemen, Manny Trillo surprised many observers by ably handling his role as a utility infielder for the Cubs in 1986. Trillo played respectably at second base and third base as well as at first base while hitting .296 in 152 at-bats.

Trillo likes the ball up-and-in and is still able to pull the ball with occasional power. His excellent bat control enabled the Cubs to hit-and-run with him. He also can sacrifice bunt or hit to the opposite field.

A career .262 hitter, Trillo stroked 10 doubles and drove in 19 runs last year in 81 games.

Trillo never has been much of a basestealing threat and at the age of 36 he doesn't figure to improve. He runs the bases well, though, and can be counted on to execute the front end of hit-and-run and sacrifice plays.

Trillo is not quite the skill player he once was defensively but he still has above-average range. Understandably, Trillo feels most comfortable defensively at second base, where he excelled as an All-Star for many years. But the presence of standout Ryne Sandberg at second means Trillo won't see much action there. Trillo played first base briefly for the first time last season and did a respectable job when regular Leon Durham was hurt.

OVERALL:

Trillo continues to keep himself in excellent physical shape and he improved his batting average 72 points from .224 in 1985, when he floundered with the Giants.

Rooker: "Manny was a big surprise last year; maybe going back to Chicago helped revive him. He still has the smoothness that has been his trademark."

CINCINNATI REDS

HITTING:

Two years ago and into the 1986 season, it looked as though Buddy Bell was finished. He didn't hit with authority. He didn't make consistent contact and his bat looked very slow. The worse matters got, the more extra time Bell spent in the batting cage. At one point, after wearing out every available batting practice pitcher, he coaxed his 14-year-old son into the task.

"I wore myself out," Bell said after his plate performance improved. "I didn't have time to think about how bad I was going. If I had, I don't know what I would have done--killed myself, probably."

By the end of June last season, Bell's hitting had improved and thoughts of him being through with baseball were set aside. His 1986 season was one of the finest of his career.

Bell puts the ball in play and hits a few home runs. He is not really a home run hitter, but he has enough extra-base power to drive in some runs. Bell's regained strength is his ability to make consistent contact.

He is another good hit-and-run man for the Reds. Bell will drive the ball into the alleys. He has more power to left-center field than anywhere else, but likes to take the outside pitch to the opposite field.

Pitchers should pitch him off the plate and inside with breaking stuff down and away.

BASERUNNING:

Bell is not fast, not a basestealing threat, but he is smart on the bases and uses good judgment. Though not fleet, he knows his opponent and will test a weak arm in the outfield, particularly when attempting to score from second.

He doesn't make mistakes or take unnecessary risks on the basepaths. When it looks as though he has blundered, you can bet someone has missed a sign.

FIELDING:

Bell is as fine a fielding third baseman as

BUDDY BELL
3B, No. 25
RR, 6'2", 185 lbs.
ML Svc: 15 years
Born: 8-27-51 in
Pittsburgh, PA

1986 STATISTICS

AVG	G	AB	R	H	2B	3B	HR	RBI	BB	SO	SB
.278	155	568	89	158	29	3	20	75	73	49	2

CAREER STATISTICS

AVG	G	AB	R	H	2B	3B	HR	RBI	BB	SO	SB
.282	2133	8068	1046	2273	392	53	177	993	732	695	50

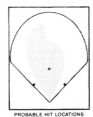

VS. RHP   VS. LHP   PROBABLE HIT LOCATIONS

there is in the National League. He still has a good, accurate arm but his range may not be quite as good as some others in the league. He catches everything he can get to.

Bell takes great pride in his fielding and credits his defense for carrying him through his worst times at the plate.

Once his hitting improved, Bell was able to breathe a sigh of relief. Despite his confusion at the plate, Bell remained confident in the field and maintained his ability to react quickly and accurately to every play at third base.

OVERALL:

Dierker: "Buddy is not finished yet. There are some people in baseball who theorize that Bell's prolonged hitting slump was simply a lengthy adjustment from American League pitching to National League pitching."

CINCINNATI REDS

PITCHING:

Most of the time when a second-year pitcher wins 14 games, everyone is more than satisfied. But Browning set some exceptional standards for himself in his rookie season by winning 20-games. He was the first National League rookie to do so since Bob Grim in 1954.

Early last season, eager to prove he would not fall to the "Sophomore Jinx," Browning departed from the mix that had made him successful the previous season. Instead of using his fastball to set up his breaking pitches, the lefthander started relying on his screwballs and curves. He did not go right after the hitters the way a pitcher should who has a 20-win season already in his pocket.

Like the rest of the Reds, Browning got off to a bad start and it led to further problems. Not finding the success he expected, Browning began to rely too heavily on his fastball, which is not an overpowering pitch. At his best, which Browning demonstrated with a two-hit shutout against the Cubs, he sets up a pair of nasty screwballs with his fastball.

He is not an extremely hard thrower, but can make good use of his fastball because he is able to put it on the corners. He'll cut the fastball and run it in on a righthanded batter. He'll also throw it straight to the outside corner.

Once Browning has established the fastball, he'll mix in a true screwball and pair that pitch with an off-speed scroogie, which reacts with less break. Along with this combination of screwballs (which is similar to that of the Dodgers' Fernando Valenzuela), Browning also has a curveball, but it's rated average and serves mostly to keep hitters guessing.

The necessity for good control is particularly the case with Browning's fastball. He has to keep that pitch off the plate. Browning is almost always in for a bad day when he keeps going to the breaking pitches. When Browning is in trouble, he gives up home runs; last season, he distributed 26 of them.

FILEDING, HITTING, BASERUNNING:

The Reds stress total production to their

TOM BROWNING
LHP, No. 32
LL, 6'1", 190 lbs.
ML Svc: 2 years
Born: 4-28-60 in
Casper, WY

1986 STATISTICS

W	L	ERA	G	GS	CG	SV	IP	H	R	ER	BB	SO
14	13	3.81	39	39	4	0	243.1	225	123	103	70	147

CAREER STATISTICS

W	L	ERA	G	GS	CG	SV	IP	H	R	ER	BB	SO
35	22	3.58	80	80	10	0	528	494	238	210	148	316

pitchers each spring. They want them to be proficient in all aspects of the game. Browning is one who takes this teaching to heart.

In the field, he is quick with the glove and heady in his fielding. He won't be caught throwing to the wrong base on a bunt or a grounder back to the mound. There is nothing flashy about his move, but simply by being a lefthander, he'll keep runners close.

Browning is a better hitter than most pitchers: he'll slash a liner through the infield on occassion, and will often bunt on his own and for base hits. The Reds began using him as a pinch-runner last season and will probably do so again this season. His speed is average--again for a pitcher--but he's extremely aggressive on the bases, more than some of the Reds' position players. It was Browning who collided with Mike Scioscia at the plate in Los Angeles last year and put the Dodger catcher out of commission with a sprained ankle.

OVERALL:

Dierker: "This season might be more indicative of what we can expect from this young pitcher. While it is doubtful that he will be a consistent 20-game winner, his eventual pattern will likely lie between 15-20 wins each year.

"One thing is for sure, he is the type of pitcher who needs a lot of runs to win. His ERA was 3.55 two years ago and 3.81 last year."

CINCINNATI REDS

HITTING:

Last season was Sal Butera's first year with the Reds and his sixth in major league baseball. Butera enjoyed a measure of celebrity after all this time and became somewhat of a cult hero in Cincinnati in 1986. A backup catcher throughout his career, it was Butera's grit as a player and personal demeanor which earned him the adoration of the fans—and not his excellence on the field. Even the scoreboard crew at Riverfront Stadium got into the Butera craze and decorated their offices with his pictures and jersey.

His role as backup was taken to its most literal extent when, during a late-season blowout Cincinnati was bound to lose, Butera even took the mound as a pitcher. He did alright.

As a hitter, Butera makes contact, can take the ball out of the park and will surprise a pitcher who takes him lightly. He's a smart hitter who stays on top of the game. Butera will hit to the opposite field when the situation requires and will hit a mistake pitch with authority.

BASERUNNING:

Butera is another slow guy who compensates for a lack of speed with a certain headiness. He has no delusions about his foot speed. While Butera is no threat to steal, his judgments are generally good and he won't bail out when he's called on to break up a double play.

FIELDING:

Butera has a soft pair of hands (one passed ball in 53 games in 1986) and a fair arm. He is not always accurate with his throws and basestealers will take advantage of his presence in a game. His throws are often short and wide of second.

Butera calls a sharp game and handles pitchers well. He's always one of the first to the ballpark each day and never misses the opposing team's batting practice, figuring he might see something that will be beneficial in the game.

SAL BUTERA
C, No. 22
RR, 6'0", 190 lbs.
ML Svc: 5 years
Born: 9-25-52 in
Richmond Hill, NY

1986 STATISTICS

AVG	G	AB	R	H	2B	3B	HR	RBI	BB	SO	SB
.239	56	113	14	27	6	1	2	16	21	10	0

CAREER STATISTICS

AVG	G	AB	R	H	2B	3B	HR	RBI	BB	SO	SB
.237	280	619	52	147	17	2	5	56	77	54	0

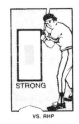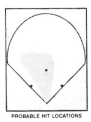

STRONG   STRONG   PROBABLE HIT LOCATIONS

VS. RHP   VS. LHP

While he is not smooth at his work, he seldom hurts his team.

OVERALL:

Butera is a very ordinary player whose effort is always the best he has to offer. That quality, as much as anything else, led to his Cincinnati Fan Club and his high marks in Rose's book. Totally team-oriented, Butera is a willing indian when so many others seek to be chief.

But when all is said and done, Butera would probably not be in the big leagues were he not a catcher. He is a backup player and a late-inning replacement. Rose likes Butera because of his workmanlike attitude and studious approach to the opposition as well as with his teammates.

Dierker: "Sal's a handy backup though he is not much more than that. He knows how to play the game of baseball, but he is physically beyond his prime (at 34 years old). He was never truly a starting player and figures to be a backup catcher again this season."

CINCINNATI REDS

HITTING:

Slated as a utility player and pinch-hitter this season, Dave Concepcion has lost much of his flair at the plate. Once a player who could damage opponents with his power and clutch hitting, Concepcion is now primarily a mistake hitter.

In the past, he could hit good pitchers, but as it appears now, pitchers can strike him out by throwing almost any good pitch, whether fastball or off-speed, inside or outside.

A high-ball hitter, Concepcion seems particularly vulnerable to high fastballs away and fastballs down-and-in. He will really flail at the high fastball off the plate. He is no longer a reliable clutch hitter.

What remains of his power is normally demonstrated to the opposite field. Once in a while, he'll connect and drive the ball into the alley or down the line.

Concepcion will generally make contact in hit-and-run situations and advance runners with ground balls in one-out situations.

BASERUNNING:

Concepcion can still run some--when he wants to. He stole 13 bases last season and can't be ignored by pitchers. A reliable baserunner, Concepcion will do the basic things and occasionally come up with a little extra. Opponents sometimes seem surprised by Concepcion's baserunning ability, partially, perhaps, because he doesn't always seem to go all-out on routine ground balls or pop-ups. He usually plays a heads-up game on the bases.

FIELDING:

Known as Señor Shortstop in Latin America, Concepcion's once sterling skills have eroded with time. His range is not as good as it once was and his arm has lost much of its strength and accuracy. He is not able to reach many of the tougher shots in the holes. When he does glove one, he no longer has the

DAVE CONCEPCION
SS, No. 13
RR, 6'1", 190 lbs.
ML Svc: 17 years
Born: 6-17-48 in
Aragua, Venezuela

1986 STATISTICS

AVG	G	AB	R	H	2B	3B	HR	RBI	BB	SO	SB
.260	90	311	42	81	13	2	3	30	26	43	13

CAREER STATISTICS

AVG	G	AB	R	H	2B	3B	HR	RBI	BB	SO	SB
.267	2300	8247	950	2198	365	48	100	909	690	1139	314

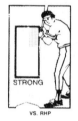

STRONG   STRONG

VS. RHP   VS. LHP   PROBABLE HIT LOCATIONS

arm to make the putout consistently.

While he is not an embarrassment at his natural position, Concepcion has worked the past three years at third base, second and first. He's adequate at all three positions and slick at third base. Some felt Concepcion was the Reds' best defensive first baseman in 1986. He'll appear at all three positions this season and may even pull duty as a third catcher in an emergency situation.

OVERALL:

Possibly in the final year of his career, Concepcion will give way to the Reds' younger shortstops, Barry Larkin and Kurt Stillwell.

Dierker: "Like Pete Rose, his best days are gone but the Reds' manager feels Concepcion will be helpful off the bench and in the development of Larkin and Stillwell."

CINCINNATI REDS

HITTING:

As a rookie in 1986, Kal Daniels displayed one of the sweetest swings in the National League, a stroke so controlled and productive that many baseball people proclaimed him "a pure hitter . . . a natural."

A grand future is most likely in store for Daniels; manager Pete Rose says he will be the Reds' starting left fielder this season. The highest praise of all for Daniels may have come during the winter meetings last year, while the Reds and San Diego Padres tried to make a deal for a starting pitcher. The Padres had pitchers to offer but insisted on Daniels' inclusion in the trade. Equally insistent, however, was the Reds' refusal to include this budding star in any swap. "Chief" Bender, the Reds' Director of Player Personnel, said, "If we were to make that trade we might be giving them the batting champions for the next eight to 10 years in Daniels and Tony Gwynn."

Daniels' promise lies in his fluid, powerful swing. He's a line drive hitter with power and true clutch ability (11-for-23 as a pinch-hitter). He'll hit the ball to all parts of the field and is not easily fooled--even by the best pitchers the league has to offer. A good situations hitter, Daniels will probably bat leadoff for the Reds this season.

BASERUNNING:

Daniels has good speed on the bases and will steal. He took 15 bases last season in 17 attempts. He'll beat out some ground balls and take the extra base on a bobble.

If there is a question regarding his baserunning, it is his intensity. Daniels, a smart baserunner, is not always as aggressive as he should be.

FIELDING:

Early last season, Daniels came under a great deal of criticism from manager Pete Rose and GM Bill Bergesch for his failures in the field. His trouble in the field and his lack of aggressiveness led to a demotion to Triple-A. Both Rose and Bergesch made it clear they did not like Daniels' work habits because they felt he concentrated so much on his hitting that his other skills were being overlooked.

KAL DANIELS
OF, No. 28
LR, 5'11", 185 lbs.
ML Svc: 1 year
Born: 8-20-63 in
Vienna, GA

1986 STATISTICS

AVG	G	AB	R	H	2B	3B	HR	RBI	BB	SO	SB
.320	74	181	34	58	10	4	6	23	22	30	15

CAREER STATISTICS

AVG	G	AB	R	H	2B	3B	HR	RBI	BB	SO	SB
.320	74	181	34	58	10	4	6	23	22	30	15

  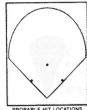

VS. RHP — STRONG VS. LHP — STRONG PROBABLE HIT LOCATIONS

After his return from the minors, Daniels showed improvement in the field. He appears to have relatively good hands, but is not blessed with a a particularly strong arm. Daniels still needs work on his defense, but he's adequate. With a little more hustle, the criticism should disappear.

OVERALL:

Daniels has the ability to be a league-leading hitter. With that kind of ability, some might say that the questions about his defense are almost inconsequential.

Dierker: "The Reds have survived with worse fielders than Kal Daniels over the years, but that still does not excuse his poor habits as a fielder. There is a bit of a squeeze on in baseball caused in part by the necessity of every player to contribute more fully in these days of the 24-man roster. And today, the owners are expecting more bang for their buck from each player.

"While there is no denying Daniels' tremendous hitting potential, he is playing for Pete Rose, a man who fashioned a 24-year career by being an all-around ballplayer. Daniels will have to dance to Pete's music."

CINCINNATI REDS

HITTING:

Reds GM Bill Bergesch refers to Kal Daniels, Barry Larkin, Tracy Jones, Kurt Stillwell and Eric Davis as the "crown jewels of the organization." Eric Davis is the most precious of them all. He is a rare blend of speed and power. In terms of all-around raw talent, Davis is in the top class in the National League.

Davis has excellent power and unparalleled speed in the league. Cardinals manager Whitey Herzog and Giants manager Roger Craig have each predicted a season in which Davis hits 50 home runs and steals 100 bases, a remarkable feat never before accomplished.

The key for Davis in 1986 was increased contact and better discipline at the plate. In 1985, his first full season with the Reds, Davis struck out once in just over every three at-bats. Last season, he was able to start making contact, to stop striking out so much and became a fairly good on-base hitter. He also hit more home runs and started drawing more walks.

Blessed with extremely fast hands, Davis has power to all fields. He'll hit home runs to the opposite field and make it look easy. More often than not, Davis' home runs are line drive shots that are still rising as they clear the outfield fence. Generally, he will hit the ball hard from left-center around to right-center.

His speed is such that a topped ground ball is often a base hit and a drive to left-center that would normally be a double can result in a triple. National League outfielders who are otherwise content to hold the ball and catch the eye of a baserunner to glare him into stopping will find that is no way to treat this extraordinary player; Davis will glare back from the next base.

The Reds face a delicious problem with Davis: whether to hit him at the top of the lineup to take advantage of his speed or in the middle of the lineup to take advantage of his power.

BASERUNNING:

Rose says Davis is unequivocally the fastest man he has ever seen in baseball; his high words of praise were not a result of a euphoric moment. His assessment was, instead, a

ERIC DAVIS
CF, No. 44
RR, 6'3", 175 lbs.
ML Svc: 3 years
Born: 5-29-62 in
Los Angeles, CA

1986 STATISTICS

AVG	G	AB	R	H	2B	3B	HR	RBI	BB	SO	SB
.277	132	415	97	115	15	3	27	71	68	100	80

CAREER STATISTICS

AVG	G	AB	R	H	2B	3B	HR	RBI	BB	SO	SB
.259	245	711	156	184	28	7	45	119	99	187	106

  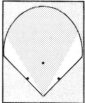

VS. RHP   VS. LHP   PROBABLE HIT LOCATIONS

result of Davis' efforts. The slender outfielder was second in the league in stolen bases (80) and he wasn't an everyday starter until June 17.

Besides having world-class speed, Davis has a definite knack for reading pitchers. If he gets a good look at a pitcher and gauges his move, he is able to get a good jump. Once that happens, he is impossible to throw out. Last season, Davis was caught stealing just 11 times.

FIELDING:

With this kind of speed, Davis runs down a lot of balls in the outfield. He isn't a natural in the field and doesn't always get a great jump, but he simply outruns his mistakes.

Davis has a strong arm--not the best--but it's good and generally accurate. He'll stick to the fundamentals and look for his cutoff men.

OVERALL:

Dierker: "Big things are expected of Davis in virtually every element of the game. His teammate Dave Parker said, 'I'm gonna play this game a couple more years, and then I'm gonna sit back and watch Eric Davis rewrite the record books in this game.'."

CINCINNATI REDS

PITCHING:

John Denny is a control pitcher whose lack of control off the mound got him in trouble with the Reds and forced him into the job market. He got into a fracas with a sportswriter and tossed a bat at a television camera; the affair ended up in court and ultimately contributed to Denny's release from the Reds.

When Denny was occupied with throwing baseballs, he showed signs of being an exceptional control pitcher. He mixed a fastball and good curve with what some baseball people say was one of the best change-ups around.

On his good days Denny will use the change-up and his curveball as his out pitch. His curveball is really a good pitch when he has it working. He keeps the ball down and moves it back and forth from one corner to the other, changing speeds often.

On occasion, Denny has pinpoint control with his big looping curve, but when he's off with it, he pays. Over the past couple of years, arm problems have prevented him from maintaining consistency on his curveball, and he had periods during which he makes too many mistakes up in the strike zone or out over the plate.

Denny has had shoulder and elbow problems and last year didn't pitch after August 18th because of a sprained wrist.

Though Denny's best years are probably behind him, he is still a pitcher with a warrior-like spirit. He is an uncompromising pitcher who will not give in to a hitter.

FILEDING, HITTING, BASERUNNING:

Denny remains a good fielder with an exceptional move to first for a righthander. Baserunners won't take liberties with him and

JOHN DENNY
RHP, No. 40
RR, 6'3", 190 lbs.
ML Svc: 12 years
Born: 11-8-52 in
Prescott, AZ

1986 STATISTICS

W	L	ERA	G	GS	CG	SV	IP	H	R	ER	BB	SO
11	10	4.20	27	27	2	0	171.1	179	89	80	56	115

CAREER STATISTICS

W	L	ERA	G	GS	CG	SV	IP	H	R	ER	BB	SO
123	108	3.58	325	322	62	0	2149.2	2093	967	856	778	1146

he'll glove most playable balls that come his way. He's heady as a pitcher and won't make the mental mistake that lengthens an inning.

He is a good-hitting pitcher (he injured his wrist last August during a 2-for-3 day against the Padres) and is an effective bunter.

He has relatively good speed for a pitcher and will steal a base if he gets a chance. As a baserunner, he is extremely aggressive on the bases. He is not afraid of anything: hitters, their line drives; hard tags and definitely not sportswriters.

OVERALL:

Probably on the tail end of his career, Denny can still put together the kind of days which earned him the Cy Young Award in 1983, but not on a consistent basis. The Reds were not interested in re-signing the veteran. His salary was too high and they were troubled by his off-field difficulties. When Denny left the Reds in September, he suggested to pitching coach Scott Breeden that he might retire.

CINCINNATI REDS

HITTING:

Bo Diaz is the first real everyday catcher the Reds have had since Johnny Bench gave up the position and eventually retired. Unfortunately, the Reds acquired Diaz after his peak years.

At age 34 and after nine years in major league baseball, Diaz is hobbled by bad knees but remains one of the better clutch-hitting and performance-oriented catchers in the league. He'll drive in the run when it counts and move runners along the bases with right-side ground outs and deep fly balls.

Manager Pete Rose claims Diaz is one of the finest hit-and-run men in the National League because of his ability to put the bat on the ball. Diaz is a good hit-and-run man whether he is facing either a left- or a righthanded pitcher.

Diaz has some power and will hit a few home runs each season. In spite of his poor speed, he will drive the ball to the alleys for doubles. He likes the ball on the inside portion of the plate and is vulnerable to breaking pitches away.

Diaz becomes a better hitter when the competition is keenest. He will seldom provide his team with the big blow, but will contribute something with his at-bat.

BASERUNNING:

Diaz is a delight on the bases. He darts, jumps, fakes, hops and generally moves around like a waterbug, albeit a very slow waterbug.

Partially because of injuries to his knees and ankles over the years, Diaz is one of the slowest, if not the slowest, runners in the league. He'll seldom score from second on a single and will rarely go from first to third on a single. He's smart and aggressive at the task but totally aware of his limitations. Late in a close game, he'll most always be dropped for a pinch-runner.

FIELDING:

Diaz handles pitchers well and knows the strengths and weaknesses of the hitters around the league. Inexperienced pitchers

BO DIAZ
C, No. 6
RR, 5'11", 200 lbs.
ML Svc: 9 years
Born: 3-23-53 in
Cua, Venezuela

1986 STATISTICS

AVG	G	AB	R	H	2B	3B	HR	RBI	BB	SO	SB
.272	134	474	50	129	21	0	10	56	40	52	1

CAREER STATISTICS

AVG	G	AB	R	H	2B	3B	HR	RBI	BB	SO	SB
.259	718	2331	246	604	120	4	61	327	166	308	8

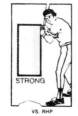

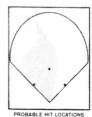

STRONG VS. RHP   STRONG VS. LHP   PROBABLE HIT LOCATIONS

praise him for his help in this area.

He can throw and gets rid of the ball smoothly and--more often than not--accurately. His mobility behind the plate, however, is restricted because of his weak knees. Last season, he was charged with 12 passed balls to rank third highest in the league among everyday catchers. He also committed 13 errors to rank among the NL's top-dropping catchers. In Diaz's case, most of his passed balls and errors are because of his inability to spring up or out quickly enough to prevent a pitch from getting away.

OVERALL:

At this point in his career, Diaz's greatest assets are his abilities as a clutch hitter and a handler of pitchers. His greatest weakness is his lack of speed. He can really clog up the bases and the same weakness hurts his defense.

Dierker: "Bo is probably a better RBI man than most of the catchers around the league, but he is getting a little older and probably is in the declining phase of his career."

CINCINNATI REDS

HITTING:

A hitter with awesome power, Nick Esasky has one problem: he is as streaky as they come. In his hot streaks, Esasky is capable of carrying a team. But in his cold periods, no one can be colder. It's in these times that Esasky, who may think too much about his hitting, has admitted he feels as though he has two strikes when he walks to the plate.

He made so much progress two years ago (21 home runs, 66 RBIs and a .262 batting average), but some of that was undone last year. He strikes out a lot (97 times in 330 at-bats last year), but the Reds simply can't give up on him because he has tremendous raw power. He can hit the ball out of any part of any ballpark.

Esasky has been a tireless worker in his efforts to improve his contact. There are glimmers of progress, but these are always followed by bad times, when Esasky is badly fooled on breaking balls and well behind on the fastball. It's almost as if Esasky has to have his pitch in his particular zone before he hits.

Even in his good times, he is not necessarily a good clutch hitter or a good two-strike hitter. He tends to hit outside of critical situations. So far, he has not been able to make enough consistent contact to be the kind of hitter the Reds hope he can be in the middle of the lineup and really doesn't have the speed to hit at the top of the lineup.

It looks as though Esasky will never hit consistently, but rather, he will be a consistently streaky hitter.

BASERUNNING:

Esasky is not considered fast, but he will surprise the opposition with his quickness. He stays alert and doesn't take unecessary chances. He won't hurt his team on the bases, but he is not a threat to steal or the man the Reds want at second with two outs, representing the tying or go-ahead run.

FIELDING:

With the exception of Pete Rose, Esasky is the Reds' most experienced first baseman. His best position, however, is at third base.

NICK ESASKY
INF/OF, No. 12
RR, 6'3", 200 lbs.
ML Svc: 4 years
Born: 2-24-60 in
Hialeah, FL

1986 STATISTICS

AVG	G	AB	R	H	2B	3B	HR	RBI	BB	SO	SB
.230	102	330	35	76	17	2	12	41	47	97	0

CAREER STATISTICS

AVG	G	AB	R	H	2B	3B	HR	RBI	BB	SO	SB
.238	425	1367	167	326	58	12	55	198	167	401	10

 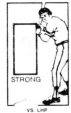 

STRONG — VS. RHP STRONG — VS. LHP PROBABLE HIT LOCATIONS

This season, it is likely that Esasky will get some action in left field.

He is a pretty decent defensive player no matter where he plays. His speed is only average, which is much more of a detriment when he is playing in the outfield, but it also contributes to his lack of range as an infielder.

Esasky has a strong, accurate arm. In the outfield, he will make the routine, expected plays but will do nothing daring. The best description of his outfield play is "careful."

OVERALL:

The best advice anyone could give Esasky as a hitter would probably be just to relax.

Dierker: "There is one clear fact: if he can develop as a hitter, the Reds will *have* to find a place for him in the lineup because he will produce a lot of runs.

"It appears as though Esasky just needs to take a few more steps forward to become a part of the 'New Red Machine.' If he doesn't take those steps, however, he will be on the fringe--playing everyday for awhile, sitting on the bench for a while."

CINCINNATI REDS

PITCHING:

John Franco is a hard-throwing, lefthanded short reliever who brings a bit of Brooklyn toughness to the mound each outing. He does not give in and he's only there to win.

He is one of the best relief pitchers around.

Franco has gained that reputation with an impressive array of pitches.

He has a good fastball (in the 88-89 MPH range) which he can spot on the corners. At times, this kind of control and power pitching is enough to get Franco a save, but *he has more.* Franco also throws a screwball and a curveball. He is a very challenging type of pitcher. He is the kind that a manager likes to have come out of the bullpen in the late innings because if he can't get the hitter one way, he'll do it another. He usually goes right after hitters with his best stuff.

Franco also has a change-up that he sets up with the fastball. He turns it over and gives it a screwball rotation. This, as much as any other, is his out pitch. He'll use this pitch to get strikeouts. He keeps his other pitches down in the zone, which generally leads to routine ground balls.

Though he was successful in 1985, Franco was not satisfied and developed a new pitch at spring training in 1986: a rising cross-seam fastball which complements his other sinking pitches. He used the pitch effectively, particularly in the last half of the season.

FILEDING, HITTING, BASERUNNING:

Franco is a quick, smart fielder with a smooth move to first. He'll catch some baserunners leaning, but generally concentrates on the hitter. He'll make the routine plays and spear some line drives back through the box. Like teammate Tom

JOHN FRANCO
LHP, No. 31
LL, 5'10", 175 lbs.
ML Svc: 3 years
Born: 9-17-60 in
Brooklyn, NY

1986 STATISTICS

W	L	ERA	G	GS	CG	SV	IP	H	R	ER	BB	SO
6	6	2.94	74	0	0	29	101	90	40	33	44	84

CAREER STATISTICS

W	L	ERA	G	GS	CG	SV	IP	H	R	ER	BB	SO
24	11	2.58	195	0	0	45	279.1	247	95	80	120	200

Browning, he takes his fielding seriously.

He can bunt, but seldom gets the chance since he enters the game as a closer. Franco is not on the bases very often and when he is, he plays it safe without being lackadaisical.

OVERALL:

With his impressive assortment of pitches and his all-around good attitude toward the game, one has to wonder if converting him to a starter at some point might be a possibility. It is unusual for a short reliever to have so many good pitches. There are many who find it unthinkable to take as successful and reliable a reliever as Franco and try to tempt fate by altering the formula, but the Reds are fortunate to have the option.

Dierker: "Though many relievers come and go quickly, there is every reason to believe Franco will be one of those who last for a while. He doesn't rely on a single pitch or a freak pitch. He has become an excellent reliever--one of the best around."

PITCHING:

This sturdy righthander was the Reds' top winner in 1986 and figures to be a big man in their starting rotation again this season. A thinking pitcher, Bill Gullickson combines a good fastball with a sinker and curveball.

He doesn't have the devastating breaking ball he had when he first came into the major leagues (in 1979), but he still throws hard--in the 90 MPH range--and he has a good idea of what he wants to do with his game plan.

Gullickson attacks a game and each hitter like a chess problem. He is a most deliberate pitcher, sometimes painfully so and will always take a game into the 2½ hour range.

Gullickson is no longer an overpowering pitcher. These days, he survives on control and wits. At this point in his career, his strong point is his durability and dependability. He will take the mound every turn and usually keeps his team in the game. Gullickson is a workhorse-type, but he has lost the "spectacular" rating given when he struck out 18 during a game his rookie season.

It is hard to say how Gullickson will attack a game now. He generally sorts through his pitches in the early part of a game until he finds what pitch or combination is working. He's learned after seven years in the big leagues to work an angle. He doesn't try to muscle his way through an assignment.

FIELDING, HITTING, BASERUNNING:

Gullickson is a fair fielder, surehanded but slow afoot. He'll have some troubles coming off the mound and won't make any daring plays in the field. His move is decent, but slow feet hinder him some in this area. He has to be

BILL GULLICKSON
RHP, No. 34
RR, 6'3", 220 lbs.
ML Svc: 7 years
Born: 2-20-59 in Marshall, MN

1986 STATISTICS

W	L	ERA	G	GS	CG	SV	IP	H	R	ER	BB	SO
15	12	3.38	37	37	6	0	244.2	245	103	92	60	121

CAREER STATISTICS

W	L	ERA	G	GS	CG	SV	IP	H	R	ER	BB	SO
87	73	3.43	213	207	37	0	1430.2	1394	597	545	348	799

careful in his pitch selection with baserunners at first who are capable of stealing.

On an already-slow Reds team, Gullickson is perhaps the slowest member. He moves around the bases one at a time. He'll get some hits once in a while and can bunt. Gullickson is reliable when it comes to moving the runner over with a bunt.

OVERALL:

Gullickson probably won't win 20 for a team, but if given sufficient run support, he will win more than he loses. A rigorous off-season workout program which he undertook this winter may strengthen him in 1987, although preparing his body for seven or nine innings is not his problem.

Dierker: "Bill is more of a journeyman pitcher at this point, but he does have the capacity to pitch some complete games, something most pitchers can't do these days."

CINCINNATI REDS

HITTING:

Tracy Jones is the first to admit that if looks and style determined success, he would be out of luck. "I'm not supposed to hold the bat the way I do," he said. "I'm not supposed to swing the bat the way I do. But, what can I say, it works for me."

Jones, sidelined the last half of the 1986 season with a torn tendon in his left hand, begins a rather stiff, short swing holding the bat in the very middle of his body--more like a flag-bearer than a hitter. He often appears to be flailing at the ball. Yet, like he says, it works for him.

He is a line drive hitter who will use the entire field although he pulls the ball more often than not. He has good size, strength and hits with power. He is not really a home run hitter at this point in his career, however, but he does show good ability to hit in the clutch.

Jones pretty much attacks the ball; his swing is anything but fluid, but the short stroke helps him adjust to off-speed pitches. But like most players early in their careers, he has some trouble with pitchers who specialize in breaking balls.

He has the speed to beat out ground balls in the infield, but usually slashes the ball into the alleys.

BASERUNNING:

Jones' style at the plate provides some insight into his character, but it's on the bases that one really gets an idea of what this youngster is all about. His desire takes him farther than his ability alone should allow. Jones has good speed, but it is not basestealing-type speed. Yet he steals bases, using a gangly, gangbuster style with success.

Jones seems to drive himself around the bases by determination. Occasionally, his desire will lead him into an unnecessary gamble and he will get burned.

FIELDING:

Jones prides himself on his fielding and is most comfortable in left field. He has a strong, accurate arm and the kind of speed that makes him adequate in center field. He doesn't always get the best jump or "read" on

TRACY JONES
OF, No. 29
RR, 6'3", 180 lbs.
ML Svc: 1 year
Born: 3-31-61 in
Hawthorne, CA

1986 STATISTICS

AVG	G	AB	R	H	2B	3B	HR	RBI	BB	SO	SB
.349	46	86	16	130	3	0	2	10	9	5	7

CAREER STATISTICS

AVG	G	AB	R	H	2B	3B	HR	RBI	BB	SO	SB
.349	46	86	16	130	3	0	2	10	9	5	7

VS. RHP   VS. LHP   PROBABLE HIT LOCATIONS

the ball and can make some plays more exciting than they should be.

A fundamentally strong outfielder, Jones doesn't make errors in judgment, such as missing the cutoff man or throwing to the wrong base.

The Reds had planned for Jones to learn first base during winter ball this past year, but he aggravated his hand injury late in the season, which made it impossible for him to play in Latin America. He will probably do some work at that position in spring training.

OVERALL:

Jones' spirit and rambunctious style is his trademark. When Jones hits the field, he's like a child knocking down the doors at recess to get outdoors. His energy for the game is boundless. There is nothing he would rather do than play this game.

Dierker: "If Jones can shed the effects of his injury, his future looks bright. He is a big, strong righthanded hitter who seems to have a lot of raw talent."

"It's hard to say if he will be successful with the approach he uses; he hit pretty well last year, but he didn't look good doing it."

CINCINNATI REDS

HITTING:

A line drive, contact hitter who surged onto the Reds' scene last August, Barry Larkin played impressively enough in 41 games to receive some votes for Rookie of the Year.

Unlike Kurt Stillwell, who appeared a bit intimidated by big league pitching, Larkin was surprisingly polished and poised as a hitter. He did, however, have a similar difficulty with off-speed pitches but not to the degree that Stillwell did. Larkin displayed a good eye and performed well as a leadoff hitter.

Larkin will drive the ball to the alley in left and generally hits from the left field alley around to right-center. He will hit in the clutch but isn't considered a home run threat. His skills as a hitter are refined enough that he will make contact when the situation requires. He has the bat control to hit behind the runner.

The question regarding his hitting is how he will do once pitchers have seen him enough to figure out his weaknesses. Last season, Larking had only 159 at-bats. The Reds are betting he will get better the more he plays.

BASERUNNING:

Larkin is fast and smart. He'll steal a base and will beat out some ground balls. He is a good all-around athlete (his brother Mike was a standout linebacker at Notre Dame, while another brother, Byron, is an excellent basketball player at Xavier University) and will do whatever it takes on the bases. He'll take out the pivot man on a double play and isn't afraid to take on a catcher who is attempting to block the plate.

FIELDING:

Larkin is slick in the field with good range, good hands and a strong, accurate arm. Like Stillwell, he is not flamboyant in the field in the way Chicago's Shawon Dunston is, but he makes the plays. Larkin appears to be better going to his left than his right and has the knack of making accurate throws while off balance.

BARRY LARKIN
SS, No. 24
RR, 6'0", 185 lbs.
ML Svc: *less than one year*
Born: 4-28-64 in
Cincinnati, OH

1986 STATISTICS

AVG	G	AB	R	H	2B	3B	HR	RBI	BB	SO	SB
.233	41	159	27	45	4	3	3	19	9	21	8

CAREER STATISTICS

AVG	G	AB	R	H	2B	3B	HR	RBI	BB	SO	SB
.233	41	159	27	45	4	3	3	19	9	21	8

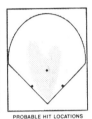

VS. RHP   VS. LHP   PROBABLE HIT LOCATIONS

Originally, the Reds planned for Larkin to learn to play second base, leaving shortstop to Stillwell. Larkin, it was believed, could make the adjustment to a new position more smoothly and quickly. But after his strong performance in 1986, the organization's thinking has shifted. Executives fear that if Larkin is moved to second, it will adversely affect his offensive production.

OVERALL:

Late in the 1986 season, Dave Concepcion was asked whom he felt should be the Reds' shortstop this year. He did not hesitate at all when he replied, "Barry Larkin. He is ready for the job."

That must have thrilled young Larkin: a Cincinnati native, Barry grew up watching Dave Concepcion and dreamed of becoming the Reds's shortstop someday.

Whether it is at shortstop or at second base, Larkin figures to be a mainstay with the Reds for years to come.

CINCINNATI REDS

HITTING:

Known for his defense, Eddie Milner broke through and had a great offensive September last year. He hit in 21 straight games and closed the season with a career-high 15 home runs.

However, his hitting streak and late home run surge came after he had been moved from the leadoff spot to the sixth position in the lineup, where he could loosen up and swing from his heels. In the leadoff and No. 2 spots, where his speed can be better utilized, Milner falls a bit short.

Milner is a guy who just has never blossomed for the Reds as they hoped he would. He has not become the contact hitter that he needs to be. He shows just a little bit of power--enough to tease him and to keep him swinging hard and trying to pull the ball, which is something he shouldn't do.

Milner is basically a pull hitter who hits the ball up with a big swing. He'll take the ball to right field and right-center most of the time and will occasionally spray one to left-center. He should be a straight spray hitter, but he is not. He needs to shorten up his big swing a little bit. His oversized swing leaves Milner somewhat vulnerable to good breaking pitches.

BASERUNNING:

Milner has good speed--better than average--but he's not in the class with Eric Davis. He has the speed to steal a lot of bases, but doesn't because he rarely gets a good jump. Last season he stole 18 bases and was caught 11 times. Milner commits himself too early, gets caught leaning and is vulnerable to a good pickoff move.

Otherwise, Milner is strong on the bases, displaying good speed and good judgment.

FIELDING:

There are some, including the Reds' Dave Parker, who firmly believe Milner is the best

**EDDIE MILNER
CF, No. 20
LL, 5'11", 170 lbs.
ML Svc: 7 years
Born: 5-21-55 in
Columbus, OH**

1986 STATISTICS

AVG	G	AB	R	H	2B	3B	HR	RBI	BB	SO	SB
.259	145	424	70	110	22	6	15	47	36	56	18

CAREER STATISTICS

AVG	G	AB	R	H	2B	3B	HR	RBI	BB	SO	SB
.255	680	2130	335	544	96	28	38	174	258	238	133

  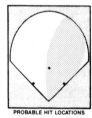

center fielder in the National League. Milner's speed is complemented by his uncanny knack to get a great jump on the ball off the bat. He has equal range to right- and left-center. He catches a lot of balls that probably should be handled by Parker in right and Kal Daniels or Nick Esasky in left.

Milner's arm is graded average for a center fielder, but he compensates by getting rid of the ball quickly and accurately. Baserunners, particularly those attempting to score, will try to take advantage of Milner's arm.

OVERALL:

It is easy to appreciate Milner's defensive ability but one must also recognize his offensive difficulties.

Dierker: "Until he makes better contact, he probably will be a backup type of player. He needs to improve his on-base percentage as well."

CINCINNATI REDS

PITCHING:

Rob Murphy is the second of the Reds' two standout lefthanded relievers (John Franco is the other).

Murphy makes it look easy.

After joining the Reds at midseason last year, he didn't lose one game and gave up only 26 hits in 50 1/3 innings.

He is a fastball, sinker, slider pitcher, who nervously pitches with a style reminiscent of Al "The Mad Hungarian" Hrabosky. He tugs at the bill of his cap, stares out at the outfield, fidgets with the rosin bag and finally goes at the hitter as if his life depended on it.

Murphy has a very compact motion. He releases the ball from a point just behind his ear, more like a quarterback throwing a football than a pitcher. The odd-looking motion and release point are essential to his success. When Murphy extends his arm, he loses some control and bite on his pitches. At any rate, the Reds have no intention of changing anything about him. "I'd be a fool to mess with Murph," Pete Rose said.

Last season, Murphy performed admirably as a set-up man for relievers Ron Robinson and John Franco. He'll probably open the season in that same capacity, but is apt to do some short work as well.

Opponents haven't found a way to get to Murphy yet, but they might find an edge in rifling his equipment bag. A genuinely superstitious sort, Murphy never pitches without wearing a special pair of black underwear. "I tried once," he admitted, "and I just didn't feel, well, right."

FIELDING, HITTING, BASERUNNING:

Murphy is a slick, quick fielder who enjoys the challenge of playing defense. He comes off the mound quickly and fields the ball well on the third- or first-base sides of the mound.

He rarely gets a chance to hit, and doesn't do much when he does. He can bunt, but is not proficient in that area.

ROB MURPHY
LHP, No. 46
LL, 6'2", 200 lbs.
ML Svc: 1 year plus
Born: 5-26-60 in
Miami, FL

1986 STATISTICS

W	L	ERA	G	GS	CG	SV	IP	H	R	ER	BB	SO
6	0	0.72	34	0	0	1	50.1	26	4	4	21	36

CAREER STATISTICS

W	L	ERA	G	GS	CG	SV	IP	H	R	ER	BB	SO
6	0	1.01	36	0	0	1	53.1	28	6	6	23	37

For a pitcher, he has pretty good speed and displays a certain intensity on the bases, much like teammate Tom Browning.

OVERALL:

Reds General Manager Bill Bergesch doesn't mention Murphy's name when he talks about the "crown jewels" of the Reds organization, but there is no reason why the reliever shouldn't be mentioned in the same breath with Eric Davis, Kal Daniels, Tracy Jones, Barry Larkin and Kurt Stillwell. For Murphy doesn't do anything for this young club but win.

Though from the way he looks on the mound, it doesn't appear as though Murphy needs baseball to make a buck. He has blended an interest in thoroughbred horses with a knack for computers to design his own genealogical study of thoroughbred horses. He advises horse buyers throughout the country based on his own research.

Dierker: "He's definitely an important part of the Reds' future. He throws the ball hard and is a challenging pitcher with a good breaking ball. He faces mostly lefthanded hitters and seems to just breeze the ball right by them."

CINCINNATI REDS

HITTING:

Ron Oester is as spirited and as intense as they come. Some Reds executives call him the "backbone" of the team. Yet, they were ready to trade the switch-hitter this winter to make room for 21-year-old Kurt Stillwell.

Oester's problem is his offensive production. He hits well enough but not often enough when it counts. He's questionable in the clutch and vulnerable to pitches down in the strike zone, a weakness he displays hitting both right-and lefthanded.

He is, by far, more effective hitting from the left side of the plate and can take the ball out of the park from both sides. He has some power, but not enough to keep opposing pitchers awake at night.

Oester has never been able to hit with either one of the two things a manager looks for: scoring production or RBI production. He does not have enough power to drive in runs and not enough speed to score runs. He will hit a ground ball most of the time but doesn't have the speed to beat it out unless it's really a high chopper.

BASERUNNING:

Oester has average speed and is always aggressive on the bases, sometimes to a fault. He will run into outs. His zeal will sometimes lead him to blunder and he has been known to run through signs in his eagerness to contribute.

FIELDING:

Oester has good hands and good actions, but his range is not the best. He won't make too many dramatic plays in the holes. He's smooth on the double play and has a superior arm (one of the best in the Reds' organization). While he will have trouble in

RON OESTER
2B, No. 16
SR, 6'2", 190 lbs.
ML Svc: 7 years
Born: 5-5-56 in
Cincinnati, OH

1986 STATISTICS

AVG	G	AB	R	H	2B	3B	HR	RBI	BB	SO	SB
.258	153	523	52	135	23	2	8	44	52	84	9

CAREER STATISTICS

AVG	G	AB	R	H	2B	3B	HR	RBI	BB	SO	SB
.266	980	3368	377	895	149	26	39	284	296	530	36

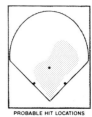

the holes, he is adept at running down pop-ups in foul territory behind first and in shallow right and center.

An excellent cutoff man, he will dazzle observers with his throws to third and the plate.

OVERALL:

Oester is not a journeyman type of player but he is not a star. With all points taken into consideration, Oester probably ranks eighth or ninth among NL second basemen.

Dierker: "Ron is a good second baseman although he doesn't stack up with the class players at his position in the National League mostly because of his lesser offense. Defensively, he has shown himself to be just adequate."

CINCINNATI REDS

HITTING:

A strong argument can be presented that no one in the National League has been as offensively productive over the past two years as Dave Parker. Since Opening Day 1985 to the end of the '86 season, he has produced 65 home runs, 241 RBIs, scored 177 runs and batted .293. In addition, he has been the Reds' inspirational leader.

Parker, 35, is one of those hitters whose skills present special problems for a pitcher. He is a good all-around hitter and handles off-speed stuff especially well. Parker really takes advantage of a pitcher who doesn't have good stuff.

There are really no holes in Parker's swing and he's one who makes adjustments with every move in the count. The best way for a pitcher to approach him is with hard stuff up and in. That, however, is not an easy thing for a pitcher to do consistently--especially with an intimidating hitter such as Parker at the plate. If a pitcher tries the up-and-in location against Parker and doesn't have absolutely everything he's got on the pitch, Parker will take it for a ride.

Always a home run threat, pitchers will try to work Parker off the plate. They don't want to give him a chance to extend his arms. Last season, many pitchers around the league decided that they simply would not throw him a good pitch. As a result, Parker fell into the trap of swinging at bad pitches late in the season. Parker's productivity is not always within his control. Last season, Buddy Bell took a long time to find himself as a hitter, and Parker was surrounded in the lineup by "easy outs." He rarely got a pitch he could drive.

Still, he's capable of taking the outside pitch to the opposite field and do it with extra-base power.

BASERUNNING:

Parker has slowed down some but still goes hard on the bases. He does his best to shake up opposing pitchers, dancing and faking off first and third, taking a long lead at second. But, when it comes right down to it, he plays it safe and uses good judgment. He tried to steal seven times last season and was thrown out six times.

DAVE PARKER
RF, No. 39
LR, 6'5", 230 lbs.
ML Svc: 13 years
Born: 6-9-51 in
Jackson, MS

1986 STATISTICS

AVG	G	AB	R	H	2B	3B	HR	RBI	BB	SO	SB
.273	162	637	89	174	31	3	31	116	56	126	1

CAREER STATISTICS

AVG	G	AB	R	H	2B	3B	HR	RBI	BB	SO	SB
.301	1779	6727	978	2024	397	69	247	1093	495	1072	140

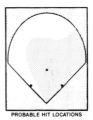

VS. RHP   VS. LHP   PROBABLE HIT LOCATIONS

FIELDING:

Once one of the best in right field, Parker has dropped off considerably. He is now a below-average outfielder. His speed is not what it once was and his arm has lost some of its strength, although not enough to dip its rating to below-average.

Parker has good instincts in the field, but sometimes seems late on the jump. He prides himself on his arm and still looks for the one-on-one challenge. Though he doesn't have the cannon anymore, runners will still pay Parker respect, seldom taking a chance against him.

OVERALL:

Parker is the leader of the Reds on the field. He seems to be improving with age and he figures to benefit as the Reds' young talent blossoms around him.

Dierker: "The end of his career looks like a it's a long way off the way he is swinging the bat. He had another outstanding season in 1986 and looks as though he has gotten his act together."

CINCINNATI REDS

PITCHING:

One of Pete Rose's principles of managing is that one should never give up on a player who has once been successful. For years to come, his prime example will be Ted Power.

Two years ago, Power was one of the most successful righthanded short relievers in the National League (27 saves, 8-6 with a 2.70 ERA). He began the 1986 season in that role and teaming with lefthander John Franco gave Rose what he felt was one of the best bullpen combinations in the league. But Power got off to a terrible start--his pitches seemed up in the strike zone--and by midseason was reassigned to middle relief.

His performance in that capacity was adequate, but Power was virtually a forgotten man until late in the season when the Reds needed a starter. John Denny was hurt and so was Mario Soto. Given a chance to start, Power performed very well. He lost his first start but then won six straight. Power's back was against the wall. He needed to prove himself. And he did.

His style as a starter is not greatly different than as a reliever, though he obviously paces himself differently.

Power is a hard thrower with an average breaking pitch. When he is right, his fastball is above average and comes at 90+ MPH. He will ride the fastball up on both righthanded and lefthanded batters and then work the corners low and away with the pitch.

The key with him is control. If he gets the breaking ball over and spots the fastball well, he is going to be successful.

As a reliever, he entered a game and threw hard from the beginning to the end of an outing. But as a starter, he sets up hitters with his breaking pitches--especially a sinker that moves down and away from lefthanded hitters--and comes back with the fastball.

TED POWER
RHP, No. 48
RR, 6'4", 225 lbs.
ML Svc: 5 years
Born: 1-31-55 in
  Guthrie, OK

1986 STATISTICS

W	L	ERA	G	GS	CG	SV	IP	H	R	ER	BB	SO
10	6	3.70	56	10	0	1	129	115	59	53	52	95

CAREER STATISTICS

W	L	ERA	G	GS	CG	SV	IP	H	R	ER	BB	SO
34	29	3.72	264	22	1	41	476.1	447	218	197	222	297

FIELDING, HITTING, BASERUNNING:

Power, a good athlete, fields his position well but is not much of a hitter or baserunner. He didn't have a hit in the major leagues until last season, when he had three. He is not fleet afoot. As a bunter, he isn't much, but he improved with increased opportunities late in the season.

OVERALL:

This is a big season for Power and the Reds. Cincinnati, loaded with questions regarding their pitching, is counting on him to be consistent. Early on, Power will have to establish that he is up to the task and can go to the mound every fourth or fifth day over the long haul.

Dierker: "He seems to enjoy his new assignment and impressed Rose with his dedication to starting. He came to the ballpark early on each day he was scheduled to start and was prepared."

GOOD CONTROL

PITCHING:

A bullish competitor, Robinson opened the season as a set-up man for what figured to be a strong bullpen and as a possible fifth starter. But when Ted Power failed in the bullpen, Robinson took over for him and did a first-rate job.

Robinson's strength is his control. He prides himself on not giving up walks. He allowed just 43 in 116 2/3 innings last year. He throws an above-average fastball and will run the fastball away from a righthanded hitter and sink it down and away from a lefthanded hitter.

Robinson mixes his fastball with a change-up, a slider and a good, short, sharp-breaking curveball. He throws all his pitches for strikes and outs. But in a jam, he'll go to the fastball-- his most reliable and difficult-to-hit pitch.

FIELDING, HITTING, BASERUNNING:

Robinson is a good, aggressive fielder who is particularly adept at gloving line drives back to the mound. A standout high school quarterback, Robinson has quick feet but is not particularly fast.

Given his role, Robinson seldom hits or reaches the bases. He's not a particularly good bunter. If he reaches base, he'll use good judgment and won't hurt his team.

RON ROBINSON
RHP, No. 33
RR, 6'4", 215 lbs.
ML Svc: 3 years
Born: 3-24-62 in
Woodlake, CA

1986 STATISTICS

W	L	ERA	G	GS	CG	SV	IP	H	R	ER	BB	SO
10	3	3.24	70	0	0	14	116.2	110	44	42	43	117

CAREER STATISTICS

W	L	ERA	G	GS	CG	SV	IP	H	R	ER	BB	SO
18	12	3.47	115	17	1	15	264.2	252	115	102	88	217

OVERALL:

A very capable short reliever, Robinson gives the Reds a needed option. Over the winter, they attempted to acquire another starter, but when those efforts failed, they considered trading for a righthanded reliever. Had they been able to get another righthander for their bullpen, they could have moved Robinson into the starting rotation.

Dierker: "Robinson is apt to show up anywhere on the Reds staff, but wherever it is he'll do a good job far more often than not.

"He really came around last year (his first full season) and became a super reliever for the Reds."

CINCINNATI REDS

HITTING:

The change in Pete Rose's bat speed from 1985, when he overtook Ty Cobb as the all-time hit leader, to 1986 was remarkable. There was a significant drop-off. Though scouts and observers around baseball remarked on this inevitable failing, the 45-year-old player-manager never agreed with his critics. However, he didn't play at all after August 17th last year and won't be eligible to play until May 15 this season as a result of his removal from the Reds' 40-man winter roster.

Some say Rose may not play again except for a showcase weekend late in the season when he will activate himself and bid the game adieu. He says he will only play this season if his services are required and younger players such as Tracy Jones and Kal Daniels do not pan out. In Rose's last at-bat in 1986 he struck out as a pinch-hitter against San Diego's Goose Gossage. "It was good morning, good afternoon, good night. Three pitches and out of there," Rose said. "I never got the ring off my bat."

Rose does not want his last major league at-bat to be a strikeout.

Heading into his 24th season, Rose is a singles hitter and only a singles hitter. Of his 52 hits last season, 10 were for extra-bases. He'll spray the ball around the field, but not with power. His extra base hits are generally while hitting lefthanded and are to the opposite field.

He will draw a walk (30 BBs last season in 237 at-bats) but took an inordinate amount of called third strikes last year. As a hitter, Rose is probably finished but then again he has already proven he is unusual among the species and he may have a few more surprises.

BASERUNNING:

He's slow. He has lost his speed, though he will never lose his hustle or his smarts. He won't make a mistake on the bases and won't overestimate his ability on the basepaths. If Rose wants to take a defenseman out of the

PETE ROSE
1B, No. 14
SR, 5'11", 200 lbs.
ML Svc: 24 years
Born: 4-14-41 in
Cincinnati, OH

1986 STATISTICS

AVG	G	AB	R	H	2B	3B	HR	RBI	BB	SO	SB
.219	72	237	15	52	8	2	0	25	30	31	3

CAREER STATISTICS

AVG	G	AB	R	H	2B	3B	HR	RBI	BB	SO	SB
.302	3562	14053	2165	4256	746	135	160	1314	1566	1143	198

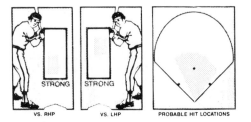

STRONG   STRONG
VS. RHP   VS. LHP   PROBABLE HIT LOCATIONS

play, he will make his hit with all the zeal he has shown throughout his career.

FIELDING:

Around the first-base bag, Rose continues to be surehanded, but he has no range and can't throw. Baserunners will take advantage of his arm. Rose can no longer get the balls in the holes and has trouble going back down the right field line for pop-ups.

OVERALL:

The great days are gone and though Rose has trouble facing the criticism he receives, there are signs he is accepting his future as a manager. As a player, his time has passed.

Dierker: "At this point he is really not a major league talent, but he's certainly the kind of guy who, if you had to use him in a pinch, you wouldn't be embarrassed by it. The Reds are hoping that their farm system will produce enough talent that they won't have to use Pete as a player in 1987."

CINCINNATI REDS

PITCHING:

Once considered one of the best starters in baseball, Mario Soto's career is now one large question mark. Troubled by arm problems the past two years, Soto has managed to win just 17 games while losing 25. He was on the disabled list twice last season with a sore shoulder and ended the year under the care of Los Angeles orthopedic surgeon Dr. Frank Jobe. Arthroscopic surgery was performed on Soto's shoulder in September and he was unable to throw until January 1st.

The Reds are hoping the righthander will make a strong comeback, but no one knows what will happen--not even Soto.

It was almost a relief for Soto to discover a tangible injury to his arm because recovery from an injury is easier to face than the thought of losing your fastball. He knows he will have to be patient and allow the healing process to dictate his progress.

Regaining the velocity on his fastball will be essential for Soto. His reputation was built on a hot fastball which he complemented with a superior change-up. But when his arm problems took something off his fastball, the change-up was not effective. Without the fastball, his pitches were too similar in speed and hitters connected with regularity.

FIELDING, HITTING, BASERUNNING:

Soto fields his position well and won't hurt his team on defense. He can hit and prides himself on his offense.

He's got a free-wheeling hack, much like that demonstrated by his countryman Joaquin Andujar. But he can also be disciplined at the plate and put down a bunt when he has to. He's relatively fast for a pitcher and has been used as a pinch-runner. He'll get around the bases without any

MARIO SOTO
RHP, No. 36
RR, 6'0", 190 lbs.
ML Svc: 10 years
Born: 7-12-56 in
Bani,
Dominican Republic

1986 STATISTICS

W	L	ERA	G	GS	CG	SV	IP	H	R	ER	BB	SO
5	10	4.71	19	19	1	0	105	113	61	55	46	67

CAREER STATISTICS

W	L	ERA	G	GS	CG	SV	IP	H	R	ER	BB	SO
94	83	3.37	277	204	69	4	1611.1	1273	665	604	617	1404

difficulty.

OVERALL:

It's a wait-and-see situation with Soto, who is as anxious about his future as anyone in the Reds' front office. If Soto had been healthy for the past two years, the clubs' fortunes might have been different (the Reds finished second in each of the last two seasons and with Soto unavailable to pitch at the end of each year).

Soto is hoping he can regain his old style of pitching, relying almost exclusively on his fastball and change-up.

Dierker: "His success or failure in his recovery from arm surgery is anybody's guess. He might not regain the velocity of his fastball until the All-Star break or later, but then he could show up at spring training popping them in at 87 MPH. If he gets his heater back, he's going to win.

"Soto has indicated that he might experiment this season with a new pitch if his arm was strong again, the split-finger fastball.

CINCINNATI REDS

HITTING:

Back in spring training of 1986, Kurt Stillwell was a hitting sensation. Of course, at the time, he was seeing mostly fastballs. When the season began, however, the 20-year-old rookie had some major problems with big league off-speed pitches. His struggles in that area led to a demotion to Triple-A, but he had no sooner arrived in Denver when Dave Concepcion injured his hand and Stillwell was back with the Reds.

Reds hitting coach Billy DeMars worked long and hard with Stillwell to enable him to wait on breaking pitches. The sessions with DeMars paid off and in the last half of the season, the switch-hitter began to make more consistent contact. Despite his improvements, Stillwell needs more time to refine his skills. DeMars, for one, felt Stillwell was rushed to the majors before he was ready for major league pitching. Good breaking balls and off-speed pitches remain more of a difficulty for him than they should be.

A line drive hitter, Stillwell hits to all fields. Though his batting average was roughly the same from both sides of the plate last season (.231 lefthanded and .226 righthanded), Reds executives say Stillwell is a better and stronger hitter when he is batting right-handed. At this stage of his career, he's not a home run threat at all.

BASERUNNING:

As a runner, Stillwell is quick, fundamentally sound on the bases and smart about his business. He is capable of stealing a base but it's not his forte. Although he is an aggressive runner, there are times when he appears a bit shy about bowling over an opponent.

FIELDING:

It is Stillwell's abilities as a fielder that have caused excitement in Cincinnati. He's not in the category with Ozzie Smith, but he'll go farther than most to make a play. He is equally effective going into the hole at third base and behind second.

Stillwell is blessed with an extremely strong arm and quick hands. His single most

KURT STILLWELL
SS, No. 11
SR, 5'11", 165 lbs.
ML Svc: 1 year
Born: 6-4-65 in
Thousand Oaks, CA

1986 STATISTICS

AVG	G	AB	R	H	2B	3B	HR	RBI	BB	SO	SB
.229	104	279	31	64	6	1	0	26	30	47	6

CAREER STATISTICS

AVG	G	AB	R	H	2B	3B	HR	RBI	BB	SO	SB
.229	104	279	31	64	6	1	0	26	30	47	6

VS. RHP

VS. LHP

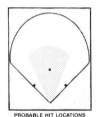

PROBABLE HIT LOCATIONS

apparent flaw in the field is a tendency to count on his arm a little too much. After making a play, he'll take a skip-step and pat the ball in his glove before throwing. As a result, some plays are far closer than they should be.

He played some at second base last year and is apt to do so again this season as Barry Larkin is likely to play a lot at shortstop. Stillwell is not as confident away from his natural position (shortstop) and his unfamiliarity shows.

OVERALL:

Stillwell looks as though he was probably rushed to the major league level and will need further big league experience to make some adjustments. He attended winter ball to work on his hitting.

Dierker: "As a hitter, Stillwell needs to make better contact than he did in 1986.

"He will fight it out with Barry Larkin for the starting shortstop position this year; if he hits better, he would give himself an edge in winning the job."

CINCINNATI REDS

HITTING:

Max Venable is a smart line drive hitter with a definite knack for getting on base. He will spray the ball all over the field, pulling the inside pitch and taking the outside pitch down the left-field line. He has some power but isn't considered a home run threat.

A role player primarily used as a late-inning pinch-hitter, Venable is most productive in this capacity when he's had some playing time. When Venable comes up in a pinch-hitting situation, always consider how long it has been since he's had some playing time.

In 1985, Venable was third in the National League, batting .371 (13-for-35), as a pinch-hitter. That year, after being called up from Triple-A in June, he appeared in 77 games and went to the plate 135 times on several occassions as a starter. Last year, he dropped off to .157 (8-for-51) as a pinch-hitter. He appeared in 108 games and batted 147 times but drew few starts. In order for Venable to stay sharp as a pinch-hitter, he has to get his at-bats in clusters.

At his best, Venable is a steady, clutch performer who can hurt an opponent when the game is on the line. Without that needed playing time, however, he isn't going to do much.

BASERUNNING:

Venable has good speed and will steal bases. His game on the bases is solid in all respects. Strong and aggressive, he'll take the extra base and the Reds won't hesitate to send him to the plate on a close play.

FIELDING:

Venable is best suited for left field, but he

MAX VENABLE
OF, No. 9
LR, 5'10", 185 lbs.
ML Svc: 8 years
Born: 6-6-57 in
Phoenix, AZ

1986 STATISTICS

AVG	G	AB	R	H	2B	3B	HR	RBI	BB	SO	SB
.211	108	147	17	31	7	1	2	15	17	24	7

CAREER STATISTICS

AVG	G	AB	R	H	2B	3B	HR	RBI	BB	SO	SB
.231	525	961	117	222	36	12	11	80	84	141	57

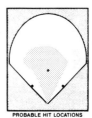

VS. RHP   VS. LHP   PROBABLE HIT LOCATIONS

can also play center field in a pinch. He has good instincts but is graded as an average outfielder. His arm is accurate but a little short in center. He won't hurt his team in the field, but is not the type of player who robs opponents of hits.

OVERALL:

A favorite of manager Pete Rose, Venable accepts his role as a part-time player and pinch-hitter.

Dierker: " He works hard at staying sharp and will generally contribute when he enters the game. He is one of those players who are good to have around."

HITTING:

Limited to a reserve role before the All-Star break, Alan Ashby regained his job as the Astros' starting catcher and hit .272 over the season's second half to spark Houston to the National League West title.

Ashby did not suffer any serious injuries in 1986, a major factor that resulted in one of his most productive years. The Astros were 60-25 in games in which Ashby caught.

A switch-hitter, Ashby hit for a higher average last season from the right side. That's unusual, because he usually is regarded as a better lefthanded hitter.

Ashby is a pull hitter from both sides of the plate. He's a line drive hitter with occasional power, particularly in clutch situations. His first four homers last season were game-winners.

Patience is one of Ashby's finest virtues as a hitter. He looks for pitches high in the strike zone and draws his share of walks. The best way to pitch Ashby is to throw breaking balls and keep the ball down.

BASERUNNING:

Although he has below-average speed, even by catchers' standards, Ashby is a smart player who seldom commits a baserunning blunder. He stole his first base in four seasons last year--a stand-up theft of third--but seldom takes the extra base.

FIELDING:

Ashby threw out less than 20% of the runners who attempted steals against him, but the Astros' pitchers don't hold runners on base very well. Having caught such pitchers as J.R. Richard, Nolan Ryan and Joe Niekro during his career, Ashby has developed a

**ALAN ASHBY
C, No. 14
SR, 6'2", 195 lbs.
ML Svc: 14 years
Born: 7-8-51 in
    Long Beach, CA**

1986 STATISTICS

AVG	G	AB	R	H	2B	3B	HR	RBI	BB	SO	SB
.257	120	315	24	81	15	0	7	38	39	56	1

CAREER STATISTICS

AVG	G	AB	R	H	2B	3B	HR	RBI	BB	SO	SB
.242	1150	3449	321	835	156	12	69	414	385	525	7

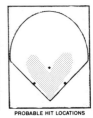

VS. RHP   VS. LHP   PROBABLE HIT LOCATIONS

superior knack for blocking pitches in the dirt and blocking the plate.

If Ashby has one outstanding trait on defense, it's his ability to handle pitchers. He knows how to call an excellent game and has caught three no-hitters during his career. He benefited greatly last year from no longer having to cope with Niekro's knuckleball.

OVERALL:

Offensively, Ashby may have peaked last season. His defensive skills are average for a 35-year-old catcher.

Dierker: "Ashby has given the Astros a very competent backstop for eight years. He is the best catcher they've got at this point. The staff responds well to him and he is a quiet leader behind the plate."

HOUSTON ASTROS

HITTING:

Once he finally was established as the Astros' starting right fielder after being shuttled between right and center, Kevin Bass really came into his own as a major league hitter. He finished fourth in the league last year with a .311 average and became the first Astro in three years to hit 20 homers and steal more than 20 bases.

Several factors led to Bass' increased effectiveness at the plate. He hit behind Denny Walling and Glenn Davis, which gave him a look at better pitches. A switch-hitter, he wasn't an easy batter to pitch around. He also learned to hit the ball to all fields.

Bass displayed more power and consistency from the right side of the plate in 1986, but he hit over .300 from both sides. He has improved each year since joining the Astros in 1982 and could become a perennial All-Star with increased discipline at the plate.

Although he is occasionally susceptible to swinging at breaking balls in the dirt and fastballs up and out of the strike zone, Bass usually gets good pitches to hit. When he does, he hits the ball hard.

Bass has become more of a contact hitter, but he does not draw many walks.

BASERUNNING:

Bass continues to improve as a baserunner. Blessed with above-average speed, he still must learn the finer points of basestealing. He needs to get a better jump and perfect his slide.

Few Astros are better at taking the extra base, but Bass could be more aggressive on the bases. He was slowed last year because of a nagging leg injury.

FIELDING:

As a center fielder, Bass left a lot to be desired. But when the Astros finally moved him to right field in mid-season, he was able to use his skills to his advantage. He had problems with the trajectory of fly balls in center, a problem that didn't surface for him

KEVIN BASS
RF, No. 17
SR, 6'0", 180 lbs.
ML Svc: 5 years
Born: 5-12-59 in
Redwood City, CA

1986 STATISTICS

AVG	G	AB	R	H	2B	3B	HR	RBI	BB	SO	SB
.311	157	591	83	184	33	5	20	79	38	72	22

CAREER STATISTICS

AVG	G	AB	R	H	2B	3B	HR	RBI	BB	SO	SB
.274	546	1689	219	462	84	18	40	195	82	228	48

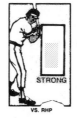

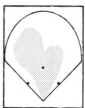

VS. RHP   VS. LHP   PROBABLE HIT LOCATIONS

in right field.

Bass gets a good jump on fly balls to the outfield and has a strong throwing arm. His throws are not always accurate, but they generally discourage most runners from trying to take the extra base. His range in the outfield is well above average. Bass underwent arthroscopic surgery on his right shoulder in December, but is scheduled to be ready for the opening of the Astros' spring exhibition season.

OVERALL:

Bass's value skyrocketed from June through October last year. He has the right combination of speed, defense and power to blossom into one of the league's top players.

Dierker: "As an outfielder, he is slightly above average. But he has improved on the bases every year. I wouldn't be surprised to see him steal 25 bases this year.

"Kevin really has started to live up to his potential. He is a guy with a lot of talent. He is a good, hard worker."

HOUSTON ASTROS

HITTING:

Jose Cruz underwent arthroscopic surgery for a knee injury he suffered in spring training last year and didn't hit full stride until mid-July. Had he been healthy all year, he may have put together another .300 season.

One of the reasons for Cruz's longevity is his unorthodox style of hitting. His ability to turn bad pitches into hits has enabled him to outlast most players his age (39). He also takes good care of himself and consistently reports to spring training in excellent physical condition.

Cruz is a difficult hitter to describe. At times, he will hit the ball with power. At other times, he will chop the ball and hit it the other way. A lefthanded hitter, he also is capable of lining the ball to left field. He has an unusual swing, but he is very strong and he has good hand-eye coordination.

Cruz struck out more frequently last year than in the past. He seems to have considerable trouble with breaking pitches low and away. He tends to be too aggressive at the plate in certain situations and hates to see lefthanders throw slow junk.

BASERUNNING:

Cruz stole fewer bases (three) last year than he had at any other time in his 16-year career in the majors. His injured knee was a big factor in his decreased output.

Cruz's biggest liability on the bases is his penchant for leaning too far and getting picked off. He has the potential for stealing 10-15 bases, however, if he enjoys an injury-free year.

FIELDING:

Cruz's range as a left fielder has diminished with age. He still has an above-average throwing arm, a big asset for a player who is projected to be the league's oldest starting

JOSE CRUZ
LF, No. 25
LL, 6'0", 185 lbs.
ML Svc: 16 years
Born: 8-8-47 in
Arroyo, PR

1986 STATISTICS

AVG	G	AB	R	H	2B	3B	HR	RBI	BB	SO	SB
.278	141	479	48	133	22	4	10	72	55	86	3

CAREER STATISTICS

AVG	G	AB	R	H	2B	3B	HR	RBI	BB	SO	SB
.287	2188	7472	980	2147	372	90	153	1032	870	958	313

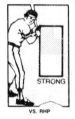

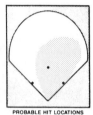

VS. RHP   VS. LHP   PROBABLE HIT LOCATIONS

outfielder in 1987.

There are times when Cruz makes easy plays look difficult and difficult plays look easy. But he usually gets a good jump on the ball.

OVERALL:

Although Cruz will turn 40 in August, he remains the best everyday player in baseball for someone his age. He hit all 10 of his homers last season after July 11, a sign that he still has plenty of pop in his bat.

Dierker: "I expect him to have another good year for the Astros, although he may have to be platooned or rested a little more often in '87 than he has been during his career.

"He is a good competitor with a good, aggressive attitude toward the game. He is above average as a left fielder and still is not a liability on the basepaths, despite his age."

HOUSTON ASTROS

PITCHING:

Having become accustomed to being both a starter and a reliever during his major league career, Danny Darwin finds himself once again cast in a starter's role in 1987. The Astros used Darwin as their fifth starter last year after they obtained him in an August trade with Milwaukee.

Darwin's fastball was consistently clocked in the 90-92 MPH range. His curveball, slider and change-up are only average, but he usually maintains good command of his pitches with a sweeping delivery that backs righthanded hitters off the plate.

One of Darwin's weaknesses in Milwaukee was his penchant for serving up home runs. That problem should be alleviated somewhat in the spacious Astrodome.

One of Darwin's biggest assets is his willingness to challenge hitters. He displayed excellent control after joining the Astros, allowing only nine walks in 58 innings pitched.

FIELDING, HITTING, BASERUNNING:

Darwin is an adequate fielder who has an average move to first base. He had trouble making contact at the plate after joining the Astros, a liability that can be traced to his days in the American League. He is an average baserunner.

DANNY DARWIN
RHP, No. 44
RR, 6'3", 190 lbs.
ML Svc: 8 years
Born: 10-25-55 in
Bonham, TX

1986 STATISTICS

W	L	ERA	G	GS	CG	SV	IP	H	R	ER	BB	SO
11	10	3.17	39	8	6	0	184.2	170	81	65	44	120

CAREER STATISTICS

W	L	ERA	G	GS	CG	SV	IP	H	R	ER	BB	SO
72	78	3.55	295	127	38	18	1241	1175	571	490	400	789

OVERALL:

Darwin could become one of the biggest keys in the Astros' attempt to successfully defend their NL West title. He is more than adequate as a fifth starter in the majors and could win 10-15 games this year.

Dierker: "He pitched especially well last year against some of the better hitters in the league. He seemed to find some extra adrenalin against guys like Dale Murphy and Dave Parker.

"He challenges hitters. He's going to be a good addition to the Astros' staff."

HOUSTON ASTROS

HITTING:

Glenn Davis has emerged as the Astros' first true power hitter in more than a decade. He was a 30-homer, 100-RBI man last season and finished second in the National League MVP balloting.

A strong righthanded hitter, Davis can hit the ball to all fields. He has the brute strength to hit the ball out of any NL stadium, although most of his homers are from left-center to the left-field line.

Despite his power potential, Davis does not strike out that much. He has had problems with breaking pitches and tends to fall in prolonged slumps. Pitchers have had their best success at pitching him low and away with change-ups or curves, particularly with two strikes. They generally pitch him high and tight early in the count to set him up for pitches low and away.

Nevertheless, Davis has shown increased discipline at the plate and has started to draw more walks. He also has improved his ability to hit pitches out of the strike zone for singles up the middle. He is a true cleanup hitter in every sense. He also is a good clutch-hitter whose power is evident in the late innings.

BASERUNNING:

Davis has average speed for a major league first baseman. But it is imperative for him to rely on snap judgment, and not natural quickness, to take the extra base.

FIELDING:

Davis showed substantial improvement last season after spending considerable time sharpening his skills over the winter. His range, hands and instincts have become assets instead of liabilities. He handled low

GLENN DAVIS
1B, No. 27
RR, 6'3", 210 lbs.
ML Svc: 2 years
Born: 3-28-61 in
Jacksonville, FL

1986 STATISTICS

AVG	G	AB	R	H	2B	3B	HR	RBI	BB	SO	SB
.265	158	574	91	152	32	3	31	101	64	72	3

CAREER STATISTICS

AVG	G	AB	R	H	2B	3B	HR	RBI	BB	SO	SB
.264	276	985	148	260	48	3	53	173	95	152	3

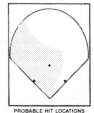

VS. RHP   VS. LHP   PROBABLE HIT LOCATIONS

throws much better, but still has problems trying to catch foul balls down the line.

OVERALL:

Davis has developed into one of the league's budding young stars. Although he may not hit 30 homers every year, he could become a perennial 100-RBI man. Defensively, he has become more of an overall player. His biggest value is the new dimension he has added to the Astros' offensive attack.

Dierker: "Glenn really came on last year and based on his 1986 performance, could be a mainstay of this club for years. He impressed everyone last season--especially with his ability to come through in clutch games."

HOUSTON ASTROS

PITCHING:

Jim Deshaies was another of the Astros' many rags-to-riches stories in 1986. He went to spring training trying to earn a spot on the roster and ended up establishing a major league record for most consecutive strikeouts (eight) at the start of a game.

Deshaies accounted for most of his damage with a rising fastball, one which helped him tie for the National League rookie lead with 12 victories. Although his fastball travels only 88-89 MPH, it has enough deception to frustrate even the most disciplined hitters.

Aside from his fastball, Deshaies throws a curveball, slider and change-up. He had problems with stamina last year, often tiring after only five or six innings. He often has trouble keeping pitches down in the strike zone.

FIELDING, HITTING, BASERUNNING:

Deshaies' reflexes are below average, thereby making him more of a liability than an asset in the field. A former American League pitcher, he did not bat until the 1986 season. Deshaies seldom made contact at the plate. When he did, he usually hit the ball to the opposite field. He is also a below-average bunter and baserunner.

JIM DESHAIES
LHP, No. 43
LL, 6'4", 222 lbs.
ML Svc: 1 year plus
Born: 6-23-60 in
Massena, NY

1986 STATISTICS

W	L	ERA	G	GS	CG	SV	IP	H	R	ER	BB	SO
12	5	3.25	26	26	1	0	144	124	58	52	59	128

CAREER STATISTICS

W	L	ERA	G	GS	CG	SV	IP	H	R	ER	BB	SO
12	6	3.56	30	28	1	0	154	139	67	61	66	135

OVERALL:

Deshaies exceeded the expectations that the Astros had for him last year. He needs to work more on his control, but his presence in the Astros' starting rotation gives Houston another quality lefthander to go with Bob Knepper.

Dierker: "Jim is a good strikeout pitcher who showed a lot of poise for a rookie. He still has some things to work on in all aspects of his game. Developing another pitch might be helpful."

HOUSTON ASTROS

HITTING:

Bill Doran is a heads-up player who knows how to combine patience and aggressiveness at the plate. He ranked among the league's leaders in walks last season, a tribute to his refusal to hit many bad pitches.

Doran's power as a switch-hitter diminished last year, as did his average and RBI total. But he still presents problems from either side of the plate. Doran is a particularly good fastball hitter and an excellent leadoff man. Most pitchers try to change speeds and pitch him low.

As a lefthanded hitter, Doran will hit to all fields. Most defenses tend to play him to pull in the outfield and straightaway in the infield. He is not quite as effective from the right side, although his tendencies are about the same.

In previous years, Doran struggled through slow starts. He overcame that habit by hitting over .300 last April. His biggest challenge is to develop more consistency at the plate and be less susceptible to prolonged slumps.

BASERUNNING:

Doran benefited greatly from the Astros' added emphasis on aggressive baserunning last year. He could have become the first Houston player since Cesar Cedeño to steal 50 bases had he not been hampered by a groin injury for three weeks.

With his natural ability and a little more experience, Doran could enhance his blossoming reputation as a baserunner. He has the potential to be one of the best.

FIELDING:

Doran has good range in the infield, great hands and a good arm. A hard-nosed player, his ability to turn the double play could be his

BILL DORAN
2B, No. 19
SR, 6'0", 175 lbs.
ML Svc: 5 years
Born: 5-28-58 in
**   Cincinnati, OH**

1986 STATISTICS

AVG	G	AB	R	H	2B	3B	HR	RBI	BB	SO	SB
.276	145	550	92	152	29	3	6	37	81	57	42

CAREER STATISTICS

AVG	G	AB	R	H	2B	3B	HR	RBI	BB	SO	SB
.274	620	2308	349	633	93	27	32	182	308	273	103

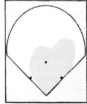

VS. RHP   VS. LHP   PROBABLE HIT LOCATIONS

best asset in the field. He most often gets into trouble when he tries too hard to make the difficult play.

OVERALL:

Simply put, Doran is an outstanding all-around player whose consistency and leadership qualities are among his superior assets.

Dierker: "Bill is one of the class second basemen in the league: he can do just about everything. He is a leader on the field because of his hard-nosed style of play."

"He is a throwback to the old days, when a player's most honored badges were mud and blood."

HOUSTON ASTROS

HITTING:

Strictly a streak hitter, Phil Garner tends to rely more on instinct than ability as he nears the end of his playing career. He started surprisingly fast at the plate last April, then cooled off considerably.

Garner represents a perplexing challenge for most pitchers. When he is hot, he will hit almost anything. When he is not, he can't hit a pitch right down the middle. But Garner is an intense competitor, the kind of player who never gives up.

He remains among the most effective Astros at the hit-and-run and can hit to the opposite field quite well. He is easily fooled, however, by breaking pitches outside the strike zone.

Garner's bat speed has slowed, forcing him to rely on his knowledge of the game for most of his power. He increased his home-run total again last year, but is regarded as more of a singles hitter.

BASERUNNING:

A deceptive player who uses savvy more than speed for success on the bases. His 12 thefts last year represented an admirable output for a 37-year-old.

Garner's biggest strength on the bases is his aggressiveness. He is good at breaking up double plays, taking the extra base and scoring from third on fly balls.

FIELDING:

Garner's best position is second base, a fact which has been underlined by his diminishing skills at third. His arm is strong but erratic, and his range is limited. He also

PHIL GARNER
3B, No. 3
RR, 5'10", 175 lbs.
ML Svc: 13 years
Born: 4-30-49 in
Jefferson City, TN

1986 STATISTICS

AVG	G	AB	R	H	2B	3B	HR	RBI	BB	SO	SB
.265	107	313	43	83	14	3	9	41	30	45	12

CAREER STATISTICS

AVG	G	AB	R	H	2B	3B	HR	RBI	BB	SO	SB
.262	1732	5885	751	1543	290	82	104	714	535	795	219

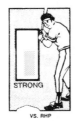  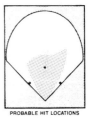

STRONG   STRONG

VS. RHP   VS. LHP   PROBABLE HIT LOCATIONS

has a tendency to misplay routine grounders and commit hasty errors by trying to compensate for his poor reflexes.

OVERALL:

Garner remains a useful player, but has a greater value as a reserve. His leadership qualities and his ability to hit in the clutch are his biggest assets as he enters the twilight of his career.

Dierker: "Phil has been associated with winning clubs throughout his career and provides intangibles to this club by his indomitable spirit. He is an intense competitor."

HOUSTON ASTROS

HITTING:

Billy Hatcher started slowly last year in his first season with the Astros. He was obtained in a trade with the Chicago Cubs at the end of the 1985 season and tried too hard to impress his new team during spring training. There were times when he didn't look as if would fit in offensively or defensively.

Hatcher's biggest problem at the plate was his tendency to lunge at pitches. He would swing wildly while off-balance, a habit that kept his average way down. He had trouble making contact, especially with breaking pitches.

As the season progressed, however, Hatcher worked diligently on altering his stance and swing. He improved to the point where he replaced Bill Doran as the Astros' leadoff hitter for almost a month, but then settled back into the No. 2 spot in the order.

A righthanded hitter, Hatcher still needs to discipline himself a little more at the plate. He still swings at too many bad pitches, but he has surprising power for a player with such a compact swing.

BASERUNNING:

If he continues to improve, Hatcher could become the best base stealer on a team which stresses aggressiveness on the bases. He has great speed and has received several tips during the early stages of his career from Davey Lopes.

Hatcher stole 38 bases as a part-time player last season. He could steal as many as 50-60 bases in years to come.

FIELDING:

Although Hatcher doesn't always get a good jump on the ball, he compensates for most of his mistakes with his natural quickness. He has a good throwing arm, but he could improve his accuracy.

Hatcher was acquired by the Astros for his

BILLY HATCHER
CF, No. 28
RR, 5'9", 175 lbs.
ML Svc: 1 year plus
Born: 10-4-60 in
Williams, AZ

1986 STATISTICS

AVG	G	AB	R	H	2B	3B	HR	RBI	BB	SO	SB
.258	127	419	55	108	15	4	6	36	22	52	38

CAREER STATISTICS

AVG	G	AB	R	H	2B	3B	HR	RBI	BB	SO	SB
.252	188	591	80	149	27	5	8	46	31	64	42

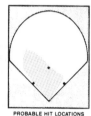

STRONG   STRONG

VS. RHP   VS. LHP   PROBABLE HIT LOCATIONS

ability as a center fielder. He could become a fixture there because of his range.

OVERALL:

This could be a pivotal year for Hatcher, who must show that his improved hitting and baserunning over the final half of the '86 season was no fluke.

Dierker: "He reminds you a little of Bill Madlock in terms of the compact, quick swing he has. Once in a while when he catches one, he can hit it a long way. I think it probably does him more harm than good because he should be the kind of player who hits the ball all over the park.

"I think Billy has the ability to improve over the years with regular play in terms of pitch selection and the ability to draw some walks. Once in a while, he has shown the ability to hit behind the runner with a runner on second base, so you know he can go that way if he wants to."

HOUSTON ASTROS

PITCHING:

Shifted from a starting role to the bullpen before the 1986 season, Charlie Kerfeld emerged as one of the National League's best set-up men. He was a big factor in Dave Smith's ability to earn 33 saves while Kerfeld won 11 of 13 decisions.

Kerfeld doesn't try to fool hitters, he comes right after them. His imposing 6'6" frame aids his fastball, which has been clocked in the 90-95 MPH range. Kerfeld also throws a deceptive slider that appears to slow down before it reaches the plate, causing hitters to swing early.

Kerfeld frequently pitched only one or two innings at a time last year and was particularly effective against righthanded hitters. He also has a change-up which he uses whenever he has to go several innings.

Once Kerfeld gets in a groove, he is very difficult to solve. He loves to challenge hitters, but occasionally has trouble getting any of his pitches in the strike zone.

FIELDING, HITTING, BASERUNNING:

Kerfeld is only an average fielder, although he has more athletic ability than one may think. He is a below-average runner. He needs to improve his bunting.

CHARLIE KERFELD
RHP, No. 37
RR, 6'6", 257 lbs.
ML Svc: 2 years
Born: 9-28-63 in
Knobnoster, MO

1986 STATISTICS

W	L	ERA	G	GS	CG	SV	IP	H	R	ER	BB	SO
11	2	2.59	61	0	0	7	93.2	71	32	27	42	77

CAREER STATISTICS

W	L	ERA	G	GS	CG	SV	IP	H	R	ER	BB	SO
15	4	3.07	72	6	0	7	138	115	54	47	67	107

OVERALL:

Kerfeld came through with a big year last season after dropping 40 pounds. If he stays in shape, he could be just as effective in '87.

Dierker: "He is extremely strong and wants the ball, the kind of pitcher you would like to have in short relief. He really likes to get in there and go after them.

"Charlie could be used as a starting pitcher again later in his career. If so, he will need to work more on his change-up."

HOUSTON ASTROS

PITCHING:

Almost two months into last season, Bob Knepper was ahead of Denny McLain's 31-victory pace of 1968. Knepper struggled during the season's final six weeks but his 17 victories tied a club record for lefthanders.

The two usual ingredients for Knepper's success are finesse and control. He doesn't try to blow the ball past hitters and must pitch inside to be effective.

Knepper throws a sinker and a cut fastball which runs in on righthanded hitters. He mixes those pitches with a slow curveball, a short curveball and a sinking fastball which he throws at two or three different speeds. He likes to nibble at the corners of the plate.

His delivery is almost effortless which is a major reason he is among the league leaders in innings-pitched each year. Control and durability are his biggest assets. When Knepper is at the top of his game, he gets a lot of ground balls.

FIELDING, HITTING, BASERUNNING:

Knepper does not have a good move to first base for a lefthander but is an above-average fielder. He is most prone to fielding mistakes when he is pitching poorly.

Although he doesn't hit for a high average by pitcher's standards, Knepper does have occasional power. He is an average bunter

BOB KNEPPER
LHP, No. 39
LL, 6'2", 210 lbs.
ML Svc: 10 years
Born: 5-25-54 in
Akron, OH

1986 STATISTICS

W	L	ERA	G	GS	CG	SV	IP	H	R	ER	BB	SO
17	12	3.14	40	38	8	0	258	232	100	90	62	143

CAREER STATISTICS

W	L	ERA	G	GS	CG	SV	IP	H	R	ER	BB	SO
114	118	3.44	338	322	73	1	2145.2	2109	944	819	592	1206

but slightly below average on the bases.

OVERALL:

Knepper has emerged as one of the league's most consistent lefthanders by winning 47 games over the last three years. He has improved steadily during that span as a result of improved control. He is a potential 20-game winner.

Dierker: "He has been a little streaky during his career but when he gets in a groove, he's one of the best. When he gets behind in the count, he has to come in over the plate and gets hit. However, he usually doesn't put too many people on that don't hit their way on."

PITCHING:

After he joined the Astros as a free agent last June, Aurelio Lopez showed why he has been a steady reliever in professional baseball for almost two decades. He did whatever was asked of him, whether it was short or middle relief, and usually did the job well.

A streaky pitcher, Lopez goes after hitters with a 88-90 MPH fastball he throws on the corners. He also has a good slider. One of his biggest assets last year was his ability to control his screwball, a pitch he had trouble throwing in recent years.

When Lopez was effective, he was a big plus for the Astros--and he was effective most of the time. But when he struggled, he was hit hard. He is a loose pitcher, one who is not afraid of pressure situations.

Lopez has a short, simple delivery and a rubber arm. He can pitch an inning or two in four consecutive games. Or he can pitch as many as four innings in one day. He must pitch often to be at the top of his game.

FIELDING, HITTING, BASERUNNING:

Lopez is an adequate fielder but nothing flashy. He has a fair pickoff move and does a good job of holding runners on base. He hasn't had that many opportunities to hit in

AURELIO LOPEZ
RHP, No. 35
RR, 6'0", 225 lbs.
ML Svc: 9 years
Born: 9-5-48 in
Tecamachalco,
Mexico

1986 STATISTICS

W	L	ERA	G	GS	CG	SV	IP	H	R	ER	BB	SO
3	3	3.46	45	0	0	7	78	64	32	30	25	44

CAREER STATISTICS

W	L	ERA	G	GS	CG	SV	IP	H	R	ER	BB	SO
60	35	3.52	433	9	0	92	872	746	370	341	345	614

recent years but he still remains an average bunter. Baserunning is not his strong suit.

OVERALL:

Lopez is a valuable man to have in a bullpen for several reasons. He can pitch often, can be a short or middle reliever, and wants the ball. He's an aggressive sort, the type of player who thrives on challenges.

Dierker: "He can be hot and cold. But he was hot about 75% of the time last year and really shut people down. He picked up some saves and some wins and did a good job."

HOUSTON ASTROS

HITTING:

Terry Puhl injured his ankle in spring training and never really reached peak form all of last year. He was coming off an injury-plagued year in 1985, so it has been two years since Puhl has been one of the Astros' established outfielders.

As a result of his inactivity, Puhl finished with a .244 average, his worst in 10 major league seasons. He is the kind of player who must play regularly to be productive. The Astros would like to give him more playing time if he is not traded, and there is a chance he could be platooned with Jose Cruz in left field this year.

The Astros attempted to transform Puhl into a power hitter at one stage during his career, but the idea flopped when his average decreased. Puhl is at his best when he is spraying the ball to all fields as a contact hitter and draws a lot of walks.

Puhl is a disciplined hitter who doesn't strike out a lot. Most pitchers tend to work him inside and low.

BASERUNNING:

Because of his history of injuries in recent years, Puhl's baserunning abilities have slipped to the point where he stole only three bases last year. He has become more tentative on the bases and has slowed a step or two as a result. He still has the potential to steal 15-20 bases if he can avoid injury.

FIELDING:

One of the league's steadiest fielders, Puhl owns one of the highest career fielding percentages among active outfielders in the majors. He has only an average arm, but his throws are very accurate.

Puhl has primarily played right and center field during his career with the Astros, but his

TERRY PUHL
RF, No. 21
LR, 6'2", 200 lbs.
ML Svc: 10 years
Born: 7-8-56 in
   Saskatchewan, Canada

1986 STATISTICS

AVG	G	AB	R	H	2B	3B	HR	RBI	BB	SO	SB
.244	81	172	17	42	10	0	3	14	15	24	3

CAREER STATISTICS

AVG	G	AB	R	H	2B	3B	HR	RBI	BB	SO	SB
.281	1155	4086	579	1150	198	50	57	363	414	413	184

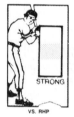

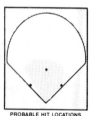

VS. RHP   VS. LHP   PROBABLE HIT LOCATIONS

future with them likely will be as a left fielder. If so, such a move might be beneficial at this stage of his career.

OVERALL:

When healthy, Puhl is an asset. But his reputation for being injury prone has left the impression that his best years may be behind him.

Dierker: "If Terry continues to try and hit the ball to all fields instead of trying to pull the ball, I think he still has a lot of good years left in him. Playing every day would be to his advantage.

"Terry's age (30) shouldn't be a detriment at this stage of his career. But he might be a possible trade candidate if the Astros' other outfielders perform well this year."

HOUSTON ASTROS

HITTING:

A steady player during much of his career, Craig Reynolds contributed much of his offense as a pinch-hitter last year. He was platooned at shortstop for much of the season with Dickie Thon, but enhanced his overall average by hitting .409 as a pinch-hitter.

Reynolds is an average hitter for a shortstop, but a below-average hitter for a major league player. He is a good contact hitter and hits the ball to all fields. He has occasional power, but rarely walks.

A lefthanded hitter, Reynolds is an unorthodox batter who has a long, slow swing. Since he has to start his swing earlier than most hitters, he often ends up swinging at bad pitches. But he has good hand-eye coordination that allows him to make contact with low pitches that normally result in strikeouts for the majority of hitters.

One of Reynolds' outstanding qualities is his leadership ability. He is aggressive at the plate and in the field, traits that compensate for whatever limitations he has in terms of natural ability.

BASERUNNING:

Reynolds is not a basestealing threat, nor is he particularly adept at taking the extra base. He relies strictly on his intelligence, a factor that helps him break up double plays.

His biggest attribute as a baserunner is his knack of beating out infield hits. If he played his home games on grass instead of Astroturf, he would be better able to use his ability as a bunter.

FIELDING:

Once an above-average defensive shortstop, Reynolds is probably average in terms of hands and arm and below average in terms of range. He rarely makes a mistake on an easy play and is extremely good at playing bad-hop grounders.

CRAIG REYNOLDS
SS, No. 12
LR, 6'1", 175 lbs.
ML Svc: 11 years
Born: 12-27-52 in Houston, TX

1986 STATISTICS

AVG	G	AB	R	H	2B	3B	HR	RBI	BB	SO	SB
.249	114	313	32	78	7	3	6	41	12	31	3

CAREER STATISTICS

AVG	G	AB	R	H	2B	3B	HR	RBI	BB	SO	SB
.259	1177	3742	409	968	115	62	35	321	170	321	49

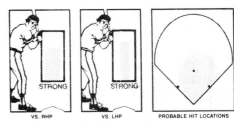

VS. RHP   VS. LHP   PROBABLE HIT LOCATIONS

Reynolds expanded his fielding horizons last year when he was asked to play first base in infrequent reserve roles. He also has played third and even pitched one inning last season. He did not have any chances on the mound, so his fielding ability as a pitcher is a question mark.

OVERALL:

Reynolds is strictly a team man, the type of player who works hard and strives to reach the maximum of his potential. His best years may be behind him, but he still performs well as a role player.

Dierker: "He and Dickie Thon form a good tandem at shortstop. Reynolds is not an everyday shortstop; his hitting is not good enough overall and he doesn't have the blazingly fast reactions to play the position as regular starter. If he continues to be used on a platoon basis, Craig will give the club everything he's got."

HOUSTON ASTROS

PITCHING:

Only a select few pitchers in baseball history have been able to throw as long and as hard as Nolan Ryan has during his Hall of Fame-bound career. But he could be a big question mark this year since he pitched the entire 1986 season suffering from elbow problems.

Ryan was on the disabled list twice last year and was limited to 100 pitches in several starts late in the year so as not to place too great a strain on his ailing elbow. The limit actually seemed to help him--he pitched better as the season progressed.

Although Ryan no longer approaches the 100-MPH barrier with his fastball, he can still bring on his heat in the 93-95 MPH range. He maintained good velocity last season, even when his elbow pained him the most, but his injury prevented from getting a good, sharp break on his curveball. As a result, hitters laid off the fastball and pounded his other pitches.

Ryan averaged more than nine strikeouts per nine innings pitched last year for only the second time in his seven seasons with the Astros. He relied on a change-up about 10% of the time, one which tends to fade away from lefthanded hitters.

Although surgery on his elbow was recommended, Ryan decided to try to let his elbow heal with rest over the winter. He fully expects to pitch this year. If healthy, he could be a very big asset in the Astros bid to recapture the pennant in the National League West.

FIELDING, HITTING, BASERUNNING:

One of Ryan's weaknesses over the years has been his inability to hold runners on base.

NOLAN RYAN
RHP, No. 34
RR, 6'2", 210 lbs.
ML Svc: 19 years
Born: 1-31-47 in
Refugio, TX

1986 STATISTICS

W	L	ERA	G	GS	CG	SV	IP	H	R	ER	BB	SO
12	8	3.34	30	30	1	0	178	119	72	66	82	194

CAREER STATISTICS

W	L	ERA	G	GS	CG	SV	IP	H	R	ER	BB	SO
253	226	3.15	611	577	203	2	4115.1	2990	1643	1440	2268	4277

His pickoff move is only average.

He is not a good hitter, even though he collected the first game-winning hit of his career last year, but he has made himself into a reasonably good bunter. He surprised himself by stealing the first base of his career last year when he missed a sign.

OVERALL:

Ryan remains one of the greatest pitchers of his era. He was superb over the final two months of the 1986 season and is looking forward to his 20th season in the majors this year. Now 40, he still overpowers hitters better than most pitchers half his age.

Dierker: "Even with his problems, Nolan had an excellent season in 1986. He's still one of the best.

"His season finale in the playoffs against the Mets when he was pitching in considerable pain was one of the year's highlights.

"Nevertheless, any report on Nolan Ryan hinges on the condition of his elbow this year."

HOUSTON ASTROS

PITCHING:

Mike Scott has developed one of baseball's most feared weapons, a pitch that travels as fast as a fastball with the movement of a knuckleball. As a result of his ability to master the split-finger fastball, he became the league's most dominant pitcher last year.

Remarkably, Scott has only two pitches, a fastball and a split-finger fastball. His fastball acts in one of several ways. It rides up and away from a righthanded hitter, up and in on a lefthanded hitter, or, it sinks. The split-finger pitch, the one that prompted the most controversy last season, can drop as much 1½ feet as it approaches the plate. Bruce Sutter had similar movement on his pitches at the height of his career.

The secret to Scott's success is velocity coupled with movement. His pitches are consistently clocked at a peak of 92-94 MPH and he has excellent control. He was so effective last year that he allowed fewer than four runs in 32 of his last 33 starts.

Scott has consistently denied that he scuffs the ball to give his pitch added and unpredictable movement. Despite the submission from players and managers to league officials of sandpaper allegedly found near the mound after he has pitched, and game balls with supposed scuff marks collected and displayed by opposing teams, Scott has never been caught altering the ball illegally.

But one thing that can't be denied: the ultimate psych out is in effect. Often the illusion of trickery is better than the reality. Scott uses the controversy to his advantage by getting hitters to think about something other than their own abilities every time they step to the plate.

MIKE SCOTT
RHP, No. 33
RR, 6'3", 215 lbs.
ML Svc: 8 years
Born: 4-26-55 in
Santa Monica, CA

1986 STATISTICS

W	L	ERA	G	GS	CG	SV	IP	H	R	ER	BB	SO
18	10	2.22	37	37	7	0	275.1	182	73	68	72	306

CAREER STATISTICS

W	L	ERA	G	GS	CG	SV	IP	H	R	ER	BB	SO
65	62	3.70	212	185	16	3	1160	1112	541	477	363	750

FIELDING, HITTING, BASERUNNING:

Scott doesn't hold runners on base very well. But then again, he didn't have many runners to worry about last year. His hitting is only average and he is a below-average bunter.

He is a smart baserunner, but no threat to take the extra base.

OVERALL:

Scott has earned a repuation as one of baseball's premier pitchers. He easily could have won 24 games last year had he received an average amount of offensive support from his teammates. He could maintain his dominance if he continues to throw his split-finger pitch effectively and stays healthy.

Dierker: "Good control has been one of Mike's prime assets all the way through his career. He never has walked many hitters and last year was no exception. When you don't let them hit it and you don't walk them, you are going to win a few. And Scott figures to win a bunch."

HOUSTON ASTROS

PITCHING:

Dave Smith finally received the recognition he deserved as one of baseball's best relief pitchers last year. He set a club record with 33 saves and was named to the All-Star team for the first time in his career.

Smith has a wide pitch selection. He is one of the few relievers who changes speeds and location with the same type of pitch. He'll cut the fastball in on a lefthanded hitter and run it away from a righthanded hitter. Simply put, he can do a lot of things with a baseball.

Smith basically throws a fastball, sinker, cut fastball and forkball. He also has a good curveball. His forkball is one of his best pitches when he's at the top of his game. Hitters rarely know what's coming. They have to be prepared, too, because Smith seldom walks hitters.

Smith usually doesn't pitch more than one inning, two at the most. He has the perfect temperament for a reliever in that he wants the ball and isn't fazed by anyone. He loves pressure situations.

FIELDING, HITTING, BASERUNNING:

Smith does an above-average job of keeping runners honest. He needs to work on his bunting and baserunning.

DAVE SMITH
RHP, No. 45
RR, 6'1", 195 lbs.
ML Svc: 7 years
Born: 1-21-55 in
San Francisco, CA

1986 STATISTICS

W	L	ERA	G	GS	CG	SV	IP	H	R	ER	BB	SO
4	7	2.73	54	0	0	33	56		39	17	17	22	46

CAREER STATISTICS

W	L	ERA	G	GS	CG	SV	IP	H	R	ER	BB	SO
38	29	2.61	361	1	0	93	526.2	453	177	153	181	337

OVERALL:

Smith's dependability has increased over the last two years to the extent he has become a very effective pitcher. He is a superlative closer, the type of reliever a team must have to contend for a division title.

Dierker: "He is an uncompromising pitcher who doesn't walk many. He usually can get a ground ball or a strikeout when he needs it. Whether or not the Astros repeat in 1987 will, in large part, be related to how well Smith and Charlie Kerfeld perform."

HOUSTON ASTROS

HITTING:

One of the game's most courageous players, Dickie Thon has continued to progress at the plate after suffering a career-threatening eye injury three years ago.

Instead of pampering him last year, the Astros gave Thon a chance to play every day. He started quickly, but soon had familiar problems against righthanders. His best success comes against lefthanded fastball pitchers.

Although his vision has improved steadily over the last two years, Thon has had to adjust his style of hitting. He has become more of a contact hitter instead of swinging for power. He used to be a pull hitter, but now hits the ball all over the park.

Thon could increase his effectiveness at the plate by cutting back on his swing and becoming more of a slap hitter. He is at his best when he remains patient at the plate and tries to go to the opposite field.

BASERUNNING:

Once one of the league's biggest stolen-base threats, Thon stole only six bases last year. He has good speed and is capable of taking the extra base, but he has become more conservative as a baserunner since the injury.

FIELDING:

Without question, Thon has made a full recovery from his injury as far as his defensive skills are concerned. He has an above-

DICKIE THON
SS, No. 10
RR, 5'11", 175 lbs.
ML Svc: 8 years
Born: 6-20-58 in
South Bend, IN

1986 STATISTICS

AVG	G	AB	R	H	2B	3B	HR	RBI	BB	SO	SB
.248	106	278	24	69	13	1	3	21	29	49	6

CAREER STATISTICS

AVG	G	AB	R	H	2B	3B	HR	RBI	BB	SO	SB
.272	649	2079	258	565	99	24	32	192	162	214	98

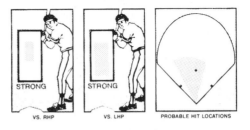

VS. RHP   VS. LHP   PROBABLE HIT LOCATIONS

average arm and good range. He doesn't make many mistakes on routine chances and is excellent at turning the double play.

OVERALL:

Dierker: "Although he likely will never approach the hitting form he displayed before his injury, Thon remains an above-average major league shortstop. His biggest improvement could come in the area of stealing more bases."

HOUSTON ASTROS

HITTING:

Denny Walling had his best season last year, when he developed into one of the league's most consistent hitters. He platooned much of the year with Phil Garner at third, playing mostly against righthanded pitchers.

Always regarded as a player with power potential, Walling nearly doubled his previous major league high for home runs and established career highs in several offensive categories. He improved his average from .270 in 1985 to .312 last year and enhanced his reputation as an excellent clutch-hitter.

A lefthanded hitter, Walling doesn't strike out much. He sprays the ball between the foul lines and is not fooled very often by off-speed pitches. He excelled as a No. 3 hitter in the Astros' lineup last year because he has enough pop to drive in runs and gets on base often enough for the heavy hitters coming up behind him.

Walling likes to swing at the first pitch, which makes him an outstanding pinch-hitter. He hit .387 as a pinch-hitter last year. His willingness to be more selective in certain situations, however, has made him a much tougher out. Lefthanders still give him problems, as do pitchers who change speeds well and keep the ball low and outside.

BASERUNNING:

Walling has only average speed. He is not the type of player who will beat out many infield grounders for hits, but he still can take the occasional extra base on hits to right field.

FIELDING:

At one time, Walling's best defensive position was first base. He also has spent considerable time in the outfield. But last year, Walling found a new home in the field.

As a result of dedication and hard work,

DENNY WALLING
3B, No. 29
LR, 6'1", 185 lbs.
ML Svc: 9 years
Born: 4-17-54 in
Neptune, NJ

1986 STATISTICS

AVG	G	AB	R	H	2B	3B	HR	RBI	BB	SO	SB
.312	130	382	54	119	23	1	13	58	36	31	1

CAREER STATISTICS

AVG	G	AB	R	H	2B	3B	HR	RBI	BB	SO	SB
.278	903	2133	287	594	95	24	41	294	229	219	39

  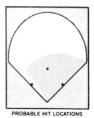

VS. RHP   VS. LHP   PROBABLE HIT LOCATIONS

Walling was considered by many scouts as the most improved defensive third baseman in the majors last year. He improved his range and smoothness and seldom made an errant throw. His strong throwing arm is another big asset.

OVERALL:

Given increased playing time last year, Walling finally became an all-around player. He is the type of veteran who can contribute as a starter or as a reserve and at the plate or in the field. His biggest challenge is improving his consistency against lefthanded pitching.

Dierker: "Walling has made himself more important to the Astros through hard work and determination. His fielding improved tremendously and he can now do so many things, that he has become more valuable to the club in view of the acceptance of the 24-man roster."

LARRY ANDERSEN
RHP, No. 47
RR, 6'3", 205 lbs.
ML Svc: 7 years
Born: 5-6-53 in
Portland, OR

PITCHING, FIELDING, HITTING, BASERUNNING:

Released by the Phillies last May, Larry Andersen signed on with the Astros and became an integral part of their bullpen. He was used primarily in middle relief and seemed to get better as the season progressed.

Andersen usually was limited to about two innings in each of his appearances with the Astros. His longest stint was 3 2/3 innings. He pitched well in the clutch, allowing only 10 of the 33 runners he inherited to score.

Primarily an off-speed pitcher, Andersen isn't going to stand on the mound and try to throw the ball past many hitters. He uses a three-quarters delievery and relies on his slider as his bread-and-butter pitch.

When Andersen is at the top of his game, he uses his slider to get ground balls against left- and righthanded hitters. Otherwise, he tends to struggle.

Andersen is the best fielder among Astros relievers. He is quick in fielding bunts. He is not a good hitter and is only an average bunter. Andersen has average speed for a pitcher.

OVERALL:

When Andersen became a free agent at the end of the 1986 season, Astros manager Hal Lanier said publicly that his team needed Andersen back in the bullpen as a middle reliever in '87. Andersen excelled in that role last year, gaining confidence in the season's final months.

Dierker: "His pitches need to have a lot of movement or he has trouble with lefthanded hitters. He is really a lot more effective overall against righthanded hitters."

TY GAINEY
OF, No. 24
LL, 6'1", 190 lbs.
ML Svc: less than one year
Born: 10-25-60 in
Cheraw, SC

HITTING, BASERUNNING, FIELDING:

Ty Gainey finally earned a chance to prove himself at the major league level last year. He showed signs of rising to the occasion by hitting .300 as a reserve and spot starter during the final half of the season.

Gainey led the Pacific Coast League in hitting last year with a .351 average. He displayed power to all fields, a trait that was conspicuous by its absence when he reached the majors.

Many scouts are still high on Gainey's potential. But he seldom pulled the ball as a lefthanded hitter, prompting several defenses to shift their second baseman behind the bag when Gainey came to the plate. His only home run in 1986 cleared the left field fence inside the the foul pole.

Gainey has exceptional speed, but he is susceptible to baserunning blunders committed by most young players.

Until now, Gainey's usual position has been center field. Although he has good range, his arm is only average in terms of strength and accuracy; he would be best used in left field.

OVERALL:

Gainey never has appeared comfortable in the majors, a problem that added experience could remedy. For Gainey to realize his full potential, he must improve his baserunning skills and work more on pulling the ball toward right field. Getting more playing time might be the key.

HOUSTON ASTROS

DAVEY LOPES
OF/INF, No. 11
RR, 5'9", 170 lbs.
ML Svc: 14 years
Born: 5-3-46 in
E. Providence, RI

HITTING, BASERUNNING, FIELDING:

The Astros' need for a veteran righthanded hitter off the bench prompted them to trade for Davey Lopes last July, a move that helped them solidify their role as division contenders in the National League West.

Although Lopes' average dipped from .299 to .275 after the trade, he still delivered several hits in critical situations. Now 40, Lopes relies more on his knowledge than pure athletic ability. Nevertheless, he still keeps himself in excellent shape.

Lopes still is regarded as a good contact hitter with occasional power. He doesn't strike out much and is good at advancing the runners.

He set a record for most stolen bases by a player 40 years or older last year (25), so he remains an extraordinary baserunner for his age. He could steal 15-20 bases again this year, depending on the amount of playing time he receives.

Lopes played third base, left field and center field for the Astros during the second half of last season. He had trouble in the field in the one game he played at third and didn't show adequate range in center. His best position at this stage of his career undoubtedly is left field, where his speed helps nullify his other shortcomings.

OVERALL:

Lopes has had a remarkable career, much like Jose Cruz. If he can continue to steal a few bases and improve on his .211 pinch-hitting average with the Astros, he could prove to be a big asset.

Dierker: "Davey is a veteran and a guy who knows how to win. He has been on a lot of winning teams and still has some ability left."

JIM PANKOVITS
INF, No. 20
RR, 5'10", 174 lbs.
ML Svc: 2 years
Born: 8-6-55 in
Pennington Gap, VA

HITTING, BASERUNNING, FIELDING:

One of the Astros' unsung heroes, Jim Pankovits made the most of his hitting opportunities off the bench last year. He was particularly effective as a pinch-hitter against lefthanders.

Pankovits isn't known as a contact hitter, but he hits the ball hard for a middle infielder. An aggressive hitter, many of his hits are to left field or up the middle. Seldom will he hit a pitch down the right field line.

Most pitchers try to keep the ball down in the strike zone and fool Pankovits with an assortment of breaking pitches. The Astros are regarded as one of baseball's best fastball-hitting teams and Pankovits is a classic example.

Pankovits plays aggressively, but his speed is only average. He has stolen only one base in each of the last two seasons and is more valuable on going from first to third.

A good utilityman, Pankovits' best position is second base. He has excelled defensively when asked to fill in for starting second baseman Bill Doran. Pankovits also can play third base and shortstop and has been given occasional playing time in left field.

He is a below-average fielder everywhere but second base, where his hands, arm, and range are considered average.

OVERALL:

Dierker: "Over the years, Pankovits has learned to accept his supporting role. But he does receive top billing as a righthanded pinch-hitter against lefthanded pitchers."

HOUSTON ASTROS

ROBBIE WINE
C, No. 7
RR, 6'1", 190 lbs..
ML Svc: less than
one year
Born: 7-22-62 in
Philadelphia, PA

HITTING, BASERUNNING, FIELDING:

During his career at Oklahoma State, Robbie Wine earned the reputation as one of the finest power hitters at the college level. The son of former Phillies shortstop and Braves manager Bobby Wine, he continued to hit tape-measure homers during the early stages of his professional training.

Soon, however, Wine found himself overmatched by minor league pitchers who changed speeds. Instructors worked with Wine on shortening his swing to decrease his power and increase his average as a righthanded hitter.

Wine has above-average speed for a catcher, but he is not a threat to steal. He has the necessary quickness to take the occasional extra base.

Wine's ability behind the plate has been the biggest reason he has been able to climb the ladder in the Astros' minor league system. He has a superior arm and does an excellent job of blocking the plate. Like his father, he has earned the reputation of being a good fielder and a below-average hitter.

OVERALL:

Wine displayed the raw tools he needs to become a quality major league catcher during the final month of the '86 season, but he needs to polish several aspects of his game. He needs to become more of a contact hitter and cut down on his strikeouts. He already possesses the defensive skills necessary for him to be a regular catcher in the majors.

LOS ANGELES DODGERS

HITTING:

Whether it was caused by the distraction of a bitter, spring-training contract squabble, or the absence of his countryman and mentor, Pedro Guerrero, or simple complacency, Mariano Duncan regressed in 1986 instead of improving on his surprising rookie showing.

He started slowly last year (.201 in April and May) and lost the youthful good humor that made him so special in 1985, when he was rushed to the big leagues to fill in for injured Steve Sax.

Duncan was upset to hear teammates and reporters questioning his guts when he missed three weeks with what appeared to be a minor ankle sprain. After breaking a toe in August and aggravating the injury by continuing to play, Duncan blamed a reporter, saying negative stories goaded him into proving his fortitude.

Duncan underwent knee surgery after a winter-league injury but is expected to be fit for spring training.

Duncan, introduced to switch-hitting only four years ago, batted just .205 from the left side. He is a low-ball hitter from that side and tends to overswing. As a righthanded hitter, he likes the pitch a bit higher up in the strike zone, more toward the belt.

He rarely takes advantage of his speed by bunting. The Dodgers sent Duncan to the Arizona instructional league to learn to bunt and were happy with his progress and determination.

BASERUNNING:

If the saying, "You can't steal first base," weren't around already, Duncan would have inspired it. He had an on-base percentage under .300 for the second straight year but finished fourth in the National League with 48 steals in 61 attempts.

FIELDING:

Spectacular, yes, but does Tommy Lasorda still place Duncan in the Ozzie Smith-Shawon Dunston class? Among NL

MARIANO DUNCAN
SS, No. 25
SR, 6'0", 175 lbs.
ML Svc: 2 years
Born: 3-13-63 in
San Pedro de Macoris,
Dominican Republic

1986 STATISTICS

AVG	G	AB	R	H	2B	3B	HR	RBI	BB	SO	SB
.229	109	407	47	93	7	0	8	30	30	78	48

CAREER STATISTICS

AVG	G	AB	R	H	2B	3B	HR	RBI	BB	SO	SB
.237	251	969	121	230	31	6	14	69	68	191	86

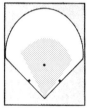

VS. RHP — STRONG   VS. LHP — STRONG   PROBABLE HIT LOCATIONS

shortstops playing at least 80 games, Duncan posted the lowest fielding percentage in each of his two seasons.

He tends to showboat and throw flat-footed, a bad habit Duncan blames on lapses of concentration. He seems to reach fewer balls than he has in previous seasons, and the numbers bear this out.

OVERALL:

Which came first, the sour attitude or the disappointing play? Duncan faltered on the field in 1986, but his lack of progress is likely not an indicator of his future. He remains a player with talent, though clearly one who will need some patience.

Dierker: "Duncan was not disciplined at the plate and was swinging at too many bad pitches last year. He swung at pitchers' pitches, not his, and got himself out on a lot of off-speed stuff and a lot of junk. Has the talent to get a better command of the strike zone because he has a quick bat."

LOS ANGELES DODGERS

HITTING:

Pedro Guerrero's severe, spring-training knee injury shattered the Dodgers' 1986 season. His five home runs in 61 at-bats after coming off the disabled list for the second time in September gave them hope that one of the game's great hitting talents will return to full strength this year.

Nobody was hotter at the plate in 1985 than Guerrero, when, despite back and wrist injuries and struggling to play third base much of the season, Guerrero led the National League in both slugging and on-base percentage.

But the injury to the tendon below the left kneecap was so serious that it hadn't fully healed by the time Guerrero headed back to his native Dominican Republic after last season for a winter of rest. It has cast his future in doubt just as he appeared to be moving into his prime.

Even the cocky Guerrero was frightened and embarrassed by his futility (0-for-7, with four strikeouts) after being activated prematurely in late July. A proud man, he demanded to return to the DL.

If he's as good as new this season, Guerrero can be expected to produce at least one torrid streak like the one-month, 15-homer explosion that destroyed the National League West two years ago. There's no correct way to pitch to Guerrero when he's that hot--but don't dare throw the ball up in the strike zone.

When he's slumping, Guerrero will chase fastballs up-and-in and breaking balls down-and-away. Because of his short stroke and strong wrists, he is able to handle pitches most anywhere in the strike zone when he is hot. The stroke also allows him to wait on pitches longer than most batters.

BASERUNNING:

Guerrero is quick to point out he hurt himself not by sliding but by trying not to slide at the last second on a busted hit-and-run play.

He's not the worst slider in the big leagues, just the most apprehensive. That's been true ever since Guerrero fractured an ankle sliding into second in the minors in 1977; he also

PEDRO GUERRERO
LF, No. 28
RR, 6'0", 195 lbs.
ML Svc: 8 years
Born: 6-29-56 in
San Pedro de Macoris,
Dominican Republic

1986 STATISTICS

AVG	G	AB	R	H	2B	3B	HR	RBI	BB	SO	SB
.246	31	61	7	15	3	0	5	10	2	19	0

CAREER STATISTICS

AVG	G	AB	R	H	2B	3B	HR	RBI	BB	SO	SB
.304	825	2842	448	865	137	21	139	461	318	493	75

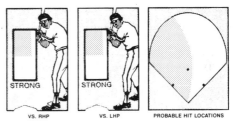

VS. RHP   VS. LHP   PROBABLE HIT LOCATIONS

sprained a knee sliding back into second on a pickoff play in 1980. Shoulder problems preclude sliding head-first.

FIELDING:

The Dodgers, hoping to limit the wear and tear on their star's knee, plan to use Guerrero in left field and move Franklin Stubbs back to first base. Guerrero is less a liability at either of those positions than at third base.

OVERALL:

Guerrero is always late for spring training, takes batting practice when he wishes, gets his pick of clubhouse music--and the fact that management and teammates put up with such eccentricities is testament to his value to the Dodgers.

Dierker: "If he is able to come back to full speed, he'll be a big help to Los Angeles. If he's lost a step of speed, they'll lose a little bit of the advantage they had with his baserunning and his left-fielding, and he will become a one-dimensional player."

LOS ANGELES DODGERS

HITTING:

Dodger management originally hoped to let Jeff Hamilton have a full season of experience in the minors in 1986, but injuries to Bill Madlock and Dave Anderson brought the then 22-year-old third baseman to Los Angeles in June. The fast rise--Hamilton spent the rest of the year with the Dodgers-- was both a blessing and a curse for this young player.

The first impressions observers had of Hamilton couldn't have been less accurate than the actual case. Hamilton drove in a run with a fly ball in his first big league at-bat, and singled sharply to left in his third. Reality came the next night, however, when Nolan Ryan struck out Hamilton in three straight at-bats.

Hamilton turned Dodger heads with his glove and arm and got a crash course in the ways of the big leagues. He also turned Dodger stomachs with his hitting: 43 strikeouts and two walks (one intentional) in 147 at-bats do not a third baseman of the future make. Hamilton was dispatched to winter ball after the 1986 season to work with Dodgers batting coach Manny Mota on hitting breaking balls and off-speed pitches. In the Dominican Republic, though, he wound up hitting in the low .200s, and the club prayed Hamilton was simply tired and homesick.

Hamilton seems to be able to hit high pitches better than those thrown low in the strike zone, though there were times during his time with the Dodgers last year where he was simply unable to hit anything at all.

When the Dodgers traded for Madlock in 1985, they expected to phase out the veteran this season and install Hamilton in the hot corner. The club is so desperate for defense at third base that the youngster must only show promise with the bat to win the job.

His best home run year came at Double-A, where he hit 13 in 1985. The Dodgers, though, hope he could eventually hit 25 for this club in transition.

BASERUNNING:

Hamilton has a little speed but is no threat on the basepaths--14 steals in four professional seasons.

JEFF HAMILTON
3B, No. 33
RR, 6'3", 205 lbs.
ML Svc: 1 year
Born: 3-19-64 in Flint, MI

1986 STATISTICS

AVG	G	AB	R	H	2B	3B	HR	RBI	BB	SO	SB
.224	71	147	22	33	5	0	5	19	2	43	0

CAREER STATISTICS

AVG	G	AB	R	H	2B	3B	HR	RBI	BB	SO	SB
.224	71	147	22	33	5	0	5	19	2	43	0

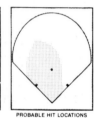

STRONG VS. RHP   STRONG VS. LHP   PROBABLE HIT LOCATIONS

FIELDING:

The Dodger front office, which may be overselling another prospect, compares Hamilton's throwing with that of the Cubs' Shawon Dunston.

Hamilton's range isn't phenomenal, but his soft hands and his good--but not great--arm make quite a package.

OVERALL:

Hamilton felt that he did not have much to learn by remaining at the Triple-A level last season and the Dodgers were forced to bring him up to Los Angeles. Hamilton might not be an Opening Day starter, but he is almost certain to play often this year--if only because Madlock needs so much R-and-R.

Dierker: "Hamilton struggled a little bit with big league pitching last year, mostly with the breaking stuff and pitches away. He was swinging at pitches out of the strike zone. With another year of maturity, he could develop into a fine hitter."

LOS ANGELES DODGERS

PITCHING:

Not long after Orel Hershiser was awarded a $1 million salary in arbitration last spring, a veteran teammate tabbed him as the Dodger most likely to struggle in 1986.

Hershiser wasn't the only Dodger disappointment or the biggest LA flop last season, but after going 19-3 with a 2.03 ERA in 1985, he slipped to 14-14 and 3.85 and had to admit he wasn't pitching as well as he had the previous year.

The sharpest criticism of Hershiser's 1986 performance came from one of Hershiser's best friends, Sid Bream, who played for the Dodgers before being traded to the Pirates in 1985. Bream made three points:

Hershiser was "choking his curveball and trying to emphasize turning the ball over." He therefore wasn't throwing as hard. And in a case of which-came-first, Bream noticed that Hershiser no longer displayed his usual healthy "cockiness" on the mound.

Hershiser's meek pitching was very much a part of Hershiser I, the relief pitcher who was so intimidated by big league hitters in 1984 that the Dodgers nearly gave up on him. Back then, Hershiser was accused of trying to make his pitches too fine instead of cutting loose. Hershiser II was the 1985 version, and last year, Hershiser III appeared. He denied that his poor performance last season was related to any pressure he might have felt because of that $788,000 raise the Dodgers gave him.

He was certainly confused but he did not panic and blamed his tendency to throw hittable pitches on 0-and-2 counts (a cardinal sin in Tommy Lasorda's book) for his less-than-spectacular year.

Because he displayed such outstanding stuff in 1985--his best pitches are a sinking fastball and a sharp-breaking curve--it's

OREL HERSHISER
RHP, No. 55
RR, 6'3", 195 lbs.
ML Svc: 3 years
Born: 9-16-58 in
Buffalo, NY

1986 STATISTICS

W	L	ERA	G	GS	CG	SV	IP	H	R	ER	BB	SO
14	14	3.85	35	35	8	0	231.1	213	112	99	86	153

CAREER STATISTICS

W	L	ERA	G	GS	CG	SV	IP	H	R	ER	BB	SO
44	25	2.85	124	89	25	3	668.2	559	255	212	210	465

assumed 1986 was an off-year and the real Hershiser lies somewhere in between.

FIELDING, HITTING, BASERUNNING:

A gifted if oddly built athlete who also excels at hockey and golf, Hershiser improved his fielding last year after leading all major league pitchers with seven errors in 1985. He still holds runners poorly.

Hershiser is an excellent hitting pitcher. In 1986 he led the Dodger staff in batting average (.239), runs batted in and sacrifice bunts. He was also Lasorda's first choice among the pitchers to pinch-run.

OVERALL:

Intelligent, analytical and easygoing, Hershiser is the kind of young man who will get the most out of his talent.

Dierker: "Hershiser has excellent control overall and is a good competitor. He did not have a good year in 1986, but the Dodgers as a whole were struggling and the team's plight probably affected him as well."

LOS ANGELES DODGERS

PITCHING:

In most cases, it's a good bet that a pitcher's career is in the balance when he experiments with a knuckleball.

Not in the case of Rick Honeycutt, who began throwing the novelty pitch in the middle of a June hot streak that put him atop the National League ERA rankings for a short time last year.

He tailed off after recording a 2.31 ERA in May and a 0.50 in June, but Honeycutt's fast start convinced the doubting Thomases (Lasorda among them) that the lefthander's 1984-85 shoulder trouble was over.

Honeycutt used the Charlie Hough-taught knuckleball as an off-speed pitch (as if he really needs another slow pitch) and it drew some double takes from veteran batters who were surprised by his flutterer.

Pitching without pain in the shoulder, Honeycutt was able to come over the top again in delivering his wicked sinker and slider.

He enjoyed a huge increase in strikeouts (to a career-high 100) and had a three-year low in walks (45).

Honeycutt, perhaps more than any other Dodgers pitcher, hopes for an improved bullpen. He has completed only one game in the last two seasons. Lasorda routinely pulls him at the first hint of trouble after the fifth inning.

FIELDING, HITTING, BASERUNNING:

Honeycutt, who was All-America as a first baseman at the University of Tennessee, is a good fielder and might be a very good hitting

RICK HONEYCUTT
LHP, No. 40
LL, 6'1", 193 lbs.
ML Svc: 10 years
Born: 6-29-54 in
Chattanooga, TN

1986 STATISTICS

W	L	ERA	G	GS	CG	SV	IP	H	R	ER	BB	SO
11	9	3.32	32	28	0	0	171	164	71	63	45	100

CAREER STATISTICS

W	L	ERA	G	GS	CG	SV	IP	H	R	ER	BB	SO
87	105	3.76	275	244	46	1	1562.1	1618	750	653	453	649

pitcher had he not spent three-plus years in the American League. He's not a good hitter.

Like most pitchers in the Tommy John/Geoff Zahn/soft-throwing/lefthanded mold, Honeycutt is very tough to run against.

OVERALL:

Honeycutt was back to his old ways in 1986--great start, poor finish. But it was an improvement over the year before, when he started 2-5 and never reached .500. His spot in the rotation (probably as the fourth man) seems secure this spring.

Dierker: "Honeycutt is a smart enough pitcher to know that he has to complement his bread-and-butter pitch, the sinker, with something to show when it's off. He induces a lot of ground balls, which may not be the best thing to do with this club, but when he has got the sinkerball working right, not many batters will get a piece of it anyway."

LOS ANGELES DODGERS

90+ FASTBALL

PITCHING:

Ken Howell is a very talented, hard-throwing righthander who's still learning to pitch in the major leagues.

Howell was proclaimed the Dodgers' bullpen ace after a rookie year (1984) in which he issued just five unintentional walks in 51 1/3 innings after a fast rise through the Dodgers' farm system.

Last season, after a sensational start, he wound up walking 63 batters in 97 2/3 innings, with a 6.30 ERA average in the second half. He was an emotional wreck by October.

The Dodgers would like to see Howell lose weight (he was listed at 228 pounds at the end of 1986 and is aiming for 205-210), correct a tendency to throw across his body and not be afraid to throw his 95 MPH fastball for strikes.

In exhibition games last spring, Dodger coaches had Howell draw a line on the mound with his toe to remind him not to plant his left foot too far to the right.

Howell, convinced batters have adjusted to his pitches since his brilliant rookie year, tries to nibble at the corners with his fastball and outstanding slider but just hasn't had the control to do so.

Pitching coach Ron Perranoski feels that everything will straighten out for Howell once he learns to throw the breaking ball for strikes.

FIELDING, HITTING, BASERUNNING:

Howell is a good fielder for a big man but must learn how to hold runners on base better. Last summer, he nearly decapitated

KEN HOWELL
RHP, No. 43
RR, 6'3", 216 lbs.
ML Svc: 3 years
Born: 11-28-60 in
Detroit, MI

1986 STATISTICS

W	L	ERA	G	GS	CG	SV	IP	H	R	ER	BB	SO
6	12	3.87	62	0	0	12	97.2	86	48	42	63	104

CAREER STATISTICS

W	L	ERA	G	GS	CG	SV	IP	H	R	ER	BB	SO
15	24	3.71	150	1	0	30	235	203	110	97	107	243

Bill Madlock with a 95 MPH "toss" to first base.

Howell is now 0-for-14 as a big league batter.

OVERALL:

"He could be a star," Dodgers Vice President Al Campanis says. Though that's certainly true, Howell must develop the maturity to pull out of his inevitable slumps, which tend to be disastrous. His ERAs for the last two Septembers: 6.41 and 7.36.

Dierker: "When he throws pitches that are anywhere near the proper location, Howell is almost an impossible pitcher to hit. But he finds himself getting behind in the count and throws down the middle of the plate. At this point, he is walking too many batters. He is not so unbelievably talented that he can get away with being wild."

LOS ANGELES DODGERS

HITTING:

Ken Landreaux was reduced to platooning with Reggie Williams in center field in 1986. And the 10-year veteran's role could diminish even further this season.

Landreaux's swing is simple and smooth but has become less and less productive over the past several seasons. He hasn't hit .270 for three years, doesn't have a lot of power and neither walks nor steals much.

A streak hitter, he was hottest in the middle of the summer for the second straight season. A .301 streak in July pushed Landreaux's average only as high as .267. Surgery to repair torn knee cartilage put him on the disabled list for August.

Landreaux can pull the ball out of the park if he gets a fastball on the inside part of the plate. In general, he prefers pitches thrown just below the belt. He has trouble, however, timing pitches that start in the middle of the strike zone and sink.

BASERUNNING:

Landreaux is quick but not intelligent on the bases. He had 61 steals between 1982 and 1983 but doesn't run as often now.

FIELDING:

Tommy Lasorda was so dumbfounded by a 1985 incident in which Landreaux actually covered his head while chasing a warning-track fly ball that the manager refused to discuss the play, saying, "I was getting a drink of water." Lasorda was fibbing, but Landreaux's defense does drive the Dodgers to drink.

Worse, the one-time American League All-Star doesn't see his own shortcomings, perhaps the result of the 1985 association with arrogant Al Oliver, one of the series of

KEN LANDREAUX
CF, No. 44
LR, 5'11", 179 lbs.
ML Svc: 10 years
Born: 12-22-54 in
Los Angeles, CA

1986 STATISTICS
AVG	G	AB	R	H	2B	3B	HR	RBI	BB	SO	SB
.261	103	283	34	74	13	2	4	29	22	39	10

CAREER STATISTICS
AVG	G	AB	R	H	2B	3B	HR	RBI	BB	SO	SB
.271	1149	3919	505	1062	176	45	85	456	283	393	140

VS. RHP

VS. LHP

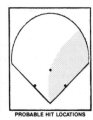

PROBABLE HIT LOCATIONS

veteran "mentors" the Dodgers hoped would have a steadying influence on Landreaux.

OVERALL:

Dodgers vice president Al Campanis listed center field as the club's No. 2 weakness--behind the bullpen--but was rebuffed in his attempts to acquire a center fielder at the winter meetings. He hoped to complete a trade by Opening Day.

Dierker: "He just has a nice swing and is going to get a lot of hits but not produce as much as the Dodgers would like from an outfielder.

"Landreaux seems to have reached the point in his career where he is not an everyday center fielder."

LOS ANGELES DODGERS

PITCHING:

Long before Dwight Gooden's arrival, Tim Leary was the young pitcher who made everybody's eyes pop when he showed up in the New York Mets' camp in 1981. With only one year of Double-A ball to his credit, Leary impressed everyone with his live fastball and won a spot in the Mets' starting rotation. The success story didn't last very long, however. Leary strained a muscle in his arm in his first major league start and spent the next four years coming back from arm problems.

Because of his arm problems, Leary has never lived up to the advance billing, but he looks as though he may be salvaging something of his career after having moderate success with the Milwaukee Brewers in 1986. He appeared to be throwing almost as hard as he had been in 1981, but he wasn't able to put everything together to become a consistent major league pitcher. In one game, he would appear to be one of the top pitchers in the league, but he wasn't able to follow up a good performance with another quality effort.

Leary's fastball is still his best pitch, but at times last year, he seemed to forget that and relied too much on his breaking pitches. His slider is his best breaking pitch but he's inconsistent with his control of it.

He has a long, loose motion that may have something to do with his inconsistency. With that kind of delivery, more things are subject to go wrong. Perhaps he should try to develop a more compact motion, which would cut down on the mechanical problems.

FIELDING:

Leary's move to first base is average and he will throw to first to keep runners honest. He fields his position adequately and gets over to

TIM LEARY
RHP, No. 39
RR, 6'3", 190 lbs.
ML Svc: 2 years
Born: 12-23-58 in
Santa Monica, CA

1986 STATISTICS

W	L	ERA	G	GS	CG	SV	IP	H	R	ER	BB	SO
12	12	4.21	33	30	3	0	188.1	216	97	88	53	110

CAREER STATISTICS

W	L	ERA	G	GS	CG	SV	IP	H	R	ER	BB	SO
17	20	4.09	61	45	4	0	288	332	153	131	84	180

first base well on balls hit to the right side of the infield.

OVERALL:

Leary appears to have overcome his arm problems and has been left with a fastball that is still above average. It has taken him a long time to come back, however, and he must become more consistent to be a successful pitcher in the major leagues.

He has been a starting pitcher for most of his career and that probably is the best spot for him, but with his live fastball, he could pitch in short relief.

Kaat: "Concentration, control and durability are things he has to improve on this year if he is to become anywhere near what people thought he would be when he first came up.

"He needs to be more of a challenging pitcher, to use his fastball more and not pitch too cautiously."

LOS ANGELES DODGERS

HITTING:

Believing that a well-conditioned Bill Madlock would be a durable Bill Madlock, the Dodgers put him on a Nautilus-and-running program before the 1986 season. It backfired.

After that winter regimen and the Dodgers' rigorous spring training, Madlock, then 35, said he began a season tired for the first time in his long career.

Madlock strained his left hip and went on the disabled list in April, was in and out of the lineup, and was batting .230 at the All-Star break before coming alive with a .322 second half.

Madlock may have to fight to keep Jeff Hamilton from taking the third-base job away from him this year.

The August 31, 1985, trade for Madlock secured the division championship for Los Angeles. He hit .360 down the stretch and was a force in the clubhouse. He hit three homers in the championship series loss to St. Louis.

The Dodgers realize now, though, that this lifetime .307 hitter is on his last legs, and those legs need frequent rest. Madlock wouldn't fight a trade to the American League, where grass fields and/or the designated hitter rule could prolong his career.

Madlock uses a small bat and a short stroke that allows him to pull fastballs and line breaking pitches to the right-center-field alley.

BASERUNNING:

The thick muscles in Madlock's legs are subject to tears and pulls and the frequent injuries have robbed him of the speed that once guaranteed him 15 to 20 steals a year. He's an intelligent, aggressive runner with just enough stamina to leg out a double.

FIELDING:

Every Doggie (his nickname) has his day,

BILL MADLOCK
3B, No. 12
RR, 5'11", 212 lbs.
ML Svc: 14 years
Born: 1-12-51 in
Memphis, TN

1986 STATISTICS

AVG	G	AB	R	H	2B	3B	HR	RBI	BB	SO	SB
.280	111	379	38	106	17	0	10	60	30	43	3

CAREER STATISTICS

AVG	G	AB	R	H	2B	3B	HR	RBI	BB	SO	SB
.307	1698	6207	859	1906	330	34	146	803	571	460	170

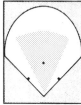

VS. RHP VS. LHP PROBABLE HIT LOCATIONS

like the one in June when, on his toes because soft-throwing Rick Honeycutt was pitching, Madlock made five sensational plays at third base. But shoulder and elbow problems have weakened his arm and the nagging leg injuries leave him with little range. Madlock's .910 fielding percentage in 1986 was the lowest among major leaguers playing 100 or more games at third.

OVERALL:

Madlock is in the last year of his contract, just as he was when he won three of his four National League batting titles.

Dierker: "Madlock is on the downside of his career. Unless he can have a comeback type of season in 1987, I think the Dodgers will be a little bit below average at third base with Madlock playing everyday."

LOS ANGELES DODGERS

HITTING:

When he's healthy, Mike Marshall is capable of 11 home runs in a month, as he hit in September 1985, or 18 homers in a half-season, as he had by the All-Star break in 1986. But he's never stayed healthy.

Last year, a mysterious back stiffness--believed related to a 1985 appendectomy that weakened his stomach muscles--limited Marshall to 44 at-bats and three hits in the second half.

A winter program of running, swimming, biking and weight-lifting had Marshall fit enough to swing a bat again in December. He gave up golf on the advice of doctors who felt the twisting action was bad for his back. Marshall was also fitted for eyeglasses in the offseason to correct his astigmatism and underwent "eye training," a crash course in focusing through lenses. It is expected that he will be a "new" Mike Marshall in 1987.

The glasses may help him to improve his walks-to-strikeouts ratio. Marshall is a very aggressive hitter who is still learning the strike zone and could threaten the Dodgers record for strikeouts in a season (149 by Billy Grabarkewitz). The Dodgers will accept the strikeouts, of course, because he could just as easily break the Los Angeles club's record for homers (33 by Steve Garvey and Pedro Guerrero).

Marshall bats in a slight crouch and, despite a 1983 beaning by Jeff Reardon, crowds the plate and likes pitches up. He can hammer the ball to right field, which is the one big reason many people in baseball compare him to Atlanta's Dale Murphy.

BASERUNNING:

Marshall has been thrown out on 14 of 21 basestealing attempts over the last two years. His back problem won't make him any faster.

FIELDING:

He would rather play first base, but Marshall never loafs in right field, where he's

MIKE MARSHALL
RF, No. 5
RR, 6'5", 220 lbs.
ML Svc: 6 years
Born: 1-12-60 in
Libertyville, IL

1986 STATISTICS

AVG	G	AB	R	H	2B	3B	HR	RBI	BB	SO	SB
.233	103	330	47	77	11	0	19	53	27	90	4

CAREER STATISTICS

AVG	G	AB	R	H	2B	3B	HR	RBI	BB	SO	SB
.268	575	1928	246	516	88	3	90	288	161	474	20

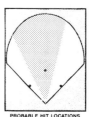

STRONG   STRONG

VS. RHP   VS. LHP   PROBABLE HIT LOCATIONS

mastered the sliding catch of bloopers near the line and isn't afraid to crash into walls. He has a strong, accurate arm.

OVERALL:

Marshall still must prove himself to many in Los Angeles, partly because he can look so bad at the plate when he's slumping and striking out a lot, and partly because many are skeptical of all his injuries.

The skeptics--including teammate Bill Russell, who confronted Marshall on this point--wondered if he "rested" his back longer than necessary in August and September to protect his numbers.

Dierker: "There is really not a single best way to pitch him except to look at him in the same sense as Dale Murphy: when he's hot, be careful with him, but when he's not, go after him and mix it up and move it around in the strike zone."

LOS ANGELES DODGERS

PITCHING:

The home run cannonade that began with the 1985 playoff game-winner by St. Louis' Ozzie Smith continued into early June last season, as Tom Niedenfuer suffered his worst season in the major leagues in 1986.

From the playoff homers by Smith and Jack Clark through grand slams by the Mets' George Foster and the Pirates' Jim Morrison, the big Dodger righthander gave up nine home runs in a 31 1/3-inning stretch.

Said teammate Bill Russell: "If he tried to say, "Here, hit the ball out,' I don't think he could do it as well."

Niedenfuer insisted he wasn't throwing all that poorly--just a bad pitch, and boom, home run--but some thought his rising fastball wasn't as fast. (His strikeouts were down dramatically.) The other view, held by Tommy Lasorda, was that Niedenfuer was still throwing his best stuff, but that he wasn't able to get his pitches anywhere *near* where he wanted to place them. Niedenfuer's location in 1986 was terrible.

After giving up nine homers in the first three months of 1986, however, Niedenfuer did settle down, and allowed just two for the rest of the season. He recorded a 1.80 ERA in August before going on the disabled list with a hamstring strain.

Niedenfuer, who was the National League's best reliever in 1983 (8-3, 1.90) but had a series of elbow ailments in 1984, is subject to fatigue and injury if he is overworked. Lasorda needs to pick this pitcher's spots carefully.

Niedenfuer throws a fastball in the low- to mid-90s and has an outstanding slider. Last season, he continued to experiment with a split-finger fastball as an off-speed pitch.

TOM NIEDENFUER
RHP, No. 49
RR, 6'5", 230 lbs.
ML Svc: 6 years
Born: 8-13-59 in
St. Louis Park, MN

1986 STATISTICS

W	L	ERA	G	GS	CG	SV	IP	H	R	ER	BB	SO
6	6	3.71	60	0	0	11	80	86	35	33	29	55

CAREER STATISTICS

W	L	ERA	G	GS	CG	SV	IP	H	R	ER	BB	SO
29	28	2.76	295	0	0	63	424	362	136	130	136	340

FIELDING, HITTING, BASERUNNING:

Niedenfuer has an average move to first base and a slow delivery to the plate. He is a solid fielder, however. (His only error over the last two years came immediately after the brawl with Ray Knight that followed the Foster grand slam in May.)

He is uncomfortable at the plate but did manage to hit a single twice in four at-bats last year.

OVERALL:

For the third straight winter, Niedenfuer was part of rumored trades for a center fielder, especially after the Dodgers acquired reliever Matt Young from Seattle.

Dierker: "He's a challenging type of pitcher, the kind of guy you like to have come in and take charge. He had his problems last year and some injuries, but I think he'll come back and pitch better for the Dodgers this season."

LOS ANGELES DODGERS

PITCHING:

A Dodger scout in the Dominican Republic reported that Alejandro Pena was throwing 92 MPH in the seventh inning of winter league games last December. If that's true, it would represent the longest and hardest that this former fireballer has been able to throw since he underwent shoulder surgery in February 1985.

It would also make Pena a challenger for the fifth spot in the Dodger rotation this season, which tentatively belonged to Tim Leary.

In 1984, before damaging the cartilage in his right shoulder and missing virtually all of September, Pena had a 95 MPH fastball and the National League's lowest ERA (2.48). The injury had some in the Dodger organization doubting he would ever pitch in the big leagues again. After a long rehabilitation, though, Pena started one game in September 1985.

He did not make smooth progress last spring and began the season on the disabled list before being sent to the minors on a rehabilitaion assignment. His numbers there (0-2, 7.47 ERA, 22 hits in 15 2/3 innings) bore testimony to Pena's inconsistency.

The Dodgers were anxious to see if Pena could pitch effectively if tried in consecutive appearances last year. He did that in early July, coming back five days after a strong, 5 2/3-inning outing against Cincinnati to shut out St. Louis for five innings and collect his first victory in nearly two years.

Pena has worked hard to smooth out his delivery, which, if successful, would allow him to continue to throw his slider.

The problem is that Pena's lack of stamina limits his effectiveness as a starter and the

ALEJANDRO PENA
RHP, No. 26
RR, 6'1", 205 lbs.
ML Svc: 4 years
Born: 6-25-59 in
    Cambiaso,
        Dominican Republic

1986 STATISTICS

W	L	ERA	G	GS	CG	SV	IP	H	R	ER	BB	SO
1	2	4.89	24	10	0	1	70	74	40	38	30	46

CAREER STATISTICS

W	L	ERA	G	GS	CG	SV	IP	H	R	ER	BB	SO
26	21	3.13	131	65	12	3	511.1	474	211	178	162	337

time it takes him to get loose--about 15 minutes, normally--precludes using him as a reliever.

FIELDING, HITTING, BASERUNNING:

Pena throws to first base often but his delivery, which is slower now than ever before, keeps him from holding runners on base very well. He's an erratic fielder.

As a batter, Pena is not afraid to swing, for better or worse.

OVERALL:

Pena's quiet, unemotional demeanor, which has made it tough for Dodger trainers to monitor his progress, has also helped him to endure a series of disappointments since the surgery several years ago.

If Pena could come back this year (the Dodgers don't even want to wish out loud that he might be back to full strength), he would boost a club that could use it this year.

LOS ANGELES DODGERS

PITCHING:

The Dodgers no longer expect Jerry Reuss to live up to his $1 million salary. They no longer expect to be able to trade him. They *do* hope,. however, that he can bounce back from an injury-ravaged season as he did in 1985, when he won 14 games.

After acquiring Tim Leary from Milwaukee at the winter meetings, Dodgers Vice President Al Campanis said the newcomer would battle Alejandro Pena for the fifth starter job. And what about Reuss? "Reuss," Campanis said, "will have to prove to us that he can still be a starter."

By anybody's standards, especially a 194-game winner's, 1986 was a terrible year for Reuss, who gave up 96 hits (including 13 home runs) in 74 innings. The question is: how much of the trouble was caused by bone chips in the left elbow that required arthroscopic surgery in July, and how much was the result of his advancing age. Reuss, for one, is convinced that his career as a major league pitcher is not over. He plans to become a four-decade major leaguer by pitching for another four years.

Reuss had surgery to remove a bone fragment from his elbow in January 1984 and pitched that season with bone spurs in both of his heels. But after having the spurs removed, Reuss came back in 1985 with a sinking fastball that, though nowhere near its prime velocity, was low and effective. He used his slow curve and change-up more often to keep hitters off balance.

A switch to the bullpen is unlikely to satisfy either Reuss or the Dodgers. He was forced to make 15 relief appearances in 1984; he hated it and it showed--he was pretty bad as a reliever.

JERRY REUSS
LHP, No. 41
LL, 6'5", 227 lbs.
ML Svc: 17 years
Born: 6-19-49 in
St. Louis, MO

1986 STATISTICS

W	L	ERA	G	GS	CG	SV	IP	H	R	ER	BB	SO
2	6	5.84	19	13	0	1	74	96	57	48	17	29

CAREER STATISTICS

W	L	ERA	G	GS	CG	SV	IP	H	R	ER	BB	SO
194	163	3.50	537	468	123	11	3219.1	3206	1438	1251	1018	1744

FIELDING, HITTING, BASERUNNING:

Dodger pitching coach Ron Perranoski ran fielding drills early last season for Reuss because the pitcher is prone to wild throws. Whatever the technique for alteration the coach offered, it seems to have worked: Reuss didn't commit an error all year last season.

Reuss has a fine move to first base. In 1985, he was the toughest National League pitcher to run on.

He's a good hitting pitcher but a poor bunter.

OVERALL:

With his contract due to expire, Reuss needs a big year this season to keep the Dodgers interested.

Dierker: "A cut fastball is his devastating pitch. It runs away from lefthanded batters and in on righthanders. Reuss needs to maintain his velocity on that pitch to make it effective; he simply didn't have it last year."

LOS ANGELES DODGERS

HITTING:

Several years ago, Steve Sax was so erratic the Dodgers took steps to see if their second baseman had a drug problem. He didn't. He just needed time to settle down and grow into his role as a major leaguer.

Sax was so consistent in 1986 that despite leading the team in hitting by 53 points, he wasn't voted "Dodger of the Month" by local reporters until September. His averages for the first four months were .333, .315, .319 and .348. During the course of the season, someone on the team was more spectacular--but none were steadier. Only once did Sax go three games without a hit last year.

Continuing a turnaround that saw him bat .311 in the last half of 1985, he came within two points of the National League batting title and added some much-needed power to his game. He became only the fourth man to collect 200 hits while playing half his games at Dodger Stadium.

Sax, whose good looks and charm have led to television work and to the authoring of a book, said he blocked out outside distractions better last season than he has been able to in the past. But he made technical improvements, too.

Sax stopped trying to pull everything and started driving balls up the middle. He stopped "muscling up," rotated his hips more and gripped the bat more loosely to put some snap in his swing. The result: Sax hit the ball farther. After having only 13 extra-base hits in 1985, fewest among major leaguers who qualified for the batting title, he hit a career-high six homers last season and was second in the NL with 43 doubles.

Sax likes high fastballs that he can punch up the middle or over the second baseman. He doesn't chase as many bad pitches as he used to.

Sax batted at the top of the order for most of 1986, though the Dodgers would prefer to lead off with Mariano Duncan to take advantage of the shortstop's great speed.

BASERUNNING:

Sax was the only member of the Dodgers'

STEVE SAX
2B, No. 3
RR, 5'11", 185 lbs.
ML Svc: 6 years
Born: 1-29-60 in
   West Sacramento, CA

1986 STATISTICS

AVG	G	AB	R	H	2B	3B	HR	RBI	BB	SO	SB
.332	157	633	91	210	43	4	6	56	59	58	40

CAREER STATISTICS

AVG	G	AB	R	H	2B	3B	HR	RBI	BB	SO	SB
.284	774	3070	420	872	118	24	19	230	274	294	211

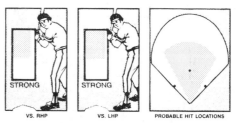

hoped-for starting eight who didn't go on the disabled list in 1986, but he played with a bone spur in his right heel. Despite the discomfort, Sax stole 40 bases in 57 attempts. He's a smarter baserunner now than he was in previous seasons.

FIELDING:

Confidence at the plate has led to confidence in the field, and Sax has put the throwing "yips" of 1983 behind him. That doesn't make him more than an adequate second baseman, though, and there are those in baseball who claim that he is the worst defensive second baseman in the league.

Sax's first step is frequently in the wrong direction and, though he makes many diving stops, he gets rid of the ball slowly. He is often prone to strategic blunders.

OVERALL:

Dierker: "Steve has become a real asset to the Dodgers. His hitting improved awfully well last season and I expect that he will hit at least as well for many seasons to come."

LOS ANGELES DODGERS

HITTING:

Mike Scioscia has about as much speed as Tommy Lasorda and abysmal power for a 220-pound man. All Scioscia does is get on base--a lot.

A lingering ankle injury last season cost Scioscia a shot at hitting in the .290s for the second straight year. In sum, 1986 was Scioscia's worst season since a 1983 rotator-cuff tear threatened his career.

Scioscia has a very level swing that puts backspin on the ball and helps it carry. Unlike most lefthanded hitters, he likes the ball above the belt. He often yanks pitches into the right-field corner for doubles.

Scioscia has exceptional knowledge of the strike zone. He's walked 191 times and fanned just 70 times in the last three years.

Lasorda likes to use Scioscia anywhere from sixth to eighth in the Dodger lineup, though some members of his coaching staff argued the catcher's bat control, bunting ability and patience make him the club's best available No. 2 hitter. Scioscia would prefer to bat there, too, and supported his case by reaching base in six of his first seven plate appearances in the No. 2 spot in 1986.

But Lasorda scrapped the idea, fearful the slow-footed Scioscia would clog the bases.

BASERUNNING:

Well, Lasorda's right. He would clog the bases.

FIELDING:

Scioscia has the respect of the Dodger pitching staff for both his glovework and brainwork behind the plate. And he has the respect of National League baserunners for his bravery in front of the plate. If you've seen any ballpark highlights videos the last three years, you know about Scioscia's plate-blocking prowess.

He tends to have throwing slumps unrelated to the 1983 shoulder injury.

MIKE SCIOSCIA
C, No. 14
LR, 6'2", 220 lbs.
ML Svc: 7 years
Born: 11-27-58 in
Upper Darby, PA

1986 STATISTICS

AVG	G	AB	R	H	2B	3B	HR	RBI	BB	SO	SB
.251	122	374	36	94	18	1	5	26	62	23	3

CAREER STATISTICS

AVG	G	AB	R	H	2B	3B	HR	RBI	BB	SO	SB
.264	665	1968	181	519	91	6	26	199	288	130	11

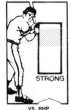

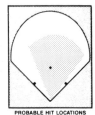

VS. RHP　　VS. LHP　　PROBABLE HIT LOCATIONS

Scioscia blamed poor footwork--which can be traced to the ankle problem--for a rash of throwing errors last season.

Ironically, Scioscia suffered the torn membrane in his right ankle in an innocuous-looking play at the plate, when Cincinnati pitcher Tom Browning slid under him on June 9th last year.

OVERALL:

Scioscia's defense makes him a key to Dodger success. But he must either maintain a very high on-base percentage or develop some power to be a great asset offensively.

Dierker: "Mike is an asset in the lineup in the sense that by getting on base more, you turn the lineup over more often. I think the Dodgers would rather have him get on base less and hit with more power, but sometimes you've got to go with the tools you've got."

LOS ANGELES DODGERS

HITTING:

About once a year, through a combination of luck and a fertile farm system, the Dodgers discover a star because of injury to an established player. Fernando Valenzuela, Steve Sax and Mariano Duncan got their breaks that way, and last year, it was Franklin Stubbs' turn.

Stubbs would have been the last player cut from the Opening Day roster had Pedro Guerrero not torn his knee on the last day of spring training in Florida. Stubbs, a natural first baseman, responded well to the challenge of playing left field.

He had 15 home runs at the All-Star break before tailing off badly as pitchers began to jam him with fastballs up-and-in and keep him off balance with change-ups and breaking balls. Stubbs stands upright at the plate and likes pitches above the belt. What Stubbs has to find now is consistency.

Stubbs was rushed to the major leagues in 1984 and suffered for it, striking out nearly one-third of the time and losing his confidence in the shuffle. The Dodgers kept him in the minors in 1985 and he hit 32 homers.

Stubbs still hasn't solved the strike zone. Last year he fanned a team-high 107 times, but walked just 37 times, which is not enough for such a dangerous hitter.

The combination of power and surprising speed give Stubbs the potential to be an outstanding offensive player.

BASERUNNING:

Stubbs is pretty quick for a guy only five pounds lighter than Mike Scioscia. He stole 23 bases in the minors in 1985 and seven in eight tries for the Dodgers last year.

FIELDING:

Stubbs doesn't have the range of an experienced left fielder and he made a lot of mistakes in the field last year. But he threw

FRANKLIN STUBBS
INF, No. 22
LL, 6'2", 215 lbs.
ML Svc: 3 years
Born: 10-21-60 in
Laurinburg, NC

1986 STATISTICS

AVG	G	AB	R	H	2B	3B	HR	RBI	BB	SO	SB
.226	132	420	55	95	11	1	23	58	37	107	7

CAREER STATISTICS

AVG	G	AB	R	H	2B	3B	HR	RBI	BB	SO	SB
.215	229	646	77	139	13	4	31	77	61	173	9

VS. RHP   VS. LHP   PROBABLE HIT LOCATIONS

out runners who took too much license and looked more comfortable than several veterans the Dodgers have tried out there in recent years.

Stubbs isn't as good a first baseman as Greg Brock. "Adequate," said Monty Basgall, the Dodgers' longtime infield tutor, describing Stubbs' ability as a first baseman.

OVERALL:

With Greg Brock out of the picture and Guerrero ticketed for left field, Stubbs will go to spring training as the Dodgers' first baseman. The stability should help his hitting.

Dierker: "He's got a tremendous amount of hitting potential, as he showed in the first half of last season, but he also has a few holes, as he showed in the second half. He does have raw power and is dangerous when you make a mistake."

LOS ANGELES DODGERS

PITCHING:

Tommy Lasorda's standing joke about Fernando Valenzuela's toughness is, "He doesn't even know we have a bullpen." Yet the lefthander's determination to finish everything he starts has caused some concern within the Los Angeles organization in recent years, when his late-season slumps, tinged with rumors of a sore shoulder, twice cost him 20 victories in a season.

So in 1986, Lasorda took several opportunities to rest his ace, pulling him from games the Dodgers led comfortably. Valenzuela still led the National League with 20 complete games and ran second with 269 1/3 innings, but he had enough left to go 4-2 in September and October and become the Dodgers' first 20-game winner since Tommy John in 1977.

Valenzuela got little help along the way from the rest of the club, both offensively and defensively.

To beat Fernando, you've got to get to him early, though even when he bends early, he rarely breaks. In his signature performances, Valenzuela struggles to find his control in the first inning, pitches out of trouble repeatedly and doesn't begin to blow batters away until late in the game.

Valenzuela throws a fastball (in the mid- to high-80s), curveball and slider, but what sets him apart are two types of screwballs--a hard one that tails away from righthanded hitters and an off-speed one. He tries to paint the corners of the plate with each delivery.

When he doesn't have outstanding control, he'll walk batters and get in trouble. But he'll usually find a way out of any jam.

FIELDING, HITTING, BASERUNNING:

Valenzuela is an outstanding, daring fielder who handles bunts as well as any pitcher in the league. He even "hiked" a throw to first

FERNANDO VALENZUEL
LHP, No. 34
LL, 5'11", 200 lbs.
ML Svc: 6 years
Born: 11-1-60 in
  Navajoa, Sonora,
  Mexico

1986 STATISTICS

W	L	ERA	G	GS	CG	SV	IP	H	R	ER	BB	SO
21	11	3.14	34	34	20	0	269.1	226	104	94	85	242

CAREER STATISTICS

W	L	ERA	G	GS	CG	SV	IP	H	R	ER	BB	SO
99	68	2.94	210	200	84	1	1554.2	1295	589	507	540	1274

base after gloving a dribbler along the line in an August game against Houston last year. He has a sneaky move to first and is one of the toughest pitchers to steal against.

Although Valenzuela lost the pitching staff's spirited batting race to Orel Hershiser in 1986, he is one of the best all-around offensive players at his position in the major leagues. He struck out just 11 times in 109 at-bats, one of four Dodgers to fan 10% of the time or less. Though you wouldn't know it to look at him, Valenzuela is a very good baserunner.

OVERALL:

Fernando, whose unswerving good humor makes him a favorite of teammates and Los Angeles fans, is an excellent investment for the Dodgers at $1.85 million, which is the highest salary for a pitcher this season.

Dierker: "Fernando is just a great all-around baseball player, the type of guy who can beat you so many ways. He'll help himself with his bat and his glove. He managed to win 21 games last season for a club that wasn't very good; that achievement alone speaks volumes about this prize pitcher."

LOS ANGELES DODGERS

PITCHING:

Don't be deceived by Bob Welch's first losing season since 1979. Look at his ERA, which was second on the team to Fernando Valenzuela's.

Welch was cheated out of more victories than any other Dodger pitcher by the Dodgers offense last year. Ten times in his first 20 starts, he gave up two or fewer earned runs--and his record was only 2-3. In his 13 defeats, Welch's teammates produced a total of 21 runs.

Ever since he was a junior at Eastern Michigan University, Welch has pitched during the spring with pain in his right elbow, the result of bone spurs. In 1985, the spurs led to tendinitis and Welch missed most of the first two months of the season. He came back to have his finest season (14-4, 2.31 ERA) that year.

Hoping to avoid the annual flareup, Dodger doctors ordered Welch to throw over the winter following the '85 season for the first time in his career and to give up batting practice, which they felt put undue strain on the elbow.

Welch responded with a fine start (3-1, 1.44 ERA in April), but then didn't win again until July. That's partly a reflection of his pitching--he had trouble finding his rhythm and his control--but mostly it was the Dodger offense (or lack of it, in this case).

The Dodgers are still waiting for Welch, who will be 31 this year, to become a star. He's still an over-the-top power pitcher with a fastball and curveball, but became another convert to the split-finger fastball in 1985, and that gives him an effective change-up.

BOB WELCH
RHP, No. 35
RR, 6'3", 192 lbs.
ML Svc: 9 years
Born: 11-3-56 in Detroit, MI

1986 STATISTICS

W	L	ERA	G	GS	CG	SV	IP	H	R	ER	BB	SO
7	13	3.28	33	33	7	0	253.2	227	95	86	55	183

CAREER STATISTICS

W	L	ERA	G	GS	CG	SV	IP	H	R	ER	BB	SO
100	77	3.09	257	232	41	8	1587	1427	608	545	479	1096

FIELDING, HITTING, BASERUNNING:

Welch has a quick move to first base and is better than average at holding runners on base. He's a good fielder.

What Welch does best at the plate is bunt, because that's about all he's allowed to do in batting practice now.

OVERALL:

Many thought that Welch, not Pedro Guerrero, was the key to the Dodgers' success in 1985. The club must keep him healthy--and supplied with runs.

Dierker: "I think he succumbed to the overall negative play of Los Angeles last season and wasn't able to rise above it, though he is an outstanding talent. I will be very surprised if he doesn't have a better year this year."

LOS ANGELES DODGERS

HITTING:

Reggie Williams did nothing spectacularly but everything well enough to help the Dodgers out of a tough spot last year. Williams, kept on the Opening Day roster as a fourth outfielder, wound up playing 128 games because of all the Dodger injuries last year and was hitting .304 at the All-Star break.

Williams, whose fireplug physique led fans to mistake him for Bill Madlock, also displayed Madlock's affinity for hitting the ball where it's pitched, spraying it to all fields.

The rookie learned fast, as cum laude honors at Southern University would suggest, and he adjusted quickly to major-league pitching. After looking bad on two Cecilio Guante curveballs, Williams knocked a third curve out of the park to win a July game at Pittsburgh last year. His first two homers came on curveballs. That's tough--very tough--for a rookie big league hitter to do.

Williams seemed almost embarrassed by the homers and might show more power this year if he doesn't concentrate so hard on hitting line drives.

The alternative is to learn to walk more, improve his on-base rate to take better advantage of his speed.

BASERUNNING:

Williams was bothered by a bone spur in his heel and bone chips in his ankle but managed to steal nine bases in 12 attempts. The scout who signed him called Williams "a human jet."

FIELDING:

Williams made several spectacular diving catches in center field last year and has a good

REGGIE WILLIAMS
OF, No. 21
RR, 5'10", 180 lbs.
ML Svc: 1 year
Born: 8-29-60 in
Memphis, TN

1986 STATISTICS

AVG	G	AB	R	H	2B	3B	HR	RBI	BB	SO	SB
.277	128	303	35	84	14	2	4	32	23	57	9

CAREER STATISTICS

AVG	G	AB	R	H	2B	3B	HR	RBI	BB	SO	SB
.279	150	312	39	87	14	2	4	32	23	61	10

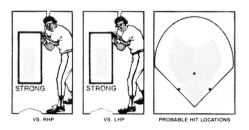

VS. RHP — VS. LHP — PROBABLE HIT LOCATIONS

arm. Aside from some trouble judging fly balls in unfamiliar stadiums, he was the Dodgers' steadiest outfielder in 1986.

OVERALL:

With the expected return to health of Pedro Guerrero and Mike Marshall, management's excitement about Ralph Bryant and the Dodgers' continued confidence in Jose Gonzalez, it's hard to say where the quiet, businesslike Williams fits in.

Dierker: "If Williams doesn't show the Dodgers more than just an ability to hit .270-.280 with no walks or home runs, he probably won't impress them enough to get a lot of playing time this season."

LOS ANGELES DODGERS

PITCHING:

After being a starter throughout his career, Matt Young was shifted to the bullpen early last summer and that now appears to be the best place for him. Never a big winner as a starter, Young showed flashes of brilliance coming out of the bullpen, but he still wasn't consistent enough.

He saved 13 games last year--more than twice as many as any other pitcher on the Mariner staff. But he had a chance to save 19 others and didn't. Maybe he will be better now that he has had basically one full season behind him.

Only two pitchers in the American League had fastballs clocked at 95 MPH at the Kingdome last year. Roger Clemens was one and Matt Young was the other.

Besides having an outstanding fastball, Young has a slider that runs in hard on righthanded batters and sharply away from lefthanders. His curveball is acceptable, but could be better.

For some reason, Young's control is much better as a reliever than it was as a starter. Perhaps it has something to do with concentration. He walked 13 in 20 innings as a starter while striking out 10. In 60 relief appearances, he struck out 72 in 83 innings and walked 33. As a starter, he had a tendency to nibble too much, but he seemed to conquer that as a reliever, reflected by the fewer number of walks he allowed coming out of the bullpen.

A 20-game stretch in June and July made one sit up and take notice of Young. He was 3-0 with 8 saves and had a .1.05 ERA during a two-month streak of superb relief.

FIELDING:

Any time Young catches a comebacker and has to throw the ball to first base, it is an adventure. He will run to the base and toss

MATT YOUNG
LHP, No. 40
LL, 6'3", 205 lbs.
ML Svc: 4 years
Born: 8-9-58 in
Pasadena, CA

1986 STATISTICS
W	L	ERA	G	GS	CG	SV	IP	H	R	ER	BB	SO
8	6	3.82	65	5	1	13	103.2	108	50	44	46	82

CAREER STATISTICS
W	L	ERA	G	GS	CG	SV	IP	H	R	ER	BB	SO
37	48	4.35	157	94	12	14	639	669	352	309	258	421

the ball underhanded, rather than throwing overhand after he makes the play. He has a mental block about throwing the ball overhand to first base and has been known to throw balls almost directly into the ground. That is not a good trait for any pitcher-- *especially* a reliever.

Although he's a lefthander, Young's pickoff move to first base is not very good. He has a high leg-kick, which only makes stealing a base against him that much easier.

OVERALL:

Up to now, Young has been one of those can't-miss prospects who has somehow managed to miss. The Dodgers are hopeful that he can become the best lefthanded short reliever they've had since Steve Howe.

Killebrew: "He throws over the top with a herky-jerky motion which I think is to his advantage. It's tough for hitters to pick up his pitches. He uses his change-up against the good hitters. He is not afraid to pitch inside to righthanded hitters and that's important for a lefthander. He has a tendency to be wild, but I feel his future is as a reliever."

DAVE ANDERSON
INF, No. 10
RR, 6'2", 185 lbs.
ML Svc: 4 years
Born: 8-1-60 in
Louisville, KY

HITTING, BASERUNNING, FIELDING:

The Dodgers kept Dave Anderson and dumped Bob Bailor in spring training in 1986, believing the younger utility man would be more versatile. The Dodgers were right. Anderson, who had to prove his value after signing a non-guaranteed contract, even volunteered to be the club's union representative and "emergency" third-string catcher.

Though Anderson filled in adequately last season for Bill Madlock at third base and Mariano Duncan at shortstop, he remained the Dodgers' biggest disappointment among recent Albuquerque grads. He lacks the power to start at third base and the range to start at short on an everyday basis.

Last season, Dodgers hitting instructor Ben Hines worked on getting Anderson to attack the ball more aggressively. A straightaway hitter who likes the ball up but is no home run threat, Anderson spent this winter trying to simplify his stroke and produce more line drives.

He once stole 43 bases in Albuquerque (in 1982, the year he batted .343.). Although he claims no lingering effects of the 1985 back trouble, Anderson tried to steal only six times last season.

OVERALL:

Dierker: "Anderson's job is safe this spring following the retirement of Bill Russell and the departure of Enos Cabell. As long as injury-prone Madlock and Duncan man the left side of the infield, Los Angeles will need Anderson on the bench."

RALPH BRYANT
OF, No. 46
LR, 6'2", 205 lbs.
ML Svc: less than
one year
Born: 5-20-61 in
Ft. Gaines, GA

HITTING, BASERUNNING, FIELDING:

Soon after Ralph Bryant was recalled from the minors for the first time in July last year, it became clear why Dodger scouts said he has the "fastest bat in the organization." His bat is rarely slowed by contact with the ball.

When Bryant doesn't strike out, the ball goes a long way. When he was recalled in September, he had six homers, two triples and four doubles among 19 hits, all against righthanded pitching. Bryant tends to uppercut but is not strictly a pull hitter. Half his September homers, in fact, went to the opposite field.

Bryant's name was on the lips of Dodgers vice president Al Campanis all winter as the lefthanded swinger threatened Dominican Republic Winter League power records. The problem: How to use him in Los Angeles? The Dodgers' outfield opening is in center field, but Bryant is no better than an average defensive player, despite his fair speed.

He seems unlikely to wilt under the heat of Dodger expectations. Bryant doesn't get down on himself. Distracted by the Astrodome ceiling in his first indoor game last season, Bryant committed a four-base error and a two-base error and played an out into a triple, all in the span of two innings, and heard laughter from the Houston fans. Bryant laughed about it, too, though, and regarded it as a learning experience.

OVERALL:

Dodger management has always valued hitting over defense, so Bryant may get a chance at the major leagues in 1987 after just two seasons in the minors at Albuquerque.

LOS ANGELES DODGERS

ENOS CABELL
1B, No. 23
RR, 6'5", 190 lbs.
ML Svc: 14 years
Born: 10-18-49 in
Fort Riley, KS

HITTING, BASERUNNING, FIELDING:

Enos Cabell endured a frustrating 1986 season. In the spring, he was one of seven players threatened with one-season suspensions by baseball commissioner Peter Ueberroth for past drug abuse. In the summer, he was forced to play the outfield for long stretches, forced to ignore his aches and pains while he suspected young teammates of babying their own injuries. Cabell, who has survived in the major leagues in recent years on wits alone, was offended more than any other Dodger by the club's lack of common sense on defense.

To top it off in the winter, Los Angeles didn't offer Cabell a 1987 contract, making him a 37-year-old free agent with declining physical skills.

Perhaps paradoxically, he is a fearless batter who swings at everything. He doesn't walk, but doesn't strike out often, either. He is particularly successful against lefthanders. Cabell still has just enough power to bloop the ball over the infield in any direction.

He can no longer run as fast as he did between 1976 and 1980, when he stole 166 total bases, but Cabell rarely gets thrown out unnecessarily.

OVERALL:

Dierker: "Cabell's great enthusiasm, clubhouse presence and feel for the game make him a candidate to perhaps manage a team someday, but the drug stigma that continues to follow him may delay that."

JOSE GONZALES
OF, No. 47
RR, 6'2", 190 lbs.
ML Svc: less than
one year
Born: 11-23-64 in
Puerto Plata,
Dominican
Republic

HITTING, BASERUNNING, FIELDING:

In a July 1986 game at Wrigley Field, right fielder Jose Gonzalez caught a fly ball near the foul line and, as a Cubs runner broke for home, let loose a throw that sailed clear over the third-base dugout, into the stands. The 350-foot throw said a lot about the 22-year-old Dodger: he is a great but unrefined talent.

For the second straight year, Gonzalez is rated the Dodgers' top prospect by *Baseball America*. Whether he fulfills that promise depends on whether he learns to hit major league breaking pitches.

The Dodgers originally planned to leave Gonzalez in the minors all season last year, hope they didn't stunt his progress by recalling him in July to replace injured Mike Marshall.

A sore knee held him to 11 steals at Albuqerque, but nobody doubts Gonzalez's speed, which has captured the 60-yard-dash championship in the last three Dodger camps. Nobody questions his arm or ability to hit fastballs over the plate, either.

OVERALL:

The Dodgers see him hitting 25 homers, stealing 50 bases and driving in 100 runs some day.

Dierker: "Right now, he's a platoon center fielder at best. The longer Gonzalez must work to solve the mysteries of breaking pitches, the less he'll learn to apply his more abundant physical gifts."

LOS ANGELES DODGERS

LEN MATUSZEK
PH, No. 17
LR, 6'2", 205 lbs.
ML Svc: 5 years
Born: 9-27-54 in
Toledo, OH

HITTING, BASERUNNING, FIELDING:

Injuries, which cost Len Matuszek a chance to win the first-base job for the Phillies in 1984, also cost him the first two months of the 1986 season. The healing process of rotator cuff surgery kept him on the disabled list until May 24.

Matuszek, a low-ball hitter, has trouble with hard stuff up-and-in. Last year, he was not very good as a pinch-hitter, which is the role the Dodgers envisioned for him when they acquired him in a 1985 trade with the Toronto Blue Jays. Matuszek's 4-for-25 contributed to the club's .184 pinch-hitting average, the worst in the National League.

After returning to the roster, Matuszek enjoyed two excellent months at the plate and, between fill-in stints in the outfield, showed the Dodgers some sharp defense at first base. Putting Matuszek in the outfield for 37 games was simply unfair; he doesn't run well and his throws didn't always reach the cutoff man.

OVERALL

The Dodgers were impressed with Matuszek's honesty in revealing the shoulder pain before signing a 1986 contract, even though his uncertain condition lowered his value.

Dierker: "Matuszek is just one of many would-be first basemen with the Dodgers and will probably have to live with being their top lefthanded pinch-hitter."

ALEX TREVINO
C, No. 29
RR, 5'11", 170 lbs.
ML Svc: 8 years
Born: 8-26-57 in
Monterrey, Mexico

HITTING, BASERUNNING, FIELDING:

It may seem the Dodgers were robbed when they gave up Candy Maldonado to get Alex Trevino in December 1985. But the Dodgers' braintrust knew Maldonado would never blossom in Los Angeles and felt certain that Trevino would prove an ideal backup for Mike Scioscia behind the plate. They were right on both counts.

Trevino batted .306 with three homers in June, when Scioscia hurt his ankle, and though his catching is suspect, Trevino handled the Dodger staff intelligently, working especially well with Fernando Valenzuela, forming what's believed to be the major leagues' first all-Mexican battery.

A free-swinger who can hit the ball down either line and runs reasonably well, Trevino has hit 10 home runs over the last two years after hitting only five homers in his first seven full seasons.

OVERALL:

Trevino was thrilled to join the Dodgers after spending parts of nine major league seasons with four teams, none of which finished above .500. Though the Dodgers' record in 1986 was no better, the whole team will try again this season.

LOS ANGELES DODGERS

ED VANDE BERG
LHP, No. 31
RL, 6'2", 180 lbs.
ML Svc: 5 years
Born: 10-26-58 in
Redlands, CA

PITCHING, FIELDING:

Ed Vande Berg's trouble started when manager Tom Lasorda spotted his new reliever at a Dodger winter workout and said with surprise, "I thought he'd be bigger." The Dodgers, trying again to replace Steve Howe, thought they were getting a hard-thrower. When Vande Berg showed up as a curveball/slider pitcher with a quirky delivery, Dodger management tried to change him.

The club asked him to junk the slider and tried to convince the skinny lefthander he has an above-average fastball, though it won't crack 90 MPH. The recommendations only confused Vande Berg.

Vande Berg is quick with the glove and has a good move to first base.

His best attribute is durability.

OVERALL:

A California native, Vande Berg admitted being "awed" by pitching for the Dodgers in April. A horrible start, especially in pressure situations, dropped him into a long-relief role. Vande Berg feuded with Dodgers vice president Al Campanis and even a satisfactory finish couldn't save him after that gaffe. Los Angeles didn't renew his contract.

Whoever picks him up will have to leave Vande Berg's pitching style alone, use him to get key lefthanded batters, and hope for the best.

MONTREAL EXPOS

HITTING:

When he takes a cut at the ball, Hubie Brooks whips his fingers so violently that it gives the tendons a nasty twist around the base of his thumbs. His troublesome hands forced Brooks to the disabled list twice in 1986, and when he tore ligaments outside the base of his thumb while swinging on August 1st, he was gone for the season.

Prior to his medical woes, Brooks handled pitchers impressively; he was in contention for the batting title and showed good power (12 HR in his first 166 AB). At one time, both right- and lefthanded pitchers had success against him when they kept the ball down, but Brooks is adjusting to that tactic. His closed stance lends the impression that a pitcher can tie him up by pitching him tight, but that really doesn't work, either.

One of the better curveball hitters on the Expos, Brooks needs to have a quick swing to be effective: that's where the thumb problems come in. When his thumb is bothering him, almost everything he hits is to right field.

BASERUNNING:

Brooks doesn't do much running, although he really shouldn't be considered a lead foot. He is not a slow runner, he is just not a basestealer. He will steal just about once a month.

FIELDING:

There were rumblings in the off-season that if the Expos traded Tim Wallach they would have Brooks switch back to third base, the position he played for the Mets before coming to Montreal. Brooks has said privately he would oppose such a move because he's worked hard to smooth his rough edges at shortstop.

Actually, Brooks made the transition from third to shortstop quite well, though initially he was weak on the pivot. He has made great

HUBIE BROOKS
SS, No. 7
RR, 6'0", 190 lbs.
ML Svc: 7 years
Born: 9-24-56 in
Los Angeles, CA

1986 STATISTICS

AVG	G	AB	R	H	2B	3B	HR	RBI	BB	SO	SB
.340	80	306	50	104	18	5	14	58	25	60	4

CAREER STATISTICS

AVG	G	AB	R	H	2B	3B	HR	RBI	BB	SO	SB
.278	787	2954	313	822	137	23	55	377	187	464	28

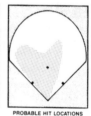

VS. RHP   VS. LHP   PROBABLE HIT LOCATIONS

strides and now moves nicely on that play.

He has good range and a strong throwing arm. It is really the routine plays that sometimes give him more trouble than the more challenging ones.

OVERALL:

The Expos are a vulnerable team without Brooks in the lineup. His uncanny ability to drive in runs in crucial situations is important for those hitting all around him.

Rooker: "His swing puts a heck of a strain on his fingers, but even the Expos' team doctor shakes his head and says he's never seen anything like it. There has been some thought of taping his fingers together, but the club has decided to leave a .340 hitter to his own devices."

"Hubie was having an MVP year until the injuries intervened. But last winter's rest should bring him back and raring to go."

MONTREAL EXPOS

PITCHING:

When his slider and sinking fastball are working properly, Tim Burke is an imposing reliever. But in 1986, he had considerable difficulty throwing his slider for strikes. Batters learned to lay off Burke's money pitch, forcing the reliever to come in with a fastball that lacked the zip it had the previous season.

A large part of Burke's reduced effectiveness can be traced to a tender elbow early in the year, and in the final month, tendinitis in his right shoulder. Making 30 appearances in the Expos' first 53 games also was a workload that probably took an early toll on Burke.

Burke was twice pressed into service as a starter and in doing so, seemed to establish the rhythm which wasn't always evident in his relief stints. Although he had nine victories, four saves and a 2.93 ERA last season, the statistics are somewhat misleading because Burke frequently left baserunners for others to handle in 1986.

FIELDING, HITTING, BASERUNNING:

Burke is the flashiest fielding pitcher in Montreal. Tall and well coordinated, he's able to grab some of the high bouncers other pitchers cannot get to. He also breaks well off the mound to handle bunts, and he'll come up with the truly outstanding play at a critical moment.

TIM BURKE
RHP, No. 44
RR, 6'3", 200 lbs.
ML Svc: 2 years
Born: 2-19-59 in Omaha, NE

1986 STATISTICS

W	L	ERA	G	GS	CG	SV	IP	H	R	ER	BB	SO
9	7	2.93	68	2	0	4	101.1	103	37	33	46	82

CAREER STATISTICS

W	L	ERA	G	GS	CG	SV	IP	H	R	ER	BB	SO
18	11	2.64	146	2	0	12	221.2	189	69	65	90	169

OVERALL:

Burke may be paying the price for the large number of appearances he's had to make over the last two seasons. He has pitched in 146 games over the past two years and is often warmed up without getting into the game. Last season he complained that his arm felt tired, and that's a bad sign for a slider pitcher.

Rooker: "A well rested, pain-free Burke should be able to again throw that nasty slider that paralyzed batters in his rookie year. If he's healthy, look for big things to happen. He has the stuff to succeed, and his delivery--keeping the ball well hidden until the last second--keeps hitters off balance."

MONTREAL EXPOS

HITTING:

Dave Collins' bags are always packed. The Tigers acquired him following the 1985 season to add versatility to their lineup. They wanted his stolen base speed on their side.

Collins managed 27 steals (in 38 attempts), fought leg injuries early in the season, was forced to play against lefthanders more than Sparky Anderson would have liked and wound up with 419 at-bats, which Anderson admitted was too many to give him.

So Collins was released after the 1986 season. He has resurfaced with the Montreal Expos, his sixth team in the past seven seasons and the eighth of his major league career.

Collins is a switch-hitting slap hitter with no home run power from either side of the plate. Typical of small players, he likes low pitches from the left side and high pitches from the right side. He is a superior hitter from the left side, partly because his speed can be put to greater use.

One rap against Collins is his lack of pitch selection. He does not work pitchers for walks, as a good leadoff hitter should. Instead, he frequently swings at the first pitch.

He is also prone to fatigue, which the Tigers discovered last season. His average hovered around .300 into August, only to wind up at .270. Collins managed to score only 44 runs. Part of the reason was that he yielded the leadoff spot to Lou Whitaker and, instead, frequently batted sixth or seventh.

BASERUNNING:

The National League probably will be a better setting for Collins than Tiger Stadium. He can better utilize his speed and batting style on the artificial surface of Olympic Stadium.

Collins' legs butter his bread. He cannot subject himself to the same leg injuries he experienced with the Tigers and expect to be successful.

DAVE COLLINS
LF, No. 29
SL, 5'10", 175 lbs.
ML Svc: 12 years
Born: 10-20-52 in
Rapid City, SD

1986 STATISTICS

AVG	G	AB	R	H	2B	3B	HR	RBI	BB	SO	SB
.270	124	419	44	113	18	2	1	27	44	49	27

CAREER STATISTICS

AVG	G	AB	R	H	2B	3B	HR	RBI	BB	SO	SB
.274	1368	4484	612	1231	171	50	32	344	422	594	369

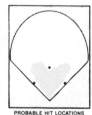

VS. RHP   VS. LHP   PROBABLE HIT LOCATIONS

FIELDING:

Defensively, Collins has limitations. His range is fair but he does not go back well. His speed can be an asset in cutting off balls hit into the alleys on artificial turf.

OVERALL:

Speed has kept Collins in the major leagues. The uncertainty surrounding the status of Tim Raines and Andre Dawson over the winter contributed to the Expos' decision to bring Collins to Canada. Collins' speed, however, seems to be diminishing and his traveling days may be reaching an end.

Kaat: "His best years are behind him, though he is still useable as a part-time player, pinch-hitter and pinch-runner."

MONTREAL EXPOS

HITTING:

Few hitters can get behind in the count as quickly as Andre Dawson. A free-swinger, he figures that he is going to see the pitcher's best stuff early.

At the start of last season, Dawson vowed that he would accept more walks, but managed only 37, relatively few for the number three hitter. As the elder statesman on a young, inexperienced team, he sometimes tries to do too much. It leads to an overanxious, rather than controlled, swing. Pitchers can get him to chase pitches out of the strike zone though Dawson can really burn any pitcher who gets the ball up. He has tremendous strength in his wrists; few players can rocket a ball out of the park faster.

Dawson's fragile knees held up well in 1986, but a hamstring pull in June last year put him on the DL for the first time in his career. It was several weeks after his return before he regained his batting form.

BASERUNNING:

Dawson was a half a step slower going down the line last season than in 1985. Though he claims that his knees felt better last year than they had in a long time, clearly, he is not the same runner. He will only steal in a critical situation; he is successful 40% of the time. His speed is more evident on runs from first-to-third and in the outfield.

FIELDING:

Dawson continues to be one of the finest right fielders in the National League. He combines swiftness with an excellent glove and a powerful throwing arm. He is sometimes too intent on making things happen, and rushes throws which sail past the cutoff man and allow runners an extra base. But word of Dawson's prowess in the field has long since been relayed, and you won't find too many runners who will challenge him.

ANDRE DAWSON
RF, No. 10
RR, 6'3", 195 lbs.
ML Svc: 11 years
Born: 7-10-54 in Miami, FL

1986 STATISTICS

AVG	G	AB	R	H	2B	3B	HR	RBI	BB	SO	SB
.284	130	496	65	141	32	2	20	78	37	79	18

CAREER STATISTICS

AVG	G	AB	R	H	2B	3B	HR	RBI	BB	SO	SB
.280	1443	5628	828	1575	295	67	225	838	354	896	253

  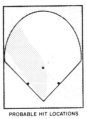

VS. RHP   VS. LHP   PROBABLE HIT LOCATIONS

OVERALL:

Dawson is a proud man who privately still bears the scars of the Gary Carter era in Montreal, when Dawson felt the salary gap between him and the catcher was unfair.

Rooker: "While Dawson's peak seasons are behind him, there remains plenty of production in him. He always furnishes a maximum effort; he will consistently hit between .275-.280, belt 20-25 homers and knock in 80 or more runs.

"Andre is the type of leader that every team would like to have. As he looks to his future, taking care of his knees is a primary concern and playing on an artificial surface as his home field is not doing him any good."

MONTREAL EXPOS

HITTING:

The Expos were certain that Mike Fitzgerald was better than the woeful .207 average he mustered in 1985. Like Fitzgerald, they can take a bow because the gritty catcher added 75 points to his average last year to emerge as the team's most improved hitter.

At midseason last year, Fitzgerald was hitting close to .400 with runners in scoring position. Then, late in July, his spikes caught in the turf while swinging a bat and he reinjured the right knee which had been surgically repaired the previous year.

While that injury did not prove serious, the first day of August was not so kind: a foul tip fractured his index finger, putting a premature end to his season.

Fitzgerald's offensive breakthrough can be attributed to his new-found ability to wait on both the curveball and the breaking ball. Often overanxious in the past, he stayed back in the batter's box more and learned to hammer the ball to all parts of the field.

Fitzgerald's statistics are all the more remarkable in that he batted eighth in the batting order; with an Expos pitching staff that is more anemic at bat than most clubs, Fitzgerald really didn't see many quality pitches.

BASERUNNING:

You don't have to worry about Fitzgerald doing too much running, but whether it's breaking up a double play at second or creating a collision at home trying to score a run, he is going to do things with intensity.

FIELDING:

While there was a dramatic offensive boost by Fitzgerald last season, defensively, that kind of improvement was missing. He threw out just 13 runners and allowed 58 successful stolen bases for a mediocre 18.3% kill ratio.

Not all of the blame belongs to Mike. The Expos pitching staff, for the most part, is very poor at holding runners on base and a

MIKE FITZGERALD
C, No. 20
RR, 6'0", 198 lbs.
ML Svc: 3 years
Born: 7-13-60 in
Long Beach, CA

1986 STATISTICS

AVG	G	AB	R	H	2B	3B	HR	RBI	BB	SO	SB
.282	73	209	20	59	13	1	6	37	27	34	3

CAREER STATISTICS

AVG	G	AB	R	H	2B	3B	HR	RBI	BB	SO	SB
.236	301	884	66	209	35	3	14	106	92	166	9

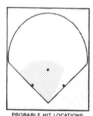

VS. RHP   VS. LHP   PROBABLE HIT LOCATIONS

number of steals charged against Fitzgerald are actually more the fault of the pitcher.

In addition, Fitzgerald spent the first month of the season in the minors, rehabilitating the shoulder he injured in spring training. It was well into the season before his shoulder was 100%.

OVERALL:

Fitzgerald now must prove that he can get through a season in one piece. In his two years with the Expos, he has visited the doctor almost as much as the pitcher's mound. His injuries have impeded his progress, though it is hoped his fortunes are about to turn.

Rooker: "The Montreal staff likes to work with Mike--he takes charge and calls an excellent game. Bryn Smith says that Mike kicks a pitcher in the butt a bit. Sometimes, a pitcher needs that.

"Fitzgerald comes to play baseball. He is a good hitter and getting better. He will occasionally sting you with the long ball."

HITTING:

When Tom Foley first arrived in Montreal from the Phillies in July last year, Expos' batting instructor Bobby Winkles worked with him to correct his uppercut swing, which was turning a lot of potential line drive singles into routine fly-ball outs.

Winkles found in Foley a tireless worker who was willing to spend a lot of extra time in the batting cage. Foley worked on learning to hit the ball where it's pitched and the results were productive enough for Foley to muscle his way into a spot in the infield against righthanded pitching.

Foley is basically a good low-ball hitter. He is able to leg out a lot of infield hits. Infielders also have to be on their toes because Foley will bunt frequently.

Foley hits home runs by accident; he is more of a singles and doubles hitter.

BASERUNNING:

A former scrambling quarterback in high school, Foley has natural running ability. He breaks well from the batter's box, and because he breaks from the lefthander's box, infielders cannot afford to be complacent on his grounders.

Foley had ten stolen bases last season, but that figure should more than double if he retains his share of the platoon job.

FIELDING:

Although he can play shortstop and third base, Foley seems more comfortable at second. He handled 116 chances there for the Expos last season making only one error.

Foley has those "soft" infielder's hands: the type that make handling nasty hops seem routine. He is also fluid around the bag when turning the double play. He does not really have the range or the quick release required for shortstop, but he is more than adequate at second base.

TOM FOLEY
INF, No. 11
LR, 6'1", 175 lbs.
ML Svc: 4 years
Born: 9-9-59 in
Columbus, GA

1986 STATISTICS

AVG	G	AB	R	H	2B	3B	HR	RBI	BB	SO	SB
.266	103	263	26	70	15	3	1	23	30	37	10

CAREER STATISTICS

AVG	G	AB	R	H	2B	3B	HR	RBI	BB	SO	SB
.248	366	888	83	220	40	8	9	82	86	124	16

  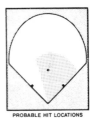

VS. RHP   VS. LHP   PROBABLE HIT LOCATIONS

OVERALL:

Foley had been a regular with the Phillies until he broke his wrist in spring training 1986 and was not able to displace Steve Jeltz upon his return. The Expos acquired Foley for pitcher Dan Schatzeder and felt they had made an exceptional deal.

Naturally ambidextrous, Foley threw with both his right and left hand back in his college quarterbacking days, yet he does not switch-hit. While at this point in his career, the development of switch-hitting is unlikely, it would surely be a help if he wants permanent employment.

Rooker: "Tom has been around a while now and the knowledge and skills he has acquired in the last few years could be extremely helpful to the Expos. The move to Montreal provided him with a fresh start, and Foley is likely to make the best of it."

MONTREAL EXPOS

HITTING:

While it is difficult to be completely sold on Andres Galarraga as a power man, there is no doubt that when he connects, he really crushes the baseball. Last season, he hit some tape-measure home runs off the National League's best pitchers.

Hard-throwing pitchers give Galarraga some trouble--especially righthanders. Last season was his first full season in the majors, and like most rookies, he was often overmatched by big league curveballs. He likes the ball from the middle of the plate toward the inside corner, so pitchers have a better chance of getting him out with curves and sliders on the outside of the plate, since Galarraga will chase a bad pitch.

Galarraga is predominantly a pull hitter to left field, but some of his more mammoth homers were to straightaway center. He still has some work to do on simply going with the pitch and using the opposite field.

For a big and powerful player, Galarraga gets his share of infield hits. While he could be made to chase bad pitches when he was trying for the fences, he also showed that he was able to hold off when he had to, coaxing a walk once every 11 at-bats.

BASERUNNING:

In situations where he has to go from first to third or from second to home, Galarraga should be a more aggressive baserunner. He is a hulking, strong young player and could use his build to be more of an intimidating force on the bases.

He might be even less of a threat to steal after some knee problems slowed him down last year.

FIELDING:

With the unquestioned exception of Keith Hernandez, Galarraga plays the bag at first as smoothly and efficiently as anyone in the National League. He moves well to both sides

ANDRES GALARRAGA
1B, No. 52
RR, 6'3", 230 lbs.
ML Svc: one year plus
Born: 6-18-61 in
**   Caracas, Venezuela**

1986 STATISTICS

AVG	G	AB	R	H	2B	3B	HR	RBI	BB	SO	SB
.271	105	321	39	87	13	0	10	42	30	79	6

CAREER STATISTICS

AVG	G	AB	R	H	2B	3B	HR	RBI	BB	SO	SB
.255	129	396	48	101	14	0	12	46	33	97	7

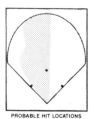

STRONG / VS. RHP   STRONG / VS. LHP   PROBABLE HIT LOCATIONS

and he has good positional instincts.

Early last season, Galarraga had difficulty scooping up throws in the dirt, but he appears to be constantly improving. He still has a few problems judging high throws from infielders, which is why he sometimes makes a catch with his right foot on the bag and his left foot in foul territory.

OVERALL:

Galarraga will be under close scrutiny this season. Time spent on the disabled list last year for torn knee cartilage and injured ribs prevented him from having a true full season.

Rooker: "For a while it looked as though the pitchers had begun to figure Galarraga out and were pitching him effectively. But September is usually a month when one can see rookie puzzles solved and Galarraga hit .340 that month. This year should be a more revealing season for him."

MONTREAL EXPOS

PITCHING:

Neal Heaton got new life last summer when Cleveland traded him to Minnesota for John Butcher, a pitcher whom the Indians released at the end of the season. No longer would there be disagreements with Pat Corrales about when Heaton should be removed from games, debates that often left both parties angry and may have kept Heaton from thinking about his real problem: living up to the potential he showed at the University of Miami.

The lefthander made some strides last year that didn't show up in his once-again poor won-loss record. Heaton got his hits-per-inning ratio near one and seemed to give up on the notion that he can overpower batters with his fastball.

Heaton spent time last season working on his breaking pitches and threw a slider that seemed to be a bit sharper in 1986 than in past years. His 88 MPH fastball would look better if he threw a more effective change-up. There are still times when he falls behind in the count and feels compelled to use his fastball.

On a given day, Heaton seems to have either everything working or nothing at all. Upon coming to Minnesota, he quickly lost a pair of 1-0 games to Baltimore, and there were several others over the course of the season that could have been victories had there been better offensive support. At the other extreme, there were starts when it looked as though every hitter Heaton faced was Wade Boggs.

Those who are optimistic about Heaton's future dismiss his career record by pointing out that he was rushed to the majors by a pitching-poor organization. His quick rise was similar to that of Frank Viola, who spent two years in the minors and two years in the Twins rotation getting rocked before developing into a winning pitcher. A lot of pitchers are still trying to break into the majors at Heaton's age instead of having more than four years of experience.

Whether Heaton is destined to mature into a winning pitcher remains to be seen. He needs to be less distracted when things go

NEAL HEATON
LHP, No. 44
LL, 6'1", 205 lbs.
ML Svc: 4 years
Born: 3-3-60 in
Jamaica, NY

1986 STATISTICS

W	L	ERA	G	GS	CG	SV	IP	H	R	ER	BB	SO
7	15	4.08	33	29	5	1	198.2	201	102	90	81	90

CAREER STATISTICS

W	L	ERA	G	GS	CG	SV	IP	H	R	ER	BB	SO
39	56	4.64	154	116	18	8	785.1	865	449	405	296	336

wrong and to develop more confidence in his off-speed pitches. Improvements such as these would make him more of a battler when he doesn't have his best stuff.

FIELDING:

Last season, Heaton's fielding faults did not stand out much because Twins pitchers, in general, are fundamentally flawed fielders. For the record, his slow motion helps basestealers to get a better break off the base and Heaton tends to fall off the mound, leaving himself out of position for grounders up the middle.

OVERALL:

Common baseball wisdom has it that lefties are late bloomers. If Heaton continues to concentrate on improving his all-around skills, he could blossom into the winning pitcher Cleveland gave up on. Not being among the anchors of the rotation, a position he held almost from the start in Cleveland, may also be to his benefit.

Killebrew: "Heaton is being given new life in an organization that needs him badly, and perhaps he'll be up to the challenge being presented. Everyone knows he has a good arm, so maybe *this* will be the year that Heaton finally puts it all together."

MONTREAL EXPOS

PITCHING:

Joe Hesketh's season ended in the first week of July last year--just about a month earlier than it had in 1985. His latest ailment was an impinged nerve which led to muscle deterioration in the back of his shoulder blade. Surgery was required last August to free the nerve. Hesketh still faces a lengthy rehabilitation.

The benching was especially unfortunate last season because after a horrible 0-3 start during which he carried a whopping 9.17 ERA, Hesketh had just begun to get back on track. When sidelined, he had just won four of his last five starts and compiled a more than repectable 2.25 ERA in those games.

The turnaround coincided with his regaining command of his slider, the pitch that keeps the batters honest. Combined with a fastball which he throws consistently in the 86-87 MPH range, the slider gets Hesketh plenty of strikeouts.

Hesketh has to be frequently reminded to maintain his aggressiveness on the mound because he has a tendency to ease up against certain hitters. He doesn't bear down against the hitters in the lower part of the batting order, a oversight which drives manager Buck Rodgers crazy.

FIELDING, HITTING, BASERUNNING:

Tall and reed-like, Hesketh is agile on the mound, pouncing on slow infield choppers hit to either side of the mound. His delivery to the plate is such that he is usually in a good position to field comebackers.

He does not get much chance to run the bases; for him a walk constitutes a hitting streak.

How dreadful a hitter is he? Very. Throw the ball and strike him out. His career batting average is .060. On the positive side, he was working to improve his bunting ability. Good thing.

JOE HESKETH
LHP, No. 38
LL, 6'1", 170 lbs.
ML Svc: 2 years
Born: 2-15-59 in
Lackawanna, NY

1986 STATISTICS

W	L	ERA	G	GS	CG	SV	IP	H	R	ER	BB	SO
6	5	5.01	15	15	0	0	82.2	92	46	46	31	67

CAREER STATISTICS

W	L	ERA	G	GS	CG	SV	IP	H	R	ER	BB	SO
18	12	3.12	51	45	3	1	283	255	110	98	91	212

OVERALL:

Last season was not meant to be Hesketh's season. Later in the year, when his role on the team had been reduced to that of cheerleader, he reached into the clubhouse refrigerator for a snack, caught his finger on a sharp object and ripped it open.

Entering the 1987 season, the Expos were not counting on Hesketh to be in the starting rotation. The victim of two major injuries in each of his first two big league seasons have left observers wondering whether he is destined to be a promising athlete whose career is curtailed by misfortune.

Quality lefthanders are among the most prized possessions in baseball, and in the National League East there are more than a few clubs who do poorly against lefthanders. The loss of Hesketh is a loss of a potential 15-game winner. Barring another NL East runaway, it could mean the difference for the Expos.

Rooker: "Hesketh will be 28 years old on Opening Day. He is at an age when prospects should have begun to prosper. He maintains a positive outlook, however, and seems to be the type who will work to overcome adversity. The Expos need him every bit as much as he needs them."

MONTREAL EXPOS

HITTING:

Vance Law, an unheralded infielder, endured a series of unsettling family difficulties during the 1986 season which affected him at the plate. He is the type of player who approaches the game in the spirit of a true professional and has quietly overcome whatever challenge he has had to face throughout his career.

Law protects the plate well and because he has a good eye, he draws a lot of walks. He hits to the opposite field often--especially with curveballs. He is also a fine hit-and-run man because of his excellent bat control.

It's best to keep the ball down on him. If a pitcher gets the ball up, Law has enough power to pull it out of the park or line it for extra bases.

BASERUNNING:

Law's speed on the bases is deceptive, even though he had only three steals in 1986. Of course, the Expos would likely run him more if he was batting second and Tim Raines was leading off.

A student of the game, Law is a smart baserunner, especially in situations which call for a quick assessment of opponents' throwing arms when trying to grab an extra base.

FIELDING:

What Law can get to, he can play. The statistics bear this out: he had 457 chances at second base last year and made only three errors. At first base, he had 104 more chances and committed one error.

Law is a shrewd positional player and while he does not have exceptional range, not many balls scoot by him.

He is a handy man to have around because he can capably play any of the four infield positions in a pinch.

VANCE LAW
2B, No. 2
RR, 6'3", 190 lbs.
ML Svc: 7 years
Born: 10-1-56 in
Boise, ID

1986 STATISTICS

AVG	G	AB	R	H	2B	3B	HR	RBI	BB	SO	SB
.225	112	360	37	81	17	2	5	44	37	66	3

CAREER STATISTICS

AVG	G	AB	R	H	2B	3B	HR	RBI	BB	SO	SB
.250	522	1608	192	402	76	10	31	199	155	243	14

VS. RHP

VS. LHP

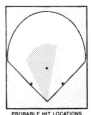

PROBABLE HIT LOCATIONS

OVERALL:

In listing Law's assets, one can't overlook the fact he had the second-best ERA (yes, that's *ERA*) on the Montreal staff last year. That only covers three mop-up relief outings to be sure, but it's indicative that the man is a versatile performer. He is willing to play anywhere, except perhaps catch, which is the only position he hasn't played in the majors.

Rooker: "With his family matters seemingly on the upswing, look for Law to return to the grind-it-out style which made him so successful offensively in 1985. He has a challenge awaiting him, however, since the Expos have indicated he may have to platoon at second base with the lefthanded-hitting Tom Foley.

"You pull for a guy like Vance Law. He works hard in all phases of the game and is a true professional."

MONTREAL EXPOS

PITCHING:

Dennis Martinez was in the Baltimore minor league system recovering from tendinitis in his right shoulder when the Expos obtained him last June. At the time, tendinitis or not, there were doubts whether Martinez was still capable of getting out big league hitters.

Once in Montreal, Martinez was a study in contrasts. One game he'd toss a sterling five-hitter and yet in the next outing he'd be unable to survive the fifth inning.

But his fastball was back in the high-80 MPH range for most of the time, and his problems usually were traced to a lack of movement.

Generally, there are a lot of fly-ball outs with Martinez, whose fastball moves outside to lefthanded batters and runs in on the righthanders. Martinez will mix the speed of his fastball and he'll also throw the curveball, slider and change-up. He needs to get the fastball to sink in order to be effective.

Part of Martinez's inconsistency last year was because of a flaw in his delivery. He sometimes doesn't turn his hip enough when delivering the ball, and the result is a hanging curveball. When pitching from the stretch, Martinez's pitching motion does not appear to have fluidity.

FIELDING, HITTING, BASERUNNING:

If Martinez has any problems in the field, it's that he doesn't cover first base as quickly as most members of the Expo staff (as explanation, one might suggest a trained over-reliance on Baltimore first baseman Eddie Murray's defense). His delivery to the plate, although slow at times, usually leaves him in a good position to field balls hit back through the middle. He also has a sneaky pickoff move.

At the plate, Martinez was as overwhelmed as one might expect of a former American Leaguer suddenly thrust into an offensive

DENNIS MARTINEZ
RHP, No. 30
RR, 6'1", 180 lbs.
ML Svc: 10 years
Born: 5-14-55 in
**   Granada, Nicaragua**

1986 STATISTICS

W	L	ERA	G	GS	CG	SV	IP	H	R	ER	BB	SO
3	6	4.73	23	19	1	0	104.2	114	57	55	30	65

CAREER STATISTICS

W	L	ERA	G	GS	CG	SV	IP	H	R	ER	BB	SO
111	99	4.18	338	262	70	5	1873.1	1925	951	870	611	921

role. He needs a lot of work, not so much on swinging the bat as bunting.

Martinez isn't endowed with much speed on the bases, but that isn't nearly as large a priority as improving his skills with the bat.

OVERALL:

When the 1986 season ended, Martinez was a free agent. He showed enough in his half-season in Montreal to secure employment as a fifth starter on the Expo staff. Although he can still be moody at times (after one game last year he openly criticized an outfielder for failing to reach a ball he thought should have been caught), Martinez has enough stuff to win 10-12 games for a team.

Martinez hinted that he might retire after a few ineffective outings with the Expos, but to his credit, he persevered to overcome adversity. He just has to maintain a higher concentration level, paying special attention to his delivery.

Rooker: "Dennis has to keep the ball down better than he did last year. The other pitches he throws will have to be quality stuff to complement a fastball that may be losing some of its zip."

MONTREAL EXPOS

HITTING:

Tim Raines has improved as a hitter during each of his last five major league seasons. Last year, he became more selective at the plate; he progressed from a good fastball hitter to a hitter who can handle good breaking stuff as well. That refinement helped to earn him the National League batting title.

He leans over the plate as though he is a father protecting a small child. When he's swinging the bat well, most of Raines' hits are stinging shots up the middle.

While he shows no glaring weaknesses as a hitter, when he is batting from the left side, Raines can be jammed. When he is batting righthanded, pitchers should keep everything away. He breaks from the batter's box like a bullet; his speed enables him to avoid prolonged slumps.

If Raines could master the bunt, he'd have no trouble hitting .350. Despite going to the Florida Instructional League prior to the start of the 1986 season, he had no bunt hits last year.

Statistically, Raines remains one of the best leadoff batters ever to play the game, but with Hubie Brooks out of the lineup in the second half of last season, the Expos needed Raines' punch batting third. He is such a catalyst batting leadoff it would seem to the Expos' benefit to return him there.

BASERUNNING:

Raines is more likely to get picked off base by a pitcher than he is to be caught stealing by a catcher. Entering this season, Raines has been nabbed by pitchers 35 times in his career, and by catchers, 33.

Most of Raines' problems on the basepaths are with lefthanded pitchers. Last year, even lefties with average moves seemed able to shorten his lead from first base. Raines does not appear to be as aggressive a basestealer as he's been in the past, perhaps concerned about his steals/caught stealing ratio.

TIM RAINES
LF, No. 30
SR, 5'8", 180 lbs.
ML Svc: 6 years
Born: 9-16-59 in
Sanford, FL

1986 STATISTICS

AVG	G	AB	R	H	2B	3B	HR	RBI	BB	SO	SB
.334	151	580	91	194	35	10	9	62	78	60	70

CAREER STATISTICS

AVG	G	AB	R	H	2B	3B	HR	RBI	BB	SO	SB
.305	882	3372	604	1028	180	55	48	314	469	376	461

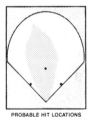

VS. RHP   VS. LHP   PROBABLE HIT LOCATIONS

FIELDING:

Raines continues to display an arm that is gaining in strength and accuracy. His speed enables him to get quickly to balls and to launch his throws on the run. There are still times, however, when he has trouble judging line drives hit to the outfield, and he still does not appear comfortable playing against the wall. He is capable of making brilliant catches and throws, but needs to become more consistent.

OVERALL:

Rooker: "Some players run when they can. Tim runs when he wants to. He can dominate a pitcher in a lot of ways. If he returns to the leadoff spot full-time this season, his 100+ stolen-base year may be at hand."

MONTREAL EXPOS

HITTING:

Jeff Reed wants to be a slugger, but has found out that he only hurts himself by swinging for the fences. That lesson was painfully clear a couple of years ago when he showed up for spring training with a new batting stance, did little but hit infield pop-ups and found himself spending another season in the minors when he had expected to make the Twins roster.

Reed spent most of last season in the majors and got increased playing time as the season progressed. He showed flashes of competence at the plate, but seems to be the sort of guy who's going to be yanked for a pinch-hitter in important late-inning situations. He needs to keep working on developing a quick stroke and hitting to the opposite field.

If Reed could hit around .250, he would probably start against righthanded pitchers because he is a very good defensive catcher. If he could bat .270 (an unlikely prospect), he could become the everyday catcher.

Reed has a pretty good eye and can usually be counted on to make contact, even if it isn't solid, and he keeps the ball in the air. He grounded into only two double plays in 165 at-bats last year.

BASERUNNING:

He is another typical catcher on the bases. Reed has limited speed but doesn't make bad moves to expose that weakness. He doesn't get out of the batter's box quickly and isn't apt to beat out many grounders.

FIELDING:

Reed, a first-round draft choice in 1980, had been projected as the Twins "catcher of the future" because of his skills behind the plate (he was the most feared catcher in the International League for several seasons). But the Twins pitchers, with a couple of exceptions, were not known for their ability to

JEFF REED
C, No. 10
LR, 6'2", 190 lbs.
ML Svc: 1 year plus
Born: 11-12-62 in
Joliet, IL

1986 STATISTICS

AVG	G	AB	R	H	2B	3B	HR	RBI	BB	SO	SB
.236	68	165	13	39	6	1	2	9	16	19	1

CAREER STATISTICS

AVG	G	AB	R	H	2B	3B	HR	RBI	BB	SO	SB
.224	93	196	18	44	9	1	2	10	18	28	1

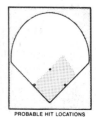

VS. RHP   VS. LHP   PROBABLE HIT LOCATIONS

hold runners on base, and as a result, Reed did not have the chance to show if he could or couldn't throw out basestealers in the majors. He isn't afraid to take charge of the pitching staff.

OVERALL:

This is the season that Reed would, once and for all, like to end his shuttle between the majors and the minors. He is being given the chance to battle Mike Fitzgerald for the full-time catcher's job this season. He has the opportunity to show his new club if he is as good as he thinks he is.

Killebrew: "It will be awfully hard to justify giving him the starting catcher's job if he does not hit better than he has to date. Jeff has to concentrate on the things he does best--his defensive skills and making contact at the plate. This could finally be the year he's been waiting for."

MONTREAL EXPOS

PITCHING:

In nine of his last 11 starts last season, Bob Sebra went six innings or more. All of his appearances have to be considered quality outing. He pitched two complete games against the Mets and allowed only one run (a ninth-inning home run).

The Expos have reason to be encouraged by the performance of Sebra (who was the player obtained from the Texas Rangers for Pete Incaviglia). Sebra was recalled to Montreal from Triple-A in late July last season and his improvement was steady.

A strong youngster with a lot of stamina, Sebra must have his curveball working early in the game if he is going to be effective. It is the curveball which sets the tone for the rest of the game because if Sebra can give the batters a good look at it in their first at-bat, he can play the fastball against it later.

Sebra is an aggressive pitcher and often gets ahead in the count quickly. The fastball is his only other pitch, and Sebra should be working to add another pitch so he won't have to be at the mercy of his ordinary fastball when he can't get the curve over for strikes.

He should also work on his pitching motion, which is not as fluid as it should be and causes him to leave his curveball hanging. Surprisingly, he wasn't burned too badly in 1986 by gopher balls and not singed by walks either.

FIELDING, HITTING, BASERUNNING:

Sebra has a good pickoff move and good defensive instincts; in 1986, he handled all of his fielding chores flawlessly. He was the only Expo pitcher to start at least two double plays.

BOB SEBRA
RHP, No. 48
RR, 6'2", 195 lbs.
ML Svc: one year plus
Born: 12-11-61 in
Ridgewood, NJ

1986 STATISTICS

W	L	ERA	G	GS	CG	SV	IP	H	R	ER	BB	SO
5	5	3.55	17	13	3	0	91.1	82	39	36	25	66

CAREER STATISTICS

W	L	ERA	G	GS	CG	SV	IP	H	R	ER	BB	SO
5	7	4.27	24	17	3	0	111.2	108	56	53	39	79

He is no pushover at the plate, either, and his .207 batting average was the highest among Expo starting pitchers last year. Like the rest of the staff, however, Sebra should work to polish his bunt.

OVERALL:

Last year had to be a confidence builder for Sebra, especially in light of the brilliant way he ended the season: allowing only two earned runs in 22 innings, which included a two-hit shutout over the Mets.

In one of his outings, he walked in the winning run with the bases loaded last season and was the picture of total dejection in the clubhouse. But he showed his mettle by using the adversity as a learning experience.

Rooker: "Sebra doesn't usually beat himself. If he has got the curve working in the early innings, you can expect him to go seven. He has a lively arm and should be able to permanently crack the Expos' rotation. He could be this year's sleeper."

MONTREAL EXPOS

PITCHING:

For a pitcher who has always prided himself on his good control, Bryn Smith was issuing close to two more walks than usual per game last season. His loss of control partially explains his sub-par year.

He spent much of the year with a stiffness in his arm that affected his rhythm. He was often pitching from behind in the count and was forced to come in with his less-than-good fastball.

Normally, Smith throws an assortment of pitches, keeping opponents off balance with his curveball, slider and palmball. He uses his palmball as his change-up.

Smith is a perceptive pitcher with a knack for determining what is working well for him in the early innings. He establishes his game plan as quickly as he can.

The best-laid plans had gone awry by the end of the season, however. Smith was on the disabled list with a fractured bone spur in his right elbow. There is now a large concern he will miss a substantial portion of the 1987 season.

FIELDING, HITTING, BASERUNNING:

Probably no pitcher on the Montreal staff has better fielding reflexes than Smith; he is like an extra infielder. He routinely grabs sharp ground balls other pitchers would watch skip into center field.

Smith is quick at getting off the mound to cover the bag at first base on balls hit to the right side and he rarely makes a fundamental mistake.

As pitchers go, Smith is also a decent baserunner who shows good instincts in sizing up the game's situation.

At the plate, Smith's one home run and seven RBIs tied him with Floyd Youmans for the pitching staff lead. Smith spends a lot of

**BRYN SMITH
RHP, No. 28
RR, 6'2", 205 lbs.
ML Svc: 5 years
Born: 8-11-55 in
Marietta, GA**

1986 STATISTICS
W	L	ERA	G	GS	CG	SV	IP	H	R	ER	BB	SO
10	8	3.94	30	30	1	0	187.1	182	101	82	63	105

CAREER STATISTICS
W	L	ERA	G	GS	CG	SV	IP	H	R	ER	BB	SO
49	41	3.27	193	103	14	6	836.1	790	356	304	224	493

time on the golf course (and hits in the low 70s); he carries some of his swinging habits with him to the ballpark. He could, however, use improvement with his bunting.

OVERALL:

Last year was the first time that Smith had entered a major league season shouldering the responsibility of being the staff ace and stopper. He admitted that he may have allowed the burden to bother him. This season, Smith may be helped by the fact that Floyd Youmans will be sharing ace billing along with him.

Smith went 28 starts before completing his first game in 1986--a drought which was just as uncharacteristic as the lack of ground ball outs he was getting. When Smith is at the top of his game, it is generally a busy day for the infielders.

Rooker: "If he is physically sound, Smith is still the kind of pitcher who can lead a a staff. Other pitchers can learn by watching the way he sets up the hitters."

MONTREAL EXPOS

PITCHING:

In his first five starts as an Expo last season, Jay Tibbs was humming along with a 3-0 record and a 1.25 ERA. There was good cause for high hopes. Expos management imagined that Tibbs would provide the club with the 15 victories they had come to expect from traded-away Bill Gullickson.

From the end of April until the middle of July, however, Tibbs was 1-5, a stretch categorized by mediocrity. His ineffectiveness forced him into the bullpen for a short while and chipped away at his confidence. He finished the season with a 7-9 record. He has the basic stuff, however, to be much better than that record would indicate.

Tibbs throws a fastball, curveball, slider and change-up. His best pitch is the fastball, which is usually in the 87-90 MPH range. He does not get the kind of movement on his fastball he should. All too often the fastball stays flat rather than tailing away from the hitter.

He worked hard to introduce off-speed pitches to his repertoire, but the flatness of his 1986 fastball negated any effectiveness the slower stuff may have set up.

Tibbs needs to use the inside portion of the plate more often and to show the batters who's the boss. Tibbs was in his 456th major league inning last season when he finally hit his first batter with a pitch (for trivia buffs, it was the Pirates' Jim Morrison). His first hit-batsman can be taken as the slightest indication that perhaps Tibbs is ready to pitch inside. He *must* come inside if he is to become as effective as he can be.

He also needs to work on pitching from the stretch, a delivery with which he does not appear to be very comfortable.

FIELDING, HITTING, BASERUNNING:

Tibbs fields his position well; he was not charged with an error in 38 fielding chances all season. He has quick reactions when the ball

JAY TIBBS
RHP, No. 39
RR, 6'1", 180 lbs.
ML Svc: 3 years
Born: 1-4-62 in
*   Birmingham, AL*

1986 STATISTICS

W	L	ERA	G	GS	CG	SV	IP	H	R	ER	BB	SO
7	9	3.97	35	31	3	0	190.1	181	96	84	70	117

CAREER STATISTICS

W	L	ERA	G	GS	CG	SV	IP	H	R	ER	BB	SO
23	27	3.73	84	79	11	0	509	484	241	211	186	255

is hit back to the mound or down either of the baselines.

His pickoff move to first base improved last season but there is still some work to do because runners take all sorts of liberties with him.

Any Tibbs hit is a bonus. He led the pitching staff last year with 31 strikeouts in 54 at-bats. He should join his teammates in learning how to bunt.

OVERALL:

Tibbs must develop a longer span of concentration. He has mental lapses in the middle of the game and when runs are scored against him, they usually come in bunches. The early innings appear to be his most trying time; he'll give up three runs and then settle down for six or seven spotless innings. He thinks too much on the mound and spends too much time analyzing errors which are out of his hands.

This season, Tibbs is on his own. He is not the staff ace and might figure out a way to slide in successfully as the number three or four man in the rotation.

Rooker: "Jay has the stuff it takes to be a winner, especially if he can do some work on his third and fourth pitches (the curve and the slider). The Expos need to stick with him."

MONTREAL EXPOS

HITTING:

It appeared as though Tim Wallach had two seasons in 1986. In the first half, he was on a home run and RBI pace that might have surpassed his career-best year of 1982. But in the second half, he hit a tepid .162 with just 22 RBIs.

An accounting? Some claim he is too placid, that he lacks motivation, others point to needed adjustments in his swing, still others point to his obvious disappointment at not being selected to the 1986 All-Star team. While any of these is possible, the fact remains that Wallach's offensive slide coincided with the absence of Hubie Brooks and Andres Galarraga, a pair of power threats who normally bat ahead of and behind him in the order. With these two heavyweights gone, Wallach was pitched to differently.

Wallach handles low pitches better than he does pitches from the waist up. His uppercut swing leads to a lot of harmless pop-ups and fly balls when he gets in a rut. Wallach is a streaky hitter, who will use right and right-center field when he's hot. When he hits a cold spell, however, it can last for an agonizingly long time. In a slump, he lunges helplessly at curves and sliders outside the strike zone.

BASERUNNING:

Wallach is not much on the basepaths, but since the Expos now have more punch at the bottom of the batting order, look for him to be going from time to time. His speed is average, but he does seem to be getting a better jump than he has in the past.

FIELDING:

Hard work has made Wallach one of the game's best at the hot corner. He has the edge on Mike Schmidt defensively, last season notwithstanding. His arm is powerful and usually accurate--even from a kneeling position. Wallach also has eye-opening reflexes. It isn't unusual to see him make a

TIM WALLACH
3B, No. 29
RR, 6'3", 200 lbs.
ML Svc: 6 years
Born: 9-14-57 in
Huntington Park, CA

1986 STATISTICS

AVG	G	AB	R	H	2B	3B	HR	RBI	BB	SO	SB
.233	134	480	50	112	22	1	18	71	44	72	8

CAREER STATISTICS

AVG	G	AB	R	H	2B	3B	HR	RBI	BB	SO	SB
.254	839	3031	338	771	156	15	110	406	239	470	26

  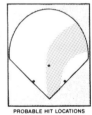

VS. RHP   VS. LHP   PROBABLE HIT LOCATIONS

spectacular diving grab of a sure double down the line.

Last year, five of the 16 errors Wallach made all season came in the first nine games, when he was still feeling the effects of a broken toe suffered during spring training which affected his throws to first base.

Wallach won the Gold Glove at third base in 1985 and he felt the pressure to duplicate the feat. He admitted that it took a pep talk from manager Buck Rodgers to settle him down defensively.

OVERALL:

Rooker: "There's no question about Tim's rise as a third baseman. Only Mike Schmidt puts up better power numbers offensively, but Wallach may be ready to explode. The second half of last year is not indicative of his abilities. He needs to bear down and concentrate to reach his very real potential."

MONTREAL EXPOS

HITTING:

Perhaps because he had smashed a surprising 11 homers in 212 at-bats in 1985, Mitch Webster went for the fences early last season but produced nothing more than frustration. What Webster does best is contact hitting and in that role, he is the Expos' most consistent hitter behind Tim Raines.

A switch-hitter, Webster is a good fastball hitter who likes the ball down and in from a righthanded pitcher and up from a southpaw. He is a better fastball hitter than he is against the off-speed and breaking ball, although as he matures, Webster seems to be adapting nicely.

He has the tendency to guess at the first couple of pitches, but becomes more analytical as the battle progresses, often forcing a pitcher to work extra hard.

Webster is a diligent worker who will do anything to make himself a better hitter. Last season, he added bunting to his list of skills and, together with his deceptive speed, delivered 12 bunt hits and beat out 27 infield hits.

BASERUNNING:

Webster's determination and aggressiveness compensate for his lack of blazing speed. He was caught stealing 15 times last season, often because he was simply outplayed. He needs to read lefthanded pitchers better. Still, Webster led the National League with 13 triples last season and is capable of a 50-stolen base season--especially with Tim Raines in the lineup.

FIELDING:

Good instincts have made Webster a well-rounded center fielder. He positions himself well, gets a good jump on the ball and is almost always in a good position to throw. His perceptive play makes his average throwing

MITCH WEBSTER
OF, No. 23
SL, 6'1", 185 lbs.
ML Svc: 2 years
Born: 5-16-59 in
Larned, KS

1986 STATISTICS

AVG	G	AB	R	H	2B	3B	HR	RBI	BB	SO	SB
.290	151	576	89	167	31	13	8	49	57	78	36

CAREER STATISTICS

AVG	G	AB	R	H	2B	3B	HR	RBI	BB	SO	SB
.282	266	822	132	232	41	16	19	83	79	119	51

  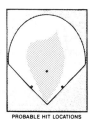

VS. RHP   VS. LHP   PROBABLE HIT LOCATIONS

arm look better.

He tracks down the line drives in the gap well and does not show any fear of the fences. If he has any problem in the outfield it is probably that he has a tendency to have the occasional mental lapse when the game isn't close.

OVERALL:

Manager Buck Rodgers feels that Webster was the Expos' most improved player last year.

Rooker: "When he was swinging for the fences early last year, Webster was striking out too often for a leadoff man, but he is quickly becoming a much better player. He will benefit from squeezing in somewhat unnoticed between the other, more powerful hitters in the Expos' lineup."

PITCHING:

Floyd Youmans was actually banished to the bullpen after a pair of ineffective starts last April, and he wasn't that far away from being told to pack for the minors. His major problem was a lack of control, which got him into a lot of first-inning trouble.

With the other Expo starters also struggling, manager Buck Rodgers restored Youmans to the rotation after just one relief outing. His patience was rewarded, as Youmans, discarding a curveball he was unable to control, started to mix a dandy change-up with his overpowering fastball and hard slider.

By the end of the year, the Expos had themselves a 13-game winner. Youmans might have recorded more wins, but he suffered three one-run losses, two by 2-1 and another by 3-1.

The 90+ fastball is Youmans' bread-and-butter pitch. In most games in which Youmans threw 100 pitches, between 60-70% of his fastballs exceeded 90 MPH. His fastest recorded fastball was 96 MPH and appeared in a game in which he was pumped up and facing former high school teammate Dwight Gooden.

Youmans does not nibble. He is fully prepared to match power against power, but he is a heady pitcher, quickly learning how to keep a hitter off balance by inserting off-speed stuff at an opportune moment.

FIELDING, HITTING, BASERUNNING:

Youmans does not hold runners on base very well. Last year, 31 baserunners tested him and 28 were successful. That is as close to a sure bet as it gets. The word on him is: *When on first, go!*

He takes too much time between pitches. If he can pick up his pace, runners will likely be reluctant to take that extra step on this fireballer.

Youmans' fielding can use polish. He is, however, an exceptional athlete who will get better with experience.

FLOYD YOUMANS
RHP, No. 33
RR, 6'0", 180 lbs.
ML Svc: 2 years
Born: 5-11-64 in Tampa, FL

1986 STATISTICS

W	L	ERA	G	GS	CG	SV	IP	H	R	ER	BB	SO
13	12	3.53	33	32	6	0	219	145	93	86	118	202

CAREER STATISTICS

W	L	ERA	G	GS	CG	SV	IP	H	R	ER	BB	SO
17	15	3.25	47	44	6	0	296	202	120	107	167	256

He is no patsy at the plate. He may flail away at times like any pitcher, but he loves to hit and takes delight each time he reaches base by his own prowess. He hit one home run last season and drove in seven runs, which tied him for the team lead among the pitching staff.

OVERALL:

Based on the progress he displayed in what actually amounted to his rookie season last year, it is reasonable to predict that Youmans could be a 20-game winner as early as this year.

Youmans is a carefree sort who rarely allows developments in a game to discourage or excite him. As long as he continues to throw the change-up effectively, he is going to get the strikeouts he needs.

He certainly has the stamina to go with his sizzling fastball. He is usually clocked at the same 93-95 MPH in the seventh inning as he was in the first inning.

Rooker: "Youmans yielded a meager 5.96 hits per nine innings pitched; a hair's breadth behind Mike Scott for the National League lead. When a pitcher is that stingy, he's going to win a lot of games. He has all the tools to be a great one. If he stays away from throwing the high fastball, Floyd will frustrate a lot of batters."

MONTREAL EXPOS

DANN BILARDELLO
C, No. 11
RR, 6'0", 190 lbs.
ML Svc: 4 years
Born: 5-26-59 in
Santa Cruz, CA

HITTING, BASERUNNING, FIELDING:

Last year was the time for Dann Bilardello to show he could play. When regular catcher Mike Fitzgerald was injured in spring training, the temporary catcher's job was up for grabs, but the brass ring eluded Bilardello.

Never a heavyweight at bat--his career average was .216--Dann dropped below that mark, managing only .194 and striking out once in every six at-bats. He is not aggressive at the plate and pitchers exploit his tentativeness by feeding him a diet of curveballs which leave him confused and frustrated.

Perhaps because he had some early success power-wise, Bilardello altered his swing a bit. The result, however, was a bat that was virtually silent for most of the year.

On the bases, Bilardello has average speed for a catcher, which means the opposition can rest easy.

Bilardello's slump extended to his defense. He made eight errors behind the plate in 437 chances, had six passed balls and was not able to establish a great rapport with the pitchers.

Among the five catchers used by the Expos last season, however, Bilardello probably has the best arm for throwing out runners, although getting into games on such an infrequent basis reduces the effectiveness.

OVERALL:

Light-hitting catchers with a decent throwing arm can sometimes find a spot on teams where the first-stringer is going to play 140 games or so. Since Mike Fitzgerald has been injury-prone, they may need a backup who can deliver more punch than Bilardello.

Rooker: "Dann is destined to serve as a backup catcher for as long as he remains in the majors."

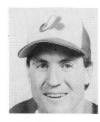

CASEY CANDAELE
INF, No. 9
SR, 5'9", 160 lbs.
ML Svc: less than
one year
Born: 1-12-61 in
Lompoc, CA

HITTING, BASERUNNING, FIELDING:

If Casey Candaele is to remain with the Expos in 1987, he must force more walks out of opposing pitchers. And as he stands at just 5'9", it really shouldn't be so difficult. Yet last year, Candaele walked only five times in 104 at-bats, a ratio which disturbed manager Buck Rodgers. Candaele also needs to bunt more often to make maximum use of his better-than-average speed.

Candaele has a chance to stick with a club as a platoon second baseman against lefthanded pitching. A switch-hitter, he is more effective batting from the right side than from the left, where he can be overpowered.

As a baserunner, Candaele still has much to learn about getting the proper lead and jump--opposing catchers nabbed him five times in eight attempts.

In the field, Candaele showed flashes of brilliance at times last season, but he lacks consistency. He has a tough time with routine plays. In his favor, Candaele is versatile and plays three infield positions as well as the outfield.

OVERALL:

Candaele is the type who would run through a barrage of baseballs to get the job done, an attitude that managers are looking for. But he has to remind himself that he shouldn't go beyond his limits in trying to impress the decision-makers.

WALLACE JOHNSON
OF, No. 63
SR, 5'11", 185 lbs.
ML Svc: 2 years
Born: 12-25-56 in
Gary, IN

HITTING, BASERUNNING, FIELDING:

Wallace Johnson may have finally secured a spot on the Expos' roster with his timely pinch-hits last year. As pinch-hitting goes, it doesn't get much better than his 13-for-30 record (a .433 average) after July 30th.

The major change in Johnson at the plate is confidence. He does not seem to be the tentative batter he was in other, less impressive stints with the Expos. In the past, a steady diet of curveballs was enough to outwit Johnson, but he seems determined not to waste what is likely his last shot at the majors.

Johnson is the type of baserunner who keeps a pitcher on guard--he will steal a base when the club needs one. He also has the speed to turn singles into doubles and doubles into triples.

In the field, he is somewhat of a risk--not the type a manager would want in the latter part of a close game. If Wallace remains in the majors, it will be on the strength of his pinch-hitting, not his fielding.

OVERALL:

Rooker: "Since 1981, Johnson has been brought up from or sent down to the minors eight times by the Expos. But it now seems that as long as he can deliver as a pinch-hitter even close to last year's performance, he could be the 24th man on the roster."

WAYNE KRENCHICKI
INF, No. 15
LR, 6'1", 180 lbs.
ML Svc: 8 years
Born: 9-17-54 in
Trenton, NJ

HITTING, BASERUNNING, FIELDING:

If the *First-ball, Fastball Hitters Club* is searching for a president, Wayne Krenchicki is their man. He doesn't like to be cheated on his swings.

He likes the ball up and in from both right- and lefthanded pitchers, although his at-bats against southpaws are infrequent. But Krenchicki has also had some success with pitches out and away, taking them to the opposite field. For the most part, however, he likes to pull the ball and has extra-base power when he gets a fastball to his liking.

On the bases, Krenchicki has average speed, but he knows how to pick his spots for a stolen base. He may show less speed this season: a lingering effect of a bone fracture in his foot late last year. Though he spends time on the bench, he is a student of the game and that has helped him do the little things that win ball games.

While Krenchicki does not have outstanding range in the field, he is a smooth fielder on any ball he can reach. He can also surprise the opposition with a true fielding gem when least expected. He can play either first or third base, although he appears less comfortable at third than he used to be. He can even play the outfield in an emergency.

OVERALL:

Krenchicki isn't flashy, but he is a good fill-in for a week or so. His mind is always on the game and he might make excellent coaching, even managerial material.

Rooker: "Krenchicki can do so many things coming off the bench, but it appears that his ability as a pinch-hitter is what will keep him around a few more seasons."

**CHARLIE LEA
RHP, No. 53
RR, 6'4", 205 lbs.
ML Svc: 6 years
Born: 12-25-58 in
    Orleans, France**

PITCHING, FIELDING:

If Charlie Lea throws even one pitch in a spring training game, it will be one more than he's thrown in either of the last two exhibition seasons. It was in the spring of 1985 that he reported to camp with tendinitis in his right shoulder. Eventually, the tendinitis was diagnosed as a rotator cuff tear, a career-threatening injury for a pitcher. Lea had surgery in May 1985, and has been on a rehabilitation program ever since.

It has been a long and uncertain way back for the man who was described by Pete Rose in 1984, as "one of the five toughest pitchers I've ever had to face. He reminds me a lot of Juan Marichal when he was with the Giants. He can throw four or five different pitches, and he's effective with all of them."

In his prime, Lea could get you out with his 90+ MPH fastball, the slider, curveball or change-up. He also had tremendous poise, usually finishing among the league-leaders for clutch pitching with men on base.

Although he sometimes looks a little awkward as a fielder, Lea is strong fundamentally and usually handles anything hit his way. His hitting has never been good and it's doubtful that he is concerned with improving either his plate or baserunning skills at this point.

OVERALL:

He was able to throw for a short while without straining himself last summer, but he couldn't throw hard for long. The Expos' medical personnel are optimistic Lea can do some pitching this spring, although management is not counting him in its plans. Anything will be a welcome surprise.

**BOB McCLURE
LHP, No. 10
SL, 5'11", 170 lbs.
ML Svc: 10 years
Born: 4-29-53 in
    Oakland, CA**

PITCHING, FIELDING:

Manager Buck Rodgers summoned Bob McClure to Montreal last season for the specific purpose of getting out a lefthanded hitter here and there.

The longest outing for McClure is usually one inning, a contrast to the days when he was an occasional starter and frequent set-up man with the Brewers. When there's a tough lefthanded hitter due up in the seventh or eighth inning, the call goes out to McClure.

McClure remains effective against the lefties because he can freeze them with a sharp-breaking curveball, which is his major league meal ticket. He also throws the fastball in the 85-90 MPH range, which means that batters can't just set themselves up for the curve.

Although McClure is a two-pitch pitcher, he still throws both with quality and savvy. The pressure situations don't bother him, although he sometimes can exasperate a manager on the way to producing a happy conclusion.

National League baserunners saw McClure's pickoff move for the first time last season and it was enough to make opponents wary. His move to first is quick and runners are advised not to let their lead extend much beyond three steps.

McClure also does all the little things well on the mound, alertly grabbing bunts and unhesitatingly throwing to the proper base. He covers first base well.

MONTREAL EXPOS

ANDY McGAFFIGAN
RHP, No. 27
RR, 6'3", 195 lbs.
ML Svc: 4 years
Born: 10-25-56 in West Palm Beach, FL

PITCHING, FIELDING:
HITTING, BASERUNNING:

Already armed with a moving fastball and a sneaky slider, Andy McGaffigan added a change-up last year, and it was effective in keeping batters off balance.

As a starter, he is less successful once he's had a couple of turns through the batting order. Hitters warm up to him and he runs out of gas after about five innings. He is better-suited to a relief role. After August 1st last year, McGaffigan allowed only six earned runs as a long and middle reliever, a stretch of almost 50 innings, which resulted in a glittering 1.09 ERA.

A McGaffigan trademark is his habit of throwing to first base on pickoff attempts. His effort to hold runners close is often counterproductive, however, since his concentration on the hitter suffers. McGaffigan is a poor fielder and most of his errors are on throws--yes, on *throws*--some of which even occur on pickoff attempts. He's adequate in fielding balls hit in the vicinity of the mound.

At bat, he's not good for much other than an occasional bunt. As a baserunner, he is average.

OVERALL:

There are outings during which McGaffigan comes out of the bullpen ready to pitch aggressively and well. At other times, however, he is a defensive pitcher who loses his concentration too quickly.

His successes during the latter part of the season lead one to think his aggressive days are here to stay.

Rooker: "Everything points to the fact that McGaffigan is best-suited for a middle relief, perhaps even a stopper role out of the Montreal bullpen.

"He needs a little kick every once in a while, but with McGaffigan's stuff, he can either win or save a lot of games for you."

LUIS RIVERA
INF, No. 57
RR, 5'9", 165 lbs.
ML Svc: 1 year
Born: 1-3-64 in Cidra, PR

HITTING, BASERUNNING, FIELDING:

At first glance, the .205 average which Luis Rivera left as his calling card in 1986 wouldn't seem to get him an invitation back to the big leagues. But Montreal manager Rodgers believes that Rivera can be at least a .250 hitter if he can learn to hit the ball to the opposite field.

At the moment, Rivera isn't a match for major league pitchers, who have quickly learned that he will succumb to hard stuff which is kept down and on the outside part of the plate.

While Rivera displays good speed when hustling down the first base line, he isn't much of a threat to steal.

It is Rivera's fielding that attracts the eye, however. If the Expos do trade Tim Wallach and move Hubie Brooks to third, Rivera would likely inherit the shortstop job. He covers more ground than the incumbent and can make the truly dazzling play, although he sometimes lays back too long on slow or high choppers.

OVERALL:

There does not seem to be much doubt that the Expos are grooming Rivera as their shortstop of the future.

Rooker: "Rivera headed to the winter league in the Dominican Republic as soon as the major league season ended, with specific instructions to learn to spray the ball. He may have to expand the learning process to another year at Triple-A."

MONTREAL EXPOS

RANDY ST. CLAIRE
RHP, No. 51
RR, 6'3", 190 lbs.
ML Svc: 1 year plus
Born: 8-23-60 in
 Glens Falls, NY

PITCHING, FIELDING:

It was a new Randy St. Claire who reported to the Expos after his recall from the minors last September. Even when he strode to the mound, you noticed the difference. Unlike most major leaguers who wear their socks under the pants legs of their uniform, St. Claire pulled his over the cuffs, a throwback to another era. But that wasn't the only new approach by St. Claire.

He had worked on his fastball and especially his slider at Indianapolis, and he finally was determined to challenge big league hitters with his best stuff. He only pitched in six games in September, but the 15 strikeouts and 1.41 ERA he recorded had to be a source of encouragement, both to himself and to the ballclub. The more success he had, the more confident St. Claire became, expertly mixing his pitches to keep batters guessing.

St. Claire also helps himself in the field. He has the instincts of an infielder, and he's fearless, whether it comes to blocking home plate when the catcher is chasing a wild pitch or outracing a baserunner galumphing down the first-base line.

OVERALL:

Rooker: "Randy has been back and forth to the minors several times over the past few years and has lacked the intensity it takes to hold on to a major league job. But he seems to have developed a more determined outlook to the game and has a fire in his eyes that could help make him stick this time."

HERMAN
 WINNINGHAM
OF, No. 3
LR, 5'11", 175 lbs.
ML Svc: 2 years
Born: 12-1-61 in
 Orangeburg, SC

HITTING, BASERUNNING, FIELDING:

Two seasons ago, Herman Winningham was considered by the Expos as one of their prime prospects. By July of last year, he was in the minors.

As a hitter, his problem is that his front elbow comes up too high when he swings, giving a lift to his swing and turning too many balls into easy fly ball outs. While Winningham did make some adjustments, he has to remind himself to maintain a compact swing and to chop the ball through the infield to make use of his better-than-average speed.

He was overmatched by nearly all types of pitches he saw in the big leagues last year, nearly striking out once in every four at-bats.

On the bases, Winningham is still a valuable asset, although he has to study pitchers more. With his good speed, getting the proper jump would mean a lot more stolen bases.

It is Winningham's poor defense that really needs work: he frequently throws to the wrong base. It was his inability to play "heads-up ball" which led to his exile in the minor leagues. He will, however, chase down anything in the outfield, but his average arm and mental errors make his future uncertain.

OVERALL:

Winningham is an easygoing, almost complacent player who might benefit from a more competitive on-the-field outlook.

Rooker: "Winningham is still young enough to adjust, but he needs a lot more work. Fortunately, his attitude remains keen, but with Mitch Webster playing ahead of him, Winningham is likely to learn more in the minors."

PITCHING:

Rick Aguilera struggled early in the season and felt like a fifth wheel in the Mets' powerful starting rotation. While the fans at Shea were posting Ks for Gooden, Ss for Sid, loving Darling and getting to know Ojeda, Aguilera was getting his pitches up in the strike zone and giving up home runs (on May 1st in Atlanta, he served up 4 gopher balls in 3 1/3 innings). His demotion to the bullpen was intended to relax him by taking the pressure off, but it served to upset him further and he had a difficult time adjusting. Given a shot as a starter again in early July when Bruce Berenyi couldn't cut it, Aguilera came on strong to salvage a respectable season. He went on to win six decisions in a row, including five straight starts. He allowed just five home runs in his last 116 innings.

Aguilera throws five pitches, but his essential pitches are the sinker and the slider. He must have those pitches working down low in the strike zone and forcing ground ball outs. He also throws a good curveball and change-up as well as an above-average fastball. He has plenty of pitches in his arsenal and can have stretches where he throws them all for strikes, thus keeping hitters off balance. The intangible aspect--confidence--must also be in place, however, if he is to be successful.

FIELDING, HITTING, BASERUNNING:

Because of his training as an infielder (he was a third baseman at Brigham Young University and played on the same team with Chicago pitcher Scott Nielsen, Cleveland outfielder Cory Snyder and California first

RICK AGUILERA
RHP, No. 38
RR, 6'4", 200 lbs.
ML Svc: 2 years
Born: 12-31-61 in
San Gabriel, CA

1986 STATISTICS

W	L	ERA	G	GS	CG	SV	IP	H	R	ER	BB	SO
10	7	3.88	28	20	2	0	141.2	145	70	61	36	104

CAREER STATISTICS

W	L	ERA	G	GS	CG	SV	IP	H	R	ER	BB	SO
20	14	2.58	49	39	4	0	264	263	119	105	73	178

baseman Wally Joyner) and his natural abilities as an athlete, Aguilera is a fine fielder.

He is the most accomplished hitter among Mets pitchers, with a .212 average, two home runs and eight RBIs in 85 career at-bats. He is a decent baserunner.

OVERALL:

Aguilera became a pitcher during his sophomore year in college, which was only six years ago. He is still developing his pitching skills. Considering his limited experience, his development has been extraordinary.

Rooker: "The key for Rick is having control of his slider and sinker. When he has both of them working well, he is one of the game's best pitchers. He has the right stuff and composure to rank among the game's elite. He has the ability to catch up with the other stars on the Mets and have a big year in 1987."

NEW YORK METS

HITTING:

Four years ago, Wally Backman was going nowhere in the Mets organization. The club's brain trust at the time had not only awarded the second-base job to Brian Giles, but demoted Backman to Triple-A, where he was told to convert to third base.

But then-Tidewater manager Davey Johnson, a former All-Star second baseman, showed confidence in Backman and switched him back to second. Backman has never forgotten the favor. He also never has stopped working to repay it by making himself into a better player.

A switch-hitter, Backman compiled a career-best .340 average against righthanded pitching last season when he batted .320 overall. He became one of baseball's premier table setters along with teammates Lenny Dykstra and Mookie Wilson.

A fastball hitter from both sides, Backman can punch the ball to all fields, but he has good gap power when he gets the low-ball from a righthander. He is weak as a righthanded hitter (last season, in 52 righty at-bats against southpaw pitching, he hit just .192). Batting righthanded, he is primarily a high-ball hitter.

Backman is a gritty performer who will do what it takes to get on base, an approach reflected by the fact he has built himself into one of the game's more accomplished bunters. He legged out 10 of 20 bunt attempts last season.

BASERUNNING:

A tough player to double up, Backman has good speed and rarely grounds into double plays. He was hampered by a thigh injury which nagged him much of the early part of last season and limited his basestealing ability. Though the injury wasn't serious enough to keep him out of the lineup, he never used it as an excuse for his subpar basestealing.

FIELDING:

Backman has made himself into one of the

WALLY BACKMAN
2B, No. 6
SR, 5'9", 160 lbs.
ML Svc: 5 years
Born: 9-22-59 in
Hillsboro, OR

1986 STATISTICS

AVG	G	AB	R	H	2B	3B	HR	RBI	BB	SO	SB
.320	124	387	67	124	18	2	1	27	36	32	13

CAREER STATISTICS

AVG	G	AB	R	H	2B	3B	HR	RBI	BB	SO	SB
.285	572	1775	272	506	77	13	6	125	194	243	86

VS. RHP

VS. LHP

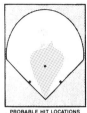

PROBABLE HIT LOCATIONS

National League's most dependable second baseman. He has turned a weakness into a strength by improving his footwork and timing on the double play pivot.

His personal highlight of the season was a diving stab he made to knock down Terry Pendleton's smash up the middle and start a game-ending double play against the Cardinals in late April. The play helped the Mets sweep four straight from the defending NL East champs at a time when the Mets were staking out the league title by making the Cardinals roll over.

OVERALL:

Rooker: "He had a great year with the bat last season. Though he still likes the ball pitched away, he is beginning to handle the inside pitch better now.

"There may be more talented players, but few play the game harder and approach it with better work habits. Backman's flinty, aggressive style has won him much respect."

NEW YORK METS

HITTING:

A classic cleanup hitter, Gary Carter is aggressive to a fault. He often swings at the first pitch. He is easily jammed by pitches up and in and often chases breaking balls down and away. He chased bad pitches more often this season than in the past; his strikeout total was up and his .255 average was his lowest in six seasons. Righthanders with good breaking balls give him trouble as do lefthanders with decent movement on their fastballs or curveballs. A weakness that Carter has imposed on himself with his aggressive style is that he does not take advantage of the right field and right-center opportunities which overcompensating defenses allow him.

A dead pull hitter, Carter continues, however, to pull a lot of weight in the power-packed Mets' order. He has proven himself Timex-tough, withstanding a gauntlet of punishment throughout his distinguished 12-year career. When the Mets put him on the disabled list last August, they did it to protect him from himself as much as to rest his injured ligaments in his left thumb. Amazingly, it was only the second time in his career that Carter has done time on the DL.

BASERUNNING:

His surgery-scarred right knee is a ball and chain on the bases. He slides aggressively, but the bottom line is that his plodding speed caused him to hit into 21 double plays, the most ever by a Met.

FIELDING:

Carter's strength as a signal caller is disputed by some. But he knows the hitters. Newcomer Bob Ojeda credited Carter as a key to his success early last season.

Dodgers' catcher Mike Scioscia has a slight edge on Carter in the business of plate-blocking, but baserunners heading for home against the Mets' backstop know they're heading for a brick wall. He will brutalize the less kamikaze among them. He is a rock and inflicts as much hurt as he absorbs. He is

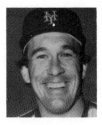

GARY CARTER
C, No. 8
RR, 6'2", 210 lbs.
ML Svc: 12 years
Born: 4-8-54 in
Culver City, CA

1986 STATISTICS

AVG	G	AB	R	H	2B	3B	HR	RBI	BB	SO	SB
.255	132	490	81	125	14	2	24	105	62	63	1

CAREER STATISTICS

AVG	G	AB	R	H	2B	3B	HR	RBI	BB	SO	SB
.271	1689	6063	847	1646	287	26	271	999	680	765	36

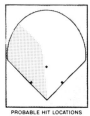

VS. RHP   VS. LHP   PROBABLE HIT LOCATIONS

equally adept at protecting the ball as well as the plate.

While Carter blamed both tendinitis and the inability of his pitchers to hold runners close, his 26% kill ratio during the regular season tells more. His battle-scarred knees prevent him from popping up as quickly as he used to and his release does not pack its former explosive force. In short, he can be run on by even mediocre baserunners.

OVERALL:

Carter has been oft criticized by the opposition for his rah-rah, fist-in-the-air playing style. If more major leaguers played like Gary Carter, however, fewer owners and fans would gripe about feeling cheated.

Rooker: "Don't stop at saying he is the best catcher in the game, he's also one of the best players in the game. He is tough to pitch to and aggressive in all phases of the game. The Mets have already had their money's worth from Carter."

NEW YORK METS

RON DARLING
RHP, No. 12
RR, 6'3", 195 lbs.
ML Svc: 3 years
Born: 8-19-60 in
Honolulu, HI

PITCHING:

The ultimate proof of Ron Darling's 1986 pitching performance is the 27-8 record the Mets compiled in games he started last season. When Darling pitches, the Mets are very likely to win. That doesn't necessarily mean that Darling will *get* the win; he led the staff in no decisions with 13. But he did his job consistently well.

Though his record could easily have been better with a little luck, his 15-6 mark was a measure of his consistency, a good follow-up to a strong 16-6 season the previous year. A measure of his improvement was the fact his walks were down by 33, his strikeouts were up by 17 despite pitching 11 fewer innings and he lowered his ERA from 2.90 in '85 to 2.81, the third-best in the league.

Darling has become more consistent, but consistency is still an area in which he can improve. While his control was better in '86, it was still a problem as he stretched the count to too many hitters. Better control and a little luck are the only things keeping him from a 20-win season.

A power pitcher who can also show finesse, Darling mixes an excellent forkball (the forefather of the split-finger fastball) with an outstanding curveball, change-up and slider.

FIELDING, HITTING, BASERUNNING:

A tremendous athlete, Darling is confident, talented and quick afield. He is also cunning and will throw out the lead runner without hesitation. Perhaps his greatest talent in the field, however, is his pickoff move, which is one of the game's best.

He has good speed, but has yet to hit well enough to make himself a threat on the bases. Darling is one of the Mets' most proficient bunters.

OVERALL:

Already established as one of the game's better pitchers, this is the year Darling joins the elite and finally wins 20 games. His stuff is sharp and he is a smart and diligent worker who responds well to pressure.

Rooker: "Darling's one problem may be he tries to be too fine. If he lets his natural talent prevail and continues to improve with his control, Darling is a sure bet to win 20 games."

1986 STATISTICS

W	L	ERA	G	GS	CG	SV	IP	H	R	ER	BB	SO
15	6	2.81	34	34	4	0	237	203	84	74	81	184

CAREER STATISTICS

W	L	ERA	G	GS	CG	SV	IP	H	R	ER	BB	SO
44	24	3.12	108	107	11	0	726	627	285	252	316	510

NEW YORK METS

HITTING:

With play-alike Wally Backman, Lenny Dykstra is the other half of the Mets' pigpen twins. Like Backman, Dykstra plays the game as if he is paid by how much dirt he gets smeared on his uniform. A tough out, he sported a .445 slugging percentage during the regular season as the Mets' leadoff man.

Perhaps the ultimate compliment paid to Dykstra's deceptive pop came when both the Astros and Red Sox accused Dykstra of corking his bat after his power production helped eliminate them in the playoffs and World Series. Dykstra batted .300 in the post-season with three home runs; one of them, a dramatic, two-run ninth-inning shot won Game Three of the playoffs. It is unlikely, however, that Dykstra will heretofore be known as a power hitter.

It took time for Davey Johnson to be convinced Dykstra had what it takes to be the Mets' everyday center fielder and leadoff man, but Dykstra finally took a headfirst slide into Johnson's heart with his kamikaze style. Besides batting .295, Dykstra had a .377 on-base average during the regular season.

A gamer who comes to play, Dykstra is a fastball hitter who can bunt the breaking ball. Dykstra also squeezes the strike zone with his crouching style and has an excellent eye.

Dykstra tries to lift the ball too much and should be hitting more on the ground. He probably flied out three times as often as he grounded out last season. He is at his best when he is trying to hit the ball from from the first-base side just to the left of second base.

He is still vulnerable to lefthanders. Dykstra batted just .225 against lefties in 1986.

BASERUNNING:

Dykstra plays the game pedal-to-the-metal whether in the outfield or on the bases, where he runs with abandon and bodysurfs into bases. As he becomes more familiar with the pitchers, he is getting better jumps. He is always a threat to take the extra base.

With his speed, Dykstra still does not hit

LENNY DYKSTRA
CF, No. 4
LL, 5'10", 160 lbs.
ML Svc: 2 years
Born: 2-10-63 in
Santa Ana, CA

1986 STATISTICS

AVG	G	AB	R	H	2B	3B	HR	RBI	BB	SO	SB
.295	147	431	77	127	27	7	8	45	58	55	31

CAREER STATISTICS

AVG	G	AB	R	H	2B	3B	HR	RBI	BB	SO	SB
.280	230	667	117	187	36	10	9	64	88	79	46

  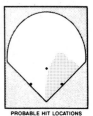

VS. RHP   VS. LHP   PROBABLE HIT LOCATIONS

the ball enough on the ground.

FIELDING:

Dykstra goes to the fence like a hockey player to the boards. He has made more than one amazing catch, but the most memorable came in May when his leaping catch at the center field wall robbed Cincinnati's Dave Parker of a probable home run.

Of all the 1986 Mets' outfielders, Dykstra showed the best judgment and rarely was caught making a fundamental mistake. His speed enables him to play deeper than most and his arm strength is above average.

OVERALL:

Rooker: "Dykstra sets an aggressive tone for the Mets at the top of their order and makes things happen. He has improved steadily as a player in all areas. His 1986 heroics during the playoffs and World Series proved that he can even perform beyond his abilities when necessary."

NEW YORK METS

PITCHING:

Maturity had always been Sid Fernandez's biggest problem along with a waistline that obeys like a spoiled child. But Fernandez matured greatly in 1986, particularly when he put aside the hurt of being passed over for a World Series start to help the Mets win the World Championship with 2 1/3 innings of hitless relief in Game 7.

Fernandez has two things to work on: his consistency and his weight. After a brilliant start which saw him post a 12-2 record and 2.67 ERA in 17 starts before the All-Star break, Fernandez slumped badly after the break, going 4-4 with a 4.69 ERA in 14 starts to finish 16-6 with 200 strikeouts. Fernandez's K-total tied Gooden for fourth highest in the league.

A hard fastball and excellent curveball notwithstanding, Fernandez's greatest weapon is his delivery. He delivers his pitches with a split-second's hesitation which gives hitters as much trouble as his pitches; this half-beat makes it difficult to time his delivery. In addition, his fastball rides and his curveball drops sharply. Fernandez can also change gears with the curveball, throwing a hard curve or a slow curve that freezes batters.

He also developed a change-up last season and became more confident with it after learning from the success Bob Ojeda enjoyed with his.

Fernandez is prone to being beaten by righthanded hitters, however. Of the 13 home runs Fernandez allowed, 12 of them were by righthanded hitters.

FIELDING, HITTING, BASERUNNING:

Fernandez worked to improve his move to first, but he can only compensate so much for his naturally slow delivery that makes him a liability against speed-oriented teams. He actually hates to bother himself with throws

SID FERNANDEZ
LHP, No. 50
LL, 6'1", 205 lbs.
ML Svc: 3 years
Born: 10-12-62 in
Honolulu, HI

1986 STATISTICS

W	L	ERA	G	GS	CG	SV	IP	H	R	ER	BB	SO
16	6	3.52	32	31	2	1	204.1	161	82	80	91	200

CAREER STATISTICS

W	L	ERA	G	GS	CG	SV	IP	H	R	ER	BB	SO
31	22	3.29	75	73	5	1	470.2	350	182	172	212	451

to first and does so only at the insistent demands of first baseman Keith Hernandez.

He is a decent enough fielder, but he is not alert defensively and doesn't concentrate enough on situations such as the bunt.

Sid can swing the bat, but is not a fast runner.

OVERALL:

Fernandez has the deceptive delivery and the stuff to make him a 20-game winner. He must continue to mature and work hard to get the most out of his talent. Slimming down is perhaps the best way to show management that he has those intentions.

Rooker: "Fernandez had an outstanding year last season. If he continues to improve, he could win the Cy Young in the not-so-distant future.

"As a pitcher, Fernandez seems to be growing up before our eyes. Almost as quickly, however, he is also growing *out*. He is so susceptible to putting on weight that he is going to have to resign himself to counting calories throughout his career. Being out of shape will not give him the kind of stamina it takes to pitch past the seventh inning."

NEW YORK METS

PITCHING:

FACT: Last season, Dwight Gooden became the first pitcher in major league history to strike out 200 or more batters in his first three seasons.

FACT: His 12 complete games stood second in the league to Fernando Valenzuela's 20; his 200 strikeouts tied teammate Sid Fernandez for fourth in the league; his 2.84 ERA tied for fourth best in the league and his 17-6 record was fifth best overall.

FICTION: Something is wrong with Dwight Gooden.

Something *is* different with Dwight Gooden, however.

His fastball was too straight and his curveball lost some of its arc last season, but give the National League hitters some credit. His utter dominance over two long seasons caused hitters enough frustration that Gooden had become public enemy number one. A good, solid hit off the 22-year-old fireballer had become a much sought-after badge of courage. Hitters learned to lay off Gooden's high fastball, and Gooden spent much of the season trying to work another angle.

Besides a disobedient fastball, his problems included getting behind in the count early and a breaking ball which proved erratic throughout the season. His successes were nowhere near as effortless as they appeared to be during his first two seasons.

Despite control problems and the overstated concern they brought, Gooden remained composed and in control of himself, if not his pitches.

He is still working to develop a change-up, which he will need to outsmart hitters when his fastball straightens out and his curveball isn't sharp. His fastball, which still rockets in at 95 MPH, and his curveball, when right, are still the class of the league.

Gooden became more of a pitcher than a smoker last season and the transition should help him over the long haul.

DWIGHT GOODEN
RHP, No. 16
RR, 6'3", 198 lbs.
ML Svc: 3 years
Born: 11-16-64 in
Tampa, FL

1986 STATISTICS

W	L	ERA	G	GS	CG	SV	IP	H	R	ER	BB	SO
17	6	2.84	33	33	12	0	250	197	92	79	80	200

CAREER STATISTICS

W	L	ERA	G	GS	CG	SV	IP	H	R	ER	BB	SO
58	19	2.28	99	99	35	0	744.2	556	215	189	222	744

FIELDING, HITTING, BASERUNNING:

He is still not quick to the plate and may never be because of his unhurried motion, but last season Gooden became more attuned to holding runners on base than he had been in the past.

He fields his position well and is quick to cover first base.

Gooden was as disappointed with his batting slump in 1986 as his pitching slump. After tying for the league-lead in hits among pitchers with 21 in 1985, he managed only seven hits last year.

OVERALL:

There are numerous theories as to why Gooden was only very successful and not sensational in 1986. Those theories range from a weight gain of 20 pounds to poor leg drive off the mound to personal problems, including a breakup with his fiance over the birth of a son by another woman.

Still, Gooden is one of the game's great talents and he has the personal makeup and competitive fire necessary to stay at the top of his game.

Rooker: "Dwight will be the pitcher who sets the standards for the '80s. He is just 22 years old but pitches as though he is 32. He experienced a bit of a transitional year and had to learn how to pitch when his best stuff wasn't working. The lessons learned will only serve to make him a better pitcher."

NEW YORK METS

HITTING:

Danny Heep had an impressive year in 1986, filling in wherever the Mets needed him in the outfield or at first base and leading the club in pinch-hitting with a .300 average. He filled the gap left when pinch-hitter deluxe Rusty Staub was not brought back last spring.

But in his free agent year, the 29-year old outfielder sought his freedom from the Mets to pursue a chance to play everyday with another club. Heep was willing to forfeit the chance to play on a winning club to take that shot, despite no guarantee of a starting job elsewhere.

Too bad.

In 1986, Heep batted .282 in a fill-in role with five homers and 33 RBIs and he hit .404 with men in scoring position. Because Davey Johnson likes to go with the hot hand, Heep got a shot to replace left fielder George Foster when Foster slumped at midseason. But after Foster was released, Heep tailed off and Kevin Mitchell and later Mookie Wilson got hot enough to take the job away.

Heep is a pull hitter and because of that there are holes in his swing on the outside part of the plate and below his thighs. He is a streak hitter who likes the ball up from righthanders. Lefthanders are his worst enemy: he batted .083 (1-for-12) against them last season.

BASERUNNING:

Heep is not as aggressive as he could be on the bases. Though he is a threat to stretch singles into doubles, he is not much of a threat to steal despite having decent speed.

FIELDING:

Heep can play all three outfield positions

DANNY HEEP
OF, No. 25
LL, 5'11", 185 lbs.
ML Svc: 7 years
Born: 7-3-57 in
San Antonio, TX

1986 STATISTICS

AVG	G	AB	R	H	2B	3B	HR	RBI	BB	SO	SB
.282	86	195	24	55	8	2	5	33	30	31	1

CAREER STATISTICS

AVG	G	AB	R	H	2B	3B	HR	RBI	BB	SO	SB
.257	560	1313	144	338	71	5	25	149	153	175	9

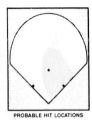

VS. RHP   VS. LHP   PROBABLE HIT LOCATIONS

well and back up at first base. He is an adequate outfielder who runs down balls it does not initially appear he will get. In addition to his good range he has a decent arm.

OVERALL:

Because of his inability to hit lefthanded pitching, Heep may be fooling himself with his obsession to become an everyday player. He is a valuable player to a winning club in the role he filled with the Mets, but he would be devalued if he was exposed to lefthanders everyday.

Rooker: "Danny tries to pull the ball a bit much. He is a good pinch-hitter and has a winning attitude. He has not shown enough ability against lefthanded pitchers to earn consideration for a full-time starting role."

NEW YORK METS

HITTING:

A career .300-plus hitter, Keith Hernandez prides himself on knowing the tendencies of the league's pitchers, catchers and even individual umpires. If his .413 on-base average (which tied for the league-lead) is not testimony to his study habits, his league-leading 94 walks are.

Though he claims that he often guess-hits, Hernandez is the consummate thinking man's hitter. He takes a pitcher to a 3-2 count so often, a Hernandez at-bat is often like a suspense thriller come to life.

He has the ability to intensify his concentration level as both the count and the stakes get higher. Despite a subpar post-season performance, he is correctly renowned as a clutch hitter. Over the past eight seasons, he has hit .333 with runners in scoring position.

A low-ball hitter early in the count, Hernandez frequently goes the other way with two strikes against him. He hits both lefthanders and righthanders equally well, as illustrated by his 1986 .307 average vs. LHP and .310 overall.

When he is hot, Hernandez has few weaknesses. The only way for a lefthanded pitcher to get even a slight edge is to pitch him inside with breaking stuff.

BASERUNNING:

No one digs harder going from first to third, but most players are faster. He is not the Pete Rose-type of baserunner who will run out everything to first base and he is not a basestealer, but he runs the bases knowing that it's the fastest way to get back in the batter's box.

FIELDING:

Hernandez ranks among the best players ever to flash a first baseman's mitt. He positively shines when fielding the bunt and stalking the lead runner. His left arm is a high-powered hunting rifle and Hernandez is a confident marksman. He turns the 3-6-3 double play better than anyone in the game.

KEITH HERNANDEZ
1B, No. 17
LL, 6'0", 195 lbs.
ML Svc: 12 years
Born: 10-20-53 in
San Francisco, CA

1986 STATISTICS

AVG	G	AB	R	H	2B	3B	HR	RBI	BB	SO	SB
.310	149	551	94	171	34	1	13	83	94	69	2

CAREER STATISTICS

AVG	G	AB	R	H	2B	3B	HR	RBI	BB	SO	SB
.302	1721	6090	969	1840	372	58	128	900	917	795	96

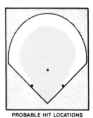

VS. RHP   VS. LHP   PROBABLE HIT LOCATIONS

His graceful style is often ballet-like; no one can leap for a ball, turn, double-pump and throw the way he can.

OVERALL:

Hernandez is the team-acknowledged MVP and leader of the Mets. Now 33, he has said he would like to play until he is 40 years old. On that point, however, his body will have the final say. A chain smoker who likes his beer, Hernandez does not exercise the kind of care most players need to enjoy that kind of longevity. His career is notorious for slow starts and slumps during the late July/early August dog days. Such predictable valleys are likely attributable to these two vices. His smoking threatens to hurt him more than any breaking-ball ace.

Rooker: "Keith is heads and shoulders above anyone else in baseball in the style he plays first base. He has more than enough range to his right and seems to know what a batter is going to do before it's done.

"He is a player's player and the Mets would not be the same team without him."

NEW YORK METS

HITTING:

Howard Johnson is a fastball fiend. He can hit the league's best heaters out of most ballparks. Unfortunately, he can be curved to death.

After two seasons with the Mets, Johnson has yet to learn to hit the breaking ball and develop into the patient, disciplined hitter the Mets intend him to become. Johnson did contribute 10 home runs and 39 RBIs, power numbers closely equivalent to his 1985 production (11 homers, 46 RBI) in 169 fewer at-bats.

A switch-hitter, Johnson's better half is the left side, where he shows more power. He is a low-ball hitter from that side and a high-ball hitter from the right side.

Johnson still chases a lot of bad pitches, and until he learns more discipline, he will only be an average hitter and a below-average pinch-hitter. He has the power and speed to be a better-than-average hitter if he ever cuts down his swing and learns to be less concerned with pulling the ball.

BASERUNNING:

Johnson is a good baserunner with decent speed. He stole eight bases last season and was caught just once.

He is a legitimate threat to stretch a single into a double and he could be a good basestealing threat if he ever develops the consistency needed to win a starting job.

FIELDING:

Defense has been a roller coaster ride for Johnson. He will routinely make the brilliant play, then have problems with the ordinary one. His range is excellent and his arm is strong. His club-high 20 errors in 98 games last season are explained by the fact that Davey Johnson used him on an experimental basis at shortstop last season. Also, Johnson

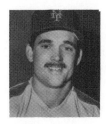

HOWARD JOHNSON
3B, No. 20
SR, 5'10", 175 lbs.
ML Svc: 5 years
Born: 11-29-60 in
Clearwater, FL

1986 STATISTICS

AVG	G	AB	R	H	2B	3B	HR	RBI	BB	SO	SB
.245	88	220	30	54	14	0	10	39	31	64	8

CAREER STATISTICS

AVG	G	AB	R	H	2B	3B	HR	RBI	BB	SO	SB
.252	411	1185	145	299	51	5	40	154	128	249	31

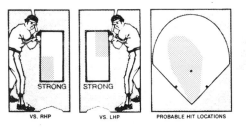

VS. RHP VS. LHP PROBABLE HIT LOCATIONS

played inconsistently because he received inconsistent playing time.

OVERALL:

Johnson has forged a reputation for getting clutch hits during his brief career. He added to that reputation with a ninth-inning, game-tying home run off hard-throwing Cardinals reliever Todd Worrell in late April and later with a game-winning three-run home run to beat the Reds in the 14th inning of a memorable July brawl-game.

Rooker: "Johnson is a positive force and coachable player who adopted gracefully to his part-time role. With Ray Knight's hot start, Johnson really never had a chance to compete. Here's a guy who can hit for power and who can steal bases. Defensively, he'll probably never be rock solid, but his clutch-hitting and baserunning will always make his resume respectable."

NEW YORK METS

HITTING:

Hitters constantly tinker with their batting stances, looking to spackle holes in their swings. But few, if any, have ever changed their stances as drastically as Ray Knight did last spring.

Desperate men do desperate things.

When Mets GM Frank Cashen held a spring training "State of the Mets" news briefing last March, he made it plain that Knight's final guaranteed year of $600,000 in 1986 was eminently chewable. The emergence of rookie Kevin Mitchell, a third baseman by trade, put Knight up against a wall.

To Knight's rescue rode hitting instructor Bill Robinson, a self-made hitter who developed late in his career with the perenially strong Pirate teams of the mid and late 1970s. Robinson convinced Knight to make a change before the Mets made one first by releasing him. Robinson had Knight abandon the crouch he had used his entire career and take a more stand-up stance which better utilized his strong hands. Robinson's solution was a stroke of genius.

With his new, improved swing, Knight went on to bat .298 for the season and distinguish himself as the National League's *Comeback Player of the Year.*

Knight is a high fastball hitter who likes the ball out over the plate. A good breaking ball from a righthanded pitcher will take the bat out of his hands. But Knight proved last season he still has the power to pull a mistake out of the ballpark--he had 11 homers during the regular season. He is still a tough out in the clutch, as evidenced by his .354 average with runners in scoring position.

BASERUNNING:

Knight is slow afoot and no threat to take the extra base. He grounded into 19 double plays last season, second only to Gary Carter on the Mets.

FIELDING:

A lack of speed limits Knight's defensive range. While his lateral movement is a liability, he is quick and aggressive fielding bunts.

His arm was written off last winter. But after two seasons spent recovering from shoulder and elbow operations, Knight's arm was finally right in 1986 and it made a healthy

RAY KNIGHT
3B, No. 22
RR, 6'2", 185 lbs.
ML Svc: 10 years
Born: 12-28-52 in
Albany, GA

1986 STATISTICS

AVG	G	AB	R	H	2B	3B	HR	RBI	BB	SO	SB
.298	137	486	51	145	24	2	11	76	40	63	2

CAREER STATISTICS

AVG	G	AB	R	H	2B	3B	HR	RBI	BB	SO	SB
.278	1240	3967	410	1102	230	25	67	497	284	459	13

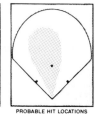

return along with his bat.

OVERALL:

While on the road to the 1986 world championship, the Mets front office had to make many decisions which were criticized by their fans. The club's decision not to go to arbitration with Ray Knight last winter was the first unpopular decision they made since October. It will not be the last.

Obviously, the Mets felt that Ray Knight is not a million-dollar-a-year third baseman. You can't blame Knight for asking but you can't blame the Mets for saying no.

When healthy, Knight has proved he can hit .300 or better in the majors, a feat few hitters ever achieve. Knight accomplished it twice, once with Cincinnati in 1979 and with Houston in 1983.

Rooker: "Ray surprised everyone last season by showing how much fight he still had in him. He's a competitive player who will turn combative when challenged.

"In the beginning of last season, Knight said he felt 'like a man without honor.' But his season came full circle when in the first World Series appearance of his 10-year major league career, he won the World Series MVP honor along with a world championship ring. Hats off to Ray Knight."

NEW YORK METS

HITTING:

Ever since Rusty Staub's retirement was forced by the advent of the 24-man roster, the Mets have sought a veteran lefthanded pinch-hitter off the bench. Danny Heep filled that gap much of last season until Lee Mazzilli was signed. And the Mets believe Lee Mazzilli is the right man for a part-time utility fielding and pinch-hitter deluxe role.

George Foster, feeling threatened by Mazzilli's August signing of a Triple-A contract with the Mets organization the week before, charged the Mets with racism. He was given his release, which he believed to be imminent, and Mazzilli took his spot the next day.

Mazzilli batted .276 for the Mets, and he contributed two critical pinch-hit singles that ignited come-from-behind wins in Games Six and Seven of the World Series.

After leaving New York to split the 1982 season between the Texas Rangers and the New York Yankees, he settled in with the Pirates in a part-time role during the past five seasons. In that time, Mazzilli matured into the role of a part-time player and pinch-hitter.

A switch-hitter, the 10-year major league veteran likes the ball down and in from righthanders and out over the plate from lefthanders. Stronger from the left side because he can go the other way and drive the ball that way, Mazzilli batted just .173 (total, including his stint with Pittsburgh) from the right side last season.

A .263 career hitter, Mazzilli has occasional pop in his bat, but his best asset is his ability to get on base as evidenced by his .401 on-base average last season and his .341 on-base average for his career. He has an excellent eye and draws a lot of walks.

BASERUNNING:

When he gets on base, Mazzilli still has the speed to steal a base. Not possessed with explosive speed, he has learned to steal off the pitcher and is a legitimate threat to take

LEE MAZZILLI
1B/OF, No. 13
SR, 6'1", 195 lbs.
ML Svc: 11 years
Born: 3-25-55 in
Brooklyn, NY

1986 STATISTICS

AVG	G	AB	R	H	2B	3B	HR	RBI	BB	SO	SB
.245	100	151	28	37	5	1	3	15	38	36	4

CAREER STATISTICS

AVG	G	AB	R	H	2B	3B	HR	RBI	BB	SO	SB
.263	1243	3758	514	987	176	23	84	406	575	562	183

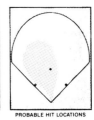

VS. RHP   VS. LHP   PROBABLE HIT LOCATIONS

STRONG   STRONG

the extra base.

FIELDING:

A first baseman/outfielder, Mazzilli's speed gives him good range in the outfield. But opponents run on his poor throwing arm, which is considered his biggest weakness.

At first base, he can do an adequate job in the part-time role of spelling Hernandez, but he is not an everyday first baseman.

OVERALL:

Rooker: "Mazzilli is ideal for what the Mets use him as: a versatile role player and switch-hitter coming off the bench to pinch-hit and fill in or start at three outfield positions as well as first base.

"Having the chance to go back to New York should add a few more years to his career."

PITCHING:

The story goes that Roger McDowell showed up at a major league tryout camp right out of high school and after he had thrown several fastballs, a scout said: "OK, let's see the fastball."

McDowell's fastball wasn't overpowering then--nor is it now. It is, however, no longer sneered at.

Through hard work and a medical miracle, his fastball has evolved into a sinister sinker that can drop as quickly as a sailor's paycheck. Three years ago, McDowell had surgery on his arm, during which doctors removed bone chips and spurs from his right elbow. There were fears he would never pitch again, but as it turns out, the physicians seem to have implanted a wicked sinker in their place. His post-operative sinker has made all the difference for this young reliever, and during teammate Jesse Orosco's inconsistencies early in 1986, some might say for the Mets as well.

McDowell has become one of the National League's most effective stoppers. Any lingering doubts about his arm strength were laid to rest by the 128 innings he pitched last season, following 127.1 innings the previous season. He recorded 22 saves in 38 save opportunities last season and his 14-9 record tied for most wins by a reliever.

The key to his fortune is consistency and the drop of the sinkerball. When he is on, the pitch drops so much and so quickly that a close-up shot of the swinging bat in relation to the ball would make the hitter look utterly foolish. It can be almost unhittable. When McDowell is going well, the shortstop and second baseman have to be on their toes, as he induces a bevy of double play balls. Last year, McDowell led the league in forcing batters to hit into DPs with 19. And of the 31 runners he inherited, only four scored.

When he simply doesn't have it in a particular outing, the sinker is a flat, slow fastball. He'll get his pitches up, and the hitters start to hit him. If you see two batters in a row hit fly balls or high line drives, the Davey Johnson hook won't be far behind. If

ROGER McDOWELL
RHP, No. 42
RR, 6'1", 175 lbs.
ML Svc: 2 years
Born: 12-21-60 in
Cincinnati, OH

1986 STATISTICS

W	L	ERA	G	GS	CG	SV	IP	H	R	ER	BB	SO
14	9	3.02	75	0	0	22	128	107	48	43	42	65

CAREER STATISTICS

W	L	ERA	G	GS	CG	SV	IP	H	R	ER	BB	SO
20	14	2.93	137	2	0	39	255.1	215	91	83	79	135

McDowell pitches as he did in 1986, however, that won't be very often.

FIELDING, HITTING, BASERUNNING:

McDowell fields his position like another shortstop, which is a big bonus since he is predominantly a ground ball pitcher. He springs off the mound with his follow-through and is in a good position to field anything hit back to him. McDowell has cat-quick reflexes and the good instincts to make any defensive play.

His speed makes him a decent baserunner. He is a fair hitter but doesn't get the opportunity to bat very often because of his role as reliever.

OVERALL:

His attitude is exceptional. McDowell reminds one of a former Met, Tug McGraw, in that he is intense on the field but has a good sense of humor that buoys his teammates and himself during tough times.

Rooker: "Roger has the uncanny ability to let a bad performance or loss roll off his back, a requisite attitude for a pitcher in such a pressure-filled role. He became a better pitcher last year and showed amazing control and consistency. He and Jesse Orosco form a great bullpen."

NEW YORK METS

HITTING:

With a dramatic surge over the final six weeks of the 1986 season, Kevin McReynolds finally reached the brink of the stardom that was predicted for him three years earlier.

McReynolds is one of the game's best "cripple shooters," a hitter who will punish the pitcher for falling behind in the count. Many of his home runs last year were on 3-0 and 3-1 pitches. He will take a 3-1 fastball right over the fence and can cream a hanging curveball or slider.

In a fashion typical of the stereotypical slugger, McReynolds strikes out a lot, but he has developed great patience at the plate and led the Padres in walks in 1986. Many pitchers would prefer to walk him rather than pit their best pitch against his strength. Observers can watch pitchers tempt McReynolds with breaking balls away, in a sort of tip-toe attempt to prevent him from extending his arms to power a fat pitch downtown.

McReynolds is a line drive hitter, home runs included. He hits to all parts of the park, though most of his homers are pulled to left field. He still is prone to slumps and doesn't seem to know how to work his way out of them.

BASERUNNING:

McReynolds is a good runner and he demonstrates that with good range in the field. But he hasn't been particularly effective on the bases, partly because he hasn't been pushed to do so. He's never stolen more than eight bases in a season, yet some people in baseball feel that he could steal 25-30 bases with a running club.

FIELDING:

He has fairly good range but should be a better outfielder in left field for the Mets than he was as a centerfielder with the Padres. Though he prefers to play center, McReynolds is better suited to the confines in left field and will play the line and the wall well.

He has the tendency to get a poor jump on the ball and will break back rather than wait for or charge a shallow fly. He plays the carom well, however, and has a very strong arm.

KEVIN McREYNOLDS
OF, No. 18
RR, 6'1", 207 lbs.
ML Svc: 4 years
Born: 10-16-59 in
Little Rock, AK

1986 STATISTICS

AVG	G	AB	R	H	2B	3B	HR	RBI	BB	SO	SB
.287	158	560	89	161	31	6	26	96	66	83	8

CAREER STATISTICS

AVG	G	AB	R	H	2B	3B	HR	RBI	BB	SO	SB
.263	496	1789	233	470	84	17	65	260	155	262	17

  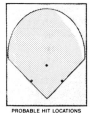

STRONG   STRONG

VS. RHP   VS. LHP   PROBABLE HIT LOCATIONS

OVERALL:

When aroused, McReynolds is one of the most dangerous hitters in the game. The only question thus far seems to be what it will take to arouse him. The Mets are hoping that the fans at Shea Stadium and a blockbuster lineup around him will do the trick.

McReynolds appears more nonchalant than he is, but he needs a swift kick every once in a while to get going (that's where the New York crowd comes in). Last season he responded to criticism by going on a six-week tear in which he drove in 35 runs and slugged six homers.

McReynolds' presence in the lineup means a lot for the Mets. Perhaps the most obvious advantage will be to take the pressure off Darryl Strawberry to produce the monster shots. But by the same token, it also helps to put the squeeze on Strawberry to produce more than he has to date.

Dierker: "McReynolds has learned to be a little more selective with the bat and draw more walks. He has great raw power and doesn't have to swing hard to hit a home run. He showed last year that he is not as fooled by breaking pitches as in the past. Overall, a good, solid hitter and a great pickup for the Mets."

NEW YORK METS

PITCHING:

The Mets outmaneuvered the Boston Red Sox twice within the same year. First they picked Boston's pocket by trading for Bob Ojeda in the '85-86 off-season; the second time was in October at Shea Stadium when they stole the championship out from under the BoSox' nose. Down on the streets, they call it "the bump and roll."

After compiling a 44-39 record in four seasons with Boston, Ojeda went 18-5, finished second in the league with a 2.57 ERA and made a most impressive transition from the American League.

Ojeda has been called the non-smoker on a staff of power pitchers. But he is more than that. Crafty, sly and fiercely competitive, he is a pitcher's pitcher. He works the corners, changes speeds and uses the ground ball as his most expedient way out of trouble.

Ojeda was knocked for his inconsistency with the Red Sox, yet his consistency was his most shining asset with the Mets in 1986.

Ojeda's fastball is a sneaky one which doesn't get much hotter than 87 MPH though it appears faster because he sets it up so well. He prepares the hitter by using an excellent change-up, a breaking ball and, occasionally, a screwball.

Ojeda can paint the corners with the best of them and his only weakness is that his control has to be sharp for him to be effective. It usually was in 1986.

FIELDING, HITTING, BASERUNNING:

Underrated as a fielder in the American League, Ojeda is a good fielder with quick reflexes and a steely nerve. Like the other Mets pitchers, Ojeda benefits from Hernandez's aggressive tone and is not afraid

BOB OJEDA
LHP, No. 43
LL, 6'1", 190 lbs.
ML Svc: 5 years
Born: 12-17-57 in
Los Angeles, CA

1986 STATISTICS

W	L	ERA	G	GS	CG	SV	IP	H	R	ER	BB	SO
18	5	2.57	32	30	7	0	217.1	185	72	62	52	148

CAREER STATISTICS

W	L	ERA	G	GS	CG	SV	IP	H	R	ER	BB	SO
62	44	3.83	172	143	27	1	936	919	435	398	337	573

to stalk the lead runner.

Ojeda's move to first is decent, but his high leg kick negates much of the advantage he has as a lefthander.

With fair speed, Ojeda is a smart baserunner, but not a baserunning or basestealing threat. He is not much of a hitter after spending four seasons as a non-hitting pitcher in the American League.

OVERALL:

He is the perfect complement to the rest of the Mets' staff and joins Fernandez to add balance to the left side of the Mets' rotation.

The transition to the deeper dimensions of the National League parks have helped him pitch with confidence, particularly since he came from the tight confines of Fenway, where he was 20-13 for his career.

Rooker: "Those who are simply waiting for the rest of the National League to catch up to Ojeda are fooling themselves. He is a winner whose competitive edge was sharpened by joining a winning team."

NEW YORK METS

PITCHING:

Doubts concerning Jesse Orosco's effectiveness first surfaced during the 1985 season when he revealed he had pitched part of the campaign with a tender left elbow. But he dispelled most maligning whispers last October when he retired 16 of 18 batters during the World Series. It would seem that Orosco passed his ultimate stress test with flying colors.

Concerns lingered throughout much of 1986 as his fastball seemed to lose something, and many believed that he was no longer the same reliever that he used to be. In the past, his fastball had been clocked at 89 MPH, but last year it came in most often around 86. And while you may try to convince the highway patrol that 3 MPH is not much, sir, it sure makes a difference to a major league fastball. Also, his strikeouts were down slightly during the regular season.

Orosco appeared at spring training fit (his weight was down by 15 lbs.) and pitched well throughout much of the first half of the season. He hit a brick wall, however, just before the All-Star break and was not able to surmount the obstacle for about a month. His slider lacked the nasty bite it should have and often looked more like a sweeping curveball. He was shaking off catcher Gary Carter quite a bit and stopped talking to the press for a time.

But then it all came together again, and he ended the season with impressive numbers: 21 saves in 29 save opportunities and a 2.33 ERA (his lowest ERA since 1983, when it was an incredible 1.47). Of the 37 runners he inherited during the regular season, only nine scored.

Orosco throws two sliders: one is a hard one and the other is an off-speed one which he uses almost like a change-up. Because of the drop in velocity, his fastball is no longer a reliable strikeout weapon. He now uses it more as a set-up pitch, while his hard slider is his out pitch. In August, Orosco began to try a split-finger fastball as a change-up (he had thrown that pitch in 1981-82) and took a few

JESSE OROSCO
LHP, No. 47
RL, 6'2", 185 lbs.
ML Svc: 6 years
Born: 4-21-57 in
Santa Barbara, CA

1986 STATISTICS

W	L	ERA	G	GS	CG	SV	IP	H	R	ER	BB	SO
8	6	2.33	58	0	0	21	81	64	23	21	35	62

CAREER STATISTICS

W	L	ERA	G	GS	CG	SV	IP	H	R	ER	BB	SO
44	38	2.48	314	4	0	91	518.1	402	166	143	209	428

days to get back in the groove with it. He did not use it much, however.

FIELDING, HITTING, BASERUNNING:

A gifted athlete, Orosco fields his position well. He has a decent move to first base and is a good baserunner. Though he is also a good hitter, he does not get many opportunities as a late-inning reliever.

OVERALL:

When Orosco sagged during the mid-summer, the Mets experimented by bringing up smoke-throwing lefty Randy Myers from Triple-A. Orosco responded to the competitive challenge and finished strong, particularly in the post-season.

It is evident, however, that Orosco is no longer the top stopper of the Mets' staff who can expect to be used in that role. The stopper job is now a role shared by McDowell and Orosco. The reliever on a roll will fill the role.

Rooker: "He is using the breaking ball more and more. He pitched well last season and is learning to do without a terrific fastball. But you certainly have to wonder about his fastball and whether Jesse can continue to throw slider after slider without augmenting it with a better heater."

NEW YORK METS

HITTING:

For a light hitter, Rafael Santana loves to pull the ball. But last season, his bat pulled him down instead.

Santana didn't crack the .200 mark until late August. A high fastball hitter, Santana is susceptible to anything low, particularly away. Last year, he was even vulnerable to fastballs, often overpowered and over-matched and batted just .218. With his average down 40 points from the previous season, Santana can argue that he is capable of doing better. He better hope that's true.

Santana was the weak-link in an otherwise powerful Mets order, and while the Mets could afford to hide his bat last season, he will have to show immediate signs of improvement this spring in order to keep his job.

BASERUNNING:

His speed is average, but Santana did not hurt the Mets on the bases, though he does not have the quickness to help them there, either. Incredibly, he did not attempt a stolen base all season.

FIELDING:

Defense is Santana's strong suit. He handles his position with commendable consistency and his arm is more powerful than he lets on.

Santana never tries to gun a runner or show off, though it is clear he has a strong arm. His range isn't what it could be up the middle, but he is strong going to his right.

Few shortstops in baseball handle the double play pivot and exchange with better

RAFAEL SANTANA
SS, No. 3
RR, 6'1", 160 lbs.
ML Svc: 3 years
Born: 1-31-58 in
    La Romana,
        Dominican Republic

1986 STATISTICS

AVG	G	AB	R	H	2B	3B	HR	RBI	BB	SO	SB
.218	139	394	38	86	11	0	1	28	36	43	0

CAREER STATISTICS

AVG	G	AB	R	H	2B	3B	HR	RBI	BB	SO	SB
.245	374	1089	94	267	41	2	3	71	76	116	1

STRONG   STRONG

VS. RHP   VS. LHP   PROBABLE HIT LOCATIONS

precision.

OVERALL:

Santana's deficient offense may cause the Mets to take a long look at another shortstop, unless he can rediscover with his bat the consistency he shows with his glove.

Rooker: "With so many good hitters in the Mets lineup last year, the pitchers saw Rafael step to the plate and went for the jugular. He succumbed.

"Defensively, however, Rafael is as much as the Mets could want. But if they have the chance to get a better-hitting shortstop, they just might take the opportunity."

NEW YORK METS

PITCHING:

Doug Sisk continues to try to get it together. Last season was one of rebuilding for him. He had bone spurs and chips removed from his pitching elbow in September 1985 and underwent a rehabilitation program which was scheduled to last through spring training 1986. Just two months after the surgery, however, he decided to play doctor and, against the advice of his physical therapist, removed the wraps from his elbow. He began pitching on a high school field near his home in Tacoma, Washington. By the start of spring training in February, Sisk was throwing nearly as hard as he ever has. If he was feeling pain, he didn't tell anyone about it. He was the last cut in spring training but pitched his way back to Shea by mid-May.

Sisk's problem was not the chips and spurs but his lack of control and the subsequent lack of confidence. Sisk is a ground ball pitcher who throws a sinker, slider and fastball. His sinker should be his out pitch. His control seemed sharper last season and he began to show his old good movement on his pitches. He generally approaches each hitter with a well-thought-out plan. An encouraging sign is the fact that last season he did not allow a home run in 70.2 innings pitched. That is especially important for a pitcher like him who comes into the game in the later innings.

FIELDING, HITTING, BASERUNNING:

Not the smoothest or quickest fielder, Sisk knows what to do with the ball when it comes his way, especially a double play ground ball.

DOUG SISK
RHP, No. 39
RR, 6'2", 210 lbs.
ML Svc: 4 years
Born: 9-26-57 in
Renton, WA

1986 STATISTICS

W	L	ERA	G	GS	CG	SV	IP	H	R	ER	BB	SO
4	2	3.06	41	0	0	1	70.2	77	31	24	31	31

CAREER STATISTICS

W	L	ERA	G	GS	CG	SV	IP	H	R	ER	BB	SO
14	15	3.01	208	0	0	30	334.1	313	142	112	188	126

He holds runners well. He has a quick move to first and a fast delivery.

In his relief role, he doesn't get to hit often.

OVERALL:

Back in late 1983 and 1984, Sisk and Jesse Orosco were a great bullpen duo and not many batters got a hit off either one. Sisk showed flashes of that form last year, though the jury is still out. His comeback is continuing: after recording 15 saves and a 2.03 ERA in 1984, he was completely lost in 1985. He had no control and lost his sinker, his job and his confidence. But it appeared as though Sisk could now be on his way back.

Rooker: "When right, Sisk is a tough pitcher to hit. If his elbow is completely sound, then he can continue to throw his good sinker. His continued resurrection as a reliever will make the Mets' bullpen deep in its balance of powerful ground ball pitchers."

NEW YORK METS

HITTING:

When it comes to raw baseball talent, Darryl Strawberry has won the lottery. Yet his talent has been both a blessing and a curse. The problem with lottery winners is they don't have to work hard. Some choose to. Many don't.

Strawberry should be a better, more consistent hitter after four years in the major leagues. At age 25, he is still young, though that excuse is getting old.

Hard work and concentration are two areas Strawberry needs to apply if he is really ever to air out his remarkable talent. Until he does, he will be fair game for the New York boo birds who so upset him late last season.

A low-ball hitter, Strawberry has learned to go to the opposite field, though he does not do so consistently. He can take anyone out of the yard at any time. But he has done it far fewer times against lefthanders and good breaking ball pitchers, two enemies he must master if he is ever to come close to having the monster season his talent promises. Strawberry hit just .212 against lefties last season, and his 141 strikeouts in 475 regular season at-bats attest to a batter who is easily frozen by a breaking ball. The strikeout total was his highest by far in four major league seasons, and his batting average dipped 18 points from a high of .277 the previous season.

Strawberry adjusted somewhat by moving in on the plate late last season, a strategy that improved his success against lefthanders and breaking balls. He finished strong, only to grope through the post-season, a boom-or-bust microcosm of his inconsistent career.

BASERUNNING:

Baserunning is one of his many strengths. Strawberry has better-than-average speed and is an aggressive basestealer. He has learned to be smarter on the basepaths after getting caught trying to steal third with two outs once too often in his younger, more inexperienced years.

FIELDING:

Strawberry has developed into one of the

DARRYL STRAWBERRY
RF, No. 18
LL, 6'6", 190 lbs.
ML Svc: 4 years
Born: 3-12-62 in
Los Angeles, CA

1986 STATISTICS

AVG	G	AB	R	H	2B	3B	HR	RBI	BB	SO	SB
.259	136	475	76	123	27	5	27	93	72	141	28

CAREER STATISTICS

AVG	G	AB	R	H	2B	3B	HR	RBI	BB	SO	SB
.260	516	1810	292	471	84	20	108	343	267	496	100

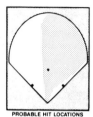

VS. RHP   VS. LHP   PROBABLE HIT LOCATIONS

better outfielders in the National League. His range is well above average and so is his arm, which is, however, stronger than it is accurate. He still suffers lapses in concentration, occasionally getting late jumps on balls and trying to strong-arm a runner when he should be throwing to another base. But his mistakes afield are fewer and further between than in the past.

OVERALL:

One of the most feared home run hitters in the game, Strawberry hits the ball unprecedented distances and can dominate a game at any time. His career will take off like one of his home runs when Darryl Strawberry decides to wed hard work and concentration to his awesome skills.

Rooker: "A possible MVP, he could do it all. If he matures, the sky is the limit. He can carry a team and dominate the game, but will he ever want to enough to put it all together?"

NEW YORK METS

HITTING:

The transition to the National League wasn't as smooth as Tim Teufel had hoped.

He was pitched more outside than he had expected and it took Teufel much of the season to catch up to the style of the National League pitchers and to learn to go the other way. He eventually made the adjustment and began to use the whole field and to sting the ball more consistently late in the summer.

Teufel also had to adjust to a platoon situation and spot duty as the righthanded-hitting half of the Mets' second base platoon with Wally Backman.

When Teufel was under the most pressure --at the eye of an off-field storm following a Houston barroom scuffle that led to the arrest of four Mets--he responded by playing his best baseball of the season.

He still tries to pull the ball and hit for extra-base power instead of staying within himself. He usually pops up or flies out when he tries to force things. He did, however, account for the Mets' only two pinch-hit home runs; one of them was a grand slam.

A dead fastball hitter, Teufel can be jammed and is vulnerable to breaking stuff, especially when pitched away.

BASERUNNING:

A smart runner who lacks speed, Teufel is not a threat to take the extra base. He has good instincts on the basepaths.

FIELDING:

Defense was called Teufel's biggest weakness when he played for the Twins. But Teufel proved better than adequate as a defensive second baseman by working hard to improve his footwork on the pivot. His range is only fair and Teufel doesn't always appear to get low enough to the ground. By learning the National League hitters, he can compensate for what he lacks in speed and

TIM TEUFEL
2B, No. 11
RR, 6'0", 175 lbs.
ML Svc: 4 years
Born: 7-7-58 in
Greenwich, CT

1986 STATISTICS

AVG	G	AB	R	H	2B	3B	HR	RBI	BB	SO	SB
.247	93	279	35	69	20	1	4	31	32	42	1

CAREER STATISTICS

AVG	G	AB	R	H	2B	3B	HR	RBI	BB	SO	SB
.261	409	1359	180	355	81	8	31	148	158	193	6

STRONG
VS. RHP

STRONG
VS. LHP

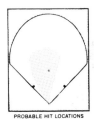

PROBABLE HIT LOCATIONS

range.

OVERALL:

A slow transition, the Houston affair and a costly error in Game 1 of the World Series clouded Teufel's season. But because he took the heat and played with a quiet, intense pride, he proved his mettle under fire and finished strong by batting .444 in the Series with a home run in Game 5.

Rooker: "Teufel teamed with Backman at second base to create good righty/lefty punch. Last season, he often looked as though he was overswinging, though that might have been a carry-over from his time spent playing in the Homer-Metrodome in Minneapolis.

"The Mets proved a good judge of character in getting Teufel and he is working hard at rewarding them."

NEW YORK METS

HITTING:

Mookie Wilson overcame a freak eye injury, which threatened his sight in spring training, to enjoy arguably his finest season at the plate. There was considerable concern that Wilson might never play again, let alone be the same player, after he was struck above the right eye by a thrown ball during a routine baserunning drill. But after missing the first month of the season, the switch-hitter bounced back to pound both lefthanders and righthanders. He also batted .373 with runners in scoring position.

Wilson is still regarded as a free-swinger who strikes out too often and doesn't get on base as frequently as an ideal leadoff hitter should. Those factors, plus the emergence of Lenny Dykstra, influenced Davey Johnson's decision to award Dykstra the leadoff and starting center field jobs in late July.

Wilson likes the ball up from lefthanded pitchers and down from righthanders. He is stronger from the left side, where he makes better use of his speed. But Wilson has resisted harnessing his speed by utilizing the bunt as a weapon.

A guess hitter, Wilson is a better fastball hitter. He is prone to low-and-away breaking stuff.

BASERUNNING:

Wilson has blazing speed. The sight of Wilson racing to third on a triple is a thing of rare beauty.

His 25 steals ranked third highest on the Mets last season. But the total was less than half his 1985 output of 52 steals accumulated in 30 fewer games.

Still, Wilson is aggressive on the basepaths, slides hard and runs with intelligence.

FIELDING:

While his speed is a strength in the outfield, his twice-surgically repaired throwing arm is a weakness. But Wilson showed his arm is not

MOOKIE WILSON
CF, No. 1
SR, 5'10", 168 lbs.
ML Svc: 7 years
Born: 2-9-56 in
Bamberg, SC

1986 STATISTICS

AVG	G	AB	R	H	2B	3B	HR	RBI	BB	SO	SB
.289	123	381	61	110	17	5	9	45	32	72	25

CAREER STATISTICS

AVG	G	AB	R	H	2B	3B	HR	RBI	BB	SO	SB
.277	800	3015	451	834	124	49	40	249	168	497	238

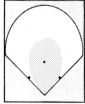

STRONG — VS. RHP   STRONG — VS. LHP   PROBABLE HIT LOCATIONS

powerless, by collecting two assists in the World Series, including throwing Dwight Evans out at the plate in Game 1.

OVERALL:

When Johnson awarded the starting job to Dykstra, Wilson accepted his benching gracefully. That he made the situation a temporary one by playing the most consistently impressive baseball of his career to win back the center field starting job against lefthanded pitchers and the left field job against righties is credit to Wilson's character.

Rooker: "There are two puzzling things about Mookie: his disregard for the bunt as an effective means of getting on base and his continued misjudgment of the strike zone. If he could hold back from swinging at bad pitches and control the bat enough to place bunts well, he would be much more difficult to displace from the lineup."

NEW YORK METS

KEVIN ELSTER
INF, No. 44
RR, 6'2", 180 lbs.
ML Svc: less than one
year
Born: 8-3-64 in
San Pedro, CA

HITTING, BASERUNNING, FIELDING:

Kevin Elster is a banjo hitter who is weaker with the bat than Rafael Santana, the Mets' light-hitting regular shortstop. Elster is primarily a fastball hitter who will go up the middle or to the opposite field. He likes the ball up and out over the plate. He is prone to breaking stuff and to being jammed inside with hard stuff.

Elster is not especially fast, yet he probably has the speed to take the extra base and his instincts are good on the bases.

His strength is his glove and his soft hands. Elster has good range, though not exceptional nor that much better than Santana's. His arm is strong and accurate. But Elster needs work on the double play pivot, which he does not execute smoothly yet.

OVERALL:

Rooker: "Because Elster skipped Triple-A ball and came to the Mets directly from Double-A, he was obviously playing out of his element. No doubt that any shortcomings we saw last year could be attributed to his nervousness at playing at the major league level. It is therefore difficult to evaluate his strengths and weaknesses fairly.

"He needs to develop some body strength and that could make a difference."

ED HEARN
C, No. 49
RR, 6'3", 215 lbs.
ML Svc: less than
one year
Born: 8-23-60 in
Stuart, FL

HITTING, BASERUNNING, FIELDING:

Ed Hearn opened a lot of eyes last year with his quiet self-confidence and handling of the bat.

He proved himself disciplined at the plate and went well to the opposite field, showing occasional power. Hearn's one weakness may be that his power is not consistent with his size.

Still, he batted .265 with four homers and 10 RBIs, which was a pleasant surprise to Mets management, which had long sought an offensive-minded backup catcher to spell Gary Carter.

Hearn can go the other way with the breaking ball, but likes the fastball up and over the plate. He is vulnerable to breaking stuff low and to being jammed up and in.

No threat to steal a base or stretch, Hearn is a capable runner who knows his way around the bases and will slide hard. His defense was adequate, but he could use work to polish that aspect of his game. He needs to become more accurate with his throws.

OVERALL:

A tough scrapper who hung on in the minors because of his bat, Hearn's hitting proved the key to unlock his chance at a major league opportunity. He surprised plenty of people by doing a solid job.

Rooker: "Hearn is a good backup for Carter. He still needs work on defense and that's tough to get in the bullpen."

NEW YORK METS

RANDY NIEMANN
LHP, No. 40
LL, 6'5", 215 lbs.
ML Svc: 4 years
Born: 11-15-55 in
Scotia, CA

PITCHING, FIELDING, HITTING, BASERUNNING:

A journeyman reliever who has pitched for the Astros, Pirates and White Sox, Randy Niemann is an effective staff filler because he is lefthanded and a reliever.

He contributed two impressive outings to the Mets' success in 1986. Niemann pitched 3 2/3 innings of scoreless relief in a mid-May game against the Dodgers to preserve a 5-4 lead in an eventual 8-4 Mets' win. Then, he ended a four-game Mets' losing streak by holding the Cardinals to one earned run and five hits over six innings during a spot start in August. While neither outing was the highlight of the Mets' season, the two instances proved Niemann can do the job under pressure.

Niemann is a ground ball pitcher who mixes a slider and forkball with a curveball and fastball. His slider is his best pitch and the one he generally uses to force ground ball outs.

Fair as a fielder, Niemann has a slight problem with bunts because his 6'5" frame takes a while to unfold, bend and throw.

He has an average move to first.

Niemann proved better than average with the bat, going 2-for-6 in his limited hitting opportunities. But he is not fast afoot.

OVERALL:

Rooker: "Randy has average ability, relies too much on the forkball and doesn't throw enough strikes. He will have to fight to make the team this year."

GENE WALTER
LHP, No. 48
LL, 6'4", 200 lbs.
ML Svc: 1 year plus
Born: 11-22-60 in
Chicago, IL

PITCHING, FIELDING, HITTING, BASERUNNING:

His numbers last year were underwhelming, but Gene Walter provided one valuable commodity to the Padres in 1986: the ability to get lefthanded hitters out. He often was called upon to face only one batter and consequently had few enough innings pitched that it took only one bad outing to send his ERA spiraling upward.

His best strength is his deceptiveness. At 6'4", Walter has a strange, gangling delivery and protects the ball well prior to releasing it. The unusual motion couples with his big breaking ball to induce hitters to swing at pitches that are well out of the strike zone.

While that served Walter well during his first tour of the NL last season, the word was out on this sidearmed thrower by his second pass-through: make him throw a strike. When batters showed the discipline to wait him out and get ahead in the count last season, they were usually rewarded with an average-speed strike-zone fastball there for the hitting.

Walter hurts himself time and again with his inability to hold runners on base. He takes a big stretch, throws to first only casually and has such a pronounced delivery that runners are half way to second by the time he releases the ball. It's difficult for a person of his size to perfect a compact delivery, but Walter needs to try.

OVERALL:

The Mets insisted that Walter be included in the Kevin McReynolds trade.

Dierker: "Walter has the tools, but but he must throw his breaking ball for a strike more often. The Mets probably plan to use him as the Padres did: to face one lefthanded hitter in advance of a closer."

PHILADELPHIA PHILLIES

HITTING:

It's hard to judge Luis Aguayo's 1986 offensive season since he was not used properly. A bench player needs to be given a start every ten days or so to keep sharp but that didn't happen with Aguayo. His 133 at-bats came in bunches. Early in the year, he made 13 straight starts at second base while regular Juan Samuel was out with an injury. Later in the year, he made some starts at shortstop. In between, he didn't play, making it extremely difficult for him to fill in capably when he was called on.

Aguayo is a dead pull hitter with a lot of power for a little man. He likes fastballs up and out over the plate. Because Aguayo is a pull hitter, he's susceptible to breaking balls thrown down-and-away. Aguayo hit .211 in 133 at-bats last year, but he hit .500 with a home run as a pinch-hitter.

Aguayo uses an upright, closed stance and crowds the plate; he was hit by pitches three times last year. He is not a patient hitter and walked only eight times in 146 plate appearances last season. He likes to hit early in the count and does not spend a whole lot of time working a pitcher. If he did, he'd hit for a better average, although it's hard to argue with his 11 extra-base hits in so few at-bats.

BASERUNNING:

Aguayo has below-average speed and is not a threat to steal. When he gets on base, he is conservative and does not make many mistakes.

FIELDING:

Defensively, second base is Aguayo's best position. He doesn't have much range or a great arm and isn't spectacular at turning double plays. But he's capable of a workmanlike performance at second. He does not have the arm or the range to play shortstop on an everyday basis. He has played some at third base, but doesn't have

LUIS AGUAYO
INF, No. 16
RR, 5'9", 190 lbs.
ML Svc: 7 years
Born: 3-13-59 in
Vega Baja, PR

1986 STATISTICS

AVG	G	AB	R	H	2B	3B	HR	RBI	BB	SO	SB
.211	62	133	17	28	6	1	4	13	8	26	1

CAREER STATISTICS

AVG	G	AB	R	H	2B	3B	HR	RBI	BB	SO	SB
.251	328	561	89	141	23	8	18	67	52	95	5

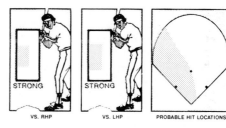

VS. RHP   VS. LHP   PROBABLE HIT LOCATIONS

the reflexes or the arm to do the job over any length of time.

OVERALL:

Aguayo's future remains as a bench player, but the Phillies didn't help him--or any of their bench guys--by sitting him for long periods of time.

If Aguayo is going to be effective this year, manager John Felske is going to have to find a way to get him a start once in awhile. There is absolutely no way a player can be expected to perform after sitting for three weeks at a time.

Rooker: "He is one of the best utility infielders in the National League. His best position is at second base but he can fill in at shortstop or at third base.

"He likes the high fastball and he likes to hit the first pitch. With his versatility and acceptance of being a part-time player, Aguayo should be around for quite awhile."

PHILADELPHIA PHILLIES

PITCHING:

There's no more drastic change for a pitcher than to go from a starter's role to late-inning relief, which was the switch Steve Bedrosian made last year.

Bedrosian wasn't completely new to the bullpen, having been a late-inning stopper from 1982 through 1984 with the Braves. But he experienced late-season arm problems during those seasons, so he became a starter in 1985 on the theory that pitching once every five days would be easier on his arm than pitching one or two innings every other day.

Despite his previous relief experience, it took him almost half of 1986 to adjust to late-inning work. Because Bedrosian was coming off arm trouble and he needed time to ease into the role of bullpen stopper, the Phillies nursed him early in the year.

Part of the adjustment Bedrosian had to make was mechanical. He has a compact delivery, but uses a high leg kick. There were times when his left leg seemed to take on a life of its own and he'd wind up planting his foot somewhere in the vicinity of first base instead of toward home plate. This habit tended to make his arm drag behind his body and rob his fastball of velocity.

Basically, Bedrosian is a one-pitch pitcher. He has an excellent fastball that has been clocked in the mid-90s. He throws a slider, but it's not a particularly good pitch and he does not have great command of it. At the end of last season, Bedrosian was considering resurrecting the change-up he used when he was a starting pitcher.

When everything was working mechanically, and when Bedrosian wasn't over-psyched, he was as effective as any late-inning reliever in the National League last year. When he rushed himself, which usually occurred when Bedrosian let his emotions get the better of him, he got hit hard. He was susceptible to the gopher ball; he allowed 12 home runs in 90 1/3 innings.

STEVE BEDROSIAN
RHP, No. 40
RR, 6'3", 195 lbs.
ML Svc: 5 years
Born: 12-6-57 in
Methuen, MA

1986 STATISTICS

W	L	ERA	G	GS	CG	SV	IP	H	R	ER	BB	SO
8	6	3.39	68	0	0	29	90.1	79	39	34	34	82

CAREER STATISTICS

W	L	ERA	G	GS	CG	SV	IP	H	R	ER	BB	SO
42	45	3.27	294	46	0	70	662.1	559	266	241	301	543

Bedrosian had some problems with concentration. Of the 34 earned runs he allowed, 15 were scored in the 14 appearances he made with a lead of more than two runs. That says Bedrosian didn't take those three- and four-run leads seriously enough when he was brought in to protect them.

FIELDING, HITTING, BASERUNNING:

Bedrosian has an average move to first base. Even with his high leg kick, he gets the ball to the plate quickly enough to keep opposing baserunners honest. He is an average fielder who covers first well. He does not bat often enough to be judged as a hitter or a baserunner.

OVERALL:

Rooker: "He needs to develop control as well as another pitch to go along with his fastball. If he can get a handle on his slider and start throwing it for strikes, he'll become more consistent as a bullpen stopper.

"If he does, 40 saves aren't out of the question. Bedrosian is at the peak of his career."

PHILADELPHIA PHILLIES

PITCHING:

In what became one of the all-time why-didn't-they-think-of-that-sooner moves, the Phillies converted Don Carman from a reliever into a starter last July.

Before the switch, Carman struggled mightily as the tablesetter for Steve Bedrosian and occasional bullpen stopper. In 34 relief appearances, Carman was 3-2 with a 4.97 ERA and one save in 11 save opportunities. After the switch, he was nothing short of a revelation, going 7-3 with a 2.43 ERA and allowing an amazingly low 68 hits in 92 2/3 innings. Included among his 14 starts were a one-hit shutout of the Giants in which he took a perfect game into the ninth inning, five starts of less than eight innings in which he did not allow a run and a complete game shutout of the Pirates.

Not bad for a one-pitch pitcher.

Carman's one pitch is a fastball. It's not a 90 MPH fastball, but it has excellent movement, tailing away from righthanded hitter. He also hides the ball extremely well. He has no breaking ball to speak of and throws a change-up about once a month. All of this would make it seem that Carman is tailor-made for the bullpen.

But mentally, Carman is much better suited to starting. He tends to carry the failure of one bullpen outing into his next appearance. As a starter, he has four days to get over whatever problems occurred during his game.

Of course, Carman is going to have to develop his breaking ball and change-up to continue to be effective as a starter. He was able to fool a lot of hitters with his fastball for half a season last year. Over the course of a full schedule, the hitters will adjust and force him to break camp from the outside corner of the plate. An effective breaking ball will keep them honest.

FIELDING, HITTING, BASERUNNING:

Carman has an average move to first for a lefthander but gets the ball to the plate

DON CARMAN
LHP, No. 42
LL, 6'3", 190 lbs.
ML Svc: 2 years
Born: 8-14-59 in
Oklahoma City, OK

1986 STATISTICS

W	L	ERA	G	GS	CG	SV	IP	H	R	ER	BB	SO
10	5	3.22	50	14	2	1	134.1	113	50	48	52	98

CAREER STATISTICS

W	L	ERA	G	GS	CG	SV	IP	H	R	ER	BB	SO
19	10	2.91	133	14	2	9	235	179	84	76	96	201

quickly. He is an average fielder. As a hitter, he's the pits. He went *0-for-1986* at the plate last year in 36 at-bats.

OVERALL:

In mid-September last season, Carman developed some soreness in his left shoulder and missed a turn. He came back to throw five shutout innings two weeks later, then packed it in for the season. After examining his shoulder, Phillies medical personnel recommended that he be returning to the bullpen because relieving would put less strain on his shoulder.

But Carman balked at the idea of return to relief work and the Phillies' team physician gave his consent for Carman to continue working as a starter as long as he is not overused. Which means Carman won't be completing many games this year.

Rooker: "Don could be a big winner. There are times when he goes into the seventh inning with just his fastball. If he could get the curveball and slider going longer and more often, he could win 15-20 games if the Phillies keep him in the starting rotation."

PHILADELPHIA PHILLIES

HITTING:

After missing the majority of 1984 and 1985 with a pinched nerve in his neck that affected his throwing, Darren Daulton began last season injury-free. Finally healthy, Daulton showed he had an excellent arm. He was good at blocking balls in the dirt. His pitchers liked him as a receiver and he called a decent game. He was good and he was going to get better.

Then, in Steve Carlton's last game as a Phillie (June 21), the Cardinals' Mike Heath slid into Daulton on a play at the plate, tearing the cruciate ligament of Daulton's left knee. Daulton underwent reconstructive surgery a few days later and began rehabilitation in September. He is not expected to be ready to play until June 1987 at the earliest. There is a good chance he won't be coming back at all.

As a hitter, Daulton has shown excellent power. He has opened his stance slightly, but remains pretty much a pull hitter. At the time of his injury, he had eight home runs (second on the club behind Mike Schmidt), four doubles and 21 RBIs. He also was sixth in the league in walks with 38.

The rap on him has been that he was too passive at the plate and spent too much time guessing instead of hacking. Last year, however, Daulton showed considerable patience and though he didn't hit for average, his on-base percentage was excellent (.391) and he surprised some people with his power.

Like most lefthanders, he is a low-ball hitter. Pitchers generally try to feed him breaking balls and off-speed stuff away, or to climb the ladder on him with fastballs.

BASERUNNING:

Before his knee injury, Daulton was an excellent baserunner with fine speed for a catcher. He was actually a threat to run in certain situations (he stole two bases in three attempts).

FIELDING:

Daulton is an excellent catcher. He won the starting catcher's spot in spring training after

DARREN DAULTON
C, No. 10
LR, 6'2", 190 lbs.
ML Svc: 2 years
Born: 1-3-62 in
Arkansas City, KS

1986 STATISTICS

AVG	G	AB	R	H	2B	3B	HR	RBI	BB	SO	SB
.225	49	138	18	31	4	0	8	21	38	41	2

CAREER STATISTICS

AVG	G	AB	R	H	2B	3B	HR	RBI	BB	SO	SB
.217	87	244	33	53	7	1	12	32	55	79	5

  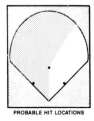

VS. RHP VS. LHP PROBABLE HIT LOCATIONS

the Phillies dealt away their regular catcher, Ozzie Virgil. With very little experience and almost no knowledge of the hitters, Daulton managed to gain the confidence of his pitchers. He showed that, given time, he would develop into an excellent defensive catcher.

OVERALL:

The injury has put Daulton's career on the line. An athlete is never the same after reconstructive knee surgery. Some don't make it back at all. For a catcher to come back and be able to crouch for nine innings seems next to impossible. Daulton has his youth and his determination going for him in his attempt to come back. Unfortunately, that may not be enough.

Rooker: "Until his knee injury, it looked as though the Phillies had found a regular catcher. He is a pull hitter with good power. Darren is a fine receiver, throws well and was just on the verge of learning the ins and outs of his pitching staff."

PHILADELPHIA PHILLIES

HITTING:

"The Hit Man." Mike Easler's moniker says plenty about his offensive ability. Easler is a craftsman when it comes to hitting.

He has a quick, well-honed stroke and has long been regarded as an exceptional low-ball hitter. Pitchers must stay away from pitching anything low and inside, especially fastballs. Easler will sometimes swing through high fastballs as well as breaking balls away. He is able to make adjustments with each plate appearance and, with his vast experience, pitchers are hard-pressed to outwit him.

Easler has power to left- and right-center field. He fell into the Yankee Stadium trap early in the 1986 campaign, attempting to pull everything into the short right-field porch and briefly losing sight of the things that had always worked for him.

Easler is ordinarily a spray hitter and, with that style in Philadelphia, will be able to hit home runs to all fields. The move away from Yankee Stadium will help him offensively.

BASERUNNING:

Baserunning is not Easler's strong suit. "The Hit Man" is a hitter; nobody ever said he could run.

FIELDING:

Philadelphia gambled that Easler can be an adequate everyday left fielder in acquiring him from the Yankees for disappointing pitcher Charlie Hudson.

The task requires a major adjustment by Easler, who was a designated hitter with Boston and the Yankees. Easler is a hard worker and that's what it will take for him to meet this challenge.

Easler will have a relatively small amount of ground to cover in left field at Veterans Stadium. He played the outfield occasionally

**MIKE EASLER
DH, No. 17
LR, 6'1", 196 lbs.
ML Svc: 9 years
Born: 11-29-50 in
Cleveland, OH**

1986 STATISTICS

AVG	G	AB	R	H	2B	3B	HR	RBI	BB	SO	SB
.302	146	490	64	148	26	2	14	78	49	87	3

CAREER STATISTICS

AVG	G	AB	R	H	2B	3B	HR	RBI	BB	SO	SB
.294	1053	3400	445	1000	179	25	113	491	301	644	19

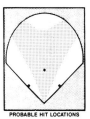

VS. RHP   VS. LHP   PROBABLE HIT LOCATIONS

with the Yankees and didn't hurt the cause. Although no play was easy for him, the catches were made.

Easler has a poor arm. Opponents can definitely challenge him.

OVERALL:

Easler was under substantial pressure in New York after being acquired from Boston in exchange for clubhouse favorite Don Baylor. As Baylor's power and leadership helped the Red Sox to their first division title since 1975, the heat was turned up on Easler. It was an unfair burden because Easler is a completely different type of player and personality.

Kaat: "Easler is a first-class individual. He can be a good influence and be important to a ballclub."

PHILADELPHIA PHILLIES

HITTING:

Greg Gross is a consummate bench player with the ability to play all three outfield positions as well as at first base without embarrassing himself. He is also one of the best lefthanded pinch-hitters in the National League.

He led the Phillies last year with 13 pinch-hits and tied Gates Brown for eighth on the all-time pinch-hit list with 108. But Gross was not a happy ballplayer last year. He had only 101 at-bats, which was one less than his total during the strike-shortened 1981 season. In order for bench players to be effective, an occasional start is necessary once in a while, yet Gross did not start *even one game* after the All-Star break. Manager John Felske buried his role players last season and Gross was one of those down under.

That Gross was walked 12 times as a pinch-hitter is testimony to the respect he commands around the league. It also says something about the way Felske used him. Gross is a lefthanded singles hitter, a contact guy with an inside-out swing who takes everything the other way. He is a low-ball hitter who likes the ball from the middle of the plate out. As a pinch-hitter, his greatest value would seem to lie in leading off innings. But Gross was used a lot as a sacrificial lamb. Whenever a situation arose with runners in scoring position and first base open, Felske invariably used Gross ahead of Ron Roenicke. A case can be made for that strategy, since Roenicke is a switch-hitter with some power and a greater ability to produce a fly ball. But the effect of the strategy was to take the bat out of Gross' hands, a heavy price to pay for the percentage of Roenicke producing a fly ball. He is an excellent bunter.

BASERUNNING:

Gross is slow on the bases and no threat to steal. But he is a smart baserunner who's never caught trying to do something he is not capable of doing.

FIELDING:

Gross is adequate no matter where you put him. He has no speed, so he doesn't have

GREG GROSS
OF, No. 21
LL, 5'11", 175 lbs.
ML Svc: 13 years
Born: 8-1-52 in
York, PA

1986 STATISTICS

AVG	G	AB	R	H	2B	3B	HR	RBI	BB	SO	SB
.248	87	101	11	25	5	0	0	8	21	11	1

CAREER STATISTICS

AVG	G	AB	R	H	2B	3B	HR	RBI	BB	SO	SB
.292	1537	3404	423	993	125	45	6	287	471	229	39

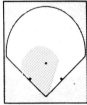

VS. RHP   VS. LHP   PROBABLE HIT LOCATIONS

much range in the outfield. His arm is average, at best. But he does all the fundamental things right. He never makes a mistake judging a fly ball and if he can get to it, it's caught.

He charges the ball extremely well, gets rid of it very quickly and always hits the cutoff man. If they ever make a film on the fundamentals of playing outfield defense, Gross is the player who should be used as an example.

OVERALL:

Despite his discontent, Gross decided not to ask for a trade at the end of last year. He is 34 years old and in the last year of his contract. He is going to be a pinch-hitter no matter where he plays. Since his home is in the Philadelphia area, he might as well pinch-hit for the Phillies.

Rooker: "Greg is a valuable pinch-hitter who can play a little defense. He is adequate in the outfield because he does all the little things right.

"He is a good worker, very professional about his job."

PHILADELPHIA PHILLIES

PITCHING:

If a disappointing 1986 season did nothing else, it should have helped Kevin Gross to mature. After winning 15 games for a fifth-place team the year before, Gross went into spring training as the Phillies' righthanded ace. He had an excellent spring and was on schedule to start on Opening Day. But at the last minute, the Phillies bowed to the wishes of an aging Steve Carlton and gave him the Opening Day assignment. Gross was bitterly disappointed by the move, and he let it bother him for some time afterward.

A persistent lack of poise has become a real problem for this pitcher. In 1985, Gross was especially adept at adjusting in games when he did not have his best stuff. Back then, he was a young pitcher hoping to prove himself, but last season, he was expected to win consistently and when he didn't, he became one very agitated pitcher.

All too often now, Gross allows himself to be easily frustrated. If he is satisfied with the quality of his pitches and nothing has gone awry in the game, Gross can be counted on to keep his team competitive. But if he detects a flaw or if a teammate commits an error, Gross has shown that he can lose it mentally in a hurry.

Mechanically, Gross is fine. He uses all four of his pitches--fastball, curveball, slider and change-up--at any point in the count. When he has his best stuff, he is tough.

Gross did have some problems with his location, especially with his curveball, and that contributed heavily to the 28 home runs he allowed last year.

His slider is his fourth-best pitch and he never uses it as his out pitch. He developed a cut fastball during the year and by September he was using it in place of his slider. He also

KEVIN GROSS
RHP, No. 46
RR, 6'5", 203 lbs.
ML Svc: 4 years
Born: 6-8-61 in
Downey, CA

1986 STATISTICS

W	L	ERA	G	GS	CG	SV	IP	H	R	ER	BB	SO
12	12	4.02	37	36	7	0	241.2	240	115	108	94	154

CAREER STATISTICS

W	L	ERA	G	GS	CG	SV	IP	H	R	ER	BB	SO
39	36	5.59	136	98	15	1	672.1	674	313	283	254	455

experimented with a slow curve last year, but wasn't able to throw it for a strike.

FIELDING, HITTING, BASERUNNING:

Gross has a below-average move to first, and he's easy to steal against. He's an average fielder.

Gross has some power, and that makes him more dangerous than most pitchers at the plate. He's not a good bunter. As a baserunner, he is slow but adequate.

OVERALL:

Rooker: "Gross 'can't be pidgeonholed as either a power pitcher or control pitcher because he is a little bit of both. His fastball is good enough to blow away some hitters. But his best pitch, by far, is his curveball, though he has a tendency to throw it up to high. If he's throwing his curve for strikes, then all of his other pitches can operate off that. Hitters can't sit on his fastball and are susceptible to his change-up."

PHILADELPHIA PHILLIES

HITTING:

Von Hayes was poking along at a tortoise-like .183 pace at the end of April last season when he decided to scrap everything he had learned in the big leagues and go back to the way he hit in college.

He spread his stance wider than it had been, crouched lower and dropped his bat so it was almost level with the ground. The results were startling. Hayes went on to become the Phillies' first .300 hitter since 1981, to tie Tony Gwynn for the league-lead in runs scored and set a club record for doubles by a first baseman. Although he did not make the National League All-Star team, Hayes finished eighth in the MVP balloting at the end of the year.

The death of his father during spring training last year had a profound effect on Hayes. The personal tragedy seemed to mature Hayes and he put up the best numbers of his career. In the past, he had difficulty controlling his emotions on the field. A simple strikeout could send him into a rage. But last year, Hayes kept his anger largely in check. He benefited with a consistent year.

He is a low-ball hitter with two weaknesses: hard stuff up-and-in and hard stuff away. He is a very good breaking-ball hitter and is one of the few hitters around who has no trouble with novelty pitches such as the split-finger fastball because he waits so long on the ball. But lefthanders who pitch him away get him out consistently.

Hayes' approach to hitting is to take everything up the middle. He is patient and willing to take a walk. He'll go with anything on the outside part of the plate and take it to left field and has excellent power to the opposite field. He will turn on inside fastballs or hanging breaking balls and pull them. Although he is basically a line drive hitter, Hayes has outstanding power to all fields and can hit a ball out of any part of any ballpark. Hayes is a fair bunter who will occasionally lay down a drag bunt.

BASERUNNING:

Hayes improved vastly as a baserunner last year. He has above-average speed but until

VON HAYES
1B, No. 9
LR, 6'5", 185 lbs.
ML Svc: 6 years
Born: 8-31-58 in
Stockton, CA

1986 STATISTICS

AVG	G	AB	R	H	2B	3B	HR	RBI	BB	SO	SB
.305	158	610	107	186	46	2	19	98	74	77	24

CAREER STATISTICS

AVG	G	AB	R	H	2B	3B	HR	RBI	BB	SO	SB
.276	779	2728	399	753	145	22	69	366	286	388	153

  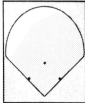

VS. RHP   VS. LHP   PROBABLE HIT LOCATIONS

last year lacked presence of mind on the bases. Both the speed and the run-producing ability of the hitters behind him in the lineup (Mike Schmidt and Glenn Wilson) accounted for Hayes' 107 runs. But he helped himself by cutting down some of his aggressiveness on the bases. Instead of running the Phillies out of innings by trying to take the extra base at the wrong time, Hayes calmed down considerably.

FIELDING:

Hayes moved from center field to first base at the beginning of the season and made himself into a competent fielder. He has trouble going to his right but became adept at digging throws out of the dirt. He is excellent at turning the 3-6-3 double play.

OVERALL:

Rooker: "Von really turned it on last year. He is just coming into his own as a player. He has all the tools to become one of the best. He needs to continue to keep his emotions in check and to treat each game as a day at the office. His natural talent will take it from there."

PHILADELPHIA PHILLIES

PITCHING:

The *Tom Hume Career Watch* is on hold. His career was on the line after an ineffective 1984 season. But now he's put together two consistent years as a long reliever, and that should guarantee him a few more seasons of gainful employment.

Granted, long relief is one step away from civilian life. But it's a job and somebody has to do it, and Hume probably was as good as anybody in the National League at doing it last year.

Hume no longer has the stuff that made him one of baseball's best late-inning relievers from 1979 to 1982. He has lost velocity on both his fastball and his slider. But his sinker is good enough to get ground balls and his control last year was good enough to make his sinker an effective pitch.

He was lost for the first three months of the season, having undergone arthroscopic surgery on his left knee in January and missed most of spring training. He started the year on the disabled list, was activated in early May and rang up a 5.40 ERA in his first 13 appearances. But for the rest of the season, he was effective. Beginning June 27, he went 4-1 with a 1.90 ERA. His 2.77 overall ERA was his lowest since 1980.

FIELDING, HITTING, BASERUNNING:

Hume is a sure fielder with an average move to first. As a hitter, he will put the ball in play and he is capable of moving runners along with a bunt. He is no speed demon on the bases, but knows what he is doing once he gets on.

TOM HUME
RHP, No. 37
RR, 6'1", 185 lbs.
ML Svc: 9 years
Born: 3-29-53 in
* Cincinnati, OH*

1986 STATISTICS

W	L	ERA	G	GS	CG	SV	IP	H	R	ER	BB	SO
4	1	2.77	48	1	0	4	94.1	89	37	29	34	51

CAREER STATISTICS

W	L	ERA	G	GS	CG	SV	IP	H	R	ER	BB	SO
55	67	3.73	494	49	5	92	1002.1	1017	467	415	341	503

OVERALL:

Hume is well past his peak as a pitcher. His greatest strengths are his experience and his knowledge of the hitters. His weakness is his stuff, which is average at best. If he doesn't have excellent control on any given day, he gets hit hard. On most days last year, his control was excellent. There's no reason to think he won't be just as good this year. Hume is not the pitcher he once was. But there's a place on every pitching staff for a guy adept at holding the fort.

Rooker: "Hume is a hard worker and is respected in the clubhouse. He doesn't let his ego get in the way of reality, and is willing to pitch in the obscurity of long relief which may also prolong his career. Quiet and soft-spoken, Hume is an excellent guy to have on a team. 1986 was a good year for him. It looks like he's made it back."

PHILADELPHIA PHILLIES

HITTING:

If Chris James had not broken a bone in his left ankle in early May last season, he might have played himself into a job in the Phillies' outfield. James is a genuine prospect with a chance to win a job this spring.

He is an alleys hitter with the power potential to hit 15-20 home runs a year. He is a fastball hitter who crowds the plate and likes the ball up-and-away from him. He has a big problem with breaking balls down-and-away, and is a wild, undisciplined swinger who's been known to take a cut at balls that bounce in the dirt. Patience and discipline as a hitter are learned traits, not completely natural, and James, who is 24 years old, has time to learn.

BASERUNNING:

James is a good baserunner and is getting better. He has the speed to turn singles into doubles and doubles into triples. He will have to learn the nuances of the NL's pitchers' moves, but looks to have the ability to steal 25-30 bases a year.

FIELDING:

James is an excellent defensive outfielder and can play in either center field or in left field. He has a strong, accurate arm and is very aggressive. Ultimately, however, his future probably lies as a third baseman. With Mike Schmidt nearing the end of his career, the Phillies must begin grooming a replacement for him at third base. James is the most qualified candidate on the club right now.

CHRIS JAMES
OF, No. 34
RR, 6'1", 190 lbs.
ML Svc: less than one year
Born: 10-4-62 in
Rusk, TX

1986 STATISTICS

AVG	G	AB	R	H	2B	3B	HR	RBI	BB	SO	SB
.283	16	46	5	13	3	0	1	5	1	13	0

CAREER STATISTICS

AVG	G	AB	R	H	2B	3B	HR	RBI	BB	SO	SB
.283	16	46	5	13	3	0	1	5	1	13	0

OVERALL:

Last year, James was named among the country's top 10 minor league prospects by *Baseball America* magazine. In 69 games last year with Portland, he hit .241 with 12 homers and 41 RBIs even though he missed two months of the season because of the broken ankle and wasn't completely healthy when he returned. The injury haunted him after he was called up in September. It never healed properly and he had to undergo surgery last October. He is expected to be healthy in time for spring training, however.

It might be best for James if he went to Triple-A and played third base full-time. He needs to get some at-bats under his belt. The worst thing the Phillies could do would be to keep him and not play him. James is a solid prospect, but there's no compelling reason to rush him.

PHILADELPHIA PHILLIES

HITTING:

Having been told to hit the pike, Steve Jeltz went home to Kansas after the 1985 season and taught himself how to switch-hit. He took up residence in a batting cage and spent that winter batting lefthanded against a pitching machine. When spring training rolled around last season, he was still being largely ignored by the Phillies, who had traded for another shortstop (Tom Foley) after Jeltz hit .189 from his natural side (the right). It seemed that the career of one good-field/no-hit shortstop had come to a dead end.

But as it turned out, the dead end was actually a crossroads. Foley sustained a fractured wrist when he was hit by a pitch during a spring training game. Jeltz was given his old job back, and this time, he kept it.

Learning to switch-hit didn't transform Jeltz into the second coming of Cal Ripken, however. Jeltz hit .217 from the left side, .221 from the right. He was patient from both sides, working 65 walks. He struck out 97 times, too often for a No. 8 hitter who is supposed to be putting the ball in play.

Whether he batted left- or righthanded, pitchers generally go after him with hard stuff. He makes them throw strikes, but guys with good fastballs can blow him away. He could improve himself as a hitter by hitting the ball on the ground more, cutting down on his swing and making contact. As a righthanded hitter, he shows an occasional willingness to go the other way with outside pitches. As a lefty, he tries to go up the middle with everything, but is rarely able to go to the opposite field.

BASERUNNING:

Jeltz is a good bunter and an excellent baserunner with above-average speed. He is capable of stealing more than the six bases he stole in nine attempts last year, but he wasn't called upon to run much.

FIELDING:

Jeltz is an excellent defensive shortstop.

STEVE JELTZ
SS, No. 30
SR, 5'11", 170 lbs.
ML Svc: 3 years
Born: 5-28-59 in
Paris, France

1986 STATISTICS

AVG	G	AB	R	H	2B	3B	HR	RBI	BB	SO	SB
.219	145	439	44	96	11	4	0	36	65	97	6

CAREER STATISTICS

AVG	G	AB	R	H	2B	3B	HR	RBI	BB	SO	SB
.208	275	711	68	148	15	7	1	56	99	165	9

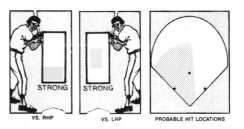

He has good range to either side, a strong, accurate arm and turns the double play well. Jeltz used to play a very shallow shortstop, mostly because his arm wasn't strong enough to throw out runners from the hole. But he lifted weights and bulked up while he was sitting on the bench at the tail end of the 1985 season and came back last year with a much stronger arm. He started playing deeper and got to a lot more balls in the hole.

Jeltz's weakness as a defensive player is his concentration. When he learns to concentrate on every hitter, he'll cut down on the 22 errors he made last year.

OVERALL:

Rooker: "Jeltz is starting to get rid of the no-hit tag. As a hitter, he likes the ball down. He is a better righthanded hitter than he is lefthanded, but then he just started to switch-hit in the majors last year. If he continues to improve with the bat, he could become one of the better shortstops in the league."

PHILADELPHIA PHILLIES

PITCHING:

Presenting Mike Maddux, who made his rookie season a tour de force in jitters.

Watching this guy warm up in the bullpen, a scout would swear he had the right stuff to get big league hitters out. He has a nice, smooth, three-quarters delivery and three decent pitches, and presumably enough minor league experience to know what to do with the ball once he gets to the mound.

The problem is, once he gets to the mound, Maddux invariably finds it impossible to calm down and to allow his stuff and his athletic instincts to take over. The result: a steady string of first-inning debacles last year. His 1986 first-inning ERA was 13.20. He reached the absolute nadir of his first-inning problems in a mid-September start against the Mets. In that game, Lenny Dykstra led off with a home run, the next three Mets reached base and Maddux was gone after just 11 pitches.

Self-confidence is difficult to gain when you're getting your brains beat out. But a lack of confidence, more than anything else, was the cause of Maddux's downfall in 1986. He is going to have to find a way to calm down and begin believing in himself or he is not going to be around long.

A lack of control was yet another problem, though it probably was related to the first. In truth, he got squeezed a few times by umpires but every young pitcher goes through that. The fact was, Maddux did a lot of nibbling instead of going after hitters and that cost him walks. And the walks cost him runs.

MIKE MADDUX
RHP, No. 44
RR, 6'2", 180 lbs.
ML Svc: 1 year
Born: 8-27-61 in Dayton, OH

1986 STATISTICS

W	L	ERA	G	GS	CG	SV	IP	H	R	ER	BB	SO
3	7	5.42	16	16	0	0	78	88	56	47	34	44

CAREER STATISTICS

W	L	ERA	G	GS	CG	SV	IP	H	R	ER	BB	SO
3	7	5.42	16	16	0	0	78	88	56	47	34	44

HITTING, FIELDING, BASERUNNING:

Maddux is an average fielder with an average move to first. He is an average hitter and below-average bunter, though he is a decent baserunner with enough speed to score from second on a single to right field.

OVERALL:

If ever there was a spring training project for pitching coach Claude Osteen, Maddux is it. If the Phillies can find a way to help him believe he belongs, he could be an effective pitcher. At this point, however, his future is murky. The Phillies need pitching, but several of their minor league prospects have already passed Maddux in the pecking order.

Rooker: "Maddux has a fastball that won't overpower anyone, but you have to respect it. Just like any other pitcher, he has to get his breaking ball over to be effective."

PHILADELPHIA PHILLIES

PITCHING:

Shane Rawley was headed for the first 20-win season of his career last year when a shoulder injury ended his season in late July.

A quick worker with a classic overhand delivery, Rawley used his control and his ability to change speeds on his fastball and slider to run up an 11-4 record and a 2.76 ERA--good enough to earn a spot on the National League All-Star team. In his first 19 starts, Rawley pitched seven complete games and only twice failed to pitch into the seventh inning.

He left a July 12 start against the Astros with a sore shoulder and sat out the All-Star Game. He made three starts after the All-Star break, but obviously was not the same pitcher. The soreness was later diagnosed as a stress fracture in his left shoulder. He spent the rest of the season and this past winter recovering and rehabilitating. The Phillies expect him to be healthy in time for spring training 1987.

Before the injury, Rawley was as good as any lefthander in the league except Fernando Valenzuela. Rawley has an above-average fastball but he doesn't try to overpower hitters with it. He relies instead on changing speeds and hitting spots. He became a master of changing speeds not only with his fastball but with his slider as well. He also has an above-average change-up, which he uses effectively.

When his control was good, which was most of the time, Rawley won. Only five times in his first 21 starts did he walk more than two batters in a game. When his control was off, his pitches were up in the strike zone and he rarely survived. If he is not going well, he'll get knocked out by the fourth inning.

Rawley will get the close calls from the umpire because he never begs strikes. Because he works the corners, he needs the close calls. Rawley doesn't fall behind in the count very often. Part of the reason for his

SHANE RAWLEY
LHP, No. 48
RL, 6'0", 180 lbs.
ML Svc: 9 years
Born: 7-27-55 in
Racine, WI

1986 STATISTICS

W	L	ERA	G	GS	CG	SV	IP	H	R	ER	BB	SO
11	7	3.54	23	23	7	0	157.2	166	67	62	50	73

CAREER STATISTICS

W	L	ERA	G	GS	CG	SV	IP	H	R	ER	BB	SO
81	79	3.80	374	137	32	40	1298	1297	599	548	510	713

success is his ability to throw any one of his three pitches for a strike. Hitters cannot go to the plate anticipating a first-pitch fastball.

Rawley's concentration is impeccable. A consummate professional, he works the hitters. Even when he pitches with a big lead, there is no sign of a let up.

FIELDING, HITTING, BASERUNNING:

Rawley has an average move to first and keeps runners close. He is an excellent athlete who fields his position well. He is quick off the mound, stops a lot of ground balls that are hit back up the middle and covers first base well. He is a good hitter, good bunter and a heads-up baserunner.

OVERALL:

Rooker: "Shane is willing to throw his slider at any time. It's an even better pitch than his fastball, and that's above average. Before the injury, he showed he was ready to be a staff leader. He is an outstanding competitor.

"What I really like about him is that he likes to finish what he starts, which is a rare attitude these days."

PHILADELPHIA PHILLIES

EXCELLENT SPEED

HITTING:

For years, the standard line on Gary Redus has been that he would make somebody a great leadoff hitter, if only he would hit the ball on the ground.

Well, Redus is 30 years old now. He has produced his unwanted fly-ball outs for two teams, the Phillies and Reds, and it's obvious that he is not suddenly going to become Vince Coleman.

Redus is on his way to becoming a journeyman, even though his tools dictate he should be more than that. The Reds traded him after he suggested late in 1985 that Pete Rose might be doing the team a disservice by keeping himself in the lineup. At the end of last year, the Phillies were shopping him around the league, mostly because they had a glut of outfield talent and, of the players they were willing to deal, he had the most value.

Redus is a pull hitter with excellent power to left and left-center field. Last season, he set career highs in doubles and extra-base hits despite missing two months after undergoing arthroscopic surgery to remove bone chips from his right elbow in May.

He likes the ball up-and-away from him. Pitchers work him down-and-in and down-and-away. They can fool him with breaking stuff and off-speed pitches. He is not a particularly patient hitter, but he knows the strike zone well enough to work a walk when he cares to do so. With his big swing, he is not a good contact hitter--he strikes out a lot.

Redus' report does not read like a description of the ideal leadoff hitter. In fact, the Phillies dropped him to sixth in the lineup last September, though he is probably best-suited to hit in the No. 3 spot in the order. But he won't be batting third for the Phillies because the spot has already been taken by Von Hayes.

BASERUNNING:

Speed is what makes Redus so attractive as a leadoff hitter. He gets out of the box extremely well, gets down to first in a hurry and has the ability to score from first on a single to right. He is an excellent basestealer with the potential to steal 50 or more bases over the course of a full season.

GARY REDUS
OF, No. 22
RR, 6'1", 180 lbs.
ML Svc: 4 years
Born: 11-1-56 in
  Limestone County, AL

1986 STATISTICS

AVG	G	AB	R	H	2B	3B	HR	RBI	BB	SO	SB
.247	90	340	62	84	22	4	11	33	47	78	25

CAREER STATISTICS

AVG	G	AB	R	H	2B	3B	HR	RBI	BB	SO	SB
.248	459	1516	284	376	80	22	42	141	219	333	171

  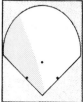

VS. RHP   VS. LHP   PROBABLE HIT LOCATIONS

FIELDING:

Redus is a below-average defensive outfielder. His good speed is nullified by his bad judgment in left field. Surgery rendered a weak arm even weaker.

OVERALL:

If there's been mistakes made somewhere, maybe they haven't all been made by Redus, who despite his uppercut swing managed a .343 on-base percentage last year, third-best on the Phillies behind Mike Schmidt and Von Hayes, who finished in the league's top 10. Maybe the first mistake was to pidgeon-hole Redus as a leadoff hitter early in his career solely on the basis of his exceptional speed.

Redus has pretty much reached his level of potential, even though he has yet to play a full season. Redus is a hybrid: a power hitter with speed. He is not going to change.

Rooker: "He can be an exciting player because he has great tools, though somewhere along the line, they've become dull. He runs extremely well and could be right up there in stolen bases with Coleman if he got on base more."

PHILADELPHIA PHILLIES

HITTING:

Ron Roenicke was a victim of the 24-man roster last spring when he was cut by the Giants. He was in the Oakland minor league system when he was salvaged by the Phillies.

Roenicke might never have seen the major leagues again if the Philadelphia outfielders hadn't started dropping like flies last year. Garry Maddox retired because of back problems, Gary Redus underwent elbow surgery and Chris James broke his ankle all in the span of just 11 days. The purchasing of Roenicke's contract turned out to be one of the best moves the Phillies made all year.

He is a good ballplayer with enough ability to be part of somebody's bench somewhere. Roenicke hits for a better average from the right side of the plate, but has a little more power from the left side. He likes the ball down-and-in from righthanders and away from lefthanders. He's an excellent bunter who led the Phillies' non-pitchers in sacrifices with four.

But between his acquisition in May and the All-Star break, Roenicke was run down by the Phillies' own minor league system. In spite of Roenicke's fine performance, the Phillies felt that home-grown Jeff Stone was more in line with their future and decided to give Stone big league experience. Even when Stone went down with an ankle injury, Roenicke sat on the bench. By that time, Redus was back in left field and Milt Thompson had begun his resurgence as a hitter. Roenicke read the handwriting on the wall. No matter how well he played as a starter, his role was on the bench.

BASERUNNING:

He has good speed and is an intelligent baserunner.

FIELDING:

Roenicke will do a workmanlike job

RON ROENICKE
OF, No. 17
SL, 6'0", 180 lbs.
ML Svc: 6 years
Born: 8-19-56 in Covina, CA

1986 STATISTICS

AVG	G	AB	R	H	2B	3B	HR	RBI	BB	SO	SB
.247	102	275	42	68	13	1	5	42	61	52	2

CAREER STATISTICS

AVG	G	AB	R	H	2B	3B	HR	RBI	BB	SO	SB
.248	450	961	128	238	47	2	16	104	172	172	23

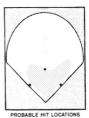

VS. RHP   VS. LHP   PROBABLE HIT LOCATIONS

defensively at all three outfield positions. He doesn't have the range to be an everyday center fielder or the arm to be an everyday right fielder. But he does all the little things well, such as charging the ball and hitting the cutoff man.

OVERALL:

While he was an occasional starter, he was their most productive bench player, a handyman who could play all three outfield positions, bat from either side of the plate and pinch-hit. He was versatile enough to fit perfectly as the 24th man.

Rooker: "Roenicke's value lies in his versatility and his ability to come off the bench. He is above average at any of the three outfield spots. The opportunity he was given last season should have caught the eye of any club looking for that 24th man."

PHILADELPHIA PHILLIES

PITCHING:

At 22 years old, Bruce Ruffin made the awesome jump from Double-A ball to the major leagues last season. In late June, he was recalled from the minors to replace Steve Carlton. The pressure of replacing a Hall of Fame pitcher in the starting rotation, his own youth and inexperience all pointed to Ruffin heading toward a rude awakening when he reached Philadelphia.

But Phillie fans were in for a huge surprise. In 21 starts, Ruffin went 9-4 with a 2.46 ERA. The ballclub was 15-6 in games he started. He allowed more than three earned runs only once and led the staff with 2.7 walks per nine innings.

What Ruffin brought to the Phillies was a hard sinker, a decent slider and poise beyond his years. He replaced Carlton without thinking twice about it (well, *maybe* twice). This is a youngster whose first start at home came before 61,475 people. He beat the Reds, 7-3.

Ruffin is a lefthander with a compact motion and a three-quarters delivery. He is an extremely fast worker (when Ruffin is pitching, count on a 2½-hour game) and specializes in ground balls. Fifty-six percent of his outs came on ground balls last year. His sinker is a very effective pitch.

Ruffin's slider is really a half-slider/half-curve that he calls a "slurve." It could use some improvement. If Ruffin improves his slider and starts jamming righthanders with it, then his sinker, which tails down and away from them, will be that much more effective.

It's easy to tell when Ruffin is losing his stuff or just doesn't have it. He gets his pitches up and those ground ball outs turn into line drives. When the line drives start coming, the

BRUCE RUFFIN
LHP, No. 47
RL, 6'2", 205 lbs.
ML Svc: less than one year
Born: 10-4-63 in Lubbock, TX

1986 STATISTICS

W	L	ERA	G	GS	CG	SV	IP	H	R	ER	BB	SO
9	4	2.46	21	21	6	0	146.1	138	53	40	44	70

CAREER STATISTICS

W	L	ERA	G	GS	CG	SV	IP	H	R	ER	BB	SO
9	4	2.46	21	21	6	0	146.1	138	53	40	44	70

only thing to do is get Ruffin out of there because, as primarily a one-pitch pitcher, there's nothing for him to fall back on.

FIELDING, HITTING, BASERUNNING:

Ruffin has an above-average move to first and keeps runners close. He is an abysmal hitter and a terrible bunter. He doesn't help himself at all at the plate. On the bases, he is slow and cautious.

OVERALL:

Rooker: "His minor league coach assured the Phillies that Bruce was mature enough to handle the major leagues. What he couldn't say, however, was whether he had enough stuff to win. But last year Bruce showed them all they needed to know.

"For a rookie, he showed excellent poise. With enough work, he could be a big winner. He is a great example of: it's not what you throw, but where you throw it."

PHILADELPHIA PHILLIES

HITTING:

Three years ago, John Russell failed to make it as an outfielder. Two years ago, he couldn't cut it as a first baseman. Last year, he was pretty much a flop as a catcher. But let's not give up on him just yet. There's still time, and he might yet improve himself enough to become an everyday catcher.

What started Russell on his nomadic life through the outfield and first base was his offense. He hasn't hit for average and probably never will. But he has awesome power.

Here's what makes it so hard to give up on Russell: In 630 big league at-bats, Russell has 68 extra-base hits, including 24 home runs and 94 RBIs. It's not likely Russell would put those numbers up in a single season, especially if he were to catch everyday, but in the parts of the three seasons he has played for the Phillies, *45% of Russell's hits have gone for extra bases.* And last year, he ranked fourth in the National League in RBIs per at-bat, with one every 5.2 at-bats. Only Mike Schmidt, Gary Carter and Candy Maldonado were ahead of him in that category.

If Russell made contact more often, he might hit 20 to 30 points higher than the .241 he hit last year. He is a high-ball, fastball, dead pull hitter who likes the ball away from him. He has a serious weakness for breaking balls away; he can be jammed with hard stuff and will chase bad pitches. Russell could help himself by cutting down on his swing with two strikes and learning some discipline at the plate.

BASERUNNING:

Russell is a slow and cautious baserunner. He is not a threat to steal.

FIELDING:

Russell was moved back to behind the plate (the position he played in college and early in his minor league career) and began the 1986 season as a part-time catcher who played almost exclusively against lefthanded pitching. But when Darren Daulton went down with a season-ending injury in late June,

JOHN RUSSELL
C, No. 6
RR, 6'0", 200 lbs.
ML Svc: 3 years
Born: 1-5-61 in
*   Oklahoma City, OK*

1986 STATISTICS

AVG	G	AB	R	H	2B	3B	HR	RBI	BB	SO	SB
.241	93	315	35	76	21	2	13	60	25	103	0

CAREER STATISTICS

AVG	G	AB	R	H	2B	3B	HR	RBI	BB	SO	SB
.240	213	630	68	151	41	3	24	94	55	208	2

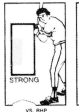

VS. RHP

VS. LHP

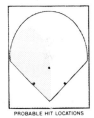

PROBABLE HIT LOCATIONS

Russell was elevated to the starting catcher's spot and given the opportunity to prove himself.

He is far from ready for prime time. His defense is lacking in virtually every phase of catching. From receiving to throwing out baserunners to getting his glove on pitches, Russell is woefully inadequate. As a signal-caller, he seems unable to put down more than one finger at a time, especially when a potential basestealer is dancing off first. The Phillies' pitchers crossed him up a lot last season, which was part of the reason why he led the NL in passed balls.

Russell does two things well, however. He blocks balls in the dirt and blocks the plate on plays at home. The rest of his game has to be, shall we say, polished up.

OVERALL:

Rooker: "His bat has improved, but he has a lot of work ahead of him as a catcher. He doesn't throw well and his mechanics are weak. He could hit 20-plus home runs a year. But the question is, how many runs will he let in?"

PHILADELPHIA PHILLIES

HITTING:

It's not exactly a state secret that Samuel is a low-ball, fastball hitter. Armed with that information, National League pitchers dutifully fed him breaking balls, off-speed stuff

Maybe someday Juan Samuel will learn the strike zone. That's the only way he will become the kind of hitter the Phillies think he can be.

and climbed the ladder on him with fastballs last season. Samuel saw perhaps three low fastballs all year. For the rest of the time, he hacked at slop or jumped out of his shoes to reach something headed for the backstop.

Samuel thinks patience belongs in a doctor's office. Does he like to swing at the first pitch? You bet he does. Samuel also likes to swing at the second, third, fourth and fifth pitches. His well-documented overaggressiveness at the plate is the reason why he struck out an awesome 142 times (and 451 strikeouts in three years), walked 26 times all year and produced an embarrassment of an on-base percentage (.302) for a hitter of his calibre.

Samuel's blazing speed makes him a natural leadoff hitter. But as the leadoff hitter in 1985, he didn't show enough discipline at the plate to hold the job and he started the 1986 season as the Phillies' No. 3 hitter. When Von Hayes caught fire, Samuel was dropped to sixth. By the end of the season, Samuel was hitting second.

With all of his faults at the plate, Samuel still managed to hit .266 in 1986, score 90 runs, drive in 78 and produce 64 extra-base hits, including 12 triples. The numbers give a clear indication that if Samuel ever disciplined himself at the plate, he'd have the potential to win a Triple Crown.

BASERUNNING:

Samuel is one of the fastest runners in baseball and gets out of the box quicker than any righthanded hitter in the game. His speed makes him an awesome threat to steal (he has stolen 167 bases in three years), but he is not a good situation runner. For instance, Samuel was never shy about running with Mike Schmidt at the plate, which merely served to

JUAN SAMUEL
2B, No. 8
RR, 5'11", 168 lbs.
ML Svc: 3 years
Born: 12-9-60 in
San Pedro de Macoris,
Dominican Republic

1986 STATISTICS

AVG	G	AB	R	H	2B	3B	HR	RBI	BB	SO	SB
.266	145	591	90	157	36	12	16	78	26	142	42

CAREER STATISTICS

AVG	G	AB	R	H	2B	3B	HR	RBI	BB	SO	SB
.268	484	2020	310	541	104	46	52	226	91	467	170

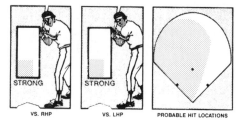

take the bat out of Schmidt's hands.

FIELDING:

Samuel is a capable, if unspectacular, defensive second baseman. In his rookie year, Samuel led all National League second basemen in errors with 33. He cut his errors to 15 in '86, but they rose to 25 last year. He has vast range but has trouble on balls hit to his right. He goes to his left extremely well, however. His arm is strong but erratic.

Last year, Samuel improved on the double play pivot and finally seemed to have perfected his footwork on that play.

OVERALL:

Great things have been expected from Samuel ever since he broke into the major leagues. He has offered glimpses of greatness as an offensive player but so far has not been consistent.

Rooker: "Juan is a player with all the tools and could be as good as Ryne Sandberg, maybe better. Samuel strikes out too much and chases far too many bad pitches. If he ever learns to concentrate all the time, he could be very, very good."

PHILADELPHIA PHILLIES

PITCHING:

What's the best way for a pitcher with declining, marginal stuff to keep a job in the National League? Be lefthanded and hit the hell out of the ball.

Schatzeder started the 1986 season with Montreal but the Phillies were looking for a reliever who could get out lefthanders, and if Schatzeder was nothing else as a pitcher, he was tough on lefthanders. So in late July they dealt shortstop Tom Foley to the Expos and got Schatzeder. They're still talking about what a great deal it was in Montreal.

Schatzeder spent the season pitching with tendinitis in his left shoulder. It had an effect, of course. Schatzeder had to be given extra time in the bullpen to warm up and there were some days when he couldn't get loose at all.

None of Schatzeder's four pitches are the stuff of legend, but there's a job open in the Phillies' bullpen for him. They would prefer to have two lefthanders in their bullpen to complement righthanders Steve Bedrosian, Kent Tekulve and Tom Hume. Schatzeder could be one of them. He would be the long man, or the guy to get out a couple lefthanders in the middle innings. It's the role he played last year with limited success. Considering he pitched in pain most of the year, it would be unfair to say he was ineffective. He gave the Phillies what he had.

FIELDING, HITTING, BASERUNNING:

If his arm ever betrays him, it's not inconceivable that Schatzeder could make his living as a pinch-hitter. He is that good. Schatzeder has some power and hit .385 with

DAN SCHATZEDER
LHP, No. 35
LL, 5'11", 204 lbs.
ML Svc: 9 years
Born: 12-1-54 in
Elmhurst, IL

1986 STATISTICS

W	L	ERA	G	GS	CG	SV	IP	H	R	ER	BB	SO
6	5	3.26	55	0	0	2	88.1	81	43	32	35	47

CAREER STATISTICS

W	L	ERA	G	GS	CG	SV	IP	H	R	ER	BB	SO
58	59	3.59	328	117	18	6	1076.2	978	473	429	378	584

one home run in 26 at-bats in 1986. He hit .417 (5-for-12) as a pinch-hitter. His five pinch-hits were the most by a National League pitcher since Don Newcombe had five in 1959.

Schatzeder has a good move to first and holds runners well. He is an above-average fielder and good baserunner.

OVERALL:

If he were righthanded, Schatzeder probably would be selling real estate right now. But there's always a job somewhere for a lefthander, which means Schatzeder should be able to hang in there as a long man and lefty specialist indefinitely.

Rooker: "He has four basic pitches and must use them all. Dan will have to be satisfied with a role as a long man. He's lost some zip on his fastball but his breaking stuff saves him. The condition of his arm may be questionable, however."

PHILADELPHIA PHILLIES

HITTING:

Mike Schmidt adjusted his hitting style back in June 1985 and returned to prominence as one of the game's premier players almost immediately. The pre-1985 Schmidt stood as far off the plate as the rules allowed, the better to avoid being jammed, and swung with a huge uppercut. He was a low-ball hitter.

In early 1985, he moved closer to the plate and leveled off his swing a little bit. The change enabled him to hit the high fastball. These modifications represented more than a mere fine-tuning; they were major alterations for a player whose hitting style had been established for years.

Schmidt's Most Valuable Player season in 1986, however, was due to more than a stance adjustment. From the start of spring training in 1986, Mike Schmidt was a man on a mission. For one thing, he was looking to avenge critics who held his anemic .215 batting average over the first two months of 1985 responsible for the Phillies' hasty fadeaway from the pennant race. But beyond that, Schmidt was also looking at the horizon and seeing the end of his career. A proud athlete, Schmidt wants to leave the game while he is on top.

The result was one of the most consistent seasons of his career. A notorious streak hitter, Schmidt went two consecutive starts without a hit just twice all season. He hit .285 in the first half of the season and .295 in the second.

One of the greatest improvements Schmidt made as a hitter last season was cutting down his strikeouts to a career-low 89, fully 38 less than the average for his career. He cut down on his swing with two strikes and went more for base hits instead of trying to take every pitch deep.

Schmidt has always been a patient hitter with an excellent knowledge of the strike zone as well as of his own hitting zone. He works a pitcher as well as anyone and usually will not swing at a pitch that isn't a strike or in his power zone. However, pitchers were still occasionally able to climb the ladder on him and fool him last year. When he was caught guessing, it was usually a fastball coming at a time when he was expecting something off-speed.

MIKE SCHMIDT
3B, No. 20
RR, 6'2", 203 lbs.
ML Svc: 14 years
Born: 9-27-49 in Dayton, OH

1986 STATISTICS

AVG	G	AB	R	H	2B	3B	HR	RBI	BB	SO	SB
.290	160	552	97	160	29	1	37	119	89	84	1

CAREER STATISTICS

AVG	G	AB	R	H	2B	3B	HR	RBI	BB	SO	SB
.268	2107	7292	1347	1954	352	57	495	1392	1354	1744	169

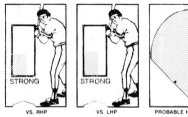

STRONG STRONG

VS. RHP   VS. LHP   PROBABLE HIT LOCATIONS

BASERUNNING:

Both time and an arthritic condition in his knees have eroded Schmidt's ability as a baserunner. He never had great speed, but now he is slow and no threat whatsoever to steal.

FIELDING:

Because both of his knees are weak, Schmidt has lost some of his range at third base. Nevertheless, he made only eight errors all year (six at third base and two at first) and was in line to win the Gold Glove. His arm is strong and accurate.

OVERALL:

Schmidt's contract expires at the end of the 1987 season. He has considered retiring, though he will probably not make a decision until the end of this year. If the Phillies look as though they might contend for the pennant in 1988, if his family is amenable and if he is healthy, Schmidt might play beyond this season.

Rooker: "Schmidt has adjusted to the high pitch and now both left- and righthanders have to pitch him inside more. For a home run hitter, Schmidt is unusually patient and could easily have another great year."

PHILADELPHIA PHILLIES

HITTING:

Rick Schu has spent his first two years in the big leagues serving as an insurance policy to Mike Schmidt at third base.

Being Schmidt's understudy at third base has meant that Schu doesn't play very much. Schu started only 42 games and got 208 at-bats last year--half his total for 1985. Yet even with limited action, he hit eight home runs and drove in 25 runs, which was one more homer and one more RBI than he had in 1985.

He is a high-ball, fastball hitter with power to left and left-center field. Schu likes to pull the ball and, like most young hitters, has trouble with breaking balls away. He can be struck out with the generic in-out, up-down pitching pattern. But he'll hurt a pitcher who makes a mistake with a fastball or who hangs a slider.

Schu could probably use more patience at the plate and bring a pitcher to full counts more often. But it's understandable that a player who bats an average of eight times a week would be a little anxious when he gets to the plate.

Even though he showed the Phillies more power than he did in his rookie year, Schu continued to struggle when he was hitting with runners in scoring position. Overall, he hit .274, but with runners in scoring position, he was a .167 hitter, a tremendous disappointment.

BASERUNNING:

Schu has good speed and is an excellent baserunner. He's not much of a threat to steal, but he knows what he's doing once he gets on base.

FIELDING:

Schu's greatest defensive improvement was on charge plays. As a rookie in 1985, he *never* made the play. Last year, however, he executed it consistently.

He worked hard on his defense during the season, concerned mostly with his balance. Schu tended to fold himself into too much of a crouch and get up on his toes. This habit slowed his reaction time considerably and third base is a reflex position. He remained a

RICK SCHU
3B, No. 15
RR, 6'0", 170 lbs.
ML Svc: 2 years
Born: 1-26-62 in
Philadelphia, PA

1986 STATISTICS

AVG	G	AB	R	H	2B	3B	HR	RBI	BB	SO	SB
.274	92	208	32	57	10	1	8	25	18	44	2

CAREER STATISTICS

AVG	G	AB	R	H	2B	3B	HR	RBI	BB	SO	SB
.260	221	653	98	170	33	6	17	54	62	128	10

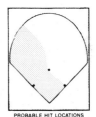

STRONG — VS. RHP   STRONG — VS. LHP   PROBABLE HIT LOCATIONS

two-step and dive third baseman to either side on ground balls, with a heavy weakness to his right.

An off-season weightlifting program after 1985 not only increased Schu's power, it made his arm better. Accuracy was never a problem, but he needed to improve his arm if he was planning to become an everyday third baseman.

OVERALL:

Schu hasn't reached his peak as a player, but he is 25 years old and he wants to be given a chance to prove himself as an everyday player. At the end of last season, he would have welcomed a trade. But as long as the Phillies needed someone as a hedge against an injury to Mike Schmidt, they weren't sending Schu anywhere.

Rooker: "He is a fastball hitter who likes the ball up-and-away. Schu has better-than-average speed and could steal a few bases if he played more often. He can make all the plays at third, but he is a little slow to his right. His biggest problem is being behind Mike Schmidt. It looks like he is going to have to wait a little longer for his chance."

PHILADELPHIA PHILLIES

HITTING:

Jeff Stone is an opposite field hitter who likes the ball pitched down-and-away from him. He is basically a singles hitter although he has excellent power to left field. He is a first-ball, fastball hitter with a big hole in his strike zone up-and-in. Both righties and lefties should try to jam him; Stone will hit anything low in the strike zone. He is not a patient hitter and would benefit by becoming more selective.

Stone is one of the few lefthanded hitters who has no trouble with lefthanded pitching. Last year, he hit .317 against lefthanders and .277 overall.

After losing the everyday job in left field in 1985, Stone started last year in the minors. When the Phillies brought him up in May, he was used as a leadoff or No. 2 hitter. But he does not get on base enough for a leadoff hitter and is lousy with runners in scoring position. Stone is at his best when he doesn't have to lead off an inning or bat with runners in scoring position, which quickly narrows down his value as an offensive player.

BASERUNNING:

Stone's greatest asset is his speed, which is exceptional. He should be a good basestealer, but he is not. Those 27 bases Stone stole in 51 games as a rookie in 1984 were the product of pure speed. Once pitchers learned that Stone could be flushed by holding the ball, they took away his best weapon. Stone has stolen a total of 34 bases in the last two years, far fewer than he should have stolen.

It was incumbent upon him to learn the pitchers and adjust to their moves. But he has been unable to do that. Lefthanders are real trouble for him. He seems unable to pick up the keys in their deliveries that would let him know when to run.

FIELDING:

Stone is a weak defensive player. His great speed allows him to get to a lot of balls but he has a lot of trouble judging fly balls. He doesn't

JEFF STONE
OF, No. 26
LR, 6'0", 175 lbs.
ML Svc: 2 years
Born: 12-26-60 in
Kennett, MO

1986 STATISTICS

AVG	G	AB	R	H	2B	3B	HR	RBI	BB	SO	SB
.277	82	249	32	69	6	4	6	19	20	52	19

CAREER STATISTICS

AVG	G	AB	R	H	2B	3B	HR	RBI	BB	SO	SB
.298	230	702	97	209	14	15	10	48	44	129	65

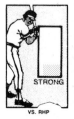  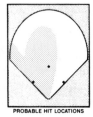

VS. RHP   VS. LHP   PROBABLE HIT LOCATIONS

charge ground balls well and has shown very little arm strength.

While in the minors last year, he was put in center field and, surprisingly, was a much better defensive player there. He had played center before in the minors and said he was much more comfortable roaming in the middle of the range. As a center fielder, his judgment was fine. He made several spectacular, diving catches and his arm, while not great, proved to be adequate.

OVERALL:

Stone wasn't happy with his role as sometime left fielder, sometime center fielder and sometime pinch-hitter (he was 7-for-21 as a pinch-hitter). At the end of the year, he was hoping the Phillies would trade him to a team that would accept his faults and play him everyday.

Rooker: "He has very good speed and should steal more bases than he does. He could learn to be a little more selective at the plate. This year could be decision time on Stone. A change might help him."

PHILADELPHIA PHILLIES

PITCHING:

Kent Tekulve found a home last year as a set-up man for Steve Bedrosian. As a past master of late-inning relief, Tekulve could have demanded a trade and tried to revive a flagging career somewhere other than in Philadelphia. But Tekulve didn't get to be 39 years old last year without doing some growing up. He realized that if he insisted on working as a bullpen stopper, he might not be working at all.

So after a disastrous 1985, he readily accepted moving to the middle innings, where he became a *Comeback Player of the Year* candidate. Tekulve went 11-5 with a 2.54 ERA as a tablesetter. Only the Mets' Roger McDowell had more victories (14) among National League relievers. Tekulve made 73 appearances, guaranteeing through a clause in his contract that he would return for 1987, and breaking Elroy Face's league record for career appearances.

Tekulve throws a sinker and a slider with a submarine motion. He has lost a lot off his fastball over the years, but made up for that last season with excellent control and an encyclopedic knowledge of the hitters. His experience made him particularly effective when he entered games with runners on base. Of the 47 baserunners he inherited, only nine scored.

His submarine motion causes his slider to rise rather than to drop, making him naturally tough on righthanded hitters. He developed a change-up that helped him against left-handers, who have been traditionally his nemesis. By the end of the year, Tekulve was using his change-up against both left- and righthanded batters. The new pitch also served to make his sinker a more effective pitch.

But the change-up wasn't what made Tekulve an effective pitcher in 1986. His sinker regained its old authority and his slider broke with more bite than it did in 1985. The reason, Tekulve said, was because he was used regularly in '86 and wasn't the previous season.

He had a point. Tekulve is the kind of pitcher who has always thrived on work and

KENT TEKULVE
RHP, No. 27
RR, 6'4", 185 lbs.
ML Svc: 12 years
Born: 3-5-47 in
Cincinnati, OH

1986 STATISTICS

W	L	ERA	G	GS	CG	SV	IP	H	R	ER	BB	SO
11	5	2.54	73	0	0	4	110	99	35	31	25	57

CAREER STATISTICS

W	L	ERA	G	GS	CG	SV	IP	H	R	ER	BB	SO
85	76	2.69	853	0	0	176	1119.1	1066	419	358	417	645

who has always put up good numbers when he's pitched close to 100 innings a year. He pitched 110 innings last year (his most since 1982, when he saved 20 games for the Pirates).

FIELDING, HITTING, BASERUNNING:

Tekulve has a below-average move to first but holds runners on by both throwing to first and stepping off the rubber. He is an average fielder who covers first quickly but doesn't stop many grounders hit back up the middle. As a hitter, he is below average and is conservative on the bases.

OVERALL:

It's understood that Tekulve is close to the end of his career. His contract expires at the end of this season. He says he's not interested in any more multi-year contracts, but wants to continue his career on a year-to-year basis. He has a rubber arm that isn't likely to snap anytime soon. So physically, he should be able to pitch for one or two more years.

Rooker: "Teke has made the transition from stopper to set-up man in spectacular fashion. His value lies in his durability and that gives him a chance to pitch maybe two or three more years. He is an excellent guy to have in a clubhouse."

PHILADELPHIA PHILLIES

HITTING:

There's a misconception about Milt Thompson that needs clearing up.

He is not a young prospect waiting to burst on the scene. Thompson is a middle-of-the-road, 28-year-old outfielder with more than seven years of minor league time under his belt. He is an average defensive center fielder with an average arm. He has some speed, so he covers a lot of ground out there. He is a good, fast baserunner. He is a contact hitter who doesn't make enough contact. Almost any pitcher in the National League can jam him at will.

What he has going for him is his speed and his attitude: Thompson is willing to learn. He's willing to do whatever it takes to make it as an everyday center fielder.

So that's Milt Thompson, a guy with, at best, average tools as a hitter, excellent speed, a great attitude and not much time left to prove himself.

When he was in the Braves' minor league system, the party line was that Thompson had been held up by the presence of Dale Murphy in center field. But Thompson's time in the minors had more to do with Milt Thompson than with Dale Murphy. Thompson had a slow bat. He couldn't hit the inside fastball. Not just Dwight Gooden's inside fastball, *anybody's* inside fastball.

So it shouldn't have surprised the Phillies when Thompson hit .207 in his first 53 games. As a lefthanded hitter with speed who gets out of the box extremely well, Thompson should have picked up a lot of infield hits. He didn't because all his ground balls to the infield went to the right side.

After watching Thompson struggle to make contact, the Phillies sent him to Triple-A in early July. In his six weeks there, Thompson hit well, which boosted his confidence. He changed his approach to hitting: he started using an inside-out swing and trying to take everything to left field, which is what the Phillies had wanted him to do from the beginning.

When he returned to the majors in the middle of August, he was a vastly improved hitter. The flood of ground balls to second base slowed to a trickle. He hit .294 after

MILT THOMPSON
OF, No. 28
LR, 5'11", 160 lbs.
ML Svc: 2 years
Born: 1-5-59 in
**   Washington, D.C.**

1986 STATISTICS

AVG	G	AB	R	H	2B	3B	HR	RBI	BB	SO	SB
.251	96	299	38	75	7	1	6	23	26	62	19

CAREER STATISTICS

AVG	G	AB	R	H	2B	3B	HR	RBI	BB	SO	SB
.276	194	580	71	160	15	3	8	33	44	109	42

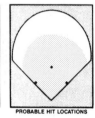

VS. RHP   VS. LHP   PROBABLE HIT LOCATIONS

returning from Portland and was declared the everyday center fielder for 1987.

BASERUNNING:

Thompson is an excellent baserunner with above-average speed. He was the Phillies' most effective basestealer, stealing 19 times in 23 attempts. He's a rotten bunter, however, with no conception of how to lay down a drag bunt for a hit.

FIELDING:

Thompson's defense isn't good enough to keep him in a lineup.

OVERALL:

Rooker: "If he is going to play everyday, he's going to have to learn how to get on base and be patient at the plate. He has to continue to go to the opposite field. He also could help himself by learning how to bunt. His speed is his strength right now. He should be able to steal 40-50 bases."

PHILADELPHIA PHILLIES

HITTING:

Glenn Wilson spent the majority of his 1986 season climbing out of a hole he dug for himself in April and May, when he got off to a *slow* start. How slow? How about .181 with three homers and 19 RBIs through May 31?

Wilson was a victim of his own winter of content. After driving in 102 runs in 1985, Wilson did not work out in the off-season. When he went to spring training, he was without the fire and drive that made him an exceptional offensive player the previous year.

Wilson does not not have a lot of self-confidence, so the first two months of the season took their toll. But to his credit, he snapped out of it. From June on, he hit .303 with 12 homers and 65 RBIs.

What Wilson did to turn his season around was finally to stop worrying about repeating as an All-Star or driving in another 100 runs, and to start taking his year on a game-by-game basis. He wasn't able to concentrate early in the year because he was pressing for a second All-Star spot and another 100-RBI season. When it was certain that neither would happen, he did his best to salvage the season and came away with fairly respectable numbers. His .271 average in 1986 is only four points lower than what he hit in 1985.

In some respects, Wilson actually improved as a hitter in 1986. His walks were up, his strikeouts down. He led the team by grounding into 15 double plays, but that is still nine fewer than he had previous year.

Wilson remains a high-ball, fastball hitter who likes pitches away. Pitchers get him out by bringing their fastballs up higher and higher in the strike zone or by getting him to pull breaking balls away. Wilson could improve himself as a hitter by going to right field more often than he does and by concentrating during every at-bat. He has a tendency to kiss off at-bats when there are no runners on base or when a game is out of hand.

BASERUNNING:

Wilson has average speed, but is an above-average baserunner who will steal on occasion.

GLENN WILSON
RF, No. 12
RR, 6'1", 190 lbs.
ML Svc: 5 years
Born: 12-22-58 in
Baytown, TX

1986 STATISTICS

AVG	G	AB	R	H	2B	3B	HR	RBI	BB	SO	SB
.271	155	584	70	158	30	4	15	84	42	91	5

CAREER STATISTICS

AVG	G	AB	R	H	2B	3B	HR	RBI	BB	SO	SB
.270	676	2358	265	636	130	19	58	316	134	394	22

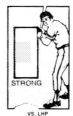
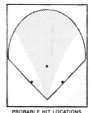

STRONG · VS. RHP   STRONG · VS. LHP   PROBABLE HIT LOCATIONS

FIELDING:

Wilson is one of the best defensive right fielders in the National League and established himself as a Gold Glove candidate by leading the league in assists with 20 last year. Not many outfielders can throw a runner out at first, but Wilson did just that to the Cubs' Keith Moreland last year.

Wilson's greatest improvement in 1986 came in his consistency; he cut his errors from 12 the previous season to four. He is an aggressive outfielder and is especially good at running down balls in the gap. He is willing to challenge walls and charges balls well. He loves to play defense and gets a personal thrill from throwing out baserunners.

OVERALL:

Wilson is an exciting, gung-ho player who is just beginning to come into his own. At the end of the year, he vowed to train as hard as he did going into the 1985 season.

Rooker: "Along with Andy Van Slyke, Glenn is the best-throwing right fielder in the league. As a hitter, he likes the ball up from both lefties and righties. He is a gamer who's willing to play in pain."

PHILADELPHIA PHILLIES

MARVIN FREEMAN
RHP, No. 48
RR, 6'6", 182 lbs.
ML Svc: less than
one year
Born: 4-10-63 in
Chicago, IL

PITCHING, FIELDING, HITTING, BASERUNNING:

Marvin Freeman is a very tall, very thin righthander with a very bright future.

He spent most of 1986 pitching in Double-A where he finished second in the Eastern League in victories with 13. He made three starts for the Phillies in September and was impressive, allowing six hits in 16 innings. His best performance came on September 21, when he one-hit the Mets (who were using their regular lineup that game) for seven innings.

Freeman has a 93 MPH fastball and a good, hard slider (clocked at 86 MPH). But he has problems throwing strikes. In his three starts, he walked 10 and struck out only eight batters. He particularly had problems throwing his slider for strikes. But it often takes tall guys more time to gain coordination. As Freeman matures, he should be able to smooth out the kinks in his delivery. When that happens, he'll find the strike zone. And when that happens, he could become one *very* nasty pitcher.

During spring training in 1986, Freeman really didn't pitch well enough even to make the Double-A roster. But the organization decided to put him there anyway to see what he could do. He had all kinds of control problems early in the year and junked his curveball for a few starts. Then, in July, he started to come around. He started getting his curve over and his confidence grew. By the time the Phillies called him up, he had matured a great deal.

OVERALL:

Rooker: "Freeman will have to work on his control and changing speeds to improve, but the potential is there for him to be successful at the major league level. He will probably start 1987 in Triple-A. But if he stays healthy, look for him to be a member of the Phillies' starting rotation before 1988."

RONN REYNOLDS
C, No. 29
RR, 6'0", 200 lbs.
ML Svc: less than
one year
Born: 9-28-58 in
Wichita, KS

HITTING, BASERUNNING, FIELDING:

Ronn Reynolds spent the 1985 season as the backup catcher to the Mets' Gary Carter, which really means he did not play much. Noting that he was 27 years old and not about to beat out Carter for the everyday job, Reynolds asked the Mets to deal him. They obliged in January 1986.

Reynolds began the season in the minors, but was called up by the Phillies after Darren Daulton went down for the season with a knee injury. Then he was backup to John Russell, but when it became clear that Russell's defense was lacking, Reynolds was used often.

Reynolds is a high-ball, fastball hitter with excellent power to left field. He likes pitches away from him. Teams play him to pull and pitchers generally work him inside. He's selective enough at the plate, but with a big, uppercut swing, he doesn't make contact often enough. If Reynolds would quit trying to pull everything, he might add a few points to his average. He needs to add about 25 points to his average to qualify offensively as a catcher who can play everyday.

Defensively, there's nothing wrong with Reynolds: he's a fine receiver and knows how to call a game. He's not Jody Davis or Tony Pena, but he has a strong, accurate arm. He does everything a major league catcher should do.

PITTSBURGH PIRATES

HITTING:

Now fully settled into a utility role, Bill Almon saw his batting tumble from a respectable .270 in 1985 to .219 last year, mostly because he was used more sporadically by Pirate manager Jim Leyland than he had been by the club's previous skipper, Chuck Tanner.

Despite getting 48 fewer at-bats in 1986, Almon's production actually increased. He hit more home runs than the season before and drove in almost as many runs.

Almon, who seems to wait longer when he's hitting than most batters, is a high fastball hitter who looks to pull the ball. Early in the season he showed good power but then fell off in the season's later stages, especially when Mike Diaz took over the left field job.

Almon is a streak hitter but never had the chance to see a hot streak through. Last season's emergence of rookie Barry Bonds in center field and the experimentation with Mike Diaz in left field kept Almon from starting enough games consecutively to fuel any fire in his bat.

BASERUNNING:

Almon will fool you with his speed. At 34, he can still steal a base, being successful on 11 of 15 tries last year. A graduate of Brown University, he is an extremely intelligent baserunner. He is an aggressive baserunner who is willing to go in hard at second base to break up a double play.

FIELDING:

Almon is known as one of the game's most versatile players, able to perform adequately everywhere but as pitcher or catcher. Last season, he played at five different positions:

BILL ALMON
INF, No. 34
RR, 6'3", 191 lbs.
ML Svc: 10 years
Born: 11-21-52 in
Providence, RI

1986 STATISTICS

AVG	G	AB	R	H	2B	3B	HR	RBI	BB	SO	SB
.219	102	196	29	43	7	2	7	27	30	38	11

CAREER STATISTICS

AVG	G	AB	R	H	2B	3B	HR	RBI	BB	SO	SB
.256	1148	3230	376	826	132	25	36	290	238	604	127

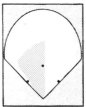

left field (52 games), third base (28), shortstop (19), first base (4) and right field (2).

As an infielder, Almon has good hands but his throwing arm can be erratic. As an outfielder, he is best suited to left field and was used often as a defensive replacement there.

OVERALL:

Thirteen years ago, Almon was the nation's No. 1 draft pick. He never became the star many thought he would be but has been smart enough to realize that his versatility can make him more valuable and prolong his career.

Rooker: "Bill is the kind of player who would fit in extremely well as a bench player for a club looking to win a pennant."

PITTSBURGH PIRATES

HITTING:

Rafael Belliard surprised everyone by making the team in spring training last season and then won the shortstop job from one-time No. 1 draft pick Sammy Khalifa at midseason.

Belliard's biggest problem as a hitter is that, despite standing only 5'6" and weighing no more than 152 lbs., he likes to hit high fastballs. *Power hitters* are supposed to go after high fastballs, not guys built like Belliard. His high, hard fastball habit leads to too many weak fly balls. The Pirates have tried getting him to choke up more on the bat to cut down on his swing, but Belliard still goes after pitches too high in the strike zone. He must learn to hit the ball on the ground more to take advantage of his speed.

Belliard needs the bunt. Already good at it, he should work on it even more to bunt for base hits. He shows very little power or the ability to hit the ball hard: he had only seven extra-base hits in 309 at-bats last season.

Hitting in the No. 8 spot in the batting order, Belliard was impressive in clutch situations. He had a number of hits when there were two outs and drove in a number of important RBIs.

BASERUNNING:

If Belliard can find a way to raise his average 30 or 40 points and draw a few walks (he had only 20 non-intentional walks last season), he could become a basestealing threat. He is a lithe and extremely fast runner and was successful in 12 of 14 attempts.

FIELDING:

Belliard's defense is what got him on the roster last year and just might keep him there. Wresting the shortstop job at midseason from the disappointing Sammy Khalifa, Belliard has excellent range and sure hands. His arm is capable of making the throw from the hole.

Initially unfamiliar with the rhythm of playing next to second baseman Johnny Ray, Belliard settled down soon enough. Once the

RAFAEL BELLIARD
INF, No. 38
RR, 5'6", 152 lbs.
ML Svc: 2 years
Born: 10-24-61 in
Pueblo Nuevo,
Dominican Republic

1986 STATISTICS

AVG	G	AB	R	H	2B	3B	HR	RBI	BB	SO	SB
.233	117	309	33	72	5	2	0	31	26	54	12

CAREER STATISTICS

AVG	G	AB	R	H	2B	3B	HR	RBI	BB	SO	SB
.232	167	354	41	82	5	2	0	32	26	61	17

  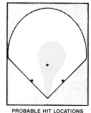

STRONG — VS. RHP STRONG — VS. LHP PROBABLE HIT LOCATIONS

two found their synchronization, they developed into a particularly good team when turning double plays.

Belliard is also a good fill-in at second, demonstrating that in 15 starts there when Ray was injured last season.

OVERALL:

One of the more pleasant surprises on the struggling Pirates last year, Belliard still cannot consider the starting shortstop's job his, however.

Rooker: "Rafael will have to come to spring training this year prepared to prove he can handle a starting role. He must work to become physically stronger to play every day at the big league level.

"Defensively, he is a very slick fielder who works well with Johnny Ray. Belliard will develop into a good, quick baserunner who might give the Pirates another form of attack they could use."

PITTSBURGH PIRATES

HITTING:

The Pirates rushed young Barry Bonds to the major leagues quicker than originally planned. The temptation to hustle him along was easy to understand: Bonds devoured the pitching of the Pacific Coast League and the club felt he had learned all he could there.

Bonds experienced a "learning season" last year. He hit just .223 with 102 strikeouts in 413 at-bats. But while he was learning, Bonds was also teaching. He showed the rest of the league that he is going to be a player to be reckoned with in the near future. He led all National League rookies in home runs (16), RBIs (48), stolen bases (36) and walks (63). He was the only major league rookie to hit at least 15 homers and steal at least 30 bases.

As a hitter, Bonds' greatest difficulty is learning to hit the inside fastball. His swing is still a bit too big and looping; while he proved able to send most any fastball to the fences, pitchers found that he couldn't cover the inside corner. Once he learns this, he should develop into more of a pull hitter who will power 30-40 home runs a year. His power is now from left- to right-center field.

For a young player, Bonds has a good eye. He won't swing at bad pitches--his strikeouts are because he just misses good ones. He should draw as many as 100 walks each season.

BASERUNNING:

Bonds has been taught by two of the game's best basestealers. Both his father and Yankee speedster Rickey Henderson have served as tutors--and it shows.

Bonds is smart and fast. He was not brought up to the majors last season until late May, yet he stole 36 bases. In a full season, he is likely to have 60-70 stolen bases. Only two of the National League's catchers (Atlanta's Ted Simmons and Mets' backup Ed Hearn) were able to throw him out all season.

FIELDING:

Bonds can make center field look small. He plays extremely shallow yet goes back on the ball so well that very few get over his head and

BARRY BONDS
OF, No. 7
LL, 6'1", 185 lbs.
ML Svc: 1 year
Born: 7-24-64 in
Riverside, CA

1986 STATISTICS

AVG	G	AB	R	H	2B	3B	HR	RBI	BB	SO	SB
.223	113	413	72	92	26	3	16	48	65	102	36

CAREER STATISTICS

AVG	G	AB	R	H	2B	3B	HR	RBI	BB	SO	SB
.223	113	413	72	92	26	3	16	48	65	102	36

  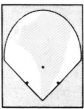

VS. RHP   VS. LHP   PROBABLE HIT LOCATIONS

remain in the park. He goes into the gap on either side equally well and takes advantage of his speed. Bonds is so smooth that he often seems to glide to the ball, making difficult catches appear routine.

His defensive weakness is a no-better-than-average arm. Oddly enough, it appears as though he doesn't seem to *like* to throw and often gets the ball caught up in the glove when he might have a chance to throw out a runner. He will not take aggressive chances to throw out advancing runners.

OVERALL:

Like his father, former major league star Bobby Bonds, Barry has speed and power. And like his father, he strikes out a lot.

Rooker: "Barry has a chance to become as good as his father, maybe even better . . . and he knows it. Bonds is thoroughly confident in his skills, so much so that some think it is arrogance.

"He was the Pirates' best choice at leadoff, though he should eventually settle in as the No. 3 hitter in the order. He should become one of the game's bright young stars."

PITTSBURGH PIRATES

HITTING:

A manager takes just one look at Bobby Bonilla, 6'3" and 210 lbs. of switch-hitter, and just *drools* thinking about his power potential. And the power is there, all right, though it has not surfaced as yet.

Like many young players, Bonilla has not learned to pull the ball to take full advantage of his power. He is a straightaway hitter with the tendency to lunge at pitches. He has been working hard to keep his weight back to wait longer on the pitch. He has power from both sides of the plate.

Bonilla hit .269 with the White Sox before the Pirates traded pitcher Jose DeLeon for him last July. Inexperienced but learning quickly, he hit just .240 with the Pirates, with only one homer.

Bonilla hits out of a crouch. In the American League he hit better lefthanded, yet in the National League he hit for a higher average from the right side.

BASERUNNING:

Because of his size, Bonilla doesn't look fast but he has deceptive speed. He can go from first to third well and is willing to break up the double play. He cannot be considered a basestealing threat at this point, but the Pirates are confident that with continued work, he will be.

FIELDING:

Bonilla played all over the place last year. He started at five different positions: all three outfield spots, first and third base. The Pirates are looking closely at him as a third baseman.

He has an outstanding throwing arm from the outfield, which makes him more suited for right field. He is already a good outfielder who will only get better if the Pirates decide to

BOBBY BONILLA
OF, No. 25
SR, 6'3", 210 lbs.
ML Svc: 1 year
Born: 2-23-63 in
New York, NY

1986 STATISTICS

AVG	G	AB	R	H	2B	3B	HR	RBI	BB	SO	SB
.256	138	426	55	109	16	4	3	43	62	48	8

CAREER STATISTICS

AVG	G	AB	R	H	2B	3B	HR	RBI	BB	SO	SB
.256	138	426	55	109	16	4	3	43	62	48	8

VS. RHP | VS. LHP | PROBABLE HIT LOCATIONS

leave him there.

OVERALL:

Bonilla is one of those youngsters for whom the cliche fits: *he has all the tools.* If he can learn to take advantage of them, he could blossom into a star as he blends size with speed and puts it together in a switch-hitting package.

Rooker: "Bobby works hard at improving himself. He overcame a badly broken ankle in 1985 to jump to the major leagues without Triple-A experience.

"The Pirates are working with his hitting mechanics. Bonilla is a coachable young man and is anxious to stick in the majors. He will get every opportunity to do so."

PITTSBURGH PIRATES

HITTING:

Sid Bream enjoyed his first full major league season in 1986; it proved to be a dream-come-true for him. He was third in the league in doubles with 37 and began to show flashes of becoming a power hitter with 16 homers and 77 RBI.

The Pirates' confidence in Bream's power potential allowed them to trade first baseman Jason Thompson to Montreal (thereby unloading a major expense from their ledger). Bream's performance made them forget Jason Thompson quickly.

Bream is an unusual lefthanded hitter in that he likes the ball up from both left- and righthanded pitchers.

Early in the season, Bream had a lot of trouble against lefthanded pitchers and found himself platooned for a while. But he came back so well and had made such substantial improvement that he erased all thoughts of his being a platoon player.

BASERUNNING:

Bream has below-average speed but is a terrific baserunner, as evidenced by his leading the Pirates with 73 runs scored. He uses the element of surprise to steal a base and finished last season with 13 stolen bases, more than any Pirate first baseman since Donn Clendenon had 22 in 1963. He has enough guts and savvy that he is not afraid to try to steal third base, a move usually reserved for the more renowned base-runners.

FIELDING:

Bream has made himself a better-than-average fielder. He has what probably is the best throwing arm among National League first baseman and set the league record for assists last season with 166, breaking Bill Buckner's mark of 161.

Bream comes in well against the sacrifice bunt, so well, in fact, that he is as good as the Mets' Keith Hernandez at that maneuver. Bream led the National League last year in total chances.

SID BREAM
1B, No. 5
LL, 6'4", 218 lbs.
ML Svc: 3 years
Born: 8-3-60 in
Carlisle, PA

1986 STATISTICS											
AVG	G	AB	R	H	2B	3B	HR	RBI	BB	SO	SB
.268	154	522	73	140	37	5	16	77	60	73	13

CAREER STATISTICS											
AVG	G	AB	R	H	2B	3B	HR	RBI	BB	SO	SB
.253	246	730	93	185	47	5	22	106	86	108	14

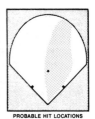

VS. RHP — STRONG   VS. LHP — STRONG   PROBABLE HIT LOCATIONS

Defensively, Bream's biggest problem is inconsistency. He needs to become more fundamentally reliable in taking throws at first, although last season, video replays of plays in which the umpire ruled his foot was off the bag at the catch proved otherwise. Nonetheless, he led first baseman in the league in errors with 17.

OVERALL:

With a full year under his belt, Sid Bream could explode in 1987. With his power, he could become a player who hits 20-25 home runs per year.

Rooker: "Sid has a marvelous attitude for the game, which helped him get through some trying times with the Dodgers before he was traded to Pittsburgh. He is still upset with the Dodgers over his treatment there and is bound and determined to prove that they made a mistake in selecting Greg Brock as their first baseman over him."

PITTSBURGH PIRATES

HITTING:

Mike Brown was the biggest disappointment the Pirates had last season. Having come to Pittsburgh from the California Angels in the John Candelaria-George Hendrick deal, Brown was supposed to solve their right field problem and provide power. A strong September in 1985 made the Pirates confident he could do the job but last year he became completely unraveled.

He showed up muscle-bound in spring training after a winter of pumping iron and it affected all areas of his game, especially his swing. Told they wanted power from him, Brown spent the year looking for fastballs he could drive--but they never came.

Previously he had had success with hitting the ball to all fields, but last year Brown forgot about that and looked for pitches he could power to left field. The pitchers saw this early and worked him with off-speed breaking stuff away. He wound up hitting only four home runs and spending time in the minor leagues.

Brown will be given another chance to prove himself, but instead of being the front-runner to win the right field job, he now has a lot of competition and must prove that he can find the power potential that left him last season.

BASERUNNING:

Brown is an adequate baserunner who is unafraid to go in and break up a double play. He is mostly a one-base-at-a-time runner who doesn't take an extra base unless it's handed to him.

FIELDING:

Brown is a better at fielding fly balls than ground balls. He gets a good jump on balls hit

MIKE BROWN
RF, No. 4
RR, 6'2", 196 lbs.
ML Svc: 4 years
Born: 12-29-59 in
San Francisco, CA

1986 STATISTICS

AVG	G	AB	R	H	2B	3B	HR	RBI	BB	SO	SB
.218	87	243	18	53	7	0	4	26	27	32	2

CAREER STATISTICS

AVG	G	AB	R	H	2B	3B	HR	RBI	BB	SO	SB
.267	297	853	101	228	47	7	23	110	76	123	5

VS. RHP — STRONG   VS. LHP — STRONG   PROBABLE HIT LOCATIONS

in the air and is confident when running them down.

On ground balls, however, he is less sure and has trouble stopping runners from taking an extra base. He has an accurate arm but he takes too long to get rid of the ball.

OVERALL:

Rooker: "This is a crucial year in the career of Mike Brown. At 26 years of age, the last problem he should be having is getting his head together, yet that is exactly what he must do if he is to live up to the potential he showed in the Angels' farm system and in his first half-season with the Pirates."

PITTSBURGH PIRATES

PITCHING:

The Yankees had to give up quality in the six-player trade with Pittsburgh that brought them Rick Rhoden and they did--Doug Drabek.

After Drabek reached the Yankees with a modicum of Triple-A experience, some observers felt he eventually could be for the Yankees what Roger Clemens was for Boston--not necessarily a 24-game winner, but a dominant pitcher who would consistently win big games.

Drabek has all the ingredients for success, starting with an outstanding fastball that moves along in the upper-80s or low-90s. Aside from the speed, it is a fastball with plenty of life. At his best, Drabek is able to throw as hard in the eighth inning as the first.

Drabek's slider and curveball are equally effective. He can hit spots with both, which is why he merits such a high rating. The change-up gives the young righthander four good pitches, something few major leaguers can boast. Drabek will improve his ability to change speeds, critical to every pitcher's development, as he logs more innings.

Perhaps Drabek's greatest quality is an aggressiveness that delighted Yankees manager Lou Piniella. There is nothing timid about Drabek. He really goes after hitters. Even after strong performances, he will analyze his errors and be determined to avoid them the next start.

FIELDING:

Drabek is a good athlete so there is no reason he shouldn't be a good major league fielder. He completely immerses himself in the game and is alert to every option on a play.

DOUG DRABEK
RHP, No.
RR, 6'1", 185 lbs.
ML Svc: 1 year
Born: 7-25-62 in
Victoria, TX

1986 STATISTICS

W	L	ERA	G	GS	CG	SV	IP	H	R	ER	BB	SO
7	8	4.10	27	21	0	0	131.2	126	64	60	50	76

CAREER STATISTICS

W	L	ERA	G	GS	CG	SV	IP	H	R	ER	BB	SO
7	8	4.10	27	21	0	0	131.2	126	64	60	50	76

Baserunners didn't see a lot of Drabek's pickoff move as a rookie, so it remains uncertain how effective he will be at holding runners. Certainly no one was taking liberties against him.

OVERALL:

The Yankees traded Drabek with the conviction that he can be a consistent winner in the major leagues. Why the deal then? Because New York, after two second-place finishes, feels it is on the verge of winning the American League East. Rhoden is the better candidate to be the pitcher who makes the difference than Drabek at this stage in their respective careers.

Kaat: "Doug is going from a contending ballclub to a club that will not be in contention this year. That might be a tough adjustment for him. How he adjusts to something like that will have a big effect on the pitcher he becomes."

PITTSBURGH PIRATES

PITCHING:

The Pittsburgh Pirates hope they can figure out what makes Brian Fisher tick. He was a mystery to his first two clubs, Atlanta and the New York Yankees, who dealt him to the Pirates over the winter in a rare six-pitcher swap.

The Yankees initially thought they had a steal of a deal when they acquired Fisher from the Braves for mediocre catcher Rick Cerone in December 1984. They converted Fisher into a reliever, and he responded with 14 saves and a glittering 2.38 ERA and was a Rookie of the Year candidate.

But he was a major disappointment in 1986. He didn't pitch nearly as well as his 9-5 record might indicate. His ERA was a truer reflection, as it soared to 4.93, more than two and a half runs higher than in his promising rookie campaign.

Still, Fisher has the chance to be a successful closer because of his outstanding fastball. He has an easy motion that deceives hitters, who find a fastball in the low- to mid-90's bearing down on them in an instant.

Fisher needs to be more aggressive with his fastball and show more confidence in it. He must challenge hitters more and use his power to quickly get ahead in the count.

Fisher has a history of control problems: these are related to his mental approach. When he gets hit, he often seems tentative about going into the strike zone on the next hitter. Instead, he nibbles at the plate, a pattern that cost him dearly in '86.

Fisher's breaking pitches need a great deal of work. When he's behind in the count, he is very hittable if batters are geared for the fastball. His slider is only fair. He does not have a curveball and doesn't have much of a change-up. Too often in 1986, Fisher was beaten by bad breaking balls rather than the fastball, his best pitch by far.

FIELDING, HITTING, BASERUNNING:

Fisher is not exceptionally quick off the

BRIAN FISHER
RHP, No. 54
RR, 6'4", 210 lbs.
ML Svc: 2 years
Born: 3-18-62 in
Honolulu, HI

1986 STATISTICS

W	L	ERA	G	GS	CG	SV	IP	H	R	ER	BB	SO
9	5	4.93	62	0	0	6	96.2	105	61	53	37	67

CAREER STATISTICS

W	L	ERA	G	GS	CG	SV	IP	H	R	ER	BB	SO
13	9	3.65	117	0	0	20	195	182	93	79	66	152

mound. He is not swift in making his judgments, either. This sometimes causes him to botch basic plays such as routine sacrifice bunts.

Fisher has an average move to first base. Because he is primarily a fastball pitcher, however, he is not easy to run on.

With the designated hitter rule in the American League, Fisher did not have to bat or run the bases for the Yankees. This will be part of his adjustment to a new team and league.

OVERALL:

The trade to Pittsburgh should greatly help Fisher. He was not a New York-type ballplayer. The turmoil in the front office--he was stunned when he was sent to Columbus for a couple of weeks in 1986--seemed to affect him more than others.

Kaat: "I think Pittsburgh made a real steal. If they can get Fisher in the right frame of mind, he could come in and be a stopper. I could definitely see him as a good late-inning pitcher for the right club."

PITTSBURGH PIRATES

HITTING:

Sammy Khalifa began the 1986 season with big expectations. He had won the shortstop job the previous year by performing exceedingly well over the final half of that season. Despite having been rushed in 1985, he had even shown some flashes of power as a hitter.

However, it all caught up with him last year. Khalifa is a fastball hitter who likes the ball up-and-away but found every pitcher in the league simply crowding him with fastballs. He started the season trying to pull the ball too much, perhaps enamored of the vision of power-hitting, and went from being the club's starting shortstop to being sent to Triple-A in Hawaii, where he seemed to put things back together.

To do well, Khalifa is going to have to go back to the basics, cut down on strikeouts and become a contact hitter who uses the hit-and-run to his advantage. He drove in only four runs in 151 at-bats.

BASERUNNING:

Although a shortstop, Khalifa has no more than average speed and is an average baserunner. He has lapses in concentration when he is on the bases and it causes him to make baserunning blunders.

FIELDING:

Khalifa is an average shortstop who should get much better. He has excellent hands but his throwing has a tendency to be erratic, more from footwork than from a weakness in the arm. If Khalifa has a major problem, it is with concentration, which forces him to make careless errors, both physical and mental.

OVERALL:

Still just 23 years old, Khalifa will be given

SAM KHALIFA
INF, No. 27
RR, 5'11", 180 lbs.
ML Svc: 1 year plus
Born: 12-5-63 in
Fontana, CA

1986 STATISTICS

AVG	G	AB	R	H	2B	3B	HR	RBI	BB	SO	SB
.185	64	151	8	28	6	0	0	4	19	28	0

CAREER STATISTICS

AVG	G	AB	R	H	2B	3B	HR	RBI	BB	SO	SB
.220	159	471	38	104	20	3	2	35	53	84	5

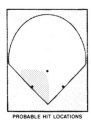

STRONG   STRONG

VS. RHP   VS. LHP   PROBABLE HIT LOCATIONS

another chance to win the shortstop job this year. To do that, however, he will have to show marked improvement. He needs to keep his head in the game at all times. Too often, he appears to be fundamentally weak, swinging at the wrong time in the count or attempting a double play with two outs. But he has spent enough time in the minors to know better. He needs to keep his head in the game and to concentrate on making big league plays all the time.

Rooker: "Last season, even after Khalifa was recalled from Hawaii, where he batted .315, manager Jim Leyland used Rafael Belliard and U.L. Washington ahead of him. He will have to work hard to restore the club's rapidly eroding confidence.

"It might not be a bad idea for Khalifa to build himself up with some kind of weight-training program."

PITTSBURGH PIRATES

PITCHING:

Most young pitchers put in an apprentice-ship during which they learn as they go. They come to the major leagues as hard throwers who don't know how to pitch and *then* are taught.

That was not the case, however, with Bob Kipper, who came to the Pirates as part of the trade with the California Angels for John Candelaria and George Hendrick. He throws a good major league fastball, but what you notice first about him is that at age 22, he tries to be a pitcher. He cuts his fastball and throws a slider and a change-up, all with a smooth delivery.

Kipper also has excellent control, which is rare for a young lefthander. He walked one batter or less in 12 of his 19 starts.

Not all is rosy with this youngster, however. He pitches with knowledge and cunning beyond his years, but his tender age and lack of experience were indicated in his tendency to get a lot of pitches up in the strike zone. This was especially true early in the season and he had trouble keeping the ball in the park.

Kipper went on the disabled list with shoulder problems but pitched well after coming back, winning six of his last 10 decisions.

BOB KIPPER
LHP, No. 51
RL, 6'2", 182 lbs.
ML Svc: 1 year
Born: 7-8-64 in
Aurora, IL

1986 STATISTICS

W	L	ERA	G	GS	CG	SV	IP	H	R	ER	BB	SO
6	8	4.03	20	19	0	0	114	123	60	51	34	81

CAREER STATISTICS

W	L	ERA	G	GS	CG	SV	IP	H	R	ER	BB	SO
7	11	4.63	27	24	0	0	142	151	84	73	44	94

FIELDING, HITTING, BASERUNNING:

Kipper is an average fielder and has an average move. He did register four pickoffs. He is a swinger, not a hitter, with a bat in his hands and still needs work on his bunting. For a pitcher, he is an average baserunner.

OVERALL:

Rooker: "The future for Bob Kipper is extremely bright if he continues to improve. Right now he is capable of winning 10 to 15 games and the Pirates believe he can eventually become a big winner."

PITTSBURGH PIRATES

PITCHING:

When healthy, he is a power pitcher with a tailing fastball, curveball, slider and forkball. He wants to be a starter but his lack of success has forced him to the bullpen, where he did show signs of pitching well at times last season, once stringing together 10 consecutive scoreless appearances.

Manager Jim Leyland wants at least two lefthanders in his bullpen and is hoping that McWilliams will come to accept being one of them.

McWilliams' career was saved five years ago when it appeared he was about to disappear from the major league scene forever. He credits Johnny Sain, then the pitching coach at the Pirates' Richmond, Va., farm team with turning his career around. Sain gave McWilliams a funky, herky-jerky, no-windup delivery, much as Sain did to prolong the career of Jim Kaat, another lefthander, a number of years back.

FIELDING, HITTING, BASERUNNING:

One of McWilliams' strengths is his ability to keep runners close. They seldom try to run on him. His quickness makes him an excellent fielder.

As a hitter, he is a liability with a .130 lifetime average but he helps himself with his

LARRY McWILLIAMS
LHP, No. 49
LL, 6'5", 176 lbs.
ML Svc: 8 years
Born: 2-10-54 in
Wichita, KS

1986 STATISTICS

W	L	ERA	G	GS	CG	SV	IP	H	R	ER	BB	SO
3	11	5.15	49	15	0	0	122.1	129	75	70	49	80

CAREER STATISTICS

W	L	ERA	G	GS	CG	SV	IP	H	R	ER	BB	SO
68	67	3.91	258	184	29	2	1240.1	1239	598	539	424	772

ability to bunt.

OVERALL:

Arm trouble over the past two seasons has left Larry McWilliams only a shell of his former self. Over that time, he has won just 10 of 30 decisions.

Rooker: "He says his arm is fine but doesn't have the consistent fastball and that has been his big problem. If he gets the strength in his arm back, he will probably start. If not, Larry could wind up in long relief. The Pirates would like to trade him but his large contract makes that difficult."

PITTSBURGH PIRATES

HITTING:

Good things really do come to those who wait. Jim Morrison spent years hanging around on the fringes, considered a top utility player but not capable of playing every day.

Last season, when rookie Denny Gonzalez's knee was not fully healed from his off-season surgery, Morrison was given the opportunity to become the Pirates' everyday third baseman and took full advantage of it.

At 33, he became the league's second-most productive third baseman (behind Mike Schmidt) with 23 homers and 88 RBIs while batting .274.

In the past, Morrison liked to sit on the fastball and try to pull it. Last season, however, he worked on going more to the opposite field and surprised a lot of people when he hit five home runs over the right field wall. If he continues to take the breaking ball and outside fastball the other way he will be an even more dangerous hitter.

Morrison was at his best with runners in scoring position, hitting .302 in such situations.

BASERUNNING:

Morrison is not a fast baserunner but he is extremely smart. He stole nine bases last year, after stealing only eight in 360 previous games. He does not not take chances on the bases.

FIELDING:

Morrison will not win any Gold Gloves at third base but he performed adequately there. His arm, which was suspect, held up over the season. He has trouble with balls to his right and with slow rollers or bunts.

Originally a second baseman, Morrison can

JIM MORRISON
INF, No. 2
RR, 5'11", 185 lbs.
ML Svc: 9 years
Born: 9-23-52 in
Pensacola, FL

1986 STATISTICS

AVG	G	AB	R	H	2B	3B	HR	RBI	BB	SO	SB
.274	154	537	58	147	35	4	23	88	47	88	9

CAREER STATISTICS

AVG	G	AB	R	H	2B	3B	HR	RBI	BB	SO	SB
.266	884	2744	302	730	140	14	97	351	173	410	40

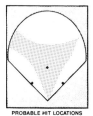

STRONG   STRONG

VS. RHP   VS. LHP   PROBABLE HIT LOCATIONS

play a number of positions; his versatility helps to make him even more valuable.

OVERALL:

All Jim Morrison ever asked for was a chance, and when he got it he became the surprise player in the National League.

Rooker: "Jim's fine performance last year eased the pressure on the Pirates in a number of areas. By hitting with power, Morrison made it less urgent that the club look for a righthanded power hitter. Further, it gave the club time: time to nurture minor league third baseman Jeff King, the nation's No. 1 draft pick in 1986."

PITTSBURGH PIRATES

HITTING:

Back in 1985, the future was looking pretty bright for Joe Orsulak. At that time, he was the only National League rookie to hit .300. A contact hitter with speed, he looked as though he could only get better.

But last year was his second full big league season and while the pitchers adjusted to him, he did not adapt along with them. His average fell more than 50 points to .249.

A fastball hitter who likes the ball pitched up-and-away, Orsulak saw a steady diet of off-speed stuff and was unable to stay back and wait.

Not a power hitter, Orsulak drove in only 19 runs in 138 games. He hit just .208 with runners in scoring position and collected only two hits in his last 26 at-bats with runners in scoring position.

Orsulak is an excellent bunter and often attempts to bunt for base hits.

BASERUNNING:

For the second straight year, Orsulak stole 24 bases in 35 tries. He could develop into a good basestealer in time. Orsulak is a hustler who runs everything out and who is not afraid to go hard into second base to break up a double play.

However, in his over-aggressiveness, he continues to take too many foolish chances and runs into his own mistakes.

FIELDING:

Orsulak has a strong and accurate arm, enough so that he led all Pirate outfielders with 11 assists. He can play all three outfield positions but seems best suited to play right field.

He is an aggressive fielder who will dive for balls or challenge walls. His aggressiveness, however, sometimes gets him in the way of

JOE ORSULAK
OF, No. 11
LL, 6'1", 186 lbs.
ML Svc: 2 years
Born: 5-31-62 in
Glen Ridge, NJ

1986 STATISTICS

AVG	G	AB	R	H	2B	3B	HR	RBI	BB	SO	SB
.249	138	401	60	100	19	6	2	19	28	38	24

CAREER STATISTICS

AVG	G	AB	R	H	2B	3B	HR	RBI	BB	SO	SB
.272	298	876	126	238	34	14	2	44	55	74	51

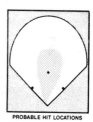

VS. RHP   VS. LHP   PROBABLE HIT LOCATIONS

other outfielders. That sort of territorial confusion should straighten out, however, the more the young Pirate outfielders work together.

OVERALL:

The development of Barry Bonds and R.J. Reynolds, along with the acquisition of Bobby Bonilla, has hurt Orsulak's chances of starting for the Pirates. Early last season, the club was looking for a quick solution to their outfield puzzle and Orsulak's inability to hit well in the first few weeks took him out of the frenzied running right away.

Rooker: "Joe's lack of power--just two home runs in two years--and his inability to drive in runs also hurt his chances. He's a hustling kid, though, whose style of play is contagious."

PITTSBURGH PIRATES

PITCHING:

Bob Patterson was two different pitchers last season and the second one may have impressed enough people to make him a candidate to win a role as one of the Pirates' five starters.

Patterson was a relief pitcher in spring training and when called to the major leagues the first time. However, after failing in that role, he was converted to a starting pitcher.

As a starter, he led the Pacific Coast League in strikeouts and won a second chance with the Pirates, where he pitched impressively. Patterson said his arm was weak early in the year but by converting to a starter he strengthened the arm.

His fastball, which is more sneaky than overpowering, did improve and merged with a good change-up and outstanding control to make him a complete pitcher.

FIELDING, HITTING, BASERUNNING:

Patterson showed just an average move when he was with the Pirates but new pitching coach Ray Miller worked on that in the Instructional League this past winter and the word is that Patterson's ability to hold runners close improved dramatically. Other

BOB PATTERSON
LHP, No. 46
RL, 6'2", 190 lbs.
ML Svc: less than one year
Born: 5-19-59 in
Jacksonville, FL

1986 STATISTICS

W	L	ERA	G	GS	CG	SV	IP	H	R	ER	BB	SO
2	3	4.95	11	5	0	0	36.1	49	20	20	5	2

CAREER STATISTICS

W	L	ERA	G	GS	CG	SV	IP	H	R	ER	BB	SO
2	3	6.92	14	5	0	0	40.1	62	31	31	8	21

than that, Patterson is an average fielder and did not show much as a hitter.

OVERALL:

Rooker: "Bob came to the Pirates from the Padres in exchange for outfielder Marvell Wynne last season. The Pirates were hoping he might develop into a lefthanded relief pitcher. However, his development as a starter at Hawaii may have served to force the veteran Larry McWilliams into the bullpen."

STRONG ARM

HITTING:

For the second season in a row Tony Pena got off to a poor start and was hitting only .241 at the All-Star break. The reason for Pena's slow starts is his free-swinging nature. Pressing to hit the long ball and try and make things happen, Pena often chases the pitcher's pitches.

Pena decided to change his batting style at midseason. He began to rest the bat on his shoulder until just before the pitch, when he would then raise it. At the same time, he was working to be more selective at the plate.

The results were startling. Pena hit .349 after the All-Star break, the highest of all National League regulars, to finish at .288. His attention to selectivity paid off as well as he drew a career-high 53 walks.

Pena likes the ball up-and-away from righthanded pitchers and up-and-in from lefthanders. He still has his own strike zone, meaning that he can handle certain pitches out of the umpire's strike zone.

BASERUNNING:

At the very least, Pena is an aggressive baserunner. He thinks that he is a better baserunner than he is and often takes foolish chances which can kill rallies. He did steal nine bases but was thrown out 10 times doing it.

FIELDING:

No catcher in the National League has a stronger throwing arm or a quicker release than Pena. He loves to throw and will not hesitate to attempt to pick runners off base, making as many as five throws a game. He'll throw from any position and has actually picked runners off second base while throwing from his knees.

His aggressive style led to an uncharacteristic 18 errors last season and baserunners had good success against him, stealing at a

TONY PENA
C, No. 6
RR, 6'0", 184 lbs.
ML Svc: 6 years
Born: 6-4-57 in
  Montecristi,
    Dominican Republic

1986 STATISTICS

AVG	G	AB	R	H	2B	3B	HR	RBI	BB	SO	SB
.288	144	510	56	147	26	3	10	52	53	69	9

CAREER STATISTICS

AVG	G	AB	R	H	2B	3B	HR	RBI	BB	SO	SB
.286	801	2872	307	821	140	16	63	340	174	372	42

  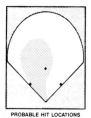

VS. RHP VS. LHP PROBABLE HIT LOCATIONS

65% rate. Pena threw out only 58 of 165 basestealers.

Pena still needs to work on calling his game. He is not the type of catcher who carefully charts a game plan for each batter. He flies by the seat of his pants a bit as opposed to being a strategist. A little more forethought in setting up the hitters might be helpful.

OVERALL:

No one enjoys playing the game of baseball more than Tony Pena. He bubbles when he's on the field, flashing a smile that is contagious.

Rooker: "Tony benefited from a bit more rest in 1986 than he had had in previous seasons, starting 133 games behind the plate and appearing four times at first base. He is among the game's best catchers, but still has some rough edges. His best years remain ahead of him."

PITTSBURGH PIRATES

HITTING:

The ultimate contact hitter, Johnny Ray is always among the toughest in the National League to strike out. A switch-hitter, he covers the strike zone well from both sides and takes what the pitcher gives him.

Thrust into the No. 3 spot in the Pirates' lineup last year, he responded with a .301 season that included a career-high 78 RBIs, the most by a Pirates' second baseman since Bill Mazeroski drove in 82 in 1966.

Always a stronger lefthanded hitter, Ray is getting better each season from the right side and hit .261 last year.

Ray drives a lot of balls into the gaps, which accounts for his being one of only three players to have 30 or more doubles over the last five years (Baltimore's Cal Ripken and Montreal's Tim Raines are the others).

BASERUNNING:

Ray does more with his baserunning than his speed would indicate. For a second baseman, he is a below-average runner but is smart and seldom makes a mistake. He gets a better-than-average lead and goes from first to third and from second to home well. He is no threat to steal.

FIELDING:

Steady is the best way to describe Johnny Ray on defense. Not possessed of great range or a strong arm, he seldom makes a mistake. Last season, he tied the major league record for fewest errors by a second baseman (5). He committed just three errors in his last 137 games.

He compensates for his lack of range by having a great knowledge of hitters. He positions himself well and knows the tendencies of each NL batter. His strength at positioning also serves to mask his below-average arm.

JOHNNY RAY
2B, No. 3
SR, 5'11", 185 lbs.
ML Svc: 6 years
Born: 3-1-57 in
Chouteau, OK

1986 STATISTICS

AVG	G	AB	R	H	2B	3B	HR	RBI	BB	SO	SB
.301	155	579	67	174	33	0	7	78	58	47	6

CAREER STATISTICS

AVG	G	AB	R	H	2B	3B	HR	RBI	BB	SO	SB
.288	808	3053	366	880	183	23	32	337	218	171	64

  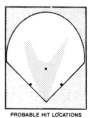

VS. RHP VS. LHP PROBABLE HIT LOCATIONS

Ray has improved tremendously over the last couple of seasons in making the double play pivot.

OVERALL:

Johnny Ray should have made the All-Star team last year. He was more affected by the snub than he let on to anyone. He was the National League Player of the Month in April and might have contended for the batting title had he not played much of the season with a hamstring injury. He played uncomplainingly with an injury which would have sidelined a less dedicated player whose team was firmly entrenched in the cellar.

Rooker: "Johnny keeps getting better every year and should just now be reaching his peak. Because the Pirate teams of recent years have been less than sparkling, he remains one of baseball's best-kept secrets."

GOOD CONTROL

PITCHING:

When Rick Reuschel's going well, he is a joy to watch pitch. He is the classic sinker/slider pitcher, with perfect control. He walked just seven men in his last nine starts and walked one or less in half of his 34 starts.

Reuschel pitches with a smooth, effortless rocking motion. He still throws hard enough to keep hitters honest but relies on the ground ball to get the job done.

A one-time 20-game winner with the Chicago Cubs (1977), Reuschel suffered through a seven-game losing streak at midseason when he seemed to be having some arm trouble. He never complained and remained in the rotation trying to work out the kinks. The losing streak matched the longest of his career.

FIELDING, HITTING, BASERUNNING:

Even though Reuschel is down 30 lbs. from his days with the Chicago Cubs (he has weighed as much as 240 lbs.), he remains a large man. Because of that, people think of him as slovenly but that is not so.

He is quick and graceful, one of the league's best fielders. He is exceptionally quick on bunts, sometimes getting to soft little pop bunts before they can even hit the ground. He also has a good move to first and a quick move to the plate that makes him tough to run

RICK REUSCHEL
RHP, No. 48
RR, 6'3", 240 lbs.
ML Svc: 14 years
Born: 5-16-49 in
*   Quincy, IL*

1986 STATISTICS

W	L	ERA	G	GS	CG	SV	IP	H	R	ER	BB	SO
9	16	3.96	35	34	4	0	215.2	232	106	95	57	125

CAREER STATISTICS

W	L	ERA	G	GS	CG	SV	IP	H	R	ER	BB	SO
162	155	3.43	436	414	81	4	2771.2	2825	1195	1056	759	1652

on.

He is a good hitter with some power, runs very well, and is often used as a pinch-runner.

OVERALL:

Reuschel had a bad season last year because of his lack of arm strength. He spent last winter throwing every week in order to correct that.

Rooker: "Despite being 38 years old this year, he expects to bounce back. If drive and determination can do it, Reuschel is sure to succeed. One of the game's classiest players."

PITTSBURGH PIRATES

PITCHING:

Despite yet another career-threatening injury, 1986 proved to be a pivotal year in the career of big, raw-boned Don Robinson. Robby came back from an early-season knee injury to win the stopper role in the bullpen.

His doctors had said that if Robinson's knee could not heal without surgery, his career probably would be over. Always a tough guy, Robinson had already undergone elbow surgery in 1977 and shoulder surgery in 1979, 1981 and 1983.

He spent more than a month on the disabled list while rehabilitating the knee, and came back wearing a knee brace that allowed him to pitch without fear.

A power pitcher who throws his fastball at better than 90 MPH in spite of four arm operations, Robinson lives with his fastball, slider and forkball.

The Pirates expect new pitching coach Ray Miller to help Robinson's forkball. If that happens, he could become unhittable. When Robinson has problems it is because he is overthrowing and loses control, falling behind in the count and walking batters who he should be making hit to get on base.

FIELDING, HITTING, BASERUNNING:

One of the best hitting pitchers in baseball, Robinson is also a dangerous power hitter. However, his new role of short reliever kept him from hitting often so his .667 average (4-for-6) is an aberration. He is a .264 lifetime hitter.

DON ROBINSON
RHP, No. 43
RR, 6'4", 235 lbs.
ML Svc: 9 years
Born: 6-8-57 in
Ashland, KY

1986 STATISTICS

W	L	ERA	G	GS	CG	SV	IP	H	R	ER	BB	SO
3	4	3.38	50	0	0	14	69.1	61	27	26	27	53

CAREER STATISTICS

W	L	ERA	G	GS	CG	SV	IP	H	R	ER	BB	SO
59	63	3.85	301	126	22	31	1137	1089	538	487	419	772

Robinson is an excellent fielder with a quick move to first base. He is slow coming to the plate because of a high leg kick but runners do not steal often because his move keeps them close.

Once, when his shoulder was bad, the Pirates sent him to the Instructional League and allowed him to play the outfield.

OVERALL:

Rooker: "Robinson is the type of man who loves a challenge, whether it be to come back from surgery when no one believes he can or to become converted from a starter to a bullpen stopper. He won the job last year after virtually all the other Pirate relievers failed in the role. He has the guts of a burglar when the game is on the line."

PITTSBURGH PIRATES

MIKE BIELECKI
RHP, No. 34
RR, 6'3", 200 lbs.
ML Svc: 1 year plus
Born: 7-31-59 in
Baltimore, MD

PITCHING, FIELDING, HITTING, BASERUNNING:

No one expected Mike Bielecki to open the season with the Pirates after undergoing surgery to repair a ruptured disc during the off-season. However, he pitched his way onto the staff in spring training.

Bielecki is the owner of a 90+ fastball and an average slider. His biggest problem is with his control. Even his fastball gives him trouble at times.

The Pirates are hoping that new pitching coach Ray Miller can help Bielecki to smooth over the rough points and to develop into the type of consistent winner they thought they had when he won 19 and lost 3 at Hawaii in 1984.

Bielecki will show flashes of brilliance, then look totally lost. He'll open a game and be unhittable for three innings, then look as though he had never been on a mound before, falling behind in the count and being afraid to throw his fastball. He began the season by ripping off three straight victories, yet could not win a game after July 9.

Bielecki must work on his move to first base and does not help himself with his hitting or his bunting. He is a competent fielder.

OVERALL:

When Bielecki learns to finish off hitters, he will be a star. He was just a thrower last year and must learn to be a pitcher.

Rooker: "I would work on changing his delivery. A pitcher cannot control the strike zone until he learns to control his body. At this point, Bielecki's body flies open as he delivers, and that's not the right way for him to pitch."

MIKE DIAZ
C, No. 10
RR, 6'2", 205 lbs.
ML Svc: 1 year
Born: 4-15-60 in
San Francisco, CA

HITTING, BASERUNNING, FIELDING:

A dead fastball hitter with power plus, Mike Diaz was tied for second among NL rookies in home runs with 12 despite being used only sparingly. He was the Pirates' best pinch-hitter with 11 hits in 33 tries and drove in 10 runs in that role.

Diaz is not a free-swinging power hitter, but is a thinking man's hitter. He has a good idea with each at-bat of what he wants to try to do. He pulls with power to left field.

Diaz seems to bear down more against the better pitchers in the league, as evidenced by home runs off John Tudor, Fernando Valenzuela, Shane Rawley, Tom Browning, Gene Garber and Floyd Youmans.

Diaz has below-average speed and is no threat to steal a base.

Defensively, Diaz's best position is on the bench. Originally a catcher, the Pirates--in need of a righthanded power hitter against lefthanders--tried to convert him into a left fielder. Despite hard work, he remains a below-average fielder. He has tried first base, but it looks as though Sid Bream is the man there.

OVERALL:

Mike Diaz could be a great designated hitter in the American League. He would hit 20 or more homers and drive in 80 or more runs. As a National Leaguer, he would probably do the same but because of his defensive limitations, he might let in as many.

Rooker: "Mike's nickname of 'Rambo' gives you some idea of the type of person he is. No one tries harder than Diaz and no one has worked on his defense more. Right now, however, he is best suited as a pinch-hitter in the National League."

PITTSBURGH PIRATES

**BENNY
  DISTEFANO
INF, No. 31
LL, 6'1", 195 lbs.
ML Svc: 1 year plus
Born: 1-23-62 in
  Brooklyn, NY**

HITTING, BASERUNNING, FIELDING:

Benny Distefano was called up to the major leagues in August to fill in as a lefthanded pinch-hitter. A free-swinger, Distefano is a dead fastball hitter who likes the ball down. He has power when he gets the fastball he is looking for but doesn't do much with off-speed stuff.

An aggressive, hustling baserunner, Distefano will break up a double play or try to take an extra base, although he is not a basestealing threat.

Distefano is a good defensive player both at first base and in right field. He has a strong, accurate arm and has earned the nickname of "Rock" because he'll run through a wall or dive across a gravel warning track to make a play.

OVERALL:

Rooker: "An aggressive, hustling youngster, Distefano plays baseball with the toughness of a street fighter. At the moment, he seems to be cast in the role of a pinch-hitter with the Pirates."

**BARRY JONES
RHP, No. 50
RR, 6'4", 210 lbs.
ML Svc: 1 year
Born: 2-15-63 in
  Centerville, IN**

PITCHING, FIELDING,
   HITTING, BASERUNNING:

Barry Jones showed a great amount of poise for a rookie when he was called up from Hawaii at midseason last year.

A fastball/slider pitcher, Jones uses his slider as his out pitch but he can blow a fastball by the hitter at times.

Not afraid to challenge the batter in the tightest of situations, he won a whole lot more battles than he lost as the league batted just .215 against him.

Jones also displayed one other attribute that few young pitchers have, and that was an ability to learn from his mistakes. He doesn't make the same mistake twice. Considering the short attention span of some other pitchers, Jones is way ahead of the game.

Jones has a good move to first base, which is vital in a relief pitcher who is being called on to hold a one-run lead late in a game. He's a good fielder who will get better with experience. He does not bat often but seems capable of making contact as a hitter. Jones bunts adequately enough and is a decent runner.

OVERALL:

Rooker: "The thing you like most about Barry is his attitude. He is perfectly suited to be a short reliever. He uses the lessons learned from a bad outing well. His fastball/slider duo and his *gimme the ball* attitude could be the answer for the Pirates' bullpen and could make Barry a star."

PITTSBURGH PIRATES

JUNIOR ORTIZ
C, No. 26
RR, 5'11, 176 lbs.
ML Svc: 4 years
Born: 10-24-59 in
Humacao, PR

HITTING, BASERUNNING, FIELDING:

One of the big surprises in baseball last year was Junior Ortiz. A lifetime .243 hitter up to that point, Ortiz hit .336 as Tony Pena's backup. He was especially effective with runners in scoring position, batting .419.

Ortiz likes the ball up and out over the plate and goes to right field a great deal. He shows good bat control and is especially good at the hit-and-run play.

Ortiz is an average baserunner with not bad speed for a catcher.

There is a lot of Tony Pena in Junior Ortiz behind the plate. Both are good receivers with excellent arms and like to throw the ball. If anything, Ortiz may even call a better game than Pena does.

OVERALL:

One of the most difficult things to do is find a backup catcher who is both capable and content with his role. Junior Ortiz is both.

Rooker: "A popular player off the field with his teammates and one of manager Jim Leyland's favorites (his autographed picture hangs in Leyland's office), Ortiz accepts his plight as a 30-game-a-year catcher."

R.J. REYNOLDS
OF, No. 39
SR, 6'0", 183 lbs.
ML Svc: 4 years
Born: 4-19-60 in
Sacramento, CA

HITTING, BASERUNNING, FIELDING:

The Pirates tried R.J. Reynolds as a leadoff hitter last year, but he didn't feel comfortable there and didn't produce. He prefers the No. 5 or 6 spot in the batting order.

A streaky hitter who strikes out too often, Reynolds was among the league's top 10 hitters at one point last year before he began slumping badly.

Reynolds is a poor hitter against righthanded pitchers and because of that weakness, will probably be platooned.

Reynolds has excellent speed and knows how to use it. He's a daring baserunner who will try to take an extra base on a sleeping outfielder who is slow in fielding a single. He is not afraid to go hard into second base. He is a legitimate basestealing threat, but must use more discretion when picking his spots.

Reynolds is not a sure outfielder and seems to make his mistakes on the routine plays, which could be a sign of a lack of concentration. His arm is average. He was one of three National League players to start 10 or more games in all three outfield positions last year.

OVERALL:

The injury jinx struck Reynolds as a pulled groin muscle sidelined him for the final month of the season. When he was with the Dodgers, numerous leg muscle pulls slowed his progress through the system.

Rooker: "R.J. is a hustling type of player who is popular with the fans, but he is going to have to put together a consistent, injury-free season to become the quality player the Pirates believe he can be."

PITTSBURGH PIRATES

JOHN SMILEY
LHP, No. 54
LL, 6'4", 180 lbs.
ML Svc: less than one year
Born: 3-17-65 in
Phoenixville, PA

PITCHING, FIELDING, HITTING, BASERUNNING:

John Smiley came out of nowhere last September to make a big impression on the Pirates. He was brought up from the Class A Prince William, Va., farm team flashing a fastball that was clocked in the mid-90s.

Smiley doesn't show much else, just the fastball, but firepower like that from a lefthander was enough. After a rocky debut, he allowed only two hits in his last 11.1 innings. None of the 10 runners he inherited scored.

Smiley was nearly unhittable--the league batted just .105 against him. His only problem was a lack of control. He walked as many batters as he allowed base hits.

Smiley did not get a chance to show whatever skills he has as a fielder, at the plate or on the bases in his brief stay with the major league team.

OVERALL:

John Smiley has a bright future as a major league reliever. He jumped from Class A to the big leagues last September without any other minor league experience. He is a free spirit, complete with a tattoo on his arm and a liking for pool halls and beaches.

Rooker: "Manager Jim Leyland brought Smiley along very, very carefully last season, initially only allowing him to pitch one-third of an inning at a time. Smiley adjusted well and did not seem to be intimidated by the big league hitters. He simply rears back and throws his heater.

"He will probably start the season in Class A or in Double-A ball. If he does as well as the Pirates are expecting, he should be in Pittsburgh before long."

BOB WALK
RHP, No. 17
RR, 6'4", 212 lbs.
ML Svc: 5 years
Born: 11-26-56 in
Van Nuys, CA

PITCHING, FIELDING, HITTING, BASERUNNING:

Bob Walk has the makings of a winning pitcher, including the type of carefree attitude which often appears to border on care*less*. Unfortunately, throughout his career, big league managers have found it difficult to take him seriously. His lighthearted approach to the business of pitching has sent him packing from Philadelphia to Atlanta to Pittsburgh as well as up and down between the majors and the minors.

Walk has an average fastball with excellent movement, a major league curveball and a slider. He has, however, always been his own worst enemy. Walk is forever fighting his control. His good stuff won't get him anywhere unless he throws his pitches for strikes.

At 30, he is at the crossroads of his career. The Pirates, in the midst of a youth movement, may feel they have enough experienced veterans on their staff and may use Walk as trade bait.

Walk is a below-average bunter but a better-than-average hitter who last season drove in seven runs with his six hits. He is a below-average fielder but helps himself with a deceptive move to first base. Last year he led the Pirates with seven pickoffs and only 10 of 19 basestealers were successful against him.

OVERALL:

Walk makes himself valuable by being a versatile pitcher who can start or work out of long or short relief.

Rooker: "Bob needs to develop more consistency; that might come from better concentration."

PITTSBURGH PIRATES

JIM WINN
RHP, No. 41
RR, 6'3", 219 lbs.
ML Svc: 2 years
Born: 9-23-59 in
Stockton, CA

PITCHING, FIELDING, HITTING, BASERUNNING:

Jim Winn is a former No. 1 draft pick who has not improved upon the raw talent that made him so highly sought after when he came out of tiny John Brown University.

Winn has been shuffled back and forth between starting and relieving throughout his career as well as bouncing up and down between the minor leagues and the major leagues.

Last summer, the Pirates began to think that he had the superior physical equipment to become a late-inning closer out of the bullpen and gave him a chance to win the stopper's job. Winn couldn't do it.

A sinkerball pitcher, Winn must learn to control the strike zone better and he must learn to get over the nervousness that plagues him when he is thrust into critical situations.

He is not a good fielder, hitter or bunter and he has trouble holding runners close to first base. Because of this, opponents take many liberties and, in close games, it beats him.

OVERALL:

Goose Gossage is Jim Winn's idol. Physically, he has Gossage's attributes but he is not at the same level mentally with Gossage.

Rooker: "He needs much, much, much more confidence if he is to succeed as a major league relief pitcher."

ST. LOUIS CARDINALS

HITTING:

One wonders if Jack Clark will *ever* play a full season again. In the last three years, injuries have caused him to miss 247 games, or nearly a season and a half.

Clark looks for the fastball at all times and makes no bones about it. His theory is that a hitter can always adjust to the breaking ball. If his home park was any other than Busch Stadium, Clark probably would hit 30 home runs a year.

Both right- and lefthanders must keep the ball away from Clark to take away his ability to pull the ball. He will not go with the pitch to the opposite field. Most of Clark's hits are from center field to the left field line. He hits balls as hard as anyone in baseball. He likes the ball belt-high and never gets cheated on his swings. He can look bad on a breaking ball, especially one down and away, but will jump all over a mistake.

Normally blessed with a good batting eye, Clark swung at many bad pitches last season as he sought to take up the slack in the Cardinals' pitiful 1986 attack. He was trying to hit five-run homers with nobody on base and as a result, pitchers quickly figured they didn't have to throw him anything close to the strike zone to evoke a big cut.

If some of the Cardinals' speedsters get on base ahead of him, Clark becomes a better hitter. Clark's power, combined with the club's speed, invariably forces a pitcher to throw nothing but fastballs in an attempt to reduce the threat of a stolen base or double steal. The problem is that the Cardinals have been unable to bring in an authoritative hitter to hit behind him: Clark rarely gets anything good to hit.

BASERUNNING:

Never a basestealing threat, Clark has become a better baserunner since joining the Cardinals, if nothing else than by osmosis. He has been concentrating on the nuances of baserunning more than he did in the past.

JACK CLARK
1B, No. 22
RR, 6'3", 205 lbs.
ML Svc: 11 years
Born: 11-10-55 in
New Brighton, PA

1986 STATISTICS

AVG	G	AB	R	H	2B	3B	HR	RBI	BB	SO	SB
.237	65	232	34	55	12	2	9	23	45	61	1

CAREER STATISTICS

AVG	G	AB	R	H	2B	3B	HR	RBI	BB	SO	SB
.275	1235	4405	702	1213	235	35	194	705	535	717	62

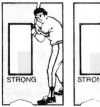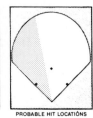

VS. RHP   VS. LHP   PROBABLE HIT LOCATIONS

FIELDING:

Clark could be an above-average outfielder if the Cardinals were not as well stocked there. He has a good throwing arm, but at first base, he doesn't have much chance to show it off. He has good hands for fielding throws but is not very good at fielding grounders to his right. It often appears as though he does not know where his territory ends and that of the second baseman starts.

OVERALL:

Rooker: "Clark is at the stage of his career when he must prove he can play without suffering serious injury. His biggest offensive year is still in him, but the Cardinals must find somebody to hit behind him and protect him if we are ever going to see Jack explode."

EXCELLENT SPEED

HITTING:

After hitting far better in 1985 than anybody had dreamed possible, Vince Coleman regressed last season, dropping 35 points to .232.

. . . He should be able to *bunt* .232.

Succinctly, Coleman hit far too many balls in the air and way too few on the ground. Herzog actually tried paying him for every ball he hit on the ground and finally, in desperation, made him use a heavier bat to weigh down his stroke. It didn't help.

When Coleman did hit ground balls last season, they went toward second base, where even *he* has little chance to beat them out. Ideally, he should be aiming for grounders to shortstop or third base, where it would take perfect handling of the play and a perfect throw to get him.

Last year, Coleman was also trying to show power that is just not there. He was muscling up and hitting fly balls which flew no farther than the warning track.

Against righthanded pitchers, the switch-hitting Coleman likes the ball down and in. That's the pitch he'll drag-bunt most effectively. When he is hitting well, Coleman's lefthanded swing is one in which he flings the bat at the ball. As a righthanded batter, Coleman likes the ball up and in. That's the pitch most likely to wind up in the air just before it lands in a glove.

Coleman continues to strike out far too often. If he is ever to realize his ambition of a 200-stolen-base season, he must develop a better idea of the strike zone and the skill to handle first-pitch breaking balls.

BASERUNNING:

If Coleman can hit at least .250, he may well break all major league basestealing records. He sports an over 80% success rate. No player has ever stolen third base better than Coleman, who gets a quarter of his steals at third. And no baserunner forces more balks when he is on first than Coleman. He takes one of the longest leads in baseball, often having both feet on the dirt surface on artificial turf fields.

VINCE COLEMAN
LF, No. 29
SR, 6'0", 170 lbs.
ML Svc: 2 years
Born: 9-22-61 in
Jacksonville, FL

1986 STATISTICS

AVG	G	AB	R	H	2B	3B	HR	RBI	BB	SO	SB
.232	154	600	94	139	13	8	0	29	60	98	107

CAREER STATISTICS

AVG	G	AB	R	H	2B	3B	HR	RBI	BB	SO	SB
.250	305	1236	201	309	33	18	1	69	110	213	217

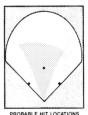

VS. RHP   VS. LHP   PROBABLE HIT LOCATIONS

FIELDING:

Coleman was a defensive disappointment last season and often appeared unsteady. There are times when he doesn't see the ball off the bat or will throw to the wrong base after making the catch. By virtue of his natural tools, however, Coleman should be among the best left fielders in the league. He plays shallow enough that he can run down the loopers and he is fast enough to get back to the warning track.

He is also one of the few left fielders who has a good enough arm and enough speed to play either center field or right field.

OVERALL:

Rooker: "One thing Coleman has going for him is his work ethic. He is aware that he must hit better to remain a big league regular. He also has the kind of competitive attitude and shows just enough swagger to make him the best at what he does."

ST. LOUIS CARDINALS

PITCHING:

Tim Conroy, a former No. 1 pick by the Oakland A's, had trouble with a weak shoulder last season and was on the disabled list twice. He first went on at the beginning of the season and the second time was in late May. When he is healthy and throwing well, Conroy is still one of the top prospects in baseball but, but at age 27, may be reaching the stage where he is more suspect than prospect.

Conroy had a terrible time in the early innings of his starts and, in fact, allowed a homer on his first pitch of the game three times. It may be, as manager Whitey Herzog suggested, that Conroy would be better as a reliever instead of knowing in advance when he was going to pitch.

Scouts, executives and even teammates continue to look for more fire from Conroy, whose demeanor is roughly the same whether he wins or loses. One of six lefthanders the Cardinals had on their staff last season, Conroy was considered to have the best stuff but his inconsistency is reflected by a 5-11 record and an abnormally high allowance of home runs-per-innings-pitched. His motion occasionally gets out of synch because of his high leg kick and the result is that he tries to rush his delivery.

This is probably the critical year for Conroy to assert himself. Management's patience wore thin with him in Oakland and it might reach that point in St. Louis as well.

FIELDING, HITTING, BASERUNNING:

Although he didn't bat in a professional game from 1978 to 1986, Conroy had the best swing on the Cardinals' staff and Herzog said he almost wished that Conroy had had a chance to play some other position earlier in

TIM CONROY
LHP, No. 39
LL, 6'1", 185 lbs.
ML Svc: 3 years
Born: 4-3-60 in
Monroeville, PA

1986 STATISTICS
W	L	ERA	G	GS	CG	SV	IP	H	R	ER	BB	SO
5	11	5.23	25	21	1	0	115.1	122	72	67	56	79

CAREER STATISTICS
W	L	ERA	G	GS	CG	SV	IP	H	R	ER	BB	SO
15	30	4.60	125	62	5	0	426.1	390	253	218	259	285

his career. His potential for hitting was such that the Cardinals sent him to the Florida Instructional League after last season to work on his hitting.

The Cardinals envision Conroy as a two-way player in these days of 24-man rosters, much like reliever Dan Schatzeder, who can pinch-hit and then stay in the game to pitch.

Conroy does not have a particularly good, or quick, move to first base and his fielding otherwise is average. As a baserunner, he shows more ability than some other pitchers.

OVERALL:

Conroy's confidence, which has been beaten down over several unsuccessful years and trips to the minors, must be built up this season if he is to succeed. When one has a fastball such as he has, it is difficult to give up hope.

Rooker: "Of all the six lefthanders on last year's Cardinals' staff, Conroy has the overall best stuff. If his elbow does not flare up again this year, Tim could be a big winner."

ST. LOUIS CARDINALS

For the first time in his major league career, Danny Cox did not have trouble with his elbow. But he did have a spring training mishap with his foot and injured it by failing to negotiate a 2½ foot jump from a sea wall. The result was a chip fracture of his ankle and about half a season of frustration as Cox, even after the ankle healed, struggled to pitch comfortably.

His early-season troubles (Cox was 2-7) can be traced to the fact that he couldn't push off his injured ankle and tried to alter his delivery in compensation; since he wasn't allowed to run between starts, Cox was not in the best shape possible.

But in the second half of the season, Cox pitched like the 18-game winner he was in 1985 and the 20-game winner he could be. The strongest of the Cardinals' pitchers, the 6'4", 225-pounder completed eight starts, more than double anybody else on the staff.

Cox is a very tough competitor and not averse to buzzing a hitter with an inside fastball if provoked.

With his herky-jerky delivery and powerful follow-through to the plate, Cox appears to be throwing considerably harder than he is. In truth, his fastball is just above average but he has a wicked slider and one of the best change-ups in baseball.

When Cox gets behind in the count, he does not give in to the hitters but will throw his breaking ball or change-up. His biggest problems occur when he is feeling his oats too much and loses his discipline. It is then that Cox tries to overthrow and his fastball is not such that he can do that.

Cox has had two straight years of earned run averages under 3.00, even though he had a losing record last season.

FIELDING, HITTING, BASERUNNING:

For a big man, Cox never has packed much

DANNY COX
RHP, No. 34
RR, 6'4", 225 lbs.
ML Svc: 4 years
Born: 9-21-59 in
** Northhampton, England**

1986 STATISTICS

W	L	ERA	G	GS	CG	SV	IP	H	R	ER	BB	SO
12	13	2.90	32	32	8	0	220	189	85	71	60	108

CAREER STATISTICS

W	L	ERA	G	GS	CG	SV	IP	H	R	ER	BB	SO
42	39	3.19	108	106	19	0	700.1	678	295	248	201	345

of a wallop at the plate, although he has become one of the pitching staff's best bunters. Cox runs reasonably well for his size but is rarely on base.

If there is a deficiency in Cox's game, it is his fielding. His follow-through carries him to the first-base side of the bag and he probably lost two or three games last year by not being able to field bouncers up the middle. With work, Cox has improved his move to first to the point it is above average.

OVERALL:

With the preponderance of lefthanders on the Cardinals' staff, Cox perhaps is the key starter in the rotation. His career has been retarded by injuries but he appears ready to break through in a big way this season.

Rooker: "With his size, a hitter would look for a hard fastball, but it's just not there. Instead, Cox will get a batter using his herky-jerky delivery to send a hard slider and excellent change-up. He goes to his off-speed stuff when he is behind in the count. He has the ability to be a 20-game winner."

ST. LOUIS CARDINALS

PITCHING:

Bill Dawley continued to slide away from his performance in 1983, when he broke in as a rookie with the Houston Astros and wound up pitching in the All-Star Game. His record with the White Sox last season was an underwhelming 0-7, but he really wasn't as bad at that mark might indicate.

The problem? He wasn't that good either. His 3.32 ERA was fine and, despite his penchant for throwing wild pitches, Dawley exhibited outstanding control.

In the clutch though, a situation in which Dawley gets paid to perform, he faltered more often than not. He throws the fastball in the 90s and also has some zip on his slider, but he was guilty of throwing too many meatballs. Dawley would let just one pitch sail and the ball would be hit into the cheap seats. He was effective for the most part and a good bet to strike out righthanders when he kept the ball down, but declining performances since his stellar rookie season may be working on him mentally. Another big problem is getting out lefthanded batters. He doesn't try to fool hitters and is most effective when he is in control of his fastball and slider.

At 6'4" and 240 pounds, Dawley is an imposing presence on the mound who can put the fear of God into a batter. Occasional arm injuries have troubled him, but not as much as the high fastball.

FIELDING:

Dawley has an average move to first base but is difficult to steal on because he gets the

BILL DAWLEY
RHP, No. 46
RR, 6'4", 240 lbs.
ML Svc: 4 years
Born: 2-6-58 in
Norwich, CT

1986 STATISTICS

W	L	ERA	G	GS	CG	SV	IP	H	R	ER	BB	SO
0	7	3.32	46	0	0	2	97.2	91	38	36	28	66

CAREER STATISTICS

W	L	ERA	G	GS	CG	SV	IP	H	R	ER	BB	SO
22	20	2.88	203	0	0	23	356.1	300	123	114	122	221

ball to the plate in a hurry.

He's a surprisingly good fielder, with a good glove and good mobility to first for a big man.

OVERALL:

Confidence and a injury-free year would work wonders for Dawley, who now must prove that he was no flash in the pan. Relief pitchers are bound to have bad outings and Dawley must be able to shake off if he is destined to return to a legitimate bullpen stopper.

Killebrew: "He throws the ball hard and really looks like he can intimidate a lot of hitters out there. He was a disappointment last season but has the tools to be a reliable closer coming out of the bullpen."

BIG, BREAKING CURVEBALL

PITCHING:

Dayley is at the crossroads of his career after a serious operation to repair his pitching elbow. Part of the operation entailed transferring a tendon from his right (non-pitching) wrist to his left arm and Dayley isn't expected to be able to pitch until June 1st of this year.

In a sense, the operation was similar to that done on Tommy John several years ago but John wasn't particularly a power pitcher before that and power pitching is Dayley's stock in trade.

When right, Dayley throws his fastball at 90 MPH and his overhand curveball is one of the best and most devastating in the league.

Dayley was bothered with elbow and shoulder problems from the day in spring training when the Cardinals made him pitch four innings, which normally is over his limit. He spent the last three months on the disabled list after compiling a remarkable streak in which he allowed only one earned run in twenty appearances.

Because of his arm problems, Dayley was limited mostly to one-inning stints when he was able to pitch.

The unfortunate thing for Dayley was that he just had established himself as one of the best relievers in the league and his confidence, which had been fragile for most of his career, was at an all-time high.

He had been a bust as a starter but seemed to thrive when summoned suddenly into tight pressure situations and there are those who will tell you the Cardinals would have been world champions in 1985 if Dayley had been allowed to finish the sixth game of the World Series.

One of the reasons for Dayley's increased confidence was the Cardinals' airtight defense. The lefthander knew that he could throw his best two pitches any time he wanted

KEN DAYLEY
LHP, No. 46
LL, 6'0", 178 lbs.
ML Svc: 5 years
Born: 2-25-59 in
Jerome, ID

1986 STATISTICS

W	L	ERA	G	GS	CG	SV	IP	H	R	ER	BB	SO
0	3	3.26	31	0	0	5	38.2	42	19	14	11	33

CAREER STATISTICS

W	L	ERA	G	GS	CG	SV	IP	H	R	ER	BB	SO
14	26	4.18	139	33	0	16	303.2	330	169	141	104	209

to because of the size of Busch Stadium and the range of his fielders.

FIELDING, HITTING, BASERUNNING:

Dayley is a career .260 hitter and was even used as a pinch-hitter last year. He is a good all-around athlete and makes all the fielding plays he should.

OVERALL:

Dayley must be careful not to rush his recuperation this season, even if it means not pitching in the majors at all this year. He is still young enough at 28 to come back.

Rooker: "There is no question that his curveball is one of the best in the National League. Add to that his ability to throw his fastball for strikes and you've got yourself one heckuva reliever.

"As he learned to trust the Cardinal defense, his own confidence increased. When he is healthy, Dayley will give the Cards a terrific lefty/righty combo with Todd Worrell."

ST. LOUIS CARDINALS

PITCHING:

Rescued from the near-dead after back surgery two years ago, Bob Forsch was the leading winner on the St. Louis staff in 1986 with 14 wins. There are two intangible factors which contributed to his winning record: one is his immense pride and the other is that Forsch stays in remarkable shape. Perhaps, too, it was that Forsch was pitching for a new contract for the first time in seven years.

Forsch is a tremendous example of smart pitching. Though he throws nowhere nearly as hard as when he came to the big leagues in 1974, Forsch is extremely intelligent and rarely throws the same pitch in the same place. Long ago, he realized the secret to retiring a hitter is to get him off balance and then keep him there.

Although the speed on his fastball might not be the same as it was earlier in his career, the good movement is there. Forsch also has come up with a split-finger pitch which now gives him, with his slider and curveball, a four-pitch arsenal.

Forsch might have earned even more victories last season but he seemed to tire late in the year under a 230-inning workload, the most asked of him in four years. He went at least six innings in 29 of his 33 starts and had to pick up the slack caused by injuries to Tim Conroy, Danny Cox and John Tudor.

The 37-year-old righthander has long been regarded as one of the St. Louis team's toughest competitors even though his mild countenance might belie that.

FIELDING, HITTING, BASERUNNING:

Forsch is one of the best-hitting pitchers in baseball. Last year, he bashed the first grand slam of his career. He also had another homer

BOB FORSCH
RHP, No. 31
RR, 6'3", 200 lbs.
ML Svc: 13 years
Born: 1-13-50 in
Sacramento, CA

1986 STATISTICS

W	L	ERA	G	GS	CG	SV	IP	H	R	ER	BB	SO
14	10	3.25	33	33	3	0	230	211	91	83	68	104

CAREER STATISTICS

W	L	ERA	G	GS	CG	SV	IP	H	R	ER	BB	SO
143	116	3.62	392	358	64	3	2371.2	2302	1088	954	697	950

in a 12-RBI season. He is especially effective against lefthanded pitching. Righthanders with good breaking balls still get him out, which is why Forsch isn't a third baseman anymore--as he once was in amateur baseball before he switched to the mound.

Forsch is an excellent fielder and improved further last season by cutting down his delivery time to the plate with runners on base by cocking his left leg before making his move home.

OVERALL:

A career that some considered to be over in 1984 might extend even several more years if Forsch can eventually move to the bullpen.

Rooker: "Bob is a terrific example for the other pitchers on the St. Louis staff. He is a very smart pitcher with excellent control who has extended his career by dedication, savvy and hard work.

"His 1986 performance will be a tough act to follow, but if anyone can do it, Forsch will."

ST. LOUIS CARDINALS

HITTING:

Who is the real Herr? The one who drove in 110 runs with a .302 average in 1985? Or the one who hit .252 with 61 RBIs last year? The answer probably lies somewhere in the middle.

Herr should hit about .275-.280 and drive in 75 runs if he continues to bat third in the Cardinals' lineup behind Vince Coleman and Willie McGee.

After a draining 1985 regular season and the World Series disappointment, Herr reported to camp somewhat sluggish last year and hit only .166 for the first two months of the season. Thereafter, trying to make the best of a lost season, he batted a more satisfactory .284.

So much of what Herr can accomplish with the Cardinals is directly related to Vince Coleman and Willie McGee that as they go, so does he. In 1986, they were all like falling dominoes.

In the scheme of the Cardinals' stolen-base offense, Herr has developed into the club's most patient and selective hitter. But the strategy is effective only if Coleman and/or McGee is on base. Without them to force pitchers to throw fastballs, Herr's average with runners in scoring position dropped from .342 in their pennant-winning 1985 season to only .215 last year.

Ordinarily, the switch-hitting Herr covers the plate better and is more disciplined from the left side, yet he batted just .212 against righthanders last year. One of the problems was that he seemed to be feeling for the ball and many of his swings resulted in looping fly balls into left field.

Herr likes the ball inside when he is batting righthanded and generally has more power that way.

BASERUNNING:

As a runner, Herr will never be the same after having had three knee operations. He is a smart runner and has stolen 53 bases over the last two seasons while being caught only 11 times. He reads pitchers well and gets a good jump.

TOM HERR
2B, No. 28
SR, 6'0", 185 lbs.
ML Svc: 8 years
Born: 4-4-56 in
Lancaster, PA

1986 STATISTICS
AVG	G	AB	R	H	2B	3B	HR	RBI	BB	SO	SB
.252	152	559	48	141	30	4	2	61	73	75	22

CAREER STATISTICS
AVG	G	AB	R	H	2B	3B	HR	RBI	BB	SO	SB
.276	873	3162	421	874	150	31	16	349	359	322	130

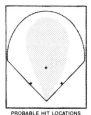

VS. RHP   VS. LHP   PROBABLE HIT LOCATIONS

FIELDING:

He has lost some range in the field, especially to his left, but Herr makes up for it with intelligent positioning. He has a strong lower body and is one of the best in baseball at standing in on a double play pivot. He never misses the routine play.

OVERALL:

This is a critical year for the 31-year-old Herr. But, given his performance in the past, there is good reason to expect him to bounce back with pride. He is and has been a winner.

Rooker: "Early last season, Tom was having a hard time staying back on the ball and was swinging way in front of everything. As a lefthanded batter, his front shoulder was flying out. It took a while to smooth out his mechanics, but he seemed to settle down later in the season."

ST. LOUIS CARDINALS

PITCHING:

Rick Horton is one of the Cardinals' most valuable commodities because he does three jobs: spot start, middle relief and late relief. There are, in fact, few pitchers in baseball as versatile.

After suffering an arm injury early last season, Horton was disabled for nearly a month. For the month following his return, he wasn't able to snap off his breaking ball as well as he wanted. But from late June to the end of the season, Horton was one of the best pitchers in the league, giving up just 10 earned runs in 67 1/3 innings.

Horton's elbow problems had caused some concern, though at the end of the season, he didn't seem to have any pain.

The lefthander's pitching motion is more of a flip than a thrust, much as if he were throwing darts. But his control of all three of his pitches, the fastball, change-up and slider, is impeccable. Considering his lack of velocity, that's a good thing.

Tim Raines, the league's top hitter, once said of Horton, "You think you're going to get a good pitch right where you want it and then when you swing, it's not there."

Horton originally was used to relieve against isolated lefthanded hitters or to start against predominantly lefthanded-hitting teams but his stuff has become good enough that he doesn't have to be hidden and can pitch against anybody.

Horton must remember that even though his fastball seems to have more movement than before, it is still not his out pitch. He must not try to overthrow with something that isn't there.

RICK HORTON
LHP, No. 49
LL, 6'2", 195 lbs.
ML Svc: 3 years
Born: 7-30-59 in
Poughkeepsie, NY

1986 STATISTICS

W	L	ERA	G	GS	CG	SV	IP	H	R	ER	BB	SO
4	3	2.24	42	9	1	3	100.1	77	25	25	26	49

CAREER STATISTICS

W	L	ERA	G	GS	CG	SV	IP	H	R	ER	BB	SO
16	9	2.91	128	30	2	5	315.2	301	108	102	99	184

FIELDING, HITTING, BASERUNNING:

After a first at-bat single against none other than Dwight Gooden in the Mets' home opener, Horton went hitless for the rest of the season. He does make consistent contact, though, striking out just three times in 18 at-bats, and he is an excellent bunter.

Horton shows intelligence and some speed on the bases and has been used as a pinch-runner. His move to first is among the best lefty moves in the NL and his follow-through is perfect to field balls hit back at him.

OVERALL:

Rooker: "Horton will never be a big winner or on the All-Star team. Because of the nature of his role on the staff, he often pitches 'anonymously.' His strength is in coming out of the bullpen and Herzog is a master at using him that way."

ST. LOUIS CARDINALS

HITTING:

Tito Landrum suffered a colossal dropoff in hitting in 1986 after a sterling 1985 season in which he was a post-season hero for the Cardinals. His stock in trade had been his ability to hit with authority against lefthanded pitching but Landrum batted just .181 against southpaws in 1986.

Part of his problem was that he played less often--especially after manager Whitey Herzog decided to let Andy Van Slyke play every day in right field. It is more difficult for an extra man to snap out of a slump when he is used infrequently and Landrum found that out firsthand. At age 32, Landrum still is one of the top defensive outfielders in the game but his slide last season raised some doubts about his abilities to sustain himself by hitting.

He didn't seem to swing the bat with as much gusto as before and instead seemed to be feeling for the ball at times, hitting more defensively than offensively. Again, little-used extra men tend to develop bad habits.

Frustrated at not being able to play more, Landrum might be more effective with a team other than the Cardinals.

A dead fastball hitter earlier in his career, Landrum has made strides in recent years in his ability to wait for the breaking pitch.

He is almost fanatical about keeping in shape. He constantly works out but his body is so tightly wound that he often suffers injury. In the last several years, he has been troubled by a bad back.

FIELDING:

Landrum can play any of the three outfield positions with proficiency, though center field probably is his weakest one. He does not seem to pick up the flight of the ball as quickly there and, in fact, had difficulty reacting to balls wherever he played last year. His arm is above average in its accuracy although he

TITO LANDRUM
OF, No. 21
RR, 5'11", 175 lbs.
ML Svc: 7 years
Born: 10-25-54 in Joplin, MO

1986 STATISTICS

AVG	G	AB	R	H	2B	3B	HR	RBI	BB	SO	SB
.210	96	205	24	43	7	1	2	17	20	41	3

CAREER STATISTICS

AVG	G	AB	R	H	2B	3B	HR	RBI	BB	SO	SB
.256	513	854	105	219	36	11	12	99	71	160	15

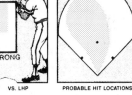

VS. RHP   VS. LHP   PROBABLE HIT LOCATIONS

sometimes takes too long to unload the ball.

BASERUNNING:

Landrum has speed but doesn't have the inclination for basestealing. He will, however, take the extra base on a hit.

OVERALL:

Landrum has indicated he is a player who can rise to the occasion. Now, he must fight for his job.

Rooker: "Tito's poor 1986 season might have been part of the whole Cardinal turnaround last year. He never seemed to get it going. He has, however, been a great defensive replacement and one of the best extra men in the game."

ST. LOUIS CARDINALS

PITCHING:

Greg Mathews is as close to being a John Tudor-clone as there is. Mathews is another smoothie who throws no harder than 86 MPH but has good enough off-speed pitches to survive a lack of speed.

Mathews probably has a better curveball than Tudor but his change-up, while good, has not progressed to the level of the Cardinal ace's. Mathews' motion is such that hitters seem to be lulled to sleep by it.

Mathews tailed off in the last five weeks of the season, when he won only one game. Hitters were beginning to adjust to his pitching and Mathews admitted to being mentally unprepared to pitch through October, the full length of the major league season (minor league seasons end by Labor Day).

As he gets older, Mathews is expected to get stronger. He completed just one of 22 starts, although the reliability of short man Todd Worrell was largely responsible for the quick Cardinal hook.

Mathews must pinpoint his pitches because if he makes a mistake, even Busch Stadium isn't spacious enough to hold it. He gave up nearly one homer per nine innings, a rather high figure considering the size of his home park.

FIELDING, HITTING, BASERUNNING:

Mathews had never batted professionally until last year and it showed. In a word, he was horrible.

At one point, he began switch-hitting but the results were dismal. He was 2-for-43

GREG MATHEWS
LHP, No. 53
SL, 6'2", 180 lbs.
ML Svc: 1 year
Born: 5-17-62 in
Harbor City, CA

1986 STATISTICS

W	L	ERA	G	GS	CG	SV	IP	H	R	ER	BB	SO
11	8	3.65	23	22	1	0	145.1	139	61	59	44	67

CAREER STATISTICS

W	L	ERA	G	GS	CG	SV	IP	H	R	ER	BB	SO
11	8	3.65	23	22	1	0	145.1	139	61	59	44	67

overall and struck out 19 times. His bunting was only somewhat better and his baserunning is unknown. He scored only one run and slid just three times.

OVERALL:

His decline at the end of the season presented some concern but Mathews seems intelligent enough to adjust this season. A 15-win season is not out of the question considering he won 11 games in four months last year.

Rooker: "With his first season under his belt, Mathews could have a good year in 1987. He might have been rushed to the majors a bit too quickly, but he adjusted and came through.

"He is another good, young arm on the Cardinals' staff, but where will they put them all?"

ST. LOUIS CARDINALS

HITTING:

In 1986 Willie McGee suffered a disastrous 97-point drop in his average from the previous year--when he was the league batting champion and its MVP. While he is not a .353 hitter, he is not a .256 batter, either.

McGee spent considerable time last season worrying about the shape of his legs, a concern which had a distracting effect on his game. McGee knows that his legs are his livelihood; a knee injury which required surgery and two hamstring pulls caused him much alarm. He feels that he is a slower healer than others and refuses to be rushed until he feels he is ready.

Oddly, McGee felt no pressure to match his 1985 MVP/batting title performance. Some of his frustrations were caused by being on a losing team. His devotion and attention to baseball suffered and he even entertained wild thoughts of quitting.

Still an impatient hitter, McGee has no advantage with a 2-0 count and is never behind at 0-2. Observations of McGee during the at-bats of just one game would give a scout every reason to report that this hitter had no idea how to work a count or pick a pitch. McGee will swing at many awful pitches and look futile as he hacks away at a fool's curveball in the dirt. But then later in the game, McGee might drive the very same pitch for an extra-base hit.

Most of McGee's power comes from the right side: he had five of his seven homers while batting righthanded even though he had 99 fewer at-bats from that side of the plate.

A switch-hitter, he prefers the ball up when he is hitting righthanded so that he can turn on it. As a lefthanded hitter, he might be more selective and prefers the ball down.

If Vince Coleman is on base, McGee will see almost all fastballs. If Coleman is not on, McGee will almost never see a fastball. Last season, Coleman had his own problems reaching first base and McGee found himself chasing breaking balls out of the strike zone.

BASERUNNING:

Because of his fragile legs, McGee wasn't nearly as aggressive on the bases as he had

WILLIE McGEE
CF, No. 51
SR, 6'1", 175 lbs.
ML Svc: 5 years
Born: 11-2-58 in
San Francisco, CA

1986 STATISTICS

AVG	G	AB	R	H	2B	3B	HR	RBI	BB	SO	SB
.256	124	497	65	127	22	7	7	48	37	82	19

CAREER STATISTICS

AVG	G	AB	R	H	2B	3B	HR	RBI	BB	SO	SB
.298	691	2703	379	806	101	52	32	311	138	404	181

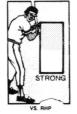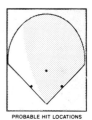

VS. RHP VS. LHP PROBABLE HIT LOCATIONS

been in the past. He stole just 19 last year and, either confused or in need of confidence, he was caught stealing an astounding 16 times.

FIELDING:

A multiple Gold Glove winner, McGee plays the deepest center field in the National League. He comes in on a ball very well but is reluctant to bang into walls. McGee has an outstanding, very accurate arm and is much better than he has been in the past at throwing to the correct base.

OVERALL:

Rooker: "Willie is at something of a crossroads in his career, considering his reconstructive knee surgery performed last October. If he is confident in his own health, he could bounce back to have another big year. He is among the many Cardinals players who were way out of synch last year."

ST. LOUIS CARDINALS

HITTING:

The Cardinals didn't expect Ozzie Smith to be their leading hitter last season but he was, almost from start to finish, batting a career-high .280.

At one time considered an "easy out" as a lefthanded batter if a pitcher simply jammed him, Smith has worked tirelessly to improve his lefty hitting. Smith can now drive the ball better than ever before. As a result, defenses have had to treat him with more respect when he bats lefthanded. Smith's left-side turnaround may someday help him to reach the .300 average he now aims for.

Smith likes the ball up when batting both right- and lefthanded and is now among the more consistent switch-hitters in baseball. He hit .282 lefthanded and .277 righthanded last year. Save for his blast off Tom Niedenfuer in Game Five of the 1985 NLCS, Smith has never had a homer lefthanded in nine seasons and nearly 3,300 at-bats from that side.

Most defenses try to bunch Smith toward the middle, although he can pull a ball with authority when the occasion demands. His best skill as a hitter is that he rarely strikes out. Over the past two seasons, he has averaged less than two strikeouts per week (58Ks/1051ABs). He has managed to stay away from the type of 2-for-40 killer slumps that used to ruin his average. At this point, Smith's problems at the plate come when he starts to feel his oats and swing for the fences; the results are mere warning track fly-ball outs.

BASERUNNING:

A very smart baserunner, Smith consistently steals at a 75-80% success rate. He is almost without peer at taking the extra base. Early last season, Smith had to adjust his sliding style to accommodate his tender shoulder. He had to remind himself to slide feet-first in situations when he might have otherwise gone in with his arm and tender shoulder leading.

OZZIE SMITH
SS, No. 1
SR, 5'10", 150 lbs.
ML Svc: 9 years
Born: 12-26-54 in
 Mobile, AL

1986 STATISTICS

AVG	G	AB	R	H	2B	3B	HR	RBI	BB	SO	SB
.280	153	514	67	144	19	4	0	54	79	27	31

CAREER STATISTICS

AVG	G	AB	R	H	2B	3B	HR	RBI	BB	SO	SB
.247	1317	4739	583	1169	179	38	13	374	528	273	303

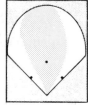

VS. RHP   VS. LHP   PROBABLE HIT LOCATIONS

FIELDING:

Smith is surely one of the most creative and innovative of fielders, and hitters actually *like* to see the ball hit to him just to see what he will do.

There was fear that a torn rotator cuff might shorten or even end Smith's career but he managed to play with pain the whole season and compensated for lack of arm strength with a quicker release. In the past, Smith had a way of throwing the ball across his body when on the run; in deference to his shoulder, he threw in a more conventional style last season.

OVERALL:

Rooker: "Ozzie continues to be utterly amazing. His shoulder healed so phenomenally fast that he is almost a medical miracle. He keeps himself in superb condition and respects his body as his stock in trade. He very well might have his .300 season this year if he remembers not to swing for the fences."

ST. LOUIS CARDINALS

HITTING:

Terry Pendleton had his second straight .240-ish season at the plate last year. It would seem that his .324 rookie season was a flash in the pan.

Traditionally, third base is an offensive position but Pendleton does not fit that mold, having hit just one homer in 1986, although driving in 59 runs. If a third baseman is not going to drive in 80 or 85 runs, he must compensate by drawing walks and stealing a lot of bases. Pendleton stole 24 bases in 30 attempts but walked just 34 times, 10 of them intentionally, and had an unacceptable .279 on-base percentage.

With more discipline, Pendleton should be a .265-.270 hitter. All too often, however, he loses his direction in an at-bat and, even if he is ahead in the count, finds himself hitting the pitcher's pitch instead of waiting for his. (He has shown particular impatience against righthanded pitching, hitting just .220 last year and drawing just 12 unintentional walks in 391 appearances.)

Against righthanded pitchers, Pendleton likes the ball down in the strike zone but he must make sure the ball is *in* the strike zone.

As a righthanded hitter, Pendleton has a little more pop in his bat. He hit .271 righthanded and averaged one RBI per eight at-bats. He does best against lefthanders with balls pitched away, both up and down.

BASERUNNING:

Pendleton is no speed burner but shows instinct and intelligence on the bases. His 80% rate of successful basestealing is more than adequate.

FIELDING:

Defensively, Pendleton has become one of the best third baseman in the game. His reflexes are cat-quick and he is especially adept at backhanding balls behind the bag and racing into the outfield or foul ground to take pop-ups over his shoulder.

TERRY PENDLETON
3B, No. 9
SR, 5'9", 180 lbs.
ML Svc: 3 years
Born: 7-16-60 in
Los Angeles, CA

1986 STATISTICS

AVG	G	AB	R	H	2B	3B	HR	RBI	BB	SO	SB
.239	159	578	56	138	26	5	1	59	34	59	24

CAREER STATISTICS

AVG	G	AB	R	H	2B	3B	HR	RBI	BB	SO	SB
.255	375	1399	149	357	58	11	7	161	87	166	61

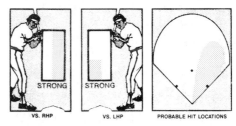

Once Mike Schmidt retires, Pendleton might have Gold Glove honors all to himself-- especially if Tim Wallach is switched from playing third base this year. A converted second baseman, Pendleton is the perfect complement to shortstop Ozzie Smith, after whom he has patterned himself greatly.

OVERALL:

Pendleton is one of the tireless workers on the Cardinals and is always trying to improve his game. He takes instruction readily but perhaps works too hard at trying to rectify his mistakes.

Rooker: "As a defensive player, Terry might be among the league's elite. He goes to his left and his right equally well and has a good strong arm.

"Offensively, because he has limited power and not much speed, he should work on developing a good bunt to add to both the Cardinals' attack as well as his average."

ST. LOUIS CARDINALS

PITCHING:

The workload of the last two seasons may have taken its toll on John Tudor last year. He was unable to shake a twinge in his shoulder, an injury which surfaced early in the season and forced him to miss the last three weeks.

Tudor has worked nearly 500 innings over the last two years although he had just three complete games last year.

Nonetheless, Tudor was six games over .500 with a team that finished three games under and his 2.92 ERA was among the league's best. That ERA was fairly remarkable inasmuch as he didn't throw any shutouts after having had 10 the year before.

Although he has absolutely no breaking ball to speak of and only a modest fastball, Tudor wins because of an exceptional change-up, impeccable control and brains.

While Tudor's fastball is not of laser-beam quality, he does have two different kinds, both of which move. His change-up makes his fastball seem faster than the 85 MPH occasionally registered on the radar gun.

Tudor is one of the most frustrating pitchers a hitter has to face. The subtlety of his stuff is so deceiving, many hitters face him fully confident that they can beat him. Tudor, however, lulls them into a false sense of superiority then comes in for the kill with the precise placement of a sucker pitch. Lefthanders have a particularly tough time handling Tudor. Keith Hernandez of the Mets considers Tudor to be one of the top five lefthanders he has ever batted against.

A winter of rest (no surgery was required) should enable Tudor to regain his 1985 form. He is 33 years old but is actually just coming into his own.

JOHN TUDOR
LHP, No. 30
LL, 6'0", 185 lbs.
ML Svc: 8 years
Born: 2-2-54 in
   Schenectady, NY

1986 STATISTICS

W	L	ERA	G	GS	CG	SV	IP	H	R	ER	BB	SO
13	7	2.92	30	30	3	0	219	197	81	71	53	107

CAREER STATISTICS

W	L	ERA	G	GS	CG	SV	IP	H	R	ER	BB	SO
85	58	3.26	204	192	44	1	1342.2	1251	544	487	366	775

FIELDING, HITTING, BASERUNNING:

Tudor is the consummate athlete and always is in shape. His pickoff move is excellent and he is cat-quick defensively. While not fast, he does not make mistakes on the bases. Tudor is not exactly a robust hitter but generally keeps the ball in play and is a good bunter.

OVERALL:

A record of 34-15 over the last two years is easy evidence of the status Tudor has achieved. Hitters have found that it is very difficult to hit against a pitcher who can get more than one pitch over at a time.

Rooker: "John uses his fastball, change-up and occasional slider very well. He pitches with his head and has great concentration on the mound. The twinge of pain he felt in his arm finally caught up with him in September, though he had probably been pitching in pain throughout the season. This winter's rest should bring him back healthy and ready to go."

STRONG ARM

HITTING:

Andy Van Slyke was having a horrific season last year; he was hitting a paltry .205 until late June when lightning struck his bat--it lit up and he hit at a .316 clip thereafter.

Van Slyke won half the Cardinals' Triple Crown, albeit a modest one. His 13 homers were a team-high and his 61 RBIs tied for the club lead. He finished second in St. Louis with a .270 batting average.

For the first time in his career, Van Slyke played against all types of pitching during the last part of the year: the results, however, were certainly mixed. His average against lefthanders was a woeful .195 for 133 at-bats. A likely explanation is the adjustment process from facing all sorts of breaking balls coming toward him at angles he hadn't seen before.

One almost thinks that Van Slyke guesses with every pitch, but when he is ahead in the count, pitchers must be careful where they spot their fastball. Van Slyke is strong enough and has quick enough hands to hit the ball out to straightaway center field. He prefers, however, to pull the ball.

The absence of the dangerous Jack Clark in the lineup last season may have been a blessing in disguise for Van Slyke. He has had trouble concentrating intently on every pitch during every at-bat in the past, but last year Van Slyke found himself having to carry a bit more of the load. He took the responsibility to heart, paying closer attention to thinking more at the plate.

Given his many skills, Van Slyke should hit around .300 with 20 HRs and 80 RBIs. But can he be consistent for six months? Van Slyke has everything going for him and he is only 26 years old.

BASERUNNING:

As unaggressive as Van Slyke sometimes appears at the plate, he is contrastingly bold on the bases. He has stolen 55 bases in 69 tries over two seasons.

ANDY VAN SLYKE
RF, No. 18
LR, 6'1", 190 lbs.
ML Svc: 4 years
Born: 12-21-60 in Utica, NY

1986 STATISTICS

AVG	G	AB	R	H	2B	3B	HR	RBI	BB	SO	SB
.270	137	418	48	113	23	7	13	61	47	85	21

CAREER STATISTICS

AVG	G	AB	R	H	2B	3B	HR	RBI	BB	SO	SB
.259	521	1512	205	392	79	22	41	204	203	274	104

  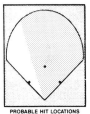

VS. RHP   VS. LHP   PROBABLE HIT LOCATIONS

FIELDING:

Despite the lack of a Gold Glove to prove it, Van Slyke could very well be the best right fielder in the league. He has a strong, accurate arm and closes off gaps quickly and precisely with his great speed.

When Willie McGee was out last season, Van Slyke also played a laudable center field and he can also look good at first base.

OVERALL:

Rooker: "Will the real Andy Van Slyke please stand up? He has everything going for him: size, speed, and power and his throws are tremendous. I don't know what he's waiting for, but I have got to believe that he *must* put it all together this year."

ST. LOUIS CARDINALS

PITCHING:

The 1986 National League *Rookie of the Year*, Todd Worrell is the prototypal "Here it comes, see if you can hit it" pitcher.

Worrell has two pitches: a hard fastball which tops out at 95 MPH and a hard slider which goes about 87 MPH. There is no mystery, no off-speed pitch. If Worrell had an off-speed pitch, he might be deemed hazardous to society.

A young pitcher like this comes along once every 10 years or so and if Worrell can stay free of arm trouble, he could be another Rich Gossage. He arguably is the best reliever in the National League already and he has been a relief pitcher only for a year and a half.

He was a bust as a minor league starter, and the Cardinals' organization made him a reliever at Louisville in 1985 when it was discovered that he would lose seven or eight miles off his fastball if he pitched more than three innings.

He never has to pitch that long in St. Louis although he did have to play in the outfield twice last year as manager Whitey Herzog maneuvered his pitchers into left/left, right/right situations.

Without Worrell, the Cardinals' season would have been a calamity. His 36 saves and nine victories represented nearly 60% of the Cardinals' victory total.

Worrell is a former bible college student but don't let that background fool you. When he comes into the game in a tight situation, he is anything but meek and polite.

His poise and attitude seem uncommon for a man who has just a year and a month of big league experience. Herzog's only concern is in not using Worrell too often and he is hoping to find a righthanded set-up man to take up some of the slack in the bullpen.

TODD WORRELL
RHP, No. 38
RR, 6'5", 200 lbs.
ML Svc: 1 year plus
Born: 9-28-59 in
Arcadia, CA

1986 STATISTICS

W	L	ERA	G	GS	CG	SV	IP	H	R	ER	BB	SO
9	10	2.08	74	0	0	36	103.2	86	29	24	41	73

CAREER STATISTICS

W	L	ERA	G	GS	CG	SV	IP	H	R	ER	BB	SO
12	10	2.27	91	0	0	41	125.1	103	36	31	48	90

FIELDING, HITTING, BASERUNNING:

Worrell got his first hit, a triple, last year. He was a small-college star as a third baseman but he really isn't that much of a threat as a big league hitter. That hit represented the only time Worrell got on base so the only thing that can be said is that he knew his way to third base.

For a big man, Worrell is fairly agile in the field. His move to first is adequate although his elongated delivery to the plate can enable runners to steal on him.

OVERALL:

Rooker: "Right now, the top relievers in the National League are Lee Smith, Jeff Reardon, Goose Gossage and Todd Worrell. Will Worrell be No. 1 soon? There is a good chance that he will.

"Todd seized the opportunity he had last year and took the bull by the horns. Before he converted to relief, he had said he was just one season away from quitting baseball. His success as a reliever is one of the best moves in baseball in the past few years."

ST. LOUIS CARDINALS

**CURT FORD
OF, No. 27
LR, 5'10", 150 lbs.
ML Svc: 1 year
Born: 10-11-60 in
Jackson, MS**

HITTING, BASERUNNING, FIELDING:

Curt Ford may have a long major league career ahead of him as an extra outfielder because he can run, play a couple of positions and is an aggressive pinch-hitter. Ford knocked in seven runs with five pinch-hits last year and showed some surprising power for a 150-pounder.

The lefthanded hitter can turn on a fastball and tries to pull most pitches. His total of 19 extra-base hits in 214 at-bats was one of the best on the team.

Ford can be pitched away because he rarely tries to hit the ball to the opposite field. If he went with the pitch as well as bunted more often, he could raise his .248 average to .280.

Like most of the Cardinals, Ford has speed and stole 13 bases in limited duty.

He played right field and left field without incident and manager Whitey Herzog is hoping that Ford, an infielder in the minors, could take a turn at third base or second base in emergency. His throwing arm is average and he rarely throws to the wrong base.

Ford probably is destined to be an extra man because of his slight build. It is thought that the heat of summer would take too much out of him on an everyday basis.

OVERALL:

Rooker: "Curt seems to be a quiet man who has the intensity Herzog likes in his bench players. He is always in the game and never is found not hustling."

**CLINT HURDLE
C/INF, No. 13
LR, 6'3", 195 lbs.
ML Svc: 6 years
Born: 7-30-57 in
Big Rapids, MI**

HITTING, BASERUNNING, FIELDING:

Clint Hurdle played five positions last season but none of them was batsman. He hit a disappointing .195, even though he was a respectable .273 as a pinch-hitter. Hurdle can still crash an occasional home run but must hit in the .230-.240 range to maintain a job.

Limited playing time may have taken away some of the skills from a man regarded as a "can't-miss" prospect eight years ago.

Hurdle is only 29 years old and his versatility may help prolong his major league career, especially since he is a fairly accomplished catcher. In recent years, however, he has not been able to hit for any kind of average.

Hurdle can still hit the down-and-in fastball with power but he can be overmatched with fastballs thrown higher in the strike zone.

Defensively, first base probably is Hurdle's best position but he won't hurt the club in left field, right field or at third base. As an outfielder, his strong arm is sort of a compensation for his lack of speed.

OVERALL:

Hurdle's career has seen its highs and lows. He approaches the sport with the proper attitude and his loose personality keeps a team relaxed. If anything, Hurdle is too modest.

Rooker: "Able to accept that he will not be the superstar he was projected to be, Hurdle is as good a team man as there is. For a benchman, that attitude is particularly important--and rare."

ST. LOUIS CARDINALS

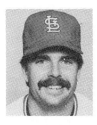

STEVE LAKE
C, No. 16
RR, 6'1", 190 lbs.
ML Svc: 4 years
Born: 3-14-57 in
Inglewood, CA

HITTING, BASERUNNING, FIELDING:

Rescued from the Chicago Cubs, where he played infrequently behind ironman Jody Davis, Steve Lake proved that he could be a solid number two catcher with the Cardinals.

Lake can hit the mediocre fastball but not the good one. He is a pull hitter and often lunges at breaking balls.

Lake is no threat to run and is mostly a station-to-station baserunner.

Last season, Lake worked on his mechanics with coach Mike Roarke and became a good thrower. In tandem with Mike LaValliere, Lake gives the Cardinals a defensively solid, although offensively weak, catching corps.

With his lack of activity in Chicago, Lake has had little chance for improvement and some of his skills might have atrophied because of that. But when one is looking for a backup player who won't complain (a rare item in baseball), Lake is that man. Happy to be in the big leagues, Lake would be a positive force on any team.

OVERALL:

He is one of the dry wits in the game and once joked that it was unfortunate that a shipment of bats came without instructions. Or then there was the time that he was scratched from the lineup in a game at Wrigley Field because the wind was blowing out and the manager thought teammate Jody Davis had a better chance of hitting a home run. "Jody doesn't need the wind," said Lake. "I do."

Rooker: "Lake is a competent defensive player and would probably be a better hitter if he were used more often. He is able, however, to occasionally turn a mistake fastball into a home run."

MIKE LaVALLIERE
C, No. 11
LR, 5'10", 200 lbs.
ML Svc: 1 year plus
Born: 8-18-60 in
Charlotte, NC

HITTING, BASERUNNING, FIELDING:

Mike LaValliere is a good backup catcher who happens to be the Cardinals' No. 1 catcher. His catching skills, especially the manner in which he receives the ball, have impressed manager Whitey Herzog so that Herzog says LaValliere is one of the best he has ever seen.

LaValliere is also a strong, accurate thrower who should get close to 40% of opposing baserunners if his pitchers cooperate by holding runners on base.

Cardinal pitchers enjoy throwing to LaValliere because he presents a low target and does not distract them by moving either his body or his glove much.

As a hitter, LaValliere will never be much more than a .240 batsman because of his very poor speed. At one point last season, LaValliere asked Herzog if he was the slowest player the manager had ever had on his team. Herzog replied, "I'm not going to say yes, for sure, but you're among them."

LaValliere is a pull hitter with little power. He seems more effective against righthanded pitching and can turn better on a ball when it is down. Against lefthanders, LaValliere batted .224 in limited exposure and did better with balls up in the strike zone.

OVERALL:

Rooker: "After a good start, LaValliere tumbled later in the season when opposing fielders began playing him deeper because of his lack of speed. 'Spanky,' as his teammates call him, must learn to hit the ball the other way more to have any chance of increasing his average."

ST. LOUIS CARDINALS

TOM LAWLESS
INF, No. 20
RR, 5'11", 165 lbs.
ML Svc: 4 years
Born: 12-19-56 in
Erie, PA

defensive replacement as an occasional pinch-hitter and especially as a pinch-runner. He stole eight bases in nine attempts.

Lawless is an accomplished second baseman and better than adequate at third base, and he started one game in left field where he made a spectacular catch. His portfolio will be further augmented this season when he becomes an emergency catcher.

HITTING, BASERUNNING, FIELDING:

A .282 hitter in 1986, Tom Lawless could have a lengthy career with the 24-man roster. He is most effective against lefthanded pitchers, against whom he batted .333. He is, however, helpless against righthanders: last year he was just 2-for-12.

Limited to a 1986 season total of just 39 at-bats, Lawless nonetheless was effective as a

OVERALL:

Lawless was the designated Steve Carlton-killer last year, going five for eight in three starts against the lefthander.

Rooker: "Many utility players chafe and complain that they should be playing regularly. Lawless, as they say, 'knows his role,' though it is a small one in the Cardinals' scheme."

JOHN MORRIS
OF, No. 33
LL, 6'1", 185 lbs.
ML Svc: 1 year
Born: 2-23-61 in
Freeport, NY

had one big series against the Mets in New York, including back-to-back game-winning hits, but leveled off later in the season. Part of the reason for that was that he was in and out of the lineup.

Morris may be destined for extra-man status but it is uncertain if he can maintain the discipline and concentration needed to be an effective pinch-hitter. He is, however, able to play all three outfield positions with proficiency.

The lefthanded hitter has some power but will not be much more than a 10-homer man if used every day.

HITTING, BASERUNNING, FIELDING:

A former No. 1 draft choice of the Kansas City Royals, John Morris still has yet to prove he can hit enough to be a regular player in the major leagues.

In the last couple of years Morris has adjusted his batting stroke in order to pull the inside pitch more to right field but he still can be jammed by hard stuff inside.

He has everything else to be a star: speed, a good throwing arm and intelligence. Morris

OVERALL:

Rooker: "Morris has the attitude to make it in the big leagues but that must be translated into more offense. With the Cardinals' wealth of young outfielders, he might be better off in another organization."

ST. LOUIS CARDINALS

JOSE OQUENDO
SS, No. 55
RR, 5'10", 160 lbs.
ML Svc: 3 years
Born: 7-4-63 in
Rio Piedras, PR

HITTING, BASERUNNING, FIELDING:

Jose Oquendo turned into one of baseball's most reliable utility infielders last season. He was even used 27 times as a pinch-hitter, which probably was 27 times more than he had been used that way previously in his career.

Batting from a crouch, Oquendo hit the ball last year with more authority than he had ever done. He had never switch-hit for a full season in the big leagues before, yet he hit a respectable .266 as a lefthanded hitter.

Still, Oquendo packs more authority in his bat when hitting righthanded. He tends to hit the ball mostly to left field as a lefthanded hitter and has trouble handling hard stuff inside.

Oquendo, though a good athlete, is not considered exceptionally fast. He does, however, show good judgment on the bases. He is not a basestealing threat, unlike most of the rest of his teammates.

Whitey Herzog considers Oquendo the second-best shortstop in the league behind his own Ozzie Smith. Oquendo probably stimulated more off-season trade interest than any other Cardinal, but as a defensive backup to Smith, Oquendo is a big safety net for St. Louis. The price to take him away would be very high.

OVERALL:

Rooker: "Though he is only 23 years old, Oquendo is an eight-season veteran of professional baseball. Given his startling improvement last season, he may be around for 10 or 15 years in the big leagues."

ST. LOUIS CARDINALS

PAT PERRY
LHP, No. 37
LL, 6'1", 170 lbs.
ML Svc: 1 year
Born: 2-4-59 in
Taylorville, IL

PITCHING, FIELDING, HITTING, BASERUNNING:

Pat Perry might be the softest thrower among the Cardinals' bevy of lefthanders.

After a bad early season, when Perry seemed to have little confidence, he was sent to Louisville for a while. When he returned, he was more sure of himself and tried to throw a curveball to augment his fastball and change-up.

Perry's change-up was his stock in trade when he had success late in the 1985 season but hitters were expecting that early last season. Cardinals manager Whitey Herzog used Perry mostly in long relief although he had to take some short turns when Ken Dayley was injured.

His effectiveness is highlighted by a hesitation in his delivery which causes hitters to jump out at him before the ball arrives. Most of his pitches are thrown from a three-quarters delivery.

Arm surgery earlier in his career probably robbed Perry of some velocity.

He rarely gets to bat because of his short stints but he is not often overmatched at the plate. He is a smooth fielder and has an above-average pickoff move.

OVERALL:

Rooker: "If Perry weren't lefthanded, he probably wouldn't be in the big leagues with his below-average stuff. But lefthanded relievers can have extremely long careers providing they throw strikes, and Perry might be in that group."

SAN DIEGO PADRES

PITCHING:

Dave Dravecky's major league career has been marked by two characteristics: excellent pitching and nagging injuries. The 1986 season was no exception. Once again Dravecky performed well when he was healthy, compiling a 3.07 ERA to go with a deceptive 9-11 record. But tendinitis in his throwing elbow put Dravecky on the bench for the year in late August. It is now uncertain as to how he'll fit into the Padres' plans this year.

After almost five full big league seasons, an obvious pattern for Dravecky has emerged. In seasons Dravecky has been called on to take a spot in the starting rotation, he has had arm problems. He suffered a shoulder injury in 1983 (when he made 28 starts and no relief appearances) that caused him to miss the last 34 games of the season. In 1984, when he split time between the rotation and the bullpen, Dravecky was fine, posting a 2.93 ERA in 156 2/3 innings. He went back into the rotation in 1985 and showed signs of tiring toward the end of the season. He started exclusively in 1986 prior to his injury.

With his sidearm delivery, excellent fastball and effective slider, Dravecky is exceptionally difficult on lefthanded batters. He uses the slider as a back-door pitch on righties and has added a forkball to his repertoire. All of his pitches have good movement. He mixes pitches well and is control-conscious, but he tires easily. As a means to keep Dravecky fresh, the Padres might limit him to pitching just 150 innings in the future.

FIELDING, HITTING, BASERUNNING:

Dravecky's fielding is above average; he's quick off the mound. He has an improving pickoff move that still needs work.

At the plate, Dravecky is hardly a threat. That's no surprise, but it is difficult to

DAVE DRAVECKY
LHP, No. 43
RL, 6'1", 193 lbs.
ML Svc: 5 years
Born: 2-14-56 in
Youngstown, OH

1986 STATISTICS

W	L	ERA	G	GS	CG	SV	IP	H	R	ER	BB	SO
9	11	3.07	26	26	3	0	161.1	149	68	55	54	87

CAREER STATISTICS

W	L	ERA	G	GS	CG	SV	IP	H	R	ER	BB	SO
50	43	3.04	169	109	22	10	827.1	741	315	279	239	396

understand why a player so well-versed in other phases of the game cannot lay down a bunt. He needs to work on it.

His alertness and good speed made him a favorite pinch-runner for the Padres in 1986. Though not a threat to steal, he can get from first to third on a single and knows how to break up a double play.

OVERALL:

Dravecky's ability to pitch as a starter, long reliever or short man, combined with his attitude and work ethic, make him a precious commodity in baseball. He would be a welcome addition to any staff. In their eagerness to get the most out of him, however, the Padres may have made a mistake in trying to start him on a regular basis. Dravecky's best season (1984) was the one in which he split time as a starter and reliever.

Dierker: "Dave is a real tough pitcher when he's healthy, but he has had arm problems over the past couple of years, and that's got to be a concern for the Padres. They're hoping he can bounce back, but that will depend on his elbow. If he's healthy, he will win."

SAN DIEGO PADRES

PITCHING:

One day last summer in Boston, there wasn't a man alive who could get a hit off Storm Davis. For 7 1/3 innings, he threw a 90+ MPH fastball, a hard-breaking curveball, a slider and a change-up. The Red Sox had no chance. Yet, just one start later, he didn't get out of the third inning. Why?

No one is quite certain. No one can explain why Davis hasn't won 20 games yet. No one can explain how he could have gone 9-12 last year and 19-21 the last two years. But his 3.62 ERA was the best among the Orioles starters last year, and he was the only one of them to keep his ERA under 4.00 all season. He is still young (25), and the switch to the National League may help him. He is still a man with great potential.

Davis *does have* all the pitches. His out pitch is his fastball, which he throws from over-the-top or three-quarters, at up to 93 MPH. It is an easy motion to follow, however, which could actually *aid* some hitters. His problem is not using his fastball enough while trying to be too fine.

His curveball is above average, though he has been known to hang a few of them. Davis has a good slider, but he didn't throw it often enough according to his former manager, Earl Weaver. His change-up, which is a kind of forkball, is still developing, but he does use it sometimes.

Davis had religiously stayed away from the home run pitch until last year when he gave up 16 in 154 innings. Most came up when he wasn't aggressive enough with his hard stuff-- and got too cute.

FIELDING:

Davis is a good athlete who is quick enough to discourage much bunting. He doesn't finish

STORM DAVIS
RHP, No. 34
RR, 6'4", 196 lbs.
ML Svc: 5 years
Born: 12-26-61 in
Dallas, TX

1986 STATISTICS

W	L	ERA	G	GS	CG	SV	IP	H	R	ER	BB	SO
9	12	3.62	25	25	2	0	154	166	70	62	49	96

CAREER STATISTICS

W	L	ERA	G	GS	CG	SV	IP	H	R	ER	BB	SO
54	40	3.65	154	121	27	1	855	819	378	347	282	586

in very good position, but he's made up for it with speed.

He does not, however, hold runners on base very well. He throws to first often, but runners do not hesitate to run on him.

OVERALL:

This guy may be ready to explode one day.

Kaat: "I think the change of scenery will do Storm some good. Going to the NL, he'll find it's more of an aggressive, hit-it-if-you-can league. If he develops that aggressive style, he can be effective. He can get lit up there, too. He has to prove to NL hitters that he can get his breaking ball over the plate. That will make his fastball that much better.

"The AL East is not a speed division, it is a power division. There will be a lot more running in the NL, so he has to improve his move. But I look for a big year out of Davis. He's got all the pitches. There's no reason he shouldn't get better. He might end up being the best pitcher on the Padres' staff."

SAN DIEGO PADRES

HITTING:

With 1986 being his third straight season above .270, Tim Flannery proved himself to be a player who has learned from his experience in the major leagues. Despite playing in more games than in any previous season, he kept his average up by avoiding the extended slump, being patient at the plate and accepting the walk.

Flannery has learned not to chase bad pitches out of the strike zone and to force the pitcher to get his breaking ball over. He still can be had, however, particularly by a 90 mph-plus fastball in tight; Flannery doesn't have the bat speed to compensate for such a heater.

Flannery led the team in being hit by pitches, was second in walks and third in on-base percentage--all of that from a player who split time at second base and filled in occasionally at shortstop and third. His only vice was the strikeout; in past seasons he was a much better bet to get wood on the ball. He knows how to lay down a bunt and can be counted on in a clutch sacrifice situation. Flannery also has a flair for the dramatic: he won six games with hits.

BASERUNNING:

Flannery never has had great speed and was caught stealing six times in nine attempts. But he has an excellent sense of where he is on the basepaths and how far he can go. As a veteran infielder, Flannery also knows how to break up a double play and he's willing to sacrifice his body to keep a rally alive.

FIELDING:

One of the best-kept secrets in the league is that Flannery finished second to Ryne Sandberg in fielding percentage for second basemen. He made only three errors in 458 chances, a .993 average. The only catch is that Flannery simply won't have a play on some balls in the hole because he doesn't have the foot speed to run them down.

He doesn't miss the ones he reaches,

TIM FLANNERY
INF, No. 11
LR, 5'11", 176 lbs.
ML Svc: 8 years
Born: 9-29-57 in
Tulsa, OK

1986 STATISTICS

AVG	G	AB	R	H	2B	3B	HR	RBI	BB	SO	SB
.280	134	368	48	103	11	2	3	28	54	61	3

CAREER STATISTICS

AVG	G	AB	R	H	2B	3B	HR	RBI	BB	SO	SB
.260	714	1897	207	493	62	20	9	162	198	211	15

  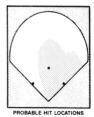

VS. RHP   VS. LHP   PROBABLE HIT LOCATIONS

though, and won't hesitate to leave his feet to stop one. Flannery is much improved on the double play pivot.

OVERALL:

Though they've never allowed him true "everyday" player status, the Padres recognize Flannery's value. He's the only player on the roster who remains from 1980, when Jack McKeon took over as GM. A player who gets the most out of his admittedly average skills, he is the kind of versatile performer winning teams must have. His excellent off-field demeanor further enhances his worth.

Dierker: "He's surehanded, got a good arm, can turn the double play, but he lacks range in the field and he lacks speed on the bases. He can do just about everything but run. Unfortunately, when you play second base in the major leagues you're expected to run fast and he can't."

SAN DIEGO PADRES

HITTING:

Steve Garvey had a strong finish that brought his numbers up to deceptively decent levels, but 1986 had to be considered one of the weaker offensive seasons in his highly successful career. His batting average was more than 40 points below his career average, he scored only about a run every three games and he was nowhere to be found during the long summer months during which the Padres faded slowly into the West's cellar.

Still a great fastball hitter, Garvey displayed an increasing impatience at the plate, drawing only 23 walks and routinely swinging at breaking pitches in the dirt. It is a wonder that pitchers ever try to put a high fastball past him; Garvey will hit that ball out of the park. He has proven time and again to be susceptible to the big curve and almost always swings at the first pitch.

His 21 home runs in 1986 was Garvey's best power production since he hit 26 for the Dodgers in 1980, but he hit only eight of those in the Padres' final 98 games. Because he still bats in the middle of the order, he will occasionally see the fastball with basestealing runners aboard and he can hit it out.

Last season it was obvious that, despite his objections, the 38-year-old first baseman no longer can be effective while playing every day. His slumps became longer and more pronounced.

BASERUNNING:

Though he doesn't possess great speed, Garvey is not a great liability on the basepaths. He probably could get away with taking more chances and under Larry Bowa, he probably will. Garvey is a heads-up player who isn't likely to get his team in trouble because of a baserunning blunder.

FIELDING:

In his early years Garvey's lame throwing arm didn't detract from the overall package. Now, though, he's also become practically stationary at first base and even his excellent glove cannot totally compensate for those

**STEVE GARVEY
1B, No. 6
RR, 5'10", 190 lbs.
ML Svc: 17 years
Born: 12-22-48 in
Tampa, FL**

1986 STATISTICS

AVG	G	AB	R	H	2B	3B	HR	RBI	BB	SO	SB
.255	155	557	58	142	22	0	21	81	23	72	1

CAREER STATISTICS

AVG	G	AB	R	H	2B	3B	HR	RBI	BB	SO	SB
.295	2305	8759	1138	2583	437	43	271	1299	478	993	83

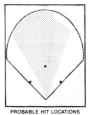

VS. RHP   VS. LHP   PROBABLE HIT LOCATIONS

two shortcomings.

Opponents always bunt toward Garvey because they know that in all but the most extreme circumstances he will not attempt a throw to any base but first. Garvey is a conservative player who always takes the sure out. Because of his severely limited range, the right side of the infield is opened up considerably when he's playing.

OVERALL:

The 17 years of wear and tear have had their effect on Garvey, but it's likely he still can be productive if placed in a platoon at first base. Because he has always prided himself on his durability, that may not sit well with him, but even Garvey should recognize the value of prolonging his career. As always, he remains a very dangerous hitter with the game on the line.

Dierker: "Garvey is still the kind of guy who will play hurt, get the big hits, make the big plays in the field and deliver a lot of leadership. He's the kind you like to have on a team."

SAN DIEGO PADRES

PITCHING:

Prior to the 1986 season, Goose Gossage's ERA had not been above 2.90 for nine consecutive years. But last season, while the Padres slid into the depths of the National League West, Gossage's concentration seemed to lag along with them. The big righthander suffered through the worst season of his otherwise illustrious career: he posted a 4.45 ERA, allowed 69 hits in 64 2/3 innings and saved only 21 games in 32 opportunities.

At age 35, Gossage can still throw a 92-93 MPH fastball with regularity. At this stage of his career, it is his regularity which can be his undoing; he so rarely deviates from his heater that batters have learned to sit back, time it, and get their share of hits. He also throws an excellent slider, and by his own admission his best seasons have been when he has mixed in his slider often enough to prevent hitters from sitting on the fastball. But Gossage did not do that last season and was beaten several times by batters who guessed fastball--and got one.

FIELDING, HITTING, BASERUNNING:

One of Gossage's greatest weaknesses is an almost nonexistent move to first base. He has never held runners on well because he concentrates more on pitching to the batter rather than on the runners on base. Last season, however, he was hit so hard that a good pickoff move might have prevented a lot more baserunners from advancing.

His delivery leaves him in such an awkward position that he's of little help defensively on the bunts and slow rollers.

Because he's been primarily a stopper, Gossage rarely gets a chance to hit. He's capable of putting down a bunt, but is never called upon to do so.

OVERALL:

Last season, Gossage's running feud with

RICH GOSSAGE
RHP, No. 54
RR, 6'3", 220 lbs.
ML Svc: 15 years
Born: 7-5-51 in
   Colorado Springs, CO

1986 STATISTICS

W	L	ERA	G	GS	CG	SV	IP	H	R	ER	BB	SO
5	7	4.45	45	0	0	21	64.2	69	36	32	20	63

CAREER STATISTICS

W	L	ERA	G	GS	CG	SV	IP	H	R	ER	BB	SO
101	89	2.81	725	37	16	278	1482.1	1196	531	463	592	1275

the Padres' front office reached a new low when he so incensed team president Ballard Smith that Smith slapped Gossage with a 20-day suspension for criticizing the club's policies. The bickering and resulting animosity undoubtedly contributed to Gossage's already-disturbing lack of rhythm.

This season, Gossage will be splitting time as the stopper with Lance McCullers. The arrangement may work to the Padres' advantage: a little competition for number one stopper honors just might be the incentive Goose needs to work hard even in games on which little is riding.

Last season, the Padres brought in Gossage to begin an inning clean; in retrospect, that probably was a mistake. Gossage, ever the aggressor and always the challenger, has been at his best when thrown directly into the pressure cooker.

Dierker: "Gossage did not appear as effective last season as he was in his prime and his days as a premier short reliever may be limited. He can still blow his fastball by hitters some of the time, but batters know it's coming and too many of them are timing him correctly. He needs to maintain his slider and to use it more frequently."

GOOD CLUTCH HITTER

HITTING:

If anyone could possibly pick a bone with the offense that Tony Gwynn delivered before last season, it was that he hadn't demonstrated enough power. In 1986, Gwynn added that dimension to his arsenal and solidified his position as one of the most productive hitters in baseball.

Prior to the season, Gwynn, who'd hit a total of 13 home runs in three previous big league seasons, said he wanted to try for 10 or more. He wound up with 14 to go with 59 RBIs, 107 runs scored and 37 stolen bases. In the Padres' lineup, he was not often asked to fill the power role, but that could change under new manager Larry Bowa.

Gwynn possesses the consummate work ethic, showing up practically every day of the season for extra batting practice. He has excellent eyesight and picks up the baseball more quickly than most hitters. His bat speed is astonishing and he guides the ball to all fields.

On top of it all, Gwynn has become one of the game's best 0-2 hitters. He stays with breaking pitches well. If he has had a fault at the plate, it is that he has been overeager and sometimes swings at bad pitches in an effort to make contact. Maturity is correcting that.

BASERUNNING:

Gwynn always had good speed, but never before used it effectively. He stole 33 bases in 1984, but that year the Padres had fleet Alan Wiggins batting ahead of him, often on base with him and creating openings for Gwynn to steal. Last year, given a perpetual "green light" from the manager, he did it all on his own. Gwynn's greatest contribution in that area, though, was probably his innate sense of when to try for the extra base on a hit. He was seldom wrong (witness 33 doubles and seven triples).

FIELDING:

The Gold Glove he received after last season was Gwynn's crowning achievement, for he said he's worked harder at improving his defense than at becoming a better hitter. He had a .989 fielding percentage and a

TONY GWYNN
RF, No. 19
LL, 5'11", 206 lbs.
ML Svc: 5 years
Born: 5-9-60 in
Los Angeles, CA

1986 STATISTICS

AVG	G	AB	R	H	2B	3B	HR	RBI	BB	SO	SB
.329	160	642	107	211	33	7	14	59	52	35	37

CAREER STATISTICS

AVG	G	AB	R	H	2B	3B	HR	RBI	BB	SO	SB
.326	612	2364	352	770	97	26	27	230	193	128	99

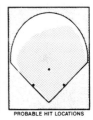

VS. RHP   VS. LHP   PROBABLE HIT LOCATIONS

personal-high 19 assists and threw out three New York Mets on the bases in one memorable game.

Gwynn covers right field completely, rarely misses the cutoff man, has a much-improved throwing arm and almost never misjudges a ball off the bat. The only place he can't seem to play is Candlestick Park, which bothers most fielders.

OVERALL:

Gwynn has developed into a complete player and one of the few whom Padres GM Jack McKeon wouldn't consider trading. Though he doesn't consider himself a leader, he has become one simply by virtue of his examples on the field. He will not be outworked and has an unflagging enthusiasm for the game. That he posted the numbers he did for a San Diego team that was so bad in 1986 is incredible.

Dierker: "He's just an outstanding hitter and a real tough problem for a pitcher because there's no way to pitch him. He could be more selective to get on base more. I expect him to do that because he is a smart ballplayer. I also expect him to hit with more power as he becomes more selective."

SAN DIEGO PADRES

PITCHING:

Just when he appeared poised to take his place among the better pitchers in baseball, Andy Hawkins suffered through a maddeningly inconsistent season in 1986. His 10-8 record was accomplished only by winning the last game of San Diego's season; prior to that, Hawkins hadn't had a decision in six weeks. It was a far cry from the 18-8 record and 3.15 ERA he posted in 1985.

At the root of his problems was the cut fastball, a pitch that is either Hawkins' greatest ally or his worst enemy. He abandoned the cut fastball several times during the year because he was having trouble throwing it for a strike--and he probably should have done without it more often.

Nonetheless, when Hawkins has the cut fastball working for him, he can shut down the opposition altogether. A big, strong overhand thrower, Hawkins possesses an above-average fastball, a decent change-up and an erratic slider.

Last season, Hawkins admitted that there were many outings when he was not really certain what he was trying to do on the mound; such lapses of concentration probably contributed as much as anything to his inconsistency.

FIELDING, HITTING, BASERUNNING:

Hawkins is extremely mobile for so tall a pitcher. He has developed a good move to first base and was rated by former Padres catcher Terry Kennedy as one of the best on the staff at holding the runners on base. His improved defensive skills helped him on several occasions last year.

Hawkins is not absolutely awful as a hitter;

ANDY HAWKINS
RHP, No. 40
RR, 6'3", 205 lbs.
ML Svc: 5 years
Born: 1-21-60 in Waco, TX

1986 STATISTICS

W	L	ERA	G	GS	CG	SV	IP	H	R	ER	BB	SO
10	8	4.30	37	35	3	0	209.1	218	111	100	75	117

CAREER STATISTICS

W	L	ERA	G	GS	CG	SV	IP	H	R	ER	BB	SO
43	37	3.80	142	119	15	0	767.1	762	372	324	287	347

he is just bad. He logged a .149 batting average last season, which does not reflect his six sacrifices. His best hitting attribute is that he knows how to bunt. Unfortunately, he sometimes gets careless and allows good bunting opportunities to pass.

OVERALL:

Hawkins is a prime candidate to learn the split-finger fastball, for he seems to be only one good "out" pitch away from achieving the success that was predicted for him after the 1985 season. A durable performer, he can be counted on to make all his starts. An added bonus is that some of Hawkins' best work since 1984 has been done out of the bullpen; he's an excellent long reliever.

Dierker: "Last year was a disappointment for Hawkins. He just didn't have the pinpoint control to succeed. When he made a mistake with his fastball, he was hit. He's going to have to improve the consistency on his breaking ball or the control on his fastball to get back to an 18-win season."

SAN DIEGO PADRES

PITCHING:

Undoubtedly, 1986 one of the most difficult years of LaMarr Hoyt's life and also his strangest season in baseball. Hoyt missed a month of spring training last season while undergoing drug rehabilitation and simply never found a groove afterward. Still bothered at the outset of the season by shoulder problems that hounded him toward the end of the 1985 season, he gave up nine runs in 3 1/3 innings in one start, and failed to throw a strike in the 13 pitches he lasted in another start.

Hoyt is a control pitcher who seems to have lost the trademark control that led him to the American League Cy Young Award in 1983. When right, Hoyt is strictly a finesse pitcher. He relies on a change-up, a big breaking ball and the occasional straight fastball to keep hitters guessing. The 68 walks he issued in 159 innings last season were a personal worst. Opposing hitters ravaged his hanging sliders, whacking 27 home runs in Hoyt's 35 games.

The off-season revelation that Hoyt has been suffering from a sleep disorder may explain some of his inability to pitch the way he used to. Without control, Hoyt is an average pitcher at best.

FIELDING, HITTING, BASERUNNING:

Hoyt is prone to wild fluctuations in his weight. When he is overweight, his mobility off the mound is greatly reduced and he is an ineffective fielder.

In general, however, he has a good glove and maintains an even keel. He rarely makes a throwing error or attempts a high-risk play that may backfire. He does not hold runners particularly well. Hoyt had six hits for the Padres last season, but recorded only three sacrifices. Like many of the San Diego pitchers, he failed to bunt in several critical situations.

OVERALL:

Hoyt has become such an unpredictable

LaMARR HOYT
RHP, No. 31
RR, 6'2", 244 lbs.
ML Svc: 7 years
Born: 1-1-55 in
Columbia, SC

1986 STATISTICS

W	L	ERA	G	GS	CG	SV	IP	H	R	ER	BB	SO
8	11	5.15	35	25	1	0	159	170	100	91	68	85

CAREER STATISTICS

W	L	ERA	G	GS	CG	SV	IP	H	R	ER	BB	SO
98	68	3.99	344	172	48	10	1311.1	1313	637	582	279	681

personality and ballplayer that it is impossible to predict what is to become of him in the 1987 season. Last year, while he was still on probation for a drug smuggling conviction, he was caught for the second time attempting to bring drugs across the Mexican border into the United States. Sentenced to a 45-day prison term for this offense, Hoyt is scheduled to be released just as spring training begins this year.

In a dramatic courtroom scene last December, it was revealed that Hoyt has been suffering from a sleep disorder which some analysts have claimed has distorted his sense of judgment and rational thought to the extent that his behavior has been downright stupid. He has spent more time in the past year fighting personal demons off the field than opposing hitters on it. Undoubtedly, he can be a great pitcher when all of the elements fall together, but his state of mind must be his primary concern now. He must regain his control and stay healthy if he is to ever again win 16 games, as he did for the Padres in 1985.

Dierker: "Hoyt always had good control until last season. It seems as though he's lost control of everything. If that's the case, it might be all over for him. However, he's still young enough that if he can get past his legal problems and get his life in shape, he could come back and be a good pitcher."

SAN DIEGO PADRES

HITTING:

In 1986, the Padres looked to an unproven rookie, Leon "Bip" Roberts, to provide the speed and disruptiveness the team was seeking at the top of the batting order. Roberts' inexperience showed and he was ineffective. Now San Diego will ask another rookie, Stanley Jefferson, to shoulder that burden. Jefferson, one of the players included in the eight-man trade that sent Kevin McReynolds to the New York Mets, has played a total of 14 major league games. Nonetheless, Padres manager Larry Bowa has indicated that, barring some collapse, Jefferson will be the team's leadoff batter and the starting center fielder.

Though Jefferson batted over .300 only once in his four minor league seasons, he demonstrated the capability to get on base. Despite playing in only 95 games with Tidewater in 1986 because of a hamstring pull, he collected 107 hits (19 of them doubles) and drew 41 walks. He also stole 25 bases.

A switch-hitter, Jefferson appears to be stronger from the right side. He is regarded as a disciplined, line drive hitter whose safeties find the outfield alleys. Good work in the Puerto Rican league over the winter may have helped prepare him for the majors, although the quality of competition there was rated as somewhere between Double- and Triple-A.

BASERUNNING:

The Padres probably value Jefferson more for his ability to stretch a single into a double than for his ability to steal bases. Jefferson appears able to do both. He stole a personal-best 45 bases for Lynchburg in 1984, then led the Texas League with 39 steals for Jackson in 1985. He collected 60 doubles and 19 triples in his last three minor league seasons.

FIELDING:

Jefferson's strength in the outfield clearly is his range. His quick feet allow him to get a good jump and run down baseballs that otherwise would fall into the gaps. He'll be

STANLEY JEFFERSON
CF, No. 13
SR, 5'11", 175 lbs.
ML Svc: less than one year
Born: 12-4-62 in
New York, NY

1986 STATISTICS

AVG	G	AB	R	H	2B	3B	HR	RBI	BB	SO	SB
.208	14	24	6	8	1	0	1	3	2	8	0

CAREER STATISTICS

AVG	G	AB	R	H	2B	3B	HR	RBI	BB	SO	SB
.208	14	24	6	8	1	0	1	3	2	8	0

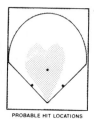

VS. RHP   VS. LHP   PROBABLE HIT LOCATIONS

especially effective working the right-center field lanes with Tony Gwynn. His glove is adequate, his throwing arm slightly above average.

OVERALL:

The Padres are placing Jefferson in a difficult spot, asking him not only to take over for McReynolds in center field but to bat leadoff and return some threat to the top of the order. However, he won't be alone. San Diego will be starting several younger players in 1987, so perhaps Jefferson won't be affected by the burdensome task assigned him.

In order to survive a rookie year in which he'll be asked to stand in against righthanders and lefties alike, Jefferson must increase still his selectiveness at the plate. Already regarded as disciplined, he will need to be even more so. As part of the Padres' youth movement, he'll be given time to progress, and that may take some of the pressure off him.

SAN DIEGO PADRES

HITTING:

It should have come as no surprise that John Kruk batted .309 in his first year in the major leagues: he has been able to hit at every professional level. Kruk's slashing, see-the-ball/hit-the-ball style was nearly as effective on the big league stage as it had been in the Pacific Coast League, where his .351 average was tops in 1985.

Kruk belted his way onto the Padres' roster by hitting .465 in spring training last year. Despite his susceptibility to breaking pitches--particularly from lefthanders--he did a good job of maintaining his consistency throughout the season. His average wasn't below .300 the entire second half.

Kruk's sweet spot is the outside part of the plate. Each of his four home runs was hit to the opposite field and when he made out, it was usually when trying to handle a tight inside pitch. His free and loose swing allows him to hit the ball to all parts of the field.

With his excellent natural stroke and ability to focus on the ball, Kruk would seem a candidate for the 200-hit club. But he logged only 278 at-bats in 1986 and it remains to be seen how he'll fare in a 550- or 600-at-bat rigor.

A bonus: he drew 45 walks despite limited plate action.

BASERUNNING:

Kruk's weight is a problem for him as a baserunner. He's carrying perhaps 15 pounds more than he should and it slows him down. He's currently not much of a threat to steal or even to take the occasional extra base, but he was fast enough to log 16 doubles in his 86 hits last season.

FIELDING:

Kruk played in left field most of last season but it's clear the Padres would prefer for him to split time at first base with Steve Garvey. To that end, Kruk went to winter baseball with the goal of becoming a better first baseman.

JOHN KRUK
OF, No. 44
LL, 5'10", 170 lbs.
ML Svc: 1 year
Born: 2-9-61 in
  Charleston, WV

1986 STATISTICS

AVG	G	AB	R	H	2B	3B	HR	RBI	BB	SO	SB
.309	122	278	33	86	16	2	4	38	45	58	2

CAREER STATISTICS

AVG	G	AB	R	H	2B	3B	HR	RBI	BB	SO	SB
.309	122	278	33	86	16	2	4	38	45	58	2

  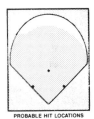

VS. RHP   VS. LHP   PROBABLE HIT LOCATIONS

He doesn't have great range, but he fields cleanly what he reaches. He's not an embarrassment in the field, but he could hardly be considered an asset; his strength is at the plate.

OVERALL:

For Kruk to break through and become an everyday player, he will have to work harder and lose some weight. New manager Larry Bowa is likely to help in those departments. Kruk is an immensely talented hitter, though he will have to become more of an RBI producer if he is to play first base regularly. He has a surprising amount of power, and should capitalize on that.

Dierker: "Kruk is just a good all-around hitter. His only liability offensively is that he is not very fast. But if he plays first base, his average speed will not hinder him defensively."

SAN DIEGO PADRES

PITCHING:

If Dave LaPoint proved anything in 1986, it was that he is of little value as a relief pitcher. Used out of the bullpen both by the Detroit Tigers and, after a July trade, the San Diego Padres, LaPoint was absolutely ineffective. He had a 5.72 ERA for the Tigers and a 4.26 mark for the Padres, while making a combined 28 relief appearances and only 12 starts.

LaPoint is the classic junkballer, a southpaw overhand thrower who tempts hitters with an excellent change-up and a decent slider. He doesn't have much zip on his fastball, however, and that's bad news for a reliever being asked to put out fires instead of starting fresh and working the hitters around a bit.

He has a tendency to be wild high in the strike zone and must control his slider to avoid getting pounded. LaPoint is a smart pitcher who knows how to bob and weave around danger, but suffered greatly from erratic and infrequent use and clearly was out of his element trying to work from the bullpen.

FIELDING, HITTING, BASERUNNING:

Quick off the mound, LaPoint made only one fielding error in 1986, and helped turn one double play to get himself out of a jam. Still, he is not as smooth a fielder as one would like.

From his years in the St. Louis system, he has learned how to bunt and last season put down four sacrifices. He could have been

**DAVE LaPOINT
LHP, No. 40
LL, 6'3", 215 lbs.
ML Svc: 5 years
Born: 7-29-59 in
Glens Falls, NY**

1986 STATISTICS

W	L	ERA	G	GS	CG	SV	IP	H	R	ER	BB	SO
4	10	5.02	40	12	0	0	129	152	86	72	56	77

CAREER STATISTICS

W	L	ERA	G	GS	CG	SV	IP	H	R	ER	BB	SO
46	49	3.97	191	131	5	1	898.2	962	453	396	358	532

useful as a bunting instructor for the rest of the Padres' inept bunch of bunters.

OVERALL:

Where LaPoint will play is anybody's guess, as the Padres cut him loose over the winter in favor of younger, less expensive talent. His history shows that he can thrive as a regular in a starting rotation. He had three straight winning seasons as a starter for the Cardinals from 1982-84. Bringing him out of the bullpen, however, is a mistake.

Dierker: "LaPoint has an outstanding change-up, but doesn't have the great fastball that would complement it. He has to have good control to be successful. Over his career, however, he has been unable to maintain that control game after game."

SAN DIEGO PADRES

PITCHING:

As one of the few consistently reliable relievers on the Padres' staff last year, Craig Lefferts received more bullpen calls than in any of his three previous major league campaigns. Unfortunately, it took its toll. Lefferts appeared in more than half the Padres' games but he wearied down the stretch. His ERA shot up more than a point (from 2.05 to 3.09) from August 1st to the season's end.

Generally regarded as one of the best screwball pitchers in the majors, Lefferts uses that weapon more often than all his other pitches combined. His fastball, slider and off-speed pitches are only fair, but if the screwball is working, he hardly needs to throw anything else.

Lefferts made the jump from obscurity to the spotlight with 10 innings of scoreless relief in 1984 post-season play, then ballooned to a 3.35 ERA in 1985--hardly spectacular for a middle reliever. With last season's performance, he seemed to reinforce the idea that he at least knows how to get batters out, although it was obvious that too much work will render him ineffective toward the end of the season.

Lefferts' value to the Padres lies in his devastating effect on lefthanded hitters. The screwball also acts as a kind of back-door slider against righties.

FIELDING, HITTING, BASERUNNING:

Lefferts was perfect as a fielder last year, making good on all 27 chances and turning three double plays. He squares around as he comes off the mound, which helps him to be prepared to field most shots that come his way.

CRAIG LEFFERTS
LHP, No. 37
LL, 6'1", 196 lbs.
ML Svc: 4 years
Born: 9-29-57 in
Munich, West Germany

1986 STATISTICS

W	L	ERA	G	GS	CG	SV	IP	H	R	ER	BB	SO
9	8	3.09	83	0	0	4	107.2	98	41	37	44	72

CAREER STATISTICS

W	L	ERA	G	GS	CG	SV	IP	H	R	ER	BB	SO
22	22	2.89	261	5	0	17	385.2	341	139	124	127	236

Though he had only eight at-bats, and just one hit, it was a memorable one: a solo home run that won a game in the 10th inning.

OVERALL:

The Padres couldn't be blamed for being a little apprehensive about Lefferts after his disappointing season in 1985, but he showed that he is a capable reliever. As long as his screwball is live, he'll get batters out. But the lesson was learned: Lefferts should be used in around 60 games, as he was in 1984, rather than 75 or 80; his arm simply can't withstand the strain of throwing the scroogie so often.

Dierker: "Sometimes Lefferts shows a good fastball and when he does he is doubly tough. He needs to have his screwball working well. When he doesn't, he battles the hitter, but really just hangs in there to stay even because the other pitches aren't good enough to get by on their own.

"He is a good guy to have on the staff because he throws strikes. He always goes out there and gives the hitter a good battle one way or the other."

SAN DIEGO PADRES

HITTING:

After two years as the Padres' starting left fielder, Carmelo Martinez played himself out of the job in 1986 with his shoddy defensive work overshadowing his capability at the plate. As a result, he was used sporadically and unpredictably, and his numbers suffered accordingly.

Martinez has outstanding power potential, as demonstrated by the 21 homers he hit in 1985. He'll hit a high fastball out of the park and has learned patience at the plate (35 walks in 244 at-bats in 1986). But he needs to play every day to work out of slumps and last year he was unable to do that.

After stumbling along at the start of the season because of a bad knee (which was compounded by the 15 extra pounds he carried), Martinez never found a groove and was benched before he had a chance to right himself. He struck out often and was little help as a pinch-hitter (8-for-36, .222).

Martinez is the type of overswinger who needs to get his hacks every day. When he was forced into a part-time role, he nearly faded out of the picture altogether.

BASERUNNING:

Martinez's weight problem prevents him from being anything but a liability on the bases. His frame is not so big that he is naturally slow, but the excess baggage is too much to carry. He is aboutely no threat to steal.

FIELDING:

The kindest thing that can be said of his work in left field is that Martinez is a natural first baseman. He played at first base every year of his baseball career until 1984, when the Padres converted him to the outfield.

Strange as it sounds, he seems to have regressed at that position and has convinced himself that he simply cannot play left field. His fielding was atrocious last year and he

CARMELO MARTINEZ
OF, No. 14
RR, 6'2", 210 lbs.
ML Svc: 4 years
Born: 7-28-60 in Dorado, PR

1986 STATISTICS

AVG	G	AB	R	H	2B	3B	HR	RBI	BB	SO	SB
.238	113	244	28	58	10	0	9	25	35	46	1

CAREER STATISTICS

AVG	G	AB	R	H	2B	3B	HR	RBI	BB	SO	SB
.249	442	1335	164	333	69	3	49	179	194	229	2

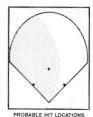

VS. RHP   VS. LHP   PROBABLE HIT LOCATIONS

missed the cutoff man with his throws so often that a trip to the bench was inevitable.

OVERALL:

Martinez can be an offensive force if he is allowed to play first base every day. Since the Padres already have Steve Garvey and John Kruk at first, that is unlikely. In 1984 and 1985, Martinez's offensive contributions outweighed his defensive liabilities. Given a 162-game playing schedule, it's a good bet he can return to that form.

Dierker: "Martinez wasn't used very much and he was in the doghouse with the Padres in '86. Still, he's a guy who is young and has a lot of talent. He's another guy who would be better off at first base because of his speed. But the Southern California teams have a glut of first basemen and a shortage of purebred outfielders."

PITCHING:

When he burst onto the scene for the Padres at the end of the 1985 season, Lance McCullers was given the nickname "Baby Goose" because his temperament, attitude and fastball all bear resemblance to teammate Rich Gossage's in his prime. Last season, McCullers did nothing to dispel that notion, and in fact established himself as Gossage's peer and likely successor as the late-inning stopper.

A hard-throwing righthander whose delivery is somewhere between sidearm and overhand, McCullers can blaze a fastball at 90 to 95 MPH a la Gossage. But he goes beyond Gossage in his ability to drop a breaking pitch or a change-up right into the strike zone. Only in Gossage's best years did he possess a slider similar to McCullers'.

His numbers were deceptively high, as the Padres were forced to insert McCullers in the starting rotation for two separate stints during the season. In the relief role, for which he is so well suited mentally, McCullers was 9-6 with five saves and a 2.13 ERA.

Like Gossage, McCullers loves to challenge the hitters and even in his first full major league season performed without intimidation or awe. He has the tremendous ego and sense of infallibility that most good firemen carry with them to the mound.

FIELDING, HITTING, BASERUNNING:

Without question, McCullers has the best pickoff move on the Padres staff. He holds runners extremely well and as a result yields few stolen bases. Though quick off the mound, his glove is still a little unpredictable and he left a few balls on the ground last

LANCE McCULLERS
RHP, No. 41
SR, 6'1", 185 lbs.
ML Svc: 1 year plus
Born: 3-8-64 in
Tampa, FL

1986 STATISTICS

W	L	ERA	G	GS	CG	SV	IP	H	R	ER	BB	SO
10	10	2.78	70	7	0	5	136	103	46	42	58	92

CAREER STATISTICS

W	L	ERA	G	GS	CG	SV	IP	H	R	ER	BB	SO
10	12	2.68	91	7	0	10	171	126	61	51	74	119

season.

As a hitter, McCullers is a dismal free-swinger, but he can bunt and laid down a couple of drag bunts for hits last season. He also has value offensively as a pinch-runner. He had two doubles, stole a base and scored four runs in 1986.

OVERALL:

McCullers appears destined for greatness, assuming he is allowed to perform solely in the role of stopper. At the age of 23, he's still a little immature as indicated by times when he will try to challenge a hitter when finesse is called for. He needs the voices of experience from the infielders around him in such situations.

Dierker: "Because he throws so hard, he needs occasional time off to stay fresh. But he certainly appears to be the heir apparent to Gossage and is a gem any club would love to have. McCullers goes right after the hitters with confidence and determination."

SAN DIEGO PADRES

HITTING:

Though he burst onto the scene last season and performed well enough to make the Padres confident enough to trade away Terry Kennedy, the fact remains that Benito Santiago is an unproven commodity in the major leagues. Nowhere is this more clearly demonstrated than at the plate, yet his talent is such that it may only be a question of time before he overcomes that liability.

Santiago batted .287 at Class AAA in Las Vegas last year, with 17 home runs in 117 games. He was a pleasant surprise upon being called up at the end of the season, recording a .290 average in 17 games for the Padres. He even showed he had a little pop in his bat, clubbing three home runs.

Santiago often swung wildly or flailed desperately at pitches that were well out of the strike zone and was overwhelmed by many of the big league pitchers he faced. At age 21, he's still a very undisciplined hitter and Manager Larry Bowa has cautioned that Santiago is green and may not hit particularly well in his first season in the majors. But he shows great promise and already can make a pitcher pay for a mistake.

BASERUNNING:

Santiago has good speed for a catcher and stole 19 bases in 26 tries at Las Vegas. Though he probably won't be called on for that talent very often, he can get from first to third on a single and seems to know what he can and cannot attempt on the paths.

FIELDING:

It was Santiago's defense that earned him the most accolades after he was called up last September. He has range, motion and flexibility similar to Tony Pena's and can throw to first or second from a crouch. He picked off a runner at second base in one of his major league starts.

Santiago's ability to call a game remains to be seen, as does how well he communicates with the members of his pitching staff. He has had trouble fielding pitches above his mask,

BENITO SANTIAGO
C, No. 10
RR, 6'1", 180 lbs.
ML Svc: less than one year
Born: 3-9-65 in
Ponce, PR

1986 STATISTICS

AVG	G	AB	R	H	2B	3B	HR	RBI	BB	SO	SB
.290	17	62	10	18	2	0	3	6	2	12	0

CAREER STATISTICS

AVG	G	AB	R	H	2B	3B	HR	RBI	BB	SO	SB
.290	17	62	10	18	2	0	3	6	2	12	0

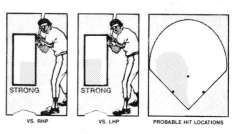

VS. RHP   VS. LHP   PROBABLE HIT LOCATIONS

appearing to momentarily lose sight of the ball. He's also still very unpolished. Overall, however, the Padres can expect to be a drastically improved defensive team with him behind the plate.

OVERALL:

Patience is probably the key here. Santiago didn't play more than one season at any level in the minor leagues and is a good bet to succeed similarly in the majors. But it won't happen overnight. The Padres have done him a huge favor by making it clear he's the No. 1 catcher; if he can learn such professional skills as laying off the big breaking pitch and accepting a walk, he will make a significant contribution.

Dierker: "Santiago looks like a real good talent, but he has a long, long way to go as a catcher. There were times when his mechanics were poor and his arm was erratic, though fairly strong. He looks like the kind of guy who has the raw talent to be a real good hitter."

SAN DIEGO PADRES

PITCHING:

In the midst of his best season as a professional ballplayer, Eric Show was shocked to discover that the pain in his right elbow was tendinitis. Not only was it the first injury he'd ever suffered, it marked the first time that Show had ever missed a scheduled start at *any* level of professional baseball.

Late last August, after retiring all seven batters he had faced, Show was removed from a game against the Mets. He did not pitch for the rest of the season. Since the Padres were already languishing in last place, his loss did not have the effect it might have in some other, more successful, year for the club. The big question now is whether the extended rest has healed Show's elbow.

Show is a hard thrower. He has a good curveball and a decent change-up, but both are set up by a fastball that gets to the plate more quickly than many batters expect it to. The tendinitis reduced Show's fastball to merely average, which makes his success last season all the more remarkable. Essentially, he was getting batters out strictly with off-speed stuff.

That is not his game. For Show to be consistently successful, he must return to the power pitching that has brought him 62 victories in five seasons.

FIELDING, HITTING, BASERUNNING:

Show is one of the best all-around athletes the Padres have, a surehanded fielder who makes the smart defensive plays and never takes unnecessary gambles. He hustles after the slow rollers, backs up well and holds runners effectively.

ERIC SHOW
RHP, No. 30
RR, 6'1", 175 lbs.
ML Svc: 6 years
Born: 5-19-56 in
Riverside, CA

1986 STATISTICS

W	L	ERA	G	GS	CG	SV	IP	H	R	ER	BB	SO
9	5	2.97	24	22	2	0	136.1	109	47	45	69	94

CAREER STATISTICS

W	L	ERA	G	GS	CG	SV	IP	H	R	ER	BB	SO
62	46	3.30	188	136	16	6	949.2	831	385	348	375	569

As a hitter, he'll never be confused with Tony Gwynn. But Show did have two doubles and scored two runs. He's fast enough on the basepaths not to be a liability.

OVERALL:

Detractors accuse Show, a highly intelligent person, of thinking too much on the mound. But he only gets in trouble when he thinks too little and lets his fastball tail high in the strike zone. When healthy, he's almost always good for seven strong innings.

One caveat: he too often allows himself to be bothered by little annoyances and sometimes lets a Texas Leaguer or bloop hit break his concentration.

Dierker: "Show is very uncompromising. He won't come in and throw the ball down the middle no matter what, in any situation, to any hitter. Sometimes I think if he were just a little more of a challenger he could be more successful. If his arm problems are behind him, I expect him to continue to win."

SAN DIEGO PADRES

HITTING:

In former manager Steve Boros' ever-changing lineup, Garry Templeton was constantly shifting positions in the batting order last season. For a free and undisciplined swinger like Templeton, it was a contributing factor to a poor year.

His batting average dipped 35 points from his 1985 number and 40 points below his career average. Templeton also was down in runs, RBIs, stolen bases and walks. He said he had trouble maintaining a high level of concentration, for reasons he couldn't fully explain. He often appeared lackadaisical, even careless at the plate.

Though always a talented hitter, Templeton is notoriously wild with the bat and often swings at pitches that are certifiably over his head or in the dirt. He's an opposite-field hitter and accomplishes that by swinging behind the pitch rather than waiting for outside offerings. As a result, he looks worse than most when he swings and misses.

BASERUNNING:

He still possesses good speed, but Templeton didn't run much in 1986. Part of that was that he batted eighth much of the season and thus didn't get many chances. He can score from second on a single, but his effectiveness may depend on the health of his chronically bad left knee.

FIELDING:

Templeton may have the strongest throwing arm of any shortstop in the league. That hard release allows him to take an instant longer than most fielders before throwing. He has excellent anticipation and can make difficult plays look routine because he reaches the ball so quickly.

His bad knee and the occasional stiff back that it produces can combine to limit his range and Templeton may not be as good as he

GARRY TEMPLETON
SS, No. 1
SR, 6'0", 192 lbs.
ML Svc: 11 years
Born: 3-24-56 in
Lockey, TX

1986 STATISTICS

AVG	G	AB	R	H	2B	3B	HR	RBI	BB	SO	SB
.247	147	510	42	126	21	2	2	44	35	86	10

CAREER STATISTICS

AVG	G	AB	R	H	2B	3B	HR	RBI	BB	SO	SB
.284	1423	5562	703	1578	240	86	44	519	256	774	215

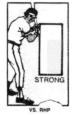  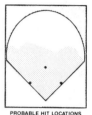

VS. RHP   VS. LHP   PROBABLE HIT LOCATIONS

once was at going after the pop fly in the shallow outfield.

OVERALL:

His best years may be behind him, but Templeton still is capable of being a productive player. He is most comfortable offensively when left in the same spot in the batting order, but even that won't cure his free-swinging habit. Even after 10 major league seasons, he needs discipline. He also needs an occasional rest--three or four games on artificial surface must be punctuated by a day off.

Dierker: "He's a wild swinger and won't take many walks, which is a shame because he has the speed to really do something if he could get on base a little more often. His average dropped off last year, but I expect it to pick up again--he's not that old."

SAN DIEGO PADRES

PITCHING:

A downhill slide that began almost as soon as he signed as a free agent with the New York Yankees two years ago continued for Ed Whitson in 1986 even after he was traded back to the Padres, the team for whom he enjoyed his greatest success (14-8, 3.24 ERA in 1984).

Whether or not the physical tools have left him remains unknown, for Whitson was such a head case after his year-and-a-half-long nightmare in New York that he never appeared to have the concentration to pitch at all last year. He had a 7.54 ERA in his time with the Yankees and a 5.59 mark in 17 appearances for the Padres.

Whitson has an average fastball and an average slider. What made the 1984 season special was a palmball that he employed for the first time back then. He hasn't been able to throw the pitch consistently enough to be of any help the past two seasons, however, and it's anybody's guess whether he can regain control of it.

Whitson's best work for the Padres came out of the bullpen, where he allowed only two earned runs in 12 innings. As a starter in 1986, he didn't seem to have any idea of what he was trying to do.

FIELDING, HITTING, BASERUNNING:

Whitson is an adequate fielder whose only downfall is a tendency to overrun slow rollers in his haste to get to them. He has a good move to first base, though he's not always as cognizant of the runner as he should be.

ED WHITSON
RHP, No. 38
RR, 6'3", 195 lbs.
ML Svc: 9 years
Born: 5-19-55 in
Johnson City, TN

1986 STATISTICS

W	L	ERA	G	GS	CG	SV	IP	H	R	ER	BB	SO
6	9	6.23	31	16	0	0	112.2	139	85	78	60	73

CAREER STATISTICS

W	L	ERA	G	GS	CG	SV	IP	H	R	ER	BB	SO
69	73	3.98	304	189	16	8	1295.2	1335	642	573	477	723

He is a mediocre batter. Worse, he is an awful bunter, a common problem among Padres pitchers. Whitson muffed several bunt opportunities last season.

OVERALL:

Whitson's destination is unknown. The Padres obviously hope that a fresh start and a full season back in San Diego will help him regain the form he showed in 1984. But his reliance on the palmball indicates that Whitson wants to trick the hitters rather than throw the ball past them, so the palmball has to be perfect for him to be successful.

Dierker: "He's a guy who once had all the pitches and was a starting pitcher who, when he had his good control, won. He hasn't had it for a couple of years and I don't know if he ever will again."

SAN DIEGO PADRES

BRUCE BOCHY
C, No. 15
RR, 6'4", 229 lbs.
ML Svc: 8 years
Born: 4-16-55 in
**   Landes de Boussac,**
**   France**

HITTING, BASERUNNING, FIELDING:

Slow afoot with so-so defensive skills, Bruce Bochy has used his brawn and his brain to establish himself as one of the best backup catchers in the game. Though he had only 127 at-bats last season, Bochy clubbed eight home runs--a power ratio that ranked third in the National League--and two of the homers came in pinch at-bats to win games.

As a pinch-hitter, Bochy was 7-for-20 (.350) with six RBIs. All eight of his home runs came off lefthanded pitchers; since 1984, 14 of his 17 homers have been off lefties. He is a dead-fastball hitter with enormous power; a steady diet of breaking pitches is advised to get him out.

Bochy is dreadfully slow and opposing infielders often dive for balls they wouldn't normally try for because they know they'll still have time to recover and throw him out. But he is rarely called upon to run well.

Defensively, Bochy is an average fielder. His strength lies in his ability to call a good game and his excellent rapport with the pitching staff. Most of the Padres pitchers love working with him.

OVERALL:

Bochy is a priceless addition to a team, an easygoing, well-liked player who can keep a clubhouse loose even in the worst of times. He is the consummate team player fully accepting of his role as a backup and will be counted on heavily to work with rookie catcher Benito Santiago, who will start ahead of him. He is ready to play every day.

Dierker: "Bochy is an outstanding backup catcher. He's very slow and perhaps not as mobile behind the plate as some, but he will catch the ball, block the plate and has a strong arm, with an average-to-below-average delivery. He's shown the ability to deliver some big hits coming off the bench."

JIMMY JONES
RHP, No. 45
RR, 6'2", 175 lbs.
ML Svc: less than one year
Born: 4-20-64 in
**   Dallas, TX**

PITCHING, FIELDING,
HITTING, BASERUNNING:

The Padres' No. 1 draft pick in 1982 (ahead of Dwight Gooden), Jimmy Jones was expected to reach the major leagues sooner than last season. But a rash of injuries, including shoulder, ankle and knee problems held him back. Finally, at the end of last season, Jones got his first call to the major leagues and responded with a one-hit, no-walk effort in his very first start. He's now tentatively penciled in as a member of the Padres' starting rotation.

Jones always had an excellent fastball but needed to add other pitches to get to the big leagues. Under the tutelage of Jack Lamabe, he's developed a good curveball and a slider: decent enough for him to get by.

As a fielder, he's quick off the mound and a heady pitcher who showed great poise in the three starts he made with the Padres. His batting skills are rudimentary, but he learned how to bunt while playing for Larry Bowa in Las Vegas in 1986.

OVERALL:

Still only 22 years old, Jones may yet become a mainstay of the Padres' staff. The biggest concern is that he stay healthy, though of his three minor league injuries only one related to his pitching arm. The current thinking among the Padres brass is to give Jones a year's worth of major league starts and see how he holds up.

SAN DIEGO PADRES

KEVIN MITCHELL
INF/OF, No. 35
RR, 5'11", 210 lbs.
ML Svc: 1 year plus
Born: 1-13-62 in
San Diego, CA

HITTING, BASERUNNING, FIELDING:

Kevin Mitchell cooled off considerably after a hot start in 1986. He was a leading candidate for the National League's *Rookie of the Year* honors until he went into a late-summer swoon that saw him bat .219 with eight home runs and 23 RBIs in 196 at bats after July 20.

Mitchell was another heat-seeking bat in the Mets' fastball-oriented order. He loves the ball up and out over the plate. He impresses observers with his ability to hit the curveball, but last year he was murdered by pitchers who hammered him with outside stuff.

A strong pull hitter, he must learn to go to the opposite field if he is to last in the majors and must learn to hit righthanders, against whom he batted .234 last season.

Mitchell has decent speed for a big man and is aggressive on the basepaths, but is not a real threat to steal.

In spite of the fact that he played at six positions, fielding is Mitchell's major flaw. Last season, he started 26 games in left field, 21 in right field, 6 in center field, 20 at shortstop, 3 at third base and 1 at first base. He doesn't play any one position exceptionally well. His glove and arm are adequate, however, and with more schooling, he could develop as a third baseman.

OVERALL:

Rooker "In the first season of the 24-man roster, Mitchell was a manager's dream. He started at six positions, but played mostly in the outfield after proving error-prone at both shortstop and third base. He's a very tough kid."

GRAIG NETTLES
3B, No. 9
LR, 6'0", 189 lbs.
ML Svc: 20 years
Born: 8-20-44 in
San Diego, CA

HITTING, BASERUNNING, FIELDING:

Though his value to a major league team has decreased dramatically, Graig Nettles is still a threat to hit the ball out of the park in any given at-bat. Unfortunately, his occasional home runs occur at the end of prolonged slumps and form part of a too-high strikeout-to-home run ratio.

Nettles was not offered a contract for 1987 from the Padres for a variety of reasons. He no longer has the range to be an effective third baseman, and subsequently, he winds up diving for (and missing) balls that he used to get on the run. He will surprise and delight the crowd by occasionally turning a sparkling defensive play, but these are few and far between.

Nettles is the ultimate streak hitter, whose only saving grace at this point is his excellent batting eye and his ability to draw a walk. He's got a good chance to reach base because of that, but the possibility of hitting into a double play or a straight whiff has become more of a probability than ever before.

A dead-fastball hitter, he cannot get around on the tremendous heaters the way he used to and can be fooled with a breaking pitch.

OVERALL:

Dierker: "Graig can still make a great play, but his is also letting some balls get by that probably wouldn't have eluded him a couple of years ago. He is on the down side of his career. He doesn't have the kind of consistency that you would like to see in a regular third baseman."

SAN DIEGO PADRES

LEON ROBERTS
INF, No. 2
SR, 5'7", 160 lbs.
ML Svc: 1 year
Born: 10-27-63 in
Berkeley, CA

HITTING, BASERUNNING, FIELDING:

Desperately searching for a player to bat leadoff and add some speed to the top of their order, the Padres rushed Leon "Bip" Roberts from Double-A to the major leagues in 1986. Unfortunately, Roberts wasn't ready for the transition, and he paid the price for the Padres' haste: an 0-for-20 slump to begin the season. Roberts never fully recovered.

Roberts is a small, compact player whose best game is to put the ball in play and hope to beat the throw to first. But the Padres found out that although he is fast, he is not particularly quick-footed; he couldn't get out of the box efficiently enough to beat out many hits.

His inexperience showed in his inability to hit the curveball. The switch-hitting Roberts also needs to learn how to bunt--mastery of this dying art could greatly enhance his value.

Roberts suffered from platooning with the lefthanded-hitting Tim Flannery: Roberts is a weaker hitter from the right side, yet that is the way he was forced to bat for most of the season. He batted .320 as a lefthanded hitter and only .203 from the right side.

Roberts' fielding skills are adequate, his arm decent and his pivot on the double play is good. His lack of height can be a disadvantage on the tantalizing loopers to shallow right field.

OVERALL:

Roberts needs to spend time in Triple-A. He has the physical tools to stick in the big leagues, but must get his confidence back after being brutalized by the top-level pitching he encountered.

MARVELL WYNNE
OF, No. 36
LL, 5'11", 176 lbs.
ML Svc: 4 years
Born: 12-17-59 in
Chicago, IL

HITTING, BASERUNNING, FIELDING:

Marvell Wynne was a perfect addition to the Padres in 1986, though it's uncertain how he'll fit into the club's drastically altered roster this season. San Diego acquired Wynne at a time when it needed a late-inning defensive replacement, someone who could hit and someone who could run.

Of those attributes, Wynne's defense clearly was the greater. He demonstrated great range in center field, a sure hand even on the difficult balls, and a throwing arm that was more than adequate. He was used often in his intended capacity, but gradually forced his way into the starting-lineup.

It was then that his weaknesses began to show. Wynne tired as the summer wore on and it became apparent that he cannot play effectively every day. He had surprising power (7 homers) but his average tailed off late in the season.

Wynne, though fast, can be a liability on the bases because he doesn't run intelligently. He got caught in a couple of senseless rundowns and was thrown out a few times trying unreasonably to stretch a hit.

OVERALL:

Wynne was a great role-player for the Padres last year and should be able to continue to contribute in that capacity. To use him in any other format would be a mistake.

Dierker: "Wynne looks like a good fourth outfielder or defensive replacement, but probably would be below average as a starting center fielder. He has speed, but is not a blinding basestealing kind of runner. He will steal some, but he'll get thrown out, too."

PATENT HITTER

HITTING:

Catcher Bob Brenly recovered from a slump-ridden 1985 season to become a more disciplined hitter last year. His patience at the plate did not go unnoticed by the Giants; Brenly has now become a valuable asset to the ballclub and integral to their plans for 1987.

In addition to supplying much needed power for the club, Brenly has fine-tuned his eye and is not afraid to get on base via a walk. In 1986, he ranked ninth in the National League with a career high of 74 bases on balls. Early in the season, however, Brenly was too willing to accept a walk and did so often; though he was getting on base, he was also cutting off his power supply. But he came on strong in the final month in terms of power (7 HRs & 19 RBIs in September) to finish with respectable stats.

The best way to minimize Brenly's power is to keep the ball down low in the strike zone and to change speeds. The strides that he has made in developing a good idea of the strike zone will make it tough now for pitchers to expect to get him out if they make bad pitches. He will hit mistakes a long way.

He prefers high pitches and has become primarily a pull hitter after hitting more straightaway in the past.

BASERUNNING:

Brenly is among the better-baserunning catchers in the major leagues. While that is not saying much, it certainly fits in well with manager Roger Craig's philosophy of emphasizing good baserunning execution.

FIELDING:

The club disguised Brenly's defensive flaws last year by having the Giants' pitchers become more responsible for holding baserunners at first base. Consequently, he nailed 36% of the runners as compared with 27% in 1985.

His league-leading .995 fielding percentage offers statistical proof that Brenly has greatly improved as a catcher. As a backstop, he made only three errors all season last year, although he did allow 10 passed balls.

Brenly has become more of a take-charge

BOB BRENLY
C, No. 15
RR, 6'2", 200 lbs.
ML Svc: 5 years
Born: 2-25-54 in
** Coshocton, OH**

1986 STATISTICS

AVG	G	AB	R	H	2B	3B	HR	RBI	BB	SO	SB
.246	149	472	60	116	26	0	16	62	74	97	10

CAREER STATISTICS

AVG	G	AB	R	H	2B	3B	HR	RBI	BB	SO	SB
.254	615	1924	242	489	88	5	67	251	24	289	33

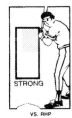  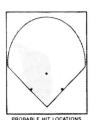

STRONG   STRONG   PROBABLE HIT LOCATIONS

VS. RHP   VS. LHP

guy with the pitching staff, but his mechanics still leave him second-best defensively to teammate Bob Melvin.

Largely because of his footspeed, Brenly can also be used at third base and in the outfield. At third base last season, he made four errors in one inning.

OVERALL:

Despite the defensive rap and a low batting average, Brenly remains among Craig's favorites because of his hustle and attitude. The veteran is a gamer who gives 110% and really cares whether the club wins or loses.

Nevertheless, the fact remains that teammate Bob Melvin would be doing a lot more catching if he were nearly as productive at the plate as Brenly is.

Dierker: "He can hurt you offensively, but he can hurt his team defensively, too. He had a respectable year in 1986 as a catcher, but is not good enough to be rock-solid reliable behind the plate. The Giants will continue to complement Brenly with Bob Melvin, though Melvin could wrestle the job from him in time."

SAN FRANCISCO GIANTS

CHRIS BROWN
3B, No. 35
RR, 6'2", 210 lbs.
ML Svc: 2 years
Born: 8-15-61 in
Jackson, MS

HITTING:

As his .317 average in an injury-plagued (what's new?) season suggests, Chris Brown is a promising hitter who can handle most pitches. He hit for a high average for the first time in 1986 and has flashed power and RBI potential in each of his two major league seasons.

An excellent pull hitter, Brown is an exceptionally good fastball hitter, but also makes good contact with off-speed and breaking stuff. The opposition can can bunch the infielders toward the left side of the field because Brown will seldom hit the other way. Still, he has the strength to hit the ball hard through a pulled around infield and is definitely a hitter who figures to get better, especially if he can remain healthy over an entire season.

Brown is an extremely proficient clutch hitter, batting .358 with runners in scoring position and .371 with men in scoring position and two out during his major league career.

Insofar as Brown has developed a nasty reputation for being a player who wants to sit on the bench for what many consider to be non-benchable types of injuries, it is surprising to note that he is unflinching at the plate as pitches head right for him; Brown has been hit by a pitch 20 times in two years.

BASERUNNING:

For a man so big, he's as surprising on the bases as he is afield: he is quick more than he is fast. The good jump he gets helped him on his way to 13 stolen bases in 1986.

FIELDING:

Brown's 10 errors and a .971 fielding percentage topped the National League in his rookie campaign of 1985, but he slipped badly in the second half of last year and finished with 18 errors and a .933 mark.

No one in the National League played the third baseman's position better than Brown did during the first half of last season. But a shoulder injury contributed to his second-half slippage.

He has above-average range, a strong and

1986 STATISTICS

AVG	G	AB	R	H	2B	3B	HR	RBI	BB	SO	SB
.317	116	416	57	132	16	3	7	49	33	43	13

CAREER STATISTICS

AVG	G	AB	R	H	2B	3B	HR	RBI	BB	SO	SB
.293	270	932	113	273	43	6	24	121	80	140	17

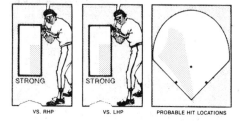

VS. RHP   VS. LHP   PROBABLE HIT LOCATIONS

accurate arm and great instincts for playing the position.

OVERALL:

It seems that Chris Brown can be about as good as he wants to be. His desire has been questioned, and many eyebrows were raised quickly last year when he left the lineup September 1st with tendinitis in his left shoulder. X-rays taken at the time were negative, which only served to fuel the ire of critics who call him a malingerer. Yet a more extensive examination at the conclusion of the season did reveal a tear, which was corrected by November surgery.

Despite rumors to the contrary, the Giants think enough of his future to render him a fixture at third base. If he stays healthy, look out. During the first half of last year, Brown's .338 average and fielding prowess earned him All-Star honors.

Dierker: "Brown is a player with unlimited talents as a third baseman, but he has had injury problems throughout his career. Until he can have a full season, it's hard to say that he can ever reach star status."

STRONG ARM

HITTING:

While there were some complaints about Will Clark's lack of offensive pop (11 homers, 41 RBIs) during his rookie campaign last year, the Giants knew what they were getting. Clark will probably never be a big home run hitter, but he has alley power and the ability to hit in the clutch. There are indications, however, that Clark will be a high-average hitter, a guy more suited to batting third in the lineup as opposed to the fourth or fifth spot.

He struck out pretty often last season, but that's not uncommon for a youngster learning the pitchers who are new to him. His .287 average pleased the Giants' brass, especially in consideration of his rapid jump to the majors after only 65 games at the Class-A level and that he had to bounce back after missing 47 games with a hyperextended left elbow.

Clark is a potential .300 hitter who has the eye to hit nearly 20 home runs in a season.

BASERUNNING:

Clark seemed like a reasonably smart baserunner last season and his intelligence compensated for his lack of great speed. Prior to his elbow injury, he was among the league leaders in runs scored. Clearly, he knows how to get around on the bases.

FIELDING:

Clark is a defensive asset to the Giants. Although he made his share of errors last year, his aggressive style of play did not hurt his overall defense.

His strength is a strong and accurate arm. He enjoys throwing the ball and charges bunts and fires the ball with accuracy to second or third base. He has a lot of confidence in his arm. And justifiably so.

WILL CLARK
1B, No. 22
LL, 6'1", 185 lbs.
ML Svc: one year
Born: 3-13-64 in
New Orleans, LA

1986 STATISTICS

AVG	G	AB	R	H	2B	3B	HR	RBI	BB	SO	SB
.287	111	408	66	117	27	2	11	41	34	76	4

CAREER STATISTICS

AVG	G	AB	R	H	2B	3B	HR	RBI	BB	SO	SB
.287	111	408	66	117	27	2	11	41	34	76	4

  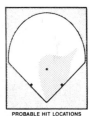

VS. RHP   VS. LHP   PROBABLE HIT LOCATIONS

OVERALL:

Clark is a jewel of a player whose rookie season justified the front office's decision to give him the starting first baseman's job during spring training of 1986. He has demonstrated a penchant for the dramatic and was nicknamed "Will the Thrill" after hitting a home run off Astros fireballer Nolan Ryan on his first major league swing. He also homered in his Candlestick Park debut.

Clark showed his toughness by batting .310 in 64 games after coming off the disabled list. He batted .315 against lefthanders and was a favorite of the San Francisco fans by hitting .336 at Candlestick.

Dierker: "Will has shown that he's a real talent. Defensively, he's one of the best first basemen to come into the league since Keith Hernandez and he looks like he can handle the bat. Clark is a real key to the Giants' future."

SAN FRANCISCO GIANTS

HITTING:

Chili Davis endured a schizophrenic 1986 season. It makes you wonder which of the two Chilis will show up in spring training this year. At the time of the All-Star break last year, Davis had hit nine home runs and had 55 RBIs, but only managed to hit four home runs and to drive in 15 thereafter. Part of Davis' RBI dropoff in the second half of the season can be attributed to the absence of power-hitting teammate Jeffrey Leonard's bat in the lineup.

When things didn't go well for Davis last season, he brooded. His dissatisfaction led him to express an interest in securing a trade.

Hard stuff inside gives him the most trouble and he has difficulty getting out of slumps because he allows himself to fall into mental slumps as well.

Davis is not a good switch-hitter. He used to be much tougher from the right side, enough so to consider abandoning switch-hitting. But he's worked hard to overcome that flaw, so now he's a much more dangerous southpaw swinger, and last year, he hit .302 as a lefthanded batter and .226 righthanded.

Davis became a more disciplined hitter last season; this was especially evident in the second half of the season when Jeffrey Leonard was out of the lineup and Davis was not getting good pitches to hit. Nonetheless, Davis managed to lead the Giants with 84 walks. When Chili's hot, he's as good as they come, but his hitting needs to develop more consistency.

BASERUNNING:

Leg problems have slowed him down and as a result, Davis is not as effective on the bases as he should be. Last season, he was caught stealing 13 times. He doesn't take advantage of all his ability on the basepaths, and as he has dropped lower in the batting order, he has concentrated more fully on power-hitting and less on basestealing.

FIELDING:

Davis is a good outfielder because he has

CHILI DAVIS
RF, No. 30
SR, 6'3", 195 lbs.
ML Svc: 5 years
Born: 1-17-60 in
  Kingston, Jamaica

1986 STATISTICS

AVG	G	AB	R	H	2B	3B	HR	RBI	BB	SO	SB
.278	153	526	71	146	28	3	13	70	84	96	16

CAREER STATISTICS

AVG	G	AB	R	H	2B	3B	HR	RBI	BB	SO	SB
.270	725	2648	352	715	122	19	77	342	289	469	79

  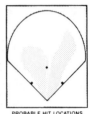

VS. RHP   VS. LHP   PROBABLE HIT LOCATIONS

good hands and makes the plays but he tends to have lapses in concentration.

Excellent defense at any of the outfield positions in the unsavory climate conditions of Candlestick Park would be difficult for even the most outstanding outfielder. For any player of average ability, such as Chili Davis, error-free defense is virtually impossible. Last season, Davis led National League outfielders in errors with nine.

OVERALL:

It is no secret that the Giants have been shopping Chili around in an attempt to accomodate his desire to be traded. But, they are not about to give him away for a song.

To Davis' credit, he played all last season with a shoulder injury that required post-season surgery. He could be the leadoff hitter the club is looking for. His .375 on-base percentage ranked eighth in the league in 1986.

Dierker: "Chili is a good all-around player who is just short of superstar status in that he's not really a 100-RBI man or a 100-runs-scored type of ballplayer. He will hit for a good batting average, will knock in 80 runs or so and make most of the defensive plays he needs to."

SAN FRANCISCO GIANTS

PITCHING:

Mark Davis remains somewhat of an enigma because he continues to lose despite having some of the best stuff in the National League.

Davis is a big strikeout pitcher and last year fanned 90 hitters in 84 1/3 innings, a very impressive ratio. He is devastating against lefthanded batters who hit just .115 against him last season and .185 in 1985.

Davis uses a wicked breaking ball. It is sort of a half-curve, half-slider type of a breaking pitch--and he throws it very hard. His fastball is above average (in the 90+ range) and his control of his heater is quite decent. His control of the strike zone, however, is a different matter, and he often makes one key misplacement that gets him into a heap of trouble.

Over the winter of 1986-87, he worked to perfect the split-finger fastball in the Arizona Instructional League.

He is going to get a lot of consideration as a possible starter for this season as the staff has been depleted by the loss of Vida Blue and the potential loss of Atlee Hammaker. Roger Craig apparently feels that Davis has the tools to blossom into a big winner.

There are a lot of clubs who like what they see in this pitcher and it was *this* Davis--and not Chili--who was the most requested Giants player during trade discussions over the winter.

FIELDING, HITTING, BASERUNNING:

Somehow, Davis went errorless in 1985, but it caught up with him last year. He made three errors in just 17 chances last season. He is especially bad at charging bunts and throwing. Astute hitters who can place a pretty bunt can take advantage of this hole in his game.

A fine athlete, Davis runs well but it hardly matters because he is such a terrible hitter. Last year, he managed only one hit and struck out four times in eight at-bats.

**MARK DAVIS
LHP, No. 13
LL, 6'4", 205 lbs.
ML Svc: 4 years
Born: 10-19-60 in
Livermore, CA**

1986 STATISTICS

W	L	ERA	G	GS	CG	SV	IP	H	R	ER	BB	SO
5	7	2.99	67	2	0	4	84.1	63	33	28	34	90

CAREER STATISTICS

W	L	ERA	G	GS	CG	SV	IP	H	R	ER	BB	SO
21	44	4.36	221	60	3	11	534.1	499	285	259	208	462

OVERALL:

The Giants'consideration of putting Davis in the starting rotation is a gamble. Last season, he was just beginning to get the hang of being the southpaw stopper in the bullpen.

Davis' biggest problem in the past has been not making the best use of his overwhelming stuff; he finds a way to lose. His mental toughness has come under scrutiny and even he admits that he is concerned with his inability to bear down and come in for the kill under pressure. Davis has become better in this regard, but it may not be enough to suit Roger Craig, who doesn't want to hear about a bullpen stopper choking. Davis' overall makeup may be better-suited to starting, yet the last time he did it (1984), he was a 17-game loser. It'll be interesting to see what develops.

Dierker: "Davis has the tendency to make that fat pitch over the middle of the plate, have it hit out of the park and ruin a performance that looked to be otherwise dominating.

"He needs to mature as a pitcher, to dodge some of the tougher hitters and to go after the easier ones to avoid those self-destructive mistakes. If he can do that, he can be an outstanding starter or reliever, though I see him more as a reliever."

SAN FRANCISCO GIANTS

PITCHING:

Kelly Downs could surprise almost everyone in baseball this season except manager Roger Craig. If all goes as planned, Downs will be in the starting rotation on Opening Day 1987.

Downs was recalled from the Giants' Triple-A club in Phoenix late last year and to the more astute and keen observers of the game, pitched outstandingly and received little notoriety. He was off to a 0-4 start with the Giants and many simply turned the other way at what appeared to be the record of a September minor leaguer with a losing ballclub.

But Downs was impressive and proved his mettle as he rounded the clubhouse turn with a 4-0 record made even more attractive by his 1.81 ERA over his last eight starts (he ended the season with a none-too-shabby 2.75 ERA).

In fact, even in his losses, Downs pitched well. He was victimized by a lack of support, getting only 24 runs while he still was in the game in his 14 starts. Downs does not have particularly great pitches, but he pitches with the maturity and poise which keeps everything moving and low in the strike zone. He is definitely more of a pitcher than a thrower and that is a compliment it takes many pitchers years to earn.

Downs' fastball approaches 90 MPH. He also throws a solid breaking ball and is (of course) learning the nuances of the split-finger fastball.

Manager Roger Craig believes that this young pitcher has the poise to help him pitch his way through rough spots and expects big things from him.

KELLY DOWNS
RHP, No. 37
RR, 6'4", 200 lbs.
ML Svc: less than one year
Born: 10-25-60 in
Ogden, UT

1986 STATISTICS

W	L	ERA	G	GS	CG	SV	IP	H	R	ER	BB	SO
4	4	2.75	14	14	1	0	88.1	78	29	27	30	64

CAREER STATISTICS

W	L	ERA	G	GS	CG	SV	IP	H	R	ER	BB	SO
4	4	2.75	14	14	1	0	88.1	78	29	27	30	64

FIELDING, HITTING, BASERUNNING:

Downs looked to be an able fielder and a capable hitter for a pitcher. In his limited major league at-bats, he placed the bat on the ball sufficiently well enough to belt five singles. Downs needs work on his bunting. He runs the bases well.

OVERALL:

Even more so than Jeff Robinson, Downs is the sleeper of the Giants' staff this year. Because he came on late, he was basically overlooked in the club's 1986 success, but Craig took notice of the consistent quality of his work.

Over the past four minor league seasons, Downs posted a horrendous record of 27-50 and justifiably considered quitting baseball out of frustration. But he seems to have made a breakthrough and it just might be a case of better late than never.

90+ FASTBALL

PITCHING:

Like teammate Mark Davis, Scott Garrelts has been shuttled back and forth between the starting rotation and the bullpen. He appears, however, to have finally found his niche as the club's ace reliever. But beyond that, he looks as though he could become one of the best stoppers in the league.

Garrelts has an above-average fastball which most often comes in at the 90-94 MPH range. He also throws a good breaking pitch that bends down through the strike zone more than it moves away from the hitter.

Last season, he did his best to comply with Roger Craig's split-finger fastball fetish, but Garrelts was not able to throw it well enough to get batters to fall for its break. His fastball and his breaking pitches are so good, however, that he really doesn't need the split-finger pitch in order to be effective.

Garrelts is a tough-guy competitor who seems to thrive in tough situations, but tends to get careless when things look easy.

FIELDING, HITTING, BASERUNNING:

Hurrying his throws and making bad ones as a result is the weakest part of Garrelts' defense. He has improved in this regard, however, and last year, made only two errors in 48 chances.

His hitting continues to improve and he made huge strides in the bunting department last year and hit seven successful sacrifice bunts in 1986. He also got a thrill when he hit his first major league home run last season. He is still a pitcher and not a hitter, of course, but at least the element of potential power is there.

SCOTT GARRELTS
RHP, No. 50
RR, 6'4", 195 lbs.
ML 3 years
Born: 10-30-61 in Urbana, IL

1986 STATISTICS

W	L	ERA	G	GS	CG	SV	IP	H	R	ER	BB	SO
13	9	3.11	53	18	2	10	173.2	144	65	60	74	125

CAREER STATISTICS

W	L	ERA	G	GS	CG	SV	IP	H	R	ER	BB	SO
26	20	3.17	154	26	3	23	360	301	149	127	187	283

His baserunning is not a strength.

OVERALL:

The Giants have undoubtedly learned, once and for all, that Scotty is better suited to bullpen work. He had his bright moments as a starter in the early part of 1986, but was much more effective when he returned full-time to the bullpen. He was 5-7 with a 3.53 ERA as a starter, for instance, but blossomed to 8-2 with a 2.29 ERA and 10 saves on his rescue missions.

Dierker: "One of the more promising developments in Garrelts is the emergence of that 'killer instinct' which is so important for a short reliever. If he can maintain that attitude, it would serve him well.

"All signs point to his becoming one of the best in the business. He is just a real talent who seems to get better every year. I expect him to be a real workhorse on the San Francisco staff in 1987."

SAN FRANCISCO GIANTS

HITTING:

Dan Gladden is still trying to find his niche as a major league hitter. His success has been erratic over the past three seasons. When he first appeared in the majors, up from Triple-A in 1984, he hit a robust .351. Greatness was predicted. It hasn't happened yet.

Following a slumping 1985 season, Gladden bounced back with respectable stats last year, yet hasn't quite filled the bill as the leadoff batter the club desperately needs. Still, his presence was missed when he left the lineup with torn ligaments in his right thumb in early June. He was sidelined afterwards for 46 games.

Gladden is a streaky hitter but provides a spark for the Giants' lineup when he is hot. He has tried a lot of things in an attempt to make more contact, including hitting with big-handled bats, choking up, trying to pull and attempting to hit the other way. Nothing has helped him recapture the magic of his 1984 season.

To his credit, however, Gladden has managed to overcome the delusions of power grandeur he suffered from in 1985.

BASERUNNING:

Gladden's excellent baserunning is one of his strengths. Despite missing 60 games over the course of the 1986 season, he once again led the club in stolen bases with 27. When he's in a basestealing groove, as he was at the start of last season, Gladden makes things happen on the basepaths and makes the Giants' offense go. If he were more of an ideal leadoff hitter who reached base more often, 50 steals wouldn't be out of the question because the speed is there.

FIELDING:

Gladden's arm is merely average, which isn't unusual among center fielders, but he really takes off like a demon on anything hit in or near his territory and he shows no fear of the outfield walls.

His speed helps to provide him with above-average range and he gets to a tremendous amount of balls.

He is, however, prone to lapses in

DAN GLADDEN
CF, No. 32
RR, 5'11", 180 lbs.
ML Svc: 4 years
Born: 7-7-57 in
San Jose, CA

1986 STATISTICS

AVG	G	AB	R	H	2B	3B	HR	RBI	BB	SO	SB
.276	102	351	55	97	16	1	4	29	39	59	27

CAREER STATISTICS

AVG	G	AB	R	H	2B	3B	HR	RBI	BB	SO	SB
.281	348	1258	196	353	50	11	16	110	117	185	94

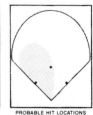

VS. RHP   VS. LHP   PROBABLE HIT LOCATIONS

concentration and sometimes will show poor judgment after making the catch. Candlestick Park is a tough park for any outfielder, and as a result, his fundamental mistakes can make a bad situation worse.

OVERALL:

The Giants were lulled into a false sense of security by Gladden's sensational big league debut. The bottom line is that he isn't selective enough (39 walks, 59 strikeouts last year) to be an ideal leadoff batter. He is also too much of a streak hitter and hurts the offense deeply when he's in a slump. If the Giants are able to come up with a more suitable leadoff hitter, Gladden will likely sit on the bench.

Dierker: "He's got the speed to steal bases and make things happen on the bases, but last year was on and off for him in that regard.

"If the Giants are going to be contenders, they're going to need him out there in center field most of the time, and they're going to need him getting on base. He has the physical skills to do it but he has to put everything together."

MOST IMPROVED

PITCHING:

This plucky righthander finally put it all together last season to shed his ".500-pitcher" reputation. Mike Krukow became the Giants' first 20-game winner since 1973.

Krukow throws an outstanding curveball and a good fastball which comes in at the 88-90 MPH range. He has developed a split-finger fastball and the addition of that to his arsenal might have been what got him over the hump of his past.

He spots his fastball well and can make it sink as it reaches the batter. He also can run it in to a lefthanded batter. Krukow is able to change speeds off his curveball and the resulting deception has been a very sneaky and effective tool for him.

In a nutshell, Krukow has finally become a complete pitcher who uses power, finesse and an assortment of pitches to get the job done. His ability to get the key games to go his way was evident last season as he was the only NL pitcher to blow off the World Champion Mets all four times he faced them.

FIELDING, HITTING, BASERUNNING:

In the past, Krukow's high leg kick has made it difficult for him to effectively hold runners on base. He improved last season and appeared better able to concentrate on the batter and keep an eye on the runners simultaneously.

As a hitter, he is above-average for a pitcher and helped himself by driving in eight runs in 1986. He laid down 12 successful sacrifice bunts last season. He is a pitcher from the old school who prides himself on his work ethic and makes an effort to be

MIKE KRUKOW
RHP, No. 39
RR, 6'4", 205 lbs.
ML Svc: 10 years
Born: 1-21-52 in
Long Beach, CA

1986 STATISTICS

W	L	ERA	G	GS	CG	SV	IP	H	R	ER	BB	SO
20	9	3.05	34	34	10	0	245	204	90	83	55	178

CAREER STATISTICS

W	L	ERA	G	GS	CG	SV	IP	H	R	ER	BB	SO
108	104	3084	311	299	37	1	1859.1	1858	900	794	672	1281

proficient in baseball skills other than pitching.

OVERALL:

Krukow led the pitching staff last year not only in statistics, but by his example as well. He sustained a midseason rib injury in a brawl with the Cardinals which threatened his bid for 20 wins, but he pitched in pain and finished tough.

He developed good work habits under the influence of Steve Carlton when they were Phillies teammates. Krukow comes to the game extremely well prepared and has a game plan for each starting assignment.

Dierker: "Mike kept the club in virtually every game in which he pitched last season, and there's no reason to expect a dropoff. He had the type of year a lot of people were expecting from him for a long time.

"I believe that the confidence he showed last year will give him the opportunity to have another good year if he stays healthy."

SAN FRANCISCO GIANTS

PITCHING:

Mike LaCoss had two dramatic seasons last year. In the first half of 1986, he looked as though he could really help the Giants in their pennant drive and at the time of the All-Star break had produced a 9-3 record and a 2.76 ERA. Immediately thereafter, however, his numbers fell flat. He was only able to win one game for the remainder of the season and his ERA for the rest of the year shot up to 4.91 as he notched ten additional losses.

His second-half downward spiral coincided with the vacation taken by the Giants' offensive production, causing the San Francisco club to fall out of orbit. In complete fairness, however, LaCoss pitched in tough luck more than any other pitcher on the staff. Nine of his 13 losses were by one run and two were by a pair of runs.

LaCoss is a fastball/forkball/curveball pitcher who can be successful when he gets them all over the plate. When he first entered the major leagues, he showed a good sinker, but he has not been able to get it breaking in the strike zone for several seasons. He must now rely on spotting his fastball in order to be effective. He lost the control of his fastball in the second half of last year, so his decline was inevitable.

FIELDING, HITTING, BASERUNNING:

LaCoss fields his position well and made just one error in 54 chances last season.

For what it is worth, he put together his best offensive season in 1986 and hit .230, drove in nine runs and belted his first two major league home runs on successive at-

MIKE LaCOSS
RHP, No. 29
RR, 6'4", 200 lbs.
ML Svc: 9 years
Born: 5-30-56 in
Glendale, CA

1986 STATISTICS

W	L	ERA	G	GS	CG	SV	IP	H	R	ER	BB	SO
10	13	3.57	37	31	4	0	204.1	179	99	81	70	86

CAREER STATISTICS

W	L	ERA	G	GS	CG	SV	IP	H	R	ER	BB	SO
61	67	4.09	281	163	21	6	1179.1	1224	614	536	487	487

bats. He is a gangly athlete and not a good baserunner.

OVERALL:

LaCoss' good first half was an unexpected bonus for the Giants last year. He was not even expected to make the club past spring training.

The Giants have a lot of young pitchers on the major league staff as well as in the system, making it doubtful that LaCoss will figure prominently in the 1987 rotation.

Dierker: "LaCoss' second-half slump last year makes it hard to justify a continuing set role. If he is with the club in 1987, he would be most effective as a jack-of-all-trades.

"He has had trouble sticking in the big leagues for the last two or three years and it is possible he has already squeezed out his last season."

SAN FRANCISCO GIANTS

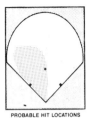

HITTING:

Jeffrey Leonard is a good, hard-nosed competitor who can handle a lot of different types of pitches. He is an aggressive hitter who would rather take his hacks than walk.

He likes the ball down and in, and has successfully become a long-ball threat in spite of the fact that he began his major league career with the expectations of being strictly a hitter for average.

When Leonard is hitting well, the Giants prosper. Last season, Leonard was clicking offensively during the first half of the season and the club was in first place. During that time, he was putting up MVP-type numbers.

A wrist injury suffered in late May began to take its toll by robbing Leonard of his power, but he continued to gut it out in spite of the pain. Finally, when he no longer was productive, the Giants placed him on the disabled list and he underwent wrist surgery in early August. He also had arthroscopic surgery on his left shoulder in mid-September. In spite of the fact that both the 1985 and 1986 seasons have been marred by injury for Leonard, he is expected to bounce back as good as new this year.

BASERUNNING:

Manager Roger Craig regards him as the best all-around baserunner on the club: Leonard's 16 steals in 19 attempts last year attest to his heady baserunning. He's at his best going for the extra base and can really fly with his long strides. If healthy, Leonard has the speed to steal 30 bases and the power to hit 30 home runs in a season.

FIELDING:

Because of his troublesome wrist last season, it would not have been evident to a first-time Giants observer that Leonard is the club's most dependable outfielder. But he is.

If he were healthy over the course of a full season, he would likely rank among the outfield assists leaders--such is the strength and accuracy of his arm. His speed is more than good enough to enable him to take over in center field should the club accomodate Chili Davis and/or if Candy Maldonado is placed in right field.

JEFFREY LEONARD
LF, No. 20
RR, 6'3", 200 lbs.
ML Svc: 9 years
Born: 9-22-55 in
** Philadelphia, PA**

1986 STATISTICS

AVG	G	AB	R	H	2B	3B	HR	RBI	BB	SO	SB
.279	89	341	48	95	11	3	6	42	20	62	16

CAREER STATISTICS

AVG	G	AB	R	H	2B	3B	HR	RBI	BB	SO	SB
.273	862	2964	379	808	127	31	81	428	228	628	120

STRONG   STRONG

VS. RHP   VS. LHP   PROBABLE HIT LOCATIONS

OVERALL:

Leonard is the key man to the San Francisco offensive attack. As evidenced last season, the team's hitting can go into a tailspin without him in the lineup. Although as things turned out, Leonard's absence gave rise to Candy Maldonado's development as an extraordinary pinch-hitter last year; in that respect, Leonard's injury was a blessing in disguise for the Giants. But Leonard offers leadership and more all-around ability than any other team member and was sorely missed. He had a .322 average and 31 RBIs through May, and the Giants were operating on all cylinders.

Dierker: "Leonard's loss was the biggest reason for the club's slide from first place to third in 1986 and the Giants' management is fully aware of it. He has the potential for greatness if he stays healthy.

"He is above-average as a left fielder in this league and his moody demeanor disguises a gamer who is respected for his ability between the lines.

"He doesn't walk much anymore, but that's the only negative aspect of his hitting."

SAN FRANCISCO GIANTS

HITTING:

Candy Maldonado really came on last year with the Giants after what turned out to be a great trade with the Dodgers. In the early part of the season, Maldonado's pinch-hitting feats were making headlines and surprising almost everyone but himself.

When the power-hitting Giants' outfielder Jeffrey Leonard went on the disabled list last year, Maldonado finally got his wish to play everyday. He continued to produce RBIs and proved that he could be the type of productive hitter he was as a Dodgers minor leaguer. Vindication was a long time in coming for Maldonado, and on the heels of his 1986 season, it is going to be difficult to keep him out of the lineup this year.

Maldonado hits the ball all over the field and does it with plenty of power. Like Leonard, he doesn't get cheated at the plate. He hates to walk and did not hit for a high average (.252) last year, but he was a tough out nevertheless.

He hangs back and waits well on curveballs and change-ups and is obviously tough on fastballs.

BASERUNNING:

He is a big, strong athlete who does not run the bases particularly well. Maldonado definitely fits into the power-hitters mold on the basepaths, and as such, is not expected to steal many bases.

FIELDING:

Maldonado's greatest defensive strength is his rocket arm. His firepower accounted for a club-high of 10 assists from the outfield in only 101 games there.

His speed is at the very best average, and his range is proportional. He doesn't chase down everything, but his arm can make up somewhat for lack of outfield quickness. He is probably never going to be a good overall defensive player, and at some point in his career will have to consider a role as a DH in the American League.

OVERALL:

The Dodgers gave up on Maldonado, but

CANDY MALDONADO
OF/PH, No. 29
RR, 5'11", 195 lbs.
ML Svc: 4 years
Born: 9-5-60 in
Humacao, Puerto Rico

1986 STATISTICS

AVG	G	AB	R	H	2B	3B	HR	RBI	BB	SO	SB
.252	133	405	49	102	31	3	18	85	20	77	4

CAREER STATISTICS

AVG	G	AB	R	H	2B	3B	HR	RBI	BB	SO	SB
.243	429	950	99	231	53	5	29	138	64	167	5

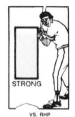

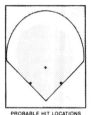

VS. RHP   VS. LHP   PROBABLE HIT LOCATIONS

he exacted sweet revenge on their misjudging him last season. He drove home his point by knocking in seven runs and powering two home runs in the season finale in Los Angeles.

Maldonado did not sashay into San Francisco already scripted by Roger Craig as a secret weapon; Candy had to prove himself to his new manager. Craig wanted him used strictly off the bench in the early part of the season and Maldonado gave him a hard time about it. Craig was steadfast, citing Maldonado's 17 pinch-hits (which set a club record) and his four pinch-homers (which tied another).

But Maldonado was able to produce as a regular player as well, ranking among the league leaders with 85 RBIs and belting a team-leading 18 home runs in only 405 at-bats. There is probably truth to both sides of this coin: Maldonado set his sights last season to make his point and accomplished his mission. He is going to have to maintain that level of desire and concentration over the full course of the 1987 season if he is going to produce the kind of numbers the Giants now want from him.

SAN FRANCISCO GIANTS

HITTING:

Bob Melvin's first full season in the big leagues produced a less-than-acceptable .224 batting average and less power than you would expect from a man of his size. His offensive failures make it difficult for the Giants to make him their everyday catcher.

He has a big, sweeping swing and was susceptible to breaking stuff and outside pitches last year. He needs to shorten his swing and make it a little more compact. He appears to have the hand-eye coordination to make enough contact and the strength to be able to hit the ball hard enough to be a good hitter.

Melvin is a straightaway hitter who has alley power, making him more of a doubles threat than a guy who'll knock it out of the park.

BASERUNNING:

He is a lumbering-type of runner because of his large size, and is simply a typical catcher running the bases. He lags far behind teammate and fellow catcher Bob Brenly as far as his ability to steal a base or take the extra base.

FIELDING:

Melvin's defensive skills are his strengths and instigated manager Roger Craig's desire to pry him from the Tigers' system two seasons ago.

Melvin gets rid of the ball quickly, is accurate with his throws and has a strong arm. He handles pitchers well from a leadership standpoint and his mechanics are sound.

Last season, he threw out 36% of the baserunners who attempted to steal on him. He was charged with only two passed balls as compared with 10 for Brenly, though Melvin made twice as many errors (6) behind the plate.

OVERALL:

Pure and simple, Melvin is going to have to

BOB MELVIN
C, No. 18
RR, 6'4", 205 lbs.
ML Svc: 2 years
Born: 10-21-61 in Palo Alto, CA

1986 STATISTICS

AVG	G	AB	R	H	2B	3B	HR	RBI	BB	SO	SB
.224	89	268	24	60	14	2	5	25	15	69	3

CAREER STATISTICS

AVG	G	AB	R	H	2B	3B	HR	RBI	BB	SO	SB
.223	130	350	34	78	18	3	5	29	18	90	3

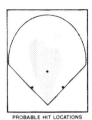

VS. RHP   VS. LHP   PROBABLE HIT LOCATIONS

become a better hitter to oust Bob Brenly from the role of starting catcher. Craig gave him every opportunity last year, but Melvin wasn't an aggressive hitter and was atrocious against righthanded pitchers, batting just .170 against them. Consequently, he'll see most of his action when southpaws are throwing because he hit them well (.311) last season.

When Melvin was with the Tigers, he played in ironman Lance Parrish's shadow. He was regarded as an outstanding prospect, but increased exposure to major league righthanders has not helped to develop the hitting skills necessary to take advantage of his fine defensive skills.

Dierker: "If Bob can shorten his swing and become a better hitter, he will really be an asset to the Giants. He needs to become hungrier at the plate. A stint in the Arizona Instructional League last fall may have ironed out some flaws. He is young enough to improve, though he needs to do so this season."

SAN FRANCISCO GIANTS

GREG MINTON
RHP, No. 38
SR, 6'2", 190 lbs.
ML Svc: 9 years
Born: 7-29-51 in
Lubbock, TX

PITCHING:

Greg Minton is on the downhill side of what has been a great career. The "Moon Man" lost his status as the main man in the Giants' bullpen long ago, and now is attempting to salvage something out of his dwindling reputation.

In his better years, he sported a nasty little sinker that hitters could only beat into the ground. Now, however, he is more of a curveball pitcher because he can't get the sinker to do what it's supposed to do most of the time.

So many borderline pitchers are looking at the success the Astros' Mike Scott has enjoyed because of the split-finger fastball that its mastery has become a coveted goal. Minton can't be blamed for looking to that pitch, but it doesn't appear to be his answer.

He is now more of a middle-inning relief pitcher. And while that may have hurt his pride, it has done no damage to his wallet.

FIELDING, HITTING, BASERUNNING:

Minton's ample belly gets in the way of his mobility as a fielder, but he is a good athlete who is better at the game than his out-of-shape appearance would indicate.

He doesn't get cheated at the plate and likes to take a big cut and hope the ball hits the bat. And with a .400 batting average (2-for-5) who's to say he should open his eyes at the plate now?

OVERALL:

Minton has been coming to camp with a

1986 STATISTICS

W	L	ERA	G	GS	CG	SV	IP	H	R	ER	BB	SO
4	4	3.93	48	0	0	5	68.2	63	35	30	34	34

CAREER STATISTICS

W	L	ERA	G	GS	CG	SV	IP	H	R	ER	BB	SO
44	52	3.22	537	7	0	124	847.1	827	352	303	366	343

new gimmick every spring, hoping to revive a sagging career. Last season, he put himself on an exotic diet which shed pounds and restored his strength. In fact, when Garrelts was made a starter, Minton reassumed the short relief role and did well at the beginning of the season. But then his recurring weight problem dragged him down.

It has reached the point in San Francisco where Minton is a fallen idol. The fans boo him at Candlestick Park, showing their understandable frustration as a fat paycheck produces meager results.

Dierker: "Minton is not able to pitch consistently well for any sustained period of time. He may even have trouble as a middle reliever now.

"He used to be one of the game's best pitchers, but that is just a memory now."

90+ FASTBALL

PITCHING:

Jeff Robinson is a very promising young pitcher. He bears close watching as a potential standout major league talent.

Robinson's out pitch is an excellent forkball. His throws his fastball in the 89-90 MPH range and his slider is effective, though he does not get a consistently good break on it.

In general, he goes primarily with a forkball/fastball combination. When he has got his forkball working well, he almost doesn't need any other pitch: it's that unhittable. Last year, he was able to control the forkball well and to make it move. He likes to throw it and will do so often.

FIELDING, HITTING, BASERUNNING:

Robinson is not a good fielder, though he seems to be improving.

The fact that he is a good runner hardly matters because he is a terrible hitter and hit just one single and one sacrifice last season.

OVERALL:

Robinson is one of the sleepers of the San Francisco staff. He has the chance for a major breakthrough this season, and it may come

JEFF ROBINSON
RHP, No. 49
RR, 6'4", 200 lbs.
ML Svc: 2 years
Born: 12-13-60 in
Santa Ana, CA

1986 STATISTICS

W	L	ERA	G	GS	CG	SV	IP	H	R	ER	BB	SO
6	3	3.36	64	1	0	8	104.1	92	46	39	32	90

CAREER STATISTICS

W	L	ERA	G	GS	CG	SV	IP	H	R	ER	BB	SO
13	18	4.16	106	34	1	8	288	303	156	133	94	200

for him as a starter or in relief.

As a strikeout specialist, he is right behind teammates Mark Davis and Scott Garrelts; last season, Robinson fanned 90 hitters in 104 1/3 innings.

Dierker: "Robinson is a pitcher blessed with natural stuff. If he masters the split-finger fastball and gets a chance to do more than long relief, he could be an extremely valuable commodity for the Giants. Given his role last year, a 6-3 record and eight saves was a major contribution to the club's success.

"What he needs right now is the experience to develop consistency."

SAN FRANCISCO GIANTS

HITTING:

Rob Thompson was a tremendous surprise for the Giants last year. He made a most successful jump to the majors by skipping Triple-A play and proceeding to Candlestick Park directly from Double-A.

Unlike so many young hitters--and especially those who have not played at Triple-A--Thompson was not intimidated by major league pitching. He posted a pro-career-high .271 average and led the club in runs (73) and hits (149). Even more telling was his strong finish, indicating that the National League pitchers were not able to figure him out and blow him off during their final confrontations with him.

Thompson handles the high pitch and the fastball well, but struck out too often because he is susceptible to breaking pitches and off-speed stuff down the middle.

He is an aggressive hitter who will look to get a hit almost any way he can and managed to keep his average at a respectable level for a second baseman because he is a hustling hitter. His deft offensive execution included a club-record 18 sacrifice bunts, including six squeezes. Only the Pirates' Barry Bonds had more RBIs among National League rookies last year.

BASERUNNING:

Thompson has average speed and will steal a base occasionally, but his strength as a baserunner is his smarts. Manager Roger Craig regards him as a natural ballplayer because of his fine instincts; Thompson's ability to react well to game situations is demonstrated by the heads-up way he runs the bases.

FIELDING:

Thompson is not a flashy second baseman, but he is highly effective because of his seemingly natural instincts for the fine points of baseball. It didn't take him long to learn how to play the hitters and he's bound to improve with more experience. His range is average, but he anticipates ground balls and

ROB THOMPSON
INF, No. 6
RR, 5'11", 170 lbs.
ML Svc: 1 year
Born: 5-10-62 in
West Palm Beach, FL

1986 STATISTICS

AVG	G	AB	R	H	2B	3B	HR	RBI	BB	SO	SB
.271	149	549	73	149	27	3	7	47	42	112	12

CAREER STATISTICS

AVG	G	AB	R	H	2B	3B	HR	RBI	BB	SO	SB
.271	149	549	73	149	27	3	7	47	42	112	12

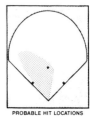

STRONG vs. RHP · STRONG vs. LHP · PROBABLE HIT LOCATIONS

line drives well and manages to get to a lot of balls. He stands in very tough on the double play.

His accurate throws and ability to get them off cleanly are a bonus for all of the other infielders; he made only two throwing errors all last year.

OVERALL:

A diamond in the rough but one who shone more brightly with each game, Thompson came out of virtually nowhere to earn *Rookie of the Year* honors from The Sporting News in 1986.

This young player can flat-out play this game. He played hurt last year and is the type of gritty ballplayer managers love.

Dierker: "He is a good-looking all-around second baseman and is on the verge of becoming a real quality player. Thompson is a tough, hard-nosed player and did not appear the least bit intimidated by big league competition. In 1986 he met the challenge presented to him both offensively and defensively."

SAN FRANCISCO GIANTS

HITTING:

Jose Uribe enjoyed a more successful season in 1986 than his .223 average would indicate. He improved his on-base percentage, became a better basestealer and hit reasonably well in the clutch. Moreover, he was the toughest player in the majors to double up, grounding into DPs only twice in 453 at-bats. If he continues to improve in 1987 and raises his average a few points, he'd be at least an average hitter for a shortstop and a valuable asset to the club.

A switch-hitter, Uribe improved on the disparity between his hitting from the right and left sides last year, but remains more effective as a lefthanded hitter (.230). Oddly enough, he shows all of his power as a righthanded hitter: his only three home runs last season were from that side.

The most surprising development in Uribe's overall play was his ability in the clutch. He batted .303 with runners in scoring position and .326 with runners in scoring position with two outs. His 43 RBIs were a career high and not a bad figure for a No. 8 hitter.

When you only bat .223, it's apparent a lot of pitches give you trouble, so there are holes in his bat for pitchers to exploit.

BASERUNNING:

Uribe stole 22 bases last season, but it must be noted that he was caught stealing 11 times. He has excellent speed but shows poor judgment. He must learn when and against which pitchers and/or catchers to attempt a stolen base. Uribe became a more confident baserunnner last year, but he now needs to become more efficient.

FIELDING:

Uribe is an above-average shortstop and as an indicator, he played in 157 games at that position last year and made just one more error (16) than the Cardinals' Ozzie Smith. Uribe has an above-average arm and is accurate with his throws. He has very good

JOSE URIBE
SS, No. 23
SR, 5'10", 165 lbs.
ML Svc: 2 years
Born: 1-21-60 in
San Cristobal,
Dominican Republic

1986 STATISTICS

AVG	G	AB	R	H	2B	3B	HR	RBI	BB	SO	SB
.223	157	453	46	101	15	1	3	43	61	76	22

CAREER STATISTICS

AVG	G	AB	R	H	2B	3B	HR	RBI	BB	SO	SB
.230	312	948	96	218	35	5	6	72	91	135	31

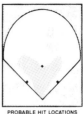

VS. RHP   VS. LHP   PROBABLE HIT LOCATIONS

range.

He became more consistent in 1986, but as happened in 1985, Uribe began to fall apart in the late stages of the season as overwork began to strain his shoulder.

He does not turn the double play particularly well, though he had a hand in 95 DPs last year (one fewer than Smith and the Cubs' Shawon Dunston, who led the league).

OVERALL:

Uribe's .977 fielding percentage last season was the best by a Giants shortstop since Chris Speier's .982 in 1975. The club has reacquired Speier to give Uribe an occasional breather and to prevent wear and tear on Uribe's arm.

Dierker: "Uribe improved a great deal last year as a hitter and as a defensive player. He's becoming at least average offensively for a shortstop, but his strength is certainly his solid defense. He has become a more consistent player."

SAN FRANCISCO GIANTS

PITCHING:

This rejuvenated, oft rejected, pitcher saved his major league career last season by pitching outstanding baseball with the Giants' Triple-A club. Cast adrift in the spring, Frank Williams wasn't counted on to help the club initially but had to be called to the majors at midseason. At the time, he was leading the Pacific Coast League in saves.

Williams arrived at the Giants and proceeded to post a 3-1 record and a miniscule 1.20 ERA, yielding runs in only four of 36 appearances.

Williams uses a sidearm delivery which helps to give him an initial edge in his battle with the hitter and is a tricky style especially helpful to a reliever.

He is tough on righthanded batters and can be tough on everyone when his control is sharp. But that's the rub. Williams has never been able to maintain his control for a long enough stretch to be considered more than a minor leaguer with major league potential.

FIELDING, HITTING, BASERUNNING:

Williams is a terrible fielder and has a lot of trouble making throws after he catches the ball. Because he's a sidearm-style pitcher, his follow-through is awkward and he never appears sure which way to throw when he fields a ball. Though he was errorless in 11 chances last year, each opportunity was an adventure.

OVERALL:

With Greg Minton slipping rapidly and his role being reduced to barely middle relief and Mark Davis being considered for the starting rotation, Williams is very likely to get a lot

FRANK WILLIAMS
RHP, No. 47
RR, 6'1", 180 lbs.
ML Svc: 3 years
Born: 2-13-58 in
Seattle, WA

1986 STATISTICS

W	L	ERA	G	GS	CG	SV	IP	H	R	ER	BB	SO
3	1	1.20	36	0	0	1	52.1	35	8	7	21	33

CAREER STATISTICS

W	L	ERA	G	GS	CG	SV	IP	H	R	ER	BB	SO
14	9	3.22	146	1	1	4	231.2	188	96	83	107	178

more work this season.

He has only average stuff and will probably not become an ace reliever, but his sidewinding delivery makes him an asset when he can find the plate. His pitching success last season might have been a fluke sustained by his unusual pitching style. His strength is that his pitches come from different angles and are difficult to pick up for righthanded batters. But odd-angles notwithstanding, Williams still needs to have pinpoint control or else the professional hitters in the National League will find him very hittable.

A long reliever often is hurt by a lack of work but Williams cleared that hurdle last year and may have found the opportunity for steady employment.

Dierker: "He can get by without great control against righthanded hitters, but when facing lefty sluggers must be much more on the mark. I would say he hasn't been able to show that control consistently and will have to prove that he can cut it as anything more than a long reliever."

SAN FRANCISCO GIANTS

HITTING:

One of the best utilitymen in the game, Joel Youngblood doesn't do anything well enough over the long haul to remain an everyday player. He hits for a fairly good average and has some power which makes him a valuable offensive tool as a spot player and pinch-hitter.

Youngblood is a good contact hitter with streaky power. He takes his job seriously and is a hard worker who keeps himself in optimum shape for when he's needed.

He became embroiled in a feud with the front office over his value to the club during the winter of 1985-86, when the Giants deemed him expendable, but the club finally reconsidered and took him back in the spring last year. The decision fared well for both parties because Youngblood's contributions made the Giants' bench among the best in the major leagues last year.

BASERUNNING:

Youngblood is a heady player who is always in the game and as a result, he will not take foolish chances or make errors of judgment on the basepaths. Still, his basestealing days have dwindled with his years in the bigs.

FIELDING:

Youngblood's defensive strengths and weaknesses vary with the position he is playing. For the most part, he is very versatile, although he is best suited as an outfielder.

He has been used satisfactorily as a second baseman, but since the Giants have secured the services of Chris Speier, a professional utility infielder, it is unlikely that Youngblood will spend much time at second base this season. It is even more unlikely that he will be used at third base--or at least he *shouldn't be*--because he is simply awful at the hot corner.

He played six different positions for the club last season, attesting to his versatility and value.

OVERALL:

Youngblood is always a good guy to have

JOEL YOUNGBLOOD
OF/PH, No. 8
RR, 5'11", 175 lbs.
ML Svc: 11 years
Born: 8-28-51 in
Houston, TX

1986 STATISTICS

AVG	G	AB	R	H	2B	3B	HR	RBI	BB	SO	SB
.255	97	184	20	47	12	0	5	28	18	34	1

CAREER STATISTICS

AVG	G	AB	R	H	2B	3B	HR	RBI	BB	SO	SB
.268	1180	3327	419	890	168	23	74	918	304	538	58

  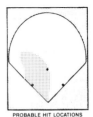

VS. RHP · VS. LHP · PROBABLE HIT LOCATIONS

on a team because he can do so many things and is very businesslike in his approach to the game. A true professional, Blood was especially valuable as a pinch-hitter last season. He came through 16 times, which would have been an all-time Giants record were it not for the emergence of Candy Maldonado as a pinch-hitter deluxe.

A bit of a worry wart, Youngblood has a tendency to get down mentally when things aren't going well, but the positive vibrations emanating from the Giants' clubhouse last year allowed him to go with the flow more comfortably.

Dierker: "He has never been excellent at one position on the field and he never has had the consistent power or the consistently high batting average to win a regular job.

"He is far from finished and could probably have almost as many more years left in baseball as he wants if he maintains himself as well as he does physically and continues to perform adequately at the plate."

SAN FRANCISCO GIANTS

MIKE ALDRETE
OF, No. 1
LL, 5'11", 180 lbs.
ML Svc: 1 year
Born: 1-29-61 in
**   Carmel, CA**

HITTING, BASERUNNING, FIELDING:

Mike Aldrete has the potential to be a solid, all-around hitter, much like Will Clark. Aldrete batted .371 in Triple-A and has the potential to hover near the .300 mark in the majors.

He struggled when he was first recalled from the minors last season, but seemed much more comfortable at the plate when he was recalled for the second time. Aldrete uses the entire field, has some power and is quite patient at the plate for a youngster, and will take his share of walks. He's not a true home run hitter, but he has enough strength to hit balls out of the park, although he's more of an alleys hitter.

A stocky, compact athlete, Aldrete is not a threat to steal a base, but he's a heady runner who won't hurt the club on the basepaths.

His lack of speed makes him a better first-base candidate than an outfielder. Aldrete made only one error in 68 games afield and it was not made during his 37 games at first base. He is a better defensive player as a first baseman, but Will Clark has that position nailed down solid at this stage, so Aldrete may have to concentrate on becoming a better outfielder. If the Giants trade away Chili Davis, Aldrete would likely platoon with Joel Youngblood in left field.

OVERALL:

Dierker: "Aldrete is an unspectacular player, but he is a solid, all-around performer who can help the club, especially since it needs lefthanded punch. He needs to continue to develop."

JUAN BERENGUER
RHP, No. 40
RR, 5'11", 215 lbs.
ML Svc: 9 years
Born: 11-30-54 in
**   Aguadulce, Panama**

PITCHING, FIELDING,
*   HITTING, BASERUNNING:*

Juan Berenguer is an extremely hard throwing pitcher who has (surprise!) come up with a split-finger pitch. There were times last season when he was able to throw it well and was simply devastating with it. But the split-finger is a fickle pickle and difficult to control. Berenguer was not able to handle it well enough consistently. When it deserted him, he reverted to his tendency to get wild and come in with fastballs which met the good part of the bat.

Berenguer also throws a slider, but the emphasis is on the heater and the split-finger pitch.

Berenguer saves his wildness until after the first batter. Last season, he retired 32 of the first batters he faced in 42 relief appearances. To his further credit, he did not make the kind of mistakes that get knocked out of the park; last year, he yielded but two homers in 56 1/3 innings of bullpen work.

But he still does not show the consistent, reliable control that can wrap up or hold onto a game.

Berenguer is not much of a fielder. He is fairly capable as a sacrifice bunter, but he is a big man who doesn't rustle up the dust when he is running the bases.

OVERALL:

A temperamental sort, Berenguer fumes when he's not working regularly; that is a trait he'll have to overcome if he's to remain with the Giants. There's so much younger talent on this club that Berenguer would be fortunate to be the 10th pitcher on the staff.

His heat can be intimidating, but at this point, he is a spare part.

SAN FRANCISCO GIANTS

JIM GOTT
RHP, No. 51
RR, 6'4", 220 lbs.
ML Svc: 5 years
Born: 8-3-59 in
    Hollywood, CA

PITCHING, FIELDING,
HITTING, BASERUNNING:

Jim Gott's career is a big question mark this season. He began the '86 season full of high hopes for a good season with the Giants. Roger Craig was hopeful, too, and believed that correcting some mechanical problems with Gott's delivery could be the key to his success.

Craig and pitching coach Norm Sherry worked with Gott to alter his delivery by making it more compact. Craig liked his stuff, but never had the chance to see very much of it because the veteran righthander appeared

in only nine games before succumbing to tendinitis in his right bicep and, later, rotator cuff surgery.

Gott has shown a 90 MPH fastball, but the rest of his repertoire is merely ordinary. That's why the delivery was changed, but the Giants may never know if it was a good move as the rotator cuff surgery might end his career.

In the past, Gott has not been a good fielder, but his first try at major league hitting with the Giants in 1985 was a three-homer success.

OVERALL:

If he does anything with the club this year, it would be a bonus. At best, if he is healthy, Gott will be used as a long reliever.

Dierker: "We saw him in 1985 and he appeared to have only average stuff. The jury is out on what is going to happen this year. It all depends on his arm."

ATLEE HAMMAKER
LHP, No. 7
LL, 6'2", 195 lbs.
ML Svc: 6 years
Born: 1-24-58 in
    Carmel, CA

PITCHING, FIELDING,
HITTING, BASERUNNING:

What a shame. Once the most promising lefthander in the National League, Atlee Hammaker spent the entire 1986 season on the disabled list and hasn't been healthy since he was the ERA champ in 1983. Following two surgeries in 1984, Hammaker had yet another operation performed on the rotator cuff last April in addition to knee surgery.

Any report on Hammaker must be read with the note that he has not pitched in the major leagues for three full seasons.

When he was healthy, he demonstrated excellent control with his fastball and breaking pitches and was able to keep the ball low in the strike zone. His stuff and fastball

were merely average, but he was precocious in that he knew how to pitch at an early age.

There have been glimpses since 1983 that indicate he can still do the job when he takes the mound, but he hasn't been able to do that often enough for a true reading.

OVERALL:

The skeptics figure he'll never pitch again, but the Giants remain mildly optimistic. Hammaker is confident because he threw without pain over the winter. *Anything* he does on the mound would be a bonus, of course, and there is always hope: the American League 1986 Cy Young Award winner, Boston's Roger Clemens had the exact same rotator cuff procedure that Atlee underwent last April. It's a wait-and-see proposition.

Dierker: "At one time, he was one of the classiest lefthanders in the league and it looked as if he would become a big winner. Now, of course, no one knows if he can ever pitch again. If Hammaker can come back and demonstrate good control and pitch well, it would be one of the most welcome surprises the Giants can hope for."

SAN FRANCISCO GIANTS

RANDY KUTCHER
INF, No. 29
RR, 6'4", 190 lbs.
ML Svc: less than
 one year
Born: 4-20-60 in
 Anchorage, AK

HITTING, BASERUNNING, FIELDING:

It took Randy Kutcher a long time to reach the majors, but he finally broke in with a bang by belting seven home runs in his first 25 games.

Then reality set in and the honeymoon was over.

Kutcher added only two more home runs over his last 46 games. His final average of .237 indicates the reason he has been buried in the minors.

Roger Craig likes his aggressiveness, however, and may keep him around as a utilityman because he can play the infield and the outfield. In fact, he looked pretty good in center field and has the ability to steal bases.

OVERALL:

There is not a very promising future in store for Kutcher, but it looks better than it did two winters ago, when he almost gave up the game to do construction work following moderate minor league success.

Last season, the Giants had a part-time job to fill and as a temporary player, Kutcher was in the right place at the right time.

Dierker: "He showed some power and also made some plays in the outfield, but his numbers at the plate show he can't do it on a regular basis. Also he's a little too old (Kutcher will be 27 years old this spring) to be starting out, so he'll likely figure in a part-time role if he's still with the club this season."

ROGER MASON
RHP, No. 19
RR, 6'6", 215 lbs.
ML Svc: 2 years
Born: 9-18-58 in
 Bellaire, MI

PITCHING, FIELDING,
HITTING, BASERUNNING:

Roger Mason experienced elbow problems last season and it is hoped that his injury-shortened 1986 season is merely an interruption on his way to a most successful career.

Mason and Roger Craig worked together when both were in the Detroit system a few seasons ago, and when Craig became the San Francisco manager, he was most anxious to bring Mason along with him.

Transformed into a regular starter last spring, Mason was off to a 2-1 start with a 2.00 ERA after five outings when he developed tendinitis in the right elbow. His 1986 season was limited to just 11 appearances.

When healthy, Mason has an effective trailing fastball and is proficient at throwing the split-finger fastball. If he's sound, he will most likely be in the rotation this year; his injury is not regarded to be as serious as those suffered by Jim Gott and Atlee Hammaker.

As a fielder, don't expect Mason to be any good. He isn't--injury or not. Nor is he a good hitter or baserunner.

OVERALL:

Craig was so confident that Mason would bounce back before the end of last season, he had mentally penciled him into the starting rotation for the second half of the year. Mason's name never reached the lineup card.

Undoubtedly, Mason could have been the pennant impetus the Giants desperately needed last year. On the very bright side, however, he is most likely to provide that for the club in 1987.

SAN FRANCISCO GIANTS

HARRY SPILMAN
INF, No. 16
LR, 6'1", 190 lbs.
ML Svc: 8 years
Born: 7-18-54 in
Albany, GA

HITTING, BASERUNNING, FIELDING:

The Giants did well by signing this journeyman after he was cut loose by the Tigers last season. Harry Spilman joined the Giants in mid-June and promptly became their top lefthanded pinch-hitter, ranking fifth in the National League at .406 and batting .287 overall.

With the club loaded with outfielders and Mike Aldrete and Bob Brenly able to give Will Clark a rest at first base, it seems that Spilman will not have much chance to be used defensively; his role will be restricted to pinch-hitting in 1987.

Spilman is a good clutch hitter with a trained eye and was the Giants' most effective hitter on the team (.441) with runners in scoring position.

As a baserunnner, he is merely adequate, but he won't hurt you with the glove at first base.

OVERALL:

When Spilman, Mike LaCoss and Vida Blue filed for free agency at the end of the 1986 season, signing Spilman was the club's top priority.

Dierker: "If Candy Maldonado is successful as a regular player, Harry would be a good bet to be the first pinch-hitter off the bench. He could enjoy that role for a long time if he continues to produce as he did last year."

PLAYER INDEX

A

B

E

F

G

H

I

J

K

L

M

T

U

V

W

Y